Agatha Christie®

The Mystery of Three Quarters

THE NEW HERCULE POIROT MYSTERY

SOPHIE HANNAH

HarperCollins*Publishers*

HarperCollins*Publishers*
1 London Bridge Street
London SE1 9GF
www.harpercollins.co.uk

Published by HarperCollins*Publishers* 2018
1

The Mystery of Three Quarters™ is a trade mark of Agatha Christie Limited
and Agatha Christie®, Poirot® and the Agatha Christie Signature
are registered trade marks of Agatha Christie Limited in the UK
and elsewhere.
Copyright © Agatha Christie Limited 2018
All rights reserved.
www.agathachristie.com

Sophie Hannah asserts the moral right
to be identified as the author of this work.

A catalogue record for this book
is available from the British Library

ISBN   978-0-00-826445-1   HB
ISBN   978-0-00-826446-8   TPB

Set in Sabon by Palimpsest Book Production Ltd,
Falkirk, Stirlingshire.

Printed and bound in Great Britain by
CPI Group (UK) Ltd, Croydon CR0 4YY

MIX
Paper from
responsible sources
FSC
www.fsc.org   **FSC™ C007454**

This book is produced from independently certified FSC™ paper
to ensure responsible forest management.
For more information visit: www.harpercollins.co.uk/green

THE MYSTERY OF THREE QUARTERS

Also by Sophie Hannah

Little Face
Hurting Distance
The Point of Rescue
The Other Half Lives
A Room Swept White
Lasting Damage
Kind of Cruel
The Carrier
The Orphan Choir
The Telling Error
Pictures Or It Didn't Happen
A Game for All the Family
The Narrow Bed
Did You See Melody?

Hercule Poirot mysteries

The Monogram Murders
Closed Casket

For Faith Tilleray,
who has gone above and beyond,
and taught me so much

Acknowledgements

I am hugely grateful to the following people:

James Prichard, Mathew Prichard and everybody at Agatha Christie Limited; David Brawn, Kate Elton and everyone at HarperCollins UK; my agent Peter Straus and his team at Rogers, Coleridge & White; my wonderful publishers William Morrow in New York, and all my Poirot publishers all over the world who have helped to distribute the books far and wide; Chris Gribble, who read and enthused at a crucial early stage; Emily Winslow who made editorial suggestions that were meticulous and invaluable, as always; Jamie Bernthal-Hooker, who did a million helpful things, from proof-reading to researching to title brainstorming; Faith Tilleray, who designed me a stunning new website and then became my marketing guru; my family— Dan, Phoebe, Guy . . . and Brewster in particular on this occasion, for reasons that will be clear to anyone who reads the book!

Thank you to competition winners Melanie Vout and

Ian Mason, who supplied the names Peter Vout and Hubert Thrubwell respectively. They are both wonderful names! A massive thank you, also, to all the readers who have loved *The Monogram Murders* and *Closed Casket*, and my other books, and have written/tweeted/messaged me to tell me so—your enthusiasm makes it all feel so worthwhile.

Contents

THE FIRST QUARTER

CHAPTER 1

Poirot is Accused

Hercule Poirot smiled to himself as his driver brought the motorcar to a stop with satisfying symmetry. As a lover of neatness and order, Poirot appreciated such perfect alignment with the entrance doors of Whitehaven Mansions where he lived. One could draw a straight line from the middle of the vehicle to the exact point where the doors met.

The luncheon from which he was returning had been *très bon divertissement*: the most excellent of food and company. He alighted, bestowed a warm thank-you upon his driver, and was about to go inside when he had a peculiar feeling that (this was how he put it to himself) something behind him was in need of his attention.

He expected, on turning, to observe nothing out of the ordinary. It was a mild day for February, but perhaps a light breeze had put a tremor in the air around him.

Poirot soon saw that the disturbance had not been caused by the weather, though the well-turned-out woman approaching at a great pace did, in spite of her fashionable pale blue coat and hat, resemble a force of nature. 'She is the whirlwind most fierce,' Poirot murmured to himself.

He disliked the hat. He had seen women in town wearing similar ones: minimal, without ornament, fitted close to the scalp like bathing caps made of cloth. A hat ought to have a brim or some manner of embellishment, thought Poirot. At least, it should do something more than cover the head. No doubt he would soon get used to these modern hats— and then, once he had, the fashion would change as it always did.

The blue-clad woman's lips twitched and curled, though no sound came from her. It was as if she was rehearsing what she would say when she finally reached Poirot's side. There was no doubt that he was her target. She looked determined to do something unpleasant to him as soon as she was close enough. He took a step back as she marched towards him in what he could only think of as a stampede—one consisting of nothing and nobody but herself.

Her hair was dark brown and lustrous. When she came to an abrupt halt directly in front of him, Poirot saw that she was not as young as she had looked from a distance. No, this woman was more than fifty years old. She was perhaps sixty. A lady in her middle age, expert at concealing the lines on her face. Her eyes were a striking blue, neither light nor dark.

'You are Hercule Poirot, are you not?' she said in the loudest of whispers. Poirot noted that she wished to convey anger but without being overheard, though there was nobody nearby.

'*Oui*, madame. I am he.'

'How *dare* you? How *dare* you send me such a letter?'

'Madame, pardon me, but I do not believe we know one another.'

'Don't act the part of the innocent with *me*! I am Sylvia Rule. As you know perfectly well.'

'Now I know, because you have told me. A moment ago, I did not know. You referred to a letter—'

'Will you force me to repeat your slander of me in a public place? Very well, then, I shall. I received a letter this morning—a most disgusting and objectionable letter, signed by *you*.' She stabbed the air with a forefinger that would have poked Poirot in the chest had he not hopped to one side to avoid it.

'*Non*, madame—' he tried to protest, but his attempt at denial was swiftly demolished.

'In this travesty of a letter, you accused me of murder. *Murder!* Me! Sylvia Rule! You claimed that you could prove my guilt, and you advised me to go at once to the police and confess to my crime. How *dare* you? You cannot prove anything against me, for the simple reason that I am innocent. I have not killed anybody. I am the least violently inclined person I have ever met. And I have never heard of a Barnabas Pandy!'

'A Barnabas—'

'It is monstrous that you accuse *me*, of all people! Simply monstrous. I shall not stand for it. I have a good mind to go to my solicitor about this, except I don't want him to know I have been so defamed. Perhaps I shall go to the police. The slur I have suffered! The insult! A woman of my standing in the world!'

Sylvia Rule went on in this manner for some time. There was a lot of hiss and fizz in her agitated whispering. She made Poirot think of the loud, turbulent waterfalls he had encountered on his travels: impressive to watch, but mainly alarming on account of their relentlessness. The flow never stopped.

As soon as he could make himself heard, he said, 'Madame, please accept my assurance that I have written no such letter. If you have received one, it was not sent by me. I too have never heard of Barnabas Pandy. That is the name of the man you are accused of murdering, by whoever wrote the letter?'

'*You* wrote it, and do not provoke me further by pretending you didn't. Eustace put you up to it, didn't he? You both know that I have killed nobody, that I am as blameless as it is possible for a person to be! You and Eustace have hatched a plan together to send me out of my wits! This is exactly the sort of thing he would do, and no doubt he will claim later that it was all a joke.'

'I know of no Eustace, madame.' Poirot continued to make his best effort, though it was plain that nothing he said made the slightest bit of difference to Sylvia Rule.

'He thinks he's so clever—quite the cleverest man in England!—with that disgusting smirk that never leaves his appalling face. How much did you pay you? I know it must have been his idea. And you did his dirty work. You, the famed Hercule Poirot, who are trusted by our loyal and hardworking police. You are a fraud! How *could* you? Slandering a woman of my good character! Eustace would do anything to defeat me. Anything! Whatever he has told you about me, it's a lie!'

If she had been willing to listen, Poirot might have told her that he would be unlikely to cooperate with any man who considered himself to be the cleverest man in England for as long as he, Hercule Poirot, resided in London.

'Please show me this letter you received, madame.'

'Do you think I *kept* it? It made me ill to hold it in my hand! I tore it into a dozen pieces and tossed it on the fire. I should like to toss Eustace on a fire! What a pity such actions are against the law. All I can say is that whoever made that particular law must never have met Eustace. If you *ever* traduce me in this way again, I shall go straight to Scotland Yard—not to confess to anything, for I am entirely innocent, but to accuse *you*, M. Poirot!'

Before Poirot could formulate a suitable response, Sylvia Rule had turned and marched away.

He did not call her back. He stood for a few seconds, shaking his head slowly. As he mounted the steps to his building, he muttered to himself, 'If she is the least violently inclined person, then I do not wish to meet the most.'

Inside his spacious and well-appointed flat, his valet awaited him. George's rather wooden smile turned to an expression of consternation when he saw Poirot's face.

'Are you quite well, sir?'

'*Non*. I am perplexed, Georges. Tell me, as one who knows much about the upper echelons of English society . . . do you know a Sylvia Rule?'

'By reputation only, sir. She is the widow of the late Clarence Rule. Extremely well connected. I believe she sits on the boards of various charities.'

'What about Barnabas Pandy?'

George shook his head. 'That name is not familiar to me. London society is my area of special knowledge, sir. If Mr Pandy lives elsewhere—'

'I do not know where he lives. I do not know *if* he lives, or if he was, perhaps, murdered. *Vraiment*, I could not know less about Barnabas Pandy than I do presently—that would be an impossibility! But do not try, Georges, to tell this to Sylvia Rule, who imagines that I know all about him! She believes I wrote a letter accusing her of his murder, a letter I now deny having written. I did not write the letter. I have sent no communication of any kind to Mrs Sylvia Rule.'

Poirot removed his hat and coat with less care than he usually took, and handed both to George. 'It is not a pleasant thing, to be accused of something one has not done. One ought to be able to brush the untruths aside, but somehow they take hold of the mind and cause a spectral form of guilt—like a ghost in the head, or in the conscience! Someone is certain that you have done this terrible thing, and so you start to feel as if you have, even though you know you have not. I begin to understand, Georges, why people confess to crimes of which they are innocent.'

George looked doubtful, as he frequently did. English discretion, Poirot had observed, had an outward appearance that suggested doubt. Many of the politest English men and women he had met over the years looked as if they had been ordered to disbelieve everything that was said to them.

'Would you like a drink, sir? A *sirop de menthe*, if I might be permitted to make a suggestion?'

'*Oui*. That is an excellent idea.'

'I should also mention, sir, that you have a visitor waiting to see you. Am I to bring your drink immediately, and ask him to wait a little longer?'

'A visitor?'

'Yes, sir.'

'What is his name? Is it Eustace?'

'No, sir. It's a Mr John McCrodden.'

'Ah! That is a relief. No Eustace. I can cherish the hope that the nightmare of Madame Rule and her Eustace has departed and will not return to Hercule Poirot! Did Monsieur McCrodden state the nature of his business?'

'No, sir. Though I should warn you, he seemed . . . displeased.'

Poirot allowed a small sigh to escape his lips. After his more than satisfactory luncheon, the afternoon was taking a disappointing turn. Still, John McCrodden was unlikely to be as vexatious as Sylvia Rule.

'I shall postpone the pleasure of *sirop de menthe* and see Monsieur McCrodden first,' Poirot told George. 'His name is familiar.'

'You might be thinking of the solicitor Rowland McCrodden, sir?'

'*Mais oui, bien sûr*. Rowland Rope, that dear friend of the hangman—though you are too polite, Georges, to call him by the *soubriquet* that suits him so well. The gallows, they are not allowed by Rowland Rope to have a moment's rest.'

'He has been instrumental in bringing several criminals to justice, sir,' agreed George, with his customary tact.

'Perhaps John McCrodden is a relation,' said Poirot. 'Allow me to settle myself and then you may bring him in.'

As it transpired, George was prevented from bringing in John McCrodden by McCrodden's determination to stride into the room without help or introduction. He overtook the valet and positioned himself in the middle of the carpet where he stopped as if frozen in the manner of one sent to play the part of a statue.

'Please, monsieur, you may sit down,' Poirot said with a smile.

'No, thank you,' said McCrodden. His tone was one of contemptuous detachment.

He was forty years old or thereabouts, Poirot guessed. He had the kind of handsome face that one rarely encountered apart from in works of art. His features might have been chiselled by a master craftsman. Poirot found it difficult to reconcile the face with the clothes, which were shabby and showed patches of dirt. Was he in the habit of sleeping on park benches? Did he have recourse to the usual domestic amenities? Poirot wondered if McCrodden had sought to cancel out the advantages that nature had bestowed upon him—the large green eyes and the golden hair—by making himself look as repellent as possible.

McCrodden glared down at Poirot. 'I received your letter,' he said. 'It arrived this morning.'

'I'm afraid I must contradict you, monsieur. I have sent you no letter.'

There was a long, uneasy silence. Poirot did not wish to leap to any hasty conclusions, but he feared he knew the direction the conversation was about to take. But it could not be! *How* could it be? Only in his dreams had he encountered this sensation before: the doom-laden knowledge that one is trapped in a predicament that makes no sense and will never make sense, no matter what one does.

'What did it say, this letter that you received?' he asked.

'You ought to know, since you wrote it,' said John McCrodden. 'You accused me of murdering a man named Barnabas Pandy.'

CHAPTER 2

Intolerable Provocation

'I must say, I was rather disappointed,' McCrodden went on. 'The famous Hercule Poirot, allowing himself to be used for such frivolities.'

Poirot waited a few moments before answering. Was it his particular choice of words that had proved so ineffective in persuading Sylvia Rule to listen to him? Then, for John McCrodden, he would make an effort to be clearer and more persuasive. 'Monsieur, *s'il vous plait*. I believe that somebody sent you a letter and that, in it, you were accused of murder. The murder of Barnabas Pandy. This part of your story I do not dispute. But—'

'You are in no position to dispute it,' said McCrodden.

'Monsieur, please believe me when I tell you that *I was not the writer of the letter you received*. To Hercule Poirot, there is nothing frivolous about murder. I would—'

'Oh, there won't have been any murder,' McCrodden interrupted again with a bitter laugh. 'Or, if there has, the police will already have caught the person responsible. This

12

is one of my father's childish games.' He frowned, as if something disturbing had occurred to him. 'Unless the old gargoyle is more sadistic than I thought and would actually risk my neck in a real and unsolved case of murder. I suppose it's possible. With his ruthless determination . . .' McCrodden broke off, then muttered, 'Yes. It *is* possible. I should have thought of that.'

'Your father is the solicitor Rowland McCrodden?' asked Poirot.

'You know he is.' John McCrodden had already declared himself disappointed, and that was how he sounded—as if Poirot was sinking lower in his estimation with each word he spoke.

'I know your father by reputation only. I have not personally made his acquaintance, nor have I ever spoken to him.'

'You have to maintain the pretence, of course,' said John McCrodden. 'I'm sure he's paid you a handsome sum to keep his name out of it.' He looked around the room he was standing in, seeming to notice it for the first time. Then he nodded as if confirming something to himself, and said, 'The rich who need money least—like you, like my father—will stop at nothing to get their hands on more of it. That's why I've never trusted it. I was right not to. Money is corrosive to character once you're accustomed to it, and you, M. Poirot, are the living proof.'

Poirot could not recall when someone had last said something so unpleasant to him, so unfair or so personally wounding. He said quietly, 'I have spent my life working for the greater good and the protection of the innocent

13

and—yes!—the wrongly accused. That group includes you, monsieur. Also, today, it includes Hercule Poirot. I too am wrongly accused. I am as innocent of writing and sending the letter you received as you are of murder. I too know no Barnabas Pandy. Not a dead Barnabas Pandy and not an alive Barnabas Pandy do I know! But here—ah! Here is where the similarities between us end, for when you insist you are innocent, I listen. I think, "This man might be telling the truth." Whereas when I—'

'Spare me the fancy words,' McCrodden cut in again. 'If you imagine I'm likely to trust dazzling rhetoric any more than I trust money, reputation or any of the other things my father holds in high regard, you're grievously mistaken. Now, since Rowland Rope will doubtless require you to relay to him my response to his sordid little scheme, please tell him this: I'm not playing. I have never heard of a Barnabas Pandy, I have killed nobody, therefore I have nothing to fear. I have enough confidence in the law of the land to trust that I won't hang for a crime I didn't commit.'

'Do you believe your father wants that to happen?'

'I don't know. It's possible. I have always thought that if Father ever runs out of guilty people to send to the gallows, he'll turn his attentions to the innocent and pretend they're guilty—both in court and in his own mind. Anything to feed his lust for the blood of his fellow human beings.'

'That is a remarkable accusation, monsieur, and not the first one you have made since you arrived.' McCrodden's brisk, business-as-usual way of speaking chilled Poirot. It lent an air of objectivity to his words, as if he was merely conveying the plain and uncontroversial facts.

The Rowland Rope about whom Poirot had heard so much over the years was not the man his son was describing. He was a strong advocate of death as a punishment for the guilty—a little too strong for Poirot's taste, for there were circumstances that called for discretion—but Poirot suspected McCrodden Senior would be as horrified as he himself would be at the prospect of an innocent man or woman being sent to the gallows. And if the man in question was his own son . . .

'Monsieur, I have not, in all my years, met a father who sought to have his son condemned to death for a murder he did not commit.'

'Ah, but you have,' John McCrodden responded swiftly. 'Despite your protests to the contrary, I know you must have met my father, or at least you have conversed with him, and the two of you have conspired to accuse me. Well, you can tell Dear Father that I no longer hate him. Now that I see how low he is willing to stoop, I pity him. He's no better than a murderer. Neither are you, M. Poirot. The same is true of anyone in favour of choking wrongdoers at the end of a rope, the way our brutal system does.'

'Is that your opinion, monsieur?'

'All my life I've been a source of embarrassment and frustration to Father: refusing to bow down, to do what he wants, think what he thinks, work in *his* chosen profession. He wants me to take up the law. He's never forgiven me for not wanting to be him.'

'May I ask what is your profession?'

'Profession?' McCrodden sneered. 'I work for a living. Nothing fancy. Nothing grand that involves playing with other people's lives. I've worked in a mine, on farms, in factories. I've made trinkets for ladies and sold them. I'm good at selling. At the moment I've got a market stall. It keeps a roof over my head, but none of that's good enough for my father. And, being Rowland McCrodden, he won't admit defeat. Never.'

'What do you mean?'

'I hoped he had given up on me. Now I see that he never will. He knows a man accused of murder will need to defend himself. It's rather clever of him, actually. He's trying to provoke me, and harbouring all sorts of fantasies, I imagine, of me insisting on defending myself against the charge of murder at the Old Bailey. To do that, I would have to take an interest in the law, wouldn't I?'

It was evident that Rowland McCrodden was to John McCrodden what Eustace was to Sylvia Rule.

'You can tell him from me that his plan has failed. I will never be the person my father wants me to be. And I would rather he didn't attempt to communicate with me again—directly, or using you or any of his other toadies as a conduit.'

Poirot rose from his chair. 'Please wait here for a few moments,' he said. He left the room, taking care to leave the door wide open.

When Poirot returned to the room, he was accompanied by his valet. He smiled at John McCrodden and said, 'You have already met Georges. You will, I hope, have heard me explain to him that I would like him to join us for a short while. I raised my voice so that you would hear everything I said to him.'

'Yes, I heard,' said McCrodden in a bored voice.

'If I had said anything else to Georges, you would have heard it too. I did not. Therefore, what he is about to tell you will, I hope, convince you that I am not your enemy. Please, Georges—speak!'

George looked astonished. He was not accustomed to receiving such vague instructions. 'About what, sir?'

Poirot turned to John McCrodden. 'You see? He does not know. I have not prepared him for this. Georges, when I returned from luncheon today, I told you about something that had just happened to me, did I not?'

'You did, sir.'

'Please repeat the story that I told you.'

'Very well, sir. You were accosted by a lady who introduced herself as Mrs Sylvia Rule. Mrs Rule mistakenly believed that you had written a letter to her in which you had accused her of murder.'

'*Merci*, Georges. Tell me, who was the supposed victim of this murder?'

'A Mr Barnabas Pandy, sir.'

'And what else did I tell you?'

'That you were not acquainted with a man of that name, sir. If there is such a gentleman, you do not know if he is alive or dead, or if he has been murdered. When you tried to explain this to Mrs Rule, she refused to listen.'

17

Poirot turned to John McCrodden in triumph. 'Monsieur, perhaps your father wishes also for Sylvia Rule to defend herself at the Old Bailey? Or are you finally willing to concede that you have misjudged and most unfairly maligned Hercule Poirot? It might interest to you to know that Madame Rule also accused me of conspiring with one of her enemies to cause her distress—a man named Eustace.'

'I still say my father is behind it all,' John McCrodden said after a short interval. He sounded markedly less certain than he had before. 'He enjoys nothing more than the challenge of an elaborate puzzle. I'm supposed to work out why Mrs Rule received the same letter I did.'

'When one has a driving preoccupation—yours with your father, or Sylvia Rule's obsession with her Eustace—it colours the way one sees the world,' said Poirot with a sigh. 'I don't suppose you have brought the letter with you?'

'No. I tore it up and sent the pieces to my father with a note telling him what I think of him, and now I'm telling you, M. Poirot. I won't stand for it. Even the great Hercule Poirot cannot accuse innocent people of murder and expect to get away with it.'

It was a considerable relief when John McCrodden finally removed himself from the room. Poirot stood by the window in order to watch his visitor's departure from the building.

'Are you ready for your *sirop de menthe* now, sir?' George asked.

'*Mon ami*, I am ready for all the *sirop de menthe* in the world.' Seeing that he might have caused confusion, he clarified. 'One glass please, Georges. Only one.'

Poirot returned to his chair in a state of agitation. What hope was there for justice or peace to prevail in the world when three people who might have made common cause— three wrongly accused people: Sylvia Rule, John McCrodden and Hercule Poirot—could not sit together and have a calm, rational discussion that might have helped them all to understand what had happened? Instead there had been anger, an almost fanatical refusal to entertain a point of view other than one's own, and the ceaseless hurling of insults. Not from Hercule Poirot, however; he had behaved impeccably in the face of intolerable provocation.

When George brought him his *sirop*, he said, 'Tell me—is there anybody else waiting to see me?'

'No, sir.'

'Nobody has telephoned to request an appointment?'

'No, sir. Are you expecting someone?'

'*Oui*. I am expecting an angry stranger, or perhaps several.'

'I'm not sure what you mean, sir.'

Just then the telephone started to ring. Poirot nodded permitted himself a small smile. When there was no other pleasure to be taken from a situation, one might as well enjoy being correct, he thought. 'There he is, Georges—or there *she* is. The third person. Third of who knows how many? Three, four, five? It could be any number.'

'Number of what, sir?'

'People who have received a letter accusing them of the murder of Barnabas Pandy—signed, fraudulently, in the name of Hercule Poirot!'

19

CHAPTER 3

The Third Person

At three o'clock the next day, Poirot was visited at Whitehaven Mansions by a Miss Annabel Treadway. As he waited for George to show her in, he found himself looking forward to the encounter. For those of a different temperament, it might have been tedious to field the same accusation time after time from a succession of strangers united in their determination not to listen to a word that was said to them; not so for Hercule Poirot. This third time, he resolved, he would succeed in making his point. He would convince Miss Annabel Treadway that he was telling the truth. Perhaps then progress might be made and some more interesting questions asked.

The puzzle of why most people, even intelligent people, were so illogical and pig-headed was one to which Poirot had devoted quite enough consideration while lying awake the previous night; he was eager to turn his attention to Barnabas Pandy himself. Of course, that was assuming that Barnabas Pandy had a self. It was possible that he did not exist, had never existed, and was no more than a figment of the letter-writer's imagination.

The door opened and George ushered in a thin woman of average height, with fair hair and dark eyes and clothes. Poirot was alarmed by his reaction to the sight of her. He felt as if he ought to bow his head and say, 'My condolences, mademoiselle.' Having no reason to believe that she had suffered a loss, he restrained himself. A letter accusing her of murder might provoke anger or fear, but it could hardly be considered a tragedy; it would not, Poirot thought, make a person sad.

As surely as John McCrodden had filled Poirot's room with cold contempt, Annabel Treadway had brought sorrow in with her. 'The aching heart,' Poirot thought. He felt it as keenly as if it were his own.

'Thank you, Georges,' he said. 'Please, sit down, mademoiselle.'

She hurried to the nearest chair and sat in a manner that cannot have been comfortable for her. Poirot observed that her most striking facial feature was a deep vertical groove that started between her eyebrows: a pronounced crease that seemed to divide her forehead into two neat halves. Poirot resolved not to look at it again, lest she should notice.

'Thank you for allowing me to come here today,' she said quietly. 'I expected you to refuse.' She looked at Poirot five or six times as she spoke, turning away quickly on each occasion as if she didn't want him to catch her in the act of observing him.

'From where have you come, mademoiselle?'

'Oh, you won't have heard of it. Nobody has. It's in the country.'

'Why did you expect me to refuse to see you?'

'Most people would go to any lengths to prevent someone they believed to be a murderer from entering their home,' she said. 'M. Poirot, what I came here to tell you is . . . Well, you might not believe me, but I am innocent. I could not murder another living soul. Never! You cannot know . . .' She broke off with a ragged gasp.

'Please continue,' said Poirot gently. 'What is it that I cannot know?'

'I have never caused pain or injury to anybody, and nor could I. I have *saved* lives!'

'Mademoiselle—'

Annabel Treadway had produced a handkerchief from her pocket and was dabbing at her eyes. 'Please forgive me if I sounded boastful. I did not mean to exaggerate my own goodness or my achievements, but it is true that I have saved a life. Many years ago.'

'A life? You said "lives".'

'I only meant that if I had the opportunity to do so again, I should save every life that I could save, even if I had to place myself in danger to do so.' Her voice trembled.

'Is that because you are especially heroic or because you think other people matter more than you do?' Poirot asked her.

'I . . . I'm not sure what you mean. We must all put

22

others before ourselves. I don't pretend to be more selfless than most, and I'm far from brave. I'm a terrible coward, in fact. Coming here to talk to you took all my courage. My sister Lenore—she's the brave one. I'm sure you are brave, M. Poirot. Wouldn't you save every life that you could, every single one?'

Poirot frowned. It was a peculiar question. The conversation so far had been unusual—even for what Poirot was calling in his mind 'the new age of Barnabas Pandy'.

'I have heard of your work and I admire you greatly,' said Annabel Treadway. 'That is why your letter pained me so. M. Poirot, you are quite wrong in your suspicions. You say you have proof against me, but I don't see how that is possible. I have committed no crime.'

'And I have sent you no letter,' Poirot told her. 'I did not accuse you—I *do* not accuse you—of the murder of Barnabas Pandy.'

Annabel Treadway blinked at Poirot in astonishment. 'But . . . I don't understand.'

'The letter you received was not written by the true Hercule Poirot. I too am innocent! An impersonator has sent these accusations, each one with my name signed at the bottom.'

'Each . . . each one? Do you mean—?'

'*Oui*. You are the third person in two days to say this very thing to me: that I have written to you and accused you of murdering a Barnabas Pandy. Yesterday it was Madame Sylvia Rule and Monsieur John McCrodden. Today it is you.' Poirot watched her closely to see if the names of her fellow accusees had any noticeable effect. There was none that he could see.

'So you didn't . . .' Her mouth moved for a while after she stopped speaking. Eventually she said, 'So you don't think I'm a killer?'

'That is correct. At the present moment, I have no reason to believe you have murdered anybody. Now, if you were the only person to come to me as you have and talk about this letter of accusation, I might wonder . . .' Deciding against sharing any more of his thoughts, Poirot smiled and said, 'It is a cruel joke that this trickster, whomever he is, has played upon us both, mademoiselle. The names Sylvia Rule and John McCrodden are not known to you?'

'I have never heard of either of them,' said Annabel Treadway. 'And jokes are supposed to be funny. This is not funny. It's appalling. Who would do it? I'm not important, but to do such a thing to a person of your reputation is shocking, M. Poirot.'

'To me you are extremely important,' he told her. 'You alone, of the three people to receive this letter, have listened. You alone believe Hercule Poirot when he says that he wrote and sent no such accusation. You do not make me feel I must be going mad, as the other two did. For that I am profoundly grateful.'

An oppressive air of sorrow still lingered in the room. If Poirot could only bring a smile to Annabel Treadway's face . . . Ah, but that was a dangerous way to think. Allow a person to affect your emotions and your judgement suffered, always. Reminding himself that Miss Treadway might, despite seeming forlorn, nevertheless have murdered a man named Barnabas Pandy, Poirot continued with less effusiveness: 'Madame Rule and Monsieur McCrodden, they did not believe Poirot. They did not listen.'

'They surely didn't accuse you of lying?'

'Unfortunately, they did.'

'But you're Hercule Poirot!'

'An undeniable truth,' Poirot agreed. 'May I ask, have you brought the letter with you?'

'No. I destroyed it at once, I'm afraid. I . . . I couldn't bear for it to exist.'

'*Dommage*. I should have liked to see it. *Eh bien*, mademoiselle, let us take the next step in our investigation. Who should want to make mischief in this particular way—for you, for me, and for Madame Rule and Monsieur McCrodden? Four people who do not know this Barnabas Pandy, if he exists at all, which, for all we know—'

'Oh!' Annabel Treadway gasped.

'What is the matter?' Poirot asked her. 'Tell me. Do not be afraid.'

She looked terrified. 'It's not true,' she whispered.

'What is not true?'

'He does exist.'

'Monsieur Pandy? Barnabas Pandy?'

'Yes. Well, he *did* exist. He's dead, you see. Not murdered, though. He fell asleep and . . . I thought . . . it was not my intention to deceive you, M. Poirot. I should have made it clear straight away . . . I simply thought . . .' Her eyes moved quickly from one part of the room

25

to another. There was, Poirot sensed, great chaos in her mind at that moment.

'You have not deceived me,' he assured her. 'Madame Rule and Monsieur McCrodden were adamant that they knew no one by the name of Barnabas Pandy, and neither do I. I made the assumption that the same must be true of you. Now, please tell me all that you know about Monsieur Pandy. He is dead, you say?'

'Yes. He died in December of last year. Three months ago.'

'And you say it was not murder—which means you know how he died?'

'Of course I do. I was there. We lived together in the same house.'

'You . . . you lived together?' This Poirot had not been expecting.

'Yes, since I was seven years old,' she said. 'Barnabas Pandy was my grandfather.'

'He was more like a parent to me than a grandparent,' Annabel Treadway told Poirot, once he had succeeded in convincing her that he was not angry with her for misleading him. 'My mother and father died when I was seven, and Grandy—that's what I called him—took us in, Lenore and me. Lenore has also been like a parent to me, in a way. I don't know what I'd do without her. Grandy was terribly old. It's sad when they leave us, of course, but old people do die, don't they? Naturally, when it's their time.'

The contrast between her matter-of-fact tone and the air

of sadness that seemed to cling to her led Poirot to conclude that, whatever was making her unhappy, it was not her grandfather's death.

Then her manner changed. There was a flash of something in her eyes as she said fiercely, 'People mind so much less when old people die, which is dreadfully unfair! "He had a good innings," they say, as if that makes it tolerable, whereas when a child dies everyone knows it's the worst kind of tragedy. I believe every death is a tragedy! Don't *you* think it's unfair, M. Poirot?'

The word 'tragedy' seemed to echo in the air. If Poirot had been ordered to pick one word to describe the essence of the woman before him, he would have chosen that one. It was almost a relief to hear it spoken aloud.

When he didn't immediately answer her question, Annabel Treadway blushed and said, 'When I spoke of old people dying and nobody caring as much as . . . well, I didn't mean . . . I was talking about really *very* old people. Grandy was ninety-four, which I'm sure is *much* older than . . . I hope I have caused no offence.'

Thus, reflected Poirot, did some reassurances cause greater alarm than the original remark upon which they sought to improve. Somewhat dishonestly, he told Annabel Treadway that he was not offended. 'How did you destroy the letter?' he asked her.

She looked down at her knees.

'You would prefer not to tell me?'

'Being accused of murder—not by you, but definitely by somebody—makes one a little nervous of revealing anything.'

'I understand. All the same, I should like to know how you disposed of it.'

She frowned. '*Alors!*' thought Poirot to himself as the crease between her eyebrows deepened. That was one mystery solved at least. Frowning was a habit of hers and had been for many years. The groove in her forehead was the proof.

'You'll think me silly and superstitious if I tell you,' she said, raising her handkerchief to just below her nose. She was not crying, but perhaps expected to be soon. 'I took a pen and scored thick black lines through every word, so that nothing of what was written remained visible. I did it to your name too, M. Poirot. Every single word! Then I tore it up and burned the pieces.'

'Three distinct methods of obliteration.' Poirot smiled. 'I am impressed. Madame Rule and Monsieur McCrodden, they were less thorough than you, mademoiselle. There is something else I should like to ask you. I sense you are unhappy, and perhaps afraid?'

'I have nothing to be afraid of,' she said quickly. 'I've told you, I'm innocent. Oh, if only it were Lenore or Ivy accusing me, I would know how to convince them. I would simply say, "I swear on Hoppy's life," and they would know I was telling the truth. They already know, of course, that I did not kill Grandy.'

'Who is Hoppy?' asked Poirot.

'Hopscotch. My dog. He's the most darling creature. I would never swear on his life and then lie. You would love him, M. Poirot. It's impossible not to love him.' For the first time since arriving, Annabel Treadway smiled, and the thick layer of sadness in the room's atmosphere lifted a little. 'I must get back to him. You'll think me foolish, but I miss him dreadfully. And I'm not afraid—truly. If the person who sent the letter wasn't willing to put his name to it, then it's not a serious accusation, is it? It's a silly trick, that's all it is, and I'm very glad to be able to see you and straighten it out. Now, I must go.'

'Please, mademoiselle, do not leave yet. I would like to ask you more questions.'

'But I must get back to Hoppy,' Annabel Treadway insisted, rising to her feet. 'He needs . . . and none of them can . . . When I'm not there, he . . . I'm so sorry. I hope whoever sent those letters causes you no further trouble. Thank you for seeing me. Good day, M. Poirot.'

'Good day, mademoiselle,' Poirot said to a room that was suddenly empty apart from himself and a lingering feeling of desolation.

CHAPTER 4

The Odd One Out?

The next morning felt peculiar to Hercule Poirot. By ten o'clock, no stranger had telephoned. Nobody had appeared at Whitehaven Mansions to accuse him of accusing them of the murder of Barnabas Pandy. He waited in until forty minutes after eleven (one never knew when a faulty alarm clock might cause an accusee to oversleep), then set off across town to Pleasant's Coffee House.

Unofficially in charge at Pleasant's was a young waitress by the name of Euphemia Spring. Everyone called her Fee for short. Poirot liked her enormously. She said the most unexpected things. Her flyaway hair defied gravity by refusing to lie flat against her head, though there was nothing floaty or flighty about her mind, which was always sharply in focus. She made the finest coffee in London, then did all she could to discourage customers from drinking it. Tea, she was fond of proclaiming, was a far superior beverage and beneficial to health, whereas coffee apparently led to sleepless nights and ruination of every sort.

Poirot continued to drink Fee's excellent coffee in spite of her warnings and entreaties, and had noticed that on many subjects (other than the aforementioned) she had much wisdom to impart. One of her areas of expertise was Poirot's friend and occasional helper Inspector Edward Catchpool—which was why he was here.

The coffee house was starting to fill with people. Moisture dripped down the insides of the windows. Fee was serving a gentleman on the other side of the room when Poirot walked in, but she waved at him with her left hand: an eloquent gesture that told him precisely where to sit and wait for her.

Poirot sat. He straightened the cutlery on the table in front of him as he always did, and tried not to look at the teapot collection that filled the high shelves on the walls. He found the sight of them unbearable: all angled differently and apparently at random. There was no logic to it. To be someone who cared about teapots, enough to collect so many, and yet not to see the need to point all the spouts in the same direction . . . Poirot had long suspected Fee of creating a deliberately haphazard arrangement solely to cause him distress. He had once, when the teapots were lined up in a more conventional fashion, remarked that one was positioned incorrectly. Each time he had come to Pleasant's since that day, there had been no pattern at all. Fee Spring did not respond well to criticism.

She appeared by his side and slammed a plate down between his knife and fork. There was a slice of cake on it, one Poirot had not ordered. 'I'll be needing your help,' she said, before he could ask her about Catchpool, 'but you'll have to eat up first.'

It was her famous Church Window Cake, so called because each slice comprised two yellow and two pink squares that were supposed to resemble the stained glass of a church window. Poirot found the name bothersome. Church windows were coloured, yes, but they were also transparent and made of glass. One might as well call it 'Chess Board Cake'—that was what it brought to Poirot's mind when he saw it: a chess board, albeit too small and in the wrong colours.

'I telephoned to Scotland Yard this morning,' he told Fee. 'They say that Catchpool is at the seaside on holiday, with his mother. This did not sound to me likely.'

'Eat,' said Fee.

'*Oui, mais*—'

'But you want to know where Edward is. Why? Has something happened?' She had started, in recent months, to refer to Catchpool as 'Edward', though never when he was present, Poirot noticed.

'Do you know where he is?' Poirot asked her.

'Might do.' Fee grinned. 'I'll gladly tell all's I know, once you've said you'll help me. Now, eat.'

Poirot sighed. 'How will it help you if I eat a slice of your cake?'

Fee sat down beside him and rested both her elbows on the table. 'It's not my cake,' she whispered, as if talking about something shameful. 'Looks the same, tastes the same, but it isn't *mine*. That's the problem.'

'I do not understand.'

'Were you ever served by a girl here, name of Philippa—all bones, teeth like a horse?'

'*Non.* She does not sound familiar.'

'She wasn't here long. I caught her pilfering food and had to have words. Not that she didn't need feeding up, but I wasn't having her taking food from plates of those who'd paid fair and square. I told her she was welcome to leftovers, but that weren't good enough for her. Didn't like being spoken to like a thief—thieves never do—and so she never came back after. Well, now she's at the new coffee house, Kemble's, near the wine merchants' place on Oxford Street. They can keep her and good luck to 'em—but then customers start telling me she's making *my* cake. I didn't believe 'em at first. How could she know the recipe? Passed down from my great-granny, it were, to my granny, then my ma, then to me. I'd cut out my own tongue before I'd tell it to anyone outside the family, and I haven't, to no one—certainly not to *her*. I've not written it down. Only way she could know's if she's secretly watched me making it . . . and when I thought carefully, I thought, yes, she might've. She'd have only needed to do it once if she'd paid attention, and I can't swear she didn't. All that time, the two of us together in a tiny kitchen . . .'

Fee pointed an accusatory finger, as if the kitchen of Pleasant's were to blame. 'Easy enough to look like she's busy with somethin' else. And she was a proper little sneak-about. Anyhow, I had to go and try it, didn't I? And I think they're right, those who've told me she's making my cake.

I think they're dead right!' Her eyes blazed with indignation.

'What would you like me to do, mademoiselle?'

'Haven't I said? Haven't I been saying? Eat that and tell me if I'm right or wrong. That's hers, not mine. I shoved it in a coat pocket when she wasn't looking. She never even knew I was in her coffee house, that's how careful I was. I went in disguise—wore a proper costume!'

Poirot did not wish to eat a slice of cake that had been in anybody's pocket. 'I have not sampled your Church Window Cake for many months,' he told Fee. 'My memory of it is not strong enough to judge. Besides, one does not remember taste accurately—it is impossible.'

'D'you think I don't know that?' said Fee impatiently. 'I'll give you a slice of mine next, won't I? I'll get it right now.' She stood up. 'Have a little bite of one, then the other. Then do it again, a little bite from each. Tell me if they couldn't all come from the same slice.'

'If I do this, you will tell me where is Catchpool?'

'No.'

'No?'

'I said I'd tell you where Edward is if you'll help me.'

'And I have agreed to taste—'

'The tasting's not the helping,' Fee said firmly. 'That'll come after.'

Hercule Poirot rarely allowed himself to be bent to the will of others, but to resist Fee Spring was a fool's enterprise. He waited until she returned with another slice of Church Window Cake that looked identical to the first and then, obediently, sampled both. To be certain, he tasted three pieces from each one.

Fee watched him closely. Finally she could control herself no longer and demanded, 'Well? Is it the same or not?'

'I can taste no difference,' Poirot told her. 'None at all. But, mademoiselle, I am afraid that there is no statute that prevents one person from making the same cake as another, if she has observed with her own eyes—'

'Oh, I'm not after using the law against her. All's I want to know is if she thinks she's stolen from me or not.'

'I see,' said Poirot. 'You are interested not in the legal offence but in the moral one.'

'I want you to go to her coffee house, order her cake, and then ask her about it. Ask where she got the recipe.'

'What if she says, "It is the one used by Fee Spring of Pleasant's"?'

'Then I'll go see her myself, and tell her what she doesn't know: that the Spring family recipe's not to be used by anyone else. If it's an honest mistake, that's how I'll treat it.'

'And what will you do if she answers more evasively?' Poirot asked. 'Or if she says boldly that she got the recipe for her cake from somewhere else, and you do not believe her?'

Fee smiled and narrowed her eyes. 'Oh, I'll soon have her regretting it,' she said, then quickly added, 'Not in a way as'd make you wish you hadn't helped me, mind.'

'I am glad to hear that, mademoiselle. If you will allow Poirot to offer you a piece of wise advice: the pursuit of revenge is rarely a good idea.'

'Neither's sitting around twiddling your thumbs when folks have made off with what's rightfully yours,' said Fee decisively. 'What I want from you's the help I've asked for, not advice I didn't asked for.'

'*Je comprends*,' said Poirot.

'Good.'

'Please. Where is Catchpool?'

Fee grinned. 'At the seaside with his ma, just like Scotland Yard said.'

Poirot's face assumed a stern look. 'I see that I have been tricked,' he said.

'Hardly! You didn't believe it when they told you. Now I'm telling you it's true, so's you know. That's where he is. Great Yarmouth, out east.'

'As I said before . . . this does not sound likely.'

'He didn't want to go but he had to, to get the old girl to leave him be. She'd found another perfect wife for him.'

'Ah!' Poirot was familiar with Catchpool's mother's ambition to see her son settled with a nice young lady.

'And this one had so much going in her favour—a right looker, Edward said she was, and from a respectable family. Kind, too, and cultivated. He found it harder than usual to say no.'

'To his mother? Or did the *jolie femme* make to him the proposal of marriage?'

Fee laughed. 'No—it was his ma's notion and that was all. It knocked the stuffing out of the old girl when he said he wasn't interested. She must've thought, "If he won't be persuaded, even for this one . . ." Edward decided he had

36

to do something to lift her spirits, and she loves Great Yarmouth, so that's where they are.'

'It is February,' said Poirot crossly. 'To go to an English seaside resort in February is to invite misery, is it not?' What a dismal time Catchpool must be having, he thought. He ought to return to London at once so that Poirot could discuss with him the matter of Barnabas Pandy.

'Excuse me, M. Poirot? M. Hercule Poirot?' A tentative voice interrupted his thoughts. He turned to find a smartly attired man beaming at him as if suffused with the greatest joy.

'Hercule Poirot, *c'est moi*,' he confirmed.

The man extended his hand. 'How delightful to meet you,' he said. 'Your reputation is formidable. It's hard to judge what one ought to say to such a great man. I'm Dockerill—Hugo Dockerill.'

Fee eyed the new arrival suspiciously. 'I'll leave you to it, then,' she said. 'Don't forget you've promised to help me,' she warned Poirot before leaving the table. He assured her that he would not forget, then invited the smiling man to sit.

Hugo Dockerill was almost completely bald, though not yet fifty, Poirot guessed.

'I'm terribly sorry to accost you in this manner,' Dockerill said, sounding jolly and not at all regretful. 'Your valet told me I might find you here. He encouraged me to make an appointment for later this afternoon, but I'm awfully anxious to clear up the misunderstanding. So I told him I'd rather seek you out sooner, and when I explained to him what it was all about, he seemed to think that you might want to see *me* rather urgently—so here I am!' He guffawed loudly, as if he'd told a hilarious anecdote.

'Misunderstanding?' Poirot said. He was starting to wonder if perhaps a fourth letter . . . but no, how could that be? Would any person, even the most enthusiastic and optimistic, beam with delight in such circumstances?

'Yes. I received your letter two days ago, and . . . well, I'm sure the fault is entirely mine and I'd hate you to think I'm levelling any sort of criticism at you—I'm absolutely not,' Hugo Dockerill chattered on. 'In fact, I'm a keen admirer of your work, from what I've heard of it, but . . . well, I must have unwittingly done something that's given you the wrong idea. For that, I apologize. I do sometimes get into a bit of a muddle. You'd only need to ask my wife Jane—she'd tell you. I planned to track you down at once, after I got your letter, but I misplaced it almost immediately—'

'Monsieur,' said Poirot sternly. 'To which letter are you referring?'

'The one about . . . well, about old Barnabas Pandy,' said Hugo Dockerill, beaming with renewed vitality now that the crucial name had been uttered. 'I wouldn't normally dare to suggest that the amazing Hercule Poirot might be wrong about something, but on this occasion . . . I'm afraid it wasn't me. I thought that . . . well, if you could tell me what has led you to believe it was, maybe between us we could get this funny mess ironed out. As I say, I'm sure the misunderstanding is entirely my fault.'

'You say it was not you, monsieur. What was not you?'

'The person who murdered Barnabas Pandy,' said Hugo Dockerill.

Having declared himself innocent of murder, Hugo Dockerill picked up an unused fork from the place setting opposite Poirot and helped himself to a chunk of Fee Spring's Church Window Cake. Or perhaps it was Philippa the pilferer's slice; Poirot could no longer remember which was which.

'You don't mind, do you?' Dockerill said. 'Shame for it to go to waste. Don't tell my wife! She's always complaining I've got the table manners of a guttersnipe. But we boys are a bit more robust when it comes to filling our bellies, eh?'

Poirot, aghast that anyone would find a half-eaten slice of cake tempting, made a tactfully non-specific noise. He permitted himself to reflect, briefly, upon similarity and difference. When many people do or say precisely the same thing, the effect is the opposite of what one might expect. Now two women and two men had come forward to communicate the same message: that they had received a letter signed in the name of Hercule Poirot and accusing them of the murder of Barnabas Pandy. Instead of pondering the similarities between these four encounters, Poirot found himself intrigued by the differences. He was now firmly of the view that if you wanted to see clearly how one person's character diverged from that of another, the most efficient method was to place both in identical situations.

Sylvia Rule was egotistical and full of proud rage. Like

John McCrodden, she was in the grip of a powerful obsession with a particular person. Both believed Poirot must have done the bidding of that person in writing the letters, be it Rowland 'Rope' McCrodden or the mysterious Eustace. John McCrodden's anger, Poirot thought, was equal to Sylvia Rule's but different: less explosive, more enduring. He would not forget, whereas she might if a new and more pressing drama occurred.

Of the four, Annabel Treadway was the hardest to fathom. She had not been angry at all, but she was withholding something. And afflicted, somehow.

Hugo Dockerill was the first and only letter-recipient to remain cheerful in the face of his predicament, and certainly the first to demonstrate a belief that all the world's problems could be solved if only decent people sat down at a table together and set things straight. If he objected to being accused of murder, he concealed it well. He was still doing his best to split his face across the middle with a radiant smile, and muttering, between mouthfuls of Church Window Cake, about how sorry he was if anything he'd done had created the impression that he might be a killer.

'Do not keep apologizing,' Poirot told him. 'You spoke of "old Barnabas Pandy" a moment ago. Why did you refer to him in that way?'

'Well, he was on his way to being a hundred years old when he died, wasn't he?'

'So you knew Monsieur Pandy?'

'I had never met him, but I knew about him, of course— because of Timothy.'

'Who is Timothy?' asked Poirot. 'I should explain, monsieur, that the letter you received did not come from me. I knew nothing of a Barnabas Pandy until I was visited by three people who were all sent the same letter. And now a fourth: you. These letters were signed "Hercule Poirot" by a deceiver. A fraud! They did not come from me. I have accused nobody of the murder of Monsieur Pandy—who, I believe, died of natural causes.'

'Golly!' Hugo Dockerill's broad smile dipped a little as his eyes filled with confusion. 'What a rum do. Silly prank, was it?'

'Who is Timothy?' Poirot asked again.

'Timothy Lavington—he's old Pandy's great-grandson. I'm his housemaster at school. Turville. Pandy himself was a pupil there, as was Timothy's father—both Old Turvillians. As am I. Only difference is, I never left the place!' Dockerill chortled.

'I see. So you are acquainted with Timothy Lavington's family?'

'Yes. But, as I say, I never met old Pandy.'

'When did Barnabas Pandy die?'

'I couldn't tell you the exact date. It was late last year, I think. November or December.' This matched what Annabel Treadway had said.

'In your capacity as housemaster, you were told, I assume, that the great-grandfather of one of your charges was deceased?'

'Yes, I was. We were all a bit glum about it. Still, the old boy lived to a ripe old age. We should all be so lucky!'

The joyous smile was back in place. 'And if one has to go, I suppose there are worse ways than drowning.'

'Drowning?'

'Yes. Poor old Pandy fell asleep in his bath and sank down under the water. Drowned. Horrible accident. There was never any talk of it being anything else.'

Annabel Treadway had spoken of her grandfather falling asleep. Poirot had assumed this meant he had died naturally in the night. She had said nothing about a bath or drowning. Had she deliberately withheld that part of the story?

'This was what you believed until you received a letter signed in the name of Hercule Poirot—that Monsieur Pandy drowned in his bathtub, accidentally?'

'It's what everybody believes,' said Hugo Dockerill. 'There was an inquest that returned a verdict of accidental death. I remember hearing Jane, my wife, commiserating with young Timothy. I suppose the inquest must have got it wrong, what?'

'Do you have the letter with you?' Poirot asked him.

'No, I'm sorry, I don't. As I said, I mislaid it. I lost it twice, in fact. I found it the first time—that's how I had your address—but then it went astray again. I looked for the blasted thing before I set off for London, but couldn't lay my hands on it. I do hope one of our boys hasn't got his grubby mitts on it. I should hate for anybody to think I stand accused of murder—especially when, as it turns out, you have accused me of no such thing!'

'Do you and your wife have children?'

'Not yet. We're hoping to. Oh—I'm speaking as a

housemaster when I say "our boys". We've got seventy-five of the little blighters! My wife is a saint to put up with them, I always say, and *she* always says that they're no trouble at all, and if she's a saint then it's for putting up with *me*.' A predictable guffaw followed.

'Perhaps you could ask your wife to help you search the house?' said Poirot. 'So far, not one person has brought me their letter. It would be very helpful if I could see at least one.'

'Of course. I should have thought of that. Jane'll find it, I have no doubt. She's tremendous! She has a talent for finding things, though she denies it. She says to me, "You'd find all the same things I find, Hugo, if you'd only open your eyes and engage your brain." She's marvellous!'

'Do you know a woman by the name of Annabel Treadway, monsieur?'

Hugo's smile widened. 'Annabel! Of course. She's Timothy's aunt, and old Pandy's—what would it be? Let me think. Timothy's mother Lenore is Pandy's grand-daughter, so . . . yes, Annabel was his . . . erm . . . She's Lenore's sister, so . . . she was also Pandy's grand-daughter.'

Poirot suspected that Hugo Dockerill was one of the stupidest people he had ever met.

'Lenore is usually accompanied by both Annabel and her daughter Ivy—Timothy's sister—when she comes to Turville, so I've got to know Annabel rather well over the years. I'm afraid, M. Poirot, that *therein lies a tale*, as they say. I proposed to Annabel some years ago. Marriage, you know.

Quite head over heels, I was. Oh—I wasn't married to my wife at the time,' Dockerill clarified.

'I am glad to hear, monsieur, that you did not make a bigamous proposal.'

'What? Golly, no. I was a bachelor then. It was peculiar, actually. To this day I can't make sense of it. Annabel seemed thrilled when I asked her, and then, almost immediately, she burst into tears and refused me. Women are nothing if not changeable, as every man knows—apart from Jane. She's tremendously reliable. But still . . . saying no seemed to upset Annabel dreadfully—so much so, I suggested to her that changing her "no" to a "yes" might make her feel more chipper.'

'What was her reaction?'

'A firm "no", I'm afraid. Ah, well, these things have a way of working out for the best, don't they? Jane's so wonderful with our boys. Annabel assured me when she rejected me that she would have been *hopeless* with them. I don't know why she thought that, devoted to Timothy and Ivy as she is. And she truly is—like a second mother to them. I've wondered more than once if she was secretly afraid of having her own children—in case it weakened her motherly bond with her niece and nephew. Or maybe it was the sheer number of boys in my house that discouraged her. They are rather like a herd of beasts sometimes, and Annabel's a quiet creature. But then, as I say, she dotes on young Timothy, who's hardly the easiest of boys. He's given us a spot of trouble over the years.'

'What kind of trouble?' asked Poirot.

'Oh, nothing serious. I'm sure he'll shake out all right. Like a lot of Turville boys, he can be rather self-congratulatory when no such congratulations are in order. Sometimes carries on as if school rules don't apply to him. As if he's above them. Jane blames it on . . .' Hugo Dockerill broke off. 'Whoops!' he laughed. 'Mustn't be indiscreet.'

'Nothing you tell me will go any further,' Poirot assured him.

'I was only going to say that as far as his mother is concerned, nothing is ever Timothy's fault. Once when I felt I absolutely had to punish him for insubordination—Jane *insisted*—I got punished myself by Lenore Lavington. She didn't speak to me for nearly six months. Not one word!'

'Do you know a John McCrodden?' Poirot asked.

'No, I'm afraid not. Should I?'

'What about Sylvia Rule?'

'Yes, I know Sylvia.' Hugo beamed, happy to be able to answer in the affirmative.

Poirot was surprised. He had been wrong again. There was nothing he found more disconcerting. He had assumed that there were two pairs of two, he mused, like the two yellow squares and two pink squares in a slice of Church Window Cake: Sylvia Rule and John McCrodden, who did not know Barnabas Pandy and had never heard his name; and the other pair, the pair who had known Pandy or at least known of him, Annabel Treadway and Hugo Dockerill.

Incorrectly, Poirot had assumed these pairs would remain neatly separate, as distinct as the yellow squares and the pink squares of the cake. Now, however, things were messy: Hugo Dockerill knew Sylvia Rule.

'How do you know her?'

'Her son Freddie is a pupil at Turville. He's in the same year as Timothy Lavington.'

'How old are these two boys?'

'Twelve, I think. Both in the Second Form, at any rate, and both in my house. Very different boys. Goodness me, they couldn't be more different! Timothy's a popular, gregarious young fellow, always surrounded by a crowd of admirers. Poor Freddie is a loner. He doesn't seem to have any friends. Spends a lot of time helping Jane, in fact. She's tremendous. "No boy here will be lonely if I've got anything to do with it," she often says. Means it, too!'

Had Sylvia Rule lied about not knowing Pandy? Poirot wondered. Would a person necessarily know the name of their son's school acquaintance's great-grandfather, particularly when the surnames were different? Timothy's last name was Lavington, not Pandy.

'So Madame Rule has a son who is in the same house at school as the great-grandson of Barnabas Pandy,' Poirot muttered, more to himself than to Hugo Dockerill.

'Golly. Does she?'

'That is what we have established, monsieur.' Perhaps it was only family relationships that Hugo Dockerill struggled with. That and knowing where things were—things like important letters.

Dockerill's smile dimmed as he struggled to make sense of Poirot's announcement. 'A son who . . . the great-grandson of . . . Of course! Yes, she does. She does indeed!'

This meant, thought Poirot, that it was not so simple as two pink squares and two yellow; it was not a case of pairs. Three recipients of the letter could be linked to Barnabas Pandy most definitively, and one could not—at least, not *yet*.

Two questions interested Poirot: had Barnabas Pandy been murdered? And was John McCrodden the odd one out? Or was he also connected to the deceased Pandy in a manner that was not yet clear?

CHAPTER 5

A Letter with a Hole in it

I am producing this account of what Poirot later decided to call 'The Mystery of Three Quarters' on a typewriter that has a faulty letter 'e'. I don't know if anyone will publish it, but if you are reading a printed version, all of the 'e's will be flawless. It is nevertheless significant that in the original typescript there is (or should I say for the benefit of future readers, was?) a small white gap in the middle of the horizontal bar of each letter 'e'—an extraordinarily tiny hole in the black ink.

Why is this important? To answer that question immediately would be to rush ahead of my own narrative. Let me explain.

My name is Edward Catchpool and I'm an inspector with Scotland Yard. I'm also the person telling this story—not only now, but from the beginning, though I have been helped by several people to fill in those parts of the drama for which I was absent. I am especially grateful to the sharp eyes and the loquaciousness of Hercule Poirot, who, when it comes to detail, misses nothing. Thanks to him, I do not feel that I, in any meaningful sense, missed the events I have so far recounted, all of which occurred before I returned from Great Yarmouth.

The less said about my infuriatingly tedious stay at the seaside, the better. The only relevant point is that I was compelled to return to London sooner than planned (you can imagine my relief) by the arrival of two telegrams. One was from Hercule Poirot, who said he urgently needed my help, and could I come back at once? The other, impossible to ignore, was from my superintendent at Scotland Yard, Nathaniel Bewes. This second telegram, though not from Poirot, was about him. Apparently he was 'making life difficult', and Bewes wanted me to stop him.

I was touched by the Super's quite unjustifiable confidence in my ability to alter the behaviour of my Belgian friend, and so, once back in Bewes's office, I sat quietly and nodded sympathetically as he gave vent to his dismay. The essence of what was at stake seemed clear enough. Poirot believed the son of Rowland 'Rope' McCrodden to be guilty of murder, and had said so, and claimed to be able to prove it. The Super didn't like this one bit because Rowland Rope was a chum of his, and he wanted me to persuade Poirot to think otherwise.

Instead of paying attention to the Super's loud and varied expressions of disgust, I was busy rehearsing my answer. Should I say, 'There's no point in my talking to Poirot about this—if he's sure he's right then he won't listen to me'? No, that would make me sound both truculent and defeatist.

And, since Poirot wanted to talk to me as a matter of urgency, presumably about this very same business, I decided to promise the Super that I would do my best to make him see sense. Then, from Poirot, I would find out why he believed Rowland Rope's son was a murderer when apparently no one else did, and convey his thoughts back to the Super. All of this seemed manageable. I saw no need to upset the apple cart at work by pointing out that 'He's my friend's son' is neither proof of innocence nor a viable defence.

Nathaniel Bewes is a mild, even-tempered and fair-minded man—apart from in the immediate aftermath of something that has especially upset him. In those rare moments he is incapable of realizing that he is greatly distressed and that his emotional state might have skewed his perspective. Because his judgement is so often sound, he assumes it will always be, and is therefore liable to make the most absurd pronouncements—things which, in his usual calm frame of mind, he would be the first to call idiotic. Once restored to sanity after one of his episodes, he never refers to the period during which he emitted a series of ridiculous statements and directives, and, as far as I know, no one else ever refers to them either. I certainly don't. Though it sounds fanciful, I am not convinced that the normal Super is aware of the existence of his deranged counterpart who occasionally understudies for him.

I nodded judiciously as the understudy ranted and growled, striding up and down his small office, pushing his spectacles back up to the bridge of his nose as they slid down with disconcerting frequency.

'Rowly's son, a murderer? Preposterous! He's the son of Rowland McCrodden! If you were the son of a man like that, Catchpool, would you take up murder as a way of passing the time? Of course you wouldn't! Only a fool would! Besides, the death of Barnabas Pandy was an accident—I've availed myself of the official record of his passing and it's all there in black and white, plain as day: *accident!* The man drowned in his bath. Ninety-four, he was. I mean, I ask you—*ninety-four!* How much longer was he likely to live? Would you risk your neck to murder a ninety-four-year-old man, Catchpool? It beggars belief. No one would. Why would they?'

'Well—'

'There could be no reason,' Bewes concluded. 'Now, I don't know what your Belgian chum thinks he's up to, but you'd better make it clear to him in no uncertain terms that he is to write to Rowly McCrodden at once and convey his most profuse apologies.' Bewes had clearly forgotten that he too was on friendly terms with Poirot.

There were, of course, many reasons why someone might murder a nonagenarian: if he had threatened to expose their shameful secret to the world the very next day, for instance. And Bewes—the real Bewes, not his unbalanced *doppelgänger*—knew as well as I did that some murders are initially mistaken for accidents. To grow up as the son of a man famous for helping to dispatch miscreants to the gallows could, arguably, warp a person's psyche to the point where he might decide to kill.

I knew there was no point saying any of this to the Super

today, though in a different mood he would have made the same good points himself. I decided to risk only a minor challenge. 'Didn't you say Poirot sent this letter of accusation to Rowland Rope's son, not to Rowland Rope himself?'

'Well, what if he did?' Bewes rounded on me angrily. 'What difference does that make?'

'How old is John McCrodden?'

'How old? What the devil are you talking about? Does his age matter?'

'Is he a man or a young boy?' I continued patiently.

'Have you taken leave of your senses, Catchpool? John McCrodden is a grown man.'

'Then wouldn't it make more sense for me to ask Poirot to apologize to *John* McCrodden, not his father? Assuming he's mistaken and John McCrodden is innocent. I mean, if John is not a minor—'

'He used to be a miner, but not any more,' said Bewes. 'He worked in a mine somewhere up in the north-east.'

'Ah,' I said, knowing that my boss's ability to understand context would return sooner if I said as little as possible.

'But that, Catchpool, is beside the point. Poor Rowly's the one we need to worry about. John is blaming him for the whole mess. Poirot must write to Rowly immediately and grovel for all he's worth. This is a monstrous accusation—an outrageous slur! Please see to it that this happens, Catchpool.'

'I'll do my best, sir.'

'Good.'

'Can you tell me any more about the particulars of the

case, sir? I don't suppose Rowland Rope mentioned *why* Poirot has got hold of this idea that—'

'How the devil should I know why, Catchpool? Man must have lost his grip on his faculties—that's the only explanation I can think of. You can read the letter for yourself, if you like!'

'Do you have it?'

'John tore it into pieces, which he sent to Rowly with a note of accusation of his own. Rowly taped the pieces together and passed the letter on to me. I don't know why John thinks Rowly's behind it. Rowly plays a straight bat. Always has. His son, of all people, should know that. If Rowly had something to say to John, he'd say it himself.'

'I'd like to see the letter if I may, sir.'

Bewes walked over to his desk, opened one of the drawers and grimaced as he pulled out the offending item. He handed it to me. 'It's the purest nonsense!' he said, in case I was unsure of his opinion of the matter. 'Malicious rubbish!'

'But Poirot is never malicious,' I nearly said; I stopped myself just in time.

I read the letter. It was brief: only one paragraph. Nevertheless, given what it sought to communicate, it could have been half the length. In a muddled and artless way, it accused John McCrodden of the murder of Barnabas Pandy and claimed that there was proof to vindicate the accusation. If McCrodden did not immediately confess to this murder, then this proof would be turned over to the police.

My gaze settled upon the signature at the bottom of the

letter. In a sloping hand was written the name '*Hercule Poirot*'.

It would have been useful if I could have recalled my friend's signature, but I could not, despite having seen it once or twice. Perhaps whoever had sent the letter had meticulously copied Poirot's handwriting. What they had not done was manage to sound at all like the man they hoped to impersonate, nor to write the sort of letter he might have written.

If Poirot believed that John McCrodden had murdered this Barnabas Pandy fellow and successfully passed his death off as an accident, he would have visited McCrodden accompanied by the police. He wouldn't have sent this letter and allowed McCrodden the chance to escape or to take his own life before Hercule Poirot had looked him in the eye and explained to him the chain of errors that had led to his unmasking. And the nasty, insinuating tone . . . No, it was impossible. There was no doubt in my mind.

I had not had time to work out what effect my revelation would have upon the Super, but I felt I must tell him at once: 'Sir, the situation seems not to be exactly what I . . . or what you . . . That is to say, I'm not sure that an apology from Poirot . . .' I was making a hash of it.

'What are you trying to say, Catchpool?'

'The letter is a fake, sir,' I said. 'I don't know who wrote it, but I can tell you for certain that it was not Hercule Poirot.'

CHAPTER 6

Rowland Rope

The Super's instructions were clear: I was to find Poirot at once and ask him to accompany me to the offices of Rowland Rope's firm of solicitors, Donaldson & McCrodden. Once there, we were to explain that the letter sent to John McCrodden had not been written by Poirot, and to apologize fulsomely for the distress caused by neither one of us.

Having already wasted too many days in Great Yarmouth, I had urgent work to catch up with and was displeased to have this task assigned to me. Surely a telephone call from Bewes to Rowland Rope would have sufficed? The two were great friends, after all. But no, the Super had insisted that McCrodden Senior was a more than usually cautious man who would require an assurance from Poirot that he had not written the offending letter. Bewes wanted me to be present so that I could report back to him that the matter had been satisfactorily dealt with.

'This should all be straightened out within an hour or

two,' I thought to myself as I set off for Whitehaven Mansions. Alas, Poirot was not at home. His valet told me he was likely to be *en route* to Scotland Yard. He was apparently as keen to locate me as I was to find him.

I made my way back to Scotland Yard and discovered that Poirot had been there, asking for me, and even waited a short while, but was now gone. There was no sign of Superintendent Bewes either, so I could not ask him how I ought to proceed. I tried Pleasant's Coffee House, but Poirot was not there either. In the end, exasperated, I decided to visit Rowland McCrodden's offices alone. I reasoned that he would prefer to know as soon as possible that his son did not stand accused of murder by Hercule Poirot; the word of a Scotland Yard inspector ought to be enough even for Rowland Rope.

Donaldson & McCrodden Solicitors occupied the top two floors of a tall stucco-fronted terrace on Henrietta Street, next to the Covent Garden Hotel. I was greeted by a smiling young woman with a pink face and dark brown hair cut into a short and severely geometrical style. She wore a white blouse and checked skirt that brought to mind a picnic blanket.

She introduced herself as Miss Mason before asking me a series of questions that prevented me from stating the nature of my business as easily as I might have if I had simply been asked 'How may I help you?' Instead, an absurd amount of time was wasted by her 'And if I might enquire as to your name, sir?', 'And if I might ask to whom you wish to speak, sir?', 'And might I enquire as to whether you have an appointment, sir?', 'And are you able to divulge the purpose of your visit?' Her method of enquiry ensured that I was only able to utter two words at a time, and all the while she stared with undisguised prurience at the envelope in my hand, which was the letter sent by somebody to John McCrodden, accusing him of murder.

By the time Miss Mason led me along a narrow corridor lined on both sides with leather-bound books about the law, I was tempted to run in the opposite direction rather than follow her anywhere. I noticed—no one could fail to—that she did not so much walk as forward-bounce, on two of the tiniest feet I have ever observed.

We reached a black-painted door with the name 'Rowland McCrodden' painted on it in white. Miss Mason knocked and a deep voice said, 'Come!' We entered, and were met by a man with curly grey hair, a vast expanse of forehead that seemed to occupy an unreasonable amount of his face, and small beady black eyes that were closer to his chin than eyes should be.

Since McCrodden had agreed to see me, I was expecting to be able to commence our conversation at once, but I had not accounted for Miss Mason's capability to hinder progress. There ensued a frustrating attempt to persuade McCrodden to allow her to enter my name in his appointments diary. 'What would be the point of that?' asked McCrodden with obvious impatience. He had a thin, reedy voice that brought to mind a woodwind instrument. 'Inspector Catchpool is already here.'

'But, sir, the rule is that no one can be admitted without an appointment.'

'Inspector Catchpool has already been admitted, Miss Mason. There he is—*you* admitted him!'

'Sir, if you're meeting Inspector Catchpool, shouldn't I make an appointment for, well, *now*, and record it in—?'

'No,' Rowland McCrodden cut her off mid-question. 'Thank you, Miss Mason, that will be all. Please be seated, Inspector—' He broke off, blinked several times, then said, 'What is it, Miss Mason?'

'I was only going to ask, sir, if Inspector Catchpool might wish to partake of some tea. Or coffee. Or perhaps a glass of water? Or if, indeed, *you* might wish to—'

'Not for me,' said McCrodden. 'Inspector?'

I could not immediately produce an answer. A cup of tea was exactly what I wanted, but it would necessitate the return of Miss Mason.

'Why don't you have a little think, Inspector Catchpool, and I'll come back in a few moments and—'

'I'm sure the inspector can make up his mind,' said McCrodden briskly.

'Nothing for me, thank you,' I said with a smile.

Finally, mercifully, Miss Mason withdrew. I was determined to waste no more time, so I pulled the letter out of the envelope, laid it on McCrodden's desk and told him that there was no question of it having come from Hercule Poirot. McCrodden asked how I could be sure of this, and I explained that both the tone and the message left me in no doubt.

'So, if Poirot did not write the letter, who did?' asked McCrodden.

'I'm afraid I don't know.'

'Does Poirot know?'

'I have not yet had the chance to speak to him.'

'And why did they pretend to be Hercule Poirot?'

'I don't know.'

'Then your general bearing, if I may say so, is erroneous.'

'I'm not sure I understand what you mean,' I confessed.

'You said you were here to clear something up, and your manner suggests that you now believe it to be cleared up: Hercule Poirot has not accused my son of murder, therefore I have nothing to worry about. Is that your opinion?'

'Well . . .' I cast about for the correct answer. 'I can see that it's an upsetting thing to happen, but if the accusation was some sort of prank, then I wouldn't concern myself unduly, if I were you.'

'I disagree. I am, if anything, more disturbed now.' McCrodden stood up and walked over to the window. He looked down at the street below for a moment before moving two steps to the right and staring at the wall. 'When I thought it was Poirot, I was confident of a proper resolution. He would eventually admit his error, I thought. I have heard that he is proud, but also honourable and, most importantly of all, amenable to reason. He treats character as if it were a concrete fact, I'm told. Is this true?'

'He certainly believes knowledge of character is essential to the solving of crime,' I said. 'Without knowing the motive, you can't solve anything, and without understanding character, motive is unknowable. I have also heard him say that no man can act in a way that is contrary to his own nature.'

'Then I would have been able to convince him that John could never commit a murder—to do so would be at odds with his principles. The idea is laughable. Now, however, I learn that Hercule Poirot is not the one I need to convince, for he did not write the letter. Furthermore, I am able to draw the inescapable conclusion that the letter's true author is a liar and a fraudster. That sort of person might stop at nothing in his quest to destroy my son.'

McCrodden returned quickly to his chair as if the wall at which he had been staring had silently instructed him to do so. 'I must know who wrote and sent the letter,' he said. 'It is imperative, if I'm to ensure John's safety. I should like to engage the services of Hercule Poirot. Do you think he would agree to investigate for me?'

'He might, but . . . it's not at all certain that the letter-writer believes what he claims to believe. What if it's no more than a horribly misjudged joke? This might be the end of it. If your son receives no further communications—'

'You are naïve in the extreme if you think that,' said McCrodden. He picked up the letter and threw it at me. It landed on the floor at my feet. 'When someone sends something like that, they mean you harm. You ignore them at your peril.'

'My superintendent tells me the death of Barnabas Pandy was an accident,' I said. 'He drowned while taking a bath.'

'That is the story, yes. Officially, there is no suspicion that the death was a murder.'

'You sound as if you think it could have been,' I said.

'Once the possibility is raised, one has a duty to consider it,' said McCrodden.

'But the likelihood is that Pandy was not murdered, and you say your son could never commit a murder, so . . .'

'I see,' said McCrodden. 'You think I am guilty of wilful paternal blindness? No, it's not that. No one knows John better than I do. He has many faults, but he would not kill.'

He had misunderstood me; I had simply wanted to say that since no one was looking for a murderer in connection with Pandy's death, and since he knew his son was innocent, McCrodden really had nothing to worry about.

'You will have heard that I am a strong advocate of the death penalty. "Rowland Rope", they call me. I do not care for the name, and no one would dare say it in my presence. Now, if they were to call me "Rowland Just and Civilized Society For the Protection of the Innocent" . . . Unfortunately, that does not trip so easily off the tongue. I'm sure you agree, Inspector, that we must all be accountable for our actions. I don't need to tell you about Plato's Ring of Gyges. I discussed it with John many times. I did everything I could to instil proper values in him, but I failed. He is so passionately against the taking of human life that he doesn't support the death penalty even for the most depraved monsters. He contends that I am as much a murderer as the bloodthirsty reprobate who slits a throat in an alleyway for the sake of a few shillings. Murder is murder, he says. So you see, he would never allow himself to kill another person. It would make him look ludicrous in his own eyes, which would be intolerable to him.'

I nodded, though I was not convinced. My experience as a police inspector has taught me that many people are able to regard themselves with inordinate fondness, no matter what heinous crimes they have committed. They care only about how they look to others, and whether they can get away with it.

'And, as you say, no one apart from our nefarious letter-writer seems to think Pandy's death was unlawful,' McCrodden went on. 'He was an extremely wealthy man—owner of the Combingham Hall Estate and former owner of several slate mines in Wales. That's how he made his fortune.'

'Mines?' I recalled my conversation with the Super, and the minor/miner misunderstanding. 'Did your son John used to work in a mine?'

'Yes. In the north, near Guisborough.'

'Not in Wales, then?'

'Never in Wales. You can abandon that idea.'

I did my best to look as if I had abandoned it.

'Pandy was ninety-four when he drowned in his bath,' said McCrodden. 'He had been a widower for sixty-five years. He and his wife had one child, a daughter, who married and had two daughters of her own before dying, along with her husband, in a house fire. Pandy took in his two orphaned grandchildren, Lenore and Annabel, who have both lived at Combingham Hall ever since. Annabel, the youngest, is not married. The older sister, Lenore, married a man by the name of Cecil Lavington. They had two children, Ivy and Timothy, in that order. Cecil died of an infection four years ago. That's all I've managed to find out, and none of it is interesting or suggestive of what steps to take next. I hope Poirot can do better.'

'There might be nothing to find out,' I said. 'They might be a quite ordinary family, in which no murder has been committed.'

'There is plenty to find out,' McCrodden corrected me. 'Who is the letter-writer, and why did he or she fix upon my son? Until we know these things, those of us who have been accused remain implicated.'

'You have been accused of nothing,' I said.

'You would not say that if you saw the note John enclosed with the letter!' He pointed at the floor, where the letter still lay by my feet. 'He accused me of putting Poirot up to it, so that John would have no choice but to take up the law in order to defend himself.'

'Why would he think you might do that?'

'John believes I hate him. It could not be further from the truth. I have been critical of the way he conducts his affairs in the past, but only because I want him to prosper. He seems to wish the opposite for himself. He has squandered every opportunity I've created for him. One of the reasons I know he cannot have killed Barnabas Pandy is that he does not have the animus to spare. All of his ill will is directed towards me—erroneously.'

I made a polite noise that I hoped was expressive of sympathy.

'The sooner I can speak to Hercule Poirot, the better,' said McCrodden. 'I hope he will be able to get to the bottom of this unsavoury business. I long ago gave up hope of changing my son's mind about me, but I should like to prove, if I can, that I had nothing do to with that letter.'

CHAPTER 7

An Old Enemy

While I was in the offices of Donaldson & McCrodden on Henrietta Street, Poirot was also in the offices of a firm of solicitors: Fuller, Fuller & Vout, only a short distance away on Drury Lane. Needless to say, I did not know this at the time.

Frustrated by his inability to find me, my Belgian friend had set about discovering all he could about Barnabas Pandy and almost the first thing he found out was that Pandy had been represented in all matters of a legal nature by Peter Vout, the firm's senior partner.

Poirot, unlike me, had made an appointment—or rather his valet, George, had made one for him. He arrived punctually and was shown into Vout's office by a girl far less obtrusive than Rowland McCrodden's Miss Mason. He tried to conceal his shock when he saw the room in which the solicitor worked.

'Welcome, welcome,' said Vout, rising from his chair to shake his visitor's hand. He had an engaging smile and

65

snow-white hair that peaked and curled in random tufts. 'You must be Herc-*ule* Poir-*ot*—is that correct?'

'*C'est parfait*,' said Poirot approvingly. Rare indeed was the Englishman who could pronounce both the Christian name and the family name correctly. Was it appropriate, however, to feel admiration for any man who could work in conditions such as these? The room was an extraordinary sight. It was large, about twenty feet by fifteen, with a high ceiling. Pushed up against the wall on the right were Vout's large mahogany desk and green leather chair. In front of those stood two straight-backed armchairs in brown leather. In the right-hand third of the room there was also a bookcase, a lamp and a fireplace. On the mantelpiece above the fire there was an invitation to a dinner of the Law Society.

The other two thirds of the available space were occupied by scruffy cardboard boxes, piled high, one atop another, to form an enormous and uneven edifice that was breathtaking in its grotesqueness. It would have been impossible to walk around or through the boxes. Effectively, their presence reduced the size of the room to a degree that any sane person would have found intolerable. Many of the boxes were open, with things spilling out of them: yellowing papers, broken picture frames, old cloths with dirt stains on them. Beyond the gargantuan box-structure was a window at which hung strips of pale yellow material that could not hope to cover the glass in front of which they dangled.

'*C'est le cauchemar*,' Poirot murmured.

'I see you've spotted the curtains.' Vout sounded

apologetic. 'One could make this room more appealing to the eye if one replaced them. They're terribly old. I'd have one of the office girls pull them down, but, as you can see, no one can reach them.'

'Because of the boxes?'

'Well, my mother died three years ago. There's much to be sorted out, and I've yet to make inroads, I'm afraid. Not all the boxes are Mama's possessions, mind you. A lot of it is my own . . . paraphernalia.' He sounded quite happy with the situation. 'Please, do be seated, M. Poirot. How may I be of assistance?'

Poirot lowered himself into one of the available armchairs. 'You do not mind working in here, with . . . the paraphernalia?' he persisted.

'I see you're fascinated by it, M. Poirot. I expect you're one of those chaps who likes everything to be ship-shape at all times, are you?'

'Most assuredly I am, monsieur. I am inordinately fond of the shape of the ship. It is necessary for me to be in a tidy environment if I am to think clearly and productively. It is not so for you?'

'I'm not going to let a few old boxes bother me.' Vout chuckled. 'I don't notice them from one day to the next. I'll tackle them at some point. Until then . . . why let them worry me?'

With a small twitch of the eyebrows, Poirot moved on to the subject he had come to discuss. Vout expressed regret at the death of his dear old friend Barnabas Pandy, and regaled Poirot with all the same facts that Rowland

McCrodden was (perhaps at that very moment) relating to me: Welsh slate mines; Combingham Hall Estate; two grand-daughters, Lenore and Annabel; two great-grandchildren, Ivy and Timothy. Vout also offered a detail about Barnabas Pandy that was absent from Rowland Rope's account: he mentioned the faithful and long-serving Kingsbury. 'More like a younger brother to Barnabas, was Kingsbury. He felt like a member of the family more than a servant— though he was always most conscientious when it came to performing his tasks. Naturally, Barnabas made arrange-ments for him to be looked after. A bequest . . .'

'Ah yes, the will,' said Poirot. 'I would like to hear about it.'

'Well, I don't see what harm it would do to tell you. Barnabas wouldn't have minded, and his testamentary affairs were very simple—just what one would expect, in fact. But . . . might I ask why you're interested?'

'It has been suggested to me—indirectly—that Monsieur Pandy was murdered.'

'Oh, I see.' Vout laughed and rolled his eyes. 'Murder, eh? No, not a bit of it. Barnabas drowned. Fell asleep while in the tub, sank under the water and, sadly . . .' He left the obvious conclusion unstated.

'That is the official story. However, the possibility has been raised that the death was made to look like an acci-dent, when in fact it was deliberate.'

Vout was shaking his head emphatically. 'Tommyrot! Goodness me, someone's been rumour-mongering for all he's worth, eh? Or she—it's usually the ladies who like to gossip. We chaps are much too sensible to waste our time stirring up trouble.'

'You are certain, then, that Monsieur Pandy's death was accidental?' asked Poirot.

'Couldn't be more so.'

'How are you able to state this with such conviction? Were you present in the bathroom when he died?'

Vout looked affronted. 'Of course I wasn't in the bathroom with him! Wasn't there at all! Seventh of December, wasn't it? My wife and I were at my nephew's wedding that day, as it happens. In Coventry.'

Poirot smiled politely. 'I simply wished to suggest that if you were not in the room when he died, and not at Combingham Hall, then you are not in a position to say definitively that the death of Monsieur Pandy was accidental. If someone had crept into the bathroom and pushed him under the water . . . How would you know this had happened, or had not happened, if you were at a wedding in Coventry?'

'It's only that I know the family,' Vout said eventually, with a concerned frown. 'I'm a dear friend to them all, as they are to me. I know who was at the Hall when the tragedy occurred: Lenore, Annabel, Ivy and Kingsbury, and I can assure you that none of them would have raised a finger against Barnabas. The idea is unthinkable! I have witnessed their grief first-hand, M. Poirot.'

Poirot mouthed to himself the words '*C'est ca.*' His suspicion had been correct. Vout was one of those people who believed in things like murder, and evil, and all forms of serious unpleasantness only when they did not affect him personally. Were he to read in a newspaper that a maniac had chopped five members of the same family into small pieces, he would not question it. Suggest to him, though, that a man he regarded as a friend might have been murdered, and you would never succeed in persuading him that it was possible.

'Please tell me about Monsieur Pandy's will,' said Poirot.

'As I say, Kingsbury was left a tidy sum: enough to be comfortable for the remainder of his days. The house and estate are left in trust for Ivy and Timothy, on the under-standing that Lenore and Annabel may continue to live there for the rest of their lives. All the money and other assets, of which there are plenty, go to Lenore and Annabel. Each is now, in her own right, an extremely wealthy woman.'

'So an inheritance might provide a motive,' said Poirot.

Vout sighed impatiently. 'M. Poirot, please hear what I'm trying to tell you. There is simply no circumstance—'

'Yes, yes, I hear. Most people would assume that a man of ninety-four will die reasonably soon. But if someone needed money immediately . . . if to wait a year would have dire consequences for that person . . .'

'I tell you, you're barking up the wrong tree, man!' There was alarm in Vout's eyes and in his voice. 'They are a delightful family.'

'You are their good friend, monsieur,' Poirot reminded him gently.

'Quite! I am! Do you think I would continue a friendship with a family that contained a murderer? Barnabas was not murdered. I can prove it. He . . .' Vout stopped. A new pinkness suffused his cheeks.

'Anything you are able to tell me will be most helpful,' said Poirot.

Vout looked glum. Having said something he hadn't intended to say, he now lacked the gumption to find an ingenious way out of it.

'Well, I suppose it won't do any harm if I tell you.' He sighed. 'I can't help thinking Barnabas knew he was going to die. I saw him shortly before his death and . . . well, he seemed to know that his time was coming to an end.'

'What gave you this impression?'

'The last time I saw him, he struck me as a man from whose shoulders a great weight had been lifted. It was as if he was at peace. He smiled in a particular way, made certain oblique remarks about the need to set certain matters straight *now* before it was too late. I had the sense that he thought death was imminent, and it turned out to be so, sadly.'

'*Dommage*,' Poirot agreed. 'Still, it is better to meet the inevitable end with a peaceful spirit, is it not? Which matters did Monsieur Pandy wish to set straight?'

'Hmmph? Oh, there was a man who had been his . . . well, his *enemy* really, if the word doesn't sound fanciful. Vincent Lobb, the chap's name was. At our last meeting, Barnabas announced that he wished to send a letter to this fellow and suggest that the two of them might perhaps be reconciled.'

'A sudden urge to forgive an old enemy,' muttered Poirot.

71

'That is interesting. If someone wanted this making of peace not to take place . . . Was this letter to Monsieur Lobb ever sent?'

'It was,' said Vout. 'I told Barnabas I thought it was an excellent initiative, and he sent it off that very day. I don't know if he received a reply. It was really only a few days later that he . . . passed on. Very sad. Though he'd had a good innings at ninety-four! I suppose an answering letter might have arrived after his death, but I think Annabel or Lenore would have told me if it had.'

'What was the cause of the ill will between Messieurs Pandy and Lobb?' Poirot asked.

'I'm afraid I can't help you there. Barnabas never told me.'

'I should be grateful if you could tell me about the family,' said Poirot. 'Was it—is it—a happy household at Combingham Hall?'

'Oh, very happy. Very happy indeed. Lenore is a tower of strength. Both Annabel and Ivy admire her enormously. Annabel adores Lenore's children—and her beloved dog, of course. Hopscotch. He's a character! A big beast. Likes to leap up and lick you! Stubborn, mind you, but very affectionate. And as for young Timothy—that boy will go far. He is possessed of a shrewd mind and heaps of determination. I can see him being Prime Minister one day. Barnabas often said so. "That boy could be anything he set out to be," he often said. "Anything at all." Barnabas was devoted to them all, and they to him.'

'Truly you describe the perfect family,' said Poirot. 'Yet

no family is without its troubles. There must have been something that was less than perfect.'

'Well . . . I wouldn't say . . . I mean, obviously life is never without its infelicities, but for the most part . . . As I said before, M. Poirot: it is ladies who enjoy scurrilous gossip. Barnabas loved his family—and Kingsbury—and they loved him back. That is all I shall say. As there is no question of the death being anything but an accident, I see no reason to delve into a good man's private life and that of his family in search of unsavoury morsels.'

Seeing that Vout had resolved to disclose no more, Poirot thanked him for his help and left.

'But there is more to be disclosed,' he said to nobody in particular as he stood on the pavement of Drury Lane. 'Most certainly, there is more, and I shall find out what it is. Not one unsavoury morsel will escape from Hercule Poirot!'

CHAPTER 8

Poirot Issues Some Instructions

I found Poirot waiting for me in my office when I returned to Scotland Yard. He appeared to be lost in thought, muttering soundlessly to himself as I entered the room. He looked as dandified as ever, his remarkable moustaches appearing particularly well tended.

'Poirot! At last!'

Startled out of his reverie, he rose to his feet. '*Mon ami* Catchpool! Where have you been? There is a matter I wish to discuss with you that is causing me much consternation.'

'Let me guess,' I said. 'A letter, signed in your name although not written or sent by you, accusing Rowland McCrodden's son John of the murder of Barnabas Pandy.'

Poirot looked dumbfounded. '*Mon cher* . . . Somehow, you know. You will tell me how, I'm sure. Ah, but you say "letter", not "letters"! Does that mean you are unaware of the others?'

'Others?'

'*Oui, mon ami.* To Mrs Sylvia Rule, Miss Annabel Treadway and Mr Hugo Dockerill.'

Annabel? I knew that I had heard the name recently, but could not think where. Then I remembered: Rowland McCrodden had told me that one of Pandy's granddaughters was called Annabel.

'Quite correct,' said Poirot, when I asked. 'Miss Treadway is indeed the granddaughter of Monsieur Pandy.'

'Then who are the other two? What were their names again?'

'Sylvia Rule and Hugo Dockerill. They are two people— and Annabel Treadway is a third, and John McCrodden a fourth—who received letters signed in my name, accusing them of the murder of Barnabas Pandy. Most of these people have presented themselves at my home to berate me for having sent these letters that I did not send, and failed to pay attention when I explained that I did not send them! It has been enervating and discouraging, *mon ami*. And not one of them has been able to show me the letter they received.'

'I might be able to help on that front,' I told him.

His eyes widened. 'Do you have one of the letters? You do! You must, then, have the one sent to John McCrodden, since his was the name you mentioned. Ah! It is a pleasure to be in your office, Catchpool. There is no unsightly mountain of boxes!'

'Boxes? Why should there be?'

'There should not, my friend. But tell me, how can you have the letter that John McCrodden received? He told me he tore it into pieces and sent those pieces to his father.'

I explained about the Super's telegram and my meeting with Rowland Rope, trying to omit nothing that might be important. He nodded eagerly as I spoke.

When I had finished, he said, 'This is most fortuitous. Without realizing it, we have been highly efficient and—how do you say it?—in concert with one another! While you were speaking to Rowland McCrodden, I was speaking to the solicitor of Barnabas Pandy.' He then told me what he had found out and what he had failed to find out. 'There is something more, perhaps a great deal more, that Peter Vout did not wish to tell me about the family of Barnabas Pandy. And, since he is absolutely certain that Pandy was not murdered, he feels no obligation to divulge what he knows. Still, I have an idea—one that Rowland Rope might be able to assist with, if he is willing. I must speak with him at the earliest opportunity. But first, show me John McCrodden's letter.'

I handed it over. Poirot's eyes blazed with anger as he read it.

'It is inconceivable that Hercule Poirot should write and send such a thing as this, Catchpool. It is so poorly formulated and inelegantly written! I am insulted to think that anyone could believe it came from me.'

I tried to cheer him: 'None of the recipients knows you. If they did, they would have known, as I did the moment I saw it, that it was not your handiwork.'

'There is much to consider. I will make a list. We must get to work, Catchpool.'

'I'm afraid *I* must get to work, Poirot. By all means, speak to Rowland Rope—he is eager to speak to you—but I'm afraid you will have to count me out if you're planning to take any further action with regard to Barnabas Pandy.'

'How can I not act, *mon ami*? Why do you think the four letters were sent? Someone wishes to put in my head the idea that Barnabas Pandy was murdered. Is it not understandable that I am curious? Now, there is something I need you to do for me.'

'Poirot—'

'Yes, yes, you need to do your work. *Je comprends*. This I will allow you to do, once you have helped me. It is only a small task, and one that can be accomplished far more easily by you than by me. Find out where all four were on the day that Barnabas Pandy died: Sylvia Rule, Hugo Dockerill, Annabel Treadway and John McCrodden. The solicitor, Vout, told me that Mademoiselle Treadway was at home when her grandfather died, at Combingham Hall. Find out if she says the same thing. Now, it is of vital importance that you ask each of them in *precisely the same way*: the same questions, in the same order. Is that clear? I have realized that this is the way to distinguish most effectively one person's character from another's. Also, I am interested in this Eustace with whom Madame Rule is so obsessed. If you could—'

I waved at him to stop, like a railway signalman in the face of an out-of-control train hurtling towards him.

'Poirot, please! Who is Eustace? No—don't answer that. I have work to do. Barnabas Pandy's death has been officially recorded as an accident. I'm afraid that means I can't very well go around demanding that people furnish me with alibis.'

'Not straightforwardly, of course,' Poirot agreed. He stood up and started to smooth imaginary creases from his clothing. 'I am sure you will find an ingenious way around the problem. Good day, *mon ami*. Come and see me when you are able to give me the information I require. And—yes, yes!—*then* you will do your work assigned to you by Scotland Yard.'

CHAPTER 9

Four Alibis

Later that same evening, John McCrodden received a telephone call at the house where he lived. His landlady answered.

'It's John McCrodden you're after, is it? Not John Webber? McCrodden, yes? All right, I'll get him. Saw him a minute ago. He's probably upstairs in his room. You need to talk to him, do you? Then I'll get him. You wait there. I'll get him.'

The caller waited nearly five minutes, imagining a startlingly inefficacious woman who could well fail to find a person in the same house as herself.

Eventually a male voice came on the line: 'McCrodden here. Who is this?'

'I'm telephoning on behalf of Inspector Edward Catchpool,' said the caller. 'From Scotland Yard.'

There was a pause. Then John McCrodden said, 'Are you now?' He sounded as if he might be amused by the notion if he were not so weary.

79

'Yes. Yes, I am.'

'And who might you be? His wife?' he asked sarcastically.

The caller would not have minded telling McCrodden who she was, but she had been given explicit instructions not to do so. She had in front of her, on small cards, the precise words she was supposed to say and she intended to stick to them.

'I've got a few questions I'd like to ask you, questions to which Inspector Catchpool would like to know the answers. If you—'

'Then why doesn't he ask me himself? What is your name? Tell me at once, or this conversation is at an end.'

'If you provide me with satisfactory answers, then Inspector Catchpool hopes it won't be necessary for him to interview you at the police station. All I want to know is this: where were you on the day that Barnabas Pandy died?'

McCrodden laughed. 'Kindly tell my father that I'm not willing to put up with his campaign of harassment for one second longer. If he will not cease his devious persecution of me, then he is strongly advised to take precautions to ensure his own safety. Tell him I haven't the slightest clue when Barnabas Pandy died because I know no Barnabas Pandy. I don't know that he lived, died or joined the circus as a trapeze artist, and I don't know *when* he did those things, if he did them at all.'

The caller had been warned that John McCrodden might respond uncooperatively. She listened patiently as he continued to address her with icy disgust.

'Additionally, you may tell him I'm not as stupid as he thinks I am, and that I'm quite certain that if Scotland Yard employs an inspector by the name of "Edward Catchpool"—which I very much doubt—then that man knows nothing about this telephone call, and that you are in no way authorized to make it. Which is why you refuse to tell me your name.'

'Barnabas Pandy died on the seventh of December last year.'

'Did he? I'm delighted to hear it.'

'Where were you on that date, sir? Inspector Catchpool believes that Mr Pandy died at his home in the country, Combingham Hall—'

'Never heard of it.'

'—so if you can tell me your whereabouts on that date, and if anyone can vouch for you, then Inspector Catchpool might not need—'

'My whereabouts? Why, of course! Seconds before Barnabas Pandy breathed his last, I was standing over his prone body with a carving knife in my hand, ready to plunge it into his heart. Is that what my father would like me to say?'

There was a loud banging sound, and then the line went dead.

On the back of one of her question cards, the caller made a note of what she felt were the essential points: that John McCrodden believed his father to be behind the telephone call, that he had questioned the existence of Edward Catchpool and—most importantly, the caller thought—that he had not known, or had claimed not to know, the date of Barnabas Pandy's death.

'No alibi given,' she wrote. 'Said he was standing over Pandy with a knife just before Pandy died, but he said it like I was not supposed to believe it.'

After twice reading through what she had written, and after thinking for a few minutes, the caller picked up her pencil again and added, 'But maybe it *was* true, and the lie was the way he made his voice sound when he said it.'

'Is that Mrs Rule? Mrs Sylvia Rule?'

'Yes it is. To whom am I speaking?'

'Good evening, Mrs Rule. I'm telephoning on behalf of Inspector Edward Catchpool. From Scotland Yard.'

'Scotland Yard?' Sylvia Rule sounded instantly frightened. 'Has something happened? Is it Mildred? Is Mildred all right?'

'This isn't about anything to do with any Mildred, ma'am.'

'She was supposed to be home by now. I was starting to worry, and then . . . Scotland Yard? Oh, dear!'

'This is about something different. There's no reason to think anything's happened to Mildred.'

'Wait!' Sylvia Rule barked, causing the caller to jerk her head away from the telephone mouthpiece. 'I think that's her. Oh, thank the heavens! Let me . . .' A few grunts and panted breaths later, Mrs Rule said, 'Yes, it's Mildred. She's safely home. Do you have children, Inspector Catchpool?'

'I said I was telephoning on *behalf* of Inspector Catchpool.

82

I am not, myself, Inspector Catchpool.' Damned fool! Did Mrs Rule not know that women could not be police inspectors, no matter how much they might want to be or how talented they were? The caller resented being compelled to reflect upon this unwelcome fact and how unfair it was. She harboured a secret belief that she would make a better police inspector than anyone she knew.

'Oh, yes. Yes, quite,' said Sylvia Rule, who sounded as if she was not fully listening. 'Well, if you have children, then you'll know as well as I do that whatever age they are, one frets about them constantly. They might be anywhere, and how would one know? And with the most despicable degenerates! *Do* you have children?'

'No.'

'Well, I'm sure you will one day. I hope and pray you never suffer what I'm suffering now! My Mildred is engaged to be married to the most detestable man . . .'

The caller looked down at the notes she had been given. She guessed that, imminently, she was about to hear the name Eustace.

'. . . and now they've set a wedding date! Next June, or so they say. Eustace is more than capable of persuading Mildred to marry him in secret before that date. Oh, he knows I'm going to spend every waking moment from now until next June trying to make the wretched girl see sense— not that she will! Who ever listens to their mother? I think he's taken the opportunity to play a cruel trick on me.'

'Mrs Rule, I have a question—'

'He wants me to believe I have a full sixteen months to

talk Mildred out of marrying him, so that I won't set about it in a hurry. Oh, I know the way his disgusting mind works! It wouldn't surprise me if he and Mildred were to turn up already married in a month's time and say, "Surprise! We've tied the knot!" That's why I'm a bag of nerves whenever she leaves the house. Eustace could make her do anything. I don't know why the silly girl is so comprehensively unable to stand up for herself.'

The caller had some ideas about why this might be.

'Mrs Rule, I need to ask you a question. It's about the death of Barnabas Pandy. If you can give me a satisfactory answer then it might not be necessary for Inspector Catchpool to interview you at the police station.'

'Barnabas Pandy? Who is he? Oh, I remember! The letter Eustace induced that dreadful continental detective to send to me—what a reprehensible little toad he is! I used to hold Hercule Poirot in high esteem, but anyone who would allow himself to be bent to Eustace's will in that way . . . I refuse even to think about him!'

'If you can give me a satisfactory answer then it might not be necessary for Inspector Catchpool to interview you at the police station,' said the caller patiently. 'Where were you on the day that Barnabas Pandy died?'

A gasp came down the telephone line. 'Where was I? You are asking me where I was?'

'Yes.'

'And you say that Inspector—what name did you say?'

'Edward Catchpool.'

It sounded as if Sylvia Rule was making a note of the

name: 'And Inspector Edward Catchpool of Scotland Yard wishes to know this?'

'Yes.'

'Why? Doesn't he know that Eustace and that foreigner have cooked up this nonsense between them?'

'If you could just tell me where you were on the day in question?'

'What day? The day a man named Barnabas Pandy was murdered—a man I don't know, whose name was unknown to me until I received that odious letter? How should I know where I was when someone killed him? I have no idea when he died.'

The caller made a note of three things: first, Sylvia Rule seemed to accept that Pandy was murdered; second, this was understandable if she believed this telephone call to have hailed from Scotland Yard; third, she professed not to know when Pandy died, which might indicate that she had not killed him.

'Mr Pandy died on the seventh of December,' said the caller.

'Wait a moment and I shall go and look at last year's diary,' said Mrs Rule. 'Incidentally, whether or not Inspector . . .' There was a pause. The caller pictured Mrs Rule glancing down at a piece of paper. 'Whether or not Inspector Catchpool judges it necessary to interview me, I should very much like to speak to him. I wish to make it clear that I have murdered nobody and am not the kind of person who would do such a thing. Once I've explained to him about Eustace, I'm sure he will see this unsavoury business for what it is: an attempt to frame me for a crime of which I am innocent. He will find it as shocking as I do, I have no doubt—a woman of my reputation and distinction! I'm rather pleased that this has happened, for I expect it to be Eustace's downfall. Obstructing the proper investigation of a murder with slanderous accusations is a crime, is it not?'

'I would have thought so,' said the caller.

'Well, then! I shall check my diary. The seventh of December last year, you say?'

'Yes.'

The caller waited, listening to the sounds of Sylvia Rule's house. There was much stomping, doors opening and closing, footsteps on stairs. When Mrs Rule returned, she said triumphantly:

'I was at Turville College on the seventh of December, from ten in the morning until supper time. My son Freddie is a pupil there, and it was the day of the Christmas Fair. I didn't leave until well past eight o'clock. What is more, there were *hundreds* present—parents, teachers and pupils— and *all* of them will confirm what I have told you. Oh, how delightful!' Sylvia Rule sighed. 'Eustace's plan is doomed to fail. Wouldn't it be simply marvellous if he were to hang for his lies and calumnies against me—the very fate he had in mind for me?'

After John McCrodden and Sylvia Rule, Annabel Treadway was a positive pleasure to interrogate. She had no obvious grudges, no Eustace equivalent, and did not speak venomously and at length about any person in whom the caller had no interest. Furthermore, she had relevant information to impart.

'I was at home on the seventh of December,' she said. 'We all were—all of us who live at Combingham Hall. Kingsbury had just returned from a few days away. He drew the bath, as he always did, and he was the one who . . . who found Grandy under the water a while later. It was upsetting for all of us, but it must have been especially awful for Kingsbury. To be the person who *discovers* such a tragedy . . . By the time Lenore, Ivy and I reached the bathroom we knew something was wrong. I won't say we were prepared—how can one ever be, for something so terrible?—but we'd had warning. The way Kingsbury cried out when he saw . . . Oh, poor Kingsbury! I shall never forget the way his voice cracked as he called out to us.'

Annabel Treadway made an anguished noise. 'Kingsbury is neither a young man nor a strong one, and since Grandy's passing, he has grown so much older and weaker. Not in actual years, of course—but he looks ten years older. He had been with Grandy for most of his life.'

'Who is Kingsbury?' This question was not on the caller's list, but she felt it would be remiss of her not to ask.

'He's Grandy's manservant. Or *was*, I should say. Such a sweet, kind man. I've known him since I was a child. Really, he is more like a member of the family. We're all terribly worried about him. We're not sure how he'll manage now Grandy's gone.'

'He lives at Combingham Hall?'

'He has a cottage in the grounds. He used to spend most

of his time with us at the hall, but since Grandy died we haven't seen nearly as much of him. He does his work and then slips away, back to his cottage.'

'Apart from Kingsbury, does anyone else live in the grounds of Combingham Hall?'

'No. We have a cook and a kitchen maid, and also two housemaids, but they live in the town.'

'And who lives at Combingham Hall?'

'There were only the four of us. And my dog, Hopscotch. And then, since Grandy died, only my sister Lenore, my niece Ivy, Hopscotch and me. Oh, and Timothy for some of the exeats and school holidays, of course, though he often goes off with some friend or other to their house.'

The caller studied the notes in front of her. She had laid everything out neatly on the table so that she could see, at the same time and without shuffling papers, all potentially useful information and also all the questions that she needed to ask each of the four suspects, if 'suspects' was an accurate description of what they were. 'Timothy's your nephew, is he, Miss Treadway?' she asked.

'Yes. He's my sister Lenore's son. Ivy's younger brother.'

'Was Timothy at Combingham Hall when your grandfather died?'

'No. He was at his school's Christmas Fair.'

The caller nodded in satisfaction as she jotted this down. The notes said that Timothy Lavington was a pupil at Turville College. It seemed that Sylvia Rule had told the truth about the school's fair taking place on the seventh of December.

'Was there anyone else at Combingham Hall when Mr Pandy died apart from you, your sister Lenore, your niece Ivy, and Kingsbury?'

'No. Nobody,' said Annabel Treadway. 'Normally our cook would have been there too, and a maid, but we had given them the day off. Lenore, Ivy and I were supposed to be going to the Christmas Fair, you see, which would have meant luncheon and supper at Turville. Though in the end we didn't go.'

The caller tried not to sound too curious as she asked why the plan to attend the Christmas Fair had been abandoned.

'I'm afraid I don't remember,' Annabel said quickly. The caller did not believe her.

'So the manservant Kingsbury found Mr Pandy dead in his bathwater at twenty minutes after five, and he cried out for help? Where were you when you heard him call out?'

'This is how I know that Grandy cannot have been murdered.' She sounded glad to have been asked the question. 'I was in my niece Ivy's bedroom, with Ivy and Lenore and Hopscotch—while Grandy was still alive *and* when he must have died. Between those two times, none of us left the room, not for a second.'

'Between which two times, Miss Treadway?'

'I'm sorry, I haven't expressed myself very well. Shortly after Lenore and I went into Ivy's bedroom to talk to her, we heard Grandy's voice. We knew he was taking his bath—I had passed the bathroom on my way to Ivy's room and seen Kingsbury preparing it. The water was running. Then a little later, when Lenore and I had been in Ivy's room for ten minutes or so, we all heard Grandy shouting—so he was certainly alive then.'

'Shouting?' asked the caller. 'Do you mean shouting for help?'

'Oh, no, nothing of the sort! He sounded quite robust. He bellowed, "Can't a fellow bathe in peace? Is this cacophony necessary?" He definitely used the word "cacophony". He meant us, I'm afraid: Lenore, Ivy and me. We were probably all talking over each other the way we do when we're in high spirits. And often when we're making a commotion, Hoppy joins in with a yelp or a bark. For a dog, you'd be amazed—he has such an impressive range of noises that he makes, but I'm afraid they all annoyed Grandy, and never more so than at that moment. After he shouted at us, the three of us remained in Ivy's bedroom with the door firmly shut until we heard Kingsbury calling out in distress.'

'How much later was that?'

'It's hard to recall at a distance of so many weeks, but I should say perhaps thirty minutes later.'

'What were you talking about, in high spirits, with your sister and your niece for all that time?' asked the caller, who by now had chosen to forget that she was not an inspector with Scotland Yard.

'Oh, I couldn't tell you that, not so long afterwards,' said Annabel Treadway. Once again, the answer came a little too fast. 'I don't expect it was important.'

The caller thought it probably was. She wrote down the

words 'Bad liar' and underlined them twice for emphasis.

'The important thing is that this proves nobody could have murdered Grandy—don't you see? He fell asleep and drowned in his bath, as any man might who was as old and infirm as he was.'

'Kingsbury could have pushed him under the water,' the caller could not resist pointing out. 'He had the opportunity.'

'What?'

'Where was Kingsbury while you three ladies were talking in your niece's bedroom with the door closed?'

'I don't know, but . . . you can't honestly think . . . I mean, Kingsbury *found* Grandy. You're not suggesting . . .'

The caller waited.

'It is impossible to think that Kingsbury murdered my grandfather,' Annabel Treadway said, once she had composed herself. 'Completely impossible.'

'How can you know if you don't know where he was or what he was doing when Mr Pandy died?'

'Kingsbury is a dear, dear friend of our family. He could never be a murderer. Never!' It sounded as if Annabel Treadway had started to cry. 'I must go. I've neglected Hoppy today—poor little boy! Please tell Inspector Catchpool . . .' She stopped, then sighed loudly.

'What?' asked the caller.

'Nothing,' said Annabel Treadway. 'It's only that . . . I wish I could make him promise not to suspect Kingsbury. And I wish I hadn't answered any of your questions. But it's too late, isn't it? It's *always* too late!'

*

'Seventh of December, eh?' said Hugo Dockerill. 'I couldn't tell you where I was. Sorry! Probably pottering about at home.'

'So you weren't at Turville College's Christmas Fair?' asked the caller.

'Christmas Fair? Of course—wouldn't miss it!—but that was much later.'

'Really? What was the date of the fair?'

'Well, I can't remember the date—don't have a head for that sort of thing, I'm afraid. But I can tell you when Christmas is: twenty-fifth of December, same as every year!' Dockerill chuckled. 'I expect the fair was the twenty-third or something. What, my dearest?'

A woman's voice could be heard in the background: brisk and slightly weary.

'Aha . . . Ah! Wait a moment!' said Hugo Dockerill. 'My wife Jane has just reminded me that we would have broken up for the Christmas holidays long before the twenty-third. Yes, of course, she's quite right. You're quite right, Jane, dear. So . . . Ah! If you'd be good enough to hold on, Jane's going to check last year's calendar to see when exactly the fair was. What's that, my dearest? Yes, yes, of course, you're absolutely correct. She's quite correct. Of course the Christmas Fair was not the day before Christmas Eve—ridiculous notion!'

The caller heard a woman's voice say, 'Seventh of December.'

'I have it on good authority that our Christmas Fair last year was on December the seventh. Now, what was the date you wanted to ask me about again? I'm rather confused.'

'December the seventh. Were you at the fair that day, Mr Dockerill?'

'Indeed I was! Jolly affair, it was. Always is. We at Turville know how to . . .' He broke off suddenly, then said, 'Jane says you won't be interested in what I'm saying and that I should stick to answering your questions.'

'From what hour until what hour were you at the fair?'

'Start to finish, I expect. There was a supper afterwards, which usually finishes . . . Jane, when does . . . ? Thank you, my dearest. Around eight o'clock, Jane says. Look here, it might be simpler if you were to speak to Jane directly.'

'I would be glad to,' said the caller. Within the space of a minute, she had all the information she needed: according to Jane Dockerill, she and Hugo had been at the Christmas Fair on the seventh of December from when it started at eleven in the morning until when the supper finished at eight. Yes, Timothy Lavington had been present too, but not his mother, aunt or sister, who had been planning to attend but cancelled at the last minute. Freddie Rule had been there too, with his mother Sylvia, his sister Mildred and his sister's fiancé Eustace.

The caller said thank you and was about to say goodbye when Mrs Dockerill said, 'Wait a moment. You don't get rid of me that easily.'

'Was there something else, ma'am?'

'Yes, there is. Hugo has twice mislaid the letter he was

sent, accusing him of murder, which I realize is distinctly unhelpful. Well, I'm pleased to say that I've found it. I shall take it to Inspector Catchpool at Scotland Yard as soon as I am free to come to London. Now, I don't know if Barnabas Pandy was murdered or not—I'm inclined to think not, since to accuse four people of the same murder strikes me as more of a parlour game than a serious accusation, particularly when one fraudulently signs the name "Hercule Poirot" at the bottom of those letters—but just in case Mr Pandy *was* murdered, and in case this is a serious investigation and not some demented person's idea of a joke, there are two things I should tell you straight away.'

'Go on,' said the caller, her note-taking pencil at the ready.

'Sylvia Rule and her future son-in-law loathe one another. And poor Mildred, trapped in between them, is understandably perplexed and distraught about it all. Something must be done to avoid the direst consequences for the whole family. Poor Freddie is quite miserable enough already. I don't know how this relates to the death of Barnabas Pandy, but you asked about the Rule family, so I thought you should know, in case it's relevant.'

'Thank you.'

'The other thing I need to tell you is about the Lavingtons—Timothy's family, the family of Barnabas Pandy. It was I who answered the telephone to Annabel on the morning of the fair. Annabel is Timothy's aunt. She lied to me.'

'About what?'

'She told me that she and her sister and niece couldn't come to the fair because of a problem with the motorcar that was supposed to bring them. I don't believe that was the truth. She sounded upset and . . . shifty. Not at all her usual self. And later, Lenore Lavington, Timothy's mother, referred to having missed the fair on account of being very tired that day. None of it added up. Now, I don't know what all this means, or how my husband has managed to get himself drawn into it, but then I'm not a police inspector, so it's not my job to find out, is it? It's your job,' said Jane Dockerill.

'Yes, ma'am,' said the caller, who, at that moment, had quite forgotten that her job was something altogether different and nothing to do with investigating crimes that might or might not have been committed.

THE SECOND QUARTER

CHAPTER 10

Some Important Questions

'What the devil possessed you, Catchpool?' Superintendent Nathaniel Bewes roared in my ear.

'What do you mean, sir?'

He had been shouting for some time about my many deficiencies, but so far it had all been rather abstract.

'Last night! The telephone call you made—or, should I say, had some woman make for you!'

Ah, so that was it.

'You told me the letter to John McCrodden was not sent by Poirot, and I fell for it! Well, I'm not falling for any more clap-trap, so you needn't bother feeding me any. Do I make myself clear? I send you to see Rowly McCrodden to straighten things out, and what do you do instead? Collude with Poirot to pester Rowly's son still further. No, don't pretend this had nothing to do with you. I know that Poirot came here to see you—'

'That was because—'

'—and I know that the woman who telephoned John

99

McCrodden and demanded to hear his alibi for the day that this Pandy fellow died said she was doing so "on behalf of Inspector Edward Catchpool of Scotland Yard". Do you think I'm an imbecile? She was not acting on your behalf at all, was she? She was doing the bidding of Hercule Poirot! Like you, she is a mere cog in his machine. Well, I won't stand for it, do you hear me? Please explain to me why you and Poirot are determined to accuse an innocent man of a murder that wasn't a murder at all. Do you understand the correct meaning of the word "alibi", Catchpool?'

'Yes, s—'

'It does not mean where someone was at a particular moment. I am presently in my office talking to you, more's the pity, but that is my *whereabouts*, not my *alibi*. Do you know why? Because *no murder has been committed* while I stand here talking to you. I shouldn't have to explain this to you!'

He was bound to be wrong, I thought. Somewhere in the world, a murder was probably being committed, or had been committed, since he had started to bellow at me some twenty minutes earlier. More than one murder, very likely— and the Super was jolly lucky not to be among this potentially large and international group of victims. If I were someone who could ever be pushed over the edge into performing an act of violence, that moment would surely have come approximately ten minutes ago. Instead, and to my great regret, I seem to be a person who can balance quietly on the edge he is pushed towards for as long as anybody feels inclined to yell at him.

'Why does John McCrodden need to offer an alibi when *the death of Barnabas Pandy is not a criminal matter?* Why?' Bewes demanded.

'Sir, if you would allow me to answer . . .' I stopped, and there followed an awkward silence. I had expected the Super to interrupt me.

'If a telephone call was made to John McCrodden last night, it had nothing to do with me,' I said. 'Nothing at all. If someone used my name in order to find out where John McCrodden was on the day Barnabas Pandy died, then I can only think that . . . well, that person must have hoped to use the authority of Scotland Yard to make McCrodden talk.'

'Poirot must be behind it,' said the Super. 'Poirot and some other little helper of his.'

'Sir, the letter to John McCrodden was not the only one. Four were sent. Three other people also received a letter— signed in Poirot's name, though not from him—accusing them of the murder of Barnabas Pandy.'

'Don't be ridiculous, Catchpool!'

I told him the names of the other three recipients, and that one of them was Pandy's granddaughter, who had been in the house with him when he died. 'I spoke to Rowland McCrodden yesterday, as you asked me to, and he was keen to find out as much as he could about who sent the letters. He wants Poirot to investigate, so if Poirot *has* had some woman ask John McCrodden for an alibi, it might be . . . you know . . . helpful to Rowland McCrodden in the long run. If it sheds any light on anything, I mean.'

The Super groaned. 'Catchpool, from whom do you imagine I heard about the call to John McCrodden?'

I was feeling relieved that he'd lowered the volume of his voice, until he bellowed, 'From Rowly, of course!' next to my ear. 'He wants to know why I've permitted someone from Scotland Yard to demand an alibi from his son instead of doing what I promised I would, which was to put a stop to the whole infernal business! You can tell Poirot that it's very likely John McCrodden was in Spain in December when Pandy died. Spain! Can't kill someone in England if you're in Spain, can you?'

I took a deep breath and said, 'Rowland McCrodden wants to understand what's going on. He might have been angry to hear that his son was asked for an alibi, but I'm sure he still wants to pursue some form of enquiry until he gets an answer. There is only one way to put a stop to this: by working out who sent the four letters, and why. If there's a chance that Barnabas Pandy was murdered—'

'If I hear you make that suggestion again, Catchpool, I might just swing for you!'

'I know his death was recorded as an accident, sir, but if someone believes that it wasn't—'

'Then that someone is wrong!' In one of his more reasonable moods, and in a circumstance that did not cause distress to 'Rowly' Rope, the Super would have conceded that of course it was possible a mistake might have been made, that a crime had gone undetected. There was no point trying to persuade him of this today, however.

'You're right about one thing, Catchpool,' he said. 'Rowly

does want answers, and quickly. Therefore, until this matter is resolved, you are relieved of all official duties. You will assist Poirot in bringing this matter to a satisfactory conclusion.'

I was unsure how I felt about this. I used to worry about not knowing how I felt in certain situations, but I had more recently decided to treat them as a convenient opportunity to feel nothing at all. The Super had made his decision, and there could be no argument.

I discovered, when he next spoke, that it was not merely a decision that had been made but also concrete arrangements: 'You will find Poirot waiting for you in your office.' Bewes glanced at his watch. 'Yes, he will certainly be there by now. The two of you are expected at Rowly's offices in fifty minutes' time. That should be long enough for you to get there. Off you go! The sooner this strange affair is resolved, the happier I shall be.' He smiled unexpectedly, as if to tempt me with a glimpse of what his future happiness might look like.

Poirot was waiting for me in my office as advertised. '*Mon pauvre ami!*' he cried when he saw me. 'You have had the down-dressing, I think, from the superintendent?' His eyes twinkled.

'How did you guess?' I asked.

'He was ready to direct his fury at me, until I suggested to him that if he did so, I would leave without delay and offer no further assistance to his good friend Rowland Rope.'

'I see,' I said testily. 'Well, you needn't worry. He got it all out of his system in the end. I don't suppose he told you about Spain, did he?'

'Spain?'

'John McCrodden might have been too obstinate to volunteer an alibi, but his father told the Super that he was probably in Spain when Pandy died.'

'Probably? No sound alibi contains the word "probably".'

'I know that. I'm only telling you what the Super said.'

As we left the building, Poirot said, 'It is another question to add to the list: was John McCrodden in Spain on 7 December or not?'

I had assumed we would walk to the offices of Donaldson & McCrodden, but Poirot had arranged for a car to take us. As we set off, he produced a small piece of paper from his pocket. 'Here, you see, is the list,' he said. 'A pencil, please, Catchpool.'

I passed him one from my pocket, and he added the newest question at the bottom of the page.

The list was headed 'Important Questions' and was so much the sort of thing that Poirot would compose—so quintessentially him—that I found the last of my annoyance dissolving away.

The list read as follows:

Important Questions
1. Was Barnabas Pandy murdered?
2. If so, by whom, and why?
3. Who wrote the four letters?
4. Does the writer of the letters sincerely suspect all four? Or does he only suspect one of them? Or does he suspect none of them?

5. If the author of the letters suspects none of the four, what was the purpose of sending the letters?
6. Why were the letters signed in the name of Hercule Poirot?
7. What information is Peter Vout withholding?
8. Why were Barnabas Pandy and Vincent Lobb enemies?
9. Where is the typewriter on which the four letters were typed?
10. Did Barnabas Pandy know he was going to die?
11. Why does Annabel Treadway seem so sad? What secrets is she keeping?
12. Did Kingsbury, Barnabas Pandy's valet, kill him? If so, why?
13. Why did Annabel Treadway and Lenore and Ivy Lavington decide not to go to the Turville College Christmas Fair?
14. Was John McCrodden in Spain when Barnabas Pandy died?

'Why do you suspect Kingsbury?' I asked Poirot. 'And why is the typewriter important? One is much the same as another, surely?'

'Aha, the typewriter!' He smiled. Then, as if he had just answered my second question, he went back to the first. 'I ask about Kingsbury because of what Annabel Treadway said on the telephone last night, *mon ami*. If she was in Ivy Lavington's bedroom with Lenore and Ivy when Monsieur Pandy died, then only Kingsbury was in the house and unobserved at the relevant time. If the death was murder, he is the most likely murderer, *non?*'

'I suppose so. But then, isn't it peculiar that he received no letter? He's the only person who had the opportunity to commit the crime, and yet four people with no opportunity are accused of it.'

'Everything that has happened is peculiar in the extreme,' said Poirot. 'I begin to think that I was wrong to rush ahead and think about alibis . . .' He shook his head.

'Now's a fine time to tell me this, after the battering my eardrums have just taken.' I could still hear the Super's rage ringing in my head.

'Yes, that is unfortunate,' said Poirot. 'Ah, well. We must not regret what we have discovered. It will all prove useful, I have no doubt. But now? Now, it is time to think more deeply. For example, if Kingsbury is our killer, then for him not to have received a letter that four *innocent* people received is perhaps not peculiar at all.'

I asked him what he meant, but he made an enigmatic noise and would say no more.

At the offices of Donaldson & McCrodden, as we climbed the stairs, I prepared for my second encounter with Miss Mason. I had not warned Poirot about her. Instead, I dared to hope for a smoother passage on this occasion, given that Rowland McCrodden was expecting us.

I was soon disappointed. The pink-faced young woman almost threw herself into my arms. 'Oh, Inspector Catchpool! Thank goodness you're here! I don't know what to do!'

'What's the matter, Miss Mason? Has something happened?'

'It's Mr McCrodden. He won't open his door. I can't get in. He must have locked it from the inside, which he *never* does. And he's not answering his telephone, and when I knock and call his name, he doesn't answer. He *must* be in there. I saw him, with my own eyes, go into his room and close the door less than thirty minutes ago.'

Miss Mason turned to Poirot. 'And now you're here, and Mr McCrodden *knows* you've got an appointment, and he still won't open his door. I can't help thinking, what if he's had a fit of some sort?'

'Catchpool, can you break down Mr McCrodden's door?' said Poirot.

I reached out to touch it, preparing to assess how hard it might be to kick it down, when the door opened and there stood Rowland McCrodden. He looked perfectly well—not at all like a man who had suffered an unexpected seizure.

'Oh, thank heavens!' said Miss Mason.

'I must leave at once,' McCrodden said. 'I'm sorry, gentlemen.' Without another word, he walked past us and out of the office. We listened as his feet descended several flights of stairs. Then a door slammed loudly.

Miss Mason rushed after him, calling out, 'Mr McCrodden, this is most irregular. You can't go. These two gentlemen are here to see you.'

'He has already gone, mademoiselle.'

Miss Mason ignored Poirot and continued to howl into the now-empty stairwell: 'Mr McCrodden! *They have an appointment!*'

CHAPTER 11

Emerald Green

When I arrived at Scotland Yard the next morning, I was advised by the Super that Rowland McCrodden was keen to meet Poirot and me at our earliest convenience, though there was one condition: it could not be at the offices of Donaldson & McCrodden. We agreed, and an arrangement was made for the three of us to meet at Pleasant's at two o'clock.

The coffee house was, for once, a suitable temperature—warm but not too hot—and smelled pleasingly of cinnamon and lemons. Our friend Fee Spring rushed over to us. I had expected to be the main focus of her attention, as I usually am, but today she had eyes only for Poirot . . . and very intensely focused eyes, too. She pushed him into his chair, demanding, 'Well? Have you done what you promised you would?'

'*Oui*, mademoiselle. But we must postpone our discussion of the Church Window Cake until later. Catchpool and I are here for an important meeting.'

'With someone who isn't here yet,' said Fee. 'There's plenty of time.'

'The two of you are going to talk about Church Window Cake?' I said, confused.

They both ignored me. 'And if we begin and are then interrupted?' said Poirot. 'I prefer to do things in a more orderly fashion, one at a time.'

'Look at the teapots,' said Fee. 'Dusted 'em all, I did. Specially for you. Put all the spouts pointing the same way. Mind you, I can easily put them back how they were before . . .'

'Please refrain from doing so, I beg of you.' Poirot looked up at the shelves where the teapots stood. '*C'est magnifique!*' he declared. 'I could not have done better myself. Very well, mademoiselle, I will tell you. I visited Kemble's Coffee House as you asked me to. There I found the waitress Philippa and I ordered a slice of the Church Window Cake. I engaged her in conversation about it. She admitted to having made it herself.'

'See!' Fee hissed. 'Even if she'd denied it, I wouldn't believe a single word that came from her.'

'I asked her where the recipe came from. She told me that it came from a friend.'

'She's no friend of mine, and hasn't ever been! Working next to someone doesn't make them your friend.'

'What is this about?' I asked. Again, Poirot and Fee ignored me. Meanwhile, Rowland Rope was late.

'I asked her what was the name of the friend who gave her the recipe,' said Poirot. 'At once, she became furtive in her bearing and turned her attention to another customer.'

'That's all the proof I need,' said Fee. 'She knows she's stolen from me, right enough—but I'll deal with her! And now, I'll bring you a slice of *my* Church Window Cake with the compliments of the house.'

I glanced at my watch. Fee said, 'He'll be here in five minutes or so, your gent with the big forehead. I told him to return at fifteen minutes after two.' She smiled and made off towards the kitchen before either of us could admonish her.

'I sometimes wonder if she is a little unhinged,' I told Poirot. 'When ever did you find time to undertake this investigation into cake recipe theft?'

'I am lucky, *mon ami*. Whether I am doing my work or pursuing my own interests, I need nothing more than the opportunity to think. Sitting amid strangers and eating, slowly, a slice of cake . . . these circumstances are most conducive to the functioning of the little grey cells. Ah, Rowland McCrodden *est arrivé.*'

So he had.

'Monsieur McCrodden.' Poirot shook his hand. 'I am Hercule Poirot. You caught a glimpse of me yesterday, but I did not have the opportunity to introduce myself.'

McCrodden looked suitably embarrassed. 'That was unfortunate,' he said. 'I hope we will make good progress this afternoon, to compensate for the time lost.'

Fee brought coffee and a slice of Church Window Cake for Poirot, tea for me and water for Rowland McCrodden, who wasted no time in getting down to business.

'Whoever sent John that letter has escalated his campaign

of persecution,' he said. 'Last night a woman telephoned, pretending to be a representative of yours, Catchpool, and of Scotland Yard. She told John the date on which Barnabas Pandy died and asked him for an alibi.'

'That is not quite accurate,' I said. Poirot and I had agreed in advance that we would tell him the truth—most of it, at any rate. 'I believe she said that she was telephoning *on behalf of Inspector Catchpool* of Scotland Yard. Which she was—though not in connection with any Scotland Yard business. She certainly did not say that she herself was an employee of the Yard.'

'What the dickens . . . ?' McCrodden scowled at me across the table. 'Do you mean to say that *you* were responsible? That you put her up to it? Who was she?'

I made a point of not looking in Fee Spring's direction. Poirot, I assume, did the same. I could have made the four telephone calls myself, but I had wanted to add a layer of protection. Knowing there was a chance the Super might end up hauling me over the coals for it, I had decided that I would more plausibly be able to deny all knowledge if the voice on the other end of the telephone was reported to have been a woman's. Coward that I am, I calculated that if Fee took care of the matter for Poirot—as that was how I thought of it—then I could happily tell myself I was so uninvolved as to be guiltless. Fee had none of my qualms about the unorthodoxy of the plan; it was instantly apparent that I had made her day by asking her to do it.

'It is I who must take responsibility, monsieur,' Poirot told Rowland McCrodden. 'Do not alarm yourself. From this point forward, the three of us will work together to solve this mystery.'

'Work together?' McCrodden recoiled. 'Do you have any idea what you have done, Poirot? John came to my house after receiving that wretched telephone call, and told me that he was no longer my son and I no longer his father. He wishes to sever ties altogether.'

'He will change his mind as soon as the true identity of the letter-writer is known. Do not distress yourself, monsieur. Instead, place your trust in Hercule Poirot. May I ask . . . why did you insist on meeting today in a different place? What is in your offices that you do not wish me to see?'

McCrodden made a strange noise. 'It's too late for that,' he said.

'What do you mean?'

'Nothing.'

Poirot tried again: 'Why did you lock yourself in your room, then free yourself, only to disappear?'

We sat in silence while he considered the question.

'Monsieur? If you could please answer.'

'The reason has nothing to do with the matter at hand,' said McCrodden stiffly. 'Will that satisfy you?'

'*Pas du tout*. If you will not explain, I will have no choice but to guess. Could it be that you are afraid we will find a typewriter?'

'A typewriter?' McCrodden looked frustrated and a little bored. 'What do you mean?'

'E!' said Poirot enigmatically.

McCrodden turned to me. 'What does he mean, Catchpool?'

'I don't know, but you'll notice his eyes have turned a striking shade of emerald green. That usually means he has worked something out.'

'Emerald?' McCrodden growled, pushing his chair back from the table. 'You know, don't you? You both know. And you're taunting me. But how *could* you know? I have spoken to nobody.'

'What is it that you think we know, monsieur? About the typewriter?'

'I don't care a tuppenny damn for your typewriter! I'm talking about the reason I couldn't bear to stay in my offices a second longer yesterday and the reason I refused to meet you there today. I'm talking about Emerald, as well you know. That's why you said "emerald green", isn't it?'

Poirot and I exchanged a look of utmost confusion.

'Monsieur . . . what is this emerald?'

'Not what. *Who.* She's the reason I cannot go to my own place of work—which is most inconvenient. Miss Emerald Mason.'

'Miss Mason?' I said. 'The lady who works for you?'

'I suppose I shall have to tell you now—not that it's any of your business. Miss Mason's Christian name is Emerald. I thought you knew. When you said "emerald green". . .'

'*Non*, monsieur. Why does the presence of this woman drive you out of your building?'

'She has done nothing wrong,' said McCrodden despondently. 'She's diligent, well turned out—in every respect the model employee. The firm's affairs seem to matter to her as much as they do to Donaldson and me. I cannot fault her.'

'And yet?' Poirot prompted.

'I find her more insufferable by the day. Yesterday, I reached the point where I could bear it no longer. I had mentioned to her that I couldn't make up my mind whether to invite a particular client to attend the forthcoming Law Society dinner as my guest—there are reasons for and against, with which Miss Mason is familiar—and she reminded me *three times* in the hour that followed that I needed to decide as a matter of urgency. I know the date of the Law Society dinner as well as she does, and, what is more, she knows I do. It was clear that if she could have compelled me to make up my mind on the spot, she would have! The third time I told her I had not yet come to a decision, she said . . .' He gritted his teeth at the memory. 'She said, "Oh, dear. Well, perhaps you should have a little think." As if I were five years old. That was the last straw. I locked my office door and thereafter, when she addressed me from the other side of it, I ignored her.'

Poirot chuckled. 'And then, Catchpool and I . . . we arrive.'

'Yes. By then it was too late. The black mood that had me in its grip was . . . well, it was quite irrational.'

'If you find Miss Mason so enervating, why do you not tell her that you have no further need of her services?' said Poirot. 'Then you could once again go to work without dread in your heart.'

McCrodden seemed disgusted by the idea. 'I have no intention of turning her out on to the street. She is conscientious and has done nothing wrong. Besides, Stanley Donaldson, the firm's other partner, has no objection to her, as far as I know. I must try to overcome my aversion to her, and stop indulging in this . . . whatever it is.'

'Indulging,' said Poirot thoughtfully. 'That is an interesting way to describe it.'

'It *is* an indulgence,' said McCrodden. 'Avoiding the office, avoiding *her*, is satisfying in a way that it ought not to be—because I know how it will frustrate her.'

'This is fascinating indeed,' said Poirot.

'No, it isn't,' said McCrodden. 'It's childish of me and not what we're here to discuss. I want to know, Poirot, how you're proposing to find out who sent that letter to my son.'

'I have several ideas. The first involves your Law Society dinner. What is the date of it? I am wondering if it might be the same one to which Barnabas Pandy's solicitor, Peter Vout, has been invited.'

'It must be,' said McCrodden. 'There is only one on the horizon. Peter Vout was this Pandy fellow's solicitor, you say? Well, well.'

'Do you know him?' asked Poirot.

'A little, yes.'

'Excellent. Then you are ideally placed.'

'For what?' McCrodden asked suspiciously.

Poirot rubbed his hands together. 'As they say, *mon ami* . . . you are going to perform for us the under-the-cover investigation!'

CHAPTER 12

Many Ruined Alibis

'That's the most atrocious idea I've ever heard,' said Rowland McCrodden, once he knew the detail of Poirot's proposed plan. 'It's out of the question.'

'You might think so now, monsieur—but as the evening of the Law Society dinner draws nearer, you will come to see that it is a most advantageous opportunity, and that you are more than capable of playing your role to perfection.'

'I will not participate in a deception, however good the cause.'

'*Mon ami*, let us not argue. If you do not wish to do as I propose, then you will not do it. I cannot insist that you do.'

'And I shan't,' said McCrodden forcefully.

'We shall see. Now, will you agree to allow Catchpool here to inspect all the typewriters used by your firm?'

McCrodden's mouth tightened to a thin line. 'Why do you return to the subject of typewriters time after time?' he asked.

Poirot produced from a pocket the letter that had been sent to John McCrodden. He passed it across the table. 'Do you notice anything about any of the letters?' he said.

'No. I can't see anything worth remarking upon.'

'Study them closely.'

'No, I . . . Wait. The letter "e" is incomplete.'

'*Précisément.*'

'There's a gap in the straight line. A small hole of white.' McCrodden dropped the letter on the table. 'I see. If you find the typewriter, you find the sender of the letter. And since you've just asked permission to search my offices, I can only conclude that you suspect me of being that person.'

'Not at all, my friend. It is a mere formality. Everybody connected to this puzzle who is in possession of a typewriter we will investigate: the home of Sylvia Rule; that of Barnabas Pandy, of course; Turville College, where Timothy Lavington and Freddie Rule are pupils and Hugo Dockerill is a housemaster . . .'

'Who are all these people?' asked Rowland McCrodden. 'I've never heard of them.'

I took the opportunity to tell him that his son had not been the only person to get an accusatory letter, then watched as he struggled to digest the information. He said nothing for some time. Then: 'But why didn't you tell John, in that case, that he wasn't the only one? Instead, you allowed him to believe that he alone stood accused.'

'I did no such thing, monsieur. Assuredly, I informed your son that he was not the sole recipient of such a letter. My valet told to him the same thing—Georges testified on my behalf that I spoke the truth—but your son would not listen. He was steadfast in his belief that you must be responsible.'

'He's a blind, stubborn fool!' McCrodden banged his fist down on the table. 'Always has been, since the day he was born. What I don't understand is *why*. Why would anybody send letters to four different people, accusing them all of the same murder, and sign them in your name instead of his own?'

'It is puzzling,' Poirot concurred.

'Is that all you have to say? May I suggest that, instead of sitting around hoping the answer falls into our laps, we use our brains and try to solve the problem?'

Poirot smiled graciously. 'I did not wait, *mon ami*. I have, in fact, started without you to use the little grey cells of the mind. But, please, join me.'

'I can think of two reasons why someone might do it,' I said. 'Reason one: if he signs the letters in your name, Poirot, they are more likely to frighten the life out of those unlucky enough to receive them: the police listen when Hercule Poirot says somebody is guilty of murder. Therefore, if the letter-writer wants to give people a nasty shock, using your name is the way to do it. Even an innocent person would worry that to be accused of murder by you might prove fatal for them.'

'I agree,' said Poirot. 'What is the second reason?'

'The letter-writer wants you to look into the matter,' I said. 'He or she thinks Barnabas Pandy was murdered, but doesn't know for sure. Or *does* know it was murder, but doesn't know who did it. He or she comes up with a plan to make you curious enough to investigate. Going to the police won't work because the official record already states that Pandy's death was accidental.'

'Very good,' said Poirot. 'Both of those reasons I had thought of myself. But tell me, *why these four people*, Catchpool?'

'Not being the letter-writer myself, I'm afraid I can't answer that one.'

Poirot said to McCrodden, 'According to Monsieur Pandy's granddaughter, Annabel Treadway, there were five people at Combingham Hall on the seventh of December: she herself; Barnabas Pandy; his other granddaughter, Lenore Lavington; her daughter, Ivy; and Monsieur Pandy's manservant, Kingsbury. Let us assume for a moment that it was indeed a murder. The obvious people who ought to have received these letters of accusation are the four who were at Combingham Hall that day and are still alive: Annabel Treadway, Lenore Lavington, Ivy Lavington, and Kingsbury. Of those, only one got a letter. The other three letters were sent to two people who, if they are to be believed, were busy all of that day at the Turville College Christmas Fair—Sylvia Rule and Hugo Dockerill—and to John McCrodden, who, so far, does not appear to be in any way connected to the deceased man.'

'John is likely to have been in Spain when Pandy died,' said his father. 'I'm sure it was early December last year that I tried to track him down at the market where he works, and was told that he had gone to Spain and would remain there for several weeks.'

'You do not sound sure,' Poirot told him.

'Well . . .' McCrodden hestitated. 'It was December, undoubtedly. There were Christmas trinkets for sale on all the market stalls: shiny, useless pieces of rubbish. It might have been later in December, I suppose.' He shook his head in apparent disgust, as if he had caught himself red-handed in the act of lying to protect his son. 'You're right,' he admitted. 'I don't know where John was when Pandy died. I *never* know where he is. Poirot, believe me, I would not allow my judgement to be clouded by sentiment. Even though he is my only child, if John committed a murder, I would be the first to notify the police and I would support his execution as I support the death penalty for all murderers.'

'Is that so, monsieur?'

'It is. One must stick by one's principles or else the fabric of society crumbles. If a child of mine deserved it, I would hang him myself. But, as I told Catchpool, John would never kill another person. This I know for a fact. Therefore, his precise whereabouts on the day in question are irrelevant. He is innocent, and that's the end of the matter.'

'Those words, "the end of the matter". . . they are only ever used when the matter in question has only just begun,' said Poirot, much to Rowland McCrodden's consternation.

'Why would John go to Spain?' I asked.

A look of disapproval passed across Rowland McCrodden's face. 'He goes there regularly. His maternal grandmother lived there for a time and, when she died, she left her house to John. It's close to the sea and the weather is far superior to our climate. John is happier in Spain than in any part of England—he has always said so. And more recently, there has been a woman . . . Disreputable, of course. Not at all the sort of girl I'd have chosen for him.'

'People need to choose for themselves in these matters,' I said before I could stop myself, thinking about the 'ideal wife in waiting' whom my mother had recently found and attempted to inflict upon me. She was probably a delightful young woman, but I would forever blame her for those dismal few days in Great Yarmouth that I had felt obliged to offer Mother as compensation.

McCrodden emitted a hollow laugh. 'Matters of the heart, do you mean? Oh, John cares not a jot for the woman in Spain. He makes use of her, that's all. It's unsavoury and immoral, the way he carries on. I've told him what I think—I've told him his mother must be weeping in her grave—and do you know what he does? He laughs at me!'

'I wonder . . .' Poirot said quietly.

'What?' I asked.

'I wonder if, by pretending he is me, the letter-writer conceals a more important identity.'

'Do you mean the identity of the murderer?' asked McCrodden. 'The murderer of Barnabas Pandy?'

Something about the way he said it, in his woodwind-instrument voice, sent a shiver through me. It is hard to warm to a man who proudly announces that he would hang his own child.

'No, my friend,' said Poirot. 'That is not what I mean.

It is another possibility that occurs to me . . . a most interesting one.'

I knew he would say no more about it for the time
being, so I asked McCrodden about his own whereabouts
on the seventh of December. Without hesitation, he said,
'I was at my club, the Athenaeum, all day—with Stanley
Donaldson. In the evening the two of us went to see *Dear
Love* at the Palace Theatre. Please feel free to confirm that
with Stanley.'

Seeing that I was surprised by how readily he had
answered my question, he said, 'As soon as I discovered the
date of Pandy's death, I asked . . .' He stopped, grimaced,
then continued, 'I asked Miss Mason to bring me last year's
appointments diary. I thought that if I recalled my own
whereabouts, it might help me to know where John was.
If it were a day on which I had attempted to communicate
with him and been rebuffed, for instance . . .' The reedy
voice shook. He tried to disguise it with a cough. 'In any
case, I am in the fortunate position of having a far better
alibi than some of the other players in this unpleasant little
drama. School Christmas Fair!' he snorted contemp-
tuously.

'You are unenthusiastic about Christmas, monsieur?
About the shiny—what did you call them?—ah, yes, the
trinkets. On the market stalls. And now also about the
Christmas Fair of Turville College.'

'I have no objection to a Christmas Fair, though I would
not attend one myself if I had a choice,' said McCrodden.
'But frankly, Poirot, the notion that someone's presence at

the Christmas Fair of a large school is any sort of alibi at all is complete and utter bunkum.'

'Why do you say so, my friend?'

'It's a long time since I last attended such an event, but I recall them only too well from my youth. I remember trying to get through the day without speaking to anyone at all. It's something I still do at large gatherings, which I loathe. I shall certainly try to do it at the Law Society dinner. The secret is to pass by everybody with a friendly smile, while looking as if you're on your way to rejoin another little group that is waiting for you just over there. No one notices if you ever *do* join those towards whom you seem to be striding so urgently. Once you've passed them, they don't notice where you go or what you do.'

Poirot was frowning. His eyes darted up and down. 'You make a valuable point, monsieur. He is correct, is he not, Catchpool? I too have attended the large gatherings of this kind. It is the easiest thing in the word to disappear and reappear some while later, and no one will notice because everybody is busy talking to somebody else. *Je suis imbécile!* Monsieur McCrodden, do you know what you have done? You have brought ruination to the alibis of many people! And now we know less than we knew before we started!'

'Come now, Poirot,' I said. 'Do not exaggerate. Who are these many people with ruined alibis? Annabel Treadway still has hers: she was with Ivy and Lenore Lavington in Ivy's bedroom—though that will need checking. John McCrodden might have been in Spain—that too needs to be established. At most, this Christmas Fair problem you're so worried about leaves only two alibis looking shaky: Sylvia Rule's and Hugo Dockerill's.'

'You are wrong, *mon ami*. Also at the Christmas Fair at Turville College on the seventh of December were Jane Dockerill, the wife of Hugo, and Timothy Lavington, Barnabas Pandy's great-grandson. Oh—and young Freddie Rule, *n'est-ce pas?*'

'Why are they relevant?' Rowland McCrodden asked. 'No one has accused them of anything.'

'No one has accused the manservant Kingsbury either,' said Poirot. 'This does not make him irrelevant. No one has accused Vincent Lobb, Barnabas Pandy's old enemy. And we must not forget Sylvia Rule's hated Eustace. He, too, might be significant. I prefer to think of everybody as relevant—all of the people whose names arise in connection with this puzzling affair—until I can prove otherwise.'

'Are you suggesting that one of the people at the Christmas Fair that day might have left the grounds of Turville College, gone to Combingham Hall, and murdered Barnabas Pandy?' I said. 'They would need to have driven, or been driven, since it's a good hour's drive. And then what? They drowned Barnabas Pandy in his bathtub, then returned to the fair, where they walked around making sure lots of people observed their presence?'

'That could have happened,' said Poirot grimly. 'All too easily.'

'We mustn't forget that Barnabas Pandy's death is likely to have been an accident,' I said.

'But if it was murder . . .' Poirot said with a faraway

expression on his face. 'If it was murder, then the murderer has a powerful incentive to cast suspicion on someone other than himself, does he not?'

'Not if no one suspects him in the first place, because the death has been accepted to be an accident,' I said.

'Ah, but perhaps not everybody has accepted it,' said Poirot. 'The killer might discover that the truth is known by at least one person, and is about to be revealed. So—he casts the suspicion! Even more ingeniously, he casts suspicion on four innocent people simultaneously. That is more effective than simply to accuse one innocent person.'

'Why?' McCrodden and I asked at the same time.

'If you accuse only one person, the matter is concluded too quickly. The accused produces his alibi, or else no proof can be found to tie him to the crime, and that is that. Whereas if you accuse four people, and sign the name of Hercule Poirot to those accusations, what happens? Chaos! Confusion! Denials from many different quarters! That is the situation in which we now find ourselves and it is assuredly the most brilliant screen of smoke, is it not? We know nothing. We see nothing!'

'You're right,' said Rowland McCrodden. 'The way the letter-writer has conducted himself . . . it's rather ingenious. He has posed a question: which one of the four is guilty? He doubtless hopes that Poirot will investigate. A question that appears to have one of only four possible answers sets up a choice with an illusory limit. In truth, many more answers might be possible, and somebody entirely other might be guilty.' McCrodden leaned forward and said urgently, 'Poirot, do you believe, as I do, that the letter-writer is likely to be Barnabas Pandy's murderer?'

'I try to make no assumptions. As Catchpool says, we do not know, yet, if Monsieur Pandy was murdered. What I fear, *mes amis*, is that we may never know. I am at a loss as to how to pursue . . .' He left the sentence unfinished and, whispering something inaudible in French, pulled the plate on the table towards him. He picked up his cake fork. Holding it over the slice of Church Window Cake, he looked up at Rowland McCrodden and said purposefully, 'It is your son John that I will pursue.'

'What?' McCrodden scowled. 'Haven't I told you—'

'You misunderstand me. I do not mean that I think he is guilty. I mean that his position in the structure fascinates me.'

'What position? What structure?'

Poirot put down his cake fork and picked up a knife. 'See here the four squares in the cake,' he said. 'In the top half, a yellow and a pink square side by side, and in the bottom half the same. For the purposes of this exercise, these four little squares, these four quarters of the one slice, represent our four letter-recipients.

'At first I thought that there were two pairs of two.' Poirot cut the slice of cake in half, to illustrate his point. 'Annabel Treadway and Hugo Dockerill were one pair, both connected to Barnabas Pandy. Sylvia Rule and John McCrodden were the other pair. They both told me that they had never heard of Monsieur Pandy. But then . . .' Poirot cut one of the halves in half again, and pushed the newly detached pink square towards the half-slice that was still intact, leaving one solitary yellow square isolated at the bottom of the plate. 'Then I discover that Sylvia Rule's son, Freddie, is at school with Timothy Lavington, Barnabas Pandy's great-grandson. So now we have *three* people with a clear link to Monsieur Pandy and to each other: Annabel Treadway refused a marriage proposal from Hugo Dockerill. Hugo Dockerill is a housemaster at the school attended by Sylvia Rule's son, who is at school with Annabel Treadway's nephew. Only John McCrodden has, as far as we can see at the moment, nothing linking him to any of the others, or to Barnabas Pandy.'

'He *might* also have a connection to Pandy, though,' I said. 'One that just hasn't emerged yet.'

'But all of these other connections are very clear to see,' said Poirot. 'They are unmistakeable, straight away visible, impossible to miss.'

'You're right,' I conceded. 'John McCrodden does rather feel like the odd one out.'

Rowland McCrodden looked stricken, but said nothing.

Poirot pushed the lone yellow square of cake off the plate and on to the tablecloth. 'I wonder if this is what the writer of the letters wants me to think about,' he said. 'I wonder if he—or she—wants me to consider, above all, the guilt of Monsieur John McCrodden.'

CHAPTER 13

The Hooks

That evening, Poirot and I sat in front of a crackling log fire in the excessively decorated and alarmingly furnished drawing room of my landlady, Blanche Unsworth. We had sat like this many times, and no longer noticed the lurid shades of pink and purple, or the quite unnecessary fringes and trims appended to the ends and edges of every lamp-shade, armchair and curtain.

We each held a drink in our hand. Neither of us had spoken for some time. Poirot had been staring into the flickering flames for nearly an hour, occasionally nodding or shaking his head. I had just filled in the last clue of my crossword puzzle when he said quietly, 'Sylvia Rule burned the letter she received.'

I waited.

'John McCrodden tore his into pieces, which he sent to his father,' Poirot went on. 'Annabel Treadway first scribbled over the words of her letter, then tore it up and then burned it, and Hugo Dockerill lost his. His wife Jane subsequently found it.'

'Are any of these facts important?' I asked.

'I do not know what matters and what does not, my friend. I sit here and think more furiously than I have ever thought before, and *I find no answer to the most important puzzle of all.*'

'Whether Pandy was murdered, you mean?'

'No. There is a question still more important than that: *Why should we pursue this matter at all?* It is not the first time I have tried to discover if an accidental death might be a murder in disguise. *Pas du tout.* This I have done many times, but only ever when a person who appears to be of reliable character tells me that all might not be as it seems, or when I have the suspicion myself, based on my own observations. None of these conditions pertains to our present problem.'

'No,' I agreed, acutely aware that while I indulged the whims of Poirot, Rowland McCrodden and the Super, work would be mounting up on my desk at Scotland Yard.

'Instead, we have the suggestion that Monsieur Pandy's death was murder coming from a character we know to be untrustworthy—a person who writes letters and signs them with a name that is not his own. We know beyond the reasonable doubt that the sender of these letters is a fraud, a liar, a maker of the mischief! If I were to decide to take no further steps and turn my attention to other things, no one could fault my decision.'

'I certainly wouldn't,' I told him.

'And yet . . . the hooks, they have been successfully planted in the mind of Hercule Poirot. I would like to know why is Mademoiselle Annabel Treadway so sad? Who sent the letters, and why? Why four? And why to these four people? Does the person responsible truly believe that Barnabas Pandy was murdered, or is it some sort of trick or trap? What if he is the murderer as well as the letter-writer? Is it one culprit I must identify, or two?'

'Well, if the author of the letters *is* also the murderer, he or she must be one of the biggest fools that ever lived and breathed! "Dear Hercule Poirot, I should like to draw to your attention to the fact that I committed a murder in December of last year and I appear to have got away with it." No one would be so idiotic.'

'Perhaps. It is possible, Catchpool, that somebody who is not at all the idiot seeks to manipulate me—to what end I cannot and do not know.'

'Why not retaliate with a manipulation of your own? Do absolutely nothing. That might provoke the mischief-maker into sending more letters. He may write to you directly the next time.'

'If I had the patience . . . but it is not in my nature to do nothing. So . . .' Poirot clapped his hands together. 'You will start immediately to check all of the alibis and all of the typewriters.'

'In the world? Or only all the typewriters in London?'

'Very amusing, *mon ami*. No, not only in London. Also at Turville College, and Combingham Hall. I want you to test every typewriter you can find that might have been used by any of the people involved in this matter. Even Eustace!'

'But, Poirot—'

'Also, you must find Vincent Lobb. Ask him why he and Barnabas Pandy were enemies for so long. And, finally—for I do not want to burden you with too many tasks—please find a way to persuade Rowland McCrodden to do what we need him to do at the Law Society dinner.'

'Can't you tackle McCrodden?' I said. 'He's more likely to listen to you than to me.'

'What is your opinion of him?' Poirot asked.

'Frankly, I've been less favourably inclined towards him since hearing him say he would be pleased to hang his own son.'

'*If* his son were a murderer . . . and Rowland McCrodden is adamant that John is not. Therefore, when he says he would willingly hang him, it is not, in his mind, his son, but a fantasy version of John. This is why he is able to say it and believe he means it. Be assured, *mon ami*: if John McCrodden ever committed a murder, his father would do everything he could to save him from punishment. He would tie himself in the complicated knots and find a way to believe that John was innocent.'

'You are probably right,' I said. 'Do you think he might have sent the four letters? Think of it this way: he deliberately places his son in hot water so that he can rush to the rescue, thereby forcing John to acknowledge that he's a devoted father and not the hateful ogre John thinks he is. If at some point soon he is able to say to John, "I set Hercule Poirot to work on your behalf and he has exonerated you," and if John can see that is undeniably true, relations between them might improve greatly.'

'And he sends the letters to three other people as well, so that it does not look as if the whole exercise is about John?' said Poirot. 'It is possible. I have been thinking of Annabel Treadway as our most likely letter-writer, but it might be Rowland McCrodden.'

'Why Annabel Treadway?' I asked.

'Do you recall, I spoke of an identity that the sender of the letters might have sought to conceal? Rowland McCrodden asked me if I meant the identity of the murderer of Barnabas Pandy.'

'Yes, I remember.'

'What I meant, *mon ami*, is the identity of the *harbourer of suspicions*. I have been developing this theory with Annabel Treadway in mind.'

I sipped my drink, waiting for him to elaborate.

'It seems to me that if anyone murdered Monsieur Pandy, the most likely person is his manservant, Kingsbury,' Poirot went on. 'From what we have been told, he had the opportunity. The three women of the household were in a room together with the door closed, probably talking in an animated fashion; they would not have seen or heard anything.

'Let us say that Mademoiselle Annabel—who did not strike me as a brave or confident woman—suspects that Kingsbury killed her grandfather. She cannot prove it, so

132

she places her faith in a gamble. She decides it is possible that Hercule Poirot might be able to prove her suspicions to be correct. Why, in that case, did she not come to me and ask more straightforwardly for help?'

'I can't think of any reason why she wouldn't do precisely that,' I told him.

'What if she was afraid of Kingsbury finding out that she had done so? She might have anticipated how difficult it would be to prove that a very old man was pushed underwater while in his bath. How could it ever be proven, if only Monsieur Pandy and Kingsbury were in the room at the time?'

'I see. So you're saying she'd have thought it likely that Kingsbury would get away with it?'

'Exactly. The law would be powerless to punish him, on account of the lack of evidence. Meanwhile, he—a murderer—would know that it was Annabel Treadway who had reported her suspicions to me. What is to stop him killing her next?'

I wasn't at all convinced by this theory, and I said so. 'If that was her fear, there was a far simpler plan of action available to her. She could have accused Kingsbury in an anonymous letter *to* you, rather than accusing herself and three other people in letters purporting to be *from* you. That would have been far more straightforward.'

'Indeed,' Poirot agreed. 'For her purposes, it would have been *too* straightforward. Kingsbury might have suspected her of writing such a letter, as she was at Combingham Hall when Monsieur Pandy died. She would have been one of three obvious suspects, and the other two would have been her sister and niece, to whom she seems devoted—she would not have wished to risk their lives either. No, no. My theory is better. The four letters having been sent to this strange collection of people, including Annabel Treadway herself, she now stands accused of her grandfather's murder. This, I think, would not lead Kingsbury to believe that she suspected him of the crime. Do you see, Catchpool?'

'Yes, but—'

'She signs the four letters as "Hercule Poirot", and, in doing so, she secures my involvement. Once I am involved, once I am successfully hooked like a fish and reeled in, then she sits back and hopes that her efforts were not in vain— that I will investigate and discover the guilt of Kingbury and a means of proving it.'

'All right, but then why accuse the three others? She could have sent *one* letter, to herself, signed in your name, accusing her and nobody else of her grandfather's murder.'

'She is a woman of extreme caution and trepidation,' said Poirot.

'Is she really?' I laughed. 'Then you've disproved your own colourful theory! No one of a cautious temperament would attempt a scheme like this.'

'Ah, but you must consider also her desperation.'

'I fear we have entered the realm of pure invention,' I told him.

'Maybe so. Then again, maybe not. I hope, one day soon, to know. The next step, in any case, is clear.'

'Not to me it isn't.'

'Yes, it is, Catchpool. I have given to you the clarity: Vincent Lobb, alibis and typewriters.'

I was relieved that persuading Rowland McCrodden to turn the Law Society dinner into a pantomime of Poirot's devising seemed to be off the list. 'And what will you be doing, while I search for faulty letter "e"s?'

'Is it not obvious?' asked Poirot. 'First thing tomorrow, I shall depart for Combingham Hall. We will see what answers I may find.'

'Be a sport and check the typewriters while you're there,' I said with a grin. 'Since you're going anyway.'

'Of course, *mon ami*. Poirot, he shall be the sport!'

CHAPTER 14

At Combingham Hall

There were many reasons, thought Poirot as he stood and stared at its façade the next day, why Combingham Hall ought to have looked appealing. The sky was bright with winter sun, and the temperature mild for February. In an apparent invitation for all visitors to enter, the front door stood half open. No one could have disputed that this was a fine and handsome building. It was surrounded by all that one might wish for: attractive lawned gardens and, further from the house, a lake, a tennis court, two cottages, an orchard and a substantial wooded area, all of which Poirot had seen from the windows of the motorcar that had brought him here from the nearest railway station.

Yet he lingered outside, reluctant to enter the Hall. One might be proud to own and live in such a building, but could one grow fond of it? The open door was more suggestive of carelessness than of active welcome. Instead of nestling in its natural environment as buildings ought to, it protruded in an ungainly fashion—loomed, almost—as

136

if an ill-wisher had reached down from above and balanced it where it stood, with the aim of tricking people into thinking it belonged there. 'Or else I am a foolish old man who imagines these things,' Poirot said to himself.

A woman of perhaps forty or a few years more, wearing a yellow dress with a thin belt, appeared in the doorway. She stared at Poirot without smiling.

'Strangeness upon strangeness,' Poirot thought to himself. The woman had something in common with the building from which she had emerged. She was undoubtedly beautiful, with golden hair and every feature perfectly designed and precisely in proportion with the others, yet she looked . . .

'Uninviting,' Poirot murmured to himself.

He produced his best smile and walked briskly towards her. 'Good afternoon, madame,' he said before introducing himself.

She extended her hand for him to shake. 'It's a pleasure to meet you,' she said, though her face remained impassive. 'I'm Lenore Lavington. Please come in. We are ready for you.'

Poirot thought this a strange thing to say: as if he was an ordeal to be endured. He followed her into a large, bare entrance hall with a staircase of dark wood on the far left and a row of three archways straight ahead. Beyond these was a vaulted corridor and then a further three archways which led into a dining hall that contained a wooden table, long and narrow, with many chairs around it.

Poirot shivered. It was colder in the house than outside. The reason for this was obvious. Where were the walls?

Where were the doors separating one room from another? From where he stood, Poirot could not see none. It was quite wrong, he decided, to walk into a house and be able to see, in the distance, its dining table.

He felt greatly relieved when Lenore Lavington led him to a small, warmer sitting room with pale green wallpaper, a lit fire and a closeable door. Two other women awaited him there: Annabel Treadway, and a much younger, broad-shouldered woman with dark hair, intelligent eyes and an untidy filigree of scars trailing down one side of her face and, along her neck under her ear. This must be Ivy Lavington, thought Poirot. She could have covered some of the scarring by arranging her hair differently, but had evidently chosen not to.

A large dog with a lot of brown, fluffy hair—curly in places—was sitting on Annabel Treadway's feet, his head balanced in her lap. When Poirot appeared, he roused himself and trotted across the room to greet the new visitor. Poirot patted him, at which the dog lifted his front paw and patted him back.

'Ah! He greets me!'

'Hoppy's the friendliest boy in the world,' said Annabel Treadway. 'Hopscotch, meet M. Hercule Poirot!'

'This is my daughter, Ivy,' said Lenore Lavington. There was no suggestion in her tone that she intended this remark as a reproach to her sister.

'Yes, of course—this is Ivy,' said Annabel.

'Hello, M. Poirot. It is an honour to meet you,' said the younger woman. Her voice was warm and deep.

Hopscotch, still at Poirot's feet and staring up at him, raised his paw and patted the air between them, as if not quite daring to touch the great detective a second time.

'Oh, how sweet! He wants you to play with him,' said Annabel. 'In a moment he'll lie on his back and expect you to stroke his tummy.'

'I'm sure M. Poirot has more important things to think about,' said her sister.

'Yes, of course. I'm sorry.'

'No apology is necessary,' Poirot told her.

The dog was now lying on his back. Poirot stepped around him and, invited by Lenore Lavington to sit, lowered himself into a chair. This could not be Combingham Hall's main drawing room, he thought. It was far too small, though perhaps it was the only part of the house warm enough for human habitation.

He was offered refreshments, which he declined. Lenore Lavington sent Ivy to find Kingsbury and instruct him to prepare something to eat and drink 'in case M. Poirot changes his mind'. Once her daughter had left the room, she said, 'There is no need to wait until Ivy returns. Perhaps you could tell me why you are here?'

'You don't mind explaining, do you?' added Annabel quickly. 'You will do it so much better than I would.'

'Do you mean to say, mademoiselle, that you have not told Madame Lavington about the letter you received?'

'*C'est vraiment incroyable*,' Poirot said silently to himself. People: their strangeness had no limits. How could one sister tell another that the famous detective Hercule Poirot was to visit them at their home and not reveal the reason for the visit? And how could the other sister not demand to know, in advance of the detective's arrival?

'Annabel has told me nothing. I should very much like to know what this is about.'

As efficiently as he could, Poirot explained the situation. As she listened, Lenore Lavington paid close attention, nodding now and then. If his story surprised her, she showed no sign of it.

When he had finished, she said, 'I see,' and then, 'An unpleasant business—though not as unpleasant, I suppose, as if there was a chance the accusations were true.'

'You are going to tell me there is no such chance?'

'None whatever. Grandfather wasn't murdered, either by my sister or by anybody else. There was no one in the house when he died apart from Annabel, me, Ivy and Kingsbury—as you know, because *you* have just told me. Annabel is quite correct: she, Ivy and I were together in Ivy's bedroom between when Grandfather called out to us and when Kingsbury alerted us and we all ran to the bathroom to find Grandfather dead. None of us left the room in between.'

Poirot noted that she referred to Barnabas Pandy as 'Grandfather', not 'Grandy', as her sister called him. 'What about Kingsbury?' he asked.

'Kingsbury? Well, he wasn't in the room with us . . . but Kingsbury, kill Grandfather? It's unthinkable. I expect you'll wish to speak to him too before you leave?'

'*Oui*, madame.'

'Then you will soon see how absurd an idea it is. May I ask why you are pursuing this investigation, M. Poirot, when no police force and no court seems to have the slightest suspicion that Grandfather's death was anything but an accident? Has someone sent you? Or are you here simply to satisfy your own curiosity?'

'I am curious, I will admit. Always, I am curious. Also, the father of Monsieur John McCrodden, who received one of the four letters, asked for my help in clearing the name of his son.'

Lenore Lavington shook her head. 'This has gone too far already,' she said. 'Clear his name? It's laughable. He wasn't here in the house when Grandfather died. There: his name is cleared, and there is no need for you or the father of this Mr McClodden to waste any more of your time.'

'Though we are happy to answer your questions, of course,' said Annabel, stroking the dog under his chin. He had returned to his mistress and was once more draped across the lower part of her legs.

'May I ask? When I arrived, the front door stood open.'

'Yes. It's always open,' said Lenore.

'It's because of Hopscotch,' said Annabel. 'He likes to come and go quite freely between the house and garden, you see. We'd like it better—Lenore would like it better—if we could let him out, or in, and then close the door, but . . . well, he barks rather loudly, I'm afraid.'

'He requires the door to be left open, and Annabel insists that we indulge him.'

'Hoppy's extremely clever, M. Poirot,' said Annabel. 'He prefers the front door to be open so that whenever he wants to go out, he can, without having first to summon one of us.'

'If the door is habitually left open, is it not possible that somebody entered the house while your grandfather was in his bath on 7 December last year?' Poirot asked.

'No. It is not.'

'No,' Annabel echoed her sister. 'Ivy's bedroom is at the front of the house. One of the three of us would have seen someone coming up the driveway, whether they were in a vehicle or on a bicycle or on foot. It's impossible that none of us would have noticed.'

'What if a person approached the house from the back?' Poirot asked.

'Why would they?' asked Annabel. 'It's far easier from the front. Oh—I suppose if they didn't want to be seen . . .'

'*Précisément.*'

'The back door is also left open most of the time, though Hoppy prefers to go in and out at the front.'

Lenore said, 'The dog would have brought down the house with his barking if someone had been prowling around. He'd have smelled a stranger.'

'He did not bark when I came into the room,' Poirot pointed out.

'That's because you came in with Lenore,' said Annabel. 'He saw that you were a welcome guest.'

Lenore Lavington raised her eyebrows a little at that. 'Let us proceed,' she said. 'Do you have more questions, M. Poirot, or are you satisfied?'

'Alas, I am not yet satisfied,' Poirot told her. 'Is there a typewriter in the house?'

'A typewriter? Yes. Why do you ask?'

'May I use it before I leave?'

'If you wish.'

'Thank you, madame. Now, I should like to ask you about Vincent Lobb. He was an acquaintance of your grandfather's.'

'We know who he was,' said Lenore. 'He and Grandfather knew each other a long time ago. They were great friends, until something happened to turn them into enemies.'

'Before you ask, we don't know what happened,' said Annabel. 'Grandy never told us.'

'Perhaps you know that not long before he died, Monsieur Pandy wrote a letter to Monsieur Lobb in which he expressed a wish to end the *froideur* that existed between them?'

The sisters exchanged a look. Then Lenore said, 'No. We did not know. Who told you that?'

'Your grandfather's lawyer, Monsieur Peter Vout.'

'I see.'

'It makes me happy to think that Grandy did that.' Annabel sighed. 'And I'm not surprised to hear it. He was terribly kind and forgiving.'

'Annabel, you do say the most puzzling things,' said her sister.

'Do I, Lenore?'

'Yes, you do. Grandfather, forgiving? Whatever Vincent Lobb did, it was fifty years ago. Grandfather held a grudge for fifty years. I'm not saying he was wrong or cruel to do so—most people hold grudges, though not you, Annabel.'

'You do, Lenore.'

'Yes, I do,' her sister agreed. 'And *you* are the one with the forgiving nature. Not Grandfather.'

'No, I'm not!' Annabel seemed distressed by the suggestion. 'Who am I to forgive anybody? I'm . . .' She blinked away tears. Then she said, 'It's true, I forgave Grandy for ignoring Hoppy, and Skittle before him, and for preferring Lenore to me. I forgave him because he forgave me! He found me to be a dreadful disappointment, but he did his best not to show it. I knew how he felt about me, but I appreciated his daily efforts to hide it.'

'My sister is upset,' Lenore Lavington told Poirot. There was a small, neat smile on her face. 'She tends to exaggerate. I wonder where Ivy has got to? I do hope she's not eating the food intended for you, M. Poirot.'

'Why did your grandfather find you disappointing?' Poirot asked Annabel.

'I think it was because I had a superior older sister,' she said.

'Oh, really, Annabel!'

'No, Lenore, it's true. You *are* superior to me. I think so, and Grandy thought so too. Lenore was always his favourite, M. Poirot, and rightly so. She's so determined and efficient and strong, just like Grandy was. And she married and gave him great-grandchildren. Continued the family line. Whereas I seemed to want spend all my time with my dogs, and, worst of all, I'm a spinster with no children.'

'Annabel received many proposals of marriage,' Lenore told Poirot. 'She wasn't short of offers.'

'Grandy thought I hid away with animals because I couldn't hold my own with people. Maybe he was right. I *do* think animals are less bothersome than people, and they're certainly more loyal. They love one in spite of one's flaws. Oh—I'm not complaining about Grandy or anybody else. I should hate you to think that! He did his best, and I let him down so badly, I let—' She stopped with a sharp intake of breath. 'Here comes Ivy,' she said. It was a rather obvious attempt to change the subject.

'What do you mean, mademoiselle?' Poirot asked, wondering why she suddenly looked so frightened—as if the ghost of Barnabas Pandy himself had walked into the room.

The door opened and Ivy Lavington entered. She saw her aunt's face and looked alarmed. 'What has happened?' she asked.

'Nothing,' said Lenore Lavington. Considering that Ivy had not yet heard Poirot's explanation of why he was at Combingham Hall, this was an inadequate answer in every respect.

'How did you let your grandfather down?' Poirot asked Annabel Treadway again.

'I've told you already,' she said in a voice that sounded choked. 'He would have liked for me to marry and have children.'

There was something that she was determined not to say, thought Poirot. He decided not to pursue the matter now. There would be an opportunity to ask her later, he hoped. Perhaps when her sister and niece were not present, she would speak more freely.

He turned to Lenore Lavington. 'If it would not be too upsetting for you, madame, would you show me the bathroom in which your grandfather drowned?'

'That's rather morbid, isn't it?' said Ivy.

Her mother ignored her. 'Yes, of course,' she said to Poirot. 'If you think it's necessary.'

Annabel stood to follow them, but Lenore said, 'No.'

Annabel accepted the command without question, and sat down again.

'Why don't you tell Ivy what's happened?' Lenore suggested to her. 'Come with me, M. Poirot.'

CHAPTER 15

The Scene of the Possible Crime

The journey to the bathroom in which Barnabas Pandy had died was a relatively long one. Poirot had been inside many large country houses, but none with corridors as seemingly endless as those of Combingham Hall. When he saw that Lenore Lavington had no intention of conversing as they walked, he took the opportunity to go over in his mind the events that had taken place in the sitting room downstairs.

It had struck Poirot immediately, upon encountering Annabel Treadway a second time, that her air of unhappiness was less pronounced today. It was not that she seemed any happier, or happy at all—she did not, in spite of the presence of the dog whom she plainly loved. No, it was more that . . .

Poirot shook his head. He could not have said what it was, and that unnerved him. His thoughts moved on to Lenore Lavington. He decided that she was one of those rare people to whom one might speak for hours and still come away knowing nothing about their character. The only thing he felt he had learned about her was that she liked to make sure events unfolded in a certain way. There was an air about her of being always on duty. Poirot wondered if she was afraid of whatever it was that her sister had stopped herself from saying.

'Ah!' he exclaimed, as Lenore led him past another sequence of doors.

She stopped. 'Did you say something?' she asked him with a polite smile.

'*Non. Pardon*, madame.'

He had not intended to make a sound, but was relieved to have worked out what it was about Annabel Treadway that had struck him: although an atmosphere of melancholy still lingered around her, she had determinedly pushed her own emotions to one side in order to think only about her sister's.

'Yes, that is it,' thought Poirot to himself with satisfaction. Both of the sisters had been so acutely aware of the other, so attuned to every word, expression or gesture coming from the other . . . Why? he asked himself. It was as if Lenore had placed Annabel—and Annabel, in turn, had placed Lenore—under a form of secret surveillance. Each sister had of course known that the other was in the room, listening to whatever she said, but both had pretended to listen in an ordinary, casual way, when in fact each one had been obsessively focused on the other.

'They share a secret,' Poirot thought. 'The two sisters share a secret, and each is afraid that the other will give it

148

away to Hercule Poirot, a stranger, who has come here to poke his nose into their private affairs!'

'M. Poirot?'

Distracted by his theorizing, he had failed to notice that Lenore Lavington had stopped walking. 'This is the bathroom in which the tragedy occurred. Please, do go in.'

'Thank you, madame.'

As they entered, the floorboards creaked, making a strained noise that sounded like someone in great pain trying not to attract attention, thought Poirot wistfully. The room was sparsely furnished: only a bathtub in the middle of the room, one chair, a shelf with a crumbling edge, and in one corner a low squat chest of drawers with elaborate carvings around the edges of each drawer. Poirot had previously heard such pieces described as 'tallboys', but that name wouldn't have suited this one, which was more of a 'shortboy'. The wood ought to have been shiny, but instead had the dull look of furniture that nobody had polished for years.

On the shelf stood one solitary item: a small bottle of purple glass. 'What is that?' Poirot asked.

'In the bottle? It's oil of olives,' said Lenore Lavington.

'In the bathroom, not the kitchen?'

'Grandfather . . .' She stopped. More quietly, she started again, 'Grandfather never bathed without oil of olives.'

'In his bathwater?'

'Yes. It was good for his skin, he said, and he liked the smell—goodness knows why.' She turned away and walked over to the window. 'I'm sorry, M. Poirot. It's surprising: I find it easy to discuss his death, but that little bottle . . .'

'*Je comprends*. It is harder to talk about the bottle because it was something he enjoyed while alive. That is the thought that makes you sad.'

'Yes, it is. I was fond of Grandfather.' She said it as though this was something that might require explanation, not a fact to be taken for granted.

'You are quite sure, madame, that you heard Monsieur Pandy speak—that you heard him, alive, and that it could only have been him? And from that moment until you saw that he had drowned in his bathwater, you were together with your sister and your daughter? Not one of you left the company of the other two, even for a few moments?'

'I am quite, quite sure,' said Lenore Lavington. 'Annabel, Ivy and I were chatting away and he called out to us that we were disturbing him. He liked the house to be quiet.'

'Mademoiselle Ivy's bedroom is near this room?'

'Yes, just across the corridor and a little to the right. We had closed the door, but it makes no difference in this house. He would have heard our conversation clearly.'

'Thank you, madame.'

'I would be grateful if you could tread carefully when you speak to Kingsbury,' she said. 'He has been rather withdrawn since Grandfather died. I hope you won't need to bother him for too long.'

'I shall make it as brief as possible,' Poirot promised.

'Nobody killed Grandfather, but if anybody had, that person could never have been Kingsbury. For one thing, his clothes would have been wet, and they weren't. Annabel, Ivy and I all heard him cry out when he found . . . when he saw what had happened and, seconds later, we were all in here together. Kingsbury's clothes were completely dry.'

'You did not try to pull your grandfather out of the water?'

'No. It was apparent that it was far too late to save him.'

'Then your sister's garments were also dry?'

Lenore seemed angered by the question. '*All* of our clothing was dry. Including Annabel's. She was wearing a blue dress with white and yellow flowers on it. Long sleeves. She stood right beside me, here. I would have noticed at once if she had water dripping from her sleeves! I am an observant person.'

'I do not doubt it,' said Poirot.

'Surely you do not take this accusation against my sister seriously, M. Poirot? The same letter was sent to four people. What if it had been sent to a hundred people? Would you consider each one a possible culprit, even if the police had no suspicions and the death had already been judged by a coroner's court to be an accident?'

Poirot started to answer, but Lenore Lavington had not yet finished. 'Besides, the idea of Annabel murdering anybody is quite ludicrous,' she said. 'My sister has the wrong constitution for any sort of unlawful action. If she broke even a minor law it would torment her for ever. She would never risk a murder. She wouldn't even risk getting a different breed of dog.'

Ivy Lavington walked into the room. 'Lots of people stick with one breed,' she said. 'Hopscotch is an Airedale and so was Skittle, the one before him,' she explained to Poirot.

'Have you been listening outside the door?' asked her mother.

'No,' said Ivy. 'Have you been saying things you don't want me to overhear?

'My sister is like a second mother to Ivy and my son Timothy, M. Poirot. They both tend to leap to her defence, having first imagined I am attacking her when I'm not.'

'Oh, Mummy, stop feeling sorry for yourself!' said Ivy with good-humoured impatience. 'It's Aunt Annabel who has been accused of murder, not you. She absolutely couldn't have done it, M. Poirot.'

Poirot decided he liked Ivy Lavington. She had a youthful energy about her, and she struck him as the only normal member of the household—though of course he had yet to meet Kingsbury. 'Was Hopscotch with the three of you in your bedroom, Mademoiselle Ivy, while your Grandfather took his bath?'

'Of course he was,' Lenore Lavington answered the question on her daughter's behalf. 'Wherever Annabel goes, the dog follows. He can go off on his own, but she isn't allowed to. The day she travelled to London to see you, he howled for nearly an hour after she left. It was horribly inconvenient.'

'Madame, may I tell you the names of the other three people who received letters accusing them of Monsieur Pandy's murder?'

'Very well.'

'John McCrodden. Hugo Dockerill. Sylvia Rule. Do you know any of these names?'

'Hugo Dockerill is Timothy's housemaster at school. I have never heard the other two names apart from when you spoke of Mr McCrodden earlier.'

'Don't be silly, Mummy.' Ivy laughed. 'Of course you know who Sylvia Rule is.'

'That's not true.' Lenore Lavington looked confused. 'Do *you* know who she is?' she asked Ivy. 'Who is she?' It was as if her daughter knowing something she did not was a prospect she found intolerable.

'She's the mother of Freddie Rule. He's in Timmy's house at school. He started at Turville about six months ago. He was horribly bullied at his last school.'

Poirot watched with interest as the colour drained from Lenore Lavington's face. 'F-Freddie?' she stammered. 'Strange, lonely Freddie? His family name is *Rule*?'

'Yes. And his mother is Sylvia. You *must* have known that! Why do you look so queer?'

'Fred-die,' her mother said again, more slowly, her eyes glazed and remote. By merely uttering the name, she managed to imbue it with a peculiar sort of horror.

'Why do you object so strongly to poor Freddie, Mummy? What harm has he ever done to you?'

Ivy's robust question ruptured the tense atmosphere.

'None,' Lenore Lavington answered crisply. She seemed restored to her old self. 'I didn't know his family name, that's all. I'm surprised you do.'

'I spoke to him once when we went to visit Timmy at school. I noticed a boy on his own looking rather glum, so I went over to speak to him. We had a long and quite interesting chat. He introduced himself as Freddie Rule. At some point he must have mentioned his mother, Sylvia, because I know that's her name.'

'That awful hermit boy is no friend of Timothy's,' Lenore Lavington told Poirot. 'I've advised Timothy to avoid him, in fact. I think he's peculiar in the head—the sort of boy who might do anything.'

'Mummy!' Ivy laughed. 'Did you really? Have you lost your wits? Freddie's the most harmless boy in the world.'

Poirot said, 'On the day your grandfather died, the two of you and Mademoiselle Annabel were supposed to be attending the Christmas Fair at your son's school. That is correct, is it not?'

'Yes,' said Lenore.

'But you did not go to the fair, in the end.'

'No.'

'Why not?'

'I can't remember.'

Poirot turned to Ivy. 'Do you recall the reason, mademoiselle?'

'Perhaps Mummy wanted to avoid Freddie Rule, and that's why she changed her mind about going.'

'Don't be absurd, Ivy,' said Lenore.

'It's only that you looked so ghastly when I mentioned his name, Mummy. Why? I know you're not going to tell me, but I should very much like to know.'

So, too, would Hercule Poirot have liked to know.

CHAPTER 16

The Opportunity Man

Kingsbury's small cottage was a short walk from the main house. Immediately outside it was a compact kitchen garden with borders of lavender, rosemary and hyssop.

Poirot approached the front door, eager to meet 'The Opportunity Man', as he had begun to think of Kingsbury. If the ladies of Combingham Hall were telling the truth, then Kingsbury was the only person who could have murdered Barnabas Pandy. Could it be as simple as that? Poirot wondered. Might he extract a confession from the manservant and solve the mystery today?

He knocked on the door, and soon afterwards heard shuffling footsteps behind it. It opened. A skeletally thin man with creased, papery skin and eyes of a peculiar yellow-tinged green stood in the doorway. He looked at least seventy years old. Poirot suspected that he believed himself to be smartly dressed, though the bottoms of his trousers were covered in dust. What little hair he had hung in isolated strands of white, as if remnants of a wig he had once worn had adhered to his scalp.

155

Poirot introduced himself to the old man and explained his presence at Combingham Hall, starting with his visit from Annabel Treadway. Kingsbury squinted and bent his head forward, as if struggling to see and hear him. It was only when Poirot referred to his conversation with Lenore Lavington and mentioned that she had sent him to the cottage that the servant's manner changed. His eyes cleared and his back straightened. He invited Poirot inside.

Once uncomfortably seated on a hard chair in a room that clearly served as both sitting room and kitchen, Poirot asked Kingsbury if he thought it possible that Barnabas Pandy had been murdered.

The old man shook his head—a movement that rearranged the white strands on his scalp. 'Couldn't have been,' he said. 'The girls were all in Miss Ivy's room having a to-do, causing a commotion, and the only other person around was me.'

'And you, naturally, had no reason to want Monsieur Pandy dead?'

'Not *him*,' said Kingsbury, with a strong emphasis on the last word.

'There is, then, somebody else that you wish to kill?'

'Not to kill. But I'll not lie to you, Mr Porrott: I've thought to myself many times since Mr Pandy's been gone, it'd be a mercy if the Lord were to take me too.'

'He was a good friend as well as your employer, *n'est-ce pas?*'

'Best friend a man could have. He was a fine fellow. I don't do much of anything, now he's gone. Doesn't feel like there's a point to doing anything. I do my work, of course,' he added hurriedly. 'But I never go up to the Hall when I'm not needed, not now he's gone.'

Watching the fluttery, bird-like movements of Kingsbury's hands as he spoke, Poirot doubted he would have the strength to drown anybody. How had he helped an even older man into his bath? Perhaps Pandy, though older, had been physically stronger and able to get in and out of the tub without assistance.

Kingsbury leaned towards Poirot and said confidingly, 'Mr Porrott, I can promise you that Mr Pandy wasn't murdered. If that's the only reason you've come to Combingham Hall . . . well, you could have saved yourself the bother.'

'I hope that you are right. All the same, if you will permit me to ask you a few questions . . . ?'

'Ask if you want, but there's no more I can tell you than what I've just said. There's nothing more to tell.'

'Where were you while Monsieur Pandy took his bath and the ladies of the house were in Mademoiselle Ivy's bedroom causing the commotion?'

'I was here, unpacking my suitcase after having been away for a short spell. I drew Mr Pandy's bath for him, and put in the oil of olives like I always did, and then knowing he liked to soak in the tub for a good forty, forty-five minutes, I thought to myself, "I know what I'll do: I'll unpack that case." So that's what I did. Then I went back over to the Hall, thinking Mr Pandy would be wanting to get dried and dressed round about then. That's when I found him.' The old man's chin trembled at the memory. 'He was lying under the water. Dead. It was a terrible sight, Mr Porrott. His eyes and mouth were open. I'll not forget that in a hurry.'

'I am told that the front door to the Hall is usually left ajar,' said Poirot.

'Oh, yes. Dog won't stand for it being shut, not before nine o'clock at night, which is his bedtime, and Miss Annabel's. He doesn't mind it being shut then.'

'Could a stranger have entered the house and drowned Monsieur Pandy while the ladies were in Ivy Lavington's room and you were here unpacking your suitcase?'

Kingsbury shook his head.

'Why not?' asked Poirot.

'Dog,' said the old man. 'He'd have gone wild. I'd have heard him from over here. A stranger, creeping around the Hall? They wouldn't get out alive, not if Hopscotch had anything to do with it.'

'I have met Hopscotch,' Poirot told him. 'He seemed to me to be an affectionate creature.'

'Oh, yes, if you're a friend to the family, or an invited guest . . . but he's quick to take fright, and he'd know something was wrong if he got wind of an intruder prowling around.'

'I understand that you have been left a significant sum of money in the will of Monsieur Pandy?'

'I was left it, but I'll not be spending it—not so much as a farthing of it will I spend. It can go to one of that Dr Barnardo's homes for poor children. Mrs Lavington's said she'll arrange it all for me. What would I do with it? Money can't bring Mr Pandy back, and if he weren't gone, I'd not have had it as a worry. And now I won't again, as I'll be giving it all away.' Kingsbury spoke with apparent sincerity and conviction, but Poirot had encountered many talented liars in the past. It would be prudent, he decided, to check in due course that the sum intended for Dr Barnardo's had ended up there and not gone astray *en route*.

'*Alors*, you found a most distressing scene when you returned to the bathroom. When you cried out in shock and the three ladies soon afterwards appeared in the bathroom, were their clothes wet or dry?'

'Dry. Why would they be wet? It wasn't any of them that was in the tub, was it?'

'You are certain you would have noticed if, for example, somebody's sleeves or dress had been wet?'

The old man shook his head. 'A flock of geese could have wandered in and I'd not have noticed—not with Mr Pandy staring up at me from under the water.'

'Then . . .' Poirot sighed quietly. 'Never mind. There is a more important question I must ask you. The loud commotion that the three ladies were making while Mr Pandy bathed—'

'It was hard on the ears, I don't mind telling you,' said Kingsbury. 'Mrs Lavington and Miss Ivy were screaming at each other, and Miss Annabel was screaming at them to stop, and crying her heart out. And then Mrs Lavington shouted at her that she wasn't Miss Ivy's mother and she'd do well to remember that. It was a terrible to-do. Mr Pandy didn't like it and I can't say as I blame him. He shouted at them to be quiet.'

'You were still in the main house when you heard this?' asked Poirot.

'No, I was outside the cottage, just about to let myself in. The bathroom window was open—he always had it open. Liked his bathwater hot, he did, and the air in the room cold. Said the two balanced each other out. Oh, I heard him loud and clear.'

'After his plea for peace and quiet, were you able to hear if the argument ended?'

'I'm afraid not. Miss Ivy's bedroom is at the front of the house. But I don't think it had finished. No, I'm sure it hadn't. Or else it stopped and then started again, 'cause it was still going when I returned to the main house. Mr Pandy's death was what stopped it. They all saw him under the water and that was that.'

'If the dog was in a room full of people screaming at one another, and if he saw his mistress was upset, is it not possible that Hopscotch might, just this once, have failed to notice that a stranger had entered the house?' Poirot asked. 'The door to Ivy Lavington's bedroom was closed, according to Mrs Lavington. Might the dog not have failed to smell or hear the intruder, preoccupied as he must have been by his mistress's unhappy state?'

Kingsbury considered it. Finally he said, 'I'll admit, I'd not considered that until now. You're right, Mr Porrott. With Miss Ivy's door being closed, he *might* not have noticed if there was a stranger in the house. He would certainly have been worried by Miss Annabel's distress, and he wouldn't have left her side with her in that state. I'd still say there's a good chance he would hear a stranger on the prowl, but I'd not swear to it.'

They sat in silence, questions hanging in the air. Instead of feeling vindicated, Poirot felt defeated. The possibilities were once again endless. Barnabas Pandy might not have been murdered at all, or he might have been killed by Kingsbury, or by anybody who could have crept into the estate's grounds and illicitly entered Combingham Hall that day: Sylvia Rule, Hugo Dockerill, Jane Dockerill, Freddie Rule, John McCrodden . . . anybody.

What this puzzle lacked, thought Poirot despairingly, was parameters. There was an abundance of suspects for something that stood every chance of not being a crime. And if Rowland McCrodden had persuaded Stanley Donaldson to provide him with a false alibi for 7 December, or if Ivy and Lenore Lavington and Annabel Treadway were lying about all being together in Ivy's room, why, then the number of potential suspects grew even larger.

'Motive,' Poirot murmured. 'It is *motive* that will lead me to the answer, when too many people had the opportunity.'

'What's that you say?' Kingsbury roused himself from his reverie—and Poirot was ready to start again.

'What can you tell me about Vincent Lobb?' he asked.

'Mr Pandy wouldn't have nothing to do with him. Not for fifty years he wouldn't. Mr Lobb let him down badly.'

161

'How so?'

'I'm not able to tell you that, I'm afraid. Mr Pandy never told me. Didn't like to talk about the particulars, though he talked a lot about the treachery of it. "You'd never betray me, would you, Kingsbury?" he'd say, and I'd tell him I never would. I wouldn't have, and I never did,' the old man concluded proudly.

'What was the subject of the argument between Annabel Treadway and Ivy and Lenore Lavington?' Poirot asked.

'Oh, Miss Annabel wasn't part of the row. That was Mrs Lavington and Miss Ivy. Miss Annabel was trying to stop it.'

'What was the cause of the problem? Were you able to hear?'

'I'm not one to eavesdrop, if that's what you're suggesting. Anyone who wasn't deaf would have heard it. Still, I did my best not to listen. And I'm not sure Mrs Lavington would want me telling you what was said between her and her daughter.'

'But it was Mrs Lavington who told me that you were the person I must speak to! And you have told me a little already, have you not?'

'Not the particulars, I haven't,' said Kingsbury. 'Mrs Lavington could have told you herself if she'd wanted you to know.'

'My friend, I would be deeply grateful if you could help me in this matter. Now that we agree that the dog might not have heard a stranger enter the house, the possibility that Barnabas Pandy was murdered . . . well, let us say that it cannot be ruled out. If he was murdered, we must not let his murderer escape justice.'

'Now there I agree,' said Kingsbury grimly. 'Wring his neck with my bare hands, I would.'

'Please do not do that. Instead, help me by telling me about this argument you could not help hearing.'

'But if a stranger killed Mr Pandy, then a little family to-do can't be important to the solving of it,' said Kingsbury.

'You must trust me,' Poirot told him. 'I have solved many cases of murder.'

'I haven't,' Kingsbury interjected, his tone gloomy. 'I've never solved even one.'

'One never knows what is of vital importance, or where the connections lie, until the solution is apparent. The most inconsequential-seeming detail can be the one that matters most.'

'Well, if you think it might help, though I can't see how it could . . . It was something that Mrs Lavington had said to Miss Ivy that Miss Ivy had taken badly. And then she'd accused Mrs Lavington of intending it badly, if you follow me? She thought she'd said it purposefully to wound her, but Mrs Lavington swore she'd done no such thing and that Miss Ivy was making too much of it. Mind you, there was probably more to it than that.'

'Why do you say that?'

'Nothing had been right at the house since that dinner a few days earlier.'

'Which dinner?'

'You're going to be disappointed, Mr Porrott, because I

didn't overhear anything at all on that occasion, but that's when the trouble started. I'd left them all at the table and gone to do my last few jobs around the Hall. I was on my way to say goodnight to the family before leaving for the night, but I never got as far as the dining hall before Miss Ivy came running at me. Ran past like a mad thing she did, sobbing. Then Miss Annabel did the same, and then Mrs Lavington marched past very quickly with a face like . . . well, I don't know how to describe it, but it shocked me. There was a look in her eyes like I'd not seen before. I tried to speak to her but she didn't see or hear me, Mr Porrott. It was the strangest thing. I thought something frightful must have happened.'

'This was only a few days before Barnabas Pandy died, you say?'

'That's right. I don't remember how many, I'm sorry to say, but it might have been three or four days. Five at the most.'

'What did you do, when you suspected something dreadful had happened?'

'I hurried to the dining table, hoping to find Mr Pandy, hardly daring to wonder what state I might find him in. He was seated at the head of the table where he always sat, and . . .' Kingsbury stopped. 'Mr Porrott, don't think I didn't hear all that you said about how much the small details matter, but there's certain things I know Mr Pandy wouldn't have wanted anyone to hear about.'

'Would he have wanted his murderer to go unpunished?' said Poirot.

The old man shook his head. 'I hope I'm not doing wrong by telling you, or else Mr Pandy might give me a good hiding when we next meet in a better place.' He blinked a few times, then said, 'There's no need for you to pass on what I'm about to tell you to anybody else, mind.'

'If it has no bearing on any criminal matter, it will go no further. You have my promise.'

'Like I said: I found Mr Pandy sitting alone at the dining table, but that's not all he was doing.' Lowering his voice, Kingsbury said, 'He was *crying*, Mr Porrott. Crying! I'd not seen him do that before, not in all the years I'd known him. It was just the one tear, but I saw it clearly by the light of the candles on the table. Mr Pandy noticed me coming towards him and shook his head. He didn't want me any closer, not with him as he was, so I came back here, to the cottage. And—this is where you'll not be pleased with me, Mr Porrott—I never got to find out what had made him shed that tear and sent everyone else running from the table. I knew Mr Pandy wouldn't want to talk about it, so I never asked. It wasn't my place to ask.'

On his return to Combingham Hall, Poirot was met by Lenore Lavington, Annabel Treadway and Hopscotch the dog, who had an orange rubber ball in his mouth. 'I hope Kingsbury was helpful?' said Lenore.

'He confirmed much of what you had both already told me,' said Poirot matter-of-factly, not wishing to reveal how much he had learned in the servant's cottage. He now had more questions to ask of both sisters, but he would need to think of a clever way to do it—one that did not endanger the old man.

Did that mean, he asked himself, that he believed one of these two women standing before him to be a murderer? If one of them had killed Pandy then the other, as well as Ivy Lavington, must be lying about all being in Ivy's room together. Instinctively, Poirot had trusted Ivy. Did that mean that he distrusted Lenore Lavington and Annabel Treadway, or was he merely ambiguous about both of them? To avoid these difficult questions, he asked an easier one.

'If I might, before I leave, use your typewriter, madame?'

Lenore Lavington nodded, from which Poirot gathered that she was about to acquiesce. Then she said, 'M. Poirot, while you were with Kingsbury, Annabel and I discussed this ludicrous and rather sordid situation in which we find ourselves—and in which you are also involved—and we both feel it necessary to put a stop to it. No one has been murdered, and no one believes anybody has been murdered. The story is pure invention, and we don't even know who invented it, or what exactly their story is, though we may surmise that they were motivated by malice.'

'All of this is true, madame, but the letter I wish to type before I leave is a different thing altogether. It is . . . a personal matter.'

'Is it? Or do you want to check if our typewriter here is the same one used to type the four letters?'

Poirot gave a little bow and smiled his most charming smile. 'You are shrewd indeed, madame. I apologize a thousand times for my little trick. However, if you would be so generous as to—'

'I would be generous if I could convince myself it was the right thing to do.'.

'Lenore's right, M. Poirot,' said Annabel. There was a pleading tone to her voice. 'I should never have come to you. I should have gone straight to the police, who could have assured me that they suspect me of having committed no crime, because, as is quite clear now, there was no crime committed.'

Her sister said, 'We understand that it must be immensely frustrating for you, M. Poirot, to have your name used in the way that it was by a devious person intent on stirring up trouble for *you* as much as for anybody else . . . but the thing to do, when something like this happens, is to ignore it and get on with one's life. Don't you agree?'

'I cannot ignore it, madame, until I understand why these letters were sent.'

'Then the letter-writer has won,' said Lenore Lavington. 'Against you, he has won. Well, I'm certainly not going to let him defeat me. Which is why, with regret, I'm afraid I must now ask you to leave.'

'But madame . . .'

'I'm sorry, M. Poirot. I have made my decision.'

Nothing Poirot said could persuade her to change her mind, and his attempts to do so seemed to cause almost physical pain to Annabel Treadway. Thirty minutes later, he left Combingham Hall without having caught so much as a glimpse of its typewriter.

CHAPTER 17

Poirot's Trick

Whenever possible, Rowland McCrodden replied in the negative to the social invitations he received. Once in a while, however, he felt duty-bound to attend events that he knew he would not enjoy, and the Law Society dinner was one such occasion. The din alone was nearly enough to make him turn on his heel and leave: all those open mouths filling the air around him with pointless chirping. Everybody seemed to be talking and no one listening, as was always the way at such gatherings. McCrodden found them draining in the extreme.

The dinner was at the Bloxham Hotel, an elegant establishment, famous for its afternoon teas. McCrodden had decided not to do what he normally did, which was to move from one part of the excessively full room to another, trying to avoid being engaged in dialogue. Tonight, he had resolved to submit rather than resist. He would stand still and allow himself to be endlessly accosted. At least that would involve less effort on his part.

'Well, well, well, if it isn't old Rowly Rope!' said a booming voice.

McCrodden turned and found himself face-to-face with a man whose name he was supposed to know but stood no chance of remembering. He had certainly never asked this man to call him Rowly—or Rowland, for that matter.

'Haven't you got a drink, old chap? You don't want to be slow off the mark when it comes to the drink—not in this company! It'll be all gone before you know it!'

From the loose-mouthed way the man spoke, McCrodden had the sense that vast quantities of liquor had already gone down his throat and were at that moment sloshing around inside his barrel-shaped form.

'Tell me, old boy, how's the lovely Mrs Rope? Haven't seen her at one of these shindigs for a long time. Seem to remember she was something of a stunner!'

McCrodden, whose wife had died many years ago, bristled. 'You are mistaking me for someone else.' At that moment, he caught sight of Peter Vout approximately eight chandeliers away, on the opposite side of the large ballroom. 'Would you please excuse me?' he said to the barrel, who was shaking his head as if preparing to mount another challenge. McCrodden walked purposefully away from him. He would not, after all, stand still—not if that meant spending his evening with the most objectionable man in the room.

He had told Poirot that he would not deceive Peter Vout, but now, with Vout within easy reach, he found himself wondering: was Poirot right? Would Vout fall for such an obvious trick? McCrodden knew that he himself could not be similarly fooled . . . or perhaps he only thought that because he knew his own aim. It is natural to imagine that one's intention is obvious when one knows it oneself. Peter Vout was unaware that Rowland McCrodden and Hercule Poirot were acquainted. Furthermore, the redness of Vout's face and the two empty champagne glasses in his hand suggested he might be less vigilant than usual.

McCrodden had stopped a short distance from where Vout was standing. He could not deny that he was tempted. He was an intellectually curious man, and wanted to see if he could win. The only thing that concerned him was the idea that to do so would be to capitulate to Poirot's will. And then Fate seemed to decide the matter, as Peter Vout caught sight of McCrodden lurking nearby.

'Rowland McCrodden!' Vout strode towards him. 'What are you doing without a drink? Waiter!' he called out. 'Champagne for this gentleman, please! And for me, if you'd be so kind.'

'None for me, thank you,' McCrodden told the young waiter. 'I'll take some water instead.'

'Water? Well, that's rather dull!'

'Champagne should be reserved for celebrations,' said McCrodden. 'I'm hardly in a celebratory mood this evening.' He said this pointedly, to suggest that there was a story to be told—one that he was only too ready to tell. So far, nothing he had said had been an outright lie. The next part would be difficult, however.

'Oh, dear! Well, that's bad luck!' Vout commiserated. 'I'm sorry to hear that. Yes, indeed. Waiter, bring two glasses of champagne anyway, if you'd be so good. You never know, I might succeed in lifting my friend's spirits, and if I don't, well . . . the extra glass won't go begging. Haha!' He slapped the waiter on the back, and the young man scurried away.

'Now, then, McCrodden, you'd better tell me how you fetched up in this disconsolate state. Whatever the problem, I'm sure it's not as bad as you think it is. Things generally aren't, you know.'

Rowland McCrodden made an effort to imagine what fortuitous and alien life experiences, so vastly divergent from his own, might induce a person to utter those words and believe them to be true.

'It is not so much a problem as an irritant,' he said. 'There's nothing to be done about it—or rather, I've already done the thing that needed doing; I've told the impertinent fellow to buzz off, except I'm afraid I didn't put it quite so politely. Still, some things leave a decidedly unpleasant taste in the mouth—one that cannot be washed away with champagne!'

Rowland McCrodden had done no acting since his school days. He had a memory of loathing it and being terrible at it. This was only going to work if he drew upon his true feelings—indignation and revulsion—to bolster the false words he was about to utter. He thought about his son being accused of murder by a coward who had not dared to sign his own name, and also about John's conviction

171

that he was hated by his father, when the opposite was true.

He said to Vout: 'A detective chap came to see me today. He bombarded me with questions about private matters involving one of my most valuable clients—a man whose affairs I have handled for years. He's an old friend, really, as much as anything else. And this intrusive, grubby little man wasn't even an officer of the law! He was some sort of sleuth-for-hire, with no good reason to offer as to why I should supply him with answers to a series of really *most* intrusive questions. I sent him on his way, as I say, but . . . one wonders how such people sleep at night, undisturbed by pangs of conscience.'

Vout looked interested.

McCrodden went on, 'My client recently, and through no fault of his own, found himself in a sensitive situation that he wouldn't wish anybody to find out about. There was a young lady involved—a charming girl—and an estate to be disposed of, and a family with particular . . . sensitivities. In fact, it's a perplexing business all round and one that I should very much like to discuss with somebody impartial and unconnected to my client, but I was hardly about to chew over the details with *that* unsavoury individual!'

Rowland McCrodden pretended to be struck by a sudden thought. 'I wonder if I might consult you about it, Vout? Not tonight, of course, but perhaps if you have a spare hour next week? I don't see any harm in telling you all about it if I don't tell you the name of the chap in question.'

An expression of delight appeared on Vout's face. 'Of course! I would be only too happy to help.'

'Thank you. That's generous of you. And I'm sorry to burden you with my woes.'

'I'm very glad you did, old fellow. It's quite remarkable— but then, coincidences do happen, don't they? I recently had a similar experience to the one you've just described.'

'You did?'

'Yes. A detective—a rather well-known one, whose name in the interests of discretion I had better not mention—came to see me and asked if a longstanding client and old friend of mine might have been *murdered*. He had not, of course. He drow—Ahem!' Vout cleared his throat to cover his mistake. 'His death was a tragic accident. There was nothing deliberate or criminal about it, and nobody—no police officer and no court in the land—thought there was, apart from this detective. I told him there was no question of it being a murder, absolutely no question. This is a respectable family we're talking about. The idea is laughable! But my visitor continued to badger me. He wished to know if there was anything else I could tell him. I told him one more thing, in the spirit of helpfulness.'

'That was very decent of you and more than he deserved,' said Rowland McCrodden.

'Hmmph? Well, I didn't see that it would do any harm. The old man—my late friend and client—seemed to have an inkling that he was not long for this world. Having always tended towards a rather fiery and combative attitude, he was suddenly overcome by a desire to make peace with a chap who had been his enemy for many years. I didn't see that it would do any harm to tell the detective that much, and so I did. Was it enough for him? No! He asked the same question again: could I give him more information, about the family, their relationships? I *could* have told him considerably more, but why on earth should I share a story that I don't entirely understand myself and that has no bearing on anything now that my client's dead? It would cause great unhappiness to certain members of his family if they were to learn the truth, and how do I know that this chap won't spread it around?'

'You absolutely do not,' said Rowland McCrodden. 'You did the right thing in saying nothing. And, of course, you mustn't feel obliged to tell me any more than you have. I wouldn't want you think that because I wish to consult you about *my* client's affairs, I expect you to reciprocate in any way. After all, *your* client is deceased, and it sounds as if there is no immediate problem to be resolved, so perhaps there is no need for you to understand whatever it is that remains unclear.'

Vout frowned. 'I should like to understand, all the same. And I never have. But you're right: there is nothing to be resolved, because the story is one of something that *didn't* happen, not something that did. If I had been inclined to confide in this detective fellow, which I was not, I'd have had to tell him of events that had failed to transpire—and what would be the point of that?'

The waiter reappeared with two glasses of champagne and one of water. McCrodden took the latter, and Vout whipped the other two off the tray in a proprietorial manner. He did not raise again the question of whether McCrodden might, after all, want some champagne.

'You've aroused my curiosity,' said McCrodden, as Vout glugged down the contents of the two glasses in quick succession. 'Unlike this ill-mannered detective, I would never ask anybody to be indiscreet . . .'

'I can't see that it would do any harm to tell you, if I keep the names out of it,' said Vout. 'Would you like to hear the story?'

Rowland McCrodden indicated that he would, without displaying anything as vulgar as enthusiasm. Was it possible that this evening might have to be remembered as the only Law Society dinner he had ever enjoyed?

'The family is not one you're likely to encounter,' said Peter Vout. 'They don't live in London. And in any case, you're not an unknown quantity in the way the detective chap was. I have no doubt I can rely on you not to spread any of this about.'

'Of course.'

'Well, then: the event that did not occur was the changing of a will.'

'I see.'

'My client was an elderly gentleman who had always planned for his two granddaughters to inherit precisely equal amounts of his considerable fortune. He had no living children, you see, and was very much a father figure to his granddaughters, who had lost their parents at a young age.'

'Tragic,' Rowland McCrodden said dutifully.

'About a week before he died, my client invited me to his home to discuss what he described as "a sensitive matter". For the first time in our long acquaintance, he was particularly—one might say—cagey. He lowered his voice and kept glancing at the drawing room door, saying, "Did you hear someone?" or "Was that footsteps on the staircase?"'

'He did not want anybody to overhear the conversation?'

'No, he didn't. Which was odd, because usually he was rather blunt about his opinions and what he wanted to happen. But in this case, he wished to make a new will that would have adversely affected one of his granddaughters.'

'Only one?' McCrodden asked.

'Yes,' said Vout. 'The other would have ended up a spectacularly wealthy woman if the new will had been made, but, as I say, that didn't happen. Barn—Ahem! My client died in a tragic accident before the new will could be drawn up and signed. And, although she is quite unaware of it, the younger of his two granddaughters would not be the rich woman she is now if her grandfather had lived a little longer, for he planned to cut her off completely, without so much as a penny!'

'Goodness me.' Rowland McCrodden forgot that he was supposed to be acting a part. His surprise was genuine. He could only hope that Vout would not sense his excitement.

The younger of his two granddaughters . . . That was Annabel Treadway. Could she be a cold-blooded killer?

McCrodden wondered. Never having met her, he had no trouble believing that she could. He had known many people who were. And in spite of Barnabas Pandy's best efforts, Miss Treadway might have learned of his intentions and decided to take drastic action to safeguard her inheritance.

'I tried to make my client see sense, but he was a stubborn old cove,' said Peter Vout. 'Wouldn't listen. Did his usual trick of arguing vigorously with me until I abandoned all attempts to persuade him. It always worked! I've never known a man so sure of his own mind and desires as Barn—Ahem! And so full of energy to defend his position, however wrong-headed it was.'

'Am I to understand that you disagreed with his decision, then? You felt he was treating the younger granddaughter unfairly?'

'I did.'

'In your opinion, she had done nothing to deserve it?'

'I don't know what she had done, because my friend did not tell me. He was peculiarly oblique in his narration—told me as little as possible. Which made no sense, since I would have needed to know the details in due course in order to arrange the new will. Perhaps he was afraid of being overheard, or perhaps he was merely considering making this change and had not yet finally decided upon it.'

'Was your client in the habit of inflicting heinous punishments upon those who did not deserve them?' asked McCrodden.

'Not as a rule, no. Though, as I say, he had one

longstanding enemy—and on the same day, the day he spoke to me about the need to draw up a new will, he announced that he also wished to broker a reconciliation with this chap. I urged him to reflect upon his eagerness to make peace with this fellow, and asked if he might not employ the same approach in relation to his granddaughter. I'm afraid he laughed at me. And then he said something I have remembered ever since.'

'What was that?' Rowland McCrodden asked.

'He said, "There is a difference, Peter, between an unforgivable *act* and a person of unforgivable *character*. What matters is not what people have done but who they are. A chap might put not a foot wrong his entire life, and do nothing outward to which the world would vociferously object, yet he might be rotten to the core."'

'What was the cause of the longstanding enmity between your client and this other man?'

'I don't know, I'm afraid. Ah, well—I don't suppose it matters, now that he is no longer with us, poor fellow. And, thankfully, his death put a stop to the plan to make a new will, with the result that both granddaughters are equally well provided for. It's a relief to think that neither of them ever suspected anything was afoot.'

'You are fond of both women?' McCrodden asked.

Vout lowered his voice and said, 'I am. The truth is, I have always felt rather sorry for poor Annab—Ahem!—for the younger granddaughter. The older one was my client's favourite, and he made no attempt to hide it. She—the eldest—made a good marriage, had two children. The younger granddaughter is . . . different. My friend found her hard to fathom and was regularly irritated by her refusal to explain herself.'

'Was there something in particular that he wished her to explain?' asked McCrodden.

'Oh, she refused numerous offers of marriage, from a range of deserving and delightful suitors,' said Vout. 'My client believed it was fear that stopped her from accepting any of them, and any sort of timidity provoked him to anger. I heard him call Annabel a coward in her presence, more than once. Each time he did, she would start weeping. The worst thing was, she would always *agree*. It was most unpleasant. I never understood how he could berate her in the way he did, even in the face of her sobbing and pleading guilty to every character flaw that he accused her of possessing.'

McCrodden waited for Vout to realize that he had spoken her name aloud, but he showed no sign of having noticed his mistake. How many glasses of champagne had he taken? He must have worked his way through a bottle by now.

'There was also the dog, which was a point of bitter contention,' he went on. 'Dogs, I should say. First Skittle and then Hopscotch.'

No anonymity was to be granted to the canines of the family, then.

'The younger granddaughter loved one and loves the other as if they were fully human members of the family,' said Vout. 'My client mocked her mercilessly, I'm afraid. Called her disgusting for allowing them to sleep on her bed, but to her they were like children. *Her* children. Once the old boy locked Skittle out of the house for a whole night. It wasn't especially cold, but the dog was used to cuddling up with his owner at night, and she thought he'd be bereft to be banished. She was nearly screaming with panic, and my client only laughed at her. In fairness, Skittle didn't seem particularly perturbed to be excluded. And, in my client's defence, it *was* the day that Skittle had . . .' Vout came to an awkward halt without finishing his sentence.

'What were you about to say?' asked McCrodden.

Vout sighed. 'It's funny, but I feel as if telling you *that* story would be to speak ill of the dead. A dead *dog*, admittedly, but . . . Poor Skittle was a lovely animal, really, and he had the best of intentions. Still, the old man was not best pleased.'

McCrodden waited to be enlightened.

Vout took a further glass of champagne from a passing tray—only one this time. He said, 'My client's great-grandaughter, Ivy, nearly drowned when she was a little girl. Oh, dear! Whoops! I've just told you her name. Ah, well, never mind. You wouldn't be able to identify her by her Christian name alone. In any case . . . her name is Ivy. She's the daughter of my client's older grand-daughter.'

Ivy, Skittle, Hopscotch, a careless and undetected 'Annabel', and an old man with a name that began with 'Barn—'; Rowland McCrodden thought these snippets might well be sufficient for identification, assuming he had cared enough to pursue the matter—and had he not already known which family Vout was talking about.

'I think Ivy was three or four years old when it happened,' said Vout. 'She was out with her aunt and the dog, walking by a river, and she fell into the water. Her aunt had to leap in after her and haul her out, risking her own life in the process. There was a strong current. They both very nearly died.'

'Her aunt—do you mean the younger granddaughter?' asked McCrodden. He was thinking that this story showed Annabel Treadway as being far from a coward.

'Yes. She was walking a little ahead and had no reason to suppose little Ivy was in any danger. And nor would she have been, except that, being a mischievous child, she decided to roll down the slope of the bank. I don't know why, but young children can never resist rolling down green slopes, can they? I was the same as a boy.'

'Unless I have missed part of the story, you have not yet spoken ill of the late Skittle,' said Rowland McCrodden.

'Nor shall I,' said Vout. 'It wasn't his fault. He was a dog, and that's all there is to it. One can't hold a dog responsible . . . yet I'm afraid my client did. You see, the aunt—the younger granddaughter—wasn't the only one who tried to save young Ivy's life. Skittle did, too. But the poor creature's efforts at rescue were more of a hindrance than a help—and he scratched Ivy's face rather badly while trying to save her. *Very* badly, I'm afraid. From what I hear, he panicked and rather lashed out. Ivy was left badly scarred. Her face . . . It was most unfortunate. It *is* unfortunate. I

181

know her mother worries that no man will want her as a wife, for instance, though I'm sure that's not true. But one can see that it might be a worry.'

'And your client blamed Skittle for Ivy's scarred face?'

Vout considered the question. 'I think he was rational enough to know that the dog meant well. It was more that, well, that he blamed Skittle for *existing*. And he blamed Annabel—whoops! Still, I trust you to be discreet, old chap—he blamed Annabel *even though she saved Ivy's life*, because if it weren't for her, there would have been no Skittle there in the first place. No one else in the family cares for dogs at all. Interestingly, though, when I last visited my client at his home, I witnessed something I had never seen before . . .'

McCrodden waited.

'I saw him give Hopscotch—the current dog—a pat on the head. I thought I must be imagining things. All I had ever seen before was him shooing the dogs away and making cruel remarks about them. Used to say they were nothing but overgrown rats. It brought tears to Annabel's eyes whenever he said it, which was a source of great amusement to him. "Grow up and stop being a baby," he would say to her. I think he hoped he could toughen her up. He loved her as much as he loved her older sister, I'm sure of it—he just didn't approve of her in the same way. And then, of course . . . well, he must have decided he didn't love her at all,' said Vout sadly.

'Because of his plan to change his will?'

'Yes. The way he spoke about her when we discussed it

. . . it was clear to me that there was no love left. Something had killed it.'

'Yet, on that same day, you saw him pat her dog on the head in an affectionate manner?'

'I did—and most peculiar it was too. He didn't merely pat Hopscotch: he stroked him under his chin and I'm sure he called him a good boy. It was most unlike him, as I say. Now, where's that young chap with the drinks?'

CHAPTER 18

Mrs Dockerill's Discovery

'You fascinate me, monsieur,' said Poirot to Rowland McCrodden. 'Time after time you insist that you will *not* do for your friend Poirot this small favour—'

'There was nothing small about it,' McCrodden protested.

'—that you will not use the method I suggested to try to extract from Peter Vout the information he is hiding. Then, having refused, you do the very thing I wanted you to do, and you play your part to perfection! No acclaimed actor could have done better!'

The three of us were at Whitehaven Mansions. I had suggested to McCrodden that Poirot and I might meet him at his firm's offices, but he wouldn't hear of it. I strongly suspected that he was once again avoiding Miss Mason.

'I'm rather ashamed that I did it,' said McCrodden. 'I do not like to behave deceitfully.'

'You did so in the best of causes, *mon ami.*'

'Yes, well . . . This new information about Pandy's will changes everything, doesn't it?'

'I should say so,' I agreed.

'You are both wrong,' Poirot told us. 'It is true that each new fact is potentially useful, but this one, as with so many others we have unearthed, does not seem to take us anywhere.'

'You are surely not serious?' said McCrodden. 'Annabel Treadway had a most persuasive reason to want to do away with her grandfather. It couldn't be clearer: he was about to alter his will and leave her penniless.'

'But Lenore and Ivy Lavington have assured me that Mademoiselle Annabel cannot have killed him.'

'Then they're lying.'

I tended to agree with McCrodden. 'However fond they were of Pandy, they might nevertheless lie to protect Annabel,' I said.

'I agree,' said Poirot. 'That they would lie to save Mademoiselle Annabel's life and that she might be capable of committing murder in order to secure her material security, given the fearfulness of her nature—both are quite possible. There is, however, a problem: she was ignorant of her grandfather's wish to alter his will. It cannot be her motive if she was unaware of it.'

'Vout might be mistaken about that,' I said.

'A "might" gets us nowhere, Catchpool. Yes, she *might* have overheard the conversation about the planned new will after all, and yes, her sister and niece *might* be lying in order to save her—but one cannot rest any certain conclusions upon two "mights" of this kind.'

He was right. When you are desperately casting about

for a solution, and suddenly you learn that a vast fortune was at risk of being lost because of a proposed change to a will, it is far too tempting to decide that that must have been the motive.'

'I should like to know what Annabel Treadway did so soon before Pandy died,' said Rowland McCrodden. 'It must have been something truly appalling and shocking to him if it induced him to make peace with an enemy he had made tens of years earlier.'

'We do not know that the two are connected,' said Poirot.

'They have to be,' said McCrodden. 'When your antipathy towards one person becomes all-consuming, you find that . . . well, you might decide to dispense with all other feuds and grudges. Nobody wishes to think of himself as having a tendency towards bitterness and hatred.'

'I find this interesting,' said Poirot. 'Please, continue, my friend.'

'Well, if an unkind impulse towards one person begins to grow inside us at a rapid rate and perhaps get rather out of control, it is only natural that we should feel the need to balance that out with a sort of . . . ostentatious benevolence. If I were to guess, I should say that, when Pandy decided to cut off Miss Treadway, he balanced this out with a few clear acts of kindliness: seeking to reconcile with his old enemy Vincent Lobb, playing with the dog he usually ignored . . .'

'To make himself appear a good and charitable man in his own eyes?' said Poirot. '*Oui, je comprend*. Then . . . we might also guess that, when he made that decision,

Monsieur Pandy's bitterness towards Mademoiselle Annabel was very great indeed.'

McCrodden nodded. 'It would need to have been, yes, for my theory to be correct.'

'It is your experience with Miss Emerald Mason that has led you to this conclusion?' Poirot asked him.

'Yes. When I was first struck by the extent to which I irrationally loathed her, I felt a need to . . . well, to relinquish a few of my less important grudges.'

'Did you have many?' I asked.

'A few. Doesn't everybody?'

'I don't,' I said. 'I can't think of a single one. Do you have any grudges, Poirot?'

He was prevented from answering by a knock at the door. The valet, George, entered the room. 'There is a lady here to see you, sir. I told her you were busy, but she said it was urgent.'

'Then, if it is urgent, we must see her. Did she tell you her name?'

'She did, sir. Most thoroughly. She identified herself as Jane Dockerill, and also as Mrs Hugo Dockerill, the wife of the housemaster of Timothy Lavington and Frederick Rule at Turville College.'

'Please show her in, Georges.'

Jane Dockerill was a tiny slip of a thing, with curly dark brown hair, glasses with severe black frames, and a large brown bag that she carried into the room with both hands. It was wider than she was. She moved and spoke quickly.

When Poirot stood and introduced himself, she shook his hand at the same time as saying, 'And who are these other two gentleman?'

'Rowland McCrodden, solicitor, and Inspector Edward Catchpool of Scotland Yard.'

'I see,' said Jane Dockerill. 'I take it you've been discussing this business in which we are all involved?'

We all nodded. It did not occur to us to hold anything back. Jane Dockerill was the most naturally commanding person I could remember being in a room with. Even the Super might have done her bidding without question.

'Good,' she said. Then, without pausing for breath, 'I came here to deliver two items: one you already know about; the other you do not. The first is Hugo's letter, the one in which he is accused of murder. I thought you would probably need it.'

'Indeed, madame. Most helpful.' Poirot had never sounded more like an obedient schoolboy.

Jane Dockerill pulled the letter out of her bag and handed it to him. He read it, then passed it to me. Apart from the recipient's name and address and the words 'Dear Mr Dockerill' at the top, it was identical to the letter received by John McCrodden, right down to the missing ink from the horizontal bar of each letter 'e'. I passed the letter on to Rowland McCrodden.

'And now for the item that you were not expecting,' said Jane Dockerill. 'Neither, I should like to say, was I expecting it. I was shocked to discover it where I did, and I sincerely hope it does not mean what I think it means.'

She produced from her bag an object that I did not immediately recognize. It was blue—or, rather, there was something blue inside it: blue with tiny flashes of white and yellow. Whatever it was, it was wrapped in cellophane to make an odd-looking parcel.

'What is inside this package, madame?' Poirot asked.

'A dress. It was wrapped when wet. I found it taped to the underside of Timothy Lavington's bed. I like to keep all the dormitories spotlessly clean, which means—if you're going to do a thorough job, which I like to—looking under the beds regularly to check there is no rubbish piled up there, or forbidden items stashed away out of sight.'

'Very commendable, madame.'

Jane Dockerill moved briskly on. 'Before yesterday, the last time I looked under the beds in Timothy's dormitory was four weeks ago. I know precisely when it was because it was my first inspection since the holidays. Four weeks ago, this package was not there. Then, yesterday, there it was—taped, as I say, to the bottom of the frame of the bed: Timothy Lavington's bed. I unwrapped it in Timothy's presence, to see if he knew what it was. He recognized the dress as belonging to his aunt, but was baffled by its presence in his dorm.' Pointedly, Jane Dockerill added, 'A stiff, badly-dried dress, still damp in places. Belonging to his aunt, Annabel Treadway.'

'This causes you to suspect something?' Poirot asked her. 'May I ask what?'

'Is it not obvious? I suspect—though I pray it's not true—that Annabel Treadway murdered Barnabas Pandy

189

by drowning him in his bath, for that was how he died. Her dress got wet in the process, and, afraid it would incriminate her, she hid it at Turville, under Timothy's bed.'

'As far as we know, Mr Pandy's death was an accident,' I felt obliged to say. 'From an official point of view—'

'Oh, that means nothing,' said Jane Dockerill. 'I now believe Mr Pandy was murdered, whatever anybody else thinks.'

'Upon what do you base this belief?' asked Poirot.

'Common sense and probability,' she told him. 'Most accidental deaths are not followed by multiple accusations of murder and strange packages taped to bed frames. This one has been—therefore it seems likely to me that it was indeed a murder.'

Poirot gave a small nod. It was not suggestive of whole-hearted agreement.

'Aren't you going to open the package?' said Mrs Dockerill.

'*Oui, bien sûr*. Catchpool, if you would be so kind.'

It was easy enough to pull off the tape and unwrap the cellophane. We all looked at the pale blue fabric as it was freed from its wrapping. The spots of yellow and white turned out to be tiny flowers. Parts of the material, deprived of air for weeks, had become slimy.

'Notice the smell,' said Jane Dockerill.

'It is the oil of olives,' said Poirot. 'I smell it distinctly. This is the dress that Annabel Treadway wore the day that Barnabas Pandy died. Lenore Lavington described it to me: blue, with flowers of white and yellow. Only in one respect is the fabric of this dress different from the one Madame Lavington described.'

'For goodness' sake, don't keep us in suspense,' said Jane Dockerill. 'How is it different?'

'This dress was clearly wrapped while it was still wet,' I said.

'*Précisément*, Catchpool. Lenore Lavington told me that the dress of his sister was not wet when they stood together in the bathroom on 7 December. She offered this as proof that her sister could not have drowned their grandfather. The dress of Annabel Treadway, according to Lenore Lavington—her blue dress, with yellow and white flowers— *was completely dry.*'

CHAPTER 19

Four More Letters

'This is quite a development, isn't it?' said Jane Dockerill.

'It is,' Poirot agreed.

'I have known Timothy's mother for many years. She would certainly lie to protect a member of her family—no question about it. Hugo and I can't say a word to Timothy without her swooping down upon us in a mist of quiet fury to make a range of exaggerated threats: she'll see to it that Hugo is fired, she'll remove Timothy and, with him, the kind donations upon which the school so relies.'

Jane Dockerill uncrossed her legs, then crossed them the other way. 'Schools are terribly unfair places, you know. There are some boys—the ones whose parents have a suitable respect for authority—who are ordered to tuck in their shirts, straighten their ties, pull up their socks, and we do our well-intentioned ordering around safe in the knowledge that no member of those boys' families will turn up in due course to make our lives a misery. Other boys—and I'm afraid both Timothy Lavington and Freddie Rule fall into this category—can walk around with their blazers torn and their ties all askew, and we all contrive not to notice. Heaven forbid that we should provoke an avoidable encounter with a parent of Lenore Lavington's stripe!'

'Madame, who could have taped the parcel containing the dress to the underneath of Timothy Lavington's bed?' Poirot asked her.

'Almost anybody. Timothy himself—though I know he didn't do it. He was as surprised to see it as I was. His mother, sister or aunt could have done it during one of their visits. I or my husband could have done it. I didn't, of course, and neither did Hugo.' She laughed. 'The very idea! Hugo would never in a thousand years have been able to find adhesive tape, even if he were to have the bright idea to stick a dress to the frame of a bed.'

'Is there anybody else?' asked Poirot.

'Oh, yes, said Jane Dockerill. 'As I said: almost everybody. Any of the boys in our house, any boy from one of the other houses who crept in when Timothy's dorm room was empty. Any teacher. Any parent.'

I heard myself sigh. Poirot murmured, 'No parameters.'

'We can narrow it down a bit, you'll be glad to hear,' Jane Dockerill said with a wry smile. 'A person not known at Turville wouldn't have stood a chance of sneaking in without being stopped and thoroughly interrogated. Like all communities, we suspect outsiders of being bent on our destruction and expel them from the premises whenever we stumble upon them.' She looked irritated by our lack of reaction. 'That was a joke.'

Obediently, but too late to please her, Poirot, McCrodden and I all laughed.

'So it could have been any person from within the school community, including the parent of a pupil?' Poirot said.

'It could, I'm afraid.'

'Have you ever, in this school community or associated with it, encountered a man by the name of John McCrodden?'

At the mention of his son's name, Rowland McCrodden twitched slightly.

'No,' said Jane Dockerill. Her denial appeared genuine.

'The family of Timothy Lavington . . . have they visited him at school since Barnabas Pandy died, and since the day you checked under the bed four weeks ago when there was no package stuck there?'

'Yes. Lenore, Annabel and Timothy's sister Ivy were at Turville about two weeks ago. Any one of them could have taped the parcel containing the wet dress to the bed frame during that visit.'

'When did Madame Sylvia Rule last come to the school?' Poirot asked.

'Last week,' said Mrs Dockerill. 'With Mildred and her fiancé, Eustace.'

'You put Freddie in the "boys who don't get ordered around" category,' I said. 'Does that mean that Sylvia Rule is as fearsome a prospect as Lenore Lavington?'

'Sylvia's unbearable,' said Jane Dockerill. 'I should explain that, having lived and worked at Turville for so long, I find approximately two thirds of the parents unbearable, in so many different ways. They are generally far more difficult than the boys. Freddie Rule, Sylvia's son, is a sweetheart. His good nature must come from his father.'

'He is a loner, is he not?' said Poirot.

'He's not a popular boy,' said Jane Dockerill with a sigh. 'He's sensitive, complicated, quiet—not a person of high social status. And he feels things very deeply. He couldn't be more different from Timothy Lavington. Timothy has no use for boys like Freddie. His friends are all like him: loud, confident show-offs. The highest rung of Turville's social ladder. It broke my heart to see Freddie on his own all the time. I decided that if those stupid boys didn't want to be his friend, then I would. And I am.' She smiled. 'Freddie has become my little helper around the house. I don't know what I'd do without him. Everybody at Turville knows now: if they bully Freddie, they will have me to deal with.'

'He has been bullied?' I asked. 'Not by Timothy Lavingon, I don't suppose?'

'No, never by Timothy, but by plenty of others.' Jane Dockerill looked angry, suddenly. 'It's terribly unfair. Freddie is seen by many as tainted. It's his mother. There are rumours about her, you see—that she, um, makes her living in a way that is both immoral and unlawful. I don't expect there's a shred of truth in these lurid stories.'

'I see. Madame Dockerill, may I ask you about the Christmas Fair on 7 December? Freddie Rule was there, yes? With his mother and sister, and Eustace?'

'Yes, they were all there.'

'And Timothy Lavington, and you and your husband?'

'Of course. I was dashing about all day like a mad creature.'

'Of the people I have listed, can you be certain that any of them were at the fair for the entire day, from when it started until it closed?'

'I've just told you: they were all there,' said Jane Dockerill.

'You were watching them, with your own eyes, for every second of the day?

She looked surprised. 'No. How could I? I was desperately busy.'

'Then, pardon me, madame, but how do you know that they were there all day?'

'Well, they were certainly all at the supper in the evening. And I saw them now and then throughout the day. Where else would they have—?' She stopped abruptly. 'Oh. I see what you mean. You're wondering if one of them might have slipped out to go and kill Barnabas Pandy, then slipped back in?'

'Is it possible?' asked Poirot.

'I suppose, in the sense that you mean . . . yes, it is possible. Any of them could have absented himself or herself for the required time. They would have needed a means of getting to Combingham Hall, of course.'

After successfully dodging her questions about what next steps he planned to take, Poirot thanked Jane Dockerill, and she left.

'She has an unhealthy attachment to the Rule boy,' said Rowland McCrodden, once she had gone.

'I don't think that's true,' I told him. 'She feels protective towards a lonely boy is how I should describe it.'

'I'd be surprised if there were not as many rumours about Mrs Dockerill and young Freddie Rule as there are about Sylvia Rule being a lady of the night,' said McCrodden.

'Catchpool, when you visit Turville College, try to hear as many of these rumours as you can,' Poirot said.

'The boys are hardly likely to say anything unseemly in the presence of a Scotland Yard inspector,' I said. 'Or am I to disguise myself as a bun in the tuck-shop?'

'You will find a way, Catchpool.'

Poirot ran his fingers along the slimy fabric of the blue dress, then produced a handkerchief to wipe his hand. 'The dress of Mademoiselle Treadway,' he murmured. 'What does it mean? Does it mean that the three ladies of Combingham Hall have lied to me, and Kingsbury also? That they all know Annabel Treadway murdered Monsieur Pandy, and seek to conceal the truth? Or . . . ?' He turned to me.

'Or,' I took my cue, 'is somebody trying to frame Annabel Treadway?'

'*Exactement!* If the aim were to protect Mademoiselle Annabel, the most sensible plan would have been to wash and dry the dress immediately.'

'What if traces of olive oil would still be detectable even after washing?' I said. 'Perhaps the dress had to disappear so that no one would ever ask the question: "Why would there be olive oil on this dress?"'

Poirot said, '*Mes amis*, we have met Jane Dockerill only once. Annabel Treadway has met her many more times, on her visits to Timothy at school. Would she not assume that Madame Dockerill would check every dormitory in her boarding house most thoroughly? Having met her once, that is what I would assume. There must be hundreds of beds at Turville. Why not choose one that belongs to a stranger?'

'You think, then, that the hiding of the dress under Timothy's bed is more likely to be an attempt to frame Miss Treadway than evidence of her guilt?' asked McCrodden.

'I do not yet know enough . . .' Poirot began thoughtfully. 'Notice that the dress is equally damp all over. Mademoiselle Annabel's clothing, if she drowned her grandfather, would not have been. The arms would have been extremely wet, but the bottom of the dress? The back of it? *Non.* These would have been much drier, perhaps not wet at all. And yet, if at the time of wrapping in the cellophane the arms were drenched, while other parts of the dress were dry, the water could have soaked through to wet the dress in its entirety.'

'We may invent as many theories as we like, Poirot, but we know nothing,' said McCrodden wearily. 'There are too many possibilities. Reluctant as I am to admit defeat—'

'You think we ought to give up?' said Poirot. 'No, no, my friend. You are quite wrong. There are indeed many possibilities—but we much closer, now, to the truth!'

'Are we?' I said. 'How? Why?'

'Catchpool, do you not see what is now clear?'

I did not. Neither did Rowland McCrodden.

Poirot laughed at us both, in our ignorance. 'Thanks to this dress, I am confident that I will soon have all the answers. I do not have them yet, but I will. I intend to set myself a challenge and put a deadline in place. Let us see if Hercule Poirot can beat the clocks!'

'What do you mean?' I asked him.

He laughed again. 'It astonishes me that neither of you sees what I see. A pity, but never mind. Soon, I will explain. *Alors, maintenant*, it is time for me compose four letters, to be sent to Sylvia Rule, Annabel Treadway, John McCrodden and Hugo Dockerill. And this time, they will be from the real Hercule Poirot!'

THE THIRD QUARTER

CHAPTER 20

The Letters Arrive

Eustace Campbell-Brown was reclining in the drawing room of his fiancée Mildred's London townhouse when Mildred's mother bustled into the room holding a letter and a torn envelope with the very tips of her fingers, as if to touch them any more thoroughly might contaminate her. Sylvia Rule gasped in horror at the sight of her future son-in-law, though she had seen him many times before, and sitting in this exact position: with a cigarette in one hand and a book in the other.

'Good morning,' said Eustace. He did not think he could get into trouble for saying something so simple.

'Where is Mildred?'

'Upstairs, getting dressed. I'm taking her out for the day.' He smiled.

Sylvia Rule stared at him for a long time. Then she said, 'How much do you want?'

'I beg your pardon?'

'To leave Mildred alone and disappear for ever. There must be an amount of money that would tempt you.'

Eustace placed his cigarette in the ashtray on the table beside him and put down his book. So, he thought to himself, it had come to this, despite his best efforts to win the esteem of his soon-to-be mother-in-law.

It was time, at last, to stop trying—to stop being polite and charming and to say what he felt like saying for once.

'Finally, an enticement of money,' he said. 'I've been wondering how long it would take you. Just think, you could have made me an offer this time last year and I'd have been out of your life long ago.'

'Then . . . there is a sum . . . ?'

'No, Sylvia, there is not. I was teasing you. The fact is, I love Mildred and she loves me. The sooner you get used to that, the happier you will be.'

'Oh, you are a vile, disgusting man!'

'I don't think I am,' said Eustace quite reasonably. 'Neither does Mildred. Have you ever considered, Sylvia, that you might be the ghastly one? You are, after all, a murderer. Mildred might not know the truth about you, but I do. Don't worry—I have no wish to distress her by telling her what I know. But I don't suppose there's any chance you might lay off me for a while, is there? In return for my keeping your secret, I mean.'

'You're a liar!' Sylvia Rule's face had turned white. She lowered herself into an armchair.

'No, I'm not,' said Eustace. 'If it were not true, you would be saying, "What do you mean?" and "What on earth are you on about?" You know perfectly well what I'm talking about.'

At that moment Mildred Rule appeared in the drawing room wearing the blank expression she always wore in the company of her mother and her fiancé. She did not ask why Sylvia looked so ashen-faced, nor why Eustace was glowing with a new, peculiar energy, one she had not seen in him before. She knew that something important had probably happened in her absence, and hoped to avoid finding out what it was. Mildred had recently decided that it was better for her to know nothing about what passed between Sylvia and Eustace, and not to enquire about her mother's loathing for the man she loved more than anything.

She noticed the letter and torn envelope that her mother was holding. 'What's that?' she asked. If her mother was upset about something other than Eustace, then Mildred was interested to know what it was.

'It's another letter from Hercule Poirot,' said Sylvia Rule.

'Accusing you of murder again, is he?' Eustace sneered.

Sylvia passed the letter to Mildred. 'Read it aloud,' she said. 'It mentions you. And *him*.'

'"Dear Madame Rule,"' read Mildred. '"It is of vital importance that you attend a meeting at Combingham Hall, home of the deceased Barnabas Pandy, on 24 February, at 2 o'clock. I will be present and so will Inspector Edward Catchpool of Scotland Yard. Others will be present as well. The mystery of the death of Barnabas Pandy, in which we are all interested parties, will be resolved, and a murderer apprehended. Please extend this same invitation to your daughter Mildred and to her fiancé Eustace. It is important that they attend also. Yours sincerely, Hercule Poirot."'

'I don't suppose we have any way of knowing if the letter's from the real Hercule Poirot this time?' said Eustace.

'What shall we do?' asked Mildred. 'Shall we go? Or shall we ignore it?' She hoped that her mother and Eustace would, for once, agree upon a course of action. If they disagreed, Mildred knew her mind would freeze and be unable to make sense of anything.

'I have no intention of attending,' said Sylvia Rule.

'We have to go,' said Eustace. 'All of us. Don't you want to know who this murderer is, Sylvia? *I* do.'

John McCrodden touched the arm of the woman in his bed. He couldn't remember her name; it might have been Annie, or Aggie. She was lying on her front, facing away from him. 'Wake up. Wake up, will you?'

'I'm awake.' She rolled over with a yawn. 'Lucky for you. I don't take kindly to being woken when it's my day off work. Though, since it's you . . .' She grinned and reached out to touch John's face.

He pushed her hand away. 'I'm not in the mood. Sorry. Look, I've got things to do, so you'd better be on your way.' A peculiar letter had arrived for him and he wanted to read it again, more carefully. He couldn't concentrate with her still here.

The woman sat up, covering herself with the bed-sheet. 'Well, you're charming, aren't you? Is this how you treat all the girls?'

'As a matter of fact, it is. I never intend them any harm, but they always take it badly. No doubt you will too.'

'I suppose you'll promise to take me out again, as soon as you can, and then I'll never hear from you again,' said the woman resentfully, tears forming in the corners of her eyes.

'No. I'm promising nothing. And I don't want to take you anywhere. I enjoyed last night, but that's all it was: one night. You won't see me again, unless by chance. You may scream at me as you leave, if it makes you feel better.'

Once he'd said that, she was out of his room in seconds. She would doubtless think him callous, but she would be wrong. The cruel thing would have been to allow her to build up her hopes. When he was much younger, John had met a woman and known within moments that here was a person he could love for ever. He had not felt that way about anybody else, before or since. Nor had he spoken of the feeling to a single soul, for it had been too powerful to describe and, in any case, no one would have believed it possible who had not personally fallen into a similar chasm of longing. Humans, as a rule, were doggedly determined not to believe in the experiences of anyone but themselves.

John dressed and took the strange letter over to the chair by the window. He read it once more, shaking his head. Instead of deciding that the four accusations sent in his name were no more than a prank, and resolving to think no more about them, Hercule Poirot had evidently assigned to himself responsibility for solving this murder.

Had anyone paid him to undertake the task? John doubted it. Like Annie or Aggie or whatever her name was,

Poirot had chosen to make life more difficult and complicated than it needed to be. He had now sent letters of
invitation to a 'meeting' about Barnabas Pandy's death to
John and no doubt many other people. Making matters
worse, his letter to John contained the unwelcome line:
'Others will be present as well, including your father,
Rowland McCrodden.'

John was no fool. He had known for some time that he
had unfairly maligned both his father and Hercule Poirot.
He now believed that neither man was responsible for the
letter in which he had been accused of murdering Barnabas
Pandy. Apologies were owed; there was no getting away
from that, but there was nothing John hated more than
admitting he had been wrong—especially to two men whose
work sometimes led to nooses being placed around people's
necks.

'I'll go to Poirot's meeting,' he thought. 'That will have
to do, by way of apology. And maybe I'll find out who sent
me that letter.'

John wrote a short note to Poirot saying that he would
be at Combingham Hall on 24 February as instructed. He
put it in an envelope, which he was about to seal when he
remembered Catalina.

Ah, Catalina, his Spanish lady-friend. Now there was a
sensible, resourceful woman. Damned attractive, too. She
let John come and go as he pleased, without ever applying
pressure or crying all over him. She enjoyed his company
but managed perfectly well without him, as he did without
her. John had not met many people, men or women, whom

he felt were his equals, but Catalina most certainly was: a brilliant woman and, now, a brilliant alibi. Good old Catalina!

John walked over to his bed and reached under it for the bundle of her letters that he kept there. Most of them were about King Alfonso XIII and the precariousness of General Miguel Primo de Rivera's hold on power. Catalina was a committed Republican. John smiled. He did not care for politics. What people claimed to stand for meant very little, he had always found, and told you nothing about their true character. It was like judging a person by their choice of socks or handkerchief.

He selected Catalina's letter dated 21 December 1929 and inserted it in the envelope he would send to Poirot. Pulling out the letter he'd just written, he added, beneath his signature, the words: 'Alibi for 7 December enclosed'.

'Oh, dear,' cried Annabel Treadway. 'Hoppy, what shall I do? A meeting, here? He doesn't say how many people he's invited. Lenore will be furious. We shall have to think about the catering, and I haven't got a head for it at all—not even to talk to Kingsbury or Cook about it. But . . . oh, goodness. I'm going to have to tell Lenore, and . . . look, he says that a murderer will be apprehended. Oh, dear!'

Hopscotch lifted his head from Annabel's lap and gave her a questioning look. They were in the morning room at Combingham Hall, having recently returned from a ball game in the meadow. Hopscotch eyed Annabel hopefully, trying to work out if her latest exclamation might mean that she would soon be ready to run back outside and play a little more.

'I'm frightened,' said Annabel. 'I'm so frightened. Of everything, except you, darling Hoppy.'

The dog rolled over, wanting his tummy to be scratched.

'What if Lenore forbids Poirot from holding his meeting here?' As she spoke these words, Annabel was struck by a sudden, powerful realization. 'Oh!' she gasped. 'Even if she forbids it, the truth will come out. There is no way to stop it, not now that Hercule Poirot is involved. Oh, Hoppy, if it weren't for you . . .'

She left the sentence unfinished, not wishing to alarm the dog by saying what she would do if she were not so reluctant to leave him alone in the world. Lenore didn't care about him. Ivy claimed to, but she didn't love him the way Annabel did, as if he were a fully-fledged member of the family—which he absolutely was. Skittle had been too. 'One day,' thought Annabel, 'the world will be a more enlightened place and we will treat dogs as well as we treat people. Oh, but—I am a dreadful hypocrite!' She started to cry.

Hopscotch rolled over and placed his paw in her hand in a consolatory manner, but she continued to weep.

'Look at this, Jane.' Hugo Dockerill tried to pass his wife the letter he'd just opened. 'That trickster is pretending to be Poirot again. I suppose I ought to tell him. Poirot, I mean.'

Jane balanced a large pile of laundry on the arm of the nearest sofa, and snatched the paper out of her husband's hand. She read aloud: "Dear Monsieur Dockerill, It is of vital importance that you and your wife Jane attend a meeting at Combingham Hall . . ." She mouthed the rest of the words silently. Looking up at Hugo, she said, 'Why do you think this isn't from the real Poirot?'

He frowned. 'Do you think it might be?'

'Yes. Look at the signature. It's quite different from the one on the other letter. *Quite* different. Having met Poirot, I should say that this could well be his handwriting: very neat, with a few fancy touches here and there.'

'Golly,' said Hugo. 'I wonder why he wants us to go to Combingham Hall?'

'Have you read the letter?'

'Yes. Twice.'

'It explains why he wants us to go.'

'Do you think he's got to the bottom of it all, then? Who else do you suppose he's invited?'

'I would imagine the other three people who were accused in the first lot of letters will be there,' said Jane.

'Yes, that would make sense. What do you think, dearest one? Shall we go?'

'What do you think, Hugo? Do you want to go?'

'Well, I . . . I mean . . . I rather thought you might take a view on that, my dear. I mean . . . Well, it's hard to know. Am I . . . Are we busy on that day?'

Jane laughed affectionately and linked her arm through his. 'I'm teasing you. We're busy every day, or at least I am, but of course we must go. I want to know what the great Hercule Poirot has worked out, and who this murderer is. I wish we didn't have to wait nearly a week. I want to know *now* what he intends to tell us all.'

CHAPTER 21

The Day of the Typewriters

The Day of the Typewriters, as I will always think of it, turned out to be more interesting than I had expected it to. For one thing, it proved Poirot right: it really is a good test of character to put several people in the exact same situation and examine the difference in their reactions. I had been making a list as I went along, and dreading the moment when I would have to show it to Poirot and hear all about how vastly superior his list would have been. Mine read as follows:

Offices of Donaldson & McCrodden Solicitors
Stanley Donaldson allowed me to test his typewriter. Its letter 'e' was not faulty. (Donaldson also confirmed that Rowland Rope was with him for the whole of Saturday 7 December, first at the Athenaeum Club and then at the Palace Theatre.) None of the typewriters that I found in the firm's offices was the one we are looking for. I tested all of them, and then Miss Emerald

Mason insisted on testing them again just to make sure.

Home of Sylvia and Mildred Rule

There was one typewriter in the house. Mrs Rule tried to forbid me from entering and told me I had no business invading her privacy and hounding her when she had done nothing wrong, but then her daughter Mildred persuaded her to cooperate. I tested the typewriter and the letter 'e' was perfectly normal.

Eustace Campbell-Brown

Finally we know his last name! Mildred told me where I would find him. I visited him at home. He seemed pleased to find me on his doorstep and was happy for me to test his typewriter. It was not the one we are looking for. As I was leaving, Mr Campbell-Brown said, 'If I wanted to send letters accusing people of murder, signed in the name of Hercule Poirot, the very first thing I should do is check that the machine I was typing them on had no irregularities that might identify me.' I did not know quite what to make of this.

John McCrodden

John McCrodden told me, in a rude and surly manner, that he does not own a typewriter. His landlady does, but she assured me that McCrodden had never used it.

Peter Vout
Mr Vout was gracious enough to allow me to check all the typewriters in his firm's offices, and I found them all to be in good working order.

All Typewriters Not Based in London
Combingham Hall typewriters—Poirot tried to check, but was prevented from doing so.

Turville College's typewriters—still need to be checked. (I shall go tomorrow.)

Vincent Lobb—does he own a typewriter? If so, it needs to be checked. Still no luck tracking down Lobb.

CHAPTER 22

The Solitary Yellow Square of Cake

'Good morning, Monsieur McCrodden. You are surprised to see me here, *non?*'

John McCrodden looked up to find Hercule Poirot peering down at him where he sat cross-legged on the floor beside his market stall, a cloth bag full of coins in his lap. There were no customers around; the market had only just opened. 'What do you want?' McCrodden asked. 'Didn't you get the letter I sent to you?'

'From a woman by the name of Catalina? Yes, it arrived.'

'Then you also received my note in which I undertook to present myself at Combingham Hall on the date you want me there—so why are you here now?'

'I wished to see you before our meeting at Combingham Hall, at which others will be present. I should like to speak to you alone.'

'I have customers to deal with.'

'You do not have them now,' said Poirot with a polite smile. 'Tell me, who is this Mademoiselle Catalina?'

McCrodden grimaced. 'What does it matter to you? She's nobody you know. If you're suggesting she isn't real and I've fabricated an alibi for myself, why don't you go to Spain and talk to her yourself? Her address is on all of her letters, including the one I sent you.'

Poirot produced the letter from his pocket. 'It is most convenient for you, this letter,' he said. 'It is dated 21 December last year, and it refers to "fourteen days ago today" when you and Mademoiselle Catalina were together in . . .'—Poirot glanced down at the paper in his hand—'. . . Ribadesella. If you were in Ribadesella on 7 December, you cannot also have been at Combingham Hall, drowning Barnabas Pandy.'

'I'm glad we agree about that,' said McCrodden. 'Since we do—since we both know that I couldn't have murdered Pandy—would you care to explain your continued interest in me? Why must I attend a meeting at Combingham Hall on 24 February? And why, when I agree to do so, do you come and pester me at my place of work? It might not be the sort of work that impresses the likes of you and my father, but it's work all the same. It's how I earn my living, and you're getting in my way.'

'But still you have no customers,' Poirot pointed out. 'I interrupt nothing.'

McCrodden sighed. 'It's slow at the moment, but it'll pick up,' he said. 'And if it doesn't, I'll do something else to earn a crust. What my father has never understood about me is that I don't much care what I do. It's only work, and life's more interesting if you try a few different things. I've tried telling him that's how I see it. You'd think he wouldn't care if I move from one employment to another, wouldn't you, when he's disapproved of every single job I've ever had? He hated me being a miner—didn't want his son getting his hands dirty digging into the cliff like a commoner—but then he didn't like it when I worked at the clean end either. Didn't like me making and selling the trinkets, didn't like me working on a farm, and doesn't like me working here at the market. Yet he complains when I move around because he only approves of people who stick at things.'

'Monsieur, I am not here to talk about your father.'

'Answer me one thing, Poirot.' John McCrodden leapt to his feet. 'Do you approve of this legal form of murder that we have in our country? Because as far as I'm concerned, you're no better than a murderer yourself if you're in favour of killing those who have committed crimes—even the most serious crimes.'

Poirot looked around. The market had started to fill with people and noise. Still nobody approached John McCrodden's stall.

'If I answer your question, will you answer one of mine?' he asked.

'I will.'

'*Bien.* I believe that the loss of life, for whatever reason, is a tragedy. However, when the most heinous of crimes has been committed, is it not fitting that the perpetrator should suffer the most severe of punishments? Does justice not demand it?'

McCrodden shook his head. 'You're just like my father.

You profess to care about justice, while not having the faintest idea of what it means.'

'Now it is my turn to ask the question,' said Poirot. 'Think carefully, please, before answering. You have told me that you were not acquainted with Barnabas Pandy.'

'I never so much as heard his name until your . . . until that letter arrived.'

'Listen to these names and tell me if any of them are familiar to you: Lenore Lavington, Ivy Lavington, Timothy Lavington.'

McCrodden shook his head. 'Never heard of any Lavingtons,' he said.

'Sylvia Rule, Freddie Rule, Mildred Rule.'

'I have heard the name Sylvia Rule, but only from you,' said McCrodden. 'Or, rather, from the man who works for you. Don't you recall? You had him come into the room and tell me that Mrs Rule had also received a letter in your name, accusing her of murder.'

'*Oui*, monsieur, I remember.'

'Then why ask me, if you know I know the name? Some sort of test?'

'What about Mildred Rule and Freddie Rule?' asked Poirot.

'I agreed to answer one question,' McCrodden reminded him. 'You've used up your allowance, mate.'

'Monsieur McCrodden, I do not understand you. You seem to disapprove of the taking of life when it is done by the law. Do you not also disapprove of the lives taken by unlawful murderers?'

219

'Of course I do.'

'Then believe me when I tell you that I am trying to catch such a person: a meticulous and careful murderer, driven not by passion but by calculation. Why should you not want to help me?'

'You sound as if you've worked out who killed this Pandy fellow. Have you?'

Poirot had not. All he knew was that there was a murderer to be caught: a dangerous and wicked person who must be stopped. He had never before announced, in advance, a date on which he would reveal facts of such importance *that he did not yet know*. Why, then, had he chosen to do so in the case of Barnabas Pandy? Poirot was not sure he knew the answer. He wondered if it might be a strange sort of prayer, disguised as an exciting and alarming challenge.

Avoiding John McCrodden's question, he said, 'I am still waiting for an answer from you.'

McCrodden cursed under his breath, then said, 'No, I've never heard of Mildred Rule or Freddie Rule.'

'What about Annabel Treadway, or Hugo and Jane Dockerill? Or Eustace Campbell-Brown?'

'No. None of these names mean anything to me. Should they?'

'Not necessarily, no. Do you know Turville College?'

'I've heard of it, naturally.'

'But you have no personal connection with the place.'

'No. My father sent me first to Eton and then to Rugby. I was expelled from both.'

'Thank you, Monsieur McCrodden. It seems that you are truly the solitary yellow square of cake, all alone at the edge of the plate. But *why*? That is the question: why?'

'Cake?' snarled John McCrodden. 'Nothing that's happened recently makes sense to me. That's why I shan't bother to ask you what I have in common with a piece of cake! I'm sure I wouldn't understand, even if you told me.'

CHAPTER 23

Meaning Harm

As I set off to Turville College two days later, in the hope of talking to Timothy Lavington and examining all available typewriters, I could not help but feel hard done by. Poirot was also travelling, and I wished I could have swapped places with him. He was on his way to Llanidloes in Wales to talk to a woman by the name of Deborah Dakin. Vincent Lobb, we had learned the day before from one of Poirot's mysterious 'helpers', had died some thirteen years earlier. Mrs Dakin, the widow of Lobb's eldest son, was the only surviving member of the family.

I should have liked to go with Poirot to speak to her. Instead, with time running away from us and Poirot's quite unnecessarily self-imposed deadline of 24 February looming, I had been assigned the Turville trip.

I did not relish the prospect of venturing inside a boys' boarding school. I attended such a school myself and, despite the education I received, I would not wish the overall experience on anybody.

I felt slightly more comfortable once I was inside Coode House, the boarding house run by Hugo and Jane Dockerill. It was large and wide with a flat façade and a symmetrical distribution of windows, like an enormous doll's house. Inside, it was warm, clean and generally tidy, though as I waited to be shown to Hugo Dockerill's study I spotted one pile of books and one of papers that had been abandoned on the floor close to the front door. Notes had been placed on top of the piles: 'Hugo, please move these' and 'Hugo, please find a proper place for these'. Both were signed 'J'.

A short, bespectacled boy appeared, the third who had helped me so far. This one, like the previous two, was wearing the full Turville uniform: maroon blazer, dark grey trousers, maroon and yellow striped tie. 'I'm to take you to Mr Dockerill's study,' he said.

I thanked him and followed him past the foot of the staircase into a wide corridor. We had turned several corners before he stopped and knocked at a door.

'Come in!' called a man's voice from within.

My pupil guide entered, mumbled something about a visitor, then ran away as if he feared there might be repercussions for his having introduced me to the room. The man, with almost no hair and a wide smile on his face, came towards me, hand extended.

'Inspector Catchpool!' he said warmly. 'I'm Hugo Dockerill, and this is my wife Jane, whom I understand you have met? Welcome to Coode House! We like to think it's the best of all the boarding houses, but of course we are biased.'

'It *is* the best,' said Jane Dockerill matter-of-factly. 'Hello again, Inspector Catchpool.' She sat in a leather armchair in the corner of the room. Books lined every wall from top to bottom, and there were many piles of them on the floor. Presumably this was where those wrongly positioned piles near Coode House's front door would eventually be moved to.

On Jane Dockerill's left, on a straight-backed sofa, sat a boy with dark hair that fell over his large brown eyes. He was a strange-looking character: he was tall, and the eyes, hair and bone structure suggested he ought to be handsome, but the lower part of his face had a clumsily-assembled look about it. He wore an embattled expression and had the bearing of someone who expected to be harangued or punished.

'Good morning, Mrs Dockerill,' I said. 'A pleasure to meet you, Mr Dockerill. Thank you for fitting me into your busy day.'

'Oh, we're delighted to have you. Delighted!' proclaimed the housemaster.

'And this is Timothy Lavington, the late Barnabas Pandy's great-grandson,' said his wife.

'Is it true that you believe Grandy was murdered?' Timothy asked without looking at me.

'Timothy . . .' There was a warning tone in Jane Dockerill's voice. She evidently feared the question might be the prelude to some impertinence on Timothy's part.

'It's perfectly all right,' I told her. 'Timothy, I want you to feel free to ask me whatever questions spring to mind. This must be horrible for you.'

'I would describe it as frustrating rather than horrible,' said the boy. 'If it was murder and not an accident, is it too late to catch whoever did it?'

'No.'

'Good,' said Timothy.

'Though I think it most unlikely that Mr Pandy was murdered. You must try not to worry.'

'I'm not worried. And, unlike you, I *don't* think it's unlikely,' he said.

'Timothy,' warned Jane Dockerill again, obviously knowing that impertinence was now inevitable

He gestured towards her without looking at her and said to me, 'As you can see, I'm prevented from speaking freely by Mrs Dockerill's desire for me to say only the sorts of things that grown-ups think boys my age *should* say.'

'Why don't you think it unlikely that your great-grand-father was murdered?' I asked him.

'Several reasons. Mother, Aunt Annabel and Ivy were supposed to come to the Christmas Fair here on the day Grandy died. They cancelled at the last moment, and couldn't explain why—not to my satisfaction. Something must have happened at home, something they all decided not to tell me. Whatever it was, that something might have led to one of them killing Grandy. Even the weakest woman could easily have pushed him under the water and held him there. Physically, he was weaker than a daddy-long-legs.'

'Go on,' I said.

'Well, then someone stuck a dress belonging to my Aunt

Annabel to the bottom of my bed here—a *soggy* dress. And Grandy died while in the bath. That's extremely suspicious—don't you think so, Inspector?'

'It's certainly something that requires an explanation,' I said.

'I'll say! And what about the letters that were sent, accusing four people of killing Grandy? One of them was sent to Aunt Annabel.'

'We perhaps should not have told Timothy as much as we did,' said Jane Dockerill ruefully.

'Ivy would have told me, if you hadn't,' Timothy said. 'Oh—Ivy won't have killed Grandy, Inspector. You can cross her off your list. And Kingsbury—it definitely won't have been him.'

'Are you suggesting that your mother or your aunt might have done it?' I asked.

'One of them must have, I suppose. They've both got heaps of money now he's dead.'

'Timothy!' said Jane Dockerill.

'Mrs Dockerill, I'm sure the inspector wants me to tell the truth—don't you, Inspector? I can quite see Mother killing anyone who crossed her. She does so like to be in charge of everything. Aunt Annabel is quite the opposite, but she's a strange lady, so who knows what she might do?'

'Strange in what respect?' I asked.

'It's difficult to describe. It's as if . . . even when she's at her happiest, one sort of feels she might be pretending. Rather like . . .' Timothy nodded to himself, as if pleased with the idea that had just struck him. 'Have you ever known anyone whose skin is ice-cold, even when they're sitting in front of a roaring fire in a swelteringly hot room? If you substitute feelings for body temperature, you've got Aunt Annabel.'

'That doesn't make an awful lot of sense, Timothy,' said Jane Dockerill.

'I think I understand,' I told her.

'It's been difficult for Timothy since his father died a few years ago, Inspector.'

'Mrs Dockerill is right,' said Timothy. 'I was sad to lose my father. That does not, however, invalidate my thoughts and observations on other matters.'

'Were you also sad to lose your great-grandfather?' I asked him.

'In a theoretical sort of way, yes.'

'What do you mean?'

'The end of any life is sad, isn't it?' said Timothy. 'I definitely *thought* it was sad that Grandy was dead, but he was old, and we weren't close. He didn't speak to me much. It was amusing, actually: sometimes, at home, he saw me coming and pretended to remember something that required him to turn and walk in the opposite direction.'

'Why would he avoid you?' I asked, feeling that I knew the answer.

'He thought I was hard work. I *am* rather hard work. He was too—which meant that he preferred to speak to Mother, Aunt Annabel, Ivy and Kingsbury. They all pandered to him.'

'It did not upset you, that he displayed a preference for your sister?'

'Hardly. Mother prefers me, so it all evens out. I'm her precious little boy who can do no wrong. We have preferences, in our family. Grandy never liked Aunt Annabel anywhere near as much as he liked Mother—while I think *I* like Aunt Annabel more. She's a far nicer woman.'

'Come now, Lavington,' said Hugo Dockerill vaguely.

'One cannot choose how one feels and about whom, Mr Dockerill. Can one, Inspector?'

I had no intention of taking sides.

'Don't look so shocked, Mrs Dockerill,' said Timothy. 'You like Freddie Rule more than all the other Coode House boys, and I'm sure you can't help that any more than I can help the way I feel.'

'That's not true, Timothy,' said Jane Dockerill. 'I would treat any boy who was lonely exactly as I treat Freddie. And you need to learn the difference between truthfulness and giving voice to every idea that passes through your mind. One is helpful; the other is not. I think you have said enough this morning. Please can you return to your lessons now?'

Once Timothy had been dismissed, I asked about typewriters. Hugo Dockerill said, 'By all means, old chap—you may inspect mine to your heart's content. Oh . . . I wonder where it is. Jane, dearest, do you happen to know?'

'I'm afraid not, Hugo. I haven't seen it for weeks. Last time I saw it, it was in this room, but it's not here now.'

I tried to look as if this piece of information was of no great interest or relevance. 'Do you remember moving the machine, Mr Dockerill?' I asked.

'No. No, I'm afraid I don't. I don't think I *did* move it. Yet it's not here. How funny.'

'Why do you need to see our typewriter?' asked his wife.

I explained to her about the faulty 'e's in the four letters, and told her that if possible I should like to examine all of Turville College's typewriters.

'I suspected as much,' she said. 'Inspector, you said your visit here today was *not* official police business.'

'That's true.'

'Then there is no Scotland Yard investigation into the sending of those four letters?'

'No. For the time being, Poirot and I are simply poking around, with your kind permission, to see if we can make sense of this perplexing business.'

'I understand, Inspector—but there's a difference between a short conversation of the kind we've just had, and allowing you to test all our typewriters. I'm not sure how the boys' parents would feel about that, or the headmaster. I think he might say that, really, you ought to supply a warrant if that is what you wish to do.'

Hugo Dockerill's missing typewriter was becoming more intriguing by the second.

'May I ask a blunt question, Mrs Dockerill? Are you hoping to protect somebody?'

She looked at me carefully before speaking. 'Whom do you think I would wish to protect? I can assure you, I have not stashed Hugo's typewriter away in a secret place. Why would I have? I could not have anticipated that you would ask to see it.'

'Nevertheless, now that I have, you might not like the idea of me finding it and perhaps identifying it as the machine on which the four letters were typed.'

'Jane, dearest, you don't imagine *I* sent those letters?' Hugo Dockerill sounded alarmed.

'*You?* Don't be ridiculous, Hugo. I am simply suggesting that Inspector Catchpool ought to speak to the headmaster. Turville is his kingdom. If he finds out that a detective was allowed to prowl around without his permission, inspecting school property, we will never hear the end of it!'

To the credit of Jane Dockerill, she did her best to convince the headmaster that cooperating with me would be the sensible and correct thing to do. He seemed amenable to her arguments until he heard of the involvement of Hercule Poirot, at which point his demeanour changed and he became as impassable as a road buried under heavy snow. He made it abundantly clear that, although there were many typewriters at Turville College, I was to be shown none of them.

As I crossed the main quadrangle on my way out, I was thinking of one of these unseen machines more than any of the others: Hugo Dockerill's. Who might have made it go missing? I wondered.

'Inspector Catchpool!'

I turned to see Timothy Lavington, satchel over one shoulder, hurrying towards me.

'Do you have any more questions you'd like to ask me?' he panted.

'I do, as a matter of fact. I'd like to ask you about the Christmas Fair.'

'You mean the day Grandy died?'

'Yes, but I'm interested in the fair.'

Timothy winced. 'Why? It's a stupid waste of time, every year. I wish they'd abolish it.'

'Were you there all day?'

'Yes. Why?'

'Did you see Freddie Rule there, and his mother? And Mr and Mrs Dockerill?'

'Yes. Why are you asking? Oh, I see! You're wondering if one of them might have murdered Grandy. No, they were all here.'

'Can you be certain they were here all day? Would you have noticed if one of them left, then returned an hour or two later?'

Timothy considered the question, then said, 'No, I don't suppose so. Mrs Rule, in particular, might have done that.'

'Why do you say that?' I asked.

'She drove herself here on the day of the fair. I saw her arrive, because Freddie rushed over to greet her. And she is hardly a paragon of virtue—though Mrs Dockerill would say "Timothy!" if she had heard me tell you that.'

'You are referring, I take it, to the rumours about Sylvia Rule?'

Timothy's eyes widened in surprise. 'Do you know about her? I didn't think you would. Who told you?'

'It is possible to pick up a lot of information wandering around a large school,' I said, pleased with my carefully-chosen words.

'Then . . . you know that she kills babies? Oh! You *didn't* know.'

I must have looked as surprised as I felt. Jane Dockerill, when she had brought the dress to Whitehaven Mansions, had said something about Mrs Rule earning money in a manner that was both illegal and immoral. Poirot, Rowland McCrodden and I had all assumed she was referring to a different sort of unlawful immorality.

'It's perfectly true, you know,' said Timothy.

'When you say that Sylvia Rule kills babies . . . ?'

'Women go to her when they're expecting babies they don't want. Only the ones who can afford to pay through the nose, of course. Mrs Rule doesn't care about them—or the babies, obviously. Only about getting richer. That's why I think she might have killed Grandy. Don't you think murder could become a habit? I mean, once a person has taken one life, why not carry on? Grandy would have been an ideal victim. The very old, like the very young, can't fight back.'

Timothy's theory struck me as fanciful. What motive might Sylvia Rule have had for murdering Barnabas Pandy?

'Could Mrs Rule have stuck the dress to the bottom of your bed?' I asked.

'Easily. Though I don't know how she'd have got hold of it. It belongs to my Aunt Annabel.'

I was about to ask Timothy if he knew the whereabouts

of his housemaster's typewriter when he said, 'I want to show you something. It concerns my father. You must promise to tell nobody, if I tell you. Especially not Mother. She doesn't deserve to know. She was always so cold to Father—never showed any affection towards him that I ever saw.

'I'm not sure I can promise to keep secrets, Timothy. If, for instance, there were to be anything criminal about—'

'Oh, it's nothing like that. It's the opposite, actually.' He opened his satchel, pulled out an envelope and passed it to me. It was addressed to him—not at Combingham Hall, but here, at Turville. 'Open it,' he said.

I pulled out the letter, unfolded it and began to read:

Dear Timmy,

I am sorry to have taken so long to write and inform you that, contrary to what you have been told, I am not dead. I am alive and well, and engaged in important work on behalf of His Majesty's Government. Our country is under threat, and must be protected. It has fallen to me to be one of its protectors. My work has placed me and others in a certain amount of danger, and so it was decided that I had to disappear. I am afraid that I cannot tell you any more than I have without endangering you too, which is the very last thing I would ever wish to do. I should not be writing to you at all, and you must promise never to tell anyone that I have. This is very important, Timmy. I do not know if I shall ever be able to return to my old life, but I will certainly write to you whenever I can. This must be our little secret. As soon as I can, I will send an address at which you can write to me. Then we can have a proper correspondence. I am immensely proud of you, Timmy, and think of you every single day.

Your loving father,
Cecil Lavington

The letter was dated 21 June 1929: nearly eight months ago.

'Goodness me,' I said, suddenly aware of my heart pounding in my chest.

'I don't think Father would mind my showing you the letter,' said Timothy. 'It's Mother and Ivy and Aunt Annabel who can't be allowed to know. He surely couldn't object to my telling a policeman. And I've been bursting to tell somebody. It was so infuriating to have to sit quietly while Mrs Dockerill explained to you that I must be so sad about my dead father. She has no idea he's as alive as you and I. They must have buried an empty coffin. Ha! Your face is a picture. I knew the letter would shock you.'

'Indeed it has,' I said quietly, staring at the words 'Coode House, Turville College' typed on the envelope. Five letter 'e's; five tiny pieces of proof. And many more in the letter itself.

The horizontal bar of each 'e' had a tiny hole in it where the white paper showed through. Many months before our Hercule Poirot impersonator had decided to accuse four people of murdering Barnabas Pandy, he or she had sent this letter to Timothy Lavington.

The question, as ever, was: why? And how did all the pieces fit together?

CHAPTER 24

Ancient Enmities

In the heart of Wales, Hercule Poirot sat at a heavily scarred kitchen table opposite Deborah Dakin, a stout woman with iron-grey hair, who had talked a lot in the short time Poirot had known her about the need to put her feet up and the impossibility of ever doing so. She had delayed the start of their conversation for nearly twenty minutes while she bustled around her kitchen, assembling a plate of cakes that a detective of Poirot's eminence might deem worthy of his gastronomic attention. Finally, she had sat down and was now rubbing her ankles, grimacing and murmuring to herself about her feet as Poirot read the letter she had placed on the table, alongside the cakes.

Finding Mrs Dakin had been no easy task. Her little cottage had turned out to be not in the town of Llanidloes, as the address had led Poirot to believe, but in a sort of forest nearby, two miles up a steep, narrow track and many miles from what could reasonably be termed 'civilization'. No other houses were visible from any of the cottage's windows, only dense trees. If he had not had the reassurance that a driver was waiting for him as close to the house as it was possible for a motorcar to park, and in a reliable vehicle that would soon take him back to a railway station, Poirot would have been feeling decidedly anxious.

He read the letter a second time. It had been sent by Barnabas Pandy to Vincent Lobb at an address in Dollgellau in Wales, late the previous year. The date on it was 5 December, just two days before Pandy had died.

Pandy had written:

Dear Vincent,

You will be surprised to receive this letter from me, I am sure. For my part, I am surprised to be writing it. I have no way of knowing if, after all these years, you will be as glad to receive it as you would once have been, or if you long ago resolved to cast me from your mind and never think of me again. I asked myself if I might do more harm than good by sending a communication of this sort after so many years, when we are both old men with not much time left to us. In the end, I felt compelled to make an attempt to repair the damage that was done so many years ago.

I wish you to know that I forgive you. I understand the choice you made, and that you would have chosen differently had you not believed yourself to be in mortal danger. I should not have blamed you so unremittingly for your weakness, particularly when you endeavoured to atone for your error by telling me the truth in due course, which is something you need not have done. It was brave of you to do it.

I wish now that I had made a greater effort to see the matter from your perspective. I wish I had, much sooner than now, admitted to myself that, in your position, I too might have been afraid and thought only of saving my own life and the lives of my family, and not about justice and the morality of the situation—and so I write to beg you to be more forgiving towards me than I have been towards you. I am sorry, Vincent, truly. I regret my unyielding condemnation of you. My lack of compassion towards you was a worse sin, I now realize, than anything that you did.

Please forgive me,

Barnabas

Poirot looked up from the letter. 'You received this only three weeks ago?' he asked Deborah Dakin.

She nodded. 'With Vincent being dead, it lay around unopened for a while, until someone decided to enquire as to whether he had family anywhere—and, before you ask me, I don't know who that someone was. All I know is, one day I came home and found it sitting on my doormat. It might easily have been lost for ever and read by no one. It's lucky it got here, if it's important—and I'll admit, Mr Prarrow, that that's the *only* lucky side to it. Otherwise, if it hadn't turned out to be important, and helpful to you . . . well, I'd prefer not to have read it.'

'What do you mean, madame?'

'Only that I nearly wept tears of joy when you told me who you were, and asked if I knew anything about a letter Mr Pandy had sent to Vincent. "The Lord truly does work in mysterious ways," I thought to myself. There was I wishing I'd never clapped eyes on the wretched thing— wishing Mr Pandy had never bothered to write it—when a famous detective tells me it might help with an important investigation! I don't mind the upset it's caused me if it helps you, Mr Prarrow. I can't pretend I'll be sorry if it turns out someone *has* murdered Mr Pandy—because I won't. Not at all. Not for *his* sake. All the same, murder's wrong and I'll willingly do my duty if there's a murderer to be caught.'

'It sounds, madame, as if I ought to ask you where you were on the day Monsieur Pandy died. You speak as if you might have hated him enough to kill him.'

'Enough?' Deborah Dakin looked puzzled. 'Oh, I hated him enough all right, Mr Prarrow. But it's not a question of "enough" or "not enough". I'd never allow myself to kill a person. It's against the law, and so I wouldn't do it. That's what the law's for, isn't it? To tell us what we can and can't do? But please don't think I didn't kill Mr Pandy on account of not hating him *enough*.'

'Why did you hate him?'

'Because of what he did to Vincent. I dare say you'll have heard *that* story already, from Mr Pandy's side.'

Poirot told her he had not.

'Oh.' She looked surprised. 'Well, it goes back to the mine. Slate mine, it was, near Llanberis. Mr Pandy had a few of them—it's how he made his money. This was . . . oh, it must have been fifty years ago. I wasn't even born.'

She was younger than fifty, then. Poirot had thought she was older.

'Mr Pandy was the owner of the mine, and Vincent worked for him as a supervisor. The two of them became good friends—the *best* of friends. What you'd call lifelong friends, except it didn't last, and that was Mr Pandy's doing.'

'He did something to destroy the friendship?' said Poirot.

'Some slate was stolen, and a young man named William Evans was blamed for it. He also worked in the mine, and Mr Pandy thought he was a good lad, by all accounts. Well, Mr Evans got sent to prison, where he took his own life— and he didn't waste any time about it either. He left behind a note saying he wouldn't allow anyone to punish him for a crime he hadn't committed. Well, that made no sense, did it? When he put that rope around his neck, he punished himself worse than the prison was punishing him. And that wasn't yet the worst of it: his grief-stricken wife followed his example and did away with herself *and* their young child.'

'*Bouleversant*,' murmured Poirot, shaking his head.

'It was a terrible tragedy: three lives lost, and all for nothing. It turned out, you see, that he was *right*. About being innocent. William Evans wasn't the guilty one. But I'm getting ahead of myself. I'll admit, Mr Prarrow, I've had no practice at talking to famous detectives in my own kitchen.'

'Please, tell me the story however you wish, madame.'

'You're very kind, Mr Prarrow. Well . . . Mr Pandy was upset by the deaths of the Evanses. Very upset indeed. He wasn't one to count his profits and not care about his workers, I'll say that for him. Fair's fair, much as I hate the man. Hated, I suppose I ought to say, since he's dead.'

'Hatred can survive long after the one who inspired it is gone,' said Poirot.

'You don't have to tell me that, Mr Prarrow! I'm the expert!'

'Was the true culprit ever identified—the one who stole the slate?'

'Oh, yes. With the Evanses dead, Vincent wasn't himself at all, and Mr Pandy noticed some strange behaviour. He wanted to know why Vincent should be so wretched about it when he and William Evans had not been particular friends. Fearing Mr Pandy had guessed the truth, Vincent told him that he'd known all along that William Evans hadn't been the one to steal the slate. The guilty party was a horrible dirty beast of a man—Vincent never told us his name. Didn't want to put it in our heads, he said. Vincent told Mr Pandy that lots of the mine men had known. It wasn't only him. They all kept quiet, though, after the thief threatened to cut their throats and their wives' and children's throats if they spoke up about what they knew.'

'An evil man,' said Poirot quietly.

'Oh, without a doubt, Mr Prarrow. Without a doubt. But that didn't make Vincent evil for not saying anything, did it? He was frightened—frightened that he and his wife and their son, my late husband, would be murdered in their beds if he told Mr Pandy what he knew. Do you see? Could you or I or any of us say we wouldn't be too afraid to speak up? And besides, Vincent *did* speak up eventually. Thanks to him, that beast got what he deserved in the end.'

'But Monsieur Pandy could not forgive him? He blamed him for the death of the Evans family?'

'That he did, Mr Prarrow. And Vincent blamed himself. And I don't deny it made sense for Mr Pandy to be angry with him at first. Anyone would have been, and there was the shock of it as much as anything else. Oh, Vincent understood the way Mr Pandy felt, all right. He never could forgive himself, and neither did Mr Pandy. He treated Vincent as if he'd murdered William Evans and his family with his own bare hands. Even after twenty, thirty years, when Vincent tried again and again to say how deeply he regretted it . . . Even then Mr Pandy wouldn't see him or read his letters. Sent them all back unopened, he did. In the end, Vincent stopped trying.'

'I am sorry, madame.'

'You should be,' Deborah Dakin said. 'Well, not you, Mr Prarrow, I don't mean *you* . . . but Mr Pandy should have been sorry—very sorry—for the way he treated poor Vincent. It destroyed him. As he grew older and life got harder, and no kind word arrived from Mr Pandy, Vincent came to see his old and once so dear friend's judgement upon him as . . . well, as a kind of doom.'

'Tragedy upon tragedy,' said Poirot.

'That makes it sound as if it's no one's fault, when it was,' said Deborah Dakin. 'It was Mr Pandy's fault. Vincent died believing himself to be damned. In the last years of his life, he barely spoke a word.'

'Then . . . pardon me, madame, but why do you describe this letter as "wretched"? Were you not pleased to read it? To know that, after so many years, Monsieur Pandy relented and forgave your father-in-law?

'No, I'm not! This letter makes the whole thing so much *worse*—surely you can see that? Either Vincent committed an unforgivable sin or else he didn't. We always thought that, to Mr Pandy, that's what it was: unforgivable. Then, suddenly, after fifty years, he decides it's no such thing? He made Vincent suffer all that time, only to decide when it was too late, and when it suited *him*, that he got it wrong?'

Poirot said, 'An interesting opinion, madame—though perhaps not entirely rational.'

Deborah Dakin looked affronted. 'What do you mean it's not rational? Of course it is! Doing the right thing much too late is worse than never doing it at all.'

The same logic could be applied to Vincent Lobb's actions, thought Poirot. Evidently this had not occurred to his daughter-in-law, and Poirot decided not to extend his visit any longer than necessary by pointing it out to her.

CHAPTER 25

Poirot Returns to Combingham Hall

Poirot had been expecting a driver to collect him from the railway station. He was surprised to alight from his train and find Lenore Lavington standing on the platform under a navy blue umbrella. She offered no conventional greetings or pleasantries, and instead said, 'I hope I won't regret allowing you to visit us again, M. Poirot.'

'I hope so too, madame.'

They walked to her motorcar in silence, followed by the porter who carried Poirot's cases.

As she started up the engine a few minutes later, Lenore Lavington said, 'Your telegram need not have been as cryptic as it was. Am I to understand that you have found evidence that Grandfather was murdered, and that you plan to expose a murderer during your stay with us? Do you already know . . . ?' She left the question unfinished.

'I will admit, madame, that the picture is not yet complete. In three days' time, however, I hope to be able to tell you and others the whole story.'

Three days. The words loomed large in Poirot's mind. 24 February had seemed a safe distance away when he had sent his letters of invitation. Since then, several interesting new pieces of information had come his way. Any one of them might prove to be the key that unlocked the mystery, but when, he wondered, would the unlocking happen? For the sake of Poirot's peace of mind, he hoped it would be soon.

'At our gathering, you will learn the truth about your grandfather's death,' he said, fervently hoping he would not be proved wrong. 'One of the assembled company will know the truth already, of course.'

'Do you mean Grandfather's murderer?' asked Lenore. 'But that person won't be among the assembled company, as you put it. The only people at the Hall will be you, me, Annabel, Ivy and Kingsbury. None of us murdered Grandfather.'

'You are wrong, I am afraid, madame. Many more people are to join us. They will arrive tomorrow. Inspector Edward Catchpool of Scotland Yard, Hugo and Jane Dockerill, Freddie Rule and his mother Sylvia. Also, there will be Freddie's sister Mildred, and her fiancé Eustace Campbell-Brown, and John McCrodden and his father Rowland McCrodden. And—please be careful!'

The motorcar swerved violently, narrowly missing another vehicle travelling in the opposite direction, then stopped by the side of the road. Lenore Lavington switched off the engine.

'And also your son Timothy,' Poirot said in a faltering

voice, producing a handkerchief from his pocket to wipe his brow.

'Do you mean to tell me you have invited an assortment of complete strangers to my home, without my permission?'

'It is irregular, I know. In my defence, I will say only that it is necessary—unless you wish a murderer to escape justice.'

'Of course I don't, but . . . that does not mean that you can fill my house with strangers and people I dislike without consulting me.'

'Whom do you dislike? Freddie Rule?'

'No. I didn't mean Freddie.'

'Yet you dislike him, do you not?'

'Not at all.' She sounded bored.

'You said when we last met that you had advised your son Timothy to stay away from him.'

'Only because he's so peculiar. I was thinking of the Dockerills, if you must know.'

'What is your objection to Hugo and Jane Dockerill?'

'They are unfair to my son. They punish him for the most minor of misdemeanours, while other boys, the ones who present an angelic façade, get away with . . .' Lenore Lavington stopped.

'Murder?' Poirot suggested.

'I shall have to have lots of bedrooms made up. How long do you plan for all these people to stay? And why so many?'

Because any one of them might have murdered Barnabas Pandy—and I do not yet know which one.

246

Poirot withheld his true answer and said instead, 'I would prefer to wait until the final pieces of the puzzle fall into place before I say any more.'

Lenore Lavington sighed. Then she started up the engine, and they were once more on their way, along narrow country roads lined with beech trees and silver birches. 'I find it quite impossible to believe that one of these people you have invited could have entered the house on the day Grandfather died without any of us noticing,' she said. 'Still . . . if you're certain, and as an inspector from Scotland Yard is taking the trouble to come to the Hall, you will have my family's full cooperation.'

'*Merci mille fois*, madame.'

'As soon as we arrive at the house, you may look at the typewriter, if you still wish to do so.'

'That would be useful.'

'We have a new one, since you were last here—the old machine was past its best.'

Poirot looked alarmed. 'Do you still have the old typewriter?'

'Yes. I've asked Kingsbury to put both machines out for you to look at. The new one was still in the shop when those horrible letters were typed, but if I don't present it for inspection, you might think I am hiding something.'

'It is sensible to be always thorough and check everything,' Poirot told her. 'Which is why I should like to ask you some questions about the day Monsieur Pandy died.'

'Are you going to ask about the discussion Ivy and I

were having while Grandfather took his bath? Go ahead. I've told you: I am willing to cooperate if it will help bring an end to all this unpleasantness and uncertainty.'

'Kingsbury described it as an argument, not a discussion,' said Poirot.

'It was a horrible row, made worse by Annabel's endless wailing at us to stop,' said Lenore. 'She cannot tolerate any sort of conflict. Nobody likes it, of course, but most of us accept that not every exchange can be a pleasant one. I'm sure Ivy and I would have resolved our dispute far sooner if Annabel had not constantly interrupted with her demands that we be kind to one another. That only inspired me to be rather unkind to *her*, as I recall. Her sympathies were with Ivy, as always, yet she took care to ingratiate herself with me too.'

'Madame, I am grateful for your frankness, but it would be more useful to me if you could tell me first the cause of the *contretemps* between you and your daughter.'

'Yes, I am being frank, aren't I?' Lenore Lavington sounded surprised. 'Franker than I've been in a long time. It's rather intoxicating.'

Yet she also sounded worried by it, Poirot thought.

'The harsh words that passed between Ivy and me in her bedroom that day were not the start of the trouble. A few days earlier, there was a family dinner that ended in disaster, and several months prior to that there was an equally ill-fated trip to the beach. That's really when it all began. And it was my fault, all of it. If I had exercised a little more self-control, none of it would have happened.'

'Tell me the story from the beginning,' said Poirot.

'I will, on one condition,' said Lenore Lavington. 'That you promise not to speak of it to Ivy. I have her permission to tell you about it, but I fear it would be dreadfully embarrassing for her if you were to raise the subject in her presence.'

By way of response, Poirot made a noise that was carefully calibrated to sound like assent. The next words he heard surprised him.

'I made an unfortunate remark about Ivy's legs, while we were at the beach together.'

'Her legs, madame?'

'Yes. I will forever regret it—but, once made, a remark cannot be cancelled out of existence, however often one apologizes. It lives on in the memory of the one wounded by it.'

'The remark was an insulting one?' Poirot asked.

'It certainly wasn't intended to be. You will have noticed, I'm sure, that Ivy's face is badly scarred. Of course you have. No one could fail to notice. As her mother, I naturally worry that the disfigurement will make it difficult if not impossible for her to attract a husband. I should like her to have one—and children. My own marriage was not a success, but Ivy would make a better choice than I did, I have no doubt. She is more realistic than I was at her age. If only she would understand that marriage is about being chosen as much as it is about choosing.'

Lenore made an impatient noise. 'It is impossible to tell

this story without saying things that you might judge to be unforgivable, M. Poirot. I'm afraid I cannot help how I feel. Ivy is lucky that most of her face is unaffected by the scarring. She could easily conceal it if she arranged her hair in the right way—which she perversely refuses to do. She could if she chose to, of course, and I have never believed that her scars would deter any man from ever taking an interest in her. Ivy has a lively and engaging way about her.'

'Most engaging,' Poirot agreed.

'I *do* think, however, that she ought not to add to the problem by eating until she's the size of a small house. What man would want a wife with scars on her face *and* a hugely fat body? If I sound angry, M. Poirot, it is only because I have never said this to Ivy, though it's often in my mind. Nothing has ever mattered more to me than my children's happiness. For *their* sake, I was a dutiful and loving wife to their father, my late husband, until the day he died. For *their* sake, I allow Annabel to fuss over them and interfere in their lives as if she's as much their mother as I am. I know how much they love her, and I have always put their needs and feelings before my own. In order not to hurt Ivy's feelings, I have sat at the dinner table night after night and watched her pile extra helpings on to her plate, and I've said *nothing*—not a word—though I can hardly bear to watch. She was a large, stocky child and will always be a well-built girl, of course. She takes after Cecil, her father. Still, I cannot help watching the way she eats and wondering what on earth she thinks she's doing.

She seems not to worry at all about her figure. I can't understand it.'

Lenore Lavington exhaled loudly. 'There. I've said it. Those are my true feelings. Do you think I'm a cruel, unloving mother, M. Poirot?'

'Not unloving, madame, but . . . if you will permit me to make an observation?'

'By all means.'

'Mademoiselle Ivy is a perfectly attractive young lady of a quite normal shape and size. You are, in my opinion, worrying unnecessarily. It is true that she does not have the exceptionally fine-boned frame that you and your sister both have, but many women do not. Look around at the world! It is not only those with the waist I could encircle between my forefinger and thumb who fall in love and make successful marriages.'

Lenore Lavington shook her head vigorously as Poirot spoke. The moment he'd finished, she said, 'If Ivy continues to heap potatoes on to her plate at her present rate, she will soon have no waist to speak of. That was what started the trouble at the disastrous dinner: she helped herself to one potato, then another, then another, until I simply couldn't stop myself.'

'From what?' asked Poirot.

'All I said was, "Ivy, two potatoes are enough, surely?" I thought I had chosen my words carefully, but she flew into the wildest rage, and all her resentments came pouring out, including the full story of what had happened on the beach. Grandfather and Annabel were terribly shocked and upset, and *I* was upset because I was made to seem like the villain of the piece, which I suppose I was—and that only made it even worse!'

'Tell me the story of the beach,' said Poirot.

'It was last summer,' said Lenore. 'A blisteringly hot day. Annabel had influenza, and couldn't even get up to play with Hopscotch in the garden. He was howling and whining at the foot of her bed, and it was causing her great distress. She asked us to take him out for the day, away from Combingham Hall. I wasn't thrilled by the prospect—I am not a dog lover, I'm afraid—but Ivy said that Annabel would recover more quickly if she wasn't worried about Hopscotch, so I agreed.

'We went to the beach. Ivy nearly drowned as a young girl—did you know that? That's how she acquired those horrible scars. She rolled down a river bank into the water. Annabel's dog before Hopscotch—Skittle, his name was—he tried to stop her from rolling into the water, but only ended up scratching her face to ribbons. It wasn't his fault, of course.'

'Mademoiselle Annabel saved your daughter's life, did she not?' said Poirot.

'Yes. If it weren't for my sister, Ivy would have drowned. They both nearly drowned. The current was easily strong enough to carry them both away, but, somehow, Annabel managed to drag Ivy out of the water and save her, and save herself too. They were very lucky. I can hardly bear to think about what might have happened. Annabel has had a strong aversion to water ever since.'

'To water,' Poirot murmured. 'This is most fascinating.'

'Ivy was also scared of water for a long time, but at the age of fourteen, she set herself the task of conquering her fear, and soon became a regular and enthusiastic swimmer. She now drives to the beach for a dip as often as she can—the same beach to which she and I took Hopscotch the day Annabel was sick.'

'Commendable.'

'Yes. Though all that swimming has given her legs and arms a rather muscular quality. And there is no need to tell me that many women with the limbs of male athletes have happy marriages, M. Poirot. I don't doubt it. I simply want my daughter to look as attractive as she can, that's all.'

Poirot said nothing.

'I am not a regular swimmer myself,' said Lenore. 'I had not seen my daughter in a bathing costume for many years, until the day we took Hopscotch to the beach. Ivy swam for half an hour, then came to sit with me. Hopscotch was playing in the waves, and Ivy and I were sitting near the trees. She was eating some sort of picnic. Then the dog came running over to us, having noticed that there were goodies available, and the strangest thing happened: Ivy turned pale and began to shake. She was staring at Hopscotch, her mouth wide open, trembling as if she might faint.

'I asked her what was wrong, but she couldn't speak. A memory had come back to her, you see—a memory of the day she nearly drowned. She was able to tell me this only later, on the way home. Having remembered hardly any of the details for so many years, she had suddenly remembered her head being under the water, and being unable to breathe or free herself from whatever was trapping her there. Suddenly, she remembered all of it vividly. She remembered there had been *trees* on the river bank, like the ones she and I were sitting near on the beach, and she remembered seeing Skittle's legs . . . How well do you know dogs, M. Poirot?'

'I have made the acquaintance of several over the years, madame. Why do you ask?'

'Have you ever known a dog like Hopscotch? One with a thick, wiry coat?'

Had he? Poirot did not think that he had. He said so.

'Hopscotch is an Airedale Terrier,' said Lenore. 'You will have noticed, I'm sure, that the hair on his four legs is fluffy and voluminous—almost as if he's wearing furry trousers.'

'*Oui*. That is a good description.'

'Skittle, the dog that tried to save Ivy, was an Airedale, just like Hopscotch. When dry, the legs of Airedale Terriers look much wider than they are—the hair fluffs out instead of lying flat. When Hopscotch ran over to Ivy that day, in the hope of sharing her picnic, his legs were wet from playing in the sea, and so they looked much thinner—like two brown sticks. It took Ivy back, in the most vivid way, to the day she nearly drowned.

'She remembered seeing Skittle's wet legs, you see, and thinking, only for a second or two, that they were brown tree trunks. Because they were so thin, she said she imagined they must be far away, and thought this meant that she was trapped far out from the bank of the river with no hope of rescue. I think she was probably delirious with fear.

'Moments later, Annabel reached her and suddenly there was hope! Ivy noticed that there was a thick tree trunk beside the thin ones—that was when she knew that the thin ones were not tree trunks at all. She realized they were moving back and forth, and that they were attached to the dog. Everything started to make sense again.'

Lenore Lavington's breathing had a jagged sound to it. 'You can imagine how distressing it was for me to hear all this, M. Poirot. It brought it all back: the shock of discovering that I had so nearly lost my daughter. If Ivy and I had not taken Hopscotch to the beach that day, if he hadn't got his legs wet in the sea, those memories might never have surfaced. I wish they hadn't, and I wish *I* hadn't said what I said afterwards, but one cannot undo the past, can one?'

'Are we coming now to the unfortunate remark about the legs?' Poirot asked. He had been wondering if she would ever get to it.

'We were driving back. After what Ivy had told me, I was not myself—not at all. I tried to concentrate on getting us home without crashing into anything. I desperately wanted her to stop talking so that I could gather my wits . . . and the words just came out! I didn't *choose* to say what I said.'

'What words came out, madame?'

'I said that Skittle wasn't the one whose legs resembled tree trunks. And I said that Ivy ought to think about doing a little less swimming, because her legs would look more and more like tree trunks the more muscular she became. I regretted it as soon as the words were out of my mouth. Still, there was one benefit: Ivy was immediately furious with me. The horrible old memories of her near-drowning were no longer in her mind. All she could think about was how much she loathed her heartless mother. I didn't say what I said to hurt her—I don't *really* think her legs look like *actual* tree trunks—I only wanted her to think about something else instead of the memories that were upsetting her. I wanted her to turn her attention to her future, not the past. I must have spent hours apologizing to her, and I thought we'd put it behind us, I really did—but then *months* later at dinner . . . well, I've already told you about that.'

'Mademoiselle Ivy told your sister and your grandfather the story of what happened at the beach, and what you had said to her?'

'Yes.'

'What was their reaction?'

'Annabel was distraught, naturally,' said Lenore with a weary impatience. 'For every tear shed by anybody else, Annabel must always produce a flood of her own.'

'And Monsieur Pandy?'

'He said nothing, but he looked terribly unhappy. I don't think it was my careless remarks so much as the thought of how frightened Ivy must have been, thinking she was about to die. She perhaps should have kept her newly discovered memories to herself. It's Annabel's influence. Ivy never used to have these outbursts of emotion. Even after a dinner had been ruined, it wasn't enough for her! On the day Grandfather died, I was walking along the landing and I heard loud sobbing. It is possible to cry quietly, you know, M. Poirot.'

'Indeed, madame.'

'I'm afraid I decided I could not tolerate such self-pity any longer. My daughter used to be a robust, sensible girl. I told her so, and she screamed at me: "How am I supposed to feel when my own mother has compared my legs to tree trunks?" Then of course Annabel dashed up the stairs to meddle where she wasn't needed, in the guise of peace-keeping, and soon afterwards Grandfather shouted from his bath that we were all making a horrible din and could we please desist? If Annabel had kept out of it and let me speak to my daughter privately, there would have been far less of a commotion, because Ivy and I had to raise our voices to make ourselves heard above her ceaseless wailing. Grandfather was no fool—he knew it as well as I did. It was Annabel he was shouting at. By then, he had already decided . . .'

Poirot turned to see why Lenore Lavington had stopped speaking. Unsightly blotches had appeared on her face. She stared straight ahead, at the road.

'Please go on,' said Poirot.

'If I do, you must promise to repeat it to nobody. No one knows apart from me, now that Grandfather is dead.'

'You are going to tell me, I think, that Monsieur Pandy had decided to make a new will?'

The car jerked dramatically. '*Sacre tonnerre!*' cried Poirot. 'You are surprised to discover that Hercule Poirot knows so much, I understand, but it is no reason to kill us both.'

'How can you know about the will? Unless . . . You must have spoken to Peter about it, Peter Vout. That's funny. Grandfather said I was only one he had told. Perhaps he meant the only one of the family. Annabel must never know, M. Poirot. You must promise me. It would destroy her. I have been saying things about her that are not entirely complimentary, I know, but nevertheless . . .'

'Nevertheless, she is your sister. And she saved the life of your daughter.'

'Quite,' said Lenore. 'After Grandfather died, it was the one thing I was thankful for: that he did not have the chance to alter his will, and so Annabel would never have to find out. I would have made sure she was well looked after, naturally, but that's hardly the point. To be cut off so brutally . . . I think she might have fallen apart.'

'Did you try to persuade Monsieur Pandy to change his mind, when he told you what he intended to do?'

'No. It would only have strengthened his resolve. To try to persuade someone out of a feeling . . .' She broke off with a firm shake of the head. 'It's the very essence of futility. It never works, whether directed at oneself or at others. Grandfather rarely, though occasionally, saw that he had been wrong about something, but never when told by somebody else.'

'I see,' said Poirot.

What was it, he asked himself, that did not fit? He knew

he had heard something that jutted out awkwardly. He knew, furthermore, that he had heard it since getting into the car with Lenore Lavington. *What was it?*

'You might be thinking that my sister had the perfect motive to commit murder,' Lenore said. 'She did—but she didn't *know* she did. Therefore, she didn't.'

'Mademoiselle Annabel has also been given the most unshakeable alibi by you and your daughter,' Poirot reminded her.

'You say that as if it's a lie. It's *not* a lie. Ivy and I were with Annabel every single second, M. Poirot. And when we all stood in the bathroom together, summoned by Kingsbury, every inch of Annabel's dress was dry. It is quite impossible that she killed Grandfather.'

'Tell me, madame: has Mademoiselle Ivy forgiven you?' Poirot asked. 'Or does she still keep alive the grievance?'

'I don't know. I have no intention of raising the subject again, but I hope that she has. The other day, for the first time, she wore a bracelet I gave her. I think that might have been a sort of peace offering. I gave it to her when Grandfather died, you see. She definitely had not forgiven me then! She told me she would rather die than wear it, and threw it across the room at me. It was a beautiful, hand-carved mourning bracelet made of jet—one I cherished. I suppose I thought that giving it to Ivy would be proof of my love for her. She knew it was precious to me—a treasured gift from a seaside holiday with my late husband Cecil—but she chose to interpret it in the worst possible way.'

'In what way did she interpret it?' The gates to the Combingham Hall Estate were now visible in the distance.

'She accused me of only ever giving her gifts that were things I already owned, not presents I had bought especially for her. She went to her bedroom and started pulling drawers out of chests, looking for a hand-held fan I had once given her—more evidence against me! The fan was also a treasured possession of mine. It had a picture on it of a beautiful lady, dancing, and of course her waist was *tiny*. Trust Ivy to remember that when I had given her the fan I'd said, "The dancing lady looks like you, darling"—because she *did,* with her black hair and pale skin. Ivy had loved the fan when I first gave it to her, and taken the comparison as the compliment I intended it to be. Suddenly, however, in the light of the unfortunate events I have already described, she decided I had been duplicitous, and had wanted her to notice the difference between the fan-lady's dainty waist and her own larger one.'

'Human relationships are extremely complicated,' said Poirot.

'People make them more complicated than they need to be,' said Lenore disapprovingly. 'Though, as I say: Ivy recently wore the mourning bracelet I gave her. She made sure that I saw her wearing it, too. It must have been her way of letting me know that she has forgiven me. What else could it mean?'

CHAPTER 26

The Typewriter Experiment

When Lenore Lavington and Poirot arrived at Combingham Hall, they found Kingsbury standing guard beside a small table in the entrance hall. On the table sat two typewriters, side by side.

'I've set up the two machines for Mr Porrott, like you asked, Mrs Lavington,' he said.

'Thank you, Kingsbury. That will be all for now.'

The manservant shuffled away. Nobody made a move to close the front door.

Poirot managed to suppress his urge to ask why, in a house the size of Combingham Hall, with so many rooms presumably empty and without function, did such things as dining and the testing of typewriters need to take place in the entrance hall? It made no sense! If Poirot had owned the building, he would have put a grand piano here where the small table had been placed. That was the only thing that might look as if it belonged in this particular spot.

'Is there a problem, M. Poirot?' Lenore Lavington asked.

'Not at all, madame.' He turned his attention to the two machines in front of him. One was new and shiny; the other had a crack in its side and a deep scratch on its front. Kingsbury had set out, next to the two typewriters, the paper and carbon paper that Poirot would need later to conduct his experiment.

Once he had made himself at home in the bedroom that had been assigned to him, and taken some refreshment, Poirot sat down at the little table and tried first one typewriter, then the other. Both had identical letter 'e's with no ink missing at all. There was no need to search for other differences, though search he did. If one did not look, one gave oneself no opportunity to spot any detail that could not have been anticipated, but was nonetheless highly significant.

In his mother tongue of French, Poirot gave thanks to a higher power when he saw that such a detail was present in this instance. He was busy comparing the two pieces of paper on which he had typed precisely the same words when first he heard and then saw Hopscotch. The dog came running down the stairs and across the hall. He leapt up to greet Poirot. Annabel Treadway ran down the stairs after him. 'Hoppy, *down*. Down, boy! M. Poirot doesn't want to have his face licked, I'm sure.'

Indeed Poirot did not. He patted the dog instead, hoping Hopscotch would accept this as a reasonable compromise.

'Look how pleased he is to see you, M. Poirot! Isn't he a lovely, affectionate boy?' Annabel managed to sound sad about it: as if no one but she could appreciate the dog's good nature.

Eventually Hopscotch remembered that he had been on his way outside, and trotted off into the garden.

Annabel, spotting the two sheets of paper in Poirot's hands, said, 'I see you've begun your typewriter investigation. Oh, don't let me interrupt you. Lenore gave me strict orders to leave you alone and let you do your detective work.'

'I have concluded the experiment, mademoiselle. Would you like to see the results? Tell me, what differences do you notice?' He passed her the two sheets of paper.

She stared at them for a while before looking up at Poirot. 'I don't see anything at all,' she said. 'Nothing worthy of note, I mean. The letter "e" is fully present and correct on both pages.'

'It is. But there is more to look at than the many letters "e".'

'The same words are typed on both sheets of paper—"I, Hercule Poirot, have arrived at Combingham Hall, and I will not leave until I have solved the mystery of the death of Barnabas Pandy." The two versions are identical in every respect, aren't they? What am I failing to notice?'

'If I were to tell you the answer, Mademoiselle, I would deprive you of the chance to work it out for yourself.'

'I don't want to work anything out. I want you to tell us if we're in danger from a murderer roaming about the place, and protect us if we are, and then . . . then all I want is to forget!'

'What do you wish to forget?'

'All of it. Grandy's murder, and the reason for it, whatever that turns out to be, and the sickening letter I can't get out of my mind, even though I burned it.'

'And a wet blue dress with white and yellow flowers on it?' Poirot asked.

She looked at him, wide-eyed and apparently uncomprehending. 'What do you mean?' she said. '*I* have a blue dress with white and yellow flowers on it. But it isn't wet.'

'Where is it?'

'In my wardrobe.'

'Are you certain it is there?'

'Where else would it be? It's the dress I wore the day Grandy died. I haven't felt like wearing it since.'

She had not, then, looked for the dress and found that it was missing. *Assuming she is telling the truth*, Poirot said to himself.

'Mademoiselle, were you aware that, before he died, your grandfather decided to make a change to his will? He did not, in the end, do so. His death prevented it. But it was his intention to alter his testamentary provisions quite considerably.'

'No, I didn't know that. Though Peter Vout, his solicitor, came to the house and the two of them secluded themselves in the drawing room to talk in private, so perhaps that was . . .'

Annabel gasped suddenly, and reeled backwards. Poirot moved quickly to catch her, in case she fell.

He helped her to a chair. 'What is the matter, mademoiselle?'

'It was me, wasn't it?' she said in a whisper. 'He wished to cut me off. That was why he summoned Peter Vout. Even though I saved Ivy's life—once he knew, he couldn't forgive me! Which means I must deserve never to be forgiven,' Annabel said fiercely. 'If Grandy was going to alter his will to punish me, that means I deserve nothing. Only to suffer. He was always fair. I never imagined he could love me the way he loved Lenore, but *he was always fair.*'

'Mademoiselle, please explain to Poirot. For what could your grandfather not forgive you?'

'No! Oh, he will get what he wanted—I won't stand in the way of his wishes—but I will never tell you or anybody. *Never!*' Sobbing, she ran up the stairs.

Poirot stared after her, bemused. Then he looked at the house's open front door, and thought about how easy it would be for him to go back to London and to Whitehaven Mansions, and never return. Officially, no crime had been committed, so he could hardly be blamed for failing to solve a murder.

But of course he would not leave. He was Hercule Poirot!

'Three days,' he said to himself. 'Only three days.'

CHAPTER 27

The Bracelet and the Fan

The next morning, Poirot was on his way to take breakfast when Ivy Lavington ambushed him in the hall. Hopscotch was at her side. He did not try to lick Poirot this time. He seemed, in fact, rather subdued.

'Where is Aunt Annabel?' Ivy demanded. 'What have you done with her?'

'Is she not at home, here in the house?' he asked.

'No. She's taken one of the cars and gone off somewhere without Hoppy—which she never does. Absolutely never. Not without saying a word to me or Mummy. Did you say something to upset her?'

'*Oui, c'est possible*,' said Poirot with a heavy heart. 'Sometimes, if lives are to be saved, one must ask unwelcome questions.'

'Whose lives must be saved?' asked Ivy. 'Are you suggesting that whoever killed Grandy intends to kill again?'

'Without doubt, a murder has been planned.'

'So is it one life, or more than one? You said "lives".'

'Mademoiselle! *Sacre tonnerre!*'

'What is it? You look as if you've seen a ghost.'

Poirot opened his mouth, but could make no words come out. He was thinking too fast to speak at all.

'Are you quite well, M. Poirot?' Ivy looked concerned. 'Did I say something that frightened you?'

'Mademoiselle, you said something that has helped me greatly! Please now say nothing for a short while. I need to follow the logic of the theory that is growing in my mind, to see if I am right. I *must* be right!'

Ivy stood, arms folded, and watched him as he put the various pieces together. Hopscotch, still by her side, also stared at him quizzically.

'Thank you,' Poirot said eventually.

'Well?' said Ivy. 'Are you right?'

'I believe so, yes.'

'Jolly good! I'm looking forward to hearing your theory. I haven't been able to think up any of my own.'

'Do not try,' Poirot advised. 'Your speculations would be based upon an entirely false premise, and so you would fail.'

'What do you mean, a false premise?'

'All in good time, mademoiselle. All in good time.'

Ivy made a face at him that suggested a mixture of annoyance and admiration. 'I expect Mummy told you all about the fight we had the day Grandy died?' She grinned. 'You'll know all about my tree-trunk legs. And Mummy will have told you not to say a word to me, for fear of upsetting me all over again.'

'Mademoiselle, if I might be permitted to say so, you are most pleasing to look at, and there is nothing at all wrong with your size or shape.'

'Well, I've got my scars,' said Ivy, pointing to her face. 'But apart from that, I agree. I am a normal, healthy person, and that suits me fine. Mummy thinks I ought to aspire to be no wider than a pipe-cleaner, but food is a madness of hers. She doesn't eat properly. Never has. Did you notice last night, at dinner?'

'I am afraid I did not,' said Poirot, who had been too busy eating his own delicious meal.

'She puts the odd sliver of something in her mouth every now and then, and swallows it grudgingly, like someone taking a prescribed medicine, but she spends most of each meal prodding things with her fork as if she suspects them of plotting against her. She imagines that the reason I was so angry with her was because I couldn't bear to hear the truth about my horrible legs. What nonsense! I'm perfectly happy with my legs. What upset me was finding out that Mummy looks at me and sees only, or mainly, a bundle of physical flaws. And her dishonesty—that also enrages me.'

'Your mother is not honest?' said Poirot.

'Oh, she can't bear the truth. She is almost allergic to it. She would do or say *anything* to keep me and Timmy happy—I think she feels it's her duty as a mother—but every so often a scrap of truthfulness slips out, and when it does, she bends over backwards afterwards to deny what is plain to see. I shall *never* believe her when she says she thinks I'm beautiful. I know it's a lie. She'd be far better off admitting that she would love it if I starved myself skinny. Instead, she lies and lies about how much she loves me the way I am, and tells herself she's keeping me happy by doing so.' Ivy spoke thoughtfully and analytically, with no trace of resentment in her voice. She was, Poirot reflected, a happier and more stable woman than either her mother or her aunt.

'The thing is, if you try to deny the truth, it creeps out in other ways. I don't suppose Mummy told you about the time she gave me a fan as a present?' Ivy laughed. 'There was a picture of a dark-haired woman on it, and Mummy said, "Doesn't she look like you, Ivy? Her hair is the same colour, and her dress." All of which was true—but the woman on the fan had the tiniest waist I had ever seen! And *I* happened to be on my way out to a dance wearing a rather attention-seeking black and red dress which, looking back, probably didn't suit me, and would have looked better on someone with a more slender figure, but I didn't care. I liked the dress, so I wore it. Mummy couldn't bear it, though, because it accentuated my waist—so she presented me with a rebuke in the guise of a gift. I imagine she hoped I would take one look at the woman on the fan, notice the contrast, and immediately decide to change into something that disguised my waist and made me look smaller.'

'Your mother told me that she gave to you also a bracelet,' said Poirot.

Ivy nodded. 'That was after Grandy died. I took one look at it and thought that I wouldn't be able to squeeze my hand through it if I tried for a hundred years. It was Mummy's, and must have fitted her perfectly, but it wasn't designed for someone of my build. As it turned out, the bracelet *did* fit me, but only just. I wore it recently, but I don't think I will again. I wanted Mummy to see it on my wrist at least once. I know she still worries that she's damaged me irreparably by allowing me to discover that she would like me to be slimmer, and I wanted to show her that I've forgiven her. She can't help being the way she is. And, in my anger, I was terribly unfair to her. The bracelet and the fan were both things she loved and would never have parted with—if she hadn't given them to me, I mean— but I accused her of giving me second-hand gifts and being unwilling to spend her money on me.'

Ivy gave a rueful smile. 'I am no more perfect than Mummy is, M. Poirot. I think it's important to understand that one's nearest and dearest are *not* perfect. If one cannot accept that . . . well, that way lies madness.'

No person, Poirot agreed, could ever be perfect. On the other hand, a puzzle and its solution, once all the loose and messy ends were neatly wrapped up . . .

'Did you know, mademoiselle, that your grandfather intended to change his will, and that he died before he could do so?'

'No.' Ivy's eyes took on a sharper look. 'How did he plan to change it?'

'Both his solicitor and your mother tell me that he intended to cut off Mademoiselle Annabel—to leave to her nothing at all.'

'Why on earth should he want to do that?' said Ivy. 'Aunt Annabel is a kind, selfless, entirely good person. There are not many people like her. I am not always kind. Are you, M. Poirot?'

'I try to be, mademoiselle. It is important to try.'

'But . . . it makes no sense,' Ivy muttered. 'It can't be true. Grandfather always favoured Mummy, but he would never have demonstrated his preference so starkly. He knew as well I do that Aunt Annabel would never hurt anybody. I always believed he felt rather guilty for finding her maddening, because he knew she had done nothing to deserve it.'

'I must ask you one more question, mademoiselle,' said Poirot. 'It is a strange one, and I apologize if it causes you distress.'

'Is it about tree trunks?' Ivy said.

'No. It concerns your late father.'

'Poor Daddy.'

'Why do you say that?'

'I don't know. I don't think Mummy loved him very much. Oh, she played the role of a good wife to perfection, but her heart was not engaged. She *might* have been able to love him more if she had only been honest from the start. Instead, their relationship followed her usual pattern: she tried to do and say whatever she thought would keep him happy, and, as a result, neither of them was able to be happy.'

'Did she deceive him about something in particular?' Poirot asked.

'No, it was worse than that,' said Ivy. 'She deceived him in their ordinary, everyday life. Mummy is terribly clever, you know. Well organized, astute, capable. She tends to assume that things will go her way. Having that attitude has often made the obstacles in her path disappear. Or rather, I should say, it has since Daddy died. Daddy would fret awfully about the tiniest things, and was forever saying they shouldn't try to do this or that because they wouldn't succeed—leaving Combingham Hall, for instance, and making a home of their own. Mummy wanted to, but Daddy didn't, and so Mummy pretended to agree with him. Knowing that she could have made it work brilliantly if she'd only had the chance must have eaten away at her. She should have told him to stop being so silly instead of pandering to his timid approach to life. I imagine it must have been rather a relief to her when he died.'

'Did she express relief?'

'Goodness me, no. She'd have died too rather than admit it. She really is terribly clever. She has thoroughly enjoyed being in charge of herself and making all her own decisions since Daddy died—but without once saying, "What a relief to be free!" as many women in her position might have. To say anything like that would be too direct for Mummy.'

Ivy smiled. 'Listen to me chattering away. What did you want to ask me about Daddy? I never gave you the chance.'

'Since your father's death, have you received any letters purporting to be from him?'

'Letters from my dead father? No. Not a one. Why do you ask?'

Poirot shook his head. 'It does not matter. Thank you for taking the time to talk to me, mademoiselle. Our conversation has been most illuminating.'

'I should say it matters quite a lot,' Ivy called after him as he set off for the dining hall, where his breakfast awaited him. 'First letters from you that aren't from you, and now letters from my dead father that can't be from him . . . I hope you're going to explain all of this, M. Poirot. I want to understand every single baffling aspect of this whole peculiar business.'

'So do I,' said Poirot to himself as he sat down to eat. 'So, very much, do I.'

CHAPTER 28

An Unconvincing Confession

I was sitting in my office at Scotland Yard, grappling with a particularly difficult crossword clue, when the Super knocked on my door. 'Sorry to interrupt, Catchpool,' he said with a smile. 'There's a Miss Annabel Treadway here to see you.'

Since learning that Rowland Rope was finally convinced that neither Poirot nor Scotland Yard had accused his son of murder, the Super had been the soul of reasonable discourse and moderation.

'I'll see Miss Treadway immediately,' I said.

The Super showed her into the small room, then made himself scarce. I took one look at the woman standing before me and wondered why she struck me so powerfully at that moment as being the embodiment of a tragic fate. It was as if the room had turned darker with her arrival. But why? She wasn't crying; she wasn't dressed in mourning garments. It was a puzzle.

'Good afternoon, Miss Treadway.'

'You're Inspector Edward Catchpool?'

'That's right. I was expecting to see you tomorrow afternoon at Combingham Hall. I was not expecting you to come to me in London.'

'I have a confession to make,' she said.

'I see.' I sat down and invited her to do the same, but she remained standing.

'I killed my grandfather. I acted alone.'

'Is that so?'

'Yes.' She raised her chin and looked almost proud. 'Three other people also received letters accusing them of his murder, but they are all innocent. I killed him.'

'You murdered Barnabas Pandy—is that what you're telling me?'

'Yes.'

'How?'

She frowned. 'I'm not sure what you are asking.'

'It's quite simple. You say you killed Mr Pandy. I'm asking how.'

'But I thought you knew. He drowned in the bathtub.'

'Don't you mean *you* drowned him?'

'I . . . Yes. I drowned him.'

'That's a different story from the one you told Hercule Poirot,' I said.

Annabel Treadway lowered her eyes. 'I'm sorry.'

'For what? Killing your grandfather? Lying to Poirot? Lying to me? All three?'

'Please don't make this any harder for me than it needs to be, Inspector.'

'You've just confessed to a murder, Miss Treadway. What were you hoping for: a mug of cocoa and a pat on the back? Your sister and niece have both told Poirot that you couldn't possibly have killed Mr Pandy—that you were with them from when the three of you heard him complain about the noise you were making until Kingsbury found him dead around thirty minutes later.'

'They must be mistaken. We were all together in Ivy's bedroom, but I left the room for a few minutes. Lenore and Ivy must have forgotten. It's hard to remember events clearly at a distance of many weeks.'

'I see. Do you remember what you were wearing when you killed your grandfather?'

'What I was wearing?'

'Yes. Your sister Lenore described a particular dress.'

'I . . . I was wearing my blue dress with the yellow and white flowers.' That, at least, tallied with her sister's account.

'Tell me, where is that dress now?' I asked.

'At home. Why does everybody keep asking me about my dress? Why does it matter? I haven't worn it since the day Grandy died.'

'Did it get wet, when you forced your grandfather's head under the bathwater?' I asked her.

She looked as if she might faint. 'Yes.'

'Your sister Lenore told Poirot that your dress was completely dry.'

'She . . . she must not have noticed.'

'And what if I were to tell you that Jane Dockerill found

this blue dress of yours—that it had been wrapped in cellophane while it was sopping wet, and taped to the underside of Timothy Lavington's bed at school?'

There was no mistaking the shock on Annabel Treadway's face.

'You're making this up, to confuse me,' she said. 'You're doing it deliberately!'

'Putting you off your well-rehearsed story, am I, with some inconvenient facts?'

'You're twisting my words! Won't you please just accept my confession?'

'Not yet. Are you sure you didn't tape the dress to the frame of your nephew's bed? You weren't worried that someone would notice that it was wet and smelled of olive oil? You didn't have the bright idea to hide it somewhere far from the house?'

She said shakily, 'All right, then: yes, I did.'

'Yet, when I asked to confirm that you'd hidden the dress under Timothy's bed, you said it was at home. Why would you lie about that when you've already confessed to murder? I don't think you would.'

'There is only one thing that matters, Inspector: I killed my grandfather. I will swear to it in court. You may arrest me immediately, and do whatever you do with criminals— but would you promise me something, in exchange for my full confession? I don't want Hoppy to be stuck at Combingham Hall once I'm gone. He wouldn't be properly attended to. Promise me you'll find someone who will love and care for him properly.'

'*You* will continue to do both,' I told her cheerfully. 'It's quite clear to me that you haven't killed anybody.'

'I did. Put a Bible in my hands and I will swear on it.'

'A Bible, eh? Would you swear on the life of your dog, Hopscotch?'

Annabel Treadway's mouth set in a hard line. Tears came to her eyes. She said nothing.

'All right, Miss Treadway, tell me: *why* did you drown your grandfather?'

'That I can answer easily.' There was tangible relief, both in her voice and in her eyes. I sensed that she might be about to speak the truth, or at least some of it. 'Grandy found out something about me. He was going to cut me out of his will because of it.'

'What did he find out?'

'I shall *never* tell you that,' said Annabel Treadway. 'And you cannot compel me to.'

'You're right. I can't.'

'Are you going to arrest me for murder?'

'Me? No. I shall consult with M. Poirot, and perhaps contact the relevant police constabulary after doing so.'

'But . . . what should I do now? I wasn't expecting to have to go home again.'

'Well, I'm afraid you will have to—unless you've got somewhere else to go. Go home, walk your dog, and wait and see if anyone turns up to arrest you for murder. I think it's pretty unlikely that anyone will, but you never know. You might be lucky!'

CHAPTER 29

An Unexpected Eel

As I turned the corner into my own street later that same evening, I saw that the door of the house where I lived was standing open and that my landlady, Mrs Blanche Unsworth, had planted herself in the doorway and looked ready to burst out of it at the first sight of me. 'Oh, no,' I muttered to myself.

She hopped from one foot to the other and waved her arms about as if someone had asked her to impersonate a tree being blown by a storm. Did she imagine that I might not yet have spotted her?

I produced my best smile, and called out, 'Hello, Mrs Unsworth! A fine evening, isn't it?'

'Am I glad you're back!' she said. As soon as I was within her reach, she pulled me into the house. 'A gentleman paid a call while you were out. I didn't like the look of him. Strange piece of goods, he was. I've known all sorts, but he was like no one I've ever met.'

'Ah,' I said. The best thing about Mrs Unsworth is that

you never need to ask her a question. Within minutes of encountering her, she will have provided you with a complete list of every thought in her head and every incident she has witnessed or been involved in since the last time you saw her.

'Stood there like a china figurine, he did. As if someone had made him from pottery! His face barely moved as he spoke. He was ever so polite—almost too polite, as if he was putting it on.'

'Ah,' I said again.

'I had a funny feeling from the moment I set eyes on him. "Don't be silly, Blanche. What are you fretting about?" I said to myself. "Gentleman's nicely turned out, nice and polite, a bit reserved, maybe, but that's nothing to be concerned about. If only every gentleman caller should be so well mannered." Then he gave me a parcel to give to you, and he said it was for Inspector Edward Catchpool, and it's addressed to you, so I've left it well alone. It's all wrapped up, and I'm sure it's nothing *too* nasty, but you just never know, do you? It looks a bit lumpy to me.'

'Where is the parcel?' I asked.

'I must say, I didn't like the look of it any more than I liked the look of him,' said Mrs Unsworth. 'I'm not sure you should open it. I wouldn't, if I were you.'

'You don't need to worry about me, Mrs Unsworth.'

'Oh, but I do! I do worry.'

'Where is the parcel?'

'Well, it's in the dining room, but . . . Wait!' She stood in front of me to prevent me from proceeding along the hall. 'I can't let you open it without warning you. What happened next put the wind up me good and proper. You need to hear the whole story.'

Did I? I tried my best to look patient.

'I asked the gentleman's name and he ignored me. Acted as if I'd never asked! That's what I mean: he tried to seem ever so polite, but would a true gentleman ignore a reasonable question like that from a lady? I'm telling you, he was a piece of goods. He had a cunning glint in his eye.'

'I'm sure he did.'

'A funny smile, too. Not the sort of smile you see every day. And then he opened his mouth and said—and I'll never forget it, as long as I live! One of the most peculiar things as ever happened to me! He said, "*Tell Inspector Catchpool that the eel feels down at heel.*"'

'What?'

Blanche Unsworth obediently repeated the words.

'The eel feels down at heel?' I said.

'Those very words! Well, I thought to myself: no point being the gracious hostess if he's going to toy with me in such an unpleasant manner. "Please tell me your name," I said, and he'll have known I hadn't taken kindly to his nonsense, but he didn't care. Just said it again, didn't he? "The eel feels down at heel."'

'I must see the parcel,' I said. This time, mercifully, my landlady stood aside and allowed me to pass.

I stopped abruptly when I saw the wrapped package on the dining room table. I knew straight away what it was.

'The eel feels down at heel! Ha!'

'Why are you laughing? Do you know what it means?' Mrs Unsworth asked.

'I think I do, yes.'

She stood back, covered her mouth with her hands and gasped as I pulled off the wrapping. Once the object was revealed she said with reverence, 'It's . . . it's a typewriter.'

'I need some paper,' I told her. 'I'll explain in due course, once I've tested this thing to find out if I'm right.'

'Paper? Well, I'm sure I . . . It's no trouble, of course, but—'

'Then please bring some, without delay.'

Soon afterwards, with Mrs Unsworth standing behind me, I inserted a sheet of writing paper into the machine. I typed, 'The eel feels down at heel'. It sounded as if it might be the first line of a funny music hall song. The next line, I thought, might be, 'He kneels beside a wheel'. I typed that too.

'Who is this eel?' asked Mrs Unsworth. 'And why, I should like to know, is he kneeling beside a wheel?'

I pulled the paper out of the typewriter and surveyed the results of my creativity. 'Yes!' I said.

'If you don't tell me what this is all about, I shan't get a wink of sleep tonight,' Mrs Unsworth threatened.

'For some time, Poirot and I have been looking for a particular typewriter. This, it turns out, is the one. It has a faulty letter "e". Look closely.' I passed her the piece of paper.

'But . . . what does that have to do with an eel?' she asked.

'Whoever delivered the typewriter obviously wanted me to test it by typing a phrase that contains lots of "e"s. That's all that matters—not the eel and not the wheel, either. They're not real. What matters is: who was the strange man who came here, and whose is this machine?'

I had been imagining how pleased Poirot would be when I told him about this new development, but in fact—as I would have realized straight away if I weren't such a cloth-headed fool—it moved us no further forward.

'I expect the man you met was merely a messenger, not the true sender,' I told Blanche Unsworth. 'It's not his name we need, it's the name of whoever put him up to it.'

I excused myself, went up to my room and lay down on the bed, feeling as down at heel as our friend the eel. Somebody was taunting me—someone who had gone to great lengths to draw my attention to my own ignorance: 'Here is the typewriter you're after. Now all you have to do is work out where it came from—which you can't, can you? And you never will, because I'm cleverer than you.' I could almost hear the words being spoken in a sneering tone of voice.

'You might be cleverer than I am,' I said, though the person I was addressing had no chance of hearing me, 'but I wouldn't assume you're cleverer than Hercule Poirot.'

CHAPTER 30

The Mystery of Three Quarters

The next day, battling against the foul weather, I travelled to Combingham Hall with Rowland McCrodden. It was not an enjoyable journey. I spent much of it pondering why it should be the case that conversations between Poirot, McCrodden and me flowed easily, while McCrodden and I, minus Poirot, couldn't seem to talk in a way that was not stilted and—on his part, at least—ill-tempered.

Combingham Hall had a bland, institutional frontage. Though it was evidently an old building, it had an oddly temporary look about it, as if it had been positioned, rather than rooted, in its surrounding landscape. I found it strange to think that, the following day, everybody involved in the peculiar puzzle surrounding the death of Barnabas Pandy would congregate here, on Poirot's orders.

Rowland McCrodden and I found the front door of the Hall ajar, in spite of the driving rain. Unsurprisingly, the front part of the tiled floor was wet, and there was some mud mixed in with the water. I immediately thought about

Poirot's poor shoes and the suffering they might already have endured. There were a few muddy paw prints dotted about—the handiwork of Hopscotch the dog, I assumed. (Or 'paws-iwork', I smiled to myself.)

There was no one to greet us. McCrodden turned to me with a dissatisfied expression and seemed about to make a complaint when we both heard a shuffling sound. An elderly man had appeared from the vaulted corridor ahead and was making slow progress towards us.

'I see you've found your way in, gentlemen,' he said. 'My name is Kingsbury. Let me take your hats and coats, and then I'll show you to your rooms. Nice rooms, you've both got. Pleasing aspect. Oh—and then Mr Porrott has requested that you both join him in Mr Pandy's study.' As he shuffled closer, I noticed that he was shivering. Still, he made no move to close the front door before inviting us to follow him upstairs.

The bedroom assigned to me was enormous, austere, uncomfortable and cold. The bed had a lumpy mattress and a lumpy pillow: a disheartening combination. The view had the potential to be delightful as soon as the rain stopped lashing at the windows.

Kingsbury had told us how to find the room he still called 'Mr Pandy's study', and once I was ready to go downstairs I knocked on McCrodden's door, which was next to mine. When I asked him if his bedroom was to his liking, he replied coldly, 'It contains a bed and a washbasin, which is all I require.' The clear implication was that only a cosseted degenerate would hope for more.

We found Poirot installed in a high-backed leather armchair in the study, with a striped blanket in orange, brown and black draped around his shoulders. He was drinking a tisane. I smelled it as soon as we entered the room and could see the steam rising from it.

'Catchpool!' he said in a tone of anguish. 'I do not understand what is the matter with you English. It is as cold in this room as it is outside!'

'I agree. This house is like a glacier with walls and a roof,' I said.

'Will you two stop fussing?' Rowland McCrodden barked. 'What's that, Poirot?' He pointed to a piece of paper that lay face-down on what Kingsbury would doubtless have called 'Mr Pandy's desk'.

'Aha!' said Poirot. 'All in good time, *mon ami*, all in good time.'

'And what's in the brown paper bag?'

'I will answer your questions *bientôt*. But first . . . I am so very sorry, my friend, but it is my duty to inform you of the most terrible news. Please, will you sit down?'

'Terrible . . .' The flesh on McCrodden's face seemed to drop. 'Is it John?'

'*Non, non.* John is perfectly well.'

'Well, what is it, then? Spit it out!'

'It is *la pauvre* Mademoiselle Mason. Emerald Mason.'

'What about her? You haven't invited her here, have you? Poirot, I will swing for you if you've—'

'Please, *mon ami*.' Poirot put his finger to his lips. 'I beg of you, silence.'

'Just tell me, for pity's sake,' McCrodden snapped. 'What has Miss Mason done now?'

'There has been the most unfortunate motorcar accident. Miss Mason was in a vehicle when a . . . a horse moved unexpectedly in front of it.'

'A horse?' I said.

'Yes, Catchpool, a horse. Please do not interrupt. Nobody else was hurt, but poor Mademoiselle Mason . . . Oh! *C'est vraiment dommage!*'

'Are you saying that Emerald Mason is dead?' asked McCrodden.

'No, my friend. It would perhaps be better for her if she were. A young lady, with her whole life ahead of her . . .'

'Poirot, I demand that you tell me at once—' began McCrodden. His face had turned as red as a beetroot.

'Of course, of course. She is to lose both legs.'

'*What?*' McCrodden exclaimed.

'Good Lord!' I said. 'That's horrible.'

'A surgeon is, at this moment, removing the two limbs. There was no way to save either one. Too much damage had been sustained.'

McCrodden produced a handkerchief and started to mop his brow. He said nothing. Then he shook his head several times. 'That . . . that is . . . How unspeakably . . . I can't believe it. *Both* legs?'

'Yes, both legs.'

'We must . . . The firm must ensure she has everything she needs. And flowers. A basket of fruit. And money, damn it! As much as she needs, and the best medical expertise available. There must be specialists who train people after accidents like this, so that they can . . .' McCrodden's mouth twisted. The redness had drained from his face. Now his skin looked almost transparent. 'Will she be able to come back to work? If she can't, it will kill her. Truly, it will. She loves her work.'

'Monsieur McCrodden, I am so sorry,' said Poirot. 'You do not care for the young woman, I know, but this must nevertheless be a terrible shock for you.'

Rowland McCrodden moved slowly to the nearest chair, lowered himself into it, and covered his face with his hands. At the very same moment, Poirot turned to me and winked.

I made a questioning face at him. He winked again. A powerful sensation of disbelief gripped me. Could this really be happening?

I made another, more severe, questioning face. Was Poirot trying to signal to me that he had told McCrodden a lie? Was Emerald Mason perfectly fine, with two functioning legs still attached to the rest of her body, and no one angling to chop them off? In which case, what on earth was Poirot up to?

I wondered if I ought to speak up. What would happen if I were to say to Rowland McCrodden, 'Poirot just winked at me twice; I think he's pulling your leg'? That would hardly be the ideal phrase to use, in the circumstances.

'*Mon ami*, would you prefer to retire to your room?' Poirot asked him. 'Catchpool and I, we can hold up the fort if you do not feel well enough to continue.'

'Continue with what? I'm sorry, I . . . This appalling news has distracted me.'

'That I can see,' said Poirot.

'Catchpool, I'm sorry,' said McCrodden, almost inaudibly.

'For what?' I asked him.

'I have been atrocious company today. You've been a saint to put up with me. I've treated you unconscionably and you did nothing to deserve it. Please accept my most sincere apologies.'

'Of course,' I said. 'It's forgotten.'

'Gentlemen, we have much to discuss,' said Poirot. 'Monsieur McCrodden, you asked me about this sheet of paper. You may look at it now if you wish. So may you, Catchpool, if our friend is too distressed.'

'He looks distressed to me,' I said pointedly. 'Doesn't he to you?'

Poirot smiled. That was when I knew for certain that Emerald Mason's legs were in no danger of being chopped off. I was cross with myself. There was nothing to stop me telling McCrodden he had been tricked, so why wasn't I speaking up? Instead, I said nothing, trusting in the grand plan of Poirot, as if he were a deity.

I walked over to the desk, picked up the piece of paper and turned it over. On it were typed six words: 'The eel feels down at heel.'

'What the blazes . . . ?' I muttered.

Poirot began to laugh.

'*You* sent me the typewriter?' I said.

'Ah! *Oui, c'etait* Poirot! I had Georges deliver it, and gave him instructions about what to say. He played his part

289

most satisfactorily. To Mrs Unsworth, he gave the message about the eel.'

'Enough games, Poirot. Why didn't you simply tell me you'd found the typewriter?'

'A thousand apologies, *mon cher*. Poirot, he has every now and then the mischievous impulse.'

'Where did you find it?'

'Where did I found the down-at-heel eel? Here at Combingham Hall. Do not breathe a word, please, Catchpool. Nobody here knows that a typewriter is missing.'

'Then . . . the four letters signed in your name were typed by somebody here?'

'The letters were typed here, yes.'

'By whom?'

'That is indeed the question! I have a suspicion—but that is all it is, and I cannot prove I am right. The certain knowledge . . .' He sighed. 'After much hard work, it still eludes me.'

'Haven't you promised to reveal all at two o'clock tomorrow?' I reminded him.

'Yes. Time is starting to run out for Poirot.' He smiled, as if the idea pleased him. 'Will he make the enormous fool of himself? No, he cannot! He must think of his reputation! He must preserve his good name—the most excellent name of Hercule Poirot. *Alors*, there is, then, only one thing to do! This mystery must be solved before two o'clock tomorrow afternoon. I am very close, my friends . . . very close. I feel it here.' He pointed to his head. 'The little grey cells are hard at work. The running out of time . . . it is invigorating, Catchpool. It inspires me! Do not worry. All will be well.'

'I'm not worried,' I told him. 'I haven't promised any answers to anybody. I was only reminding you that *you* ought to be worried.'

'Very amusing, Catchpool.'

'What's in the brown paper bag?' I asked.

'Ah, yes, the bag,' said Poirot. 'We will unwrap it now. But first, I must confess something. Monsieur McCrodden, I see that you are still unable to speak, so please listen to what I am about to say. The story I told you about Miss Mason, that she is to lose both her legs—it was not true.'

McCrodden's mouth fell open. 'Not . . . not *true*?'

'Not in the least. To the best of my knowledge, that young woman has suffered no unfortunate accident, and both of her legs are still in the condition of the mint.'

'But you . . . you said . . . *Why*, Poirot?'

I found it peculiar that McCrodden was not angry. He seemed, rather, to be in a funny sort of trance. His eyes looked glazed.

'That, *mon ami*, along with much else, I will explain at our gathering tomorrow. I am sorry to have caused you distress with my little story. In my defence, I can only say that it was absolutely necessary. You do not know it yet, but you have helped me greatly.'

McCrodden nodded vaguely.

Poirot walked over to the desk. I heard a rustling noise as he took something out of the brown paper bag. Then he stood back so that we could see what it was.

'Isn't that . . . ?' I started to say. McCrodden laughed.

It was a small plate of blue and white patterned china, with a slice of Church Window Cake on it.

'Yes, indeed—it is Mademoiselle Fee's cake. One slice. That is all I need!' said Poirot.

'To keep the wolf from the door until dinner?' said McCrodden, before letting out another delirious laugh. He had evidently undergone some kind of transformation, and Poirot was responsible, yet it was hard to know if the effect was accidental or deliberately engineered.

'It is not for the stomach but for the little grey cells,' Poirot said. 'Here, my friends, in this small slice of cake, *we have the solution to the mystery of who killed Barnabas Pandy*!'

'Goodness me, what a horrible house,' said Eustace Campbell-Brown, as he, Sylvia Rule and Mildred alighted from the car that had brought them to Combingham Hall. He stared up at the building's façade. 'A person surely couldn't *live* here? Look at it! And to think, they could sell it for a fortune and buy any number of swanky, well-appointed flats in London, Paris, New York . . .'

'I don't think it's as bad as all that,' said Mildred.

'Neither do I,' said Sylvia Rule. 'You're right, Mildred—it's a very handsome building indeed. Eustace doesn't know what he's talking about. He's only displaying his ignorance.'

Mildred looked at her mother, then at her fiancé. Then, without a word, she set off towards the house. Sylvia and

Eustace watched her walk in through the open front door.

'May I suggest a truce?' said Eustace. 'At least until we return to London.'

Sylvia turned away. 'I am allowed to think that the house is attractive if that is what I happen to think,' she said.

'Doesn't it bother you that you have, once again, driven Mildred away? Don't you mind being as unbearable as you are?' Eustace held up his hands. 'That one was my fault. I will desist from making hostile remarks if you will too. How about it? We need to think not about ourselves but about Mildred. You and I might be enjoying our little war, but I don't think she can stand much more of it.'

'You called me a murderer,' Sylvia reminded him.

'I should not have said that. I apologize.'

'Do you truly believe it? Answer me honestly.'

'I have said I'm sorry.'

'But not meant it! You have no understanding of the suffering of others—of women like me. You're a demon.'

'Now that you've got that off your chest, how about that truce?' said Eustace.

'Very well. For as long as we are at Combingham Hall, I shall try my best.'

'Thank you. I will too.'

Together, they entered the house. They found Mildred standing alone in the entrance hall. She flinched at the sight of them, then looked up at the ceiling and quietly started to sing one of her favourite songs, 'The Boy I Love Is Up in the Gallery', her arms stretched out on either side. She looked as if she wanted to fly away.

Eustace thought: 'I've got to get her away from Sylvia's influence or we'll both be driven quite mad.'

Mildred's voice shook as she sang:

'Now, If I were a Duchess who had a lot of money,
I'd give it to the boy that's going to marry me.
But I haven't got a penny, so we'll live on love and kisses,
And be just as happy as the birds on the tree.
The boy I love is up in the gallery . . .'

'Does anyone hear singing?' asked Rowland McCrodden. 'I'm sure someone's singing.'

'Poirot, how can a slice of cake be the solution to an unsolved murder?' I asked.

'Because it is a whole slice: undivided, intact. Not separated into quarters. It is the solution to what I have thought of, for some time, as the Mystery of the Three Quarters! Unless . . .'

Poirot hurried over to the cake and, producing a small knife from his pocket, cut off the yellow square in the top left-hand corner. He pushed it to the edge of the plate, separating it from the rest of the slice. 'Unless *this* is the case,' he said. 'But I do not believe it is. No, I do not believe that at all.' He pushed the yellow square back to its original position, so that it was touching the other squares.

'You are suggesting that one square is not separate, but connected to the three other squares,' I said. 'Which means that . . . all four people who received letters accusing them of murder know one another?'

'*Non, mon ami.* Not at all.'

'John does not know any of the others,' said Rowland McCrodden. 'That's what he told me, and I believe him.'

'Then what does Poirot mean by the whole, undivided slice of cake being the solution?'

We both looked at him. He smiled enigmatically. Then McCrodden said, 'Wait! I think I know what he means . . .'

'But I don't *know* where it could be,' said Hugo Dockerill in a panicked voice. 'I mean, it *might* be anywhere! All I know is that it's not here, and we're already hopelessly late. Oh, dear.'

'Hugo,' said his wife gently. 'Calm down. Nobody at Combingham Hall cares if we arrive at noon or at midnight. As long as we're there in time for tomorrow's meeting, that's all that matters.'

'Thank you for trying to make me feel better, dearest Jane. I know you're crosser about our lateness than you're letting me see.'

'I'm not cross, Hugo.' She put her hand in his. 'I wish I understood, that's all: what it must feel like to be you, the way you think and . . . carry on. I can't imagine it. I can't imagine needing to make three trips to post a letter because, on the first two trips, you forget to take the letter with you. I would never do that, and so it's hard for me to understand how it's possible.'

'Well, it got posted in the end. It's not the letter that's the problem, it's my blasted hat! Where *is* the damned thing?'

'Why don't you take a different hat?'

'I wanted to take this one. I mean, *that* one, the one that isn't here any more!'

'You said you had it in your hand very recently.'

'I'm sure I did, yes.'

'Well, then. Where did you go when you left the room a moment ago?'

'Only to the parlour.'

'Then might the hat be in the parlour?'

Hugo frowned again. Then an expression of utmost delight appeared on his face. 'It might! I shall go and have a look.'

He returned a few seconds later, hat in hand. 'Your method worked. Dearest Jane, you are marvellous. Right! Shall we go?'

Jane Dockerill sighed. 'We should—but isn't there something else we need to take with us, apart from your hat and all the things already waiting by the door?'

'No, I've got everything else. It's all in the overnight case. What else do we need?'

'Timothy Lavington and Freddie Rule?' She shook her head and smiled. 'Shall I go and find them?'

'Yes, please, darling. You'll do a better job of that than I would, I'm quite sure.'

'So am I. Hugo?'

'Yes, dearest?'

'Hold that hat in your hand the whole time I'm gone, won't you? I don't want you losing it again.'

'Absolutely. I shan't let it out of my sight.'

*

'If I'm right, Poirot, then what you mean is this,' said Rowland McCrodden. 'It's not that all four people who received letters accusing them of murder know one another. Neither is it that they all knew Barnabas Pandy. It is that they were all acquainted with the writer of the letters.'

'Yes—you are correct,' said Poirot.

McCrodden looked astonished. 'Am I?' he said. 'I wasn't expecting to be. It was only a guess.'

'It was a good one,' Poirot told him. 'At least . . . I am nearly certain that you are correct. There is still one important question I must ask, and that will require a trip to London.'

'London? But everybody's coming here,' I exclaimed. '*You've* brought them!'

'And here they must remain, until I return. Do not alarm yourself, *mon cher* Catchpool. I will be back in good time for our two o'clock appointment tomorrow.'

'But where are you going?'

'It must be . . . is it Peter Vout?' asked Rowland McCrodden.

'Another ingenious guess!' Poirot clapped his hands together.

'Hardly,' said McCrodden. 'Vout is just about the only person who might know anything who isn't here at Combingham Hall.'

'He will certainly know the answer to the question I shall ask him tomorrow morning,' said Poirot. 'He cannot fail to know it! After which, hopefully the complete picture will be clear—and just in time, too.'

*

John McCrodden arrived at Combingham Hall to find the front door standing wide open. He walked in. The floor of the entrance hall was wet and muddy. There were some unattended suitcases by the bottom of a staircase three times as large as any he had seen before.

'Hello?' he called out. 'Hello! Is there anybody here?'

No person appeared, and nobody answered his question. There was nothing John would have liked more than for it to turn out that he was, indeed, alone in this enormous building that was as cold as a grave—where he could build and light a fire in one of the rooms and spend a peaceful evening on his own—but he knew this was merely a fantasy. No doubt an assortment of affected society people would appear at any moment, and he knew he would loathe them all.

He was halfway across the hall in search of a kitchen where he could rummage for food and make himself a cup of hot, strong tea when a door to the right of him opened and at last someone appeared.

'I'm John Mc . . .' he started to say, turning. But he ran out of breath saying his own name.

No. It couldn't be. It was impossible to think clearly while his heart pounded so violently.

It couldn't be. Yet it was.

'Hello, John.'

'It's . . . it's *you*,' was all he could manage to say.

THE FOURTH QUARTER

CHAPTER 31

A Note for Mr Porrott

Freddie Rule had learned a lot since arriving at Combingham Hall yesterday. Much more than he had ever learned at school, in fact. The teachers did their best to stuff useful facts into him, and he was decent at remembering them, but hearing about something that had happened in the past, or about what some long-dead chap had worked out, wasn't the same as making the discovery yourself. When that happened—and not in a stuffy, almost-silent schoolroom, but in the course of one's everyday life—whatever it was that one had learned left a much deeper impression. Freddie was certain he would never forget the two lessons that his time at Timothy Lavington's house (as he thought of it) had so far taught him: the first was that a person only really needed one friend.

Miraculously, Timothy had decided that he liked Freddie. They'd had fun running around the garden together playing hide-and-seek, pinching food from the kitchen when Cook wasn't looking, and mocking old Dimwit Dockerill and some of the other people in the house: the Old Fossil of a butler who looked as if he might crumble to dust if he moved another inch, the Belgian that both Timothy and Freddie called 'the Egg with a Moustache', and the man who looked like a bust in a museum, with curly grey hair and the highest forehead in the world.

'People are really rather grotesque, aren't they, Freddie?' Timothy had said this morning. 'Especially when lots of them are gathered together in one place, like now—that's when I really notice it—or at school. I don't think much of our species, on the whole. *You're* all right, Freddie. And obviously I'm all right too. And I love my Aunt Annabel and Ivy and my father . . .' Here Timothy had stopped and frowned, as if thinking about his father bothered him.

'What about your mother, and all your friends at Turville?'

'I try to think well of Mummy,' Timothy had sighed. 'As for my friends at Turville, I loathe them all. They're the most insufferable dullards.'

'But then . . . ?'

'Why do I keep them as friends? Why do I spend all my time with them? Survival: that's the only reason. School is a savage place, Freddie, wouldn't you agree?'

'I . . . I'm not sure,' Freddie had stammered, looking down at his lap. 'My last school was more savage. I got my collarbone broken there, and my wrist.'

'You haven't been around long enough to notice Turville's subtle savagery. No limbs are broken—only spirits. When I started there, I immediately identified that group of boys—the group of which I'm now the leader—as the one most likely to ensure my survival. I chose correctly, I think. The fact is, I knew I wasn't strong enough to tough it out alone. That's why I admire you, Freddie.'

Freddie had been too astonished to speak and so had made no response.

'You don't feel the need to make the nauseating compromises I make in order to be popular. You spend most of your time with Dimwit Dockerill's wife, who's a good egg, all things considered. Taken you under her wing, hasn't she?'

'She is kind to me, yes.'

Freddie had found it hard to concentrate, so surprised was he by what Timothy was saying. He had barely managed to answer the question. He would have made endless nauseating compromises in order to be as popular as Timothy, but the opportunity to do so had never presented itself.

'I could be your friend at school,' he said. 'If you don't like your other friends, I mean. We don't have to speak to each other, but secretly we could know that we were friends. Only if . . .' Freddie had lost his nerve at that point, and started to mumble: 'It was just an idea. I'll understand if you don't want to.'

'Or we could be friends in the normal way, quite openly, and anyone who doesn't like it can go to the devil!' Timothy had said defiantly.

'No, you don't want to do that. You can't be seen to like me. You'd soon be as unpopular as I am.'

'I don't think that's true,' Timothy had said thoughtfully.

'I did such a good job of making myself popular when I joined the school, I'm fairly sure I can now take that popularity with me wherever I go, whatever groups I do or don't belong to. We shall see. Naturally, we'll need to make a few vital alterations to . . . well, to *you*, Freddie. Your demeanour, the way you conduct yourself at school.'

'Of course,' Freddie had hastily agreed. 'Whatever you think best.'

'Your clothes are a little too . . . I mean, there's school uniform and then there's school uniform, Freddie.'

'I see. Yes, of course.'

'Still, we needn't worry about the details now. It's funny, you know: I've always envied you. The rumours about your mother . . . I hope you don't mind my mentioning them?'

'I don't mind,' Freddie had said, though he did, very much.

'It's just that everybody thinks your mother's a baby-killer and a monster, and they all say so, while they all think *my* mother is the soul of respectability. Which she is. But that means nobody ever calls her a horror, which means I can't join in and say, "Yes, I think you might be right. I think she drove my father away with her cold-heartedness." I should like to say that, loudly and to a large crowd. I should like it very much. But *my* mother's deficiencies get no official recognition. And if I tried to explain, no one would understand or feel sorry for me.'

'The rumours about my mother are completely untrue,' said Freddie quickly and quietly. He could not have forgiven himself if he hadn't said it at all.

'As are the lack of rumours about mine,' said Timothy.

'How can a *lack* of rumours be untrue?'

'You are too literal-minded, Freddie.' Timothy smiled. 'Come on, let's see if we can find any tasty scraps in the kitchen. I'm starved!'

And so—although he feared his new-found state of delirious happiness might last only as long as he and Timothy were at Combingham Hall together, with no other boys of their age present—Freddie's life had changed beyond all recognition in the space of mere minutes. He had a friend! Mrs Dockerill, kind though she was, couldn't be his friend. She could only ever be a grown-up who pitied him and took care of him—but that didn't matter, because now Freddie had Timothy.

This was what had taught him that nobody needed more than one friend. He had only one, and it turned out to be the perfect number. He felt absolutely no need for more.

The second lesson Freddie had learned at Combingham Hall was that definitions of size, like 'big' and 'small', were relative. Until he had come here, Freddie had always thought of his own home in London as large. He knew he would not be able to think of it in this way ever again, not now that he'd seen Timothy's house, which was a mansion of the sort that a royal or aristocratic person might own, and had more extensive grounds even than Turville College. The Hall was so big, it was almost like being outside in the open air, except inside. One could run past as many doors as one would normally only see side by side on a long street, and still find new corners to turn, new staircases to climb.

Freddie had now been running for some time, looking for Timothy in their latest game of hide-and-seek. He had checked dozens of empty bedrooms and every nook and cranny he could find, and was now at the stage of simply dashing around calling out, 'Timothy! Timothy!'

He raced around another corner and nearly banged into the Old Fossil. 'Mind yourself, laddie!' the old man said. What was his name? Kingswood? Kingsmead? 'You nearly knocked me to the ground!'

'Sorry, sir,' said Freddie. Kingsbury: that was it!

'I should think so too. Now, have you by any chance seen Mr Porrott?'

'Who?'

'The French gentleman.'

The Fossil was talking about the Egg with a Moustache, Freddie realized. 'He's Belgian, isn't he? Not French.'

'No, he's French. I've heard him say French-sounding things since he got here.'

'Yes, but—'

'Have you seen him, laddie?'

At that moment, Timothy Lavington ran up behind the Fossil, shouting, 'Freddie! Found you!'

The old man staggered back. He steadied himself against the wall and put his hand on his chest. 'You boys'll put me in an early grave,' he said. Freddie nearly laughed at his use of the word 'early'. He must have been at least eighty years old.

'Why'd you have to tear around like wild things, and leap out at each other like monkeys from trees?'

'Sorry, Kingsbury,' Timothy said cheerfully. 'It won't happen again, I promise.'

'Oh, but it will, Master Timothy. I know it will.'

'You're probably right, old boy.'

'I thought I was supposed to be finding you?' Freddie said.

'And I need to find Mr Porrott, the Frenchman,' said Kingsbury. 'I've looked everywhere.'

'He's Belgian! His name's pronounced *Poirot* and he's in the drawing room,' said Timothy. 'That's where we all ought to be. It's ten minutes after two. I completely forgot that we were all supposed to be there at two o'clock. Poirot sent me to round everyone up, so here I am. Consider yourselves rounded!'

Like Timothy, Freddie had forgotten about the drawing room meeting at two o'clock. So, it seemed, had the Fossil, who nodded and said, 'It's quite true that I *haven't* looked for Mr Porrott in the drawing room since the clocks struck two. I looked for him in there nearly an hour ago, but not since. In fact, I despaired of ever finding him, so I ended up writing it all down in a note. If only I'd remembered . . . Yes, he *did* say two o'clock! Shall I get the note and take it to him, I wonder?'

'I should go straight to the drawing room if I were you,' Timothy advised. 'He's waiting for us all to turn up. Also, aren't you excited to hear what he has to say? I am! We're about to find out who murdered Grandy.'

'Do you think he *was* murdered?' Freddie asked. 'Mother says he died a perfectly innocent death and someone's trying to stir up trouble.'

'Well, let's hope not,' said Timothy. 'I miss him, of course, but . . . well, if people have to die, and it seems they do, it's far better if they're murdered. It's so much more interesting.'

'Hush, Master Timothy!' Kingsbury scolded. 'That's a wicked thing to say.'

'No, it's not,' said Timothy. 'Honestly, Freddie, every time I say anything that's true, somebody gripes about it. I sometimes feel as if the whole world is conspiring to turn me into a liar.'

CHAPTER 32

Where is Kingsbury?

Finally, all the chairs in Combingham Hall's drawing room were occupied apart from two. Since the number of chairs set out (by me, at some cost to my back) corresponded exactly to the number of people who ought to have been present for Poirot's meeting, there was no doubt that the emptiness of one of those two chairs constituted a problem. The other chair belonged to Poirot himself, because, unable to keep still on account of his mounting impatience, he was pacing up and down, looking every few seconds at the door, then at the empty chair opposite his own, then at the grandfather clock beside the window that looked on to the gardens. 'Soon it will be three o'clock!' he cried out in frustration, startling everybody. 'Why do people in this house not comprehend the importance of being punctual? I have been all the way to London and back, yet still I arrived here in good time.'

'M. Poirot, we need not wait for Kingsbury,' said Lenore Lavington. 'There is no question of his having murdered anybody or sent those foul letters. Could we not proceed without him? Perhaps you would like to tell us all why we are gathered here?'

Those gathered, aside from Poirot and me, were: Rowland McCrodden, John McCrodden, Sylvia Rule, Mildred Rule, Eustace Campbell-Brown, Lenore Lavington, Ivy Lavington, Annabel Treadway, Hugo Dockerill, Jane Dockerill, Timothy Lavington and Freddie Rule. Hopscotch the dog was also with us; he was lying on the carpet and had draped himself over Annabel's feet.

'*Non*,' said Poirot in a tone of grim determination. 'We wait. I called this meeting and it will not begin until I say so! It is essential for everyone to be here.'

'I'm so sorry, M. Poirot,' said Ivy Lavington. 'It was terribly rude of us all to keep you waiting. I am not normally late for anything. Neither is Kingsbury. This is most unlike him.'

'You, mademoiselle, were the first to arrive . . . twenty minutes after two o'clock. May I ask what delayed you?'

'I . . . I was thinking,' said Ivy. 'I must have lost myself in my thoughts more fully than I had realized.'

'I see. And the rest of you?' Poirot's eyes moved slowly from one person to another. 'What caused you all to be elsewhere at two o'clock, when you were supposed to be here?'

'Timothy and I were playing hide-and-seek. We forgot the time,' said Freddie.

'I was helping Hugo to find a pair of shoes that he eventually remembered he had left at home,' said Jane Dockerill.

'I could have sworn I packed them, darling. Beats me how I could have made a silly mistake like that.'

'I was looking after Mildred,' said Sylvia Rule. 'She had a most peculiar turn. For a long time she would not stop singing.'

'Singing, madame?' said Poirot.

'Mother, please,' murmured Mildred.

'Yes, singing,' said Sylvia Rule. 'When Eustace and I finally managed to make her stop, she was in a most irregular state and needed to lie down.'

'I was with Mildred,' Eustace told Poirot. 'I am eager to hear what you have to tell us, M. Poirot, and I would have been here as the clocks struck two, but Mildred seemed unable to speak or move for a while, and I'm afraid that was all I could think about. It put this little meeting right out of my head. I might have forgotten about it altogether if Timothy hadn't whizzed past and reminded me.'

'Well done for remembering, Timmy.' Ivy smiled at her brother.

'I didn't remember,' he said. 'I was hunting for Freddie. I thought I'd try the drawing room, even though I'd tried it already. I didn't find Freddie, but—'

'He found me,' said Poirot. 'It was past two o'clock and *nobody was here*. Only Catchpool and me. I sent Timothy to hunt not only for Freddie but for all of you.'

'I was looking for John,' said Rowland McCrodden. 'I left my bedroom with the intention of coming straight here, in fact, but as I made my way along the landing, I decided I would like to speak to my son privately first, before we joined the bigger group.'

'Why?' asked John.

'I don't know.' Rowland McCrodden lowered his eyes.

'Was there something particular that you wanted to say to me?'

'No.'

'You must have had a reason,' John insisted.

'You were perhaps hoping that you and Monsieur John could come to the meeting together, Monsieur McCrodden?' said Poirot.

'Yes. I was.'

'Why?' John asked again.

'Because you're my son!' bellowed Rowland McCrodden.

Once the shock of his outburst had subsided, John said to Poirot, 'If you're about to ask me why I was late, I decided at the last minute that perhaps I wouldn't indulge you—perhaps I would simply return home without hearing your explanation.'

'You came all the way here from London only to return home, monsieur?' Poirot raised an eyebrow.

'I did not return home, as you can see. I considered doing so, then decided against it.'

'What about you, Mademoiselle Treadway? And you, Madame Lavington? Why were you late?'

'I was out with Hoppy,' said Annabel Treadway. 'We were playing with his ball. He was having so much fun that I didn't want to disappoint him by coming inside. I . . . well, I suppose when you said two o'clock, I assumed you meant "or thereabouts". I was only a little bit late, wasn't I?'

'You were twenty-five minutes late, mademoiselle.'

'I was outside looking for Annabel,' said Lenore Lavington. 'I knew there was a danger she'd forget all about the time—she's far too soft on Hopscotch, and I knew he would want to play ball for *hours*. He always does.'

'And so, in order to prevent your sister from being late, you made yourself late.'

'As a matter of fact, I glanced in through that window when I heard the church clock strike the hour . . .'—Lenore pointed—'. . . and I saw all the empty chairs, and only you and Inspector Catchpool in here, and I thought, "Oh, well, plainly the meeting won't be starting on time." Which it didn't. I missed nothing. Now, may we please hear whatever it is that you have to say this afternoon, M. Poirot? Kingsbury is probably fast asleep in his bed. He often has a sleep in the middle of the afternoon. He is old and tires easily. Annabel and I will make sure he is informed of any developments.'

'He isn't in his cottage, or asleep,' said Timothy. 'Freddie and I talked to him upstairs, didn't we, Freddie? I told him Poirot was looking for him, and he said he'd forgotten all about this meeting, but when I reminded him, he set off for the drawing room.'

'He did,' Freddie Rule confirmed. 'He seemed upset about having forgotten and being late, and hurried off towards the stairs. I'm sure he was on his way here. He also said—'

'Stop, Freddie. Hush,' said Timothy suddenly. He stood up. 'M. Poirot, might I talk to you alone for a few moments?'

'*Oui, bien sûr*,' said Poirot.

The two of them left the drawing room together, closing the door behind them.

With Poirot gone, everyone looked at me as if they expected me to take over the proceedings. I hadn't the faintest notion of what to say, so I made a cheery remark about the fire, and how necessary it was on a cold day like today. 'I hope there's enough fuel at Combingham Hall to keep it going!' I said.

No one responded.

Thankfully, a few moments later, Poirot and Timothy Lavington returned. Poirot's eyes had a hard look about them. 'Catchpool,' he said. 'As quickly as you can, please, *check every room in the house*. The rest of us will wait here.'

'What am I looking for?' I asked, already on my feet.

'In my bedroom . . . Do you know where that is?'

I nodded.

'In my bedroom, you will look for a note that has been left for me by Kingsbury.'

I heard a gasp then: an uneven, staggered gasp. It sounded as if it came from a woman—yes, I thought, definitely a woman—but there was no way of knowing which one. Perhaps if I had been looking around the room at that moment . . . but my attention had been focused solely on Poirot.

'In my room, also, and in every room of this house, you will look for Kingsbury himself,' Poirot said. 'Quick, my friend. There is no time to lose!'

Annabel Treadway stood up. 'You're frightening me,' she

314

told Poirot. 'You sound as if you think Kingsbury is in danger.'

'I do, mademoiselle. He is in the most grave danger. Please hurry, Catchpool!'

'Then we must *all* look for him,' said Annabel.

'No!' Poirot stamped his foot on the floor. 'I forbid it. Only Catchpool. *Nobody else is to leave this room.*'

I don't know how many bedrooms there are at Combingham Hall, and my memory of my panicked dash around the place that afternoon is probably unreliable, but I would not be at all surprised if someone were to tell me that there were thirty bedrooms, or even forty. I raced from room to room, from floor to floor, feeling as if I was running around a sinister, deserted city instead of a family home. I distinctly remember an entire floor of bedrooms that were unused and almost derelict, with bare mattresses in some and, in others, bed frames without mattresses.

I discovered that I did not, in fact, know where Poirot's bedroom was. It felt like hours before I reached it, but I knew it was his as soon as I walked in and saw, laid out with geometric neatness beside a book and a cigarette case, the net he uses to protect his moustaches while he sleeps.

There was an envelope on the floor, between the bed and the door. It was sealed. In spidery handwriting, someone— presumably Kingsbury—had written 'Mr Herkl Porrott'. I put the envelope in my trouser pocket and continued with my search. 'Kingsbury!' I yelled as I ran along corridor after corridor, pushing open endless doors as I went. 'Are you here? Kingsbury!' I received no answer. All I could hear was my own words as they echoed back to me.

Eventually, after what felt like hours, I pushed open a door and found that I recognized the room behind it. It was the bathroom in which Barnabas Pandy had drowned. Poirot had insisted on showing it to me yesterday.

I was relieved to see an empty bathtub: no water and no dead body. I was busy telling myself that it was absurd to imagine I might find Kingsbury drowned in the same tub in which Pandy had died, when I noticed something on the floor. It was close to my feet, near the door. It was a towel: white with red patches and streaks.

I knew straight away that the red was blood.

I bent down to examine the towel more closely and I saw, between the feet of the bathtub, a dark shape lying on the floor behind it. The bath itself had initially blocked my view of it. I knew at once what it must be, though I prayed I would turn out to be wrong as I walked over to take a closer look.

It was Kingsbury. He lay curled on his side. His eyes were open. Around and beneath his head was a pool of red, forming an almost perfect circle. It resembled, in that moment and to my eyes at least, a sort of halo or crown— neither of which suited poor Kingsbury. One look at his face was enough to tell me he was dead.

CHAPTER 33

The Marks on the Towel

The next day, our meeting was reconvened in the drawing room of Combingham Hall. Two o'clock was again the agreed hour and, unlike on the previous day, everybody arrived promptly. Poirot confided to me later that he felt insulted by their punctuality. In his eyes, it was proof that they were all more than capable of arriving at the correct time when it mattered to them.

This meeting had been called not only by Poirot but also by a local police officer by the name of Inspector Hubert Thrubwell. 'We are treating Mr Kingsbury's death as murder for a very simple reason,' he told us all. 'There was a towel on the floor in the bathroom where he lay dead. Inspector Catchpool found the towel, and it was nowhere near the body of Mr Kingsbury. Isn't that right, Inspector Catchpool?'

'It is,' I said. 'The towel was next to the door, on the opposite side of the room. I almost trod on it as I walked in.'

Thrubwell thanked me and continued. 'When that towel

was examined by our police doctor, two distinct types of blood were found.'

'You do not mean different *types* of blood, *mon ami*,' said Poirot. 'All of the blood, if it belonged to Kingsbury, must have been of the same type. You are talking about the marks made by the blood on the towel, *n'est-ce pas*?'

'Yes, I am,' said Thrubwell. 'I am indeed!' He looked pleased to have been corrected. 'The police doctor found that Mr Kingsbury's death was the result of a serious head wound. He had either been pushed or fallen back, and hit his head hard on the sharp corner of the only cupboard in the room. Without the evidence of the towel that Inspector Catchpool found, it would have been impossible to know whether he was pushed or if he fell. Thanks to the towel, I think we can safely say that he was probably pushed—and even if he wasn't, he was certainly left to bleed to death by someone who wanted him gone. And that, in my book, is what I call murder!' Thrubwell looked at Poirot, who nodded his approval.

'I don't understand,' said Lenore Lavington. 'How does a towel prove anything?'

'Because of the two types of marks made by Mr Kingsbury's blood,' said Thrubwell. 'On one side of the towel was a large, thick, dark patch of blood, where Mr Kingsbury must have held it against his wound to try to stop the flow and save his own life. Now, if that's what he was trying to do, then why did the towel end up on the other side of the room, beyond the bathtub? I can't see that Mr Kingsbury would have had the strength to throw it all that way. It's a large room, and he was in a severely weakened state, and not the strongest of men even before he sustained his head wound. And then we come to the other blood marks. As well as the dense, dark patch of blood there were also five streaks on a quite different part of the towel. These were lighter in colour than the larger patch, and one of the five was shorter and lower down than the others.'

'Streaks?' said Ivy Lavington. She looked pale and serious. Annabel Treadway, in the chair beside Ivy's, was crying silently. Hopscotch stood next to her with one paw in her lap, occasionally whining and licking the side of her face. Most of the others present looked stunned.

'Yes, streaks,' said Inspector Thrubwell. 'It didn't take long for Mr Poirot here to figure out that they were finger marks. The shorter, lower one was made by the thumb.'

'The thumb of the person who left Mr Kingsbury to bleed to death?' asked Jane Dockerill.

'No, ma'am,' said Thrubwell. 'That person would have taken care not to touch any of the blood. The bloody finger streaks were made by the murder victim: Mr Kingsbury.'

'Here is what we believe must have happened,' said Hercule Poirot. 'The killer either pushed Kingsbury so that he fell and struck his head, or else the fall was an accident. Let us say it was an accident and give to our killer the benefit of the doubt in this one respect. Having fallen, it soon becomes apparent that Kingsbury is bleeding profusely. He is also old and weak, and has recently suffered the tragic loss of his dear friend Monsieur Pandy.

'The killer sees that Kingsbury is too weak to call for help and will probably die if nothing is done to save him. This is what the murderer wants. There is only one problem: as he fell, Kingsbury reached out for a towel that must have been draped over the side of the bathtub—a towel which he now holds in his hand and presses against his wound. This, thinks the killer, might staunch the flow of blood and save the old man's life. It becomes necessary, therefore, to snatch the towel away from Kingsbury, who suddenly finds he is no longer holding it. He tries to stop the bleeding with his hand. Now he has blood on his fingers. The killer is standing over him, perhaps taunting him with the towel, and Kingsbury reaches up to try to take hold of it again. He has no hope of retrieving it from the clutches of his strong and healthy tormenter, but he is allowed, briefly, to touch the towel before it is snatched away again, and dropped near the door as the killer leaves the bathroom—*and, in doing so, leaves Kingsbury to die.*'

'You're assuming rather a lot, aren't you?' said John McCrodden. 'What if Kingsbury got blood on his fingers *before* he ever reached for the towel? What if he *did* somehow manage to throw it across the room? Being close to death can give a person extraordinary strength.'

'He could not have thrown the towel and made it land where Inspector Catchpool found it,' Inspector Thrubwell replied. 'It would have been near impossible even for a strong man without a head wound.'

'Perhaps it would have, and perhaps it would not,' said Poirot. 'I will admit that, without all the other evidence, it might be difficult to say for certain. What you must not forget, Monsieur McCrodden, is that *I know there is a murderer among us today.* I have proof—proof that was given to me by Kingsbury himself.'

'Golly!' said Hugo Dockerill.

'I know who the killer is, and I know why that person wanted Kingsbury dead,' Poirot went on. 'That is why I am able to say to Inspector Thrubwell here that, happily, I have saved him some work. I had already solved the murder of Kingsbury before he arrived here at Combingham Hall.'

'And very grateful I am too, sir,' said Inspector Thrubwell.

'What proof was given to you by Kingsbury?' asked Rowland McCrodden. 'How can he have given you proof in the matter of his own murder while he was still alive? Or are you referring to the murder of Barnabas Pandy?'

'That is a good question,' said Poirot. 'As you know, before he died, Kingsbury was looking for me. There was something important that he wished to tell me. Unable to find me, he left a note in my bedroom. The note, when I read it, brought to mind certain facts I already knew. This meant that when I was informed of the death of Kingsbury, and told about the towel, and when I put all of these things together . . . I found that I knew who had so cruelly left Kingsbury to die. I knew it—I *know* it—beyond a doubt. That person is a cold-blooded murderer by nature, whether they pushed Kingsbury or not. What else are you, if you leave a man to die whom you might have saved?'

'Presumably the same person also murdered Barnabas

Pandy,' said Jane Dockerill. 'I hope you are not going to tell me that I'm sitting in a room with two murderers, M. Poirot? That I should find difficult to believe.'

'No, madame. There is only one.' Poirot pulled a piece of paper out of his pocket. 'This is not the note that I received from Kingsbury, but it is an exact copy of it. In it, though his use of English is flawed, Kingsbury nevertheless manages to make clear his meaning. You may all examine the copy of his letter in a moment. You will see that Kingsbury tells me that he has just overheard a conversation between Ivy Lavington and another person whose identity he does not know. Kingsbury heard this person crying, but not speaking. He believed it might have been a man or a woman. It was hard to tell, so anguished and uncontrolled was the crying.

'The conversation that Kingsbury overheard, one-sided as it was, took place in Mademoiselle Ivy's bedroom, with the door pushed closed, though not securely shut. He heard Mademoiselle Ivy say . . .'

Poirot stopped. He passed the piece of paper to me. 'Catchpool, would you please read the passage I have encircled? I find it too difficult not to make the necessary corrections. I am too much the perfectionist.'

I took the copied note from Poirot and began to read the indicated section.

'She were saying words to the effect of how carrying on like you're unfamiliar with the law isnt no defence. Theres wot your allowed to do, and theres those things your not allowed to, and pretending like you cant tell the one from the other is not going to wash with anyone. No one will believe you and being as your the only one of all of us as knows this John Modden . . .'

I stopped reading at that point and asked Poirot if Kingsbury had meant John McCrodden.

'*Oui, bien sûr*. Look around you, Catchpool. *Is* there a John Modden in the room?'

I read on:

'Being as your the only one of us all who knows this John Modden you should tell Mister Porrott the truth all of it like you told it to me. He will understand and after all no harm is done if you tell the truth now and if you dont he will.'

'Thank you, Catchpool. *Mesdames et messieurs*, you will understand, I hope, that most of what you have just heard was Kingsbury quoting what he heard Ivy Lavington say. He was not the most accurate of writers. No, he was not meticulous about the details. But in essence, on the important substance of what he overheard, he is accurate. We learn, then, that Kingsbury heard Ivy Lavington talking to somebody—we do not know whom—and warning them. *Words to the effect that ignorance of the law is no defence.* And that no one will believe in this ignorance of the law, for the person to whom Ivy Lavington was speaking is *the only one acquainted with John McCrodden*. And if that person does not tell me, Hercule Poirot, the full truth, perhaps, warned Mademoiselle Ivy, John McCrodden would do so.

'All of this seems to suggest, does it not, that Ivy Lavington was talking to the murderer of Barnabas Pandy? Or at least to the writer of the four letters signed in my name?'

'What it suggests to me is that Ivy must have been speaking to Rowland McCrodden,' said Jane Dockerill. 'If only one person here is acquainted with his son, then surely it must be him?'

'Yes, that's a reasonable assumption,' said Eustace Campbell-Brown.

'It's not true,' said Ivy Lavington. 'I will not tell you to whom I was speaking, but I can promise you that it wasn't Rowland McCrodden. Obviously he knows his own son. I meant that the person I was addressing was the only one of us who is not supposed to know John McCrodden, and yet does. I had no idea Kingbury was listening at the door, so I didn't take the trouble to be clear. Incidentally, Kingsbury's note is not accurate. He got much of it wrong. What he wrote . . . those were not my words. That was not what I said.'

Poirot beamed at her. '*Eh bien!* mademoiselle, I am delighted to hear you say that. Yes, Kingsbury got some of the words wrong. Nevertheless, he enabled Hercule Poirot to get everything right!

'In his note to me, Kingsbury also wrote that, as he listened outside Mademoiselle Lavington's door, a floorboard creaked loudly. His movement caused it to do so. He hurried away, and he heard, behind him, a door bang against the wall after being flung open—at least, this was how it sounded to Kingsbury. He believed he might have been seen. I too believe this. Kingsbury was killed—or left to die, if you prefer—for what he overheard. Minutes after he spoke to Timothy Lavington and Freddie Rule upstairs, somebody either forced him or followed him into the bathroom in which he was to die.

'Of course, his murderer did not know that, before he or she ended the old man's life, Kingsbury had left this helpful note for Poirot! Ladies and gentlemen, I can reveal that the murderer of Kingsbury is . . . the person with whom Mademoiselle Ivy was conducting this secret conversation.'

'And who was that?' John McCrodden asked bluntly.

'Ivy, what does he mean?' Timothy Lavington asked his sister. 'He seems to be saying that you were involved in a conspiracy to kill Grandy, and that your fellow conspirator then killed Kingsbury.'

'*Pas du tout*,' Poirot told Timothy. 'You will soon understand why this is not true. Mademoiselle Ivy, please tell us all: with whom were you conversing in your bedroom a short while before two o'clock yesterday afternoon?'

'I shall not tell you, and I don't mind if I'm punished for it,' said Ivy Lavington. 'M. Poirot, if you know who killed Kingsbury—or left him to die—then you know that it was not I. And if you know everything, as you claim to, then you do not need me to tell you anything.'

Annabel Treadway said, through her tears, 'It was *I* who murdered Grandy. I have already told Inspector Catchpool. Why will nobody believe me?'

'Because it isn't true,' I said.

Poirot continued: 'By forty minutes after two o'clock, we were all here in this room. Everybody, apart from Kingsbury. Catchpool and I were here at two, but no one else was. After I sent Timothy Lavington and Freddie Rule to rouse people and bring them here, at about five minutes after two, this was the order of arrival. First came Ivy Lavington at twenty minutes past two. She was very soon followed by Jane and Hugo Dockerill. Next, at twenty-five minutes after two, came Annabel Treadway, Freddie Rule and Timothy Lavington, then John McCrodden and then his father, Rowland McCrodden. The last to arrive were Mildred Rule, Eustace Campbell-Brown, Sylvia Rule and Lenore Lavington. I am afraid to say that any one of the people that I have just named could have been the one who pulled the towel out of Kingsbury's hand and left him to die. We can eliminate from suspicion only four people in this room: Inspector Thrubwell, Catchpool, me . . . and the fourth person, of course, is John McCrodden.'

'I don't see that we have eliminated Mr McCrodden,' said Sylvia Rule. 'It sounds to me as if he would have had ample time to injure Kingsbury and leave him in the bathroom to die before coming to the drawing room.'

'Ah, but think, madame,' said Poirot. 'If Kingsbury's killer is the person to whom Ivy Lavington said, "You are the only one of us who knows John McCrodden . . ."?'

'Oh, I see,' said Jane Dockerill. 'Yes, you're right. The person who said that cannot, then, be Mr McCrodden.'

'How encouraging,' said John McCrodden. 'I am no longer suspected of murder.'

'Yes, you are,' said his father. 'You are not suspected of murdering Kingsbury, but there is still Barnabas Pandy to consider.'

'Actually, *mon ami*, there is not,' said Poirot.

Everyone stared at him in astonishment.

'Barnabas Pandy died an accidental death,' he said. 'He drowned in his bathwater, as everyone first, and correctly, believed. There has been only one murder: that of poor Kingsbury, Monsieur Pandy's faithful servant. In addition to that, there has been an attempted second murder that will now, I am pleased to say, be unsuccessful. Or perhaps I should call Kingsbury's death the *second* murder and the attempted murder the first, since the attempt started long before Kingsbury died.'

'An attempted murder?' said Lenore Lavington. 'Of whom?'

'Of your sister,' Poirot told her. 'You see, madame, the writer of the four letters signed falsely in my name did everything he or she could to ensure—even though, as I have already said, he was not murdered—that *Annabel Treadway would hang for the murder of Barnabas Pandy.*'

CHAPTER 34

Rebecca Grace

'May I ask you a question, M. Poirot?' said Annabel Treadway.

'*Oui*, mademoiselle. What is it?'

'The killer of Kingsbury, the writer of the four letters, and the person who wanted me to hang for the murder of Grandy—are these three different people?'

'No. Only one person is responsible.'

'Then . . . I have unwittingly helped that person,' said Annabel. She had stopped crying. 'I have colluded in the attempted murder of myself by going to Scotland Yard and confessing to drowning Grandy in his bath.'

'Let me ask you now: did you murder your grandfather, Barnabas Pandy?'

'No. No, I did not.'

'*Bien*. Now you tell the truth. *Excellent!* It is time for the truth, finally, to be told. Mademoiselle Ivy, you believe very strongly in the power of the truth, do you not?'

'I do,' said Ivy. 'Did you really confess to a murder you

did not commit, Aunt Annabel? A murder that was not even a murder? That was foolish of you.'

Poirot said to Ivy, 'The murderer of Kingsbury told you the truth, yesterday, about his or her attempt to frame Annabel Treadway, your aunt, for the murder of your great-grandfather. You refuse to reveal that person's name. You protect a remorseless killer. Why? It is because of the power of the truth they told you!'

'Why do you assume that the person in question lacks remorse?' said Ivy.

'A contrite person would confess here and now,' said Poirot, looking around the room. Nobody spoke up, until Eustace Campbell-Brown said, 'Isn't it peculiar how, in circumstances such as these, one feels madly tempted to confess? I'm innocent, but I can't bear the silence. I feel an urge to cry out that it was *I* who killed Kingsbury. It wasn't, naturally.'

'Then be quiet, please,' Poirot told him.

'What if, instead of being remorseless, the person in question is simply more frightened than he or she has ever been?' Ivy Lavington asked Poirot

'It is gratifying to me that you seek to defend the killer of Kingsbury, mademoiselle. It confirms to me that I am right in every respect. The truth told to you by this person, while Kingsbury listened outside the door . . . it touched your heart, did it not? In spite of the inexcusable acts that you know were perpetrated by this guilty one, you cannot bring yourself to harden your heart against them.'

Ivy Lavington looked away. 'As I said before: you know

everything, M. Poirot. You do not need me to confirm what you know.'

Poirot turned to Sylvia Rule. 'Madame, with the exception of your daughter and future son-in-law, have you ever before seen the face of anybody in this room?'

'Of course I have,' she snorted. 'I have seen *your* face, M. Poirot.'

'I should have added "and apart from Hercule Poirot"! Is there anybody else in this room that you recognize?'

Sylvia Rule looked down at her hands, which were folded in her lap. After a few seconds, she said, 'Yes. I have met Mrs Lavington before—Lenore Lavington—though I did not know her true name when we met. It was thirteen years ago. She told me her name was Rebecca something. Rebecca Gray, or . . . no, Grace. Rebecca Grace.'

'Why do you think Madame Lavington felt it necessary to lie about her name? Please, do not try to hide the truth. Poirot, he knows everything.'

'Mrs Lavington was in the family way, and did not want to be,' said Sylvia Rule. 'When I was younger, I . . . helped women who found themselves in situations of that kind. I was good at what I did. I offered a service that was safe and discreet. Most of the ladies who came to me used other names, not their real ones.'

'Madame?' Poirot turned to Lenore Lavington.

'It's true,' she said. 'Cecil and I were unhappy together, and I thought it would only make things worse if we were to have another baby. In the end, however, I couldn't bring myself to go through with the procedure. At our first meeting, Mrs Rule told me that she too was expecting a baby. She wanted hers, but she said she could well imagine the distress of having to bear an unwanted child. When I heard those words—"an unwanted child"—I made my excuses and left. I never went back. My child, I realized, was not unwanted after all. I certainly could not bring myself to do away with it.'

Lenore Lavington threw a vicious look in Sylvia Rule's direction. She said, 'Mrs Rule tried to force the procedure upon me, once she saw I had changed my mind—so desperate was she not to lose a customer.'

Timothy Lavington rose unsteadily to his feet. There were tears in his eyes. 'The baby you didn't want was me, wasn't it, Mother?' he said.

'She didn't go through with it, Timmy,' said Ivy.

'I knew I would love you and want you as soon as I met you, Timmy,' Lenore told him. 'And I did. I truly did.'

'Did you tell Father that you were thinking of disposing of me in this barbaric fashion?' Timothy asked, his voice full of disgust.

'No. I told nobody.'

'Indeed,' said Poirot. 'You told nobody. This is very important.'

He gestured to me. This was my cue. I left the room, and returned a few moments later, carrying a small table, which I placed in the middle of the room so that everyone could see it. It was covered with a white sheet. Poirot had refused to tell me what was beneath the sheet, but I was pretty certain I knew what he was up to. So, from the look on his face, did Rowland McCrodden. Sure enough, Poirot lifted the sheet to reveal another slice of Church Window Cake, on a small china plate. Next to the plate was a knife. How many slices of that confounded cake, I wondered, had he brought with him to Combingham Hall? Fee Spring must have been delighted to have sold so many.

'Is this your way of telling us that solving the mystery has been a piece of cake, Poirot?' said Hugo Dockerill. 'A *piece of cake*, eh? That's a good one, isn't it?' He guffawed. His wife told him to be quiet and he fell silent, looking suitably chastened.

'I will now demonstrate to you, ladies and gentlemen, that when we solve the Mystery of Three Quarters, we are well on our way to solving the entire puzzle!'

'What is the Mystery of Three Quarters, Mr Poirot?' Inspector Thrubwell asked.

'I will explain, Inspector. You see here, as do we all, that there are four quarters to this slice of cake. On the top row, if I may call it that, we have the little yellow square and then the pink, and on the bottom row there is the pink and then the yellow. But we also have, because we have not yet used the knife, the whole slice, undivided.'

Dramatically, Poirot cut the slice into two halves, which he pushed to opposite edges of the plate. 'At first I thought that the four people who received letters from someone pretending to be me, accusing them of the murder of Barnabas Pandy, were two pairs of two: Annabel Treadway and Hugo Dockerill, who were connected to Monsieur Pandy, and Sylvia Rule and John McCrodden, who did not at first appear to be. Both told me they had never heard of Barnabas Pandy. Then I discovered from Hugo Dockerill that Madame Rule's son, Freddie, is a pupil at Turville College, the same school attended by Timothy Lavington. So! Then it appears to Poirot to be like this!' He took the knife and cut one half-slice of cake in half again.

He made a new arrangement of the yellow and pink squares on the plate: three of them close together and one alone and separate. 'This, *mes amis*, is what I referred to as the Mystery of the Three Quarters! Why is Monsieur John McCrodden the exception? Why was he—a stranger to Barnabas Pandy, a man who has never heard his name and has no obvious link to him—why was *he* chosen, when the other three choices were all people with visible connections to Monsieur Pandy or his family? Why should our composer of fraudulent letters choose these three and then this one?

'I asked myself if the writer of the letters wanted me to notice John McCrodden *in particular*. Then something occurred that puzzled me. I happened to be present when Mademoiselle Ivy mentioned the name of Freddie Rule to her mother. I noticed that Lenore Lavington looked aghast. Horrified. Almost frozen by shock. Why, I wondered, would she react so dramatically to the mention of a boy at her son's school?'

Poirot probably wanted to answer the question himself, but I could not help piping up with the one that struck me at that moment: 'Because she had not known, until you referred to Freddie Rule being at Turville College, that he was. She had no idea that the son of Sylvia Rule was at the same school as her son.'

'*Précisément!* She knew about a boy whom she described as "strange, lonely Freddie", but she did not know his family name. He had only been a pupil at Turville for a few months. Lenore Lavington was unaware that the Madame Rule she had met thirteen years earlier was the mother of strange, lonely Freddie until her daughter told her it was so. Then, in order to put me off the scent, she pretended at once to have a strong objection to Freddie, and to have warned Timothy not to associate with him. She did not wish me to suspect that it was Freddie's mother, and not Freddie himself, who had caused her to feel such horror. Later, she seemed to forget altogether that she had told me she disliked Freddie. When I next mentioned him, she displayed no animosity at all and seemed to have no interest in criticizing him. She has not objected to her son spending time with him here at Combingham Hall.

'I should say, ladies and gentlemen, that it was only once I was certain that the writer of the four letters was Lenore Lavington that this piece of the puzzle fell into place.'

'Wait,' said John McCrodden. 'If you believe that the same person killed Kingsbury, and tried to have Miss Treadway here hanged for murder . . . Are you accusing Mrs Lavington of those things too?'

'For the time being, I am saying that Madame Lavington wrote the letters accusing four people—including you, monsieur—of murder, and signed them in the name of Hercule Poirot. Madame Lavington, you were shaken by the mention of Freddie Rule because you had been so sure that the link between you and Sylvia Rule could never be known or guessed by anyone. You consulted her thirteen years ago in order to procure an illegal medical procedure. Of course, it would be in both of your interests to mention this to nobody. Then, in a most casual and coincidental manner, your daughter informs you that Mrs Rule's son, Freddie, is at school with your own son. Suddenly, a link between Sylvia Rule and Barnabas Pandy is plain for all to see.

'This, for you, was a disaster. You wanted the two-halves arrangement of the slice of cake, did you not? You wanted the recipients of your letters to be two people connected to your grandfather, and two who were completely uncon-nected. That way, no one would stand out. It would have been almost impossible to work out what was the aim of the letter-writer in those circumstances. However, thanks to the accident of Freddie Rule being a pupil at Turville, you realized to your dismay that you had unintentionally directed my attention towards John McCrodden as the special one, the *different* one. I knew then that there were only two possibilities: he was either the odd one out, or there was no odd one out—only the whole, undivided slice of cake.'

Poirot pushed the cake back together so that all four squares were once again touching. 'When I talk about the undivided slice of cake, I am referring to the possibility that the letter-writer might have had a personal connection to *all four people who received the letters*, including John McCrodden.

'You chose to sign your letters in my name, Madame Lavington. Why? You know that I am the best solver of crimes, *n'est-ce pas*? There is none better! And you wanted my attention. You wanted Hercule Poirot, after involving himself in the matter, to go to the police with a stiffened, pungent dress wrapped in cellophane and the opinion that your sister Annabel must have murdered your grandfather. Who else would sound so authoritative when saying all the things you thought you could manipulate me to say? Madame, I have never been at the same time and by the same person so flattered and so underestimated! You were foolish to believe that you could distract Hercule Poirot from the truth with a dress soaked in water and oil of olives.'

Inspector Thrubwell said, 'Mr Poirot, I'm a little confused. Are you suggesting that Mrs Lavington did *not* want you to think that Mr John McCrodden was the odd one out?'

'*Oui*, monsieur. She did not want me to wonder how he fitted into the picture. She did not wish me to ask myself: if Sylvia Rule turns out to be connected to Barnabas Pandy's family, might not the same be true of John McCrodden? Because, my friends, *Lenore Lavington is the only one in this room who personally has a link to all four people who received the letters*. She made a grave error when she constructed her plan. If she wished to accuse two complete strangers, she easily could have selected them at random from the telephone directory. Instead, she chose two people with whom she has a past connection—in both cases one that she believes is secret enough to be safe. She thinks that Poirot, he will soon discover that Sylvia Rule and John

McCrodden could not have murdered Barnabas Pandy because they were strangers to him and his family, and *nowhere near Combingham Hall on the day that he died.* They had neither motive nor opportunity. Madame Lavington imagines, therefore, that the names Rule and McCrodden will soon be eliminated from consideration.

'Ah, but this too goes wrong for her! It soon became clear to me that both Madame Rule and Monsieur McCrodden *could* have come here on the day that Barnabas Pandy died. As could Hugo Dockerill. They could have slipped in while the rest of the household was busy arguing or, in Kingsbury's case, unpacking a suitcase. They could have entered via the always-open front door, killed Monsieur Pandy, and then left in a hurry, without being seen by anybody. None of the three had strong alibis: a Christmas Fair from which it would have been easy to disappear for an hour or two without anyone noticing; a letter from a Spanish woman who might have been willing to say whatever she had been told to say.'

Poirot stared at John McCrodden. He seemed to be waiting for him to speak.

Eventually McCrodden said in a low voice, 'I did not know her real name until I arrived at this house. She introduced herself to me as Rebecca Grace, as she did to Mrs Rule. Lenore.' He looked across the room at her. 'It's an unusual name. I am glad to know your name, Lenore.'

'Monsieur McCrodden, for the benefit of us all, will you please clarify the nature of your relationship to Lenore Lavington?' said Poirot. 'You were lovers, were you not?

'Yes. We were lovers for a short time. Too short. I knew she was married. How I cursed fate, for allowing me to meet her when it was too late and she already belonged to someone else.' His voice shook. 'I loved her with all my heart,' he said. 'I still do.'

CHAPTER 35

Family Loyalty

'I'm not ashamed of it,' said John McCrodden. 'I cannot be made to feel shame, as I am sure my father will be happy to tell you. Rebecca—Lenore—is the only woman I have ever loved, though we had only three days together. I have spent every hour of every day since then wishing it could have been longer—'

'John, please don't,' said Lenore. 'What good will it do now?'

'—but she insisted on returning to her husband, who, by the sound of it, was an uninspiring individual. She did her duty.'

'How dare you say that about my father?' protested Timothy Lavington. To his mother, he said coldly, 'Did *you* tell him Father was uninspiring? What other lies did you tell about him?'

Ivy touched her mother's arm and said, 'Tell him, Mummy. You have to.'

'Your father is dead, Timmy,' said Lenore. 'The letter that you received . . . I wrote it. I sent it.'

'What letter?' asked Jane Dockerill.

'Lenore Lavington sent a fifth letter,' said Poirot. 'One that most of you do not know about. She typed it on the same machine that she used for the other four: with the faulty letter "e". This letter was not an accusation of murder, however, and in it, Madame Lavington did not pretend to be Hercule Poirot. Instead, she pretended to be her late husband, Cecil Lavington. The point of the letter was to tell his son, Timothy, that he was not dead, though everybody believed that he was. Instead, he was busy with a secret government mission.'

'How could you lie about something like that, Mother?' said Timothy. 'I believed he was alive!'

Lenore Lavington looked away. Ivy touched her arm, at the same time giving Timothy a look that ordered him to stop.

Poirot continued: 'When Timothy Lavington showed to Catchpool here this letter that was supposedly from his father, Catchpool noticed at once the "e"s with the tiny white hole in the ink. He knew that the same person had sent the four letters in the name of Hercule Poirot, and that they had been typed on the same machine. You will all understand, I am sure, why we were determined to find it.

'When I first came to Combingham Hall, I asked Madame Lavington if I might test the typewriter here. She refused to allow it. Since there was no evidence to suggest that a crime had been committed, she was under no obligation to allow me to see anything in the house. Then, when I arrived at Combingham Hall the second time, I found that she had changed her mind and wished to cooperate.'

'We all wanted to help you, M. Poirot, but you tricked us,' said Annabel Treadway. 'You led us to believe that you could prove Grandy had been murdered. Now, however, you tell us his death was an accident, exactly as we had always believed.'

'Mademoiselle, I have been careful at every stage not to say a word that was not true. I told you only that I was certain there was a guilty person, a murderer, to be caught, and that, until that happened, there remained a great danger. I referred, mademoiselle, to the danger *to you*. Your sister wished to see you hang for the murder of your grandfather. When she admitted this to Mademoiselle Ivy—the conversation overheard by Kingsbury—she had not yet successfully killed anybody. Perhaps would not have continued with her plot to frame you? I do not know. But I do know this: a very short time later, thinking herself to be at risk of discovery and exposure, *she left Kingsbury to die*. Madame Lavington, I did not lie or even twist the truth when I described you as a murderer. It is a question of *character*. You became a murderer the moment you set out to arrange your sister's death.'

Lenore Lavington looked back at Poirot expressionlessly. She said nothing.

'Why did Lenore want her sister to hang?' asked John McCrodden.

'What about the other three letters?' said Annabel Treadway. 'Whatever Lenore's intentions with regard to me, why should she sent the same letter to Mr Dockerill, Mrs Rule and Mr McCrodden?'

'Mademoiselle, monsieur—please. I have not yet finished explaining. Since one cannot finish unless one starts somewhere, please allow me to start with the typewriter. Lenore Lavington used all of her cunning to try to deceive Poirot, but it did not work. Oh, yes, she was very clever. The typewriter I was forbidden to inspect when I first came here . . . it was the one I was looking for, with the imperfect letter "e".

'Between my first visit to Combingham Hall and my second, Lenore Lavington decided it would be wise for her to appear to want to help me in any way she can. I was told, upon arrival, that I could now inspect the typewriter, but that there had been purchased recently a new machine. The old one, said Lenore Lavington, was past its best. In order to appear helpful, Madame Lavington tells me she has kept the old one, *since that must be the one I will want to examine*. Naturally, the new typewriter, still unsold in the shop when the four letters were typed, cannot be the one I seek. Madame Lavington tells me she has asked Kingsbury to present me with both machines, new and old, so that I may test both. Ah, she was clever—but not clever enough.

'One of the typewriters looks new. The other looks new apart from a few scratches and cracks—which are easily made. *Alors*, Poirot, he performs the test, and he notices something most puzzling. The letter "e" is working exactly as it should on both machines, so both can be eliminated from suspicion. But it is not only the "e" that, in each case, is flawless. *It is everything.* I noticed no difference of quality. Apart from the scratches to one, *both* might have come brand new from the shop that very morning. I thought to myself: what if Lenore Lavington has lied to me and has, instead of new and old, given me two new machines to inspect? Why would she do that?'

'She would do it if she didn't want you to check the *real* old typewriter,' said Timothy Lavington. 'And she didn't—because it would have incriminated her.'

'Timmy, don't,' said Ivy. 'You needn't be the one to say it.'

'Family loyalty is the last thing in my mind at the moment,' her brother told her. 'I'm right, aren't I, M. Poirot?'

'Yes, Timothy, you are correct. Your mother was careless. She thought that telling me the old typewriter had not been working properly would be enough. She was not afraid that I would use both machines and notice that both seemed equally new, because of the many scratches she had inflicted upon one machine.

'I was nearly fooled! I asked myself: "Is it possible that the older machine is simply in excellent condition, and works well on occasions, though not on others?" I was asking myself this question when Annabel Treadway appeared and said to me, "I see you've begun your typewriter investigation. Lenore gave me strict orders to leave you alone and let you do your detective work."

'Why would Mademoiselle Annabel see *two* typewriters and *two* pieces of paper, both with words typed upon them, and conclude that I had only *begun* my typewriter experiment, rather than completed it? I could think of only one reason: she knew there were in fact *three* typewriters in the house—the two new ones, and the old machine that Lenore Lavington had hidden away.'

'Which is why Mrs Lavington told Miss Treadway to leave you alone,' said Eustace Campbell-Brown. 'If Miss Treadway knew that two typewriters had recently been purchased, she might have given the game away.'

'*Exactement.* And, remember, Lenore Lavington could not ask her sister to lie. If she did, Mademoiselle Annabel would suspect at once who had written and sent the four letters.'

'And . . .' Annabel Treadway began hesitantly '. . . when you asked me to look carefully at the two pieces of paper, and I could see no difference between them . . .'

'You were quite correct! I told you, did I not, that I had noticed something significant? *It was the absence of difference.* Often, the important thing to be noticed is a thing that is not there. I waited until I knew Madame Lavington was downstairs and not in her bedroom, and I searched that room. As I hoped I would, I found the old typewriter. It was in a bag under her bed. A quick test revealed that it was the one with the faulty "e".'

Timothy was staring furiously at his mother. 'You were going to kill me before I was even born,' he said. 'You were unfaithful to Father. You killed Kingsbury, and you would have allowed Aunt Annabel to hang if M. Poirot here hadn't stopped you. You're a monster.'

'That's enough!' John McCrodden told him.

To Poirot, McCrodden said, 'Whatever you suspect Lenore of having done, you surely cannot think it's acceptable for a boy to address his mother in such a manner, in front of strangers?'

'I do not suspect, monsieur. I *know*. Tell me—for you are not a stranger to Lenore Lavington—what did you do to anger her?'

McCrodden looked surprised. 'Anger her? How . . . how did . . .'

'How did I know? It is simple,' said Poirot. He often said this about things that were simple to nobody but him. 'Lenore Lavington wanted Annabel Treadway to hang—but she needed to conceal her true aim. She did this by sending the same letter of accusation to three other people. You, Monsieur McCrodden, were one of the three. Knowing that it would be a most unpleasant sort of letter to receive, Madame Lavington chose three people who, in her opinion, deserved to suffer a little. Not to hang for murder—that fate, she reserved only for her sister Annabel—but to worry, perhaps, that they might soon be charged with a crime they had not committed. So, I ask again: what did you do to anger Rebecca Grace, whose real name is Lenore Lavington?'

John McCrodden looked at Lenore as he spoke. 'We met at the seaside resort of Whitby. Rebec—Lenore was holidaying there with her husband. She . . . I'm afraid there is no nice way to put it. After we met, she abandoned him to spend three days with me. I don't know what she told him. I can't remember, all these years later. I seem to recall

345

she made an excuse about having to rush off somewhere. Do you remember what it was, Lenore?'

She gave no answer. For some time, she had expressed no emotion, and done nothing but sit and stare straight ahead.

'At the end of the three days, I couldn't bear to let her go,' John McCrodden went on. 'I begged her to leave her husband and live with me. She said she couldn't do that, but that she would come to Whitby and see me whenever she could. She wanted our love affair to continue, but it was a prospect I found intolerable. The idea that she planned to stay with a man she neither loved nor desired . . . It would have been wrong. And I wasn't prepared to share her.'

'Whereas cavorting with a married woman is not wrong,' muttered Sylvia Rule.

'Be quiet,' John McCrodden told her. 'You know nothing of right and wrong, and you care even less.'

'So you forced upon Madame Lavington the stark choice?' said Poirot to McCrodden.

'Yes, I did. Him or me. She chose him, and she blamed me. To her mind, I had ended a love affair that might have continued—that she very much wanted to continue.'

'And she could not forgive you,' said Poirot. 'Just as she could not forgive Sylvia Rule for trying to force her to get rid of the baby she had decided she wanted to keep. Nor could she forgive Hugo for occasionally punishing Timothy for bad behaviour, as he had to every so often. That's why Monsieur Dockerill was chosen to receive one of the four letters.'

'How did you know that Lenore and I had had a love affair?' John McCrodden asked. 'I never said a word, not to a single soul. Neither did she, I am quite certain. It's impossible that you could know.'

'Ah, monsieur, this knowledge was not difficult to acquire. You and Madame Lavington told me yourselves, with a little help from Mademoiselle Ivy.'

'That cannot be true,' Ivy said. 'I myself only found out yesterday afternoon, when Mr McCrodden walked into the house and Mummy saw him again, and then she got so upset that I was able to force her to tell me everything. Before that happened, the name John McCrodden meant nothing to me, and you and I have barely spoken since then, M. Poirot.'

'*C'est vrai*. All the same, mademoiselle, you helped me to learn the secret without knowing it yourself. I put together things you had said with things I had heard from both your mother and Monsieur McCrodden, and—'

'What things?' John McCrodden asked. 'I'm still not sure whether to believe a single word that comes out of your mouth, Poirot.'

'You told me, if you recall, that your father disapproved of your choice of work. You referred to having worked as a miner somewhere in the north of England, on the coast, or near the coast. Your father did not approve this sort of labour, in which you got the dirty hands—but, you said, *he also did not approve when you worked at the clean end, making and selling the trinkets*. It was a strange expression, this "at the clean end". I did not know what it meant at

347

the time. It struck me as not especially important, so I did not dwell upon it.

'I also did not at first realize what you might have meant by the word "trinkets". I had heard that word used recently—by your father, in fact. He used it to mean the decorations for Christmas, I think. But the word "trinkets" has another meaning too. It can mean jewellery. As for "the clean end", I decided that you must have been referring to the clean end *of mining*, for that was the subject we had been discussing. What you were trying to tell me, Monsieur McCrodden, was that you went from working in a mine—the dirty end—to the cleaner work of making jewellery from the substance that, previously, you had mined. That substance was the Whitby jet, was it not?

'Lenore Lavington told me that she had once owned a mourning bracelet made from jet, one that she later gave to her daughter, Mademoiselle Ivy. She described the bracelet to me as a treasured possession—a gift she herself was given during a seaside holiday with her late husband Cecil. From Ivy Lavington, I learned that the marriage of Cecil and Lenore Lavington was not a happy one—not, at least, on her part. Why, then, I asked myself, would she so treasure a gift bought for her by a husband she had not loved? She would not! The bracelet of Whitby jet had been given to her instead by a man she loved passionately: John McCrodden, the lover she took while on holiday.

'There was also, I learned, a second gift that Lenore

Lavington had given to her daughter: a fan—another item she described as a treasured possession. On the fan was a picture of a dancer with hair the same colour as that of Mademoiselle Ivy—a dancer wearing *a red and black dress*. Dark hair and a dress of red and black? This sounded very much to me like a *Spanish dancer*. I have seen such illustrations on ladies' fans that have been brought back as souvenirs from the continent. I knew, thanks to Rowland McCrodden, that his son John owned a house in Spain—that he loved the country and visited it often. Could John McCrodden have given that fan to Lenore Lavington, I wondered, during the three days they had spent together? I decided it was not merely possible but probable. Why else would an ordinary fan have become a treasured possession? Lenore Lavington had not forgiven John McCrodden, as we know—yet still, she treasured those gifts he had given her. Such is the complicated character of love!'

'It's a complicated business,' agreed Inspector Hubert Thrubwell. 'Not one of us could deny that, Mr Poirot.'

'The jet bracelet, the Spanish dancer fan,' Poirot went on. 'These things might have been mere coincidences, of course. Neither was proof that John McCrodden and Lenore Lavington knew one another. Then I thought: Lenore Lavington can be linked to Sylvia Rule, via Freddie; to Annabel, her sister; to Hugo Dockerill, housemaster of her son. Why not also to John McCrodden? Instead of being the odd one out, I decided it was likely that it was a case of one whole, undivided slice of cake . . .'—Poirot pointed dramatically at the plate on the table—'. . . and no odd ones out. *Lenore Lavington knew them all.*'

'Do you have anything to say about any of this, Mrs Lavington?' Inspector Thrubwell asked her.

She did not move an inch. Still, she said nothing.

John McCrodden said fiercely, 'I won't allow the woman I love to hang for murder, whatever she has done! I don't care if you're still angry with me after all these years, Lenore. I love you as much as I did then. Say something, for God's sake!'

'Poirot, I'm still not at all clear about the need for four letters,' said Rowland McCrodden. 'If Mrs Lavington hoped to see Miss Treadway punished for her grandfather's murder, why didn't she send only one letter, to her sister?'

'Because, my friend, she wished to conceal the fact that she was the accuser—the one with the suspicions! Lenore Lavington could not guarantee that her plan would work and that Mademoiselle Annabel would be sent to the gallows. If the plan did not work, she wanted to be free to try something different, perhaps—another form of revenge. This she would be better placed to do if Mademoiselle Annabel did not know she was an enemy to be feared. If one is feared, then at once precautions are taken. Lenore Lavington did not wish such precautions to be in operation. She wanted her sister *unguarded.*

'If she had been the only one accused of murder, Annabel Treadway would have asked herself, "Who might have done such a thing to me, and why?" If, on the other hand, she hears from Hercule Poirot that *four* people have been accused of the murder of Barnabas Pandy, then it seems to her that the accuser might be some person of whom she has never heard, perhaps. It seems to Mademoiselle Annabel that the accuser would surely *not* be her sister, who knows she could not have killed their grandfather because the two of them were together in a different room when he died. *Eh bien*, Lenore Lavington is protected from suspicion of being the one who suspects, the one who accuses; her quarry remains trusting of her and therefore vulnerable, which is how Lenore Lavington wanted her.'

'Wait a moment,' said John McCrodden. 'Lenore and Annabel were in a room together when their grandfather died? Did Lenore tell you that?' He sounded excited. I could not work out why.

'*Oui, monsieur*,' said Poirot. 'All three women told me this, and it is true.'

'Then Lenore provided Annabel with an alibi,' said McCrodden 'Why would she do that, if you say she wanted her to hang?'

Poirot looked at Rowland McCrodden. 'I'm sure you can enlighten your son on this point, *mon ami*.'

'The guilty tend to try to look as if they're not doing the very thing they *are* doing—the thing they're guilty of,' said Rowland McCrodden. 'If Mrs Lavington hoped to get her sister convicted of murder, what better way to look as if she's doing the opposite than by vigorously defending Miss Treadway and providing her with an alibi?'

'Is nobody going to ask the most important question?' said Jane Dockerill impatiently.

'I will,' said Timothy Lavington. 'Why on earth should Mother wish to revenge herself upon Aunt Annabel, M. Poirot? What harm had Aunt Annabel ever done to Mother?'

CHAPTER 36

The True Culprit

Poirot turned to Annabel Treadway. 'Mademoiselle,' he said. 'You know only too well the answer to your nephew's question.'

'I do,' said Annabel Treadway. 'It is something I can never forget.'

'Indeed. It is a secret you have kept for many years, and it has cast a shadow over your whole life, a shadow of terrible guilt and regret.'

'No. Not regret,' she said. 'It was not something I decided to do. It was something that just *happened*. Oh, I know I was the one who made it happen, but how can I regret it when I can't remember making the decision?'

'Then perhaps you feel additional guilt, not knowing whether, if you found yourself in a similar situation today, you would behave differently,' said Poirot.

'Can somebody please explain?' said Jane Dockerill.

'Yes, do get it over with, M. Poirot,' said Ivy Lavington. 'For many of us, this is not a pleasant experience. I accept that it is necessary, but please digress as little as possible.'

'Very well, mademoiselle. I shall tell everybody the secret that your mother told you yesterday, before Kingsbury came to listen outside the door.

'Shortly before Barnabas Pandy died, ladies and gentlemen, there was a dinner in this house. At the table were seated Monsieur Pandy, Lenore and Ivy Lavington and Annabel Treadway. Madame Lavington chastised Mademoiselle Ivy for eating too much. During an excursion to the beach several months earlier, she had told her that her legs resembled tree-trunks, and this story was told at the dinner table by an angry Ivy Lavington, who had now been twice insulted by her mother. The meal ended in misery: all three ladies left the table in distress, and Barnabas Pandy was also unhappy. The late Kingsbury told me that he came upon Monsieur Pandy sitting alone at the dinner table, crying.

'Now I must go back to when Ivy Lavington was a little girl, and Annabel Treadway took her for a walk by a river,' Poirot went on. 'Skittle, the dog, went with them. Mademoiselle Ivy decided it would be entertaining to roll down the river bank. Skittle, immediately alert to the danger, scrambled down the bank to rescue her but failed to stop her rolling into the water. Instead, he scratched her face and caused the scarring that remains to this day. Mademoiselle Ivy was soon afterwards trapped under the water, where she nearly drowned. Annabel Treadway had to climb into these lethal waters and rescue her. The current was very strong. Mademoiselle Annabel risked her own life to save her niece.

'*Alors*, now we must leap forward in time, *mes amis*, to the trip to the beach that I have already mentioned. Lenore and Ivy Lavington had taken the dog, Hopscotch, to the beach because Annabel Treadway was confined to her bed with the influenza. Mademoiselle Ivy loves swimming in the sea. She did not allow her near-fatal accident to make her afraid of water.'

'Hopscotch?' said Eustace Campbell-Brown. 'I thought the dog was called Skittle.'

'They are two different dogs, monsieur. Skittle is no longer with us. Hopscotch, a dog of the same breed, has replaced him.'

'*Replaced* him?' Tears sprang to Annabel Treadway's eyes. 'No one could replace Skittle, just as no one will be able to replace Hopscotch when he . . . when he . . . Oh!' She buried her face in her hands.

'Apologies, mademoiselle. I spoke without thinking.'

'Very good, so they're two different dogs,' said Rowland McCrodden. 'But, really, now is no time for us to be thinking about *any* dogs.'

'You are wrong,' Poirot told him. 'Dogs—or, to be precise, the late Skittle—is the very creature about whom we must think.'

'Why, for pity's sake?'

'I am about to explain. On the day of the trip to the beach, Lenore and Ivy Lavington were sitting near some trees. Hopscotch came running towards them, after first splashing in the waves. The sight of the dog's wet legs, which looked much thinner than they do when dry, reminded Mademoiselle Ivy of the day she nearly drowned. Memories flooded back to her, memories she had been unaware of until that moment. She told her mother that, as she had struggled under the water in her state of panic, she had mistaken the dog's wet legs for tree trunks on the river bank—even though they could not have been, because they were far too thin, and moving, not still. Then Annabel Treadway came to her rescue and Mademoiselle Ivy saw the *real* tree trunks: thick and stationary. She realized that the other things she had seen were the legs of Skittle and not tree trunks at all.

'This memory came back to her most powerfully that day on the beach many years later, thanks to the wet legs of Hopscotch. She told the story to her mother, and, as she listened, Lenore Lavington realized something. It was something of which Mademoiselle Ivy herself was unaware . . . and she remained unaware of it until her mother confessed everything to her yesterday in the conversation overheard by Kingsbury.'

'*What* did Mrs Lavington realize?' asked Rowland McCrodden, by now unable to conceal his desperation to understand. I myself was feeling a similar desperation.

'Is it not obvious?' said Poirot. 'Skittle's legs would only have been on that river-bank—to be observed by Mademoiselle Ivy—if, before saving her niece, Annabel Treadway had first pulled Skittle out of the water. There is no other logical conclusion to be drawn. *She must have saved her dog first, and only afterwards saved Mademoiselle Ivy.*'

As soon as Poirot had said it, I saw precisely what he meant. 'If Skittle tried to stop Ivy Lavington from rolling into the water and failed, he wouldn't simply give up and go and wait on the bank,' I said. 'No loyal dog would do that. He would leap into the water. He wouldn't ever stop trying to save whichever family member was in danger.'

'Exactly, *mon ami*,' said Poirot. He sounded rather proud of me, which I appreciated, though we both knew I would never have worked it out on my own. 'And once his mistress, Mademoiselle Annabel, jumped into the water also, Skittle would only have become more intent upon his rescue mission. He would not have left the water by choice, not with two people he loved still in peril. His own life would have been in danger, therefore, from the strong and fast-moving current. All three of them might have died.'

'And if Skittle's legs were thin and wet when Ivy Lavington saw them on the river bank, then they must at some point have been in the water,' said Rowland McCrodden. 'You're right, Poirot. No dog would decide to save only himself and scramble back up the bank in that situation. Someone must have dragged him out of the water and . . . tethered him to something.'

'*Oui*. Annabel Treadway tethered him securely, to prevent him from leaping back into the river and placing himself in danger once more. Only then did she return to the water to save Mademoiselle Ivy. You did not realize the significance of your memory, mademoiselle, when you described it to your mother—but she knew. She knew instantly. She pictured the wet legs of Skittle on the river bank as he struggled against whatever restraint his mistress had imposed upon him. She understood exactly what it meant. But here is the dilemma. . .

'Did Lenore Lavington ask herself if her sister might have dealt with the dog first only because he was flailing so wildly in the water that her attempt to rescue her niece was impeded? If that had been the case, would not Mademoiselle Annabel have told the truth? She would have—so it must have been otherwise. Annabel Treadway must have valued the life of her dog more than that of her niece, and chosen to save Skittle first—thereby taking the most enormous risk with Mademoiselle Ivy's life. She could so easily have drowned in the time that it took for Skittle to be carried to safety.'

By now, Annabel Treadway was weeping. She made no attempt to deny any of what Poirot had said.

Poirot spoke softly to her. 'You, mademoiselle, the first time we met, told me that nobody minds when very old people die, whereas if a child dies it is seen as a tragedy. That was your guilt speaking. It pained you that the life you had risked was that of a little child with such potential and so many years ahead of her. You knew society would judge you all the more harshly for that. It is a strange coincidence . . . When I spoke to the daughter-in-law of Vincent Lobb, your grandfather's lifelong enemy with whom he sought, finally, to be reconciled, she told me that it is a most terrible thing *to do the right thing too late*. That is what you did, mademoiselle: you saved the life of your little niece, but you did it too late.'

'And I have suffered ever since,' sobbed Annabel.

'You told me in our very first conversation that you had "saved lives". You then quickly corrected yourself, or so it seemed, and suddenly it was only one life that you had saved: the life of Mademoiselle Ivy. I thought you were embarrassed to have exaggerated—that you wanted to be strictly, scrupulously accurate, and not to claim any more credit than was your due. Only much later did it occur to me that there was another possibility, equally plausible: *that you had saved more than one life, but wanted to conceal the fact.* Your initial pronouncement—*lives*, plural—was the truth.

'It was during a conversation with Mademoiselle Ivy that this struck me. Knowing that somebody had plotted to bring about the death of Annabel Treadway, I had spoken of the need to save lives. Ivy Lavington asked me if it was one life or more that needed to be saved, and I admitted that it was only one that was in danger. Of course, I did not know then that Kingsbury would be killed. I noticed that my conversation with Mademoiselle Ivy reminded me of something, and wondered what it could be. It took me only seconds, after that, to solve the mystery: it was my first encounter with Annabel Treadway of which I had been reminded, and our exchange about saving lives, or perhaps it was only one life. Suddenly, in the light of what I had deduced about the day Mademoiselle Ivy nearly drowned, Mademoiselle Annabel's remarks about saving lives made perfect sense to me.'

I could not help shaking my head, amazed at how Poirot's

brain worked. Other people looked similarly impressed. We all sat transfixed as he continued with his account.

'The first time we met, after she had received a letter that she believed was from me, accusing her of the murder of Monsieur Pandy, Annabel Treadway said something else that struck me as unusual. She said, "You cannot know . . ." then stopped herself before she said any more. She felt, you see, as if morally she deserved to receive a letter accusing her of murder, even though she had murdered nobody and Mademoiselle Ivy had not, in fact, died that day in the river. What she meant to say was that I, Hercule Poirot, *could not know* that she was guilty; it was impossible.

'She will never stop thinking of herself as guilty, ladies and gentlemen. She has tried so hard to atone. Monsieur Dockerill, you told me that she declined your offer of marriage. She said that she would not be well suited to looking after the boys of Turville College. This, too, now makes sense: she did not believe she should be entrusted with the welfare of children, and so she did not allow herself to marry and have any of her own. At the same time, she doted upon her sister's two children and poured into them all the love that she could, to compensate for her secret failure all those years ago.'

'There must have been a considerable amount of fear, as well as guilt,' said Rowland McCrodden. 'At any moment, Miss Lavington might have remembered what happened that day at the river.'

'Indeed she might have,' Poirot agreed. 'And of that,

Annabel Treadway was terrified. Then, after many years, her worst fears were realized. During the disastrous dinner, Mademoiselle Ivy told the story about the tree trunks remark, and Annabel Treadway saw in her sister's face that she knew the truth—that she had known it since the day on the beach. Monsieur Pandy also quickly understood the meaning of Mademoiselle Ivy's newly unearthed memory— and Annabel Treadway saw that too.'

Poirot turned to Ivy Lavington. 'You, mademoiselle, were the only one seated at the dinner table that night who thought that it was only legs and potatoes and your mother's opinions about your size and shape that, together, were causing such trouble. The other three people at the table were thinking about something quite different.'

'Yes, and I had no idea,' said Ivy. 'None whatsoever. Aunt Annabel, you should have told me the truth as soon as I was old enough to understand. I would have forgiven you. I *do* forgive you. Please do not feel guilty any longer—I should not be able to bear it. It's such a waste of time, and you have made yourself suffer quite enough already. I know you are sorry, and I know you love me. That is all that matters.'

'Your aunt's guilt will not, I'm afraid, be so easily banished,' Poirot told her. 'Without it, I fear she would be quite lost. She would not know herself at all. For most people, that is a prospect too frightening to contemplate.'

'You might forgive me, Ivy, but Lenore never will,' said Annabel. 'And Grandy . . . he couldn't forgive me either. He was going to cut me out of his will—leave me with nothing.'

'That was the final straw for you, was it not, mademoiselle? It was what made you decide to go to Scotland Yard and confess to the murder of Monsieur Pandy, though you knew you were innocent.'

Annabel nodded. 'I thought, "If Grandy has decided to treat me in this way, if all my kindness and devotion in the intervening years counts for nothing . . . why, then I might as well hang for murder. Perhaps it is no more than I deserve." But Ivy, darling, I would like you to know this: that day by the river, I was like a mad thing. I only realized that I had made a *choice* after I had secured Skittle to a post by his leash. It was like waking from a dream. A nightmare! And you were still thrashing around in the water, and I saved you *then*, of course, but . . . I couldn't remember, and can't remember, *deciding* not to save you first. I truly can't.'

'How old was Skittle then?' Lenore Lavington asked.

I heard a few people gasp. It was so long since she had said anything.

'He was five, wasn't he? At most he could only have lived for another seven or eight years, and I believe he died when he was ten, in fact. You risked my daughter's life, your own niece's life, to save a dog who only went on to live for another five years.'

'I'm so sorry,' Annabel said quietly. 'But . . . you mustn't pretend that you don't understand about *love*, Lenore, and what it can make a person do. After all, we have all heard about your Mr McCrodden, with whom you spent only three days. Yet you loved him passionately, did you not?

And I can see—though no one else can, because no one knows you as I do—that you *still* love him. I loved Skittle, however short his life was doomed to be.

'Love!' Annabel turned to Poirot. 'Love is the true culprit, M. Poirot. Why did my sister try to frame me for murder? Because of her determination to avenge a wrong done to her daughter many years ago—because of how much she *loves* Ivy. So many sins and crimes are committed in the name of love.'

'That may be so,' said Rowland McCrodden, 'but can we postpone our discussion of emotional matters and stick to the facts for a little longer? In his note to you, Poirot, Kingsbury wrote that he had overheard Miss Lavington saying to her interlocutor—and we now know that person was her mother, Mrs Lavington—that ignorance of the law is no defence. What, if I may ask, is the relevance of that? At what point, and in relation to what, might Mrs Lavington have pleaded ignorance of the law? I'm sorry if the question is a pedantic one.'

'Ah, my friend.' Poirot smiled at him. 'It is Hercule Poirot who must be the greater pedant. What Kingsbury wrote in his note to me was that he had heard Mademoiselle Ivy saying *words to the effect that* ignorance of the law is not an acceptable defence. That means, does it not, that the point might have been made with different words? *Words that conveyed the same meaning.* Remember, Kingsbury also wrote "John Modden" instead of "John McCrodden". He was not a person who concerned himself with precision of language or nomenclature.'

'Quite, quite,' said Rowland McCrodden, 'but however Miss Lavington might have phrased it, she must have known that her mother would have been as aware as anybody in the land that to falsely accuse someone of murder and attempt to plant evidence incriminating them is unlawful. It's hardly the sort of thing about which one might plausibly say, "Sorry, M'lud, I had no notion that such behaviour was not permitted and viewed by everybody as entirely above board."'

'Wasn't that the very point Miss Lavington was overheard making to her mother?' said Jane Dockerill. 'That ignorance of the law would *not* be accepted by any court of law as a valid defence?'

'I can see why you might think so, Madame Dockerill— just as I can see the wisdom of the point made by Monsieur McCrodden. Both sides of this particular argument are, however, irrelevant, since Lenore and Ivy Lavington did not discuss *at all* the defence of not knowing the law and whether or not it might work in this instance. Not even for a moment did they discuss it!'

'What do you mean by saying that they didn't discuss it, Mr Poirot?' asked Inspector Thrubwell. 'Mr Kingsbury wrote in his note to you that he heard—'

'Yes, yes. Let me explain what Kingsbury heard. It is startlingly simple: he heard Mademoiselle Ivy warning her mother that she would soon be found out, for she was the only person connected to all four letter-recipients. I imagine she said something of this kind: "It will soon be discovered that you and John McCrodden know one another, and

Sylvia Rule's son Freddie is at school with Timothy, *so it will be pointless to say that you don't know the Rules. That will get you nowhere. No one would believe you."'* Poirot stopped and shrugged. 'Or, as Kingsbury wrote in his most helpful note, "words to that effect".'

'The Rules,' I repeated in a whisper. 'Ivy wasn't talking about the law, she was talking about the Rule family.'

'I see,' said Rowland McCrodden. 'Thank you for clearing that up, Poirot.'

'You are most welcome, my friend. And now there remains only one more thing that must be cleared up. Madame Lavington, there is something that I must tell you. It will, I think, be of great interest to you. You have patiently sat and listened as I explained to everybody else things that you knew only too well already. But now I have a surprise for you . . .'

CHAPTER 37

The Will

'Let's hear it then, Poirot,' said John McCrodden. 'What is this final revelation?' He spoke tauntingly, as if everything Poirot had told us so far might have been a lie.

'Barnabas Pandy had no intention of cutting off Mademoiselle Annabel. None at all! The granddaughter he planned to disinherit was Lenore Lavington.'

'That can't be true,' said Annabel. 'He adored Lenore.'

'I performed a little experiment,' said Poirot. 'Not with the typewriters this time. I used, instead, human beings. There is a woman working in the offices of Rowland McCrodden—a woman he has detested for some time, with, one might say, little cause.'

'She's not the easiest of people to deal with,' I felt obliged to say.

'Her name is Emerald Mason,' said Poirot. 'To test my theory about Barnabas Pandy's attitude to Annabel Treadway and how it might have affected his behaviour towards his old enemy Vincent Lobb, I played a little trick on Monsieur McCrodden. I told him that Emerald Mason had been in a terrible motorcar accident and was to lose both her legs. This was not true, and I soon revealed that I had created this little deception. Before I did so, however, Monsieur McCrodden apologized to Catchpool for having been uncongenial when they travelled here together from London. Having been not at all amiable for the duration of the journey, Rowland McCrodden transformed himself, immediately upon hearing about poor Mademoiselle Emerald's lost legs, into a humble and contrite man who could see exactly how trying he had been until that moment.

'Why did this change take place? Because Rowland McCrodden felt terribly guilty. He realized that he had been unduly harsh towards this relatively harmless woman, and now a terrible fate had befallen her. He felt, almost, responsible—as if her tragic fate had been his fault. This led him, directly, to think of other people whom he might have treated harshly. Catchpool came immediately to mind, and so Rowland McCrodden apologized to him—something that would not have happened had I not invented the story about the legs of Mademoiselle Emerald Mason.'

'Legs again!' said Hugo Dockerill. 'Golly!'

'You are probably right, monsieur,' Poirot smiled at him. 'The subconscious influence must have been at work. In any case, when I heard Rowland McCrodden apologize to Catchpool, I knew for a certainty the reason for Barnabas Pandy's sudden lightness of spirit, noticed by his lawyer Peter Vout. I knew that it must have been caused by his understanding, finally, the pain of the timid, sad granddaughter whom for so long he had judged and found wanting. Suddenly, he comprehends how she has suffered for so many years. He regrets, profoundly, his severe judgement of her. And he finds that he no longer feels antipathy towards Vincent Lobb. He can forgive not only Annabel Treadway's weakness but also Lobb's. What he cannot tolerate, he finds, is the harsh judgement he sees in the eyes and hears in the voice of his other granddaughter, Lenore Lavington. This reminds him of his own punitive way of looking at the world until so late in his life. *Eh bien*, he resolves to ensure that Lenore Lavington does not benefit after his death—and he resolves to compensate Annabel Treadway for his years of preferential treatment towards her sister that must have greatly increased Mademoiselle Annabel's suffering.'

'What are you talking about?' said Lenore Lavington. 'It's nonsense.'

'I am explaining, madame, that you were the one your grandfather would have cut out of his will, had he survived.'

'But . . . that cannot be true,' said Annabel Treadway. She looked utterly lost.

'I was in London this morning,' said Poirot. 'I asked Monsieur Peter Vout: did Monsieur Pandy state explicitly that it was Mademoiselle Annabel whom he planned to deprive of her inheritance? I was given the answer I expected: no, he had not specified which granddaughter he had in mind for this unfortunate fate. In fact, I was told by Monsieur Vout that Monsieur Pandy had been uncharacteristically oblique when speaking of his new will. His solicitor had merely assumed, as did Lenore Lavington when he told her of his intentions without naming any names, that Mademoiselle Annabel would be the one cut off without a penny, because she had always been the least favoured granddaughter.'

'Why would Mr Pandy behave in this deliberately misleading fashion?' asked Jane Dockerill. 'Surely one would only do that if one wished to deliver a surprise punishment from beyond the grave—one that was designed to come as a great shock.'

'*Précisément*, madame. Of course, Lenore Lavington was in no doubt that she would be the one to end up twice as wealthy as she would otherwise have been as a result of this new will. How could it not be so? Had Monsieur Pandy not learned, a day or two earlier, that Annabel Treadway had left his great-granddaughter to drown in a river while saving a dog? He had! And it was she, Lenore Lavington, who had been summoned, in secret, to be told of her grandfather's plan to make this change to his will. I expect he said—to use Kingsbury's phrase again—*words to the effect of* "Everybody will get what they deserve after I die. Those who deserve nothing will get nothing."'

'You are mistaken,' Lenore Lavington said. 'Even if he was able to forgive Annabel and Vincent Lobb, Grandfather had no reason suddenly to decide to cut me off.'

'I believe he did,' said Poirot. 'At the dinner table on the evening of the unpleasantness, I believe he noticed a cruel, unforgiving glint in your eye, when you saw that he had realized the truth about Mademoiselle Ivy's accident and your sister's actions on that day. He saw you watching him closely, hoping that this new knowledge would kill any feelings of affection or loyalty that he had towards your sister once and for all. He saw in your eyes pure, unforgiving hatred. It shocked him. He found it unbearable. Shall I tell you why? Because it reminded him of himself! Suddenly, he saw how cruelly unforgiving he had been to his once good friend, Vincent Lobb. He realized, perhaps, that the very worst sin of all is the inability to forgive the sins of others. That, Madame Lavington, is why he decided you deserved nothing.'

'This is quite shameless invention on your part, Poirot,' said John McCrodden. 'Truly, I don't see how you can claim to know any of this.'

'I make deductions based upon what facts I do know, monsieur.'

Poirot turned back to Lenore Lavington. He said, 'After the disaster of the dinner, your grandfather decided to make for you a test. He wanted to test whether you—knowing that guilt had consumed the life and soul of Mademoiselle Annabel, and knowing how much she loved Mademoiselle Ivy and how sorry she must be—would beg him to reconsider and to forgive. That is why he told you about his plan to make a new will. It is the only reason he did so. If you had said, "Please, do not punish Annabel, who has already suffered enough," he would have been content to let his existing will remain in place. But you did no such thing. Instead, you showed him that you were delighted by the prospect of your sister being doomed to live in poverty. You demonstrated that you had no compassion.'

'M. Poirot, if I understand you correctly, you are saying that Mother did in fact have a substantial motive for murdering Grandy,' said Timothy Lavington. 'Except that, one, he wasn't murdered, and two, Mother *didn't know* she had a motive to kill him. She believed Aunt Annabel would be the one to lose out under the terms of the new will, not her.'

'That is precisely correct,' Poirot said. 'Barnabas Pandy was not murdered, but it was his accidental drowning that caused the murder of poor Kingsbury and the attempted murder of Mademoiselle Annabel. I do not believe that Lenore Lavington would have tried to bring about the death of her sister if Monsieur Pandy had not died. He would have changed his will, and Lenore Lavington would have assumed the change was in her favour and to the detriment of her sister. That might have been enough for her— Mademoiselle Annabel's punishment of being entirely cut off from the family fortune—at least until Monsieur Pandy eventually died and she learned the truth about the changed will.

'Instead, her grandfather died *before* making the prom-ised alterations to his testamentary affairs. This was too much for Madame Lavington to bear. Mademoiselle Annabel would not, after all, get her punishment of poverty! *That*, ladies and gentlemen, was when Lenore Lavington decided to see if she might be able to arrange for her sister to hang for a murder she did not commit. This last part, of course, is mere supposition. I cannot prove it.'

'That and the rest of what you've told us today,' said

John McCrodden coldly. 'Where is your proof that Mr Pandy would have disinherited Lenore, whom you yourself say he always favoured? Your silly experiment proves nothing.'

'Do you think so, monsieur? I disagree. I think everybody in this room who is not in love with Lenore Lavington can see the logic in what I have said. Let me tell you one more thing that might convince you: Kingsbury told me that on the night of the dinner disaster, he saw Monsieur Pandy sitting at the table and crying, once his granddaughters and great-granddaughter had left him alone. One single, solitary tear, Kingsbury said. Does this suggest that Barnabas Pandy was angry with Mademoiselle Annabel? *Non, mes amis.* One might cry from anger, but there would be a flood of passionate tears, would there not? He was not angry with Mademoiselle Annabel. He felt compassion for her. He was sad—sad and full of regret. With no knowledge of the terrible guilt she struggled with every day, he had treated her with impatience. Suddenly, this incomprehensible grand-daughter of his *made sense to him*: the invisible layer of tragedy that seemed always to surround her; her refusal to marry and bear children.

'It is not difficult to see how such thoughts—such a startling change of perspective—might lead him to reflect upon the other person whom he had treated with undue harshness: his enemy, Vincent Lobb. The analogy, when I considered it, was extremely strong, and convinced me I was right. Vincent Lobb, like Annabel Treadway, was guilty of cowardice. Too afraid of the possible consequences of choosing the right course of action, he chose the wrong one. He then felt guilty for the rest of his life—once again, like Annabel Treadway. Lobb did something terribly wrong, as did Mademoiselle Annabel, and both suffered greatly. Both were unable, thereafter, to enjoy their lives and live them to the full. In that moment, as he sat at the dinner table, Barnabas Pandy decided that he must forgive them both. It was a wise decision that he made.'

'It's all very well to spout about forgiveness, Poirot, when you are not personally the one with something to forgive,' said John McCrodden. 'You don't have children, do you? Neither do I, but I do possess an imagination. Do you believe you could ever forgive a person who left your four-year-old child to drown in a river, while saving a *dog* instead? I know I could not!'

'I know, monsieur, that I would never stick a wet dress to the bottom of a bed frame in the hope that it would be found by Hercule Poirot and result in the person I could not forgive being sent to the gallows for a murder she did not commit. That much I know.

'You made a fatal miscalculation, madame,' Poirot said to Lenore Lavington. 'The discovery of the dress provided me with a vital clue. It told me that that either your sister had murdered Monsieur Pandy, or else someone needed me to believe that she had. That was the moment when I knew there was a murderer to be caught: either one who had killed already, or one who intended to cause the death of Annabel Treadway, or perhaps both. Without the wet dress, I might not have pursued my investigation so assiduously, and the world might never have known of your guilt, madame.'

Annabel Treadway stood up. Hopscotch made a noise as he too rose from his seated position and stood by her side. It was as if he knew she had something important to say. 'My sister cannot be guilty of murder, M. Poirot. She was with me when Kingsbury was killed. Weren't you, Lenore? You were with me the whole time, between two o'clock and when we both arrived in the drawing room together. So you see, she cannot have done it.'

'I can see that you wish to follow your grandfather's example and be compassionate, mademoiselle. You intend to forgive your sister, *n'est-ce pas*, for her attempt to end your life? You cannot fool Hercule Poirot. If you and Madame Lavington had been together between two o'clock and when you arrived in the drawing room, you would have said so much sooner.'

'No, that's not true,' said Annabel. 'Lenore, tell him. We were together—don't you remember?'

Lenore Lavington ignored her sister. She looked at Poirot and said, 'I am a mother who loves her children. That is all.'

'Lenore.' John McCrodden knelt beside her and took her hand in both of his. 'You must be strong. I love you, darling. He cannot prove a damned thing, and I believe he knows it.'

A tear escaped from the corner of Lenore's eye and started, slowly, to creep down the side of her face. One single solitary tear: exactly like the one Barnabas Pandy had shed, described by Kingsbury to Poirot.

'I love you, John,' she said. 'I have never stopped loving you.'

'It turns out that you are capable of forgiveness after all, madame,' said Poirot. 'That is good. Whatever else has happened or will happen, that is always good.'

CHAPTER 38

Rowland Without a Rope

'The visitor you have been expecting has arrived, sir,' said George to Poirot late one Tuesday afternoon. Nearly two weeks had passed since Poirot and I had left Combingham Hall and returned to London.

'Monsieur Rowland McCrodden?'

'Yes, sir. Shall I show him in?'

'Yes, please, Georges.'

Rowland McCrodden entered the room moments later, looking defiant, then seemed to slump a little when he caught sight of Poirot and heard his heartfelt welcome.

'You need not be abashed,' Poirot said. 'I know what you have come to tell me. I expected it. It is quite natural that it should happen.'

'Then you've heard?' said McCrodden.

'I have heard nothing. I have been told nothing. Yet, still, I know.'

'That's impossible.'

'You have come to tell me that you will be assisting in the

376

defence of Lenore Lavington—is that not so? She is to plead not guilty to the charges of murder and attempted murder.'

'Someone *has* told you. You must have spoken to John.'

'My friend, I have spoken to no one. *You* have spoken to John at great length, though, have you not, since our time at Combingham Hall? The two of you have put aside all the unpleasantness that has passed between you, like the water under a bridge, *non*?'

'Well, yes. But I fail to see how you could have—'

'Tell me, is it possible that John will now follow you into the law, as you always hoped he would?'

'Why, yes, he . . . he expressed his intention to do so only yesterday,' said Rowland McCrodden suspiciously. 'Why won't you be straight with me, Poirot? It is simply not credible to think that anyone could guess correctly in so much detail. Even you.'

'It is not a guess. It is knowledge of human nature,' Poirot explained. 'Monsieur John, he wishes he himself could defend the woman he loves—though he is grateful for your efforts on his, and her, behalf. He shows his appreciation by deciding that, after all, it would not be such a bad thing if he were to practise the law. Especially now that his father has changed his mind about what ought to happen to those who have committed murder.'

'You talk about my own opinions and how they have changed as if you know more about it than I do,' said McCrodden.

'Not more—only the same amount,' said Poirot. 'I know what must be true, always. And in this case, it was all so easy to foresee. Your son loves Lenore Lavington, and you, *mon ami*, you love your son as any good father does. And so, although you believe that Poirot is right and that Madame Lavington is guilty, you will help to defend her. You know that if she were to hang for murder, your son's heart would break. His hopes of any future happiness would be crushed. You would do anything to prevent that, would you not? Having once lost him—seemingly irretrievably, and for so long—you will not now risk losing him again, neither on account of a disagreement about the law and its morality, nor to his own grief. And so, you help Lenore Lavington, and you change your mind about certain issues of law and justice. I imagine you now believe that no murderer should hang for his or her crime? Are we now to call you "Rowland Without a Rope"?'

'This is not what I came here to discuss, Poirot.'

'Or are you still an advocate for the death penalty in all cases apart from this one?'

'That would make me a hypocrite,' said McCrodden with a sigh. 'Isn't there another possibility? Might I not believe that Lenore Lavington is innocent?'

'No. You do not believe that.'

The two men sat for a few moments in silence. Then McCrodden said, 'I came here because I wanted to tell you in person that I shall be helping Lenore. I also want to thank you. When I first found out that John had received that horrible letter—'

'You refer to the letter sent to him *by Lenore Lavington*—the woman you intend to help?'

'I am trying to thank you, Poirot. I am grateful to you for exonerating my son.'

'He is not a murderer.'

'As you might be aware, Miss Treadway is sticking to her version of events,' said McCrodden.

'You mean she continues to insist that she was with her sister when Kingsbury died? That, too, I expected. It is her guilt at work—at work in the service of injustice. Madame Lavington is lucky indeed to have Mademoiselle Annabel to help her, and you, and your son. Less lucky are those she might kill in the future, if you all prevail. I'm sure you are aware, my friend, that once a person has allowed themselves to take one life, it is easy for them to kill again and again. This is why I pray that you will not prevail. The jury, I hope, will believe me—not because of my reputation but *because I will be telling the truth.*'

'All of the evidence against Lenore is circumstantial,' said McCrodden. 'You have nothing concrete, Poirot. No indisputable facts.'

'*Mon ami*, let us not argue the merits of our respective cases here and now. This is not a murder trial. Soon enough we will be in a courtroom, and we will see whom the jury believes.'

McCrodden nodded curtly. 'I bear you no ill will, Poirot,' he said on his way to the door. 'Quite the opposite.'

'*Merci.* And I . . .' Poirot found it hard to decide what to say. Finally he said, 'I am pleased to hear that relations between you and your son have improved. Family is very important. For your sake, I am glad that you do not find the price of reconciliation to be too high. Please do Poirot one little favour: ask yourself every day if this is the course you wish to pursue, and if it is the *right* course.'

'Kingsbury had no living relatives,' said McCrodden. 'And Annabel Treadway is not on her way to the gallows for a crime she didn't commit.'

'And so no harm is done if Lenore Lavington walks free? I disagree. When justice is deliberately distorted and denied, harm is done. You, your son, Lenore Lavington . . . and, yes, Annabel Treadway for her lies . . . if you are all lucky, you might not pay the price for your actions in this life. Beyond that, it is not up to Hercule Poirot to speculate.'

'Goodbye, Poirot. Thank you for everything you did for John.'

With these words, Rowland McCrodden turned and left.

CHAPTER 39

A New Typewriter

I am typing this final section of my account of 'The Mystery of Three Quarters' six months subsequent to the events of the preceding chapter, and on a brand new typewriter. All the letter 'e's in this last chapter are, therefore, perfect. Our friend the eel need no longer feel down at heel.

It's strange—I developed a strong aversion to the sight of those faulty 'e's as I wrote this story, but now that they are gone, I rather miss them.

The new typewriter was a gift from Poirot. A few weeks after the trial of Lenore Lavington was concluded, having noticed that I had sent him no new pages to read, he arrived at Scotland Yard with the most elegantly wrapped box I have ever seen. He said, 'You have abandoned your writing?'

I made a non-committal noise.

'Every story needs an ending, *mon ami*. Even if we do not like the resolution, it is still necessary to finish what we have started. The loose threads, they must be gathered in.'

He put the parcel down on my desk. 'This gift, I hope, will encourage you to complete your account.'

'Why does it matter?' I asked. 'There's a strong chance no one will ever read my scribblings.'

'I, Hercule Poirot, will read them.'

Once he had left my office, I unwrapped the package and stared at the shiny new machine. I was touched that he had cared enough to buy it for me, and, as always, in awe of his cleverness. Of course I would have to finish writing the story after a gesture like that. So, here I am, finishing it. Which means it is my duty to report that the trial of Lenore Lavington did not go the way I hoped it would. She was convicted of the murder of Kingsbury, and the attempted murder of Annabel Treadway, but, thanks to Rowland McCrodden's advocacy on her behalf, she was spared the gallows. I happen to know, though I should prefer not to know it, that Mrs Lavington receives regular visits in prison from a devoted John McCrodden—while poor, loyal Kingsbury lies dead.

'Do you believe justice has been done?' I asked Poirot, when we learned that Mrs Lavington would not pay with her life for the crimes she had committed.

'A jury found her guilty, *mon ami*,' he said. 'She will spend the rest of her days in prison.'

'You know as well as I do, she'd have hanged if it weren't for Rowland McCrodden's efforts, made for all the wrong reasons. Every judge in the land knows him to be the most passionate advocate of the death penalty, and suddenly he is on the side of compassion for a distraught woman who simply made a terrible mistake in a moment of weakness? That powerful speech delivered by Lenore Lavington's barrister was McCrodden's creation, and the judge knew it. The same Rowland Rope who has sent dozens of less fortunate fellows off to the gallows, without a thought for whom they might love or who might love them, purely because none of them happened to be his son! It's not right, Poirot. That isn't justice.'

He smiled at me. 'Do not torment yourself, my friend. I concern myself only with bringing to light the facts of the case, and securing the guilty verdict for the criminal, not with the punishment that follows. I leave such considerations to a higher authority. The truth has been recognized, in a court of law—that is what matters.'

We sat in silence for a few moments. Then he said, 'You perhaps do not know that there is somebody who has announced his intention to behave as if Lenore Lavington *were* dead—who has vowed never to write to her, and to burn any letters she might send to him.'

'Who?'

'Her son, Timothy. This, I think, will be an additional punishment. To be cast aside by one's own child, whatever one has done—it is a terrible thing.'

I did not know if Poirot meant, with this observation, to imply that I ought not to judge Rowland McCrodden too harshly. I decided that, if that was his intention, it would be unwise to prolong our discussion of the matter, so I said nothing.

And now, having come to the end of this account, I see that Poirot was absolutely correct: to record that a story ended unsatisfactorily is still, somehow, considerably more satisfying than to offer no resolution at all.

This, then, is the end of 'The Mystery of Three Quarters'.

Edward (with a flawless 'E'!) Catchpool

ALSO BY SOPHIE HANNAH

The Monogram Murders

'It is hate that makes people kill . . . not love.'

Hercule Poirot's quiet supper in a London coffee house is interrupted when a young woman confides to him that she is about to be murdered. She is terrified, but begs Poirot not to find and punish her killer. Once she is dead, she insists, justice will have been done.

Later that night, Poirot learns that three guests at the fashionable Bloxham Hotel have been murdered, and a cufflink has been placed in each one's mouth. Could there be a connection with the frightened woman? While Poirot struggles to connect the bizarre pieces of the puzzle, the murderer prepares a hotel bedroom for a fourth victim . . .

'Grips from the very start. Hannah gets it right in every particular.'
THE TIMES

'Immensely satisfying—an ingenious ending'
INDEPENDENT

'A highly readable locked-room mystery with a delectable twist.'
MAIL ON SUNDAY

'Superbly orchestrated . . . as exhilaratingly complicated as anything by Christie.'
SUNDAY TIMES

ALSO BY SOPHIE HANNAH

Closed Casket

'What I intend to say to you will come as a shock . . .'

Lady Athelinda Playford has planned a house party at her mansion, but it is no ordinary gathering. She announces that she has decided to change her will, cutting off her children and leaving her fortune to someone who has only weeks to live . . .

Among Lady Playford's guests are Belgian detective Hercule Poirot and Inspector Edward Catchpool of Scotland Yard, who have no idea why they have been invited . . . until Poirot starts to wonder if Lady Playford expects a murderer to strike. When the crime is committed, and the victim is not who Poirot thought it would be, will he be able to solve the mystery?

'Sparkling second outing for Hannah's reimagined Poirot'
SUNDAY TIMES

'Offers a clever twist which the Queen of Crime would have applauded'
DAILY EXPRESS

'Another satisfying addition to the Agatha Christie canon'
IRISH TIMES

'A novel fizzing with ideas and spikey dialogue'
SUNDAY EXPRESS

THE AGATHA CHRISTIE COLLECTION

Mysteries

The Man in the Brown
    Suit
The Secret of Chimneys
The Seven Dials Mystery
The Mysterious Mr Quin
The Sittaford Mystery
The Hound of Death
The Listerdale Mystery
Why Didn't They Ask
    Evans?
Parker Pyne Investigates
Murder Is Easy
And Then There Were
    None
Towards Zero
Death Comes as the End
Sparkling Cyanide
Crooked House
They Came to Baghdad
Destination Unknown
Spider's Web*
The Unexpected Guest*
Ordeal by Innocence
The Pale Horse
Endless Night
Passenger To Frankfurt
Problem at Pollensa Bay
While the Light Lasts

Poirot

The Mysterious Affair at
    Styles
The Murder on the
    Links
Poirot Investigates
The Murder of Roger
    Ackroyd
The Big Four
The Mystery of the Blue
    Train
Black Coffee*
Peril at End House
Lord Edgware Dies

Murder on the Orient
    Express
Three Act Tragedy
Death in the Clouds
The ABC Murders
Murder in Mesopotamia
Cards on the Table
Murder in the Mews
Dumb Witness
Death on the Nile
Appointment With Death
Hercule Poirot's
    Christmas
Sad Cypress
One, Two, Buckle My
    Shoe
Evil Under the Sun
Five Little Pigs
The Hollow
The Labours of
    Hercules
Taken at the Flood
Mrs McGinty's Dead
After the Funeral
Hickory Dickory Dock
Dead Man's Folly
Cat Among the Pigeons
The Adventure of the
    Christmas Pudding
The Clocks
Third Girl
Hallowe'en Party
Elephants Can
    Remember
Poirot's Early Cases
Curtain: Poirot's Last
    Case

Marple

The Murder at the
    Vicarage
The Thirteen Problems
The Body in the Library
The Moving Finger

A Murder Is Announced
They Do It With Mirrors
A Pocket Full of Rye
4.50 from Paddington
The Mirror Crack'd from
    Side to Side
A Caribbean Mystery
At Bertram's Hotel
Nemesis
Sleeping Murder
Miss Marple's Final Cases

Tommy & Tuppence

The Secret Adversary
Partners in Crime
N or M?
By the Pricking of My
    Thumbs
Postern of Fate

**Published as Mary
    Westmacott**

Giant's Bread
Unfinished Portrait
Absent in the Spring
The Rose and the Yew
    Tree
A Daughter's a Daughter
The Burden

Memoirs

An Autobiography
Come, Tell Me How You
    Live
The Grand Tour

Plays and Stories

Akhnaton
The Mousetrap and
    Other Plays
The Floating Admiral†
Star Over Bethlehem
Hercule Poirot and the
    Greenshore Folly

* novelized by Charles Osborne
† contributor

About the Authors

SOPHIE HANNAH is an internationally bestselling writer of crime fiction, published in more than 35 languages. Her novel *The Carrier* won Crime Thriller of the Year at the 2013 Specsavers National Book Awards. She lives with her husband, children and dog in Cambridge, where she is a Fellow of Lucy Cavendish College, and as a poet has been shortlisted for the TS Eliot Prize. Sophie has written two previous Hercule Poirot novels, *The Monogram Murders* and *Closed Casket,* both of which were top five *Sunday Times* bestsellers.

AGATHA CHRISTIE is known throughout the world as the Queen of Crime. Her books have sold over a billion copies in English with another billion in foreign languages. She is the most widely published author of all time, outsold only by the Bible and Shakespeare. She is the author of 80 crime novels and short story collections, more than 20 plays, and six novels written under the name Mary Westmacott.

Block Diagram

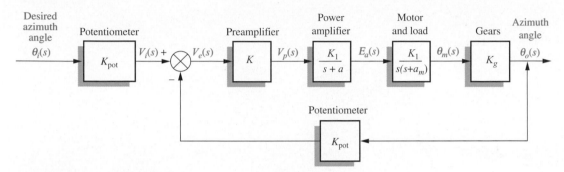

Schematic Parameters

Parameter	Configuration 1	Configuration 2	Configuration 3
V	10	10	10
n	10	1	1
K	—	—	—
K_1	100	150	100
a	100	150	100
R_a	8	5	5
J_a	0.02	0.05	0.05
D_a	0.01	0.01	0.01
K_b	0.5	1	1
K_t	0.5	1	1
N_1	25	50	50
N_2	250	250	250
N_3	250	250	250
J_L	1	5	5
D_L	1	3	3

Block Diagram Parameters

Parameter	Configuration 1	Configuration 2	Configuration 3
K_{pot}	0.318		
K	—		
K_1	100		
a	100		
K_m	2.083		
a_m	1.71		
K_g	0.1		

Note: reader may fill in Configuration 2 and Configuration 3 columns after completing the antenna control Case Study challenge problems in Chapters 2 and 10, respectively.

ANTENNA AZIMUTH POSITION CONTROL SYSTEM

Layout

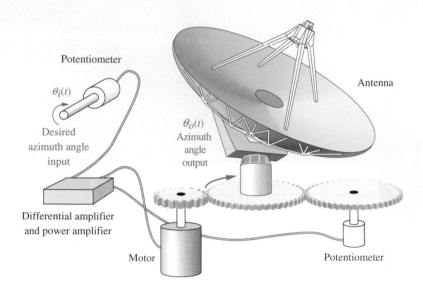

Potentiometer

$\theta_i(t)$

Desired
azimuth angle
input

$\theta_o(t)$
Azimuth
angle
output

Antenna

Differential amplifier
and power amplifier

Motor

Potentiometer

Schematic

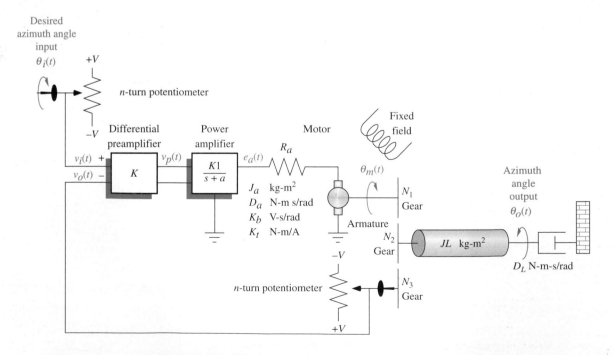

Desired
azimuth angle
input
$\theta_i(t)$

$+V$

n-turn potentiometer

$-V$

Differential
preamplifier

Power
amplifier

Motor

Fixed
field

$v_i(t)$ +

$v_o(t)$ −

K

$v_p(t)$

$\dfrac{K1}{s+a}$

$e_a(t)$

R_a

J_a kg-m^2
D_a N-m s/rad
K_b V-s/rad
K_t N-m/A

$\theta_m(t)$

N_1
Gear

Armature

N_2
Gear

$-V$

JL kg-m^2

Azimuth
angle
output
$\theta_o(t)$

D_L N-m-s/rad

n-turn potentiometer

N_3
Gear

$+V$

CONTROL SYSTEMS ENGINEERING
Fifth Edition

International Student Version

CONTROL SYSTEMS ENGINEERING
Fifth Edition

International Student Version

Norman S. Nise

California State Polytechnic University, Pomona

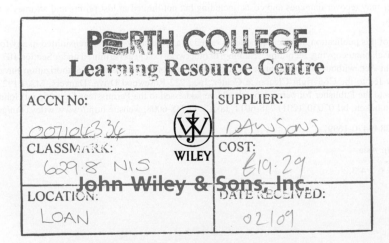
John Wiley & Sons, Inc.

To my wife, Ellen; sons, Benjamin and Alan; and daughter, Sharon.

Vice President & Executive Publisher	Don Fowley
Publisher	Daniel Sayre
Senior Acquisitions Editor	Catherine Shultz
Project Editor	Gladys Soto
Marketing Manager	Christopher Ruel
Production Manager	Dorothy Sinclair
Senior Production Editor	Sandra Dumas
Creative Director	Harry Nolan
Cover & Icons Designer	Michael St. Martine
Photo Department Manager	Hilary Newman
Photo Editor	Sheena Goldstein
Media Editor	Lauren Sapira
Editorial Assistant	Carolyn Weisman
Production Management Services	Elm Street Publishing Services
Cover Photo	William Whitehurst/Corbis
Associate Director of Education	Belinda Tan
Production Executive	Jessie Yeo
Senior Marketing Manager	Angela Teo
ISV Project Editor	Gladys Soto
ISV Production Manager	Micheline Frederick

ISBN 978-0-470-16997-1

Printed in Asia

10 9 8 7 6 5 4 3 2

CONTENTS

Web site location is www.wiley.com/college/nise.

PREFACE

This book introduces students to the theory and practice of control systems engineering. The text emphasizes the practical application of the subject to the analysis and design of feedback systems.

The study of control systems engineering is essential for students pursuing degrees in electrical, mechanical, aerospace, biomedical or chemical engineering. Control systems are found in a broad range of applications within these disciplines, from aircraft and spacecraft to robots and process control systems.

Control Systems Engineering is suitable for upper-division college and university engineering students and for those who wish to master the subject matter through self-study. The student using this text should have completed typical lower-division courses in physics and mathematics through differential equations. Other required background material, including Laplace transforms and linear algebra, is incorporated in the text, either within chapter discussions or separately in the appendixes or on the book's companion Web site. This review material can be omitted without loss of continuity if the student does not require it.

Key Features

The key features of this fifth edition are:

- Standardized chapter organization
- Qualitative and quantitative explanations
- **Examples, Skill-Assessment Exercises,** and **Case Studies** throughout the text
- WileyPLUS content management system for students and professors.
- **Cyber Exploration Laboratory** experiments
- Abundant illustrations
- Numerous end-of-chapter problems
- Emphasis on design
- Flexible coverage
- Emphasis on computer-aided analysis and design
- Icons identifying major topics

Let us look at each feature in more detail.

Standardized Chapter Organization

Each chapter begins with a list of chapter objectives, followed by a list of case study objectives that relate the chapter objectives to specific student performance in solving a practical case study problem, such as an antenna azimuth position control system.

Topics are then divided into clearly numbered and labeled sections containing explanations, examples, and, where appropriate, skill-assessment exercises with answers. These numbered sections are followed by one or more case studies, as will be outlined in a few paragraphs. Each chapter ends with a brief summary, several review questions requiring short answers, and a set of homework problems.

Qualitative and Quantitative Explanations

Explanations are clear and complete and, where appropriate, include a brief review of required background material. Topics build upon and support one another in a logical fashion. Groundwork for new concepts and terminology is carefully laid to avoid overwhelming the student and to facilitate self-study.

Although quantitative solutions are obviously important, a qualitative or intuitive understanding of problems and methods of solution is vital to producing the insight required to develop sound designs. Therefore, whenever possible, new concepts are discussed from a qualitative perspective before quantitative analysis and design are addressed. For example, in Chapter 8 the student can simply look at the root locus and describe qualitatively the changes in transient response that will occur as a system parameter, such as gain, is varied. This ability is developed with the help of a few simple equations from Chapter 4.

Examples, Skill-Assessment Exercises, and Case Studies

Explanations are clearly illustrated by means of numerous numbered and labeled **Examples** throughout the text. Where appropriate, a section concludes with **Skill-Assessment Exercises**. These are computation drills, most with answers that test comprehension and provide immediate feedback. Complete solutions can be found at www.wiley.com/college/nise.

Broader examples in the form of **Case Studies** can be found after the last numbered section of every chapter, with the exception of Chapter 1. These case studies are practical application problems that demonstrate the concepts introduced in the chapter. Each case study concludes with a ''Challenge'' problem that students may work in order to test their understanding of the material.

One of the case studies, concerning an antenna azimuth position control system, is carried throughout the book. The purpose is to illustrate the application of new material in each chapter to the same physical system, thus highlighting the continuity of the design process. Another, more challenging case study, involving an Unmannered Free-Swimming Submersible Vehicle, is developed over the course of five chapters.

WileyPLUS Content Management System for Students and Professors

WileyPLUS is an online suite of resources, including the full text, for students and instructors. For the fifth edition of Control Systems Engineering, this suite offers professors who adopt the book with WileyPLUS the ability to create homework assignments based on algorithmic problems or multi-part questions which guide the student through a problem. Instructors also have the capability to integrate assets, such as the simulations, into their lecture presentations. Students will find a Read, Study, and Practice zone to help them work through problems based on the ones offered in the text.

Control Solutions (prepared by JustAsk for the Fourth Edition), which were offered for students with the Fourth Edition, are included in the Wiley PLUS platform. The student will find simulations and Control Solutions in the Read, Study, and Practice zone. The Control Solutions are highlighted in the text with a WileyPLUS icon.

Visit www.wiley.com or contact your local Wiley representative for information.

Cyber Exploration Laboratory Experiments

Computer experiments using MATLAB®,[1] Simulink®,[2] and the Control System Toolbox are found at the end of the Problems section of Chapters 2 through 13 under the subheading **Cyber Exploration Laboratory.** The experiments allow the reader to verify the concepts covered in the chapter via simulation. The reader also can change parameters and perform "what if" exploration to gain insight into the effect of parameter and configuration changes. The experiments are written with stated Objectives, Minimum required software packages, as well as Prelab, Lab, and Postlab tasks and questions. Thus, the experiments may be used for a laboratory course that accompanies the class.

Abundant Illustrations

The ability to visualize concepts and processes is critical to the student's understanding. For this reason approximately 800 photos, diagrams, graphs, and tables appear throughout the book to illustrate the topics under discussion.

Numerous End-of-Chapter Problems

Each chapter ends with a variety of homework problems that allow students to test their understanding of the material presented in the chapter. Problems vary in degree of difficulty and complexity, and most chapters include several practical, real-life problems to help maintain students' motivation. Also, the homework problems contain a progressive analysis and design problem that uses the same practical system to demonstrate the concepts of each chapter.

Emphasis on Design

This textbook places a heavy emphasis on design. Chapters 8, 9, 11, 12, and 13 focus primarily on design. But even in chapters that emphasize analysis, simple design examples are included wherever possible.

Throughout the book, design examples involving physical systems are identified by the icon shown in the margin. End-of-chapter problems that involve the design of physical systems are included under the separate heading **Design Problems** and also, in chapters covering design, under the heading **Progressive Analysis and Design Problems**. In these examples and problems, a desired response is specified, and the student must evaluate certain system parameters, such as gain, or specify a system configuration along with parameter values. In addition, the text includes numerous design examples and problems (not identified by an icon) that involve purely mathematical systems.

Because visualization is so vital to understanding design, this text carefully relates indirect design specifications to more familiar ones. For example, the less familiar and indirect phase margin is carefully related to the more direct and familiar percent overshoot before being used as a design specification.

For each general type of design problem introduced in the text, a methodology for solving the problem is presented—in many cases in the form of a step-by-step procedure, beginning with a statement of design objectives. Example problems serve to demonstrate the methodology by following the procedure, making simplifying assumptions, and presenting the results of the design in tables or plots that compare the performance of the original system to that of the improved system. This comparison also serves as a check on the simplifying assumptions.

---

[1] MATLAB is a registered trademark of The Mathworks, Inc.

[2] Simulink is a registered trademark of The Mathworks, Inc.

Transient response design topics are covered comprehensively in the text. They include:

- Design via gain adjustment using the root locus
- Design of compensation and controllers via the root locus
- Design via gain adjustment using sinusoidal frequency response methods
- Design of compensation via sinusoidal frequency response methods
- Design of controllers in state space using pole-placement techniques
- Design of observers in state space using pole-placement techniques
- Design of digital control systems via gain adjustment on the root locus
- Design of digital control system compensation via *s*-plane design and the Tustin transformation

Steady-state error design is covered comprehensively in this textbook and includes:

- Gain adjustment
- Design of compensation via the root locus
- Design of compensation via sinusoidal frequency response methods
- Design of integral control in state space

Finally, the design of gain to yield stability is covered from the following perspectives:

- Routh-Hurwitz criterion
- Root locus
- Nyquist criterion
- Bode plots

Flexible Coverage

The material in this book can be adapted for a one-quarter or a one-semester course. The organization is flexible, allowing the instructor to select the material that best suits the requirements and time constraints of the class.

Throughout the book state-space methods are presented along with the classical approach. Chapters and sections (as well as examples, exercises, review questions, and problems) that cover state space are marked by the icon shown in the margin and can be omitted without any loss of continuity. Those wishing to add a basic introduction to state-space modeling can include Chapter 3 in the syllabus.

In one-semester course, the discussions of state-space analysis in Chapters 4, 5, 6, and 7, as well as state-space design in Chapter 12, can be covered along with the classical approach. Another option is to teach state space separately by gathering the appropriate chapters and sections marked with the **State Space** icon into a single unit that follows the classical approach. In a one-quarter course, Chapter 13, "Discrete Control Systems," could be eliminated.

Emphasis on Computer-Aided Analysis and Design

Control systems problems, particularly analysis and design problems using the root locus, can be tedious, since their solution involves trial and error. To solve these problems, students should be given access to computers or programmable calculators configured with appropriate software. In this fifth edition, MATLAB continues to be integrated into the text as an optional feature.

Many problems in this text can be solved with either a computer or a hand-held programmable calculator. For example, students can use the programmable calculator to (1) determine whether a point on the s-plane is also on the root locus, (2) find magnitude and phase frequency response data for Nyquist and Bode diagrams, and (3) convert between the following representations of a second-order system:

- Pole location in polar coordinates
- Pole location in Cartesian coordinates
- Characteristic polynomial
- Natural frequency and damping ratio
- Settling time and percent overshoot
- Peak time and percent overshoot
- Settling time and peak time

Handheld calculators have the advantage of easy accessibility for homework and exams. Please consult Appendix G, located at www.wiley.com/college/nise, for a discussion of computational aids that can be adapted to handheld calculators.

Personal computers are better suited for more computation-intensive applications, such as plotting time responses, root loci, and frequency response curves, as well as finding state-transition matrices. These computers also give the student a real-world environment in which to analyze and design control systems. Those not using MATLAB can write their own programs or use other programs, such as Program CC. Please consult Appendix G, at www.wiley.com/college/nise, for a discussion of computational aids that can be adapted for use on computers that do not have MATLAB installed.

Without access to computers or programmable calculators, students cannot obtain meaningful analysis and design results and the learning experience will be limited.

Icons Identifying Major Topics

Several icons identify coverage and optional material. The icons are summarized as follows:

Control Solutions for the student are identified with a WileyPLUS icon. These problems, developed by JustAsk, are worked in detail and offer explanations of every facet of the solution.

The MATLAB icon identifies MATLAB discussions, examples, exercises, and problems. MATLAB coverage is provided as an enhancement and is not required to use the text.

The Simulink icon identifies Simulink discussions, examples, exercises, and problems. Simulink coverage is provided as an enhancement and is not required to use the text.

The GUI Tool icon identifies MATLAB GUI Tools discussions, examples, exercises, and problems. The discussion of the tools, which includes the LTI Viewer, the Simulink LTI Viewer, and the SISO Design Tool, is provided as an enhancement and is not required to use the text.

The Symbolic Math icon identifies Symbolic Math Toolbox discussions, examples, exercises, and problems. Symbolic Math Toolbox coverage is provided as an enhancement and is not required to use the text.

State Space

Design

The State Space icon highlights state-space discussions, examples, exercises, and problems. State-space material is optional and can be omitted without loss of continuity.

The Design icon clearly identifies design problems involving physical systems.

New to This Edition

The following list describes the key changes in this fifth edition.

End-of-chapter problems   Twenty percent more problems have been added at the end of the chapters. Also, an additional Progressive Analysis and Design Problem has been added at the end of the chapter problems. The new progressive problem is Control of HIV/AIDS.

MATLAB   The use of MATLAB for computer-aided analysis and design continues to be integrated into discussions and problems as an optional feature in the fifth edition. The MATLAB tutorial has been updated to MATLAB Version 7, the Control System Toolbox Version 8, and the Symbolic Math Toolbox Version 3.2.

In addition, MATLAB code is now incorporated in the chapters in the form of sidebar boxes entitled TryIt.

MATLAB's Simulink   The use of Simulink to show the effects of nonlinearities upon the time response of open-loop and closed-loop systems appears again in this fifth edition. We also continue to use Simulink to demonstrate how to simulate digital systems. Finally, the Simulink tutorial has been updated to Simulink 6.

Cyber Exploration Laboratory   Experiments are now included in Chapters 2 and 3.

Book Companion Site (BCS) at www.wiley.com/college/nise

The BCS for the fifth edition includes various student and instructor resources. This free resource can be accessed by going to www.wiley.com/college/nise and clicking on Student Companion Site. Professors also access their password-protected resources on Instructor Companion Site available through this url. Instructors should contact their Wiley sales representative for access.

For the Student:
- All M-Files used in the MATLAB, Simulink, GUI Tools, and Symbolic Math Toolbox tutorials, as well as the new TryIt exercises
- Copies of the Cyber Exploration Laboratory experiments
- Solutions to the Skill-Assessment Exercises in the text

For the Instructor:
- PowerPoint[1] files containing the figures from the textbook
- Solutions to end-of-chapter problem sets
- Simulations, developed by JustAsk, for inclusion in lecture presentations

Topics Moved to BCS   Appendix D, MATLAB's GUI Tools, and Appendix E, MATLAB's Symbolic Math Toolbox, have been moved to the Web site.

---

[1] PowerPoint is a registered trademark of Microsoft Corporation.

Book Organization by Chapter

Many times it is helpful to understand an author's reasoning behind the organization of the course material. The following paragraphs hopefully shed light on this topic.

The primary goal of Chapter 1 is to motivate students. In this chapter students learn about the many applications of control systems in everyday life and about the advantages of study and a career in this field. Control systems engineering design objectives, such as transient response, steady-state error, and stability, are introduced, as is the path to obtaining these objectives. New and unfamiliar terms also are included in the Glossary.

Many students have trouble with an early step in the analysis and design sequence: transforming a physical system into a schematic. This step requires many simplifying assumptions based on experience the typical college student does not yet possess. Identifying some of these assumptions in Chapter 1 helps to fill the experience gap.

Chapters 2, 3, and 5 address the representation of physical systems. Chapters 2 and 3 cover modeling of open-loop systems, using frequency response techniques and state-space techniques, respectively. Chapter 5 discusses the representation and reduction of systems formed of interconnected open-loop subsystems. Only a representative sample of physical systems can be covered in a textbook of this length. Electrical, mechanical (both translational and rotational), and electromechanical systems are used as examples of physical systems that are modeled, analyzed, and designed. Linearization of a nonlinear system—one technique used by the engineer to simplify a system in order to represent it mathematically—is also introduced.

Chapter 4 provides an introduction to system analysis, that is, finding and describing the output response of a system. It may seem more logical to reverse the order of Chapters 4 and 5, to present the material in Chapter 4 along with other chapters covering analysis. However, many years of teaching control systems have taught me that the sooner students see an application of the study of system representation, the higher their motivation levels remain.

Chapters 6, 7, 8, and 9 return to control systems analysis and design with the study of stability (Chapter 6), steady-state errors (Chapter 7), and transient response of higher-order systems using root locus techniques (Chapter 8). Chapter 9 covers design of compensators and controllers using the root locus.

Chapters 10 and 11 focus on sinusoidal frequency analysis and design. Chapter 10, like Chapter 8, covers basic concepts for stability, transient response, and steady-state error analysis. However, Nyquist and Bode methods are used in place of root locus. Chapter 11, like Chapter 9, covers the design of compensators, but from the point of view of sinusoidal frequency techniques rather than root locus.

An introduction to state-space design and digital control systems analysis and design completes the text in Chapters 12 and 13, respectively. Although these chapters can be used as an introduction for students who will be continuing their study of control systems engineering, they are useful by themselves and as a supplement to the discussion of analysis and design in the previous chapters. The subject matter cannot be given a comprehensive treatment in two chapters, but the emphasis is clearly outlined and logically linked to the rest of the book.

Acknowledgments

The author would like to acknowledge the contributions of faculty and students, both at California State Polytechnic University, Pomona and across the country, whose suggestions through all editions have made a positive impact on the new edition.

I particularly want to thank the Electrical and Computer Engineering Department as well as the College of Engineering and Edward Hohmann, Dean. Their support and encouragement was vital to the completion of this volume.

I am deeply indebted to Professor Salomon Oldak, Chairman of the Electrical and Computer Engineering Department, for his authoring of the creative new problems you will find at the end of every chapter. Although under the pressure of his already busy schedule he still found time to search the literature for up-to-date and interesting systems from which to create problems and their solutions. Kudos to Professor Oldak! Additional contributions to the new problems came from Robert Wong and Robert White who deserves our sincere thanks. Finally, I want to express gratitude to my collegue, Professor Elhami T. Ibrahim, whose contributions to the development of the Web-based problems will not go unoticed by the reader.

I would like to express my appreciation to reviewers who offered valuable suggestions for this fifth edition. The reviewers Jorge Aravena, Louisiana State University; Kurt Behpour, Cal Poly SLO; Sergio Brecher, Fairleigh Dickinson University; YangQuan Chen, Utah State University; Milton Cone, Embry Riddle Aero University Prescot; Agamemnon Crassidis, RIT; Marci de Queiroz, Louisiana State University; Khaled Eltohamy, Arizona State University-Tempe; Pushkin Kachroo, Virginia Tech; Kaz Kawamura, Vanderbilt University; Farshad Khorrami, Polytechnic University; Zongli Lin, University of Virginia; Desineni Subbaram Naidu, Idaho State University-Pocatello; Charles Neuman, Carnegie Mellon University; Alexander G. Parlos, Texas A&M University; Chris Rahn, Penn State University; John Ridgely, Cal Poly SLO; Sandip Roy, Washington State University; Javad Shakib, DeVry University; Thyagarajan Srinivasan, Wilkes University; Sandra Yost, University of Detroit-Mercy; and Yih-Choung Yu, Lafayette College.

The author would like to thank John Wiley & Sons, Inc. and its staff for once again providing professional support for this project through all phases of its development. Specifically, the following are due recognition for their contributions: Don Fowley, Executive Publisher, and Daniel Sayre, Publisher, who gave full corporate support to the project; Catherine Shultz, Senior Acquisitions Editor, who along with my previous editor Bill Zobrist initiated the work on the fifth edition and continued to provide guidance and leadership; Gladys Soto, Project Editor, with whom I have had the pleasure of working closely; Chelsee Pengal and Carolyn Weisman, Editorial Assistants, whom I found very responsive to this author's requests and concerns. Others who worked behind the scenes, but who should be thanked never the less are:, Sandra Dumas, Senior Production Editor; Sheena Goldstein, Photo Editor; Hilary Newman, Photo Department Manager; Harry Nolan, Creative Director; Chris Ruel, Marketing Manager; Lauren Sapira, Media Editor; Dorothy Sinclair, Production Manager; and Michael St. Martine, Designer, who did a fantastic job on the cover.

Finally, I want to acknowledge Elm Street Publishing Services and its staff for turning the fifth edition manuscript into the finished product you are holding in your hands. Specifically, kudos go out to Heather Johnson, Senior Project Editor, who handled my concerns in the most professional manner; Angel Chavez, Art Manager; Tim Frelick, Production Manager; and Karin Kipp, Senior Project Manager. Finally, I want to express my appreciation to the copy editors whose sharp eyes and diligence prevented confusing glitches from ever reaching these printed pages.

Norman S. Nise

BASIC CONTROL SYSTEM CONCEPTS

1

CHAPTER OBJECTIVES

In this introductory chapter we will study the following:

- Control system definition and applications
- History of control systems
- The basic features and configurations of control systems
- Analysis and design objectives
- The design process
- How you can benefit from studying control systems

CASE STUDY OBJECTIVES

- You will be introduced to a running case study—an antenna azimuth position control system—that will serve to illustrate the principles in each subsequent chapter. In this chapter the system is used to demonstrate qualitatively how a control system works as well as to define performance criteria that are the basis for control systems analysis and design.

1.1 INTRODUCTION

Control systems are an integral part of modern society. Numerous applications are all around us: The rockets fire, and the space shuttle lifts off to earth orbit; in splashing cooling water, a metallic part is automatically machined; a self-guided vehicle delivering material to workstations in an aerospace assembly plant glides along the floor seeking its destination. These are just a few examples of the automatically controlled systems that we can create.

We are not the only creators of automatically controlled systems; these systems also exist in nature. Within our own bodies are numerous control systems, such as the pancreas, which regulates our blood sugar. In time of "fight or flight," our adrenaline increases along with our heart rate, causing more oxygen to be delivered to our cells. Our eyes follow a moving object to keep it in view; our hands grasp the object and place it precisely at a predetermined location.

Even the nonphysical world appears to be automatically regulated. Models have been suggested showing automatic control of student performance. The input to the model is the student's available study time, and the output is the grade. The model can be used to predict the time required for the grade to rise if a sudden increase in study time is available. Using this model, you can determine whether increased study is worth the effort during the last week of the term.

CONTROL SYSTEM DEFINITION

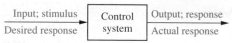

FIGURE 1.1 Simplified description of a control system

A control system consists of *subsystems* and *processes* (*or plants*) assembled for the purpose of obtaining a desired *output* with desired *performance*, given a specified *input*. Figure 1.1 shows a control system in its simplest form, where the input represents a desired output.

For example, consider an elevator. When the fourth-floor button is pressed on the first floor, the elevator rises to the fourth floor with a speed and floor-leveling accuracy designed for passenger comfort. The push of the fourth-floor button is an *input* that represents our desired *output,* shown as a step function in Figure 1.2. The *performance* of the elevator can be seen from the elevator response curve in the figure.

Two major measures of performance are apparent: (1) the transient response and (2) the steady-state error. In our example, passenger comfort and passenger patience are dependent upon the transient response. If this response is too fast, passenger comfort is sacrificed; if too slow, passenger patience is sacrificed. The steady-state error is another important performance specification since passenger safety and convenience would be sacrificed if the elevator did not properly level.

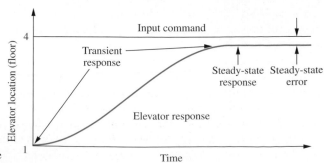

FIGURE 1.2 Elevator response

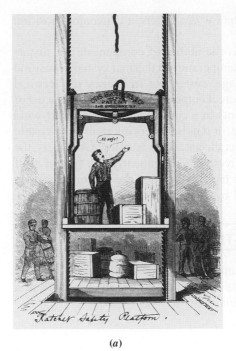

(a)   (b)

FIGURE 1.3 a. Early elevators were controlled by hand ropes or an elevator operator. Here a rope is cut to demonstrate the safety brake, an innovation in early elevators; **b.** modern Duo-lift elevators make their way up the Grande Arche in Paris, driven by one motor, with each car counterbalancing the other. Today elevators are fully automatic, using control systems to regulate position and velocity.

ADVANTAGES OF CONTROL SYSTEMS

With control systems we can move large equipment with precision that would otherwise be impossible. We can point huge antennas toward the farthest reaches of the universe to pick up faint radio signals; controlling these antennas by hand would be impossible. Because of control systems, elevators carry us quickly to our destination, automatically stopping at the right floor (Figure 1.3). We alone could not provide the power required for the load and the speed; motors provide the power, and control systems regulate the position and speed.

We build control systems for four primary reasons:

1. Power amplification
2. Remote control
3. Convenience of input form
4. Compensation for disturbances

For example, a radar antenna, positioned by the low-power rotation of a knob at the input, requires a large amount of power for its output rotation. A control system can produce the needed power amplification, or power *gain.*

Robots designed by control system principles can compensate for human disabilities. Control systems are also useful in remote or dangerous locations. For example, a remote-controlled robot arm can be used to pick up material in a radioactive environment. Figure 1.4 shows a robot arm designed to work in contaminated environments.

Control systems can also be used to provide convenience by changing the form of the input. For example, in a temperature control system,

FIGURE 1.4 *Rover* was built to work in contaminated areas at Three Mile Island in Middleton, PA, where a nuclear accident occurred in 1979. The remote-controlled robot's long arm can be seen at the front of the vehicle.

the input is a *position* on a thermostat. The output is *heat.* Thus, a convenient position input yields a desired thermal output.

Another advantage of a control system is the ability to compensate for disturbances. Typically, we control such variables as temperature in thermal systems, position and velocity in mechanical systems, and voltage, current, or frequency in electrical systems. The system must be able to yield the correct output even with a disturbance. For example, consider an antenna system that points in a commanded direction. If wind forces the antenna from its commanded position, or if noise enters internally, the system must be able to detect the disturbance and correct the antenna's position. Obviously, the system's input will not change to make the correction. Consequently, the system itself must measure the amount that the disturbance has repositioned the antenna and then return the antenna to the position commanded by the input.

1.2 A HISTORY OF CONTROL SYSTEMS

Feedback control systems are older than humanity. Numerous biological control systems were built into the earliest inhabitants of our planet. Let us now look at a brief history of human-designed control systems.[1]

LIQUID-LEVEL CONTROL

The Greeks began engineering feedback systems around 300 B.C. A water clock invented by Ktesibios operated by having water trickle into a measuring container at a constant rate. The level of water in the measuring container could be used to tell time. For water to trickle at a constant rate, the supply tank had to be kept at a constant level. This was accomplished using a float valve similar to the water-level control in today's flush toilets.

Soon after Ktesibios, the idea of liquid-level control was applied to an oil lamp by Philon of Byzantium. The lamp consisted of two oil containers configured vertically. The lower pan was open at the top and was the fuel supply for the flame. The closed upper bowl was the fuel reservoir for the pan below. The containers were interconnected by two capillary tubes and another tube, called a *vertical riser,* which was inserted into the oil in the lower pan just below the surface. As the oil burned, the base of the vertical riser was exposed to air, which forced oil in the reservoir above to flow through the capillary tubes and into the pan. The transfer of fuel from the upper reservoir to the pan stopped when the previous oil level in the pan was reestablished, thus blocking the air from entering the vertical riser. Hence, the system kept the liquid level in the lower container constant.

STEAM PRESSURE AND TEMPERATURE CONTROLS

Regulation of steam pressure began around 1681 with Denis Papin's invention of the safety valve. The concept was further elaborated on by weighting the valve top. If the upward pressure from the boiler exceeded the weight, steam was released, and the pressure decreased. If it did not exceed the weight, the valve did not open, and the pressure inside the boiler increased. Thus, the weight on the valve top set the internal pressure of the boiler.

Also in the 17th century, Cornelis Drebbel in Holland invented a purely mechanical temperature control system for hatching eggs. The device used a vial of alcohol and mercury with a floater inserted in it. The floater was connected to a damper that

---

[1] See *Bennett (1979)* and *Mayr (1970)* for definitive works on the history of control systems.

controlled a flame. A portion of the vial was inserted into the incubator to sense the heat generated by the fire. As the heat increased, the alcohol and mercury expanded, raising the floater, closing the damper, and reducing the flame. Lower temperature caused the float to descend, opening the damper and increasing the flame.

SPEED CONTROL

In 1745 speed control was applied to a windmill by Edmund Lee. Increasing winds pitched the blades farther back, so that less area was available. As the wind decreased, more blade area was available. William Cubitt improved on the idea in 1809 by dividing the windmill sail into movable louvers.

Also in the 18th century, James Watt invented the flyball speed governor to control the speed of steam engines. In this device, two spinning flyballs rise as rotational speed increases. A steam valve connected to the flyball mechanism closes with the ascending flyballs and opens with the descending flyballs, thus regulating the speed.

STABILITY, STABILIZATION, AND STEERING

Control systems theory as we know it today began to crystallize in the latter half of the 19th century. In 1868 James Clerk Maxwell published the stability criterion for a third-order system based on the coefficients of the differential equation. In 1874 Edward John Routh, using a suggestion from William Kingdon Clifford that was ignored earlier by Maxwell, was able to extend the stability criterion to fifth-order systems. In 1877 the topic for the Adams Prize was "The Criterion of Dynamical Stability." In response, Routh submitted a paper entitled *A Treatise on the Stability of a Given State of Motion* and won the prize. This paper contains what is now known as the Routh-Hurwitz criterion for stability, which we will study in Chapter 6. Alexandr Michailovich Lyapunov also contributed to the development and formulation of today's theories and practice of control system stability. A student of P. L. Chebyshev at the University of St. Petersburg in Russia, Lyapunov extended the work of Routh to nonlinear systems in his 1892 doctoral thesis, entitled *The General Problem of Stability of Motion*.

During the second half of the 1800s, the development of control systems focused on the steering and stabilizing of ships. In 1874 Henry Bessemer, using a gyro to sense a ship's motion and applying power generated by the ship's hydraulic system, moved the ship's saloon to keep it stable (whether this made a difference to the patrons is doubtful). Other efforts were made to stabilize platforms for guns as well as to stabilize entire ships, using pendulums to sense the motion.

TWENTIETH-CENTURY DEVELOPMENTS

It was not until the early 1900s that automatic steering of ships was achieved. In 1922 the Sperry Gyroscope Company installed an automatic steering system that used the elements of compensation and adaptive control to improve performance. However, much of the general theory used today to improve the performance of automatic control systems is attributed to Nicholas Minorsky, a Russian born in 1885. It was his theoretical development applied to the automatic steering of ships that led to what we call today proportional-plus-integral-plus-derivative (PID), or three-mode, controllers, which we will study in Chapters 9 and 11.

In the late 1920s and early 1930s, H. W. Bode and H. Nyquist at Bell Telephone Laboratories developed the analysis of feedback amplifiers. These contributions evolved into sinusoidal frequency analysis and design techniques currently used for feedback control systems and presented in Chapters 10 and 11.

In 1948 Walter R. Evans, working in the aircraft industry, developed a graphical technique to plot the roots of a characteristic equation of a feedback system whose parameters changed over a particular range of values. This technique, now known as the root locus, takes its place with the work of Bode and Nyquist in forming the foundation of linear control systems analysis and design theory. We will study root locus in Chapters 8, 9, and 13.

CONTEMPORARY APPLICATIONS

Today control systems find widespread application in the guidance, navigation, and control of missiles and spacecraft, as well as planes and ships at sea. For example, modern ships use a combination of electrical, mechanical, and hydraulic components to develop rudder commands in response to desired heading commands. The rudder commands, in turn, result in a rudder angle that steers the ship.

We find control systems throughout the process control industry, regulating liquid levels in tanks, chemical concentrations in vats, as well as the thickness of fabricated material. For example, consider a thickness control system for a steel plate finishing mill. Steel enters the finishing mill and passes through rollers. In the finishing mill, X rays measure the actual thickness and compare it to the desired thickness. Any difference is adjusted by a screw-down position control that changes the roll gap at the rollers through which the steel passes. This change in roll gap regulates the thickness.

Modern developments have seen widespread use of the digital computer as part of control systems. For example, computers are in control systems used for industrial robots, spacecraft, and the process control industry. It is hard to visualize a modern control system that does not use a digital computer.

The space shuttle contains numerous control systems operated by an onboard computer on a time-shared basis. Without control systems, it would be impossible to guide the shuttle to and from earth orbit or to adjust the orbit itself and support life on board. Navigation functions programmed into the shuttle's computers use data from the shuttle's hardware to estimate vehicle position and velocity. This information is fed to the guidance equations that calculate commands for the shuttle's flight control systems, which steer the spacecraft. In space the flight control system gimbals (rotates) the orbital maneuvering system (OMS) engines into a position that provides thrust in the commanded direction to steer the spacecraft. Within the earth's atmosphere, the shuttle is steered by commands sent from the flight control system to the aerosurfaces, such as the elevons.

Within this large control system represented by navigation, guidance, and control are numerous subsystems to control the vehicle's functions. For example, the elevons require a control system to ensure that their position is indeed that which was commanded, since disturbances such as wind could rotate the elevons away from the commanded position. Similarly, in space, the gimbaling of the orbital maneuvering engines requires a similar control system to ensure that the rotating engine can accomplish its function with speed and accuracy. Control systems are also used to control and stabilize the vehicle during its descent from orbit. Numerous small jets that compose the reaction control system (RCS) are used initially in the exoatmosphere, where the aerosurfaces are ineffective. Control is passed to the aerosurfaces as the orbiter descends into the atmosphere.

Inside the shuttle numerous control systems are required for power and life support. For example, the orbiter has three fuel-cell power plants that convert hydrogen and oxygen (reactants) into electricity and water for use by the crew. The fuel cells involve the use of control systems to regulate temperature and pressure. The reactant tanks are kept at constant pressure as the quantity of reactant diminishes. Sensors in the tanks send signals to the control systems to turn heaters on or off to keep the tank pressure constant (*Rockwell International, 1984*).

Control systems are not limited to science and industry. For example, a home heating system is a simple control system consisting of a thermostat containing a bimetallic material that expands or contracts with changing temperature. This expansion or contraction moves a vial of mercury that acts as a switch, turning the heater on or off. The amount of expansion or contraction required to move the mercury switch is determined by the temperature setting.

Home entertainment systems also have built-in control systems. For example, in an optical disk recording system such as a CD or DVD machine, microscopic pits representing the information are burned into the disc by a laser during the recording process (Figure 1.5).

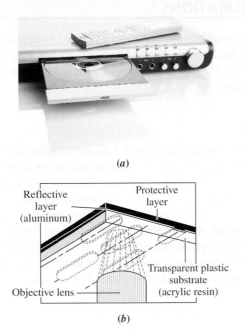

(a)

(b)

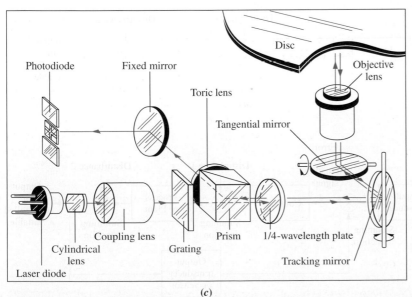

(c)

FIGURE 1.5   a. DVD player; **b.** objective lens reading pits on a DVD; **c.** optical path for playback, showing tracking mirror rotated by a control system to keep the laser beam positioned on the pits

During playback, a reflected laser beam focused on the pits changes intensity. The light intensity changes are converted to an electrical signal and processed as sound or picture. A control system keeps the laser beam positioned on the pits, which are cut as concentric circles.

There are countless other examples of control systems, from the everyday to the extraordinary. As you begin your study of control systems engineering, you will become more aware of the wide variety of applications.

1.3 SYSTEM CONFIGURATIONS

In this section we discuss two major configurations of control systems: open loop and closed loop. We can consider these configurations to be the internal architecture of the total system shown in Figure 1.1. Finally, we show how a digital computer forms part of a control system's configuration.

OPEN-LOOP SYSTEMS

A generic *open-loop system* is shown in Figure 1.6(*a*). It starts with a subsystem called an *input transducer*, which converts the form of the input to that used by the *controller*. The controller drives a *process* or a *plant*. The input is sometimes called the *reference*, while the output can be called the *controlled variable*. Other signals, such as *disturbances*, are shown added to the controller and process outputs via *summing junctions*, which yield the algebraic sum of their input signals using associated signs. For example, the plant can be a furnace or air conditioning system, where the output variable is temperature. The controller in a heating system consists of fuel valves and the electrical system that operates the valves.

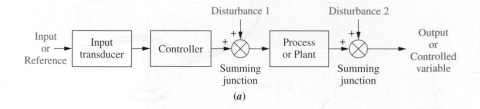

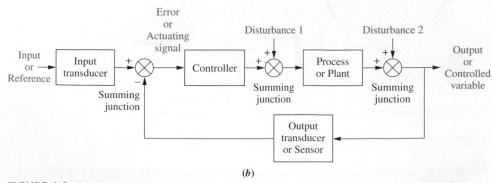

FIGURE 1.6 Block diagrams of control systems: **a.** open-loop system; **b.** closed-loop system

The distinguishing characteristic of an open-loop system is that it cannot compensate for any disturbances that add to the controller's driving signal (Disturbance 1 in Figure 1.6(*a*)). For example, if the controller is an electronic amplifier and Disturbance 1 is noise, then any additive amplifier noise at the first summing junction will also drive the process, corrupting the output with the effect of the noise. The output of an open-loop system is corrupted not only by signals that add to the controller's commands but also by disturbances at the output (Disturbance 2 in Figure 1.6(*a*)). The system cannot correct for these disturbances, either.

Open-loop systems, then, do not correct for disturbances and are simply commanded by the input. For example, toasters are open-loop systems, as anyone with burnt toast can attest. The controlled variable (output) of a toaster is the color of the toast. The device is designed with the assumption that the toast will be darker the longer it is subjected to heat. The toaster does not measure the color of the toast; it does not correct for the fact that the toast is rye, white, or sourdough, nor does it correct for the fact that toast comes in different thicknesses.

Other examples of open-loop systems are mechanical systems consisting of a mass, spring, and damper with a constant force positioning the mass. The greater the force, the greater the displacement. Again, the system position will change with a disturbance, such as an additional force, and the system will not detect or correct for the disturbance. Or assume that you calculate the amount of time you need to study for an examination that covers three chapters in order to get an A. If the professor adds a fourth chapter—a disturbance—you are an open-loop system if you do not detect the disturbance and add study time to that previously calculated. The result of this oversight would be a lower grade than you expected.

CLOSED-LOOP (FEEDBACK CONTROL) SYSTEMS

The disadvantages of open-loop systems, namely sensitivity to disturbances and inability to correct for these disturbances, may be overcome in *closed-loop systems.* The generic architecture of a closed-loop system is shown in Figure 1.6(*b*).

The input transducer converts the form of the input to the form used by the controller. An *output transducer,* or *sensor,* measures the output response and converts it into the form used by the controller. For example, if the controller uses electrical signals to operate the valves of a temperature control system, the input position and the output temperature are converted to electrical signals. The input position can be converted to a voltage by a *potentiometer,* a variable resistor, and the output temperature can be converted to a voltage by a *thermistor,* a device whose electrical resistance changes with temperature.

The first summing junction algebraically adds the signal from the input to the signal from the output, which arrives via the *feedback path,* the return path from the output to the summing junction. In Figure 1.6(*b*), the output signal is subtracted from the input signal. The result is generally called the *actuating signal.* However, in systems where both the input and output transducers have *unity gain* (that is, the transducer amplifies its input by 1), the actuating signal's value is equal to the actual difference between the input and the output. Under this condition, the actuating signal is called the *error.*

The closed-loop system compensates for disturbances by measuring the output response, feeding that measurement back through a feedback path, and comparing that response to the input at the summing junction. If there is any difference between the two responses, the system drives the plant, via the actuating signal, to make a correction. If there is no difference, the system does not drive the plant, since the plant's response is already the desired response.

Closed-loop systems, then, have the obvious advantage of greater accuracy than open-loop systems. They are less sensitive to noise, disturbances, and changes in the environment. Transient response and steady-state error can be controlled more conveniently and with greater flexibility in closed-loop systems, often by a simple adjustment of gain (amplification) in the loop and sometimes by redesigning the controller. We refer to the redesign as *compensating* the system and to the resulting hardware as a *compensator*. On the other hand, closed-loop systems are more complex and expensive than open-loop systems. A standard, open-loop toaster serves as an example: It is simple and inexpensive. A closed-loop toaster oven is more complex and more expensive since it has to measure both color (through light reflectivity) and humidity inside the toaster oven. Thus, the control systems engineer must consider the trade-off between the simplicity and low cost of an open-loop system and the accuracy and higher cost of a closed-loop system.

In summary, systems that perform the previously described measurement and correction are called closed-loop, or feedback control, systems. Systems that do not have this property of measurement and correction are called open-loop systems.

COMPUTER-CONTROLLED SYSTEMS

In many modern systems, the controller (or compensator) is a digital computer. The advantage of using a computer is that many loops can be controlled or compensated by the same computer through time sharing. Furthermore, any adjustments of the compensator parameters required to yield a desired response can be made by changes in software rather than hardware. The computer can also perform supervisory functions, such as scheduling many required applications. For example, the space shuttle main engine (SSME) controller, which contains two digital computers, alone controls numerous engine functions. It monitors engine sensors that provide pressures, temperatures, flow rates, turbopump speed, valve positions, and engine servo-valve actuator positions. The controller further provides closed-loop control of thrust and propellant mixture ratio, sensor excitation, valve actuators, spark igniters, as well as other functions (*Rockwell International, 1984*).

1.4 ANALYSIS AND DESIGN OBJECTIVES

In Section 1.1 we briefly alluded to some control system performance specifications, such as transient response and steady-state error. We now expand upon the topic of performance and place it in perspective as we define our analysis and design objectives.

Analysis is the process by which a system's performance is determined. For example, we evaluate its transient response and steady-state error to determine if they meet the desired specifications. *Design* is the process by which a system's performance is created or changed. For example, if a system's transient response and steady-state error are analyzed and found not to meet the specifications, then we change parameters or add additional components to meet the specifications.

A control system is *dynamic:* It responds to an input by undergoing a transient response before reaching a steady-state response that generally resembles the input. We have already identified these two responses and cited a position control system (an elevator) as an example. In this section we discuss three major objectives of systems analysis and design: producing the desired transient response, reducing steady-state error, and achieving stability. We also address some other design concerns, such as cost and the sensitivity of system performance to changes in parameters.

TRANSIENT RESPONSE

Transient response is important. In the case of an elevator, a slow transient response makes passengers impatient, whereas an excessively rapid response makes them uncomfortable. If the elevator oscillates about the arrival floor for more than a second, a disconcerting feeling can result. Transient response is also important for structural reasons: Too fast a transient response could cause permanent physical damage. In a computer, transient response contributes to the time required to read from or write to the computer's disk storage (see Figure 1.7). Since reading and writing cannot take place until the head stops, the speed of the read/write head's movement from one track on the disk to another influences the overall speed of the computer.

FIGURE 1.7 Computer hard disk drive, showing disks and read/write head

In this book we establish quantitative definitions for transient response. We then analyze the system for its *existing* transient response. Finally, we adjust parameters or design components to yield a *desired* transient response—our first analysis and design objective.

STEADY-STATE RESPONSE

Another analysis and design goal focuses on the steady-state response. As we have seen, this response resembles the input and is usually what remains after the transients have decayed to zero. For example, this response may be an elevator stopped near the fourth floor or the head of a disk drive finally stopped at the correct track. We are concerned about the accuracy of the steady-state response. An elevator must be level enough with the floor for the passengers to exit, and a read/write head not positioned over the commanded track results in computer errors. An antenna tracking a satellite must keep the satellite well within its beamwidth in order not to lose track. In this text we define steady-state errors quantitatively, analyze a system's steady-state error, and then design corrective action to reduce the steady-state error—our second analysis and design objective.

STABILITY

Discussion of transient response and steady-state error is moot if the system does not have *stability*. In order to explain stability, we start from the fact that the total response of a system is the sum of the *natural response* and the *forced response*. When you studied linear differential equations, you probably referred to these responses as the *homogeneous* and the *particular solutions*, respectively. Natural response describes the way the system dissipates or acquires energy. The form or nature of this response is dependent only on the system, not the input. On the other hand, the form or nature of the forced response is dependent on the input. Thus, for a *linear* system, we can write

$$\text{Total response} = \text{Natural response} + \text{Forced response} \qquad (1.1)^2$$

For a control system to be useful, the natural response must (1) eventually approach zero, thus leaving only the forced response, or (2) oscillate. In some systems, however, the natural response grows without bound rather than diminish to zero or oscillate.

---

[2] You may be confused by the words *transient* vs. *natural,* and *steady-state* vs. *forced.* If you look at Figure 1.2, you can see the transient and steady-state portions of the total response as indicated. The transient response is the sum of the natural and forced responses, while the natural response is large. If we plotted the natural response by itself, we would get a curve that is different from the transient portion of Figure 1.2. The steady-state response of Figure 1.2 is also the sum of the natural and forced responses, but the natural response is small. Thus, the transient and steady-state responses are what you actually see on the plot; the natural and forced responses are the underlying mathematical components of those responses.

Eventually, the natural response is so much greater than the forced response that the system is no longer controlled. This condition, called *instability,* could lead to self-destruction of the physical device if limit stops are not part of the design. For example, the elevator would crash through the floor or exit through the ceiling; an aircraft would go into an uncontrollable roll; or an antenna commanded to point to a target would rotate, line up with the target, but then begin to oscillate about the target with *growing* oscillations and *increasing* velocity until the motor or amplifiers reached their output limits or until the antenna was damaged structurally. A time plot of an unstable system would show a transient response that grows without bound and without any evidence of a steady-state response.

Control systems must be designed to be stable. That is, their natural response must decay to zero as time approaches infinity, or oscillate. In many systems the transient response you see on a time response plot can be directly related to the natural response. Thus, if the natural response decays to zero as time approaches infinity, the transient response will also die out, leaving only the forced response. If the system is stable, the proper transient response and steady-state error characteristics can be designed. Stability is our third analysis and design objective.

OTHER CONSIDERATIONS

The three main objectives of control system analysis and design have already been enumerated. However, other important considerations must be taken into account. For example, factors affecting hardware selection, such as motor sizing to fulfill power requirements and choice of sensors for accuracy, must be considered early in the design.

Finances are another consideration. Control system designers cannot create designs without considering their economic impact. Such considerations as budget allocations and competitive pricing must guide the engineer. For example, if your product is one of a kind, you may be able to create a design that uses more expensive components without appreciably increasing total cost. However, if your design will be used for many copies, slight increases in cost per copy can translate into many more dollars for your company to propose during contract bidding and to outlay before sales.

Another consideration is *robust* design. System parameters considered constant during the design for transient response, steady-state errors, and stability change over time when the actual system is built. Thus, the performance of the system also changes over time and will not be consistent with your design. Unfortunately, the relationship between parameter changes and their effect on performance is not linear. In some cases, even in the same system, changes in parameter values can lead to small or large changes in performance, depending on the system's nominal operating point and the type of design used. Thus, the engineer wants to create a robust design so that the system will not be sensitive to parameter changes. We discuss the concept of system sensitivity to parameter changes in Chapters 7 and 8. This concept, then, can be used to test a design for robustness.

CASE STUDY

Introduction to a Case Study

Now that our objectives are stated, how do we meet them? In this section we will look at an example of a feedback control system. The system introduced here will be used in subsequent chapters as a running case study to demonstrate the objectives of those chapters. A colored background like this will identify the case study section at the end of each chapter. Section 1.5, which follows this first case study, explores the design process that will help us build our system.

Antenna Azimuth: An Introduction to Position Control Systems

A position control system converts a position input command to a position output response. Position control systems find widespread applications in antennas, robot arms, and computer disk drives. The radio telescope antenna in Figure 1.8 is one example of a system that uses position control systems. In this section we will look in detail at an antenna azimuth position control system that could be used to position a radio telescope antenna. We will see how the system works and how we can effect changes in its performance. The discussion here will be on a qualitative level, with the objective of getting an intuitive feeling for the systems with which we will be dealing.

An antenna azimuth position control system is shown in Figure 1.9(*a*), with a more detailed layout and schematic in Figures 1.9(*b*) and 1.9(*c*), respectively. Figure 1.9(*d*) shows a *functional block diagram* of the system. The functions are shown above the blocks, and the required hardware is indicated inside the blocks. Parts of Figure 1.9 are repeated on the front endpapers for future reference.

The purpose of this system is to have the azimuth angle output of the antenna, $\theta_o(t)$, follow the input angle of the potentiometer, $\theta_i(t)$. Let us look at Figure 1.9(*d*) and

FIGURE 1.8 The search for extraterrestrial life is being carried out with radio antennas like the one pictured here. A radio antenna is an example of a system with position controls.

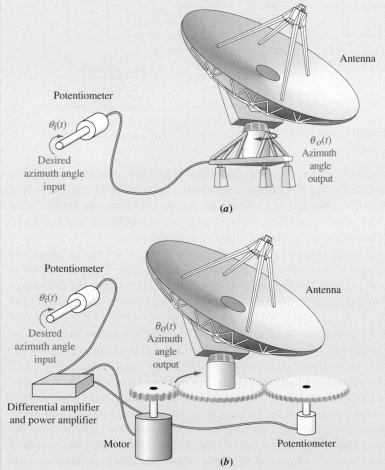

(*a*)

(*b*)

FIGURE 1.9 Antenna azimuth position control system: **a.** system concept; **b.** detailed layout (figure continues)

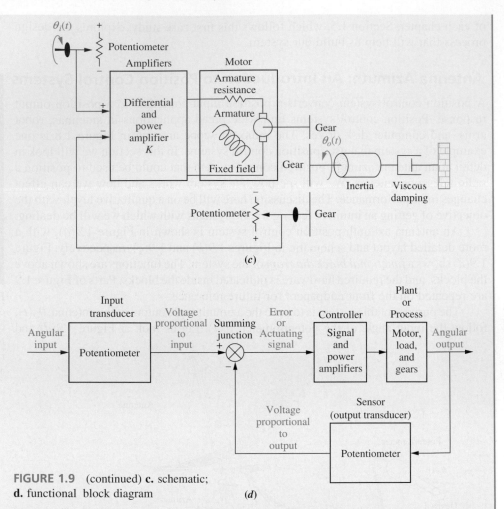

FIGURE 1.9   (continued) **c.** schematic;
d. functional block diagram   *(d)*

describe how this system works. The input command is an angular displacement. The potentiometer converts the angular displacement into a voltage. Similarly, the output angular displacement is converted to a voltage by the potentiometer in the feedback path. The signal and power amplifiers boost the difference between the input and output voltages. This amplified actuating signal drives the plant.

The system normally operates to drive the error to zero. When the input and output match, the error will be zero, and the motor will not turn. Thus, the motor is driven only when the output and the input do not match. The greater the difference between the input and the output, the larger the motor input voltage, and the faster the motor will turn.

If we increase the gain of the signal amplifier, will there be an increase in the steady-state value of the output? If the gain is increased, then for a given actuating signal, the motor will be driven harder. However, the motor will still stop when the actuating signal reaches zero, that is, when the output matches the input. The difference in the response, however, will be in the transients. Since the motor is driven harder, it turns faster toward its final position. Also, because of the increased speed, increased momentum could cause the motor to overshoot the final value and be forced by the system to return to the commanded position. Thus, the possibility exists for a transient response that consists of *damped oscillations* (that is, a sinusoidal response whose amplitude diminishes with

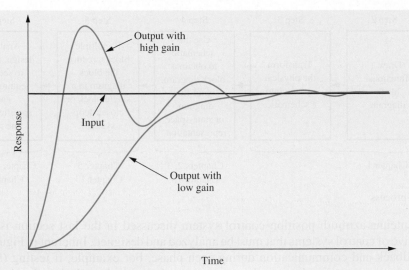

FIGURE 1.10 Response of a position control system, showing effect of high and low controller gain on the output response

time) about the steady-state value if the gain is high. The responses for low gain and high gain are shown in Figure 1.10.

We have discussed the transient response of the position control system. Let us now direct our attention to the steady-state position to see how closely the output matches the input after the transients disappear. Figure 1.10 shows zero error in the steady-state response; that is, after the transients have disappeared, the output position equals the commanded input position. In some systems the steady-state error will not be zero; for these systems a simple gain adjustment to regulate the transient response is either not effective or leads to a trade-off between the desired transient response and the desired steady-state accuracy.

To solve this problem, a controller with a dynamic response, such as an electrical filter, is used along with an amplifier. With this type of controller, it is possible to design both the required transient response and the required steady-state accuracy without the trade-off required by a simple setting of gain. However, the controller is now more complex. The filter in this case is called a compensator. Many systems also use dynamic elements in the feedback path along with the output transducer to improve system performance.

In summary, then, our design objectives and the system's performance revolve around the transient response, the steady-state error, and stability. Gain adjustments can affect performance and sometimes lead to trade-offs between the performance criteria. Compensators can often be designed to achieve performance specifications without the need for trade-offs. Now that we have stated our objectives and some of the methods available to meet those objectives, we describe the orderly progression that leads us to the final system design.

1.5 THE DESIGN PROCESS

In this section we establish an orderly sequence for the design of feedback control systems that will be followed as we progress through the rest of the book. Figure 1.11 shows the described process as well as the chapters in which the steps are discussed.

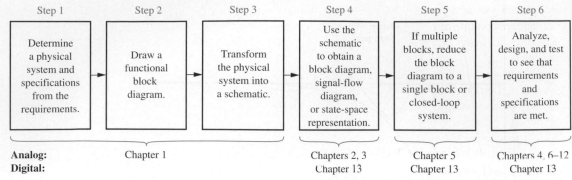

FIGURE 1.11   The control system design process

The antenna azimuth position control system discussed in the last section is representative of control systems that must be analyzed and designed. Inherent in Figure 1.11 is feedback and communication during each phase. For example, if testing (Step 6) shows that requirements have not been met, the system must be redesigned and retested. Sometimes requirements are conflicting and the design cannot be attained. In these cases, the requirements have to be respecified and the design process repeated. Let us now elaborate on each block of Figure 1.11.

STEP 1: TRANSFORM REQUIREMENTS INTO A PHYSICAL SYSTEM

We begin by transforming the requirements into a physical system. For example, in the antenna azimuth position control system, the requirements would state the desire to position the antenna from a remote location and describe such features as weight and physical dimensions. Using the requirements, design specifications, such as desired transient response and steady-state accuracy, are determined. Perhaps an overall concept, such as Figure 1.9(a), would result.

STEP 2: DRAW A FUNCTIONAL BLOCK DIAGRAM

The designer now translates a qualitative description of the system into a functional block diagram that describes the component parts of the system (that is, function and/or hardware) and shows their interconnection. Figure 1.9(d) is an example of a functional block diagram for the antenna azimuth position control system. It indicates functions such as input transducer and controller, as well as possible hardware descriptions such as amplifiers and motors. At this point the designer may produce a detailed layout of the system, such as that shown in Figure 1.9(b), from which the next phase of the analysis and design sequence, developing a schematic diagram, can be launched.

STEP 3: CREATE A SCHEMATIC

As we have seen, position control systems consist of electrical, mechanical, and electro-mechanical components. After producing the description of a physical system, the control systems engineer transforms the physical system into a schematic diagram. The control system designer can begin with the physical description, as contained in Figure 1.9(a), to derive a schematic. The engineer must make approximations about the system and neglect certain phenomena, or else the schematic will be unwieldy, making it difficult to extract a useful mathematical model during the next phase of the analysis and design sequence. The designer starts with a simple schematic representation and, at subsequent phases of the analysis and design sequence, checks the assumptions made about the physical system through analysis and computer simulation. If the schematic is too simple and does not adequately account for observed behavior, the control systems engineer adds phenomena to the schematic that were previously assumed negligible. A schematic diagram for the antenna azimuth position control system is shown in Figure 1.9(c).

When we draw the potentiometers, we make our first simplifying assumption by neglecting their friction or inertia. These mechanical characteristics yield a dynamic, rather than an instantaneous, response in the output voltage. We assume that these mechanical effects are negligible and that the voltage across a potentiometer changes instantaneously as the potentiometer shaft turns.

A differential amplifier and a power amplifier are used as the controller to yield gain and power amplification, respectively, to drive the motor. Again, we assume that the dynamics of the amplifiers are rapid compared to the response time of the motor; thus, we model them as a pure gain, K.

A dc motor and equivalent load produce the output angular displacement. The speed of the motor is proportional to the voltage applied to the motor's *armature circuit*. Both inductance and resistance are part of the armature circuit. In showing just the armature resistance in Figure 1.9(c), we assume the effect of the armature inductance is negligible for a dc motor.

The designer makes further assumptions about the load. The load consists of a rotating mass and bearing friction. Thus, the model consists of *inertia* and *viscous damping* whose resistive torque increases with speed, as in an automobile's shock absorber or a screen door damper.

The decisions made in developing the schematic stem from knowledge of the physical system, the physical laws governing the system's behavior, and *practical experience*. These decisions are not easy; however, as you acquire more design experience, you will gain the insight required for this difficult task.

STEP 4: DEVELOP A MATHEMATICAL MODEL (BLOCK DIAGRAM)

Once the schematic is drawn, the designer uses physical laws, such as Kirchhoff's laws for electrical networks and Newton's law for mechanical systems, along with simplifying assumptions, to model the system mathematically. These laws are

Kirchhoff's voltage law The sum of voltages around a closed path equals zero.

Kirchhoff's current law The sum of electric currents flowing from a node equals zero.

Newton's laws The sum of forces on a body equals zero;[3] the sum of moments on a body equals zero.

Kirchhoff's and Newton's laws lead to mathematical models that describe the relationship between the input and output of dynamic systems. One such model is the *linear, time-invariant differential equation*, Eq. (1.2):

$$\frac{d^m c(t)}{dt^n} + d_{n-1}\frac{d^{m-1}c(t)}{dt^{n-1}} + \cdots + d_0 c(t) = b_m\frac{d^m r(t)}{dt^m} + b_{m-1}\frac{d^{m-1}r(t)}{dt^{m-1}} + \cdots + b_0 r(t)$$

$$(1.2)^4$$

---

[3] Alternately, Σ forces $= Ma$. In this text the force, Ma, will be brought to the left-hand side of the equation to yield Σ forces $= 0$ (D'Alembert's principle). We can then have a consistent analogy between force and voltage, and Kirchhoff's and Newton's laws (that is, Σ forces $= 0$; Σ voltages $= 0$).

[4] The right-hand side of Eq. (1.2) indicates differentiation of the input, $r(t)$. In physical systems, differentiation of the input introduces noise. In Chapters 3 and 5 we show implementations and interpretations of Eq. (1.2) that do not require differentiation of the input.

Many systems can be approximately described by this equation, which relates the output, $c(t)$, to the input, $r(t)$, by way of the system parameters, a_i and b_j. We assume the reader is familiar with differential equations. Problems and a bibliography are provided at the end of the chapter for you to review this subject.

Simplifying assumptions made in the process of obtaining a mathematical model usually leads to a low-order form of Eq. (1.2). Without the assumptions the system model could be of high order or described with nonlinear, time-varying, or partial differential equations. These equations complicate the design process and reduce the designer's insight. Of course, all assumptions must be checked and all simplifications justified through analysis or testing. If the assumptions for simplification cannot be justified, then the model cannot be simplified. We examine some of these simplifying assumptions in Chapter 2.

In addition to the differential equation, the *transfer function* is another way of mathematically modeling a system. The model is derived from the linear, time-invariant differential equation using what we call the *Laplace transform.* Although the transfer function can be used only for linear systems, it yields more intuitive information than the differential equation. We will be able to change system parameters and rapidly sense the effect of these changes on the system response. The transfer function is also useful in modeling the interconnection of subsystems by forming a block diagram similar to Figure 1.9(d) but with a mathematical function inside each block.

Still another model is the *state-space representation.* One advantage of state-space methods is that they can also be used for systems that cannot be described by linear differential equations. Further, state-space methods are used to model systems for simulation on the digital computer. Basically, this representation turns an nth-order differential equation into n simultaneous first-order differential equations. Let this description suffice for now; we describe this approach in more detail in Chapter 3.

Finally, we should mention that to produce the mathematical model for a system, we require knowledge of the parameter values, such as equivalent resistance, inductance, mass, and damping, which is often not easy to obtain. Analysis, measurements, or specifications from vendors are sources that the control systems engineer may use to obtain the parameters.

STEP 5: REDUCE THE BLOCK DIAGRAM

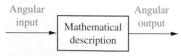

Angular input → Mathematical description → Angular output

FIGURE 1.12 Equivalent block diagram for the antenna azimuth position control system

Subsystem models are interconnected to form block diagrams of larger systems, as in Figure 1.9(d), where each block has a mathematical description. Notice that many signals, such as proportional voltages and error, are internal to the system. There are also two signals—angular input and angular output—that are external to the system. In order to evaluate system response in this example, we need to reduce this large system's block diagram to a single block with a mathematical description that represents the system from its input to its output, as shown in Figure 1.12. Once the block diagram is reduced, we are ready to analyze and design the system.

STEP 6: ANALYZE AND DESIGN

The next phase of the process, following block diagram reduction, is analysis and design. If you are interested only in the performance of an individual subsystem, you can skip the block diagram reduction and move immediately into analysis and design. In this phase the engineer analyzes the system to see if the response specifications and performance requirements can be met by simple adjustments of system parameters. If specifications cannot be met, the designer then designs additional hardware in order to effect a desired performance.

TABLE 1.1   **Test waveforms used in control systems**

Input	Function	Description	Sketch	Use
Impulse	$\delta(t)$	$\delta(t) = \infty$ for $0- < t < 0+$ $= 0$ elsewhere $\int_{0-}^{0+} \delta(t)\,dt = 1$		Transient response Modeling
Step	$u(t)$	$u(t) = 1$ for $t > 0$ $= 0$ for $t < 0$		Transient response Steady-state error
Ramp	$tu(t)$	$tu(t) = t$ for $t \geq 0$ $= 0$ elsewhere		Steady-state error
Parabola	$\frac{1}{2}t^2 u(t)$	$\frac{1}{2}t^2 u(t) = \frac{1}{2}t^2$ for $t \geq 0$ $= 0$ elsewhere		Steady-state error
Sinusoid	$\sin \omega t$			Transient response Modeling Steady-state error

Test input signals are used, both analytically and during testing, to verify the design. It is neither necessarily practical nor illuminating to choose complicated input signals to analyze a system's performance. Thus, the engineer usually selects standard test inputs. These inputs are impulses, steps, ramps, parabolas, and sinusoids, as shown in Table 1.1.

An *impulse* is infinite at $t = 0$ and zero elsewhere. The area under the unit impulse is 1. An approximation of this type of waveform is used to place initial energy into a system so that the response due to that initial energy is only the transient response of a system. From this response the designer can derive a mathematical model of the system.

A *step* input represents a *constant command,* such as position, velocity, or acceleration. Typically, the step input command is of the same form as the output. For example, if the system's output is position, as it is for the antenna azimuth position control system, the step input represents a desired position, and the output represents the actual position. If the system's output is velocity, as is the spindle speed for a video disc player, the step input represents a constant desired speed, and the output represents the actual speed. The designer uses step inputs because both the transient response and the steady-state response are clearly visible and can be evaluated.

The *ramp* input represents a *linearly increasing command.* For example, if the system's output is position, the input ramp represents a linearly increasing position, such as that found when tracking a satellite moving across the sky at constant speed. If the system's output is velocity, the input ramp represents a linearly increasing velocity. The response to an input ramp test signal yields additional information about the steady-state error. The previous discussion can be extended to *parabolic* inputs, which are also used to evaluate a system's steady-state error.

Sinusoidal inputs can also be used to test a physical system to arrive at a mathematical model. We discuss the use of this waveform in detail in Chapters 10 and 11.

We conclude that one of the basic analysis and design requirements is to evaluate the time response of a system for a given input. Throughout the book you will learn numerous methods for accomplishing this goal.

The control systems engineer must take into consideration other characteristics about feedback control systems. For example, control system behavior is altered by fluctuations in component values or system parameters. These variations can be caused by temperature, pressure, or other environmental changes. Systems must be built so that expected fluctuations do not degrade performance beyond specified bounds. A *sensitivity* analysis can yield the percentage of change in a specification as a function of a change in a system parameter. One of the designer's goals, then, is to build a system with minimum sensitivity over an expected range of environmental changes.

In this section we looked at some control systems analysis and design considerations. We saw that the designer is concerned about transient response, steady-state error, stability, and sensitivity. The text pointed out that although the basis of evaluating system performance is the differential equation, other methods, such as transfer functions and state space, will be used. The advantages of these new techniques over differential equations will become apparent as we discuss them in later chapters.

1.6 COMPUTER-AIDED DESIGN

Now that we have discussed the analysis and design sequence, let us discuss the use of the computer as a computational tool in this sequence. The computer plays an important role in the design of modern control systems. In the past, control system design was labor intensive. Many of the tools we use today were implemented through hand calculations or, at best, using plastic graphical aid tools. The process was slow, and the results not always accurate. Large mainframe computers were then used to simulate the designs.

Today we are fortunate to have computers and software that remove the drudgery from the task. At our own desktop computers, we can perform analysis, design, and simulation with one program. With the ability to simulate a design rapidly, we can easily make changes and immediately test a new design. We can play what-if games and try alternate solutions to see if they yield better results, such as reduced sensitivity to parameter changes. We can include nonlinearities and other effects and test our models for accuracy.

MATLAB

The computer is an integral part of modern control system design, and many computational tools are available for your use. In this book we use MATLAB and the MATLAB Control System Toolbox, which expands MATLAB to include control system–specific commands. In addition, presented are several MATLAB enhancements that give added functionality to MATLAB and the Control Systems Toolbox. Included are (1) Simulink, which uses a graphical user interface (GUI); (2) the LTI Viewer, which permits measurements to be made directly from time and frequency response curves; (3) the SISO Design Tool, a convenient and intuitive analysis and design tool; and (4) the Symbolic Math Toolbox, which saves labor when making symbolic calculations required in control system analysis and design. Some of these enhancements may require additional software available from The MathWorks, Inc.

MATLAB is presented as an alternate method of solving control system problems. You are encouraged to solve problems first by hand and then by MATLAB so that insight is not lost through mechanized use of computer programs. To this end, many examples throughout the book are solved by hand, followed by suggested use of MATLAB.

As an enticement to begin using MATLAB, simple program statements that you can try are suggested throughout the chapters at appropriate locations. Throughout the book various icons appear in the margin to identify MATLAB references that direct you to the proper program in the proper appendix and tell you what you will learn. Selected end-of-chapter problems and Case Study Challenges to be solved using MATLAB have also been marked with appropriate icons. The following list itemizes the specific components of MATLAB used in this book, the icon used to identify each, and the appendix in which a description can be found:

MATLAB/Control System Toolbox tutorials and code are found in Appendix B and identified in the text with the MATLAB icon shown in the margin.

Simulink tutorials and diagrams are found in Appendix C and identified in the text with the Simulink icon shown in the margin.

MATLAB GUI tools, tutorials, and examples are in Appendix D at www.wiley.com/college/nise and identified in the text with the GUI Tool icon shown in the margin. These tools consist of the LTI Viewer and the SISO Design Tool.

Symbolic Math Toolbox tutorials and code are found in Appendix E at www.wiley.com/college/nise and identified in the text with the Symbolic Math icon shown in the margin.

MATLAB code itself is not platform specific. The same code runs on PCs and workstations that support MATLAB. Although there are differences in installing and managing MATLAB files, we do not address them in this book. Also, there are many more commands in MATLAB and the MATLAB toolboxes than are covered in the appendixes. Please explore the bibliographies at the end of the applicable appendixes to find out more about MATLAB file management and MATLAB instructions not covered in this textbook.

You are encouraged to use computational aids throughout this book. Those not using MATLAB should consult Appendix G at www.wiley.com/college/nise for a discussion of other alternatives. Now that we have introduced control systems to you and established a need for computational aids to perform analysis and design, we will conclude with a discussion of your career as a control systems engineer and look at the opportunities and challenges that await you.

1.7 THE CONTROL SYSTEMS ENGINEER

Control systems engineering is an exciting field in which to apply your engineering talents, because it cuts across numerous disciplines and numerous functions within those disciplines. The control engineer can be found at the top level of large projects, engaged at the conceptual phase in determining or implementing overall system requirements. These requirements include total system performance specifications, subsystem functions, and the interconnection of these functions, including interface requirements, hardware and software design, and test plans and procedures.

Many engineers are engaged in only one area, such as circuit design or software development. However, as a control systems engineer, you may find yourself working in a board arena and interacting with people from numerous branches of engineering and the sciences. For example, if you are working on a biological system, you will need to interact with colleagues in the biological sciences, mechanical engineering, electrical engineering, and computer engineering, not to mention mathematics and physics. You will be working with these engineers at all levels of project development from concept through design and, finally, testing. At the design level the control systems engineer can be performing hardware selection, design, and interface, including total subsystem design to meet specified requirements. The control engineer can be working with sensors and motors as well as electronic, pneumatic, and hydraulic circuits.

The space shuttle provides another example of the diversity required of the systems engineer. In the previous section we showed that the space shuttle's control systems cut across many branches of science: orbital mechanics and propulsion, aerodynamics, electrical engineering, and mechanical engineering. Whether or not you work in the space program, as a control systems engineer you will apply broad-based knowledge to the solution of engineering control problems. You will have the opportunity to expand your engineering horizons beyond your university curriculum.

You are now aware of future opportunities. But for now, what advantages does this course offer to a student of control systems (other than the fact that you need it to graduate)? Engineering curricula tend to emphasize *bottom-up* design. That is, you start from the components, develop circuits, and then assemble a product. In *top-down* design, a high-level picture of the requirements is first formulated; then the functions and hardware required to implement the system are determined. You will be able to take a top-down systems approach as a result of this course.

A major reason for not teaching top-down design throughout the curriculum is the high level of mathematics initially required for the systems approach. For example, control systems theory, which requires differential equations, could not be taught as a lower-division course. However, while progressing through bottom-up design courses, it is difficult to see how such design fits logically into the large picture of the product development cycle.

After completing this control systems course, you will be able to stand back and see how your previous studies fit into the large picture. Your amplifier course or vibrations course will take on new meaning as you begin to see the role the design work plays as part of product development. For example, as engineers, we want to describe the physical world mathematically so that we can create systems that will benefit humanity. You will find that you have indeed acquired, through your previous courses, the ability to model physical systems mathematically, although at the time you might not have understood where in the product development cycle the modeling fits. This course will clarify the analysis and design procedures and show you how the knowledge you acquired fits into the total picture of system design.

Understanding control systems enables students from all branches of engineering to speak a common language and develop an appreciation and working knowledge of the other branches. You will find that there really is not much difference between the branches of engineering as far as the goals and applications are concerned. As you study control systems, you will see this commonality.

SUMMARY

Control systems contribute to every aspect of modern society. In our homes we find them in everything from toasters to heating systems to VCRs. Control systems also have widespread applications in science and industry, from steering ships and planes to guiding missiles and the space shuttle. Control systems also exist naturally; our bodies contain numerous control systems. Even economic and psychological system representations have been proposed based on control system theory. Control systems are used where power gain, remote control, or conversion of the form of the input is required.

A control system has an *input,* a *process,* and an *output.* Control systems can be *open loop* or *closed loop.* Open-loop systems do not monitor or correct the output for disturbances; however, they are simpler and less expensive than closed-loop systems. Closed-loop systems monitor the output and compare it to the input. If an error is detected, the system corrects the output and hence corrects the effects of disturbances.

Control systems analysis and design focuses on three primary objectives:

1. Producing the desired transient response
2. Reducing steady-state errors
3. Achieving stability

A system must be stable in order to produce the proper transient and steady-state response. Transient response is important because it affects the speed of the system and influences human patience and comfort, not to mention mechanical stress. Steady-state response determines the accuracy of the control system; it governs how closely the output matches the desired response.

The design of a control system follows these steps:

Step 1 Determine a physical system and specifications from requirements.
Step 2 Draw a functional block diagram.
Step 3 Represent the physical system as a schematic.
Step 4 Use the schematic to obtain a mathematical model, such as a block diagram.
Step 5 Reduce the block diagram.
Step 6 Analyze and design the system to meet specified requirements and specifications that include stability, transient response, and steady-state performance.

In the next chapter we continue through the analysis and design sequence and learn how to use the schematic to obtain a mathematical model.

REVIEW QUESTIONS

1. Name three applications for feedback control systems.
2. Name three reasons for using feedback control systems and at least one reason for not using them.

3. Give three examples of open-loop systems.

4. Functionally, how do closed-loop systems differ from open-loop systems?

5. State one condition under which the error signal of a feedback control system would not be the difference between the input and the output.

6. If the error signal is not the difference between input and output, by what general name can we describe the error signal?

7. Name two advantages of having a computer in the loop.

8. Name the three major design criteria for control systems.

9. Name the two parts of a system's response.

10. Physically, what happens to a system that is unstable?

11. Instability is attributable to what part of the total response?

12. Describe a typical control system analysis task.

13. Describe a typical control system design task.

14. Adjustments of the forward path gain can cause changes in the transient response. True or false?

15. Name three approaches to the mathematical modeling of control systems.

16. Briefly describe each of your answers to Question 15.

PROBLEMS

1. A variable resistor, called a *potentiometer*, is shown in Figure P1.1. The resistance is varied by moving a wiper arm along a fixed resistance. The resistance from A to C is fixed, but the resistance from B to C varies with the position of the wiper arm. If it takes 10 turns to move the wiper arm from A to C, draw a block diagram of the potentiometer showing the input variable, the output variable, and (inside the block) the gain, which is a constant and is the amount by which the input is multiplied to obtain the output. [Section 1.4: Introduction to a Case Study]

WileyPLUS

Control Solutions

2. An aircraft's attitude varies in roll, pitch, and yaw as defined in Figure P1.2. Draw a functional block diagram for a closed-loop system that stabilizes the roll as follows: The system measures the actual roll

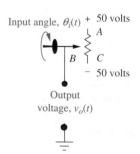

Input angle, $\theta_i(t)$

50 volts

50 volts

Output voltage, $v_o(t)$

Figure P1.1 Potentiometer

[5] The Wiley PLUS icon identifies interactive worked examples and problems. These problems, developed by JustAsk, are worked in detail and offer explanations of every facet of the solution. The identified examples and problems can be accessed at www.wiley.com/college/nise.

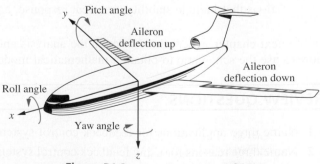

Figure P1.2 Aircraft attitude defined

angle with a gyro and compares the actual roll angle with the desired roll angle. The ailerons respond to the roll-angle error by undergoing an angular deflection. The aircraft responds to this angular deflection, producing a roll angle rate. Identify the input and output transducers, the controller, and the plant. Further, identify the nature of each signal. [Section 1.4: Introduction to a Case Study]

3. Many processes operate on rolled material that moves from a supply reel to a take-up reel. Typically, these systems, called *winders,* control the material so that it travels at a constant velocity. Besides velocity, complex winders also control tension, compensate for roll inertia while accelerating or decelerating, and regulate acceleration due to sudden changes. A winder is shown in Figure P1.3. The force transducer measures

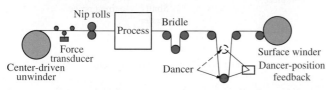

Figure P1.3 Winder

tension; the winder pulls against the nip rolls, which provide an opposing force; and the bridle provides slip. In order to compensate for changes in speed, the material is looped around a *dancer.* The loop prevents rapid changes from causing excessive slack or damaging the material. If the dancer position is sensed by a potentiometer or other device, speed variations due to buildup on the take-up reel or other causes can be controlled by comparing the potentiometer voltage to the commanded speed. The system then corrects the speed and resets the dancer to the desired position (*Ayers, 1988*). Draw a functional block diagram for the speed control system, showing each component and signal. [Section 1.4: Introduction to a Case Study]

4. In a nuclear power generating plant, heat from a reactor is used to generate steam for turbines. The rate of the fission reaction determines the amount of heat generated, and this rate is controlled by rods inserted into the radioactive core. The rods regulate the flow of neutrons. If the rods are lowered into the core, the rate of fission will diminish; if the rods are raised, the fission rate will increase. By automatically controlling the position of the rods, the amount of heat generated by the reactor can be regulated. Draw a

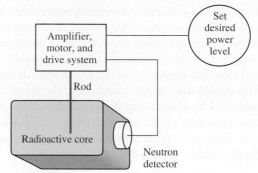

Figure P1.4 Control of a nuclear reactor

functional block diagram for the nuclear reactor control system shown in Figure P1.4. Show all blocks and signals. [Section 1.4: Introduction to a Case Study]

5. A university wants to establish a control system model that represents the student population as an output, with the desired student population as an input. The administration determines the rate of admissions by comparing the current and desired student populations. The admissions office then uses this rate to admit students. Draw a functional block diagram showing the administration and the admissions office as blocks of the system. Also show the following signals: the desired student population, the actual student population, the desired student rate as determined by the administration, the actual student rate as generated by the admissions office, the dropout rate, and the net rate of influx. [Section 1.4: Introduction to a Case Study]

6. We can build a control system that will automatically adjust a motorcycle's radio volume as the noise generated by the motorcycle changes. The noise generated by the motorcycle increases with speed. As the noise increases, the system increases the volume of the radio. Assume that the amount of noise can be represented by a voltage generated by the speedometer cable, and the volume of the radio is controlled by a dc voltage (*Hogan, 1988*). If the dc voltage represents the desired volume disturbed by the motorcycle noise, draw the functional block diagram of the automatic volume control system, showing the input transducer, the volume control circuit, and the speed transducer as blocks. Also show the following signals: the desired volume as an input, the actual volume as an output, and voltages representing speed, desired volume, and actual volume. [Section 1.4: Introduction to a Case Study]

7. Your bathtub at home is a control system that keeps the water level constant. A constant flow from the tap yields a constant water level, because the flow rate through the drain increases as the water level increases, and decreases as the water level decreases. After equilibrium has been reached, the level can be controlled by controlling the input flow rate. A low input flow rate yields a lower level, while a higher input flow rate yields a higher level. [Section 1.4: Introduction to a Case Study]

a. Sketch a control system that uses this principle to precisely control the fluid level in a tank. Show the intake and drain valves, the tank, any sensors and transducers, and the interconnection of all components.

b. Draw a functional block diagram of the system, identifying the input and output signals of each block.

8. A dynamometer is a device used to measure torque and speed and to vary the load on rotating devices. The dynamometer operates as follows to control the amount of torque: A hydraulic actuator attached to the axle presses a tire against a rotating flywheel. The greater the displacement of the actuator, the more force that is applied to the rotating flywheel. A strain gage load cell senses the force. The displacement of the actuator is controlled by an electrically operated valve whose displacement regulates fluid flowing into the actuator (*D'Souza, 1988*). Draw a functional block diagram of a closed-loop system that uses the described dynamometer to regulate the force against the tire during testing. Show all signals and systems. Include amplifiers that power the valve, the valve, the actuator and load, and the tire. [Section 1.4: Introduction to a Case Study]

9. During a medical operation an anesthesiologist controls the depth of unconsciousness by controlling the concentration of isoflurane in a vaporized mixture with oxygen and nitrous oxide. The depth of anesthesia is measured by the patient's blood pressure. The anesthesiologist also regulates ventilation, fluid balance, and the administration of other drugs. In order to free the anesthesiologist to devote more time to the latter tasks, and in the interest of the patient's safety, we wish to automate the depth of anesthesia by automating the control of isoflurane concentration. Draw a functional block diagram of the system showing pertinent signals and subsystems

(*Meier, 1992*). [Section 1.4: Introduction to a Case Study]

10. The vertical position, *x(t)*, of the grinding wheel shown in Figure P1.5 is controlled by a closed-loop system. The input to the system is the desired depth of grind, and the output is the actual depth of grind. The

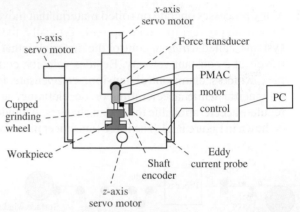

Figure P1.5 Grinder system

difference between the desired depth and the actual depth drives the motor, resulting in a force applied to the work. This force results in a feed velocity for the grinding wheel (*Jenkins, 1997*). Draw a closed-loop functional block diagram for the grinding process, showing the input, output, force, and grinder feed rate. [Section 1.4: Introduction to a Case Study]

11. A high-speed proportional solenoid valve is shown in Figure P1.6. A voltage proportional to the desired position of the spool is applied to the coil. The resulting magnetic field produced by the current in the coil causes the armature to move. A push pin connected to the armature moves the spool. A linear voltage differential transformer (LVDT) that outputs a voltage proportional to displacement senses the spool's position.

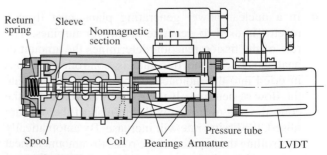

Figure P1.6 High-speed proportional solenoid valve

This voltage can be used in a feedback path to implement closed-loop operation (*Vaughan, 1996*). Draw a functional block diagram of the valve, showing input and output positions, coil voltage, coil current, and spool force. [Section 1.4: Introduction to a Case Study]

12. The human eye has a biological control system that varies the pupil diameter to maintain constant light intensity to the retina. As the light intensity increases, the optical nerve sends a signal to the brain, which commands internal eye muscles to decrease the pupil's eye diameter. When the light intensity decreases, the pupil diameter increases.

    a. Draw a functional block diagram of the light-pupil system indicating the input, output, and intermediate signals; the sensor; the controller; and the actuator. [Section 1.4: Introduction to a Case Study]

    b. Under normal conditions the incident light will be larger than the pupil, as shown in Figure P1.7(*a*). If the incident light is smaller than the diameter of the pupil as shown in Figure P1.7(*b*), the feedback path is broken (*Bechhoefer, 2005*). Modify your block diagram from Part **a** to show where the loop is broken. What will happen if the narrow beam of light varies in intensity, say in a sinusoidal fashion?

    c. It has been found (*Bechhoefer, 2005*) that it takes the pupil about 300 milliseconds to react to a change in the incident light. If light shines off center to the retina as shown in Figure P1.7(*c*), describe the response of the pupil with delay present and then without delay present.

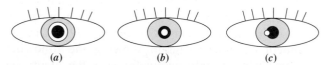

(*a*)	(*b*)	(*c*)

Figure P1.7 Pupil is shown black; light beam is shown white. **a.** Light beam diameter is larger than pupil. **b.** Light beam diameter is smaller than pupil. **c.** Narrow light beam is illuminated at pupil's edge

13. A Segway®[6] Personal Transporter (PT) (Figure P1.8) is a two-wheeled vehicle in which the human operator stands vertically on a platform. As the driver leans left, right, forward, or backward, a set of sensitive gyroscopic sensors sense the desired input. These signals are fed to a computer that amplifies them and commands motors to propel the vehicle in the

[6]Segment is a registered trademark of Segway, Inc. in the United States and/ or other countries.

Figure P1.8 The Segway Personal Transporter (PT)

desired direction. One very important feature of the HT is its safety: The system will maintain its vertical position within a specified angle despite road disturbances, such as uphills and downhills or even if the operator over-leans in any direction. Draw a functional block diagram of the HT system that keeps the system in a vertical position. Indicate the input and output signals, intermediate signals, and main subsystems. (http://segway.com)

14. In humans, hormone levels, alertness, and core body temperature are synchronized through a 24-hour circadian cycle. Daytime alertness is at its best when sleep/wake cycles are in synch with the circadian cycle. Thus alertness can be easily affected with a distributed work schedule, such as the one to which astronauts are subjected. It has been shown that the human circadian cycle can be delayed or advanced through light stimulus. To ensure optimal alertness, a system is designed to track astronauts' circadian cycles and increase the quality of sleep during missions. Core body temperature can be used as an indicator of the circadian cycle. A computer model with optimum circadian body temperature variations can be compared to an astronaut's body temperatures. Whenever a difference is detected, the astronaut is subjected to a light stimulus to advance or delay the astronaut's circadian cycle (*Mott, 2003*). Draw a functional block diagram of the system. Indicate the input and output signals, intermediate signals, and main subsystems.

15. Given the electric network shown in Figure P1.9, [Review]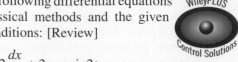

    a. Write the differential equation for the network if $v(t) = u(t)$, a unit step.

    b. Solve the differential equation for the current, $i(t)$, if there is no initial energy in the network.

    c. Make a plot of your solution if $R/L = 1$.

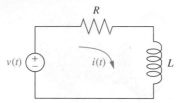

Figure P1.9 *RL* network

16. Repeat Problem 15 using the network shown in Figure P1.10. Assume $R = 1\,\Omega, L = 0.5\,\text{H}$, and $1/LC = 30$. [Review]

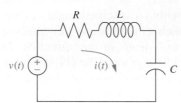

Figure P1.10 *RLC* network

17. Solve the following differential equations using classical methods. Assume zero initial conditions. [Review]

    a. $\dfrac{dx}{dt} + 7x = 5\cos 2t$

    b. $\dfrac{d^2x}{dt^2} + 6\dfrac{dx}{dt} + 8x = 5\sin 3t$

    c. $\dfrac{d^2x}{dt^2} + 8\dfrac{dx}{dt} + 25x = 10u(t)$

18. Solve the following differential equations using classical methods and the given initial conditions: [Review]

    a. $\dfrac{d^2x}{dt^2} + 2\dfrac{dx}{dt} + 2x = \sin 2t$

    $x(0) = 2;\quad \dfrac{dx}{dt}(0) = -3$

    b. $\dfrac{d^2x}{dt^2} + 2\dfrac{dx}{dt} + x = 5e^{-2t} + t$

    $x(0) = 2;\quad \dfrac{dx}{dt}(0) = 1$

    c. $\dfrac{d^2x}{dt^2} + 4x = t^2$

    $x(0) = 1;\quad \dfrac{dx}{dt}(0) = 2$

Progressive Analysis and Design Problems

19. **High-speed rail pantograph.** Some high-speed rail systems are powered by electricity supplied to a pantograph on the train's roof from a catenary overhead, as shown in Figure P1.11. The force applied by the pantograph to the catenary is regulated to avoid loss of contact due to excessive transient motion. A proposed method to regulate the force uses a closed-loop feedback system, whereby a force, F_{up}, is applied to the bottom of the pantograph, resulting in an output force applied to the catenary at the top. The contact between the head of the pantograph and the catenary is represented by a spring. The output force is proportional to the displacement of this spring, which is the difference between the catenary and pantograph head vertical positions (*O'Connor, 1997*). Draw a functional block diagram showing the following signals: the desired output force as the input; the force, F_{up}, applied to the bottom of the pantograph; the difference in displacement between the catenary

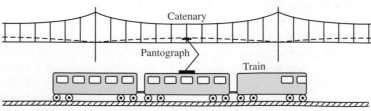

Figure P1.11 High-speed rail system showing pantograph and catenary

and pantograph head; and the output contact force. Also, show blocks representing the input transducer, controller, actuator generating F_{up}, pantograph dynamics, spring described above, and output sensor. All forces and displacements are measured from equilibrium.

20. **Contol of HIV/AIDS.** As of 2005 the number of people living worldwide with Human Immunodeficiency Virus/Acquired Immune Deficiency Syndrome (HIV/AIDS) was estimated at 40 million, with 5 million new infections per year and 3 million deaths due to the disease (*UNAIDS, 2005*). Currently there is no known cure for the disease, and the HIV cannot be completely eliminated in an infected individual. Drug combinations can be used to maintain the virus numbers at low levels, which helps prevent AIDS from developing. A common treatment for HIV is the administration of two types of drugs: reverse transcriptase inhibitors (RTIs) and protease inhibitors (PIs). The amount in which each of these drugs is administered is varied according to the amount of HIV viruses in the body (*Craig, 2004*). Draw a block diagram of a feedback system designed to control the amount of HIV viruses in an infected person. The plant input variables are the amount of RTIs and PIs dispensed. Show blocks representing the controller, the system under control, and the transducers. Label the corresponding variables at the input and output of every block.

BIBLIOGRAPHY

Ayers, J. Taking the Mystery out of Winder Controls. *Power Transmission Design*, April 1988, pp. 27–34.

Bahill, A. T. *Bioengineering: Biomedical, Medical, and Clinical Engineering*. Prentice Hall, Englewood Cliffs, NJ, 1981.

Bechhoefer, J. Feedback for Physicists: A Tutorial Essay on Control. To appear in *Review of Modern Physics,* July 2005, pp. 42–45. Also available at http://www.sfu.ca/chaos/Publications/papers/RMP_feedback.pdf.

Bennett, S. *A History of Control Engineering, 1800–1930*. Peter Peregrinus, Stevenage, UK, 1979.

Bode, H. W. *Network Analysis and Feedback Amplifier Design*. Van Nostrand, Princeton, NJ, 1945.

Cannon, R. H., Jr. *Dynamics of Physical Systems*. McGraw-Hill, New York, 1967.

Craig, I. K., Xia, X., and Venter, J. W. Introducing HIV/AIDS Education into the Electrical Engineering Curriculum at the University of Pretoria. *IEEE Transactions on Education*, vol. 47, no. 1, February 2004, pp. 65–73.

D'Azzo, J. J., and Houpis, C. H. *Feedback Control System Analysis and Synthesis*, 2d ed. McGraw-Hill, New York, 1966.

Doebelin, E. O. *Measurement Systems Application and Design*, 4th ed. McGraw-Hill, New York, 1990.

Dorf, R. C. *Modern Control Systems*, 5th ed. Addison-Wesley, Reading, MA, 1989.

D'Souza, A. F. *Design of Control Systems*. Prentice Hall, Englewood Cliffs, NJ, 1988.

Franklin, G. F., Powell, J. D., and Emami-Naeini, A. *Feedback Control of Dynamic Systems*. Addison-Wesley, Reading, MA, 1986.

Heller, H. C., Crawshaw, L. I., and Hammel, H. T. The Thermostat of Vertebrate Animals. *Scientific American*, August 1978, pp. 102–113.

Hogan, B. J. As Motorcycle's Speed Changes, Circuit Adjusts Radio's Volume. *Design News*, 18 August 1988, pp. 118–119.

Hostetter, G. H., Savant, C. J., Jr., and Stefani, R. T. *Design of Feedback Control Systems*, 2d ed. Saunders College Publishing, New York, 1989.

Jenkins, H. E., Kurfess, T. R., and Ludwick, S. J. Determination of a Dynamic Grinding Model. *Journal of Dynamic Systems, Measurements, and Control*, vol. 119, June 1997, pp. 289–293.

Klapper, J., and Frankle, J. T. *Phase-Locked and Frequency-Feedback Systems*. Academic Press, New York, 1972.

Martin, R. H., Jr. *Elementary Differential Equations with Boundary Value Problems*. McGraw-Hill, New York, 1984.

Mayr, O. The Origins of Feedback Control. *Scientific American*, October 1970, pp. 110–118.

Mayr, O. *The Origins of Feedback Control*. MIT Press, Cambridge, MA, 1970.

Meier, R., Nieuwland, J., Zbinden, A. M., and Hacisalihzade, S. S. Fuzzy Logic Control of Blood Pressure during Anesthesia. *IEEE Control Systems*, December 1992, pp. 12–17.

Mott C. et al. *Modifying the Human Circadian Pacemaker Using Model-Based Predictive Control.* Proceedings of the American Control Conference. Denver, CO, June 2003, pp. 453–458.

Novosad, J. P. *Systems, Modeling, and Decision Making.* Kendall/Hunt, Dubuque, IA, 1982.

Nyquist, H. Regeneration Theory. *Bell System Technical Journal*, January 1932.

O'Connor, D. N., Eppinger, S. D., Seering, W. P., and Wormly, D. N. Active Control of a High-Speed Pantograph. *Journal of Dynamic Systems, Measurements, and Control*, vol. 119, March 1997, pp. 1–4.

Ogata, K. *Modern Control Engineering*, 2d ed. Prentice Hall, Englewood Cliffs, NJ, 1990.

Rockwell International. *Space Shuttle Transportation System,* 1984 (press information).

Shaw, D. A., and Turnbull, G. A. Modern Thickness Control for a Generation III Hot Strip Mill. *The International Steel Rolling Conference—The Science & Technology of Flat Rolling*, vol. 1. Association Technique de la Siderurgie Francaise, Deauville, France, 1–3 June 1987.

UNAIDS. *AIDS Epidemic Update.* World Health Organization, December 2005. Available at http//www.unaids.org/Epi2005/doc/EPIupdate2005_pdf_en/epi-update2005_en.pdf. Accessed January 1, 2006.

Vaughan, N. D., and Gamble, J. B. The Modeling and Simulation of a Proportional Solenoid Valve. *Journal of Dynamic Systems, Measurements, and Control*, vol. 118, March 1996, pp. 120–125.

TRANSFER FUNCTIONS OF PHYSICAL SYSTEMS

2

CHAPTER OBJECTIVES

In this chapter you will

- Review the Laplace transform
- Learn how to find a mathematical model, called a *transfer function*, for linear, time-invariant electrical, mechanical, and electromechanical systems
- Learn how to linearize a nonlinear system in order to find the transfer function

CASE STUDY OBJECTIVES

You will be able to demonstrate your knowledge of the chapter objectives with case studies as follows:

- Given the antenna azimuth position control system shown on the front endpapers, you will be able to find the transfer function of each subsystem.
- Given a model of a human leg, or a nonlinear electrical circuit, you will be able to linearize the model and then find the transfer function.

2.1 INTRODUCTION

In Chapter 1 we discussed the analysis and design sequence that included obtaining the system's schematic and demonstrated this step for a position control system. To obtain a schematic, the control systems engineer must often make many simplifying assumptions in order to keep the ensuing model manageable and still approximate physical reality.

The next step is to develop mathematical models from schematics of physical systems. We will discuss two methods: (1) transfer functions in the frequency domain and (2) state equations in the time domain. These topics are covered in this chapter and in Chapter 3, respectively. As we proceed, we will notice that in every case the first step in developing a mathematical model is to apply the fundamental physical laws of science and engineering. For example, when we model electrical networks, Ohm's law and Kirchhoff's laws, which are basic laws of electric networks, will be applied initially. We will sum voltages in a loop or sum currents at a node. When we study mechanical systems, we will use Newton's laws as the fundamental guiding principles. Here we will sum forces or torques. From these equations we will obtain the relationship between the system's output and input.

In Chapter 1 we saw that a differential equation can describe the relationship between the input and output of a system. The form of the differential equation and its coefficients are a formulation or description of the system. Although the differential equation relates the system to its input and output, it is not a satisfying representation from a system perspective. Looking at Eq. (1.2), a general, nth-order, linear, time-invariant differential equation, we see that the system parameters, which are the coefficients, as well as the output, $c(t)$, and the input, $r(t)$, appear throughout the equation.

We would prefer a mathematical representation such as that shown in Figure 2.1(a), where the input, output, and system are distinct and separate parts. Also, we would like to represent conveniently the interconnection of several subsystems. For example, we would like to represent *cascaded* interconnections, as shown in Figure 2.1(b), where a mathematical function, called a transfer function, is inside each block, and block functions can easily be combined to yield Figure 2.1(a) for ease of analysis and design. This convenience cannot be obtained with the differential equation.

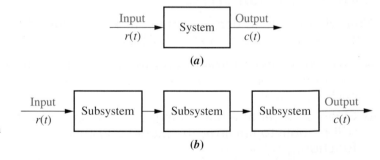

FIGURE 2.1 a. Block diagram representation of a system; **b.** block diagram representation of an interconnection of subsystems

Note: The input, $r(t)$, stands for *reference input*.
The output, $c(t)$, stands for *controlled variable*.

2.2 LAPLACE TRANSFORM REVIEW

A system represented by a differential equation is difficult to model as a block diagram. Thus, we now lay the groundwork for the Laplace transform, with which we can represent the input, output, and system as separate entities. Further, their interrelationship will be simply algebraic. Let us first define the Laplace transform and then show how it simplifies the representation of physical systems (*Nilsson, 1996*).

The Laplace transform is defined as

$$\mathscr{L}[f(t)] = F(s) = \int_{0-}^{\infty} f(t)e^{-st}\,dt \tag{2.1}$$

where $s = \sigma + j\omega$, a complex variable. Thus, knowing $f(t)$ and that the integral in Eq. (2.1) exists, we can find a function, $F(s)$, that is called the *Laplace transform* of $f(t)$.[1]

The notation for the lower limit means that even if $f(t)$ is discontinuous at $t = 0$, we can start the integration prior to the discontinuity as long as the integral converges. Thus, we can find the Laplace transform of impulse functions. This property has distinct advantages when applying the Laplace transform to the solution of differential equations where the initial conditions are discontinuous at $t = 0$. Using differential equations, we have to solve for the initial conditions after the discontinuity knowing the initial conditions before the discontinuity. Using the Laplace transform we need only know the initial conditions before the discontinuity. See *Kailath (1980)* for a more detailed discussion.

The inverse Laplace transform, which allows us to find $f(t)$ given $F(s)$, is

$$\mathscr{L}^{-1}[F(s)] = \frac{1}{2\pi j}\int_{\sigma-j\infty}^{\sigma+j\infty} F(s)e^{st}\,ds = f(t)u(t) \tag{2.2}$$

where

$$u(t) = 1 \qquad t > 0$$
$$= 0 \qquad t < 0$$

is the unit step function. Multiplication of $f(t)$ by $u(t)$ yields a time function that is zero for $t < 0$.

Using Eq. (2.1), it is possible to derive a table relating $f(t)$ to $F(s)$ for specific cases. Table 2.1 shows the results for a representative sample of functions. If we use the

TABLE 2.1   **Laplace transform table**

Item no.	$f(t)$	$F(s)$
1.	$\delta(t)$	1
2.	$u(t)$	$\dfrac{1}{s}$
3.	$tu(t)$	$\dfrac{1}{s^2}$
4.	$t^n u(t)$	$\dfrac{n!}{s^{n+1}}$
5.	$e^{-at}u(t)$	$\dfrac{1}{s+a}$
6.	$\sin \omega t\, u(t)$	$\dfrac{\omega}{s^2+\omega^2}$
7.	$\cos \omega t\, u(t)$	$\dfrac{s}{s^2+\omega^2}$

[1] The Laplace transform exists if the integral of Eq. (2.1) converges. The integral will converge if $\int_{0-}^{\infty}|f(t)|e^{-\sigma_1 t}\,dt < \infty$. If $|f(t)| < Me^{\sigma_2 t}$, $0 < t < \infty$, the integral will converge if $\infty > \sigma_1 > \sigma_2$. We call σ_2 the *abscissa of convergence,* and it is the smallest value of σ, where $s = \sigma + j\omega$, for which the integral exists.

tables, we do not have to use Eq. (2.2), which requires complex integration, to find $f(t)$ given $F(s)$. In the following example we demonstrate the use of Eq. (2.1) to find the Laplace transform of a time function.

EXAMPLE 2.1

Laplace transform of a time function

Problem: Find the Laplace transform of $f(t) = Ae^{-at}u(t)$.

SOLUTION: Since the time function does not contain an impulse function, we can replace the lower limit of Eq. (2.1) with 0. Hence,

$$F(s) = \int_0^\infty f(t)e^{-st}\,dt = \int_0^\infty Ae^{-at}e^{-st}\,dt = A\int_0^\infty e^{-(s+a)t}\,dt$$

$$= -\frac{A}{s+a}e^{-(s+a)t}\Big|_{t=0}^\infty = \frac{A}{s+a}$$

$$(2.3)$$

In addition to the Laplace transform table, Table 2.1, we can use Laplace transform theorems, listed in Table 2.2, to assist in transforming between $f(t)$ and $F(s)$. In the next example, we demonstrate the use of the Laplace transform theorems shown in Table 2.2 to find $f(t)$ given $F(s)$.

TABLE 2.2   Laplace transform theorems

Item no.	Theorem		Name
1.	$\mathscr{L}[f(t)] = F(s)$	$= \int_{0-}^\infty f(t)e^{-st}dt$	Definition
2.	$\mathscr{L}[kf(t)]$	$= kF(s)$	Linearity theorem
3.	$\mathscr{L}[f_1(t) + f_2(t)] = F_1(s) + F_2(s)$		Linearity theorem
4.	$\mathscr{L}[e^{-at}f(t)]$	$= F(s+a)$	Frequency shift theorem
5.	$\mathscr{L}[f(t-T)]$	$= e^{-sT}F(s)$	Time shift theorem
6.	$\mathscr{L}[f(at)]$	$= \dfrac{1}{a}F\left(\dfrac{s}{a}\right)$	Scaling theorem
7.	$\mathscr{L}\left[\dfrac{df}{dt}\right]$	$= sF(s) - f(0-)$	Differentiation theorem
8.	$\mathscr{L}\left[\dfrac{d^2f}{dt^2}\right]$	$= s^2F(s) - sf(0-) - f(0-)$	Differentiation theorem
9.	$\mathscr{L}\left[\dfrac{d^nf}{dt^n}\right]$	$= s^nF(s) - \sum\limits_{k=1}^n s^{n-k}f^{k-1}(0-)$	Differentiation theorem
10.	$\mathscr{L}\left[\int_{0-}^1 f(\tau)d\tau\right]$	$= \dfrac{F(s)}{s}$	Integration theorem
11.	$f(\infty)$	$= \lim\limits_{s\to 0} sF(s)$	Final value theorem[1]
12.	$f(0+)$	$= \lim\limits_{s\to\infty} sF(s)$	Initial value theorem[2]

---

[1] For this theorem to yield correct finite results, all roots of the denominator of $F(s)$ must have negative real parts, and no more than one can be at the origin.

[2] For this theorem to be valid, $f(t)$ must be continuous or have a step discontinuity at $t = 0$ (that is, no impulses or their derivatives at $t = 0$).

EXAMPLE 2.2

Inverse Laplace transform

Problem: Find the inverse Laplace transform of $F_1(s) = 1/(s+3)^2$.

SOLUTION: For this example we make use of the frequency shift theorem, Item 4 of Table 2.2, and the Laplace transform of $f(t) = tu(t)$, Item 3 of Table 2.1. If the inverse transform of $F(s) = 1/s^2$ is $tu(t)$, the inverse transform of $F(s+a) = 1/(s+a)^2$ is $e^{-at} tu(t)$. Hence, $f_1(t) = e^{-3t} tu(t)$.

PARTIAL-FRACTION EXPANSION

To find the inverse Laplace transform of a complicated function, we can convert the function to a sum of simpler terms for which we know the Laplace transform of each term. The result is called a *partial-fraction expansion*. If $F_1(s) = N(s)/D(s)$, where the order of $N(s)$ is less than the order of $D(s)$, then a partial-fraction expansion can be made. If the order of $N(s)$ is greater than or equal to the order of $D(s)$, then $N(s)$ must be divided by $D(s)$ successively until the result has a remainder whose numerator is of order less than its denominator. For example, if

$$F_1(s) = \frac{s^3 + 2s^2 + 6s + 7}{s^2 + s + 5} \tag{2.4}$$

we must perform the indicated division until we obtain a remainder whose numerator is of order less than its denominator. Hence,

$$F_1(s) = s + 1 + \frac{2}{s^2 + s + 5} \tag{2.5}$$

Taking the inverse Laplace transform, using Item 1 of Table 2.1, along with the differentiation theorem (Item 7) and the linearity theorem (Item 3 of Table 2.2), we obtain

$$f_1(t) = \frac{d\delta(t)}{dt} + \delta(t) + \mathscr{L}^{-1}\left[\frac{2}{s^2 + s + 5}\right] \tag{2.6}$$

Using partial-fraction expansion, we will be able to expand functions like $F(s) = 2/(s^2 + s + 5)$ into a sum of terms and then find the inverse Laplace transform for each term. We will now consider three cases and show for each case how an $F(s)$ can be expanded into partial fractions.

Case 1. Roots of the Denominator of F(s) Are Real and Distinct
An example of an $F(s)$ with real and distinct roots in the denominator is

$$F(s) = \frac{2}{(s+1)(s+2)} \tag{2.7}$$

The roots of the denominator are distinct, since each factor is raised only to unity power. We can write the partial-fraction expansion as a sum of terms where each factor of the original denominator forms the denominator of each term, and constants, called *residues,* form the numerators. Hence,

$$F(s) = \frac{2}{(s+1)(s+2)} = \frac{K_1}{(s+1)} + \frac{K_2}{(s+2)} \qquad (2.8)$$

To find K_1, we first multiply Eq. (2.8) by $(s+1)$, which isolates K_1. Thus,

$$\frac{2}{(s+2)} = K_1 + \frac{(s+1)K_2}{(s+2)} \qquad (2.9)$$

Letting s approach -1 eliminates the last term and yields $K_1 = 2$. Similarly, K_2 can be found by multiplying Eq. (2.8) by $(s+2)$ and then letting s approach -2; hence, $K_2 = -2$.

Each component part of Eq. (2.8) is an $F(s)$ in Table 2.1. Hence, $f(t)$ is the sum of the inverse Laplace transform of each term, or

$$f(t) = (2e^{-t} - 2e^{-2t})u(t) \qquad (2.10)$$

In general, then, given an $F(s)$ whose denominator has real and distinct roots, a partial fraction expansion,

$$F(s) = \frac{N(s)}{D(s)} = \frac{N(s)}{(s+p_1)(s+p_2)\cdots(s+p_m)\cdots(s+p_n)}$$

$$= \frac{K_1}{(s+p_1)} + \frac{K_2}{(s+p_2)} + \cdots + \frac{K_m}{(s+p_m)} + \cdots + \frac{K_n}{(s+p_n)} \qquad (2.11)$$

can be made if the order of $N(s)$ is less than the order of $D(s)$. To evaluate each residue, K_i, we multiply Eq. (2.11) by the denominator of the corresponding partial fraction. Thus, if we want to find K_m, we multiply Eq. (2.11) by $(s + p_m)$ and get

$$(s+p_m)F(s) = \frac{(s+p_m)N(s)}{(s+p_1)(s+p_2)\cdots(s+p_m)\cdots(s+p_n)}$$

$$= (s+p_m)\frac{K_1}{(s+p_1)} + (s+p_m)\frac{K_2}{(s+p_2)} + \cdots + K_m + \cdots$$

$$+ (s+p_m)\frac{K_n}{(s+p_n)} \qquad (2.12)$$

If we let s approach $-p_m$, all terms on the right-hand side of Eq. (2.12) go to zero except the term K_m, leaving

$$\frac{(s+p_m)N(s)}{(s+p_1)(s+p_2)\cdots(s+p_m)\cdots(s+p_n)}\Bigg|_{s \to -p_m} = K_m \qquad (2.13)$$

The following example demonstrates the use of the partial-fraction expansion to solve a differential equation. We will see that the Laplace transform reduces the task of finding the solution to simple algebra.

EXAMPLE 2.3

Laplace transform solution of a differential equation

Problem: Given the following differential equation, solve for $y(t)$ if all initial conditions are zero. Use the Laplace transform.

$$\frac{d^2y}{dt^2} + 12\frac{dy}{dt} + 32y = 32u(t) \tag{2.14}$$

SOLUTION: Substitute the corresponding $F(s)$ for each term in Eq. (2.14), using Item 2 in Table 2.1, Items 7 and 8 in Table 2.2, and the initial conditions of $y(t)$ and $dy(t)/dt$, given by $y(0-) = 0$ and $\dot{y}(0-) = 0$, respectively. Hence, the Laplace transform of Eq. (2.14) is

$$s^2Y(s) + 12sY(s) + 32Y(s) = \frac{32}{s} \tag{2.15}$$

Solving for the response, $Y(s)$, yields

$$Y(s) = \frac{32}{s(s^2 + 12s + 32)} = \frac{32}{s(s + 4)(s + 8)} \tag{2.16}$$

To solve for $y(t)$, we notice that Eq. (2.16) does not match any of the terms in Table 2.1. Thus, we form the partial-fraction expansion of the right-hand term and match each of the resulting terms with $F(s)$ in Table 2.1. Therefore,

$$Y(s) = \frac{32}{s(s + 4)(s + 8)} = \frac{K_1}{s} + \frac{K_2}{(s + 4)} + \frac{K_3}{(s + 8)} \tag{2.17}$$

where, from Eq. (2.13),

$$K_1 = \left.\frac{32}{(s + 4)(s + 8)}\right|_{s \to 0} = 1 \tag{2.18a}$$

$$K_2 = \left.\frac{32}{s(s + 8)}\right|_{s \to -4} = -2 \tag{2.18b}$$

$$K_3 = \left.\frac{32}{s(s + 4)}\right|_{s \to -8} = 1 \tag{2.18c}$$

Hence,

$$Y(s) = \frac{1}{s} - \frac{2}{(s + 4)} + \frac{1}{(s + 8)} \tag{2.19}$$

Since each of the three component parts of Eq. (2.19) is represented as an $F(s)$ in Table 2.1, $y(t)$ is the sum of the inverse Laplace transforms of each term. Hence,

$$y(t) = (1 - 2e^{-4t} + e^{-8t})u(t) \tag{2.20}$$

MATLAB

Students who are using MATLAB should now run ch2p1 through ch2p8 in Appendix B. This is your first MATLAB exercise. You will learn how to use MATLAB to (1) represent polynomials, (2) find roots of polynomials, (3) multiply polynomials, and (4) find partial-fraction expansions. Finally, Example 2.3 will be solved using MATLAB.

The $u(t)$ in Eq. (2.20) shows that the response is zero until $t = 0$. Unless otherwise specified, all inputs to systems in the text will not start until $t = 0$. Thus, output responses will also be zero until $t = 0$. For convenience, we will leave off the $u(t)$ notation from now on. Accordingly, we write the output response as

$$y(t) = 1 - 2e^{-4t} + e^{-8t} \tag{2.21}$$

TryIt 2.1

Use the following MATLAB and Control System Toolbox statement to form the linear, time-invariant (LTI) transfer function of Eq. (2.22).

F = zpk([], [−1 −2 −2], 2)

Case 2. Roots of the Denominator of F(s) Are Real and Repeated

An example of an $F(s)$ with real and repeated roots in the denominator is

$$F(s) = \frac{2}{(s+1)(s+2)^2} \tag{2.22}$$

The roots of $(s+2)^2$ in the denominator are repeated, since the factor is raised to an integer power higher than 1. In this case the denominator root at -2 is a *multiple root* of *multiplicity* 2.

We can write the partial-fraction expansion as a sum of terms, where each factor of the denominator forms the denominator of each term. In addition, each multiple root generates additional terms consisting of denominator factors of reduced multiplicity. For example, if

$$F(s) = \frac{2}{(s+1)(s+2)^2} = \frac{K_1}{(s+1)} + \frac{K_2}{(s+2)^2} + \frac{K_3}{(s+2)} \tag{2.23}$$

then $K_1 = 2$, which can be found as previously described. K_2 can be isolated by multiplying Eq. (2.23) by $(s+2)^2$, yielding

$$\frac{2}{s+1} = (s+2)^2 \frac{K_1}{(s+1)} + K_2 + (s+2)K_3 \tag{2.24}$$

Letting s approach -2, $K_2 = -2$. To find K_3 we see that if we differentiate Eq. (2.24) with respect to s,

TryIt 2.2

Use the following MATLAB statements to help you get Eq. (2.26).

numf = 2;
denf = poly([−1 −2 −2]);
[K, p, k] = residue...
(numf, denf)

$$\frac{-2}{(s+1)^2} = \frac{(s+2)s}{(s+1)^2}K_1 + K_3 \tag{2.25}$$

K_3 is isolated and can be found if we let s approach -2. Hence, $K_3 = -2$.

Each component part of Eq. (2.23) is an $F(s)$ in Table 2.1; hence, $f(t)$ is the sum of the inverse Laplace transform of each term, or

$$f(t) = 2e^{-t} - 2te^{-2t} - 2e^{-2t} \tag{2.26}$$

If the denominator root is of higher multiplicity than 2, successive differentiation would isolate each residue in the expansion of the multiple root.

In general, then, given an $F(s)$ whose denominator has real and repeated roots, a partial-fraction expansion,

$$
\begin{aligned}
F(s) &= \frac{N(s)}{D(s)} \\
&= \frac{N(s)}{(s+p_1)^r(s+p_2)\cdots(s+p_n)} \\
&= \frac{K_1}{(s+p_1)^r} + \frac{K_2}{(s+p_1)^{r-1}} + \cdots + \frac{K_r}{(s+p_1)} \\
&\quad + \frac{K_{r+1}}{(s+p_2)} + \cdots + \frac{K_n}{(s+p_n)}
\end{aligned}
\tag{2.27}
$$

can be made if the order of $N(s)$ is less than the order of $D(s)$ and the repeated roots are of multiplicity r at $-p_1$. To find K_1 through K_r for the roots of multiplicity greater than unity, first multiply Eq. (2.27) by $(s+p_1)^r$ getting $F_1(s)$, which is

$$
\begin{aligned}
F_1(s) &= (s+p_1)^r F(s) \\
&= \frac{(s+p_1)^r N(s)}{(s+p_1)^r(s+p_2)\cdots(s+p_n)} \\
&= K_1 + (s+p_1)K_2 + (s+p_1)^2 K_3 + \cdots + (s+p_1)^{r-1}K_r \\
&\quad + \frac{K_{r+1}(s+p_1)^r}{(s+p_2)} + \cdots + \frac{K_n(s+p_1)^r}{(s+p_n)}
\end{aligned}
\tag{2.28}
$$

Immediately, we can solve for K_1 if we let s approach $-p_1$. We can solve for K_2 if we differentiate Eq. (2.28) with respect to s and then let s approach $-p_1$. Subsequent differentiation will allow us to find K_3 through K_r. The general expression for K_1 through K_r for the multiple roots is

$$
K_i = \frac{1}{(i-1)!} \frac{d^{i-1}F_1(s)}{ds^{i-1}}\bigg|_{s\to -p_1} \qquad i = 1, 2, \ldots, r; \quad 0! = 1
\tag{2.29}
$$

Case 3. Roots of the Denominator of F(s) Are Complex or Imaginary
An example of $F(s)$ with complex roots in the denominator is

$$
F(s) = \frac{3}{s(s^2 + 2s + 5)}
\tag{2.30}
$$

This function can be expanded in the following form:

$$
\frac{3}{s(s^2 + 2s + 5)} = \frac{K_1}{s} + \frac{K_2 s + K_3}{s^2 + 2s + 5}
\tag{2.31}
$$

K_1 is found in the usual way to be $\frac{3}{5}$. K_2 and K_3 can be found by first multiplying Eq. (2.31) by the lowest common denominator, $s(s^2 + 2s + 5)$, and clearing the fractions. After simplification with $K_1 = \frac{3}{5}$, we obtain

$$
3 = \left(K_2 + \frac{3}{5}\right)s^2 + \left(K_3 + \frac{6}{5}\right)s + 3
\tag{2.32}
$$

TryIt 2.3

Use the following MATLAB and Control System Toolbox statement to form the LTI transfer function of Eq. (2.30).

`F = tf([3],[1 2 5 0])`

Balancing coefficients, $(K_2 + \frac{3}{5}) = 0$ and $(K_3 + \frac{6}{5}) = 0$. Hence $K_2 = -\frac{3}{5}$ and $K_3 = -\frac{6}{5}$. Thus,

$$F(s) = \frac{3}{s(s^2 + 2s + 5)} = \frac{3/5}{s} - \frac{3}{5}\frac{s+2}{s^2 + 2s + 5} \tag{2.33}$$

The last term can be shown to be the sum of the Laplace transforms of an exponentially damped sine and cosine. Using Item 7 in Table 2.1 and Items 2 and 4 in Table 2.2, we get

$$\mathscr{L}[Ae^{-at}\cos\omega t] = \frac{A(s+a)}{(s+a)^2 + \omega^2} \tag{2.34}$$

Similarly,

$$\mathscr{L}[Be^{-at}\sin\omega t] = \frac{B\omega}{(s+a)^2 + \omega^2} \tag{2.35}$$

Adding Eqs. (2.34) and (2.35), we get

$$\mathscr{L}[Ae^{-at}\cos\omega t + Be^{-at}\sin\omega t] = \frac{A(s+a) + B\omega}{(s+a)^2 + \omega^2} \tag{2.36}$$

We now convert the last term of Eq. (2.33) to the form suggested by Eq. (2.36) by completing the squares in the denominator and adjusting terms in the numerator without changing its value. Hence,

$$F(s) = \frac{3/5}{s} - \frac{3}{5}\frac{(s+1) + (1/2)(2)}{(s+1)^2 + 2^2} \tag{2.37}$$

Comparing Eq. (2.37) to Table 2.1 and Eq. (2.36), we find

$$f(t) = \frac{3}{5} - \frac{3}{5}e^{-t}\left(\cos 2t + \frac{1}{2}\sin 2t\right) \tag{2.38}$$

In order to visualize the solution, an alternate form of $c(t)$, obtained by trigonometric identities, is preferable. Using the amplitudes of the cos and sin terms, we factor out $\sqrt{1^2 + (1/2)^2}$ from the term in parentheses and obtain

$$c(t) = \frac{3}{5} - \frac{3}{5}\sqrt{1^2 + (1/2)^2}e^{-t}\left(\frac{1}{\sqrt{1^2 + (1/2)^2}}\cos 2t + \frac{1/2}{\sqrt{1^2 + (1/2)^2}}\sin 2t\right) \tag{2.39}$$

Letting $1/\sqrt{1^2 + (1/2)^2} = \cos\phi$ and $(1/2)/\sqrt{1^2 + (1/2)^2} = \sin\phi$,

$$c(t) = \frac{3}{5} - \frac{3}{5}\sqrt{1^2 + (1/2)^2}e^{-t}(\cos\phi\cos 2t + \sin\phi\sin 2t) \tag{2.40}$$

or

$$c(t) = 0.6 - 0.671e^{-t}\cos(2t - \phi) \tag{2.41}$$

TryIt 2.4

Use the following MATLAB and Symbolic Math Toolbox statements to get Eq. (2.38) from Eq. (2.30).

```
syms s
f = ilaplace...
(3/(s*(s^2 + 2*s + 5)));
pretty(f)
```

where $\phi = \arctan 0.5 = 26.57°$. Thus, $c(t)$ is a constant plus an exponentially damped sinusoid.

In general, then, given an $F(s)$ whose denominator has complex or purely imaginary roots, a partial-fraction expansion,

$$F(s) = \frac{N(s)}{D(s)} = \frac{N(s)}{(s + p_1)(s^2 + as + b) \cdots}$$

$$= \frac{K_1}{(s + p_1)} + \frac{(K_2 s + K_3)}{(s^2 + as + b)} + \cdots \qquad (2.42)$$

can be made if the order of $N(s)$ is less than the order of $D(s)$, p_1 is real, and $(s^2 + as + b)$ has complex or purely imaginary roots. The complex or imaginary roots are expanded with $(K_2 s + K_3)$ terms in the numerator rather than just simply K_i, as in the case of real roots. The K_i's in Eq. (2.42) are found through balancing the coefficients of the equation after clearing fractions. After completing the squares on $(s^2 + as + b)$ and adjusting the numerator, $(K_2 s + K_3)/(s^2 + as + b)$ can be put into the form shown on the right-hand side of Eq. (2.36).

Finally, the case of purely imaginary roots arises if $a = 0$ in Eq. (2.42). The calculations are the same.

Another method that follows the technique used for the partial-fraction expansion of $F(s)$ with real roots in the denominator can be used for complex and imaginary roots. However, the residues of the complex and imaginary roots are themselves complex conjugates. Then, after taking the inverse Laplace transform, the resulting terms can be identified as

$$\frac{e^{j\theta} + e^{-j\theta}}{2} = \cos\theta \qquad (2.43)$$

and

$$\frac{e^{j\theta} - e^{-j\theta}}{2j} = \sin\theta \qquad (2.44)$$

For example, the previous $F(s)$ can also be expanded in partial fractions as

$$F(s) = \frac{3}{s(s^2 + 2s + 5)} = \frac{3}{s(s + 1 + j2)(s + 1 - j2)}$$

$$= \frac{K_1}{s} + \frac{K_2}{s + 1 + j2} + \frac{K_3}{s + 1 - j2} \qquad (2.45)$$

Finding K_2,

$$K_2 = \frac{3}{s(s + 1 - j2)} \bigg|_{s \to -1 - j2} = -\frac{3}{20}(2 + j1) \qquad (2.46)$$

Similarly, K_3 is found to be the complex conjugate of K_2, and K_1 is found as previously described. Hence,

$$F(s) = \frac{3/5}{s} - \frac{3}{20}\left(\frac{2 + j1}{s + 1 + j2} + \frac{2 - j1}{s + 1 - j2}\right) \qquad (2.47)$$

TryIt 2.5

Use the following MATLAB statements to help you get Eq. (2.47).

```
numf = 3
denf = [1 2 5 0]
[K, p, k] = residue...
(numf, denf)
```

from which

$$f(t) = \frac{3}{5} - \frac{3}{20}\Big[(2+j1)e^{-(1+j2)t} + (2-j1)e^{-(1-j2)t}\Big]$$

$$= \frac{3}{5} - \frac{3}{20}e^{-t}\left[4\left(\frac{e^{j2t} + e^{-j2t}}{2}\right) + 2\left(\frac{e^{j2t} - e^{-j2t}}{2j}\right)\right] \qquad (2.48)$$

Using Eqs. (2.43) and (2.44), we get

$$f(t) = \frac{3}{5} - \frac{3}{5}e^{-t}\left(\cos 2t + \frac{1}{2}\sin 2t\right) = 0.6 - 0.671e^{-t}\cos(2t - \phi) \qquad (2.49)$$

where $\phi = \arctan 0.5 = 26.57°$.

Students who are performing the MATLAB exercises and want to explore the added capability of MATLAB's Symbolic Math Toolbox should now run ch2sp1 and ch2sp2 in Appendix E at www.wiley.com/college/nise. You will learn how to construct symbolic objects and then find the inverse Laplace and Laplace transforms of frequency and time functions, respectively. The examples in Case 2 and Case 3 in this section will be solved using the Symbolic Math Toolbox.

SKILL-ASSESSMENT EXERCISE 2.1

Problem: Find the Laplace transform of $f(t) = te^{-5t}$.

ANSWER: $F(s) = 1/(s+5)^2$

The complete solution is at www.wiley.com/college/nise.

SKILL-ASSESSMENT EXERCISE 2.2

Problem: Find the inverse Laplace transform of $F(s) = 10/[s(s+2)(s+3)^2]$.

ANSWER: $f(t) = \frac{5}{9} - 5e^{-2t} + \frac{10}{3}te^{-3t} + \frac{40}{9}e^{-3t}$

The complete solution is at www.wiley.com/college/nise.

2.3 THE TRANSFER FUNCTION

In the previous section we defined the Laplace transform and its inverse. We presented the idea of the partial-fraction expansion and applied the concepts to the solution of differential equations. We are now ready to formulate the system representation shown in Figure 2.1 by establishing a viable definition for a function that algebraically relates a system's output to its input. This function will allow separation of the input, system, and output into three separate and distinct parts, unlike the differential equation. The function will also allow us to *algebraically* combine mathematical representations of subsystems to yield a total system representation.

Let us begin by writing a general nth-order, linear, time-invariant differential equation,

$$a_n \frac{d^n c(t)}{dt^n} + a_{n-1} \frac{d^{n-1} c(t)}{dt^{n-1}} + \cdots + a_0 c(t) = b_m \frac{d^m r(t)}{dt^m} + b_{m-1} \frac{d^{m-1} r(t)}{dt^{m-1}} + \cdots + b_0 r(t)$$

$$(2.50)$$

where $c(t)$ is the output, $r(t)$ is the input, and the a_i's, b_i's, and the form of the differential equation represent the system. Taking the Laplace transform of both sides,

$$a_n s^n C(s) + a_{n-1} s^{n-1} C(s) + \cdots + a_0 C(s) + \text{initial condition}$$
$$\text{terms involving } c(t)$$
$$= b_m s^m R(s) + b_{m-1} s^{m-1} R(s) + \cdots + b_0 R(s) + \text{initial condition}$$
$$\text{terms involving } r(t) \quad (2.51)$$

Equation (2.51) is a purely algebraic expression. If we assume that *all initial conditions are zero*, Eq. (2.51) reduces to

$$(a_n s^n + a_{n-1} s^{n-1} + \cdots + a_0) C(s) = (b_m s^m + b_{m-1} s^{m-1} + \cdots + b_0) R(s) \quad (2.52)$$

Now form the ratio of the output transform, $C(s)$, divided by the input transform, $R(s)$:

$$\boxed{\frac{C(s)}{R(s)} = G(s) = \frac{(b_m s^m + b_{m-1} s^{m-1} + \cdots + b_0)}{(a_n s^n + a_{n-1} s^{n-1} + \cdots + a_0)}} \quad (2.53)$$

Notice that Eq. (2.53) separates the output, $C(s)$, the input, $R(s)$, and the system, the ratio of polynomials in s on the right. We call this ratio, $G(s)$, the *transfer function* and evaluate it with *zero initial conditions*.

The transfer function can be represented as a block diagram, as shown in Figure 2.2, with the input on the left, the output on the right, and the system transfer function inside the block. Notice that the denominator of the transfer function is identical to the characteristic polynomial of the differential equation. Also, we can find the output, $C(s)$, by using

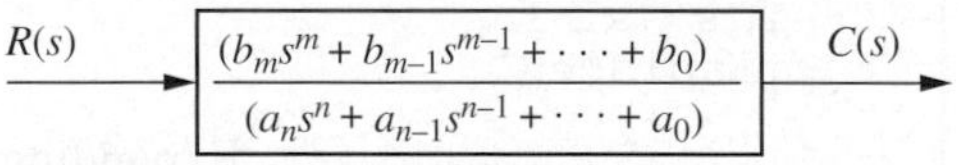

FIGURE 2.2 Block diagram of a transfer function

$$\boxed{C(s) = R(s)G(s)} \quad (2.54)$$

Let us apply the concept of a transfer function to an example and then use the result to find the response of the system.

EXAMPLE 2.4

Transfer function for a differential equation

Problem: Find the transfer function represented by

$$\frac{dc(t)}{dt} + 2c(t) = r(t) \quad (2.55)$$

SOLUTION: Taking the Laplace transform of both sides, assuming zero initial conditions, we have

$$sC(s) + 2C(s) = R(s) \quad (2.56)$$

The transfer function, $G(s)$, is

$$G(s) = \frac{C(s)}{R(s)} = \frac{1}{s+2} \tag{2.57}$$

Students who are using MATLAB should now run ch2p9 through ch2p12 in Appendix B. You will learn how to use MATLAB to create transfer functions with numerators and denominators in polynomial or factored form. You will also learn how to convert between polynomial and factored forms. Finally, you will learn how to use MATLAB to plot time functions.

Students who are performing the MATLAB exercises and want to explore the added capability of MATLAB's Symbolic Math Toolbox, should now run ch2sp3 in Appendix E at www.wiley.com/college/nise. You will learn how to use the Symbolic Math Toolbox to simplify the input of complicated transfer functions as well as improve readability. You will learn how to enter a symbolic transfer function and convert it to a linear, time-invariant (LTI) object as presented in Appendix B, ch2p9.

▉▉▉ EXAMPLE 2.5 ▉▉▉

System response from the transfer function

TryIt 2.6

Use the following MATLAB and Symbolic Math Toolbox statements to help you get Eq. (2.60).

```
syms s
C = 1/(s*(s + 2))
c = ilaplace(C)
```

TryIt 2.7

Use the following MATLAB statements to plot Eq. (2.60) for t from 0 to 1 s at intervals of 0.01 s.

```
t = 0:0.01:1;
plot...
(t, (1/2 – 1/2*exp(–2*t)))
```

Problem: Use the result of Example 2.4 to find the response, $c(t)$, to an input, $r(t) = u(t)$, a unit step, assuming zero initial conditions.

SOLUTION: To solve the problem, we use Eq. (2.54), where $G(s) = 1/(s+2)$ as found in Example 2.4. Since $r(t) = u(t)$, $R(s) = 1/s$, from Table 2.1. Since the initial conditions are zero,

$$C(s) = R(s)G(s) = \frac{1}{s(s+2)} \tag{2.58}$$

Expanding by partial fractions, we get

$$C(s) = \frac{1/2}{s} - \frac{1/2}{s+2} \tag{2.59}$$

Finally, taking the inverse Laplace transform of each term yields

$$c(t) = \frac{1}{2} - \frac{1}{2}e^{-2t} \tag{2.60}$$

▉▉▉ SKILL-ASSESSMENT EXERCISE 2.3 ▉▉▉

Problem: Find the transfer function, $G(s) = C(s)/R(s)$, corresponding to the differential equation $\dfrac{d^3c}{dt^3} + 3\dfrac{d^2c}{dt^2} + 7\dfrac{dc}{dt} + 5c = \dfrac{d^2r}{dt^2} + 4\dfrac{dr}{dt} + 3r$.

ANSWER: $G(s) = \dfrac{C(s)}{R(s)} = \dfrac{s^2 + 4s + 3}{s^3 + 3s^2 + 7s + 5}$

The complete solution is at www.wiley.com/college/nise.

==

SKILL-ASSESSMENT EXERCISE 2.4

Problem: Find the differential equation corresponding to the transfer function,

$$G(s) = \frac{2s+1}{s^2+6s+2}.$$

ANSWER: $\dfrac{d^2c}{dt^2} + 6\dfrac{dc}{dt} + 2c = 2\dfrac{dr}{dt} + r$

The complete solution is at www.wiley.com/college/nise.

==

SKILL-ASSESSMENT EXERCISE 2.5

Problem: Find the ramp response for a system whose transfer function is

$$G(s) = \frac{s}{(s+4)(s+8)}.$$

ANSWER: $c(t) = \dfrac{1}{32} - \dfrac{1}{16}e^{-4t} + \dfrac{1}{32}e^{-8t}$

The complete solution is at www.wiley.com/college/nise.

WileyPLUS

Control Solutions

==

In general, a physical system that can be represented by a linear, time-invariant differential equation can be modeled as a transfer function. The rest of this chapter will be devoted to the task of modeling individual subsystems. We will learn how to represent electrical networks, translational mechanical systems, rotational mechanical systems, and electromechanical systems as transfer functions. As the need arises, the reader can consult the Bibliography at the end of the chapter for discussions of other types of systems, such as pneumatic, hydraulic, and heat-transfer systems (*Cannon, 1967*).

2.4 ELECTRICAL NETWORK TRANSFER FUNCTIONS

In this section we formally apply the transfer function to the mathematical modeling of electric circuits including passive networks and operational amplifier circuits. Subsequent sections cover mechanical and electromechanical systems.

Equivalent circuits for the electric networks that we work with first consist of three passive linear components: resistors, capacitors, and inductors.[2] Table 2.3 summarizes

TABLE 2.3 Voltage-current, voltage-charge, and impedance relationships for capacitors, resistors, and inductors

Component	Voltage-current	Current-voltage	Voltage-charge	Impedance $Z(s) = V(s)/I(s)$	Admittance $Y(s) = I(s)/V(s)$
⊣⊢ Capacitor	$v(t) = \dfrac{1}{C}\displaystyle\int_0^1 i(\tau)d\tau$	$i(t) = C\dfrac{dv(t)}{dt}$	$v(t) = \dfrac{1}{C}q(t)$	$\dfrac{1}{Cs}$	Cs
⊸⋀⋀⋀⊸ Resistor	$v(t) = Ri(t)$	$i(t) = \dfrac{1}{R}v(t)$	$v(t) = R\dfrac{dq(t)}{dt}$	R	$\dfrac{1}{R} = G$
⎓⎓⎓ Inductor	$v(t) = L\dfrac{di(t)}{dt}$	$i(t) = \dfrac{1}{L}\displaystyle\int_0^1 v(\tau)\,d\tau$	$v(t) = L\dfrac{d^2q(t)}{dt^2}$	Ls	$\dfrac{1}{Ls}$

Note: The following set of symbols and units is used throughout this book: $v(t) = $ V (volts), $i(t) = $ A (amps), $q(t) = $ Q (coulombs), $C = $ F (farads), $R = \Omega$ (ohms), $G = \Omega$ (mhos), $L = H$ (henries).

[2] *Passive* means that there is no internal source of energy.

the components and the relationships between voltage and current and between voltage and charge under zero initial conditions.

We now combine electrical components into circuits, decide on the input and output, and find the transfer function. Our guiding principles are Kirchhoff's laws. We sum voltages around loops or sum currents at nodes, depending on which technique involves the least effort in algebraic manipulation, and then equate the result to zero. From these relationships we can write the differential equations for the circuit. Then we can take the Laplace transforms of the differential equations and finally solve for the transfer function.

SIMPLE CIRCUITS VIA MESH ANALYSIS

Transfer functions can be obtained using Kirchhoff's voltage law and summing voltages around loops or meshes.[3] We call this method *loop* or *mesh analysis* and demonstrate it in the following example.

EXAMPLE 2.6

Transfer function—single loop via the differential equation

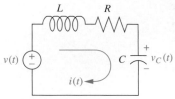

FIGURE 2.3 *RLC* network

Problem: Find the transfer function relating the capacitor voltage, $V_C(s)$, to the input voltage, $V(s)$, in Figure 2.3.

SOLUTION: In any problem the designer must first decide what the input and output should be. In this network several variables could have been chosen to be the output—for example, the inductor voltage, the capacitor voltage, the resistor voltage, or the current. The problem statement, however, is clear in this case: We are to treat the capacitor voltage as the output and the applied voltage as the input.

Summing the voltages around the loop, assuming zero initial conditions, yields the integrodifferential equation for this network as

$$L\frac{di(t)}{dt} + Ri(t) + \frac{1}{C}\int_0^t i(\tau)\,d\tau = v(t) \tag{2.61}$$

Changing variables from current to charge using $i(t) = dq(t)/dt$ yields

$$L\frac{d^2q(t)}{dt^2} + R\frac{dq(t)}{dt} + \frac{1}{C}q(t) = v(t) \tag{2.62}$$

From the voltage-charge relationship for a capacitor in Table 2.3,

$$q(t) = Cv_C(t) \tag{2.63}$$

Substituting Eq. (2.63) into Eq. (2.62) yields

$$LC\frac{d^2v_C(t)}{dt^2} + RC\frac{dv_C(t)}{dt} + v_C(t) = v(t) \tag{2.64}$$

---

[3] A particular loop that resembles the spaces in a screen or fence is called a *mesh*.

Taking the Laplace transform assuming zero initial conditions, rearranging terms, and simplifying yields

$$(LCs^2 + RCs + 1)V_C(s) = V(s) \quad (2.65)$$

Solving for the transfer function, $V_C(s)/V(s)$, we obtain

$$\frac{V_C(s)}{V(s)} = \frac{1/LC}{s^2 + \frac{R}{L}s + \frac{1}{LC}} \quad (2.66)$$

as shown in Figure 2.4.

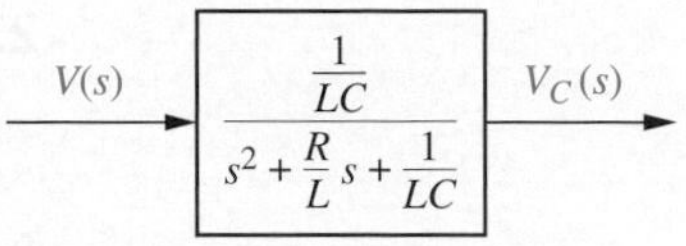

FIGURE 2.4 Block diagram of series RLC electrical network

Let us now develop a technique for simplifying the solution for future problems. First, take the Laplace transform of the equations in the voltage-current column of Table 2.3 assuming zero initial conditions.

For the capacitor,

$$V(s) = \frac{1}{Cs}I(s) \quad (2.67)$$

For the resistor,

$$V(s) = RI(s) \quad (2.68)$$

For the inductor,

$$V(s) = LsI(s) \quad (2.69)$$

Now define the following transfer function:

$$\frac{V(s)}{I(s)} = Z(s) \quad (2.70)$$

Notice that this function is similar to the definition of resistance, that is, the ratio of voltage to current. But, unlike resistance, this function is applicable to capacitors and inductors and carries information on the dynamic behavior of the component, since it represents an equivalent differential equation. We call this particular transfer function *impedance*. The impedance for each of the electrical elements is shown in Table 2.3.

Let us now demonstrate how the concept of impedance simplifies the solution for the transfer function. The Laplace transform of Eq. (2.61), assuming zero initial conditions, is

$$\left(Ls + R + \frac{1}{Cs}\right)I(s) = V(s) \quad (2.71)$$

Notice that Eq. (2.71), which is in the form

$$[\text{Sum of impedances}]I(s) = [\text{Sum of applied voltages}] \quad (2.72)$$

suggests the series circuit shown in Figure 2.5. Also notice that the circuit of Figure 2.5 could have been obtained immediately from the circuit of Figure 2.3 simply by replacing each element with its impedance. We call this altered circuit the *transformed circuit*. Finally, notice that the transformed circuit leads immediately to Eq. (2.71) if we add impedances in series as we add resistors in series. Thus, rather than writing the differential equation first and then taking the Laplace transform, we can draw the transformed circuit and obtain the Laplace transform of the

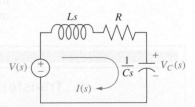

FIGURE 2.5 Laplace-transformed network

differential equation simply by applying Kirchhoff's voltage law to the transformed circuit. We summarize the steps as follows:

1. Redraw the original network showing all time variables, such as $v(t)$, $i(t)$, and $v_C(t)$, as Laplace transforms $V(s)$, $I(s)$, and $V_C(s)$, respectively.

2. Replace the component values with their impedance values. This replacement is similar to the case of dc circuits, where we represent resistors with their resistance values.

We now redo Example 2.6 using the transform methods just described and bypass the writing of the differential equation.

■ EXAMPLE 2.7 ■

Transfer function—single loop via transform methods

Problem: Repeat Example 2.6 using mesh analysis and transform methods without writing a differential equation.

SOLUTION: Using Figure 2.5 and writing a mesh equation using the impedances as we would use resistor values in a purely resistive circuit, we obtain

$$\left(Ls + R + \frac{1}{Cs}\right)I(s) = V(s) \tag{2.73}$$

Solving for $I(s)/V(s)$,

$$\frac{I(s)}{V(s)} = \frac{1}{Ls + R + \dfrac{1}{Cs}} \tag{2.74}$$

But the voltage across the capacitor, $V_C(s)$, is the product of the current and the impedance of the capacitor. Thus,

$$V_C(s) = I(s)\frac{1}{Cs} \tag{2.75}$$

Solving Eq. (2.75) for $I(s)$, substituting $I(s)$ into Eq. (2.74), and simplifying yields the same result as Eq. (2.66).

SIMPLE CIRCUITS VIA NODAL ANALYSIS

Transfer functions also can be obtained using Kirchhoff's current law and summing currents flowing from nodes. We call this method *nodal analysis*. We now demonstrate this principle by redoing Example 2.6 using Kirchhoff's current law and the transform methods just described to bypass writing the differential equation.

■ EXAMPLE 2.8 ■

Transfer function—single node via transform methods

Problem: Repeat Example 2.6 using nodal analysis and without writing a differential equation.

SOLUTION: The transfer function can be obtained by summing currents flowing out of the node whose voltage is $V_C(s)$ in Figure 2.5. We assume that currents leaving the node are positive and currents entering the node are negative. The currents consist of the current through the capacitor and the current flowing through the series resistor and inductor. From Eq. (2.70), each $I(s) = V(s)/Z(s)$. Hence,

$$\frac{V_C(s)}{1/Cs} + \frac{V_C(s) - V(s)}{R + Ls} = 0 \tag{2.76}$$

where $V_C(s)/(1/Cs)$ is the current flowing out of the node through the capacitor, and $[V_C(s) - V(s)]/(R + Ls)$ is the current flowing out of the node through the series resistor and inductor. Solving Eq. (2.76) for the transfer function, $V_C(s)/V(s)$, we arrive at the same result as Eq. (2.66).

SIMPLE CIRCUITS VIA VOLTAGE DIVISION

Example 2.6 can be solved directly by using voltage division on the transformed network. We now demonstrate this technique.

EXAMPLE 2.9

Transfer function—single loop via voltage division

Problem: Repeat Example 2.6 using voltage division and the transformed circuit.

SOLUTION: The voltage across the capacitor is some proportion of the input voltage, namely the impedance of the capacitor divided by the sum of the impedances. Thus,

$$V_C(s) = \frac{1/Cs}{\left(Ls + R + \dfrac{1}{Cs}\right)} V(s) \tag{2.77}$$

Solving for the transfer function, $V_C(s)/V(s)$, yields the same result as Eq. (2.66).

Review Examples 2.6 through 2.9. Which method do you think is easiest for this circuit?

The previous example involves a simple, single-loop electrical network. Many electrical networks consist of multiple loops and nodes, and for these circuits we must write and solve simultaneous differential equations in order to find the transfer function, or solve for the output.

COMPLEX CIRCUITS VIA MESH ANALYSIS

To solve complex electrical networks—those with multiple loops and nodes—using mesh analysis, we can perform the following steps:

1. Replace passive element values with their impedances.

2. Replace all sources and time variables with their Laplace transform.

3. Assume a transform current and a current direction in each mesh.

4. Write Kirchhoff's voltage law around each mesh.

5. Solve the simultaneous equations for the output.

6. Form the transfer function.

Let us look at an example.

▮ EXAMPLE 2.10 ▮

Transfer function—multiple loops

Problem: Given the network of Figure 2.6(a), find the transfer function, $I_2(s)/V(s)$.

SOLUTION: The first step in the solution is to convert the network into Laplace transforms for impedances and circuit variables, assuming zero initial conditions. The result is shown in Figure 2.6(b). The circuit with which we are dealing requires two simultaneous equations to solve for the transfer function. These equations can be found by summing voltages around each mesh through which the assumed currents, $I_1(s)$ and $I_2(s)$, flow. Around Mesh 1, where $I_1(s)$ flows,

$$R_1 I_1(s) + Ls I_1(s) - Ls I_2(s) = V(s) \tag{2.78}$$

Around Mesh 2, where $I_2(s)$ flows,

$$Ls I_2(s) + R_2 I_2(s) + \frac{1}{Cs} I_2(s) - Ls I_1(s) = 0 \tag{2.79}$$

Combining terms, Eqs. (2.78) and (2.79) become simultaneous equations in $I_1(s)$ and $I_2(s)$:

$$(R_1 + Ls)I_1(s) - Ls I_2(s) = V(s) \tag{2.80a}$$

$$-Ls I_1(s) + \left(Ls + R_2 + \frac{1}{Cs}\right)I_2(s) = 0 \tag{2.80b}$$

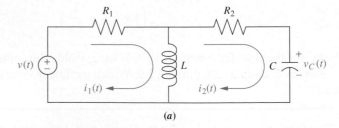

(a)

(b)

FIGURE 2.6
a. Two-loop electrical network;
b. transformed two-loop electrical network;
c. block diagram

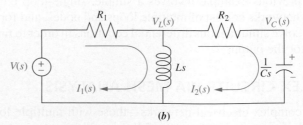

(c)

We can use Cramer's rule (or any other method for solving simultaneous equations) to solve Eqs. (2.80) for $I_2(s)$.[4] Hence,

$$I_2(s) = \frac{\begin{vmatrix} (R_1 + Ls) & V(s) \\ -Ls & 0 \end{vmatrix}}{\Delta} = \frac{LsV(s)}{\Delta} \qquad (2.81)$$

where

$$\Delta = \begin{vmatrix} (R_1 + Ls) & -Ls \\ -Ls & \left(Ls + R_2 + \dfrac{1}{Cs}\right) \end{vmatrix}$$

Forming the transfer function, $G(s)$, yields

$$G(s) = \frac{I_2(s)}{V(s)} = \frac{Ls}{\Delta} = \frac{LCs^2}{(R_1 + R_2)LCs^2 + (R_1 R_2 C + L)s + R_1} \qquad (2.82)$$

as shown in Figure 2.6(c).

We have succeeded in modeling a physical network as a transfer function: The network of Figure 2.6(a) is now modeled as the transfer function of Figure 2.6(c). Before leaving the example, we notice a pattern first illustrated by Eq. (2.72). The form that Eqs. (2.80) take is

$$\begin{bmatrix} \text{Sum of} \\ \text{impedances} \\ \text{around Mesh 1} \end{bmatrix} I_1(s) - \begin{bmatrix} \text{Sum of} \\ \text{impedances} \\ \text{common to the} \\ \text{two meshes} \end{bmatrix} I_2(s) = \begin{bmatrix} \text{Sum of applied} \\ \text{voltages around} \\ \text{Mesh 1} \end{bmatrix}$$

$$(2.83a)$$

$$- \begin{bmatrix} \text{Sum of} \\ \text{impedances} \\ \text{common to the} \\ \text{two meshes} \end{bmatrix} I_1(s) + \begin{bmatrix} \text{Sum of} \\ \text{impedances} \\ \text{around Mesh 2} \end{bmatrix} I_2(s) = \begin{bmatrix} \text{Sum of applied} \\ \text{voltages around} \\ \text{Mesh 2} \end{bmatrix}$$

$$(2.83b)$$

Recognizing the form will help us write such equations rapidly; for example, mechanical equations of motion (covered in Sections 2.5 and 2.6) have the same form.

Students who are performing the MATLAB exercises and want to explore the added capability of MATLAB's Symbolic Math Toolbox should now run ch2sp4 in Appendix E at www.wiley.com/college/nise, where Example 2.10 is solved. You will learn how to use the Symbolic Math Toolbox to solve simultaneous equations using Cramer's rule. Specifically, the Symbolic Math Toolbox will be used to solve for the transfer function in Eq. (2.82) using Eqs. (2.80).

Symbolic Math

---

[4] See Appendix F (Section F.4) at www.wiley.com/college/nise for Cramer's rule.

COMPLEX CIRCUITS VIA NODAL ANALYSIS

Often, the easiest way to find the transfer function is to use nodal analysis rather than mesh analysis. The number of simultaneous differential equations that must be written is equal to the number of nodes whose voltage is unknown. In the previous example we wrote simultaneous mesh equations using Kirchhoff's voltage law. For multiple nodes we use Kirchhoff's current law and sum currents flowing from each node. Again, as a convention, currents flowing from the node are assumed to be positive, and currents flowing into the node are assumed to be negative.

Before progressing to an example, let us first define *admittance*, $Y(s)$, as the reciprocal of impedance, or

$$Y(s) = \frac{1}{Z(s)} = \frac{I(s)}{V(s)} \tag{2.84}$$

When writing nodal equations, it can be more convenient to represent circuit elements by their admittance. Admittances for the basic electrical components are shown in Table 2.3. Let us look at an example.

EXAMPLE 2.11

Transfer function—multiple nodes

Problem: Find the transfer function, $V_C(s)/V(s)$, for the circuit in Figure 2.6(*b*). Use nodal analysis.

SOLUTION: For this problem we sum currents at the nodes rather than sum voltages around the meshes. From Figure 2.6(*b*) the sum of currents flowing from the nodes marked $V_L(s)$ and $V_C(s)$ are, respectively,

$$\frac{V_L(s) - V(s)}{R_1} + \frac{V_L(s)}{Ls} + \frac{V_L(s) - V_C(s)}{R_2} = 0 \tag{2.85a}$$

$$CsV_C(s) + \frac{V_C(s) - V_L(s)}{R_2} = 0 \tag{2.85b}$$

Rearranging and expressing the resistances as conductances,[5] $G_1 = 1/R_1$ and $G_2 = 1/R_2$, we obtain,

$$\left(G_1 + G_2 + \frac{1}{Ls}\right)V_L(s) \qquad - G_2V_C(s) = V(s)G_1 \tag{2.86a}$$

$$-G_2V_L(s) + (G_2 + Cs)V_C(s) = 0 \tag{2.86b}$$

Solving for the transfer function, $V_C(s)/V(s)$, yields

$$\frac{V_C(s)}{V(s)} = \frac{\frac{G_1G_2}{C}s}{(G_1 + G_2)s^2 + \frac{G_1G_2L + C}{LC}s + \frac{G_2}{LC}} \tag{2.87}$$

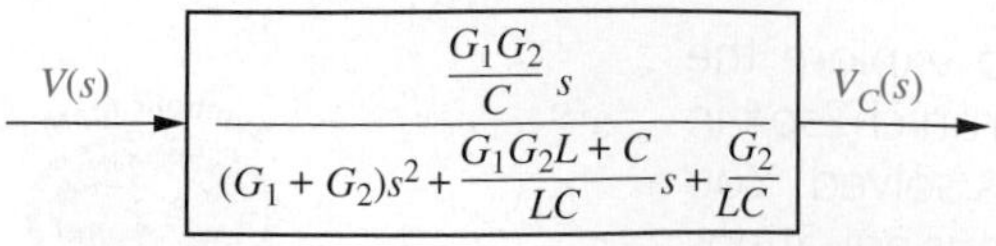

as shown in Figure 2.7.

FIGURE 2.7 Block diagram of the network of Figure 2.6

[5] In general, admittance is complex. The real part is called conductance and the imaginary part is called susceptance. But when we take the reciprocal of resistance to obtain the admittance, a purely real quantity results. The reciprocal of resistance is called conductance.

Another way to write node equations is to replace voltage sources by current sources. A voltage source presents a constant voltage to any load; conversely, a current source delivers a constant current to any load. Practically, a current source can be constructed from a voltage source by placing a large resistance in series with the voltage source. Thus, variations in the load do not appreciably change the current, because the current is determined approximately by the large series resistor and the voltage source. Theoretically, we rely on *Norton's theorem*, which states that a voltage source, $V(s)$, in series with an impedance, $Z_s(s)$, can be replaced by a current source, $I(s) = V(s)/Z_s(s)$, in parallel with $Z_s(s)$.

In order to handle multiple-node electrical networks, we can perform the following steps:

1. Replace passive element values with their admittances.

2. Replace all sources and time variables with their Laplace transform.

3. Replace transformed voltage sources with transformed current sources.

4. Write Kirchhoff's current law at each node.

5. Solve the simultaneous equations for the output.

6. Form the transfer function.

Let us look at an example.

EXAMPLE 2.12

Transfer function—multiple nodes with current sources

Problem: For the network of Figure 2.6, find the transfer function, $V_C(s)/V(s)$, using nodal analysis and a transformed circuit with current sources.

SOLUTION: Convert all impedances to admittances and all voltage sources in series with an impedance to current sources in parallel with an admittance using Norton's theorem.

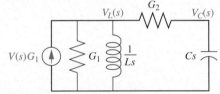

FIGURE 2.8 Transformed network ready for nodal analysis

Redrawing Figure 2.6(*b*) to reflect the changes, we obtain Figure 2.8, where $G_1 = 1/R_1$, $G_2 = 1/R_2$, and the node voltages—the voltages across the inductor and the capacitor—have been identified as $V_L(s)$ and $V_C(s)$, respectively. Using the general relationship, $I(s) = Y(s)V(s)$, and summing currents at the node $V_L(s)$,

$$G_1 V_L(s) + \frac{1}{Ls} V_L(s) + G_2[V_L(s) - V_C(s)] = V(s)G_1 \qquad (2.88)$$

Summing the currents at the node $V_C(s)$ yields

$$Cs V_C(s) + G_2[V_C(s) - V_L(s)] = 0 \qquad (2.89)$$

Combining terms, Eqs. (2.88) and (2.89) become simultaneous equations in $V_C(s)$ and $V_L(s)$, which are identical to Eqs. (2.86) and lead to the same solution as Eq. (2.87).

An advantage of drawing this circuit lies in the form of Eqs. (2.86) and its direct relationship to Figure 2.8, namely

$$\begin{bmatrix} \text{Sum of admittances} \\ \text{connected to Node 1} \end{bmatrix} V_L(s) - \begin{bmatrix} \text{Sum of admittances} \\ \text{common to the two} \\ \text{nodes} \end{bmatrix} V_C(s) = \begin{bmatrix} \text{Sum of applied} \\ \text{currents at Node 1} \end{bmatrix}$$

$$(2.90a)$$

$$-\begin{bmatrix} \text{Sum of admittances} \\ \text{common to the two} \\ \text{nodes} \end{bmatrix} V_L(s) + \begin{bmatrix} \text{Sum of admittances} \\ \text{connected to Node 2} \end{bmatrix} V_C(s) = \begin{bmatrix} \text{Sum of applied} \\ \text{currents at Node 2} \end{bmatrix}$$

$$(2.90b)$$

A PROBLEM-SOLVING TECHNIQUE

In all of the previous examples, we have seen a repeating pattern in the equations that we can use to our advantage. If we recognize this pattern, we need not write the equations component by component; we can sum impedances around a mesh in the case of mesh equations or sum admittances at a node in the case of node equations. Let us now look at a three-loop electrical network and write the mesh equations by inspection to demonstrate the process.

EXAMPLE 2.13

Mesh equations via inspection

Problem: Write, but do not solve, the mesh equations for the network shown in Figure 2.9.

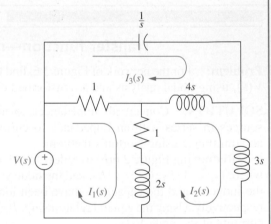

FIGURE 2.9   Three-loop electrical network

SOLUTION: Each of the previous problems has illustrated that the mesh equations and nodal equations have a predictable form. We use that knowledge to solve this three-loop problem. The equation for Mesh 1 will have the following form:

$$\begin{bmatrix} \text{Sum of} \\ \text{impedances} \\ \text{around Mesh 1} \end{bmatrix} I_1(s) - \begin{bmatrix} \text{Sum of} \\ \text{impedances} \\ \text{common to} \\ \text{Mesh 1 and} \\ \text{Mesh 2} \end{bmatrix} I_2(s)$$

$$- \begin{bmatrix} \text{Sum of} \\ \text{impedances} \\ \text{common to} \\ \text{Mesh 1 and} \\ \text{Mesh 3} \end{bmatrix} I_3(s) = \begin{bmatrix} \text{Sum of applied} \\ \text{voltages around} \\ \text{Mesh 1} \end{bmatrix}$$

$$(2.91)$$

Similarly, Meshes 2 and 3, respectively, are

$$-\begin{bmatrix} \text{Sum of} \\ \text{impedances} \\ \text{common to} \\ \text{Mesh 1 and} \\ \text{Mesh 2} \end{bmatrix} I_1(s) + \begin{bmatrix} \text{Sum of} \\ \text{impedances} \\ \text{around Mesh 2} \end{bmatrix} I_2(s)$$

$$-\begin{bmatrix} \text{Sum of} \\ \text{impedances} \\ \text{common to} \\ \text{Mesh 2 and} \\ \text{Mesh 3} \end{bmatrix} I_3(s) = \begin{bmatrix} \text{Sum of applied} \\ \text{voltages around} \\ \text{Mesh 2} \end{bmatrix}$$

(2.92)

and

$$-\begin{bmatrix} \text{Sum of} \\ \text{impedances} \\ \text{common to} \\ \text{Mesh 1 and} \\ \text{Mesh 3} \end{bmatrix} I_1(s) - \begin{bmatrix} \text{Sum of} \\ \text{impedances} \\ \text{common to} \\ \text{Mesh 2 and} \\ \text{Mesh 3} \end{bmatrix} I_2(s)$$

$$+\begin{bmatrix} \text{Sum of} \\ \text{impedances} \\ \text{around Mesh 3} \end{bmatrix} I_3(s) = \begin{bmatrix} \text{Sum of applied} \\ \text{voltages around} \\ \text{Mesh 3} \end{bmatrix}$$

(2.93)

Substituting the values from Figure 2.9 into Eqs. (2.91) through (2.93) yields

$$+(2s+2)I_1(s) - (2s+1)I_2(s) \qquad\qquad - I_3(s) = V(s) \qquad (2.94a)$$

$$-(2s+1)I_1(s) + (9s+1)I_2(s) \qquad\qquad -4sI_3(s) = 0 \qquad (2.94b)$$

$$-I_1(s) \qquad -4sI_2(s) + \left(4s+1+\tfrac{1}{s}\right)I_3(s) = 0 \qquad (2.94c)$$

which can be solved simultaneously for any desired transfer function, for example, $I_3(s)/V(s)$.

> **TryIt 2.8**
>
> Use the following MATLAB and Symbolic Math Toolbox statements to help you solve for the electrical currents in Eqs. (2.94).
>
> ```
> syms s I1 I2 I3 V
> A = [(2*s + 2) -(2*s + 1) -1
>      -(2*s + 1)(9*s + 1) -4*s
>      -1 -4*s (4*s + 1 + 1/s)];
> B = [I1
>      I2
>      I3];
> C = [V
>      0
>      0];
> B = inv(A)*C;
> pretty(B)
> ```

Passive electrical circuits were the topic of discussion up to this point. We now discuss a class of active circuits that can be used to implement transfer functions. These are circuits built around an operational amplifier.

OPERATIONAL AMPLIFIERS

An *operational amplifier,* pictured in Figure 2.10(a), is an electronic amplifier used as a basic building block to implement transfer functions. It has the following characteristics:

1. Differential input, $v_2(t) - v_1(t)$

2. High input impedance, $Z_i = \infty$ (ideal)

3. Low output impedance, $Z_o = 0$ (ideal)

4. High constant gain amplification, $A = \infty$ (ideal)

FIGURE 2.10
a. Operational amplifier;
b. schematic for an inverting
operational amplifier;
c. inverting operational
amplifier configured for
transfer function realization.
Typically, the amplifier gain,
A, is omitted

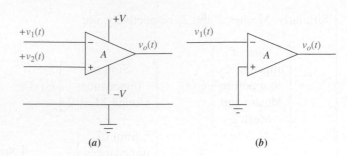

(a)   (b)

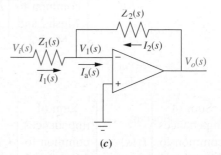

(c)

The output, $v_o(t)$, is given by

$$v_o(t) = A(v_2(t) - v_1(t)) \tag{2.95}$$

INVERTING OPERATIONAL AMPLIFIER

If $v_2(t)$ is grounded, the amplifier is called an *inverting operational amplifier,* as shown
in Figure 2.10(b). For the inverting operational amplifier, we have

$$v_o(t) = -Av_1(t) \tag{2.96}$$

If two impedances are connected to the inverting operational amplifier as shown in
Figure 2.10(c), we can derive an interesting result if the amplifier has the characteristics
mentioned in the beginning of this subsection. If the input impedance to the amplifier is
high, then by Kirchhoff's current law $I_a(s) = 0$ and $I_1(s) = -I_2(s)$. Also, since the gain
A is large, $v_1(t) \approx 0$. Thus, $I_1(s) = V_i(s)/Z_1(s)$, and $-I_2(s) = -V_o(s)/Z_2(s)$. Equating
the two currents, $V_o(s)/Z_2(s) = -V_i(s)/Z_1(s)$, or the transfer function of the inverting
operational amplifier configured as shown in Figure 2.10(c) is

$$\frac{V_o(s)}{V_i(s)} = -\frac{Z_2(s)}{Z_1(s)} \tag{2.97}$$

EXAMPLE 2.14

Transfer function—inverting operational amplifier circuit

Problem: Find the transfer function, $V_o(s)/V_i(s)$, for the circuit given in Figure 2.11.

SOLUTION: The transfer function of the operational amplifier circuit is given by
Eq. (2.97). Since the admittances of parallel components add, $Z_1(s)$ is the reciprocal of

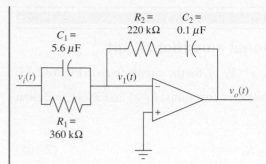

FIGURE 2.11 Inverting operational amplifier circuit for Example 2.14

the sum of the admittances, or

$$Z_1(s) = \frac{1}{C_1 s + \dfrac{1}{R_1}} = \frac{1}{5.6 \times 10^{-6} s + \dfrac{1}{360 \times 10^3}} = \frac{360 \times 10^3}{2.016 s + 1} \qquad (2.98)$$

For $Z_2(s)$ the impedances add, or

$$Z_2(s) = R_2 + \frac{1}{C_2 s} = 220 \times 10^3 + \frac{10^7}{s} \qquad (2.99)$$

Substituting Eqs. (2.98) and (2.99) into Eq. (2.97) and simplifying, we get

$$\frac{V_o(s)}{V_i(s)} = -1.232 \frac{s^2 + 45.95 s + 22.55}{s} \qquad (2.100)$$

The resulting circuit is called a PID controller and can be used to improve the performance of a control system. We explore this possibility further in Chapter 9.

NONINVERTING OPERATIONAL AMPLIFIER

Another circuit that can be analyzed for its transfer function is the noninverting operational amplifier circuit shown in Figure 2.12. We now derive the transfer function. We see that

$$V_o(s) = A(V_i(s) - V_1(s)) \qquad (2.101)$$

But, using voltage division,

$$V_1(s) = \frac{Z_1(s)}{Z_1(s) + Z_2(s)} V_o(s) \qquad (2.102)$$

Substituting Eq. (2.102) into Eq. (2.101), rearranging, and simplifying, we obtain

$$\frac{V_o(s)}{V_i(s)} = \frac{A}{1 + AZ_1(s)/(Z_1(s) + Z_2(s))} \qquad (2.103)$$

For large A, we disregard unity in the denominator and Eq. (2.103) becomes

$$\boxed{\frac{V_o(s)}{V_i(s)} = \frac{Z_1(s) + Z_2(s)}{Z_1(s)}} \qquad (2.104)$$

Let us now look at an example.

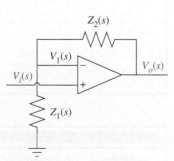

FIGURE 2.12 General noninverting operational amplifier circuit

EXAMPLE 2.15

Transfer function—noninverting operational amplifier circuit

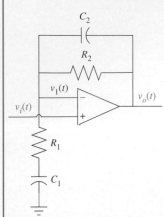

Problem: Find the transfer function, $V_o(s)/V_i(s)$, for the circuit given in Figure 2.13.

SOLUTION: We find each of the impedance functions, $Z_1(s)$ and $Z_2(s)$, and then substitute them into Eq. (2.104). Thus,

$$Z_1(s) = R_1 + \frac{1}{C_1 s} \tag{2.105}$$

and

$$Z_2(s) = \frac{R_2(1/C_2 s)}{R_2 + (1/C_2 s)} \tag{2.106}$$

Substituting Eqs. (2.105) and (2.106) into Eq. (2.104) yields

$$\frac{V_o(s)}{V_i(s)} = \frac{C_2 C_1 R_2 R_1 s^2 + (C_2 R_2 + C_1 R_2 + C_1 R_1)s + 1}{C_2 C_1 R_2 R_1 s^2 + (C_2 R_2 + C_1 R_1)s + 1} \tag{2.107}$$

FIGURE 2.13 Noninverting operational amplifier circuit for Example 2.15

SKILL-ASSESSMENT EXERCISE 2.6

Problem: Find the transfer function, $G(s) = V_L(s)/V(s)$, for the circuit given in Figure 2.14. Solve the problem two ways—mesh analysis and nodal analysis. Show that the two methods yield the same result.

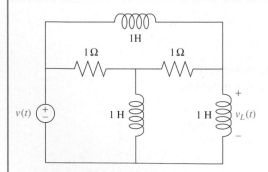

FIGURE 2.14 Electric circuit for Skill-Assessment Exercise 2.6

ANSWER: $V_L(s)/V(s) = (s^2 + 2s + 1)/(s^2 + 5s + 2)$

The complete solution is at www.wiley.com/college/nise.

SKILL-ASSESSMENT EXERCISE 2.7

Problem: If $Z_1(s)$ is the impedance of a 10 μF capacitor and $Z_2(s)$ is the impedance of a 100 kΩ resistor, find the transfer function, $G(s) = V_o(s)/V_i(s)$, if these components are used with (a) an inverting operational amplifier and (b) a noninverting amplifier as shown in Figures 2.10(c) and 2.12, respectively.

ANSWER: $G(s) = -s$ for an inverting operational amplifier; $G(s) = s + 1$ for a noninverting operational amplifier.

The complete solution is at www.wiley.com/college/nise.

In this section we found transfer functions for multiple-loop and multiple-node electrical networks, as well as operational amplifier circuits. We developed mesh and nodal equations, noted their form, and wrote them by inspection. In the next section we begin our work with mechanical systems. We will see that many of the concepts applied to electrical networks can also be applied to mechanical systems via analogies—from basic concepts to writing the describing equations by inspection. This revelation will give you the confidence to move beyond this textbook and study systems not covered here, such as hydraulic or pneumatic systems.

2.5 TRANSLATIONAL MECHANICAL SYSTEM TRANSFER FUNCTIONS

We have shown that electrical networks can be modeled by a transfer function, $G(s)$, that algebraically relates the Laplace transform of the output to the Laplace transform of the input. Now we will do the same for mechanical systems. In this section we concentrate on translational mechanical systems. In the next section we extend the concepts to rotational mechanical systems. Notice that the end product, shown in Figure 2.2, will be mathematically indistinguishable from an electrical network. Hence, an electrical network can be interfaced to a mechanical system by cascading their transfer functions, provided that one system is not loaded by the other.[6]

Mechanical systems parallel electrical networks to such an extent that there are analogies between electrical and mechanical components and variables. Mechanical systems, like electrical networks, have three passive, linear components. Two of them, the spring and the mass, are energy-storage elements; one of them, the viscous damper, dissipates energy. The two energy-storage elements are analogous to the two electrical energy-storage elements, the inductor and capacitor. The energy dissipator is analogous to electrical resistance. Let us take a look at these mechanical elements, which are shown in Table 2.4. In the table, K, f_v, and M are called *spring constant, coefficient of viscous friction*, and *mass*, respectively.

We now create analogies between electrical and mechanical systems by comparing Tables 2.3 and 2.4. Comparing the force-velocity column of Table 2.4 to the voltage-current column of Table 2.3, we see that mechanical force is analogous to electrical voltage and mechanical velocity is analogous to electrical current. Comparing the force-displacement column of Table 2.4 with the voltage-charge column of Table 2.3 leads to the analogy between the mechanical displacement and electrical charge. We also see that the spring is analogous to the capacitor, the viscous damper is analogous to the resistor, and the mass is analogous to the inductor. Thus, summing forces written in terms of velocity is analogous to summing voltages written in terms of current, and the resulting mechanical differential equations are analogous to mesh equations. If the forces are written in terms of displacement, the resulting mechanical equations resemble, but are not analogous to, the mesh equations. We, however, will use this model for mechanical systems so that we can write equations directly in terms of displacement.

---

[6] The concept of loading is explained further in Chapter 5.

TABLE 2.4   **Force-velocity, force-displacement, and impedance translational relationships for springs, viscous dampers, and mass**

Component	Force-velocity	Force-displacement	Impedence $Z_M(s) = F(s)/X(s)$
Spring K	$f(t) = K \int_0^t v(\tau)d\tau$	$f(t) = Kx(t)$	K
Viscous damper f_v	$f(t) = f_v v(t)$	$f(t) = f_v \dfrac{dx(t)}{dt}$	$f_v s$
Mass	$f(t) = M \dfrac{dv(t)}{dt}$	$f(t) = M \dfrac{d^2x(t)}{dt^2}$	Ms^2

Note: The following set of symbols and units is used throughout this book: $f(t) = $ N (newtons), $x(t) = $ m (meters), $v(t) = $ m/s (meters/second), $K = $ N/m (newtons/meter), $f_v = $ N-s/m(newton-seconds/meter), $M = $ kg(kilograms $= $ newton-seconds^2/meter).

Another analogy can be drawn by comparing the force-velocity column of Table 2.4 to the current-voltage column of Table 2.3 in reverse order. Here the analogy is between force and current and between velocity and voltage. Also, the spring is analogous to the inductor, the viscous damper is analogous to the resistor, and the mass is analogous to the capacitor. Thus, summing forces written in terms of velocity is analogous to summing currents written in terms of voltage and the resulting mechanical differential equations are analogous to nodal equations. We will discuss these analogies in more detail in Section 2.9.

We are now ready to find transfer functions for translational mechanical systems. Our first example, shown in Figure 2.15(a), is similar to the simple *RLC* network of Example 2.6 (see Figure 2.3). The mechanical system requires just one differential equation, called the *equation of motion*, to describe it. We will begin by assuming a positive direction of motion, for example, to the right. This assumed positive direction of motion is similar to assuming a current direction in an electrical loop. Using our assumed direction of positive motion, we first draw a free-body diagram, placing on the body all forces that act on the body either in the direction of motion or opposite to it. Next we use Newton's law to form a differential equation of motion by summing the forces and setting the sum equal to zero. Finally, assuming zero initial conditions, we take the Laplace transform of the differential equation, separate the variables, and arrive at the transfer function. An example follows.

EXAMPLE 2.16

Transfer function—one equation of motion

Problem: Find the transfer function, $X(s)/F(s)$, for the system of Figure 2.15(a).

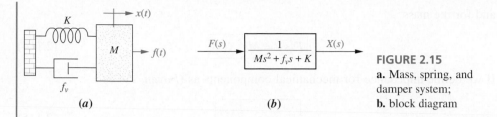

FIGURE 2.15
a. Mass, spring, and damper system;
b. block diagram

SOLUTION: Begin the solution by drawing the free-body diagram shown in Figure 2.16(*a*). Place on the mass all forces felt by the mass. We assume the mass is traveling toward the right. Thus, only the applied force points to the right; all other forces impede the motion and act to oppose it. Hence, the spring, viscous damper, and the force due to acceleration point to the left.

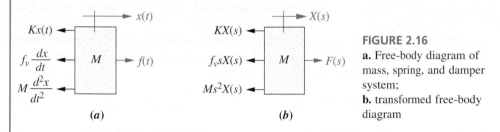

FIGURE 2.16
a. Free-body diagram of mass, spring, and damper system;
b. transformed free-body diagram

We now write the differential equation of motion using Newton's law to sum to zero all of the forces shown on the mass in Figure 2.16(*a*):

$$M\frac{d^2x(t)}{dt^2} + f_v\frac{dx(t)}{dt} + Kx(t) = f(t) \tag{2.108}$$

Taking the Laplace transform, assuming zero initial conditions,

$$Ms^2X(s) + f_vsX(s) + KX(s) = F(s) \tag{2.109}$$

or

$$(Ms^2 + f_vs + K)X(s) = F(s) \tag{2.110}$$

Solving for the transfer function yields

$$G(s) = \frac{X(s)}{F(s)} = \frac{1}{Ms^2 + f_vs + K} \tag{2.111}$$

which is represented in Figure 2.15(*b*).

Now can we parallel our work with electrical networks by circumventing the writing of differential equations and by defining impedances for mechanical components? If so, we can apply to mechanical systems the problem-solving techniques learned in the previous section. Taking the Laplace transform of the force-displacement column in Table 2.4, we obtain for the spring

$$\boxed{F(s) = KX(s)} \tag{2.112}$$

for the viscous damper

$$\boxed{F(s) = f_vsX(s)} \tag{2.113}$$

and for the mass

$$F(s) = Ms^2 X(s)$$

(2.114)

If we define impedance for mechanical components as (*Raven, 1995*)

$$Z_M(s) = \frac{F(s)}{X(s)}$$

(2.115)

and apply the definition to Eqs. (2.112) through (2.114), we arrive at the impedances of each component as summarized in Table 2.4.[7]

Replacing each force in Figure 2.16(*a*) by its Laplace transform, which is in the format

$$F(s) = Z_M(s)X(s)$$

(2.116)

we obtain Figure 2.16(*b*), from which we could have obtained Eq. (2.109) immediately without writing the differential equation. From now on we use this approach.

Finally, notice that Eq. (2.110) is of the form

$$[\text{Sum of impedances}]X(s) = [\text{Sum of applied forces}]$$

(2.117)

which is similar, but not analogous, to a mesh equation (see footnote 7).

Many mechanical systems are similar to multiple-loop and multiple-node electrical networks, where more than one simultaneous differential equation is required to describe the system. In mechanical systems, the number of equations of motion required is equal to the number of *linearly independent* motions. Linear independence implies that a point of motion in a system can still move if all other points of motion are held still. Another name for the number of linearly independent motions is the number of *degrees of freedom*. This discussion is not meant to imply that these motions are not coupled to one another; in general, they are. For example, in a two-loop electrical network, each loop current depends on the other loop current, but if we open-circuit just one of the loops, the other current can still exist if there is a voltage source in that loop. Similarly, in a mechanical system with two degrees of freedom, one point of motion can be held still while the other point of motion moves under the influence of an applied force.

In order to work such a problem, we draw the free-body diagram for each point of motion and then use superposition. For each free-body diagram we begin by holding all other points of motion still and finding the forces acting on the body due only to its own motion. Then we hold the body still and activate the other points of motion one at a time, placing on the original body the forces created by the adjacent motion.

Using Newton's law, we sum the forces on each body and set the sum to zero. The result is a system of simultaneous equations of motion. As Laplace transforms, these equations are then solved for the output variable of interest in terms of the input variable from which the transfer function is evaluated. Example 2.17 demonstrates this problem-solving technique.

---

[7] Notice that the impedance column of Table 2.4 is not a direct analogy to the impedance column of Table 2.3, since the denominator of Eq. (2.115) is displacement. A direct analogy could be derived by defining mechanical impedance in terms of velocity as $F(s)/V(s)$. We chose Eq. (2.115) as a convenient definition for writing the equations of motion in terms of displacement, rather than velocity. The alternative, however, is available.

EXAMPLE 2.17

Transfer function—two degrees of freedom

Problem: Find the transfer function, $X_2(s)/F(s)$, for the system of Figure 2.17(a).

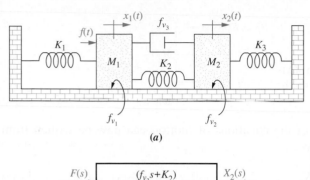

(a)

$$\frac{(f_{v_3}s+K_2)}{\Delta}$$

$F(s)$ → → $X_2(s)$

(b)

FIGURE 2.17
a. Two-degrees-of-freedom translational mechanical system;[8]
b. block diagram

SOLUTION: The system has two degrees of freedom, since each mass can be moved in the horizontal direction while the other is held still. Thus, two simultaneous equations of motion will be required to describe the system. The two equations come from free-body diagrams of each mass. Superposition is used to draw the free-body diagrams. For example, the forces on M_1 are due to (1) its own motion and (2) the motion of M_2 transmitted to M_1 through the system. We will consider these two sources separately.

If we hold M_2 still and move M_1 to the right, we see the forces shown in Figure 2.18(a). If we hold M_1 still and move M_2 to the right, we see the forces shown in Figure 2.18(b). The total force on M_1 is the superposition, or sum, of the forces just discussed. This result is shown in Figure 2.18(c). For M_2, we proceed in a similar fashion: First we move M_2 to the right while holding M_1 still; then we move M_1 to the right and hold M_2 still. For each case we evaluate the forces on M_2. The results appear in Figure 2.19.

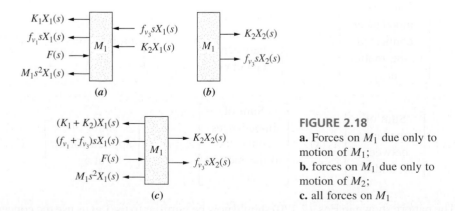

FIGURE 2.18
a. Forces on M_1 due only to motion of M_1;
b. forces on M_1 due only to motion of M_2;
c. all forces on M_1

---

[8] Friction shown here and throughout the book, unless otherwise indicated, is viscous friction. Thus, f_{v_1} and f_{v_2} are not Coulomb friction, but arise because of a viscous interface.

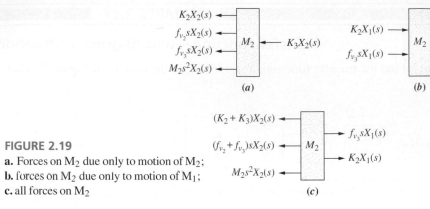

FIGURE 2.19
a. Forces on M_2 due only to motion of M_2;
b. forces on M_2 due only to motion of M_1;
c. all forces on M_2

The Laplace transform of the equations of motion can now be written from Figures 2.18(c) and 2.19(c) as

$$[M_1 s^2 + (f_{v_1} + f_{v_3})s + (K_1 + K_2)]X_1(s) - (f_{v_3}s + K_2)X_2(s) = F(s) \qquad (2.118a)$$

$$-(f_{v_3}s + K_2)X_1(s) + [M_2 s^2 + (f_{v_2} + f_{v_3})s + (K_2 + K_3)]X_2(s) = 0 \qquad (2.118b)$$

From this, the transfer function, $X_2(s)/F(s)$, is

$$\frac{X_2(s)}{F(s)} = G(s) = \frac{(f_{v_3}s + K_2)}{\Delta} \qquad (2.119)$$

as shown in Figure 2.17(b) where

$$\Delta = \begin{vmatrix} [M_1 s^2 + (f_{v_1} + f_{v_3})s + (K_1 + K_2)] & -(f_{v_3}s + K_2) \\ -(f_{v_3}s + K_2) & [M_2 s^2 + (f_{v_2} + f_{v_3})s + (K_2 + K_3)] \end{vmatrix}$$

Notice again, in Eqs. (2.118), that the form of the equations is similar to electrical mesh equations:

$$\begin{bmatrix} \text{Sum of} \\ \text{impedances} \\ \text{connected} \\ \text{to the motion} \\ \text{at } x_1 \end{bmatrix} X_1(s) - \begin{bmatrix} \text{Sum of} \\ \text{impedances} \\ \text{between} \\ x_1 \text{ and } x_2 \end{bmatrix} X_2(s) = \begin{bmatrix} \text{Sum of} \\ \text{applied forces} \\ \text{at } x_1 \end{bmatrix} \qquad (2.120a)$$

$$-\begin{bmatrix} \text{Sum of} \\ \text{impedances} \\ \text{between} \\ x_1 \text{ and } x_2 \end{bmatrix} X_1(s) + \begin{bmatrix} \text{Sum of} \\ \text{impedances} \\ \text{connected} \\ \text{to the motion} \\ \text{at } x_2 \end{bmatrix} X_2(s) = \begin{bmatrix} \text{Sum of} \\ \text{applied forces} \\ \text{at } x_2 \end{bmatrix} \qquad (2.120b)$$

The pattern shown in Eqs. (2.120) should now be familiar to us. Let us use the concept to write the equations of motion of a three-degrees-of-freedom mechanical network by inspection, without drawing the free-body diagram.

▌ EXAMPLE 2.18 ▌

Equations of motion by inspection

Problem: Write, but do not solve, the equations of motion for the mechanical network of Figure 2.20.

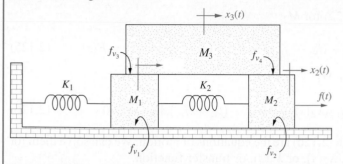

FIGURE 2.20
Three-degrees-of-freedom translational mechanical system

SOLUTION: The system has three degrees of freedom, since each of the three masses can be moved independently while the others are held still. The form of the equations will be similar to electrical mesh equations. For M_1,

$$
\begin{bmatrix} \text{Sum of} \\ \text{impedances} \\ \text{connected} \\ \text{to the motion} \\ \text{at } x_1 \end{bmatrix} X_1(s) - \begin{bmatrix} \text{Sum of} \\ \text{impedances} \\ \text{between} \\ x_1 \text{ and } x_2 \end{bmatrix} X_2(s)
$$
$$
- \begin{bmatrix} \text{Sum of} \\ \text{impedances} \\ \text{between} \\ x_1 \text{ and } x_3 \end{bmatrix} X_3(s) = \begin{bmatrix} \text{Sum of} \\ \text{applied forces} \\ \text{at } x_1 \end{bmatrix}
\tag{2.121}
$$

Similarly, for M_2 and M_3, respectively,

$$
- \begin{bmatrix} \text{Sum of} \\ \text{impedances} \\ \text{between} \\ x_1 \text{ and } x_2 \end{bmatrix} X_1(s) + \begin{bmatrix} \text{Sum of} \\ \text{impedances} \\ \text{connected} \\ \text{to the motion} \\ \text{at } x_2 \end{bmatrix} X_2(s)
$$
$$
- \begin{bmatrix} \text{Sum of} \\ \text{impedances} \\ \text{between} \\ x_2 \text{ and } x_3 \end{bmatrix} X_3(s) = \begin{bmatrix} \text{Sum of} \\ \text{applied forces} \\ \text{at } x_2 \end{bmatrix}
\tag{2.122}
$$

$$
- \begin{bmatrix} \text{Sum of} \\ \text{impedances} \\ \text{between} \\ x_1 \text{ and } x_3 \end{bmatrix} X_1(s) - \begin{bmatrix} \text{Sum of} \\ \text{impedances} \\ \text{between} \\ x_2 \text{ and } x_3 \end{bmatrix} X_2(s)
$$
$$
+ \begin{bmatrix} \text{Sum of} \\ \text{impedances} \\ \text{connected} \\ \text{to the motion} \\ \text{at } x_3 \end{bmatrix} X_3(s) = \begin{bmatrix} \text{Sum of} \\ \text{applied forces} \\ \text{at } x_3 \end{bmatrix}
\tag{2.123}
$$

M_1 has two springs, two viscous dampers, and mass associated with its motion. There is one spring between M_1 and M_2 and one viscous damper between M_1 and M_3. Thus, using Eq. (2.121),

$$[M_1s^2 + (f_{v_1} + f_{v_3})s + (K_1 + K_2)]X_1(s) - K_2X_2(s) - f_{v_3}sX_3(s) = 0 \qquad (2.124)$$

Similarly, using Eq. (2.122) for M_2,

$$-K_2X_1(s) + [M_2s^2 + (f_{v_2} + f_{v_4})s + K_2]X_2(s) - f_{v_4}sX_3(s) = F(s) \qquad (2.125)$$

and using Eq. (2.123) for M_3,

$$-f_{v_3}sX_1(s) - f_{v_4}sX_2(s) + [M_3s^2 + (f_{v_3} + f_{v_4})s]X_3(s) = 0 \qquad (2.126)$$

Equations (2.124) through (2.126) are the equations of motion. We can solve them for any displacement, $X_1(s)$, $X_2(s)$, or $X_3(s)$, or transfer function.

▌ SKILL-ASSESSMENT EXERCISE 2.8 ▌

Problem: Find the transfer function, $G(s) = X_2(s)/F(s)$, for the translational mechanical system shown in Figure 2.21.

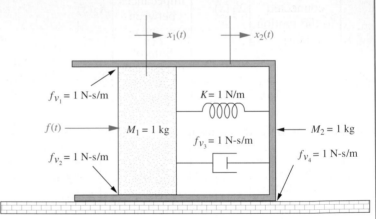

FIGURE 2.21 Translational mechanical system for Skill-Assessment Exercise 2.8

ANSWER: $G(s) = \dfrac{3s + 1}{s(s^3 + 7s^2 + 5s + 1)}$

The complete solution is at www.wiley.com/college/nise.

2.6 ROTATIONAL MECHANICAL SYSTEM TRANSFER FUNCTIONS

Having covered electrical and translational mechanical systems, we now move on to consider rotational mechanical systems. Rotational mechanical systems are handled the same way as translational mechanical systems, except that torque replaces force and angular displacement replaces translational displacement. The mechanical components for rotational systems are the same as those for translational systems, except that the

TABLE 2.5 **Torque-angular velocity, torque-angular displacement, and impedance rotational relationships for springs, viscous dampers, and inertia**

Component	Torque-angular velocity	Torque-angular displacement	Impedance $Z_M(s) = T(s)/\theta(s)$
Spring $T(t)\ \theta(t)$ K	$T(t) = K \int_0^t \omega(\tau)d\tau$	$T(t) = K\theta(t)$	K
Viscous damper $T(t)\ \theta(t)$ D	$T(t) = D\omega(t)$	$T(t) = D\dfrac{d\theta(t)}{dt}$	Ds
Inertia $T(t)\ \theta(t)$ J	$T(t) = J\dfrac{d\omega(t)}{dt}$	$T(t) = J\dfrac{d^2\theta(t)}{dt^2}$	Js^2

Note: The following set of symbols and units is used throughout this book: $T(t)$ = N-m (newton-meters), $\theta(t)$ = rad (radians), $\omega(t)$ = rad/s (radians/second), K = N-m/rad (newton-meters/radian), D = N-m-s/rad (newton-meters-seconds/radian). J = kg-m^2 (kilograms-meters^2 = newton-meters-seconds^2/radian).

components undergo rotation instead of translation. Table 2.5 shows the components along with the relationships between torque and angular velocity, as well as angular displacement. Notice that the symbols for the components look the same as translational symbols, but they are undergoing rotation and not translation.

Also notice that the term associated with the mass is replaced by inertia. The values of K, D, and J are called *spring constant, coefficient of viscous friction,* and *moment of inertia,* respectively. The impedances of the mechanical components are also summarized in the last column of Table 2.5. The values can be found by taking the Laplace transform, assuming zero initial conditions, of the torque-angular displacement column of Table 2.5.

The concept of degrees of freedom carries over to rotational systems, except that we test a point of motion by *rotating* it while holding still all other points of motion. The number of points of motion that can be rotated while all others are held still equals the number of equations of motion required to describe the system.

Writing the equations of motion for rotational systems is similar to writing them for translational systems; the only difference is that the free-body diagram consists of torques rather than forces. We obtain these torques using superposition. First, we rotate a body while holding all other points still and place on its free-body diagram all torques due to the body's own motion. Then, holding the body still, we rotate adjacent points of motion one at a time and add the torques due to the adjacent motion to the free-body diagram. The process is repeated for each point of motion. For each free-body diagram, these torques are summed and set equal to zero to form the equations of motion.

Two examples will demonstrate the solution of rotational systems. The first one uses free-body diagrams; the second uses the concept of impedances to write the equations of motion by inspection.

■ **EXAMPLE 2.19** ■

Transfer function—two equations of motion

Problem: Find the transfer function, $\theta_2(s)/T(s)$, for the rotational system shown in Figure 2.22(*a*). The rod is supported by bearings at either end and is undergoing torsion. A torque is applied at the left, and the displacement is measured at the right.

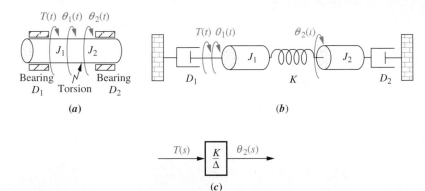

FIGURE 2.22
a. Physical system;
b. schematic;
c. block diagram

SOLUTION: First, obtain the schematic from the physical system. Even though torsion occurs throughout the rod in Figure 2.22(*a*),[9] we approximate the system by assuming that the torsion acts like a spring concentrated at one particular point in the rod, with an inertia J_1 to the left and an inertia J_2 to the right.[10] We also assume that the damping inside the flexible shaft is negligible. The schematic is shown in Figure 2.22(*b*). There are two degrees of freedom, since each inertia can be rotated while the other is held still. Hence, it will take two simultaneous equations to solve the system.

Next, draw a free-body diagram of J_1, using superposition. Figure 2.23(*a*) shows the torques on J_1 if J_2 is held still and J_1 rotated. Figure 2.23(*b*) shows the torques on J_1 if J_1 is held still and J_2 rotated. Finally, the sum of Figures 2.23(*a*) and 2.23(*b*) is shown in Figure 2.23(*c*), the final free-body diagram for J_1. The same process is repeated in Figure 2.24 for J_2.

FIGURE 2.23
a. Torques on J_1 due only to the motion of J_1;
b. torques on J_1 due only to the motion of J_2;
c. final free-body diagram for J_1

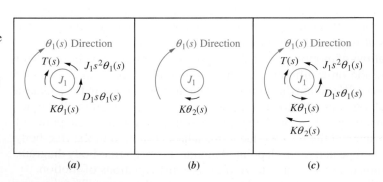

---

[9] In this case the parameter is referred to as a *distributed* parameter.
[10] The parameter is now referred to as a *lumped* parameter.

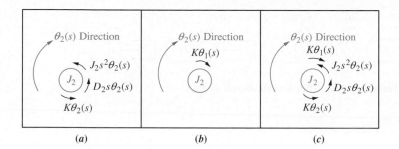

FIGURE 2.24
a. Torques on J_2 due only to the motion of J_2;
b. torques on J_2 due only to the motion of J_1;
c. final free-body diagram for J_2

Summing torques respectively from Figures 2.23(c) and 2.24(c) we obtain the equations of motion,

$$(J_1s^2 + D_1s + K)\theta_1(s) \qquad\qquad - K\theta_2(s) = T(s) \qquad (2.127a)$$

$$-K\theta_1(s) + (J_2s^2 + D_2s + K)\theta_2(s) = 0 \qquad (2.127b)$$

from which the required transfer function is found to be

$$\frac{\theta_2(s)}{T(s)} = \frac{K}{\Delta} \qquad (2.128)$$

as shown in Figure 2.22(c), where

$$\Delta = \begin{vmatrix} (J_1s^2 + D_1s + K) & -K \\ -K & (J_2s^2 + D_2s + K) \end{vmatrix}$$

Notice that Eqs. (2.127) have that now well-known form

$$\begin{bmatrix} \text{Sum of} \\ \text{impedances} \\ \text{connected} \\ \text{to the motion} \\ \text{at } \theta_1 \end{bmatrix} \theta_1(s) - \begin{bmatrix} \text{Sum of} \\ \text{impedances} \\ \text{between} \\ \theta_1 \text{ and } \theta_2 \end{bmatrix} \theta_2(s) = \begin{bmatrix} \text{Sum of} \\ \text{applied torques} \\ \text{at } \theta_1 \end{bmatrix} \quad (2.129a)$$

$$-\begin{bmatrix} \text{Sum of} \\ \text{impedances} \\ \text{between} \\ \theta_1 \text{ and } \theta_2 \end{bmatrix} \theta_1(s) + \begin{bmatrix} \text{Sum of} \\ \text{impedances} \\ \text{connected} \\ \text{to the motion} \\ \text{at } \theta_2 \end{bmatrix} \theta_2(s) = \begin{bmatrix} \text{Sum of} \\ \text{applied torques} \\ \text{at } \theta_2 \end{bmatrix} \quad (2.129b)$$

TryIt 2.9

Use the following MATLAB and Symbolic Math Toolbox statements to help you get Eq. (2.128).

```
syms s J1 D1 K T J2 D2...
theta1 theta2
A = [(J1*s^2+D1*s + K) −K
    −K (J2*s^2+D2*s+K)];
B = [theta1
    theta2];
C = [T
    0];
B = inv(A)*C;
theta2 = B(2);
'Theta2'
pretty(theta2)
```

■■■■■■■■■ **EXAMPLE 2.20** ■■■■■■■■■

Equations of motion by inspection

Problem: Write, but do not solve, the Laplace transform of the equations of motion for the system shown in Figure 2.25.

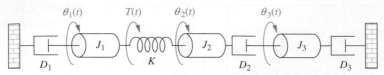

FIGURE 2.25   Three-degrees-of-freedom rotational system

SOLUTION: The equations will take on the following form, similar to electrical mesh equations:

$$
\begin{bmatrix} \text{Sum of} \\ \text{impedances} \\ \text{connected} \\ \text{to the motion} \\ \text{at } \theta_1 \end{bmatrix} \theta_1(s) - \begin{bmatrix} \text{Sum of} \\ \text{impedances} \\ \text{between} \\ \theta_1 \text{ and } \theta_2 \end{bmatrix} \theta_2(s)
$$

$$
- \begin{bmatrix} \text{Sum of} \\ \text{impedances} \\ \text{between} \\ \theta_1 \text{ and } \theta_3 \end{bmatrix} \theta_3(s) = \begin{bmatrix} \text{Sum of} \\ \text{applied torques} \\ \text{at } \theta_1 \end{bmatrix} \tag{2.130a}
$$

$$
- \begin{bmatrix} \text{Sum of} \\ \text{impedances} \\ \text{between} \\ \theta_1 \text{ and } \theta_2 \end{bmatrix} \theta_1(s) + \begin{bmatrix} \text{Sum of} \\ \text{impedances} \\ \text{connected} \\ \text{to the motion} \\ \text{at } \theta_2 \end{bmatrix} \theta_2(s)
$$

$$
- \begin{bmatrix} \text{Sum of} \\ \text{impedances} \\ \text{between} \\ \theta_2 \text{ and } \theta_3 \end{bmatrix} \theta_3(s) = \begin{bmatrix} \text{Sum of} \\ \text{applied torques} \\ \text{at } \theta_2 \end{bmatrix} \tag{2.130b}
$$

$$
- \begin{bmatrix} \text{Sum of} \\ \text{impedances} \\ \text{between} \\ \theta_1 \text{ and } \theta_3 \end{bmatrix} \theta_1(s) - \begin{bmatrix} \text{Sum of} \\ \text{impedances} \\ \text{between} \\ \theta_2 \text{ and } \theta_3 \end{bmatrix} \theta_2(s)
$$

$$
+ \begin{bmatrix} \text{Sum of} \\ \text{impedances} \\ \text{connected} \\ \text{to the motion} \\ \text{at } \theta_3 \end{bmatrix} \theta_3(s) = \begin{bmatrix} \text{Sum of} \\ \text{applied torques} \\ \text{at } \theta_3 \end{bmatrix} \tag{2.130c}
$$

Hence,

$$(J_1 s^2 + D_1 s + K)\theta_1(s) \qquad\qquad - K\theta_2(s) \qquad\qquad\qquad - 0\theta_3(s) = T(s)$$

$$-K\theta_1(s) + (J_2 s^2 + D_2 s + K)\theta_2(s) \qquad\qquad - D_2 s\theta_3(s) = 0$$

$$-0\theta_1(s) \qquad\qquad - D_2 s\theta_2(s) + (J_3 s^2 + D_3 s + D_2 s)\theta_3(s) = 0$$

$$(2.131\text{a,b,c})$$

SKILL-ASSESSMENT EXERCISE 2.9

Problem: Find the transfer function, $G(s) = \theta_2(s)/T(s)$, for the rotational mechanical system shown in Figure 2.26.

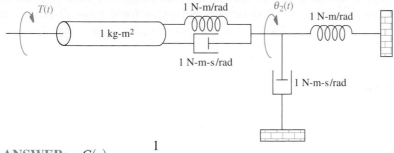

FIGURE 2.26 Rotational mechanical system for Skill-Assessment Exercise 2.9

ANSWER: $G(s) = \dfrac{1}{2s^2 + s + 1}$

The complete solution is at www.wiley.com/college/nise.

2.7 TRANSFER FUNCTIONS FOR SYSTEMS WITH GEARS

Now that we are able to find the transfer function for rotational systems, we realize that these systems, especially those driven by motors, are rarely seen without associated gear trains driving the load. This section covers this important topic.

Gears provide mechanical advantage to rotational systems. Anyone who has ridden a 10-speed bicycle knows the effect of gearing. Going uphill, you shift to provide more torque and less speed. On the straightaway, you shift to obtain more speed and less torque. Thus, gears allow you to match the drive system and the load—a trade-off between speed and torque.

For many applications, gears exhibit *backlash,* which occurs because of the loose fit between two meshed gears. The drive gear rotates through a small angle before making contact with the meshed gear. The result is that the angular rotation of the output gear does not occur until a small angular rotation of the input gear has occurred. In this section, we idealize the behavior of gears and assume that there is no backlash.

The linearized interaction between two gears is depicted in Figure 2.27. An input gear with radius r_1 and N_1 teeth is rotated through angle $\theta_1(t)$ due to a torque, $T_1(t)$. An output gear with radius r_2 and N_2 teeth responds by rotating through angle $\theta_2(t)$ and delivering a torque, $T_2(t)$. Let us now find the relationship between the rotation of Gear 1, $\theta_1(t)$, and Gear 2, $\theta_2(t)$.

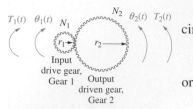

FIGURE 2.27 A gear system

From Figure 2.27, as the gears turn, the distance traveled along each gear's circumference is the same. Thus,

$$r_1\theta_1 = r_2\theta_2 \tag{2.132}$$

or

$$\boxed{\frac{\theta_2}{\theta_1} = \frac{r_1}{r_2} = \frac{N_1}{N_2}} \tag{2.133}$$

since the ratio of the number of teeth along the circumference is in the same proportion as the ratio of the radii. We conclude that the ratio of the angular displacement of the gears is inversely proportional to the ratio of the number of teeth.

What is the relationship between the input torque, T_1, and the delivered torque, T_2? If we assume the gears do not absorb or store energy, the energy into Gear 1 equals the energy out of Gear 2.[11] Since the translational energy of force times displacement becomes the rotational energy of torque times angular displacement,

$$T_1\theta_1 = T_2\theta_2 \tag{2.134}$$

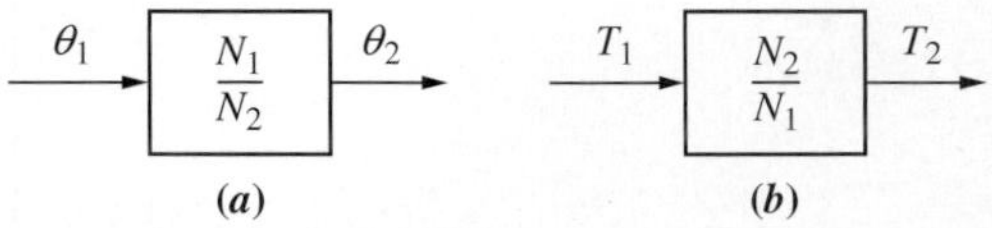

Solving Eq. (2.134) for the ratio of the torques and using Eq. (2.133), we get

$$\boxed{\frac{T_2}{T_1} = \frac{\theta_1}{\theta_2} = \frac{N_2}{N_1}} \tag{2.135}$$

$$\theta_1 \longrightarrow \boxed{\frac{N_1}{N_2}} \longrightarrow \theta_2$$

$$(a)$$

$$T_1 \longrightarrow \boxed{\frac{N_2}{N_1}} \xrightarrow{T_2}$$

$$(b)$$

FIGURE 2.28

Transfer functions for
a. angular displacement in lossless gears and
b. torque in lossless gears

Thus, the torques are directly proportional to the ratio of the number of teeth. All results are summarized in Figure 2.28.

Let us see what happens to mechanical impedances that are driven by gears. Figure 2.29(a) shows gears driving a rotational inertia, spring, and viscous damper. For clarity, the gears are shown by an end-on view. We want to represent Figure 2.29(a) as an equivalent system at θ_1 without the gears. In other words, can the mechanical impedances be reflected from the output to the input, thereby eliminating the gears?

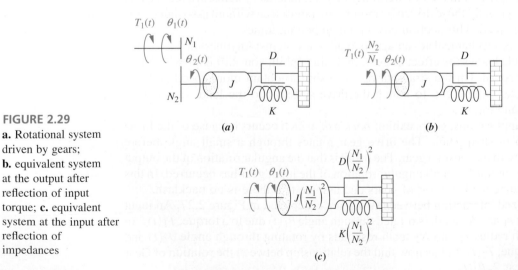

FIGURE 2.29
a. Rotational system driven by gears;
b. equivalent system at the output after reflection of input torque; **c.** equivalent system at the input after reflection of impedances

[11] This is equivalent to saying that the gears have negligible inertia and damping.

From Figure 2.28(*b*), T_1 can be reflected to the output by multiplying by N_2/N_1. The result is shown in Figure 2.29(*b*), from which we write the equation of motion as

$$(Js^2 + Ds + K)\theta_2(s) = T_1(s)\frac{N_2}{N_1} \tag{2.136}$$

Now convert $\theta_2(s)$ into an equivalent $\theta_1(s)$, so that Eq. (2.136) will look as if it were written at the input. Using Figure 2.28(*a*) to obtain $\theta_2(s)$ in terms of $\theta_1(s)$, we get

$$(Js^2 + Ds + K)\frac{N_1}{N_2}\theta_1(s) = T_1(s)\frac{N_2}{N_1} \tag{2.137}$$

After simplification,

$$\left[J\left(\frac{N_1}{N_2}\right)^2 s^2 + D\left(\frac{N_1}{N_2}\right)^2 s + K\left(\frac{N_1}{N_2}\right)^2\right]\theta_1(s) = T_1(s) \tag{2.138}$$

which suggests the equivalent system at the input and without gears shown in Figure 2.29(*c*). Thus, the load can be thought of as having been reflected from the output to the input.

Generalizing the results, we can make the following statement: *Rotational mechanical impedances can be reflected through gear trains by multiplying the mechanical impedance by the ratio*

$$\left(\frac{\text{Number of teeth of gear on } \textit{destination } \text{shaft}}{\text{Number of teeth of gear on } \textit{source } \text{shaft}}\right)^2$$

where the impedance to be reflected is attached to the source shaft and is being reflected to the destination shaft. The next example demonstrates the application of the concept of reflected impedances as we find the transfer function of a rotational mechanical system with gears.

EXAMPLE 2.21

Transfer function—system with lossless gears

Problem: Find the transfer function, $\theta_2(s)/T_1(s)$, for the system of Figure 2.30(*a*).

SOLUTION: It may be tempting at this point to search for two simultaneous equations corresponding to each inertia. The inertias, however, do not undergo linearly independent motion, since they are tied together by the gears. Thus, there is only one degree of freedom and hence one equation of motion.

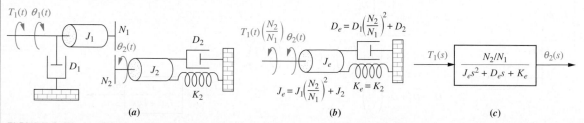

(a)   (b)   (c)

FIGURE 2.30 **a.** Rotational mechanical system with gears; **b.** system after reflection of torques and impedances to the output shaft; **c.** block diagram

Let us first reflect the impedances (J_1 and D_1) and torque (T_1) on the input shaft to the output as shown in Figure 2.30(b), where the impedances are reflected by $(N_2/N_1)^2$ and the torque is reflected by (N_2/N_1). The equation of motion can now be written as

$$(J_e s^2 + D_e s + K_e)\theta_2(s) = T_1(s)\frac{N_2}{N_1} \tag{2.139}$$

where

$$J_e = J_1\left(\frac{N_2}{N_1}\right)^2 + J_2; \quad D_e = D_1\left(\frac{N_2}{N_1}\right)^2 + D_2; \quad K_e = K_2$$

Solving for $\theta_2(s)/T_1(s)$, the transfer function is found to be

$$G(s) = \frac{\theta_2(s)}{T_1(s)} = \frac{N_2/N_1}{J_e s^2 + D_e s + K_e} \tag{2.140}$$

as shown in Figure 2.30(c).

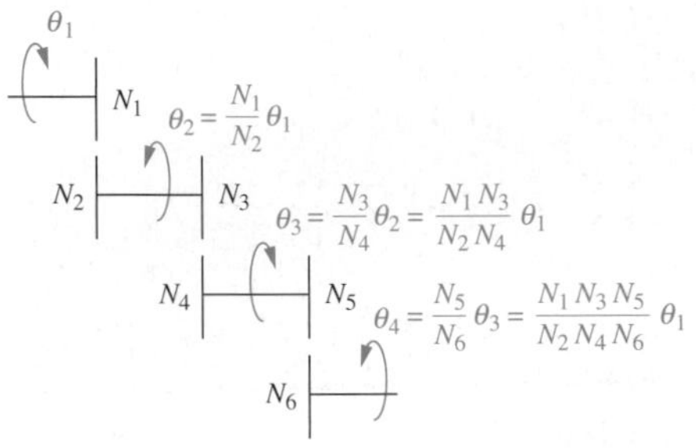

FIGURE 2.31   Gear train

In order to eliminate gears with large radii, a *gear train* is used to implement large gear ratios by cascading smaller gear ratios. A schematic diagram of a gear train is shown in Figure 2.31. Next to each rotation, the angular displacement relative to θ_1 has been calculated. From Figure 2.31,

$$\theta_4 = \frac{N_1 N_3 N_5}{N_2 N_4 N_6}\theta_1 \tag{2.141}$$

For gear trains, we conclude that the equivalent gear ratio is the product of the individual gear ratios. We now apply this result to solve for the transfer function of a system that does not have lossless gears.

EXAMPLE 2.22

Transfer function—gears with loss

Problem: Find the transfer function, $\theta_1(s)/T_1(s)$, for the system of Figure 2.32(a).

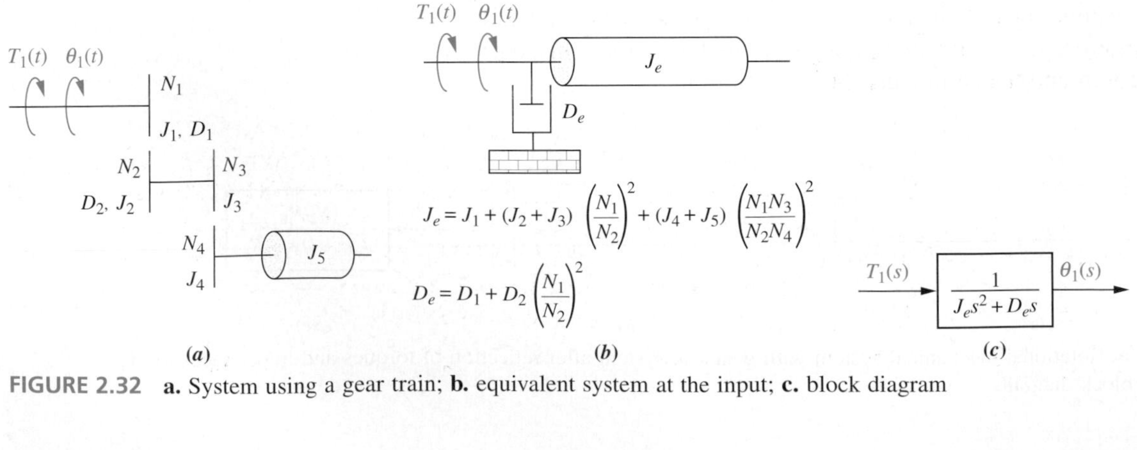

FIGURE 2.32   a. System using a gear train; **b.** equivalent system at the input; **c.** block diagram

SOLUTION: This system, which uses a gear train, does not have lossless gears. All of the gears have inertia, and for some shafts there is viscous friction. To solve the problem, we want to reflect all of the impedances to the input shaft, θ_1. The gear ratio is not the same for all impedances. For example, D_2 is reflected only through one gear ratio as $D_2(N_1/N_2)^2$, whereas J_4 plus J_5 is reflected through two gear ratios as $(J_4 + J_5)[(N_3/N_4)(N_1/N_2)]^2$. The result of reflecting all impedances to θ_1 is shown in Figure 2.32(b), from which the equation of motion is

$$(J_e s^2 + D_e s)\theta_1(s) = T_1(s) \tag{2.142}$$

where

$$J_e = J_1 + (J_2 + J_3)\left(\frac{N_1}{N_2}\right)^2 + (J_4 + J_5)\left(\frac{N_1 N_3}{N_2 N_4}\right)^2$$

and

$$D_e = D_1 + D_2\left(\frac{N_1}{N_2}\right)^2$$

From Eq. (2.142), the transfer function is

$$G(s) = \frac{\theta_1(s)}{T_1(s)} = \frac{1}{J_e s^2 + D_e s} \tag{2.143}$$

as shown in Figure 2.32(c).

SKILL-ASSESSMENT EXERCISE 2.10

Problem: Find the transfer function, $G(s) = \theta_2(s)/T(s)$, for the rotational mechanical system with gears shown in Figure 2.33.

FIGURE 2.33 Rotational mechanical system with gears for Skill-Assessment Exercise 2.10

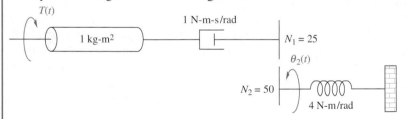

ANSWER: $G(s) = \dfrac{1/2}{s^2 + s + 1}$

The complete solution is at www.wiley.com/college/nise.

2.8 ELECTROMECHANICAL SYSTEM TRANSFER FUNCTIONS

In the last section we talked about rotational systems with gears, which completed our discussion of purely mechanical systems. Now, we move to systems that are hybrids of electrical and mechanical variables, the *electromechanical systems*. We have seen one application of an electromechanical system in Chapter 1, the antenna azimuth position control system. Other applications for systems with electromechanical components are

FIGURE 2.34 NASA flight simulator robot arm with electromechanical control system components

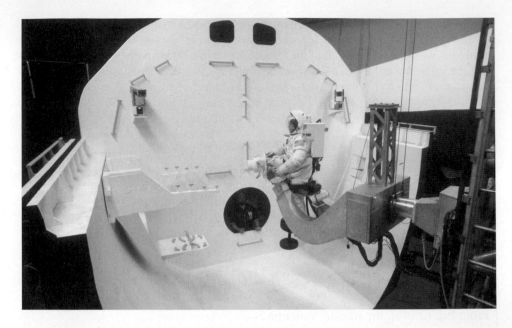

robot controls, sun and star trackers, and computer tape and disk-drive position controls. An example of a control system that uses electromechanical components is shown in Figure 2.34.

A motor is an electromechanical component that yields a displacement output for a voltage input, that is, a mechanical output generated by an electrical input. We will derive the transfer function for one particular kind of electromechanical system, the armature-controlled dc servomotor (*Mablekos, 1980*). The motor's schematic is shown in Figure 2.35(*a*), and the transfer function we will derive appears in Figure 2.35(*b*).

In Figure 2.35(*a*) a magnetic field is developed by stationary permanent magnets or a stationary electromagnet called the *fixed field*. A rotating circuit called the *armature*, through which current $i_a(t)$ flows, passes through this magnetic field at right angles and feels a force, $F = Bli_a(t)$, where B is the magnetic field strength and l is the length of the conductor. The resulting torque turns the *rotor*, the rotating member of the motor.

There is another phenomenon that occurs in the motor: A conductor moving at right angles to a magnetic field generates a voltage at the terminals of the conductor equal to $e = Blv$, where e is the voltage and v is the velocity of the conductor normal to the

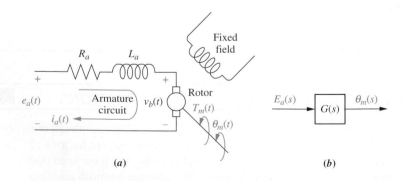

FIGURE 2.35 DC motor:
a. schematic;[12]
b. block diagram

[12] See Appendix H at www.wiley.com/college/nise for a derivation of this schematic and its parameters.

magnetic field. Since the current-carrying armature is rotating in a magnetic field, its voltage is proportional to speed. Thus,

$$v_b(t) = K_b \frac{d\theta_m(t)}{dt} \qquad (2.144)$$

We call $v_b(t)$ the *back electromotive force (back emf)*; K_b is a constant of proportionality called the back emf constant; and $d\theta_m(t)/dt = \omega_m(t)$ is the angular velocity of the motor. Taking the Laplace transform, we get

$$V_b(s) = K_b s \theta_m(s) \qquad (2.145)$$

The relationship between the armature current, $i_a(t)$, the applied armature voltage, $e_a(t)$, and the back emf, $v_b(t)$, is found by writing a loop equation around the Laplace transformed armature circuit (see Figure 3.5(a)):

$$R_a I_a(s) + L_a s I_a(s) + V_b(s) = E_a(s) \qquad (2.146)$$

The torque developed by the motor is proportional to the armature current; thus,

$$T_m(s) = K_t I_a(s) \qquad (2.147)$$

where T_m is the torque developed by the motor, and K_t is a constant of proportionality, called the motor torque constant, which depends on the motor and magnetic field characteristics. In a consistent set of units, the value of K_t is equal to the value of K_b. Rearranging Eq. (2.147) yields

$$I_a(s) = \frac{1}{K_t} T_m(s) \qquad (2.148)$$

To find the transfer function of the motor, we first substitute Eqs. (2.145) and (2.148) into (2.146), yielding

$$\frac{(R_a + L_a s)T_m(s)}{K_t} + K_b s \theta_m(s) = E_a(s) \qquad (2.149)$$

Now we must find $T_m(s)$ in terms of $\theta_m(s)$ if we are to separate the input and output variables and obtain the transfer function, $\theta_m(s)/E_a(s)$.

Figure 2.36 shows a typical equivalent mechanical loading on a motor. J_m is the equivalent inertia at the armature and includes both the armature inertia and, as we will see later, the load inertia reflected to the armature. D_m is the equivalent viscous damping at the armature and includes both the armature viscous damping and, as we will see later, the load viscous damping reflected to the armature. From Figure 2.36,

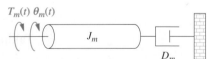

FIGURE 2.36 Typical equivalent mechanical loading on a motor

$$T_m(s) = (J_m s^2 + D_m s)\theta_m(s) \qquad (2.150)$$

Substituting Eq. (2.150) into Eq. (2.149) yields

$$\frac{(R_a + L_a s)(J_m s^2 + D_m s)\theta_m(s)}{K_t} + K_b s \theta_m(s) = E_a(s) \qquad (2.151)$$

If we assume that the armature inductance, L_a, is small compared to the armature resistance, R_a, which is usual for a dc motor, Eq. (2.151) becomes

$$\left[\frac{R_a}{K_t}(J_m s + D_m) + K_b\right] s\theta_m(s) = E_a(s) \tag{2.152}$$

After simplification, the desired transfer function, $\theta_m(s)/E_a(s)$, is found to be

$$\frac{\theta_m(s)}{E_a(s)} = \frac{K_t/(R_a J_m)}{s\left[s + \dfrac{1}{J_m}\left(D_m + \dfrac{K_t K_b}{R_a}\right)\right]} \tag{2.153}{}^{[13]}$$

Even though the form of Eq. (2.153) is relatively simple, namely

$$\frac{\theta_m(s)}{E_a(s)} = \frac{K}{s(s + \alpha)} \tag{2.154}$$

the reader may be concerned about how to evaluate the constants.

Let us first discuss the mechanical constants, J_m and D_m. Consider Figure 2.37, which shows a motor with inertia J_a and damping D_a at the armature driving a load consisting of inertia J_L and damping D_L. Assuming that all inertia and damping values shown are known, J_L and D_L can be reflected back to the armature as some equivalent inertia and damping to be added to J_a and D_a, respectively. Thus, the equivalent inertia, J_m, and equivalent damping, D_m, at the armature are

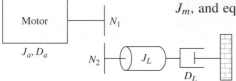

$$J_m = J_a + J_L\left(\frac{N_1}{N_2}\right)^2; \quad D_m = D_a + D_L\left(\frac{N_1}{N_2}\right)^2 \tag{2.155}{}^{[14]}$$

FIGURE 2.37　DC motor driving a rotational mechanical load

Now that we have evaluated the mechanical constants, J_m and D_m, what about the electrical constants in the transfer function of Eq. (2.153)? We will show that these constants can be obtained through a *dynamometer* test of the motor, where a dynamometer measures the torque and speed of a motor under the condition of a constant applied voltage. Let us first develop the relationships that dictate the use of a dynamometer.

Substituting Eqs. (2.145) and (2.148) into Eq. (2.146), with $L_a = 0$, yields

$$\frac{R_a}{K_t}T_m(s) + K_b s\theta_m(s) = E_a(s) \tag{2.156}$$

Taking the inverse Laplace transform, we get

$$\frac{R_a}{K_t}T_m(t) + K_b \omega_m(t) = e_a(t) \tag{2.157}$$

where the inverse Laplace transform of $s\theta_m(s)$ is $d\theta_m(t)/dt$ or, alternately, $\omega_m(t)$.

---

[13] The units for the electrical constants are K_t = N-m-A (newton-meters/ampere), and K_b = V-s/rad (volt-seconds/radian).

[14] If the values of the mechanical constants are not known, motor constants can be determined through laboratory testing using transient response or frequency response data. The concept of transient response is covered in Chapter 4; frequency response is covered in Chapter 10.

If a dc voltage, e_a, is applied, the motor will turn at a constant angular velocity, ω_m, with a constant torque, T_m. Hence, dropping the functional relationship based on time from Eq. (2.157), the following relationship exists when the motor is operating at steady state with a dc voltage input:

$$\frac{R_a}{K_t} T_m + K_b \omega_m = e_a \tag{2.158}$$

Solving for T_m yields

$$T_m = -\frac{K_b K_t}{R_a} \omega_m + \frac{K_t}{R_a} e_a \tag{2.159}$$

Equation (2.159) is a straight line, T_m vs. ω_m, and is shown in Figure 2.38. This plot is called the *torque-speed curve*. The torque axis intercept occurs when the angular velocity reaches zero. That value of torque is called the *stall torque*, T_{stall}. Thus,

$$T_{\text{stall}} = \frac{K_t}{R_a} e_a \tag{2.160}$$

The angular velocity occurring when the torque is zero is called the *no-load speed*, $\omega_{\text{no-load}}$. Thus,

$$\omega_{\text{no-load}} = \frac{e_a}{K_b} \tag{2.161}$$

The electrical constants of the motor's transfer function can now be found from Eqs. (2.160) and (2.161) as

$$\frac{K_t}{R_a} = \frac{T_{\text{stall}}}{e_a} \tag{2.162}$$

and

$$K_b = \frac{e_a}{\omega_{\text{no-load}}} \tag{2.163}$$

The electrical constants, K_t/R_a and K_b, can be found from a dynamometer test of the motor, which would yield T_{stall} and $\omega_{\text{no-load}}$ for a given e_a.

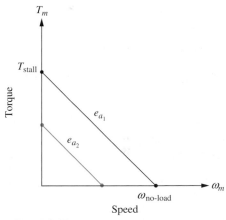

FIGURE 2.38 Torque-speed curves with an armature voltage, e_a, as a parameter

---

EXAMPLE 2.23

Transfer function—dc motor and load

Problem: Given the system and torque-speed curve of Figure 2.39(a) and (b), find the transfer function, $\theta_L(s)/E_a(s)$.

SOLUTION: Begin by finding the mechanical constants, J_m and D_m, in Eq. (2.153). From Eqs. (2.155), the total inertia at the armature of the motor is

$$J_m = J_a + J_L\left(\frac{N_1}{N_2}\right)^2 = 5 + 700\left(\frac{1}{10}\right)^2 = 12 \tag{2.164}$$

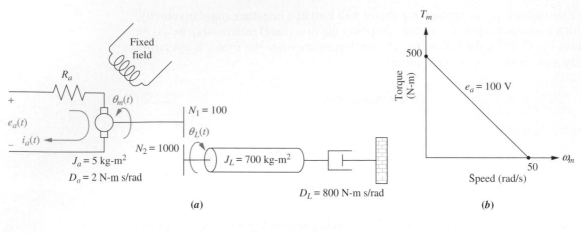

FIGURE 2.39
a. Dc motor and load;
b. torque-speed curve;
c. block diagram

(c)

and the total damping at the armature of the motor is

$$D_m = D_a + D_L \left(\frac{N_1}{N_2}\right)^2 = 2 + 800 \left(\frac{1}{10}\right)^2 = 10 \tag{2.165}$$

Now we will find the electrical constants, K_t/R_a and K_b. From the torque-speed curve of Figure 2.39(b),

$$T_{\text{stall}} = 500 \tag{2.166}$$

$$\omega_{\text{no-load}} = 50 \tag{2.167}$$

$$e_a = 100 \tag{2.168}$$

Hence the electrical constants are

$$\frac{K_t}{R_a} = \frac{T_{\text{stall}}}{e_a} = \frac{500}{100} = 5 \tag{2.169}$$

and

$$K_b = \frac{e_a}{\omega_{\text{no-load}}} = \frac{100}{50} = 2 \tag{2.170}$$

Substituting Eqs. (2.164), (2.165), (2.169), and (2.170) into Eq. (2.153) yields

$$\frac{\theta_m(s)}{E_a(s)} = \frac{5/12}{s\left\{s + \dfrac{1}{12}[10 + (5)(2)]\right\}} = \frac{0.417}{s(s + 1.667)} \tag{2.171}$$

In order to find $\theta_L(s)/E_a(s)$, we use the gear ratio, $N_1/N_2 = 1/10$, and find

$$\frac{\theta_L(s)}{E_a(s)} = \frac{0.0417}{s(s + 1.667)} \tag{2.172}$$

as shown in Figure 2.39(c).

| SKILL-ASSESSMENT EXERCISE 2.11 |

Problem: Find the transfer function, $G(s) = \theta_L(s)/E_a(s)$, for the motor and load shown in Figure 2.40. The torque-speed curve is given by $T_m = -8\omega_m + 200$ when the input voltage is 100 volts.

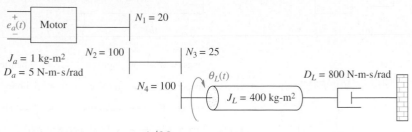

$J_a = 1$ kg-m^2
$D_a = 5$ N-m-s/rad

FIGURE 2.40 Electromechanical system for Skill-Assessment Exercise 2.11

ANSWER: $G(s) = \dfrac{1/20}{s[s+(15/2)]}$

The complete solution is at www.wiley.com/college/nise.

2.9 ELECTRIC CIRCUIT ANALOGS

In this section we show the commonality of systems from the various disciplines by demonstrating that the mechanical systems with which we worked can be represented by equivalent electric circuits. We have pointed out the similarity between the equations resulting from Kirchhoff's laws for electrical systems and the equations of motion of mechanical systems. We now show this commonality even more convincingly by producing electric circuit equivalents for mechanical systems. The variables of the electric circuits behave exactly as the analogous variables of the mechanical systems. In fact, converting mechanical systems to electrical networks before writing the describing equations is a problem-solving approach that you may want to pursue.

An electric circuit that is analogous to a system from another discipline is called an electric circuit *analog*. Analogs can be obtained by comparing the describing equations, such as the equations of motion of a mechanical system, with either electrical mesh or nodal equations. When compared with mesh equations, the resulting electrical circuit is called a *series analog*. When compared with nodal equations, the resulting electrical circuit is called a *parallel analog*.

SERIES ANALOG

Consider the translational mechanical system shown in Figure 2.41(*a*), whose equation of motion is

$$(Ms^2 + f_v s + K)X(s) = F(s) \tag{2.173}$$

Kirchhoff's mesh equation for the simple series *RLC* network shown in Figure 2.41(*b*) is

$$\left(Ls + R + \frac{1}{Cs}\right)I(s) = E(s) \tag{2.174}$$

As we previously pointed out, Eq. (2.173) is not directly analogous to Eq. (2.174) because displacement and current are not analogous. We can create a direct analogy by

FIGURE 2.41　Development of series analog: **a.** mechanical system; **b.** desired electrical representation; **c.** series analog; **d.** parameters for series analog

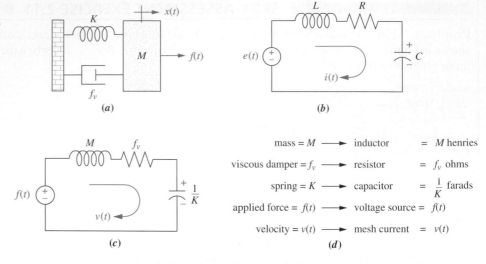

operating on Eq. (2.173) to convert displacement to velocity by dividing and multiplying the left-hand side by s, yielding

$$\frac{Ms^2 + f_v s + K}{s} sX(s) = \left(Ms + f_v + \frac{K}{s}\right) V(s) = F(s) \qquad (2.175)$$

Comparing Eqs. 2.174 and 2.175, we recognize the sum of impedances and draw the circuit shown in Figure 2.41(c). The conversions are summarized in Figure 2.41(d).

When we have more than one degree of freedom, the impedances associated with a motion appear as series electrical elements in a mesh, but the impedances between adjacent motions are drawn as series electrical impedances between the two corresponding meshes. We demonstrate with an example.

■ EXAMPLE 2.24 ■

Converting a mechanical system to a series analog

Problem:　Draw a series analog for the mechanical system of Figure 2.17(a).

SOLUTION:　Equations 2.118 are analogous to electrical mesh equations after conversion to velocity. Thus,

$$\left[M_1 s + (f_{v_1} + f_{v_3}) + \frac{(K_1 + K_2)}{s}\right] V_1(s) - \left(f_{v_3} + \frac{K_2}{s}\right) V_2(s) = F(s) \qquad (2.176a)$$

$$-\left(f_{v_3} + \frac{K_2}{s}\right) V_1(s) + \left[M_2 s + (f_{v_2} + f_{v_3}) + \frac{(K_2 + K_3)}{s}\right] V_2(s) = 0 \qquad (2.176b)$$

Coefficients represent sums of electrical impedance. Mechanical impedances associated with M_1 form the first mesh, where impedances between the two masses are common to the two loops. Impedances associated with M_2 form the second mesh. The result is shown in Figure 2.42, where $v_1(t)$ and $v_2(t)$ are the velocities of M_1 and M_2, respectively.

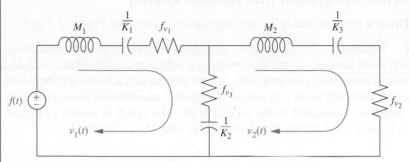

FIGURE 2.42

Series analog of mechanical system of Figure 2.17(a)

PARALLEL ANALOG

A system can also be converted to an equivalent parallel analog. Consider the translational mechanical system shown in Figure 2.43(a), whose equation of motion is given by Eq. (2.175). Kirchhoff's nodal equation for the simple parallel *RLC* network shown in Figure 2.43(b) is

$$\left(Cs + \frac{1}{R} + \frac{1}{Ls}\right)E(s) = I(s) \tag{2.177}$$

Comparing Eqs. (2.175) and (2.177), we identify the sum of admittances and draw the circuit shown in Figure 2.43(c). The conversions are summarized in Figure 2.43(d).

When we have more than one degree of freedom, the components associated with a motion appear as parallel electrical elements connected to a node, but the components of adjacent motions are drawn as parallel electrical elements between two corresponding nodes. We demonstrate with an example.

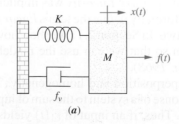

(a)

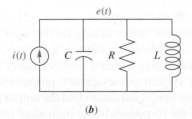

(b)

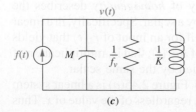

(c)

mass = M	$\longrightarrow$	capacitor	= M farads
viscous damper = f_v	$\longrightarrow$	resistor	= $\frac{1}{f_v}$ ohms
spring = K	$\longrightarrow$	inductor	= $\frac{1}{K}$ henries
applied force = $f(t)$	$\longrightarrow$	current source = $f(t)$	
velocity = $v(t)$	$\longrightarrow$	node voltage = $v(t)$	

(d)

FIGURE 2.43

Development of parallel analog:
a. mechanical system;
b. desired electrical representation;
c. parallel analog;
d. parameters for parallel analog

EXAMPLE 2.25

Converting a mechanical system to a parallel analog

Problem: Draw a parallel analog for the mechanical system of Figure 2.17(*a*).

SOLUTION: Equations (2.176) are also analogous to electrical node equations. Coefficients represent sums of electrical admittances. Admittances associated with M_1 form the elements connected to the first node, where mechanical admittances between the two masses are common to the two nodes. Mechanical admittances associated with M_2 form the elements connected to the second node. The result is shown in Figure 2.44, where $v_1(t)$ and $v_2(t)$ are the velocities of M_1 and M_2, respectively.

FIGURE 2.44   Parallel analog of mechanical system of Figure 2.17(*a*)

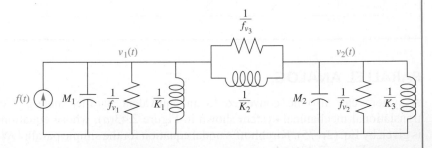

SKILL-ASSESSMENT EXERCISE 2.12

Problem: Draw a series and parallel analog for the rotational mechanical system of Figure 2.22.

ANSWER: The complete solution is at www.wiley.com/college/nise.

2.10 NONLINEARITIES

The models thus far are developed from systems that can be described approximately by linear, time-invariant differential equations. An assumption of *linearity* was implicit in the development of these models. In this section we formally define the terms *linear* and *nonlinear* and show how to distinguish between the two. In Section 2.11 we show how to approximate a nonlinear system as a linear system so that we can use the modeling techniques previously covered in this chapter (*Hsu, 1968*).

A linear system possesses two properties: superposition and homogeneity. The property of *superposition* means that the output response of a system to the sum of inputs is the sum of the responses to the individual inputs. Thus, if an input of $r_1(t)$ yields an output of $c_1(t)$ and an input of $r_2(t)$ yields an output of $c_2(t)$, then an input of $r_1(t) + r_2(t)$ yields an output of $c_1(t) + c_2(t)$. The property of *homogeneity* describes the response of the system to a multiplication of the input by a scalar. Specifically, in a linear system, the property of homogeneity is demonstrated if for an input of $r_1(t)$ that yields an output of $c_1(t)$, an input of $Ar_1(t)$ yields an output of $Ac_1(t)$; that is, multiplication of an input by a scalar yields a response that is multiplied by the same scalar.

We can visualize linearity as shown in Figure 2.45. Figure 2.45(*a*) is a linear system where the output is always $\frac{1}{2}$ the input, or $f(x) = 0.5x$, regardless of the value of x. Thus each of the two properties of linear systems applies. For example, an input of 1 yields an output of $\frac{1}{2}$ and an input of 2 yields an output of 1. Using superposition, an input that is the sum of the original inputs, or 3, should yield an output that is the sum of the individual outputs, or 1.5. From Figure 2.45(a), an input of 3 does indeed yield an output of 1.5.

To test the property of homogeneity, assume an input of 2, which yields an output of 1. Multiplying this input by 2 should yield an output of twice as much, or 2. From Figure 2.45(a), an input of 4 does indeed yield an output of 2. The reader can verify that the properties of linearity certainly do not apply to the relationship shown in Figure 2.45(b).

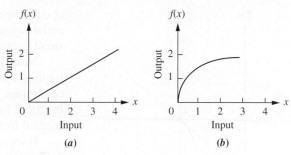

FIGURE 2.45   a. Linear system; **b.** nonlinear system

Figure 2.46 shows some examples of physical nonlinearities. An electronic amplifier is linear over a specific range but exhibits the nonlinearity called *saturation* at high input voltages. A motor that does not respond at very low input voltages due to frictional forces exhibits a nonlinearity called *dead zone.* Gears that do not fit tightly exhibit a nonlinearity called *backlash:* The input moves over a small range without the output responding. The reader should verify that the curves shown in Figure 2.46 do not fit the definitions of linearity over their entire range. Another example of a nonlinear subsystem is a phase detector, used in a phase-locked loop in an FM radio receiver, whose output response is the sine of the input.

A designer can often make a linear approximation to a nonlinear system. Linear approximations simplify the analysis and design of a system and are used as long as the results yield a good approximation to reality. For example, a linear relationship can be established at a point on the nonlinear curve if the range of input values about that point is small and the origin is translated to that point. Electronic amplifiers are an example of physical devices that perform linear amplification with small excursions about a point.

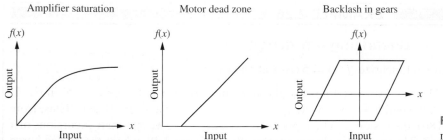

FIGURE 2.46   Some physical nonlinearities

2.11 LINEARIZATION

The electrical and mechanical systems covered thus far were assumed to be linear. However, if any nonlinear components are present, we must linearize the system before we can find the transfer function. In the last section we defined and discussed nonlinearities; in this section we show how to obtain linear approximations to nonlinear systems in order to obtain transfer functions.

The first step is to recognize the nonlinear component and write the nonlinear differential equation. When we linearize a nonlinear differential equation, we linearize it for small-signal inputs about the steady-state solution when the small-signal input is equal to zero. This steady-state solution is called *equilibrium* and is selected as the second step in the linearization process. For example, when a pendulum is at rest, it is

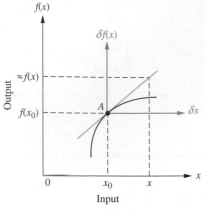

FIGURE 2.47   Linearization about a point A

at equilibrium. The angular displacement is described by a nonlinear differential equation, but it can be expressed with a linear differential equation for small excursions about this equilibrium point.

Next we linearize the nonlinear differential equation, and then we take the Laplace transform of the linearized differential equation, assuming zero initial conditions. Finally, we separate input and output variables and form the transfer function. Let us first see how to linearize a function; later, we will apply the method to the linearization of a differential equation.

If we assume a nonlinear system operating at point A, $[x_0, f(x_0)]$ in Figure 2.47, small changes in the input can be related to changes in the output about the point by way of the slope of the curve at the point A. Thus, if the slope of the curve at point A is m_a, then small excursions of the input about point A, δx, yield small changes in the output, $\delta f(x)$, related by the slope at point A. Thus,

$$[f(x) - f(x_0)] \approx m_a(x - x_0) \tag{2.178}$$

from which

$$\delta f(x) \approx m_a \delta x \tag{2.179}$$

and

$$f(x) \approx f(x_0) + m_a(x - x_0) \approx f(x_0) + m_a \delta x \tag{2.180}$$

This relationship is shown graphically in Figure 2.47, where a new set of axes, δx and $\delta f(x)$, is created at the point A, and $f(x)$ is approximately equal to $f(x_0)$, the ordinate of the new origin, plus small excursions, $m_a \delta x$, away from point A. Let us look at an example.

EXAMPLE 2.26

Linearizing a function

Problem: Linearize $f(x) = 5 \cos x$ about $x = \pi/2$.

SOLUTION: We first find that the derivative of $f(x)$ is $df/dx = (-5 \sin x)$. At $x = \pi/2$, the derivative is -5. Also $f(x_0) = f(\pi/2) = 5 \cos(\pi/2) = 0$. Thus, from Eq. (2.180), the system can be represented as $f(x) = -5 \delta x$ for small excursions of x about $\pi/2$. The process is shown graphically in Figure 2.48, where the cosine curve does indeed look like a straight line of slope -5 near $\pi/2$.

The previous discussion can be formalized using the Taylor series expansion, which expresses the value of a function in terms of the value of that function at a particular point, the excursion away from that point, and derivatives evaluated at that point. The Taylor series is shown in Eq. (2.181).

$$f(x) = f(x_0) + \frac{df}{dx}\bigg|_{x=x_0} \frac{(x - x_0)}{1!} + \frac{d^2 f}{dx^2}\bigg|_{x=x_0} \frac{(x - x_0)^2}{2!} + \cdots \tag{2.181}$$

For small excursions of x from x_0, we can neglect higher-order terms. The resulting approximation yields a straight-line relationship between the change in $f(x)$ and the excursions away from x_0. Neglecting the higher-order terms in Eq. (2.181).

FIGURE 2.48   Linearization of $5\cos x$ about $x = \pi/2$

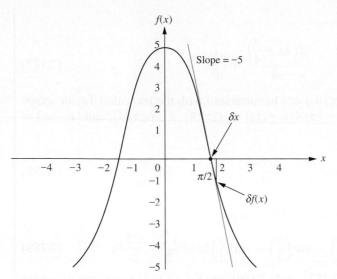

we get

$$f(x) - f(x_0) \approx \left.\frac{df}{dx}\right|_{x=x_0} (x - x_0) \qquad (2.182)$$

or

$$\delta f(x) \approx m|_{x=x_0} \,\delta x \qquad (2.183)$$

which is a linear relationship between $\delta f(x)$ and δx for small excursions away from x_0. It is interesting to note that Eqs. (2.182) and (2.183) are identical to Eqs. (2.178) and (2.179), which we derived intuitively. The following examples illustrate linearization. The first example demonstrates linearization of a differential equation, and the second example applies linearization to finding a transfer function.

EXAMPLE 2.27

Linearizing a differential equation

Problem: Linearize Eq. (2.184) for small excursions about $x = \pi/4$.

$$\frac{d^2x}{dt^2} + 2\frac{dx}{dt} + \cos x = 0 \qquad (2.184)$$

SOLUTION: The presence of the term $\cos x$ makes this equation nonlinear. Since we want to linearize the equation about $x = \pi/4$, we let $x = \delta x + \pi/4$, where δx is the small excursion about $\pi/4$, and substitute x into Eq. (2.184):

$$\frac{d^2\left(\delta x + \dfrac{\pi}{4}\right)}{dt^2} + 2\frac{d\left(\delta x + \dfrac{\pi}{4}\right)}{dt} + \cos\left(\delta x + \frac{\pi}{4}\right) = 0 \qquad (2.185)$$

But

$$\frac{d^2\left(\delta x + \dfrac{\pi}{4}\right)}{dt^2} = \frac{d^2\delta x}{dt^2} \qquad (2.186)$$

and

$$\frac{d\left(\delta x + \frac{\pi}{4}\right)}{dt} = \frac{d\delta x}{dt} \tag{2.187}$$

Finally, the term $\cos(\delta x + (\pi/4))$ can be linearized with the truncated Taylor series. Substituting $f(x) = \cos(\delta x + (\pi/4))$, $f(x_0) = f(\pi/4) = \cos(\pi/4)$, and $(x - x_0) = \delta x$ into Eq. (2.182) yields

$$\cos\left(\delta x + \frac{\pi}{4}\right) - \cos\left(\frac{\pi}{4}\right) = \frac{d\cos x}{dx}\bigg|_{x=\frac{\pi}{4}} \delta x = -\sin\left(\frac{\pi}{4}\right)\delta x \tag{2.188}$$

Solving Eq. (2.188) for $\cos(\delta x + (\pi/4))$, we get

$$\cos\left(\delta x + \frac{\pi}{4}\right) = \cos\left(\frac{\pi}{4}\right) - \sin\left(\frac{\pi}{4}\right)\delta x = \frac{\sqrt{2}}{2} - \frac{\sqrt{2}}{2}\delta x \tag{2.189}$$

Substituting Eqs. (2.186), (2.187), and (2.189) into Eq. (2.185) yields the following linearized differential equation:

$$\frac{d^2\delta x}{dt^2} + 2\frac{d\delta x}{dt} - \frac{\sqrt{2}}{2}\delta x = -\frac{\sqrt{2}}{2} \tag{2.190}$$

This equation can now be solved for δx, from which we can obtain $x = \delta x + (\pi/4)$.

Even though the nonlinear Eq. (2.184) is homogeneous, the linearized Eq. (2.190) is not homogeneous. Eq. (2.190) has a forcing function on its right-hand side. This additional term can be thought of as an input to a system represented by Eq. (2.184).

Another observation about Eq. (2.190) is the negative sign on the left-hand side. The study of differential equations tells us that since the roots of the characteristic equation are positive, the homogeneous solution grows without bound instead of diminishing to zero. Thus, this system linearized around $x = \pi/4$ is not stable.

EXAMPLE 2.28

Transfer function—nonlinear electrical network

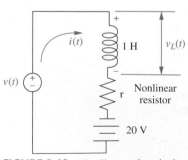

FIGURE 2.49 Nonlinear electrical network

Problem: Find the transfer function, $V_L(s)/V(s)$, for the electrical network shown in Figure 2.49, which contains a nonlinear resistor whose voltage-current relationship is defined by $i_r = 2e^{0.1v_r}$, where i_r and v_r are the resistor current and voltage, respectively. Also, $v(t)$ in Figure 2.49 is a small-signal source.

SOLUTION: We will use Kirchhoff's voltage law to sum the voltages in the loop to obtain the nonlinear differential equation, but first we must solve for the voltage across the nonlinear resistor. Taking the natural log of the resistor's current-voltage relationship, we get $v_r = 10 \ln\frac{1}{2}i_r$. Applying Kirchhoff's voltage law around the loop, where $i_r = i$, yields

$$L\frac{di}{dt} + 10\ln\frac{1}{2}i - 20 = v(t) \tag{2.191}$$

Next, let us evaluate the equilibrium solution. First, set the small-signal source, $v(t)$, equal to zero. Now evaluate the steady-state current. With $v(t) = 0$, the circuit consists of a 20 V battery in series with the inductor and nonlinear resistor. In the steady state the voltage across the inductor will be zero, since $v_L(t) = L\,di/dt$ and di/dt is zero in the steady state, given a constant battery source. Hence, the resistor voltage, v_r, is 20 V. Using the characteristics of the resistor, $i_r = 2e^{0.1v_r}$, we find that $i_r = i = 14.78$ amps. This current, i_0, is the equilibrium value of the network current. Hence $i = i_0 + \delta i$. Substituting this current into Eq. (2.191) yields

$$L\frac{d(i_0 + \delta i)}{dt} + 10 \ln\frac{1}{2}(i_0 + \delta i) - 20 = v(t) \tag{2.192}$$

Using Eq. (2.182) to linearize $\ln\frac{1}{2}(i_0 + \delta i)$, we get

$$\ln\frac{1}{2}(i_0 + \delta i) - \ln\frac{1}{2}i_0 = \left.\frac{d(\ln\frac{1}{2}i)}{di}\right|_{i=i_0}\delta i = \left.\frac{1}{i}\right|_{i=i_0}\delta i = \frac{1}{i_0}\delta i \tag{2.193}$$

or

$$\ln\frac{1}{2}(i_0 + \delta i) = \ln\frac{i_0}{2} + \frac{1}{i_0}\delta i \tag{2.194}$$

Substituting into Eq. (2.192), the linearized equation becomes

$$L\frac{d\delta i}{dt} + 10\left(\ln\frac{i_0}{2} + \frac{1}{i_0}\delta i\right) - 20 = v(t) \tag{2.195}$$

Letting $L = 1$ and $i_0 = 14.78$, the final linearized differential equation is

$$\frac{d\delta i}{dt} + 0.677\delta i = v(t) \tag{2.196}$$

Taking the Laplace transform with zero initial conditions and solving for $\delta i(s)$, we get

$$\delta i(s) = \frac{V(s)}{s + 0.677} \tag{2.197}$$

But the voltage across the inductor about the equilibrium point is

$$v_L(t) = L\frac{d}{dt}(i_0 + \delta i) = L\frac{d\delta i}{dt} \tag{2.198}$$

Taking the Laplace transform,

$$V_L(s) = Ls\delta i(s) = s\delta i(s) \tag{2.199}$$

Substituting Eq. (2.197) into Eq. (2.199) yields

$$V_L(s) = s\frac{V(s)}{s + 0.677} \tag{2.200}$$

from which the final transfer function is

$$\frac{V_L(s)}{V(s)} = \frac{s}{s + 0.677} \tag{2.201}$$

for small excursions about $i = 14.78$ or, equivalently, about $v(t) = 0$.

SKILL-ASSESSMENT EXERCISE 2.13

Problem: Find the linearized transfer function, $G(s) = V(s)/I(s)$, for the electrical network shown in Figure 2.50. The network contains a nonlinear resistor whose voltage-current relationship is defined by $i_r = e^{v_r}$. The current source, $i(t)$, is a small-signal generator.

ANSWER:

$$G(s) = \frac{1}{s+2}$$

The complete solution is at www.wiley.com/college/nise.

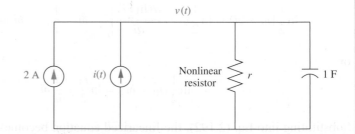

FIGURE 2.50 Nonlinear electric circuit for Skill-Assessment Exercise 2.13

CASE STUDIES

Antenna Control: Transfer Functions

This chapter showed that physical systems can be modeled mathematically with transfer functions. Typically, systems are composed of subsystems of different types, such as electrical, mechanical, and electromechanical.

The first case study uses our ongoing example of the antenna azimuth position control system to show how to represent each subsystem as a transfer function.

Problem: Find the transfer function for each subsystem of the antenna azimuth position control system schematic shown on the front endpapers. Use Configuration 1.

SOLUTION: First, we identify the individual subsystems for which we must find transfer functions; they are summarized in Table 2.6. We proceed to find the transfer function for each subsystem.

TABLE 2.6 **Subsystems of the antenna azimuth position control system**

Subsystem	Input	Output
Input potentiometer	Angular rotation from user, $\theta_i(t)$	Voltage to preamp, $v_i(t)$
Preamp	Voltage from potentiometers, $v_e(t) = v_i(t) - v_o(t)$	Voltage to power amp, $v_p(t)$
Power amp	Voltage from preamp, $v_p(t)$	Voltage to motor, $e_a(t)$
Motor	Voltage from power amp, $e_a(t)$	Angular rotation to load, $\theta_o(t)$
Output potentiometer	Angular rotation from load, $\theta_o(t)$	Voltage to preamp, $v_o(t)$

INPUT POTENTIOMETER; OUTPUT POTENTIOMETER   Since the input and output potentiometers are configured in the same way, their transfer functions will be the same. We *neglect* the dynamics for the potentiometers and simply find the relationship between the output voltage and the input angular displacement. In the center position the output voltage is zero. Five turns toward either the positive 10 volts or the negative 10 volts yields a voltage change of 10 volts. Thus, the transfer function, $V_i(s)/\theta_i(s)$, for the potentiometers is found by dividing the voltage change by the angular displacement:

$$\frac{V_i(s)}{\theta_i(s)} = \frac{10}{10\pi} = \frac{1}{\pi} \tag{2.202}$$

PREAMPLIFIER; POWER AMPLIFIER   The transfer functions of the amplifiers are given in the problem statement. Two phenomena are *neglected*. First, we *assume* that saturation is never reached. Second, the dynamics of the preamplifier are *neglected*, since its speed of response is typically much greater than that of the power amplifier. The transfer functions of both amplifiers are given in the problem statement and are the ratio of the Laplace transforms of the output voltage divided by the input voltage. Hence, for the preamplifier,

$$\frac{V_p(s)}{V_e(s)} = K \tag{2.203}$$

and for the power amplifier,

$$\frac{E_a(s)}{V_p(s)} = \frac{100}{s + 100} \tag{2.204}$$

MOTOR AND LOAD   The motor and its load are next. The transfer function relating the armature displacement to the armature voltage is given in Eq. (2.153). The equivalent inertia, J_m, is

$$J_m = J_a + J_L\left(\frac{25}{250}\right)^2 = 0.02 + 1\frac{1}{100} = 0.03 \tag{2.205}$$

where $J_L = 1$ is the load inertia at θ_o. The equivalent viscous damping, D_m, at the armature is

$$D_m = D_a + D_L\left(\frac{25}{250}\right)^2 = 0.01 + 1\frac{1}{100} = 0.02 \tag{2.206}$$

where D_L is the load viscous damping at θ_o. From the problem statement, $K_t = 0.5$ N-m/A, $K_b = 0.5$ V-s/rad, and the armature resistance $R_a = 8$ ohms. These quantities along with J_m and D_m are substituted into Eq. (2.153), yielding the transfer function of the motor from the armature voltage to the armature displacement, or

$$\frac{\theta_m(s)}{E_a(s)} = \frac{K_t/(R_a J_m)}{s\left[s + \dfrac{1}{J_m}\left(D_m + \dfrac{K_t K_b}{R_a}\right)\right]} = \frac{2.083}{s(s + 1.71)} \tag{2.207}$$

To complete the transfer function of the motor, we multiply by the gear ratio to arrive at the transfer function relating load displacement to armature voltage:

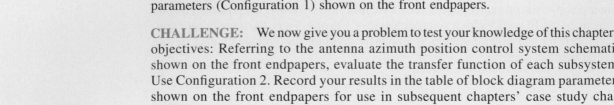

$$\frac{\theta_o(s)}{E_a(s)} = 0.1 \frac{\theta_m(s)}{E_a(s)} = \frac{0.2083}{s(s+1.71)} \qquad (2.208)$$

The results are summarized in the block diagram and table of block diagram parameters (Configuration 1) shown on the front endpapers.

CHALLENGE: We now give you a problem to test your knowledge of this chapter's objectives: Referring to the antenna azimuth position control system schematic shown on the front endpapers, evaluate the transfer function of each subsystem. Use Configuration 2. Record your results in the table of block diagram parameters shown on the front endpapers for use in subsequent chapters' case study challenges.

Transfer Function of a Human Leg

In this case study we find the transfer function of a biological system. The system is a human leg, which pivots from the hip joint. In this problem the component of weight is nonlinear, so the system requires linearization before the evaluation of the transfer function.

Problem: The transfer function of a human leg relates the output angular rotation about the hip joint to the input torque supplied by the leg muscle. A simplified model for the leg is shown in Figure 2.51. The model *assumes* an applied muscular torque, $T_m(t)$, viscous damping, D, at the hip joint, and inertia, J, around the hip joint.[15] Also, a component of the weight of the leg, Mg, where M is the mass of the leg and g is the acceleration due to gravity, creates a nonlinear torque. If we *assume* that the leg is of uniform density, the weight can be applied at $L/2$, where L is the length of the leg (*Milsum, 1966*). Do the following:

a. Evaluate the nonlinear torque.
b. Find the transfer function, $\theta(s)/T_m(s)$, for small angles of rotation, where $\theta(s)$ is the angular rotation of the leg about the hip joint.

SOLUTION: First, calculate the torque due to the weight. The total weight of the leg is Mg acting vertically. The component of the weight in the direction of rotation is $Mg \sin \theta$. This force is applied at a distance $L/2$ from the hip joint. Hence the torque in the direction of rotation, $T_W(t)$, is $Mg(L/2)\sin \theta$. Next, draw a free-body diagram of the leg, showing the applied torque, $T_m(t)$, the torque due to the weight, $T_W(t)$, and the opposing torques due to inertia and viscous damping (see Figure 2.52).

Summing torques, we get

$$J\frac{d^2\theta}{dt^2} + D\frac{d\theta}{dt} + Mg\frac{L}{2}\sin\theta = T_m(t) \qquad (2.209)$$

We linearize the system about the equilibrium point, $\theta = 0$, the vertical position of the leg. Using Eq. (2.182), we get

$$\sin\theta - \sin 0 = (\cos 0)\,\delta\theta \qquad (2.210)$$

from which, $\sin \theta = \delta\theta$. Also, $J\,d^2\theta/dt^2 = J\,d^2\delta\theta/dt^2$ and $D\,d\theta/dt = D\,d\delta\theta/dt$. Hence Eq. (2.209) becomes

$$J\frac{d^2\delta\theta}{dt^2} + D\frac{d\delta\theta}{dt} + Mg\frac{L}{2}\delta\theta = T_m(t) \qquad (2.211)$$

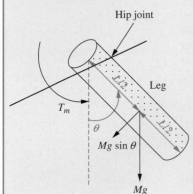

FIGURE 2.51 Cylinder model of a human leg

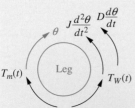

FIGURE 2.52 Free-body diagram of leg model

---

[15] For emphasis, J is not around the center of mass, as we previously assumed for inertia in mechanical rotation.

Notice that the torque due to the weight approximates a spring torque on the leg. Taking the Laplace transform with zero initial conditions yields

$$\left(Js^2 + Ds + Mg\frac{L}{2}\right)\delta\theta(s) = T_m(s) \tag{2.212}$$

from which the transfer function is

$$\frac{\delta\theta(s)}{T_m(s)} = \frac{1/J}{s^2 + \frac{D}{J}s + \frac{MgL}{2J}} \tag{2.213}$$

for small excursions about the equilibrium point, $\theta = 0$.

Challenge: We now introduce a case study challenge to test your knowledge of this chapter's objectives. Although the physical system is different from a human leg, the problem demonstrates the same principles—linearization followed by transfer function evaluation.

Given the nonlinear electrical network shown in Figure 2.53, find the transfer function relating the output nonlinear resistor voltage, $V_r(s)$, to the input source voltage, $V(s)$.

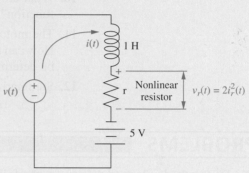

FIGURE 2.53   Nonlinear electric circuit

SUMMARY

In this chapter we discussed how to find a mathematical model, called a *transfer function,* for linear, time-invariant electrical, mechanical, and electromechanical systems. The transfer function is defined as $G(s) = C(s)/R(s)$, or the ratio of the Laplace transform of the output to the Laplace transform of the input. This relationship is algebraic and also adapts itself to modeling interconnected subsystems.

We realize that the physical world consists of more systems than we illustrated in this chapter. For example, we could apply transfer function modeling to hydraulic, pneumatic, heat, and even economic systems. Of course, we must assume these systems to be linear, or make linear approximations, in order to use this modeling technique.

Now that we have our transfer function, we can evaluate its response to a specified input. System response will be covered in Chapter 4. For those pursuing the state-space approach, we continue our discussion of modeling in Chapter 3, where we use the time domain rather than the frequency domain.

REVIEW QUESTIONS

1. What mathematical model permits easy interconnection of physical systems?
2. To what classification of systems can the transfer function be best applied?
3. What transformation turns the solution of differential equations into algebraic manipulations?
4. Define the transfer function.
5. What assumption is made concerning initial conditions when dealing with transfer functions?

6. What do we call the mechanical equations written in order to evaluate the transfer function?

7. If we understand the form the mechanical equations take, what step do we avoid in evaluating the transfer function?

8. Why do transfer functions for mechanical networks look identical to transfer functions for electrical networks?

9. What function do gears perform?

10. What are the component parts of the mechanical constants of a motor's transfer function?

11. The motor's transfer function relates armature displacement to armature voltage. How can the transfer function that relates load displacement and armature voltage be determined?

12. Summarize the steps taken to linearize a nonlinear system.

PROBLEMS

1. Derive the Laplace transform for the following time functions: [Section: 2.2]

   a. $u(t)$

   b. $tu(t)$

   c. $\sin \omega t\, u(t)$

   d. $\cos \omega t\, u(t)$

2. Using the Laplace transform pairs of Table 2.1 and the Laplace transform theorems of Table 2.2, derive the Laplace transforms for the following time functions: [Section: 2.2]

   a. $e^{-at} \sin \omega t\, u(t)$

   b. $e^{-at} \cos \omega t\, u(t)$

   c. $t^3 u(t)$

3. Repeat Problem 17 in Chapter 1, using Laplace transforms. Assume that the forcing functions are zero prior to $t = 0-$. [Section: 2.2]

4. Repeat Problem 18 in Chapter 1, using Laplace transforms. Assume that the forcing functions are zero prior to $t = 0-$. [Section: 2.2]

5. Use MATLAB and the Symbolic Math Toolbox to find the Laplace transform of the following time functions: [Section: 2.2]

   a. $f(t) = 5t^2 \cos(3t + 45°)$

   b. $f(t) = 5te^{-2t} \sin(4t + 60°)$

6. Use MATLAB and the Symbolic Math Toolbox to find the inverse Laplace transform of the following frequency functions: [Section: 2.2]

   a. $G(s) = \dfrac{(s^2 + 3s + 7)(s + 2)}{(s + 3)(s + 4)(s^2 + 2s + 100)}$

   b. $G(s) = \dfrac{s^3 + 4s^2 + 6s + 5}{(s + 8)(s^2 + 8s + 3)(s^2 + 5s + 7)}$

7. A system is described by the following differential equation:

$$\frac{d^3y}{dt^3} + 5\frac{d^2y}{dt^2} + 7\frac{dy}{dt} + y = \frac{d^3x}{dt^3} + 2\frac{d^2x}{dt^2} + 3\frac{dx}{dt} + 7x$$

Find the expression for the transfer function of the system, $Y(s)/X(s)$.

8. For each of the following transfer functions, write the corresponding differential equation. [Section: 2.3]

   a. $\dfrac{X(s)}{F(s)} = \dfrac{1}{s^2 + 2s + 7}$

   b. $\dfrac{X(s)}{F(s)} = \dfrac{10}{(s + 7)(s + 8)}$

   c. $\dfrac{X(s)}{F(s)} = \dfrac{s + 2}{s^3 + 8s^2 + 9s + 15}$

9. Write the differential equation for the system shown in Figure P2.1.

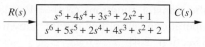

$$\frac{s^5+4s^4+3s^3+2s^2+1}{s^6+5s^5+2s^4+4s^3+s^2+2}$$

R(s) → ... → C(s)

Figure P2.1

10. Write the differential equation that is mathematically equivalent to the block diagram shown in Figure P2.2. Assume that $r(t) = t^3$.

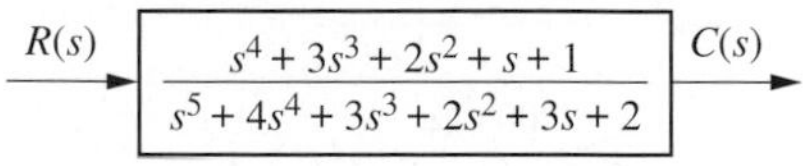

R(s) → $\dfrac{s^4+3s^3+2s^2+s+1}{s^5+4s^4+3s^3+2s^2+3s+2}$ → C(s)

Figure P2.2

11. A system is described by the following differential equation: [Section 2.3]

$$\frac{d^2x}{dt^2} + 2\frac{dx}{dt} + 3x = 1$$

with the initial conditions $x(0) = 1, \dot{x}(0) = -1$. Show a block diagram of the system, giving its transfer function and all pertinent inputs and outputs. (Hint: the initial conditions will show up as added inputs to an effective system with zero initial conditions.)

12. Use MATLAB to generate the transfer function [Section: 2.3]

$$G(s) =$$

$$\frac{5(s+15)(s+26)(s+72)}{s(s+55)(s^2+5s+30)(s+56)(s^2+27s+52)}$$

in the following ways:

a. the ratio of factors;

b. the ratio of polynomials.

13. Repeat Problem 12 for the following transfer function: [Section: 2.3]

$$G(s) = \frac{s^4+25s^3+20s^2+15s+42}{s^5+13s^4+9s^3+37s^2+35s+50}$$

14. Use MATLAB to generate the partial-fraction expansion of the following function: [Section: 2.3]

$$F(s) = \frac{10^4(s+10)(s+60)}{s(s+40)(s+50)(s^2+7s+100)(s^2+6s+90)}$$

15. Use MATLAB and the Symbolic Math Toolbox to input and form LTI objects in polynomial and factored form for the following frequency functions: [Section: 2.3] Symbolic Math

a. $G(s) = \dfrac{45(s^2+37s+74)(s^3+28s^2+32s+16)}{(s+39)(s+47)(s^2+2s+100)(s^3+27s^2+18s+15)}$

b. $G(s) = \dfrac{56(s+14)(s^3+49s^2+62s+53)}{(s^3+81s^2+76s+65)(s^2+88s+33)(s^2+56s+77)}$

16. Find the transfer function, $G(s) = V_o(s)/V_i(s)$, for each network shown in Figure P2.3. [Section: 2.4]

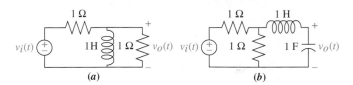

Figure P2.3

17. Find the transfer function, $G(s) = V_L(s)/V(s)$, for each network shown in Figure P2.4. [Section: 2.4]

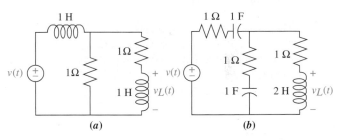

Figure P2.4

18. Find the transfer function, $G(s)=V_o(s)/V_i(s)$, for each network shown in Figure P2.5. Solve the problem using mesh analysis. [Section: 2.4] WileyPLUS Control Solutions

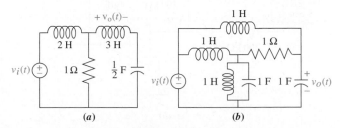

Figure P2.5

19. a. Write, but do not solve, the mesh and nodal equations for the network of Figure P2.6. [Section: 2.4]

    b. Use MATLAB, the Symbolic Math Toolbox, and the equations found in part a to solve for the transfer function, $G(s) = V_o(s)/V(s)$. Use both the mesh and nodal equations and show that either set yields the same transfer function. [Section: 2.4]

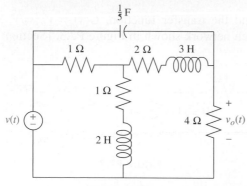

Figure P2.6

20. Find the transfer function, $G(s) = V_o(s)/V_i(s)$, for each operational amplifier circuit shown in Figure P2.7. [Section: 2.4]

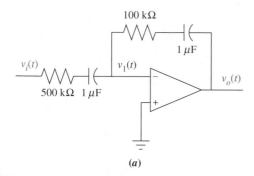

(a)

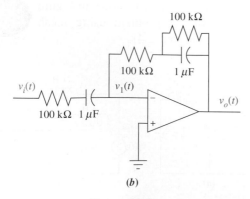

(b)

Figure P2.7

21. Find the transfer function, $G(s) = V_o(s)/V_i(s)$, for each operational amplifier circuit shown in Figure P2.8. [Section: 2.4]

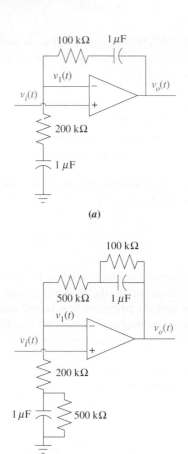

(a)

(b)

Figure P2.8

22. Find the transfer function, $G(s) = X_1(s)/F(s)$, for the translational mechanical system shown in Figure P2.9. [Section: 2.5]

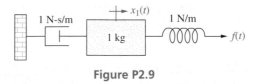

Figure P2.9

23. Find the transfer function, $G(s) = X_2(s)/F(s)$, for the translational mechanical network shown in Figure P2.10. [Section: 2.5]

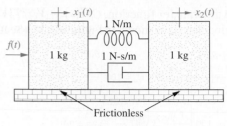

Figure P2.10

24. Find the transfer function, $G(s) = X_2(s)/F(s)$, for the translational mechanical system shown in Figure P2.11. (Hint: Place a zero mass at $x_2(t)$.)

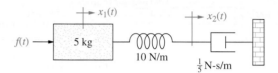

Figure P2.11

25. For the system of Figure P2.12 find the transfer function, $G(s) = X_1(s)/F(s)$. [Section: 2.5]

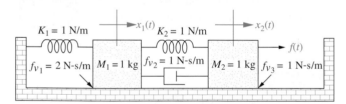

Figure P2.12

26. Find the transfer function, $G(s) = X_3(s)/F(s)$, for the translational mechanical system shown in Figure P2.13.

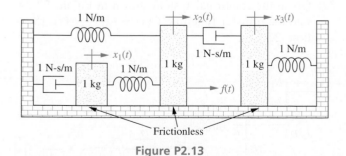

Figure P2.13

27. Find the transfer function, $X_3(s)/F(s)$, for each system shown in Figure P2.14. [Section: 2.5]

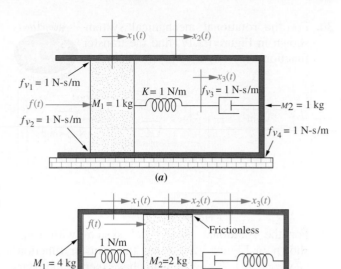

Figure P2.14

28. Write, but do not solve, the equations of motion for the translational mechanical system shown in Figure P2.15.

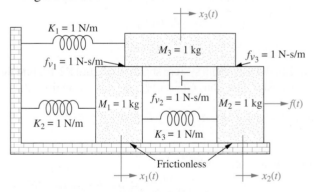

Figure P2.15

29. For each of the rotational mechanical systems shown in Figure P2.16, write, but do not solve, the equations of motion. [Section: 2.6]

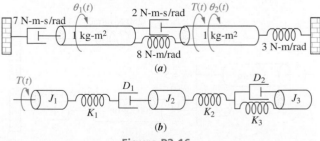

Figure P2.16

30. For the rotational mechanical system shown in Figure P2.17, find the transfer function $G(s) = \theta_2(s)/T(s)$ [Section: 2.6]

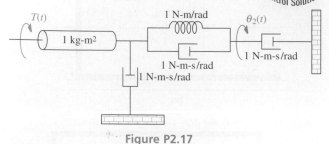

Figure P2.17

31. For the rotational mechanical system with gears shown in Figure P2.18, find the transfer function, $G(s) = \theta_3(s)/T(s)$. The gears have inertia and bearing friction as shown. [Section: 2.7]

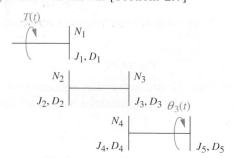

Figure P2.18

32. For the rotational system shown in Figure P2.19, find the transfer function, $G(s) = \theta_2(s)/T(s)$. [Section: 2.7]

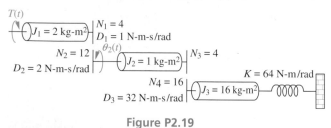

Figure P2.19

33. Find the transfer function, $G(s) = \theta_2(s)/T(s)$, for the rotational mechanical system shown in Figure P2.20.

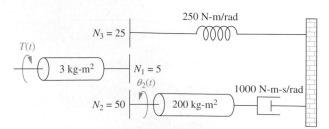

Figure P2.20

34. Find the transfer function, $G(s) = \theta_4(s)/T(s)$, for the rotational system shown in Figure P2.21. [Section: 2.7]

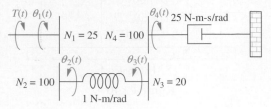

Figure P2.21

35. For the rotational system shown in Figure P2.22, find the transfer function, $G(s) = \theta_L(s)/T(s)$. [Section: 2.7]

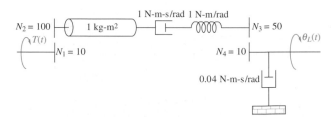

Figure P2.22

36. For the rotational system shown in Figure P2.23, write the equations of motion from which the transfer function, $G(s) = \theta_1(s)/T(s)$, can be found. [Section: 2.7]

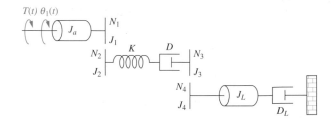

Figure P2.23

37. Given the rotational system shown in Figure P2.24, find the transfer function, $G(s) = \theta_6(s)/\theta_1(s)$. [Section: 2.7]

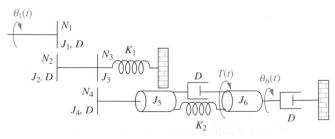

Figure P2.24

38. In the system shown in Figure P2.25, the inertia, J, of radius, r, is constrained to move only about the stationary axis A. A viscous damping force of translational value f_v exists between the bodies J and M. If an external force, $f(t)$, is applied to the mass, find the transfer function, $G(s) = \theta(s)/F(s)$. [Sections: 2.5; 2.6]

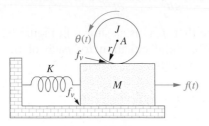

Figure P2.25

39. For the combined translational and rotational system shown in Figure P2.26, find the transfer function, $G(s) = X(s)/T(s)$. [Sections: 2.5; 2.6; 2.7]

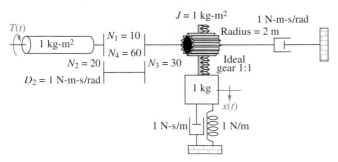

Figure P2.26

40. Given the combined translational and rotational system shown in Figure P2.27, find the transfer function, $G(s) = X(s)/T(s)$. [Sections: 2.5; 2.6]

WileyPLUS

Control Solutions

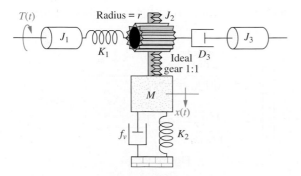

Figure P2.27

41. For the motor, load, and torque-speed curve shown in Figure P2.28, find the transfer function, $G(s) = \theta_L(s)/E_a(s)$. [Section: 2.8]

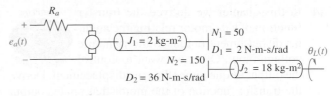

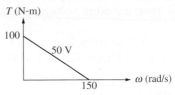

Figure P2.28

42. The motor whose torque-speed characteristics are shown in Figure P2.29 drives the load shown in the diagram. Some of the gears have inertia. Find the transfer function, $G(s) = \theta_2(s)/E_a(s)$. [Section: 2.8]

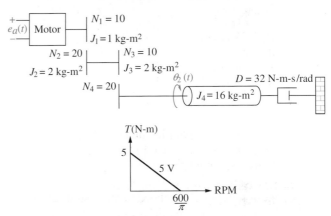

Figure P2.29

43. A dc motor develops 50 N-m of torque at a speed of 500 rad/s when 10 volts are applied. It stalls out at this voltage with 100 N-m of torque. If the inertia and damping of the armature are 5 kg-m^2 and 1 N-m-s/rad, respectively, find the transfer function, $G(s) = \theta_L(s)/E_a(s)$, of this motor if it drives an inertia load of 100 kg-m^2 through a gear train, as shown in Figure P2.30. [Section: 2.8]

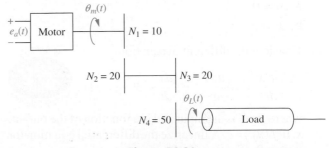

Figure P2.30

44. In this chapter we derived the transfer function of a dc motor relating the angular displacement output to the armature voltage input. Often we want to control the output torque rather than the displacement. Derive the transfer function of the motor that relates output torque to input armature voltage. [Section: 2.8]

45. Find the transfer function, $G(s) = X(s)/E_a(s)$, for the system shown in Figure P2.31. [Sections: 2.5–2.8]

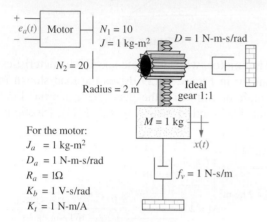

For the motor:
$J_a = 1$ kg-m^2
$D_a = 1$ N-m-s/rad
$R_a = 1\Omega$
$K_b = 1$ V-s/rad
$K_t = 1$ N-m/A

Figure P2.31

46. Find the series and parallel analogs for the rotational mechanical systems shown in Figure P2.16(b) in the problems. [Section: 2.9]

47. A system's output, c, is related to the system's input, r, by the straight-line relationship, $c = 5r + 7$. Is the system linear? [Section: 2.10]

48. Consider the differential equation

$$\frac{d^2x}{dt^2} + 3\frac{dx}{dt} + 2x = f(x)$$

where $f(x)$ is the input and is a function of the output, x. If $f(x) = \sin x$, linearize the differential equation for small excursions. [Section: 2.10]

a. $x = 0$

b. $x = \pi$

49. Consider the differential equation

$$\frac{d^3x}{dt^3} + 10\frac{d^2x}{dt^2} + 31\frac{dx}{dt} + 30x = f(x)$$

where $f(x)$ is the input and is a function of the output, x. If $f(x) = e^{-x}$, linearize the differential equation for x near 0. [Section: 2.10]

50. Many systems are *piecewise* linear. That is, over a *large* range of variable values, the system can be described linearly. A system with amplifier saturation is one such example. Given the differential equation

$$\frac{d^2x}{dt^2} + 15\frac{dx}{dt} + 50x = f(x)$$

assume that $f(x)$ is as shown in Figure P2.32. Write the differential equation for each of the following ranges of x: [Section: 2.10]

a. $-\infty < x < -2$

b. $-2 < x < 2$

c. $2 < x < \infty$

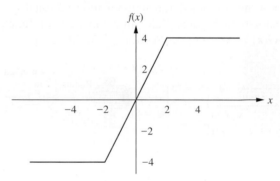

Figure P2.32

51. For the translational mechanical system with a nonlinear spring shown in Figure P2.33, find the transfer function, $G(s) = X(s)/F(s)$, for small excursions around $f(t) = 1$. The spring is defined by $x_s(t) = 1 - e^{-f_s(t)}$, where $x_s(t)$ is the spring displacement and $f_s(t)$ is the spring force. [Section: 2.10]

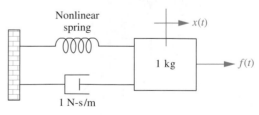

Figure P2.33

52. Consider the restaurant plate dispenser shown in Figure P2.34, which consists of a vertical stack of dishes supported by a compressed spring. As each plate is removed, the reduced weight on the dispenser causes

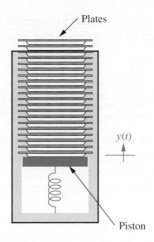

Figure P2.34 Plate dispenser

the remaining plates to rise. Assume that the mass of the system minus the top plate is M, the viscous friction between the piston and the sides of the cylinder is f_v, the spring constant is K, and the weight of a single plate is W_D. Find the transfer function, $Y(s)/F(s)$, where $F(s)$ is the step reduction in force felt when the top plate is removed, and $Y(s)$ is the vertical displacement of the dispenser in an upward direction.

53. Each inner ear in a human has a set of three nearly perpendicular semicircular canals of about 0.28 mm in diameter filled with fluid. Hair-cell transducers that deflect with skull movements and whose main purpose is to work as attitude sensors as well as help us maintain our sense of direction and equilibrium are attached to the canals. As the hair cells move, they deflect a waterproof flap called the *cupula*. It has been shown that the skull and cupula movements are related by the following equation (*Milsum, 1966*):

$$J\ddot{\phi} + b\dot{\phi} + k\phi = (aJ)\ddot{\psi}$$

where

J = moment of inertia of the fluid in the thin tube (constant)

b = torque per unit relative angular velocity (constant)

k = torque per unit relative angular displacement (constant)

a = constant

$\phi(t)$ = angular deflection of the cupula (output)

$\ddot{\psi}(t)$ = skull's angular acceleration (input)

Find the transfer function $\dfrac{\Phi(s)}{\ddot{\Psi}(s)}$.

54. Diabetes is an illness that has risen to epidemic proportions, affecting about 3% of the total world population

in 2003. A differential equation model that describes the total population size of diabetics is

$$\frac{dC(t)}{dt} = -(\lambda + \mu + \delta + \gamma + v)C(t) + \lambda N(t)$$

$$\frac{dN(t)}{dt} = -(v + \delta)C(t) - \mu N(t) + I(t)$$

with the initial conditions $C(0) = C_0$ and $N(0) = N_0$ and

$I(t)$ = the system input: the number of new cases of diabetes

$C(t)$ = number of diabetics with complications

$N(t)$ = the system output: the total number of diabetics with and without complications

μ = natural mortality rate (constant)

λ = probability of developing a complication (constant)

δ = mortality rate due to complications (constant)

v = rate at which patients with complications become severely disabled (constant)

γ = rate at which complications are cured (constant)

Assume the following values for parameters: $v = \delta = 0.05/yr$, $\mu = 0.02/yr$, $\gamma = 0.08/yr$, $\lambda = 0.7$, with initial conditions $C_0 = 47{,}000{,}500$ and $N_0 =$, $61{,}100{,}500$. Assume also that diabetic incidence is constant $I(t) = I = 6 \times 10^6$ (*Boutayeb, 2004*).

a. Draw a block diagram of the system showing the output $N(s)$, the input $I(s)$, the transfer function, and the initial conditions.

b. Use any method to find the analytic expression for $N(t)$ for $t \geq 0$.

55. The circuit shown in Figure P2.35(*a*) is excited with the pulse shown in Figure P2.35(*b*).

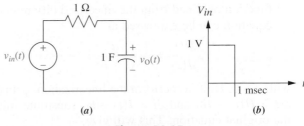

(*a*)   (*b*)

Figure P2.35

The Laplace transform can be used to calculate $v_o(t)$ in two different ways: The "exact" method is performed by writing $v_i(t) = u(t) - u(t - 0.001)$, from which we use the Laplace transform to obtain

$$V_{in}(s) = \frac{1 - e^{-0.001s}}{s}.$$

(Hint: look at Item 5 in Table 2.2, the time shift theorem.) In the second approach the pulse is approximated by an impulse input having the same area (energy) as the original input. From Figure P2.35(b): $v_{in}(t) \approx (1 \text{ V})(1 \text{ msec})\delta(t) = 0.001\delta(t)$. In this case, $V_{in}(s) = 0.001$. This approximation can be used as long as the width of the pulse of Figure P2.35(b) is much smaller than the circuit's smallest time constant. (Here, $\tau = RC = (1\,\Omega)(1\,\text{F}) = 1 \text{ sec} \gg 1 \text{ msec}$.)

a. Assuming the capacitor is initially discharged, obtain an analytic expression for $v_o(t)$ using both methods.

b. Plot the results of both methods using any means available to you, and compare both outputs. Discuss the differences.

56. In a magnetic levitation experiment a metallic object is held up in the air suspended under an electromagnet. The vertical displacement of the object can be described by the following nonlinear differential equation (*Galvão, 2003*):

$$m\frac{d^2H}{dt^2} = mg - k\frac{I^2}{H^2}$$

where

$m =$ mass of the metallic object
$g =$ gravity acceleration constant
$k =$ a positive constant
$H =$ distance between the electromagnet and the metallic object (output signal)
$I =$ electromagnet's current (input signal)

a. Show that a system's equilibrium will be achieved when $H_0 = I_0\sqrt{\dfrac{k}{mg}}$.

b. Linearize the equation about the equilibrium point found in Part **a** and show that the resulting transfer function obtained from the linearized differential equation can be expressed as

$$\frac{\delta H(s)}{\delta I(s)} = -\frac{a}{s^2 - b^2}$$

with $a > 0$. Hint: to perform the linearization, define $\delta H = H(t) - H_0$ and $\delta I = I(t) - I_0$; substitute into the original equation. This will give

$$m\frac{d^2(H_0 + \delta H)}{dt^2} = mg - k\frac{(I_0 + \delta I)^2}{(H_0 + \delta H)^2} = \gamma$$

Now get a first-order Taylor's series approximation on the right-hand side of the equation. Namely, calculate

$$m\frac{d^2\delta H}{dt^2} = \left.\frac{\partial\gamma}{\partial\delta H}\right|_{\delta H = 0, \delta I = 0} \delta H + \left.\frac{\partial\gamma}{\partial\delta I}\right|_{\delta H = 0, \delta I = 0} \delta I$$

57. Figure P2.36 shows a quarter-car model commonly used for analyzing suspension systems. The car's tire is considered to act as a spring without damping, as shown. The parameters of the model are (*Lin, 1997*)

$M_b =$ car's body mass
$M_{us} =$ wheel's mass
$K_a =$ strut's spring constant
$K_t =$ tire's spring constant
$f_v =$ strut's damping constant
$r =$ road disturbance (input)
$x_s =$ car's vertical displacement
$x_w =$ wheel's vertical displacement

Obtain the transfer function from the road disturbance to the car's vertical displacement $\dfrac{X_s(s)}{R(s)}$.

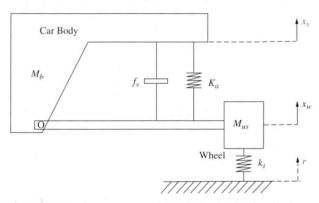

Figure P2.36   Quarter-car model used for suspension design (© 1997 IEEE)

58. Enzymes are large proteins that biological systems use to increase the rate at which reactions occur. For example, food is usually composed of large molecules that are hard to digest; enzymes break down the large molecules into small nutrients as part of the digestive process. One such enzyme is amylase, contained in human saliva. It is commonly known that if you place a piece of uncooked pasta in your mouth its taste will change from paper-like to sweet as amylase breaks down the carbohydrates into sugars. Enzyme breakdown is often expressed by the following relation:

$$S + E \overset{k_s}{\underset{k_1}{\rightleftarrows}} C \overset{k_2}{\rightarrow} P$$

In this expression a substrate (S) interacts with an enzyme (E) to form a combined product (C) at a rate k_1. The intermediate compound is reversible and gets disassociated at a rate k_{-1}. Simultaneously some of the compound is transformed into the final product (P) at a rate k_2. The kinetics describing this reaction are known as the Michaelis-Menten equations and consist of four nonlinear differential equations. However, under some conditions these equations can be simplified. Let E_0 and S_0 be the initial concentrations of enzyme and substrate, respectively. It is generally accepted that under some energetic conditions or when the enzyme concentration is very big $(E_0 \gg S_0)$, the kinetics for this reaction are given by (*Schnell, 2004*)

$$\frac{dS}{dt} = k_\psi(\tilde{K}_s C - S)$$

$$\frac{dC}{dt} = k_\psi(S - \tilde{K}_M C)$$

$$\frac{dP}{dt} = k_2 C$$

where the following constant terms are used:

$$k_\psi = k_1 E_0$$
$$\tilde{K}_s = \frac{k_{-1}}{k_\psi}$$

and

$$\tilde{K}_M = \tilde{K}_s + \frac{k_2}{k_\psi}$$

a. Assuming the initial conditions for the reaction are $S(0) = S_0$, $E(0) = E_0$, $C(0) = P(0) = 0$, find the Laplace transform expressions for S, C, and P: $\mathscr{L}\{S\}$, $\mathscr{L}\{C\}$, and $\mathscr{L}\{P\}$, respectively.

b. Use the final theorem to find $S(\infty)$, $C(\infty)$, and $P(\infty)$.

59. Humans are able to stand on two legs through a complex feedback system that includes several sensory inputs—equilibrium and visual along with muscle actuation. In order to gain a better understanding of the workings of the postural feedback mechanism, an individual is asked to stand on a platform to which sensors are attached at the base. Vibration actuators are attached with straps to the individual's calves. As the vibration actuators are stimulated, the individual sways and movements are recorded. It was hypothesized that the human postural dynamics are analogous to those of a cart

with a balancing standing pole attached (inverted pendulum). In that case the dynamics can be described by the following two equations:

$$J\frac{d^2\theta}{dt^2} = mgl\sin\theta(t) + T_{\text{bal}} + T_d(t)$$

$$T_{\text{bal}}(t) = -mgl\sin\theta(t) - kJ\theta(t) - \eta J\dot{\theta}(t)$$

$$- \rho J \int_0^t \theta(t)\, dt$$

where m is the individual's mass; l is the height of the individual's center of gravity; g is the gravitational constant; J is the individual's equivalent moment of inertia; η, ρ, and k are constants given by the body's postural control system; $\theta(t)$ is the individual's angle with respect to a vertical line; $T_{\text{bal}}(t)$ is the torque generated by the body muscles to maintain balance; and $T_d(t)$ is the external torque input disturbance. Find the transfer function $\dfrac{\Theta(s)}{T_d(s)}$ (*Johansson, 1988*).

60. Figure P2.37 shows a crane hoisting a load. Although the actual system's model is highly nonlinear, if the rope is considered to be stiff with a fixed length L, the system can be modeled using the following equations:

$$m_L \ddot{x}_{La} = m_L g\phi$$
$$m_T \ddot{x}_T = f_T - m_L g\phi$$
$$x_{La} = x_T - x_L$$
$$x_L = L\phi$$

where m_L is the mass of the load, m_T is the mass of the cart, x_T and x_L are displacements as defined in the figure, ϕ is the rope angle with respect to the vertical, and f_T is the force applied to the cart (*Marttinen, 1990*).

a. Obtain the transfer function from cart velocity to rope angle $\dfrac{\Phi(s)}{V_T(s)}$.

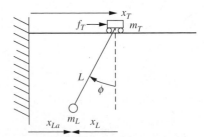

Figure P2.37 (©1990 IEEE)

b. Assume that the cart is driven at a constant velocity V_0 and obtain an expression for the resulting $\phi(t)$. Show that under this condition, the load will sway with a frequency $\omega_0 = \sqrt{\dfrac{g}{L}}$.

c. Find the transfer function from the applied force to the cart's position, $\dfrac{X_T(s)}{F_T(s)}$.

d. Show that if a constant force is applied to the cart, its velocity will increase without bound as $t \to \infty$.

61. In 1978 Malthus developed a model for human growth population that is also commonly used to model bacterial growth as follows. Let $N(t)$ be the population density observed at time t. Let K be the rate of reproduction per unit time. Neglecting population deaths, the population density at a time $t + \Delta t$ (with small Δt) is given by

$$N(t + \Delta t) \approx N(t) + KN(t)\Delta t$$

which also can be written as

$$\frac{N(t + \Delta t) - N(t)}{\Delta t} = KN(t)$$

Since $N(t)$ can be considered to be a very large number, letting $\Delta t \to 0$ gives the following differential equation (*Edelstein-Keshet, 2005*):

$$\frac{dN(t)}{dt} = KN(t)$$

a. Assuming an initial population $N(0) = N_0$, solve the differential equation by finding $N(t)$.

b. Find the time at which the population is double the initial population.

62. Blood vessel blockages can in some instances be diagnosed through noninvasive techniques such as the use of sensitive microphones to detect flow acoustic anomalies. In order to predict the sound properties of the left coronary artery, a model has been developed that partitions the artery into 14 segments, as shown in Figure P2.38(*a*).

Each segment is then modeled through the analogous electrical circuit of Figure P2.38(*b*), resulting in the total model shown in Figure P2.38(*c*), where eight terminal resistances (Z) have been added. In the electrical model pressure is analogous to voltage and blood flow is analogous to current. As an example, for segment 3 it was experimentally verified that $R_3 = 4176\,\Omega$, $C_3 = 0.98\,\mu\text{F}$, $L_3 = 140.6\,\text{H}$, and $Z_3 = 308{,}163\,\Omega$ (*Wang, 1990*).

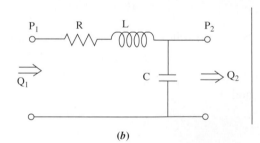

(b)

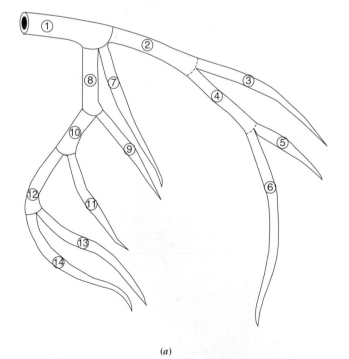

(a)

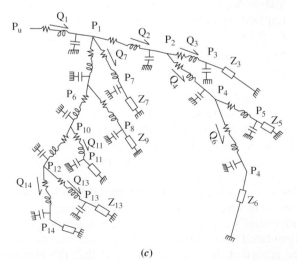

(c)

Figure P2.38   (©1990 IEEE)

a. For segment 3, find the transfer function from input pressure to blood flow through Z_3, $\dfrac{Q_{03}(s)}{P_2(s)}$.

b. It is well known in circuit analysis that if a constant input is applied to a circuit such as the one of Figure P2.38(b), the capacitor can be substituted by an open circuit and the inductor can be substituted by a short circuit as time approaches infinity. Use this fact to calculate the flow through Z_3 after a constant unit pressure pulse is applied and time approaches infinity.

c. Verify the result obtained in Part **b** using the transfer function obtained in Part **a** and applying the final value theorem.

63. The Gompertz growth model is commonly used to model tumor cell growth. Let $v(t)$ be the tumor's volume, then

$$\frac{dv(t)}{dt} = \lambda e^{-\alpha t} v(t)$$

where λ and α are two appropriate constants (*Edelstein-Keshet, 2005*).

a. Verify that the solution to this equation is given by $v(t) = v_0 e^{\lambda/\alpha(1-e^{-\alpha t})}$, where v_0 is the initial tumor volume.

b. This model takes into account the fact that when nutrients and oxygen are scarce at the tumor's core, its growth is impaired. Find the final predicted tumor volume (let $t \to \infty$).

c. For a specific mouse tumor, it was experimentally found that $\lambda = 2.5$ days, $\alpha = 0.1$ days with $v_0 = 50 \times 10^{-3}$ mm^3 (*Chignola, 2005*). Use any method available to make a plot of $v(t)$ vs. t.

d. Check the result obtained in Part **b** with the results from the graph from Part **c.**

Progressive Analysis and Design Problems

64. **High-speed rail pantograph.** Problem 19 in Chapter 1 discusses active control of a pantograph mechanism for high-speed rail systems. The diagram for the pantograph and catenary coupling is shown in Figure P2.39(a). Assume the simplified model shown in Figure P2.39(b), where the catenary is represented by the spring, K_{ave} (*O'Connor, 1997*).

a. Find the transfer function, $G_1(s) = Y_{cat}(s)/F_{up}(s)$, where $y_{cat}(t)$ is the catenary displacement

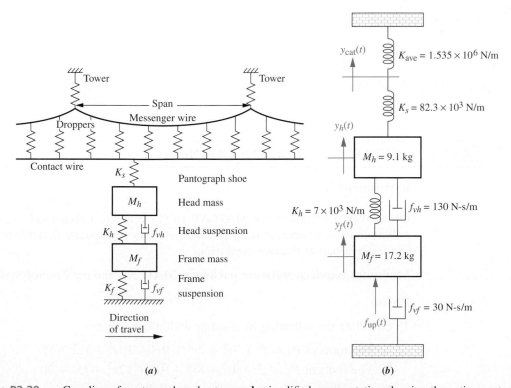

(a)

(b)

Figure P2.39 **a.** Coupling of pantograph and catenary; **b.** simplified representation showing the active-control force

and $f_{up}(t)$ is the upward force applied to the pantograph under active control.

b. Find the transfer function $G_2(s) = Y_h(s)/F_{up}(s)$, where $y_h(t)$ is the pantograph head displacement.

c. Find the transfer function, $G(s) = (Y_h(s) - Y_{cat}(s))/F_{up}(s)$.

65. Control of HIV/AIDS. HIV inflicts its damage by infecting healthy CD4+ T cells (a type of white blood cell) that are necessary to fight infection. As the virus embeds in a T cell and the immune system produces more of these cells to fight the infection, the virus propagates in an opportunistic fashion. As we now develop a simple HIV model, refer to Figure P2.40. Normally T cells are produced at a rate s and die at a rate d. The HIV virus is present in the bloodstream in the infected individual. These viruses in the bloodstream, called *free viruses*, infect healthy T cells at a rate β. Also, the viruses reproduce through the T cell multiplication process or otherwise at a rate

k. Free viruses die at a rate c. Infected T cells die at a rate μ.

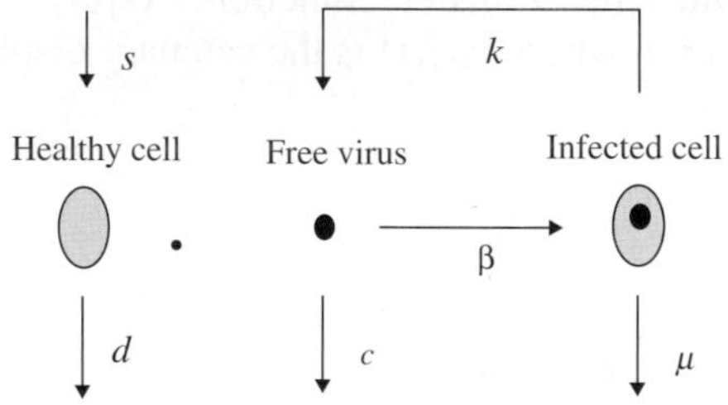

A simple mathematical model that illustrates these interactions is given by the following equations (*Craig, 2004*):

$$\frac{dT}{dt} = s - dT - \beta Tv$$

$$\frac{dT^*}{dt} = \beta Tv - \mu T^*$$

$$\frac{dv}{dt} = kT^* - cv$$

where

T = number of healthy T cells
T^* = number of infected T cells
v = number of free viruses

a. The system is nonlinear; thus linearization is necessary to find transfer functions as you will do in subsequent chapters. The nonlinear nature of this model can be seen from the above equations. Determine which of these equations are linear, which are nonlinear, and explain why.

b. The system has two equilibrium points. Show that these are given by

$$(T_0, T_0^*, v_0) = \left(\frac{s}{d}, 0, 0\right)$$

and

$$(T_0, T_0^*, v_0) = \left(\frac{c\mu}{\beta k}, \frac{s}{\mu} - \frac{cd}{\beta k}, \frac{sk}{c\mu} - \frac{d}{\beta}\right)$$

Figure P2.40 (©2004 IEEE)

CYBER EXPLORATION LABORATORY

Experiment 2.1

Objectives To learn to use MATLAB to (1) generate polynomials, (2) manipulate polynomials, (3) generate transfer functions, (4) manipulate transfer functions, and (5) perform partial-fraction expansions.

Minimum required software packages MATLAB and the Control System Toolbox

Prelab

1. Calculate the following by hand or with a calculator:

a. The roots of $P_1 = s^6 + 7s^5 + 2s^4 + 9s^3 + 10s^2 + 12s + 15$

b. The roots of $P_2 = s^6 + 9s^5 + 8s^4 + 9s^3 + 12s^2 + 15s + 20$

c. $P_3 = P_1 + P_2; P_4 = P_1 - P_2; P_5 = P_1 P_2$

2. Calculate by hand or with a calculator the polynomial

$$P_6 = (s + 7)(s + 8)(s + 3)(s + 5)(s + 9)(s + 10)$$

3. Calculate by hand or with a calculator the following transfer functions:

a. $G_1(s) = \dfrac{20(s + 2)(s + 3)(s + 6)(s + 8)}{s(s + 7)(s + 9)(s + 10)(s + 15)}$,

represented as a numerator polynomial divided by a denominator polynomial.

b. $G_2(s) = \dfrac{s^4 + 17s^3 + 99s^2 + 223s + 140}{s^5 + 32s^4 + 363s^3 + 2092s^2 + 5052s + 4320}$,

expressed as factors in the numerator divided by factors in the denominator, similar to the form of $G_1(s)$ in Prelab **3a**.

c. $G_3(s) = G_1(s) + G_2(s)$; $G_4(s) = G_1(s) - G_2(s)$; $G_5(s) = G_1(s)G_2(s)$ expressed as factors divided by factors and expressed as polynomials divided by polynomials.

4. Calculate by hand or with a calculator the partial fraction expansion of the following transfer functions:

a. $G_6 = \dfrac{5(s + 2)}{s(s^2 + 8s + 15)}$

b. $G_7 = \dfrac{5(s + 2)}{s(s^2 + 6s + 9)}$

c. $G_8 = \dfrac{5(s + 2)}{s(s^2 + 6s + 34)}$

Lab

1. Use MATLAB to find P_3, P_4, and P_5 in Prelab 1.

2. Use only one MATLAB command to find P_6 in Prelab 2.

3. Use only two MATLAB commands to find $G_1(s)$ in Prelab **3a** represented as a polynomial divided by a polynomial.

4. Use only two MATLAB commands to find $G_2(s)$ expressed as factors in the numerator divided by factors in the denominator.

5. Using various combinations of $G_1(s)$ and $G_2(s)$, find $G_3(s)$, $G_4(s)$, and $G_5(s)$. Various combinations implies mixing and matching $G_1(s)$ and $G_2(s)$ expressed as factors and polynomials. For example, in finding $G_3(s)$, $G_1(s)$ can be expressed in factored form and $G_2(s)$ can be expressed in polynomial form. Another combination is $G_1(s)$ and $G_2(s)$ both expressed as polynomials. Still another combination is $G_1(s)$ and $G_2(s)$ both expressed in factored form.

6. Use MATLAB to evaluate the partial fraction expansions shown in Prelab 4.

Postlab

1. Discuss your findings for Lab 5. What can you conclude?

2. Discuss the use of MATLAB to manipulate transfer functions and polynomials. Discuss any shortcomings in using MATLAB to evaluate partial fraction expansions.

Experiment 2.2

Objectives To learn to use MATLAB and the Symbolic Math Toolbox to (1) find Laplace transforms for time functions, (2) find time functions from Laplace transforms, (3) create LTI transfer functions from symbolic transfer functions, and (4) perform solutions of symbolic simultaneous equations.

Minimum required software packages MATLAB, the Symbolic Math Toolbox, and the Control System Toolbox

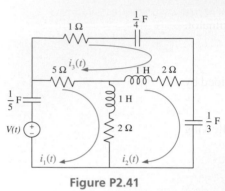

Figure P2.41

Prelab

1. Using a hand calculation, find the Laplace transform of

$$f(t) = 0.0075 - 0.00034\,e^{-2.5t}\cos(22t) + 0.087\,e^{-2.5t}\sin(22t) - 0.0072\,e^{-8t}$$

2. Using a hand calculation, find the inverse Laplace transform of

$$F(s) = \frac{2(s+3)(s+5)(s+7)}{s(s+8)(s^2+10s+100)}$$

3. Use a hand calculation to solve the circuit for the loop currents shown in Figure P2.41.

Lab

1. Use MATLAB and the Symbolic Math Toolbox to

   a. Generate symbolically the time function $f(t)$ shown in Prelab 1.

   b. Generate symbolically $F(s)$ shown in Prelab 2. Obtain your result symbolically in both factored and polynomial forms.

   c. Find the Laplace transform of $f(t)$ shown in Prelab 1.

   d. Find the inverse Laplace transform of $F(s)$ shown in Prelab 2.

   e. Generate an LTI transfer function for your symbolic representation of $F(s)$ in Prelab 2 in both polynomial form and factored form. Start with the $F(s)$ you generated symbolically.

   f. Solve for the loop currents in Prelab 3.

Postlab

1. Discuss the advantages and disadvantages between the Symbolic Math Toolbox and MATLAB alone to convert a transfer function from factored form to polynomial form and vice versa.

2. Discuss the advantages and disadvantages of using the Symbolic Math Toolbox to generate LTI transfer functions.

3. Discuss the advantages of using the Symbolic Math Toolbox to solve simultaneous equations of the type generated by the electrical network in Prelab 3. Is it possible to solve the equations via MATLAB alone? Explain.

4. Discuss any other observations you had using the Symbolic Math Toolbox.

BIBLIOGRAPHY

Aggarwal, J. K. *Notes on Nonlinear Systems*. Van Nostrand Reinhold, New York, 1972.

Boutayeb, A., Twizell, E. H., Achouayb, K., and Chetouani, A. Mathematical Model for the Burden of Diabetes and Its Complications. *BioMedical Engineering OnLine*, 2004 3:20 or http://www.bio-medical-engineering-online.com/content/3/1/20, pp. 1–19.

Cannon, R. H., Jr., *Dynamics of Physical Systems*. McGraw-Hill, New York, 1967.

Carlson, L. E., and Griggs, G. E. *Aluminum Catenary System Quarterly Report*. Technical Report Contract Number DOT-FR-9154, U.S. Department of Transportation, 1980.

Chignola, R., and Foroni, R. I. Estimating the Growth Kinetics of Experimental Tumors from as Few as Two Determinations of Tumor Size: Implications for Clinical Oncology. *IEEE Transactions on Biomedical Engineering*, vol. 52, no. 5, May 2005, pp. 808–815.

Cochin, I. *Analysis and Design of Dynamic Systems*. Harper and Row, New York, 1980.

Cook, P. A. *Nonlinear Dynamical Systems*. Prentice Hall, United Kingdom, 1986.

Craig, I. K., Xia, X., and Venter, J. W. Introducing HIV/AIDS Education into the Electrical Engineering Curriculum at the University of Pretoria. *IEEE Transactions on Education*, vol. 47, no. 1, February 2004, pp. 65–73.

Davis, S. A., and Ledgerwood, B. K. *Electromechanical Components for Servomechanisms*. McGraw-Hill, New York, 1961.

Doebelin, E. O. *Measurement Systems Application and Design*. McGraw-Hill, New York, 1983.

Dorf, R. *Introduction to Electric Circuits*, 2d ed. Wiley, New York, 1993.

D'Souza, A. *Design of Control Systems*. Prentice Hall, Englewood Cliffs, NJ, 1988.

Edelstein-Keshet, L. *Mathematical Models in Biology*. Society for Industrial and Applied Mathematics, Philadelphia, PA, 2005.

Elkins, J. A. *A Method for Predicting the Dynamic Response of a Pantograph Running at Constant Speed under a Finite Length of Overhead Equipment*. Technical Report TN DA36, British Railways, 1976.

Franklin, G. F., Powell, J. D., and Emami-Naeini, A. *Feedback Control of Dynamic Systems*. Addison-Wesley, Reading, MA, 1986.

Galvão, R. K. H., Yoneyama, T., and de Araújo, F. M. U. A Simple Technique for Identifying a Linearized Model for a Didactic Magnetic Levitation System. *IEEE Transactions on Education*, vol. 46, no. 1, February 2003, pp. 22–25.

Hsu, J. C., and Meyer, A. U. *Modern Control Principles and Applications*. McGraw-Hill, New York, 1968.

Johansson, R., Magnusson, M., and Åkesson, M. Identification of Human Postural Dynamics. *IEEE Transactions on Biomedical Engineering*, vol. 35, no. 10, October 1988, pp. 858–869.

Kailath, T. *Linear Systems*. Prentice Hall, Englewood Cliffs, NJ, 1980.

Kermurjian, A. From the Moon Rover to the Mars Rover. *The Planetary Report*, July/August 1990, pp. 4–11.

Kuo, F. F. *Network Analysis and Synthesis*. Wiley, New York, 1966.

Lago, G., and Benningfield, L. M. *Control System Theory*. Ronald Press, New York, 1962.

Lin, J.-S., and Kanellakopoulos I. Nonlinear Design of Active Suspensions. *IEEE Control Systems Magazine*, vol. 17, issue 3, June 1997, pp. 45–59.

Mablekos, V. E. *Electric Machine Theory for Power Engineers*. Harper & Row, Cambridge, MA, 1980.

Marttinen, A., Virkkunen, J., and Salminen, R. T. Control Study with Pilot Crane. *IEEE Transactions on Education*, vol. 33, no. 3, August 1990, pp. 298–305.

Milsum, J. H. *Biological Control Systems Analysis*. McGraw-Hill, New York, 1966.

Minorsky, N. *Theory of Nonlinear Control Systems*. McGraw-Hill, New York, 1969.

Nilsson, J. W., and Riedel, S. A. *Electric Circuits*, 5th ed. Addison-Wesley, Reading, MA, 1996.

O'Connor, D. N., Eppinger, S. D., Seering, W. P., and Wormly, D. N. Active Control of a High-Speed Pantograph. *Journal of Dynamic Systems, Measurements, and Control*, vol. 119, March 1997, pp. 1–4.

Ogata, K. *Modern Control Engineering*, 2d ed. Prentice Hall, Englewood Cliffs, NJ, 1990.

Raven, F. H. *Automatic Control Engineering*, 5th ed. McGraw-Hill, New York, 1995.

Schnell, S., and Mendoza, C. The Condition for Pseudo-First-Order Kinetics in Enzymatic Reactions Is Independent of the Initial Enzyme Concentration. *Biophysical Chemistry* (107), 2004, pp. 165–174.

VanValkenburg, M. E. *Network Analysis*. Prentice Hall, Englewood Cliffs, NJ, 1974.

Vidyasagar, M. *Nonlinear Systems Analysis*. Prentice Hall, Englewood Cliffs, NJ, 1978.

Wang, J. Z., Tie, B., Welkowitz, W., Semmlow, J. L., and Kostis, J. B. Modeling Sound Generation in Stenosed Coronary Arteries. *IEEE Transactions on Biomedical Engineering*, vol. 37, no. 11, November 1990, pp. 1087–1094.

STATE EQUATIONS FOR PHYSICAL SYSTEMS

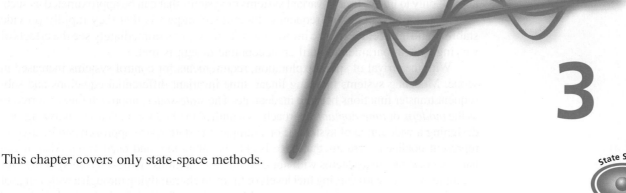

3

This chapter covers only state-space methods.

State Space

CHAPTER OBJECTIVES

In this chapter you will learn the following:

- How to find a mathematical model, called a *state-space* representation, for a linear, time-invariant system
- How to convert between transfer function and state-space models
- How to linearize a state-space representation

CASE STUDY OBJECTIVES

You will be able to demonstrate your knowledge of the chapter objectives with case studies as follows:

- Given the antenna azimuth position control system shown on the front endpapers, you will be able to find the state-space representation of each subsystem.
- Given a description of the way a pharmaceutical drug flows through a human being, you will be able to find the state-space representation to determine drug concentrations in specified compartmentalized blocks of the process and of the human body. You will also be able to apply the same concepts to an aquifer to find water level.

3.1 INTRODUCTION

Two approaches are available for the analysis and design of feedback control systems. The first, which we began to study in Chapter 2, is known as the *classical*, or *frequency-domain*, technique. This approach is based on converting a system's differential equation to a transfer function, thus generating a mathematical model of the system that *algebraically* relates a representation of the output to a representation of the input. Replacing a differential equation with an algebraic equation not only simplifies the representation of individual subsystems but also simplifies modeling interconnected subsystems.

The primary disadvantage of the classical approach is its limited applicability: It can be applied only to linear, time-invariant systems or systems that can be approximated as such.

A major advantage of frequency-domain techniques is that they rapidly provide stability and transient response information. Thus, we can immediately see the effects of varying system parameters until an acceptable design is met.

With the arrival of space exploration, requirements for control systems increased in scope. Modeling systems by using linear, time-invariant differential equations and subsequent transfer functions became inadequate. The *state-space,* approach (also referred to as the *modern,* or *time-domain,* approach) is a unified method for modeling, analyzing, and designing a wide range of systems. For example, the state-space approach can be used to represent nonlinear systems that have backlash, saturation, and dead zone. Also, it can handle, conveniently, systems with nonzero initial conditions. Time-varying systems, (for example, missiles with varying fuel levels or lift in an aircraft flying through a wide range of altitudes) can be represented in state space. Many systems do not have just a single input and a single output. Multiple-input, multiple-output systems (such as a vehicle with input direction and input velocity yielding an output direction and an output velocity) can be compactly represented in state space with a model similar in form and complexity to that used for single-input, single-output systems. The time-domain approach can be used to represent systems with a digital computer in the loop or to model systems for digital simulation. With a simulated system, system response can be obtained for changes in system parameters—an important design tool. The state-space approach is also attractive because of the availability of numerous state-space software packages for the personal computer.

The time-domain approach can also be used for the same class of systems modeled by the classical approach. This alternate model gives the control systems designer another perspective from which to create a design. While the state-space approach can be applied to a wide range of systems, it is not as intuitive as the classical approach. The designer has to engage in several calculations before the physical interpretation of the model is apparent, whereas in classical control a few quick calculations or a graphic presentation of data rapidly yields the physical interpretation.

In this book the coverage of state-space techniques is to be regarded as an introduction to the subject, a springboard to advanced studies, and an alternate approach to frequency-domain techniques. We will limit the state-space approach to linear, time-invariant systems or systems that can be linearized by the methods of Chapter 2. The study of other classes of systems is beyond the scope of this book. Since state-space analysis and design rely on matrices and matrix operations, you may want to review this topic in Appendix F, located at www.wiley.com/college/nise, before continuing.

3.2 SOME OBSERVATIONS

We proceed now to establish the state-space approach as an alternate method for representing physical systems. This section sets the stage for the formal definition of the state-space representation by making some observations about systems and their variables. In the discussion that follows, some of the development has been placed in footnotes to avoid clouding the main issues with an excess of equations and to ensure that the concept is clear. Although we use two electrical networks to illustrate the concepts, we could just as easily have used a mechanical or any other physical system.

We now demonstrate that for a system with many variables, such as inductor voltage, resistor voltage, and capacitor charge, we need to use differential equations only to solve for a selected subset of system variables because all other remaining system variables can be evaluated algebraically from the variables in the subset. Our examples take the following approach:

1. We select a particular *subset* of all possible system variables and call the variables in this subset *state variables*.

2. For an *n*th-order system, we write *n simultaneous, first-order differential equations* in terms of the state variables. We call this system of simultaneous differential equations *state equations*.

3. If we know the initial condition of all of the state variables at t_0 as well as the system input for $t \geq t_0$, we can solve the simultaneous differential equations for the state variables for $t \geq t_0$.

4. We *algebraically* combine the state variables with the system's input and find all of the other system variables for $t \geq t_0$. We call this algebraic equation the *output equation*.

5. We consider the state equations and the output equations a viable representation of the system. We call this representation of the system a *state-space representation*.

Let us now follow these steps through an example. Consider the *RL* network shown in Figure 3.1 with an initial current of $i(0)$.

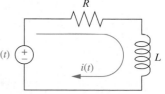

FIGURE 3.1 *RL* network

1. We select the current, $i(t)$, for which we will write and solve a differential equation using Laplace transforms.

2. We write the loop equation,

$$L\frac{di}{dt} + Ri = v(t) \tag{3.1}$$

3. Taking the Laplace transform, using Table 2.2, Item 7 and including the initial conditions, yields

$$L[sI(s) - i(0)] + RI(s) = V(s) \tag{3.2}$$

Assuming the input, $v(t)$, to be a unit step, $u(t)$, whose Laplace transform is $V(s) = 1/s$, we solve for $I(s)$ and get

$$I(s) = \frac{1}{R}\left(\frac{1}{s} - \frac{1}{s + \dfrac{R}{L}}\right) + \frac{i(0)}{s + \dfrac{R}{L}} \tag{3.3}$$

from which

$$i(t) = \frac{1}{R}\left(1 - e^{-(R/L)t}\right) + i(0)e^{-(R/L)t} \tag{3.4}$$

The function $i(t)$ is a subset of all possible network variables that we are able to find from Eq. (3.4) if we know its initial condition, $i(0)$, and the input, $v(t)$. Thus, $i(t)$ is a state variable, and the differential equation (3.1) is a *state equation*.

4. We can now solve for all of the other network variables *algebraically* in terms of $i(t)$ and the applied voltage, $v(t)$. For example, the voltage across the resistor is

$$v_R(t) = Ri(t) \tag{3.5}$$

The voltage across the inductor is

$$v_L(t) = v(t) - Ri(t) \tag{3.6}[1]$$

The derivative of the current is

$$\frac{di}{dt} = \frac{1}{L}[v(t) - Ri(t)] \tag{3.7}[2]$$

Thus, knowing the state variable, $i(t)$, and the input, $v(t)$, we can find the value, or *state*, of any network variable at any time, $t \geq t_0$. Hence, the algebraic equations, Eqs. (3.5) through (3.7), are *output equations*.

5. Since the variables of interest are completely described by Eq. (3.1) and Eqs. (3.5) through (3.7), we say that the combined state equation (3.1) and the output equations (3.5 through 3.7) form a viable representation of the network, which we call a *state-space representation*.

Equation (3.1), which describes the dynamics of the network, is not unique. This equation could be written in terms of any other network variable. For example, substituting $i = v_R/R$ into Eq. (3.1) yields

$$\frac{L}{R}\frac{dv_R}{dt} + v_R = v(t) \tag{3.8}$$

which can be solved knowing that the initial condition $v_R(0) = Ri(0)$ and knowing $v(t)$. In this case, the state variable is $v_R(t)$. Similarly, all other network variables can now be written in terms of the state variable, $v_R(t)$, and the input, $v(t)$. Let us now extend our observations to a second-order system, such as that shown in Figure 3.2.

1. Since the network is of second order, two simultaneous, first-order differential equations are needed to solve for two state variables. We select $i(t)$ and $q(t)$, the charge on the capacitor, as the two state variables.

2. Writing the loop equation yields

$$L\frac{di}{dt} + Ri + \frac{1}{C}\int i\,dt = v(t) \tag{3.9}$$

Converting to charge, using $i(t) = dq/dt$, we get

$$L\frac{d^2q}{dt^2} + R\frac{dq}{dt} + \frac{1}{C}q = v(t) \tag{3.10}$$

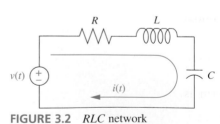

FIGURE 3.2   *RLC* network

---

[1] Since $v_L(t) = v(t) - v_R(t) = v(t) - Ri(t)$.

[2] Since $\frac{di}{dt} = \frac{1}{L}v_L(t) = \frac{1}{L}[v(t) - Ri(t)]$.

But an *n*th-order differential equation can be converted to *n* simultaneous first-order differential equations, with each equation of the form

$$\frac{dx_i}{dt} = a_{i1}x_1 + a_{i2}x_2 + \cdots + a_{in}x_n + b_i f(t) \qquad (3.11)$$

where each x_i is a state variable, and the a_{ij}'s and b_i are constants for linear, time-invariant systems. We say that the right-hand side of Eq. (3.11) is a *linear combination* of the state variables and the input, $f(t)$.

We can convert Eq. (3.10) into two simultaneous, first-order differential equations in terms of $i(t)$ and $q(t)$. The first equation can be $dq/dt = i$. The second equation can be formed by substituting $\int i \, dt = q$ into Eq. (3.9) and solving for di/dt. Summarizing the two resulting equations, we get

$$\frac{dq}{dt} = i \qquad (3.12a)$$

$$\frac{di}{dt} = -\frac{1}{LC}q - \frac{R}{L}i + \frac{1}{L}v(t) \qquad (3.12b)$$

3. These equations are the state equations and can be solved simultaneously for the state variables, $q(t)$ and $i(t)$, using the Laplace transform and the methods of Chapter 2, if we know the initial conditions for $q(t)$ and $i(t)$ and if we know $v(t)$, the input.

4. From these two state variables, we can solve for all other network variables. For example, the voltage across the inductor can be written in terms of the solved state variables and the input as

$$v_L(t) = -\frac{1}{C}q(t) - Ri(t) + v(t) \qquad (3.13)^3$$

Equation (3.13) is an *output equation;* we say that $v_L(t)$ is a *linear combination* of the state variables, $q(t)$ and $i(t)$, and the input, $v(t)$.

5. The combined state equations (3.12) and the output equation (3.13) form a viable representation of the network, which we call a *state-space representation*.

Another choice of two state variables can be made, for example, $v_R(t)$ and $v_C(t)$, the resistor and capacitor voltage, respectively. The resulting set of simultaneous, first-order differential equations follows:

$$\frac{dv_R}{dt} = -\frac{R}{L}v_R - \frac{R}{L}v_C + \frac{R}{L}v(t) \qquad (3.14a)^4$$

$$\frac{dv_C}{dt} = \frac{1}{RC}v_R \qquad (3.14b)$$

Again, these differential equations can be solved for the state variables if we know the initial conditions along with $v(t)$. Further, all other network variables can be found as a linear combination of these state variables.

---

[3] Since $v_L(t) = L \, (di/dt) = -(1/C)q - Ri + v(t)$, where di/dt can be found from Eq. (3.9), and $\int i \, dt = q$.

[4] Since $v_R(t) = i(t)R$, and $v_C(t) = (1/C) \int i \, dt$, differentiating $v_R(t)$ yields $dv_R/dt = R \, (di/dt) = (R/L)v_L = (R/L)[v(t) - v_R - v_C]$, and differentiating $v_C(t)$ yields $dv_C/dt = (1/C)i = (1/RC)v_R$.

Is there a restriction on the choice of state variables? Yes! Typically, the minimum number of state variables required to describe a system equals the order of the differential equation. Thus, a second-order system requires a minimum of two state variables to describe it. We can define more state variables than the minimal set; however, within this minimal set the state variables must be linearly independent. For example, if $v_R(t)$ is chosen as a state variable, then $i(t)$ cannot be chosen, because $v_R(t)$ can be written as a linear combination of $i(t)$, namely $v_R(t) = Ri(t)$. Under these circumstances we say that the state variables are *linearly dependent*. State variables must be *linearly independent;* that is, no state variable can be written as a linear combination of the other state variables, or else we would not have enough information to solve for all other system variables, and we could even have trouble writing the simultaneous equations themselves.

The state and output equations can be written in vector-matrix form if the system is linear. Thus, Eqs. (3.12), the state equations, can be written as

$$\dot{\mathbf{x}} = \mathbf{A}\mathbf{x} + \mathbf{B}u \qquad (3.15)$$

where

$$\dot{\mathbf{x}} = \begin{bmatrix} dq/dt \\ di/dt \end{bmatrix}; \quad \mathbf{A} = \begin{bmatrix} 0 & 1 \\ -1/LC & -R/L \end{bmatrix}$$

$$\mathbf{x} = \begin{bmatrix} q \\ i \end{bmatrix}; \quad \mathbf{B} = \begin{bmatrix} 0 \\ 1/L \end{bmatrix}; \ u = v(t)$$

Equation (3.13), the output equation, can be written as

$$y = \mathbf{C}\mathbf{x} + Du \qquad (3.16)$$

where

$$y = v_L(t); \quad \mathbf{C} = [-1/C \quad -R]; \quad \mathbf{x} = \begin{bmatrix} q \\ i \end{bmatrix}; \quad D = 1; \quad u = v(t)$$

We call the combination of Eqs. (3.15) and (3.16) a *state-space representation* of the network of Figure 3.2. A state-space representation, therefore, consists of (1) the simultaneous, first-order differential equations from which the state variables can be solved and (2) the algebraic output equation from which all other system variables can be found. A state-space representation is not unique, since a different choice of state variables leads to a different representation of the same system.

In this section we used two electrical networks to demonstrate some principles that are the foundation of the state-space representation. The representations developed in this section were for single-input, single-output systems, where y, D, and u in Eqs. (3.15) and (3.16) are scalar quantities. In general, systems have multiple inputs and multiple outputs. For these cases, y and u become vector quantities, and D becomes a matrix. In Section 3.3 we will generalize the representation for multiple-input, multiple-output systems and summarize the concept of the state-space representation.

3.3 THE GENERAL STATE-SPACE REPRESENTATION

Now that we have represented a physical network in state space and have a good idea of the terminology and the concept, let us summarize and generalize the representation for linear differential equations. First we formalize some of the definitions that we came across in the last section.

Linear combination. A linear combination of n variables, x_i, for $i = 1$ to n, is given by the following sum, S:

$$S = K_n x_n + K_{n-1} x_{n-1} + \cdots + K_1 x_1 \tag{3.17}$$

where each K_i is a constant.

Linear independence. A set of variables is said to be linearly independent if none of the variables can be written as a linear combination of the others. For example, given x_1, x_2, and x_3, if $x_2 = 5x_1 + 6x_3$, then the variables are not linearly independent, since one of them can be written as a linear combination of the other two. Now, what must be true so that one variable cannot be written as a linear combination of the other variables? Consider the example $K_2 x_2 = K_1 x_1 + K_3 x_3$. If no $x_i = 0$, then any x_i can be written as a linear combination of other variables, unless all $K_i = 0$. Formally, then, variables x_i, for $i = 1$ to n, are said to be linearly independent if their linear combination, S, equals zero *only* if every $K_i = 0$ and *no* $x_i = 0$ for all $t \geq 0$.

System variable. Any variable that responds to an input or initial conditions in a system.

State variables. The smallest set of linearly independent system variables such that the values of the members of the set at time t_0 along with known forcing functions completely determine the value of all system variables for all $t \geq t_0$.

State vector. A vector whose elements are the state variables.

State space. The n-dimensional space whose axes are the state variables. This is a new term and is illustrated in Figure 3.3, where the state variables are assumed to be a resistor voltage, v_R, and a capacitor voltage, v_C. These variables form the axes of the *state space*. A trajectory can be thought of as being mapped out by the state vector, $\mathbf{x}(t)$, for a range of t. Also shown is the state vector at the particular time $t = 4$.

State equations. A set of n simultaneous, first-order differential equations with n variables, where the n variables to be solved are the state variables.

Output equation. The algebraic equation that expresses the output variables of a system as linear combinations of the state variables and the inputs.

Now that the definitions have been formally stated, we define the state-space representation of a system. A system is represented in state space by the following equations:

$$\boxed{\dot{\mathbf{x}} = \mathbf{A}\mathbf{x} + \mathbf{B}\mathbf{u}} \tag{3.18}$$

$$\boxed{\mathbf{y} = \mathbf{C}\mathbf{x} + \mathbf{D}\mathbf{u}} \tag{3.19}$$

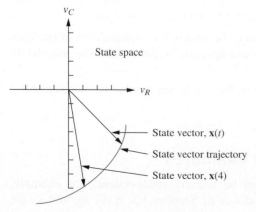

FIGURE 3.3 Graphic representation of state space and a state vector

for $t \geq t_0$ and initial conditions, $\mathbf{x}(t_0)$, where

$$\mathbf{x} = \text{state vector}$$
$$\dot{\mathbf{x}} = \text{derivative of the state vector with respect to time}$$
$$\mathbf{y} = \text{output vector}$$
$$\mathbf{u} = \text{input or control vector}$$
$$\mathbf{A} = \text{system matrix}$$
$$\mathbf{B} = \text{input matrix}$$
$$\mathbf{C} = \text{output matrix}$$
$$\mathbf{D} = \text{feedforward matrix}$$

Equation (3.18) is called the *state equation*, and the vector $\mathbf{x}$, the *state vector*, contains the state variables. Equation (3.18) can be solved for the state variables, which we demonstrate in Chapter 4. Equation (3.19) is called the *output equation*. This equation is used to calculate any other system variables. This representation of a system provides complete knowledge of all variables of the system at any $t \geq t_0$.

As an example, for a linear, time-invariant, second-order system with a single input $v(t)$, the state equations could take on the following form:

$$\frac{dx_1}{dt} = a_{11}x_1 + a_{12}x_2 + b_1 v(t) \tag{3.20a}$$

$$\frac{dx_2}{dt} = a_{21}x_1 + a_{22}x_2 + b_2 v(t) \tag{3.20b}$$

where x_1 and x_2 are the state variables. If there is a single output, the output equation could take on the following form:

$$y = c_1 x_1 + c_2 x_2 + d_1 v(t) \tag{3.21}$$

The choice of state variables for a given system is not unique. The requirement in choosing the state variables is that they be linearly independent and that a minimum number of them be chosen.

3.4 APPLYING THE STATE-SPACE REPRESENTATION

In this section we apply the state-space formulation to the representation of more complicated physical systems. The first step in representing a system is to select the state vector, which must be chosen according to the following considerations:

1. A minimum number of state variables must be selected as components of the state vector. This minimum number of state variables is sufficient to describe completely the state of the system.

2. The components of the state vector (that is, this minimum number of state variables) must be linearly independent.

Let us review and clarify these statements.

LINEARLY INDEPENDENT STATE VARIABLES

The components of the state vector must be linearly independent. For example, following the definition of linear independence in Section 3.3, if x_1, x_2, and x_3 are chosen as state variables, but $x_3 = 5x_1 + 4x_2$, then x_3 is not linearly independent of x_1 and x_2, since knowledge of the values of x_1 and x_2 will yield the value of x_3. Variables and their successive derivatives are linearly independent. For example, the voltage across an inductor, v_L, is linearly independent of the current through the inductor, i_L, since $v_L = L \, di_L/dt$. Thus, v_L cannot be evaluated as a linear combination of the current, i_L.

MINIMUM NUMBER OF STATE VARIABLES

How do we know the minimum number of state variables to select? Typically, the minimum number required equals the order of the differential equation describing the system. For example, if a third-order differential equation describes the system, then three simultaneous, first-order differential equations are required along with three state variables. From the perspective of the transfer function, the order of the differential equation is the order of the denominator of the transfer function after canceling common factors in the numerator and denominator.

In most cases another way to determine the number of state variables is to count the number of independent energy-storage elements in the system.[5] The number of these energy-storage elements equals the order of the differential equation and the number of state variables. In Figure 3.2 there are two energy-storage elements, the capacitor and the inductor. Hence, two state variables and two state equations are required for the system.

If too few state variables are selected, it may be impossible to write particular output equations, since some system variables cannot be written as a linear combination of the reduced number of state variables. In many cases it may be impossible even to complete the writing of the state equations, since the derivatives of the state variables cannot be expressed as linear combinations of the reduced number of state variables.

If you select the minimum number of state variables but they are not linearly independent, at best you may not be able to solve for all other system variables. At worst you may not be able to complete the writing of the state equations.

Often the state vector includes more than the minimum number of state variables required. Two possible cases exist. Often state variables are chosen to be physical variables of a system, such as position and velocity in a mechanical system. Cases arise where these variables, although linearly independent, are also *decoupled*. That is, some linearly independent variables are not required in order to solve for any of the other linearly independent variables or any other dependent system variable. Consider the case of a mass and viscous damper whose differential equation is $M \, dv/dt + Dv = f(t)$, where v is the velocity of the mass. Since this is a first-order equation, one state equation is all that is required to define this system in state space with velocity as the state variable. Also, since there is only one energy-storage element, mass, only one state variable is required to represent this system in state space. However, the mass also has an associated position, which is linearly independent of velocity. If we want to include position in the state vector along with velocity, then we add position as a state variable that is linearly independent of the other state variable, velocity. Figure 3.4 illustrates what is happening. The first block is the transfer function equivalent to $M \, dv(t)/dt + Dv(t) = f(t)$. The second block shows that we integrate the output velocity to yield output displacement (see Table 2.2, Item 10). Thus, if we

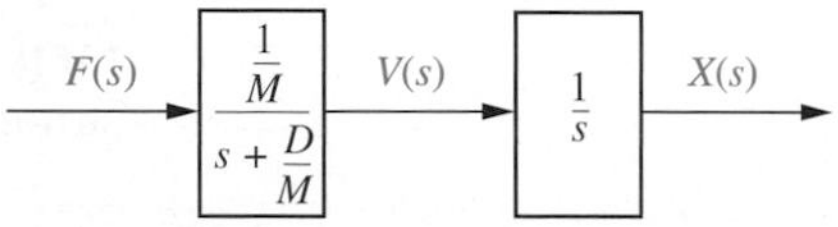

FIGURE 3.4 Block diagram of a mass and damper

---

[5]Sometimes it is not apparent in a schematic how many independent energy-storage elements there are. It is possible that more than the minimum number of energy-storage elements could be selected, leading to a state vector whose components number more than the minimum required and are not linearly independent. Selecting additional dependent energy-storage elements results in a system matrix of higher order and more complexity than required for the solution of the state equations.

want displacement as an output, the denominator, or characteristic equation, has increased in order to 2, the product of the two transfer functions. Many times, the writing of the state equations is simplified by including additional state variables.

Another case that increases the size of the state vector arises when the added variable is not linearly independent of the other members of the state vector. This usually occurs when a variable is selected as a state variable but its dependence on the other state variables is not immediately apparent. For example, energy-storage elements may be used to select the state variables, and the dependence of the variable associated with one energy-storage element on the variables of other energy-storage elements may not be recognized. Thus, the dimension of the system matrix is increased unnecessarily, and the solution for the state vector, which we cover in Chapter 4, is more difficult. Also, adding dependent state variables affects the designer's ability to use state-space methods for design.[6]

We saw in Section 3.2 that the state-space representation is not unique. The following example demonstrates one technique for selecting state variables and representing a system in state space. Our approach is to write the simple derivative equation for each energy-storage element and solve for each derivative term as a linear combination of any of the system variables and the input that are present in the equation. Next we select each differentiated variable as a state variable. Then we express all other system variables in the equations in terms of the state variables and the input. Finally, we write the output variables as linear combinations of the state variables and the input.

▮▮▮▮▮ EXAMPLE 3.1 ▮▮▮▮▮

Representing an electrical network

Problem: Given the electrical network of Figure 3.5, find a state-space representation if the output is the current through the resistor.

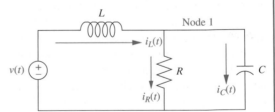

FIGURE 3.5 Electrical network for representation in state space

SOLUTION: The following steps will yield a viable representation of the network in state space.

Step 1   Label all of the branch currents in the network. These include i_L, i_R, and i_C, as shown in Figure 3.5.

Step 2   Select the state variables by writing the derivative equation for all energy-storage elements, that is, the inductor and the capacitor. Thus,

$$C\frac{dv_C}{dt} = i_C \tag{3.22}$$

$$L\frac{di_L}{dt} = v_L \tag{3.23}$$

---

[6]See Chapter 12 for state-space design techniques.

From Eqs. (3.22) and (3.23), choose the state variables as the quantities that are differentiated, namely v_C and i_L. Using Eq. (3.20) as a guide, we see that the state-space representation is complete if the right-hand sides of Eqs. (3.22) and (3.23) can be written as linear combinations of the state variables and the input.

Since i_C and v_L are not state variables, our next step is to express i_C and v_L as linear combinations of the state variables, v_C and i_L, and the input, $v(t)$.

Step 3 Apply network theory, such as Kirchhoff's voltage and current laws, to obtain i_C and v_L in terms of the state variables, v_C and i_L. At Node 1,

$$\begin{aligned} i_C &= -i_R + i_L \\ &= -\frac{1}{R} v_C + i_L \end{aligned} \tag{3.24}$$

which yields i_C in terms of the state variables, v_C and i_L.

Around the outer loop,

$$v_L = -v_C + v(t) \tag{3.25}$$

which yields v_L in terms of the state variable, v_C, and the source, $v(t)$.

Step 4 Substitute the results of Eqs. (3.24) and (3.25) into Eqs. (3.22) and (3.23) to obtain the following state equations:

$$C\frac{dv_C}{dt} = -\frac{1}{R} v_C + i_L \tag{3.26a}$$

$$L\frac{di_L}{dt} = -v_C + v(t) \tag{3.26b}$$

or

$$\frac{dv_C}{dt} = -\frac{1}{RC} v_C + \frac{1}{C} i_L \tag{3.27a}$$

$$\frac{di_L}{dt} = -\frac{1}{L} v_C + \frac{1}{L} v(t) \tag{3.27b}$$

Step 5 Find the output equation. Since the output is $i_R(t)$,

$$i_R = \frac{1}{R} v_C \tag{3.28}$$

The final result for the state-space representation is found by representing Eqs. (3.27) and (3.28) in vector-matrix form as follows:

$$\begin{bmatrix} \dot{v}_C \\ \dot{i}_L \end{bmatrix} = \begin{bmatrix} -1/(RC) & 1/C \\ -1/L & 0 \end{bmatrix} \begin{bmatrix} v_C \\ i_L \end{bmatrix} + \begin{bmatrix} 0 \\ 1/L \end{bmatrix} v(t) \tag{3.29a}$$

$$i_R = \begin{bmatrix} 1/R & 0 \end{bmatrix} \begin{bmatrix} v_C \\ i_L \end{bmatrix} \tag{3.29b}$$

where the dot indicates differentiation with respect to time.

In order to clarify the representation of physical systems in state space, we will look at two more examples. The first is an electrical network with a dependent source. Although we will follow the same procedure as in the previous problem, this problem will yield increased complexity in applying network analysis to find the state equations. For the second example, we find the state-space representation of a mechanical system.

EXAMPLE 3.2

Representing an electrical network with a dependent source

Problem: Find the state and output equations for the electrical network shown in Figure 3.6 if the output vector is $\mathbf{y} = \begin{bmatrix} v_{R_2} & i_{R_2} \end{bmatrix}^T$, where T means transpose.[7]

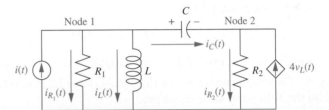

FIGURE 3.6 Electrical network for Example 3.2

SOLUTION: Immediately notice that this network has a voltage-dependent current source.

Step 1 Label all of the branch currents on the network, as shown in Figure 3.6.

Step 2 Select the state variables by listing the voltage-current relationships for all of the energy-storage elements:

$$L\frac{di_L}{dt} = v_L \tag{3.30a}$$

$$C\frac{dv_C}{dt} = i_C \tag{3.30b}$$

From Eqs. (3.30) select the state variables to be the differentiated variables. Thus, the state variables, x_1 and x_2, are

$$x_1 = i_L; \quad x_2 = v_C \tag{3.31}$$

Step 3 Remembering that the form of the state equation is

$$\dot{\mathbf{x}} = \mathbf{A}\mathbf{x} + \mathbf{B}\mathbf{u} \tag{3.32}$$

we see that the remaining task is to transform the right-hand side of Eqs. (3.30) into linear combinations of the state variables and input source current. Using Kirchhoff's voltage and current laws, we find v_L and i_C in terms of the state variables and the input current source.

---

[7]See Appendix F for a discussion of the transpose. Appendix F is located at www.wiley.com/college/nise.

Around the mesh containing L and C,

$$v_L = v_C + v_{R_2} = v_C + i_{R_2} R_2 \tag{3.33}$$

But at Node 2, $i_{R_2} = i_C + 4v_L$. Substituting this relationship for i_{R_2} into Eq. (3.33) yields

$$v_L = v_C + (i_C + 4v_L)R_2 \tag{3.34}$$

Solving for v_L, we get

$$v_L = \frac{1}{1 - 4R_2}(v_C + i_C R_2) \tag{3.35}$$

Notice that since v_C is a state variable, we only need to find i_C in terms of the state variables. We will then have obtained v_L in terms of the state variables.

Thus, at Node 1 we can write the sum of the currents as

$$\begin{aligned}
i_C &= i(t) - i_{R_1} - i_L \\
&= i(t) - \frac{v_{R_1}}{R_1} - i_L \\
&= i(t) - \frac{v_L}{R_1} - i_L
\end{aligned} \tag{3.36}$$

where $v_{R_1} = v_L$. Equations (3.35) and (3.36) are two equations relating v_L and i_C in terms of the state variables i_L and v_C. Rewriting Eqs. (3.35) and (3.36), we obtain two simultaneous equations yielding v_L and i_C as linear combinations of the state variables i_L and v_C:

$$(1 - 4R_2)v_L - R_2 i_C = v_C \tag{3.37a}$$

$$-\frac{1}{R_1}v_L - i_C = i_L - i(t) \tag{3.37b}$$

Solving Eqs. (3.37) simultaneously for v_L and i_C yields

$$v_L = \frac{1}{\Delta}[R_2 i_L - v_C - R_2 i(t)] \tag{3.38}$$

and

$$i_C = \frac{1}{\Delta}\left[(1 - 4R_2)i_L + \frac{1}{R_1}v_C - (1 - 4R_2)i(t)\right] \tag{3.39}$$

where

$$\Delta = -\left[(1 - 4R_2) + \frac{R_2}{R_1}\right] \tag{3.40}$$

Substituting Eqs. (3.38) and (3.39) into (3.30), simplifying, and writing the result in vector-matrix form renders the following state equation:

$$\begin{bmatrix} \dot{i}_L \\ \dot{v}_C \end{bmatrix} = \begin{bmatrix} R_2/(L\Delta) & -1/(L\Delta) \\ (1 - 4R_2)/(C\Delta) & 1/(R_1 C\Delta) \end{bmatrix} \begin{bmatrix} i_L \\ v_C \end{bmatrix} \\ + \begin{bmatrix} -R_2/(L\Delta) \\ -(1 - 4R_2)/(C\Delta) \end{bmatrix} i(t) \tag{3.41}$$

Step 4 Derive the output equation. Since the specified output variables are v_{R_2} and i_{R_2}, we note that around the mesh containing C, L, and R_2,

$$v_{R_2} = -v_C + v_L \tag{3.42a}$$

$$i_{R_2} = i_C + 4v_L \tag{3.42b}$$

Substituting Eqs. (3.38) and (3.39) into (3.42), v_{R_2} and i_{R_2} are obtained as linear combinations of the state variables, i_L and v_C. In vector-matrix form, the output equation is

$$\begin{bmatrix} v_{R_2} \\ i_{R_2} \end{bmatrix} = \begin{bmatrix} R_2/\Delta & -(1 + 1/\Delta) \\ 1/\Delta & (1 - 4R_1)/(\Delta R_1) \end{bmatrix} \begin{bmatrix} i_L \\ v_C \end{bmatrix} + \begin{bmatrix} -R_2/\Delta \\ -1/\Delta \end{bmatrix} i(t) \tag{3.43}$$

In the next example we find the state-space representation for a mechanical system. It is more convenient when working with mechanical systems to obtain the state equations directly from the equations of motion rather than from the energy-storage elements. For example, consider an energy-storage element such as a spring, where $F = Kx$. This relationship does not contain the derivative of a physical variable as in the case of electrical networks, where $i = C\,dv/dt$ for capacitors, and $v = L\,di/dt$ for inductors. Thus, in mechanical systems we change our selection of state variables to be the position and velocity of each point of linearly independent motion. In the example we will see that although there are three energy-storage elements, there will be four state variables; an additional linearly independent state variable is included for the convenience of writing the state equations. It is left to the student to show that this system yields a fourth-order transfer function if we relate the displacement of either mass to the applied force, and a third-order transfer function if we relate the velocity of either mass to the applied force.

EXAMPLE 3.3

Representing a translational mechanical system

Problem: Find the state equations for the translational mechanical system shown in Figure 3.7.

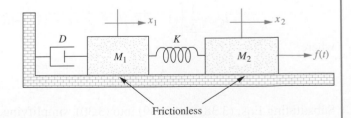

FIGURE 3.7 Translational mechanical system

Frictionless

SOLUTION: First write the differential equations for the network in Figure 3.7, using the methods of Chapter 2 to find the Laplace-transformed equations of motion. Next take the inverse Laplace transform of these equations, assuming zero initial conditions, and obtain

$$M_1 \frac{d^2 x_1}{dt^2} + D \frac{dx_1}{dt} + Kx_1 - Kx_2 = 0 \tag{3.44}$$

$$-Kx_1 + M_2\frac{d^2x_2}{dt^2} + Kx_2 = f(t) \qquad (3.45)$$

Now let $d^2x_1/dt^2 = dv_1/dt$, and $d^2x_2/dt^2 = dv_2/dt$, and then select x_1, v_1, x_2, and v_2 as state variables. Next form two of the state equations by solving Eq. (3.44) for dv_1/dt and Eq. (3.45) for dv_2/dt. Finally, add $dx_1/dt = v_1$ and $dx_2/dt = v_2$ to complete the set of state equations. Hence,

$$\frac{dx_1}{dt} = \qquad\qquad +v_1 \qquad\qquad (3.46a)$$

$$\frac{dv_1}{dt} = -\frac{K}{M_1}x_1 - \frac{D}{M_1}v_1 + \frac{K}{M_1}x_2 \qquad (3.46b)$$

$$\frac{dx_2}{dt} = \qquad\qquad\qquad +v_2 \qquad\qquad (3.46c)$$

$$\frac{dv_2}{dt} = +\frac{K}{M_2}x_1 \qquad\qquad -\frac{K}{M_2}x_2 \qquad +\frac{1}{M_2}f(t) \qquad (3.46d)$$

In vector-matrix form,

$$\begin{bmatrix} \dot{x}_1 \\ \dot{v}_1 \\ \dot{x}_2 \\ \dot{v}_2 \end{bmatrix} = \begin{bmatrix} 0 & 1 & 0 & 0 \\ -K/M_1 & -D/M_1 & K/M_1 & 0 \\ 0 & 0 & 0 & 1 \\ K/M_2 & 0 & -K/M_2 & 0 \end{bmatrix} \begin{bmatrix} x_1 \\ v_1 \\ x_2 \\ v_2 \end{bmatrix} + \begin{bmatrix} 0 \\ 0 \\ 0 \\ 1/M_2 \end{bmatrix} f(t) \qquad (3.47)$$

where the dot indicates differentiation with respect to time. What is the output equation if the output is $x(t)$?

SKILL-ASSESSMENT EXERCISE 3.1

Problem: Find the state-space representation of the electrical network shown in Figure 3.8. The output is $v_o(t)$.

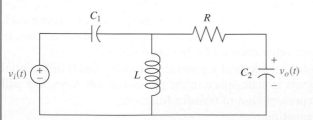

FIGURE 3.8 Electric circuit for Skill-Assessment Exercise 3.1

ANSWER:

$$\dot{\mathbf{x}} = \begin{bmatrix} 1/C_1 & 1/C_1 & -1/C_1 \\ -1/L & 0 & 0 \\ 1/C_2 & 0 & -1/C_2 \end{bmatrix} \mathbf{x} + \begin{bmatrix} 0 \\ 1 \\ 0 \end{bmatrix} v_i(t)$$

$$y = \begin{bmatrix} 0 & 0 & 1 \end{bmatrix}\mathbf{x}$$

The complete solution is at www.wiley.com/college/nise.

SKILL-ASSESSMENT EXERCISE 3.2

Problem: Represent the translational mechanical system shown in Figure 3.9 in state space, where $x_3(t)$ is the output.

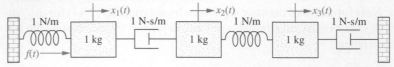

FIGURE 3.9   Translational mechanical system for Skill-Assessment Exercise 3.2

ANSWER:

$$\dot{\mathbf{z}} = \begin{bmatrix} 0 & 1 & 0 & 0 & 0 & 0 \\ -1 & -1 & 0 & 1 & 0 & 0 \\ 0 & 0 & 0 & 1 & 0 & 0 \\ 0 & 1 & -1 & -1 & 1 & 0 \\ 0 & 0 & 0 & 0 & 0 & 1 \\ 0 & 0 & 1 & 0 & -1 & -1 \end{bmatrix} \mathbf{z} + \begin{bmatrix} 0 \\ 1 \\ 0 \\ 0 \\ 0 \\ 0 \end{bmatrix} f(t)$$

$$y = \begin{bmatrix} 0 & 0 & 0 & 0 & 1 & 0 \end{bmatrix} \mathbf{z}$$

where

$$\mathbf{z} = \begin{bmatrix} x_1 & \dot{x}_1 & x_2 & \dot{x}_2 & x_3 & \dot{x}_3 \end{bmatrix}^T$$

The complete solution is at www.wiley.com/college/nise.

3.5 CONVERTING A TRANSFER FUNCTION TO STATE SPACE

In the last section we applied the state-space representation to electrical and mechanical systems. We learn how to convert a transfer function representation to a state-space representation in this section. One advantage of the state-space representation is that it can be used for the simulation of physical systems on the digital computer. Thus, if we want to simulate a system that is represented by a transfer function, we must first convert the transfer function representation to state space.

At first we select a set of state variables, called *phase variables,* where each subsequent state variable is defined to be the derivative of the previous state variable. In Chapter 5 we show how to make other choices for the state variables.

Let us begin by showing how to represent a general, nth-order, linear differential equation with constant coefficients in state space in the phase-variable form. We will then show how to apply this representation to transfer functions.

Consider the differential equation

$$\frac{d^n y}{dt^n} + a_{n-1}\frac{d^{n-1} y}{dt^{n-1}} + \cdots + a_1 \frac{dy}{dt} + a_0 y = b_0 u \tag{3.48}$$

A convenient way to choose state variables is to choose the output, $y(t)$, and its $(n-1)$ derivatives as the state variables. This choice is called the *phase-variable choice.* Choosing the state variables, x_i, we get

$$x_1 = y \tag{3.49a}$$

$$x_2 = \frac{dy}{dt} \tag{3.49b}$$

$$x_3 = \frac{d^2y}{dt^2} \tag{3.49c}$$

$$\vdots$$

$$x_n = \frac{d^{n-1}y}{dt^{n-1}} \tag{3.49d}$$

and differentiating both sides yields

$$\dot{x}_1 = \frac{dy}{dt} \tag{3.50a}$$

$$\dot{x}_2 = \frac{d^2y}{dt^2} \tag{3.50b}$$

$$\dot{x}_3 = \frac{d^3y}{dt^3} \tag{3.50c}$$

$$\vdots$$

$$\dot{x}_n = \frac{d^ny}{dt^n} \tag{3.50d}$$

where the dot above the x signifies differentiation with respect to time.

Substituting the definitions of Eqs. (3.49) into Eqs. (3.50), the state equations are evaluated as

$$\dot{x}_1 = x_2 \tag{3.51a}$$

$$\dot{x}_2 = x_3 \tag{3.51b}$$

$$\vdots$$

$$\dot{x}_{n-1} = x_n \tag{3.51c}$$

$$\dot{x}_n = -a_0x_1 - a_1x_2 \cdots -a_{n-1}x_n + b_0u \tag{3.51d}$$

where Eq. (3.51d) was obtained from Eq. (3.48) by solving for d^ny/dt^n and using Eqs. (3.49). In vector-matrix form, Eqs. (3.51) become

$$
\begin{bmatrix} \dot{x}_1 \\ \dot{x}_2 \\ \dot{x}_3 \\ \vdots \\ \dot{x}_{n-1} \\ \dot{x}_n \end{bmatrix} = \begin{bmatrix} 0 & 1 & 0 & 0 & 0 & 0 & \cdots & 0 \\ 0 & 0 & 1 & 0 & 0 & 0 & \cdots & 0 \\ 0 & 0 & 0 & 1 & 0 & 0 & \cdots & 0 \\ \vdots & & & & & & & \\ 0 & 0 & 0 & 0 & 0 & 0 & \cdots & 1 \\ -a_0 & -a_1 & -a_2 & -a_3 & -a_4 & -a_5 & \cdots & -a_{n-1} \end{bmatrix} \begin{bmatrix} x_1 \\ x_2 \\ x_3 \\ \vdots \\ x_{n-1} \\ x_n \end{bmatrix} + \begin{bmatrix} 0 \\ 0 \\ 0 \\ \vdots \\ 0 \\ b_0 \end{bmatrix} u
$$

$$\tag{3.52}$$

Equation (3.52) is the phase-variable form of the state equations. This form is easily recognized by the unique pattern of 1's and 0's and the negative of the coefficients of the differential equation written in reverse order in the last row of the system matrix.

Finally, since the solution to the differential equation is $y(t)$, or x_1, the output equation is

$$y = \begin{bmatrix} 1 & 0 & 0 & \cdots & 0 \end{bmatrix} \begin{bmatrix} x_1 \\ x_2 \\ x_3 \\ \vdots \\ x_{n-1} \\ x_n \end{bmatrix} \tag{3.53}$$

In summary, then, to convert a transfer function into state equations in phase-variable form, we first convert the transfer function to a differential equation by cross-multiplying and taking the inverse Laplace transform, assuming zero initial conditions. Then we represent the differential equation in state space in phase-variable form. An example illustrates the process.

EXAMPLE 3.4

Converting a transfer function with constant term in numerator

Problem: Find the state-space representation in phase-variable form for the transfer function shown in Figure 3.10(a).

SOLUTION:

Step 1 Find the associated differential equation. Since

$$\frac{C(s)}{R(s)} = \frac{24}{(s^3 + 9s^2 + 26s + 24)} \tag{3.54}$$

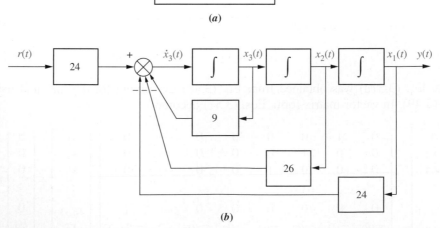

(a)

(b)

FIGURE 3.10   **a.** Transfer function; **b.** equivalent block diagram showing phase variables. Note: $y(t) = c(t)$

cross-multiplying yields

$$(s^3 + 9s^2 + 26s + 24)C(s) = 24R(s) \tag{3.55}$$

The corresponding differential equation is found by taking the inverse Laplace transform, assuming zero initial conditions:

$$\dddot{c} + 9\ddot{c} + 26\dot{c} + 24c = 24r \tag{3.56}$$

Step 2 Select the state variables.
Choosing the state variables as successive derivatives, we get

$$x_1 = c \tag{3.57a}$$

$$x_2 = \dot{c} \tag{3.57b}$$

$$x_3 = \ddot{c} \tag{3.57c}$$

Differentiating both sides and making use of Eqs. (3.57) to find $\dot{x}_1$ and $\dot{x}_2$, and Eq. (3.56) to find $\dddot{c} = \dot{x}_3$, we obtain the state equations. Since the output is $c = x_1$, the combined state and output equations are

$$\dot{x}_1 = \qquad\qquad x_2 \tag{3.58a}$$

$$\dot{x}_2 = \qquad\qquad\qquad x_3 \tag{3.58b}$$

$$\dot{x}_3 = -24x_1 - 26x_2 - 9x_3 + 24r \tag{3.58c}$$

$$y = c = x_1 \tag{3.58d}$$

In vector-matrix form,

$$\begin{bmatrix} \dot{x}_1 \\ \dot{x}_2 \\ \dot{x}_3 \end{bmatrix} = \begin{bmatrix} 0 & 1 & 0 \\ 0 & 0 & 1 \\ -24 & -26 & -9 \end{bmatrix} \begin{bmatrix} x_1 \\ x_2 \\ x_3 \end{bmatrix} + \begin{bmatrix} 0 \\ 0 \\ 24 \end{bmatrix} r \tag{3.59a}$$

$$y = \begin{bmatrix} 1 & 0 & 0 \end{bmatrix} \begin{bmatrix} x_1 \\ x_2 \\ x_3 \end{bmatrix} \tag{3.59b}$$

Notice that the third row of the system matrix has the same coefficients as the denominator of the transfer function but negative and in reverse order.

At this point we can create an equivalent block diagram of the system of Figure 3.10(a) to help visualize the state variables. We draw three integral blocks as shown in Figure 3.10(b) and label each output as one of the state variables, $x_i(t)$, as shown. Since the input to each integrator is $\dot{x}_i(t)$, use Eqs. (3.58a), (3.58b), and (3.58c) to determine the combination of input signals to each integrator. Form and label each input. Finally, use Eq. (3.58d) to form and label the output, $y(t) = c(t)$. The final result of Figure 3.10(b) is a system equivalent to Figure 3.10(a) that explicitly shows the state variables and gives a vivid picture of the state-space representation.

Students who are using MATLAB should now run ch3p1 through ch3p4 in Appendix B. You will learn how to represent the system matrix **A**, the input matrix **B**, and the output matrix **C** using MATLAB. You will learn how to convert a transfer function to the state-space representation in phase-variable form. Finally, Example 3.4 will be solved using MATLAB.

The transfer function of Example 3.4 has a constant term in the numerator. If a transfer function has a polynomial in s in the numerator that is of order less than the polynomial in the denominator, as shown in Figure 3.11(a), the numerator and denominator can be handled separately. First separate the transfer function into two cascaded transfer functions, as shown in Figure 3.11(b); the first is the denominator, and the second is just the numerator. The first transfer function with just the denominator is converted to the phase-variable representation in state space as demonstrated in the last example. Hence, phase variable x_1 is the output, and the rest of the phase variables are the internal variables of the first block, as shown in Figure 3.11(b). The second transfer function with just the numerator yields

$$Y(s) = C(s) = (b_2 s^2 + b_1 s + b_0)X_1(s) \tag{3.60}$$

where, after taking the inverse Laplace transform with zero initial conditions,

$$y(t) = b_2 \frac{d^2 x_1}{dt^2} + b_1 \frac{dx_1}{dt} + b_0 x_1 \tag{3.61}$$

But the derivative terms are the definitions of the phase variables obtained in the first block. Thus, writing the terms in reverse order to conform to an output equation,

$$y(t) = b_0 x_1 + b_1 x_2 + b_2 x_3 \tag{3.62}$$

Hence, the second block simply forms a specified linear combination of the state variables developed in the first block.

From another perspective, the denominator of the transfer function yields the state equations, while the numerator yields the output equation. The next example demonstrates the process.

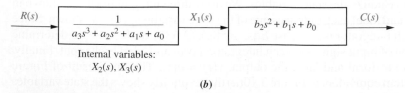

FIGURE 3.11 Decomposing a transfer function

████████ **EXAMPLE 3.5** ████████

Converting a transfer function with polynomial in numerator

Problem: Find the state-space representation of the transfer function shown in Figure 3.12(*a*).

SOLUTION: This problem differs from Example 3.4 since the numerator has a polynomial in *s* instead of just a constant term.

Step 1 Separate the system into two cascaded blocks, as shown in Figure 3.12(*b*). The first block contains the denominator, and the second block contains the numerator.

Step 2 Find the state equations for the block containing the denominator. We notice that the first block's numerator is 1/24 that of Example 3.4. Thus, the state equations are the same except that this system's input matrix is 1/24 that of Example 3.4. Hence, the state equation is

$$\begin{bmatrix} \dot{x}_1 \\ \dot{x}_2 \\ \dot{x}_3 \end{bmatrix} = \begin{bmatrix} 0 & 1 & 0 \\ 0 & 0 & 1 \\ -24 & -26 & -9 \end{bmatrix} \begin{bmatrix} x_1 \\ x_2 \\ x_3 \end{bmatrix} + \begin{bmatrix} 0 \\ 0 \\ 1 \end{bmatrix} r \qquad (3.63)$$

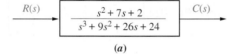

(*a*)

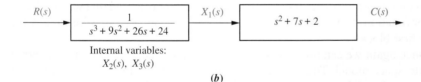

Internal variables:
$X_2(s),\ X_3(s)$

(*b*)

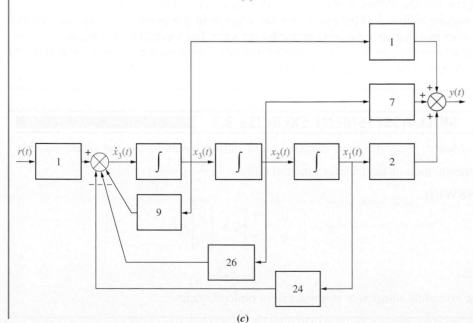

(*c*)

FIGURE 3.12
a. Transfer function;
b. decomposed transfer function;
c. equivalent block diagram.
Note: $y(t) = c(t)$

Step 3 Introduce the effect of the block with the numerator. The second block of Figure 3.12(b), where $b_2 = 1$, $b_1 = 7$, and $b_0 = 2$, states that

$$C(s) = (b_2 s^2 + b_1 s + b_0)X_1(s) = (s^2 + 7s + 2)X_1(s) \qquad (3.64)$$

Taking the inverse Laplace transform with zero initial conditions, we get

$$c = \ddot{x}_1 + 7\dot{x}_1 + 2x_1 \qquad (3.65)$$

But

$$\begin{aligned} x_1 &= x_1 \\ \dot{x}_1 &= x_2 \\ \ddot{x}_1 &= x_3 \end{aligned}$$

Hence,

$$y = c(t) = b_2 x_3 + b_1 x_2 + b_0 x_1 = x_3 + 7x_2 + 2x_1 \qquad (3.66)$$

Thus, the last box of Figure 3.11(b) "collects" the states and generates the output equation. From Eq. (3.66),

$$y = \begin{bmatrix} b_0 & b_1 & b_2 \end{bmatrix} \begin{bmatrix} x_1 \\ x_2 \\ x_3 \end{bmatrix} = \begin{bmatrix} 2 & 7 & 1 \end{bmatrix} \begin{bmatrix} x_1 \\ x_2 \\ x_3 \end{bmatrix} \qquad (3.67)$$

Although the second block of Figure 3.12(b) shows differentiation, this block was implemented without differentiation because of the partitioning that was applied to the transfer function. The last block simply collected derivatives that were already formed by the first block.

Once again we can produce an equivalent block diagram that vividly represents our state-space model. The first block of Figure 3.12(b) is the same as Figure 3.10(a) except for the different constant in the numerator. Thus, in Figure 3.12(c) we reproduce Figure 3.10(b) except for the change in the numerator constant, which appears as a change in the input multiplying factor. The second block of Figure 3.12(b) is represented using Eq. (3.66), which forms the output from a linear combination of the state variables, as shown in Figure 3.12(c).

TryIt 3.1

Use the following MATLAB statements to form an LTI state-space representation from the transfer function shown in Figure 3.12(a). The **A** matrix and **B** vector are shown in Eq. (3.63). The **C** vector is shown in Eq. (3.67).

```
num = [1 7 2];
den = [1 9 26 24];
[A,B,C,D] = tf2ss...
  (num,den);
P = [0 0 1; 0 1 0; 1 0 0];
A = inv(P)*A*P
B = inv(P)*B
C = C*P
```

SKILL-ASSESSMENT EXERCISE 3.3

WileyPLUS

Control Solutions

Problem: Find the state equations and output equation for the phase-variable representation of the transfer function $G(s) = \dfrac{2s + 1}{s^2 + 7s + 9}$.

ANSWER:

$$\dot{\mathbf{x}} = \begin{bmatrix} 0 & 1 \\ -9 & -7 \end{bmatrix} \mathbf{x} + \begin{bmatrix} 0 \\ 1 \end{bmatrix} r(t)$$

$$y = \begin{bmatrix} 1 & 2 \end{bmatrix} \mathbf{x}$$

The complete solution is at www.wiley.com/college.nise.

3.6 CONVERTING FROM STATE SPACE TO A TRANSFER FUNCTION

In Chapters 2 and 3, we have explored two methods of representing systems: the transfer function representation and the state-space representation. In the last section we united the two representations by converting transfer functions into state-space representations. Now we move in the opposite direction and convert the state-space representation into a transfer function.

Given the state and output equations

$$\dot{\mathbf{x}} = \mathbf{Ax} + \mathbf{Bu} \tag{3.68a}$$

$$\mathbf{y} = \mathbf{Cx} + \mathbf{Du} \tag{3.68b}$$

take the Laplace transform assuming zero initial conditions:[8]

$$s\mathbf{X}(s) = \mathbf{AX}(s) + \mathbf{BU}(s) \tag{3.69a}$$

$$\mathbf{Y(s)} = \mathbf{CX}(s) + \mathbf{DU(s)} \tag{3.69b}$$

Solving for $\mathbf{X}(s)$ in Eq. (3.69a),

$$(s\mathbf{I} - \mathbf{A})\mathbf{X}(s) = \mathbf{BU}(s) \tag{3.70}$$

or

$$\mathbf{X}(s) = (s\mathbf{I} - \mathbf{A})^{-1}\mathbf{BU}(s) \tag{3.71}$$

where $\mathbf{I}$ is the identity matrix.

Substituting Eq. (3.71) into Eq. (3.69*b*) yields

$$\mathbf{Y}(s) = \mathbf{C}(s\mathbf{I} - \mathbf{A})^{-1}\mathbf{BU}(s) + \mathbf{DU}(s) = [\mathbf{C}(s\mathbf{I} - \mathbf{A})^{-1}\mathbf{B} + \mathbf{D}]\mathbf{U}(s) \tag{3.72}$$

We call the matrix $[\mathbf{C}(s\mathbf{I} - \mathbf{A})^{-1}\mathbf{B} + \mathbf{D}]$ the transfer function matrix, since it relates the output vector, $\mathbf{Y}(s)$, to the input vector, $\mathbf{U}(s)$. However, if $\mathbf{U}(s) = U(s)$ and $\mathbf{Y}(s) = Y(s)$ are scalars, we can find the transfer function,

$$\boxed{T(s) = \frac{Y(s)}{U(s)} = \mathbf{C}(s\mathbf{I} - \mathbf{A})^{-1}\mathbf{B} + \mathbf{D}} \tag{3.73}$$

Let us look at an example.

---

[8] The Laplace transform of a vector is found by taking the Laplace transform of each component. Since $\dot{\mathbf{x}}$ consists of the derivatives of the state variables, the Laplace transform of $\dot{\mathbf{x}}$ with zero initial conditions yields each component with the form $sX_i(s)$, where $X_i(s)$ is the Laplace transform of the state variable. Factoring out the complex variable, s, in each component yields the Laplace transform of $\dot{\mathbf{x}}$ as $s\mathbf{X}(s)$, where $\mathbf{X}(s)$ is a column vector with components $X_i(s)$.

▮ EXAMPLE 3.6 ▮

State-space representation to transfer function

Problem: Given the system defined by Eqs. (3.74), find the transfer function, $T(s) = Y(s)/U(s)$, where $U(s)$ is the input and $Y(s)$ is the output.

$$\dot{\mathbf{x}} = \begin{bmatrix} 0 & 1 & 0 \\ 0 & 0 & 1 \\ -1 & -2 & -3 \end{bmatrix} \mathbf{x} + \begin{bmatrix} 10 \\ 0 \\ 0 \end{bmatrix} u \qquad (3.74a)$$

$$y - \begin{bmatrix} 1 & 0 & 0 \end{bmatrix} \mathbf{x} \qquad (3.74b)$$

SOLUTION: The solution revolves around finding the term $(s\mathbf{I} - \mathbf{A})^{-1}$ in Eq. (3.73).[9] All other terms are already defined. Hence, first find $(s\mathbf{I} - \mathbf{A})$:

$$(s\mathbf{I} - \mathbf{A}) = \begin{bmatrix} s & 0 & 0 \\ 0 & s & 0 \\ 0 & 0 & s \end{bmatrix} - \begin{bmatrix} 0 & 1 & 0 \\ 0 & 0 & 1 \\ -1 & -2 & -3 \end{bmatrix} = \begin{bmatrix} s & -1 & 0 \\ 0 & s & -1 \\ 1 & 2 & s+3 \end{bmatrix} \qquad (3.75)$$

Now form $(s\mathbf{I} - \mathbf{A})^{-1}$:

$$(s\mathbf{I} - \mathbf{A})^{-1} = \frac{\text{adj}(s\mathbf{I} - \mathbf{A})}{\det(s\mathbf{I} - \mathbf{A})} = \frac{\begin{bmatrix} (s^2 + 3s + 2) & s+3 & 1 \\ -1 & s(s+3) & s \\ -s & -(2s+1) & s^2 \end{bmatrix}}{s^3 + 3s^2 + 2s + 1} \qquad (3.76)$$

Substituting $(s\mathbf{I} - \mathbf{A})^{-1}$, **B**, **C**, and **D** into Eq. (3.73), where

$$\mathbf{B} = \begin{bmatrix} 10 \\ 0 \\ 0 \end{bmatrix}$$

$$\mathbf{C} = \begin{bmatrix} 1 & 0 & 0 \end{bmatrix}$$

$$\mathbf{D} = 0$$

we obtain the final result for the transfer function:

$$T(s) = \frac{10(s^2 + 3s + 2)}{s^3 + 3s^2 + 2s + 1} \qquad (3.77)$$

Students who are using MATLAB should now run ch3p5 in Appendix B. You will learn how to convert a state-space representation to a transfer function using MATLAB. You can practice by writing a MATLAB program to solve Example 3.6.

Students who are performing the MATLAB exercises and want to explore the added capability of MATLAB's Symbolic Math Toolbox should now run ch3sp1 in Appendix E located at www.wiley.com/college/nise. You will learn how to use the Symbolic Math Toolbox to write matrices and vectors. You will see that the Symbolic Math Toolbox yields an alternative way to use MATLAB to solve Example 3.6.

---

[9] See Appendix F. It is located at www.wiley.com/college/nise and discusses the evaluation of the matrix inverse.

SKILL-ASSESSMENT EXERCISE 3.4

Problem: Convert the state and output equations shown in Eqs. (3.78) to a transfer function.

$$\dot{\mathbf{x}} = \begin{bmatrix} -4 & -1.5 \\ 4 & 0 \end{bmatrix}\mathbf{x} + \begin{bmatrix} 2 \\ 0 \end{bmatrix}u(t) \tag{3.78a}$$

$$y = \begin{bmatrix} 1.5 & 0.625 \end{bmatrix}\mathbf{x} \tag{3.78b}$$

ANSWER:

$$G(s) = \frac{3s + 5}{s^2 + 4s + 6}$$

The complete solution is located at www.wiley.com/college/nise.

TryIt 3.2

Use the following MATLAB and the Control System Toolbox statements to obtain the transfer function shown in Skill-Assessment Exercise 3.4 from the state-space representation of Eqs. (3.78).

```
A = [-4 - 1.5; 4 0];
B = [2 0]';
C = [1.5 0.625];
D = 0;
T = ss(A,B,C,D);
T = tf(T)
```

In Example 3.6 the state equations in phase-variable form were converted to transfer functions. In Chapter 5 we will see that other forms besides the phase-variable form can be used to represent a system in state space. The method of finding the transfer function representation for these other forms is the same as that presented in this section.

3.7 LINEARIZATION

A prime advantage of the state-space representation over the transfer function representation is the ability to represent systems with nonlinearities, such as the one shown in Figure 3.13. The ability to represent nonlinear systems does not imply the ability to solve their state equations for the state variables and the output. Techniques do exist for the solution of some nonlinear state equations, but this study is beyond the scope of this course. However, in Appendix G located at www.wiley.com/college/nise, you can see how to use the digital computer to solve state equations. This method also can be used for nonlinear state equations.

FIGURE 3.13 Walking robots, such as *Hannibal* shown here, can be used to explore hostile environments and rough terrain, such as that found on other planets or inside volcanoes.

If we are interested in small perturbations about an equilibrium point, as we were when we studied linearization in Chapter 2, we can also linearize the state equations about the equilibrium point. The key to linearization about an equilibrium point is, once again, the Taylor series. In the following example we write the state equations for a simple pendulum, showing that we can represent a nonlinear system in state space; then we linearize the pendulum about its equilibrium point, the vertical position with zero velocity.

EXAMPLE 3.7

Representing a nonlinear system

Problem: First represent the simple pendulum shown in Figure 3.14(*a*) (which could be a simple model for the leg of the robot shown in Figure 3.13) in state space: Mg is the weight, T is an applied torque in the θ direction, and L is the length of the pendulum. Assume the mass is evenly distributed, with the center of mass at $L/2$. Then linearize the state equations about the pendulum's equilibrium point—the vertical position with zero angular velocity.

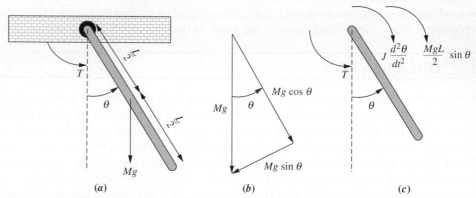

FIGURE 3.14   a. Simple pendulum; **b.** force components of Mg; **c.** free-body diagram

SOLUTION: First draw a free-body diagram as shown in Figure 3.14(*c*). Summing the torques, we get

$$J\frac{d^2\theta}{dt^2} + \frac{MgL}{2}\sin\theta = T \tag{3.79}$$

where J is the moment of inertia of the pendulum around the point of rotation. Select the state variables x_1 and x_2 as phase variables. Letting $x_1 = \theta$ and $x_2 = d\theta/dt$, we write the state equations as

$$\dot{x}_1 = x_2 \tag{3.80a}$$

$$\dot{x}_2 = -\frac{MgL}{2J}\sin x_1 + \frac{T}{J} \tag{3.80b}$$

where $\dot{x}_2 = d^2\theta/dt^2$ is evaluated from Eq. (3.79).

Thus, we have represented a nonlinear system in state space. It is interesting to note that the nonlinear Eqs. (3.80) represent a valid and complete model of the pendulum in state space even under nonzero initial conditions and even if parameters are time varying. However, if we want to apply classical techniques and convert these state equations to a transfer function, we must linearize them.

Let us proceed now to linearize the equation about the equilibrium point, $x_1 = 0$, $x_2 = 0$, that is, $\theta = 0$ and $d\theta/dt = 0$. Let x_1 and x_2 be perturbed about the equilibrium point, or

$$x_1 = 0 + \delta x_1 \tag{3.81a}$$

$$x_2 = 0 + \delta x_2 \tag{3.81b}$$

Using Eq. (2.182), we obtain

$$\sin x_1 - \sin 0 = \left.\frac{d(\sin x_1)}{dx_1}\right|_{x_1 = 0} \delta x_1 = \delta x_1 \tag{3.82}$$

from which

$$\sin x_1 = \delta x_1 \tag{3.83}$$

Substituting Eqs. (3.81) and (3.83) into (3.80) yields the following state equations:

$$\dot{\delta x_1} = \delta x_2 \tag{3.84a}$$

$$\dot{\delta x_2} = -\frac{MgL}{2J}\delta x_1 + \frac{T}{J} \tag{3.84b}$$

which are linear and a good approximation to Eqs. (3.80) for small excursions away from the equilibrium point. What is the output equation?

SKILL-ASSESSMENT EXERCISE 3.5

Problem: Represent the translational mechanical system shown in Figure 3.15 in state space about the equilibrium displacement. The spring is nonlinear, where the relationship between the spring force, $f_s(t)$, and the spring displacement, $x_s(t)$, is $f_s(t) = 2x_s^2(t)$. The applied force is $f(t) = 10 + \delta f(t)$, where $\delta f(t)$ is a small force about the 10 N constant value.

Assume the output to be the displacement of the mass, $x(t)$.

ANSWER:

$$\mathbf{x} = \begin{bmatrix} 0 & 1 \\ -4\sqrt{5} & 0 \end{bmatrix}\mathbf{x} + \begin{bmatrix} 0 \\ 1 \end{bmatrix}\delta f(t)$$

$$y = \begin{bmatrix} 1 & 0 \end{bmatrix}\mathbf{x}$$

The complete solution is located at www.wiley.com/college/nise.

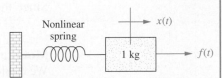

FIGURE 3.15 Nonlinear translational mechanical system for Skill-Assessment Exercise 3.5

Antenna Control: State-Space Representation

We have covered the state-space representation of individual physical subsystems in this chapter. In Chapter 5 we will assemble individual subsystems into feedback control systems and represent the entire feedback system in state space. Chapter 5 also shows how the state-space representation, via signal-flow diagrams, can be used to interconnect these subsystems and permit the state-space representation of the whole closed-loop system. In the following case study, we look at the antenna azimuth position control system and demonstrate the concepts of this chapter by representing each subsystem in state space.

Problem: Find the state-space representation in phase-variable form for each dynamic subsystem in the antenna azimuth position control system shown on the front endpapers, *Configuration 1*. By *dynamic,* we mean that the system does not reach the steady state instantaneously. For example, a system described by a differential equation of first order or higher is a dynamic system. A pure gain, on the other hand, is an example of a nondynamic system, since the steady state is reached instantaneously.

SOLUTION: In the case study problem of Chapter 2, each subsystem of the antenna azimuth position control system was identified. We found that the power amplifier and the motor and load were dynamic systems. The preamplifier and the potentiometers are pure gains and so respond instantaneously. Hence, we will find the state-space representations only of the power amplifier and of the motor and load.

Power amplifier: The transfer function of the power amplifier is given on the front endpapers as $G(s) = 100/(s + 100)$. We will convert this transfer function to its state-space representation. Letting $v_p(t)$ represent the power amplifier input and $e_a(t)$ represent the power amplifier output,

$$G(s) = \frac{E_a(s)}{V_p(s)} = \frac{100}{(s + 100)} \tag{3.85}$$

Cross-multiplying, $(s + 100)E_a(s) = 100V_p(s)$, from which the differential equation can be written as

$$\frac{de_a}{dt} + 100e_a = 100v_p(t) \tag{3.86}$$

Rearranging Eq. (3.86) leads to the state equation with e_a as the state variable:

$$\frac{de_a}{dt} = -100e_a + 100v_p(t) \tag{3.87}$$

Since the output of the power amplifier is $e_a(t)$, the output equation is

$$y = e_a \tag{3.88}$$

Motor and load: We now find the state-space representation for the motor and load. We could of course use the motor and load block shown in the block diagram on the front endpapers to obtain the result. However, it is more informative to derive the state-space representation directly from the physics of the motor without first deriving the transfer function. The elements of the derivation were covered in Section 2.8 but are repeated here for continuity. Starting with Kirchhoff's voltage equation around the armature circuit, we find

$$e_a(t) = i_a(t)R_a + K_b \frac{d\theta_m}{dt} \tag{3.89}$$

where $e_a(t)$ is the armature input voltage, $i_a(t)$ is the armature current, R_a is the armature resistance, K_b is the armature constant, and θ_m is the angular displacement of the armature.

The torque, $T_m(t)$, delivered by the motor is related separately to the armature current and the load seen by the armature. From Section 2.8,

$$T_m(t) = K_t i_a(t) = J_m \frac{d^2\theta_m}{dt^2} + D_m \frac{d\theta_m}{dt} \tag{3.90}$$

where J_m is the equivalent inertia as seen by the armature, and D_m is the equivalent viscous damping as seen by the armature.

Solving Eq. (3.90) for $i_a(t)$ and substituting the result into Eq. (3.89) yields

$$e_a(t) = \left(\frac{R_a J_m}{K_t}\right) \frac{d^2\theta_m}{dt^2} + \left(\frac{D_m R_a}{K_t} + K_b\right) \frac{d\theta_m}{dt} \tag{3.91}$$

Defining the state variables x_1 and x_2 as

$$x_1 = \theta_m \tag{3.92a}$$

$$x_2 = \frac{d\theta_m}{dt} \tag{3.92b}$$

and substituting into Eq. (3.91), we get

$$e_a(t) = \left(\frac{R_a J_m}{K_t}\right) \frac{dx_2}{dt} + \left(\frac{D_m R_a}{K_t} + K_b\right) x_2 \tag{3.93}$$

Solving for dx_2/dt yields

$$\frac{dx_2}{dt} = -\frac{1}{J_m}\left(D_m + \frac{K_t K_b}{R_a}\right) x_2 + \left(\frac{K_t}{R_a J_m}\right) e_a(t) \tag{3.94}$$

Using Eqs. (3.92) and (3.94), the state equations are written as

$$\frac{dx_1}{dt} = x_2 \tag{3.95a}$$

$$\frac{dx_2}{dt} = -\frac{1}{J_m}\left(D_m + \frac{K_t K_b}{R_a}\right) x_2 + \left(\frac{K_t}{R_a J_m}\right) e_a(t) \tag{3.95b}$$

The output, $\theta_o(t)$, is 1/10 the displacement of the armature, which is x_1. Hence, the output equation is

$$y = 0.1x_1 \tag{3.96}$$

In vector-matrix form,

$$\dot{\mathbf{x}} = \begin{bmatrix} 0 & 1 \\ 0 & -\dfrac{1}{J_m}\left(D_m + \dfrac{K_t K_b}{R_a}\right) \end{bmatrix}\mathbf{x} + \begin{bmatrix} 0 \\ \dfrac{K_t}{R_a J_m} \end{bmatrix} e_a(t) \qquad (3.97a)$$

$$y = \begin{bmatrix} 0.1 & 0 \end{bmatrix}\mathbf{x} \qquad (3.97b)$$

But from the case study problem in Chapter 2, $J_m = 0.03$ and $D_m = 0.02$. Also, $K_t/R_a = 0.0625$ and $K_b = 0.5$. Substituting the values into Eqs. (3.97), we obtain the final state-space representation:

$$\dot{\mathbf{x}} = \begin{bmatrix} 0 & 1 \\ 0 & -1.71 \end{bmatrix}\mathbf{x} + \begin{bmatrix} 0 \\ 2.083 \end{bmatrix} e_a(t) \qquad (3.98a)$$

$$y = \begin{bmatrix} 0.1 & 0 \end{bmatrix}\mathbf{x} \qquad (3.98b)$$

Challenge: You are now given a problem to test your knowledge of this chapter's objectives. Referring to the antenna azimuth position control system shown on the front endpapers, find the state-space representation of each dynamic subsystem. Use Configuration 2.

Pharmaceutical Drug Absorption

An advantage of state-space representation over the transfer function representation is the ability to focus on component parts of a system and write n simultaneous, first-order differential equations rather than attempt to represent the system as a single, nth-order differential equation, as we have done with the transfer function. Also, multiple-input, multiple-output systems can be conveniently represented in state space. This case study demonstrates both of these concepts.

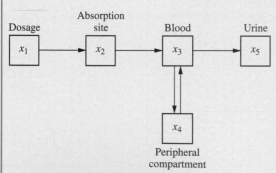

FIGURE 3.16   Pharmaceutical drug-level concentrations in a human

Problem: In the pharmaceutical industry we want to describe the distribution of a drug in the body. A simple model divides the process into compartments: the dosage, the absorption site, the blood, the peripheral compartment, and the urine. The rate of change of the amount of a drug in a compartment is equal to the input flow rate diminished by the output flow rate. Figure 3.16 summarizes the system. Here each x_i is the amount of drug in that particular compartment (*Lordi, 1972*). Represent the system in state space, where the outputs are the amounts of drug in each compartment.

SOLUTION: The flow rate of the drug into any given compartment is proportional to the concentration of the drug in the previous compartment, and the flow rate out of a given compartment is proportional to the concentration of the drug in its own compartment. We now write the flow rate for each compartment. The dosage is released to the absorption site at a rate proportional to the dosage concentration, or

$$\frac{dx_1}{dt} = -K_1 x_1 \qquad (3.99)$$

The flow into the absorption site is proportional to the concentration of the drug at the dosage site. The flow from the absorption site into the blood is proportional to the concentration of the drug at the absorption site. Hence,

$$\frac{dx_2}{dt} = K_1 x_1 - K_2 x_2 \qquad (3.100)$$

Similarly, the net flow rate into the blood and peripheral compartment is

$$\frac{dx_3}{dt} = K_2 x_2 - K_3 x_3 + K_4 x_4 - K_5 x_3 \qquad (3.101)$$

$$\frac{dx_4}{dt} = \qquad K_5 x_3 - K_4 x_4 \qquad (3.102)$$

where $(K_4 x_4 - K_5 x_3)$ is the net flow rate into the blood from the peripheral compartment. Finally, the amount of the drug in the urine is increased as the blood releases the drug to the urine at a rate proportional to the concentration of the drug in the blood. Thus,

$$\frac{dx_5}{dt} = K_3 x_3 \qquad (3.103)$$

Equations (3.99) through (3.103) are the state equations. The output equation is a vector that contains each of the amounts, x_i. Thus, in vector-matrix form,

$$\dot{\mathbf{x}} = \begin{bmatrix} -K_1 & 0 & 0 & 0 & 0 \\ K_1 & -K_2 & 0 & 0 & 0 \\ 0 & K_2 & -(K_3 + K_5) & K_4 & 0 \\ 0 & 0 & K_5 & -K_4 & 0 \\ 0 & 0 & K_3 & 0 & 0 \end{bmatrix} \mathbf{x} \qquad (3.104a)$$

$$\mathbf{y} = \begin{bmatrix} 1 & 0 & 0 & 0 & 0 \\ 0 & 1 & 0 & 0 & 0 \\ 0 & 0 & 1 & 0 & 0 \\ 0 & 0 & 0 & 1 & 0 \\ 0 & 0 & 0 & 0 & 1 \end{bmatrix} \mathbf{x} \qquad (3.104b)$$

You may wonder how there can be a solution to these equations if there is no input. In Chapter 4, when we study how to solve the state equations, we will see that initial conditions will yield solutions without forcing functions. For this problem an initial condition on the amount of dosage, x_1, will generate drug quantities in all other compartments.

Challenge: We now give you a problem to test your knowledge of this chapter's objectives. The problem concerns the storage of water in aquifers. The principles are similar to those used to model pharmaceutical drug absorption.

Underground water supplies, called aquifers, are used in many areas for agricultural, industrial, and residential purposes. An aquifer system consists of a number of interconnected natural storage tanks. Natural water flows through the sand and sandstone of the aquifer system, changing the water levels in the tanks on its way to the sea. A water conservation policy can be established whereby water is pumped between tanks to prevent its loss to the sea.

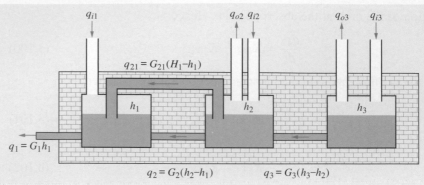

FIGURE 3.17 Aquifer system model

A model for the aquifer system is shown in Figure 3.17. In this model the aquifer is represented by three tanks, with water level h_i called the *head*. Each q_n is the natural water flow to the sea and is proportional to the difference in head between two adjoining tanks, or $q_n = G_n(h_n - h_{n-1})$, where G_n is a constant of proportionality and the units of q_n are m^3/yr.

The engineered flow consists of three components, also measured in m^3/yr: (1) flow from the tanks for irrigation, industry, and homes, q_{on}; (2) replenishing of the tanks from wells, q_{in}; and (3) flow, q_{21}, created by the water conservation policy to prevent loss to the sea. In this model, water for irrigation and industry will be taken only from Tank 2 and Tank 3. Water conservation will take place only between Tank 1 and Tank 2, as follows. Let H_1 be a reference head for Tank 1. If the water level in Tank 1 falls below H_1, water will be pumped from Tank 2 to Tank 1 to replenish the head. If h_1 is higher than H_1, water will be pumped back to Tank 2 to prevent loss to the sea. Calling this *flow for conservation* q_{21}, we can say this flow is proportional to the difference between the head of Tank 1, h_1, and the reference head, H_1, or $q_{21} = G_{21}(H_1 - h_1)$.

The net flow into a tank is proportional to the rate of change of head in each tank. Thus,

$$C_n dh_n/dt = q_{in} - q_{on} + q_{n+1} - q_n + q_{(n+1)n} - q_{n(n-1)}$$

(Kandel, 1973).

Represent the aquifer system in state space, where the state variables and the outputs are the heads of each tank.

SUMMARY

This chapter has dealt with the state-space representation of physical systems, which took the form of a state equation,

$$\dot{\mathbf{x}} = \mathbf{A}\mathbf{x} + \mathbf{B}\mathbf{u} \tag{3.105}$$

and an output equation,

$$\mathbf{y} = \mathbf{C}\mathbf{x} + \mathbf{D}\mathbf{u} \tag{3.106}$$

for $t \geq t_0$, and initial conditions $\mathbf{x}(t_0)$. Vector $\mathbf{x}$ is called the *state vector* and contains variables, called *state variables*. The state variables can be combined algebraically with the input to form the output equation, Eq. (3.106), from which any other system variables can be found. State variables, which can represent physical quantities such as current or voltage, are chosen to be linearly independent. The choice of state variables is not unique and affects how the matrices **A, B, C,** and **D** look. We will solve the state and output equations for **x** and **y** in Chapter 4.

In this chapter transfer functions were represented in state space. The form selected was the phase-variable form, which consists of state variables that are successive derivatives of each other. In three-dimensional state space, the resulting system matrix, **A,** for the phase-variable representation is of the form

$$\begin{bmatrix} 0 & 1 & 0 \\ 0 & 0 & 1 \\ -a_0 & -a_1 & -a_2 \end{bmatrix} \tag{3.107}$$

where the a_i's are the coefficients of the characteristic polynomial or denominator of the system transfer function. We also discussed how to convert from a state-space representation to a transfer function.

In conclusion, then, for linear, time-invariant systems, the state-space representation is simply another way of mathematically modeling them. One major advantage of applying the state-space representation to such linear systems is that it allows computer simulation. Programming the system on the digital computer and watching the system's response is an invaluable analysis and design tool. Simulation is covered in Appendix G located at www.wiley.com/college/nise.

REVIEW QUESTIONS

1. Give two reasons for modeling systems in state space.
2. State an advantage of the transfer function approach over the state-space approach.
3. Define *state variables*.
4. Define *state*.
5. Define *state vector*.
6. Define *state space*.
7. What is required to represent a system in state space?
8. An eighth-order system would be represented in state space with how many state equations?
9. If the state equations are a system of first-order differential equations whose solution yields the state variables, then the output equation performs what function?
10. What is meant by *linear independence*?
11. What factors influence the choice of state variables in any system?
12. What is a convenient choice of state variables for electrical networks?
13. If an electrical network has three energy-storage elements, is it possible to have a state-space representation with more than three state variables? Explain.
14. What is meant by the phase-variable form of the state-equation?

PROBLEMS

1. Represent the electrical network shown in Figure P3.1 in state space, where $v_o(t)$ is the output. [Section: 3.4]

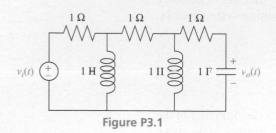

Figure P3.1

2. Represent the electrical network shown in Figure P3.2 in state space, where $i_R(t)$ is the output.

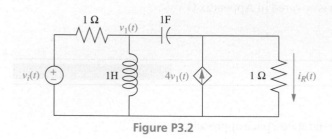

Figure P3.2

3. Find the state-space representation of the network shown in Figure P3.3 if the output is $v_o(t)$.

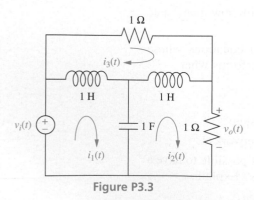

Figure P3.3

4. Represent the system shown in Figure P3.4 in state space where the output is $x_3(t)$. [Section: 3.4]

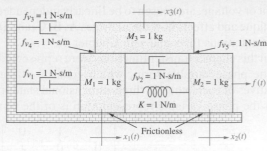

Figure P3.4

5. Represent the translational mechanical system shown in Figure P3.5 in state space, where $x_1(t)$ is the output. [Section: 3.4]

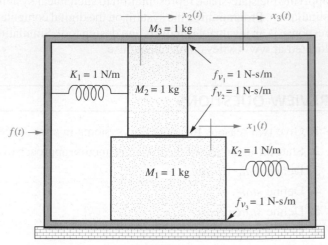

Figure P3.5

6. Represent the rotational mechanical system shown in Figure P3.6 in state space, where $\theta_1(t)$ is the output. [Section: 3.4]

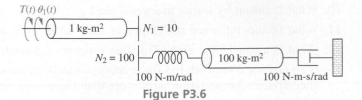

Figure P3.6

7. Represent the system shown in Figure P3.7 in state space where the output is $\theta_L(t)$. [Section: 3.4]

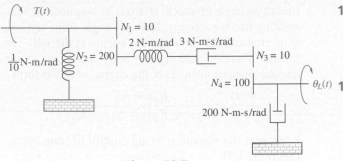

Figure P3.7

8. Show that the system of Figure 3.7 in the text yields a fourth-order transfer function if we relate the displacement of either mass to the applied force, and a third-order one if we relate the velocity of either mass to the applied force. [Section: 3.4]

9. Find the state-space representation in phase-variable form for each of the systems shown in Figure P3.8. [Section: 3.5]

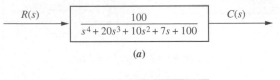

(a)

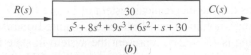

(b)

Figure P3.8

10. For each system shown in Figure P3.9, write the state equations and the output equation for the phase-variable representation. [Section: 3.5]

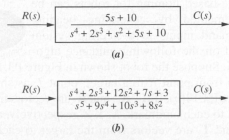

(a)

(b)

Figure P3.9

11. Represent the following transfer function in state space. Give your answer in vector-matrix form. [Section: 3.5]

$$T(s) = \frac{(s^2 + 3s + 7)}{(s + 1)(s^2 + 5s + 4)}$$

12. Find the transfer function $G(s)=Y(s)/R(s)$ for each of the following systems represented in state space: [Section: 3.6]

a. $\dot{\mathbf{x}} = \begin{bmatrix} 0 & 1 & 0 \\ 0 & 0 & 1 \\ -3 & -2 & -5 \end{bmatrix} \mathbf{x} + \begin{bmatrix} 0 \\ 0 \\ 10 \end{bmatrix} r$

$y = \begin{bmatrix} 1 & 0 & 0 \end{bmatrix} \mathbf{x}$

b. $\dot{\mathbf{x}} = \begin{bmatrix} 2 & -3 & -8 \\ 0 & 5 & 3 \\ -3 & -5 & -4 \end{bmatrix} \mathbf{x} + \begin{bmatrix} 1 \\ 4 \\ 6 \end{bmatrix} r$

$y = \begin{bmatrix} 1 & 3 & 6 \end{bmatrix} \mathbf{x}$

c. $\dot{\mathbf{x}} = \begin{bmatrix} 3 & -5 & 2 \\ 1 & -8 & 7 \\ -3 & -6 & 2 \end{bmatrix} \mathbf{x} + \begin{bmatrix} 5 \\ -3 \\ 2 \end{bmatrix} r$

$y = \begin{bmatrix} 1 & -4 & 3 \end{bmatrix} \mathbf{x}$

13. Use MATLAB to find the transfer function, $G(s) = Y(s)/R(s)$, for each of the following systems represented in state space: [Section: 3.6]

a. $\dot{\mathbf{x}} = \begin{bmatrix} 0 & 1 & 3 & 0 \\ 0 & 0 & 1 & 0 \\ 0 & 0 & 0 & 1 \\ -7 & -9 & -2 & -3 \end{bmatrix} \mathbf{x} + \begin{bmatrix} 0 \\ 5 \\ 8 \\ 2 \end{bmatrix} r$

$y = \begin{bmatrix} 1 & 3 & 4 & 6 \end{bmatrix} \mathbf{x}$

b. $\dot{\mathbf{x}} = \begin{bmatrix} 3 & 1 & 0 & 4 & -2 \\ -3 & 5 & -5 & 2 & -1 \\ 0 & 1 & -1 & 2 & 8 \\ -7 & 6 & -3 & -4 & 0 \\ -6 & 0 & 4 & -3 & 1 \end{bmatrix} \mathbf{x} + \begin{bmatrix} 2 \\ 7 \\ 6 \\ 5 \\ 4 \end{bmatrix} r$

$y = \begin{bmatrix} 1 & -2 & -9 & 7 & 6 \end{bmatrix} \mathbf{x}$

14. Repeat Problem 13 using MATLAB, the Symbolic Math Toolbox, and Eq. (3.73). [Section: 3.6]

15. Gyros are used on space vehicles, aircraft, and ships for inertial navigation. The gyro shown in Figure P3.10 is a rate gyro restrained by springs connected

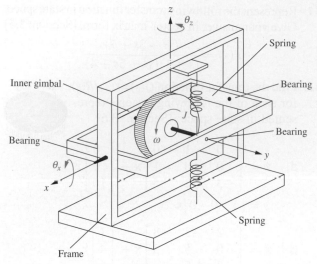

Figure P3.10   Gyro system

between the inner gimbal and the outer gimbal (frame) as shown. A rotational rate about the z-axis causes the rotating disk to precess about the x-axis. Hence, the input is a rotational rate about the z-axis, and the output is an angular displacement about the x-axis. Since the outer gimbal is secured to the vehicle, the displacement about the x-axis is a measure of the vehicle's angular rate about the z-axis. The equation of motion is

$$J_x \frac{d^2\theta_x}{dt^2} + D_x \frac{d\theta_x}{dt} + K_x\theta_x = J\omega \frac{d\theta_z}{dt}$$

Represent the gyro in state space. [Section: 3.4]

16. A missile in flight, as shown in Figure P3.11, is subject to several forces: thrust, lift, drag, and gravity. The missile

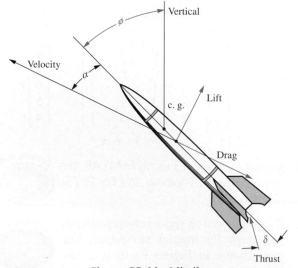

Figure P3.11   Missile

flies at an angle of attack, α, from its longitudinal axis, creating lift. For steering, the body angle from vertical, ϕ, is controlled by rotating the engine at the tail. The transfer function relating the body angle, ϕ, to the angular displacement, δ, of the engine is of the form

$$\frac{\Phi(s)}{\delta(s)} = \frac{K_a s + K_b}{K_3 s^3 + K_2 s^2 + K_1 s + K_0}$$

Represent the missile steering control in state space. [Section: 3.5]

17. Given the dc servomotor and load shown in Figure P3.12, represent the system in state space, where the state variables are the armature current, i_a, load displacement, θ_L, and load angular velocity, ω_L. Assume that the output is the angular displacement of the armature. Do not neglect armature inductance. [Section: 3.4]

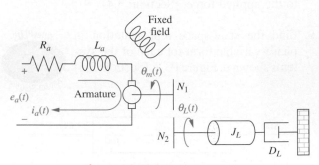

Figure P3.12   Motor and load

18. Consider the mechanical system of Figure P3.13. If the spring is nonlinear, and the force, F_s, required to stretch the spring is $F_s = 2x_1^2$, represent the system in state space linearized about $x_1 = 1$ if the output is x_2. [Section: 3.7]

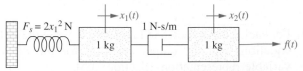

Figure P3.13   Nonlinear mechanical system

19. Image-based homing for robots can be implemented by generating heading command inputs to a steering system based on the following guidance algorithm. Suppose the robot shown in Figure P3.14(a) is to go from point R to a target, point T, as shown in Figure P3.14(b). If $\mathbf{R}_x$, $\mathbf{R}_y$, and $\mathbf{R}_z$ are vectors from the robot to each landmark, X, Y, Z, respectively, and $\mathbf{T}_x$, $\mathbf{T}_y$, and $\mathbf{T}_z$ are vectors from the target to each landmark, respectively, then heading commands would

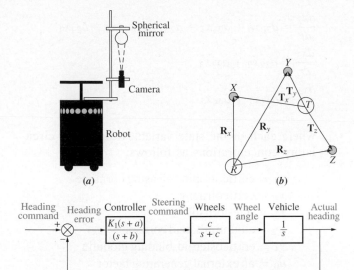

(a)

(b)

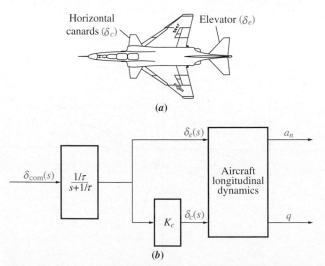

(c)

Figure P3.14   **a.** Robot with television imaging system; **b.** vector diagram showing concept behind image-based homing; **c.** heading control system (©1992 IEEE)

drive the robot to minimize $\mathbf{R}_x - \mathbf{T}_x$, $\mathbf{R}_y - \mathbf{T}_y$, and $\mathbf{R}_z - \mathbf{T}_z$ simultaneously, since the differences will be zero when the robot arrives at the target (*Hong, 1992*). If Figure P3.14(*c*) represents the control system that steers the robot, represent each block—the controller, wheels, and vehicle—in state space. [Section: 3.5]

20. Given the F4-E military aircraft shown in Figure P3.15(*a*), where normal acceleration, a_n, and pitch rate, q, are controlled by elevator deflection, δ_e, on

Figure P3.15   **a.** F4-E with canards; **b.** open-loop flight control system

the horizontal stabilizers and by canard deflection, δ_e. A commanded deflection, δ_{com}, as shown in Figure P3.15(*b*), is used to effect a change in both δ_e and δ_c. The relationships are

$$\frac{\delta_e(s)}{\delta_{com}(s)} = \frac{1/\tau}{s + 1/\tau}$$

$$\frac{\delta_c(s)}{\delta_{com}(s)} = \frac{K_c/\tau}{s + 1/\tau}$$

These deflections yield, via the aircraft longitudinal dynamics, a_n and q. The state equations describing the effect of δ_{com} on a_n and q is given by (*Cavallo, 1992*)

$$\begin{bmatrix} \dot{a}_n \\ \dot{q} \\ \dot{\delta}_e \end{bmatrix} = \begin{bmatrix} -1.702 & 50.72 & 263.38 \\ 0.22 & -1.418 & -31.99 \\ 0 & 0 & -14 \end{bmatrix} \begin{bmatrix} a_n \\ q \\ \delta_e \end{bmatrix}$$
$$+ \begin{bmatrix} -272.06 \\ 0 \\ 14 \end{bmatrix} \delta_{com}$$

Find the following transfer functions: [Section: 3.5]

$$G_1(s) = \frac{A_n(s)}{\delta_{com}(s)}$$

$$G_2(s) = \frac{Q(s)}{\delta_{com}(s)}$$

21. Modern robotic manipulators that act directly upon their target environments must be controlled so that impact forces as well as steady-state forces do not damage the targets. At the same time, the manipulator must provide sufficient force to perform the task. In order to develop a control system to regulate these forces, the robotic manipulator and target environment must be modeled. Assuming the model shown in Figure P3.16, represent in state space the manipulator and its environment under the following conditions (*Chiu, 1997*): [Section: 3.5]

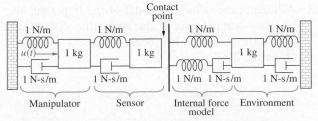

Figure P3.16   Robotic manipulator and target environment (©1997 IEEE)

a. The manipulator is not in contact with its target environment.

b. The manipulator is in constant contact with its target environment.

22. In the past, Type-1 diabetes patients had to inject themselves with insulin three to four times a day. New delayed-action insulin analogues such as insulin Glargine require a single daily dose. A similar procedure to the one described in the Pharmaceutical Drug Absorption case study of this chapter is used to find a model for the concentration-time evolution of plasma for insulin Glargine. For a specific patient, state-space model matrices are given by (*Tarín, 2005*)

$$\mathbf{A} = \begin{bmatrix} -0.435 & 0.209 & 0.02 \\ 0.268 & -0.394 & 0 \\ 0.227 & 0 & -0.02 \end{bmatrix}; \quad \mathbf{B} = \begin{bmatrix} 1 \\ 0 \\ 0 \end{bmatrix};$$

$$\mathbf{C} = \begin{bmatrix} 0.0003 & 0 & 0 \end{bmatrix}; \quad \mathbf{D} = 0$$

where the state vector is given by

$$\mathbf{x} = \begin{bmatrix} x_1 \\ x_2 \\ x_3 \end{bmatrix}.$$

The state variables are

$x_1 =$ insulin amount in plasma compartment

$x_2 =$ insulin amount in liver compartment

$x_3 =$ insulin amount in interstitial (in body tissue) compartment

The system's input is $u =$ external insulin flow. The system's output is $y =$ plasma insulin concentration.

a. Find the system's transfer function.

b. Verify your result using MATLAB.

23. A linear, time-invariant model of the hypothalamic-pituitary-adrenal axis of the endocrine system with five state variables has been proposed as follows (*Kyrylov, 2005*):

$$\frac{dx_0}{dt} = a_{00}x_0 + a_{02}x_2 + d_0$$

$$\frac{dx_1}{dt} = a_{10}x_0 + a_{11}x_1 + a_{12}x_2$$

$$\frac{dx_2}{dt} = a_{20}x_0 + a_{21}x_1 + a_{22}x_2 + a_{23}x_3 + a_{24}x_4$$

$$\frac{dx_3}{dt} = a_{32}x_2 + a_{33}x_3$$

$$\frac{dx_4}{dt} = a_{42}x_2 + a_{44}x_4$$

where each of the state variables represents circulatory concentrations as follows:

$x_0 =$ corticotropin-releasing hormone

$x_1 =$ corticotropin

$x_2 =$ free cortisol

$x_3 =$ albumin-bound cortisol

$x_4 =$ corticosteroid-binding globulin

$d_0 =$ an external generating factor

Express the system in the form $\dot{\mathbf{x}} = \mathbf{Ax} + \mathbf{Bu}$.

24. In this chapter, we described the state-space representation of single-input, single-output systems. In general, systems can have multiple inputs and multiple outputs. An autopilot is to be designed for a submarine as shown in Figure P3.17 to maintain a constant depth under severe wave disturbances. We will see that this system has two inputs and two outputs and thus the scaler u becomes a vector, $\mathbf{u}$, and the scaler y becomes a vector, $\mathbf{y}$, in the state equations.

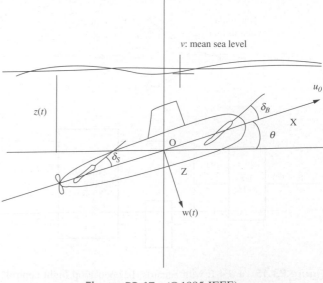

Figure P3.17   (©1995 IEEE)

It has been shown that the system's linearized dynamics under neutral buoyancy and at a given constant speed are given by (*Liceaga-Castro, 1995*):

$$\dot{\mathbf{x}} = \mathbf{A}\mathbf{x} + \mathbf{B}\mathbf{u}$$

$$\mathbf{y} = \mathbf{C}\mathbf{x}$$

where

$$\mathbf{x} = \begin{bmatrix} w \\ q \\ z \\ \theta \end{bmatrix}; \quad \mathbf{y} = \begin{bmatrix} z \\ \theta \end{bmatrix}; \quad \mathbf{u} = \begin{bmatrix} \delta_B \\ \delta_S \end{bmatrix}$$

$$\mathbf{A} = \begin{bmatrix} -0.038 & 0.896 & 0 & 0.0015 \\ 0.0017 & -0.092 & 0 & -0.0056 \\ 1 & 0 & 0 & -3.086 \\ 0 & 1 & 0 & 0 \end{bmatrix};$$

$$\mathbf{B} = \begin{bmatrix} -0.0075 & -0.023 \\ 0.0017 & -0.0022 \\ 0 & 0 \\ 0 & 0 \end{bmatrix}; \quad \mathbf{C} = \begin{bmatrix} 0 & 0 & 1 & 0 \\ 0 & 0 & 0 & 1 \end{bmatrix}$$

and where

w = the heave velocity
q = the pitch rate
z = the submarine depth
θ = the pitch angle
δ_B = the bow hydroplane angle
δ_S = the stern hydroplane angle

Since this system has two inputs and two outputs, four transfer functions are possible.

MATLAB

a. Use MATLAB to calculate the system's matrix transfer function.

b. Using the results from Part **a**, write the transfer functions $\dfrac{z(s)}{\delta_B(s)}$, $\dfrac{z(s)}{\delta_S(s)}$, $\dfrac{\theta(s)}{\delta_B(s)}$, and $\dfrac{\theta(s)}{\delta_S(s)}$.

25. Experiments to identify precision grip dynamics between the index finger and thumb have been performed using a ball-drop experiment. A subject holds a device with a small receptacle into which an object is dropped, and the response is measured (*Fagergren, 2000*). Assuming a step input, it has been found that the response of the motor subsystem together with the sensory system is of the form

$$G(s) = \frac{Y(s)}{R(s)} = \frac{s + c}{(s^2 + as + b)(s + d)}$$

Convert this transfer function to a state-space representation.

26. State-space representations are, in general, not unique. One system can be represented in several possible ways. For example, consider the following systems:

a. $\begin{aligned} \dot{x} &= -5x + 3u \\ y &= 7x \end{aligned}$

b. $\begin{bmatrix} \dot{x}_1 \\ \dot{x}_2 \end{bmatrix} = \begin{bmatrix} -5 & 0 \\ 0 & -1 \end{bmatrix} \begin{bmatrix} x_1 \\ x_2 \end{bmatrix} + \begin{bmatrix} 3 \\ 1 \end{bmatrix} u$

$y = \begin{bmatrix} 7 & 0 \end{bmatrix} \begin{bmatrix} x_1 \\ x_2 \end{bmatrix}$

c. $\begin{bmatrix} \dot{x}_1 \\ \dot{x}_2 \end{bmatrix} = \begin{bmatrix} -5 & 0 \\ 0 & -1 \end{bmatrix} \begin{bmatrix} x_1 \\ x_2 \end{bmatrix} + \begin{bmatrix} 3 \\ 0 \end{bmatrix} u$

$y = \begin{bmatrix} 7 & 3 \end{bmatrix} \begin{bmatrix} x_1 \\ x_2 \end{bmatrix}$

Show that these systems will result in the same transfer function. We will explore this phenomenon in more detail in Chapter 5.

Progressive Analysis and Design Problems

27. **High-speed rail pantograph.** A translational mechanical system model for a high-speed rail pantograph, used to supply electricity to a train from an overhead catenary, is shown in Figure P2.39(*b*) (*O'Connor, 1979*). Represent the pantograph in state space, where the output is the displacement of the top of the pantograph, $y_h(t) - y_{cat}(t)$.

28. **Control of HIV/AIDS.** Problem 65 in Chapter 2 introduced a model for HIV infection. If retroviral drugs, RTIs and PIs as discussed in Problem 20 in Chapter 1, are used, the model is modified as follows (*Craig, 2004*):

$$\frac{dT}{dt} = s - dT - (1 - u_1)\beta Tv$$

$$\frac{dT^*}{dt} = (1 - u_1)\beta Tv - \mu T^*$$

$$\frac{dv}{dt} = (1 - u_2)kT^* - cv$$

where $0 \le u_1 \le 1$, $0 \le u_2 \le 1$ represent the effectiveness of the RTI and PI medication, respectively.

a. Obtain a state-space representation of the HIV/AIDS model by linearizing the equations about the

$$(T_0, T_0^*, v_0) = \left(\frac{c\mu}{\beta k}, \frac{s}{\mu} - \frac{cd}{\beta k}, \frac{sk}{c\mu} - \frac{d}{\beta} \right)$$

equilibrium with $u_{10} = u_{20} = 0$. This equilibrium represents the asymptomatic HIV-infected patient. Note that each one of the above equations is of the form $\dot{x}_i = f_i(x_i, u_1, u_2) i = 1, 2, 3$.

b. If Matrices **A** and **B** are given by

$$\mathbf{A} = \begin{bmatrix} \dfrac{\partial f_1}{\partial x_1} & \dfrac{\partial f_1}{\partial x_2} & \dfrac{\partial f_1}{\partial x_3} \\ \dfrac{\partial f_2}{\partial x_1} & \dfrac{\partial f_2}{\partial x_2} & \dfrac{\partial f_2}{\partial x_3} \\ \dfrac{\partial f_3}{\partial x_1} & \dfrac{\partial f_3}{\partial x_2} & \dfrac{\partial f_3}{\partial x_3} \end{bmatrix}_{T_0, T_0^*, v_0} ; \quad \mathbf{B} = \begin{bmatrix} \dfrac{\partial f_1}{\partial u_1} & \dfrac{\partial f_1}{\partial u_2} \\ \dfrac{\partial f_2}{\partial u_1} & \dfrac{\partial f_2}{\partial u_2} \\ \dfrac{\partial f_3}{\partial u_1} & \dfrac{\partial f_3}{\partial u_2} \end{bmatrix}_{T_0, T_0^*, v_0}$$

and we are interested in the number of free HIV viruses as the system's output,

$$\mathbf{C} = \begin{bmatrix} 0 & 0 & 1 \end{bmatrix}$$

show that

$$\mathbf{A} = \begin{bmatrix} -(d + \beta v_0) & 0 & -\beta T_0 \\ \beta v_0 & -\mu & \beta T_0 \\ 0 & k & -c \end{bmatrix} ; \quad \mathbf{B} = \begin{bmatrix} \beta T_0 v_0 & 0 \\ -\beta T_0 v_0 & 0 \\ 0 & -k T_0^* \end{bmatrix}$$

c. Typical parameter values and descriptions for the HIV/AIDS model are shown in the following table.

t	Time	days
d	Death of uninfected T cells	0.02/day
k	Rate of free viruses produced per infected T cell	100 counts/cell
s	Source term for uninfected T cells	$10/\text{mm}^3/\text{day}$
β	Infectivity rate of free virus particles	$2.4 \times 10^{-5}/\text{mm}^3/\text{day}$
c	Death rate of viruses	2.4/day
μ	Death rate of infected T cells	0.24/day

(©2004 IEEE)

Substitute the values from the table into your model and write as

$$\dot{\mathbf{x}} = \mathbf{A}\mathbf{x} + \mathbf{B}\mathbf{u}$$
$$\mathbf{y} = \mathbf{C}\mathbf{x}$$

CYBER EXPLORATION LABORATORY

Experiment 3.1

Objectives To learn to use MATLAB to (1) generate an LTI state-space representation of a system and (2) convert an LTI state-space representation of a system to an LTI transfer function.

Minimum required software packages MATLAB and the Control System Toolbox

Prelab

1. Derive the state-space representation of the translational mechanical system shown in Skill-Assessment Exercise 3.2 if you have not already done so. Consider the output to be $x_3(t)$.

2. Derive the transfer function, $\dfrac{X_3(s)}{F(s)}$, from the equations of motion for the translational mechanical system shown in Skill-Assessment Exercise 3.2.

Lab

1. Use MATLAB to generate the LTI state-space representation derived in Prelab 1.

2. Use MATLAB to convert the LTI state-space representation found in Lab 1 to the LTI transfer function found in Prelab 2.

Postlab

1. Compare your transfer functions as found from Prelab 2 and Lab 2.

2. Discuss the use of MATLAB to create LTI state-space representations and the use of MATLAB to convert these representations to transfer functions.

Experiment 3.2

Objectives To learn to use MATLAB and the Symbolic Math Toolbox to (1) find a symbolic transfer function from the state-space representation and (2) find a state-space representation from the equations of motion.

Minimum required software packages MATLAB, the Symbolic Math Toolbox, and the Control System Toolbox

Prelab

1. Perform Prelab 1 and 2 of Experiment 3.1 if you have not already done so.

2. Using the equation $T(s) = \mathbf{C}(s\mathbf{I} - \mathbf{A})^{-1}\mathbf{B}$ to find a transfer function from a state-space representation, write a MATLAB program using the Symbolic Math Toolbox to find the symbolic transfer function from the state-space representation of the translational mechanical system shown in Skill-Assessment Exercise 3.2 and found in Prelab 1.

3. Using the equations of motion of the translational mechanical system shown in Skill-Assessment Exercise 3.2 and found as a step in Prelab 1, write a symbolic MATLAB program to find the transfer function, $\dfrac{X_3(s)}{F(s)}$, for this system.

Lab

1. Run the programs composed in Prelabs 2 and 3 and obtain the symbolic transfer functions by the two methods.

Postlab

1. Compare the symbolic transfer function obtained from $T(s) = \mathbf{C}(s\mathbf{I} - \mathbf{A})^{-1}\mathbf{B}$ with the symbolic transfer function obtained from the equations of motion.

2. Discuss the advantages and disadvantages between the two methods.

3. Describe how you would obtain an LTI state-space representation and an LTI transfer function from your symbolic transfer function.

BIBLIOGRAPHY

Carlson, L. E., and Griggs, G. E. *Aluminum Catenary System Quarterly Report*. Technical Report Contract Number DOT-FR-9154, U.S. Department of Transportation, 1980.

Cavallo, A., De Maria, G., and Verde, L. Robust Flight Control Systems: A Parameter Space Design. *Journal of Guidance, Control, and Dynamics*, vol. 15, no. 5, September–October 1992, pp. 1207–1215.

Cereijo, M. R. State Variable Formulations. *Instruments and Control Systems*, December 1969, pp. 87–88.

Chiu, D. K., and Lee, S. Design and Experimentation of a Jump Impact Controller. *IEEE Control Systems*, June 1997, pp. 99–106.

Cochin, I. *Analysis and Design of Dynamic Systems*. Harper & Row, New York, 1980.

Craig, I. K., Xia, X., and Venter, J. W. Introducing HIV/AIDS Education into the Electrical Engineering Curriculum at the University of Pretoria. *IEEE Transactions on Education*, vol. 47, no. 1, February 2004, pp. 65–73.

Elkins, J. A. *A Method for Predicting the Dynamic Response of a Pantograph Running at Constant Speed under a Finite Length of Overhead Equipment*. Technical Report TN DA36, British Railways, 1976.

Fagergren, A., Ekeberg, Ö., and Forssberg, H. Precision Grip Force Dynamics: A System Identification Approach. *IEEE Transactions on Biomedical Engineering*, vol. 47, no. 10, 2000, pp. 1366–1375.

Franklin, G. F., Powell, J. D., and Emami-Naeini, A. *Feedback Control of Dynamic Systems*. Addison-Wesley, Reading, MA, 1986.

Hong, J., Tan, X., Pinette, B., Weiss, R., and Riseman, E. M. Image-Based Homing. *IEEE Control Systems*, February 1992, pp. 38–45.

Inigo, R. M. Observer and Controller Design for D.C. Positional Control Systems Using State Variables. *Transactions, Analog/Hybrid Computer Educational Society*, December 1974, pp. 177–189.

Kailath, T. *Linear Systems*. Prentice Hall, Englewood Cliffs, NJ, 1980.

Kandel, A. Analog Simulation of Groundwater Mining in Coastal Aquifers. *Transactions, Analog/Hybrid Computer Educational Society*, November 1973, pp. 175–183.

Kyrylov, V., Severyanova, L. A., and Vieira, A. Modeling Robust Oscillatory Behavior of the Hypothalamic-Pituitary-Adrenal Axis. *IEEE Transactions on Biomedical Engineering*, vol. 52, no. 12, 2005, pp. 1977–1983.

Liceage-Castro, E., and van der Molen, G. M. Submarine H^∞ Depth Control Under Wave Disturbances. *IEEE Transactions on Control Systems Technology*, vol. 3, no. 3, 1995, pp. 338–346.

Lordi, N. G. Analog Computer Generated Lecture Demonstrations in Pharmacokinetics. *Transactions, Analog/Hybrid Computer Educational Society*, November 1972, pp. 217–222.

O'Connor, D. N., Eppinger, S. D., Seering, W. P., and Wormly, D. N. Active Control of a High-Speed Pantograph. *Journal of Dynamic Systems, Measurements, and Control*, vol. 119, March 1997, pp. 1–4.

Philco Technological Center. *Servomechanism Fundamentals and Experiments*. Prentice Hall, Englewood Cliffs, NJ, 1980.

Riegelman, S. et al. Shortcomings in Pharmacokinetic Analysis by Conceiving the Body to Exhibit Properties of a Single Compartment. *Journal of Pharmaceutical Sciences*, vol. 57, no. 1, 1968, pp. 117–123.

Tarin, C., Teufel, E., Picó, J., Bondia, J., and Pfleiderer, H. J. Comprehensive Pharmacokinetic Model of Insulin Glargine and Other Insulin Formulations. *IEEE Transactions on Biomedical Engineering*, vol. 52, no. 12, 2005, pp. 1994–2005.

Timothy, L. K., and Bona, B. E. *State Space Analysis: An Introduction*. McGraw-Hill, New York, 1968.

TRANSIENT RESPONSE

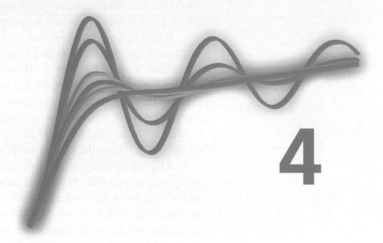

4

CHAPTER OBJECTIVES

In this chapter you will learn the following:

- How to find the time response from the transfer function
- How to use poles and zeros to determine the response of a control system
- How to describe quantitatively the transient response of first- and second-order systems
- How to approximate higher-order systems as first or second order
- How to view the effects of nonlinearities on the system time response
- How to find the time response from the state-space representation

CASE STUDY OBJECTIVES

You will be able to demonstrate your knowledge of the chapter objectives with case studies as follows:

- Given the antenna azimuth position control system shown on the front endpapers, you will be able to (1) predict, by inspection, the form of the open-loop angular velocity response of the load to a step voltage input to the power amplifier; (2) describe quantitatively the transient response of the open-loop system; (3) derive the expression for the open-loop angular velocity output for a step voltage input; (4) obtain the open-loop state-space representation; (5) plot the open-loop velocity step response using a computer simulation.

- Given the block diagram for the Unmanned Free-Swimming Submersible (UFSS) vehicle's pitch control system shown on the back endpapers, you will be able to predict, find, and plot the response of the vehicle dynamics to a step input command. Further, you will be able to evaluate the effect of system zeros and higher-order poles on the response. You will also be able to evaluate the roll response of a ship at sea.

4.1 INTRODUCTION

In Chapter 2 we saw how transfer functions can represent linear, time-invariant systems. In Chapter 3 systems were represented directly in the time domain via the state and output equations. After the engineer obtains a mathematical representation of a subsystem, the subsystem is analyzed for its transient and steady-state responses to see if these characteristics yield the desired behavior. This chapter is devoted to the analysis of system transient response.

It may appear more logical to continue with Chapter 5, which covers the modeling of closed-loop systems, rather than to break the modeling sequence with the analysis presented here in Chapter 4. However, the student should not continue too far into system representation without knowing the application for the effort expended. Thus, this chapter demonstrates applications of the system representation by evaluating the transient response from the system model. Logically, this approach is not far from reality, since the engineer may indeed want to evaluate the response of a subsystem prior to inserting it into the closed-loop system.

After describing a valuable analysis and design tool, poles and zeros, we begin analyzing our models to find the step response of first- and second-order systems. The order refers to the order of the equivalent differential equation representing the system—the order of the denominator of the transfer function after cancellation of common factors in the numerator or the number of simultaneous first-order equations required for the state-space representation.

4.2 POLES, ZEROS, AND SYSTEM RESPONSE

The output response of a system is the sum of two responses: the *forced response* and the *natural response*.[1] Although many techniques, such as solving a differential equation or taking the inverse Laplace transform, enable us to evaluate this output response, these techniques are laborious and time-consuming. Productivity is aided by analysis and design techniques that yield results in a minimum of time. If the technique is so rapid that we feel we derive the desired result by inspection, we sometimes use the attribute *qualitative* to describe the method. The use of poles and zeros and their relationship to the time response of a system is such a technique. Learning this relationship gives us a qualitative "handle" on problems. The concept of poles and zeros, fundamental to the analysis and design of control systems, simplifies the evaluation of a system's response. The reader is encouraged to master the concepts of poles and zeros and their application to problems throughout this book. Let us begin with two definitions.

POLES OF A TRANSFER FUNCTION

The *poles* of a transfer function are (1) the values of the Laplace transform variable, s, that cause the transfer function to become infinite or (2) any roots of the denominator of the transfer function that are common to roots of the numerator.

---

[1] The forced response is also called the *steady-state response* or *particular solution*. The natural response is also called the *homogeneous solution*.

Strictly speaking, the poles of a transfer function satisfy part (1) of the definition. For example, the roots of the characteristic polynomial in the denominator are values of s that make the transfer function infinite, so they are thus poles. However, if a factor of the denominator can be canceled by the same factor in the numerator, the root of this factor no longer causes the transfer function to become infinite. In control systems we often refer to the root of the canceled factor in the denominator as a pole even though the transfer function will not be infinite at this value. Hence, we include part (2) of the definition.

ZEROS OF A TRANSFER FUNCTION

The *zeros* of a transfer function are (1) the values of the Laplace transform variable, s, that cause the transfer function to become zero, or (2) any roots of the numerator of the transfer function that are common to roots of the denominator.

Strictly speaking, the zeros of a transfer function satisfy part (1) of this definition. For example, the roots of the numerator are values of s that make the transfer function zero and are thus zeros. However, if a factor of the numerator can be canceled by the same factor in the denominator, the root of this factor no longer causes the transfer function to become zero. In control systems we often refer to the root of the canceled factor in the numerator as a zero even though the transfer function will not be zero at this value. Hence, we include part (2) of the definition.

POLES AND ZEROS OF A FIRST-ORDER SYSTEM: AN EXAMPLE

Given the transfer function $G(s)$ in Figure 4.1(a), a pole exists at $s = -5$, and a zero exists at -2. These values are plotted on the complex s-plane in Figure 4.1(b), using an $\times$ for the pole and a $\bigcirc$ for the zero. To show the properties of the poles and zeros, let us find the unit step response of the system. Multiplying the transfer function of Figure 4.1(a) by a step function yields

$$C(s) = \frac{(s+2)}{s(s+5)} = \frac{A}{s} + \frac{B}{s+5} = \frac{2/5}{s} + \frac{3/5}{s+5} \qquad (4.1)$$

where

$$A = \frac{(s+2)}{(s+5)}\Bigg|_{s \to 0} = \frac{2}{5}$$

$$B = \frac{(s+2)}{s}\Bigg|_{s \to -5} = \frac{3}{5}$$

Thus,

$$c(t) = \frac{2}{5} + \frac{3}{5}e^{-5t} \qquad (4.2)$$

From the development summarized in Figure 4.1(c), we draw the following conclusions:

1. A pole of the input function generates the form of the *forced response* (that is, the pole at the origin generated a step function at the output).

2. A pole of the transfer function generates the form of the *natural response* (that is, the pole at -5 generated e^{-5t}).

3. A pole on the real axis generates an *exponential* response of the form $e^{-\alpha t}$, where $-\alpha$ is the pole location on the real axis. Thus, the farther to the left a pole is on the negative real axis, the faster the exponential transient response will decay to zero (again, the pole at -5 generated e^{-5t}; see Figure 4.2 for the general case).

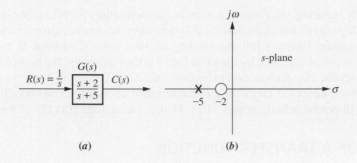

(a)

(b)

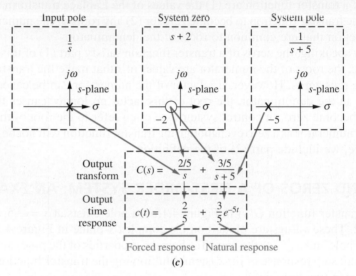

Input pole   System zero   System pole

Output transform

Output time response

Forced response   Natural response

(c)

FIGURE 4.1   a. System showing input and output; **b.** pole-zero plot of the system; **c.** evolution of a system response. Follow blue arrows to see the evolution of the response component generated by the pole or zero

4. The zeros and poles generate the *amplitudes* for both the forced and natural responses (this can be seen from the calculation of A and B in Eq. (4.1)).

Let us now look at an example that demonstrates the technique of using poles to obtain the form of the system response. We will learn to write the form of the response by inspection. Each pole of the system transfer function that is on the real axis generates an exponential response that is a component of the natural response. The input pole generates the forced response.

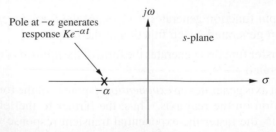

FIGURE 4.2   Effect of a real-axis pole upon transient response.

◼ EXAMPLE 4.1 ◼

Evaluating response using poles

Problem: Given the system of Figure 4.3, write the output, $c(t)$, in general terms. Specify the forced and natural parts of the solution.

SOLUTION: By inspection, each system pole generates an exponential as part of the natural response. The input's pole generates the forced response. Thus,

$$C(s) \equiv \underbrace{\frac{K_1}{s}}_{\substack{\text{Forced} \\ \text{response}}} + \underbrace{\frac{K_2}{(s+2)} + \frac{K_3}{(s+4)} + \frac{K_4}{(s+5)}}_{\substack{\text{Natural} \\ \text{response}}} \qquad (4.3)$$

Taking the inverse Laplace transform, we get

$$c(t) \equiv \underbrace{K_1}_{\substack{\text{Forced} \\ \text{response}}} + \underbrace{K_2 e^{-2t} + K_3 e^{-4t} + K_4 e^{-5t}}_{\substack{\text{Natural} \\ \text{response}}} \qquad (4.4)$$

$$R(s) = \frac{1}{s} \longrightarrow \boxed{\frac{(s+3)}{(s+2)(s+4)(s+5)}} \xrightarrow{\ C(s)\ }$$

FIGURE 4.3   System for Example 4.1

◼ SKILL-ASSESSMENT EXERCISE 4.1 ◼

Problem: A system has a transfer function, $G(s) = \dfrac{10(s+4)(s+6)}{(s+1)(s+7)(s+8)(s+10)}$.
Write, by inspection, the output, $c(t)$, in general terms if the input is a unit step.

ANSWER: $c(t) \equiv A + Be^{-t} + Ce^{-7t} + De^{-8t} + Ee^{-10t}$

In this section we learned that poles determine the nature of the time response: Poles of the input function determine the form of the forced response, and poles of the transfer function determine the form of the natural response. Zeros and poles of the input or transfer function contribute to the amplitudes of the component parts of the total response. Finally, poles on the real axis generate exponential responses.

4.3 FIRST-ORDER SYSTEMS

We now discuss first-order systems without zeros to define a performance specification for such a system. A first-order system without zeros can be described by the transfer function shown in Figure 4.4(*a*). If the input is a unit step, where $R(s) = 1/s$, the Laplace transform of the step response is $C(s)$, where

$$C(s) = R(s)G(s) = \frac{a}{s(s+a)} \qquad (4.5)$$

Taking the inverse transform, the step response is given by

$$\boxed{c(t) = c_f(t) + c_n(t) = 1 - e^{-at}} \qquad (4.6)$$

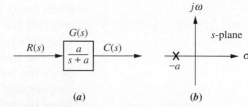

FIGURE 4.4   **a.** First-order system; **b.** pole plot

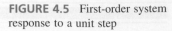

FIGURE 4.5 First-order system
response to a unit step

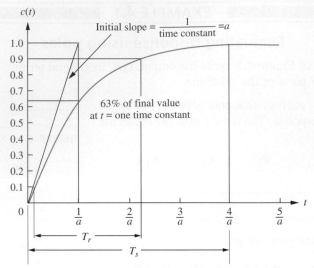

where the input pole at the origin generated the forced response $c_f(t) = 1$, and the system pole at $-a$, as shown in Figure 4.4(b), generated the natural response $c_n(t) = -e^{-at}$. Equation (4.6) is plotted in Figure 4.5.

Let us examine the significance of parameter a, the only parameter needed to describe the transient response. When $t = 1/a$,

$$e^{-at}|_{t=1/a} = e^{-1} = 0.37 \tag{4.7}$$

or

$$c(t)|_{t=1/a} = 1 - e^{-at}|_{t=1/a} = 1 - 0.37 = 0.63 \tag{4.8}$$

We now use Eqs. (4.6), (4.7), and (4.8) to define three transient response performance specifications.

TIME CONSTANT

We call $1/a$ the *time constant* of the response. From Eq. (4.7) the time constant can be described as the time for e^{-at} to decay to 37% of its initial value. Alternately, from Eq. (4.8) the time constant is the time it takes for the step response to rise to 63% of its final value (see Figure 4.5).

The reciprocal of the time constant has the units (1/seconds), or frequency. Thus, we can call the parameter a the *exponential frequency*. Since the derivative of e^{-at} is $-a$ when $t = 0$, a is the initial rate of change of the exponential at $t = 0$. Thus, the time constant can be considered a transient response specification for a first-order system, since it is related to the speed at which the system responds to a step input.

The time constant can also be evaluated from the pole plot (see Figure 4.4(b)). Since the pole of the transfer function is at $-a$, we can say the pole is located at the *reciprocal* of the time constant, and the farther the pole from the imaginary axis, the faster the transient response.

Let us look at other transient response specifications, such as rise time, T_r, and settling time, T_s, as shown in Figure 4.5.

RISE TIME, T_r

Rise time is defined as the time for the waveform to go from 0.1 to 0.9 of its final value. Rise time is found by solving Eq. (4.6) for the difference in time at $c(t) = 0.9$ and $c(t) = 0.1$. Hence,

$$T_r = \frac{2.31}{a} - \frac{0.11}{a} = \frac{2.2}{a} \qquad (4.9)$$

SETTLING TIME, T_s

Settling time is defined as the time for the response to reach, and stay within, 2% of its final value.[2] Letting $c(t) = 0.98$ in Eq. (4.6) and solving for time, t, we find the settling time to be

$$T_s = \frac{4}{a} \qquad (4.10)$$

FIRST-ORDER TRANSFER FUNCTIONS VIA TESTING

Often it is not possible or practical to obtain a system's transfer function analytically. Perhaps the system is closed, and the component parts are not easily identifiable. Since the transfer function is a representation of the system from input to output, the system's step response can lead to a representation even though the inner construction is not known. With a step input, we can measure the time constant and the steady-state value, from which the transfer function can be calculated.

Consider a simple first-order system, $G(s) = K/(s + a)$, whose step response is

$$C(s) = \frac{K}{s(s + a)} = \frac{K/a}{s} - \frac{K/a}{(s + a)} \qquad (4.11)$$

If we can identify K and a from laboratory testing, we can obtain the transfer function of the system.

For example, assume the unit step response given in Figure 4.6. We determine that it has the first-order characteristics we have seen thus far, such as no overshoot and

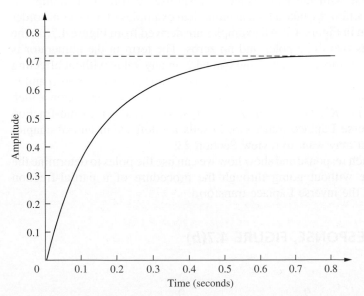

FIGURE 4.6 Laboratory results of a system step response test

---

[2] Strictly speaking, this is the definition of the 2% *setting time*. Other percentages, for example 5%, also can be used. We will use *settling time* throughout the book to mean 2% settling time.

nonzero initial slope. From the response, we measure the time constant, that is, the time for the amplitude to reach 63% of its final value. Since the final value is about 0.72, the time constant is evaluated where the curve reaches $0.63 \times 0.72 = 0.45$, or about 0.13 second. Hence, $a = 1/0.13 = 7.7$.

To find K, we realize from Eq. (4.11) that the forced response reaches a steady-state value of $K/a = 0.72$. Substituting the value of a, we find $K = 5.54$. Thus, the transfer function for the system is $G(s) = 5.54/(s + 7.7)$. It is interesting to note that the response of Figure 4.6 was generated using the transfer function $G(s) = 5/(s + 7)$.

SKILL-ASSESSMENT EXERCISE 4.2

Problem: A system has a transfer function, $G(s) = \dfrac{50}{s + 50}$. Find the time constant, T_c, settling time, T_s, and rise time, T_r.

ANSWERS: $T_c = 0.02$ s, $T_s = 0.08$ s, and $T_r = 0.044$ s.

The complete solution is located at www.wiley.com/college/nise.

4.4 SECOND-ORDER SYSTEMS: INTRODUCTION

Let us now extend the concepts of poles and zeros and transient response to second-order systems. Compared to the simplicity of a first-order system, a second-order system exhibits a wide range of responses that must be analyzed and described. Whereas varying a first-order system's parameter simply changes the speed of the response, changes in the parameters of a second-order system can change the *form* of the response. For example, a second-order system can display characteristics much like a first-order system or, depending on component values, display damped or pure oscillations for its transient response.

To become familiar with the wide range of responses before formalizing our discussion in the next section, we take a look at numerical examples of the second-order system responses shown in Figure 4.7. All examples are derived from Figure 4.7(*a*), the general case, which has two finite poles and no zeros. The term in the numerator is simply a scale or input multiplying factor that can take on any value without affecting the form of the derived results. By assigning appropriate values to parameters a and b, we can show all possible second-order transient responses. The unit step response then can be found using $C(s) = R(s)G(s)$, where $R(s) = 1/s$, followed by a partial-fraction expansion and the inverse Laplace transform. Details are left as an end-of-chapter problem, for which you may want to review Section 2.2.

We now explain each response and show how we can use the poles to determine the nature of the response without going through the procedure of a partial-fraction expansion followed by the inverse Laplace transform.

OVERDAMPED RESPONSE, FIGURE 4.7(*b*)

For this response,

$$C(s) = \frac{9}{s(s^2 + 9s + 9)} = \frac{9}{s(s + 7.854)(s + 1.146)} \tag{4.12}$$

FIGURE 4.7 Second-order systems, pole plots, and step responses

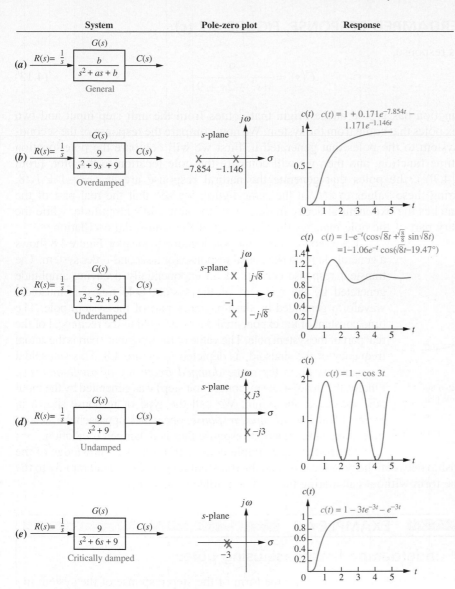

This function has a pole at the origin that comes from the unit step input and two real poles that come from the system. The input pole at the origin generates the constant forced response; each of the two system poles on the real axis generates an exponential natural response whose exponential frequency is equal to the pole location. Hence, the output initially could have been written as $c(t) = K_1 + K_2 e^{-7.854t} + K_3 e^{-1.146t}$. This response, shown in Figure 4.7(b), is called *overdamped*.[3] We see that the poles tell us the form of the response without the tedious calculation of the inverse Laplace transform.

---

[3] So named because *overdamped* refers to a large amount of energy absorption in the system, which inhibits the transient response from overshooting and oscillating about the steady-state value for a step input. As the energy absorption is reduced, an overdamped system will become underdamped and exhibit overshoot.

UNDERDAMPED RESPONSE, FIGURE 4.7 (c)

For this response,

$$C(s) = \frac{9}{s(s^2 + 2s + 9)} \tag{4.13}$$

This function has a pole at the origin that comes from the unit step input and two complex poles that come from the system. We now compare the response of the second-order system to the poles that generated it. First we will compare the pole location to the time function, and then we will compare the pole location to the plot. From Figure 4.7(c), the poles that generate the natural response are at $s = -1 \pm j\sqrt{8}$. Comparing these values to $c(t)$ in the same figure, we see that the real part of the pole matches the exponential decay frequency of the sinusoid's amplitude, while the imaginary part of the pole matches the frequency of the sinusoidal oscillation.

Let us now compare the pole location to the plot. Figure 4.8 shows a general, damped sinusoidal response for a second-order system. The transient response consists of an exponentially decaying amplitude generated by the real part of the system pole times a sinusoidal waveform generated by the imaginary part of the system pole. The time constant of the exponential decay is equal to the reciprocal of the real part of the system pole. The value of the imaginary part is the actual frequency of the sinusoid, as depicted in Figure 4.8. This sinusoidal frequency is given the name *damped frequency of oscillation, ω_d*. Finally, the steady-state response (unit step) was generated by the input pole located at the origin. We call the type of response shown in Figure 4.8 an *underdamped response,* one which approaches a steady-state value via a transient response that is a damped oscillation.

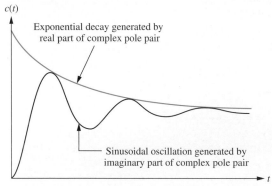

FIGURE 4.8   Second-order step response components generated by complex poles

The following example demonstrates how a knowledge of the relationship between the pole location and the transient response can lead rapidly to the response form without calculating the inverse Laplace transform.

EXAMPLE 4.2

Form of underdamped response using poles

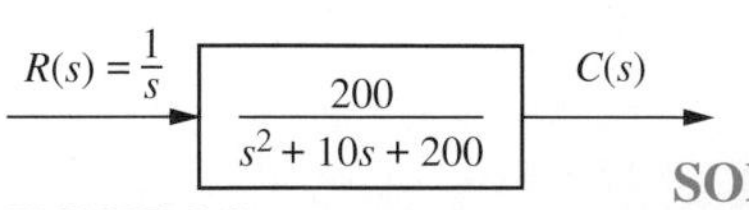

$$R(s) = \frac{1}{s} \longrightarrow \boxed{\dfrac{200}{s^2 + 10s + 200}} \longrightarrow C(s)$$

FIGURE 4.9   System for Example 4.2

Problem: By inspection, write the form of the step response of the system in Figure 4.9.

SOLUTION: First we determine that the form of the forced response is a step. Next we find the form of the natural response. Factoring the denominator of the transfer function in Figure 4.9, we find the poles to be $s = -5 \pm j13.23$. The real part, -5, is the exponential frequency for the damping. It is also the reciprocal of the time constant of the decay of the oscillations. The imaginary part, 13.23, is the radian frequency for the sinusoidal oscillations. Using our previous discussion and Figure 4.7(c) as a guide, we obtain $c(t) = K_1 + e^{-5t}(K_2 \cos 13.23t + K_3 \sin 13.23t) = K_1 + K_4 e^{-5t}$ $(\cos 13.23t - \phi)$, where $\phi = \tan^{-1} K_3/K_2$, $K_4 = \sqrt{K_2^2 + K_3^2}$, and $c(t)$ is a constant plus an exponentially damped sinusoid.

We will revisit the second-order underdamped response in Sections 4.5 and 4.6, where we generalize the discussion and derive some results that relate the pole position to other parameters of the response.

UNDAMPED RESPONSE, FIGURE 4.7(*d*)

For this response,

$$C(s) = \frac{9}{s(s^2 + 9)} \tag{4.14}$$

This function has a pole at the origin that comes from the unit step input and two imaginary poles that come from the system. The input pole at the origin generates the constant forced response, and the two system poles on the imaginary axis at $\pm j3$ generate a sinusoidal natural response whose frequency is equal to the location of the imaginary poles. Hence, the output can be estimated as $c(t) = K_1 + K_4 \cos(3t - \phi)$. This type of response, shown in Figure 4.7(*d*), is called *undamped*. Note that the absence of a real part in the pole pair corresponds to an exponential that does not decay. Mathematically, the exponential is $e^{-0t} = 1$.

CRITICALLY DAMPED RESPONSE, FIGURE 4.7(e)

For this response,

$$C(s) = \frac{9}{s(s^2 + 6s + 9)} = \frac{9}{s(s + 3)^2} \tag{4.15}$$

This function has a pole at the origin that comes from the unit step input and two multiple real poles that come from the system. The input pole at the origin generates the constant forced response, and the two poles on the real axis at -3 generate a natural response consisting of an exponential and an exponential multiplied by time, where the exponential frequency is equal to the location of the real poles. Hence, the output can be estimated as $c(t) = K_1 + K_2 e^{-3t} + K_3 t e^{-3t}$. This type of response, shown in Figure 4.7(*e*), is called *critically damped*. Critically damped responses are the fastest possible without the overshoot that is characteristic of the underdamped response.

We now summarize our observations. In this section we defined the following natural responses and found their characteristics:

1. *Overdamped responses*

Poles: Two real at $-\sigma_1, -\sigma_2$

Natural response: Two exponentials with time constants equal to the reciprocal of the pole locations, or

$$c(t) = K_1 e^{-\sigma_1 t} + K_2 e^{-\sigma_2 t}$$

2. *Underdamped responses*

Poles: Two complex at $-\sigma_d \pm j\omega_d$

Natural response: Damped sinusoid with an exponential envelope whose time constant is equal to the reciprocal of the pole's real part. The radian frequency of the sinusoid, the damped frequency of oscillation, is equal to the imaginary part of the poles, or

$$c(t) = Ae^{-\sigma_d t}\cos(\omega_d t - \phi)$$

3. *Undamped responses*

Poles: Two imaginary at $\pm j\omega_1$

Natural response: Undamped sinusoid with radian frequency equal to the imaginary part of the poles, or

$$c(t) = A\cos(\omega_1 t - \phi)$$

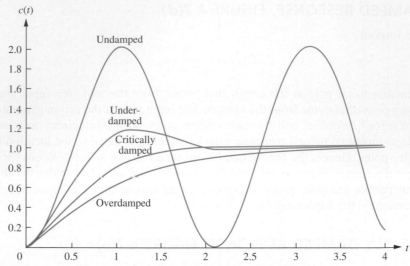

FIGURE 4.10   Step responses for second-order system damping cases

4. *Critically damped responses*

Poles: Two real at $-\sigma_1$

Natural response: One term is an exponential whose time constant is equal to the reciprocal of the pole location. Another term is the product of time, t, and an exponential with time constant equal to the reciprocal of the pole location, or

$$c(t) = K_1 e^{-\sigma_1 t} + K_2 t e^{-\sigma_1 t}$$

The step responses for the four cases of damping discussed in this section are superimposed in Figure 4.10. Notice that the critically damped case is the division between the overdamped cases and the underdamped cases and is the fastest response without overshoot.

SKILL-ASSESSMENT EXERCISE 4.3

Problem: For each of the following transfer functions, write, by inspection, the general form of the step response:

a. $G(s) = \dfrac{400}{s^2 + 12s + 400}$

b. $G(s) = \dfrac{900}{s^2 + 90s + 900}$

c. $G(s) = \dfrac{225}{s^2 + 30s + 225}$

d. $G(s) = \dfrac{625}{s^2 + 625}$

ANSWERS:

a. $c(t) = A + Be^{-6t}\cos(19.08t + \phi)$

b. $c(t) = A + Be^{-78.54t} + Ce^{-11.46t}$

c. $c(t) = A + Be^{-15t} + Cte^{-15t}$

d. $c(t) = A + B\cos(25t + \phi)$

The complete solution is located at www.wiley.com/college/nise.

In the next section we will formalize and generalize our discussion of second-order responses and define two specifications used for the analysis and design of second-order systems. In Section 4.6 we will focus on the *underdamped* case and derive some specifications unique to this response that we will use later for analysis and design.

4.5 THE GENERAL SECOND-ORDER SYSTEM

Now that we have become familiar with second-order systems and their responses, we generalize the discussion and establish quantitative specifications defined in such a way that the response of a second-order system can be described to a designer without the need for sketching the response. In this section we define two physically meaningful specifications for second-order systems. These quantities can be used to describe the characteristics of the second-order transient response just as time constants describe the first-order system response. The two quantities are called natural frequency and damping ratio. Let us formally define them.

NATURAL FREQUENCY, ω_n

The *natural frequency* of a second-order system is the frequency of oscillation of the system without damping. For example, the frequency of oscillation of a series *RLC* circuit with the resistance shorted would be the natural frequency.

DAMPING RATIO, ζ

Before we state our next definition, some explanation is in order. We have already seen that a second-order system's underdamped step response is characterized by damped oscillations. Our definition is derived from the need to quantitatively describe this damped oscillation regardless of the time scale. Thus, a system whose transient response goes through three cycles in a millisecond before reaching the steady state would have the same measure as a system that went through three cycles in a millennium before reaching the steady state. For example, the underdamped curve in Figure 4.10 has an associated measure that defines its shape. This measure remains the same even if we change the time base from seconds to microseconds or to millennia.

A viable definition for this quantity is one that compares the exponential decay frequency of the envelope to the natural frequency. This ratio is constant regardless of the time scale of the response. Also, the reciprocal, which is proportional to the ratio of the natural period to the exponential time constant, remains the same regardless of the time base.

We define the *damping ratio, ζ,* to be

$$\zeta = \frac{\text{Exponential decay frequency}}{\text{Natural frequency (rad/second)}} = \frac{1}{2\pi} \frac{\text{Natural period (seconds)}}{\text{Exponential time constant}}$$

Let us now revise our description of the second-order system to reflect the new definitions. The general second-order system shown in Figure 4.7(*a*) can be transformed to show the quantities ζ and ω_n. Consider the general system

$$G(s) = \frac{b}{s^2 + as + b} \tag{4.16}$$

Without damping, the poles would be on the $j\omega$-axis, and the response would be an undamped sinusoid. For the poles to be purely imaginary, $a = 0$. Hence,

$$G(s) = \frac{b}{s^2 + b} \tag{4.17}$$

By definition, the natural frequency, ω_n, is the frequency of oscillation of this system. Since the poles of this system are on the $j\omega$-axis at $\pm j\sqrt{b}$,

$$\omega_n = \sqrt{b} \tag{4.18}$$

Hence,

$$b = \omega_n^2 \tag{4.19}$$

Now what is the term a in Eq. (4.16)? Assuming an underdamped system, the complex poles have a real part, σ, equal to $-a/2$. The magnitude of this value is then the exponential decay frequency described in Section 4.4. Hence,

$$\zeta = \frac{\text{Exponential decay frequency}}{\text{Natural frequency (rad/second)}} = \frac{|\sigma|}{\omega_n} = \frac{a/2}{\omega_n} \tag{4.20}$$

from which

$$a = 2\zeta\omega_n \tag{4.21}$$

Our general second-order transfer function finally looks like this:

$$G(s) = \frac{\omega_n^2}{s^2 + 2\zeta\omega_n s + \omega_n^2} \tag{4.22}$$

In the following example we find numerical values for ζ and ω_n by matching the transfer function to Eq. (4.22).

EXAMPLE 4.3

Finding ζ and ω_n for a second-order system

Problem: Given the transfer function of Eq. (4.23), find ζ and ω_n.

$$G(s) = \frac{36}{s^2 + 4.2s + 36} \tag{4.23}$$

SOLUTION: Comparing Eq. (4.23) to (4.22), $\omega_n^2 = 36$, from which $\omega_n = 6$. Also, $2\zeta\omega_n = 4.2$. Substituting the value of ω_n, $\zeta = 0.35$.

Now that we have defined ζ and ω_n, let us relate these quantities to the pole location. Solving for the poles of the transfer function in Eq. (4.22) yields

$$s_{1,2} = -\zeta\omega_n \pm \omega_n\sqrt{\zeta^2 - 1} \tag{4.24}$$

From Eq. (4.24) we see that the various cases of second-order response are a function of ζ; they are summarized in Figure 4.11.[4]

In the following example we find the numerical value of ζ and determine the nature of the transient response.

---

[4] The student should verify Figure 4.11 as an exercise.

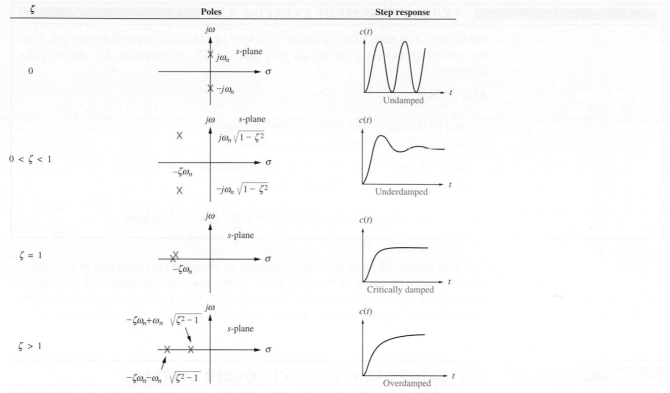

FIGURE 4.11 Second-order response as a function of damping ratio

---

EXAMPLE 4.4

Characterizing response from the value of ζ

Problem: For each of the systems shown in Figure 4.12, find the value of ζ and report the kind of response expected.

SOLUTION: First match the form of these systems to the forms shown in Eqs. (4.16) and (4.22). Since $a = 2\zeta\omega_n$ and $\omega_n = \sqrt{b}$,

$$\zeta = \frac{a}{2\sqrt{b}} \tag{4.25}$$

Using the values of a and b from each of the systems of Figure 4.12, we find $\zeta = 1.155$ for system (a), which is thus overdamped, since $\zeta > 1$; $\zeta = 1$ for system (b), which is thus critically damped; and $\zeta = 0.894$ for system (c), which is thus underdamped, since $\zeta < 1$.

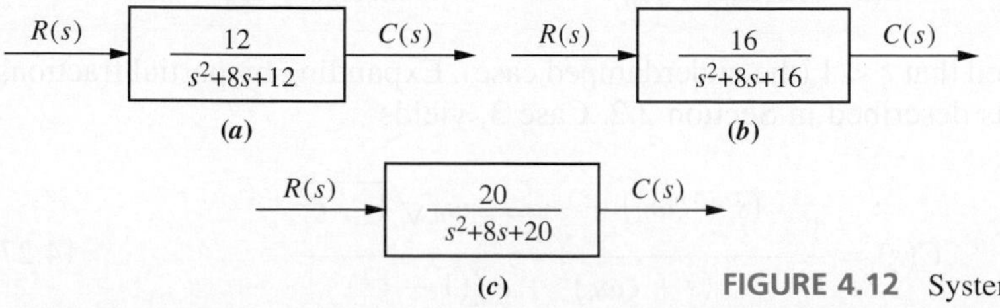

$$R(s) \longrightarrow \boxed{\dfrac{12}{s^2+8s+12}} \longrightarrow C(s) \qquad R(s) \longrightarrow \boxed{\dfrac{16}{s^2+8s+16}} \longrightarrow C(s)$$

$$(a) \qquad\qquad\qquad\qquad (b)$$

$$R(s) \longrightarrow \boxed{\dfrac{20}{s^2+8s+20}} \longrightarrow C(s)$$

$$(c)$$

FIGURE 4.12 Systems for Example 4.4

SKILL-ASSESSMENT EXERCISE 4.4

Problem: For each of the transfer functions in Skill-Assessment Exercise 4.3, do the following: (1) Find the values of ζ and ω_n; (2) characterize the nature of the response.

ANSWERS:

a. $\zeta = 0.3$, $\omega_n = 20$; system is underdamped

b. $\zeta = 1.5$, $\omega_n = 30$; system is overdamped

c. $\zeta = 1$, $\omega_n = 15$; system is critically damped

d. $\zeta = 0$, $\omega_n = 25$; system is undamped

The complete solution is located at www.wiley.com/college/nise.

This section defined two specifications, or parameters, of second-order systems: natural frequency, ω_n, and damping ratio, ζ. We saw that the nature of the response obtained was related to the value of ζ. Variations of damping ratio alone yield the complete range of overdamped, critically damped, underdamped, and undamped responses.

4.6 UNDERDAMPED SECOND-ORDER SYSTEMS

Now that we have generalized the second-order transfer function in terms of ζ and ω_n, let us analyze the step response of an *underdamped* second-order system. Not only will this response be found in terms of ζ and ω_n, but more specifications indigenous to the underdamped case will be defined. The underdamped second-order system, a common model for physical problems, displays unique behavior that must be itemized; a detailed description of the underdamped response is necessary for both analysis and design. Our first objective is to define transient specifications associated with underdamped responses. Next we relate these specifications to the pole location, drawing an association between pole location and the form of the underdamped second-order response. Finally, we tie the pole location to system parameters, thus closing the loop: Desired response generates required system components.

Let us begin by finding the step response for the general second-order system of Eq. (4.22). The transform of the response, $C(s)$, is the transform of the input times the transfer function, or

$$C(s) = \frac{\omega_n^2}{s(s^2 + 2\zeta\omega_n s + \omega_n^2)} = \frac{K_1}{s} + \frac{K_2 s + K_3}{s^2 + 2\zeta\omega_n s + \omega_n^2} \tag{4.26}$$

where it is assumed that $\zeta < 1$ (the underdamped case). Expanding by partial fractions, using the methods described in Section 2.2, Case 3, yields

$$C(s) = \frac{1}{s} - \frac{(s + \zeta\omega_n) + \dfrac{\zeta}{\sqrt{1-\zeta^2}}\omega_n\sqrt{1-\zeta^2}}{(s + \zeta\omega_n)^2 + \omega_n^2(1-\zeta^2)} \tag{4.27}$$

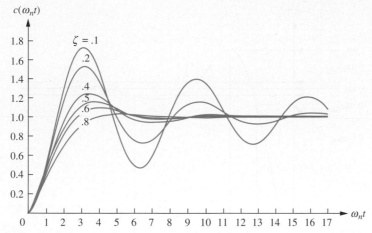

FIGURE 4.13 Second-order underdamped responses for damping ratio values

Taking the inverse Laplace transform, which is left as an exercise for the student, produces

$$
\begin{aligned}
c(t) &= 1 - e^{-\zeta\omega_n t}\left(\cos\omega_n\sqrt{1-\zeta^2}\,t + \frac{\zeta}{\sqrt{1-\zeta^2}}\sin\omega_n\sqrt{1-\zeta^2}\,t\right) \\
&= 1 - \frac{1}{\sqrt{1-\zeta^2}}e^{-\zeta\omega_n t}\cos\left(\omega_n\sqrt{1-\zeta^2}\,t - \phi\right)
\end{aligned}
\tag{4.28}
$$

where $\phi = \tan^{-1}(\zeta/\sqrt{1-\zeta^2})$.

A plot of this response appears in Figure 4.13 for various values of ζ, plotted along a time axis normalized to the natural frequency. We now see the relationship between the value of ζ and the type of response obtained: The lower the value of ζ, the more oscillatory the response. The natural frequency is a time-axis scale factor and does not affect the nature of the response other than to scale it in time.

We have defined two parameters associated with second-order systems, ζ and ω_n. Other parameters associated with the underdamped response are rise time, peak time, percent overshoot, and settling time. These specifications are defined as follows (see also Figure 4.14):

1. *Rise time, T_r.* The time required for the waveform to go from 0.1 of the final value to 0.9 of the final value.

2. *Peak time, T_P.* The time required to reach the first, or maximum, peak.

3. *Percent overshoot, %OS.* The amount that the waveform overshoots the steady-state, or final, value at the peak time, expressed as a percentage of the steady-state value.

4. *Settling time, T_s.* The time required for the transient's damped oscillations to reach and stay within ±2% of the steady-state value.

Notice that the definitions for settling time and rise time are basically the same as the definitions for the first-order response. All definitions are also valid for systems of order higher than 2, although analytical expressions for these parameters cannot be found unless the response of the higher-order system can be approximated as a second-order system, which we do in Sections 4.7 and 4.8.

Rise time, peak time, and settling time yield information about the speed of the transient response. This information can help a designer determine if the speed and the

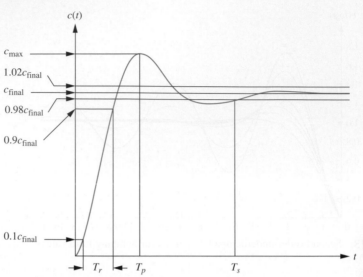

FIGURE 4.14 Second-order underdamped response specifications

nature of the response do or do not degrade the performance of the system. For example, the speed of an entire computer system depends on the time it takes for a floppy disk drive head to reach steady state and read data; passenger comfort depends in part on the suspension system of a car and the number of oscillations it goes through after hitting a bump.

We now evaluate T_p, $\%OS$, and T_s as functions of ζ and ω_n. Later in this chapter we relate these specifications to the location of the system poles. A precise analytical expression for rise time cannot be obtained; thus, we present a plot and a table showing the relationship between ζ and rise time.

EVALUATION OF T_p

T_p is found by differentiating $c(t)$ in Eq. (4.28) and finding the first zero crossing after $t = 0$. This task is simplified by "differentiating" in the frequency domain by using Item 7 of Table 2.2. Assuming zero initial conditions and using Eq. (4.26), we get

$$\mathscr{L}[\dot{c}(t)] = sC(s) = \frac{\omega_n^2}{s^2 + 2\zeta\omega_n s + \omega_n^2} \tag{4.29}$$

Completing squares in the denominator, we have

$$\mathscr{L}[\dot{c}(t)] = \frac{\omega_n^2}{(s + \zeta\omega_n)^2 + \omega_n^2(1 - \zeta^2)} = \frac{\dfrac{\omega_n}{\sqrt{1 - \zeta^2}}\omega_n\sqrt{1 - \zeta^2}}{(s + \zeta\omega_n)^2 + \omega_n^2(1 - \zeta^2)} \tag{4.30}$$

Therefore,

$$\dot{c}(t) = \frac{\omega_n}{\sqrt{1 - \zeta^2}} e^{-\zeta\omega_n t} \sin \omega_n \sqrt{1 - \zeta^2}\, t \tag{4.31}$$

Setting the derivative equal to zero yields

$$\omega_n \sqrt{1 - \zeta^2}\, t = n\pi \tag{4.32}$$

or

$$t = \frac{n\pi}{\omega_n\sqrt{1-\zeta^2}} \tag{4.33}$$

Each value of n yields the time for local maxima or minima. Letting $n = 0$ yields $t = 0$, the first point on the curve in Figure 4.14 that has zero slope. The first peak, which occurs at the peak time, T_p, is found by letting $n = 1$ in Eq. (4.33):

$$T_p = \frac{\pi}{\omega_n\sqrt{1-\zeta^2}} \tag{4.34}$$

EVALUATION OF %OS

From Figure 4.14 the percent overshoot, $\%OS$, is given by

$$\%OS = \frac{c_{max} - c_{final}}{c_{final}} \times 100 \tag{4.35}$$

The term c_{max} is found by evaluating $c(t)$ at the peak time, $c(T_p)$. Using Eq. (4.34) for T_p and substituting into Eq. (4.28) yields

$$c_{max} = c(T_p) = 1 - e^{-(\zeta\pi/\sqrt{1-\zeta^2})}\left(\cos\pi + \frac{\zeta}{\sqrt{1-\zeta^2}}\sin\pi\right) \tag{4.36}$$

$$= 1 + e^{-(\zeta\pi/\sqrt{1-\zeta^2})}$$

For the unit step used for Eq. (4.28),

$$c_{final} = 1 \tag{4.37}$$

Substituting Eqs. (4.36) and (4.37) into Eq. (4.35), we finally obtain

$$\%OS = e^{-(\zeta\pi/\sqrt{1-\zeta^2})} \times 100 \tag{4.38}$$

Notice that the percent overshoot is a function only of the damping ratio, ζ.

Whereas Eq. (4.38) allows one to find $\%OS$ given ζ, the inverse of the equation allows one to solve for ζ given $\%OS$. The inverse is given by

$$\zeta = \frac{-\ln(\%OS/100)}{\sqrt{\pi^2 + \ln^2(\%OS/100)}} \tag{4.39}$$

The derivation of Eq. (4.39) is left as an exercise for the student. Equation (4.38) (or, equivalently, (4.39)) is plotted in Figure 4.15.

EVALUATION OF T_s

In order to find the settling time, we must find the time for which $c(t)$ in Eq. (4.28) reaches and stays within $\pm2\%$ of the steady-state value, c_{final}. Using our definition, the settling time is the time it takes for the amplitude of the decaying sinusoid in Eq. (4.28) to reach 0.02, or

$$e^{-\zeta\omega_n t}\frac{1}{\sqrt{1-\zeta^2}} = 0.02 \tag{4.40}$$

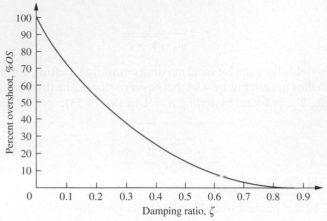

FIGURE 4.15 Percent overshoot versus damping ratio

This equation is a conservative estimate, since we are assuming that $\cos(\omega_n\sqrt{1-\zeta^2}t - \phi) = 1$ at the settling time. Solving Eq. (4.40) for t, the settling time is

$$T_s = \frac{-\ln(0.02\sqrt{1-\zeta^2})}{\zeta\omega_n} \tag{4.41}$$

You can verify that the numerator of Eq. (4.41) varies from 3.91 to 4.74 as ζ varies from 0 to 0.9. Let us agree on an approximation for the settling time that will be used for all values of ζ; let it be

$$\boxed{T_s = \frac{4}{\zeta\omega_n}} \tag{4.42}$$

EVALUATION OF T_r

A precise analytical relationship between rise time and damping ratio, ζ, cannot be found. However, using a computer and Eq. (4.28), the rise time can be found. We first designate $\omega_n t$ as the normalized time variable and select a value for ζ. Using the

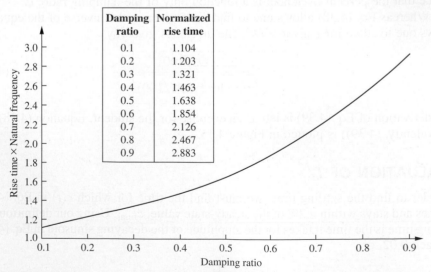

Damping ratio	Normalized rise time
0.1	1.104
0.2	1.203
0.3	1.321
0.4	1.463
0.5	1.638
0.6	1.854
0.7	2.126
0.8	2.467
0.9	2.883

FIGURE 4.16 Normalized rise time versus damping ratio for a second-order underdamped response

computer, we solve for the values of $\omega_n t$ that yield $c(t) = 0.9$ and $c(t) = 0.1$. Subtracting the two values of $\omega_n t$ yields the normalized rise time, $\omega_n T_r$, for that value of ζ. Continuing in like fashion with other values of ζ, we obtain the results plotted in Figure 4.16.[5] Let us look at an example.

EXAMPLE 4.5

Finding T_p, %OS, T_s, and T_r from a transfer function

Problem: Given the transfer function

$$G(s) = \frac{100}{s^2 + 15s + 100} \tag{4.43}$$

find T_p, %OS, T_s, and T_r.

SOLUTION: ω_n and ζ are calculated as 10 and 0.75, respectively. Now substitute ζ and ω_n into Eqs. (4.34), (4.38), and (4.42) and find, respectively, that $T_p = 0.475$ second, %OS $= 2.838$, and $T_s = 0.533$ second. Using the table in Figure 4.16, the normalized rise time is approximately 2.3 seconds. Dividing by ω_n yields $T_r = 0.23$ second. This problem demonstrates that we can find T_p, %OS, T_s, and T_r without the tedious task of taking an inverse Laplace transform, plotting the output response, and taking measurements from the plot.

We now have expressions that relate peak time, percent overshoot, and settling time to the natural frequency and the damping ratio. Now let us relate these quantities to the location of the poles that generate these characteristics.

The pole plot for a general, underdamped second-order system, previously shown in Figure 4.11, is reproduced and expanded in Figure 4.17 for focus. We see from the Pythagorean theorem that the radial distance from the origin to the pole is the natural frequency, ω_n, and the $\cos\theta = \zeta$.

Now, comparing Eqs. (4.34) and (4.42) with the pole location, we evaluate peak time and settling time in terms of the pole location. Thus,

$$T_p = \frac{\pi}{\omega_n\sqrt{1-\zeta^2}} = \frac{\pi}{\omega_d} \tag{4.44}$$

$$T_s = \frac{4}{\zeta\omega_n} = \frac{4}{\sigma_d} \tag{4.45}$$

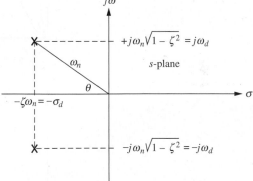

FIGURE 4.17 Pole plot for an underdamped second-order system

where ω_d is the imaginary part of the pole and is called the *damped frequency of oscillation,* and σ_d is the magnitude of the real part of the pole and is the *exponential damping frequency.*

Equation (4.44) shows that T_p is inversely proportional to the imaginary part of the pole. Since horizontal lines on the s-plane are lines of constant imaginary value, they are also lines of constant peak time. Similarly, Eq. (4.45) tells us that settling time is inversely proportional to the real part of the pole. Since vertical lines on the s-plane are

---

[5] Figure 4.16 can be approximated by the following polynomials: $\omega_n T_r = 1.76\zeta^3 - 0.417\zeta^2 + 1.039\zeta + 1$ (maximum error less than $\frac{1}{2}$% for $0 < \zeta < 0.9$), and $\zeta = 0.115(\omega_n T_r)^3 - 0.883(\omega_n T_r)^2 + 2.504(\omega_n T_r) - 1.738$ (maximum error less than 5% for $0.1 < \zeta < 0.9$). The polynomials were obtained using MATLAB's **polyfit** function.

FIGURE 4.18 Lines of constant peak time, T_p, settling time, T_s, and percent overshoot, %OS. Note: $T_{s_2} < T_{s_1}$; $T_{p_2} < T_{p_1}$; %OS_1 < %OS_2

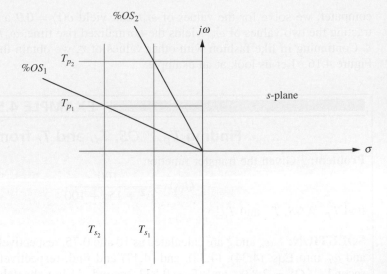

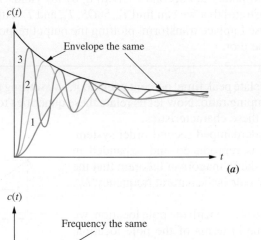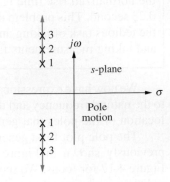

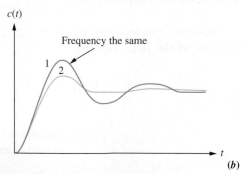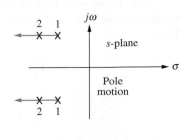

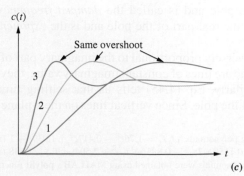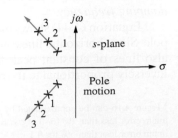

FIGURE 4.19 Step responses of second-order underdamped systems as poles move: **a.** with constant real part; **b.** with constant imaginary part; **c.** with constant damping ratio

lines of constant real value, they are also lines of constant settling time. Finally, since $\zeta = \cos\theta$, radial lines are lines of constant ζ. Since percent overshoot is only a function of ζ, radial lines are thus lines of constant percent overshoot, $\%OS$. These concepts are depicted in Figure 4.18, where lines of constant T_p, T_s, and $\%OS$ are labeled on the s-plane.

At this point we can understand the significance of Figure 4.18 by examining the actual step response of comparative systems. Depicted in Figure 4.19(a) are the step responses as the poles are moved in a vertical direction, keeping the real part the same. As the poles move in a vertical direction, the frequency increases, but the envelope remains the same since the real part of the pole is not changing. The figure shows a constant exponential envelope, even though the sinusoidal response is changing frequency. Since all curves fit under the same exponential decay curve, the settling time is virtually the same for all waveforms. Note that as overshoot increases, the rise time decreases.

Let us move the poles to the right or left. Since the imaginary part is now constant, movement of the poles yields the responses of Figure 4.19(b). Here the frequency is constant over the range of variation of the real part. As the poles move to the left, the response damps out more rapidly, while the frequency remains the same. Notice that the peak time is the same for all waveforms because the imaginary part remains the same.

Moving the poles along a constant radial line yields the responses shown in Figure 4.19(c). Here the percent overshoot remains the same. Notice also that the responses look exactly alike, except for their speed. The farther the poles are from the origin, the more rapid the response.

We conclude this section with some examples that demonstrate the relationship between the pole location and the specifications of the second-order underdamped response. The first example covers analysis. The second example is a simple design problem consisting of a physical system whose component values we want to design to meet a transient response specification.

EXAMPLE 4.6

Finding T_p, $\%OS$, and T_s from pole location

Problem: Given the pole plot shown in Figure 4.20, find ζ, ω_n, T_p, $\%OS$, and T_s.

SOLUTION: The damping ratio is given by $\zeta = \cos\theta = \cos[\arctan(7/3)] = 0.394$. The natural frequency, ω_n, is the radial distance from the origin to the pole, or $\omega_n = \sqrt{7^2 + 3^2} = 7.616$. The peak time is

$$T_p = \frac{\pi}{\omega_d} = \frac{\pi}{7} = 0.449 \text{ second} \tag{4.46}$$

The percent overshoot is

$$\%OS = e^{-(\zeta\pi/\sqrt{1-\zeta^2})} \times 100 = 26\% \tag{4.47}$$

The approximate settling time is

$$T_s = \frac{4}{\sigma_d} = \frac{4}{3} = 1.333 \text{ seconds} \tag{4.48}$$

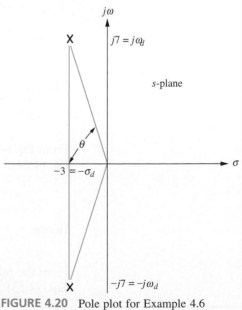

FIGURE 4.20 Pole plot for Example 4.6

MATLAB

Students who are using MATLAB should now run ch4p1 in Appendix B. You will learn how to generate a second-order polynomial from two complex poles as well as extract and use the coefficients of the polynomial to calculate T_p, %OS, and T_s. This exercise uses MATLAB to solve the problem in Example 4.6.

EXAMPLE 4.7

Design

Transient response through component design

Problem: Given the system shown in Figure 4.21, find J and D to yield 20% overshoot and a settling time of 2 seconds for a step input of torque $T(t)$.

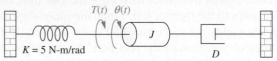

$T(t)$ $\theta(t)$

$K = 5$ N-m/rad

D

J

FIGURE 4.21 Rotational mechanical system for Example 4.7

SOLUTION: First, the transfer function for the system is

$$G(s) = \frac{1/J}{s^2 + \dfrac{D}{J}s + \dfrac{K}{J}} \qquad (4.49)$$

From the transfer function,

$$\omega_n = \sqrt{\frac{K}{J}} \qquad (4.50)$$

and

$$2\zeta\omega_n = \frac{D}{J} \qquad (4.51)$$

But, from the problem statement,

$$T_s = 2 = \frac{4}{\zeta\omega_n} \qquad (4.52)$$

or $\zeta\omega_n = 2$. Hence,

$$2\zeta\omega_n = 4 = \frac{D}{J} \qquad (4.53)$$

Also, from Eqs. (4.50) and (4.52),

$$\zeta = \frac{4}{2\omega_n} = 2\sqrt{\frac{J}{K}} \qquad (4.54)$$

From Eq. (4.39), a 20% overshoot implies $\zeta = 0.456$. Therefore, from Eq. (4.54),

$$\zeta = 2\sqrt{\frac{J}{K}} = 0.456 \qquad (4.55)$$

Hence,

$$\frac{J}{K} = 0.052 \qquad (4.56)$$

From the problem statement, $K = 5$ N-m/rad. Combining this value with Eqs. (4.53) and (4.56), $D = 1.04$ N-m-s/rad, and $J = 0.26$ kg-m^2.

SECOND-ORDER TRANSFER FUNCTIONS VIA TESTING

Just as we obtained the transfer function of a first-order system experimentally, we can do the same for a system that exhibits a typical underdamped second-order response. Again, we can measure the laboratory response curve for percent overshoot and settling time, from which we can find the poles and hence the denominator. The numerator can be found, as in the first-order system, from a knowledge of the measured and expected steady-state values. A problem at the end of the chapter illustrates the estimation of a second-order transfer function from the step response.

SKILL-ASSESSMENT EXERCISE 4.5

Problem: Find ζ, ω_n, T_s, T_p, T_r, and %OS for a system whose transfer function is $G(s) = \dfrac{361}{s^2 + 16s + 361}$.

ANSWERS: $\zeta = 0.421$, $\omega_n = 19$, $T_s = 0.5$ s, $T_p = 0.182$ s, $T_r = 0.079$ s, and %OS $= 23.3\%$.

The complete solution is located at www.wiley.com/college/nise.

WileyPLUS

Control Solutions

TryIt 4.1

Use the following MATLAB statements to calculate the answers to Skill-Assessment Exercise 4.5. Ellipses mean code continues on next line.

```
numg=361;
deng=[1 16 361];
omegan=sqrt(deng(3)...
   /deng(1))
zeta=(deng(2)/deng(1))...
   /(2*omegan)
Ts=4/(zeta*omegan)
Tp=pi/(omegan*sqrt
   (1-zeta^2))
pos=100*exp(-zeta*
   pi/sqrt(1-zeta^2))
Tr=(1.768*zeta^3-...
0.417*zeta^2+1.039*
   zeta+1)/omegan
```

Now that we have analyzed systems with two poles, how does the addition of another pole affect the response? We answer this question in the next section.

4.7 SYSTEM RESPONSE WITH ADDITIONAL POLES

In the last section we analyzed systems with one or two poles. It must be emphasized that the formulas describing percent overshoot, settling time, and peak time were derived only for a system with two complex poles and no zeros. If a system such as that shown in Figure 4.22 has more than two poles or has zeros, we cannot use the formulas to calculate the performance specifications that we derived. However, under certain conditions, a system with more than two poles or with zeros can be approximated as a second-order system that has just two complex *dominant poles*. Once we justify this approximation, the formulas for percent overshoot, settling time, and peak time can be applied to these higher-order systems by using the location of the dominant poles. In this section we investigate the effect of an additional pole on the second-order response. In the next section we analyze the effect of adding a zero to a two-pole system.

Let us now look at the conditions that would have to exist in order to approximate the behavior of a three-pole system as that of a two-pole system. Consider a three-pole system with complex poles and a third pole on the real axis. Assuming that the complex poles

FIGURE 4.22 The Cybermotion SR3 security robot on patrol. The robot navigates by ultrasound and path programs transmitted from a computer, eliminating the need for guide strips on the floor. It has video capabilities as well as temperature, humidity, fire, intrusion, and gas sensors.

are at $-\zeta\omega_n \pm j\omega_n\sqrt{1-\zeta^2}$ and the real pole is at $-\alpha_r$, the step response of the system can be determined from a partial-fraction expansion. Thus, the output transform is

$$C(s) = \frac{A}{s} + \frac{B(s+\zeta\omega_n) + C\omega_d}{(s+\zeta\omega_n)^2 + \omega_d^2} + \frac{D}{s+\alpha_r} \tag{4.57}$$

or, in the time domain,

$$c(t) = Au(t) + e^{-\zeta\omega_n t}(B\cos\omega_d t + C\sin\omega_d t) + De^{-\alpha_r t} \tag{4.58}$$

The component parts of *c(t)* are shown in Figure 4.23 for three cases of α_r. For Case I, $\alpha_r = \alpha_{r_1}$ and is not much larger than $\zeta\omega_n$; for Case II, $\alpha_r = \alpha_{r_2}$ and is much larger than $\zeta\omega_n$; and for Case III, $\alpha_r = \infty$.

Let us direct our attention to Eq. (4.58) and Figure 4.23. If $\alpha_r \gg \zeta\omega_n$ (Case II), the pure exponential will die out much more rapidly than the second-order underdamped step response. If the pure exponential term decays to an insignificant value at the time of the first overshoot, such parameters as percent overshoot, settling time, and peak time will be generated by the second-order underdamped step response component. Thus, the total response will approach that of a pure second-order system (Case III).

If α_r is not much greater than $\zeta\omega_n$ (Case I), the real pole's transient response will not decay to insignificance at the peak time or settling time generated by the second-order pair. In this case, the exponential decay is significant, and the system cannot be represented as a second-order system.

The next question is, How much farther from the dominant poles does the third pole have to be for its effect on the second-order response to be negligible? The answer of course depends on the accuracy for which you are looking. However, this book assumes that the exponential decay is negligible after five time constants. Thus, if the real pole is five times farther to the left than the dominant poles, we assume that the system is represented by its dominant second-order pair of poles.

What about the magnitude of the exponential decay? Can it be so large that its contribution at the peak time is not negligible? We can show, through a partial-fraction

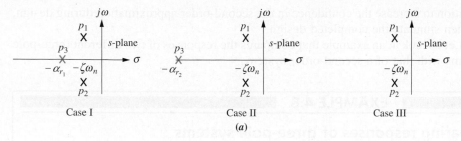

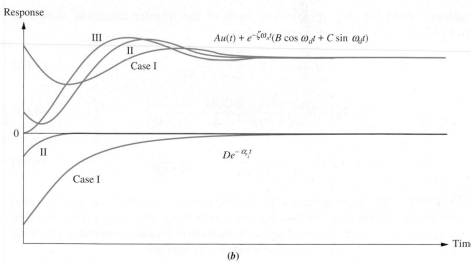

FIGURE 4.23 Component responses of a three-pole system: **a.** pole plot; **b.** component responses: Nondominant pole is near dominant second-order pair (Case I), far from the pair (Case II), and at infinity (Case III)

expansion, that the residue of the third pole, in a three-pole system with dominant second-order poles and no zeros, will actually decrease in magnitude as the third pole is moved farther into the left half-plane. Assume a step response, $C(s)$, of a three-pole system:

$$C(s) = \frac{bc}{s(s^2 + as + b)(s + c)} = \frac{A}{s} + \frac{Bs + C}{s^2 + as + b} + \frac{D}{s + c} \qquad (4.59)$$

where we assume that the nondominant pole is located at $-c$ on the real axis and that the steady-state response approaches unity. Evaluating the constants in the numerator of each term,

$$A = 1; \qquad\qquad B = \frac{ca - c^2}{c^2 + b - ca} \qquad (4.60a)$$

$$C = \frac{ca^2 - c^2 a - bc}{c^2 + b - ca}; \quad D = \frac{-b}{c^2 + b - ca} \qquad (4.60b)$$

As the nondominant pole approaches ∞, or $c \to \infty$,

$$A = 1; \quad B = -1; \quad C = -a; \quad D = 0 \qquad (4.61)$$

Thus, for this example, D, the residue of the nondominant pole and its response, becomes zero as the nondominant pole approaches infinity.

The designer can also choose to forgo extensive residue analysis, since all system designs should be simulated to determine final acceptance. In this case the control systems engineer can use the "five times" rule of thumb as a necessary but not sufficient condition to increase the confidence in the second-order approximation during design, but then simulate the completed design.

　　Let us look at an example that compares the responses of two different three-pole systems with that of a second-order system.

EXAMPLE 4.8

Comparing responses of three-pole systems

Problem: Find the step response of each of the transfer functions shown in Eqs. (4.62) through (4.64) and compare them.

$$T_1(s) = \frac{24.542}{s^2 + 4s + 24.542} \tag{4.62}$$

$$T_2(s) = \frac{245.42}{(s + 10)(s^2 + 4s + 24.542)} \tag{4.63}$$

$$T_3(s) = \frac{73.626}{(s + 3)(s^2 + 4s + 24.542)} \tag{4.64}$$

SOLUTION: The step response, $C_i(s)$, for the transfer function, $T_i(s)$, can be found by multiplying the transfer function by $1/s$, a step input, and using partial-fraction expansion followed by the inverse Laplace transform to find the response, $c_i(t)$. With the details left as an exercise for the student, the results are

$$c_1(t) = 1 - 1.09e^{-2t}\cos(4.532t - 23.8°) \tag{4.65}$$

$$c_2(t) = 1 - 0.29e^{-10t} - 1.189e^{-2t}\cos(4.532t - 53.34°) \tag{4.66}$$

$$c_3(t) = 1 - 1.14e^{-3t} + 0.707e^{-2t}\cos(4.532t + 78.63°) \tag{4.67}$$

The three responses are plotted in Figure 4.24. Notice that $c_2(t)$, with its third pole at -10 and farthest from the dominant poles, is the better approximation of $c_1(t)$, the pure second-order system response; $c_3(t)$, with a third pole close to the dominant poles, yields the most error.

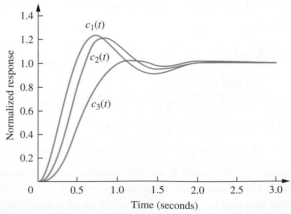

FIGURE 4.24 Step responses of system $T_1(s)$, system $T_2(s)$, and system $T_3(s)$

Students who are using MATLAB should now run ch4p2 in Appendix B. You will learn how to generate a step response for a transfer function and how to plot the response directly or collect the points for future use. The example shows how to collect the points and then use them to create a multiple plot, title the graph, and label the axes and curves to produce the graph in Figure 4.24 to solve Example 4.8.

System responses can alternately be obtained using Simulink. Simulink is a software package that is integrated with MATLAB to provide a graphical user interface (GUI) for defining systems and generating responses. The reader is encouraged to study Appendix C, which contains a tutorial on Simulink as well as some examples. One of the illustrative examples, Example C.1, solves Example 4.8 using Simulink.

Another method to obtain systems responses is through the use of MATLAB's LTI Viewer. An advantage of the LTI Viewer is that it displays the values of settling time, peak time, rise time, maximum response, and the final value on the step response plot. The reader is encouraged to study Appendix D on the Wiley web site at www.wiley.com/college/nise, which contains a tutorial on the LTI Viewer as well as some examples. Example D.1 solves. Example 4.8 using the LTI Viewer.

SKILL-ASSESSMENT EXERCISE 4.6

Problem: Determine the validity of a second-order approximation for each of these two transfer functions:

a. $G(s) = \dfrac{700}{(s+15)(s^2+4s+100)}$

b. $G(s) = \dfrac{360}{(s+4)(s^2+2s+90)}$

ANSWERS:

a. The second-order approximation is valid.

b. The second-order approximation is not valid.

The complete solution is located at www.wiley.com/college/nise.

TryIt 4.2

Use the following MATLAB and Control System Toolbox statements to investigate the effect of the additional pole in Skill-Assessment Exercise 4.6(a). Move the higher-order pole originally at -15 to other values by changing "a" in the code.

```
a = 15
numga = 100*a;
denga = conv([1 a],...
  [1 4 100]);
Ta = tf(numga, denga);
numg = 100;
deng = [1 4 100];
T = tf(numg, deng);
step(Ta,',',T,'-')
```

4.8 SYSTEM RESPONSE WITH ZEROS

Now that we have seen the effect of an additional pole, let us add a zero to the second-order system. In Section 4.2 we saw that the zeros of a response affect the residue, or amplitude, of a response component but do not affect the nature of the response—exponential, damped sinusoid, and so on. In this section we add a real-axis zero to a two-pole system. The zero will be added first in the left half-plane and then in the right half-plane and its effects noted and analyzed. We conclude the section by talking about pole-zero cancellation.

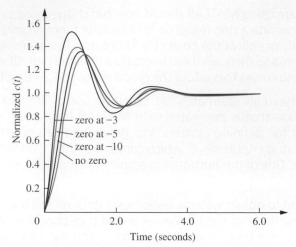

FIGURE 4.25   Effect of adding a zero to a two-pole system

Starting with a two-pole system with poles at $(-1 \pm j2.828)$, we consecutively add zeros at -3, -5, and -10. The results, normalized to the steady-state value, are plotted in Figure 4.25. We can see that the closer the zero is to the dominant poles, the greater its effect on the transient response. As the zero moves away from the dominant poles, the response approaches that of the two-pole system. This analysis can be reasoned via the partial-fraction expansion. If we assume a group of poles and a zero far from the poles, the residue of each pole will be affected the same by the zero. Hence, the relative amplitudes remain appreciably the same. For example, assume the partial-fraction expansion shown in Eq. (4.68):

$$
\begin{aligned}
T(s) &= \frac{(s+a)}{(s+b)(s+c)} = \frac{A}{s+b} + \frac{B}{s+c} \\
&= \frac{(-b+a)/(-b+c)}{s+b} + \frac{(-c+a)/(-c+b)}{s+c}
\end{aligned}
\tag{4.68}
$$

If the zero is far from the poles, then a is large compared to b and c, and

$$
T(s) \approx a\left[\frac{1/(-b+c)}{s+b} + \frac{1/(-c+b)}{s+c}\right] = \frac{a}{(s+b)(s+c)}
\tag{4.69}
$$

Hence, the zero looks like a simple gain factor and does not change the relative amplitudes of the components of the response.

Another way to look at the effect of a zero, which is more general, is as follows (*Franklin, 1991*): Let $C(s)$ be the response of a system, $T(s)$, with unity in the numerator. If we add a zero to the transfer function, yielding $(s+a)T(s)$, the Laplace transform of the response will be

$$
\boxed{(s+a)C(s) = sC(s) + aC(s)}
\tag{4.70}
$$

Thus, the response of a system with a zero consists of two parts: the derivative of the original response and a scaled version of the original response. If a, the negative of the zero, is very large, the Laplace transform of the response is approximately $aC(s)$, or a scaled version of the original response. If a is not very large, the response has an additional component consisting of the derivative of the original response. As a

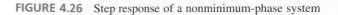

FIGURE 4.26 Step response of a nonminimum-phase system

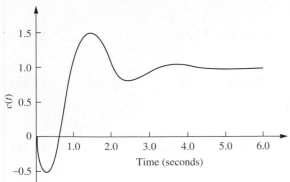

becomes smaller, the derivative term contributes more to the response and has a greater effect. For step responses, the derivative is typically positive at the start of a step response. Thus, for small values of a, we can expect more overshoot in second-order systems because the derivative term will be additive around the first overshoot. This reasoning is borne out by Figure 4.25.

An interesting phenomenon occurs if a is negative, placing the zero in the right half-plane. From Eq. (4.70) we see that the derivative term, which is typically positive initially, will be of opposite sign from the scaled response term. Thus, if the derivative term, $sC(s)$, is larger than the scaled response, $aC(s)$, the response will initially follow the derivative in the opposite direction from the scaled response. The result for a second-order system is shown in Figure 4.26, where the sign of the input was reversed to yield a positive steady-state value. Notice that the response begins to turn toward the negative direction even though the final value is positive. A system that exhibits this phenomenon is known as a *nonminimum-phase* system. If a motorcycle or airplane was a non-minimum-phase system, it would initially veer left when commanded to steer right.

Let us now look at an example of an electrical nonminimum-phase network.

EXAMPLE 4.9

Transfer function of a nonminimum-phase system

Problem:

a. Find the transfer function, $V_o(s)/V_i(s)$, for the operational amplifier circuit shown in Figure 4.27.

b. If $R_1 = R_2$, this circuit is known as an all-pass filter, since it passes sine waves of a wide range of frequencies without attenuating or amplifying their magnitude (*Dorf, 1993*). We will learn more about frequency response in Chapter 10. For now, let $R_1 = R_2$, $R_3C = 1/10$, and find the step response of the filter. Show that component parts of the response can be identified with those in Eq. (4.70).

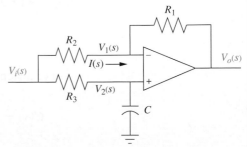

FIGURE 4.27 Nonminimum-phase electric circuit

SOLUTION:

a. Remembering from Chapter 2 that the operational amplifier has a high input impedance, the current, $I(s)$, through R_1 and R_2, is the same and is equal to

$$I(s) = \frac{V_i(s) - V_o(s)}{R_1 + R_2} \tag{4.71}$$

Also,

$$V_o(s) = A(V_2(s) - V_1(s)) \tag{4.72}$$

But

$$V_1(s) = I(s)R_1 + V_o(s) \tag{4.73}$$

Substituting Eq. (4.71) into (4.73),

$$V_1(s) = \frac{1}{R_1 + R_2}(R_1 V_i(s) + R_2 V_0(s)) \tag{4.74}$$

Using voltage division,

$$V_2(s) = V_i(s)\frac{1/Cs}{R_3 + \dfrac{1}{Cs}} \tag{4.75}$$

Substituting Eqs. (4.74) and (4.75) into Eq. (4.72) and simplifying yields

$$\frac{V_o(s)}{V_i(s)} = \frac{A(R_2 - R_1 R_3 Cs)}{(R_3 Cs + 1)(R_1 + R_2(1 + A))} \tag{4.76}$$

Since the operational amplifier has a large gain, A, let A approach infinity. Thus, after simplification

$$\frac{V_o(s)}{V_i(s)} = \frac{R_2 - R_1 R_3 Cs}{R_2 R_3 Cs + R_2} = -\frac{R_1}{R_2}\frac{\left(s - \dfrac{R_2}{R_1 R_3 C}\right)}{\left(s + \dfrac{1}{R_3 C}\right)} \tag{4.77}$$

b. Letting $R_1 = R_2$ and $R_3 C = 1/10$,

$$\frac{V_o(s)}{V_i(s)} = -\frac{\left(s - \dfrac{1}{R_3 C}\right)}{\left(s + \dfrac{1}{R_3 C}\right)} = -\frac{(s - 10)}{(s + 10)} \tag{4.78}$$

For a step input we evaluate the response as suggested by Eq. (4.70):

$$C(s) = -\frac{(s - 10)}{s(s + 10)} = -\frac{1}{s + 10} + 10\frac{1}{s(s + 10)} = sC_o(s) - 10C_o(s) \tag{4.79}$$

where

$$C_o(s) = -\frac{1}{s(s + 10)} \tag{4.80}$$

is the Laplace transform of the response without a zero. Expanding Eq. (4.79) into partial fractions,

$$C(s) = -\frac{1}{s + 10} + 10\frac{1}{s(s + 10)} = -\frac{1}{s + 10} + \frac{1}{s} - \frac{1}{s + 10} = \frac{1}{s} - \frac{2}{s + 10} \tag{4.81}$$

or the response with a zero is

$$c(t) = -e^{-10t} + 1 - e^{-10t} = 1 - 2e^{-10t} \tag{4.82}$$

Also, from Eq. (4.80),

$$C_o(s) = -\frac{1/10}{s} + \frac{1/10}{s + 10} \tag{4.83}$$

or the response without a zero is

$$c_o(t) = -\frac{1}{10} + \frac{1}{10}e^{-10t} \tag{4.84}$$

The normalized responses are plotted in Figure 4.28. Notice the immediate reversal of the nonminimum-phase response, $c(t)$.

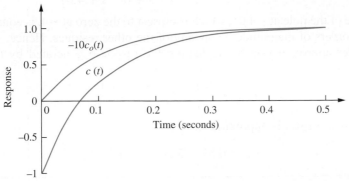

FIGURE 4.28 Step response of the nonminimum-phase network of Figure 4.27 ($c(t)$) and normalized step response of an equivalent network without the zero ($-10c_o(t)$)

We conclude this section by talking about pole-zero cancellation and its effect on our ability to make second-order approximations to a system. Assume a three-pole system with a zero as shown in Eq. (4.85). If the pole term, $(s + p_3)$, and the zero term, $(s + z)$, cancel out, we are left with

$$T(s) = \frac{K(s + z)}{(s + p_3)(s^2 + as + b)} \tag{4.85}$$

as a second-order transfer function. From another perspective, if the zero at $-z$ is very close to the pole at $-p_3$, then a partial fraction expansion of Eq. (4.85) will show that the residue of the exponential decay is much smaller than the amplitude of the second-order response. Let us look at an example.

EXAMPLE 4.10

Evaluating pole-zero cancellation using residues

Problem: For each of the response functions in Eqs. (4.86) and (4.87), determine whether there is cancellation between the zero and the pole closest to the zero.

TryIt 4.4

Use the following MATLAB and Symbolic Math Toolbox statements to evaluate the effect of higher-order poles by finding the component parts of the time response of $c_1(t)$ and $c_2(t)$ in Example 4.10.

```
syms s
C1=26.25*(s+4)/...
  (s*(s+3.5)*...
(s+5)*(s+6));
C2=26.25*(s+4)/...
  (s*(s+4.01)*...
(s+5)*(s+6));
c1=ilaplace(C1);
c1=vpa(c1,3);
pretty(c1)
c2=ilaplace(C2);
c2=vpa(c2,3);
pretty(c2);
```

For any function for which pole-zero cancellation is valid, find the approximate response.

$$C_1(s) = \frac{26.25(s+4)}{s(s+3.5)(s+5)(s+6)} \tag{4.86}$$

$$C_2(s) = \frac{26.25(s+4)}{s(s+4.01)(s+5)(s+6)} \tag{4.87}$$

SOLUTION: The partial-fraction expansion of Eq. (4.86) is

$$C_1(s) = \frac{1}{s} - \frac{3.5}{s+5} + \frac{3.5}{s+6} - \frac{1}{s+3.5} \tag{4.88}$$

The residue of the pole at -3.5, which is closest to the zero at -4, is equal to 1 and is not negligible compared to the other residues. Thus, a second-order step response approximation cannot be made for $C_1(s)$. The partial-fraction expansion for $C_2(s)$ is

$$C_2(s) = \frac{0.87}{s} - \frac{5.3}{s+5} + \frac{4.4}{s+6} + \frac{0.033}{s+4.01} \tag{4.89}$$

The residue of the pole at -4.01, which is closest to the zero at -4, is equal to 0.033, about two orders of magnitude below any of the other residues. Hence, we make a second-order approximation by neglecting the response generated by the pole at -4.01:

$$c_2(s) \approx \frac{0.87}{s} - \frac{5.3}{s+5} + \frac{4.4}{s+6} \tag{4.90}$$

and the response $c_2(t)$ is approximately

$$c_2(t) \approx 0.87 - 5.3e^{-5t} + 4.4e^{-6t} \tag{4.91}$$

WileyPLUS

Control Solutions

SKILL-ASSESSMENT EXERCISE 4.7

Problem: Determine the validity of a second-order step-response approximation for each transfer function shown below.

a. $G(s) = \dfrac{185.71(s+7)}{(s+6.5)(s+10)(s+20)}$

b. $G(s) = \dfrac{197.14(s+7)}{(s+6.9)(s+10)(s+20)}$

ANSWERS:

a. A second-order approximation is not valid.

b. A second-order approximation is valid.

The complete solution is located at www.wiley.com/college/nise.

In this section we have examined the effects of additional transfer function poles and zeros upon the response. In the next section we add nonlinearities of the type discussed in Section 2.10 and see what effects they have on system response.

4.9 EFFECTS OF NONLINEARITIES UPON TIME RESPONSE

In this section we qualitatively examine the effects of nonlinearities upon the time response of physical systems. In the following examples we insert nonlinearities, such as saturation, dead zone, and backlash, as shown in Figure 2.46, into a system to show the effects of these nonlinearities upon the linear responses.

The responses were obtained using Simulink, a simulation software package that is integrated with MATLAB to provide a graphical user interface (GUI). Readers who would like to learn how to use Simulink to generate nonlinear responses should consult the Simulink tutorial in Appendix C. Simulink block diagrams are included with all responses that follow.

Let us assume the motor and load from the Antenna Control Case Study of Chapter 2 and look at the load angular velocity, $\omega_o(s)$, where $\omega_o(s) = 0.1s\theta_m(s) = 0.2083E_a(s)/(s + 1.71)$ from Eq. (2.208). If we drive the motor with a step input through an amplifier of unity gain that saturates at ± 5 volts, Figure 4.29 shows that the effect of amplifier saturation is to limit the obtained velocity.

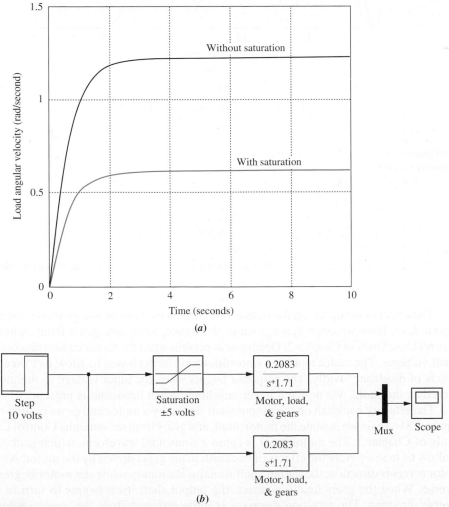

FIGURE 4.29 **a.** Effect of amplifier saturation on load angular velocity response; **b.** Simulink block diagram

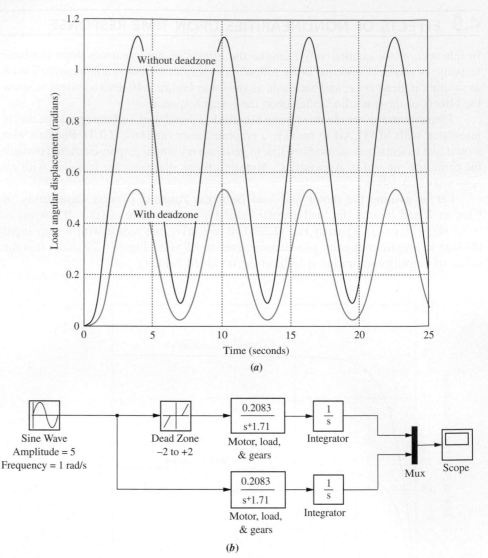

FIGURE 4.30 **a.** Effect of deadzone on load angular displacement response; **b.** Simulink block diagram

The effect of deadzone on the output shaft driven by a motor and gears is shown in Figure 4.30. Here we once again assume the motor, load, and gears from Antenna Control Case Study of Chapter 2. Deadzone is present when the motor cannot respond to small voltages. The motor input is a sinusoidal waveform chosen to allow us to see the effects of deadzone vividly. The response begins when the input voltage to the motor exceeds a threshold. We notice a lower amplitude when deadzone is present.

The effect of backlash on the output shaft driven by a motor and gears is shown in Figure 4.31. Again we assume the motor, load, and gears from the Antenna Control Case Study of Chapter 2. The motor input is again a sinusoidal waveform, which is chosen to allow us to see vividly the effects of backlash in the gears driven by the motor. As the motor reverses direction, the output shaft remains stationary while the motor begins to reverse. When the gears finally connect, the output shaft itself begins to turn in the reverse direction. The resulting response is quite different from the linear response without backlash.

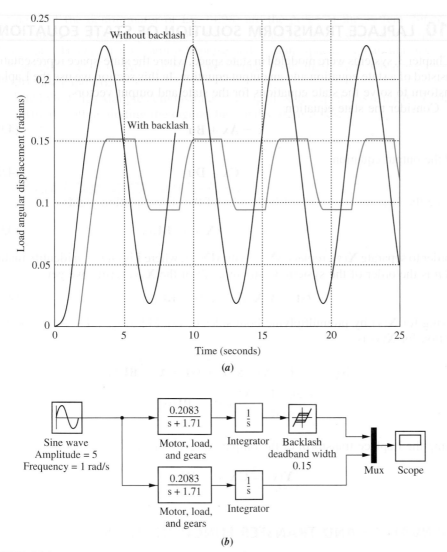

FIGURE 4.31   **a.** Effect of backlash on load angular displacement response; **b.** Simulink block diagram

---

SKILL-ASSESSMENT EXERCISE 4.8

Problem: Use MATLAB's Simulink to reproduce Figure 4.31.

ANSWER: See Figure 4.31.

Now that we have seen the effects of nonlinearities on the time response, let us return to linear systems. Our coverage so far for linear systems has dealt with finding the time response by using the Laplace transform in the frequency domain. Another way to solve for the response is to use state-space techniques in the time domain. This topic is the subject of the next two sections.

and

$$(s\mathbf{I} - \mathbf{A})^{-1} = \frac{\begin{bmatrix} (s^2 + 9s + 26) & (s+9) & 1 \\ -24 & s^2 + 9s & s \\ -24s & -(26s + 24) & s^2 \end{bmatrix}}{s^3 + 9s^2 + 26s + 24} \tag{4.102}$$

Since $\mathbf{U}(s)$ (the Laplace transform for e^{-t}) is $1/(s+1)$, $\mathbf{X}(s)$ can be calculated. Rewriting Eq. (4.96) as

$$\mathbf{X}(s) = (s\mathbf{I} - \mathbf{A})^{-1}[\mathbf{x}(0) + \mathbf{B}\mathbf{U}(s)] \tag{4.103}$$

and using $\mathbf{B}$ and $\mathbf{x}(0)$ from Eqs. (4.99a) and (4.99c), respectively, we get

$$X_1(s) = \frac{(s^3 + 10s^2 + 37s + 29)}{(s+1)(s+2)(s+3)(s+4)} \tag{4.104a}$$

$$X_2(s) = \frac{(2s^2 - 21s - 24)}{(s+1)(s+2)(s+3)(s+4)} \tag{4.104b}$$

$$X_3(s) = \frac{s(2s^2 - 21s - 24)}{(s+1)(s+2)(s+3)(s+4)} \tag{4.104c}$$

The output equation is found from Eq. (4.99b). Performing the indicated addition yields

$$Y(s) = \begin{bmatrix} 1 & 1 & 0 \end{bmatrix} \begin{bmatrix} X_1(s) \\ X_2(s) \\ X_3(s) \end{bmatrix} = X_1(s) + X_2(s) \tag{4.105}$$

or

$$\begin{aligned} Y(s) &= \frac{(s^3 + 12s^2 + 16s + 5)}{(s+1)(s+2)(s+3)(s+4)} \\ &= \frac{-6.5}{s+2} + \frac{19}{s+3} - \frac{11.5}{s+4} \end{aligned} \tag{4.106}$$

where the pole at -1 canceled a zero at -1. Taking the inverse Laplace transform,

$$y(t) = -6.5e^{-2t} + 19e^{-3t} - 11.5e^{-4t} \tag{4.107}$$

b. The denominator of Eq. (4.102), which is $\det(s\mathbf{I} - \mathbf{A})$, is also the denominator of the system's transfer function. Thus, $\det(s\mathbf{I} - \mathbf{A}) = 0$ furnishes both the poles of the system and the eigenvalues -2, -3, and -4.

Students who are performing the MATLAB exercises and want to explore the added capability of MATLAB's Symbolic Toolbox should now run ch4sp1 in Appendix E on the Wiley website at www.wiley.com/college/nise. You will learn how to solve state equations for the output response using the Laplace transform. Example 4.11 will be solved using MATLAB and the Symbolic Math Toolbox.

SKILL-ASSESSMENT EXERCISE 4.9

Problem: Given the system represented in state space by Eqs. (4.108),

$$\dot{\mathbf{x}} = \begin{bmatrix} 0 & 2 \\ -3 & -5 \end{bmatrix}\mathbf{x} + \begin{bmatrix} 0 \\ 1 \end{bmatrix}e^{-t} \qquad (4.108a)$$

$$y = \begin{bmatrix} 1 & 3 \end{bmatrix}\mathbf{x} \qquad (4.108b)$$

$$\mathbf{x}(0) = \begin{bmatrix} 2 \\ 1 \end{bmatrix} \qquad (4.108c)$$

do the following:

a. Solve for $y(t)$ using state-space and Laplace transform techniques.
b. Find the eigenvalues and the system poles.

ANSWERS:

a. $y(t) = -0.5e^{-t} - 12e^{-2t} + 17.5e^{-3t}$
b. $-2, -3$

The complete solution is located at www.wiley.com/college/nise.

TryIt 4.5

Use the following MATLAB and Symbolic Math Toolbox statements to solve Skill-Assessment Exercise 4.9.

```
symss
A=[0 2; -3 -5]; B=[0; 1];
C=[1 3]; X0=[2; 1];
U=1/(s+1);
I=[1 0; 0 1];
X=((s*I-A)^-1)*...
  (X0+B*U);
Y=C*X;
Y=simplify(Y);
y=ilaplace(Y);
pretty(y)
eig(A)
```

4.11 TIME DOMAIN SOLUTION OF STATE EQUATIONS

We now look at another technique for solving the state equations. Rather than using the Laplace transform, we solve the equations directly in the time domain using a method closely allied to the classical solution of differential equations. We will find that the final solution consists of two parts that are different from the forced and natural responses.

The solution in the time domain is given directly by

$$\mathbf{x}(t) = e^{\mathbf{A}t}\mathbf{x}(0) + \int_0^t e^{\mathbf{A}(t-\tau)}\mathbf{B}\mathbf{u}(\tau)\,d\tau$$

$$= \mathbf{\Phi}(t)\mathbf{x}(0) + \int_0^t \mathbf{\Phi}(t-\tau)\mathbf{B}\mathbf{u}(\tau)\,d\tau \qquad (4.109)$$

where $\mathbf{\Phi}(t) = e^{\mathbf{A}t}$ by definition, and which is called the *state-transition matrix*. Eq. (4.109) is derived in Appendix I located at www.wiley.com/college/nise. Readers who are not familiar with this equation or who may want to refresh their memory should consult Appendix I before proceeding.

Notice that the first term on the right-hand side of the equation is the response due to the initial state vector, $x(0)$. Notice also that it is the only term dependent on the initial state vector and not the input. We call this part of the response the *zero-input response,* since it is the total response if the input is zero. The second term, called the *convolution integral,* is dependent only on the input, **u**, and the input matrix, **B**, not the initial state vector. We call this part of the response the *zero-state response,* since it is the total response if the initial state vector is zero. Thus, there is a partitioning of the response different from the forced/natural response we have seen when solving differential equations. In differential equations, the arbitrary constants of the natural response are evaluated based on the initial conditions and the initial values of the forced response and its derivatives. Thus, the natural response's amplitudes are a function of the initial conditions of the output and the input. In Eq. (4.109), the zero-input response is not dependent on the initial values of the input and its derivatives. It is dependent only on the initial conditions of the state vector. The next example vividly shows the difference in partitioning. Pay close attention to the fact that in the final result the zero-state response contains not only the forced solution but also pieces of what we previously called the natural response. We will see in the solution that the natural response is distributed through the zero-input response and the zero-state response.

Before proceeding with the example, let us examine the form the elements of $\mathbf{\Phi}(t)$ take for linear, time-invariant systems. The first term of Eq. (4.96), the Laplace transform of the response for unforced systems, is the transform of $\mathbf{\Phi}(t)\mathbf{x}(0)$, the zero-input response from Eq. (4.109). Thus, for the unforced system

$$\mathscr{L}[\mathbf{x}(t)] = \mathscr{L}[\mathbf{\Phi}(t)\mathbf{x}(0)] = (s\mathbf{I} - \mathbf{A})^{-1}\mathbf{x}(0) \tag{4.110}$$

from which we can see that $(s\mathbf{I} - \mathbf{A})^{-1}$ *is the Laplace transform of the state-transition matrix,* $\mathbf{\Phi}(t)$. We have already seen that the denominator of $(s\mathbf{I} - \mathbf{A})^{-1}$ is a polynomial in s whose roots are the system poles. This polynomial is found from the equation det $(s\mathbf{I} - \mathbf{A}) = 0$. Since

$$\boxed{\mathscr{L}^{-1}[(s\mathbf{I} - \mathbf{A})^{-1}] = \mathscr{L}^{-1}\left[\frac{\text{adj}\,(s\mathbf{I} - \mathbf{A})}{\det\,(s\mathbf{I} - \mathbf{A})}\right] = \mathbf{\Phi}(t)} \tag{4.111}$$

each term of $\mathbf{\Phi}(t)$ would be the sum of exponentials generated by the system's poles.

Let us summarize the concepts with two numerical examples. The first example solves the state equations directly in the time domain. The second example uses the Laplace transform to solve for the state-transition matrix by finding the inverse Laplace transform of $(s\mathbf{I} - \mathbf{A})^{-1}$.

EXAMPLE 4.12

Time domain solution

Problem: For the state equation and initial state vector shown in Eqs. (4.112), where $u(t)$ is a unit step, find the state-transition matrix and then solve for $\mathbf{x}(t)$.

$$\dot{\mathbf{x}}(t) = \begin{bmatrix} 0 & 1 \\ -8 & -6 \end{bmatrix}\mathbf{x}(t) + \begin{bmatrix} 0 \\ 1 \end{bmatrix}u(t) \tag{4.112a}$$

$$\mathbf{x}(0) = \begin{bmatrix} 1 \\ 0 \end{bmatrix} \tag{4.112b}$$

SOLUTION: Since the state equation is in the form

$$\dot{\mathbf{x}}(t) = \mathbf{A}\mathbf{x}(t) + \mathbf{B}u(t) \tag{4.113}$$

find the eigenvalues using det $(s\mathbf{I} - \mathbf{A}) = 0$. Hence, $s^2 + 6s + 8 = 0$, from which $s_1 = -2$ and $s_2 = -4$. Since each term of the state-transition matrix is the sum of responses generated by the poles (eigenvalues), we assume a state-transition matrix of the form

$$\mathbf{\Phi}(t) = \begin{bmatrix} (K_1 e^{-2t} + K_2 e^{-4t}) & (K_3 e^{-2t} + K_4 e^{-4t}) \\ (K_5 e^{-2t} + K_6 e^{-4t}) & (K_7 e^{-2t} + K_8 e^{-4t}) \end{bmatrix} \tag{4.114}$$

In order to find the values of the constants, we make use of the properties of the state-transition matrix derived in Appendix I located at www.wiley.com/college/nise.

$$\mathbf{\Phi}(0) = \mathbf{I} \tag{4.115}$$

$$K_1 + K_2 = 1 \tag{4.116a}$$

$$K_3 + K_4 = 0 \tag{4.116b}$$

$$K_5 + K_6 = 0 \tag{4.116c}$$

$$K_7 + K_8 = 1 \tag{4.116d}$$

and since

$$\dot{\mathbf{\Phi}}(0) = \mathbf{A} \tag{4.117}$$

then

$$-2K_1 - 4K_2 = 0 \tag{4.118a}$$

$$-2K_3 - 4K_4 = 1 \tag{4.118b}$$

$$-2K_5 - 4K_6 = -8 \tag{4.118c}$$

$$-2K_7 - 4K_8 = -6 \tag{4.118d}$$

The constants are solved by taking two simultaneous equations four times. For example, Eq. (4.116a) can be solved simultaneously with Eq. (4.118a) to yield the values of K_1 and K_2. Proceeding similarly, all of the constants can be found. Therefore,

$$\mathbf{\Phi}(t) = \begin{bmatrix} (2e^{-2t} - e^{-4t}) & \left(\frac{1}{2}e^{-2t} - \frac{1}{2}e^{-4t}\right) \\ (-4e^{-2t} + 4e^{-4t}) & (-e^{-2t} + 2e^{-4t}) \end{bmatrix} \tag{4.119}$$

Also,

$$\mathbf{\Phi}(t - \tau)\mathbf{B} = \begin{bmatrix} \left(\frac{1}{2}e^{-2(t-\tau)} - \frac{1}{2}e^{-4(t-\tau)}\right) \\ (-e^{-2(t-\tau)} + 2e^{-4(t-\tau)}) \end{bmatrix} \tag{4.120}$$

Hence, the first term of Eq. (4.109) is

$$\boldsymbol{\Phi}(t)\mathbf{x}(0) = \begin{bmatrix} (2e^{-2t} - e^{-4t}) \\ (-4e^{-2t} + 4e^{-4t}) \end{bmatrix} \qquad (4.121)$$

The last term of Eq. (4.109) is

$$\int_0^t \boldsymbol{\Phi}(t - \tau)\mathbf{B}\mathbf{u}(\tau)\,d\tau = \begin{bmatrix} \dfrac{1}{2}e^{-2t}\int_0^t e^{2\tau}d\tau - \dfrac{1}{2}e^{-4t}\int_0^t e^{4\tau}d\tau \\[3mm] -e^{-2t}\int_0^t e^{2\tau}d\tau + 2e^{-4t}\int_0^t e^{\Lambda\tau}d\tau \end{bmatrix}$$

$$= \begin{bmatrix} \dfrac{1}{8} - \dfrac{1}{4}e^{-2t} + \dfrac{1}{8}e^{-4t} \\[3mm] \dfrac{1}{2}e^{-2t} - \dfrac{1}{2}e^{-4t} \end{bmatrix} \qquad (4.122)$$

Notice, as promised, that Eq. (4.122), the zero-state response, contains not only the forced response, $1/8$, but also terms of the form Ae^{-2t} and Be^{-4t} that are part of what we previously called the natural response. However, the coefficients, A and B, are not dependent on the initial conditions.

The final result is found by adding Eqs. (4.121) and (4.122). Hence,

$$\mathbf{x}(t) = \boldsymbol{\Phi}(t)\mathbf{x}(0) + \int_0^t \boldsymbol{\Phi}(t - \tau)\mathbf{B}\mathbf{u}(\tau)\,d\tau = \begin{bmatrix} \dfrac{1}{8} + \dfrac{7}{4}e^{-2t} - \dfrac{7}{8}e^{-4t} \\[3mm] -\dfrac{7}{2}e^{-2t} + \dfrac{7}{2}e^{-4t} \end{bmatrix} \qquad (4.123)$$

◼ EXAMPLE 4.13 ◼

State-transition matrix via Laplace transform

Problem: Find the state-transition matrix of Example 4.12, using $(s\mathbf{I} - \mathbf{A})^{-1}$.

SOLUTION: We use the fact that $\boldsymbol{\Phi}(t)$ is the inverse Laplace transform of $(s\mathbf{I} - \mathbf{A})^{-1}$. Thus, first find $(s\mathbf{I} - \mathbf{A})$ as

$$(s\mathbf{I} - \mathbf{A}) = \begin{bmatrix} s & -1 \\ 8 & (s+6) \end{bmatrix} \qquad (4.124)$$

from which

$$(s\mathbf{I} - \mathbf{A})^{-1} = \dfrac{\begin{bmatrix} s+6 & 1 \\ -8 & s \end{bmatrix}}{s^2 + 6s + 8} = \begin{bmatrix} \dfrac{s+6}{s^2 + 6s + 8} & \dfrac{1}{s^2 + 6s + 8} \\[3mm] \dfrac{-8}{s^2 + 6s + 8} & \dfrac{s}{s^2 + 6s + 8} \end{bmatrix} \qquad (4.125)$$

Expanding each term in the matrix on the right by partial fractions yields

$$(s\mathbf{I} - \mathbf{A})^{-1} = \begin{bmatrix} \left(\dfrac{2}{s+2} - \dfrac{1}{s+4}\right) & \left(\dfrac{1/2}{s+2} - \dfrac{1/2}{s+4}\right) \\[2ex] \left(\dfrac{-4}{s+2} + \dfrac{4}{s+4}\right) & \left(\dfrac{-1}{s+2} + \dfrac{2}{s+4}\right) \end{bmatrix} \qquad (4.126)$$

Finally, taking the inverse Laplace transform of each term, we obtain

$$\mathbf{\Phi}(t) = \begin{bmatrix} \left(2e^{-2t} - e^{-4t}\right) & \left(\dfrac{1}{2}e^{-2t} - \dfrac{1}{2}e^{-4t}\right) \\[2ex] \left(-4e^{-2t} + 4e^{-4t}\right) & \left(-e^{-2t} + 2e^{-4t}\right) \end{bmatrix} \qquad (4.127)$$

Students who are performing the MATLAB exercises and want to explore the added capability of MATLAB's Symbolic Toolbox should now run ch4sp2 in Appendix E on the Wiley website at www.wiley.com/college/nise. You will learn how to solve state equations for the output response using the convolution integral. Examples 4.12 and 4.13 will be solved using MATLAB and the Symbolic Math Toolbox.

Symbolic Math

Systems represented in state space can be simulated on the digital computer. Programs such as MATLAB can be used for this purpose. Alternately, the user can write specialized programs, as discussed in Appendix G.1 located at www.wiley.com/college/nise.

Students who are using MATLAB should now run ch4p3 in Appendix B. This exercise uses MATLAB to simulate the step response of systems represented in state space. In addition to generating the step response, you will learn how to specify the range on the time axis for the plot.

MATLAB

SKILL-ASSESSMENT EXERCISE 4.10

Problem: Given the system represented in state space by Eqs. (4.128):

$$\dot{\mathbf{x}} = \begin{bmatrix} 0 & 2 \\ -2 & -5 \end{bmatrix} \mathbf{x} + \begin{bmatrix} 0 \\ 1 \end{bmatrix} e^{-2t} \qquad (4.128a)$$

$$y = \begin{bmatrix} 2 & 1 \end{bmatrix} \mathbf{x} \qquad (4.128b)$$

$$\mathbf{x}(0) = \begin{bmatrix} 1 \\ 2 \end{bmatrix} \qquad (4.128c)$$

WileyPLUS

Control Solutions

do the following:

a. Solve for the state-transition matrix.
b. Solve for the state vector using the convolution integral.
c. Find the output, $y(t)$.

We found that the poles of the input generate the forced response, whereas the system poles generate the transient response. If the system poles are real, the system exhibits *overdamped* behavior. These exponential responses have time constants equal to the reciprocals of the pole locations. Purely imaginary poles yield *undamped* sinusoidal oscillations whose radian frequency is equal to the magnitude of the imaginary pole. Systems with complex poles display *underdamped* responses. The real part of the complex pole dictates the exponential decay envelope, and the imaginary part dictates the sinusoidal radian frequency. The exponential decay envelope has a time constant equal to the reciprocal of the real part of the pole, and the sinusoid has a radian frequency equal to the imaginary part of the pole.

For all second-order cases, we developed specifications called the *damping ratio, ζ,* and *natural frequency, ω_n.* The damping ratio gives us an idea about the nature of the transient response and how much overshoot and oscillation it undergoes, regardless of time scaling. The natural frequency gives an indication of the speed of the response.

We found that the value of ζ determines the form of the second-order natural response:

- If $\zeta = 0$, the response is undamped.
- If $\zeta < 1$, the response is underdamped.
- If $\zeta = 1$, the response is critically damped.
- If $\zeta > 1$, the response is overdamped.

The natural frequency is the frequency of oscillation if all damping is removed. It acts as a scaling factor for the response, as can be seen from Eq. (4.28), in which the independent variable can be considered to be $\omega_n t$.

For the underdamped case we defined several transient response specifications, including these:

- Percent overshoot, %*OS*
- Peak time, T_p
- Settling time, T_s
- Rise time, T_r

The peak time is inversely proportional to the imaginary part of the complex pole. Thus, horizontal lines on the *s*-plane are lines of constant peak time. Percent overshoot is a function of only the damping ratio. Consequently, radial lines are lines of constant percent overshoot. Finally, settling time is inversely proportional to the real part of the complex pole. Hence, vertical lines on the *s*-plane are lines of constant settling time.

We found that peak time, percent overshoot, and settling time are related to pole location. Thus, we can design transient responses by relating a desired response to a pole location and then relating that pole location to a transfer function and the system's components.

The effects of nonlinearities, such as saturation, deadzone, and backlash were explored using MATLAB's Simulink.

In this chapter we also evaluated the time response using the state-space approach. The response found in this way was separated into the *zero-input response,* and the *zero-state response,* whereas the frequency response method yielded a total response divided into *natural response* and *forced response* components.

In the next chapter we will use the transient response specifications developed here to analyze and design systems that consist of the interconnection of multiple sub-systems. We will see how to reduce these systems to a single transfer function in order to apply the concepts developed in Chapter 4.

REVIEW QUESTIONS

1. Name the performance specification for first-order systems.

2. What does the performance specification for a first-order system tell us?

3. In a system with an input and an output, what poles generate the steady-state response?

4. In a system with an input and an output, what poles generate the transient response?

5. The imaginary part of a pole generates what part of a response?

6. The real part of a pole generates what part of a response?

7. What is the difference between the natural frequency and the damped frequency of oscillation?

8. If a pole is moved with a constant imaginary part, what will the responses have in common?

9. If a pole is moved with a constant real part, what will the responses have in common?

10. If a pole is moved along a radial line extending from the origin, what will the responses have in common?

11. List five specifications for a second-order underdamped system.

12. For Question 11 how many specifications completely determine the response?

13. What pole locations characterize (1) the underdamped system, (2) the overdamped system, and (3) the critically damped system?

14. Name two conditions under which the response generated by a pole can be neglected.

15. How can you justify pole-zero cancellation?

16. Does the solution of the state equation yield the output response of the system? Explain.

17. What is the relationship between $(s\mathbf{I} - \mathbf{A})$, which appeared during the Laplace transformation solution of the state equations, and the state-transition matrix, which appeared during the classical solution of the state equation?

18. Name a major advantage of using time domain techniques for the solution of the response.

19. Name a major advantage of using frequency domain techniques for the solution of the response.

20. What three pieces of information must be given in order to solve for the output response of a system using state-space techniques?

21. How can the poles of a system be found from the state equations?

State Space

State Space

State Space

State Space

State Space

PROBLEMS

1. Find the output response, $c(t)$, for each of the systems shown in Figure P4.1. Also find the time constant, rise time, and settling time for each case. [Sections: 4.2, 4.3]

WileyPLUS

Control Solutions

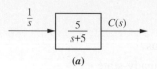

(a)

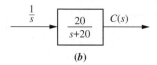

(b)

Figure P4.1

2. Find the capacitor voltage in the network shown in Figure P4.2 if the switch closes at $t = 0$. Assume zero initial conditions. Also find the time constant, rise time, and settling time for the capacitor voltage. [Sections: 4.2, 4.3]

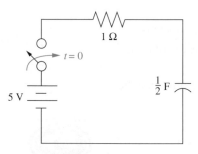

Figure P4.2

3. Plot the step response for Problem 2 using MATLAB. From your plots, find the time constant, rise time, and settling time.

MATLAB

4. Find the displacement, $x(t)$, in Figure P4.3 if the applied force is a unit step. Assume zero initial conditions and neglect the mass of all components. Also, find the time constant, rise time, and settling time for the displacement.

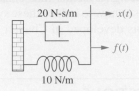

Figure P4.3

5. Plot the step response for Problem 4 using MATLAB. From your plots, find the time constant, rise time, and settling time.

MATLAB

6. For each of the transfer functions shown below, find the locations of the poles and zeros, plot them on the s-plane, and then write an expression for the general form of the step response without solving for the inverse Laplace transform. State the nature of each response (overdamped, underdamped, and so on).

a. $T(s) = \dfrac{2}{s + 2}$

b. $T(s) = \dfrac{5}{(s + 3)(s + 6)}$

c. $T(s) = \dfrac{10(s + 7)}{(s + 10)(s + 20)}$

d. $T(s) = \dfrac{20}{s^2 + 6s + 144}$

e. $T(s) = \dfrac{s + 2}{s^2 + 9}$

f. $T(s) = \dfrac{(s + 5)}{(s + 10)^2}$

7. Use MATLAB to find the poles of

$$T(s) = \frac{s^2 + 2s + 2}{s^4 + 7s^3 + 3s^2 + 5s + 3}$$

MATLAB

8. Find the transfer function and poles of the system represented in state space here: [Section: 4.10]

$$\dot{\mathbf{x}} = \begin{bmatrix} 8 & -4 & 1 \\ -3 & 2 & 0 \\ 5 & 7 & -9 \end{bmatrix} \mathbf{x} + \begin{bmatrix} 1 \\ 3 \\ 7 \end{bmatrix} u(t)$$

$$y = \begin{bmatrix} 2 & 8 & -3 \end{bmatrix} \mathbf{x}; \quad x(0) = \begin{bmatrix} 0 \\ 0 \\ 0 \end{bmatrix}$$

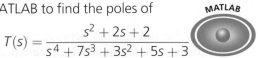

9. Repeat Problem 8 using MATLAB. [Section: 4.10].

10. Write the general form of the capacitor voltage for the electrical network shown in Figure P4.4. [Section: 4.4].

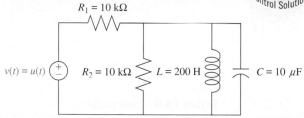

$R_1 = 10 \text{ k}\Omega$

$v(t) = u(t)$ $R_2 = 10 \text{ k}\Omega$ $L = 200 \text{ H}$ $C = 10 \ \mu\text{F}$

Figure P4.4

11. Use MATLAB to plot the capacitor voltage in Problem 10. [Section: 4.4].

12. Solve for $x(t)$ in the system shown in Figure P4.5 if $f(t)$ is a unit step. [Section: 4.4].

$M = 1 \text{ kg}$
$K_s = 5 \text{ N/m}$
$f_v = 1 \text{ N-s/m}$
$f(t) = u(t) \text{ N}$

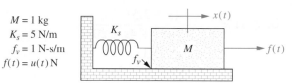

$x(t)$

K_s

M

f_v

$f(t)$

Figure P4.5

13. The system shown in Figure P4.6 has a unit step input. Find the output response as a function of time. Assume the system is underdamped. Notice that the result will be Eq. (4.28). [Section: 4.6].

$R(s)$ $\dfrac{\omega_n^2}{s^2 + 2\zeta\omega_n s + \omega_n^2}$ $C(s)$

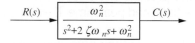

Figure P4.6

14. Derive the relationship for damping ratio as a function of percent overshoot, Eq. (4.39). [Section: 4.6].

15. Calculate the exact response of each system of Problem 6 using Laplace transform techniques, and compare the results to those obtained in that problem. [Sections: 4.3, 4.4].

16. Find the damping ratio and natural frequency for each second-order system of Problem 6 and show that the value of the damping ratio conforms to the type of response (underdamped, overdamped, and so on) predicted in that problem. [Section: 4.5].

17. A system has a damping ratio of 0.5, a natural frequency of 100 rad/s, and a dc gain of 1. Find the response of the system to a unit step input. [Section: 4.6].

18. For each of the second-order systems that follow, find ζ, ω_n, T_s, T_p, T_r, and $\%OS$. [Section: 4.6].

a. $T(s) = \dfrac{16}{s^2 + 3s + 16}$

b. $T(s) = \dfrac{0.04}{s^2 + 0.02s + 0.04}$

c. $T(s) = \dfrac{1.05 \times 10^7}{s^2 + 1.6 \times 10^3 s + 1.05 \times 10^7}$

19. Repeat Problem 18 using MATLAB. Have the computer program estimate the given specifications and plot the step responses. Estimate the rise time from the plots. [Section: 4.6].

20. Use MATLAB's LTI Viewer and obtain settling time, peak time, rise time, and percent overshoot for each of the systems in Problem 18. [Section: 4.6].

21. For each pair of second-order system specifications below, find the location of the second-order pair of poles.

a. $\%OS = 10\%$; $T_s = 0.5$ second

b. $\%OS = 15\%$; $T_p = 0.25$ second

c. $T_s = 5$ seconds; $T_p = 2$ seconds

22. Find the transfer function of a second-order system that yields a 12.3% overshoot and a settling time of 1 second. [Section: 4.6]

23. For the system shown in Figure P4.7, do the following: [Section: 4.6]

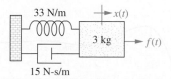

33 N/m

$x(t)$

3 kg

$f(t)$

15 N-s/m

Figure P4.7

a. Find the transfer function $G(s) = X(s)/F(s)$.

b. Find ζ, ω_n, $\%OS$, T_s, T_p, and T_r.

24. For the system shown in Figure P4.8, a step torque is applied at $\theta_1(t)$. Find

a. The transfer function, $G(s) = \theta_2(s)/T(s)$.

b. The percent overshoot, settling time, and peak time for $\theta_2(t)$. [Section: 4.6]

Figure P4.8

25. Derive the unit step response for each transfer function in Example 4.8. [Section: 4.7].

26. Find the percent overshoot, settling time, rise time, and peak time for

$$T(s) = \frac{14.145}{(s^2 + 1.204s + 2.829)(s + 5)} \quad \text{[Section: 4.7]}$$

27. For each of the unit step responses shown in Figure P4.9, find the transfer function of the system. [Sections: 4.3, 4.6].

WileyPLUS

Control Solutions

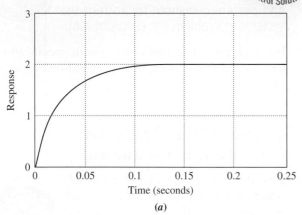

(a)

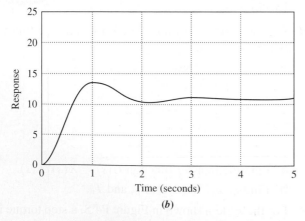

(b)

Figure P4.9 (figure continues)

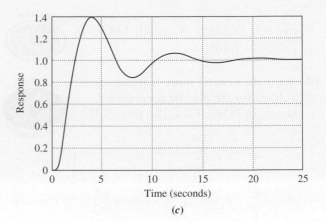

(c)

Figure P4.9 (continued)

28. For the following response functions, determine if pole-zero cancellation can be approximated. If it can, find percent overshoot, settling time, rise time, and peak time. [Section: 4.8].

a. $C(s) = \dfrac{(s+3)}{s(s+2)(s^2 + 3s + 10)}$

b. $C(s) = \dfrac{(s+2.5)}{s(s+2)(s^2 + 4s + 20)}$

c. $C(s) = \dfrac{(s+2.1)}{s(s+2)(s^2 + s + 5)}$

d. $C(s) = \dfrac{(s+2.01)}{s(s+2)(s^2 + 5s + 20)}$

29. Using MATLAB, plot the time response of Problem 28(a) and from the plot determine percent overshoot, settling time, rise time, and peak time. [Section: 4.8]

MATLAB

30. Find peak time, settling time, and percent overshoot for only those responses below that can be approximated as second-order responses. [Section: 4.8].

a. $c(t) = 0.003500 - 0.001524e^{-4t}$
$\qquad - 0.001976e^{-3t}\cos(22.16t)$
$\qquad - 0.0005427e^{-3t}\sin(22.16t)$

b. $c(t) = 0.05100 - 0.007353e^{-8t}$
$\qquad - 0.007647e^{-6t}\cos(8t)$
$\qquad - 0.01309e^{-6t}\sin(8t)$

c. $c(t) = 0.009804 - 0.0001857e^{-5.1t}$
$\qquad - 0.009990e^{-2t}\cos(9.796t)$
$\qquad - 0.001942e^{-2t}\sin(9.796t)$

d. $c(t) = 0.007000 - 0.001667e^{-10t}$
$- 0.008667e^{-2t}\cos(9.951t)$
$- 0.0008040e^{-2t}\sin(9.951t)$

31. For each of the following transfer functions with zeros, find the component parts of the unit step response: (1) the derivative of the response without a zero and (2) the response without a zero, scaled to the negative of the zero value. Also, find and plot the total response. Describe any nonminimum-phase behavior. [Section: 4.8].

a. $G(s) = \dfrac{s+2}{s^2+3s+36}$

b. $G(s) = \dfrac{s-2}{s^2+3s+36}$

32. Use MATLAB's Simulink to obtain the step response of a system,

Simulink

$$G(s) = \dfrac{1}{s^2+3s+10}$$

under the following conditions: [Section: 4.9]

a. The system is linear and driven by an amplifier whose gain is 10.

b. An amplifier whose gain is 10 drives the system. The amplifier saturates at ±0.25 volts. Describe the effect of the saturation on the system's output.

c. An amplifier whose gain is 10 drives the system. The amplifier saturates at ±0.25 volts. The system drives a 1:1 gear train that has backlash. The deadband width of the backlash is 0.02 rad. Describe the effect of saturation and backlash on the system's output.

33. A system is represented by the state and output equations that follow. Without solving the state equation, find the poles of the system. [Section: 4.10]

State Space

$$\dot{\mathbf{x}} = \begin{bmatrix} -2 & -1 \\ -3 & -5 \end{bmatrix}\mathbf{x} + \begin{bmatrix} 1 \\ 2 \end{bmatrix}u(t)$$
$$y = \begin{bmatrix} 3 & 2 \end{bmatrix}\mathbf{x}$$

34. A system is represented by the state and output equations given below. Without solving the state equation, find

WileyPLUS
Control Solutions

a. the characteristic equation

b. the poles of the system

$$\dot{\mathbf{x}} = \begin{bmatrix} 0 & 1 & 2 \\ 0 & 3 & 4 \\ 1 & 3 & 2 \end{bmatrix}\mathbf{x} + \begin{bmatrix} 0 \\ 0 \\ 1 \end{bmatrix}u(t)$$
$$y = \begin{bmatrix} 1 & 1 & 0 \end{bmatrix}\mathbf{x}$$

35. Given the following state-space representation of a system, find $Y(s)$: [Section: 4.10]

State Space

$$\dot{\mathbf{x}} = \begin{bmatrix} 1 & 2 \\ -3 & -1 \end{bmatrix}\mathbf{x} + \begin{bmatrix} 1 \\ 1 \end{bmatrix}\sin 3t$$
$$y = \begin{bmatrix} 1 & 2 \end{bmatrix}\mathbf{x}; \quad \mathbf{x}(0) = \begin{bmatrix} 2 \\ 1 \end{bmatrix}$$

36. Given the following system represented in state space, solve for $Y(s)$ using the Laplace transform method for solution of the state equation: [Section: 4.10]

State Space

$$\dot{\mathbf{x}} = \begin{bmatrix} 0 & 1 & 0 \\ -2 & -4 & 1 \\ 0 & 0 & -6 \end{bmatrix}\mathbf{x} + \begin{bmatrix} 0 \\ 0 \\ 1 \end{bmatrix}e^{-t}$$
$$y = \begin{bmatrix} 1 & 0 & 0 \end{bmatrix}\mathbf{x}; \quad \mathbf{x}(0) = \begin{bmatrix} 0 \\ 0 \\ 0 \end{bmatrix}$$

37. Solve the following state equation and output equation for $y(t)$, where $u(t)$ is the unit step. Use the Laplace transform method. [Section: 4.10]

State Space

$$\dot{\mathbf{x}} = \begin{bmatrix} -2 & 0 \\ -1 & -1 \end{bmatrix}\mathbf{x} + \begin{bmatrix} 1 \\ 1 \end{bmatrix}u(t)$$
$$y = \begin{bmatrix} 0 & 1 \end{bmatrix}\mathbf{x}; \quad \mathbf{x}(0) = \begin{bmatrix} 1 \\ 0 \end{bmatrix}$$

38. Solve for $y(t)$ for the following system represented in state space, where $u(t)$ is the unit step. Use the Laplace

State Space

transform approach to solve the state equation. [Section: 4.10]

$$\dot{x} = \begin{bmatrix} -3 & 1 & 0 \\ 0 & -6 & 1 \\ 0 & 0 & -5 \end{bmatrix} x + \begin{bmatrix} 0 \\ 1 \\ 1 \end{bmatrix} u(t)$$

$$y = \begin{bmatrix} 0 & 1 & 1 \end{bmatrix} x; \quad x(0) = \begin{bmatrix} 0 \\ 0 \\ 0 \end{bmatrix}$$

39. Use MATLAB to plot the step response of Problem 38. [Section: 4.10]

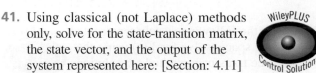

40. Repeat Problem 38 using MATLAB's Symbolic Math Toolbox and Eq. (4.96). In addition, run your program with an initial condition, $x(0) = \begin{bmatrix} 1 \\ 1 \\ 0 \end{bmatrix}$. [Section: 4.10]

41. Using classical (not Laplace) methods only, solve for the state-transition matrix, the state vector, and the output of the system represented here: [Section: 4.11]

$$\dot{x} = \begin{bmatrix} 0 & 1 \\ -1 & -5 \end{bmatrix} x; \quad y = \begin{bmatrix} 1 & 2 \end{bmatrix} x;$$

$$x(0) = \begin{bmatrix} 1 \\ 0 \end{bmatrix}$$

42. Using classical (not Laplace) methods only, solve for the state-transition matrix, the state vector, and the output of the system represented below, where $u(t)$ is the unit step.

$$\dot{x} = \begin{bmatrix} 0 & 1 \\ -1 & 0 \end{bmatrix} x + \begin{bmatrix} 0 \\ 1 \end{bmatrix} u(t)$$

$$y = \begin{bmatrix} 3 & 2 \end{bmatrix} x; \quad x(0) = \begin{bmatrix} 0 \\ 0 \end{bmatrix}$$

43. Solve for $y(t)$ for the following system represented in state space, where $u(t)$ is the unit step. Use the classical approach to solve the state equation. [Section: 4.11]

$$\dot{x} = \begin{bmatrix} -2 & 1 & 0 \\ 0 & 0 & 1 \\ 0 & -6 & -1 \end{bmatrix} x + \begin{bmatrix} 1 \\ 0 \\ 0 \end{bmatrix} u(t)$$

$$y = \begin{bmatrix} 1 & 0 & 0 \end{bmatrix} x; \quad x(0) = \begin{bmatrix} 0 \\ 0 \\ 0 \end{bmatrix}$$

44. Repeat Problem 43 using MATLAB's Symbolic Math Toolbox and Eq. (4.109). In addition, run your program with an initial condition, $x(0) = \begin{bmatrix} 1 \\ 1 \\ 0 \end{bmatrix}$. [Section: 4.11].

45. Using methods described in Appendix G.1 located at www.wiley.com/college/nise simulate the following system and plot the step response. Verify the expected values of percent overshoot, peak time, and settling time.

$$T(s) = \frac{1}{s^2 + 0.8s + 1}$$

46. Using methods described in Appendix G.1 located at www.wiley.com/college/nise simulate the following system and plot the output, $y(t)$, for a step input:

$$\dot{x} = \begin{bmatrix} 0 & 1 & 0 \\ -10 & -7 & 1 \\ 0 & 0 & -2 \end{bmatrix} x + \begin{bmatrix} 0 \\ 0 \\ 1 \end{bmatrix} u(t)$$

$$y(t) = \begin{bmatrix} 1 & 1 & 0 \end{bmatrix} x; \quad x(0) = \begin{bmatrix} -1 \\ 0 \\ 0 \end{bmatrix}$$

47. A human responds to a visual cue with a physical response, as shown in Figure P4.10. The transfer function that relates the output physical response, $P(s)$, to the input visual command, $V(s)$, is

$$G(s) = \frac{P(s)}{V(s)} = \frac{(s + 0.5)}{(s + 2)(s + 5)}$$

(*Stefani, 1973*). Do the following:

a. Evaluate the output response for a unit step input using the Laplace transform.

b. Represent the transfer function in state space.

c. Use MATLAB to simulate the system and obtain a plot of the step response.

48. Industrial robots are used for myriad applications. Figure P4.11 shows a robot used to move 55-pound

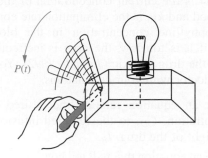

Step 1: Light source on   Step 2: Recognize light source   Step 3: Respond to light source

Figure P4.10   Steps in determining the transfer function relating output physical response to the input visual command

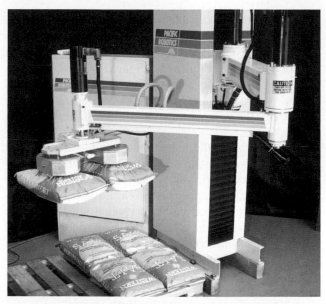

Figure P4.11   Vacuum robot lifts two bags of salt

bags of salt pellets; a vacuum head lifts the bags before positioning. The robot can move as many as 12 bags per minute (*Schneider, 1992*). Assume a model for the open-loop swivel controller and plant of

$$G_e(s) = \frac{\omega_o(s)}{V_i(s)} = \frac{K}{(s+10)(s^2+4s+10)}$$

where $\omega_o(s)$ is the Laplace transform of the robot's output swivel velocity and $V_i(s)$ is the voltage applied to the controller.

a. Evaluate percent overshoot, settling time, peak time, and rise time of the response of the open-loop swivel velocity to a step-voltage input. Justify all second-order assumptions.

State Space

b. Represent the open-loop system in state space.

c. Use MATLAB or any other computer program to simulate the system and compare your results to (a).

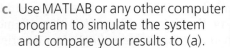

49. Anesthesia induces muscle relaxation (paralysis) and unconsciousness in the patient. Muscle relaxation can be monitored using electromyogram signals from nerves in the hand; unconsciousness can be monitored using the cardiovascular system's mean arterial pressure. The anesthetic drug is a mixture of isoflurane and atracurium. An approximate model relating muscle relaxation to the percent isoflurane in the mixture is

$$\frac{P(s)}{U(s)} = \frac{7.63 \times 10^{-2}}{s^2 + 1.15s + 0.28}$$

where $P(s)$ is muscle relaxation measured as a fraction of total paralysis (normalized to unity) and $U(s)$ is the percent mixture of isoflurane (*Linkens, 1992*). [Section: 4.6]

a. Find the damping ratio and the natural frequency of the paralysis transient response.

b. Find the maximum possible percent paralysis if a 2% mixture of isoflurane is used.

c. Plot the step response of paralysis if a 1% mixture of isoflurane is used.

d. What percent isoflurane would have to be used for 100% paralysis?

50. To treat acute asthma, the drug theophylline is infused intravenously. The rate of change of the drug concentration in the blood is equal to the difference between the infused concentration and the eliminated concentration. The infused concentration is $i(t)/V_d$, where $i(t)$ is the rate of flow of the drug by weight and V_d is the apparent volume and depends on the patient. The eliminated concentration is given by $k_{10}c(t)$,

where $c(t)$ is the current concentration of the drug in the blood and k_{10} is the elimination rate constant. The theophylline concentration in the blood is critical—if it is too low, the drug is ineffective; if too high, the drug is toxic (*Jannett, 1992*). You will help the doctor with your calculations.

a. Derive an equation relating the desired blood concentration, C_D, to the required infusion rate by weight of the drug, I_R.

b. Derive an equation that will tell how long the drug must be administered to reach the desired blood concentration. Use both rise time and settling time.

c. Find the infusion rate of theophylline if $V_D = 600$ ml, $k_{10} = 0.07$ h^{-1}, and the required blood level of the drug is 12 mcg/ml ("mcg" means micrograms). See *Jannett (1992)* for a description of parameter values.

d. Find the rise and settling times for the constants in (c).

51. Upper motor neuron disorder patients can benefit and regain useful function through the use of functional neuroprostheses. The design requires a good understanding of muscle dynamics. In an experiment to determine muscle responses, the identified transfer function was (*Zhou, 1995*)

$$M(s) = \frac{2.5e^{-0.008s}(1 + 0.172s)(1 + 0.008s)}{(1 + 0.07s)^2(1 + 0.05s)^2}$$

Find the unit step response of this transfer function.

52. When electrodes are attached to the mastoid bones (right behind the ears) and current pulses are applied, a person will sway forward and backward. It has been found that the transfer function from the current to the subject's angle (in degrees) with respect to the vertical is given by (*Nashner, 1974*)

$$\frac{\theta(s)}{I(s)} = \frac{5.8(0.3s + 1)e^{-0.1s}}{(s + 1)(s^2/1.2^2 + 0.6s/1.2 + 1)}$$

a. Determine whether a dominant pole approximation can be applied to this transfer function.

b. Find the body sway caused by a 250 μA pulse of 150 msec duration.

53. A MOEMS (optical MEMS) is a MEMS (Micro Electromechanical Systems) with an optical fiber channel that takes light generated from a laser diode. It also has a photodetector that measures light intensity variations and outputs voltage variations proportional to small mechanical device deflections. Additionally, a

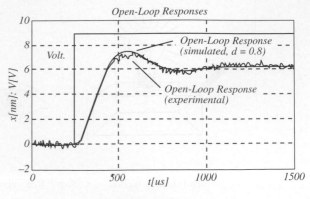

Figure P4.12

voltage input is capable of deflecting the device. The apparatus can be used as an optical switch or as a variable optical attenuator, and it does not exceed 2000 μm in any dimension. Figure P4.12 shows input-output signal pairs used to identify the parameters of the system. Assume a second-order transfer function and find the system's transfer function (*Borovic, 2005*).

54. The response of the deflection of a fluid-filled catheter to changes in pressure can be modeled using a second-order model. Knowledge of the parameters of the model is important because in cardiovascular applications the undamped natural frequency should be close to five times the heart rate. However, due to sterility and other considerations, measurement of the parameters is difficult. A method to obtain transfer functions using measurements of the amplitudes of two consecutive peaks of the response and their timing has been developed (*Glantz, 1979*). Assume that Figure P4.13 is obtained from catheter measurements. Using the information shown and assuming a second-order model excited by a unit step input, find the corresponding transfer function.

55. Several factors affect the workings of the kidneys. For example, Figure P4.14 shows how a step change in arterial flow pressure affects renal blood flow in rats. In the "hot tail" part of the experiment, peripheral thermal receptor stimulation is achieved by inserting the rat's tail in heated water. Variations between different test subjects are indicated by the vertical lines. It has been argued that the "control" and "hot tail" responses are identical except for their steady-state values (*DiBona, 2005*).

a. Using Figure P4.14, obtain the normalized ($c_{\text{final}} = 1$) transfer functions for both responses.

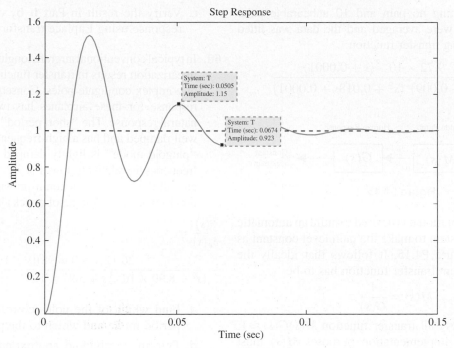

Figure P4.13

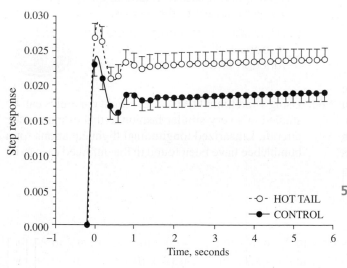

Figure P4.14

b. Use MATLAB to prove or disprove the assertion about the "control" and "hot tail" responses.

56. The transfer function of a nano-positioning device capable of translating biological samples within a few μm uses a piezoelectric actuator and a linear variable differential transformer (LDVT) as a displacement sensor. The transfer function from input to displacement has been found to be (*Salapaka, 2002*)

$$G(s) = \frac{9.7 \times 10^4 (s^2 - 14400s + 106.6 \times 10^6)}{(s^2 + 3800s + 23.86 \times 10^6)(s^2 + 240s + 2324.8 \times 10^3)}$$

Use a dominant-pole argument to find an equivalent transfer function with the same numerator but only three poles. Use MATLAB to find the actual size and approximate system unit step responses, plotting them on the same graph. Explain the differences between both responses given that both pairs of poles are so far apart.

57. At some point in their lives most people will suffer from at least one onset of low back pain. This disorder can trigger excruciating pain and temporary disability, but its causes are hard to diagnose. It is well known that low back pain alters motor trunk patterns; thus it is of interest to study the causes for these alterations and their extent. Due to the different possible causes of this type of pain, a "control" group of people is hard to obtain for laboratory studies. However, pain can be stimulated in healthy people and muscle movement ranges can be compared. Controlled back pain can be induced by injecting saline solution directly into related muscles or ligaments. The transfer function from infusion rate to pain response was obtained experimentally by injecting a 5% saline solution at six different infusion rates over a period of 12 minutes. Subjects verbally rated their pain every 15 sec on a scale from 0 to 10, with 0 indicating no pain and 10 unbearable pain. Several trials were averaged and the data was fitted to the following transfer function:

$$G(s) = \frac{9.72 \times 10^{-8}(s + 0.0001)}{(s + 0.009)^2(s^2 + 0.018s + 0.0001)}$$

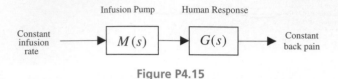

Infusion Pump   Human Response

Constant infusion rate → $M(s)$ → $G(s)$ → Constant back pain

Figure P4.15

For experimentation it is desired to build an automatic dispensing system to make the pain level constant as shown in Figure P4.15. It follows that ideally the injection system transfer function has to be

$$M(s) = \frac{1}{G(s)}$$

to obtain an overall transfer function $M(s)G(s) \approx 1$. However, for implementation purposes $M(s)$ must have at least one more pole than zeros (*Zedka, 1999*). Find a suitable transfer function, $M(s)$, by inverting $G(s)$ and adding poles that are far from the imaginary axis.

58. An artificial heart works in closed loop by varying its pumping rate according to changes in signals from the recipient's nervous system. For feedback compensation design it is important to know the heart's open-loop transfer function. To identify this transfer function, an artificial heart is implanted in a calf while the main parts of the original heart are left in place. Then the atrial pumping rate in the original heart is measured while step input changes are effected on the artificial heart. It has been found that, in general, the obtained response closely resembles that of a second-order system. In one such experiment it was found that the step response has a %OS = 30% and a time of first peak $T_p = 127$ sec (*Nakamura, 2002*). Find the corresponding transfer function.

59. An observed transfer function from voltage potential to force in skeletal muscles is given by (*Ionescu, 2005*)

$$T(s) = \frac{450}{(s + 5)(s + 20)}$$

a. Obtain the system's impulse response.

b. Integrate the impulse response to find the step response.

c. Verify the result in Part **b** by obtaining the step response using Laplace transform techniques.

60. In typical conventional aircraft, longitudinal flight model linearization results in transfer functions with two pairs of complex conjugate poles. Consequently, the natural response for these airplanes has two modes in their natural response. The "short period" mode is relatively well-damped and has a high-frequency oscillation. The "plugoid mode" is lightly damped and its oscillation frequency is relatively low. For example, in a specific aircraft the transfer function from wing elevator deflection to nose angle (angle of attack) is (*McRuer, 1973*)

$$\frac{\theta(s)}{\delta_e(s)} =$$
$$-\frac{26.12(s + 0.0098)(s + 1.371)}{(s^2 + 8.99 \times 10^{-3} s + 3.97 \times 10^{-3})(s^2 + 4.21s + 18.23)}$$

a. Find which of the poles correspond to the short period mode and which to the phugoid mode.

b. Peform a "phugoid approximation" (dominant-pole approximation), retaining the two poles and the zero closest to the; ω-axis.

c. Use MATLAB to compare the step responses of the original transfer function and the approximation.

61. Using wind tunnel tests, insect flight dynamics can be studied in a very similar fashion to that of man-made aircraft. Linearized longitudinal flight equations for a bumblebee have been found in the unforced case to be

$$\begin{bmatrix} \dot{u} \\ \dot{w} \\ \dot{q} \\ \dot{\theta} \end{bmatrix} =$$
$$\begin{bmatrix} -8.792 \times 10^{-3} & 0.56 \times 10^{-3} & -1.0 \times 10^{-3} & -13.79 \times 10^{-3} \\ -0.347 \times 10^{-3} & -11.7 \times 10^{-3} & -0.347 \times 10^{-3} & 0 \\ 0.261 & -20.8 \times 10^{-3} & -96.6 \times 10^{-3} & 0 \\ 0 & 0 & 1 & 0 \end{bmatrix} \begin{bmatrix} u \\ w \\ q \\ \theta \end{bmatrix}$$

where u = forward velocity, w = vertical velocity, q = angular pitch rate at center of mass, and θ = pitch angle between the flight direction and the horizontal (*Sun, 2005*).

a. Use MATLAB to obtain the system's eigenvalues.

b. Write the general form of the state-transition matrix. How many constants would have to be found?

62. A dc-dc converter is a device that takes as an input an unregulated dc voltage and provides a regulated dc voltage as its output. The output voltage may be lower (buck converter), higher (boost converter), or the same as the input voltage. Switching dc-dc converters have a semiconductor active switch (BJT or FET) that is closed periodically with a duty cycle d in a pulse width modulated (PWM) manner. For a boost converter, averaging techniques can be used to arrive at the following state equations (*Van Dijk, 1995*):

$$L\frac{di_L}{dt} = -(1-d)u_c + E_s$$

$$C\frac{du_C}{dt} = (1-d)i_L - \frac{u_C}{R}$$

where L and C are respectively the values of internal inductance and capacitance; i_L is the current through the internal inductor; R is the resistive load connected to the converter; E_s is the dc input voltage; and the capacitor voltage, u_C, is the converter's output.

a. Write the converter's equations in the form

$$\dot{\mathbf{x}} = \mathbf{A}\mathbf{x} + \mathbf{B}u$$
$$\mathbf{y} = \mathbf{C}\mathbf{x}$$

assuming d is a constant.

b. Using the **A**, **B**, and **C** matrices of Part **a**, obtain the converter's transfer function $\frac{U_C(s)}{E_s(s)}$.

63. An IPMC (Ionic Polymer-Metal Composite) is a Nafion sheet plated with gold on both sides. An IPMC bends when an electric field is applied across its thickness. IPMCs have been used as robotic actuators in several applications and as active catheters in biomedical applications. With the aim of improving actuator settling times, a state-space model has been developed for a 20 mm × 10 mm ×0.2 mm polymer sample (*Mallavarapu, 2001*):

$$\begin{bmatrix} \dot{x}_1 \\ \dot{x}_2 \end{bmatrix} = \begin{bmatrix} -8.34 & -2.26 \\ 1 & 0 \end{bmatrix} \begin{bmatrix} x_1 \\ x_2 \end{bmatrix} + \begin{bmatrix} 1 \\ 0 \end{bmatrix} u$$

$$y = \begin{bmatrix} 12.54 & 2.26 \end{bmatrix} \begin{bmatrix} x_1 \\ x_2 \end{bmatrix}$$

where u is the applied input voltage and y is the deflection at one of the material's tips when the sample is tested in a cantilever arrangement.

a. Find the state-transition matrix for the system.

b. From Eq. (4.109) in the text, it follows that if a system has zero initial conditions the system output for any input can be directly calculated from the state-space representation and the state-transition matrix using

$$y(t) = \mathbf{C}\mathbf{x}(t) = \int \mathbf{C}\Phi(t-\tau)\mathbf{B}u(\tau)\,d\tau$$

Use this equation to find the zero initial condition unit step response of the IPMC material sample.

c. Use MATLAB to verify that your step response calculation in Part **b** is correct.

Design Problems

64. Find an equation that relates 2% settling time to the value of f_v for the translational mechanical system shown in Figure P4.16. Neglect the mass of all components. [Section: 4.6]

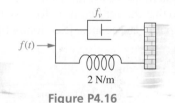

Figure P4.16

65. Consider the translational mechanical system shown in Figure P4.17. A 1-pound force, $f(t)$, is applied at $t = 0$. If $M = 1$, find K and f_v such that the response is characterized by a 20% overshoot and a damped frequency of oscillation of 10 rad/s.

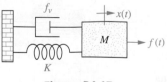

Figure P4.17

66. Given the translational mechanical system of Figure P4.17, where $K = 1$ and $f(t)$ is a unit step, find the values of M and hr f_v to yield a response with 30% overshoot and a settling time of 10 seconds

67. Find J and K in the rotational system shown in Figure P4.18 to yield a 30% overshoot and a settling time of 4 seconds for a step input in torque. [Section: 4.6]

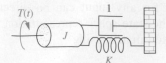

Figure P4.18

68. Given the system shown in Figure P4.19, find the damping, D, to yield a 30% overshoot in output angular displacement for a step input in torque. [Section: 4.6]

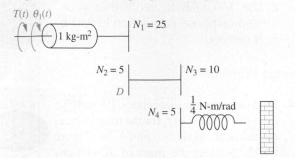

Figure P4.19

69. For the system shown in Figure P4.20, find N_1/N_2 so that the settling time for a step torque input is 16 seconds. [Section: 4.6]

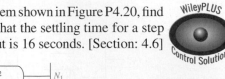

Figure P4.20

70. Find M and K, shown in the system of Figure P4.21, to yield $x(t)$ with 10% overshoot and 10 seconds

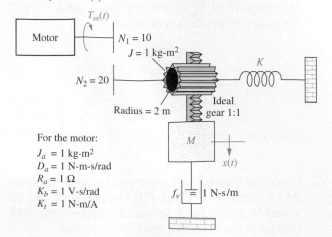

Figure P4.21

settling time for a step input in motor torque, $T_m(t)$. [Section: 4.6]

71. If $v_i(t)$ is a step voltage in the network shown in Figure P4.22, find the value of the resistor such that a 20% overshoot in voltage will be seen across the capacitor if $C = 10^{-6}$ F and $L = 1$ H. [Section: 4.6]

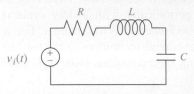

Figure P4.22

72. If $v_i(t)$ is a step voltage in the network shown in Figure P4.22, find the values of R and C to yield a 20% overshoot and a 1 ms settling time for $v_c(t)$ if $L = 1$H. [Section: 4.6]

73. Given the circuit of Figure P4.22, where $C = 10\,\mu$F, find R and L to yield 15% overshoot with a settling time of 2 ms for the capacitor voltage. The input, $v(t)$, is a unit step. [Section: 4.6]

74. For the circuit shown in Figure P4.23, find the values of R_2 and C to yield 15% overshoot with a settling time of 1 ms for the voltage across the capacitor, with $v_i(t)$ as a step input. [Section: 4.6]

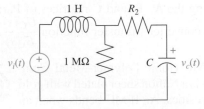

Figure P4.23

75. Hydraulic pumps are used as inputs to hydraulic circuits to supply pressure, just as voltage sources supply potential to electric circuits. Applications for hydraulic circuits can be found in the robotics and aircraft industries, where hydraulic actuators are used to move component parts. Figure P4.24 shows the internal parts of the pump. A barrel containing equally spaced pistons rotates about the i-axis. A swashplate, set at an angle, causes the slippers at the ends of the pistons to move the pistons in and out. When the pistons are moving across the intake port, they are extending, and when they are moving across the discharge port, they are retracting and pushing fluid from the port. The large and small actuators at the top and

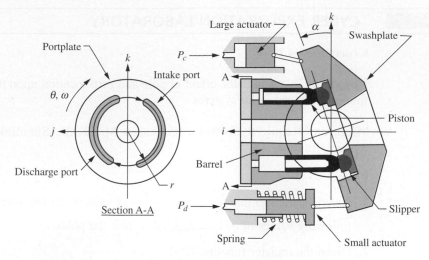

Figure P4.24 Pump diagram

bottom, respectively, control the angle of the swashplate, α. The swashplate angle affects the piston stroke length. Thus, by controlling the swashplate angle, the pump discharge flow rate can be regulated. Assume the state equation for the hydraulic pump is

$$\dot{\mathbf{x}} = \begin{bmatrix} (3.45 - 14000 K_c) & -0.255 \times 10^{-9} \\ 0.499 \times 10^{11} & -3.68 \end{bmatrix} \mathbf{x}$$
$$+ \begin{bmatrix} -3.45 + 14000 K_c \\ -0.499 \times 10^{11} \end{bmatrix} \alpha_0,$$

where $\mathbf{x} = \begin{bmatrix} \alpha \\ P_d \end{bmatrix}$

and P_d is the pump discharge pressure (*Manring, 1996*). Find the value of controller flow gain, K_c, so that the damping ratio of the system's poles is 0.9.

Progressive Analysis and Design Problems

76. **High-speed rail pantograph.** Problem 64(c) in Chapter 2 asked you to find $G(s) = (Y_h(s) - Y_{cat}(s))/ F_{up}(s)$ (*O'Connor, 1997*).

   a. Use the dominant poles from this transfer function and estimate percent overshoot, damping ratio, natural frequency, settling time, peak time, and rise time.

   b. Determine if the second-order approximation is valid.

   c. Obtain the step response of $G(s)$ and compare the results to Part **a**.

MATLAB

State Space

77. **Control of HIV/AIDS.** In Chapter 3, Problem 28, we developed a linearized state-space model of HIV infection. The

model assumed that two different drugs were used to combat the spread of the HIV virus. Since this book focuses on single-input, single-output systems, only one of the two drugs will be considered. We will assume that only RTIs are used as an input. Thus, in the equations of Chapter 3, Problem 28, $u_2 = 0$ (*Craig, 2004*).

a. Show that when using only RTIs in the linearized system of Problem 28 and substituting the typical parameter values given in the table of Problem 28(c), the resulting state-space representation for the system is given by

$$\begin{bmatrix} \dot{T} \\ \dot{T}^* \\ \dot{v} \end{bmatrix} = \begin{bmatrix} -0.04167 & 0 & -0.0058 \\ 0.0217 & -0.24 & 0.0058 \\ 0 & 100 & -2.4 \end{bmatrix}$$
$$\times \begin{bmatrix} T \\ T^* \\ v \end{bmatrix} + \begin{bmatrix} 5.2 \\ -5.2 \\ 0 \end{bmatrix} u_1$$
$$y = \begin{bmatrix} 0 & 0 & 1 \end{bmatrix} \begin{bmatrix} T \\ T^* \\ v \end{bmatrix}$$

b. Obtain the transfer function from RTI efficiency to virus count; namely find $\dfrac{Y(s)}{U_1(s)}$.

c. Assuming RTIs are 100% effective, what will be the steady-state change of virus count in a given infected patient? Express your answer in virus copies per mL of plasma. Approximately how much time will the medicine take to reach its maximum possible effectiveness?

CYBER EXPLORATION LABORATORY

Experiment 4.1

Objective To evaluate the effect of pole and zero location upon the time response of first- and second-order systems.

Minimum Required Software Packages MATLAB, Simulink, and the Control System Toolbox

Prelab

1. Given the transfer function $G(s) = \dfrac{a}{s+a}$: Evaluate settling time and rise time for the following values of a: 1, 2, 3, 4. Also, plot the poles.

2. Given the transfer function $G(s) = \dfrac{b}{s^2 + as + b}$:

   a. Evaluate percent overshoot, settling time, peak time, and rise time for the following values: $a = 4$, $b = 25$. Also, plot the poles.

   b. Calculate the values of a and b so that the imaginary part of the poles remains the same but the real part is increased 2 times over that of Prelab 2(a), and repeat Prelab 2(a).

   c. Calculate the values of a and b so that the imaginary part of the poles remains the same but the real part is decreased $\frac{1}{2}$ time over that of Prelab 2(a), and repeat Prelab 2(a).

3. a. For the system of Prelab 2(a), calculate the values of a and b so that the real part of the poles remains the same but the imaginary part is increased 2 times over that of Prelab 2(a), and repeat Prelab 2(a).

   b. For the system of Prelab 2(a), calculate the values of a and b so that the real part of the poles remains the same but the imaginary part is increased 4 times over that of Prelab 2(a), and repeat Prelab 2(a).

4. a. For the system of Prelab 2(a), calculate the values of a and b so that the damping ratio remains the same but the natural frequency is increased 2 times over that of Prelab 2(a), and repeat Prelab 2(a).

   b. For the system of Prelab 2(a), calculate the values of a and b so that the damping ratio remains the same but the natural frequency is increased 4 times over that of Prelab 2(a), and repeat Prelab 2(a).

5. Briefly describe the effects on the time response as the poles are changed in each of Prelabs 2, 3, and 4.

Lab

1. Using Simulink, set up the systems of Prelab 1 and plot the step response of each of the four transfer functions on a single graph by using the Simulink LTI Viewer. Also, record the values of settling time and rise time for each step response.

2. Using Simulink, set up the systems of Prelab 2. Using the Simulink LTI Viewer, plot the step response of each of the three transfer functions on a single graph. Also, record the values of percent overshoot, settling time, peak time, and rise time for each step response.

3. Using Simulink, set up the systems of Prelab 2(a) and Prelab 3. Using the Simulink LTI Viewer, plot the step response of each of the three transfer functions on a single graph. Also, record the values of percent overshoot, settling time, peak time, and rise time for each step response.

4. Using Simulink, set up the systems of Prelab 2(a) and Prelab 4. Using the Simulink LTI Viewer, plot the step response of each of the three transfer functions on a single graph. Also, record the values of percent overshoot, settling time, peak time, and rise time for each step response.

Postlab

1. For the first-order systems, make a table of calculated and experimental values of settling time, rise time, and pole location.

2. For the second-order systems of Prelab 2, make a table of calculated and experimental values of percent overshoot, settling time, peak time, rise time, and pole location.

3. For the second-order systems of Prelab 2(a) and Prelab 3, make a table of calculated and experimental values of percent overshoot, settling time, peak time, rise time, and pole location.

4. For the second-order systems of Prelab 2(a) and Prelab 4, make a table of calculated and experimental values of percent overshoot, settling time, peak time, rise time, and pole location.

5. Discuss the effects of pole location upon the time response for both first- and second-order systems. Discuss any discrepancies between your calculated and experimental values.

Experiment 4.2

Objective To evaluate the effect of additional poles and zeros upon the time response of second-order systems.

Minimum Required Software Packages MATLAB, Simulink, and the Control System Toolbox

Prelab

1. **a.** Given the transfer function $G(s) = \dfrac{25}{s^2 + 4s + 25}$: Evaluate the percent overshoot, settling time, peak time, and rise time. Also, plot the poles.

   b. Add a pole at -200 to the system of Prelab 1(a). Estimate whether the transient response in Prelab 1(a) will be appreciably affected.

   c. Repeat Prelab 1(b) with the pole successively placed at -20, -10, and -2.

2. A zero is added to the system of Prelab 1(a) at -200 and then moved to -50, -20, -10, -5, and -2. List the values of zero location in the order of the greatest to the least effect upon the pure second-order transient response.

3. Given the transfer function $G(s) = \dfrac{(25b/a)(s+a)}{(s+b)(s^2 + 4s + 25)}$: Let $a = 3$ and $b = 3.01$, 3.1, 3.3, 3.5, and 4.0. Which values of b will have minimal effect upon the pure second-order transient response?

4. Given the transfer function $G(s) = \dfrac{(2500b/a)(s+a)}{(s+b)(s^2+40s+2500)}$: Let $a = 30$ and $b = 30.01, 30.1, 30.5, 31, 35,$ and 40. Which values of b will have minimal effect upon the pure second-order transient response?

Lab

1. Using Simulink, add a pole to the second-order system of Prelab 1(a) and plot the step responses of the system when the higher-order pole is nonexistent, at -200, -20, -10, and -2. Make your plots on a single graph, using the Simulink LTI Viewer. Normalize all plots to a steady-state value of unity. Record percent overshoot, settling time, peak time, and rise time for each response.

2. Using Simulink, add a zero to the second-order system of Prelab 1(a) and plot the step responses of the system when the zero is nonexistent, at $-200, -50, -20, -10$, -5, and -2. Make your plots on a single graph, using the Simulink LTI Viewer. Normalize all plots to a steady-state value of unity. Record percent overshoot, settling time, peak time, and rise time for each response.

3. Using Simulink and the transfer function of Prelab 3 with $a = 3$, plot the step responses of the system when the value of b is $3, 3.01, 3.1, 3.3, 3.5,$ and 4.0. Make your plots on a single graph using the Simulink LTI Viewer. Record percent overshoot, settling time, peak time, and rise time for each response.

4. Using Simulink and the transfer function of Prelab 4 with $a = 30$, plot the step responses of the system when the value of b is $30, 30.01, 30.1, 30.5, 31, 35,$ and 40. Make your plots on a single graph, using the Simulink LTI Viewer. Record percent overshoot, settling time, peak time, and rise time for each response.

Postlab

1. Discuss the effect upon the transient response of the proximity of a higher-order pole to the dominant second-order pole pair.

2. Discuss the effect upon the transient response of the proximity of a zero to the dominant second-order pole pair. Explore the relationship between the length of the vector from the zero to the dominant pole and the zero's effect upon the pure second-order step response.

3. Discuss the effect of pole-zero cancellation upon the transient response of a dominant second-order pole pair. Allude to how close the canceling pole and zero should be and the relationships of (1) the distance between them and (2) the distance between the zero and the dominant second-order poles.

BIBLIOGRAPHY

Borovic, B., Liu, A. Q., Popa, D., and Lewis, F. L. Open-Loop versus Closed-Loop Control of MEMS Devices: Choices and Issues. *Journal of Micromechanics, Microengineering*, vol. 15, 2005, pp. 1917–1924.

Craig, I. K., Xia, X., and Venter, J. W.; Introducing HIV/AIDS Education into the Electrical Engineering Curriculum at the University of Pretoria. *IEEE Transactions on Education*, vol. 47, no. 1, February 2004, pp. 65–73.

DiBona, G. F. Physiology in Perspective: The Wisdom of the Body. Neural Control of the Kidney. *American Journal of Physiology–Regulatory, Integrative and Comparative Physiology*, vol. 289, 2005, pp. R633–R641.

Dorf, R. C. *Introduction to Electric Circuits*, 2d ed. Wiley, New York, 1993.

Franklin, G. F., Powell, J. D., and Emami-Naeini, A. *Feedback Control of Dynamic Systems*, 2d ed. Addison-Wesley, Reading, MA, 1991.

Glantz, A. S., and Tyberg, V. J. Determination of Frequency Response from Step Response: Application to Fluid-Filled Catheters. *American Journal of Physiology*, vol. 2, 1979, pp. H376–H378.

Good, M. C., Sweet, L. M., and Strobel, K. L. Dynamic Models for Control System Design of Integrated Robot and Drive Systems. *Journal of Dynamic Systems, Measurement, and Control*, March 1985, pp. 53–59.

Ionescu, C., and De Keyser, R. Adaptive Closed-Loop Strategy for Paralyzed Skeletal Muscles. Proceedings of the IASTED International Conference on Biomedical Engineering, 2005.

Jannett, T. C., and Aragula, S. Simulation of Adaptive Control of Theophylline Concentrations. *IEEE Control Systems*, December 1992, pp. 32–37.

Johnson, H. et al. *Unmanned Free-Swimming Submersible (UFSS) System Description*. NRL Memorandum Report 4393. Naval Research Laboratory, Washington, DC, 1980.

Kuo, B. C. *Automatic Control Systems*, 5th ed. Prentice Hall, Englewood Cliffs, NJ, 1987.

Linkens, D. A. Adaptive and Intelligent Control in Anesthesia. *IEEE Control Systems*, December 1992, pp. 6–11.

Mallavarapu, K., Newbury, K., and Leo, D. J. *Feedback Control of the Bending Response of Ionic Polymer-Metal Composite Actuators*. Proceedings of the SPIE, vol. 4329, 2001, pp. 301–310.

Manring, N. D., and Johnson, R. E. Modeling and Designing a Variable-Displacement Open-Loop Pump. *Journal of Dynamic Systems, Measurements, and Control*, vol. 118, June 1996, pp. 267–271.

McRuer, D., Ashkenas, I., and Graham, D. *Aircraft Dynamics and Automatic Control*. Princeton University Press, 1973.

Nakamura, M. et al. Transient Response of Remnant Atrial Heart Rate to Step Changes in Total Artificial Heart Output. *Journal of Artificial Organs*, vol. 5, 2002, pp. 6–12.

Nashner, L. M., and Wolfson, P. Influence of Head Position and Proprioceptive Cues on Short Latency Postural Reflexes Evoked by Galvanic Stimulation of the Human Labyrinth. *Brain Research*, vol. 67, 1974, pp. 255–268.

O'Connor, D. N., Eppinger, S. D., Seering, W. P., and Wormly, D. N. Active Control of a High-Speed Pantograph. *Journal of Dynamic Systems, Measurements, and Control*, vol. 119, March 1997, pp. 1–4.

Ogata, K. *Modern Control Engineering*, 2d ed. Prentice Hall, Englewood Cliffs, NJ, 1990.

Philips, C. L., and Nagle, H. T. *Digital Control Systems Analysis and Design*. Prentice Hall, Englewood Cliffs, NJ, 1984.

Salapaka, S., Sebastian, A.,Cleveland, J. P., and Salapaka, M. V. High Bandwidth Nano-Positioner: A Robust Control Approach. *Review of Scientific Instruments*, vol. 73, No. 9, 2002, pp. 3232–3241.

Sawusch, M. R., and Summers, T. A. *1001 Things to Do with Your Macintosh*. TAB Books, Blue Ridge Summit, PA, 1984.

Schneider, R. T. Pneumatic Robots Continue to Improve. *Hydraulics & Pneumatics*, October 1992, pp. 38–39.

Stefani, R. T. *Modeling Human Response Characteristics*. COED Application Note No. 33. Computers in Education Division of ASEE, 1973.

Sun, M., and Xiong, Y. Dynamic Flight Stability of a Hovering Bumblebee. *Journal of Experimental Biology*, vol. 208, 2005, pp. 447–459.

Timothy, L. K., and Bona, B. E. *State Space Analysis: An Introduction.* McGraw-Hill, New York, 1968.

Van Dijk, E., Spruijt, J. N., O'Sullivan, D. M., and Klaasens, J. B. PWM-Switch Modeling of DC-DC Converters. *IEEE Transactions on Power Electronics,* vol. 10, 1995, pp. 659–665.

Zedka, M., Prochazka, A., Knight, B., Gillard, D., and Gauthier, M. Voluntary and Reflex Control of Human Back Muscles During Induced Pain. *Journal of Physiology,* vol. 520, 1999, pp. 591–604.

Zhou, B. H., Baratta, R. V., Solomonow, M., and D'Ambrosia, R. D. The Dynamic Response of the Cat Ankle Joint During Load-Moving Contractions. *IEEE Transactions on Biomedical Engineering,* vol. 42, no. 4, 1995, pp. 386–393.

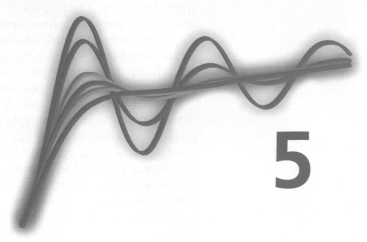

EQUIVALENT SYSTEMS

5

CHAPTER OBJECTIVES

In this chapter you will learn the following:

- How to reduce a block diagram of multiple subsystems to a single block representing the transfer function from input to output
- How to analyze and design transient response for a system consisting of multiple subsystems
- How to represent in state space a system consisting of multiple subsystems
- How to convert between alternate representations of a system in state space

CASE STUDY OBJECTIVES

You will be able to demonstrate your knowledge of the chapter objectives with case studies as follows:

- Given the antenna azimuth position control system shown on the front endpapers, you will be able to (a) find the closed-loop transfer function that represents the system from input to output; (b) find a state-space representation for the closed-loop system; (c) predict, for a simplified system model, the percent overshoot, settling time, and peak time of the closed-loop system for a step input; (d) calculate the step response for the closed-loop system; and (e) for the simplified model, design the system gain to meet a transient response requirement.

- Given the block diagrams for the UFSS vehicle's pitch and heading control systems on the back endpapers, you will be able to represent each control system in state space.

5.1 INTRODUCTION

We have been working with individual subsystems represented by a block with its input and output. More complicated systems, however, are represented by the interconnection of many subsystems. Since the response of a single transfer function can be calculated, we want to represent multiple subsystems as a single transfer function. We can then apply the analytical techniques of the previous chapters and obtain transient response information about the entire system.

In this chapter multiple subsystems are represented in two ways: as block diagrams and as signal-flow graphs. Although neither representation is limited to a particular analysis and design technique, block diagrams are usually used for frequency-domain analysis and design, and signal-flow graphs for state-space analysis.

Signal-flow graphs represent transfer functions as lines, and signals as small-circular nodes. Summing is implicit. To show why it is convenient to use signal-flow graphs for state-space analysis and design, consider Figure 3.10. A graphical representation of a system's transfer function is as simple as Figure 3.10(*a*). However, a graphical representation of a system in state space requires representation of each state variable, as in Figure 3.10(*b*). In this example, a single-block transfer function requires seven blocks and a summing junction to show the state variables explicitly. Thus, signal-flow graphs have advantages over block diagrams, such as Figure 3.10(*b*): they can be drawn more quickly, they are more compact, and they emphasize the state variables.

We will develop techniques to reduce each representation to a single transfer function. Block diagram algebra will be used to reduce block diagrams and Mason's rule to reduce signal-flow graphs. Again, it must be emphasized that these methods are typically used as described. As we shall see, however, either method can be used for frequency-domain or state-space analysis and design.

5.2 BLOCK DIAGRAMS

As you already know, a subsystem is represented as a block with an input, an output, and a transfer function. Many systems are composed of multiple subsystems, as in Figure 5.1. When multiple subsystems are interconnected, a few more schematic elements must be added to the block diagram. These new elements are *summing junctions* and *pickoff points.* All component parts of a block diagram for a linear, time-invariant system are shown in Figure 5.2. The characteristic of the summing junction shown in Figure 5.2(*c*) is that the output signal, $C(s)$, is the algebraic sum of the input signals, $R_1(s)$, $R_2(s)$, and $R_3(s)$. The figure shows three inputs, but any number can be present. A pickoff point, as shown in Figure 5.2(*d*), distributes the input signal, $R(s)$, undiminished, to several output points.

We will now examine some common topologies for interconnecting subsystems and derive the single transfer function representation for each of them. These common topologies will form the basis for reducing more complicated systems to a single block.

CASCADE FORM

Figure 5.3(*a*) shows an example of cascaded subsystems. Intermediate signal values are shown at the output of each subsystem. Each signal is derived from the product of the input times the transfer function. The equivalent transfer function, $G_e(s)$, shown in

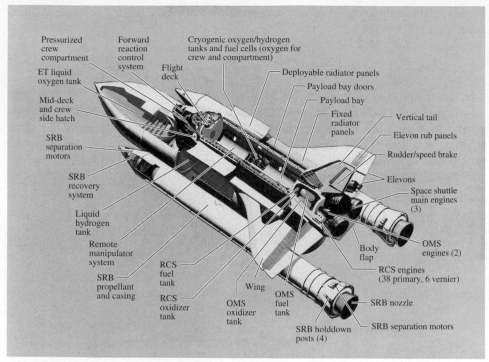

FIGURE 5.1 The space shuttle consists of multiple subsystems. Can you identify those that are control systems or parts of control systems?

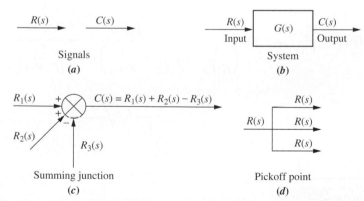

FIGURE 5.2 Components of a block diagram for a linear, time-invariant system

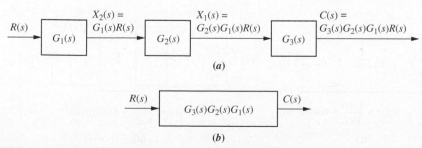

FIGURE 5.3 **a.** Cascaded subsystems; **b.** equivalent transfer function

Figure 5.3(b), is the output Laplace transform divided by the input Laplace transform from Figure 5.3(a), or

$$G_e(s) = G_3(s)G_2(s)G_1(s) \tag{5.1}$$

which is the product of the subsystems' transfer functions.

Equation 5.1 was derived under the assumption that interconnected subsystems do not load adjacent subsystems. That is, a subsystem's output remains the same whether or not the subsequent subsystem is connected. If there is a change in the output, the subsequent subsystem loads the previous subsystem, and the equivalent transfer function is not the product of the individual transfer functions. The network of Figure 5.4(a) demonstrates this concept. Its transfer function is

$$G_1(s) = \frac{V_1(s)}{V_i(s)} = \frac{\dfrac{1}{R_1 C_1}}{s + \dfrac{1}{R_1 C_1}} \tag{5.2}$$

Similarly, the network of Figure 5.4(b) has the following transfer function:

$$G_2(s) = \frac{V_2(s)}{V_1(s)} = \frac{\dfrac{1}{R_2 C_2}}{s + \dfrac{1}{R_2 C_2}} \tag{5.3}$$

If the networks are placed in cascade, as in Figure 5.4(c), you can verify that the transfer function found using loop or node equations is

$$G(s) = \frac{V_2(s)}{V_i(s)} = \frac{\dfrac{1}{R_1 C_1 R_2 C_2}}{s^2 + \left(\dfrac{1}{R_1 C_1} + \dfrac{1}{R_2 C_2} + \dfrac{1}{R_2 C_1}\right)s + \dfrac{1}{R_1 C_1 R_2 C_2}} \tag{5.4}$$

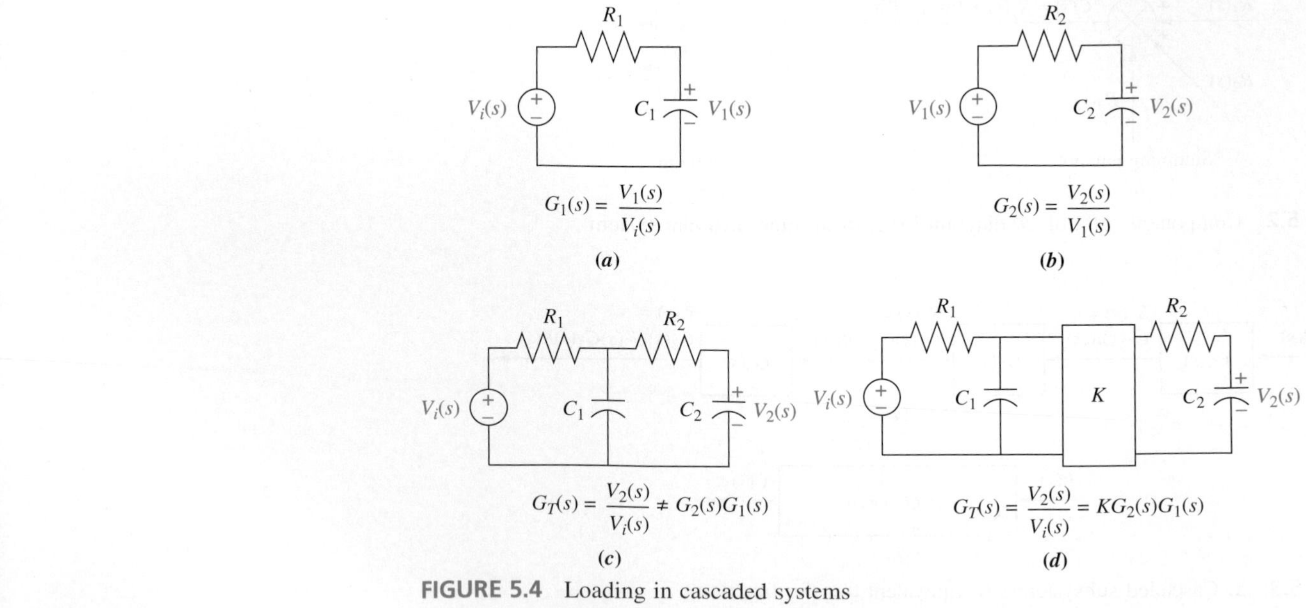

$$G_1(s) = \frac{V_1(s)}{V_i(s)}$$

(a)

$$G_2(s) = \frac{V_2(s)}{V_1(s)}$$

(b)

$$G_T(s) = \frac{V_2(s)}{V_i(s)} \neq G_2(s)G_1(s)$$

(c)

$$G_T(s) = \frac{V_2(s)}{V_i(s)} = KG_2(s)G_1(s)$$

(d)

FIGURE 5.4 Loading in cascaded systems

But, using Eq. (5.1),

$$G(s) = G_2(s)G_1(s) = \dfrac{\dfrac{1}{R_1C_1R_2C_2}}{s^2 + \left(\dfrac{1}{R_1C_1} + \dfrac{1}{R_2C_2}\right)s + \dfrac{1}{R_1C_1R_2C_2}} \tag{5.5}$$

Equations (5.4) and (5.5) are not the same: Eq. (5.4) has one more term for the coefficient of s in the denominator and is correct.

One way to prevent loading is to use an amplifier between the two networks, as shown in Figure 5.4(d). The amplifier has a high-impedance input, so that it does not load the previous network. At the same time it has a low-impedance output, so that it looks like a pure voltage source to the subsequent network. With the amplifier included, the equivalent transfer function is the product of the transfer functions and the gain, K, of the amplifier.

PARALLEL FORM

Figure 5.5 shows an example of parallel subsystems. Again, by writing the output of each subsystem, we can find the equivalent transfer function. Parallel subsystems have a common input and an output formed by the algebraic sum of the outputs from all of the subsystems. The equivalent transfer function, $G_e(s)$, is the output transform divided by the input transform from Figure 5.5(a), or

$$\boxed{G_e(s) = \pm G_1(s) \pm G_2(s) \pm G_3(s)} \tag{5.6}$$

which is the algebraic sum of the subsystems' transfer functions; it appears in Figure 5.5(b).

FEEDBACK FORM

The third topology is the feedback form, which will be seen repeatedly in subsequent chapters. The feedback system forms the basis for our study of control systems engineering. In Chapter 1 we defined open-loop and closed-loop systems and pointed

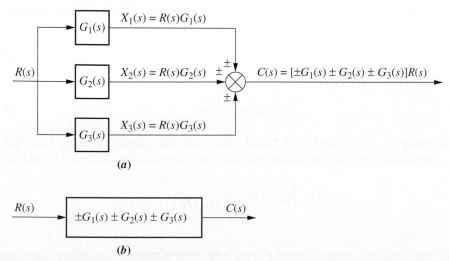

(a)

(b)

FIGURE 5.5 **a.** Parallel subsystems; **b.** equivalent transfer function

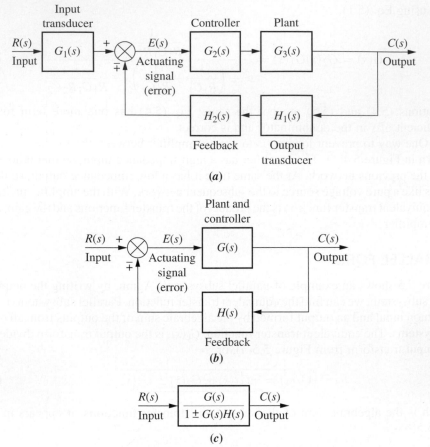

FIGURE 5.6 **a.** Feedback control system; **b.** simplified model; **c.** equivalent transfer function

out the advantage of closed-loop, or feedback control, systems over open-loop systems. As we move ahead, we will focus on the analysis and design of feedback systems.

Let us derive the transfer function that represents the system from its input to its output. The typical feedback system, described in detail in Chapter 1, is shown in Figure 5.6(a); a simplified model is shown in Figure 5.6(b).[1] Directing our attention to the simplified model,

$$E(s) = R(s) \mp C(s)H(s) \tag{5.7}$$

But since $C(s) = E(s)G(s)$,

$$E(s) = \frac{C(s)}{G(s)} \tag{5.8}$$

Substituting Eq. (5.8) into Eq. (5.7) and solving for the transfer function, $C(s)/R(s) = G_e(s)$, we obtain the equivalent, or *closed-loop*, transfer function shown in Figure 5.6(c),

$$G_e(s) = \frac{G(s)}{1 \pm G(s)H(s)} \tag{5.9}$$

---

[1] The system is said to have *negative feedback* if the sign at the summing junction is negative and *positive feedback* if the sign is positive.

The product, $G(s)H(s)$, in Eq. (5.9) is called the *open-loop transfer function,* or *loop gain.*

So far, we have explored three different configurations for multiple subsystems. For each, we found the equivalent transfer function. Since these three forms are combined into complex arrangements in physical systems, recognizing these topologies is a prerequisite to obtaining the equivalent transfer function of a complex system. In this section we will reduce complex systems composed of multiple subsystems to single transfer functions.

MOVING BLOCKS TO CREATE FAMILIAR FORMS

Before we begin to reduce block diagrams, it must be explained that the familiar forms (cascade, parallel, and feedback) are not always apparent in a block diagram. For example, in the feedback form, if there is a pickoff point after the summing junction, you cannot use the feedback formula to reduce the feedback system to a single block. That signal disappears, and there is no place to reestablish the pickoff point.

This subsection will discuss basic block moves that can be made in order to establish familiar forms when they almost exist. In particular, it will explain how to move blocks left and right past summing junctions and pickoff points.

Figure 5.7 shows equivalent block diagrams formed when transfer functions are moved left or right past a summing junction, and Figure 5.8 shows equivalent block diagrams formed when transfer functions are moved left or right past a pickoff point. In the diagrams the symbol $\equiv$ means "equivalent to." These equivalences, along with the forms studied earlier in this section, can be used to reduce a block diagram to a single transfer function. In each case of Figures 5.7 and 5.8, the equivalence can be verified by tracing the signals at the input through to the output and recognizing that the output signals are identical. For example, in Figure 5.7(a), signals $R(s)$ and $X(s)$ are multiplied by $G(s)$ before reaching the output. Hence, both block diagrams are equivalent, with

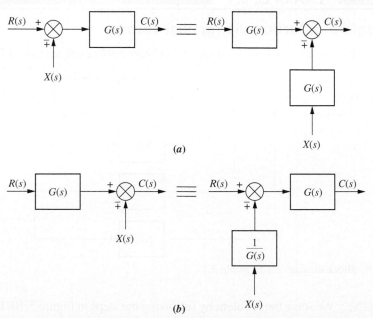

FIGURE 5.7 Block diagram algebra for summing junctions—equivalent forms for moving a block **a.** to the left past a summing junction; **b.** to the right past a summing junction

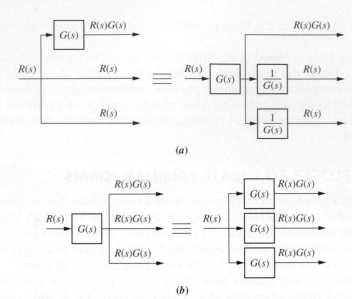

(a)

(b)

FIGURE 5.8 Block diagram algebra for pickoff points—equivalent forms for moving a block **a.** to the left past a pickoff point; **b.** to the right past a pickoff point

$C(s) = R(s)G(s) \mp X(s)G(s)$. In Figure 5.7(*b*), $R(s)$ is multiplied by $G(s)$ before reaching the output, but $X(s)$ is not. Hence, both block diagrams in Figure 5.7(*b*) are equivalent, with $C(s) = R(s)G(s) \mp X(s)$. For pickoff points, similar reasoning yields similar results for the block diagrams of Figure 5.8(*a*) and (*b*).

Let us now put the whole story together with examples of block diagram reduction.

EXAMPLE 5.1

Block diagram reduction via familiar forms

Problem: Reduce the block diagram shown in Figure 5.9 to a single transfer function.

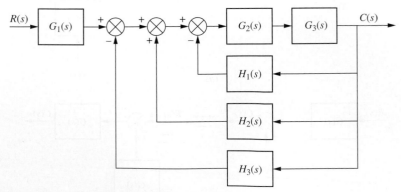

FIGURE 5.9 Block diagram for Example 5.1

SOLUTION: We solve the problem by following the steps in Figure 5.10. First, the three summing junctions can be collapsed into a single summing junction, as shown in Figure 5.10(*a*).

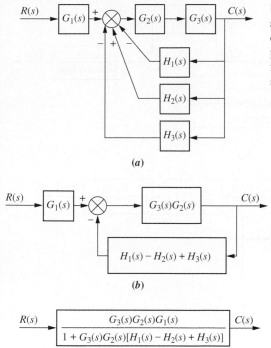

FIGURE 5.10 Steps in solving Example 5.1: **a.** Collapse summing junctions; **b.** form equivalent cascaded system in the forward path and equivalent parallel system in the feedback path; **c.** form equivalent feedback system and multiply by cascaded $G_1(s)$

Second, recognize that the three feedback functions, $H_1(s)$, $H_2(s)$, and $H_3(s)$, are connected in parallel. They are fed from a common signal source, and their outputs are summed. The equivalent function is $H_1(s) - H_2(s) + H_3(s)$. Also recognize that $G_2(s)$ and $G_3(s)$ are connected in cascade. Thus, the equivalent transfer function is the product, $G_3(s)G_2(s)$. The results of these steps are shown in Figure 5.10(*b*).

Finally, the feedback system is reduced and multiplied by $G_1(s)$ to yield the equivalent transfer function shown in Figure 5.10(*c*).

EXAMPLE 5.2

Block diagram reduction by moving blocks

Problem: Reduce the system shown in Figure 5.11 to a single transfer function.

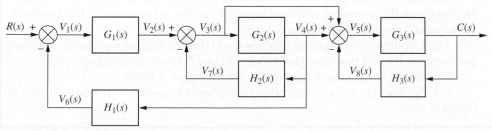

FIGURE 5.11   Block diagram for Example 5.2

SOLUTION: In this example we make use of the equivalent forms shown in Figures 5.7 and 5.8. First, move $G_2(s)$ to the left past the pickoff point to create parallel

FIGURE 5.12 Steps in the block diagram reduction for Example 5.2

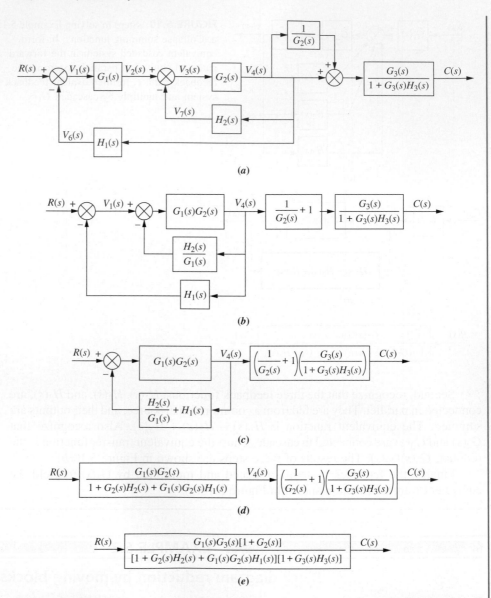

(a)

(b)

(c)

(d)

(e)

subsystems, and reduce the feedback system consisting of $G_3(s)$ and $H_3(s)$. This result is shown in Figure 5.12(*a*).

Second, reduce the parallel pair consisting of $1/G_2(s)$ and unity, and push $G_1(s)$ to the right past the summing junction, creating parallel subsystems in the feedback. These results are shown in Figure 5.12(*b*).

Third, collapse the summing junctions, add the two feedback elements together, and combine the last two cascaded blocks. Figure 5.12(*c*) shows these results.

Fourth, use the feedback formula to obtain Figure 5.12(*d*).

Finally, multiply the two cascaded blocks and obtain the final result, shown in Figure 5.12(*e*).

MATLAB

Students who are using MATLAB should now run ch5p1 in Appendix B to perform block diagram reduction.

SKILL-ASSESSMENT EXERCISE 5.1

Problem: Find the equivalent transfer function, $T(s) = C(s)/R(s)$, for the system shown in Figure 5.13.

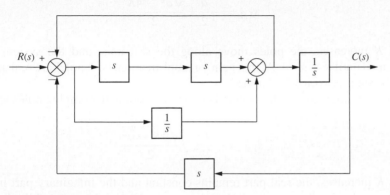

FIGURE 5.13   Block diagram for Skill-Assessment Exercise 5.1

ANSWER:

$$T(s) = \frac{s^3 + 1}{2s^4 + s^2 + 2s}$$

The complete solution is at www.wiley.com/college/nise.

TryIt 5.1

Use the following MATLAB and Control System Toolbox statements to find the closed-loop transfer function of the system in Example 5.2 if all $G_i(s) = 1/(s + 1)$ and all $H_i(s) = 1/(s)$.

```
G1=tf(1,[1 1]);
G2=G1;G3=G1;
H1=tf(1,[1 0]);
H2=H1;H3=H1;
System=append ...
(G1,G2,G3,H1,H2,H3);
input=1; output=3;
Q=[1 -4  0  0  0
   2  1 -5  0  0
   3  2  1 -5 -6
   4  2  0  0  0
   5  2  0  0  0
   6  3  0  0  0];
T=connect(System,...
Q,input,output);
T=tf(T);T=minreal(T)
```

In this section we examined the equivalence of several block diagram configurations containing signals, systems, summing junctions, and pickoff points. These configurations were the cascade, parallel, and feedback forms. During block diagram reduction, we attempt to produce these easily recognized forms and then reduce the block diagram to a single transfer function. In the next section we will examine some applications of block diagram reduction.

5.3 ANALYSIS AND DESIGN OF FEEDBACK SYSTEMS

An immediate application of the principles of Section 5.2 is the analysis and design of feedback systems that reduce to second-order systems. Percent overshoot, settling time, peak time, and rise time can then be found from the equivalent transfer function.

Consider the system shown in Figure 5.14, which can model a control system such as the antenna azimuth position control system. For example, the transfer function, $K/s(s + a)$, can model the amplifiers, motor, load, and gears. From Eq. (5.9), the closed-loop transfer function, $T(s)$, for this system is

$$T(s) = \frac{K}{s^2 + as + K} \qquad (5.10)$$

where K models the amplifier gain, that is, the ratio of the output voltage to the input voltage. As K varies, the poles move through the

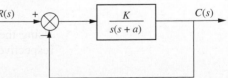

FIGURE 5.14   Second-order feedback control system

three ranges of operation of a second-order system: overdamped, critically damped, and underdamped. For example, for K between 0 and $a^2/4$, the poles of the system are real and are located at

$$s_{1,2} = -\frac{a}{2} \pm \frac{\sqrt{a^2 - 4K}}{2} \tag{5.11}$$

As K increases, the poles move along the real axis, and the system remains overdamped until $K = a^2/4$. At that gain, or amplification, both poles are real and equal, and the system is critically damped.

For gains above $a^2/4$, the system is underdamped, with complex poles located at

$$s_{1,2} = -\frac{a}{2} \pm j\frac{\sqrt{4K - a^2}}{2} \tag{5.12}$$

Now as K increases, the real part remains constant and the imaginary part increases. Thus, the peak time decreases and the percent overshoot increases, while the settling time remains constant.

Let us look at two examples that apply the concepts to feedback control systems. In the first example we determine a system's transient response. In the second example we design the gain to meet a transient response requirement.

EXAMPLE 5.3

Finding transient response

Problem: For the system shown in Figure 5.15, find the peak time, percent overshoot, and settling time.

SOLUTION: The closed-loop transfer function found from Eq. (5.9) is

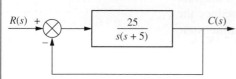

$R(s)$ $+$ $\bigotimes$ $\dfrac{25}{s(s+5)}$ $C(s)$ $-$

FIGURE 5.15   Feedback system for Example 5.3

$$T(s) = \frac{25}{s^2 + 5s + 25} \tag{5.13}$$

From Eq. (4.18),

$$\omega_n = \sqrt{25} = 5 \tag{5.14}$$

From Eq. (4.21),

$$2\zeta\omega_n = 5 \tag{5.15}$$

Substituting Eq. (5.14) into (5.15) and solving for ζ yields

$$\zeta = 0.5 \tag{5.16}$$

Using the values for ζ and ω_n along with Eqs. (4.34), (4.38), and (4.42), we find, respectively,

$$T_p = \frac{\pi}{\omega_n\sqrt{1 - \zeta^2}} = 0.726 \text{ second} \tag{5.17}$$

$$\%OS = e^{-\zeta\pi/\sqrt{1-\zeta^2}} \times 100 = 16.303 \qquad (5.18)$$

$$T_s = \frac{4}{\zeta\omega_n} = 1.6\,\text{seconds} \qquad (5.19)$$

Students who are using MATLAB should now run ch5p2 in Appendix B. You will learn how to perform block diagram reduction followed by an evaluation of the closed-loop system's transient response by finding, T_p, $\%OS$, and T_s. Finally, you will learn how to use MATLAB to generate a closed-loop step response. This exercise uses MATLAB to do Example 5.3.

MATLAB's Simulink provides an alternative method of simulating feedback systems to obtain the time response. Students who are performing the MATLAB exercises and want to explore the added capability of MATLAB's Simulink should now consult Appendix C, "MATLAB's Simulink Tutorial" located at www.wiley.com/college/nise. Example C.3 includes a discussion about, and an example of, the use of Simulink to simulate feedback systems with nonlinearities.

EXAMPLE 5.4

Gain design for transient response

Problem: Design the value of gain, K, for the feedback control system of Figure 5.16 so that the system will respond with a 10% overshoot.

SOLUTION: The closed-loop transfer function of the system is

$$T(s) = \frac{K}{s^2 + 5s + K} \qquad (5.20)$$

From Eq. (5.20),

$$2\zeta\omega_n = 5 \qquad (5.21)$$

and

$$\omega_n = \sqrt{K} \qquad (5.22)$$

Thus,

$$\zeta = \frac{5}{2\sqrt{K}} \qquad (5.23)$$

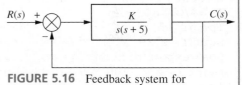

FIGURE 5.16 Feedback system for Example 5.4

Since percent overshoot is a function only of ζ, Eq. (5.23) shows that the percent overshoot is a function of K.

A 10% overshoot implies that $\zeta = 0.591$. Substituting this value for the damping ratio into Eq. (5.23) and solving for K yields

$$K = 17.9 \qquad (5.24)$$

Although we are able to design for percent overshoot in this problem, we could not have selected settling time as a design criterion because, regardless of the value of K, the real parts, -2.5, of the poles of Eq. (5.20) remain the same.

WileyPLUS

Control Solutions

TryIt 5.2

Use the following MATLAB and Control System Toolbox statements to find $\zeta, \omega_n, \%OS,$ $T_s, T_p,$ and T_r for the closed-loop unity feedback system described in Skill-Assessment Exercise 5.2. Start with $a = 2$ and try some other values. A step response for the closed-loop system will also be produced.

```
a = 2;
numg = 16;
deng = poly([0 −a]);
G = tf(numg, deng);
T = feedback(G, 1);
[numt, dent] = ...
tfdata (T, 'v');
wn = sqrt(dent(3))
z = dent(2)/(2*wn)
Ts = 4/(z*wn)
Tp = pi/(wn*...
sqrt(1 − z^2))
pos = exp(−z*pi...
/sqrt(1 − z^2))*100
Tr = (1.76*z^3 − ...
0.417*z^2 + 1.039*...
z + 1)/wn
step (T)
```

■ SKILL-ASSESSMENT EXERCISE 5.2 ■

Problem: For a unity feedback control system with a forward-path transfer function $G(s) = \dfrac{16}{s(s + a)}$, design the value of a to yield a closed-loop step response that has 5% overshoot.

ANSWER:

$$a = 5.52$$

The complete solution is at www.wiley.com/college/nise.

5.4 SIGNAL-FLOW GRAPHS

Signal-flow graphs are an alternative to block diagrams. Unlike block diagrams, which consist of blocks, signals, summing junctions, and pickoff points, a signal-flow graph consists only of *branches,* which represent systems, and *nodes,* which represent signals. These elements are shown in Figure 5.17(a) and (b), respectively. A system is represented by a line with an arrow showing the direction of signal flow through the system. Adjacent to the line we write the transfer function. A signal is a node with the signal's name written adjacent to the node.

Figure 5.17(c) shows the interconnection of the systems and the signals. Each signal is the sum of signals flowing into it. For example, the signal $V(s) = R_1(s)G_1(s) - R_2(s)G_2(s) + R_3(s)G_3(s)$. The signal $C_2(s) = V(s)G_5(s) = R_1(s)G_1(s)G_5(s) - R_2(s)G_2(s)G_5(s) + R_3(s)G_3(s)G_5(s)$. The signal $C_3(s) = -V(s)G_6(s) = -R_1(s)G_1(s)G_6(s) + R_2(s)G_2(s)G_6(s) - R_3(s)G_3(s)G_6(s)$. Notice that in summing negative signals we associate the negative sign with the system and not with a summing junction, as in the case of block diagrams.

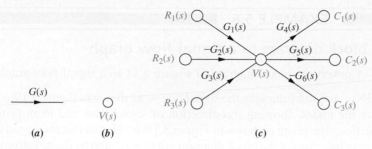

FIGURE 5.17 Signal-flow graph components: **a.** system; **b.** signal; **c.** interconnection of systems and signals

To show the parallel between block diagrams and signal-flow graphs, we will take some of the block diagram forms from Section 5.2 and convert them to signal-flow graphs in Example 5.5. In each case we will first convert the signals to nodes and then interconnect the nodes with system branches. In Example 5.6 we will convert an intricate block diagram to a signal-flow graph.

EXAMPLE 5.5

Converting common block diagrams to signal-flow graphs

Problem: Convert the cascaded, parallel, and feedback forms of the block diagrams shown in Figures 5.3(a), 5.5(a), and 5.6(b), respectively, into signal-flow graphs.

SOLUTION: In each case we start by drawing the signal nodes for that system. Next we interconnect the signal nodes with system branches. The signal nodes for the cascaded, parallel, and feedback forms are shown in Figure 5.18(a), (c), and (e), respectively. The interconnection of the nodes with branches that represent the subsystems is shown in Figure 5.18(b), (d), and (f) for the cascaded, parallel, and feedback forms, respectively.

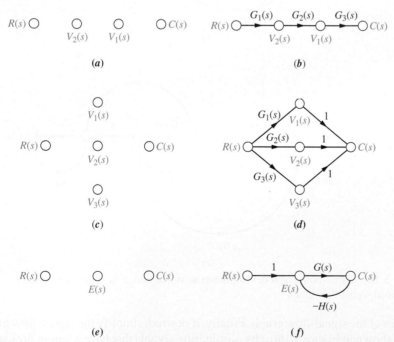

FIGURE 5.18 Building signal-flow graphs: **a.** cascaded system nodes (from Figure 5.3(a)); **b.** cascaded system signal-flow graph; **c.** parallel system nodes (from Figure 5.5(a)); **d.** parallel system signal-flow graph; **e.** feedback system nodes (from Figure 5.6(b)); **f.** feedback system signal-flow graph

EXAMPLE 5.6

Converting a block diagram to a signal-flow graph

Problem: Convert the block diagram of Figure 5.11 to a signal-flow graph.

SOLUTION: Begin by drawing the signal nodes, as shown in Figure 5.19(*a*). Next, interconnect the nodes, showing the direction of signal flow and identifying each transfer function. The result is shown in Figure 5.19(*b*). Notice that the negative signs at the summing junctions of the block diagram are represented by the negative transfer

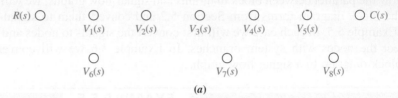

(*a*)

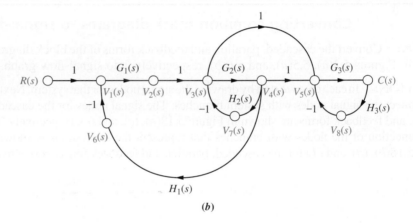

(*b*)

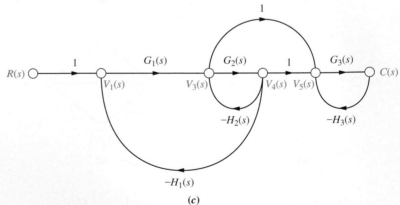

(*c*)

FIGURE 5.19   Signal-flow graph development: **a.** signal nodes; **b.** signal-flow graph; **c.** simplified signal-flow graph

functions of the signal-flow graph. Finally, if desired, simplify the signal-flow graph to the one shown in Figure 5.19(*c*) by eliminating signals that have a single flow in and a single flow out, such as $V_2(s)$, $V_6(s)$, $V_7(s)$, and $V_8(s)$.

5.5 MASON'S RULE

Earlier in this chapter, we discussed how to reduce block diagrams to single transfer functions. Now we are ready to discuss a technique for reducing signal-flow graphs to single transfer functions that relate the output of a system to its input.

The block diagram reduction technique we studied in Section 5.2 requires successive application of fundamental relationships in order to arrive at the system transfer function. On the other hand, Mason's rule for reducing a signal-flow graph to a single transfer function requires the application of one formula. The formula was derived by S. J. Mason when he related the signal-flow graph to the simultaneous equations that can be written from the graph (*Mason, 1953*).

In general, it can be complicated to implement the formula without making mistakes. Specifically, the existence of what we will later call nontouching loops increases the complexity of the formula. However, many systems do not have non-touching loops. For these systems, you may find Mason's rule easier to use than block diagram reduction.

Mason's formula has several components that must be evaluated. First, we must be sure that the definitions of the components are well understood. Then we must exert care in evaluating the components. To that end, we discuss some basic definitions applicable to signal-flow graphs; then we state Mason's rule and do an example.

DEFINITIONS

Loop gain. The product of branch gains found by traversing a path that starts at a node and ends at the same node, following the direction of the signal flow, without passing through any other node more than once. For examples of loop gains, see Figure 5.20. There are four loop gains:

1. $G_2(s)H_1(s)$ (5.25a)
2. $G_4(s)H_2(s)$ (5.25b)
3. $G_4(s)G_5(s)H_3(s)$ (5.25c)
4. $G_4(s)G_6(s)H_3(s)$ (5.25d)

Forward-path gain. The product of gains found by traversing a path from the input node to the output node of the signal-flow graph in the direction of signal flow.

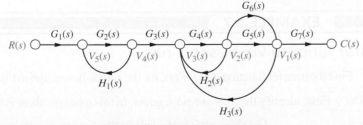

FIGURE 5.20 Signal-flow graph for demonstrating Mason's rule

Examples of forward-path gains are also shown in Figure 5.20. There are two forward-path gains:

1. $G_1(s)G_2(s)G_3(s)G_4(s)G_5(s)G_7(s)$ (5.26a)
2. $G_1(s)G_2(s)G_3(s)G_4(s)G_6(s)G_7(s)$ (5.26b)

Nontouching loops. Loops that do not have any nodes in common. In Figure 5.20, loop $G_2(s)H_1(s)$ does not touch loops $G_4(s)H_2(s)$, $G_4(s)G_5(s)H_3(s)$, and $G_4(s)G_6(s)$ $H_3(s)$.

Nontouching-loop gain. The product of loop gains from nontouching loops taken two, three, four, or more at a time. In Figure 5.20 the product of loop gain $G_2(s)H_1(s)$ and loop gain $G_4(s)H_2(s)$ is a nontouching-loop gain taken two at a time. In summary, all three of the nontouching-loop gains taken two at a time are

1. $[G_2(s)H_1(s)][G_4(s)H_2(s)]$ (5.27a)
2. $[G_2(s)H_1(s)][G_4(s)G_5(s)H_3(s)]$ (5.27b)
3. $[G_2(s)H_1(s)][G_4(s)G_6(s)H_3(s)]$ (5.27c)

The product of loop gains $[G_4(s)G_5(s)H_3(s)][G_4(s)G_6(s)H_3(s)]$ is not a nontouching-loop gain since these two loops have nodes in common. In our example there are no nontouching-loop gains taken three at a time since three nontouching loops do not exist in the example.

We are now ready to state Mason's rule.

MASON'S RULE

The transfer function, $C(s)/R(s)$, of a system represented by a signal-flow graph is

$$G(s) = \frac{C(s)}{R(s)} = \frac{\sum_k T_k \Delta_k}{\Delta} \qquad (5.28)$$

where

k = number of forward paths

T_k = the kth forward-path gain

$\Delta = 1 - \sum$ loop gains $+ \sum$ nontouching-loop gains taken two at a time $- \sum$ nontouching-loop gains taken three at a time $+ \sum$ nontouching-loop gains taken four at a time $- \cdots$

$\Delta_k = \Delta - \sum$ loop gain terms in Δ that touch the kth forward path. In other words, Δ_k is formed by eliminating from Δ those loop gains that touch the kth forward path.

Notice the alternating signs for the components of Δ. The following example will help clarify Mason's rule.

EXAMPLE 5.7

Transfer function via Mason's rule

Problem: Find the transfer function, $C(s)/R(s)$, for the signal-flow graph in Figure 5.21.

SOLUTION: First, identify the *forward-path gains*. In this example there is only one:

$$G_1(s)G_2(s)G_3(s)G_4(s)G_5(s) \qquad (5.29)$$

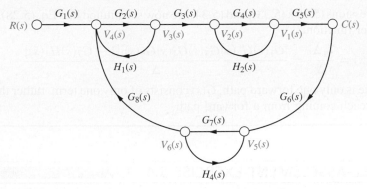

FIGURE 5.21 Signal-flow graph for Example 5.7

Second, identify the *loop gains*. There are four, as follows:

1. $G_2(s)H_1(s)$ (5.30a)
2. $G_4(s)H_2(s)$ (5.30b)
3. $G_7(s)H_4(s)$ (5.30c)
4. $G_2(s)G_3(s)G_4(s)G_5(s)G_6(s)G_7(s)G_8(s)$ (5.30d)

Third, identify the *nontouching loops taken two at a time*. From Eqs. (5.30) and Figure 5.21, we can see that loop 1 does not touch loop 2, loop 1 does not touch loop 3, and loop 2 does not touch loop 3. Notice that loops 1, 2, and 3 all touch loop 4. Thus, the combinations of nontouching loops taken two at a time are as follows:

$$\text{Loop 1 and loop 2}: G_2(s)H_1(s)G_4(s)H_2(s) \qquad (5.31a)$$

$$\text{Loop 1 and loop 3}: G_2(s)H_1(s)G_7(s)H_4(s) \qquad (5.31b)$$

$$\text{Loop 2 and loop 3}: G_4(s)H_2(s)G_7(s)H_4(s) \qquad (5.31c)$$

Finally, the *nontouching loops taken three at a time* are as follows:

$$\text{Loops 1, 2, and 3}: G_2(s)H_1(s)G_4(s)H_2(s)G_7(s)H_4(s) \qquad (5.32)$$

Now, from Eq. (5.28) and its definitions, we form Δ and Δ_k. Hence,

$$
\begin{aligned}
\Delta = 1 - &[G_2(s)H_1(s) + G_4(s)H_2(s) + G_7(s)H_4(s) \\
&\qquad\qquad + G_2(s)G_3(s)G_4(s)G_5(s)G_6(s)G_7(s)G_8(s)] \\
+&[G_2(s)H_1(s)G_4(s)H_2(s) + G_2(s)H_1(s)G_7(s)H_4(s) \\
&\qquad\qquad + G_4(s)H_2(s)G_7(s)H_4(s)] \\
-&[G_2(s)H_1(s)G_4(s)H_2(s)G_7(s)H_4(s)]
\end{aligned}
$$

$$(5.33)$$

We form Δ_k by eliminating from Δ the loop gains that touch the kth forward path:

$$\Delta_1 = 1 - G_7(s)H_4(s) \qquad (5.34)$$

Expressions (5.29), (5.33), and (5.34) are now substituted into Eq. (5.28), yielding the transfer function:

$$G(s) = \frac{T_1 \Delta_1}{\Delta} = \frac{[G_1(s)G_2(s)G_3(s)G_4(s)G_5(s)][1 - G_7(s)H_4(s)]}{\Delta} \tag{5.35}$$

Since there is only one forward path, $G(s)$ consists of only one term, rather than a sum of terms, each coming from a forward path.

SKILL-ASSESSMENT EXERCISE 5.4

Problem: Use Mason's rule to find the transfer function of the signal-flow diagram shown in Figure 5.19(c). Notice that this is the same system used in Example 5.2 to find the transfer function via block diagram reduction.

ANSWER:

$$T(s) = \frac{G_1(s)G_3(s)[1 + G_2(s)]}{[1 + G_2(s)H_2(s) + G_1(s)G_2(s)H_1(s)][1 + G_3(s)H_3(s)]}$$

The complete solution is at www.wiley.com/college/nise.

5.6 SIGNAL-FLOW GRAPHS OF STATE EQUATIONS

In this section we draw signal-flow graphs from state equations. At first this process will help us visualize state variables. Later we will draw signal-flow graphs and then write alternate representations of a system in state space.

Consider the following state and output equations:

$$\dot{x}_1 = 2x_1 - 5x_2 + 3x_3 + 2r \tag{5.36a}$$

$$\dot{x}_2 = -6x_1 - 2x_2 + 2x_3 + 5r \tag{5.36b}$$

$$\dot{x}_3 = x_1 - 3x_2 - 4x_3 + 7r \tag{5.36c}$$

$$y = -4x_1 + 6x_2 + 9x_3 \tag{5.36d}$$

First, identify three nodes to be the three state variables, x_1, x_2, and x_3; also identify three nodes, placed to the left of each respective state variable, to be the derivatives of the state variables, as in Figure 5.22(a). Also identify a node as the input, r, and another node as the output, y.

Next interconnect the state variables and their derivatives with the defining integration, $1/s$, as shown in Figure 5.22(b). Then using Eqs. (5.36), feed to each node the indicated signals. For example, from Eq. (5.36a), $\dot{x}_1$ receives $2x_1 - 5x_2 + 3x_3 + 2r$, as shown in Figure 5.22(c). Similarly, $\dot{x}_2$ receives $-6x_1 - 2x_2 + 2x_3 + 5r$, as shown in Figure 5.22(d), and $\dot{x}_3$ receives $x_1 - 3x_2 - 4x_3 + 7r$, as shown in Figure 5.22(e). Finally, using Eq. (5.36d), the output, y, receives $-4x_1 + 6x_2 + 9x_3$, as shown in Figure 5.19(f), the final phase-variable representation, where the state variables are the outputs of the integrators.

SKILL-ASSESSMENT EXERCISE 5.5

Problem: Draw a signal-flow graph for the following state and output equations:

$$\dot{\mathbf{x}} = \begin{bmatrix} -2 & 1 & 0 \\ 0 & -3 & 1 \\ -3 & -4 & -5 \end{bmatrix} \mathbf{x} + \begin{bmatrix} 0 \\ 0 \\ 1 \end{bmatrix} r$$

$$y = \begin{bmatrix} 0 & 1 & 0 \end{bmatrix} \mathbf{x}$$

ANSWER: The complete solution is at www.wiley.com/college/nise.

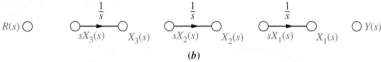

(a)

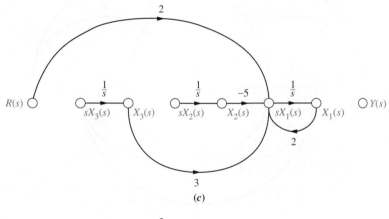

(b)

(c)

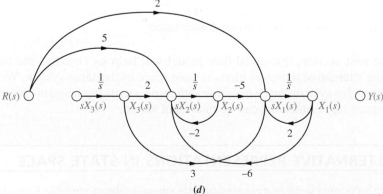

(d)

FIGURE 5.22   Stages of development of a signal-flow graph for the system of Eqs. 5.36:
a. Place nodes; **b.** interconnect state variables and derivatives; **c.** form dx_1/dt; **d.** form dx_2/dt;
(figure continues)

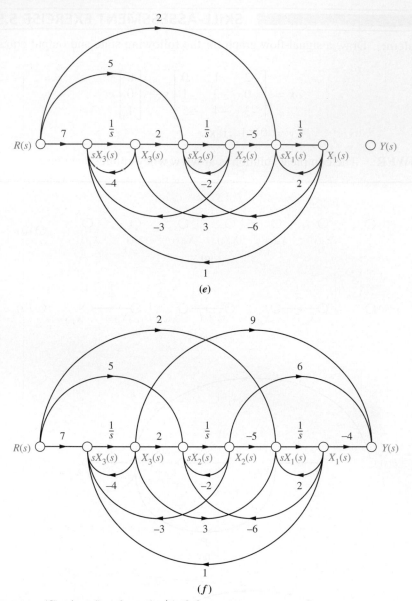

FIGURE 5.22   (Continued) **e.** form dx_3/dt; **f.** form output

In the next section, the signal-flow model will help us visualize the process of determining alternative representations in state space of the same system. We will see that even though a system can be the same with respect to its input and output terminals, the state-space representations can be many and varied.

5.7 ALTERNATIVE REPRESENTATIONS IN STATE SPACE

In Chapter 3 systems were represented in state space in phase-variable form. However, system modeling in state space can take on many representations other than the phase-variable form. Although each of these models yields the same output for a given input, an engineer may prefer a particular one for several reasons. For example, one set of state variables, with its unique representation, can model actual physical variables of a system, such as amplifier and filter outputs.

Another motive for choosing a particular set of state variables and state-space model is ease of solution. As we will see, a particular choice of state variables can decouple the system of simultaneous differential equations. Here each equation is written in terms of only one state variable, and the solution is effected by solving n first-order differential equations individually.

Ease of modeling is another reason for a particular choice of state variables. Certain choices may facilitate converting the subsystem to the state-variable representation by using recognizable features of the model. The engineer learns quickly how to write the state and output equations and draw the signal-flow graph, both by inspection. These converted subsystems generate the definition of the state variables.

We will now look at a few representative forms and show how to generate the state-space representation for each.

CASCADE FORM

We have seen that systems can be represented in state space with the state variables chosen to be the phase variables, that is, variables that are successive derivatives of each other. This is by no means the only choice. Returning to the system of Figure 3.10(*a*), the transfer function can be represented alternately as

$$\frac{C(s)}{R(s)} = \frac{24}{(s+2)(s+3)(s+4)} \tag{5.37}$$

Figure 5.23 shows a block diagram representation of this system formed by cascading each term of Eq.(5.37). The output of each first-order system block has been labeled as a state variable. These state variables are not the phase variables.

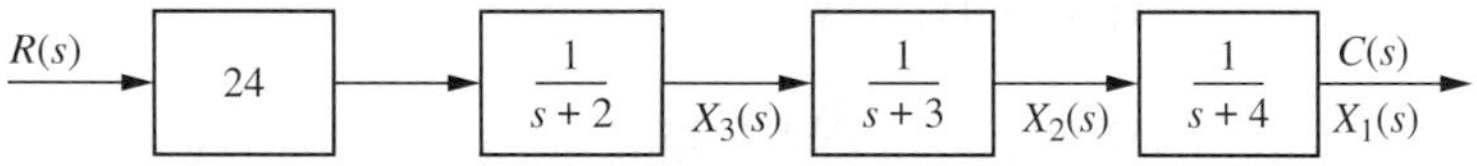

FIGURE 5.23   Representation of Figure 3.10 system as cascaded first-order systems

We now show how the signal-flow graph can be used to obtain a state-space representation of this system. In order to write the state equations with our new set of state variables, it is helpful to draw a signal-flow graph first, using Figure 5.23 as a guide. The signal flow for each first-order system of Figure 5.23 can be found by transforming each block into an equivalent differential equation. Each first-order block is of the form

$$\frac{C_i(s)}{R_i(s)} = \frac{1}{(s+a_i)} \tag{5.38}$$

Cross-multiplying, we get

$$(s+a_i)C_i(s) = R_i(s) \tag{5.39}$$

After taking the inverse Laplace transform, we have

$$\frac{dc_i(t)}{dt} + a_i c_i(t) = r_i(t) \tag{5.40}$$

The output equation is found by summing the signals that give $c(t)$:

$$y = c(t) = x_1 + x_2 + x_3 \tag{5.48}$$

In vector-matrix form Eqs. (5.47) and (5.48) become

$$\dot{\mathbf{x}} = \begin{bmatrix} -2 & 0 & 0 \\ 0 & -3 & 0 \\ 0 & 0 & -4 \end{bmatrix} \mathbf{x} + \begin{bmatrix} 12 \\ -24 \\ 12 \end{bmatrix} r \tag{5.49}$$

and

$$y = \begin{bmatrix} 1 & 1 & 1 \end{bmatrix} \mathbf{x} \tag{5.50}$$

Thus, our third representation of the system of Figure 3.10(a) yields a diagonal system matrix. What is the advantage of this representation? Each equation is a first-order differential equation in only one variable. Thus, we would solve these equations independently. The equations are said to be *decoupled*.

Students who are using MATLAB should now run ch5p3 in Appendix B. You will learn how to use MATLAB to convert a transfer function to state space in a specified form. The exercise solves the previous example by representing the transfer function in Eq. (5.45) by the state-space representation in parallel form of Eq. (5.49).

If the denominator of the transfer function has repeated real roots, the parallel form can still be derived from a partial-fraction expansion. However, the system matrix will not be diagonal. For example, assume the system

$$\frac{C(s)}{R(s)} = \frac{(s+3)}{(s+1)^2(s+2)} \tag{5.51}$$

which can be expanded as partial fractions:

$$\frac{C(s)}{R(s)} = \frac{2}{(s+1)^2} - \frac{1}{(s+1)} + \frac{1}{(s+2)} \tag{5.52}$$

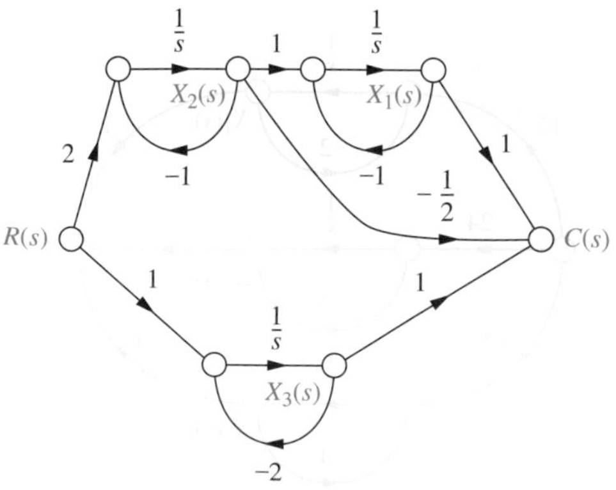

Proceeding as before, the signal-flow graph for Eq. (5.52) is shown in Figure 5.26. The term $-1/(s+1)$ was formed by creating the signal flow from $X_2(s)$ to $C(s)$. Now the state and output equations can be written by inspection from Figure 5.26 as follows:

$$\dot{x}_1 = -x_1 \quad + x_2 \tag{5.53a}$$

$$\dot{x}_2 = \qquad\quad -x_2 \quad\quad + 2r \tag{5.53b}$$

$$\dot{x}_3 = \qquad\qquad\qquad -2x_3 + r \tag{5.53c}$$

$$y = c(t) = \quad x_1 - \frac{1}{2}x_2 + x_3 \tag{5.53d}$$

FIGURE 5.26 Signal-flow representation of Eq. (5.52)

or, in vector-matrix form,

$$\dot{\mathbf{x}} = \begin{bmatrix} -1 & 1 & 0 \\ 0 & -1 & 0 \\ 0 & 0 & -2 \end{bmatrix} \mathbf{x} + \begin{bmatrix} 0 \\ 2 \\ 1 \end{bmatrix} r \tag{5.54a}$$

$$y = \begin{bmatrix} 1 & -\dfrac{1}{2} & 1 \end{bmatrix} \mathbf{x} \tag{5.54b}$$

This system matrix, although not diagonal, has the system poles along the diagonal. Notice the 1 off the diagonal for the case of the repeated root. The form of the system matrix is known as the *Jordan canonical form.*

CONTROLLER CANONICAL FORM

Another representation that uses phase variables is called the *controller canonical form,* so named for its use in the design of controllers, which is covered in Chapter 12. This form is obtained from the phase-variable form simply by ordering the phase variables in the reverse order. For example, consider the transfer function

$$G(s) = \frac{C(s)}{R(s)} = \frac{s^2 + 7s + 2}{s^3 + 9s^2 + 26s + 24} \tag{5.55}$$

The phase-variable form was derived in Example 3.5 as

$$\begin{bmatrix} \dot{x}_1 \\ \dot{x}_2 \\ \dot{x}_3 \end{bmatrix} = \begin{bmatrix} 0 & 1 & 0 \\ 0 & 0 & 1 \\ -24 & -26 & -9 \end{bmatrix} \begin{bmatrix} x_1 \\ x_2 \\ x_3 \end{bmatrix} + \begin{bmatrix} 0 \\ 0 \\ 1 \end{bmatrix} r \tag{5.56a}$$

$$y = \begin{bmatrix} 2 & 7 & 1 \end{bmatrix} \begin{bmatrix} x_1 \\ x_2 \\ x_3 \end{bmatrix} \tag{5.56b}$$

where $y = c(t)$. Renumbering the phase variables in reverse order yields

$$\begin{bmatrix} \dot{x}_3 \\ \dot{x}_2 \\ \dot{x}_1 \end{bmatrix} = \begin{bmatrix} 0 & 1 & 0 \\ 0 & 0 & 1 \\ -24 & -26 & -9 \end{bmatrix} \begin{bmatrix} x_3 \\ x_2 \\ x_1 \end{bmatrix} + \begin{bmatrix} 0 \\ 0 \\ 1 \end{bmatrix} r \tag{5.57a}$$

$$y = \begin{bmatrix} 2 & 7 & 1 \end{bmatrix} \begin{bmatrix} x_3 \\ x_2 \\ x_1 \end{bmatrix} \tag{5.57b}$$

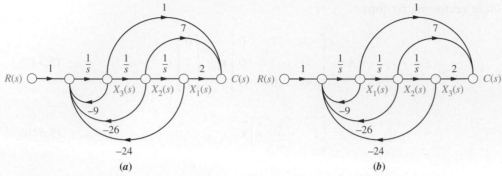

FIGURE 5.27 Signal-flow graphs for obtaining forms for $G(s) = C(s)/R(s) = (s^2 + 7s + 2)/(s^3 + 9s^2 + 26s + 24)$: **a.** phase-variable form; **b.** controller canonical form

Finally, rearranging Eqs. (5.57) in ascending numerical order yields the controller canonical form[3] as

$$\begin{bmatrix} \dot{x}_1 \\ \dot{x}_2 \\ \dot{x}_3 \end{bmatrix} = \begin{bmatrix} -9 & -26 & -24 \\ 1 & 0 & 0 \\ 0 & 1 & 0 \end{bmatrix} \begin{bmatrix} x_1 \\ x_2 \\ x_3 \end{bmatrix} + \begin{bmatrix} 1 \\ 0 \\ 0 \end{bmatrix} r \tag{5.58a}$$

$$y = \begin{bmatrix} 1 & 7 & 2 \end{bmatrix} \begin{bmatrix} x_1 \\ x_2 \\ x_3 \end{bmatrix} \tag{5.58b}$$

Figure 5.27 shows the steps we have taken on a signal-flow graph. Notice that the controller canonical form is obtained simply by renumbering the phase variables in the opposite order. Equations (5.56) can be obtained from Figure 5.27(*a*), and Eqs. (5.58) from Figure 5.27(*b*).

Notice that the phase-variable form and the controller canonical form contain the coefficients of the characteristic polynomial in the bottom row and in the top row, respectively. System matrices that contain the coefficients of the characteristic polynomial are called *companion matrices* to the characteristic polynomial. The phase-variable and controller canonical forms result in a lower and an upper companion system matrix, respectively. Companion matrices can also have the coefficients of the characteristic polynomial in the left or right column. In the next subsection, we discuss one of these representations.

OBSERVER CANONICAL FORM

The *observer canonical form,* so named for its use in the design of observers (covered in Chapter 12), is a representation that yields a left companion system matrix. As an example, the system modeled by Eq. (5.55) will be represented in this form. Begin by dividing all terms in the numerator and denominator by the highest power of s, s^3, and obtain

$$\frac{C(s)}{R(s)} = \frac{\dfrac{1}{s} + \dfrac{7}{s^2} + \dfrac{2}{s^3}}{1 + \dfrac{9}{s} + \dfrac{26}{s^2} + \dfrac{24}{s^3}} \tag{5.59}$$

Cross-multiplying yields

$$\left[\frac{1}{s} + \frac{7}{s^2} + \frac{2}{s^3} \right] R(s) = \left[1 + \frac{9}{s} + \frac{26}{s^2} + \frac{24}{s^3} \right] C(s) \tag{5.60}$$

---

[3] Students who are using MATLAB to convert from transfer functions to state space using the command **tf2ss** will notice that MATLAB reports the results in controller canonical form.

TryIt 5.3

Use the following MATLAB and Control System Toolbox statements to convert the transfer function of Eq. (5.55) to the controller canonical state-space representation of Eqs. (5.58).

```
numg = [1 7 2];
deng = [1 9 26 24];
[Acc, Bcc, Ccc, Dcc]...
= tf2ss(numg, deng)
```

Combining terms of like powers of integration gives

$$C(s) = \frac{1}{s}[R(s) - 9C(s)] + \frac{1}{s^2}[7R(s) - 26C(s)] + \frac{1}{s^3}[2R(s) - 24C(s)] \quad (5.61)$$

or

$$C(s) = \frac{1}{s}\left[[R(s) - 9C(s)] + \frac{1}{s}\left([7R(s) - 26C(s)] + \frac{1}{s}[2R(s) - 24C(s)]\right)\right] \quad (5.62)$$

Equation (5.61) or (5.62) can be used to draw the signal-flow graph. Start with three integrations, as shown in Figure 5.28(a).

Using Eq. (5.61), the first term tells us that output $C(s)$ is formed, in part, by integrating $[R(s) - 9C(s)]$. We thus form $[R(s) - 9C(s)]$ at the input to the integrator closest to the output, $C(s)$, as shown in Figure 5.28(b). The second term tells us that the term $[7R(s) - 26C(s)]$ must be integrated twice. Now form $[7R(s) - 26C(s)]$ at the input to the second integrator. Finally, the last term of Eq. (5.61) says $[2R(s) - 24C(s)]$ must be integrated three times. Form $[2R(s) - 24C(s)]$ at the input to the first integrator.

Identifying the state variables as the outputs of the integrators, we write the following state equations:

$$\dot{x}_1 = -9x_1 + x_2 \qquad\qquad + r \qquad\qquad (5.63a)$$

$$\dot{x}_2 = -26x_1 \qquad\quad + x_3 + 7r \qquad\quad (5.63b)$$

$$\dot{x}_3 = -24x_1 \qquad\qquad\quad + 2r \qquad\qquad (5.63c)$$

The output equation from Figure 5.28(b) is

$$y = c(t) = x_1 \qquad\qquad\qquad (5.64)$$

In vector-matrix form Eqs. (5.63) and (5.64) become

$$\dot{\mathbf{x}} = \begin{bmatrix} -9 & 1 & 0 \\ -26 & 0 & 1 \\ -24 & 0 & 0 \end{bmatrix}\mathbf{x} + \begin{bmatrix} 1 \\ 7 \\ 2 \end{bmatrix}r \qquad (5.65a)$$

$$y = \begin{bmatrix} 1 & 0 & 0 \end{bmatrix}\mathbf{x} \qquad\qquad (5.65b)$$

TryIt 5.4

Use the following MATLAB and Control System Toolbox statements to convert the transfer function of Eq. (5.55) to the observer canonical state-space representation of Eqs. (5.65).

```
numg=[1 7 2];
deng=[1 9 26 24];
[Acc,Bcc,Ccc,Dcc]...
=tf2ss(numg,deng);
Aoc=transpose(Acc)
Boc=transpose(Ccc)
Coc=transpose(Bcc)
```

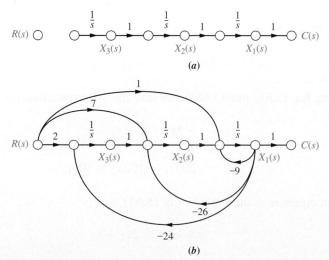

FIGURE 5.28   Signal-flow graph for observer canonical form variables: **a.** planning; **b.** implementation

Notice that the form of Eqs. (5.65) is similar to the phase-variable form, except that the coefficients of the denominator of the transfer function are in the first column, and the coefficients of the numerator form the input matrix, **B**. Also notice that the observer canonical form has an **A** matrix that is the transpose of the controller canonical form, a **B** vector that is the transpose of the controller canonical form's **C** vector, and a **C** vector that is the transpose of the controller canonical form's **B** vector. We therefore say that these two forms are *duals*. Thus, if a system is described by **A**, **B**, and **C**, its dual is described by $\mathbf{A_D} = \mathbf{A}^T$, $\mathbf{B_D} = \mathbf{C}^T$, $\mathbf{C_D} = \mathbf{B}^T$. You can verify the significance of duality by comparing the signal-flow graphs of a system and its dual, Figures 5.27(*b*) and 5.28(*b*), respectively. The signal-flow graph of the dual can be obtained from that of the original by reversing all arrows, changing state variables to their derivatives and vice versa, and interchanging $C(s)$ and $R(s)$, thus reversing the roles of the input and the output.

We conclude this section with an example that demonstrates the application of the previously discussed forms to a feedback control system.

EXAMPLE 5.8

State-space representation of feedback systems

Problem: Represent the feedback control system shown in Figure 5.29 in state space. Model the forward transfer function in cascade form.

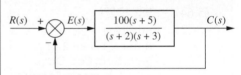

FIGURE 5.29 Feedback control system for Example 5.8

SOLUTION: First we model the forward transfer function in cascade form. The gain of 100, the pole at -2, and the pole at -3 are shown cascaded in Figure 5.30(*a*). The zero at -5 was obtained using the method for implementing zeros for a system represented in phase-variable form, as discussed in Section 3.5.

Next add the feedback and input paths, as shown in Figure 5.30(*b*). Now, by inspection, write the state equations:

$$\dot{x}_1 = -3x_1 + x_2 \tag{5.66a}$$

$$\dot{x}_2 = \quad -2x_2 + 100(r - c) \tag{5.66b}$$

But, from Figure 5.30(*b*),

$$c = 5x_1 + (x_2 - 3x_1) = 2x_1 + x_2 \tag{5.67}$$

Substituting Eq. (5.67) into (5.66*b*), we find the state equations for the system:

$$\dot{x}_1 = \quad -3x_1 \quad + x_2 \tag{5.68a}$$

$$\dot{x}_2 = -200x_1 - 102x_2 + 100r \tag{5.68b}$$

The output equation is the same as Eq. (5.67), or

$$y = c(t) = 2x_1 + x_2 \tag{5.69}$$

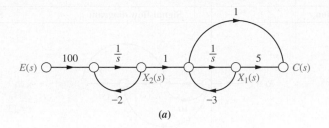

(a)

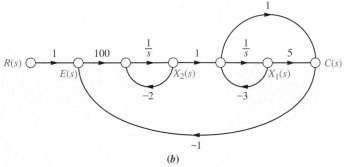

(b)

FIGURE 5.30 Creating a signal-flow graph for the Figure 5.29 system: **a.** forward transfer function; **b.** complete system

In vector-matrix form

$$\dot{\mathbf{x}} = \begin{bmatrix} -3 & 1 \\ -200 & -102 \end{bmatrix} \mathbf{x} + \begin{bmatrix} 0 \\ 100 \end{bmatrix} r \qquad (5.70\text{a})$$

$$y = \begin{bmatrix} 2 & 1 \end{bmatrix} \mathbf{x} \qquad (5.70\text{b})$$

SKILL-ASSESSMENT EXERCISE 5.6

Problem: Represent the feedback control system shown in Figure 5.29 in state space. Model the forward transfer function in controller canonical form.

ANSWER:

$$\dot{\mathbf{x}} = \begin{bmatrix} -105 & -506 \\ 1 & 0 \end{bmatrix} \mathbf{x} + \begin{bmatrix} 1 \\ 0 \end{bmatrix} r$$

$$y = \begin{bmatrix} 100 & 500 \end{bmatrix} \mathbf{x}$$

The complete solution is at www.wiley.com/college/nise.

In this section we used transfer functions and signal-flow graphs to represent systems in parallel, cascade, controller canonical, and observer canonical forms, in addition to the phase-variable form. Using the transfer function $C(s)/R(s) = (s + 3)/[(s + 4)(s + 6)]$ as an example, Figure 5.31 compares the aforementioned forms. Notice the duality of the controller and observer canonical forms, as demonstrated by their respective signal-flow graphs and state equations. In the next section we will

Form	Transfer function	Signal-flow diagram	State equations
Phase variable	$\dfrac{1}{(s^2 + 10s + 24)} * (s + 3)$		$\dot{\mathbf{x}} = \begin{bmatrix} 0 & 1 \\ -24 & -10 \end{bmatrix}\mathbf{x} + \begin{bmatrix} 0 \\ 1 \end{bmatrix} r$ $y = [3 \ 1]\mathbf{x}$
Parallel	$\dfrac{-1/2}{(s + 4)} + \dfrac{3/2}{s + 6}$		$\dot{\mathbf{x}} = \begin{bmatrix} -4 & 0 \\ 0 & -6 \end{bmatrix}\mathbf{x} + \begin{bmatrix} -\frac{1}{2} \\ \frac{3}{2} \end{bmatrix} r$ $y = [1 \ 1]\mathbf{x}$
Cascade	$\dfrac{1}{(s + 4)} * \dfrac{(s + 3)}{(s + 6)}$		$\dot{\mathbf{x}} = \begin{bmatrix} -6 & 1 \\ 0 & -4 \end{bmatrix}\mathbf{x} + \begin{bmatrix} 0 \\ 1 \end{bmatrix} r$ $y = [-3 \ 1]\mathbf{x}$
Controller canonical	$\dfrac{1}{(s^2 + 10s + 24)} * (s + 3)$		$\dot{\mathbf{x}} = \begin{bmatrix} -10 & -24 \\ 1 & 0 \end{bmatrix}\mathbf{x} + \begin{bmatrix} 1 \\ 0 \end{bmatrix} r$ $y = [1 \ 3]\mathbf{x}$
Observer canonical	$\dfrac{\dfrac{1}{s} + \dfrac{3}{s^2}}{1 + \dfrac{10}{s} + \dfrac{24}{s^2}}$		$\dot{\mathbf{x}} = \begin{bmatrix} -10 & 1 \\ -24 & 0 \end{bmatrix}\mathbf{x} + \begin{bmatrix} 1 \\ 3 \end{bmatrix} r$ $y = [1 \ 0]\mathbf{x}$

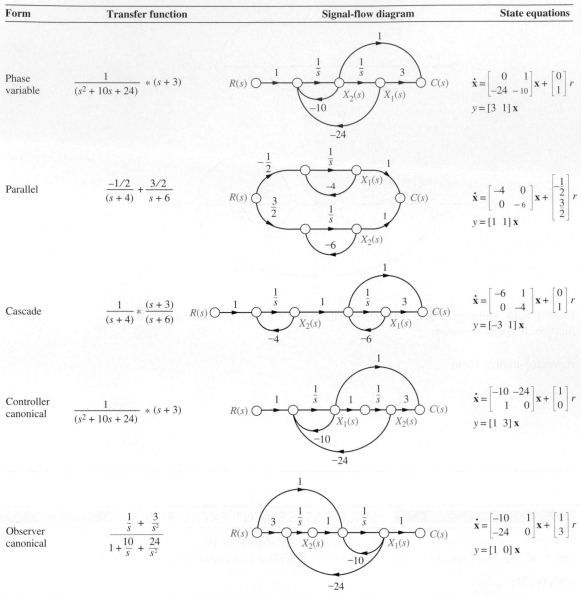

FIGURE 5.31   State-space forms for $C(s)/R(s) = (s + 3)/[(s + 4)(s + 6)]$. Note: $y = c(t)$

explore the possibility of transforming between representations without using transfer functions and signal-flow graphs.

5.8 SIMILARITY TRANSFORMATIONS

In Section 5.7 we saw that systems can be represented with different state variables even though the transfer function relating the output to the input remains the same. The various forms of the state equations were found by manipulating the transfer function, drawing a signal-flow graph, and then writing the state equations from the signal-flow graph. These systems are called *similar systems*. Although their state-space representations are different, similar systems have the same transfer function and hence the same poles and eigenvalues.

We can make transformations between similar systems from one set of state equations to another without using the transfer function and signal-flow graphs. The results are presented in this section along with examples. Students who have not broached this subject in the past or who wish to refresh their memories are encouraged to study Appendix K at www.wiley.com/college/nise for the derivation. The result of the derivation states: A system represented in state space as

$$\dot{\mathbf{x}} = \mathbf{A}\mathbf{x} + \mathbf{B}\mathbf{u} \tag{5.71a}$$

$$\mathbf{y} = \mathbf{C}\mathbf{x} + \mathbf{D}\mathbf{u} \tag{5.71b}$$

can be transformed to a similar system,

$$\dot{\mathbf{z}} = \mathbf{P}^{-1}\mathbf{A}\mathbf{P}\mathbf{z} + \mathbf{P}^{-1}\mathbf{B}\mathbf{u} \tag{5.72a}$$

$$\mathbf{y} = \mathbf{C}\mathbf{P}\mathbf{z} + \mathbf{D}\mathbf{u} \tag{5.72b}$$

where, for 2-space,

$$\mathbf{P} = [\mathbf{U}_{\mathbf{z}_1}\mathbf{U}_{\mathbf{z}_2}] = \begin{bmatrix} p_{11} & p_{12} \\ p_{21} & p_{22} \end{bmatrix} \tag{5.72c}$$

$$\mathbf{x} = \begin{bmatrix} p_{11} & p_{12} \\ p_{21} & p_{22} \end{bmatrix} \begin{bmatrix} z_1 \\ z_2 \end{bmatrix} = \mathbf{P}\mathbf{z} \tag{5.72d}$$

and

$$\mathbf{z} = \mathbf{P}^{-1}\mathbf{x} \tag{5.72e}$$

Thus, **P** is a transformation matrix whose columns are the coordinates of the basis vectors of the z_1z_2 space expressed as linear combinations of the x_1x_2 space. Let us look at an example.

EXAMPLE 5.9

Similarity transformations on state equations

Problem: Given the system represented in state space by Eqs. (5.73),

$$\dot{\mathbf{x}} = \begin{bmatrix} 0 & 1 & 0 \\ 0 & 0 & 1 \\ -2 & -5 & -7 \end{bmatrix} \mathbf{x} + \begin{bmatrix} 0 \\ 0 \\ 1 \end{bmatrix} u \tag{5.73a}$$

$$y = [1 \quad 0 \quad 0]\mathbf{x} \tag{5.73b}$$

transform the system to a new set of state variables, $\mathbf{z}$, where the new state variables are related to the original state variables, $\mathbf{x}$, as follows:

$$z_1 = 2x_1 \tag{5.74a}$$

$$z_2 = 3x_1 + 2x_2 \tag{5.74b}$$

$$z_3 = x_1 + 4x_2 + 5x_3 \tag{5.74c}$$

SOLUTION: Expressing Eqs. (5.74) in vector-matrix form,

$$\mathbf{z} = \begin{bmatrix} 2 & 0 & 0 \\ 3 & 2 & 0 \\ 1 & 4 & 5 \end{bmatrix} \mathbf{x} = \mathbf{P}^{-1}\mathbf{x} \tag{5.75}$$

Using Eqs. (5.72) as a guide,

$$\mathbf{P}^{-1}\mathbf{A}\mathbf{P} = \begin{bmatrix} 2 & 0 & 0 \\ 3 & 2 & 0 \\ 1 & 4 & 5 \end{bmatrix} \begin{bmatrix} 0 & 1 & 0 \\ 0 & 0 & 1 \\ -2 & -5 & -7 \end{bmatrix} \begin{bmatrix} 0.5 & 0 & 0 \\ -0.75 & 0.5 & 0 \\ 0.5 & -0.4 & 0.2 \end{bmatrix}$$

$$= \begin{bmatrix} -1.5 & 1 & 0 \\ -1.25 & 0.7 & 0.4 \\ -2.5 & 0.4 & -6.2 \end{bmatrix} \tag{5.76}$$

$$\mathbf{P}^{-1}\mathbf{B} = \begin{bmatrix} 2 & 0 & 0 \\ 3 & 2 & 0 \\ 1 & 4 & 5 \end{bmatrix} \begin{bmatrix} 0 \\ 0 \\ 1 \end{bmatrix} = \begin{bmatrix} 0 \\ 0 \\ 5 \end{bmatrix} \tag{5.77}$$

$$\mathbf{C}\mathbf{P} = \begin{bmatrix} 1 & 0 & 0 \end{bmatrix} \begin{bmatrix} 0.5 & 0 & 0 \\ -0.75 & 0.5 & 0 \\ 0.5 & -0.4 & 0.2 \end{bmatrix} = \begin{bmatrix} 0.5 & 0 & 0 \end{bmatrix} \tag{5.78}$$

Therefore, the transformed system is

$$\dot{\mathbf{z}} = \begin{bmatrix} -1.5 & 1 & 0 \\ -1.25 & 0.7 & 0.4 \\ -2.55 & 0.4 & -6.2 \end{bmatrix} \mathbf{z} + \begin{bmatrix} 0 \\ 0 \\ 5 \end{bmatrix} u \tag{5.79a}$$

$$y = \begin{bmatrix} 0.5 & 0 & 0 \end{bmatrix} \mathbf{z} \tag{5.79b}$$

Students who are using MATLAB should now run ch5p4 in Appendix B. You will learn how to perform similarity transformations. This exercise uses MATLAB to do Example 5.9.

Thus far we have talked about transforming systems between basis vectors in a different state space. One major advantage of finding these similar systems is apparent in the transformation to a system that has a diagonal matrix.

DIAGONALIZING A SYSTEM MATRIX

In Section 5.7 we saw that the parallel form of a signal-flow graph can yield a diagonal system matrix. A diagonal system matrix has the advantage that each state equation is a function of only one state variable. Hence, each differential equation can be solved independently of the other equations. We say that the equations are *decoupled*.

Rather than using partial fraction expansion and signal-flow graphs, we can decouple a system using matrix transformations. If we find the correct matrix, $\mathbf{P}$, the transformed system matrix, $\mathbf{P}^{-1}\mathbf{AP}$, will be a diagonal matrix. Thus, we are looking for a transformation to another state space that yields a diagonal matrix in that space. This new state space also has basis vectors that lie along its state variables. We give a special name to any vectors that are collinear with the basis vectors of the new system that yields a diagonal system matrix: they are called *eigenvectors*. Thus, the coordinates of the eigenvectors form the columns of the transformation matrix, $\mathbf{P}$, as we demonstrate in Eq. (K.7) in Appendix K on the accompanying CD-ROM.

First, let us formally define eigenvectors from another perspective and then show that they have the property just described. Then we will define eigenvalues. Finally, we will show how to diagonalize a matrix.

DEFINITIONS

Eigenvector. The eigenvectors of the matrix $\mathbf{A}$ are all vectors, $\mathbf{x_i} \neq \mathbf{0}$, which under the transformation $\mathbf{A}$ become multiples of themselves; that is,

$$\boxed{\mathbf{Ax_i} = \lambda_i\mathbf{x_i}} \tag{5.80}$$

where λ_i's are constants.

Figure 5.32 shows this definition of eigenvectors. If $\mathbf{Ax}$ is not collinear with $\mathbf{x}$ after the transformation, as in Figure 5.32(*a*), $\mathbf{x}$ is not an eigenvector. If $\mathbf{Ax}$ is collinear with $\mathbf{x}$ after the transformation, as in Figure 5.32(*b*), $\mathbf{x}$ is an eigenvector.

Eigenvalue. The eigenvalues of the matrix $\mathbf{A}$ are the values of λ_i that satisfy Eq. (5.80) for $\mathbf{x_i} \neq \mathbf{0}$.

To find the eigenvectors, we rearrange Eq. (5.80). Eigenvectors, $\mathbf{x_i}$, satisfy

$$\mathbf{0} = (\lambda_i\mathbf{I} - \mathbf{A})\mathbf{x_i} \tag{5.81}$$

Solving for $\mathbf{x_i}$ by premultiplying both sides by $(\lambda_i\mathbf{I} - \mathbf{A})^{-1}$ yields

$$\mathbf{x_i} = (\lambda_i\mathbf{I} - \mathbf{A})^{-1}\mathbf{0} = \frac{\text{adj}\,(\lambda_i\mathbf{I} - \mathbf{A})}{\det\,(\lambda_i\mathbf{I} - \mathbf{A})}\mathbf{0} \tag{5.82}$$

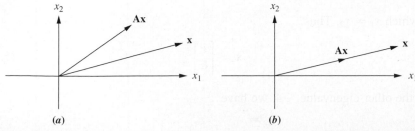

(*a*)   (*b*)

FIGURE 5.32 To be an eigenvector, the transformation $\mathbf{Ax}$ must be collinear with $\mathbf{x}$; thus, in (*a*), $\mathbf{x}$ is not an eigenvector; in (*b*), it is

Since $\mathbf{x_i} \neq \mathbf{0}$, a nonzero solution exists if

$$\boxed{\det\left(\lambda_i\,\mathbf{I} - \mathbf{A}\right) = \mathbf{0}} \tag{5.83}$$

from which λ_i, the eigenvalues, can be found.

We are now ready to show how to find the eigenvectors, $\mathbf{x_i}$. First we find the eigenvalues, λ_i, using $\det\left(\lambda_i\,\mathbf{I} - \mathbf{A}\right) = \mathbf{0}$, and then we use Eq. (5.80) to find the eigenvectors.

■ EXAMPLE 5.10 ■

Finding eigenvectors

Problem: Find the eigenvectors of the matrix

$$\mathbf{A} = \begin{bmatrix} -3 & 1 \\ 1 & -3 \end{bmatrix} \tag{5.84}$$

SOLUTION: The eigenvectors, $\mathbf{x_i}$, satisfy Eq. (5.81). First, use $\det\left(\lambda_i\,\mathbf{I} - \mathbf{A}\right) = 0$ to find the eigenvalues, λ_i, for Eq. (5.81):

$$
\begin{aligned}
\det\left(\lambda\,\mathbf{I} - \mathbf{A}\right) &= \left| \begin{bmatrix} \lambda & 0 \\ 0 & \lambda \end{bmatrix} - \begin{bmatrix} -3 & 1 \\ 1 & -3 \end{bmatrix} \right| \\
&= \begin{vmatrix} \lambda+3 & -1 \\ -1 & \lambda+3 \end{vmatrix} \\
&= \lambda^2 + 6\lambda + 8
\end{aligned} \tag{5.85}
$$

from which the eigenvalues are $\lambda = -2$, and -4.

Using Eq. (5.80) successively with each eigenvalue, we have

$$\mathbf{A}\mathbf{x_i} = \lambda\mathbf{x_i}$$

$$\begin{bmatrix} -3 & 1 \\ 1 & -3 \end{bmatrix} \begin{bmatrix} x_1 \\ x_2 \end{bmatrix} = -2 \begin{bmatrix} x_1 \\ x_2 \end{bmatrix} \tag{5.86}$$

or

$$-3x_1 + x_2 = -2x_1 \tag{5.87a}$$

$$x_1 - 3x_2 = -2x_2 \tag{5.87b}$$

from which $x_1 = x_2$. Thus,

$$\mathbf{x} = \begin{bmatrix} c \\ c \end{bmatrix} \tag{5.88}$$

Using the other eigenvalue, -4, we have

$$\mathbf{x} = \begin{bmatrix} c \\ -c \end{bmatrix} \tag{5.89}$$

Using Eqs. (5.88) and (5.89), one choice of eigenvectors is

$$\mathbf{x_1} = \begin{bmatrix} 1 \\ 1 \end{bmatrix} \quad \text{and} \quad \mathbf{x_2} = \begin{bmatrix} 1 \\ -1 \end{bmatrix} \tag{5.90}$$

We now show that if the eigenvectors of the matrix $\mathbf{A}$ are chosen as the basis vectors of a transformation, $\mathbf{P}$, the resulting system matrix will be diagonal. Let the transformation matrix $\mathbf{P}$ consist of the eigenvectors of $\mathbf{A}$, $\mathbf{x_i}$.

$$\mathbf{P} = [\mathbf{x_1}, \mathbf{x_2}, \mathbf{x_3}, \ldots, \mathbf{x_n}] \tag{5.91}$$

Since $\mathbf{x_i}$ are eigenvectors, $\mathbf{Ax_i} = \lambda_i \mathbf{x_i}$, which can be written equivalently as a set of equations expressed by

$$\mathbf{AP} = \mathbf{PD} \tag{5.92}$$

where $\mathbf{D}$ is a diagonal matrix consisting of λ_i's, the eigenvalues, along the diagonal, and $\mathbf{P}$ is as defined in Eq. (5.91). Solving Eq. (5.92) for $\mathbf{D}$ by premultiplying by $\mathbf{P}^{-1}$, we get

$$\mathbf{D} = \mathbf{P}^{-1}\mathbf{AP} \tag{5.93}$$

which is the system matrix of Eq. (5.72).

In summary, under the transformation $\mathbf{P}$, consisting of the eigenvectors of the system matrix, the transformed system is diagonal, with the eigenvalues of the system along the diagonal. The transformed system is identical to that obtained using partial-fraction expansion of the transfer function with distinct real roots.

In Example 5.10 we found eigenvectors of a second-order system. Let us continue with this problem and diagonalize the system matrix.

EXAMPLE 5.11

Diagonalizing a system in state space

Problem: Given the system of Eqs. (5.94), find the diagonal system that is similar.

$$\dot{\mathbf{x}} = \begin{bmatrix} -3 & 1 \\ 1 & -3 \end{bmatrix} \mathbf{x} + \begin{bmatrix} 1 \\ 2 \end{bmatrix} u \tag{5.94a}$$

$$y = [2 \quad 3]\mathbf{x} \tag{5.94b}$$

SOLUTION: First find the eigenvalues and the eigenvectors. This step was performed in Example 5.10. Next form the transformation matrix $\mathbf{P}$, whose columns consist of the eigenvectors.

$$\mathbf{P} = \begin{bmatrix} 1 & 1 \\ 1 & -1 \end{bmatrix} \tag{5.95}$$

Finally, form the similar system's system matrix, input matrix, and output matrix, respectively.

$$\mathbf{P}^{-1}\mathbf{A}\mathbf{P} = \begin{bmatrix} 1/2 & 1/2 \\ 1/2 & -1/2 \end{bmatrix} \begin{bmatrix} -3 & 1 \\ 1 & -3 \end{bmatrix} \begin{bmatrix} 1 & 1 \\ 1 & -1 \end{bmatrix} = \begin{bmatrix} -2 & 0 \\ 0 & -4 \end{bmatrix}$$

(5.96a)

$$\mathbf{P}^{-1}\mathbf{B} = \begin{bmatrix} 1/2 & 1/2 \\ 1/2 & -1/2 \end{bmatrix} \begin{bmatrix} 1 \\ 2 \end{bmatrix} = \begin{bmatrix} 3/2 \\ -1/2 \end{bmatrix}$$

(5.96b)

$$\mathbf{C}\mathbf{P} = \begin{bmatrix} 2 & 3 \end{bmatrix} \begin{bmatrix} 1 & 1 \\ 1 & -1 \end{bmatrix} = \begin{bmatrix} 5 & -1 \end{bmatrix}$$

(5.96c)

Substituting Eqs. (5.96) into Eqs. (5.72), we get

$$\dot{\mathbf{z}} = \begin{bmatrix} -2 & 0 \\ 0 & -4 \end{bmatrix} \mathbf{z} + \begin{bmatrix} 3/2 \\ -1/2 \end{bmatrix} u$$

(5.97a)

$$y = \begin{bmatrix} 5 & -1 \end{bmatrix} \mathbf{z}$$

(5.97b)

Notice that the system matrix is diagonal, with the eigenvalues along the diagonal.

Students who are using MATLAB should now run ch5p5 in Appendix B. This problem, which uses MATLAB to diagonalize a system, is similar (but not identical) to Example 5.11.

SKILL-ASSESSMENT EXERCISE 5.7

Problem: For the system represented in state space as follows:

$$\dot{\mathbf{x}} = \begin{bmatrix} 1 & 3 \\ -4 & -6 \end{bmatrix} \mathbf{x} + \begin{bmatrix} 1 \\ 3 \end{bmatrix} u$$

$$y = \begin{bmatrix} 1 & 4 \end{bmatrix} \mathbf{x}$$

convert the system to one where the new state vector, **z**, is

$$\mathbf{z} = \begin{bmatrix} 3 & -2 \\ 1 & -4 \end{bmatrix} \mathbf{x}$$

ANSWER:

$$\dot{\mathbf{z}} = \begin{bmatrix} 6.5 & -8.5 \\ 9.5 & -11.5 \end{bmatrix} \mathbf{z} + \begin{bmatrix} -3 \\ -11 \end{bmatrix} u$$

$$y = \begin{bmatrix} 0.8 & -1.4 \end{bmatrix} \mathbf{z}$$

The complete solution is at www.wiley.com/college/nise.

SKILL-ASSESSMENT EXERCISE 5.8

Problem: For the original system of Skill-Assessment Exercise 5.7, find the diagonal system that is similar.

ANSWER:

$$\dot{\mathbf{z}} = \begin{bmatrix} -2 & 0 \\ 0 & -3 \end{bmatrix} \mathbf{z} + \begin{bmatrix} 18.39 \\ 20 \end{bmatrix} u$$

$$y = \begin{bmatrix} -2.121 & 2.6 \end{bmatrix} \mathbf{z}$$

The complete solution is at www.wiley.com/college/nise.

TryIt 5.5

Use the following MATLAB and Control System Toolbox statements to do Skill-Assessment Exercise 5.8.

```
A = [1   3; -4 - 6];
B = [1; 3];
C = [1   4];
D = 0; S = ss(A, B, C, D);
Sd = canon(S, 'modal')
```

In this section we learned how to move between different state-space representations of the same system via matrix transformations rather than transfer function manipulation and signal-flow graphs. These different representations are called *similar*. The characteristics of similar systems are that the transfer functions relating the output to the input are the same, as are the eigenvalues and poles. A particularly useful transformation was converting a system with distinct, real eigenvalues to a diagonal system matrix.

We now summarize the concepts of block diagram and signal-flow representations of systems, first through case study problems and then in a written summary. Our case studies include the antenna azimuth position control system and the Unmanned Free-Swimming Submersible vehicle (UFSS). Block diagram reduction is important for the analysis and design of these systems as well as the control systems on board *Alvin* (Figure 5.33), used to explore the wreckage of the *Titanic* 13,000 feet under the Atlantic in July 1986 (*Ballard, 1987*).

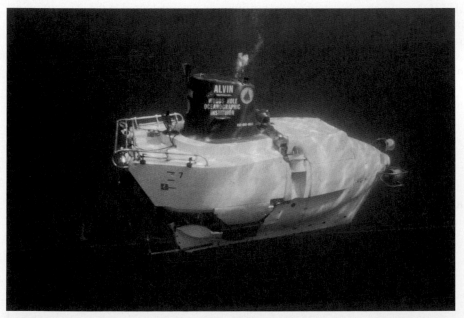

FIGURE 5.33 *Alvin,* a manned submersible, explored the wreckage of the *Titanic* with a tethered robot, *Jason Junior.*

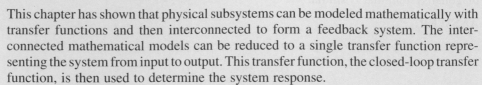

CASE STUDIES

Antenna Control: Designing a Closed-Loop Response

This chapter has shown that physical subsystems can be modeled mathematically with transfer functions and then interconnected to form a feedback system. The interconnected mathematical models can be reduced to a single transfer function representing the system from input to output. This transfer function, the closed-loop transfer function, is then used to determine the system response.

The following case study shows how to reduce the subsystems of the antenna azimuth position control system to a single, closed-loop transfer function in order to analyze and design the transient response characteristics.

Problem: Given the antenna azimuth position control system shown on the front endpapers, Configuration 1, do the following:

a. Find the closed-loop transfer function using block diagram reduction.

b. Represent each subsystem with a signal-flow graph and find the state-space representation of the closed-loop system from the signal-flow graph.

c. Use the signal-flow graph found in (b) along with Mason's rule to find the closed-loop transfer function.

d. Replace the power amplifier with a transfer function of unity and evaluate the closed-loop peak time, percent overshoot, and settling time for $K = 1000$.

e. For the system of (d), derive the expression for the closed-loop step response of the system.

f. For the simplified model of (d), find the value of K that yields a 10% overshoot.

SOLUTION: Each subsystem's transfer function was evaluated in the case study in Chapter 2. We first assemble them into the closed-loop, feedback control system block diagram shown in Figure 5.34(a).

a. The steps taken to reduce the block diagram to a single, closed-loop transfer function relating the output angular displacement to the input angular displacement are shown in Figure 5.34(a)–(d). In Figure 5.34(b) the input potentiometer was pushed to the right past the summing junction, creating a unity feedback system. In Figure 5.34(c) all the blocks of the forward transfer function are multiplied together, forming the equivalent forward transfer function. Finally, the feedback formula is applied, yielding the closed-loop transfer function in Figure 5.34(d).

b. In order to obtain the signal-flow graph of each subsystem, we use the state equations derived in the case study of Chapter 3. The signal-flow graph for the power amplifier is drawn from the state equations of Eqs. (3.87) and (3.88), and the signal-flow graph of the motor and load is drawn from the state equation of Eq. (3.98). Other subsystems are pure gains. The signal-flow graph for Figure 5.34 (a) is shown in Figure 5.35 and consists of the interconnected subsystems.

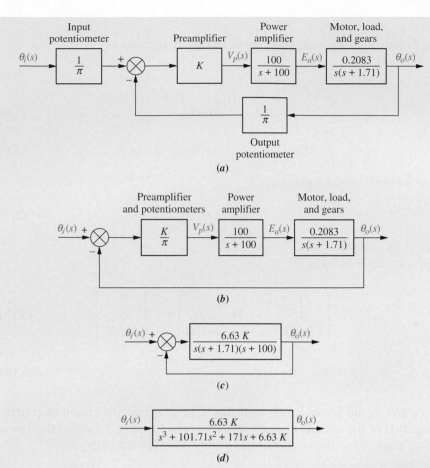

FIGURE 5.34 Block diagram reduction for the antenna azimuth position control system:
a. original; **b.** pushing input potentiometer to the right past the summing junction; **c.** showing equivalent forward transfer function; **d.** final closed-loop transfer function

The state equations are written from Figure 5.35. First define the state variables as the outputs of the integrators. Hence, the state vector is

$$\mathbf{x} = \begin{bmatrix} x_1 \\ x_2 \\ e_a \end{bmatrix} \tag{5.98}$$

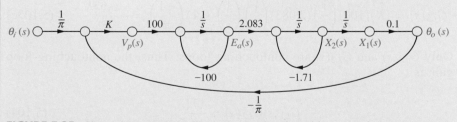

FIGURE 5.35 Signal-flow graph for the antenna azimuth position control system

Using Figure 5.35, we write the state equations by inspection:

$$\dot{x}_1 = \qquad\qquad + x_2 \tag{5.99a}$$

$$\dot{x}_2 = \qquad\quad -1.71x_2 + 2.083e_a \tag{5.99b}$$

$$\dot{e}_a = -3.18Kx_1 \qquad - \quad 100e_a + 31.8K\theta_i \tag{5.99c}$$

along with the output equation,

$$y = \theta_o = 0.1x_1 \tag{5.100}$$

where $1/\pi = 0.318$.

In vector-matrix form,

$$\dot{\mathbf{x}} = \begin{bmatrix} 0 & 1 & 0 \\ 0 & -1.71 & 2.083 \\ -3.18K & 0 & -100 \end{bmatrix} \mathbf{x} + \begin{bmatrix} 0 \\ 0 \\ 31.8K \end{bmatrix} \theta_i \tag{5.101a}$$

$$y = \begin{bmatrix} 0.1 & 0 & 0 \end{bmatrix} \mathbf{x} \tag{5.101b}$$

c. We now apply Mason's rule to Figure 5.35 to derive the closed-loop transfer function of the antenna azimuth position control system. First find the forward-path gains. From Figure 5.35 there is only one forward-path gain:

$$T_1 = \left(\frac{1}{\pi}\right)(K)(100)\left(\frac{1}{s}\right)(2.083)\left(\frac{1}{s}\right)\left(\frac{1}{s}\right)(0.1) = \frac{6.63K}{s^3} \tag{5.102}$$

Next identify the closed-loop gains. There are three: the power amplifier loop, $G_{L1}(s)$, with e_a at the output; the motor loop, $G_{L2}(s)$, with x_2 at the output; and the entire system loop, $G_{L3}(s)$, with θ_0 at the output.

$$G_{L1}(s) = \frac{-100}{s} \tag{5.103a}$$

$$G_{L2}(s) = \frac{-1.71}{s} \tag{5.103b}$$

$$G_{L3}(s) = (K)(100)\left(\frac{1}{s}\right)(2.083)\left(\frac{1}{s}\right)\left(\frac{1}{s}\right)(0.1)\left(\frac{-1}{\pi}\right) = \frac{-6.63K}{s^3} \tag{5.103c}$$

Only $G_{L1}(s)$ and $G_{L2}(s)$ are nontouching loops. Thus, the nontouching-loop gain is

$$G_{L1}(s)G_{L2}(s) = \frac{171}{s^2} \tag{5.104}$$

Forming Δ and Δ_k in Eq. (5.28), we have

$$\Delta = 1 - [G_{L1}(s) + G_{L2}(s) + G_{L3}(s)] + [G_{L1}(s)G_{L2}(s)]$$

$$= 1 + \frac{100}{s} + \frac{1.71}{s} + \frac{6.63K}{s^3} + \frac{171}{s^2} \tag{5.105}$$

and

$$\Delta_1 = 1 \tag{5.106}$$

Substituting Eqs. (5.102), (5.105), and (5.106) into Eq. (5.28), we obtain the closed-loop transfer function as

$$T(s) = \frac{C(s)}{R(s)} = \frac{T_1 \Delta_1}{\Delta} = \frac{6.63K}{s^3 + 101.71s^2 + 171s + 6.63K} \tag{5.107}$$

d. Replacing the power amplifier with unity gain and letting the preamplifier gain, K, in Figure 5.34(b) equal 1000 yield a forward transfer function, $G(s)$, of

$$G(s) = \frac{66.3}{s(s + 1.71)} \tag{5.108}$$

Using the feedback formula to evaluate the closed-loop transfer function, we obtain

$$T(s) = \frac{66.3}{s^2 + 1.71s + 66.3} \tag{5.109}$$

From the denominator, $\omega_n = 8.14$, $\zeta = 0.105$. Using Eqs. (4.34), (4.38), and (4.42), the peak time $= 0.388$ second, the percent overshoot $= 71.77\%$, and the settling time $= 4.68$ seconds.

e. The Laplace transform of the step response is found by first multiplying Eq. (5.109) by $1/s$, a unit-step input, and expanding into partial fractions:

$$C(s) = \frac{66.3}{s(s^2 + 1.71s + 66.3)} = \frac{1}{s} - \frac{s + 1.71}{s^2 + 1.71s + 66.3}$$

$$= \frac{1}{s} - \frac{(s + 0.855) + 0.106(8.097)}{(s + 0.855)^2 + (8.097)^2} \tag{5.110}$$

Taking the inverse Laplace transform, we find

$$c(t) = 1 - e^{-0.855r}(\cos 8.097t + 0.106 \sin 8.097t) \tag{5.111}$$

f. For the simplified model we have

$$G(s) = \frac{0.0663K}{s(s + 1.71)} \tag{5.112}$$

from which the closed-loop transfer function is calculated to be

$$T(s) = \frac{0.0663K}{s^2 + 1.71s + 0.0663K} \tag{5.113}$$

From Eq. (4.39) a 10% overshoot yields $\zeta = 0.591$. Using the denominator of Eq. (5.113), $\omega_n = \sqrt{0.0663K}$ and $2\zeta\omega_n = 1.71$. Thus,

$$\zeta = \frac{1.71}{2\sqrt{0.0663K}} = 0.591 \tag{5.114}$$

from which $K = 31.6$.

Challenge: You are now given a problem to test your knowledge of this chapter's objectives: Referring to the antenna azimuth position control system shown on the front endpapers, Configuration 2, do the following:

a. Find the closed-loop transfer function using block diagram reduction.

b. Represent each subsystem with a signal-flow graph and find the state-space representation of the closed-loop system from the signal-flow graph.

c. Use the signal-flow graph found in (b) along with Mason's rule to find the closed-loop transfer function.

d. Replace the power amplifier with a transfer function of unity and evaluate the closed-loop percent overshoot, settling time, and peak time for $K = 5$.

e. For the system used for (d), derive the expression for the closed-loop step response.

f. For the simplified model in (d), find the value of preamplifier gain, K, to yield 15% overshoot.

UFSS Vehicle: Pitch-Angle Control Representation

We return to the Unmanned Free-Swimming Submersible vehicle introduced in the case studies in Chapter 4 (*Johnson, 1980*). We will represent in state space the pitch-angle control system that is used for depth control.

Problem: Consider the block diagram of the pitch control loop of the UFSS vehicle shown on the back endpapers. The pitch angle, θ, is controlled by a commanded pitch angle, θ_e, which along with pitch-angle and pitch-rate feedback determines the elevator deflection, δ_e, which acts through the vehicle dynamics to determine the pitch angle. Let $K_1 = K_2 = 1$ and do the following:

a. Draw the signal-flow graph for each subsystem, making sure that pitch angle, pitch rate, and elevator deflection are represented as state variables. Then interconnect the subsystems.

b. Use the signal-flow graph obtained in (a) to represent the pitch control loop in state space.

SOLUTION:

a. The vehicle dynamics are split into two transfer functions, from which the signal-flow graph is drawn. Figure 5.36 shows the division along with the elevator actuator. Each block is drawn in phase-variable form to meet the requirement that particular system variables be state variables. This result is

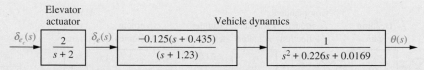

FIGURE 5.36 Block diagram of the UFSS vehicle's elevator and vehicle dynamics, from which a signal-flow graph can be drawn

shown in Figure 5.37(a). The feedback paths are then added to complete the signal-flow graph, which is shown in Figure 5.37(b).

b. By inspection, the derivatives of state variables x_1 through x_4 are written as

$$\dot{x}_1 = \qquad\qquad\qquad x_2 \tag{5.115a}$$

$$\dot{x}_2 = -0.0169x_1 - 0.226x_2 + 0.435x_3 - 1.23x_3 - 0.125x_4 \tag{5.115b}$$

$$\dot{x}_3 = \qquad\qquad\qquad\qquad -1.23x_3 - 0.125x_4 \tag{5.115c}$$

$$\dot{x}_4 = \quad 2x_1 \quad + 2x_2 \qquad\qquad\qquad -2x_4 - 2\theta c \tag{5.115d}$$

Finally, the output $y = x_1$.

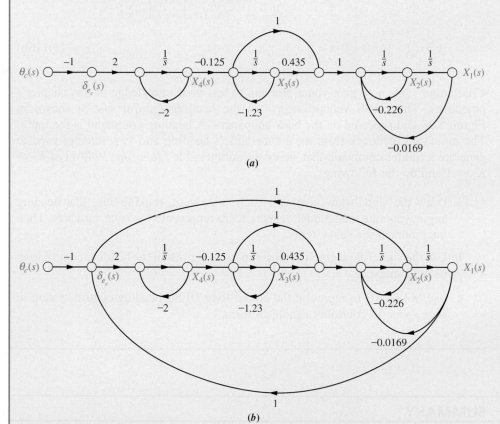

FIGURE 5.37 Signal-flow graph representation of the UFSS vehicle's pitch control system: **a.** without position and rate feedback; **b.** with position and rate feedback. (Note: Explicitly required variables are $x_1 = \theta, x_2 = d\theta/dt$, and $x_4 = \delta_e$.)

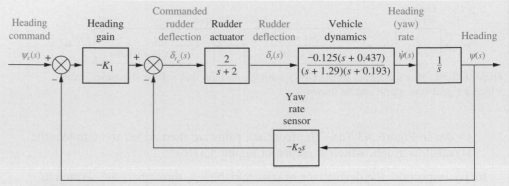

FIGURE 5.38   Block diagram of the heading control system for the UFSS vehicle

In vector-matrix form the state and output equations are

$$\dot{\mathbf{x}} = \begin{bmatrix} 0 & 1 & 0 & 0 \\ -0.0169 & -0.226 & -0.795 & -0.125 \\ 0 & 0 & -1.23 & -0.125 \\ 2 & 2 & 0 & -2 \end{bmatrix} \mathbf{x} + \begin{bmatrix} 0 \\ 0 \\ 0 \\ -2 \end{bmatrix} \theta_c \qquad (5.116a)$$

$$y = \begin{bmatrix} 1 & 0 & 0 & 0 \end{bmatrix} \mathbf{x} \qquad (5.116b)$$

Challenge: We now give you a problem to test your knowledge of this chapter's objectives. The UFSS vehicle steers via the heading control system shown in Figure 5.38 and repeated on the back endpapers. A heading command is the input. The input and feedback from the submersible's heading and yaw rate are used to generate a rudder command that steers the submersible (*Johnson, 1980*). Let $K_1 = K_2 = 1$ and do the following:

   a. Draw the signal-flow graph for each subsystem, making sure that heading angle, yaw rate, and rudder deflection are represented as state variables. Then interconnect the subsystems.

   b. Use the signal-flow graph obtained in (a) to represent the heading control loop in state space.

   c. Use MATLAB to represent the closed-loop UFSS heading control system in state space in controller canonical form.

SUMMARY

One objective of this chapter has been for you to learn how to represent multiple subsystems via block diagrams or signal-flow graphs. Another objective has been to be able to reduce either the block diagram representation or the signal-flow graph representation to a single transfer function.

We saw that the block diagram of a linear, time-invariant system consisted of four elements: *signals, systems, summing junctions,* and *pickoff points.* These elements were assembled into three basic forms: *cascade, parallel,* and *feedback.* Some basic operations were then derived: moving systems across summing junctions and across pickoff points.

Once we recognized the basic forms and operations, we could reduce a complicated block diagram to a single transfer function relating input to output. Then we applied the methods of Chapter 4 for analyzing and designing a second-order system for transient behavior. We saw that adjusting the gain of a feedback control system gave us partial control of the transient response.

The signal-flow representation of linear, time-invariant systems consists of two elements: nodes, which represent signals, and lines with arrows, which represent subsystems. Summing junctions and pickoff points are implicit in signal-flow graphs. These graphs are helpful in visualizing the meaning of the state variables. Also, they can be drawn first as an aid to obtaining the state equations for a system.

Mason's rule was used to derive the system's transfer function from the signal-flow graph. This formula replaced block diagram reduction techniques. Mason's rule seems complicated, but its use is simplified if there are no nontouching loops. In many of these cases, the transfer function can be written by inspection, with less labor than in the block diagram reduction technique.

Finally, we saw that systems in state space can be represented using different sets of variables. In the last three chapters, we have covered *phase-variable, cascade, parallel, controller canonical,* and *observer canonical* forms. A particular representation may be chosen because one set of state variables has a different physical meaning than another set, or because of the ease with which particular state equations can be solved.

In the next chapter we discuss system stability. Without stability we cannot begin to design a system for the desired transient response. We will find out how to tell whether a system is stable and what effect parameter values have on a system's stability.

REVIEW QUESTIONS

1. Name the four components of a block diagram for a linear, time-invariant system.
2. Name three basic forms for interconnecting subsystems.
3. For each of the forms in Question 2, state (respectively) how the equivalent transfer function is found.
4. Besides knowing the basic forms as discussed in Questions 2 and 3, what other equivalents must you know in order to perform block diagram reduction?
5. For a simple, second-order feedback control system of the type shown in Figure 5.14, describe the effect that variations of forward-path gain, K, have on the transient response.
6. For a simple, second-order feedback control system of the type shown in Figure 5.14, describe the changes in damping ratio as the gain, K, is increased over the underdamped region.
7. Name the two components of a signal-flow graph.
8. How are summing junctions shown on a signal-flow graph?
9. If a forward path touched all closed loops, what would be the value of Δ_k?
10. Name five representations of systems in state space.

State Space

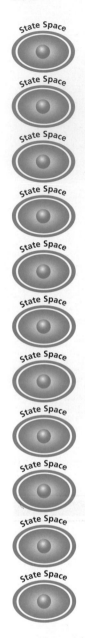

State Space

State Space

State Space

State Space

State Space

State Space

State Space

State Space

State Space

State Space

State Space

11. Which two forms of the state-space representation are found using the same method?

12. Which form of the state-space representation leads to a diagonal matrix?

13. When the system matrix is diagonal, what quantities lie along the diagonal?

14. What terms lie along the diagonal for a system represented in Jordan canonical form?

15. What is the advantage of having a system represented in a form that has a diagonal system matrix?

16. Give two reasons for wanting to represent a system by alternative forms.

17. For what kind of system would you use the observer canonical form?

18. Describe state-vector transformations from the perspective of different bases.

19. What is the definition of an eigenvector?

20. Based upon your definition of an eigenvector, what is an eigenvalue?

21. What is the significance of using eigenvectors as basis vectors for a system transformation?

PROBLEMS

1. Reduce the block diagram shown in Figure P5.1 to a single transfer function, $T(s) = C(s)/R(s)$ Use the following methods:

   a. Block diagram reduction [Section: 5.2]
   b. MATLAB

   MATLAB

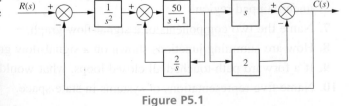

Figure P5.1

2. Find the closed-loop transfer function, $T(s) = C(s)/R(s)$ for the system shown in Figure P5.2, using block diagram reduction. [Section: 5.2]

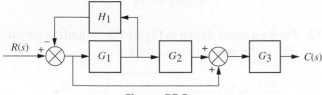

Figure P5.2

3. Find the equivalent transfer function, $T(s) = C(s)/R(s)$, for the system shown in Figure P5.3. [Section: 5.2]

WileyPLUS

Control Solutions

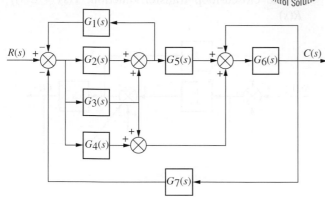

Figure P5.3

4. Reduce the system shown in Figure P5.4 to a single transfer function, $T(s) = C(s)/R(s)$. [Section: 5.2]

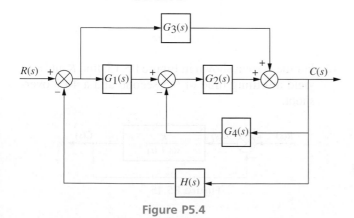

Figure P5.4

5. Find the transfer function, $T(s) = C(s)/R(s)$, for the system shown in Figure P5.5. Use the following methods:

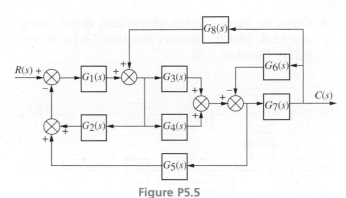

Figure P5.5

a. Block diagram reduction [Section: 5.2]

b. MATLAB. Use the following transfer functions: $G_1(s) = 1/(s+7)$, $G_2(s) = 1/(s^2 + 2s + 3)$, $G_3(s) = 1/(s+4)$, $G_4(s) = 1/s$, $G_5(s) = 5/(s+7)$, $G_6(s) = 1/(s^2 + 5s + 10)$, $G_7(s) = 3/(s+2)$, $G_8(s) = 1/(s+6)$. Hint: Use the **append** and **connect** commands in MATLAB's Control System Toolbox.

MATLAB

6. Reduce the block diagram shown in Figure P5.6 to a single block, $T(s) = C(s)/R(s)$. [Section: 5.2]

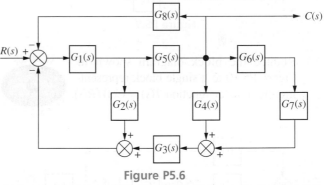

Figure P5.6

7. Find the unity feedback system that is equivalent to the system shown in Figure P5.7.

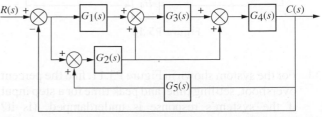

Figure P5.7

8. Given the block diagram of a system shown in Figure P5.8, find the transfer function $G(s) = \theta_{22}(s)/\theta_{11}(s)$. [Section: 5.2]

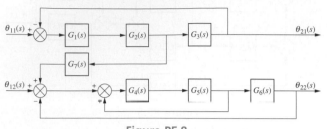

Figure P5.8

9. Reduce the block diagram shown in Figure P5.9 to a single transfer function, $T(s) = C(s)/R(s)$. [Section: 5.2]

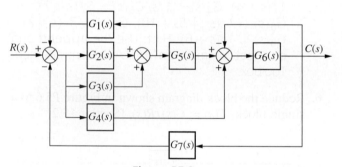

Figure P5.9

10. Reduce the block diagram shown in Figure P5.10 to a single block representing the transfer function $T(s) = C(s)/R(s)$.

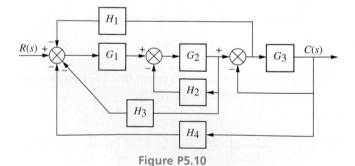

Figure P5.10

11. For the system shown in Figure P5.11, find the percent overshoot, settling time, and peak time for a step input if the system's response is underdamped. (Is it? Why?)

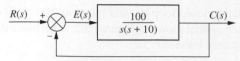

Figure P5.11

12. For the system shown in Figure P5.12, find the output, $c(t)$, if the input, $r(t)$, is a unit step.

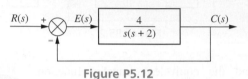

Figure P5.12

13. For the system shown in Figure P5.13, find the poles of the closed-loop transfer function, $T(s) = C(s)/R(s)$.

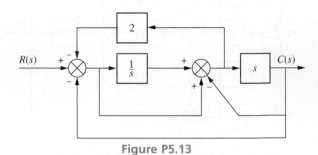

Figure P5.13

14. For the system of Figure P5.14, find the value of K that yields 20% overshoot for a step input. [Section: 5.3]

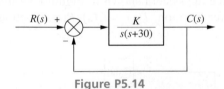

Figure P5.14

15. For the system shown in Figure P5.15, find K and α to yield a settling time of 0.5 second and a 40% overshoot.

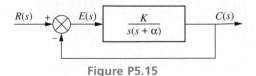

Figure P5.15

16. For the system of Figure P5.16, find the values of K_1 and K_2 to yield a peak time of 1 second and a settling time of 2 seconds for the closed-loop system's step response. [Section: 5.3]

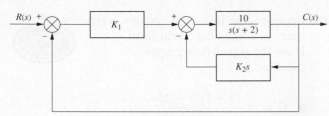

Figure P5.16

17. Find the following for the system shown in Figure P5.17: [Section: 5.3]

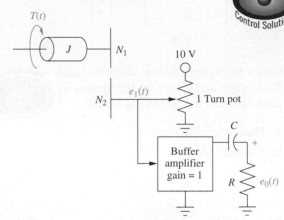

20. Find $G(s) = E_0(s)/T(s)$ for the system shown in Figure P5.20.

Figure P5.20

a. The equivalent single block that represents the transfer function, $T(s) = C(s)/R(s)$.

b. The damping ratio, natural frequency, percent overshoot, settling time, peak time, rise time, and damped frequency of oscillation.

21. Find the transfer function, $G(s) = E_o(s)/T(s)$, for the system shown in Figure P5.21.

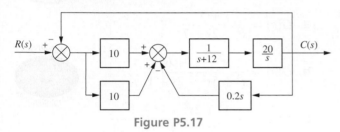

Figure P5.17

18. For the system shown in Figure P5.18, find ζ, ω_n, percent overshoot, peak time, and settling time.

19. A motor and generator are set up to drive a load as

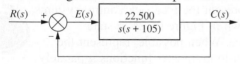

Figure P5.18

shown in Figure P5.19. If the generator output voltage is $e_g(t) = K_f i_f(t)$, where $i_f(t)$ is the generator's field current, find the transfer function $G(s) = \theta_o(s)/E_i(s)$. For the generator, $K_f = 2\ \Omega$. For the motor, $K_t = 1$ N-m/A, and $K_b = 1$ V-s/rad.

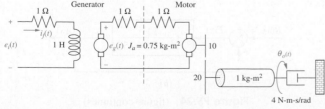

Figure P5.19

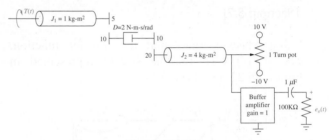

Figure P5.21

22. Label signals and draw a signal-flow graph for each of the block diagrams shown in the following problems: [Section: 5.4]

a. Problem 1

b. Problem 3

c. Problem 5

23. Draw a signal-flow graph for each of the following state equations: [Section: 5.6]

a. $\dot{\mathbf{x}} = \begin{bmatrix} 0 & 1 & 0 \\ 0 & 0 & 1 \\ -2 & -4 & -6 \end{bmatrix} \mathbf{x} + \begin{bmatrix} 0 \\ 0 \\ 1 \end{bmatrix} r$

$y = \begin{bmatrix} 1 & 1 & 0 \end{bmatrix} \mathbf{x}$

b. $\dot{\mathbf{x}} = \begin{bmatrix} 0 & 1 & 0 \\ 0 & -3 & 1 \\ -3 & -4 & -5 \end{bmatrix} \mathbf{x} + \begin{bmatrix} 0 \\ 1 \\ 1 \end{bmatrix} r$

$y = \begin{bmatrix} 1 & 2 & 0 \end{bmatrix} \mathbf{x}$

c. $\dot{\mathbf{x}} = \begin{bmatrix} 7 & 1 & 0 \\ -3 & 2 & -1 \\ -1 & 0 & 2 \end{bmatrix} \mathbf{x} + \begin{bmatrix} 1 \\ 2 \\ 1 \end{bmatrix} r$

$y = \begin{bmatrix} 1 & 3 & 2 \end{bmatrix} \mathbf{x}$

24. Given the system below, draw a signal-flow graph and represent the system in state space in the following forms:

  a. Phase-variable form

  b. Cascade form

$$G(s) = \frac{5}{s(s+6)(s+8)}$$

25. Repeat Problem 24 for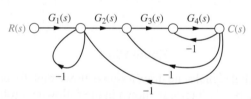

$$G(s) = \frac{20}{s(s-2)(s+5)(s+8)}$$

[Section: 5.7]

26. Using Mason's rule, find the transfer function, $T(s) = C(s)/R(s)$, for the system represented in Figure P5.22. [Section: 5.5]

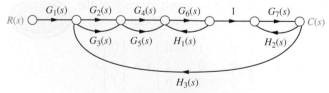

Figure P5.22

27. Using Mason's rule, find the transfer function, $T(s) = C(s)/R(s)$, for the system represented by Figure P5.23. [Section: 5.5]

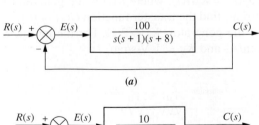

Figure P5.23

28. Use block diagram reduction to find the transfer function of Figure 5.21 in the text, and compare your answer with that obtained by Mason's rule. [Section: 5.5]

29. Represent the following systems in state space in Jordan canonical form. Draw the signal-flow graphs. [Section: 5.7]

  a. $G(s) = \dfrac{(s+1)(s+2)}{(s+3)^2(s+4)}$

  b. $G(s) = \dfrac{(s+2)}{(s+5)^2(s+7)^2}$

  c. $G(s) = \dfrac{(s+3)}{(s+2)^2(s+4)(s+5)}$

30. Represent the systems below in state space in phase-variable form. Draw the signal-flow graphs. [Section: 5.7]

  a. $G(s) = \dfrac{s+3}{s^2+2s+7}$

  b. $G(s) = \dfrac{s^2+2s+6}{s^3+5s^2+2s+1}$

  c. $G(s) = \dfrac{s^3+2s^2+7s+1}{s^4+3s^3+5s^2+6s+4}$

31. Repeat Problem 30 and represent each system in controller canonical and observer canonical forms. [Section: 5.7]

32. Represent the feedback control systems shown in Figure P5.24 in state space. When possible, represent the open-loop transfer functions separately in cascade and complete the feedback loop with the signal path from output to input. Draw your

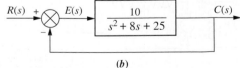

(a)

(b)

Figure P5.24   (figure continues)

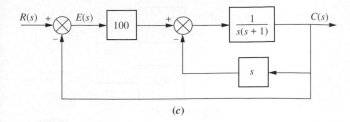

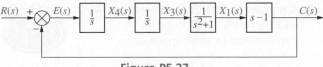

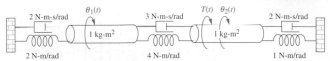

Figure P5.27

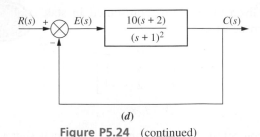

(d)

Figure P5.24 (continued)

36. Consider the rotational mechanical system shown in Figure P5.28.

   a. Represent the system as a signal-flow graph.

   b. Represent the system in state space if the output is $\theta_2(t)$.

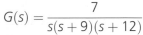

Figure P5.28

signal-flow graph (as closely as possible) to be in one-to-one correspondence to the block diagrams.

37. Given a unity feedback system with the forward-path transfer function

$$G(s) = \frac{7}{s(s+9)(s+12)}$$

33. You are given the system shown in Figure P5.25. [Section: 5.7]

use MATLAB to represent the closed-loop system in state space in

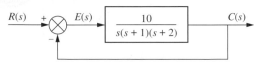

   a. phase-variable form;

Figure P5.25

   b. parallel form.

   a. Represent the system in state space in phase-variable form.

   b. Represent the system in state space in any other form besides phase-variable.

38. Consider the cascaded subsystems shown in Figure P5.29. If $G_1(s)$ is represented in state space as

$$\dot{\mathbf{x}}_1 = \mathbf{A}_1\mathbf{x}_1 + \mathbf{B}_1 r$$
$$y_1 = \mathbf{C}_1\mathbf{x}_1$$

34. Repeat Problem 33 for the system shown in Figure P5.26. [Section: 5.7]

and $G_2(s)$ is represented in state space as

$$\dot{\mathbf{x}}_2 = \mathbf{A}_2\mathbf{x}_2 + \mathbf{B}_2 y_1$$
$$y_2 = \mathbf{C}_2\mathbf{x}_2$$

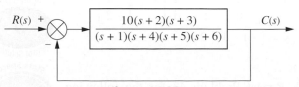

Figure P5.26

show that the entire system can be represented in state space as

$$\begin{bmatrix} \dot{\mathbf{x}}_1 \\ \dot{\mathbf{x}}_2 \end{bmatrix} = \begin{bmatrix} \mathbf{A}_1 & 0 \\ \mathbf{B}_2\mathbf{C}_1 & \mathbf{A}_2 \end{bmatrix} \begin{bmatrix} \mathbf{x}_1 \\ \mathbf{x}_2 \end{bmatrix} + \begin{bmatrix} \mathbf{B}_1 \\ 0 \end{bmatrix} r$$

$$y_2 = \begin{bmatrix} 0 & \mathbf{C}_2 \end{bmatrix} \begin{bmatrix} \mathbf{x}_1 \\ \mathbf{x}_2 \end{bmatrix}$$

35. Represent the system shown in Figure P5.27 in state space where $x_1(t)$, $x_3(t)$, and $x_4(t)$, as shown, are among the state variables, $c(t)$ is the output, and $x_2(t)$ is internal to $X_1(s)/X_3(s)$. [Section: 5.7]

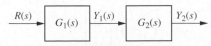

Figure P5.29

39. Consider the parallel subsystems shown in Figure P5.30. If $G_1(s)$ is represented in state space as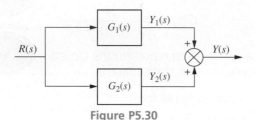

$$\dot{x} = A_1x_1 + B_1r$$
$$y_1 = C_1x_1$$

and $G_2(s)$ is represented in state space as

$$\dot{x}_2 = A_2x_2 + B_2r$$
$$y_2 = C_2x_2$$

show that the entire system can be represented in state space as

$$\begin{bmatrix} \dot{x}_1 \\ \dot{x}_2 \end{bmatrix} = \begin{bmatrix} A_1 & \vdots & 0 \\ 0 & \vdots & A_2 \end{bmatrix} \begin{bmatrix} x_1 \\ x_2 \end{bmatrix} + \begin{bmatrix} B_1 \\ B_2 \end{bmatrix} r$$

$$y = \begin{bmatrix} C_1 & \vdots & C_2 \end{bmatrix} \begin{bmatrix} x_1 \\ x_2 \end{bmatrix}$$

Figure P5.30

40. Consider the subsystems shown in Figure P5.31 and connected to form a feedback system. If $G(s)$ is represented in state space as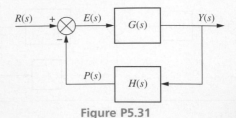

$$\dot{x}_1 = A_1x_1 + B_1e$$
$$y = C_1x_1$$

and $H_2(s)$ is represented in state space as

$$\dot{x}_2 = A_2x_2 + B_2y$$
$$p = C_2x_2$$

show that the closed-loop system can be represented in state space as

$$\begin{bmatrix} \dot{x}_1 \\ \dot{x}_2 \end{bmatrix} = \begin{bmatrix} A_1 & \vdots & -B_1C_2 \\ B_2C_1 & \vdots & A_2 \end{bmatrix} \begin{bmatrix} x_1 \\ x_2 \end{bmatrix} + \begin{bmatrix} B_1 \\ 0 \end{bmatrix} r$$

$$y = \begin{bmatrix} C_1 & \vdots & 0 \end{bmatrix} \begin{bmatrix} x_1 \\ x_2 \end{bmatrix}$$

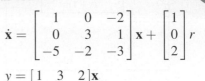

Figure P5.31

41. Given the system represented in state space as follows: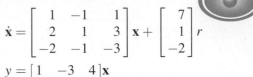

$$\dot{x} = \begin{bmatrix} 1 & 0 & -2 \\ 0 & 3 & 1 \\ -5 & -2 & -3 \end{bmatrix} x + \begin{bmatrix} 1 \\ 0 \\ 2 \end{bmatrix} r$$

$$y = \begin{bmatrix} 1 & 3 & 2 \end{bmatrix} x$$

convert the system to one where the new state vector, **z**, is

$$z = \begin{bmatrix} 1 & 3 & -2 \\ 4 & -1 & 0 \\ 2 & 5 & 1 \end{bmatrix} x$$

42. Repeat Problem 41 for the following system: [Section: 5.8]

$$\dot{x} = \begin{bmatrix} 1 & -1 & 1 \\ 2 & 1 & 3 \\ -2 & -1 & -3 \end{bmatrix} x + \begin{bmatrix} 7 \\ 1 \\ -2 \end{bmatrix} r$$

$$y = \begin{bmatrix} 1 & -3 & 4 \end{bmatrix} x$$

and the following state-vector transformation:

$$z = \begin{bmatrix} 4 & -1 & 0 \\ 2 & 3 & -2 \\ 8 & 5 & 1 \end{bmatrix} x$$

43. Diagonalize the following system: [Section: 5.8]

$$\dot{x} = \begin{bmatrix} -5 & -5 & 4 \\ 2 & 0 & -2 \\ 0 & -2 & -1 \end{bmatrix} x + \begin{bmatrix} -1 \\ 2 \\ -2 \end{bmatrix} r$$

$$y = \begin{bmatrix} -1 & 1 & 2 \end{bmatrix} x$$

44. Repeat Problem 43 for the following system: [Section: 5.8]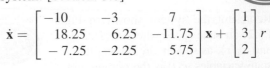

$$\dot{x} = \begin{bmatrix} -10 & -3 & 7 \\ 18.25 & 6.25 & -11.75 \\ -7.25 & -2.25 & 5.75 \end{bmatrix} x + \begin{bmatrix} 1 \\ 3 \\ 2 \end{bmatrix} r$$

$$y = \begin{bmatrix} 1 & -2 & 4 \end{bmatrix} x$$

45. Diagonalize the system in Problem 44 using MATLAB.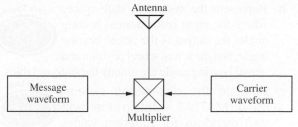

46. During ascent the space shuttle is steered by commands generated by the computer's guidance calculations. These commands are in the form of vehicle attitude, attitude rates, and attitude accelerations obtained through measurements made by the vehicle's inertial measuring unit, rate gyro assembly, and accelerometer assembly, respectively. The ascent digital autopilot uses the errors between the actual and commanded attitude, rates, and accelerations to gimbal the space shuttle main engines (called thrust vectoring) and the solid rocket boosters to effect the desired vehicle attitude. The space shuttle's attitude control system employs the same method in the pitch, roll, and yaw control systems. A simplified model of the pitch control system is shown in Figure P5.32.[4]

a. Find the closed-loop transfer function relating actual pitch to commanded pitch. Assume all other inputs are zero.

b. Find the closed-loop transfer function relating actual pitch rate to commanded pitch rate. Assume all other inputs are zero.

c. Find the closed-loop transfer function relating actual pitch acceleration to commanded pitch acceleration. Assume all other inputs are zero.

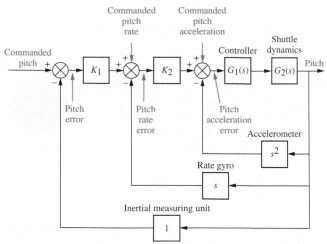

Figure P5.32 Space shuttle pitch control system (simplified)

47. An AM radio modulator generates the product of a carrier waveform

State Space

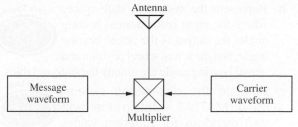

Antenna

Message waveform → Multiplier ← Carrier waveform

Figure P5.33 AM modulator

and a message waveform, as shown in Figure P5.33 (*Kurland, 1971*). Represent the system in state space if the carrier is a sinusoid of frequency $\omega = a$, and the message is a sinusoid of frequency $\omega = b$. Note that this system is nonlinear because of the multiplier.

48. A model for human eye movement consists of the closed-loop system shown in Figure P5.34, where an object's position is the input and the eye position is the output. The brain sends signals to the muscles that move the eye. These signals consist of the difference between the object's position and the position and rate information from the eye sent by the muscle spindles. The eye motion is modeled as an inertia and viscous damping and assumes no elasticity (spring) (*Milhorn, 1966*). Assuming that the delays in the brain and nervous system are negligible, find the closed-loop transfer function for the eye position control.

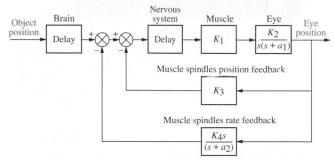

Figure P5.34 Feedback control system representing human eye movement

49. A HelpMate transport robot, shown in Figure P5.35(*a*), is used to deliver goods in a hospital setting. The robot can deliver food, drugs, laboratory materials, and patients' records (*Evans, 1992*). Given the simplified block diagram of the robot's bearing angle control system, as shown in Figure P5.35(*b*), do the following:

WileyPLUS

Control Solutions

a. Find the closed-loop transfer function.

[4]Source of background information for this problem: Rockwell International.

b. Represent the system in state space, where the input is the desired bearing angle, the output is the actual bearing angle, and the actual wheel position and actual bearing angle are among the state variables.

c. Simulate the closed-loop system using MATLAB. Obtain the unit step response for different values of K that yield responses from overdamped to underdamped to unstable.

a. Model the system in state space.

b. Simulate the step response using MATLAB. Is the response predominantly first or second order? Describe the characteristics of the response that need correction.

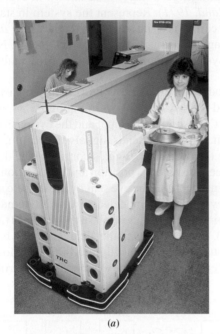

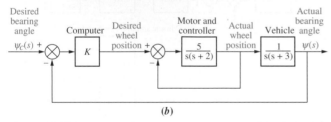

Figure P5.35 a. HelpMate robot used for in-hospital deliveries; **b.** simplified block diagram for bearing angle control

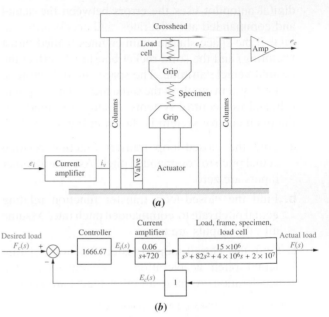

Figure P5.36 a. Load tester (© 1992 IEEE); **b.** approximate block diagram

50. Automatically controlled load testers can be used to test product reliability under real-life conditions. The tester consists of a load frame and specimen as shown in Figure P5.36(*a*). The desired load is input via a voltage, $e_i(t)$, to a current amplifier. The output load is measured via a voltage, $e_i(t)$, from a load cell measuring the load on the specimen. Figure P5.36(*b*) shows an approximate model of a load testing system without compensation (*Bailey, 1992*).

51. Consider the F4-E aircraft of Problem 20, Chapter 3. If the open-loop transfer function relating normal acceleration, $A_n(s)$, to the input deflection command, $\delta_c(s)$, is approximated as

$$\frac{A_n(s)}{\delta_c(s)} = \frac{-272(s^2 + 1.9s + 84)}{(s + 14)(s - 1.8)(s + 4.9)}$$

(*Cavallo, 1992*), find the state-space representation in

a. Phase-variable form

b. Controller canonical form

c. Observer canonical form

d. Cascade form

e. Parallel form

52. Find the closed-loop transfer function of the Unmanned Free-Swimming Submersible vehicle's pitch control system shown on the back endpapers (*Johnson, 1980*).

53. Repeat Problem 52 using MATLAB.

54. Use Simulink to plot the effects of non-linearities upon the closed-loop step response of the antenna azimuth position control system shown on the front endpapers, Configuration 1. In particular, consider individually each of the following nonlinearities: saturation (± 5 volts), backlash (deadband width 0.15), deadzone (-2 to $+2$), as well as the linear response. Assume the preamplifier gain is 100 and the step input is 2 radians.

55. Problem 11 in Chapter 1 describes a high-speed proportional solenoid valve. A subsystem of the valve is the solenoid coil shown in Figure P5.37. Current through the coil, L, generates a magnetic field that produces a force to operate the valve. Figure P5.37 can be represented as a block diagram (*Vaughan, 1996*)

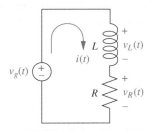

Figure P5.37 Solenoid coil circuit

a. Derive a block diagram of a feedback system that represents the coil circuit, where the applied voltage, $v_g(t)$, is the input, the coil voltage, $v_L(t)$, is the error voltage, and the current, $i(t)$, is the output.

b. For the block diagram found in Part **a**, find the Laplace transform of the output current, $I(s)$.

c. Solve the circuit of Figure P5.37 for $I(s)$, and compare to your result in Part **b**.

56. Ktesibios' water clock (see Section 1.2) is probably the first man-made system in which feedback was used in a deliberate manner. Its operations are shown in Figure P5.38(*a*). The clock indicates time progressively on scale D as water falls from orifice A toward vessel B. Clock accuracy depends mainly on water height h_f in the water reservoir G, which must be maintained at a constant level h_r by means of the conical float F that moves up or down to control the water inflow. Figure P5.38(*b*) shows a block diagram describing the system (*Lepschy, 1992*).

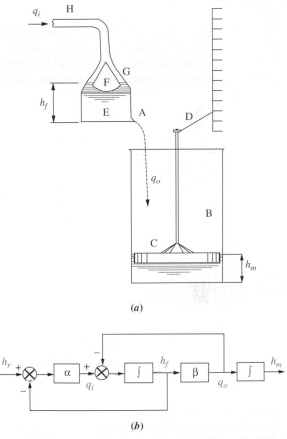

(*a*)

(*b*)

Figure P5.38 a. Ktesibios' water clock; **b.** Water clock block diagram (© 1992 IEEE)

Let $q_i(t)$ and $q_o(t)$ represent the input and output water flow, respectively, and h_m the height of water in vessel B. Use Mason's rule to find the following transfer functions, assuming α and β are constants:

a. $\dfrac{H_m(s)}{H_r(s)}$

b. $\dfrac{H_f(s)}{H_r(s)}$

c. $\dfrac{Q_i(s)}{H_r(s)}$

d. $\dfrac{Q_o(s)}{H_r(s)}$

e. Using the above transfer functions, show that if $h_r(t) = $ constant, then $q_o(t) = $ constant and $h_m(t)$ increases at a constant speed.

57. Some robotic applications can benefit from actuators in which load position as well as exerted force are controlled. Figure P5.39 shows the block diagram of such an actuator, where u_1 and u_2 are voltage inputs to two coils, each of which controls a pneumatic piston, and y represents the load displacement.

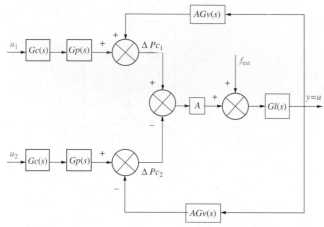

Figure P5.39   Actuator block diagram (© 1995 IEEE)

The system's output is u, the differential pressure acting on the load. The system also has a disturbance input f_{ext}, which represents external forces that are not system generated, but are acting on the load. A is a constant. (*Ben-Dov, 1995*). Use any method to obtain:

a. An expression for the system's output in terms of the inputs u_1 and u_2. (Assume $f_{ext} = 0$.)

b. An expression for the effect of f_{ext} on the output u. (Assume u_1 and $u_2 = 0$.)

c. What condition on the inputs u_1 and u_2 will result in $u = 0$?

58. Figure P5.40 shows a noninverting operational amplifier.

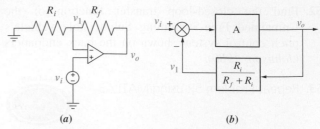

Figure P5.40   a. Noninverting amplifier; **b.** block diagram

Assuming the operational amplifier is ideal,

a. Verify that the system can be described by the following two equations:

$$v_o = A(v_i - v_o)$$
$$v_1 = \frac{R_i}{R_i + R_f} v_o$$

b. Check that these equations can be described by the block diagram of Figure P5.40(b)

c. Use Mason's rule to obtain the closed-loop system transfer function $\dfrac{V_o(s)}{V_i(s)}$.

d. Show that when $A \to \infty$, $\dfrac{V_o(s)}{V_i(s)} = 1 + \dfrac{R_f}{R_i}$.

59. Figure P5.41 shows the diagram of an inverting operational amplifier.

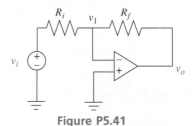

Figure P5.41

a. Assuming an ideal operational amplifier, use a similar procedure to the one outlined in Problem 58 to find the system equations.

b. Draw a corresponding block diagram and obtain the transfer function $\dfrac{V_o(s)}{V_i(s)}$.

c. Show that when $A \to \infty$, $\dfrac{V_o(s)}{V_i(s)} = -\dfrac{R_f}{R_i}$.

60. Figure P5.42(*a*) shows an *n*-channel enhancement-mode MOSFET source follower circuit. Figure P5.42(*b*)

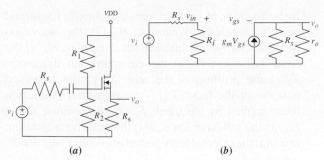

(a)   (b)

Figure P5.42 a. An *n*-channel enhancement-mode MOSFET Source Follower circuit; **b.** small-signal equivalent

shows its small-signal equivalent (where $R_i = R_1 \| R_2$) (*Neamen, 2001*).

a. Verify that the equations governing this circuit are

$$\frac{v_{in}}{v_i} = \frac{R_i}{R_i + R_s}; \quad v_{gs} = v_{in} - v_o; \quad v_o = g_m(R_s \| r_o)v_{gs}$$

b. Draw a block diagram showing the relations between the equations.

c. Use the block diagram in Part **b** to find $\frac{V_o(s)}{V_i(s)}$.

61. A car active suspension system adds an active hydraulic actuator in parallel with the passive damper and spring to create a dynamic impedance that responds to road variations. The block diagram of Figure P5.43 depicts such an actuator with closed-loop control.

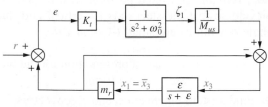

Figure P5.43   (©1997 IEEE)

In the figure, K_t is the spring constant of the tire, M_{US} is the wheel mass, r is the road disturbance, x_1 is the vertical car displacement, x_3 is the wheel vertical displacement, $\omega_0^2 = \frac{K_L}{M_{US}}$ is the natural frequency of the unsprung system and ε is a filtering parameter to be judiciously chosen (*Lin, 1997*). Find the two transfer functions of interest:

a. $\dfrac{X_3(s)}{R(s)}$

b. $\dfrac{X_1(s)}{R(s)}$

62. The basic unit of skeletal and cardiac muscle cells is a *sarcomere*, which is what gives such cells a striated (parallel line) appearance. For example, one bicep cell has about 10^5 sarcomeres. In turn, sarcomeres are composed of protein complexes. Feedback mechanisms play an important role in sarcomeres and thus muscle contraction. Namely, Fenn's law says that the energy liberated during muscle contraction depends on the initial conditions and the load encountered. The following linearized model describing sarcomere contraction has been developed for cardiac muscle:

$$\begin{bmatrix} \dot{A} \\ \dot{T} \\ \dot{U} \\ \dot{SL} \end{bmatrix} = \begin{bmatrix} -100.2 & -20.7 & -30.7 & 200.3 \\ 40 & -20.22 & 49.95 & 526.1 \\ 0 & 10.22 & -59.95 & -526.1 \\ 0 & 0 & 0 & 0 \end{bmatrix} \begin{bmatrix} A \\ T \\ U \\ SL \end{bmatrix} + \begin{bmatrix} 208 \\ -208 \\ -108.8 \\ -1 \end{bmatrix} u(t)$$

$$y = \begin{bmatrix} 0 & 1570 & 1570 & 59400 \end{bmatrix} \begin{bmatrix} A \\ T \\ U \\ SL \end{bmatrix} - 6240u(t)$$

where

$A =$ density of regulatory units with bound calcium and adjacent weak cross bridges (μM)

$T =$ density of regulatory units with bound calcium and adjacent strong cross bridges (M)

$U =$ density of regulatory units without bound calcium and adjacent strong cross bridges (M)

$SL =$ sarcomere length (m)

The system's input is $u(t) =$ the shortening muscle velocity in meters/second and the output is $y(t) =$ muscle force output in Newtons (*Yaniv, 2006*).

Do the following:

a. Use MATLAB to obtain the transfer function $\dfrac{Y(s)}{U(s)}$.
MATLAB

b. Use MATLAB to obtain a partial-fraction expansion for $\dfrac{Y(s)}{U(s)}$.
MATLAB

c. Draw a signal-flow diagram of the system in parallel form.

State Space

d. Use the diagram of Part **c** to express the system in state-variable form with decoupled equations.
State Space

63. An electric ventricular assist device (EVAD) has been designed to help patients with diminished but still functional heart pumping action to work in parallel with the natural heart. The device consists of a brushless dc electric motor that actuates on a pusher plate. The plate movements help the ejection of blood in systole and sac filling in diastole. System dynamics during systolic mode have been found to be:

$$
\begin{bmatrix} \dot{x} \\ \dot{v} \\ \dot{P}_{ao} \end{bmatrix} = \begin{bmatrix} 0 & 1 & 0 \\ 0 & -68.3 & -7.2 \\ 0 & 3.2 & -0.7 \end{bmatrix} \begin{bmatrix} x \\ v \\ P_{ao} \end{bmatrix} + \begin{bmatrix} 0 \\ 425.4 \\ 0 \end{bmatrix} e_m
$$

The state variables in this model are x, the pusher plate position, v, the pusher plate velocity, and P_{ao}, the aortic blood pressure. The input to the system is e_m, the motor voltage (*Tasch, 1990*).

a. Use MATLAB to find a similarity transformation to diagonalize the system.

b. Use MATLAB and the obtained similarity transformation of Part **a** to obtain a diagonalized expression for the system.

64. In an experiment to measure and identify postural arm reflexes, subjects hold with their hands a linear hydraulic manipulator. A load cell is attached to the actuator handle to measure resulting forces. At the application of a force, subjects try to maintain a fixed posture. Figure P5.44 shows a block diagram for the combined arm-environment system.

In the diagram, $H_r(s)$ represents the reflexive length and velocity feedback dynamics; $H_{act}(s)$ the activation dynamics, $H_i(s)$ the intrinsic act dynamics; $H_h(s)$ the hand dynamics; $H_e(s)$ the environmental dynamics; $X_a(s)$ the position of the arm; $X_h(s)$ the measured position of the hand; $F_h(s)$ the measured interaction force applied by the hand; $F_{int}(s)$ the intrinsic force; $F_{ref}(s)$ the reflexive force; $A(s)$ the reflexive activation; and $D(s)$ the external force perturbation (*de Vlugt, 2002*).

a. Obtain a signal-flow diagram from the block diagram.

b. Find $\dfrac{F_h(s)}{D(s)}$.

65. A simplified second-order transfer function model for bicycle dynamics is given by

$$
\frac{\varphi(s)}{\delta(s)} = \frac{aV}{bh} \frac{\left(s + \dfrac{V}{a} \right)}{\left(s^2 - \dfrac{g}{h} \right)}
$$

The input is $\delta(s)$, the steering angle, and the output is $\varphi(s)$, the tilt angle (between the floor and the bicycle longitudinal plane). In the model parameter a is the horizontal distance from the center of the back wheel to the bicycle center of mass; b is the horizontal distance between the centers of both wheels; h is the vertical distance from the center of mass to the floor; V is the rear wheel velocity (assumed constant); and g is the gravity constant. It is also assumed that the rider remains at a fixed position with respect to the bicycle so that the steer axis is vertical and that all angle deviations are small (*Åstrom, 2005*).

a. Obtain a state-space representation for the bicycle model in phase-variable form.

b. Find system eigenvalues and eigenvectors.

c. Find an appropriate similarity transformation matrix to diagonalize the system and obtain the state-space system's diagonal representation.

66. It is shown in Figure 5.6(*c*) that when negative feedback is used, the overall transfer function for the system of Figure 5.6(*b*) is

$$
\frac{C(s)}{R(s)} = \frac{G(s)}{1 + G(s)H(s)}
$$

Develop the block diagram of an alternative feedback system that will result in the same closed-loop transfer

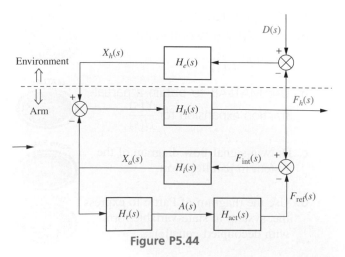

Figure P5.44

function, $C(s)/R(s)$, with $G(s)$ unchanged and un-moved. In addition, your new block diagram must have unity gain in the feedback path. You can add input transducers and/or controllers in the main forward path as required.

Design Problems

67. The motor and load shown in Figure P5.45(*a*) are used as part of the unity feedback system shown in Figure P5.45(*b*). Find the value of the coefficient of viscous damping, D_L, that must be used in order to yield a closed-loop transient response having a 20% overshoot.

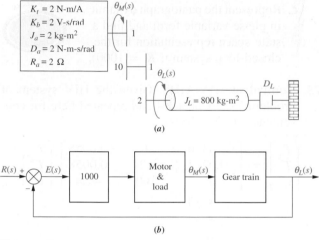

(a)

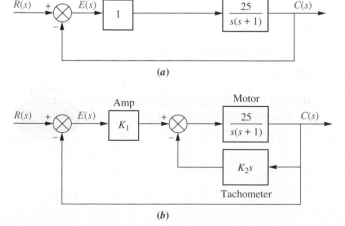

(b)

Figure P5.45 Position control: **a.** motor and load; **b.** block diagram

68. Assume that the motor whose transfer function is shown in Figure P5.46(*a*) is used as the forward path of a closed-loop, unity feedback system.

a. Calculate the percent overshoot and settling time that could be expected.

b. You want to improve the response found in Part **a**. Since the motor and the motor constants cannot be changed, an amplifier and a tachometer (voltage generator) are inserted into the loop, as shown in Figure P5.46. Find the values of K_1 and K_2 to yield a 25% overshoot and a settling time of 0.2 second.

69. The system shown in Figure P5.47 will have its transient response altered by adding a tachometer. Design K and K_2 in the system to yield a damping ratio of 0.5. The natural frequency of the system before the addition of the tachometer is 10 rad/s.

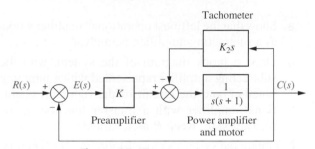

Figure P5.47 Position control

70. The mechanical system shown in Figure P5.48(*a*) is used as part of the unity feedback system shown in Figure P5.48(*b*). Find the values of M and D to yield 20% overshoot and 2 seconds settling time.

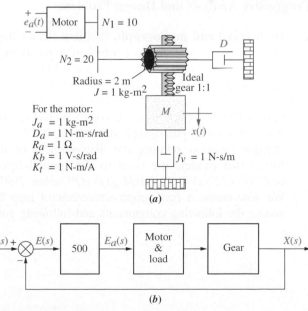

Figure P5.48 **a.** Motor and load; **b.** Motor and load in feedback system

71. Assume ideal operational amplifiers in the circuit of Figure P5.49.

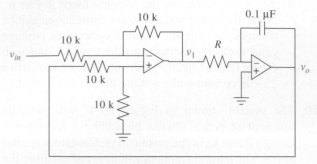

Figure P5.49

a. Show that the leftmost operational amplifier works as a subtracting amplifier. Namely, $v_1 = v_o - v_{in}$.

b. Draw a block diagram of the system, with the subtracting amplifier represented with a summing junction, and the circuit of the rightmost operational amplifier with a transfer function in the forward path. Keep R as a variable.

c. Obtain the system's closed-loop transfer function.

d. For a unit step input, obtain the value of R that will result in a settling time $T_s = 1$ msec.

e. Using the value of R calculated in Part **d**, make a sketch of the resulting unit step response.

Progressive Analysis and Design Problems

72. High-speed rail pantograph. Problem 19 in Chapter 1 discusses the active control of a pantograph mechanism for high-speed rail systems. In this problem you found a functional block diagram relating the output force (*actual*) to the input force (*desired* output). In Problem 64, Chapter 2, you found the transfer function for the pantograph dynamics, that is, the transfer function relating the displacement of the spring that models the head to the applied force, or $G(s) = (Y_h(s) - Y_{cat}(s))/F_{up}(s)$ (*O'Connor, 1997*). We now create a pantograph active-control loop by adding the following components and following your

functional block diagram found in Problem 19, Chapter 1: input transducer ($G_i(s) = 1/100$), controller ($G_c(s) = K$), actuator ($G_a(s) = 1/1000$), pantograph spring ($K_s = 82.3 \times 10^3 \text{N/m}$), and sensor ($H_o(s) = 1/100$).

a. Using the functional block diagram from your solution of Problem 19 in Chapter 1, and the pantograph dynamics, $G(s)$, found in Problem 64, Chapter 2, assemble a block diagram of the active pantograph control system.

b. Find the closed-loop transfer function for the block diagram found in Part **a** if $K = 1000$.

c. Represent the pantograph dynamics in phase-variable form and find a state-space representation for the closed-loop system if $K = 1000$).

73. Control of HIV/AIDS. Given the HIV system of Problem 77 in Chapter 4 and repeated here for convenience (*Craig, 2004*):

$$\begin{bmatrix} \dot{T} \\ \dot{T}^* \\ \dot{v} \end{bmatrix} = \begin{bmatrix} -0.04167 & 0 & -0.0058 \\ 0.0217 & -0.24 & 0.0058 \\ 0 & 100 & -2.4 \end{bmatrix} \begin{bmatrix} T \\ T^* \\ v \end{bmatrix}$$
$$+ \begin{bmatrix} 5.2 \\ -5.2 \\ 0 \end{bmatrix} u_1$$

$$y = \begin{bmatrix} 0 & 0 & 1 \end{bmatrix} \begin{bmatrix} T \\ T^* \\ v \end{bmatrix}$$

Express the system in the following forms:

a. Phase-variable form

b. Controller canonical form

c. Observer canonical form

Finally,

d. Use MATLAB to obtain the system's diagonalized representation.

CYBER EXPLORATION LABORATORY

Experiment 5.1

Objectives To verify the equivalency of the basic forms, including cascade, parallel, and feedback forms. To verify the equivalency of the basic moves, including moving blocks past summing junctions, and moving blocks past pickoff points.

Minimum Required Software Packages MATLAB, Simulink, and the Control System Toolbox

Prelab

1. Find the equivalent transfer function of three cascaded blocks, $G_1(s) = \dfrac{1}{s+1}$, $G_2(s) = \dfrac{1}{s+4}$, and $G_3(s) = \dfrac{s+3}{s+5}$.

2. Find the equivalent transfer function of three parallel blocks, $G_1(s) = \dfrac{1}{s+4}$, $G_2(s) = \dfrac{1}{s+4}$, and $G_3(s) = \dfrac{s+3}{s+5}$.

3. Find the equivalent transfer function of the negative feedback system of Figure P5.50 if $G(s) = \dfrac{s+1}{s(s+2)}$ and $H(s) = \dfrac{s+3}{s+4}$.

4. For the system of Prelab 3, push $H(s)$ to the left past the summing junction and draw the equivalent system.

5. For the system of Prelab 3, push $H(s)$ to the right past the pickoff point and draw the equivalent system.

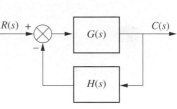

Figure P5.50

Lab

1. Using Simulink, set up the cascade system of Prelab 1 and the equivalent single block. Make separate plots of the step response of the cascaded system and its equivalent single block. Record the values of settling time and rise time for each step response.

2. Using Simulink, set up the parallel system of Prelab 2 and the equivalent single block. Make separate plots of the step response of the parallel system and its equivalent single block. Record the values of settling time and rise time for each step response.

3. Using Simulink, set up the negative feedback system of Prelab 3 and the equivalent single block. Make separate plots of the step response of the negative feedback system and its equivalent single block. Record the values of settling time and rise time for each step response.

4. Using Simulink, set up the negative feedback systems of Prelabs 3, 4, and 5. Make separate plots of the step response of each of the systems. Record the values of settling time and rise time for each step response.

Postlab

1. Using your lab data, verify the equivalent transfer function of blocks in cascade.

2. Using your lab data, verify the equivalent transfer function of blocks in parallel.

3. Using your lab data, verify the equivalent transfer function of negative feedback systems.

4. Using your lab data, verify the moving of blocks past summing junctions and pickoff points.

5. Discuss your results. Were the equivalencies verified?

BIBLIOGRAPHY

Åstrom, K., Klein, R. E., and Lennartsson, A. Bicycle Dynamics and Control. *IEEE Control Systems,* August 2005, pp. 26–47.

Bailey, F. N., Cockburn, J. C., and Dee, A. Robust Control for High-Performance Materials Testing. *IEEE Control Systems,* April 1992, pp. 63–70.

Ballard, R. D. *The Discovery of the Titanic,* Warner Books, New York, 1987.

Ben-Dov, D., and Salcudean, S. E. A Force-Controlled Pneumatic Actuator. *IEEE Transactions on Robotics and Automation,* vol. 11, 1995, pp. 906–911.

Cavallo, A., De Maria, G., and Verde, L. Robust Flight Control Systems: A Parameter Space Design. *Journal of Guidance, Control, and Dynamics,* vol. 15, no. 5, September–October 1992, pp. 1207–1215.

Craig, I. K., Xia, X., and Venter, J. W., Introducing HIV/AIDS Education into the Electrical Engineering Curriculum at the University of Pretoria, *IEEE Transactions on Education,* vol. 47, no. 1, February 2004, pp. 65–73.

de Vlugt, E., Schouten, A. C., and van der Helm, F. C. T. Adaptation of Reflexive Feedback during Arm Posture to Different Environments. *Biological Cybernetics,* vol. 87, 2002, pp. 10–26.

Evans, J., Krishnamurthy, B., Barrows, B., Skewis, T., and Lumelsky, V. Handling Real-World Motion Planning: A Hospital Transport Robot. *IEEE Control Systems,* February 1992, pp. 15–20.

Hostetter, G. H., Savant, C. J., Jr., and Stefani, R. T. *Design of Feedback Control Systems.* 2d ed. Saunders College Publishing, New York, 1989.

Johnson, H. et al. *Unmanned Free-Swimming Submersible (UFSS) System Description.* NRL Memorandum Report 4393. Naval Research Laboratory, Washington, DC, 1980.

Kurland, M., and Papson, T. P. Analog Computer Simulation of Linear Modulation Systems. *Transactions of the Analog/Hybrid Computer Educational Society,* January 1971, pp. 9–18.

Lepschy, A. M., Mian, G. A., and Viaro, U. Feedback Control in Ancient Water and Mechanical Clocks. *IEEE Transactions on Education,* vol. 35, 1992, pp 3–10.

Lin, J.-S., and Kanellakopoulos, I., Nonlinear Design of Active Suspensions. *IEEE Control Systems,* vol. 17, issue 3, June 1997, pp. 45–59.

Mason, S. J. Feedback Theory—Some Properties of Signal-Flow Graphs. *Proc. IRE,* September 1953, pp. 1144–1156.

Milhorn, H. T., Jr. *The Application of Control Theory to Physiological Systems.* W. B. Saunders, Philadelphia, 1966.

Neamen, D. A. *Electronic Circuit Analysis and Design.* McGraw-Hill, 2d ed., 2001, p. 334.

O'Connor, D. N., Eppinger, S. D., Seering, W. P., and Wormly, D. N. Active Control of a High-Speed Pantograph. *Journal of Dynamic Systems, Measurements, and Control,* vol. 119, March 1997, pp. 1–4.

Tasch, U., Koontz, J. W., Ignatoski, M. A., and Geselowitz, D. B. An Adaptive Aortic Pressure Observer for the Penn State Electric Ventricular Assist Device. *IEEE Transactions on Biomedical Engineering,* vol. 37, 1990, pp. 374–383.

Timothy, L. K., and Bona, B. E. *State Space Analysis: An Introduction.* McGraw-Hill, New York, 1968.

Vaughan, N. D., and Gamble, J. B. The Modeling and Simulation of a Proportional Solenoid Valve. *Journal of Dynamic Systems, Measurements, and Control,* vol. 118, March 1996, pp. 120–125.

Yaniv, Y., Sivan, R., and Landesberg, A. Stability, Controllability and Observability of the "Four State" Model for the Sarcomeric Control of Contraction. *Annals of Biomedical Engineering,* vol. 34, 2006, pp. 778–789.

TRANSIENT RESPONSE
STABILITY

6

CHAPTER OBJECTIVES

In this chapter you will learn the following:

- How to determine the stability of a system represented as a transfer function
- How to determine the stability of a system represented in state space
- How to determine system parameters to yield stability

CASE STUDY OBJECTIVES

You will be able to demonstrate your knowledge of the chapter objectives with case studies as follows:

- Given the antenna azimuth position control system shown on the front endpapers, you will be able to find the range of preamplifier gain to keep the system stable.
- Given the block diagrams for the UFSS vehicle's pitch and heading control systems on the back endpapers, you will be able to determine the range of gain for stability of the pitch or heading control system.

6.1 INTRODUCTION

In Chapter 1 we saw that three requirements enter into the design of a control system: transient response, stability, and steady-state errors. Thus far we have covered transient response, which we will revisit in Chapter 8. We are now ready to discuss the next requirement, stability.

Stability is the most important system specification. If a system is unstable, transient response and steady-state errors are moot points. An unstable system cannot be designed for a specific transient response or steady-state error requirement. What, then, is stability? There are many definitions for stability, depending upon the kind of system or the point of view. In this section we limit ourselves to linear, time-invariant systems.

In Section 1.5 we discussed that we can control the output of a system if the steady-state response consists of only the forced response. But the total response of a system is the sum of the forced and natural responses, or

$$c(t) = c_{\text{forced}}(t) + c_{\text{natural}}(t) \tag{6.1}$$

Using these concepts, we present the following definitions of stability, instability, and marginal stability:

A linear, time-invariant system is *stable* if the natural response approaches zero as time approaches infinity.

A linear, time-invariant system is *unstable* if the natural response grows without bound as time approaches infinity.

A linear, time-invariant system is *marginally stable* if the natural response neither decays nor grows but remains constant or oscillates as time approaches infinity.

Thus, the definition of stability implies that only the forced response remains as the natural response approaches zero.

These definitions rely on a description of the natural response. When one is looking at the total response, it may be difficult to separate the natural response from the forced response. However, we realize that if the input is bounded and the total response is not approaching infinity as time approaches infinity, then the natural response is obviously not approaching infinity. If the input is unbounded, we see an unbounded total response, and we cannot arrive at any conclusion about the stability of the system; we cannot tell whether the total response is unbounded because the forced response is unbounded or because the natural response is unbounded. Thus, our alternate definition of *stability*, one that regards the total response and implies the first definition based upon the natural response, is this:

A system is stable if *every* bounded input yields a bounded output.

We call this statement the bounded-input, bounded-output (BIBO) definition of stability.

Let us now produce an alternate definition for instability based on the total response rather than the natural response. We realize that if the input is bounded but the total response is unbounded, the system is unstable, since we can conclude that the natural response approaches infinity as time approaches infinity. If the input is unbounded, we will see an unbounded total response, and we cannot draw any conclusion about the stability of the system; we cannot tell whether the total response is unbounded because the forced response is unbounded or because the natural response is unbounded. Thus, our alternate definition of *instability,* one that regards the total response, is this:

A system is unstable if *any* bounded input yields an unbounded output.

These definitions help clarify our previous definition of *marginal stability,* which really means that the system is stable for some bounded inputs and unstable for others. For example, we will show that if the natural response is undamped, a bounded sinusoidal input of the same frequency yields a natural response of growing oscillations. Hence, the system appears stable for all bounded inputs except this one sinusoid. Thus, marginally stable systems by the natural response definitions are included as unstable systems under the BIBO definitions.

Let us summarize our definitions of stability for linear, time-invariant systems. Using the natural response:

1. A system is stable if the natural response approaches zero as time approaches infinity.

2. A system is unstable if the natural response approaches infinity as time approaches infinity.

3. A system is marginally stable if the natural response neither decays nor grows but remains constant or oscillates.

Using the total response (BIBO):

1. A system is stable if *every* bounded input yields a bounded output.

2. A system is unstable if *any* bounded input yields an unbounded output.

Physically, an unstable system whose natural response grows without bound can cause damage to the system, to adjacent property, or to human life. Many times systems are designed with limit stops to prevent total runaway. From the perspective of the time response plot of a physical system, instability is displayed by transients that grow without bound and, consequently, a total response that does not approach a steady-state value or other forced response.[1]

How do we determine if a system is stable? Let us focus on the natural response definitions of stability. Recall from our study of system poles that poles in the left half-plane (lhp) yield either pure exponential decay or damped sinusoidal natural responses. These natural responses decay to zero as time approaches infinity. Thus, if the closed-loop system poles are in the left half of the plane and hence have a negative real part, the system is stable. That is, *stable systems have closed-loop transfer functions with poles only in the left half-plane.*

Poles in the right half-plane (rhp) yield either pure exponentially increasing or exponentially increasing sinusoidal natural responses. These natural responses approach infinity as time approaches infinity. Thus, if the closed-loop system poles are in the right half of the *s*-plane and hence have a positive real part, the system is unstable. Also, poles of multiplicity greater than 1 on the imaginary axis lead to the sum of responses of the form $At^n\cos(\omega t + \phi)$, where $n = 1, 2, \ldots$, which also approaches infinity as time approaches infinity. Thus, *unstable systems have closed-loop transfer functions with at least one pole in the right half-plane and/or poles of multiplicity greater than 1 on the imaginary axis.*

Finally, a system that has imaginary axis poles of multiplicity 1 yields pure sinusoidal oscillations as a natural response. These responses neither increase nor

---

[1] Care must be taken here to distinguish between natural responses growing without bound and a forced response, such as a ramp or exponential increase, that also grows without bound. A system whose forced response approaches infinity is stable as long as the natural response approaches zero.

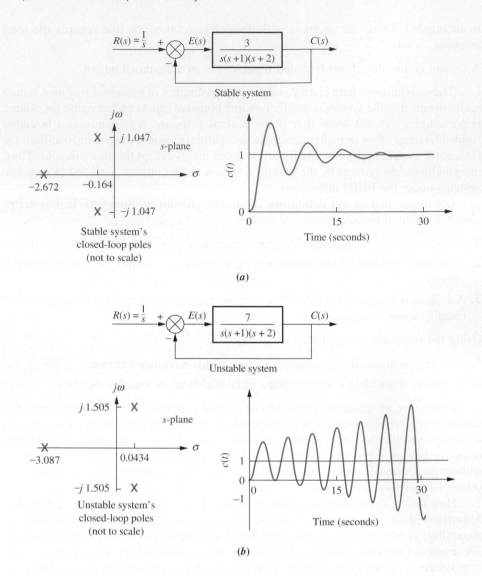

FIGURE 6.1 Closed-loop poles and response:
a. stable system;
b. unstable system

decrease in amplitude. Thus, *marginally stable systems have closed-loop transfer functions with only imaginary axis poles of multiplicity 1 and poles in the left half-plane.*

As an example, the unit step response of the stable system of Figure 6.1(*a*) is compared to that of the unstable system of Figure 6.1(*b*). The responses, also shown in Figure 6.1, show that while the oscillations for the stable system diminish, those for the unstable system increase without bound. Also notice that the stable system's response in this case approaches a steady-state value of unity.

It is not always a simple matter to determine if a feedback control system is stable. Unfortunately, a typical problem that arises is shown in Figure 6.2. Although we know the poles of the forward transfer function in Figure 6.2(*a*), we do not know the location of the poles of the equivalent closed-loop system of Figure 6.2(*b*) without factoring or otherwise solving for the roots.

However, under certain conditions, we can draw some conclusions about the stability of the system. First, if the closed-loop transfer function has only left-half-plane poles, then the factors of the denominator of the closed-loop system transfer function consist of products of terms such as $(s + a_i)$, where a_i is real and positive, or complex

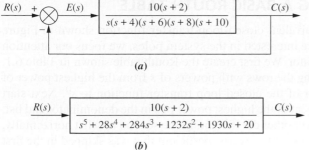

FIGURE 6.2 Common cause of problems in finding closed-loop poles:
a. original system;
b. equivalent system

with a positive real part. The product of such terms is a polynomial with all positive coefficients.[2] No term of the polynomial can be missing, since that would imply cancellation between positive and negative coefficients or imaginary axis roots in the factors, which is not the case. Thus, a sufficient condition for a system to be unstable is that all signs of the coefficients of the denominator of the closed-loop transfer function are not the same. If powers of s are missing, the system is either unstable or, at best, marginally stable. Unfortunately, if all coefficients of the denominator are positive and not missing, we do not have definitive information about the system's pole locations.

If the method described in the previous paragraph is not sufficient, then a computer can be used to determine the stability by calculating the root locations of the denominator of the closed-loop transfer function. Today some hand-held calculators can evaluate the roots of a polynomial. There is, however, another method to test for stability without having to solve for the roots of the denominator. We discuss this method in the next section.

6.2 ROUTH-HURWITZ CRITERION

In this section we learn a method that yields stability information without the need to solve for the closed-loop system poles. Using this method, we can tell how many closed-loop system poles are in the left half-plane, in the right half-plane, and on the $j\omega$-axis. (Notice that we say *how many,* not *where.*) We can find the number of poles in each section of the s-plane, but we cannot find their coordinates. The method is called the *Routh-Hurwitz criterion* for stability (*Routh, 1905*).

The method requires two steps: (1) Generate a data table called a *Routh table* and (2) interpret the Routh table to tell how many closed-loop system poles are in the left half-plane, the right half-plane, and on the $j\omega$-axis. You might wonder why we study the Routh-Hurwitz criterion when modern calculators and computers can tell us the exact location of system poles. The power of the method lies in design rather than analysis. For example, if you have an unknown parameter in the denominator of a transfer function, it is difficult to determine via a calculator the range of this parameter to yield stability. You would probably rely on trial and error to answer the stability question. We shall see later that the Routh-Hurwitz criterion can yield a closed-form expression for the range of the unknown parameter.

In this section we make and interpret a basic Routh table. In the next section we consider two special cases that can arise when generating this data table.

---

[2] The coefficients can also be made all negative by multiplying the polynomial by -1. This operation does not change the root location.

GENERATING A BASIC ROUTH TABLE

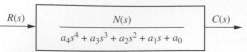

FIGURE 6.3   Equivalent closed-loop transfer function

Look at the equivalent closed-loop transfer function shown in Figure 6.3. Since we are interested in the system poles, we focus our attention on the denominator. We first create the Routh table shown in Table 6.1. Begin by labeling the rows with powers of s from the highest power of the denominator of the closed-loop transfer function to s^0. Next start with the coefficient of the highest power of s in the denominator and list, horizontally in the first row, every other coefficient. In the second row list horizontally, starting with the next highest power of s, every coefficient that was skipped in the first row.

The remaining entries are filled in as follows. Each entry is a negative determinant of entries in the previous two rows divided by the entry in the first column directly above the calculated row. The left-hand column of the determinant is always the first column of the previous two rows, and the right-hand column is the elements of the column above and to the right. The table is complete when all of the rows are completed down to s^0. Table 6.2 is the completed Routh table. Let us look at an example.

TABLE 6.1   Initial layout for Routh table

s^4	a_4	a_2	a_0
s^3	a_3	a_1	0
s^2			
s^1			
s^0			

TABLE 6.2   Completed Routh table

s^4	a_4	a_2	a_0
s^3	a_3	a_1	0
s^2	$\dfrac{-\begin{vmatrix} a_4 & a_2 \\ a_3 & a_1 \end{vmatrix}}{a_3} = b_1$	$\dfrac{-\begin{vmatrix} a_4 & a_0 \\ a_3 & 0 \end{vmatrix}}{a_3} = b_2$	$\dfrac{-\begin{vmatrix} a_4 & 0 \\ a_3 & 0 \end{vmatrix}}{a_3} = 0$
s^1	$\dfrac{-\begin{vmatrix} a_3 & a_1 \\ b_1 & b_2 \end{vmatrix}}{b_1} = c_1$	$\dfrac{-\begin{vmatrix} a_3 & 0 \\ b_1 & 0 \end{vmatrix}}{b_1} = 0$	$\dfrac{-\begin{vmatrix} a_3 & 0 \\ b_1 & 0 \end{vmatrix}}{b_1} = 0$
s^0	$\dfrac{-\begin{vmatrix} b_1 & b_2 \\ c_1 & 0 \end{vmatrix}}{c_1} = d_1$	$\dfrac{-\begin{vmatrix} b_1 & 0 \\ c_1 & 0 \end{vmatrix}}{c_1} = 0$	$\dfrac{-\begin{vmatrix} b_1 & 0 \\ c_1 & 0 \end{vmatrix}}{c_1} = 0$

EXAMPLE 6.1

Creating a Routh table

Problem: Make the Routh table for the system shown in Figure 6.4(*a*).

SOLUTION: The first step is to find the equivalent closed-loop system because we want to test the denominator of this function, not the given forward transfer function, for pole location. Using the feedback formula, we obtain the equivalent system of Figure 6.4(*b*). The Routh-Hurwitz criterion will be applied to this

FIGURE 6.4   a. Feedback system for Example 6.1; **b.** equivalent closed-loop system

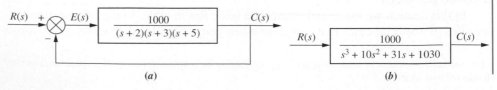

TABLE 6.3   Completed Routh table for Example 6.1

s^3	1	31	0
s^2	~~10~~ 1	~~1030~~ 103	0
s^1	$-\dfrac{\begin{vmatrix} 1 & 31 \\ 1 & 103 \end{vmatrix}}{1} = -72$	$-\dfrac{\begin{vmatrix} 1 & 0 \\ 0 & 0 \end{vmatrix}}{1} = 0$	$-\dfrac{\begin{vmatrix} 1 & 0 \\ 1 & 0 \end{vmatrix}}{1} = 0$
s^0	$-\dfrac{\begin{vmatrix} 1 & 103 \\ -72 & 0 \end{vmatrix}}{-72} = 103$	$-\dfrac{\begin{vmatrix} 1 & 0 \\ -72 & 0 \end{vmatrix}}{-72} = 0$	$-\dfrac{\begin{vmatrix} 1 & 0 \\ -72 & 0 \end{vmatrix}}{-72} = 0$

denominator. First label the rows with powers of s from s^3 down to s^0 in a vertical column, as shown in Table 6.3. Next form the first row of the table, using the coefficients of the denominator of the closed-loop transfer function. Start with the coefficient of the highest power and skip every other power of s. Now form the second row with the coefficients of the denominator skipped in the previous step. Subsequent rows are formed with determinants, as shown in Table 6.2.

For convenience any row of the Routh table can be multiplied by a positive constant without changing the values of the rows below. This can be proved by examining the expressions for the entries and verifying that any multiplicative constant from a previous row cancels out. In the second row of Table 6.3, for example, the row was multiplied by $1/10$. We see later that care must be taken not to multiply the row by a negative constant.

INTERPRETING THE BASIC ROUTH TABLE

Now that we know how to generate the Routh table, let us see how to interpret it. The basic Routh table applies to systems with poles in the left and right half-planes. Systems with imaginary poles and the kind of Routh table that results will be discussed in the next section. Simply stated, the Routh-Hurwitz criterion declares that *the number of roots of the polynomial that are in the right half-plane is equal to the number of sign changes in the first column.*

If the closed-loop transfer function has all poles in the left half of the s-plane, the system is stable. Thus, a system is stable if there are no sign changes in the first column of the Routh table. For example, Table 6.3 has two sign changes in the first column. The first sign change occurs from 1 in the s^2 row to -72 in the s^1 row. The second occurs from -72 in the s^1 row to 103 in the s^0 row. Thus, the system of Figure 6.4 is unstable since two poles exist in the right half-plane.

SKILL-ASSESSMENT EXERCISE 6.1

Problem: Make a Routh table and tell how many roots of the following polynomial are in the right half-plane and in the left half-plane.

$$P(s) = 3s^7 + 9s^6 + 6s^5 + 4s^4 + 7s^3 + 8s^2 + 2s + 6$$

ANSWER: Four in the right half-plane (rhp), three in the left half-plane (lhp)

The complete solution is at www.wiley.com/college/nise.

WileyPLUS

Control Solutions

Now that we have described how to generate and interpret a basic Routh table, let us look at two special cases that can arise.

6.3 ROUTH-HURWITZ CRITERION: SPECIAL CASES

Two special cases can occur: (1) The Routh table sometimes will have a zero *only in the first column* of a row, or (2) the Routh table sometimes will have an *entire row* that consists of zeros. Let us examine the first case.

ZERO ONLY IN THE FIRST COLUMN

If the first element of a row is zero, division by zero would be required to form the next row. To avoid this phenomenon, an epsilon, ϵ, is assigned to replace the zero in the first column. The value ϵ is then allowed to approach zero from either the positive or the negative side, after which the signs of the entries in the first column can be determined. Let us look at an example.

EXAMPLE 6.2

Stability via epsilon method

Problem: Determine the stability of the closed-loop transfer function

$$T(s) = \frac{10}{s^5 + 2s^4 + 3s^3 + 6s^2 + 5s + 3} \tag{6.2}$$

SOLUTION: The solution is shown in Table 6.4. We form the Routh table by using the denominator of Eq. (6.2). Begin by assembling the Routh table down to the row where a zero appears *only* in the first column (the s^3 row). Next replace the zero by a small number, ϵ, and complete the table. To begin the interpretation, we must first assume a sign, positive or negative, for the quantity ϵ. Table 6.5 shows the first column of Table 6.4 along with the resulting signs for choices of ϵ positive and ϵ negative.

TryIt 6.1

Use the following MATLAB statement to find the poles of the closed-loop transfer function in Eq. (6.2).

```
roots([1 2 3 6 5 3])
```

TABLE 6.4   Completed Routh table for Example 6.2

s^5	1	3	5
s^4	2	6	3
s^3	$\cancel{0}\ \ \epsilon$	$\dfrac{7}{2}$	0
s^2	$\dfrac{6\epsilon - 7}{\epsilon}$	3	0
s^1	$\dfrac{42\epsilon - 49 - 6\epsilon^2}{12\epsilon - 14}$	0	0
s^0	3	0	0

TABLE 6.5   Determining signs in first column of a Routh table with zero as first element in a row

Label	First column	$\epsilon = +$	$\epsilon = -$
s^5	1	+	+
s^4	2	+	+
s^3	$\cancel{0}\ \ \epsilon$	+	−
s^2	$\dfrac{6\epsilon - 7}{\epsilon}$	−	+
s^1	$\dfrac{42\epsilon - 49 - 6\epsilon^2}{12\epsilon - 14}$	+	+
s^0	3	+	+

If ϵ is chosen positive, Table 6.5 will show a sign change from the s^3 row to the s^2 row, and there will be another sign change from the s^2 row to the s^1 row. Hence, the system is unstable and has two poles in the right half-plane.

Alternatively, we could choose ϵ negative. Table 6.5 would then show a sign change from the s^4 row to the s^3 row. Another sign change would occur from the s^3 row to the s^2 row. Our result would be exactly the same as that for a positive choice for ϵ. Thus, the system is unstable, with two poles in the right half-plane.

Symbolic Math

Students who are performing the MATLAB exercises and want to explore the added capability of MATLAB's Symbolic Math Toolbox should now run ch6sp1 in Appendix E at www.wiley.com/college/nise. You will learn how to use the Symbolic Math Toolbox to calculate the values of cells in a Routh table even if the table contains symbolic objects, such as ϵ. You will see that the Symbolic Math Toolbox and MATLAB yield an alternate way to generate the Routh table for Example 6.2.

Another method that can be used when a zero appears only in the first column of a row is derived from the fact that a polynomial that has the reciprocal roots of the original polynomial has its roots distributed the same—right half-plane, left half-plane, or imaginary axis—because taking the reciprocal of the root value does not move it to another region. Thus, if we can find the polynomial that has the reciprocal roots of the original, it is possible that the Routh table for the new polynomial will not have a zero in the first column. This method is usually computationally easier than the epsilon method just described.

We now show that the polynomial we are looking for, the one with the reciprocal roots, is simply the original polynomial with its coefficients written in reverse order (*Phillips, 1991*). Assume the equation

$$s^n + a_{n-1}s^{n-1} + \cdots + a_1 s + a_0 = 0 \tag{6.3}$$

If s is replaced by $1/d$, then d will have roots which are the reciprocal of s. Making this substitution in Eq. (6.3),

$$\left(\frac{1}{d}\right)^n + a_{n-1}\left(\frac{1}{d}\right)^{n-1} + \cdots + a_1\left(\frac{1}{d}\right) + a_0 = 0 \tag{6.4}$$

Factoring out $(1/d)^n$,

$$\left(\frac{1}{d}\right)^n \left[1 + a_{n-1}\left(\frac{1}{d}\right)^{-1} + \cdots + a_1\left(\frac{1}{d}\right)^{(1-n)} + a_0\left(\frac{1}{d}\right)^{-n}\right]$$

$$= \left(\frac{1}{d}\right)^n [1 + a_{n-1}d + \cdots + a_1 d^{(n-1)} + a_0 d^n] = 0 \tag{6.5}$$

Thus, the polynomial with reciprocal roots is a polynomial with the coefficients written in reverse order. Let us redo the previous example to show the computational advantage of this method.

EXAMPLE 6.3

Stability via reverse coefficients

Problem: Determine the stability of the closed-loop transfer function

$$T(s) = \frac{10}{s^5 + 2s^4 + 3s^3 + 6s^2 + 5s + 3} \tag{6.6}$$

SOLUTION: First write a polynomial that has the reciprocal roots of the denominator of Eq. (6.6). From our discussion this polynomial is formed by writing the denominator of Eq. (6.6) in reverse order. Hence,

$$D(s) = 3s^5 + 5s^4 + 6s^3 + 3s^2 + 2s + 1 \tag{6.7}$$

We form the Routh table as shown in Table 6.6 using Eq. (6.7). Since there are two sign changes, the system is unstable and has two right-half-plane poles. This is the same as the result obtained in Example 6.2. Notice that Table 6.6 does not have a zero in the first column.

TABLE 6.6   Routh table for Example 6.3

s^5	3	6	2
s^4	5	3	1
s^3	4.2	1.4	
s^2	1.33	1	
s^1	−1.75		
s^0	1		

ENTIRE ROW IS ZERO

We now look at the second special case. Sometimes while making a Routh table, we find that an entire row consists of zeros because there is an even polynomial that is a factor of the original polynomial. This case must be handled differently from the case of a zero in only the first column of a row. Let us look at an example that demonstrates how to construct and interpret the Routh table when an entire row of zeros is present.

EXAMPLE 6.4

Stability via Routh table with row of zeros

Problem: Determine the number of right-half-plane poles in the closed-loop transfer function

$$T(s) = \frac{10}{s^5 + 7s^4 + 6s^3 + 42s^2 + 8s + 56} \tag{6.8}$$

SOLUTION: Start by forming the Routh table for the denominator of Eq. (6.8) (see Table 6.7). At the second row we multiply through by 1/7 for convenience. We stop at the third row, since the entire row consists of zeros, and use the following procedure.

TABLE 6.7 Routh table for Example 6.4

s^5		1		6		8
s^4	~~7~~ 1		~~42~~ 6		~~56~~ 8	
s^3	~~0~~ ~~4~~ 1		~~0~~ ~~12~~ 3		~~0~~ ~~0~~ 0	
s^2	3		8		0	
s^1	$\dfrac{1}{3}$		0		0	
s^0	8		0		0	

First we return to the row immediately above the row of zeros and form an auxiliary polynomial, using the entries in that row as coefficients. The polynomial will start with the power of s in the label column and continue by skipping every other power of s. Thus, the polynomial formed for this example is

$$P(s) = s^4 + 6s^2 + 8 \tag{6.9}$$

Next we differentiate the polynomial with respect to s and obtain

$$\frac{dP(s)}{ds} = 4s^3 + 12s + 0 \tag{6.10}$$

Finally, we use the coefficients of Eq. (6.10) to replace the row of zeros. Again, for convenience the third row is multiplied by 1/4 after replacing the zeros.

The remainder of the table is formed in a straightforward manner by following the standard form shown in Table 6.2. Table 6.7 shows that all entries in the first column are positive. Hence, there are no right-half-plane poles.

Let us look further into the case that yields an entire row of zeros. An entire row of zeros will appear in the Routh table when a purely even or purely odd polynomial is a factor of the original polynomial. For example, $s^4 + 5s^2 + 7$ is an even polynomial; it has only even powers of s. Even polynomials only have roots that are symmetrical about the origin.[3] This symmetry can occur under three conditions of root position: (1) The roots are symmetrical and real, (2) the roots are symmetrical and imaginary, or (3) the roots are quadrantal. Figure 6.5 shows examples of these cases. Each case or combination of these cases will generate an even polynomial.

It is this even polynomial that causes the row of zeros to appear. Thus, the row of zeros tells us of the existence of an even polynomial whose roots are symmetric about the origin. Some of these roots could be on the $j\omega$-axis. On the other hand, since $j\omega$ roots are symmetric about the origin, if we do not have a row of zeros, we cannot possibly have $j\omega$ roots.

Another characteristic of the Routh table for the case in question is that the row previous to the row of zeros contains the even polynomial that is a factor of the original polynomial. Finally, everything from the row containing the even polynomial down to the end of the Routh table is a test of only the even polynomial. Let us put these facts together in an example.

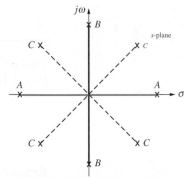

A: Real and symmetrical about the origin ——
B: Imaginary and symmetrical about the origin ——
C: Quadrantal and symmetrical about the origin ----

FIGURE 6.5 Root positions to generate even polynomials: A, B, C, or any combination

[3] The polynomial $s^5 + 5s^3 + 7s$ is an example of an odd polynomial; it has only odd powers of s. Odd polynomials are the product of an even polynomial and an odd power of s. Thus, the constant term of an odd polynomial is always missing.

EXAMPLE 6.5

Pole distribution via Routh table with row of zeros

Problem: For the transfer function

$$T(s) = \frac{20}{s^8 + s^7 + 12s^6 + 22s^5 + 39s^4 + 59s^3 + 48s^2 + 38s + 20} \tag{6.11}$$

tell how many poles are in the right half-plane, in the left half-plane, and on the $j\omega$-axis.

SOLUTION: Use the denominator of Eq. (6.11) and form the Routh table in Table 6.8. For convenience the s^6 row is multiplied by $1/10$, and the s^5 row is multiplied by $1/20$. At the s^3 row we obtain a row of zeros. Moving back one row to s^4, we extract the even polynomial, $P(s)$, as

$$P(s) = s^4 + 3s^2 + 2 \tag{6.12}$$

TABLE 6.8 Routh table for Example 6.5

s^8	1	12	39	48	20
s^7	1	22	59	38	0
s^6	~~-10~~ -1	~~-20~~ -2	~~10~~ 1	~~20~~ 2	0
s^5	~~20~~ 1	~~60~~ 3	~~40~~ 2	0	0
s^4	1	3	2	0	0
s^3	~~0~~ ~~4~~ 2	~~0~~ ~~6~~ 3	~~0~~ ~~0~~ 0	0	0
s^2	~~$\frac{3}{2}$~~ 3	~~2~~ 4	0	0	0
s^1	$\frac{1}{3}$	0	0	0	0
s^0	4	0	0	0	0

This polynomial will divide evenly into the denominator of Eq. (6.11) and thus is a factor. Taking the derivative with respect to s to obtain the coefficients that replace the row of zeros in the s^3 row, we find

$$\frac{dP(s)}{ds} = 4s^3 + 6s + 0 \tag{6.13}$$

Replace the row of zeros with 4, 6, and 0 and multiply the row by $1/2$ for convenience. Finally, continue the table to the s^0 row, using the standard procedure.

How do we now interpret this Routh table? Since all entries from the even polynomial at the s^4 row down to the s^0 row are a test of the even polynomial, we begin to draw some conclusions about the roots of the even polynomial. No sign changes exist from the s^4 row down to the s^0 row. Thus, the even polynomial does not have right-half-plane poles. Since there are no right-half-plane poles, no left-half-plane poles are present because of the requirement for symmetry. Hence, the even polynomial, Eq. (6.12), must have all four of its poles on the $j\omega$-axis.[4] These results are summarized in the first column of Table 6.9.

---

[4] A necessary condition for stability is that the $j\omega$ roots have unit multiplicity. The even polynomial must be checked for multiple $j\omega$ roots. For this case, the existence of multiple $j\omega$ roots would lead to a perfect, fourth-order square polynomial. Since Eq. (6.12) is not a perfect square, the four $j\omega$ roots are distinct.

TABLE 6.9 Summary of pole locations for Example 6.5

| Location | Polynomial | | |
	Even (fourth-order)	Other (fourth-order)	Total (eighth-order)
Right half-plane	0	2	2
Left half-plane	0	2	2
$j\omega$	4	0	4

The remaining roots of the total polynomial are evaluated from the s^8 row down to the s^4 row. We notice two sign changes: one from the s^7 row to the s^6 row and the other from the s^6 row to the s^5 row. Thus, the other polynomial must have two roots in the right half-plane. These results are included in Table 6.9 under "Other." The final tally is the sum of roots from each component, the even polynomial and the other polynomial, as shown under "Total" in Table 6.9. Thus, the system has two poles in the right half-plane, two poles in the left half-plane, and four poles on the $j\omega$-axis; it is unstable because of the right-half-plane poles.

We now summarize what we have learned about polynomials that generate entire rows of zeros in the Routh table. These polynomials have a purely even factor with roots that are symmetrical about the origin. The even polynomial appears in the Routh table in the row directly above the row of zeros. Every entry in the table from the even polynomial's row to the end of the chart applies only to the even polynomial. Therefore, the number of sign changes from the even polynomial to the end of the table equals the number of right-half-plane roots of the even polynomial. Because of the symmetry of roots about the origin, the even polynomial must have the same number of left-half-plane roots as it does right-half-plane roots. Having accounted for the roots in the right and left half-planes, we know the remaining roots must be on the $j\omega$-axis.

Every row in the Routh table from the beginning of the chart to the row containing the even polynomial applies only to the other factor of the original polynomial. For this factor the number of sign changes, from the beginning of the table down to the even polynomial, equals the number of right-half-plane roots. The remaining roots are left-half-plane roots. There can be no $j\omega$ roots contained in the other polynomial.

SKILL-ASSESSMENT EXERCISE 6.2

Problem: Use the Routh-Hurwitz criterion to find how many poles of the following closed-loop system, $T(s)$, are in the rhp, in the lhp, and on the $j\omega$-axis:

$$T(s) = \frac{s^3 + 7s^2 - 21s + 10}{s^6 + s^5 - 6s^4 + 0s^3 - s^2 - s + 6}$$

ANSWER: Two rhp, two lhp, and two $j\omega$

The complete solution is at www.wiley.com/college/nise.

Let us demonstrate the usefulness of the Routh-Hurwitz criterion with a few additional examples.

6.4 ROUTH-HURWITZ CRITERION: ADDITIONAL EXAMPLES

The previous two sections have introduced the Routh-Hurwitz criterion. Now we need to demonstrate the method's application to a number of analysis and design problems.

EXAMPLE 6.6

Standard Routh-Hurwitz

Problem: Find the number of poles in the left half-plane, the right half-plane, and on the $j\omega$ axis for the system of Figure 6.6

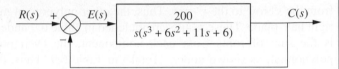

FIGURE 6.6 Feedback control system for Example 6.6

SOLUTION: First find the closed-loop transfer function as

$$T(s) = \frac{200}{s^4 + 6s^3 + 11s^2 + 6s + 200} \tag{6.14}$$

The Routh table for the denominator of Eq. (6.14) is shown as Table 6.10. For clarity we leave most zero cells blank. At the s^1 row there is a negative coefficient; thus, there are two sign changes. The system is unstable, since it has two right-half-plane poles and two left-half-plane poles. The system cannot have $j\omega$ poles since a row of zeros did not appear in the Routh table.

TABLE 6.10 **Routh table for Example 6.6**

s^4	1	11	200
s^3	~~6~~ 1	~~6~~ 1	
s^2	~~10~~ 1	~~200~~ 20	
s^1	−19		
s^0	20		

The next example demonstrates the occurrence of a zero in only the first column of a row.

EXAMPLE 6.7

Routh-Hurwitz with zero in first column

Problem: Find the number of poles in the left half-plane, the right half-plane, and on the $j\omega$-axis for the system of Figure 6.7.

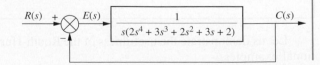

FIGURE 6.7 Feedback control system for Example 6.7

SOLUTION: The closed-loop transfer function is

$$T(s) = \frac{1}{2s^5 + 3s^4 + 2s^3 + 3s^2 + 2s + 1} \tag{6.15}$$

Form the Routh table shown as Table 6.11, using the denominator of Eq. (6.15). A zero appears in the first column of the s^3 row. Since the entire row is not zero, simply replace the zero with a small quantity, ϵ, and continue the table. Permitting ϵ to be a small, positive quantity, we find that the first term of the s^2 row is negative. Thus, there are two sign changes, and the system is unstable, with two poles in the right half-plane. The remaining poles are in the left half-plane.

TABLE 6.11   Routh table for Example 6.7

s^5	2	2	2
s^4	3	3	1
s^3	$\cancel{0}$ ϵ	$\dfrac{4}{3}$	
s^2	$\dfrac{3\epsilon - 4}{\epsilon}$	1	
s^1	$\dfrac{12\epsilon - 16 - 3\epsilon^2}{9\epsilon - 12}$		
s^0	1		

We also can use the alternative approach, where we produce a polynomial whose roots are the reciprocal of the original. Using the denominator of Eq. (6.15), we form a polynomial by writing the coefficients in reverse order,

$$s^5 + 2s^4 + 3s^3 + 2s^2 + 3s + 2 \tag{6.16}$$

The Routh table for this polynomial is shown as Table 6.12. Unfortunately, in this case we also produce a zero only in the first column at the s^2 row. However, the table is easier to work with than Table 6.11. Table 6.12 yields the same results as Table 6.11—three poles in the left half-plane and two poles in the right half-plane. The system is unstable.

TABLE 6.12   Alternative Routh table for Example 6.7

s^5	1	3	3
s^4	2	2	2
s^3	2	2	
s^2	$\cancel{0}$ ϵ	2	
s^1	$\dfrac{2\epsilon - 4}{\epsilon}$		
s^0	2		

Students who are using MATLAB should now run ch6p1 in Appendix B. You will learn how to perform block diagram reduction to find $T(s)$, followed by an evaluation of the closed-loop system's poles to determine stability. This exercise uses MATLAB to do Example 6.7.

MATLAB

In the next example we see an entire row of zeros appear along with the possibility of imaginary roots.

EXAMPLE 6.8

Routh-Hurwitz with row of zeros

Problem: Find the number of poles in the left half-plane, the right half-plane, and on the $j\omega$-axis for the system of Figure 6.8. Draw conclusions about the stability of the closed-loop system.

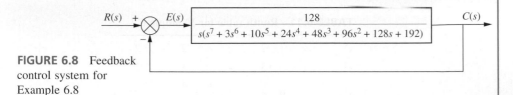

FIGURE 6.8 Feedback control system for Example 6.8

SOLUTION: The closed-loop transfer function for the system of Figure 6.8 is

$$T(s) = \frac{128}{s^8 + 3s^7 + 10s^6 + 24s^5 + 48s^4 + 96s^3 + 128s^2 + 192s + 128} \quad (6.17)$$

Using the denominator, form the Routh table shown as Table 6.13. A row of zeros appears in the s^5 row. Thus, the closed-loop transfer function denominator must have an even polynomial as a factor. Return to the s^6 row and form the even polynomial:

$$P(s) = s^6 + 8s^4 + 32s^2 + 64 \quad (6.18)$$

TABLE 6.13   Routh table for Example 6.8

s^8		1		10		48		128	128
s^7	~~3~~ 1		~~24~~ 8		~~96~~ 32		~~192~~ 64		
s^6	~~2~~ 1		~~16~~ 8		~~64~~ 32		~~128~~ 64		
s^5	~~0~~ ~~6~~ 3		~~0~~ ~~32~~ 16		~~0~~ ~~64~~ 32		~~0~~ ~~0~~ 0		
s^4	$\frac{8}{3}$ 1		$\frac{64}{3}$ 8		64 24				
s^3	~~8~~ -1		~~40~~ -5						
s^2	~~3~~ 1		~~24~~ 8						
s^1	3								
s^0	8								

Differentiate this polynomial with respect to s to form the coefficients that will replace the row of zeros:

$$\frac{dP(s)}{ds} = 6s^5 + 32s^3 + 64s + 0 \quad (6.19)$$

Replace the row of zeros at the s^5 row by the coefficients of Eq. (6.19) and multiply through by $1/2$ for convenience. Then complete the table.

TABLE 6.14 Summary of pole locations for Example 6.8

Location	Polynomial		
	Even (sixth-order)	Other (second-order)	Total (eighth-order)
Right half-plane	2	0	2
Left half-plane	2	2	4
$j\omega$	2	0	2

We note that there are two sign changes from the even polynomial at the s^6 row down to the end of the table. Hence, the even polynomial has two right-half-plane poles. Because of the symmetry about the origin, the even polynomial must have an equal number of left-half-plane poles. Therefore, the even polynomial has two left-half-plane poles. Since the even polynomial is of sixth order, the two remaining poles must be on the $j\omega$-axis.

There are no sign changes from the beginning of the table down to the even polynomial at the s^6 row. Therefore, the rest of the polynomial has no right-half-plane poles. The results are summarized in Table 6.14. The system has two poles in the right half-plane, four poles in the left half-plane, and two poles on the $j\omega$-axis, which are of unit multiplicity. The closed-loop system is unstable because of the right-half-plane poles.

The Routh-Hurwitz criterion gives vivid proof that changes in the gain of a feedback control system result in differences in transient response because of changes in closed-loop pole locations. The next example demonstrates this concept. We will see that for control systems, such as those shown in Figure 6.9, gain variations can move poles from stable regions of the s-plane onto the $j\omega$-axis and then into the right half-plane.

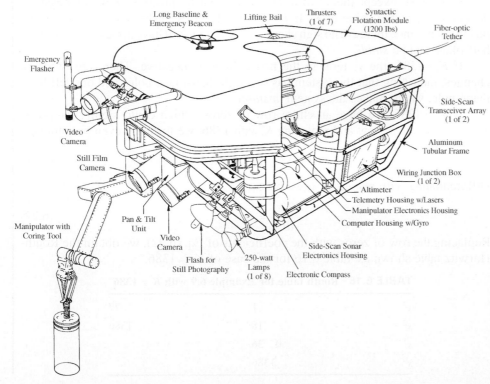

FIGURE 6.9 *Jason* is an underwater, remote-controlled vehicle that has been used to explore the wreckage of the *Lusitania*. The manipulator and cameras comprise some of the vehicle's control systems.

◼ **EXAMPLE 6.9** ◼

Stability design via Routh-Hurwitz

Problem: Find the range of gain, K, for the system of Figure 6.10 that will cause the system to be stable, unstable, and marginally stable. Assume $K > 0$.

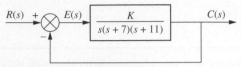

FIGURE 6.10   Feedback control system for Example 6.9

SOLUTION: First find the closed-loop transfer function as

$$T(s) = \frac{K}{s^3 + 18s^2 + 77s + K} \tag{6.20}$$

Next form the Routh table shown as Table 6.15.

TABLE 6.15   Routh table for Example 6.9

s^3	1	77
s^2	18	K
s^1	$\dfrac{1386 - K}{18}$	
s^0	K	

Since K is assumed positive, we see that all elements in the first column are always positive except the s^1 row. This entry can be positive, zero, or negative, depending upon the value of K. If $K < 1386$, all terms in the first column will be positive, and since there are no sign changes, the system will have three poles in the left half-plane and be *stable*.

If $K > 1386$, the s^1 term in the first column is negative. There are two sign changes, indicating that the system has two right-half-plane poles and one left-half-plane pole, which makes the system *unstable*.

If $K = 1386$, we have an entire row of zeros, which could signify $j\omega$ poles. Returning to the s^2 row and replacing K with 1386, we form the even polynomial

$$P(s) = 18s^2 + 1386 \tag{6.21}$$

Differentiating with respect to s, we have

$$\frac{dP(s)}{ds} = 36s + 0 \tag{6.22}$$

Replacing the row of zeros with the coefficients of Eq. (6.22), we obtain the Routh-Hurwitz table shown as Table 6.16 for the case of $K = 1386$.

TABLE 6.16   Routh table for Example 6.9 with $K = 1386$

s^3	1	77
s^2	18	1386
s^1	Ø 36	
s^0	1386	

Since there are no sign changes from the even polynomial (s^2 row) down to the bottom of the table, the even polynomial has its two roots on the $j\omega$-axis of unit multiplicity. Since there are no sign changes above the even polynomial, the remaining root is in the left half-plane. Therefore the system is *marginally stable*.

MATLAB

Students who are using MATLAB should now run ch6p2 in Appendix B. You will learn how to set up a loop to search for the range of gain to yield stability. This exercise uses MATLAB to do Example 6.9.

Symbolic Math

Students who are performing the MATLAB exercises and want to explore the added capability of MATLAB's Symbolic Math Toolbox should now run ch6sp2 in Appendix E at www.wiley.com/college/nise. You will learn how to use the Symbolic Math Toolbox to calculate the values of cells in a Routh table even if the table contains symbolic objects, such as a variable gain, K. You will see that the Symbolic Math Toolbox and MATLAB yield an alternative way to solve Example 6.9.

The Routh-Hurwitz criterion is often used in limited applications to factor polynomials containing even factors. Let us look at an example.

EXAMPLE 6.10

Factoring via Routh-Hurwitz

Problem: Factor the polynomial

$$s^4 + 3s^3 + 30s^2 + 30s + 200 \tag{6.23}$$

SOLUTION: Form the Routh table of Table 6.17. We find that the s^1 row is a row of zeros. Now form the even polynomial at the s^2 row:

$$P(s) = s^2 + 10 \tag{6.24}$$

TABLE 6.17   Routh table for Example 6.10

s^4		1		30	200
s^3	~~3~~ 1		~~30~~ 10		
s^2	~~20~~ 1		~~200~~ 10		
s^1	~~0~~ 2		~~0~~ 0		
s^0		10			

This polynomial is differentiated with respect to s in order to complete the Routh table. However, since this polynomial is a factor of the original polynomial in Eq. (6.23), dividing Eq. (6.23) by (6.24) yields ($s^2 + 3s + 20$) as the other factor. Hence,

$$s^4 + 3s^3 + 30s^2 + 30s + 200 = (s^2 + 10)(s^2 + 3s + 20)$$

$$= (s + j3.1623)(s - j3.1623) \tag{6.25}$$

$$\times (s + 1.5 + j4.213)(s + 1.5 - j4.213)$$

SKILL-ASSESSMENT EXERCISE 6.3

Problem: For a unity feedback system with the forward transfer function

$$G(s) = \frac{K(s + 20)}{s(s + 2)(s + 3)}$$

find the range of K to make the system stable.

ANSWER: $0 < K < 2$

The complete solution is at www.wiley.com/college/nise.

6.5 STABILITY IN STATE SPACE

Up to this point we have examined stability from the s-plane viewpoint. Now we look at stability from the perspective of state space. In Section 4.10, we mentioned that the values of the system's poles are equal to the eigenvalues of the system matrix, **A**. We stated that the eigenvalues of the matrix **A** were solutions of the equation $\det(s\mathbf{I} - \mathbf{A}) = 0$, which also yielded the poles of the transfer function. Eigenvalues appeared again in Section 5.8, where they were formally defined and used to diagonalize a matrix. Let us now formally show that the eigenvalues and the system poles have the same values.

Reviewing Section 5.8, the eigenvalues of a matrix, **A**, are values of λ that permit a nontrivial solution (other than **0**) for **x** in the equation

$$\mathbf{Ax} = \lambda\mathbf{x} \tag{6.26}$$

In order to solve for the values of λ that do indeed permit a solution for **x**, we rearrange Eq. (6.26) as follows:

$$\lambda\mathbf{x} - \mathbf{Ax} = \mathbf{0} \tag{6.27}$$

or

$$(\lambda\mathbf{I} - \mathbf{A})\mathbf{x} = \mathbf{0} \tag{6.28}$$

Solving for **x** yields

$$\mathbf{x} = (\lambda\mathbf{I} - \mathbf{A})^{-1}\mathbf{0} \tag{6.29}$$

or

$$\mathbf{x} = \frac{\operatorname{adj}(\lambda\mathbf{I} - \mathbf{A})}{\det(\lambda\mathbf{I} - \mathbf{A})}\mathbf{0} \tag{6.30}$$

We see that all solutions will be the null vector except for the occurrence of zero in the denominator. Since this is the only condition where elements of **x** will be $0/0$, or indeterminate, it is the only case where a nonzero solution is possible.

The values of λ are calculated by forcing the denominator to zero:

$$\det(\lambda\mathbf{I} - \mathbf{A}) = 0 \tag{6.31}$$

This equation determines the values of λ for which a nonzero solution for **x** in Eq. (6.26) exists. In Section 5.8 we defined **x** as *eigenvectors* and the values of λ as the *eigenvalues* of the matrix **A**.

Let us now relate the eigenvalues of the system matrix, **A**, to the system's poles. In Chapter 3 we derived the equation of the system transfer function, Eq. (3.73), from the state equations. The system transfer function has $\det(s\mathbf{I} - \mathbf{A})$ in the denominator because of the presence of $(s\mathbf{I} - \mathbf{A})^{-1}$. Thus,

$$\det(s\mathbf{I} - \mathbf{A}) = 0 \tag{6.32}$$

is the characteristic equation for the system from which the system poles can be found.

Since Eqs. (6.31) and (6.32) are identical apart from a change in variable name, we conclude that the eigenvalues of the matrix **A** are identical to the system's poles before cancellation of common poles and zeroes in the transfer function. Thus, we can determine the stability of a system represented in state space by finding the eigenvalues of the system matrix, **A**, and determining their locations on the *s*-plane.

EXAMPLE 6.11

Stability in state space

Problem: Given the system

$$\dot{\mathbf{x}} = \begin{bmatrix} 0 & 3 & 1 \\ 2 & 8 & 1 \\ -10 & -5 & -2 \end{bmatrix}\mathbf{x} + \begin{bmatrix} 10 \\ 0 \\ 0 \end{bmatrix}u \tag{6.33a}$$

$$y = \begin{bmatrix} 1 & 0 & 0 \end{bmatrix}\mathbf{x} \tag{6.33b}$$

find out how many poles are in the left half-plane, in the right half-plane, and on the *jω*-axis.

SOLUTION: First form $(s\mathbf{I} - \mathbf{A})$:

$$(s\mathbf{I} - \mathbf{A}) = \begin{bmatrix} s & 0 & 0 \\ 0 & s & 0 \\ 0 & 0 & s \end{bmatrix} - \begin{bmatrix} 0 & 3 & 1 \\ 2 & 8 & 1 \\ -10 & -5 & -2 \end{bmatrix} = \begin{bmatrix} s & -3 & -1 \\ -2 & s-8 & -1 \\ 10 & 5 & s+2 \end{bmatrix} \tag{6.34}$$

Now find the $\det(s\mathbf{I} - \mathbf{A})$:

$$\det(s\mathbf{I} - \mathbf{A}) = s^3 - 6s^2 - 7s - 52 \tag{6.35}$$

Using this polynomial, form the Routh table of Table 6.18.

TABLE 6.18   Routh table for Example 6.11

s^3	1		−7
s^2	~~−6~~ −3		~~−52~~ −26
s^1	$-\dfrac{47}{3}$ −1		~~0~~ 0
s^0	−26		

Since there is one sign change in the first column, the system has one right-half-plane pole and two left-half-plane poles. It is therefore unstable. Yet, you may question the possibility that if a nonminimum-phase zero cancels the unstable pole, the system will be stable. However, in practice, the nonminimum-phase zero or unstable pole will shift due to a slight change in the system's parameters. This change will cause the system to become unstable.

MATLAB

Students who are using MATLAB should now run ch6p3 in Appendix B. You will learn how to determine the stability of a system represented in state space by finding the eigenvalues of the system matrix. This exercise uses MATLAB to do Example 6.11.

SKILL-ASSESSMENT EXERCISE 6.4

WileyPLUS

Control Solutions

TryIt 6.3

Use the following MATLAB statements to find the eigenvalues of the system described in Skill-Assessment Exercise 6.4.

```
A=[2  1  1
    1  7  1
   -3  4  -5];

Eig=eig (A)
```

Problem: For the following system represented in state space, find out how many poles are in the left half-plane, in the right half-plane, and on the $j\omega$-axis.

$$\dot{\mathbf{x}} = \begin{bmatrix} 2 & 1 & 1 \\ 1 & 7 & 1 \\ -3 & 4 & -5 \end{bmatrix} \mathbf{x} + \begin{bmatrix} 0 \\ 0 \\ 1 \end{bmatrix} r$$

$$y = \begin{bmatrix} 0 & 1 & 0 \end{bmatrix} \mathbf{x}$$

ANSWER: Two rhp and one lhp

The complete solution is at www.wiley.com/college/nise.

In this section we have evaluated the stability of feedback control systems from the state-space perspective. Since the closed-loop poles and the eigenvalues of a system are the same, the stability requirement of a system represented in state space dictates that the eigenvalues cannot be in the right half of the s-plane nor be multiple on the $j\omega$-axis.

We can obtain the eigenvalues from the state equations without first converting to a transfer function to find the poles: The equation $\det(s\mathbf{I} - \mathbf{A}) = 0$ yields the eigenvalues directly. If $\det(s\mathbf{I} - \mathbf{A})$, a polynomial in s, cannot be factored easily, we can apply the Routh-Hurwitz criterion to it to evaluate how many eigenvalues are in each region of the s-plane.

We now summarize this chapter, first with case studies and then with a written summary. Our case studies include the antenna azimuth position control system and the UFSS. Stability is as important to these systems as it is to the system shown in Figure 6.11.

FIGURE 6.11 The FANUC M-410iB™ has 4 axes of motion. It is seen here moving and stacking sacks of chocolate.

CASE STUDIES

Antenna Control: Stability Design via Gain

This chapter has covered the elements of stability. We saw that stable systems have their closed-loop poles in the left half of the s-plane. As the loop gain is changed, the locations of the poles are also changed, creating the possibility that the poles can move into the right half of the s-plane, which yields instability. Proper gain settings are essential for the stability of closed-loop systems. The following case study demonstrates the proper setting of the loop gain to ensure stability.

Problem: You are given the antenna azimuth position control system shown on the front endpapers, Configuration 1. Find the range of preamplifier gain required to keep the closed-loop system stable.

SOLUTION: The closed-loop transfer function was derived in the case studies in Chapter 5 as

$$T(s) = \frac{6.63K}{s^3 + 101.71s^2 + 171s + 6.63K} \tag{6.36}$$

Using the denominator, create the Routh table shown as Table 6.19. The third row of the table shows that a row of zeros occurs if $K = 2623$. This value of K makes the system marginally stable. Therefore, there will be no sign changes in the first column if $0 < K < 2623$. We conclude that, for stability, $0 < K < 2623$.

TABLE 6.19 Routh table for antenna control case study

s^3	1	171
s^2	101.71	6.63K
s^1	17392.41 − 6.63K	0
s^0	6.63K	

Challenge: We now give you a problem to test your knowledge of this chapter's objectives. Refer to the antenna azimuth position control system shown on the front endpapers, Configuration 2. Find the range of preamplifier gain required to keep the closed-loop system stable.

UFSS Vehicle: Stability Design via Gain

Design

For this case study we return to the UFSS vehicle and study the stability of the pitch control system, which is used to control depth. Specifically, we find the range of pitch gain that keeps the pitch control loop stable.

Problem: The pitch control loop for the UFSS vehicle (*Johnson, 1980*) is shown on the back endpapers. Let $K_2 = 1$ and find the range of K_1 that ensures that the closed-loop pitch control system is stable.

SOLUTION: The first step is to reduce the pitch control system to a single, closed-loop transfer function. The equivalent forward transfer function, $G_e(s)$, is

$$G_e(s) = \frac{0.25K_1(s + 0.435)}{s^4 + 3.456s^3 + 3.457s^2 + 0.719s + 0.0416} \tag{6.37}$$

With unity feedback the closed-loop transfer function, $T(s)$, is

$$T(s) = \frac{0.25K_1(s+0.435)}{s^4 + 3.456s^3 + 3.457s^2 + (0.719 + 0.25K_1)s + (0.0416 + 0.109K_1)} \tag{6.38}$$

The denominator of Eq. (6.38) is now used to form the Routh table shown as Table 6.20.

TABLE 6.20　Routh table for UFSS case study

s^4	1	3.457	$0.0416 + 0.109K_1$
s^3	3.456	$0.719 + 0.25K_1$	
s^2	$11.228 - 0.25K_1$	$0.144 + 0.377K_1$	
s^1	$\dfrac{-0.0625K_1^2 + 1.324K_1 + 7.575}{11.228 - 0.25K_1}$		
s^0	$0.144 + 0.377K_1$		

Note: Some rows have been multiplied by a positive constant for convenience.

　　Looking at the first column, the s^4 and s^3 rows are positive. Thus, all elements of the first column must be positive for stability. For the first column of the s^2 row to be positive, $-\infty < K_1 < 44.91$. For the first column of the s^1 row to be positive, the numerator must be positive, since the denominator is positive from the previous step. The solution to the quadratic term in the numerator yields roots of $K_1 = -4.685$ and 25.87. Thus, for a positive numerator, $-4.685 < K_1 < 25.87$. Finally, for the first column of the s^0 row to be positive, $-0.382 < K_1 < \infty$. Using all three conditions, stability will be ensured if $-0.382 < K_1 < 25.87$.

Challenge: You are now given a problem to test your knowledge of this chapter's objectives. For the UFSS vehicle (*Johnson, 1980*) heading control system shown on the back endpapers and introduced in the UFSS case study challenge in Chapter 5, do the following:

MATLAB

　　a. Find the range of heading gain that ensures the vehicle's stability. Let $K_2 = 1$.

　　b. Repeat Part **a** using MATLAB.

In our case studies we calculated the ranges of gain to ensure stability. The student should be aware that although these ranges yield stability, setting gain within these limits may not yield the desired transient response or steady-state error characteristics. In Chapters 9 and 11, we will explore design techniques, other than simple gain adjustment, that yield more flexibility in obtaining desired characteristics.

SUMMARY

In this chapter we explored the concepts of system stability from both the classical and the state-space viewpoints. We found that for linear systems, *stability* is based on a natural response that decays to zero as time approaches infinity. On the other hand, if the natural response increases without bound, the forced response is overpowered by the natural response, and we lose control. This condition is known as *instability*. A third possibility exists: The natural response may neither decay nor grow without bound but oscillate. In this case the system is said to be *marginally stable*.

We also used an alternative definition of stability when the natural response is not explicitly available. This definition is based on the total response and says that a system is stable if every bounded input yields a bounded output (BIBO) and unstable if any bounded input yields an unbounded output.

Mathematically, stability for linear, time-invariant systems can be determined from the location of the closed-loop poles:

- If the poles are only in the left half-plane, the system is stable.
- If any poles are in the right half-plane, the system is unstable.
- If the poles are on the $j\omega$-axis and in the left half-plane, the system is marginally stable as long as the poles on the $j\omega$-axis are of unit multiplicity; it is unstable if there are any multiple $j\omega$ poles.

Unfortunately, although the open-loop poles may be known, we found that in higher-order systems it is difficult to find the closed-loop poles without a computer program.

The *Routh-Hurwitz criterion* lets us find how many poles are in each of the sections of the *s*-plane without giving us the coordinates of the poles. Just knowing that there are poles in the right half-plane is enough to determine that a system is unstable. Under certain limited conditions, when an even polynomial is present, the Routh table can be used to factor the system's characteristic equation.

Obtaining stability from the state-space representation of a system is based on the same concept—the location of the roots of the characteristic equation. These roots are equivalent to the eigenvalues of the system matrix and can be found by solving $\det(s\mathbf{I} - \mathbf{A}) = 0$. Again, the Routh-Hurwitz criterion can be applied to this polynomial. The point is that the state-space representation of a system need not be converted to a transfer function in order to investigate stability. In the next chapter we will look at steady-state errors, the last of three important control system requirements we emphasize.

REVIEW QUESTIONS

1. What part of the output response is responsible for determining the stability of a linear system?
2. What happens to the response named in Question 1 that creates instability?

3. What would happen to a physical system that becomes unstable?

4. Why are marginally stable systems considered unstable under the BIBO definition of stability?

5. Where do system poles have to be to ensure that a system is not unstable?

6. What does the Routh-Hurwitz criterion tell us?

7. Under what conditions would the Routh-Hurwitz criterion easily tell us the actual location of the system's closed-loop poles?

8. What causes a zero to show up only in the first column of the Routh table?

9. What causes an entire row of zeros to show up in the Routh table?

10. Why do we sometimes multiply a row of a Routh table by a positive constant?

11. Why do we not multiply a row of a Routh table by a negative constant?

12. If a Routh table has two sign changes above the even polynomial and five sign changes below the even polynomial, how many right-half-plane poles does the system have?

13. Does the presence of an entire row of zeros always mean that the system has $j\omega$ poles?

14. If a seventh-order system has a row of zeros at the s^3 row and two sign changes below the s^4 row, how many $j\omega$ poles does the system have?

15. Is it true that the eigenvalues of the system matrix are the same as the closed-loop poles?

16. How do we find the eigenvalues?

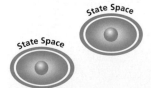

PROBLEMS

1. Tell how many roots of the following polynomial are in the right half-plane, in the left half-plane, and on the $j\omega$-axis: [Section: 6.2]

$$P(s) = s^5 + 3s^4 + 5s^3 + 4s^2 + s + 3$$

2. Tell how many roots of the following polynomial are in the right half-plane, in the left half-plane, and on the $j\omega$-axis: [Section: 6.3]

$$P(s) = s^5 + 6s^3 + 5s^2 + 8s + 20$$

3. Using the Routh table, tell how many poles of the following function are in the right half-plane, in the left half-plane, and on the $j\omega$-axis: [Section: 6.3]

$$T(s) = \frac{s+8}{s^5 - s^4 + 4s^3 - 4s^2 + 3s - 2}$$

4. The closed-loop transfer function of a system is [Section: 6.3]

$$T(s) = \frac{s^3 + 2s^2 + 7s + 21}{s^5 - 2s^4 + 3s^3 - 6s^2 + 2s - 4}$$

Determine how many closed-loop poles lie in the right half-plane, in the left half-plane, and on the $j\omega$-axis.

5. How many poles are in the right half-plane, the left half-plane, and on the $j\omega$-axis for the open-loop system of Figure P6.1?

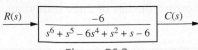

Figure P6.1

6. How many poles are in the right half-plane, the left half-plane, and on the $j\omega$-axis for the open-loop system of Figure P6.2? [Section: 6.3]

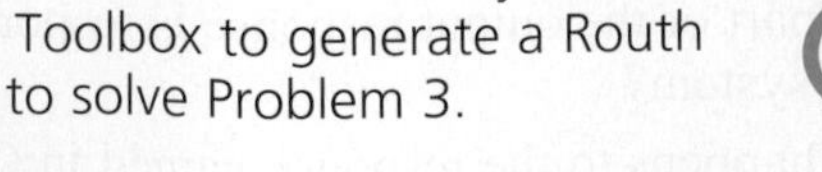

Figure P6.2

7. Use MATLAB and the Symbolic Math Toolbox to generate a Routh table to solve Problem 3.

8. Determine whether the unity feedback system of Figure P6.3 is stable if [Section: 6.2]

$$G(s) = \frac{240}{(s+1)(s+2)(s+3)(s+4)}$$

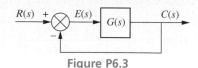

Figure P6.3

9. Consider the unity feedback system of Figure P6.3 with

$$G(s) = \frac{1}{4s^2(s^2+1)}$$

Using the Routh-Hurwitz criterion, find the region of the s-plane where the poles of the closed-loop system are located. [Section: 6.3]

10. In the system of Figure P6.3, let

$$G(s) = \frac{K(s+2)}{s(s-1)(s+3)}$$

Find the range of K for closed-loop stability. [Section: 6.4]

11. Given the unity feedback system of Figure P6.3 with [Section: 6.3]

$$G(s) = \frac{84}{s(s^7 + 5s^6 + 12s^5 + 25s^4 + 45s^3 + 50s^2 + 82s + 60)}$$

tell how many poles of the closed-loop transfer function lie in the right half-plane, in the left half-plane, and on the $j\omega$-axis. [Section: 6.3]

12. Using the Routh-Hurwitz criterion and the unity feedback system of Figure P6.3 with

$$G(s) = \frac{1}{2s^4 + 5s^3 + s^2 + 2s}$$

tell whether or not the closed-loop system is stable. [Section: 6.2]

13. Given the unity feedback system of Figure P6.3 with

$$G(s) = \frac{8}{s(s^6 - 2s^5 - s^4 + 2s^3 + 4s^2 - 8s - 4)}$$

tell how many closed-loop poles are located in the right half-plane, in the left half-plane, and on the $j\omega$-axis. [Section: 6.3]

14. Repeat Problem 13 using MATLAB.

15. Consider the following Routh table. Notice that the s^5 row was originally all zeros. Tell how many roots of the original polynomial were in the right half-plane, in the left half-plane, and on the $j\omega$-axis. [Section: 6.3]

s^7	1	2	−1	−2
s^6	1	2	−1	−2
s^5	3	4	−1	0
s^4	1	−1	−3	0
s^3	7	8	0	0
s^2	−15	−21	0	0
s^1	−9	0	0	0
s^0	−21	0	0	0

16. For the system of Figure P6.4, tell where the closed-loop poles are located (i.e., right half-plane, left half-plane, $j\omega$-axis). Notice that there is positive feedback.

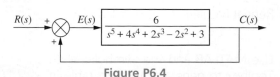

Figure P6.4

17. Using the Routh-Hurwitz criterion, tell how many closed-loop poles of the system shown in Figure P6.5 lie in the left half-plane, in the right half-plane, and on the $j\omega$-axis. [Section: 6.3]

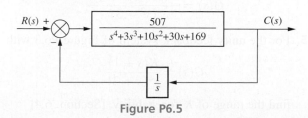

Figure P6.5

18. Determine if the unity feedback system of Figure P6.3 with

$$G(s) = \frac{K(s^2 + 1)}{(s+1)(s+2)}$$

can be unstable. [Section: 6.4]

19. For the unity feedback system of Figure P6.3 with

$$G(s) = \frac{K(s+6)}{s(s+1)(s+3)}$$

determine the range of K to ensure stability. [Section: 6.4]

20. In the system of Figure P6.3, let

$$G(s) = \frac{K(s-a)}{s(s-b)}$$

Find the range of K for closed-loop stability when: [Section: 6.4]

a. $a < 0, \quad b < 0$

b. $a < 0, \quad b > 0$

c. $a > 0, \quad b < 0$

d. $a > 0, \quad b > 0$

21. For the unity feedback system of Figure P6.3 with

$$G(s) = \frac{K(s+1)}{s(s+2)(s+3)(s+4)}$$

determine the range of K for stability.

22. Repeat Problem 21 using MATLAB.

23. Use MATLAB and the Symbolic Math Toolbox to generate a Routh table in terms of K to solve Problem 21.

24. Find the range of K for stability for the unity feedback system of Figure P6.3 with [Section: 6.4]

$$G(s) = \frac{K(s+2)(s-2)}{(s^2 + 3)}$$

25. For the unity feedback system of Figure P6.3 with

$$G(s) = \frac{K(s+1)}{s^4(s+2)}$$

find the range of K for stability. [Section: 6.4]

26. Find the range of gain, K, to ensure stability in the unity feedback system of Figure P6.3 with [Section: 6.4]

$$G(s) = \frac{K(s-2)(s+4)(s+5)}{(s^2 + 3)}$$

27. Find the range of gain, K, to ensure stability in the unity feedback system of Figure P6.3 with [Section: 6.4]

$$G(s) = \frac{K(s+2)}{(s^2 + 1)(s+4)(s-1)}$$

28. Using the Routh-Hurwitz criterion, find the value of K that will yield oscillations for the unity feedback system of Figure P6.3 with [Section: 6.4]

$$G(s) = \frac{K}{(s+15)(s+27)(s+38)}$$

29. Use the Routh-Hurwitz criterion to find the range of K for which the system of Figure P6.6 is stable. [Section: 6.4]

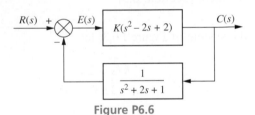

Figure P6.6

30. Repeat Problem 29 for the system of Figure P6.7. [Section: 6.4]

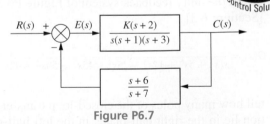

Figure P6.7

31. Given the unity feedback system of Figure P6.3 with

$$G(s) = \frac{K(s+4)}{s(s+1)(s+2)}$$

find the following: [Section: 6.4]

a. The range of K that keeps the system stable

b. The value of K that makes the system oscillate

c. The frequency of oscillation when K is set to the value that makes the system oscillate

32. Repeat Problem 31 for [Section: 6.4]

$$G(s) = \frac{K(s-1)(s-2)}{(s+2)(s^2+2s+2)}$$

33. For the system shown in Figure P6.8, find the value of gain, K, that will make the system oscillate. Also, find the frequency of oscillation. [Section: 6.4]

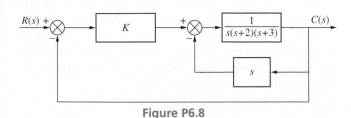

Figure P6.8

34. Given the unity feedback system of Figure P6.3 with [Section: 6.4]

WileyPLUS
Control Solutions

$$G(s) = \frac{Ks(s+2)}{(s^2-4s+8)(s+3)}$$

a. Find the range of K for stability.

b. Find the frequency of oscillation when the system is marginally stable.

MATLAB

35. Repeat Problem 34 using MATLAB.

36. For the unity feedback system of Figure P6.3 with

$$G(s) = \frac{K(s+2)}{(s^2+1)(s+4)(s-1)}$$

find the range of K for which there will be only two closed-loop, right-half-plane poles. [Section: 6.4]

37. For the unity feedback system of Figure P6.3 with [Section: 6.4]

$$G(s) = \frac{K}{(s+1)^3(s+4)}$$

a. Find the range of K for stability.

b. Find the frequency of oscillation when the system is marginally stable.

38. Given the unity feedback system of Figure P6.3 with [Section: 6.4]

$$G(s) = \frac{K}{(s+10)(s^2+4s+5)}$$

a. Find the range of K for stability.

b. Find the frequency of oscillation when the system is marginally stable.

39. Using the Routh-Hurwitz criterion and the unity feedback system of Figure P6.3 with [Section: 6.4]

$$G(s) = \frac{K}{s(s+1)(s+2)(s+5)}$$

a. Find the range of K for stability.

b. Find the value of K for marginal stability.

c. Find the actual location of the closed-loop poles when the system is marginally stable.

40. Find the range of K to keep the system shown in Figure P6.9 stable. [Section: 6.4]

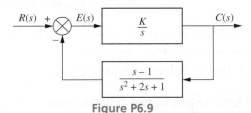

Figure P6.9

41. Find the value of K in the system of Figure P6.10 that will place the closed-loop poles as shown. [Section: 6.4]

WileyPLUS
Control Solutions

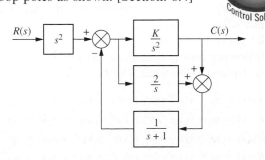

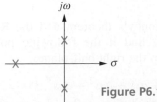

Figure P6.10 Closed-loop system with pole plot

42. The closed-loop transfer function of a system is

$$T(s) = \frac{s^2 + K_1 s + K_2}{s^4 + K_1 s^3 + K_2 s^2 + 5s + 1}$$

Determine the range of K_1 in order for the system to be stable. What is the relationship between K_1 and K_2 for stability? [Section: 6.4]

43. For the transfer function below, find the constraints on K_1 and K_2 such that the function will have only two $j\omega$ poles. [Section: 6.4]

$$T(s) = \frac{K_1 s + K_2}{s^4 + K_1 s^3 + s^2 + K_2 s + 1}$$

44. The transfer function relating the output engine fan speed (rpm) to the input main burner fuel flow rate (lb/h) in a short takeoff and landing (STOL) fighter aircraft, ignoring the coupling between engine fan speed and the pitch control command, is (*Schierman, 1992*) [Section: 6.4]

$$G(s) = \frac{1.3s^7 + 90.5s^6 + 1970s^5 + 15,000s^4 + 3120s^3 - 41,300s^2 - 5000s - 1840}{s^8 + 103s^7 + 1180s^6 + 4040s^5 + 2150s^4 - 8960s^3 - 10,600s^2 - 1550s - 415}$$

a. Find how many poles are in the right half-plane, in the left half-plane, and on the $j\omega$-axis.

b. Is this open-loop system stable?

45. An interval polynomial is of the form

$$P(s) = a_0 + a_1 s + a_2 s^2 + a_3 s^3 + a_4 s^4 + a_5 s^5 + \cdots$$

with its coefficients belonging to intervals $x_i \leq a_i \leq y_i$, where x_i, y_i are prescribed constants. Kharitonov's theorem says that an interval polynomial has all its roots in the left half-plane if each one of the following four polynomials have its roots in the left half-plane (*Minichelli, 1989*):

$$K_1(s) = x_0 + x_1 s + y_2 s^2 + y_3 s^3 + x_4 s^4 + x_5 s^5 + y_6 s^6 + \cdots$$
$$K_2(s) = x_0 + y_1 s + y_2 s^2 + x_3 s^3 + x_4 s^4 + y_5 s^5 + y_6 s^6 + \cdots$$
$$K_3(s) = y_0 + x_1 s + x_2 s^2 + y_3 s^3 + y_4 s^4 + x_5 s^5 + x_6 s^6 + \cdots$$
$$K_4(s) = y_0 + y_1 s + x_2 s^2 + x_3 s^3 + y_4 s^4 + y_5 s^5 + x_6 s^6 + \cdots$$

Use Kharitonov's theorem and the Routh-Hurwitz criterion to find if the following polynomial has any zeros in the right half-plane.

$$P(s) = a_0 + a_1 s + a_2 s^2 + a_3 s^3$$
$$2 \leq a_0 \leq 4; \quad 1 \leq a_1 \leq 2; \quad 4 \leq a_2 \leq 6; \quad a_3 = 1$$

46. A linearized model of a torque-controlled crane hoisting a load with a fixed rope length is

$$P(s) = \frac{X_T(s)}{F_T(s)} = \frac{1}{m_T} \frac{s^2 + \omega_0^2}{s^2(s^2 + a\omega_0^2)}$$

where $\omega_0 = \sqrt{\frac{g}{L}}$, $L =$ the rope length, $m_T =$ the mass of the car, $a =$ the combined rope and car mass, $f_T =$ the force input applied to the car, and $x_T =$ the resulting rope displacement (*Marttinen, 1990*). If the system is controlled in a feedback configuration by placing it in a loop as shown in Figure P6.11, with $K > 0$, where will the closed-loop poles be located?

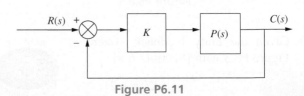

Figure P6.11

47. The read/write head assembly arm of a computer hard disk drive (HDD) can be modeled as a rigid rotating body with inertia I_b. Its dynamics can be described with the transfer function

$$P(s) = \frac{X(s)}{F(s)} = \frac{1}{I_b s^2}$$

where $X(s)$ is the displacement of the read/write head and $F(s)$ is the applied force (*Yan, 2003*). Show that if the HDD is controlled in the configuration shown in Figure P6.11, the arm will oscillate and cannot be positioned with any precision over a HDD track. Find the oscillation frequency.

48. A system is represented in state space as

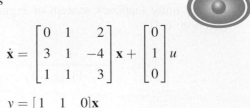

$$\dot{\mathbf{x}} = \begin{bmatrix} 0 & 1 & 2 \\ 3 & 1 & -4 \\ 1 & 1 & 3 \end{bmatrix} \mathbf{x} + \begin{bmatrix} 0 \\ 1 \\ 0 \end{bmatrix} u$$

$$y = [1 \quad 1 \quad 0]\mathbf{x}$$

Determine how many eigenvalues are in the right half-plane, in the left half-plane, and on the $j\omega$-axis.

49. Use MATLAB to find the eigenvalues of the following system:

$$\dot{x} = \begin{bmatrix} 0 & 1 & 0 \\ 0 & 1 & -4 \\ -1 & 1 & 3 \end{bmatrix} x + \begin{bmatrix} 0 \\ 0 \\ 1 \end{bmatrix} u$$

$$y = \begin{bmatrix} 0 & 0 & 1 \end{bmatrix} x$$

50. The following system in state space represents the forward path of a unity feedback system. Use the Routh-Hurwitz criterion to determine if the closed-loop system is stable. [Section: 6.5]

$$\dot{x} = \begin{bmatrix} 0 & 1 & 0 \\ 0 & 1 & 3 \\ -3 & -4 & -5 \end{bmatrix} x + \begin{bmatrix} 0 \\ 0 \\ 1 \end{bmatrix} u$$

$$y = \begin{bmatrix} 0 & 1 & 1 \end{bmatrix} x$$

51. Repeat Problem 50 using MATLAB.

52. A Butterworth polynomial is of the form

$$B_n(s) = 1 + (-1)^n \left(\frac{s}{\omega_c} \right)^{2n}, n > 0.$$

Use the Routh-Hurwitz criteria to find the zeros of a Butterworth polynomial for:

a. $n = 1$;

b. $n = 2$

Design Problems

53. A model for an airplane's pitch loop is shown in Figure P6.12. Find the

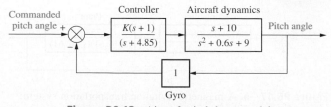

Figure P6.12 Aircraft pitch loop model

range of gain, K, that will keep the system stable. Can the system ever be unstable for positive values of K?

54. A common application of control systems is in regulating the temperature of a chemical process (Figure P6.13). The flow of chemical reactant to a process is controlled by an actuator and valve. The reactant causes the temperature in the vat to change. This temperature is sensed and compared to a desired set-point temperature in a closed loop, where the flow of reactant is adjusted to yield the desired temperature. In Chapter 9 we will learn how a PID controller is used to improve the performance of such process control systems. Figure P6.13 shows the control system prior to the addition of the PID controller. The PID controller is replaced by the shaded box with a gain of unity. For this system, prior to the design of the PID controller, find the range of amplifier gain, K, to keep the system stable.

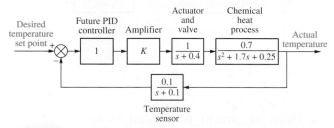

Figure P6.13 Block diagram of a chemical process control system

55. A robot arm called ISAC (Intelligent Soft Arm Control) can be used as part of a system to feed people with disabilities (see Figure P6.14(a)). The control system guides the spoon to the food and then to a position near the person's mouth. The arm uses a special pneumatically controlled actuator called a rubbertuator. Rubbertuators consist of rubber tubes covered with fiber cord. The actuator contracts in length when pneumatic pressure is increased and expands in length when pressure is decreased. This expansion and contraction in length can drive a pulley or other device. A video camera provides the sight for the robot and the tracking loop (*Kara, 1992*). Assume the simplified block diagram shown in Figure P6.14(b) for regulating the spoon at a distance from the mouth. Find the range of K for stability. (Use of a program with symbolic capability is recommended.)

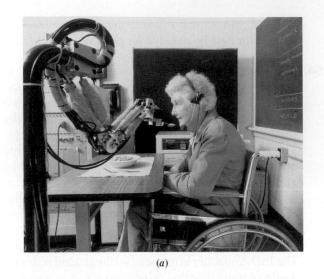

(a)

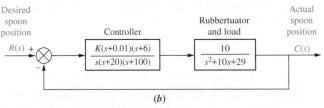

(b)

Figure P6.14 **a.** ISAC used for feeding (Courtesy of Kazuniko Kawamura, Vanderbilt University); **b.** simplified block diagram

56. Often an aircraft is required to tow another vehicle, such as a practice target or glider. To stabilize the towed vehicle and prevent it from rolling, pitching, and yawing, an autopilot is built into the towed vehicle. Assume the block diagram shown in Figure P6.15 represents the autopilot roll control system (*Cochran, 1992*). Find the range of K to keep the roll angle stable.

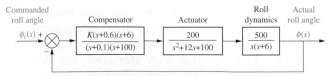

Figure P6.15 Towed vehicle roll control

57. Cutting forces should be kept constant during machining operations to prevent changes in spindle speeds or work position. Such changes would deteriorate the accuracy of the work's dimensions. A control system is proposed to control the cutting force. The plant is difficult to model, since the factors that affect cutting force are time varying and not easily predicted.

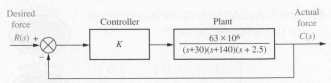

Figure P6.16 Cutting force control system

However, assuming the simplified force control model shown in Figure P6.16, use the Routh-Hurwitz criterion to find the range of K to keep the system stable (*Rober, 1997*).

58. Transportation systems that use magnetic levitation can reach very high speeds, since contact friction at the rails is eliminated (see Figure P6.17(*a*)). Electromagnets can produce the force to elevate the vehicle. Figure P6.17(*b*) is a simulation model of a control system that can be used to regulate the magnetic gap. In the figure $Z_{vin}(s)$ represents a voltage proportional to the desired amount of levitation, or gap. $Z_{vout}(s)$ represents a voltage proportional to the actual amount of levitation. The plant models the dynamic response of the vehicle to signals from the controller (*Bittar, 1998*). Use the Routh-Hurwitz criterion to find the range of gain, K, to keep the closed-loop system stable.

(a)

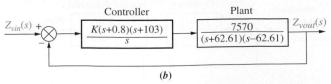

(b)

Figure P6.17 **a.** A magnetic levitation transportation system; **b.** simplified block diagram (© 1998 IEEE)

59. A transfer function from indoor radiator power, $\dot{Q}(s)$, to room temperature, $T(s)$, in an $11\,m^2$ room is

$$P(s) = \frac{T(s)}{\dot{Q}(s)} = \frac{1 \times 10^{-6}s^2 + 1.314 \times 10^{-9}s + 2.66 \times 10^{-13}}{s^3 + 0.00163s^2 + 5.272 \times 10^{-7}s + 3.538 \times 10^{-11}}$$

where $\dot{Q}$ is in watts and T is in °C. (*Thomas, 2005*). The room's temperature will be controlled by embedding it in a closed loop, such as that of Figure P6.11. Find the range of K for closed-loop stability.

60. During vertical spindle surface grinding, adjustments are made on a multi-axis CNC machine by measuring the applied force with a dynamometer and applying appropriate corrections. This feedback force control results in higher homogeneity and better tolerances in the resulting finished product. In a specific experiment with an extremely high feed rate, the transfer function from the desired depth of cut (DOC) to applied force was

$$\frac{F(s)}{DOC(s)} = \frac{K_C}{1 + \dfrac{K_C}{ms^2 + bs + k} - \dfrac{K_C}{K_f}\dfrac{1}{Ts + 1}}$$

where $k = 2.1 \times 10^4$ N/m, $b = 0.78$ Ns/m, $m = 1.2 \times 10^{-4}$ Kg, $K_C = 1.5 \times 10^4$ N/mm and $T = 0.044$ s. K_f is a parameter that is varied to adjust the system. Find the range of K_f under which the system is stable (*Hekman, 1999*).

61. Figure P6.18 depicts the schematic diagram of a phase shift oscillator.

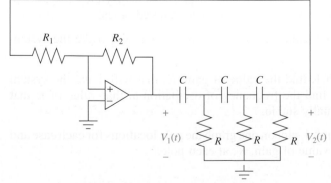

Figure P6.18 Phase shift oscillator.

The circuit will oscillate if it is designed to have poles on the $j\omega$-axis.

a. Show that the transfer function for the passive network in the circuit is given by

$$\frac{V_2(s)}{V_1(s)} = \frac{-1}{\left(1 + \dfrac{1}{sRC}\right)\left(2 + \dfrac{1}{sRC}\right)^2 - 3 - \dfrac{2}{sRC}}$$

b. Show that the oscillator's characteristic equation is given by

$$1 - K\frac{1}{\left(1 + \dfrac{1}{sRC}\right)\left(2 + \dfrac{1}{sRC}\right)^2 - 3 - \dfrac{2}{sRC}} = 0,$$

where $K = \dfrac{R_2}{R_1}$

c. Use the Routh-Hurwitz criterion to obtain the oscillation condition and the oscillation frequency.

62. Look-ahead information can be used to automatically steer a bicycle in a closed-loop configuration. A line is drawn in the middle of the lane to be followed, and an arbitrary point is chosen in the vehicle's longitudinal axis. A look-ahead offset is calculated by measuring the distance between the look-ahead point and the reference line and is used by the system to correct the vehicle's trajectory. A linearized model of a particular bicycle traveling on a straight-line path at a fixed longitudinal speed is

$$\begin{bmatrix} \dot{V} \\ \dot{r} \\ \dot{\psi} \\ \dot{Y}_g \end{bmatrix} = \begin{bmatrix} -11.7 & 6.8 & 61.6K & 7.7K \\ -3.5 & -24 & -66.9K & 8.4K \\ 0 & 1 & 0 & 0 \\ 1 & 0 & -10 & 0 \end{bmatrix} \begin{bmatrix} V \\ r \\ \psi \\ Y_g \end{bmatrix}$$

In this model V = bicycle's lateral velocity, r = bicycle's yaw velocity, ψ = bicycle's yaw acceleration, and Y_g = bicycle's center of gravity coordinate on the y-axis. K is a controller parameter to be chosen by the designer (*Özgüner, 1995*). Use the Routh-Hurwitz criterion to find the range of K for which the system is closed-loop stable.

Progressive Analysis and Design Problems

63. **High-speed rail pantograph.** Problem 19 in Chapter 1 discusses active control of a pantograph mechanism for high-speed rail systems. In Problem 72(*a*), Chapter 5, you found the block diagram for the active

pantograph control system. Using your solution for Problem 72(a) in Chapter 5 and the Routh-Hurwitz criterion, find the range of controller gain, K, that will keep the system stable (*O'Connor, 1997*).

64. **Control of HIV/AIDS.** The HIV infection linearized model developed in Problem 77, Chapter 4 can be shown to have the transfer function

$$P(s) = \frac{Y(s)}{U_1(s)} = \frac{-520s - 10.3844}{s^3 + 2.6817s^2 + 0.11s + 0.0126}$$

It is desired to develop a policy for drug delivery to maintain the virus count at prescribed levels. For the purpose of obtaining an appropriate $u_1(t)$,

feedback will be used as shown in Figure P6.19 (*Craig, 2004*).

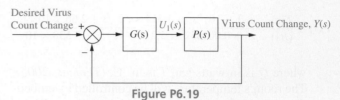

Figure P6.19

As a first approach, consider $G(s) = K$, a constant to be selected. Use the Routh-Hurwitz criteria to find the range of K for which the system is closed-loop stable.

CYBER EXPLORATION LABORATORY

Experiment 6.1

Objectives To verify the effect of pole location upon stability. To verify the effect upon stability of loop gain in a negative feedback system.

Minimum Required Software Packages MATLAB, Simulink, and the Control System Toolbox

Prelab

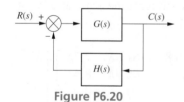

Figure P6.20

1. Find the equivalent transfer function of the negative feedback system of Figure P6.20 if

$$G(s) = \frac{K}{s(s+2)^2} \text{ and } H(s) = 1.$$

2. For the system of Prelab 1, find two values of gain that will yield closed-loop, overdamped, second-order poles. Repeat for underdamped poles.

3. For the system of Prelab 1, find the value of gain, K, that will make the system critically damped.

4. For the system of Prelab 1, find the value of gain, K, that will make the system marginally stable. Also, find the frequency of oscillation at that value of K that makes the system marginally stable.

5. For each of Prelab 2 through 4, plot on one graph the pole locations for each case and write the corresponding value of gain, K, at each pole.

Lab

1. Using Simulink, set up the negative feedback system of Prelab 1. Plot the step response of the system at each value of gain calculated to yield overdamped, underdamped, critically damped, and marginally stable responses.

2. Plot the step responses for two values of gain, K, above that calculated to yield marginal stability.

3. At the output of the negative feedback system, cascade the transfer function

$$G_1(s) = \frac{1}{s^2 + 4}$$

Set the gain, K, at a value below that calculated for marginal stability and plot the step response. Repeat for K calculated to yield marginal stability.

Postlab

1. From your plots, discuss the conditions that lead to unstable responses.

2. Discuss the effect of gain upon the nature of the step response of a closed-loop system.

BIBLIOGRAPHY

Ballard, R. D. The Riddle of the *Lusitania*. *National Geographic,* April 1994, National Geographic Society, Washington, DC, 1994, pp. 68–85.

Bittar, A., and Sales, R. M. H_2 and H_2 Control for MagLev Vehicles. *IEEE Control Systems*, vol. 18, no. 4, August 1998, pp. 18–25.

Cochran, J. E., Innocenti, M., No, T. S., and Thukral, A. Dynamics and Control of Maneuverable Towed Flight Vehicles. *Journal of Guidance, Control, and Dynamics*, vol. 15, no. 5, September–October 1992, pp. 1245–1252.

Craig, I. K., Xia, X., and Venter, J. W. Introducing HIV/AIDS Education into the Electrical Engineering Curriculum at the University of Pretoria, *IEEE Transactions on Education*, vol. 47, no. 1, February 2004, pp. 65–73

D'Azzo, J., and Houpis, C. H. *Linear Control System Analysis and Design,* 3d ed. McGraw-Hill, New York, 1988.

Dorf, R. C. *Modern Control Systems,* 5th ed. Addison-Wesley, Reading, MA, 1989.

Hekman, K. A., and Liang, S. Y. Compliance Feedback Control for Part Parallelism in Grinding. *International Journal of Manufacturing Technology*, vol. 15, 1999, pp. 64–69.

Hostetter, G. H., Savant, C. J., Jr., and Stefani, R. T. *Design of Feedback Control Systems,* 2d ed. Saunders College Publishing, New York, 1989.

Johnson, H. et al. *Unmanned Free-Swimming Submersible (UFSS) System Description.* NRL Memorandum Report 4393. Naval Research Laboratory, Washington, DC, 1980.

Kara, A., Kawamura, K., Bagchi, S., and El-Gamal, M. Reflex Control of a Robotic Aid System to Assist the Physically Disabled. *IEEE Control Systems*, June 1992, pp. 71–77.

Marttinen, A., Virkkunen, J., and Salminen, R. T. Control Study with Pilot Crane. *IEEE Transactions on Education*, vol. 33, no. 3, August 1990, pp. 298–305.

Minnichelli, R. J., Anagnost, J. J., and Desoer, C. A. An Elementary Proof of Kharitonov's Stability Theorem with Extensions. *IEEE Transactions on Automatic Control*, vol. 34, 1989, pp. 995–998.

O'Connor, D. N., Eppinger, S. D., Seering, W. P., and Wormly, D. N. Active Control of a High-Speed Pantograph. *Journal of Dynamic Systems, Measurements, and Control*, vol. 119, March 1997, pp. 1–4.

Özgüner, Ű., Űnyelioglu, K. A., and Haptipoğlu, C. An Analytical Study of Vehicle Steering Control. Proceedings of the 4th IEEE Conference Control Applications, 1995, pp. 125–130.

Phillips, C. L., and Harbor, R. D. *Feedback Control Systems,* 2d ed. Prentice Hall, Englewood Cliffs, NJ, 1991.

Rober, S. J., Shin, Y. C., and Nwokah, O. D. I. A Digital Robust Controller for Cutting Force Control in the End Milling Process. *Journal of Dynamic Systems, Measurement, and Control*, vol. 119, June 1997, pp. 146–152.

Routh, E. J. *Dynamics of a System of Rigid Bodies,* 6th ed. Macmillan, London, 1905.

Schierman, J. D., and Schmidt, D. K. Analysis of Airframe and Engine Control Interactions and Integrated Flight/Propulsion Control. *Journal of Guidance, Control, and Dynamics*, vol. 15, no. 6, November–December 1992, pp. 1388–1396.

Thomas, B., Soleimani-Mosheni, M., and Fahlén, P. Feed-Forward in Temperature Control of Buildings. *Energy and Buildings*, vol. 37, 2005, pp. 755–761.

Timothy, L. K., and Bona, B. E. *State Space Analysis: An Introduction.* McGraw-Hill, New York, 1968.

Yan, T., and Lin, R. Experimental Modeling and Compensation of Pivot Nonlinearity in Hard Disk Drives. *IEEE Transactions on Magnetics*, vol. 39, 2003, pp. 1064–1069.

FORCED RESPONSE ERRORS

7

CHAPTER OBJECTIVES

In this chapter you will learn the following:

- How to find the steady-state error for a unity feedback system
- How to specify a system's steady-state error performance
- How to find the steady-state error for disturbance inputs
- How to find the steady-state error for nonunity feedback systems
- How to design system parameters to meet steady-state error performance specifications
- How to find the steady-state error for systems represented in state space

CASE STUDY OBJECTIVES

You will be able to demonstrate your knowledge of the chapter objectives with case studies as follows:

- Given the antenna azimuth position control system shown on the front endpapers, you will be able to find the preamplifier gain to meet steady-state error performance specifications.
- Given a video laser disc recorder, you will be able to find the gain required to permit the system to record on a warped disc.

7.1 INTRODUCTION

In Chapter 1 we saw that control systems analysis and design focus on three specifications: (1) transient response, (2) stability, and (3) steady-state errors, taking into account the robustness of the design along with economic and social considerations. Elements of transient analysis were derived in Chapter 4 for first- and second-order systems. These concepts are revisited in Chapter 8, where they are extended to higher-order systems. Stability was covered in Chapter 6, where we saw that forced responses were overpowered by natural responses that increase without bound if the system is unstable. Now we are ready to examine steady-state errors. We define the errors and derive methods of controlling them. As we progress, we find that control system design entails trade-offs between desired transient response, steady-state error, and the requirement that the system be stable.

DEFINITION AND TEST INPUTS

Steady-state error is the difference between the input and the output for a prescribed test input as $t \rightarrow \infty$. Test inputs used for steady-state error analysis and design are summarized in Table 7.1.

In order to explain how these test signals are used, let us assume a position control system, where the output position follows the input commanded position. Step inputs represent constant position and thus are useful in determining the ability of the control system to position itself with respect to a stationary target, such as a

TABLE 7.1 Test waveforms for evaluating steady-state errors of position control systems

Waveform	Name	Physical interpretation	Time function	Laplace transform
$r(t)$	Step	Constant position	1	$\dfrac{1}{s}$
$r(t)$	Ramp	Constant velocity	t	$\dfrac{1}{s^2}$
$r(t)$	Parabola	Constant acceleration	$\dfrac{1}{2}t^2$	$\dfrac{1}{s^3}$

satellite in geostationary orbit (see Figure 7.1). An antenna position control is an example of a system that can be tested for accuracy using step inputs.

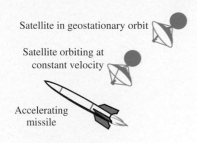

Ramp inputs represent constant-velocity inputs to a position control system by their linearly increasing amplitude. These wave-forms can be used to test a system's ability to follow a linearly increasing input or, equivalently, to track a constant-velocity target. For example, a position control system that tracks a satellite that moves across the sky at a constant angular velocity, as shown in Figure 7.1, would be tested with a ramp input to evaluate the steady-state error between the satellite's angular position and that of the control system.

Finally, parabolas, whose second derivatives are constant, represent constant-acceleration inputs to position control systems and can be used to represent accelerating targets, such as the missile in Figure 7.1, to determine the steady-state error performance.

APPLICATION TO STABLE SYSTEMS

FIGURE 7.1 Test inputs for steady-state error analysis and design vary with target type

Since we are concerned with the difference between the input and the output of a feedback control system after the steady state has been reached, our discussion is limited to stable systems, where the natural response approaches zero as $t \rightarrow \infty$. Unstable systems represent loss of control in the steady state and are not acceptable for use at all. The expressions we derive to calculate the steady-state error can be applied erroneously to an unstable system. Thus, the engineer must check the system for stability while performing steady-state error analysis and design. However, in order to focus on the topic, we assume that all the systems in examples and problems in this chapter are stable. For practice you may want to test some of the systems for stability.

EVALUATING STEADY-STATE ERRORS

Let us examine the concept of steady-state errors. In Figure 7.2(*a*) a step input and two possible outputs are shown. Output 1 has zero steady-state error, and output 2 has a finite steady-state error, $e_2(\infty)$. A similar example is shown in Figure 7.2(*b*), where a ramp input is compared with output 1, which has zero steady-state error, and output 2, which has a finite steady-state error, $e_2(\infty)$, as measured vertically between the input and output 2 after the transients have died down. For the ramp input another possibility exists. If the output's slope is different from that of the input, then output 3, shown in Figure 7.2(*b*), results. Here the steady-state error is infinite as measured vertically between the input and output 3 after the transients have died down, and t approaches infinity.

Let us now look at the error from the perspective of the most general block diagram. Since the error is the difference between the input and the output of a system, we assume a closed-loop transfer function, $T(s)$, and form the error, $E(s)$, by taking the difference between the input and the output, as shown in Figure 7.3(*a*). Here we are interested in the steady-state, or final, value of $e(t)$. For unity feedback systems, $E(s)$ appears as shown in Figure 7.3(*b*). In this chapter we study and derive expressions for the steady-state error for unity feedback systems first and then expand to nonunity feedback systems. Before we begin our study of steady-state errors for unity feedback systems, let us look at the sources of the errors with which we deal.

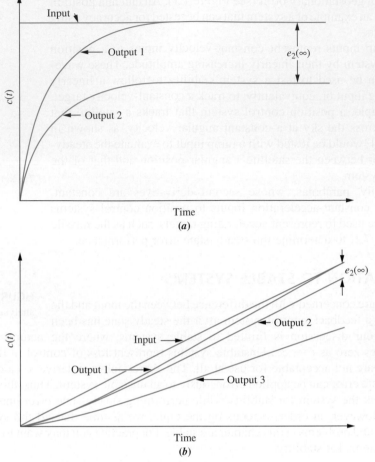

FIGURE 7.2 Steady-state error: **a.** step input; **b.** ramp input

SOURCES OF STEADY-STATE ERROR

Many steady-state errors in control systems arise from nonlinear sources, such as backlash in gears or a motor that will not move unless the input voltage exceeds a threshold. Nonlinear behavior as a source of steady-state errors, although a viable topic for study, is beyond the scope of a text on linear control systems. The steady-state errors we study here are errors that arise from the configuration of the system itself and the type of applied input.

For example, look at the system of Figure 7.4(a), where $R(s)$ is the input, $C(s)$ is the output, and $E(s) = R(s) - C(s)$ is the error. Consider a step input. In the steady state, if $c(t)$ equals $r(t)$, $e(t)$ will be zero. But with a pure gain, K, the error, $e(t)$, cannot be zero if

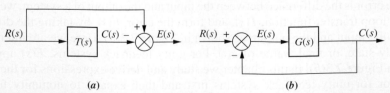

FIGURE 7.3 Closed-loop control system error: **a.** general representation; **b.** representation for unity feedback systems

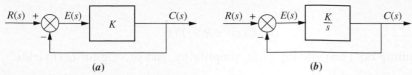

FIGURE 7.4 System with **a.** finite steady-state error for a step input; **b.** zero steady-state error for step input

$c(t)$ is to be finite and nonzero. Thus, by virtue of the configuration of the system (a pure gain of K in the forward path), an error must exist. If we call $c_{\text{steady-state}}$ the steady-state value of the output and $e_{\text{steady-state}}$ the steady-state value of the error, then $c_{\text{steady-state}} = Ke_{\text{steady-state}}$, or

$$e_{\text{steady-state}} = \frac{1}{K} c_{\text{steady-state}} \tag{7.1}$$

Thus, the larger the value of K, the smaller the value of $e_{\text{steady-state}}$ would have to be to yield a similar value of $c_{\text{steady-state}}$. The conclusion we can draw is that with a pure gain in the forward path, there will always be a steady-state error for a step input. This error diminishes as the value of K increases.

If the forward-path gain is replaced by an integrator, as shown in Figure 7.4(*b*), there will be zero error in the steady state for a step input. The reasoning is as follows: As $c(t)$ increases, $e(t)$ will decrease, since $e(t) = r(t) - c(t)$. This decrease will continue until there is zero error, but there will still be a value for $c(t)$ since an integrator can have a constant output without any input. For example, a motor can be represented simply as an integrator. A voltage applied to the motor will cause rotation. When the applied voltage is removed, the motor will stop and remain at its present output position. Since it does not return to its initial position, we have an angular displacement output without an input to the motor. Therefore, a system similar to Figure 7.4(*b*), which uses a motor in the forward path, can have zero steady-state error for a step input.

We have examined two cases qualitatively to show how a system can be expected to exhibit various steady-state error characteristics, depending upon the system configuration. We now formalize the concepts and derive the relationships between the steady-state errors and the system configuration generating these errors.

7.2 STEADY-STATE ERROR FOR UNITY FEEDBACK SYSTEMS

Steady-state error can be calculated from a system's closed-loop transfer function, $T(s)$, or the open-loop transfer function, $G(s)$, for unity feedback systems. We begin by deriving the system's steady-state error in terms of the closed-loop transfer function, $T(s)$, in order to introduce the subject and the definitions. Next we obtain insight into the factors affecting steady-state error by using the open-loop transfer function, $G(s)$, in unity feedback systems for our calculations. Later in the chapter we generalize this discussion to nonunity feedback systems.

STEADY-STATE ERROR IN TERMS OF *T(s)*

Consider Figure 7.3(*a*). To find $E(s)$, the error between the input, $R(s)$, and the output, $C(s)$, we write

$$E(s) = R(s) - C(s) \tag{7.2}$$

But

$$C(s) = R(s)T(s) \tag{7.3}$$

Substituting Eq. (7.3) into Eq. (7.2), simplifying, and solving for $E(s)$ yields

$$E(s) = R(s)[1 - T(s)] \tag{7.4}$$

Although Eq. (7.4) allows us to solve for $e(t)$ at any time, t, we are interested in the final value of the error, $e(\infty)$. Applying the final value theorem,[1] which allows us to use the final value of $e(t)$ without taking the inverse Laplace transform of $E(s)$, and then letting t approach infinity, we obtain

$$e(\infty) = \lim_{t \to \infty} e(t) = \lim_{s \to 0} sE(s) \tag{7.5}[2]$$

Substituting Eq. (7.4) into Eq. (7.5) yields

$$e(\infty) = \lim_{s \to 0} sR(s)[1 - T(s)] \tag{7.6}$$

Let us look at an example.

EXAMPLE 7.1

Steady-state error in terms of T(s)

Problem: Find the steady-state error for the system of Figure 7.3(a) if $T(s) = 5/(s^2 + 7s + 10)$ and the input is a unit step.

SOLUTION: From the problem statement, $R(s) = 1/s$ and $T(s) = 5/(s^2 + 7s + 10)$. Substituting into Eq. (7.4) yields

$$E(s) = \frac{s^2 + 7s + 5}{s(s^2 + 7s + 10)} \tag{7.7}$$

Since $T(s)$ is stable and, subsequently, $E(s)$ does not have right-half-plane poles or $j\omega$ poles other than at the origin, we can apply the final value theorem. Substituting Eq. (7.7) into Eq. (7.5) gives $e(\infty) = 1/2$.

---

[1] The final value theorem is derived from the Laplace transform of the derivative. Thus,

$$\mathscr{L}[\dot{f}(t)] = \int_{0-}^{\infty} \dot{f}(t)e^{-st}\,dt = sF(s) - f(0-)$$

As $s \to 0$,

$$\int_{0-}^{\infty} \dot{f}(t)dt = f(\infty) - f(0-) = \lim_{s \to 0} sF(s) - f(0-)$$

or

$$f(\infty) = \lim_{s \to 0} sF(s)$$

For finite steady-state errors, the final value theorem is valid only if $F(s)$ has poles only in the left half-plane and, at most, one pole at the origin. However, correct results that yield steady-state errors that are infinite can be obtained if $F(s)$ has more than one pole at the origin (see *D'Azzo and Houpis, 1988*). If $F(s)$ has poles in the right half-plane or poles on the imaginary axis other than at the origin, the final value theorem is invalid.

[2] Valid only if (1) $E(s)$ has poles only in the left half-plane and at the origin, and (2) the closed-loop transfer function, $T(s)$, is stable. Notice that by using Eq. (7.5), numerical results can be obtained for unstable systems. These results, however, are meaningless.

STEADY-STATE ERROR IN TERMS OF $G(s)$

Many times we have the system configured as a unity feedback system with a forward transfer function, $G(s)$. Although we can find the closed-loop transfer function, $T(s)$, and then proceed as in the previous subsection, we find more insight for analysis and design by expressing the steady-state error in terms of $G(s)$ rather than $T(s)$.

Consider the feedback control system shown in Figure 7.3(b). Since the feedback, $H(s)$, equals 1, the system has unity feedback. The implication is that $E(s)$ is actually the error between the input, $R(s)$, and the output, $C(s)$. Thus, if we solve for $E(s)$, we will have an expression for the error. We will then apply the final value theorem, Item 11 in Table 2.2, to evaluate the steady-state error.

Writing $E(s)$ from Figure 7.3(b), we obtain

$$E(s) = R(s) - C(s) \tag{7.8}$$

But

$$C(s) = E(s)G(s) \tag{7.9}$$

Finally, substituting Eq. (7.9) into Eq. (7.8) and solving for $E(s)$ yields

$$E(s) = \frac{R(s)}{1 + G(s)} \tag{7.10}$$

We now apply the final value theorem, Eq. (7.5). At this point in a numerical calculation, we must check to see whether the closed-loop system is stable, using, for example, the Routh-Hurwitz criterion. For now, though, assume that the closed-loop system is stable and substitute Eq. (7.10) into Eq. (7.5), obtaining

$$e(\infty) = \lim_{s \to 0} \frac{sR(s)}{1 + G(s)} \tag{7.11}$$

Equation (7.11) allows us to calculate the steady-state error, $e(\infty)$, given the input, $R(s)$, and the system, $G(s)$. We now substitute several inputs for $R(s)$ and then draw conclusions about the relationships that exist between the open-loop system, $G(s)$, and the nature of the steady-state error, $e(\infty)$.

The three test signals we use to establish specifications for a control system's steady-state error characteristics are shown in Table 7.1. Let us take each input and evaluate its effect on the steady-state error by using Eq. (7.11).

Step Input. Using Eq. (7.11) with $R(s) = 1/s$, we find

$$e(\infty) = e_{\text{step}}(\infty) = \lim_{s \to 0} \frac{s(1/s)}{1 + G(s)} = \frac{1}{1 + \lim_{s \to 0} G(s)} \tag{7.12}$$

The term

$$\lim_{s \to 0} G(s)$$

is the dc gain of the forward transfer function, since s, the frequency variable, is approaching zero. In order to have zero steady-state error,

$$\lim_{s \to 0} G(s) = \infty \tag{7.13}$$

Hence, to satisfy Eq. (7.13), $G(s)$ must take on the following form:

$$G(s) \equiv \frac{(s + z_1)(s + z_2) \cdots}{s^n(s + p_1)(s + p_2) \cdots} \tag{7.14}$$

and for the limit to be infinite, the denominator must be equal to zero as s goes to zero. Thus, $n \geq 1$; that is, at least one pole must be at the origin. Since division by s in the frequency domain is integration in the time domain (see Table 2.2, Item 10), we are also saying that at least one pure integration must be present in the forward path. The steady-state response for this case of zero steady-state error is similar to that shown in Figure 7.2(a), output 1.

If there are no integrations, then $n = 0$. Using Eq. (7.14), we have

$$\lim_{s \to 0} G(s) = \frac{z_1 z_2 \cdots}{p_1 p_2 \cdots} \tag{7.15}$$

which is finite and yields a finite error from Eq. (7.12). Figure 7.2(a), output 2, is an example of this case of finite steady-state error.

In summary, for a step input to a unity feedback system, the steady-state error will be zero if there is at least one pure integration in the forward path. If there are no integrations, then there will be a nonzero finite error. This result is comparable to our qualitative discussion in Section 7.1, where we found that a pure gain yields a constant steady-state error for a step input, but an integrator yields zero error for the same type of input. We now repeat the development for a ramp input.

Ramp Input. Using Eq. (7.11) with, $R(s) = 1/s^2$, we obtain

$$e(\infty) = e_{\text{ramp}}(\infty) = \lim_{s \to 0} \frac{s(1/s^2)}{1 + G(s)} = \lim_{s \to 0} \frac{1}{s + sG(s)} = \frac{1}{\lim_{s \to 0} sG(s)} \tag{7.16}$$

To have zero steady-state error for a ramp input, we must have

$$\lim_{s \to 0} sG(s) = \infty \tag{7.17}$$

To satisfy Eq. (7.17), $G(s)$ must take the same form as Eq. (7.14), except that $n \geq 2$. In other words, there must be at least two integrations in the forward path. An example of zero steady-state error for a ramp input is shown in Figure 7.2(b), output 1.

If only one integration exists in the forward path, then, assuming Eq. (7.14),

$$\lim_{s \to 0} sG(s) = \frac{z_1 z_2 \cdots}{p_1 p_2 \cdots} \tag{7.18}$$

which is finite rather than infinite. Using Eq. (7.16), we find that this configuration leads to a constant error, as shown in Figure 7.2(b), output 2.

If there are no integrations in the forward path, then

$$\lim_{s \to 0} sG(s) = 0 \tag{7.19}$$

and the steady-state error would be infinite and lead to diverging ramps, as shown in Figure 7.2(b), output 3. Finally, we repeat the development for a parabolic input.

Parabolic Input. Using Eq. (7.11) with $R(s) = 1/s^3$, we obtain

$$e(\infty) = e_{\text{parabola}}(\infty) = \lim_{s \to 0} \frac{s(1/s^3)}{1 + G(s)} = \lim_{s \to 0} \frac{1}{s^2 + s^2 G(s)} = \frac{1}{\lim_{s \to 0} s^2 G(s)} \qquad (7.20)$$

In order to have zero steady-state error for a parabolic input, we must have

$$\lim_{s \to 0} s^2 G(s) = \infty \qquad (7.21)$$

To satisfy Eq. (7.21), $G(s)$ must take on the same form as Eq. (7.14), except that $n \geq 3$. In other words, there must be at least three integrations in the forward path.

If there are only two integrations in the forward path, then

$$\lim_{s \to 0} s^2 G(s) = \frac{z_1 z_2 \cdots}{p_1 p_2 \cdots} \qquad (7.22)$$

is finite rather than infinite. Using Eq. (7.20), we find that this configuration leads to a constant error.

If there is only one or less integration in the forward path, then

$$\lim_{s \to 0} s^2 G(s) = 0 \qquad (7.23)$$

and the steady-state error is infinite. Two examples demonstrate these concepts.

EXAMPLE 7.2

Steady-state errors for systems with no integrations

Problem: Find the steady-state errors for inputs of $5u(t)$, $5tu(t)$, and $5t^2 u(t)$ to the system shown in Figure 7.5. The function $u(t)$ is the unit step.

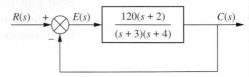

FIGURE 7.5 Feedback control system for Example 7.2

SOLUTION: First we verify that the closed-loop system is indeed stable. For this example we leave out the details. Next, for the input $5u(t)$, whose Laplace transform is $5/s$, the steady-state error will be five times as large as that given by Eq. (7.12), or

$$e(\infty) = e_{\text{step}}(\infty) = \frac{5}{1 + \lim_{s \to 0} G(s)} = \frac{5}{1 + 20} = \frac{5}{21} \qquad (7.24)$$

which implies a response similar to output 2 of Figure 7.2(*a*).

For the input $5tu(t)$, whose Laplace transform is $5/s^2$, the steady-state error will be five times as large as that given by Eq. (7.16), or

$$e(\infty) = e_{\text{ramp}}(\infty) = \frac{5}{\lim_{s \to 0} sG(s)} = \frac{5}{0} = \infty \qquad (7.25)$$

which implies a response similar to output 3 of Figure 7.2(*b*).

For the input $5t^2u(t)$, whose Laplace transform is $10/s^3$, the steady-state error will be 10 times as large as that given by Eq. (7.20), or

$$e(\infty) = e_{\text{parabola}}(\infty) = \frac{10}{\lim_{s \to 0} s^2 G(s)} = \frac{10}{0} = \infty \qquad (7.26)$$

EXAMPLE 7.3

Steady-state errors for systems with one integration

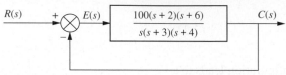

FIGURE 7.6   Feedback control system for Example 7.3

Problem: Find the steady-state errors for inputs of $5u(t)$, $5tu(t)$, and $5t^2u(t)$ to the system shown in Figure 7.6. The function $u(t)$ is the unit step.

SOLUTION: First verify that the closed-loop system is indeed stable. For this example we leave out the details. Next note that since there is an integration in the forward path, the steady-state errors for some of the input waveforms will be less than those found in Example 7.2. For the input $5u(t)$, whose Laplace transform is $5/s$, the steady-state error will be five times as large as that given by Eq. (7.12), or

$$e(\infty) = e_{\text{step}}(\infty) = \frac{5}{1 + \lim_{s \to 0} G(s)} = \frac{5}{\infty} = 0 \qquad (7.27)$$

which implies a response similar to output 1 of Figure 7.2(*a*). Notice that the integration in the forward path yields zero error for a step input, rather than the finite error found in Example 7.2.

For the input $5tu(t)$, whose Laplace transform is $5/s^2$, the steady-state error will be five times as large as that given by Eq. (7.16), or

$$e(\infty) = e_{\text{ramp}}(\infty) = \frac{5}{\lim_{s \to 0} sG(s)} = \frac{5}{100} = \frac{1}{20} \qquad (7.28)$$

which implies a response similar to output 2 of Figure 7.2(*b*). Notice that the integration in the forward path yields a finite error for a ramp input, rather than the infinite error found in Example 7.2.

For the input, $5t^2u(t)$, whose Laplace transform is $10/s^3$, the steady-state error will be 10 times as large as that given by Eq. (7.20), or

$$e(\infty) = e_{\text{parabola}}(\infty) = \frac{10}{\lim_{s \to 0} s^2 G(s)} = \frac{10}{0} = \infty \qquad (7.29)$$

Notice that the integration in the forward path does not yield any improvement in steady-state error over that found in Example 7.2 for a parabolic input.

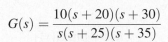

SKILL-ASSESSMENT EXERCISE 7.1

Problem: A unity feedback system has the following forward transfer function:

$$G(s) = \frac{10(s+20)(s+30)}{s(s+25)(s+35)}$$

a. Find the steady-state error for the following inputs: $15u(t)$, $15tu(t)$, and $15t^2u(t)$.

b. Repeat for

$$G(s) = \frac{10(s+20)(s+30)}{s^2(s+25)(s+35)(s+50)}$$

ANSWERS:

a. The closed-loop system is stable. For $15u(t)$, $e_{step}(\infty) = 0$; for $15tu(t)$, $e_{ramp}(\infty) = 2.1875$; for $15(t^2)u(t)$, $e_{parabola}(\infty) = \infty$.

b. The closed-loop system is unstable. Calculations cannot be made.

The complete solution is at www.wiley.com/college/nise.

7.3 STATIC ERROR CONSTANTS AND SYSTEM TYPE

We continue our focus on unity negative feedback systems and define parameters that we can use as steady-state error performance specifications, just as we defined damping ratio, natural frequency, settling time, percent overshoot, and so on as performance specifications for the transient response. These steady-state error performance specifications are called *static error constants*. Let us see how they are defined, how to calculate them, and, in the next section, how to use them for design.

STATIC ERROR CONSTANTS

In the previous section we derived the following relationships for steady-state error. For a step input, $u(t)$,

$$e(\infty) = e_{step}(\infty) = \frac{1}{1 + \lim_{s \to 0} G(s)} \tag{7.30}$$

For a ramp input, $tu(t)$,

$$e(\infty) = e_{ramp}(\infty) = \frac{1}{\lim_{s \to 0} sG(s)} \tag{7.31}$$

For a parabolic input, $\frac{1}{2}t^2u(t)$,

$$e(\infty) = e_{parabola}(\infty) = \frac{1}{\lim_{s \to 0} s^2G(s)} \tag{7.32}$$

The three terms in the denominator that are taken to the limit determine the steady-state error. We call these limits *static error constants*. Individually, their names are

position constant, K_p, where

$$K_p = \lim_{s \to 0} G(s) \qquad (7.33)$$

velocity constant, K_v, where

$$K_v = \lim_{s \to 0} sG(s) \qquad (7.34)$$

acceleration constant, K_a, where

$$K_a = \lim_{s \to 0} s^2 G(s) \qquad (7.35)$$

As we have seen, these quantities, depending upon the form of $G(s)$, can assume values of zero, finite constant, or infinity. Since the static error constant appears in the denominator of the steady-state error, Eqs. (7.30) through (7.32), the value of the steady-state error decreases as the static error constant increases.

In Section 7.2 we evaluated the steady-state error by using the final value theorem. An alternate method makes use of the static error constants. A few examples follow.

EXAMPLE 7.4

Steady-state error via static error constants

Problem: For each system of Figure 7.7, evaluate the static error constants and find the expected error for the standard step, ramp, and parabolic inputs.

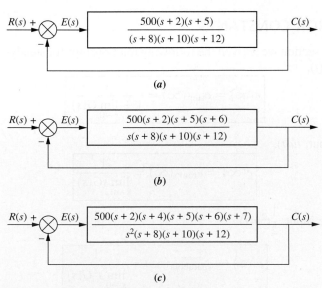

FIGURE 7.7   Feedback control systems for Example 7.4

SOLUTION: First verify that all closed-loop systems shown are indeed stable. For this example we leave out the details. Next, for Figure 7.7(*a*),

$$K_p = \lim_{s \to 0} G(s) = \frac{500 \times 2 \times 5}{8 \times 10 \times 12} = 5.208 \tag{7.36}$$

$$K_v = \lim_{s \to 0} sG(s) = 0 \tag{7.37}$$

$$K_a = \lim_{s \to 0} s^2 G(s) = 0 \tag{7.38}$$

Thus, for a step input,

$$e(\infty) = \frac{1}{1 + K_p} = 0.161 \tag{7.39}$$

For a ramp input,

$$e(\infty) = \frac{1}{K_v} = \infty \tag{7.40}$$

For a parabolic input,

$$e(\infty) = \frac{1}{K_a} = \infty \tag{7.41}$$

Now, for Figure 7.7(*b*),

$$K_p = \lim_{s \to 0} G(s) = \infty \tag{7.42}$$

$$K_v = \lim_{s \to 0} sG(s) = \frac{500 \times 2 \times 5 \times 6}{8 \times 10 \times 12} = 31.25 \tag{7.43}$$

and

$$K_a = \lim_{s \to 0} s^2 G(s) = 0 \tag{7.44}$$

Thus, for a step input,

$$e(\infty) = \frac{1}{1 + K_p} = 0 \tag{7.45}$$

For a ramp input,

$$e(\infty) = \frac{1}{K_v} = \frac{1}{31.25} = 0.032 \tag{7.46}$$

For a parabolic input,

$$e(\infty) = \frac{1}{K_a} = \infty \tag{7.47}$$

Finally, for Figure 7.7(*c*),

$$K_p = \lim_{s \to 0} G(s) = \infty \tag{7.48}$$

$$K_v = \lim_{s \to 0} sG(s) = \infty \tag{7.49}$$

and

$$K_a = \lim_{s \to 0} s^2 G(s) = \frac{500 \times 2 \times 4 \times 5 \times 6 \times 7}{8 \times 10 \times 12} = 875 \qquad (7.50)$$

Thus, for a step input,

$$e(\infty) = \frac{1}{1 + K_p} = 0 \qquad (7.51)$$

For a ramp input,

$$e(\infty) = \frac{1}{K_v} = 0 \qquad (7.52)$$

For a parabolic input,

$$e(\infty) = \frac{1}{K_a} = \frac{1}{875} = 1.14 \times 10^{-3} \qquad (7.53)$$

Students who are using MATLAB should now run ch7p1 in Appendix B. You will learn how to test the system for stability, evaluate static error constants, and calculate steady-state error using MATLAB. This exercise applies MATLAB to solve Example 7.4 with system (b).

SYSTEM TYPE

Let us continue to focus on a unity negative feedback system. The values of the static error constants, again, depend upon the form of $G(s)$, especially the number of pure integrations in the forward path. Since steady-state errors are dependent upon the number of integrations in the forward path, we give a name to this system attribute. Given the system in Figure 7.8, we define *system type* to be the value of n in the denominator or, equivalently, the number of pure integrations in the forward path. Therefore, a system with $n = 0$ is a Type 0 system. If $n = 1$ or $n = 2$, the corresponding system is a Type 1 or Type 2 system, respectively.

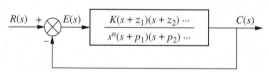

FIGURE 7.8 Feedback control system for defining system type

Table 7.2 ties together the concepts of steady-state error, static error constants, and system type. The table shows the static error constants and the steady-state errors as functions of input waveform and system type.

TABLE 7.2   **Relationships between input, system type, static error constants, and steady-state errors**

Input	Steady-state error formula	Type 0 Static error constant	Type 0 Error	Type 1 Static error constant	Type 1 Error	Type 2 Static error constant	Type 2 Error
Step, $u(t)$	$\dfrac{1}{1 + K_p}$	$K_p =$ Constant	$\dfrac{1}{1 + K_p}$	$K_p = \infty$	0	$K_p = \infty$	0
Ramp, $tu(t)$	$\dfrac{1}{K_v}$	$K_v = 0$	∞	$K_v =$ Constant	$\dfrac{1}{K_v}$	$K_v = \infty$	0
Parabola, $\frac{1}{2}t^2 u(t)$	$\dfrac{1}{K_a}$	$K_a = 0$	∞	$K_a = 0$	∞	$K_a =$ Constant	$\dfrac{1}{K_a}$

SKILL-ASSESSMENT EXERCISE 7.2

Problem: A unity feedback system has the following forward transfer function:

$$G(s) = \frac{1000(s+8)}{(s+7)(s+9)}$$

a. Evaluate system type, K_p, K_v, and K_a.

b. Use your answers to (a) to find the steady-state errors for the standard step, ramp, and parabolic inputs.

ANSWERS:

a. The closed-loop system is stable. System type = Type 0. $K_p = 127$, $K_v = 0$, and $K_a = 0$.

b. $e_{\text{step}}(\infty) = 7.8 \times 10^{-3}$, $e_{\text{ramp}}(\infty) = \infty$, and $e_{\text{parabola}}(\infty) = \infty$

The complete solution is at www.wiley.com/college/nise.

TryIt 7.1

Use MATLAB, the Control System Toolbox, and the following statements to find K_p, $e_{\text{step}}(\infty)$, and the closed-loop poles to check for stability for the system of Skill-Assessment Exercise 7.2.

```
numg=1000*[1 8];
deng=poly([-7 -9]);
G=tf(numg,deng);
Kp=dcgain(G)
estep=1/(1+Kp)
T=feedback(G,1);
poles=pole(T)
```

In this section we defined steady-state errors, static error constants, and system type. Now the specifications for a control system's steady-state errors will be formulated, followed by some examples.

7.4 STEADY-STATE ERROR SPECIFICATIONS

Static error constants can be used to specify the steady-state error characteristics of control systems, such as that shown in Figure 7.9. Just as damping ratio, ζ, settling time, T_s, peak time, T_p, and percent overshoot, $\%OS$, are used as specifications for a control

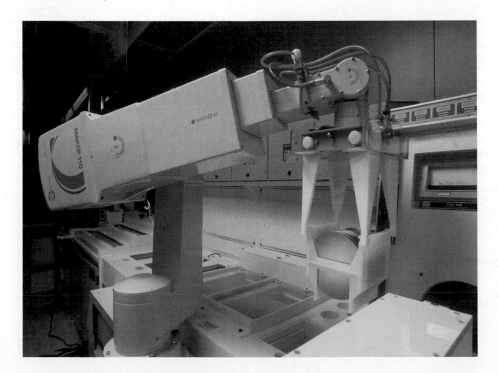

FIGURE 7.9   A robot used in the manufacturing of semiconductor random-access memories (RAMs) similar to those in personal computers. Steady-state error is an important design consideration for assembly-line robots.

system's transient response, so the position constant, K_p, velocity constant, K_v, and acceleration constant, K_a, can be used as specifications for a control system's steady-state errors. We will soon see that a wealth of information is contained within the specification of a static error constant.

For example, if a control system has the specification $K_v = 1000$, we can draw several conclusions:

1. The system is stable.

2. The system is of Type 1, since only Type 1 systems have K_v's that are finite constants. Recall that $K_v = 0$ for Type 0 systems, whereas $K_v = \infty$ for Type 2 systems.

3. A ramp input is the test signal. Since K_v is specified as a finite constant, and the steady-state error for a ramp input is inversely proportional to K_v, we know the test input is a ramp.

4. The steady-state error between the input ramp and the output ramp is $1/K_v$ per unit of input slope.

Let us look at two examples that demonstrate analysis and design using static error constants.

EXAMPLE 7.5

Interpreting the steady-state error specification

Problem: What information is contained in the specification $K_p = 1000$?

SOLUTION: The system is stable. The system is Type 0, since only a Type 0 system has a finite K_p. Type 1 and Type 2 systems have $K_p = \infty$. The input test signal is a step, since K_p is specified. Finally, the error per unit step is

$$e(\infty) = \frac{1}{1 + K_p} = \frac{1}{1 + 1000} = \frac{1}{1001} \tag{7.54}$$

EXAMPLE 7.6

Gain design to meet a steady-state error specification

Problem: Given the control system in Figure 7.10, find the value of K so that there is 10% error in the steady state.

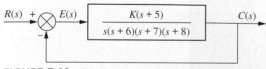

FIGURE 7.10   Feedback control system for Example 7.6

SOLUTION: Since the system is Type 1, the error stated in the problem must apply to a ramp input; only a ramp yields a finite error in a Type 1 system. Thus,

$$e(\infty) = \frac{1}{K_v} = 0.1 \tag{7.55}$$

Therefore,

$$K_v = 10 = \lim_{s \to 0} sG(s) = \frac{K \times 5}{6 \times 7 \times 8} \tag{7.56}$$

which yields

$$K = 672 \tag{7.57}$$

Applying the Routh-Hurwitz criterion, we see that the system is stable at this gain.

Although this gain meets the criteria for steady-state error and stability, it may not yield a desirable transient response. In Chapter 9 we will design feedback control systems to meet all three specifications.

Students who are using MATLAB should now run ch7p2 in Appendix B. You will learn how to find the gain to meet a steady-state error specification using MATLAB. This exercise solves Example 7.6 using MATLAB.

SKILL-ASSESSMENT EXERCISE 7.3

Problem: A unity feedback system has the following forward transfer function:

$$G(s) = \frac{K(s + 12)}{(s + 14)(s + 18)}$$

Find the value of K to yield a 10% error in the steady state.

ANSWER: $K = 189$

The complete solution is at www.wiley.com/college/nise.

TryIt 7.2

Use MATLAB, the Control System Toolbox, and the following statements to solve Skill-Assessment Exercise 7.3 and check the resulting system for stability.

```
numg=[1 12];
deng=poly([-14 -18]);
G=tf(numg,deng);
Kpdk=dcgain(G);
estep=0.1;
K=(1/estep-1)/Kpdk
T=feedback(G,1);
poles=pole(T)
```

This example and exercise complete our discussion of unity feedback systems. In the remaining sections we will deal with the steady-state errors for disturbances and the steady-state errors for feedback control systems in which the feedback is not unity.

7.5 STEADY-STATE ERROR FOR DISTURBANCES

Feedback control systems are used to compensate for disturbances or unwanted inputs that enter a system. The advantage of using feedback is that regardless of these disturbances, the system can be designed to follow the input with small or zero error, as we now demonstrate. Figure 7.11 shows a feedback control system with a disturbance, $D(s)$, injected between the controller and the plant. We now re-derive the expression for steady-state error with the disturbance included.

The transform of the output is given by

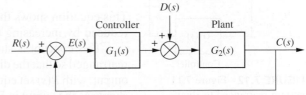

FIGURE 7.11 Feedback control system showing disturbance

$$C(s) = E(s)G_1(s)G_2(s) + D(s)G_2(s) \tag{7.58}$$

But

$$C(s) = R(s) - E(s) \qquad (7.59)$$

Substituting Eq. (7.59) into Eq. (7.58) and solving for $E(s)$, we obtain

$$E(s) = \frac{1}{1 + G_1(s)G_2(s)} R(s) - \frac{G_2(s)}{1 + G_1(s)G_2(s)} D(s) \qquad (7.60)$$

where we can think of $1/[1 + G_1(s)G_2(s)]$ as a transfer function relating $E(s)$ to $R(s)$ and $-G_2(s)/[1 + G_1(s)G_2(s)]$ as a transfer function relating $E(s)$ to $D(s)$.

To find the steady-state value of the error, we apply the final value theorem[3] to Eq. (7.60) and obtain

$$e(\infty) = \lim_{s \to 0} sE(s) = \lim_{s \to 0} \frac{s}{1 + G_1(s)G_2(s)} R(s) - \lim_{s \to 0} \frac{sG_2(s)}{1 + G_1(s)G_2(s)} D(s)$$
$$= e_R(\infty) + e_D(\infty) \qquad (7.61)$$

where

$$e_R(\infty) = \lim_{s \to 0} \frac{s}{1 + G_1(s)G_2(s)} R(s)$$

and

$$e_D(\infty) = -\lim_{s \to 0} \frac{sG_2(s)}{1 + G_1(s)G_2(s)} D(s)$$

The first term, $e_R(\infty)$, is the steady-state error due to $R(s)$, which we have already obtained. The second term, $e_D(\infty)$, is the steady-state error due to the disturbance. Let us explore the conditions on $e_D(\infty)$ that must exist to reduce the error due to the disturbance.

At this point we must make some assumptions about $D(s)$, the controller, and the plant. First we assume a step disturbance, $D(s) = 1/s$. Substituting this value into the second term of Eq. (7.61), $e_D(\infty)$, the steady-state error component due to a step disturbance is found to be

$$e_D(\infty) = -\frac{1}{\displaystyle\lim_{s \to 0} \frac{1}{G_2(s)} + \lim_{s \to 0} G_1(s)} \qquad (7.62)$$

This equation shows that the steady-state error produced by a step disturbance can be reduced by increasing the dc gain of $G_1(s)$ or decreasing the dc gain of $G_2(s)$.

This concept is shown in Figure 7.12, where the system of Figure 7.11 has been rearranged so that the disturbance, $D(s)$, is depicted as the input and the error, $E(s)$, as the output, with $R(s)$ set equal to zero. If we want to minimize the steady-state value of $E(s)$, shown as the output in Figure 7.12, we must either increase the dc gain of $G_1(s)$ so that a lower value of $E(s)$ will be fed back to match the steady-state value of $D(s)$, or decrease

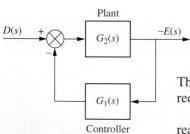

FIGURE 7.12 Figure 7.11 system rearranged to show disturbance as input and error as output, with $R(s) = 0$

---

[3] Remember that the final value theorem can be applied only if the system is stable, with the roots of $[1 + G_1(s)G_2(s)]$ in the left half-plane.

the dc value of $G_2(s)$, which then yields a smaller value of $e(\infty)$ as predicted by the feedback formula.

Let us look at an example and calculate the numerical value of the steady-state error that results from a disturbance.

EXAMPLE 7.7

Steady-state error due to step disturbance

Problem: Find the steady-state error component due to a step disturbance for the system of Figure 7.13.

SOLUTION: The system is stable. Using Figure 7.12 and Eq. (7.62), we find

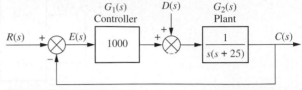

FIGURE 7.13 Feedback control system for Example 7.7

$$e_D(\infty) = -\frac{1}{\lim\limits_{s \to 0} \dfrac{1}{G_2(s)} + \lim\limits_{s \to 0} G_1(s)} = -\frac{1}{0 + 1000} = -\frac{1}{1000} \qquad (7.63)$$

The result shows that the steady-state error produced by the step disturbance is inversely proportional to the dc gain of $G_1(s)$. The dc gain of $G_2(s)$ is infinite in this example.

SKILL-ASSESSMENT EXERCISE 7.4

Problem: Evaluate the steady-state error component due to a step disturbance for the system of Figure 7.14.

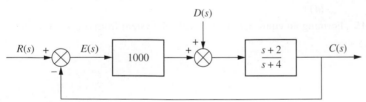

FIGURE 7.14 System for Skill-Assessment Exercise 7.4

ANSWER: $e_D(\infty) = -9.98 \times 10^{-4}$

The complete solution is at www.wiley.com/college/nise.

7.6 STEADY-STATE ERROR FOR NONUNITY FEEDBACK SYSTEMS

Control systems often do not have unity feedback because of the compensation used to improve performance or because of the physical model for the system. The feedback path can be a pure gain other than unity or have some dynamic representation.

A general feedback system, showing the input transducer, $G_1(s)$, controller and plant, $G_2(s)$, and feedback, $H_1(s)$, is shown in Figure 7.15(a). Pushing the input

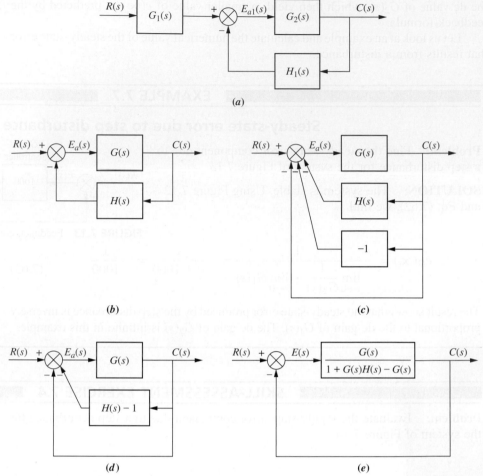

FIGURE 7.15 Forming an equivalent unity feedback system from a general nonunity feedback system

transducer to the right past the summing junction yields the general nonunity feedback system shown in Figure 7.15(b), where $G(s) = G_1(s)G_2(s)$ and $H(s) = H_1(s)/G_1(s)$. Notice that unlike a unity feedback system, where $H(s) = 1$, the error is not the difference between the input and the output. For this case we call the signal at the output of the summing junction the *actuating signal, $E_a(s)$*. If $r(t)$ and $c(t)$ have the same units, we can find the steady-state error, $e(\infty) = r(\infty) - c(\infty)$. The first step is to show explicitly $E(s) = R(s) - C(s)$ on the block diagram.

Take the nonunity feedback control system shown in Figure 7.15(b) and form a unity feedback system by adding and subtracting unity feedback paths, as shown in Figure 7.15(c). This step requires that input and output units be the same. Next combine $H(s)$ with the negative unity feedback, as shown in Figure 7.15(d). Finally, combine the feedback system consisting of $G(s)$ and $[H(s) - 1]$, leaving an equivalent forward path and a unity feedback, as shown in Figure 7.15(e). Notice that the final figure shows $E(s) = R(s) - C(s)$ explicitly.

The following example summarizes the concepts of steady-state error, system type, and static error constants for nonunity feedback systems.

EXAMPLE 7.8

Steady-state error for nonunity feedback systems

Problem: For the system shown in Figure 7.16, find the system type, the appropriate error constant associated with the system type, and the steady-state error for a unit step input. Assume input and output units are the same.

SOLUTION: After determining that the system is indeed stable, one may impulsively declare the system to be Type 1. This may not be the case, since there is a nonunity feedback element, and the plant's actuating signal is not the difference between the input and the output. The first step in solving the problem is to convert the system of Figure 7.16 into an equivalent unity feedback system. Using the equivalent forward transfer function of Figure 7.15(e) along with

$$G(s) = \frac{100}{s(s+10)} \tag{7.64}$$

and

$$H(s) = \frac{1}{(s+5)} \tag{7.65}$$

we find

$$G_e(s) = \frac{G(s)}{1 + G(s)H(s) - G(s)} = \frac{100(s+5)}{s^3 + 15s^2 - 50s - 400} \tag{7.66}$$

Thus, the system is Type 0, since there are no pure integrations in Eq. (7.66). The appropriate static error constant is then K_p, whose value is

$$K_p = \lim_{s \to 0} G_e(s) = \frac{100 \times 5}{-400} = -\frac{5}{4} \tag{7.67}$$

The steady-state error, $e(\infty)$, is

$$e(\infty) = \frac{1}{1 + K_p} = \frac{1}{1 - (5/4)} = -4 \tag{7.68}$$

The negative value for steady-state error implies that the output step is larger than the input step.

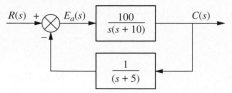

FIGURE 7.16 Nonunity feedback control system for Example 7.8

TryIt 7.3

Use MATLAB, the Control System Toolbox, and the following statements to find $G_e(s)$ in Example 7.8.

```
G = zpk([ ], [0 −10], 100);
H = zpk([ ], − 5, 1);
Ge = feedback...
(G, (H − 1));
'Ge(s)'
Ge = tf (Ge)
T = feedback (Ge, 1);
'Poles of T(s)'
pole (T)
```

To continue our discussion of steady-state error for systems with nonunity feedback, let us look at the general system of Figure 7.17, which has both a disturbance and nonunity feedback. We will derive a general equation for the steady-state error and then determine the parameters of the system in order to drive the error to zero for step inputs and step disturbances.[4]

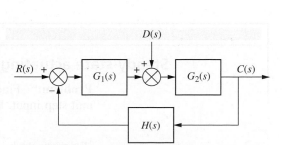

FIGURE 7.17 Nonunity feedback control system with disturbance

---

[4] Details of the derivation are included as a problem at the end of this chapter.

The steady-state error for this system, $e(\infty) = r(\infty) - c(\infty)$, is

$$
e(\infty) = \lim_{s \to 0} sE(s) = \lim_{s \to 0} s \left\{ \left[1 - \frac{G_1(s)G_2(s)}{1 + G_1(s)G_2(s)H(s)} \right] R(s) \right.
$$
$$
\left. - \left[\frac{G_2(s)}{1 + G_1(s)G_2(s)H(s)} D(s) \right] \right\}
$$

(7.69)

Now limiting the discussion to step inputs and step disturbances, where $R(s) = D(s) = 1/s$, Eq. (7.69) becomes

$$
e(\infty) = \lim_{s \to 0} sE(s) = \left\{ \left[1 - \frac{\lim\limits_{s \to 0} [G_1(s)G_2(s)]}{\lim\limits_{s \to 0} [1 + G_1(s)G_2(s)H(s)]} \right] \right.
$$
$$
\left. - \left[\frac{\lim\limits_{s \to 0} G_2(s)}{\lim\limits_{s \to 0} [1 + G_1(s)G_2(s)H(s)]} \right] \right\}
$$

(7.70)

For zero error,

$$
\frac{\lim\limits_{s \to 0} [G_1(s)G_2(s)]}{\lim\limits_{s \to 0} [1 + G_1(s)G_2(s)H(s)]} = 1 \quad \text{and} \quad \frac{\lim\limits_{s \to 0} G_2(s)}{\lim\limits_{s \to 0} [1 + G_1(s)G_2(s)H(s)]} = 0
$$

(7.71)

Equations (7.71) can always be satisfied if (1) the system is stable, (2) $G_1(s)$ is a Type 1 system, (3) $G_2(s)$ is a Type 0 system, and (4) $H(s)$ is a Type 0 system with a dc gain of unity.

To conclude this section, we discuss finding the steady-state value of the actuating signal, $E_{a1}(s)$, in Figure 7.15(a). For this task there is no restriction that the input and output units be the same, since we are finding the steady-state difference between signals at the summing junction, which do have the same units.[5] The steady-state actuating signal for Figure 7.15(a) is

$$
e_{a1}(\infty) = \lim_{s \to 0} \frac{sR(s)G_1(s)}{1 + G_2(s)H_1(s)}
$$

(7.72)

The derivation is left to the student in the problem set at the end of this chapter.

EXAMPLE 7.9

Steady-state actuating signal for nonunity feedback systems

Problem: Find the steady-state actuating signal for the system of Figure 7.16 for a unit step input. Repeat for a unit ramp input.

---

[5] For clarity, steady-state error is the steady-state difference between the input and the output. Steady-state actuating signal is the steady-state difference at the output of the summing junction. In questions asking for steady-state error in problems, examples, and skill-assessment exercises, it will be assumed that input and output units are the same.

SOLUTION: Use Eq. (7.72) with $R(s) = 1/s$, a unit step input, $G_1(s) = 1$, $G_2(s) = 100/[s(s+10)]$, and $H_1(s) = 1/(s+5)$. Also, realize that $e_{a1}(\infty) = e_a(\infty)$, since $G_1(s) = 1$. Thus,

$$e_a(\infty) = \lim_{s \to 0} \frac{s\left(\dfrac{1}{s}\right)}{1 + \left(\dfrac{100}{s(s+10)}\right)\left(\dfrac{1}{(s+5)}\right)} = 0 \qquad (7.73)$$

Now use Eq. (7.72) with $R(s) = 1/s^2$, a unit ramp input, and obtain

$$e_a(\infty) = \lim_{s \to 0} \frac{s\left(\dfrac{1}{s^2}\right)}{1 + \left(\dfrac{100}{s(s+10)}\right)\left(\dfrac{1}{(s+5)}\right)} = \frac{1}{2} \qquad (7.74)$$

SKILL-ASSESSMENT EXERCISE 7.5

Problem:

a. Find the steady-state error, $e(\infty) = r(\infty) - c(\infty)$, for a unit step input given the nonunity feedback system of Figure 7.18. Repeat for a unit ramp input. Assume input and output units are the same.

b. Find the steady-state actuating signal, $e_a(\infty)$, for a unit step input given the nonunity feedback system of Figure 7.18. Repeat for a unit ramp input.

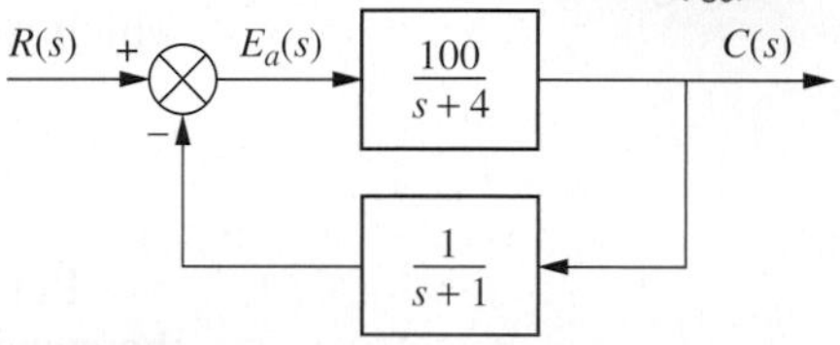

FIGURE 7.18 Nonunity feedback system for Skill-Assessment Exercise 7.5

ANSWERS:

a. $e_{step}(\infty) = 3.846 \times 10^{-2}; e_{ramp}(\infty) = \infty$

b. For a unit step input, $e_a(\infty) = 3.846 \times 10^{-2}$; for a unit ramp input, $e_a(\infty) = \infty$

The complete solution is at www.wiley.com/college/nise.

In this section we have applied steady-state error analysis to nonunity feedback systems. When nonunity feedback is present, the plant's actuating signal is not the actual error or difference between the input and the output. With nonunity feedback we may choose to (1) find the steady-state error for systems where the input and output units are the same or (2) find the steady-state actuating signal.

We also derived a general expression for the steady-state error of a nonunity feedback system with a disturbance. We used this equation to determine the attributes of the subsystems so that there was zero error for step inputs and step disturbances.

Before concluding this chapter, we will discuss a topic that is not only significant for steady-state errors but generally useful throughout the control systems design process.

7.7 SENSITIVITY

During the design process the engineer may want to consider the extent to which changes in system parameters affect the behavior of a system. Ideally, parameter changes due to heat or other causes should not appreciably affect a system's performance. The degree to which changes in system parameters affect system transfer functions, and hence performance, is called *sensitivity*. A system with zero sensitivity (that is, changes in the system parameters have no effect on the transfer function) is ideal. The greater the sensitivity, the less desirable the effect of a parameter change.

For example, assume the function $F = K/(K + a)$. If $K = 10$ and $a = 100$, then $F = 0.091$. If parameter a triples to 300, then $F = 0.032$. We see that a fractional change in parameter a of $(300 - 100)/100 = 2$ (a 200% change), yields a change in the function F of $(0.032 - 0.091)/0.091 = -0.65$ (-65% change). Thus, the function F has reduced sensitivity to changes in parameter a. As we proceed, we will see that another advantage of feedback is that in general it affords reduced sensitivity to parameter changes.

Based upon the previous discussion, let us formalize a definition of sensitivity: *Sensitivity* is the ratio of the fractional change in the function to the fractional change in the parameter as the fractional change of the parameter approaches zero. That is,

$$S_{F:P} = \lim_{\Delta P \to 0} \frac{\text{Fractional change in the function}, F}{\text{Fractional change in the parameter}, P}$$

$$= \lim_{\Delta P \to 0} \frac{\Delta F/F}{\Delta P/P}$$

$$= \lim_{\Delta P \to 0} \frac{P}{F} \frac{\Delta F}{\Delta P}$$

which reduces to

$$\boxed{S_{F:P} = \frac{P}{F} \frac{\delta F}{\delta P}} \tag{7.75}$$

Let us now apply the definition, first to a closed-loop transfer function and then to the steady-state error.

■ EXAMPLE 7.10 ■

Sensitivity of a closed-loop transfer function

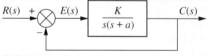

FIGURE 7.19 Feedback control system for Examples 7.10 and 7.11

Problem: Given the system of Figure 7.19, calculate the sensitivity of the closed-loop transfer function to changes in the parameter a. How would you reduce the sensitivity?

SOLUTION: The closed-loop transfer function is

$$T(s) = \frac{K}{s^2 + as + K} \tag{7.76}$$

Using Eq. (7.75), the sensitivity is given by

$$S_{T:a} = \frac{a}{T} \frac{\delta T}{\delta a} = \frac{a}{\left(\dfrac{K}{s^2 + as + K} \right)} \left(\frac{-Ks}{(s^2 + as + K)^2} \right) = \frac{-as}{s^2 + as + K} \tag{7.77}$$

which is, in part, a function of the value of s. For any value of s, however, an increase in K reduces the sensitivity of the closed-loop transfer function to changes in the parameter a.

EXAMPLE 7.11

Sensitivity of steady-state error with ramp input

Problem: For the system of Figure 7.19, find the sensitivity of the steady-state error to changes in parameter K and parameter a with ramp inputs.

SOLUTION: The steady-state error for the system is

$$e(\infty) = \frac{1}{K_v} = \frac{a}{K} \tag{7.78}$$

The sensitivity of $e(\infty)$ to changes in parameter a is

$$S_{e:a} = \frac{a}{e}\frac{\delta e}{\delta a} = \frac{a}{a/K}\left[\frac{1}{K}\right] = 1 \tag{7.79}$$

The sensitivity of $e(\infty)$ to changes in parameter K is

$$S_{e:K} = \frac{K}{e}\frac{\delta e}{\delta K} = \frac{K}{a/K}\left[\frac{-a}{K^2}\right] = -1 \tag{7.80}$$

Thus, changes in either parameter a or parameter K are directly reflected in $e(\infty)$, and there is no reduction or increase in sensitivity. The negative sign in Eq. (7.80) indicates a decrease in $e(\infty)$ for an increase in K. Both of these results could have been obtained directly from Eq. (7.78) since $e(\infty)$ is directly proportional to parameter a and inversely proportional to parameter K.

EXAMPLE 7.12

Sensitivity of steady-state error with step input

Problem: Find the sensitivity of the steady-state error to changes in parameter K and parameter a for the system shown in Figure 7.20 with a step input.

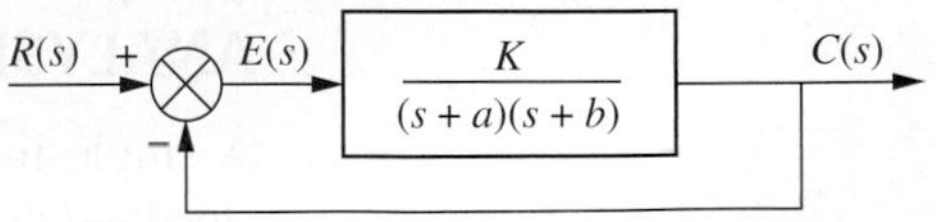

SOLUTION: The steady-state error for this Type 0 system is

$$e(\infty) = \frac{1}{1 + K_p} = \frac{1}{1 + \dfrac{K}{ab}} = \frac{ab}{ab + K} \tag{7.81}$$

The sensitivity of $e(\infty)$ to changes in parameter a is

$$S_{e:a} = \frac{a}{e}\frac{\delta e}{\delta a} = \frac{a}{\left(\dfrac{ab}{ab+K}\right)}\frac{(ab+K)b - ab^2}{(ab+K)^2} = \frac{K}{ab+K} \tag{7.82}$$

The sensitivity of $e(\infty)$ to changes in parameter K is

$$S_{e:K} = \frac{K}{e}\frac{\delta e}{\delta K} = \frac{K}{\left(\dfrac{ab}{ab+K}\right)}\frac{-ab}{(ab+K)^2} = \frac{-K}{ab+K} \tag{7.83}$$

FIGURE 7.20 Feedback control system for Example 7.12

TryIt 7.4

Use MATLAB, the Symbolic Math Toolbox, and the following statements to find $S_{e:a}$ in Example 7.12.

```
syms K a b s
G=K/((s+a)*(s+b));
Kp=subs(G,s,o);
e=1/(1+Kp);
Sea=(a/e)*diff(e,a);
Sea=simple(Sea);
'Sea'
pretty(Sea)
```

Equations (7.82) and (7.83) show that the sensitivity to changes in parameter K and parameter a is less than unity for positive a and b. Thus, feedback in this case yields reduced sensitivity to variations in both parameters.

SKILL-ASSESSMENT EXERCISE 7.6

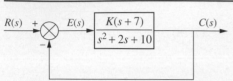

FIGURE 7.21   System for Skill-Assessment Exercise 7.6

Problem: Find the sensitivity of the steady-state error to changes in K for the system of Figure 7.21.

ANSWER: $S_{e:k} = \dfrac{-7K}{10 + 7K}$

The complete solution is at www.wiley.com/college/nise.

In this section we defined sensitivity and showed that in some cases feedback reduces the sensitivity of a system's steady-state error to changes in system parameters. The concept of sensitivity can be applied to other measures of control system performance, as well; it is not limited to the sensitivity of the steady-state error performance.

7.8 STEADY-STATE ERROR FOR SYSTEMS IN STATE SPACE

Up to this point we have evaluated the steady-state error for systems modeled as transfer functions. In this section we will discuss how to evaluate the steady-state error for systems represented in state space. Two methods for calculating the steady-state error will be covered: (1) analysis via final value theorem and (2) analysis via input substitution. We will consider these methods individually.

ANALYSIS VIA FINAL VALUE THEOREM

A single-input, single-output system represented in state space can be analyzed for steady-state error using the final value theorem and the closed-loop transfer function, Eq. (3.73), derived in terms of the state-space representation. Consider the closed-loop system represented in state space:

$$\dot{\mathbf{x}} = \mathbf{A}\mathbf{x} + \mathbf{B}r \tag{7.84a}$$

$$y = \mathbf{C}\mathbf{x} \tag{7.84b}$$

The Laplace transform of the error is

$$E(s) = R(s) - Y(s) \tag{7.85}$$

But

$$Y(s) = R(s)T(s) \tag{7.86}$$

where $T(s)$ is the closed-loop transfer function. Substituting Eq. (7.86) into (7.85), we obtain

$$E(s) = R(s)[1 - T(s)] \tag{7.87}$$

Using Eq. (3.73) for $T(s)$, we find

$$E(s) = R(s)[1 - \mathbf{C}(s\mathbf{I} - \mathbf{A})^{-1}\mathbf{B}] \qquad (7.88)$$

Applying the final value theorem, we have

$$\lim_{s \to 0} sE(s) = \lim_{s \to 0} sR(s)[1 - \mathbf{C}(s\mathbf{I} - \mathbf{A})^{-1}\mathbf{B}] \qquad (7.89)$$

Let us apply the result to an example.

EXAMPLE 7.13

Steady-state error using the final value theorem

Problem: Evaluate the steady-state error for the system described by Eqs. (7.90) for unit step and unit ramp inputs. Use the final value theorem.

$$\mathbf{A} = \begin{bmatrix} -5 & 1 & 0 \\ 0 & -2 & 1 \\ 20 & -10 & 1 \end{bmatrix}; \qquad \mathbf{B} = \begin{bmatrix} 0 \\ 0 \\ 1 \end{bmatrix}; \qquad \mathbf{C} = \begin{bmatrix} -1 & 1 & 0 \end{bmatrix} \qquad (7.90)$$

SOLUTION: Substituting Eqs. (7.90) into (7.89), we obtain

$$e(\infty) = \lim_{s \to 0} sR(s)\left(1 - \frac{s+4}{s^3 + 6s^2 + 13s + 20}\right)$$

$$= \lim_{s \to 0} sR(s)\left(\frac{s^3 + 6s^2 + 12s + 16}{s^3 + 6s^2 + 13s + 20}\right) \qquad (7.91)$$

For a unit step, $R(s) = 1/s$, and $e(\infty) = 4/5$. For a unit ramp, $R(s) = 1/s^2$, and $e(\infty) = \infty$. Notice that the system behaves like a Type 0 system.

TryIt 7.5

Use MATLAB, the Symbolic Math Toolbox, and the following statements to find the steady-state error for a step input to the system of Example 7.13.

```
syms s
A=[-5 1 0
    0 -2 1
    20 -10 1];
B=[0; 0; 1];
C=[-1 1 0];
I=[1 0 0
   0 1 0
   0 0 1];
E=(1/s)*[1 - C*...
   [(s*I - A)^-1]*B];
%New command:
%subs(X,old,new):
%Replace old in ...
%X(old) with new.
error=subs(s*E,s,0)
```

ANALYSIS VIA INPUT SUBSTITUTION

Another method for steady-state analysis avoids taking the inverse of $(s\mathbf{I} - \mathbf{A})$ and can be expanded to multiple-input, multiple-output systems; it substitutes the input along with an assumed solution into the state equations (*Hostetter, 1989*). We will derive the results for unit step and unit ramp inputs.

Step Inputs. Given the state Eqs. (7.84), if the input is a unit step where $r = 1$, a steady-state solution, $\mathbf{x}_{ss}$, for $\mathbf{x}$, is

$$\mathbf{x}_{ss} = \begin{bmatrix} V_1 \\ V_2 \\ \vdots \\ V_n \end{bmatrix} = \mathbf{V} \qquad (7.92)$$

where V_i is constant. Also,

$$\dot{\mathbf{x}}_{ss} = \mathbf{0} \tag{7.93}$$

Substituting $r = 1$, a unit step, along with Eqs. (7.92) and (7.93), into Eqs. (7.84) yields

$$\mathbf{0} = \mathbf{AV} + \mathbf{B} \tag{7.94a}$$

$$y_{ss} = \mathbf{CV} \tag{7.94b}$$

where y_{ss} is the steady state output. Solving for $\mathbf{V}$ yields

$$\mathbf{V} = -\mathbf{A}^{-1}\mathbf{B} \tag{7.95}$$

But the steady-state error is the difference between the steady-state input and the steady-state output. The final result for the steady-state error for a unit step input into a system represented in state space is

$$\boxed{e(\infty) = 1 - y_{ss} = 1 - \mathbf{CV} = 1 + \mathbf{CA}^{-1}\mathbf{B}} \tag{7.96}$$

Ramp Inputs. For unit ramp inputs, $r = t$, a steady-state solution for $\mathbf{x}$ is

$$\mathbf{x}_{ss} = \begin{bmatrix} V_1 t + W_1 \\ V_2 t + W_2 \\ \vdots \\ V_n t + W_n \end{bmatrix} = \mathbf{V}t + \mathbf{W} \tag{7.97}$$

where V_i and W_i are constants. Hence,

$$\dot{\mathbf{x}}_{ss} = \begin{bmatrix} V_1 \\ V_2 \\ \vdots \\ V_n \end{bmatrix} = \mathbf{V} \tag{7.98}$$

Substituting $r = t$ along with Eqs. (7.97) and (7.98) into Eqs. (7.84) yields

$$\mathbf{V} = \mathbf{A}(\mathbf{V}t + \mathbf{W}) + \mathbf{B}t \tag{7.99a}$$

$$y_{ss} = \mathbf{C}(\mathbf{V}t + \mathbf{W}) \tag{7.99b}$$

In order to balance Eq. (7.99a), we equate the matrix coefficients of t, $\mathbf{AV} = -\mathbf{B}$, or

$$\mathbf{V} = -\mathbf{A}^{-1}\mathbf{B} \tag{7.100}$$

Equating constant terms in Eq. (7.99a), we have $\mathbf{AW} = \mathbf{V}$, or

$$\mathbf{W} = \mathbf{A}^{-1}\mathbf{V} \tag{7.101}$$

Substituting Eqs. (7.100) and (7.101) into (7.99b) yields

$$y_{ss} = \mathbf{C}[-\mathbf{A}^{-1}\mathbf{B}t + \mathbf{A}^{-1}(-\mathbf{A}^{-1}\mathbf{B})] = -\mathbf{C}[\mathbf{A}^{-1}\mathbf{B}t + (\mathbf{A}^{-1})^2\mathbf{B}] \qquad (7.102)$$

The steady-state error is therefore

$$e(\infty) = \lim_{t\to\infty}(t - y_{ss}) = \lim_{t\to\infty}[(1 + \mathbf{C}\mathbf{A}^{-1}\mathbf{B})t + \mathbf{C}(\mathbf{A}^{-1})^2\mathbf{B}] \qquad (7.103)$$

Notice that in order to use this method, $\mathbf{A}^{-1}$ must exist. That is, det $\mathbf{A} \neq 0$.

We now demonstrate the use of Eqs. (7.96) and (7.103) to find the steady-state error for step and ramp inputs.

EXAMPLE 7.14

Steady-state error using input substitution

Problem: Evaluate the steady-state error for the system described by Eqs. (7.90) for unit step and unit ramp inputs. Use input substitution.

SOLUTION: For a unit step input, the steady-state error given by Eq. (7.96) is

$$e(\infty) = 1 + \mathbf{C}\mathbf{A}^{-1}\mathbf{B} = 1 - 0.2 = 0.8 \qquad (7.104)$$

where $\mathbf{C}$, $\mathbf{A}$, and $\mathbf{B}$ are as follows:

$$\mathbf{A} = \begin{bmatrix} -5 & 1 & 0 \\ 0 & -2 & 1 \\ 20 & -10 & 1 \end{bmatrix}; \quad \mathbf{B} = \begin{bmatrix} 0 \\ 0 \\ 1 \end{bmatrix}; \quad \mathbf{C} = \begin{bmatrix} -1 & 1 & 0 \end{bmatrix} \qquad (7.105)$$

For a ramp input, using Eq. (7.103), we have

$$e(\infty) = [\lim_{t\to\infty}[(1 + \mathbf{C}\mathbf{A}^{-1}\mathbf{B})]t + \mathbf{C}(\mathbf{A}^{-1})^2\mathbf{B}] = \lim_{t\to\infty}(0.8t + 0.08) = \infty \qquad (7.106)$$

SKILL-ASSESSMENT EXERCISE 7.7

Problem: Find the steady-state error for a step input given the system represented in state space below. Calculate the steady-state error using both the final value theorem and input substitution methods.

$$\mathbf{A} = \begin{bmatrix} 0 & 1 \\ -3 & -6 \end{bmatrix}; \quad \mathbf{B} = \begin{bmatrix} 0 \\ 1 \end{bmatrix}; \quad \mathbf{C} = \begin{bmatrix} 1 & 1 \end{bmatrix}$$

ANSWER:

$$e_{step}(\infty) = \frac{2}{3}$$

The complete solution is at www.wiley.com/college/nise.

In this chapter we covered the evaluation of steady-state error for systems represented by transfer functions as well as systems represented in state space. For systems represented in state space, two methods were presented: (1) final value theorem and (2) input substitution.

CASE STUDIES

Antenna Control: Steady-State Error Design via Gain

Design

This chapter showed how to find steady-state errors for step, ramp, and parabolic inputs to a closed-loop feedback control system. We also learned how to evaluate the gain to meet a steady-state error requirement. This ongoing case study uses our antenna azimuth position control system to summarize the concepts.

Problem: For the antenna azimuth position control system shown on the front endpapers, Configuration 1,

    a. Find the steady-state error in terms of gain, K, for step, ramp, and parabolic inputs.

    b. Find the value of gain, K, to yield a 10% error in the steady state.

SOLUTION:

    a. The simplified block diagram for the system is shown on the front endpapers. The steady-state error is given by

$$e(\infty) = \lim_{s \to 0} sE(s) = \lim_{s \to 0} \frac{sR(s)}{1 + G(s)} \tag{7.107}$$

From the block diagram, after pushing the potentiometer to the right past the summing junction, the equivalent forward transfer function is

$$G(s) = \frac{6.63K}{s(s + 1.71)(s + 100)} \tag{7.108}$$

        To find the steady-state error for a step input, use $R(s) = 1/s$ along with Eq. (7.108), and substitute these in Eq. (7.107). The result is $e(\infty) = 0$.
        To find the steady-state error for a ramp input, use $R(s) = 1/s^2$ along with Eq. (7.108), and substitute these in Eq. (7.107). The result is $e(\infty) = 25.79/K$.
        To find the steady-state error for a parabolic input, use $R(s) = 1/s^3$ along with Eq. (7.108), and substitute these in Eq. (7.107). The result is $e(\infty) = \infty$.

    b. Since the system is Type 1, a 10% error in the steady-state must refer to a ramp input. This is the only input that yields a finite, nonzero error. Hence, for a unit ramp input,

$$e(\infty) = 0.1 = \frac{1}{K_v} = \frac{(1.71)(100)}{6.63K} = \frac{25.79}{K} \tag{7.109}$$

from which $K = 257.9$. You should verify that the value of K is within the range of gains that ensures system stability. In the antenna control case study in the last chapter, the range of gain for stability was found to be $0 < K < 2623.29$. Hence, the system is stable for a gain of 257.9.

Challenge: You are now given a problem to test your knowledge of this chapter's objectives: Referring to the antenna azimuth position control system shown on the front endpapers, Configuration 2, do the following:

a. Find the steady-state errors in terms of gain, K, for step, ramp, and parabolic inputs.

b. Find the value of gain, K, to yield a 20% error in the steady state.

Video Laser Disc Recorder: Steady-State Error Design via Gain

As a second case study, let us look at a video laser disc focusing system for recording.

Problem: In order to record on a video laser disc, a 0.5μm laser spot must be focused on the recording medium to burn pits that represent the program material. The small laser spot requires that the focusing lens be positioned to an accuracy of $\pm0.1\mu$m. A model of the feedback control system for the focusing lens is shown in Figure 7.22.

The detector detects the distance between the focusing lens and the video disc by measuring the degree of focus as shown in Figure 7.23(a). Laser light reflected from the disc, D, is split by beam splitters B_1 and B_2 and focused behind aperture A. The remainder is reflected by the mirror and focuses in front of aperture A. The amount of light of each beam that passes through the aperture depends on how far the beam's focal point is from the aperture. Each side of the split photodiode, P, measures the intensity of each beam. Thus, as the disc's distance from the recording objective lens changes, so does the focal point of each beam. As a result, the relative voltage detected by each part of the split photodiode changes. When the beam is out of focus, one side of the photodiode outputs a larger voltage. When the beam is in focus, the voltage outputs from both sides of the photodiode are equal.

A simplified model for the detector is a straight line relating the differential voltage output from the two elements to the distance of the laser disc from nominal focus. A linearized plot of the detector input-output relationship is shown in Figure 7.23(b) (*Isailović, 1985*). Assume that a warp on the disc yields a worst-case disturbance in the focus of $10t^2\mu$m. Find the value of $K_1K_2K_3$ in order to meet the focusing accuracy required by the system.

SOLUTION: Since the system is Type 2, it can respond to parabolic inputs with finite error. We can assume that the disturbance has the same effect as an input of $10t^2\mu$m. The Laplace transform of $10t^2$ is $20/s^3$, or 20 units greater than the unit

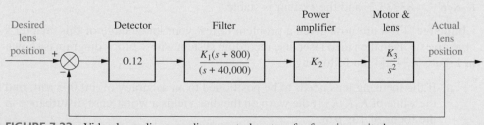

FIGURE 7.22   Video laser disc recording: control system for focusing write beam

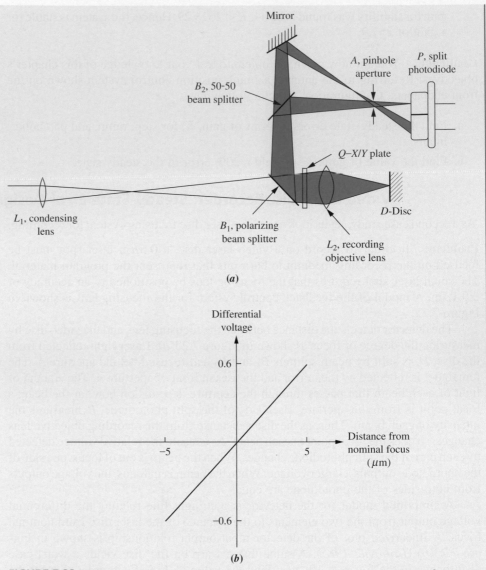

FIGURE 7.23 Video disc laser recording: **a.** focus detector optics; **b.** linearized transfer function for focus detector

acceleration used to derive the general equation of the error for a parabolic input. Thus, $e(\infty) = 20/K_a$. But $K_a = \lim\limits_{s \to 0} s^2 G(s)$.

From Figure 7.22, $K_a = 0.0024K_1K_2K_3$. Also, from the problem statement, the error must be no greater than 0.1μm. Hence, $e(\infty) = 8333.33/K_1K_2K_3 = 0.1$. Thus, $K_1K_2K_3 \geq 83333.3$, and the system is stable.

Challenge You are now given a problem to test your knowledge of this chapter's objectives: Given the video laser disc recording system whose block diagram is shown in Figure 7.24, do the following:

    a. If the focusing lens needs to be positioned to an accuracy of $\pm 0.005\ \mu$m, find the value of $K_1K_2K_3$ if the warp on the disc yields a worst-case disturbance in the focus of $15t^2\mu$m.

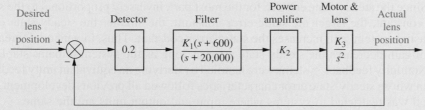

FIGURE 7.24 Video laser disc recording focusing system

b. Use the Routh-Hurwitz criterion to show that the system is stable when the conditions of (a) are met.

c. Use MATLAB to show that the system is stable when the conditions of (a) are met.

SUMMARY

This chapter covered the analysis and design of feedback control systems for steady-state errors. The steady-state errors studied resulted strictly from the system configuration. On the basis of a system configuration and a group of selected test signals, namely steps, ramps, and parabolas, we can analyze or design for the system's steady-state error performance. The greater the number of pure integrations a system has in the forward path, the higher the degree of accuracy, assuming the system is stable.

The steady-state errors depend upon the type of test input. Applying the final value theorem to stable systems, the steady-state error for unit step inputs is

$$e(\infty) = \frac{1}{1 + \lim_{s \to 0} G(s)} \tag{7.110}$$

The steady-state error for ramp inputs of unit velocity is

$$e(\infty) = \frac{1}{\lim_{s \to 0} sG(s)} \tag{7.111}$$

and for parabolic inputs of unit acceleration, it is

$$e(\infty) = \frac{1}{\lim_{s \to 0} s^2 G(s)} \tag{7.112}$$

The terms taken to the limit in Eqs. (7.110) through (7.112) are called *static error constants*. Beginning with Eq. (7.110), the terms in the denominator taken to the limit are called the *position constant, velocity constant,* and *acceleration constant,* respectively. The static error constants are the steady-state error specifications for control systems. By specifying a static error constant, one is stating the number of pure integrations in the forward path, the test signal used, and the expected steady-state error.

Another definition covered in this chapter was that of *system type*. The system type is the number of pure integrations in the forward path, assuming a unity feedback system. Increasing the system type decreases the steady-state error as long as the system remains stable.

Since the steady-state error is, for the most part, inversely proportional to the static error constant, the larger the static error constant, the smaller the steady-state error. Increasing system gain increases the static error constant. Thus, in general, increasing system gain decreases the steady-state error as long as the system remains stable.

Nonunity feedback systems were handled by deriving an equivalent unity feedback system whose steady-state error characteristics followed all previous development. The method was restricted to systems where input and output units are the same.

We also saw how feedback decreases a system's steady-state error caused by disturbances. With feedback, the effect of a disturbance can be reduced by system gain adjustments.

Finally, for systems represented in state space, we calculated the steady-state error using the final value theorem and input substitution methods.

In the next chapter we will examine the root locus, a powerful tool for the analysis and design of control systems.

REVIEW QUESTIONS

1. Name two sources of steady-state errors.
2. A position control, tracking with a constant difference in velocity, would yield how much position error in the steady state?
3. Name the test inputs used to evaluate steady-state error.
4. How many integrations in the forward path are required in order for there to be zero steady-state error for each of the test inputs listed in Question 3?
5. Increasing system gain has what effect upon the steady-state error?
6. For a step input the steady-state error is approximately the reciprocal of the static error constant if what condition holds true?
7. What is the exact relationship between the static error constants and the steady-state errors for ramp and parabolic inputs?
8. What information is contained in the specification $K_p = 10,000$?
9. Define *system type*.
10. The forward transfer function of a control system has three poles at -1, -2, and -3. What is the system type?
11. What effect does feedback have upon disturbances?
12. For a step input disturbance at the input to the plant, describe the effect of controller and plant gain upon minimizing the effect of the disturbance.
13. Is the forward-path actuating signal the system error if the system has nonunity feedback?
14. How are nonunity feedback systems analyzed and designed for steady-state errors?
15. Define, in words, *sensitivity* and describe the goal of feedback-control-system engineering as it applies to sensitivity.
16. Name two methods for calculating the steady-state error for systems represented in state space.

PROBLEMS

1. For the unity feedback system shown in Figure P7.1, where

$$G(s) = \frac{450(s+8)(s+12)(s+15)}{s(s+38)(s^2+2s+28)}$$

find the steady-state errors for the following test inputs: $25u(t)$, $37tu(t)$, $47t^2u(t)$. [Section: 7.2]

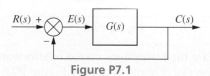

Figure P7.1

2. Figure P7.2 shows the ramp input $r(t)$ and the output $c(t)$ of a system. Assuming the output's steady state can be approximated by a ramp, find [Section: 7.1]

   a. the steady-state error;

   b. the steady-state error if the input becomes $r(t) = tu(t)$.

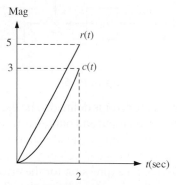

Figure P7.2

3. For the unity feedback system shown in Figure P7.1, where

$$G(s) = \frac{20(s+3)(s+4)(s+8)}{s^2(s+2)(s+15)}$$

find the steady-state error if the input is $30t^2u(t)$. [Section: 7.2]

4. For the system shown in Figure P7.3, what steady-state error can be expected for an input of $15u(t)$?

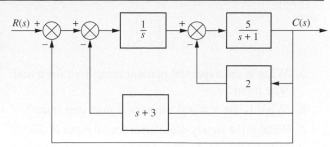

Figure P7.3

5. For the unity feedback system shown in Figure P7.1, where

$$G(s) = \frac{500}{(s+20)(s^2+4s+10)}$$

find the steady-state error for inputs of $40u(t)$, $70tu(t)$, and $80t^2u(t)$. [Section: 7.3]

6. An input of $t^3u(t)$ is applied to the input of a Type 3 unity feedback system, as shown in Figure P7.1, where

$$G(s) = \frac{30(s+1)(s+2)(s+3)}{s^3(s+5)(s+10)}$$

Find the steady-state error in position.

7. The steady-state error in velocity of a system is defined to be

$$\left.\left(\frac{dr}{dt} - \frac{dc}{dt}\right)\right|_{t\to\infty}$$

where r is the system input, and c is the system output. Find the steady-state error in velocity for an input of $t^3u(t)$ to a unity feedback system with a forward transfer function of [Section: 7.2]

$$G(s) = \frac{100(s+1)(s+2)}{s^2(s+3)(s+10)}$$

8. What is the steady-state error for a step input of 10 units applied to the unity feedback system of Figure P7.1, where

$$G(s) = \frac{(s+1)(s+2)(s+3)}{(s+6)(s+7)(s+8)}$$

9. For the unity feedback system shown in Figure P7.1, where

$$G(s) = \frac{1250}{s(s+50)}$$

   a. What is the expected percent overshoot for a unit step input?
   b. What is the settling time for a unit step input?
   c. What is the steady-state error for an input of $5u(t)$?
   d. What is the steady-state error for an input of $5tu(t)$?
   e. What is the steady-state error for an input of $5t^2u(t)$?

10. Given the unity feedback system shown in Figure P7.1, where

$$G(s) = \frac{100(s+2)(s+9)}{s(s+18)(s+\alpha)(s+10)}$$

   find the value of α to yield a $K_v = 1000$.

11. For the unity feedback system of Figure P7.1, where

$$G(s) = \frac{K(s+2)(s+4)(s+6)}{s^2(s+5)(s+7)}$$

   WileyPLUS

   Control Solutions

   find the value of K to yield a static error constant of 10,000. [Section: 7.4]

12. For the system shown in Figure P7.4

   a. Find K_p, K_v, and K_a.
   b. Find the steady-state error for an input of $50u(t)$, $50tu(t)$, and $50t^2u(t)$.
   c. State the system type.

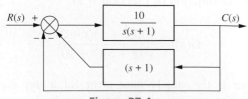

Figure P7.4

13. A Type 3 unity feedback system has $r(t) = t^3$ applied to its input. Find the steady-state position error for this input if the forward transfer function is [Section: 7.3]

$$G(s) = \frac{1000(s^2+4s+20)(s^2+20s+15)}{s^3(s+2)(s+10)}$$

14. Find the system type for the system of Figure P7.5.

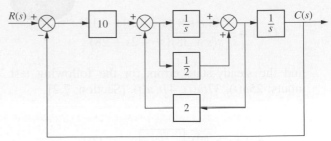

Figure P7.5

15. What are the restrictions on the feedforward transfer function $G_2(s)$ in the system of Figure P7.6 to obtain zero steady-state error for step inputs if: [Section: 7.3]

   a. $G_1(s)$ is a Type 0 transfer function;
   b. $G_1(s)$ is a Type 1 transfer function;
   c. $G_1(s)$ is a Type 2 transfer function?

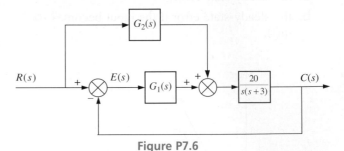

Figure P7.6

16. The steady-state error is defined to be the difference in position between input and output as time approaches infinity. Let us define a steady-state velocity error, which is the difference in velocity between input and output. Derive an expression for the error in velocity, $\dot{e}(\infty) = \dot{r}(\infty) - \dot{c}(\infty)$, and complete Table P7.1 for the error in velocity. [Sections: 7.2, 7.3]

TABLE P7.1

		Type		
		0	1	2
Input	Step			
	Ramp			
	Parabola			

17. For the system shown in Figure P7.7

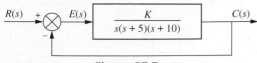

$$R(s) \xrightarrow{+} \bigotimes \xrightarrow{E(s)} \boxed{\frac{K}{s(s+5)(s+10)}} \xrightarrow{C(s)}$$

Figure P7.7

a. What value of K will yield a steady-state error in position of 0.01 for an input of $(1/10)t$?

b. What is the K_v for the value of K found in (a)?

c. What is the minimum possible steady-state position error for the input given in (a)?

18. Given the unity feedback system of Figure P7.1, where

$$G(s) = \frac{K(s+a)}{s(s+1)(s+10)}$$

find the value of Ka so that a ramp input of slope 15 will yield an error of 0.003 in the steady state when compared to the output. [Section: 7.4]

19. Given the system of Figure P7.8, design the value of K so that for an input of $100tu(t)$, there will be a 0.01 error in the steady state. [Section: 7.4]

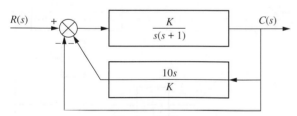

Figure P7.8

20. Find the value of K for the unity feedback system shown in Figure P7.1, where

$$G(s) = \frac{K(s+2)}{s^2(s+4)}$$

if the input is $10t^2u(t)$, and the desired steady-state error is 0.01 for this input. [Section: 7.4]

21. The unity feedback system of Figure P7.1, where

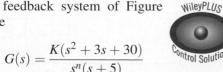

$$G(s) = \frac{K(s^2+3s+30)}{s^n(s+5)}$$

is to have $1/6000$ error between an input of $10tu(t)$ and the output in the steady state. [Section: 7.4]

a. Find K and n to meet the specification.

b. What are K_p, K_v, and K_a?

22. For the unity feedback system of Figure P7.1, where [Section: 7.3]

$$G(s) = \frac{K(s^2+2s+5)}{(s+2)^2(s+3)}$$

a. Find the system type.

b. What error can be expected for an input of $10u(t)$?

c. What error can be expected for an input of $10tu(t)$?

23. For the unity feedback system of Figure P7.1, where

$$G(s) = \frac{K(s+10)(s+15)}{s(s+3)(s+7)(s+20)}$$

find the value of K to yield a steady-state error of 0.1 for a ramp input of $25tu(t)$. [Section: 7.4]

24. Given the unity feedback system of Figure P7.1, where

$$G(s) = \frac{K(s+4)}{(s+1)(s^2+10s+26)}$$

find the value of K to yield a steady-state error of 5%. [Section: 7.4]

25. For the unity feedback system of Figure P7.1, where

$$G(s) = \frac{K}{s(s+4)(s+8)}$$

find the minimum possible steady-state position error if a unit ramp is applied. What places the constraint upon the error?

26. The unity feedback system of Figure P7.1, where

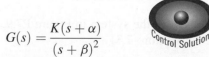

$$G(s) = \frac{K(s+\alpha)}{(s+\beta)^2}$$

is to be designed to meet the following specifications: steady-state error for a unit step input $= 0.1$; damping ratio $= 0.5$; natural frequency $= \sqrt{10}$. Find K, α, and β. [Section: 7.4]

27. A second-order, unity feedback system is to follow a ramp input with the following specifications: the steady-state output position shall differ from the input position by 0.01 of the input velocity; the natural frequency of the closed-loop system shall be 10 rad/s. Find the following:

a. The system type

b. The exact expression for the forward-path transfer function

c. The closed-loop system's damping ratio

28. The unity feedback system of Figure P7.1, where

$$G(s) = \frac{K(s+\alpha)}{s(s+\beta)}$$

is to be designed to meet the following requirements: The steady-state position error for a unit ramp input equals $1/10$; the closed-loop poles will be located at $-1 \pm j1$. Find K, α, and β in order to meet the specifications. [Section: 7.4]

29. Given the unity feedback control system of Figure P7.1, where

$$G(s) = \frac{K}{s^n(s+a)}$$

find the values of n, K, and a in order to meet specifications of 10% overshoot and $K_v = 100$. [Section: 7.4]

30. Given the unity feedback control system of Figure P7.1, where

$$G(s) = \frac{K}{s(s+a)}$$

find the following: [Section: 7.4]

a. K and a to yield $K_v = 1000$ and a 20% overshoot

b. K and a to yield a 1% error in the steady state and a 10% overshoot

31. Given the system in Figure P7.9, find the following: [Section: 7.3]

a. The closed-loop transfer function

b. The system type

c. The steady-state error for an input of $5u(t)$

d. The steady-state error for an input of $5tu(t)$

e. Discuss the validity of your answers to Parts **c** and **d**.

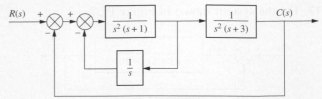

Figure P7.9

32. Repeat Problem 31 for the system shown in Figure P7.10. [Section: 7.3]

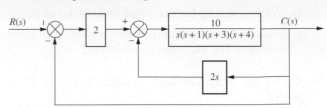

Figure P7.10

33. For the system shown in Figure P7.11, use MATLAB to find the following: [Section: 7.3]

MATLAB

a. The system type

b. K_p, K_v, and K_a

c. The steady-state error for inputs of $30u(t)$, $30tu(t)$, and $30t^2u(t)$

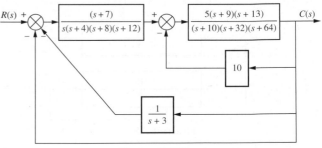

Figure P7.11

34. The system of Figure P7.12 is to have the following specifications: $K_v = 10$; $\zeta = 0.5$. Find the values of K_1 and K_f required for the specifications of the system to be met. [Section: 7.4]

WileyPLUS

Control Solutions

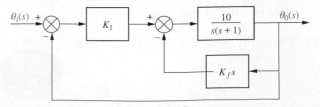

Figure P7.12

35. The transfer function from elevator deflection to altitude change in a Tower Trainer 60 Unmanned Aerial Vehicle is

$$P(s) = \frac{h(s)}{\delta(s)_e}$$

$$= \frac{-34.16s^3 - 144.4s^2 + 7047s + 557.2}{s^5 + 13.18s^4 + 95.93s^3 + 14.61s^2 + 31.94s}$$

An autopilot is built around the aircraft as shown in Figure P7.13, with $F(s) = H(s) = 1$ and

$$G(s) = \frac{0.00842(s + 7.895)(s^2 + 0.108s + 0.3393)}{(s + 0.07895)(s^2 + 4s + 8)}$$

(*Barkana, 2005*). The steady-state error for a ramp input in this system is $e_{ss} = 25$. Find the slope of the ramp input.

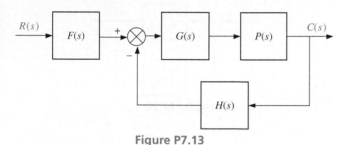

Figure P7.13

36. A block diagram representing the Ktesibios' water clock discussed in Section 1.2 is shown in Chapter 5, Problem 56, Figure P5.38(*b*) (*Lepschy, 1992*).

   a. Find the system's type.
   b. For $h_r(t) = u(t)$, find the steady-state value of $e(t) = h_r(t) - h_f(t)$.

37. Find the total steady-state error due to a unit step input and a unit step disturbance in the system of Figure P7.14. [Section: 7.5]

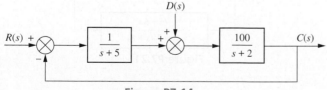

Figure P7.14

38. Design the values of K_1 and K_2 in the system of Figure P7.15 to meet the following specifications: Steady-state error component due to a unit step

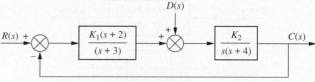

Figure P7.15

disturbance is -0.000012; steady-state error component due to a unit ramp input is 0.003. [Section: 7.5]

39. In Figure P7.16, let $G(s) = 5$ and $P(s) = \dfrac{7}{s+2}$.

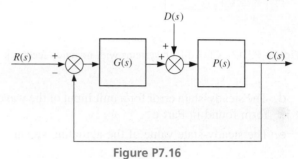

Figure P7.16

   a. Calculate the steady-state error due to a command input $R(s) = \dfrac{3}{s}$ with $D(s) = 0$. **Simulink**
   b. Verify the result of Part **a** using Simulink.
   c. Calculate the steady-state error due to a disturbance input $D(s) = -\dfrac{1}{s}$ with $R(s) = 0$. **Simulink**
   d. Verify the result of Part **c** using Simulink.
   e. Calculate the total steady-state error due to a command input $R(s) = \dfrac{3}{s}$ and a disturbance $D(s) = -\dfrac{1}{s}$ applied simultaneously. **Simulink**
   f. Verify the result of Part **e** using Simulink.

40. Derive Eq. (7.72) in the text, the final value of the actuating signal for nonunity feedback systems. [Section: 7.6]

41. For each of the systems shown in Figure P7.17, find the following: [Section: 7.6]

   a. The system type
   b. The appropriate static error constant
   c. The input waveform to yield a constant error

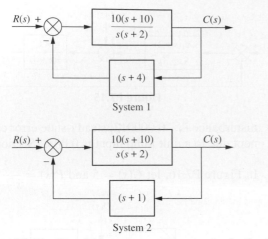

System 1

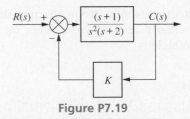

Figure P7.19

44. For the system shown in Figure P7.20, [Section: 7.6]

     a. What is the system type?

     b. What is the appropriate static error constant?

     c. What is the value of the appropriate static error constant?

     d. What is the steady-state error for a unit step input?

System 2

Figure P7.17   Closed-loop systems with nonunity feedback

     d. The steady-state error for a unit input of the wave-form found in Part **c**

     e. The steady-state value of the actuating signal

42. For each of the systems shown in Figure P7.18, find the appropriate static error constant as well as the steady-state error, $r(\infty) - c(\infty)$, for unit step, ramp, and parabolic inputs.

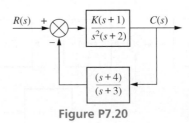

Figure P7.20

45. For the system shown in Figure P7.21, use MATLAB to find the following for $K = 10$, and $K = 10^6$: [Section: 7.6]

     a. The system type

     b. K_p, K_v, and K_a

     c. The steady-state error for inputs of $30u(t)$, $30tu(t)$, and $30t^2u(t)$

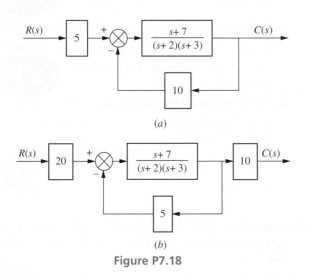

(a)

(b)

Figure P7.18

43. Given the system shown in Figure P7.19, find the following: [Section: 7.6]

     a. The system type

     b. The value of K to yield 0.1% error in the steady state

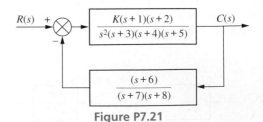

Figure P7.21

46. A dynamic voltage restorer (DVR) is a device that is connected in series to a power supply. It continuously monitors the voltage delivered to the load, and compensates voltage sags by applying the necessary extra voltage to maintain the load voltage constant.

In the model shown in Figure P7.22, u_r represents the desired reference voltage, u_o is the output voltage, and Z_L is the load impedance. All other parameters are internal to the DVR (*Lam, 2004*).

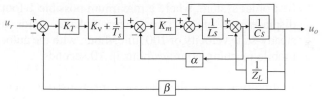

Figure P7.22 DVR Model

a. Assuming $Z_L = \dfrac{1}{sC_L}$, and $\beta \neq 1$, find the system's type.

b. Find the steady-state error to a unit step input as a function of β.

47. Given the system shown in Figure P7.23, do the following: [Section: 7.6]

a. Derive the expression for the error, $E(s) = R(s) - C(s)$, in terms of $R(s)$ and $D(s)$.

b. Derive the steady-state error, $e(\infty)$, if $R(s)$ and $D(s)$ are unit step functions.

c. Determine the attributes of $G_1(s)$, $G_2(s)$, and $H(s)$ necessary for the steady-state error to become zero.

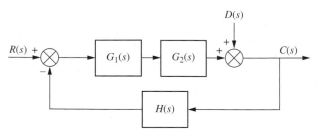

Figure P7.23 System with input and disturbance

48. Given the system shown in Figure P7.24, find the sensitivity of the steady-state error to parameter a.

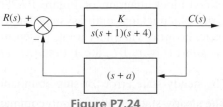

Figure P7.24

Assume a step input. Plot the sensitivity as a function of parameter a. [Section: 7.7]

49. a. Show that the sensitivity to plant changes in the system of Figure P7.13 is

$$S_{T:P} = \frac{P}{T}\frac{\delta T}{\delta P} = \frac{1}{1 + L(s)}$$

where $L(s) = G(s)P(s)H(s)$ and $T(s) = \dfrac{C(s)}{R(s)} = \dfrac{F(s)L(s)}{1 + R(s)}$.

b. Show that $S_{T:P}(s) + \dfrac{T(s)}{F(s)} = 1$ for all values of s.

50. In Figure P7.13, $P(s) = \dfrac{2}{s}$, $T(s) = \dfrac{C(s)}{R(s)} = \dfrac{14K}{(s+1)(s+2)(s^2+5s+14)}$, and $S_{T:P} = \dfrac{P}{T}\dfrac{\delta T}{\delta P} = \dfrac{s^2+5s}{s^2+5s+14}$.

a. Find $F(s)$ and $G(s)$.

b. Find the value of K that will result in zero steady-state error for a unit step input.

51. For the system shown in Figure P7.25, find the sensitivity of the steady-state error for changes in K_1 and in K_2, when $K_1 = 100$ and $K_2 = 0.1$. Assume step inputs for both the input and the disturbance. [Section: 7.7]

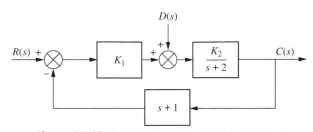

Figure P7.25 System with input and disturbance

52. Given the block diagram of the active suspension system shown in Figure P5.43 (*Lin, 1997*):

a. Find the transfer function from a road disturbance r to the error signal e.

b. Use the transfer function in Part **a** to find the steady-state value of e for a unit step road disturbance.

c. Use the transfer function in Part **a** to find the steady-state value of e for a unit ramp road disturbance.

d. From your results in Parts **b** and **c**, what is the system's type for e?

53. For each of the following closed-loop systems, find the steady-state error for unit step and unit ramp inputs. Use both the final value theorem and input substitution methods. [Section: 7.8]

a. $\dot{\mathbf{x}} = \begin{bmatrix} -5 & -4 & -2 \\ -3 & -10 & 0 \\ -1 & 1 & -5 \end{bmatrix} \mathbf{x} + \begin{bmatrix} 1 \\ 1 \\ 0 \end{bmatrix} r; \quad y = \begin{bmatrix} -1 & 2 & 1 \end{bmatrix} \mathbf{x}$

b. $\dot{\mathbf{x}} = \begin{bmatrix} 0 & 1 & 0 \\ -5 & -9 & 7 \\ -1 & 0 & 0 \end{bmatrix} \mathbf{x} + \begin{bmatrix} 0 \\ 0 \\ 1 \end{bmatrix} r; \quad y = \begin{bmatrix} 1 & 0 & 0 \end{bmatrix} \mathbf{x}$

c. $\dot{\mathbf{x}} = \begin{bmatrix} -9 & -5 & -1 \\ 1 & 0 & -2 \\ -3 & -2 & -5 \end{bmatrix} \mathbf{x} + \begin{bmatrix} 2 \\ 3 \\ 5 \end{bmatrix} r; \quad y = \begin{bmatrix} 1 & -2 & 4 \end{bmatrix} \mathbf{x}$

54. An automobile guidance system yields an actual output distance, $X(s)$, for a desired input distance, $X_e(s)$, as shown in Figure P7.26(a). Any difference, $X_e(s)$, between the commanded distance and the actual distance is converted into a velocity command, $V_c(s)$, by the controller and applied to the vehicle accelerator. The vehicle responds to the velocity command with a velocity, $V(s)$, and a displacement, $X(s)$, is realized. The velocity control, $G_2(s)$, is itself a closed-loop system, as shown in Figure P7.26(b). Here the difference, $V_e(s)$, between the commanded velocity, $V_c(s)$,

and the actual vehicle velocity, $V(s)$, drives a motor that displaces the automobile's accelerator by $Y_c(s)$ (*Stefani, 1978*). Find the steady-state error for the velocity control loop if the motor and amplifier transfer function $G_3(s) = K/[s(s+1)]$. Assume $G_4(s)$ to be a first-order system, where a maximum possible 1-foot displacement of the accelerator linkage yields a steady-state velocity of 100 miles/hour, with the automobile reaching 60 miles/hour in 10 seconds.

55. A simplified block diagram of a meter used to measure oxygen concentration is shown in Figure P7.27. The meter uses the paramagnetic properties of a stream of oxygen. A small body is placed in a stream of oxygen whose concentration is $R(s)$, and it is subjected to a magnetic field. The torque on the body, $K_1R(s)$, due to the magnetic field is a function of the concentration of the oxygen. The displacement of the body, $\theta(s)$, is detected, and a voltage, $C(s)$, is developed proportional to the displacement. This voltage is used to develop an electrostatic field that places a torque, $K_3C(s)$, on the body opposite to that developed by the magnetic field. When the body comes to rest, the output voltage represents the strength of the magnetic torque, which in turn is related to the concentration of the oxygen (*Chesmond, 1982*). Find the steady-state error between the output voltage, representing oxygen concentration, and the input oxygen concentration. How would you reduce the error to zero?

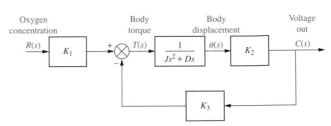

Figure P7.27 Block diagram of a paramagnetic oxygen analyzer

56. A space station, shown in Figure P7.28(a), will keep its solar arrays facing the Sun. If we assume that the simplified block diagram of Figure P7.28(b) represents the solar tracking control system that will be used to rotate the array via rotary joints called *solar alpha rotary joints* (Figure P7.28(c)). Find (*Kumar, 1992*)

a. The steady-state error for step commands

b. The steady-state error for ramp commands

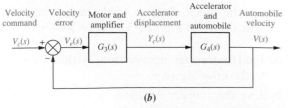

(b)

Figure P7.26 Automobile guidance system: **a.** displacement control system; **b.** velocity control loop

c. The steady-state error for parabolic commands

d. The range of K_c/J to make the system stable

Design Problems

57. The following specification applies to a position control: $K_v = 10$. On hand is an amplifier with a variable gain, K_2, with which to drive a motor. Two one-turn pots to convert shaft position into voltage are also available, where $\pm 3\pi$ volts are placed across the pots. A motor is available whose transfer function is

$$\frac{\theta_m(s)}{E_a(s)} = \frac{K}{s(s+\alpha)}$$

where $\theta_m(s)$ is the motor armature position and $E_a(s)$ is the armature voltage. The components are interconnected as shown in Figure P7.29.

The transfer function of the motor is found experimentally as follows. The motor and load are driven separately by applying a large, short square wave (a unit impulse) to the armature. An oscillograph of the response shows that the motor reached 63% of its final output value 0.5 second after application of the impulse. Furthermore, with 10 volts dc applied to the armature, the constant output speed was 100 rad/s. Draw the completed block diagram of the system, specifying the transfer function of each component of the block diagram.

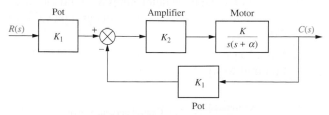

Figure P7.29 Position control system

58. A boat is circling a ship that is using a tracking radar. The speed of the boat is 20 knots, and it is circling the ship at a distance of 1 nautical mile, as shown in Figure P7.30(*a*). A simplified model of the tracking system is shown in Figure P7.30(*b*). Find the value of K so that the boat is kept in the center of the radar beam with no more than 0.1 degree error.

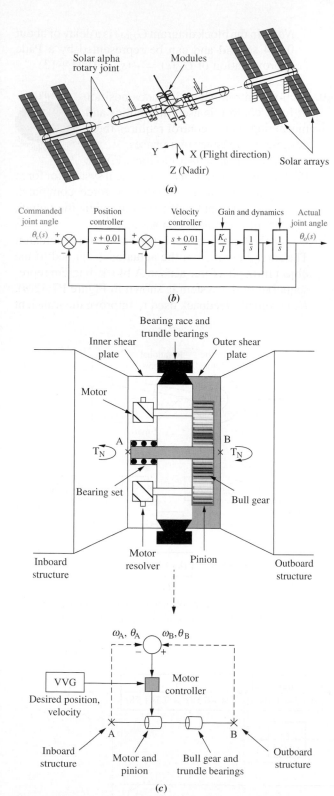

Figure P7.28 A space station: **a.** configuration (©1992 AIAA); **b.** simplified block diagram; **c.** alpha joint drive train and control system (©1992 AIAA)

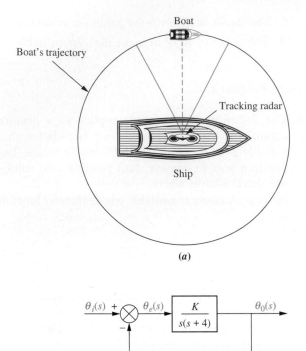

(a)

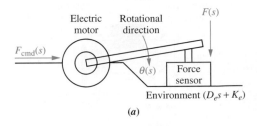

(b)

Figure P7.30   Boat tracked by ship's radar: **a.** physical arrangement; **b.** block diagram of tracking system

59. Figure P7.31 shows a simplified block diagram of a pilot in a loop to control the roll attitude of an Army UH-60A Black Hawk twin-engine helicopter with a single main rotor (*Hess, 1993*).

a. Find the system type.

b. The pilot's response determines K_1. Find the value of K_1 if an appropriate static error constant value of 700 is required.

c. Would a pilot whose K_1 is the value found in Part **b** be hired to fly the helicopter?

Note: In the block diagram $G_D(s)$ is a delay of about 0.154 second and can be represented by a Pade approximation of $G_D(s) = -(s-13)/(s+13)$.

60. Motion control, which includes position or force control, is used in robotics and machining. Force control requires the designer to consider two phases: contact and noncontact motions. Figure P7.32(*a*) is a diagram of a mechanical system for force control under contact motion. A force command, $F_{cmd}(s)$, is the input to the system, while the output, $F(s)$, is the controlled contact force.

In the figure a motor is used as the force actuator. The force output from the actuator is applied to the object through a force sensor. A block diagram representation of the system is shown in Figure P7.32(*b*). K_2 is velocity feedback used to improve the transient

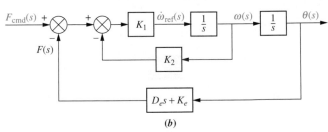

Figure P7.32   **a.** Force control mechanical loop under contact motion (©1996 IEEE); **b.** block diagram (©1996 IEEE)

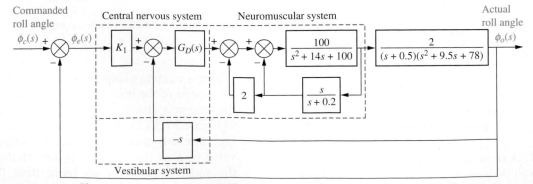

Figure P7.31   Simplified block diagram of a pilot in a loop (©1992 AIAA)

response. The loop is actually implemented by an electrical loop (not shown) that controls the armature current of the motor to yield the desired torque at the output. Recall that $T_m = K_t i_a$ (*Ohnishi, 1996*). Find an expression for the range of K_2 to keep the steady-state force error below 10% for ramp inputs of commanded force.

61. Problem 48 in Chapter 4 describes an open-loop swivel controller and plant for an industrial robot. The transfer function for the controller and plant is

$$G_e(s) = \frac{\omega_o(s)}{V_i(s)} = \frac{K}{(s+10)(s^2+4s+10)}$$

where $\omega_o(s)$ is the Laplace transform of the robot's angular swivel velocity and $V_i(s)$ is the input voltage to the controller. Assume $G_e(s)$ is the forward transfer function of a velocity control loop with an input transducer and sensor, each represented by a constant gain of 3 (*Schneider, 1992*).

a. Find the value of gain, K, to minimize the steady-state error between the input commanded angular swivel velocity and the output actual angular swivel velocity.

b. What is the steady-state error for the value of K found in Part **a**?

c. For what kind of input does the design in Part **a** apply?

62. Packet information flow in a router working under TCP/IP can be modeled using the linearized transfer function

$$P(s) = \frac{Q(s)}{p(s)} = \frac{\dfrac{C^2}{2N}e^{-sR}}{\left(s+\dfrac{2N}{R^2C}\right)\left(s+\dfrac{1}{R}\right)}$$

where

C = link capacity (packets/second).

N = load factor (number of TCP sessions)

Q = expected queue length

R = round trip time (second)

p = probability of a packet drop

The objective of an active queue management (AQM) algorithm is to automatically choose a packet-drop probability, p, so that the queue length is maintained at a desired level. This system can be represented by

the block diagram of Figure P7.13 with the plant model in the $P(s)$ block, the AQM algorithm in the $G(s)$ block, and $F(s) = H(s) = 1$. Several AQM algorithms are available, but one that has received special attention in the literature is the random early detection (RED) algorithm. This algorithm can be approximated with $G(s) = \dfrac{LK}{s+K}$, where L and K are constants (*Hollot, 2001*). Find the value of L required to obtain a 10% steady-state error for a unit step input when $C = 3750$ packets/s, $N = 50$ TCP sessions, $R = 0.1$ s, and $K = 0.005$.

63. In Figure P7.16, the plant, $P(s) = \dfrac{48,500}{s^2+2.89s}$, represents the dynamics of a robotic manipulator joint. The system's output, $C(s)$, is the joint's angular position (*Low, 2005*). The system is controlled in a closed-loop configuration as shown with $G(s) = K_P + \dfrac{K_I}{s}$, a proportional-plus-integral (PI) controller to be discussed in Chapter 9. $R(s)$ is the joint's desired angular position. $D(s)$ is an external disturbance, possibly caused by improper dynamics modeling, Coulomb friction, or other external forces acting on the joint.

a. Find the system's type.

b. Show that for a step disturbance input, $e_{ss} = 0$ when $K_I \neq 0$.

c. Find the value of K_I that will result in $e_{ss} = 5\%$ for a parabolic input.

d. Using the value of K_I found in Part **c**, find the range of K_P for closed-loop stability.

Progressive Analysis and Design Problems

64. **High-speed rail pantograph.** Problem 19 in Chapter 1 discusses the active control of a pantograph mechanism for high-speed rail systems. In Problem 72(*a*), Chapter 5, you found the block diagram for the active pantograph control system. Use your solution for Problem 72(*a*) in Chapter 5 to perform steady-state error analysis and design as follows (*O'Connor, 1997*):

a. Find the system type.

b. Find the value of controller gain, K, that minimizes the steady-state force error.

c. What is the minimum steady-state force error?

65. Control of HIV/AIDS. Consider the HIV infection model of Problem 64 in Chapter 6 and its block diagram in Figure P6.19 (*Craig, 2004*).

a. Find the system's type if $G(s)$ is a constant.

b. It was shown in Problem 64, Chapter 6 that when $G(s) = K$ the system will be stable when $K <$ 2.04×10^{-4}. What value of K will result in a unit step input steady-state error of 10%?

c. It is suggested that to reduce the steady state error the system's type should be augmented by making $G(s) = \dfrac{K}{s}$. Is this a wise choice? What is the resulting stability range for K?

CYBER EXPLORATION LABORATORY

Experiment 7.1

Objective To verify the effect of input waveform, loop gain, and system type upon steady-state errors.

Minimum Required Software Packages MATLAB, Simulink, and the Control System Toolbox

Prelab

1. What system types will yield zero steady-state error for step inputs?

2. What system types will yield zero steady-state error for ramp inputs?

3. What system types will yield infinite steady-state error for ramp inputs?

4. What system types will yield zero steady-state error for parabolic inputs?

5. What system types will yield infinite steady-state error for parabolic inputs?

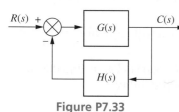

Figure P7.33

6. For the negative feedback system of Figure P7.33, where

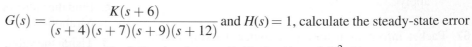

$$G(s) = \frac{K(s+6)}{(s+4)(s+7)(s+9)(s+12)} \text{ and } H(s) = 1, \text{ calculate the steady-state error}$$

in terms of K for the following inputs: $5u(t)$, $5tu(t)$, and $5t^2u(t)$.

7. Repeat Prelab 6 for $G(s) = \dfrac{K(s+6)(s+8)}{s(s+4)(s+7)(s+9)(s+12)}$ and $H(s) = 1$.

8. Repeat Prelab 6 for $G(s) = \dfrac{K(s+1)(s+6)(s+8)}{s^2(s+4)(s+7)(s+9)(s+12)}$ and $H(s) = 1$.

Lab

1. Using Simulink, set up the negative feedback system of Prelab 6. Plot on one graph the error signal of the system for an input of $5u(t)$ and $K = 50, 500, 1000,$ and 5000. Repeat for inputs of $5tu(t)$ and $5t^2u(t)$.

2. Using Simulink, set up the negative feedback system of Prelab 7. Plot on one graph the error signal of the system for an input of $5u(t)$ and $K = 50, 500, 1000,$ and 5000. Repeat for inputs of $5tu(t)$ and $5t^2u(t)$.

3. Using Simulink, set up the negative feedback system of Prelab 8. Plot on one graph the error signal of the system for an input of $5u(t)$ and $K = 200, 400, 800,$ and 1000. Repeat for inputs of $5tu(t)$ and $5t^2u(t)$.

Postlab

1. Use your plots from Lab 1 and compare the expected steady-state errors to those calculated in the Prelab. Explain the reasons for any discrepancies.

2. Use your plots from Lab 2 and compare the expected steady-state errors to those calculated in the Prelab. Explain the reasons for any discrepancies.

3. Use your plots from Lab 3 and compare the expected steady-state errors to those calculated in the Prelab. Explain the reasons for any discrepancies.

BIBLIOGRAPHY

Barkana, I. Classical and Simple Adaptive Control of Nonminimum Phase Autopilot Design. *Journal of Guidance, Control, and Dynamics*, vol. 28, 2005, pp. 631–638.

Chesmond, C. J. *Control System Technology.* E. Arnold, London,1982.

Craig, I. K., Xia, X., and Venter, J. W. Introducing HIV/AIDS Education into the Electrical Engineering Curriculum at the University of Pretoria. *IEEE Transactions on Education*, vol. 47, no. 1, February 2004, pp. 65–73.

D'Azzo, J. J., and Houpis, C. H. *Feedback Control System Analysis and Design Conventional and Modern*, 3d ed. McGraw-Hill, New York, 1988.

Hess, R. A., Malsbury, T., and Atencio, A., Jr. Flight Simulator Fidelity Assessment in a Rotorcraft Lateral Translation Maneuver. *Journal of Guidance, Control, and Dynamics*, vol. 16, no. 1, January–February 1993, pp. 79–85.

Hollot, C. V., Misra, V., Towsley, D., and Gong, W. A Control Theoretic Analysis of RED. *Proceedings of IEEE INFOCOM*, 2001, pp. 1510–1519.

Hostetter, G. H., Savant, C. J., Jr., and Stefani, R. T. *Design of Feedback Control Systems*, 2d ed. Saunders College Publishing, New York, 1989.

Isailović, J. *Videodisc and Optical Memory Systems*. Prentice Hall, Englewood Cliffs, NJ, 1985.

Kumar, R. R., Cooper, P. A., and Lim, T. W. Sensitivity of Space Station Alpha Joint Robust Controller to Structural Modal Parameter Variations. *Journal of Guidance, Control, and Dynamics*, vol. 15, no. 6, November–December 1992, pp. 1427–1433.

Lam, C. S., Wong, M. C., and Han, Y. D. Stability Study on Dynamic Voltage Restorer (DVR). *Power Electronics Systems and Applications, 2004; Proceedings First International Conference on Power Electronics*, 2004, pp. 66–71.

Lepschy, A. M., Mian, G. A., and Viaro, U. Feedback Control in Ancient Water and Mechanical Clocks. *IEEE Transactions on Education*, vol. 35, 1992, pp. 3–10.

Lin, J.-S., and Kanellakopoulos, I. Nonlinear Design of Active Suspensions. *IEEE Control Systems*, vol. 17, issue 3, June 1997, pp. 45–59.

Low, K. H., Wang, H., Liew, K. M., and Cai, Y. Modeling and Motion Control of Robotic Hand for Telemanipulation Application. *International Journal of Software Engineering and Knowledge Engineering*, vol. 15, 2005, pp. 147–152.

O'Connor, D. N., Eppinger, S. D., Seering, W. P., and Wormly, D. N. Active Control of a High-Speed Pantograph. *Journal of Dynamic Systems, Measurements, and Control*, vol. 119, March 1997, pp. 1–4.

Ohnishi, K., Shibata, M., and Murakami, T. Motion Control for Advanced Mechatronics. *IEEE/ASME Transactions on Mechatronics*, vol. 1, no. 1, March 1996, pp. 56–67.

Schneider, R. T. Pneumatic Robots Continue to Improve. *Hydraulics & Pneumatics*, October 1992, pp. 38–39.

Stefani, R. T. Design and Simulation of an Automobile Guidance and Control System. *Transactions, Computers in Education Division of ASEE*, January 1978, pp. 1–9.

A GRAPHICAL TOOL

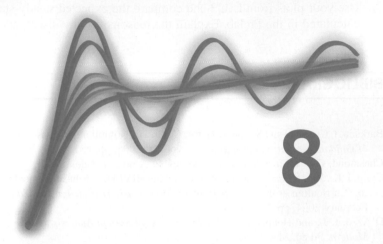

8

CHAPTER OBJECTIVES

In this chapter you will learn the following:

- The definition of a root locus
- How to sketch a root locus
- How to refine your sketch of a root locus
- How to use the root locus to find the poles of a closed-loop system
- How to use the root locus to describe qualitatively the changes in transient response and stability of a system as a system parameter is varied
- How to use the root locus to design a parameter value to meet a transient response specification for systems of order 2 and higher

CASE STUDY OBJECTIVES

You will be able to demonstrate your knowledge of the chapter objectives with case studies as follows:

- Given the antenna azimuth position control system shown on the front endpapers, you will be able to find the preamplifier gain to meet a transient response specification.
- Given the pitch or heading control system for the Unmanned Free-Swimming Submersible vehicle shown on the back endpapers, you will be able to plot the root locus and design the gain to meet a transient response specification. You will then be able to evaluate other performance characteristics.

8.1 INTRODUCTION

Root locus, a graphical presentation of the closed-loop poles as a system parameter is varied, is a powerful method of analysis and design for stability and transient response (*Evans, 1948; 1950*). Feedback control systems are difficult to comprehend from a qualitative point of view, and hence they rely heavily upon mathematics. The root locus covered in this chapter is a graphical technique that gives us the qualitative description of a control system's performance that we are looking for and also serves as a powerful quantitative tool that yields more information than the methods already discussed.

Up to this point, gains and other system parameters were designed to yield a desired transient response for only first- and second-order systems. Even though the root locus can be used to solve the same kind of problem, its real power lies in its ability to provide solutions for systems of order higher than 2. For example, under the right conditions, a fourth-order system's parameters can be designed to yield a given percent overshoot and settling time using the concepts learned in Chapter 4.

The root locus can be used to describe qualitatively the performance of a system as various parameters are changed. For example, the effect of varying gain upon percent overshoot, settling time, and peak time can be vividly displayed. The qualitative description can then be verified with quantitative analysis.

Besides transient response, the root locus also gives a graphical representation of a system's stability. We can clearly see ranges of stability, ranges of instability, and the conditions that cause a system to break into oscillation.

Before presenting root locus, let us review two concepts that we need for the ensuing discussion: (1) the control system problem and (2) complex numbers and their representation as vectors.

THE CONTROL SYSTEM PROBLEM

We have previously encountered the control system problem in Chapter 6: Whereas the poles of the open-loop transfer function are easily found (typically, they are known by inspection and do not change with changes in system gain), the poles of the closed-loop transfer function are more difficult to find (typically, they cannot be found without factoring the closed-loop system's characteristic polynomial, the denominator of the closed-loop transfer function), and further, the closed-loop poles change with changes in system gain.

A typical closed-loop feedback control system is shown in Figure 8.1(a). The open-loop transfer function was defined in Chapter 5 as $KG(s)H(s)$. Ordinarily, we can determine the poles of $KG(s)H(s)$, since these poles arise from simple cascaded first- or second-order subsystems. Further, variations in K do not affect the location of any pole of this function. On the other hand, we cannot determine the poles of $T(s) = KG(s)/[1 + KG(s)H(s)]$ unless we factor the denominator. Also, the poles of $T(s)$ change with K.

Let us demonstrate. Letting

$$G(s) = \frac{N_G(s)}{D_G(s)} \tag{8.1}$$

and

$$H(s) = \frac{N_H(s)}{D_H(s)} \tag{8.2}$$

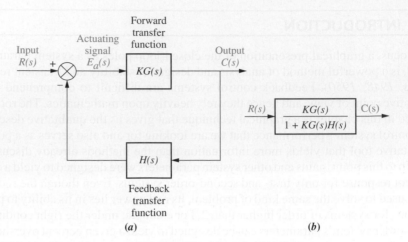

FIGURE 8.1 **a.** Closed-loop system; **b.** equivalent transfer function

then

$$T(s) = \frac{KN_G(s)D_H(s)}{D_G(s)D_H(s) + KN_G(s)N_H(s)} \qquad (8.3)$$

where N and D are factored polynomials and signify numerator and denominator terms, respectively. We observe the following: Typically, we know the factors of the numerators and denominators of $G(s)$ and $H(s)$. Also, the zeros of $T(s)$ consist of the zeros of $G(s)$ and the poles of $H(s)$. The poles of $T(s)$ are not immediately known and in fact can change with K. For example, if $G(s) = (s + 1)/[s(s + 2)]$ and $H(s) = (s + 3)/(s + 4)$, the poles of $KG(s)H(s)$ are 0, -2, and -4. The zeros of $KG(s)H(s)$ are -1 and -3. Now $T(s) = K(s + 1)(s + 4)/[s^3 + (6 + K)s^2 + (8 + 4K)s + 3K]$. Thus, the zeros of $T(s)$ consist of the zeros of $G(s)$ and the poles of $H(s)$. The poles of $T(s)$ are not immediately known without factoring the denominator, and they are a function of K. Since the system's transient response and stability are dependent upon the poles of $T(s)$, we have no knowledge of the system's performance unless we factor the denominator for specific values of K. The root locus will be used to give us a vivid picture of the poles of $T(s)$ as K varies.

VECTOR REPRESENTATION OF COMPLEX NUMBERS

Any *complex number,* $\sigma + j\omega$, described in Cartesian coordinates can be graphically represented by a vector, as shown in Figure 8.2(*a*). The complex number also can be described in polar form with magnitude M and angle θ, as $M\angle\theta$. If the complex number is substituted into a complex function, $F(s)$, another complex number will result. For example, if $F(s) = (s + a)$, then substituting the complex number $s = \sigma + j\omega$ yields $F(s) = (\sigma + a) + j\omega$, another complex number. This number is shown in Figure 8.2(*b*). Notice that $F(s)$ has a zero at $-a$. If we translate the vector a units to the left, as in Figure 8.2(*c*), we have an alternate representation of the complex number that originates at the zero of $F(s)$ and terminates on the point $s = \sigma + j\omega$.

We conclude that $(s + a)$ *is a complex number and can be represented by a vector drawn from the zero of the function to the point s.* For example, $(s + 7)|_{s \to 5+j2}$ is a complex number drawn from the zero of the function, -7, to the point s, which is $5 + j2$, as shown in Figure 8.2(*d*).

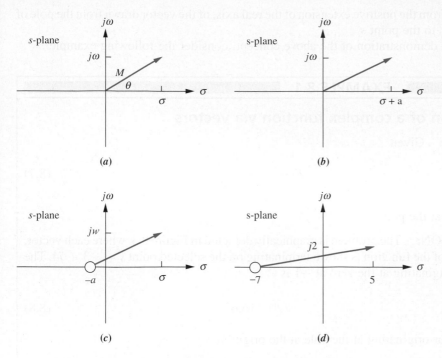

(a)

(b)

FIGURE 8.2 Vector representation of complex numbers: **a.** $s = \sigma + j\omega$; **b.** $(s + a)$; **c.** alternate representation of $(s + a)$; **d.** $(s + 7)_{s \circledast 5+j2}$

Now let us apply the concepts to a complicated function. Assume a function

$$F(s) = \frac{\prod_{i=1}^{m} (s + z_i)}{\prod_{j=1}^{n} (s + p_j)} = \frac{\prod \text{numerator's complex factors}}{\prod \text{denominator's complex factors}} \quad (8.4)$$

where the symbol $\prod$ means "product," $m = $ number of zeros, and $n = $ number of poles. Each factor in the numerator and each factor in the denominator is a complex number that can be represented as a vector. The function defines the complex arithmetic to be performed in order to evaluate $F(s)$ at any point, s. Since each complex factor can be thought of as a vector, the magnitude, M, of $F(s)$ at any point, s, is

$$M = \frac{\prod \text{zero lengths}}{\prod \text{pole lengths}} = \frac{\prod_{i=1}^{m} |(s + z_i)|}{\prod_{j=1}^{n} |(s + p_j)|} \quad (8.5)$$

where a zero length, $|(s + z_i)|$, is the magnitude of the vector drawn from the zero of $F(s)$ at $-z_i$ to the point s, and a pole length, $|(s + p_j)|$, is the magnitude of the vector drawn from the pole of $F(s)$ at $-p_j$ to the point s. The angle, θ, of $F(s)$ at any point, s, is

$$\theta = \Sigma \text{ zero angles} - \Sigma \text{ pole angles}$$
$$= \sum_{i=1}^{m} \angle(s + z_i) - \sum_{j=1}^{n} \angle(s + p_j) \quad (8.6)$$

where a zero angle is the angle, measured from the positive extension of the real axis, of a vector drawn from the zero of $F(s)$ at $-z_i$ to the point s, and a pole angle is the angle, measured from the positive extension of the real axis, of the vector drawn from the pole of $F(s)$ at $-p_j$ to the point s.

As a demonstration of the above concept, consider the following example.

▊ EXAMPLE 8.1 ▊

Evaluation of a complex function via vectors

Problem: Given

$$F(s) = \frac{(s+1)}{s(s+2)} \tag{8.7}$$

find $F(s)$ at the point $s = -3 + j4$.

SOLUTION: The problem is graphically depicted in Figure 8.3, where each vector, $(s + \alpha)$, of the function is shown terminating on the selected point $s = -3 + j4$. The vector originating at the zero at -1 is

$$\sqrt{20}\angle 116.6° \tag{8.8}$$

The vector originating at the pole at the origin is

$$5\angle 126.9° \tag{8.9}$$

The vector originating at the pole at -2 is

$$\sqrt{17}\angle 104.0° \tag{8.10}$$

Substituting Eqs. (8.8) through (8.10) into Eqs. (8.5) and (8.6) yields

$$M\angle\theta = \frac{\sqrt{20}}{5\sqrt{17}}\angle 116.6° - 126.9° - 104.0° = 0.217\angle - 114.3° \tag{8.11}$$

as the result for evaluating $F(s)$ at the point $-3 + j4$.

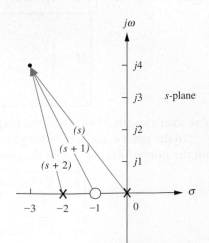

FIGURE 8.3   Vector representation of Eq. (8.7)

SKILL-ASSESSMENT EXERCISE 8.1

Problem: Given

$$F(s) = \frac{(s+2)(s+4)}{s(s+3)(s+6)}$$

find $F(s)$ at the point $s = -7 + j9$ the following ways:

a. Directly substituting the point into $F(s)$

b. Calculating the result using vectors

ANSWER:

$$-0.0339 - j0.0899 = 0.096\angle - 110.7°$$

The complete solution is at www.wiley.com/college/nise.

TryIt 8.1

Use the following MATLAB statements to solve the problem given in Skill-Assessment Exercise 8.1.

```
s=-7+9j;
G=(s+2)*(s+4)/...
    (s*(s+3)*(s+6));
Theta=(180/pi)*...
    angle(G)
M=abs(G)
```

We are now ready to begin our discussion of the root locus.

8.2 DEFINING THE ROOT LOCUS

A video camera system similar to that shown in Figure 8.4(*a*) can automatically follow a subject. The tracking system consists of a dual sensor and a transmitter, where one

(*a*)

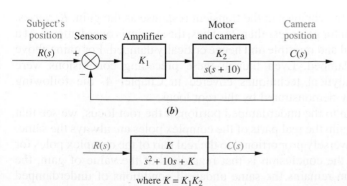

(*b*)

(*c*)

FIGURE 8.4   a. The CameraMan® Presenter Camera System automatically follows a subject who wears infrared sensors on the front and back (the front sensor is also a microphone); tracking commands and audio are relayed to CameraMan via a radio frequency link from a unit worn by the subject; **b.** block diagram; **c.** closed-loop transfer function

TABLE 8.1 Pole location as function of gain for the system of Figure 8.4

K	Pole 1	Pole 2
0	-10	0
5	-9.47	-0.53
10	-8.87	-1.13
15	-8.16	-1.84
20	-7.24	-2.76
25	-5	-5
30	$-5 + j2.24$	$-5 - j2.24$
35	$-5 + j3.16$	$-5 - j3.16$
40	$-5 + j3.87$	$-5 - j3.87$
45	$-5 + j4.47$	$-5 - j4.47$
50	$-5 + j5$	$-5 - j5$

component is mounted on the camera, and the other worn by the subject. An imbalance between the outputs of the two sensors receiving energy from the transmitter causes the system to rotate the camera to balance out the difference and seek the source of energy.

The root locus technique can be used to analyze and design the effect of loop gain upon the system's transient response and stability. Assume the block diagram representation of a tracking system as shown in Figure 8.4(b), where the closed-loop poles of the system change location as the gain, K, is varied. Table 8.1, which was formed by applying the quadratic formula to the denominator of the transfer function in Figure 8.4(c), shows the variation of pole location for different values of gain, K. The data of Table 8.1 is graphically displayed in Figure 8.5(a), which shows each pole and its gain.

As the gain, K, increases in Table 8.1 and Figure 8.5(a), the closed-loop pole, which is at -10 for $K = 0$, moves toward the right, and the closed-loop pole, which is at 0 for $K = 0$, moves toward the left. They meet at -5, break away from the real axis, and move into the complex plane. One closed-loop pole moves upward while the other moves downward. We cannot tell which pole moves up or which moves down. In Figure 8.5(b) the individual closed-loop pole locations are removed and their paths are represented with solid lines. It is this *representation of the paths of the closed-loop poles as the gain is varied* that we call a *root locus*. For most of our work, the discussion will be limited to positive gain, or $K \geq 0$.

The root locus shows the changes in the transient response as the gain, K, varies. First of all, the poles are real for gains less than 25. Thus, the system is overdamped. At a gain of 25, the poles are real and multiple and hence critically damped. For gains above 25, the system is underdamped. Even though these preceding conclusions were available through the analytical techniques covered in Chapter 4, the following conclusions are graphically demonstrated by the root locus.

Directing our attention to the underdamped portion of the root locus, we see that regardless of the value of gain, the real parts of the complex poles are always the same. Since the settling time is inversely proportional to the real part of the complex poles for this second-order system, the conclusion is that regardless of the value of gain, the settling time for the system remains the same under all conditions of underdamped responses.

FIGURE 8.5 a. Pole plot from
Table 8.1; **b.** root locus

(a)

(b)

Also, as we increase the gain, the damping ratio diminishes, and the percent overshoot increases. The damped frequency of oscillation, which is equal to the imaginary part of the pole, also increases with an increase in gain, resulting in a reduction of the peak time. Finally, since the root locus never crosses over into the right half-plane, the system is always stable, regardless of the value of gain, and can never break into a sinusoidal oscillation.

These conclusions for such a simple system may appear to be trivial. What we are about to see is that the analysis is applicable to systems of order higher than 2. For these systems, it is difficult to tie transient response characteristics to the pole location. The root locus will allow us to make that association and will become an important technique in the analysis and design of higher-order systems.

8.3 PROPERTIES OF THE ROOT LOCUS

In Section 8.2 we arrived at the root locus by factoring the second-order polynomial in the denominator of the transfer function. Consider what would happen if that polynomial were of fifth or tenth order. Without a computer, factoring the polynomial would be quite a problem for numerous values of gain.

We are about to examine the properties of the root locus. From these properties we will be able to make a rapid *sketch* of the root locus for higher-order systems without having to factor the denominator of the closed-loop transfer function.

The properties of the root locus can be derived from the general control system of Figure 8.1(*a*). The closed-loop transfer function for the system is

$$T(s) = \frac{KG(s)}{1 + KG(s)H(s)} \tag{8.12}$$

From Eq. (8.12), a pole, *s*, exists when the characteristic polynomial in the denominator becomes zero, or

$$KG(s)H(s) = -1 = 1\angle(2k+1)180° \quad k = 0, \pm 1, \pm 2, \pm 3, \ldots \tag{8.13}$$

where −1 is represented in polar form as $1\angle(2k+1)180°$. Alternately, a value of *s* is a closed-loop pole if

$$|KG(s)H(s)| = 1 \tag{8.14}$$

and

$$\angle KG(s)H(s) = (2k+1)180° \tag{8.15}$$

Equation (8.13) implies that if a value of *s* is substituted into the function $KG(s)H(s)$, a complex number results. If the angle of the complex number is an odd multiple of 180°, that value of *s* is a system pole for some particular value of *K*. What value of *K*? Since the angle criterion of Eq. (8.15) is satisfied, all that remains is to satisfy the magnitude criterion, Eq. (8.14). Thus,

$$K = \frac{1}{|G(s)||H(s)|} \tag{8.16}$$

We have just found that a pole of the closed-loop system causes the angle of $KG(s)H(s)$, or simply $G(s)H(s)$ since *K* is a scalar, to be an odd multiple of 180°. Furthermore, the magnitude of $KG(s)H(s)$ must be unity, implying that the value of *K* is the reciprocal of the magnitude of $G(s)H(s)$ when the pole value is substituted for *s*.

Let us demonstrate this relationship for the second-order system of Figure 8.4. The fact that closed-loop poles exist at −9.47 and −0.53 when the gain is 5 has already been established in Table 8.1. For this system,

$$KG(s)H(s) = \frac{K}{s(s+10)} \tag{8.17}$$

Substituting the pole at −9.47 for *s* and 5 for *K* yields $KG(s)H(s) = -1$. The student can repeat the exercise for other points in Table 8.1 and show that each case yields $KG(s)H(s) = -1$.

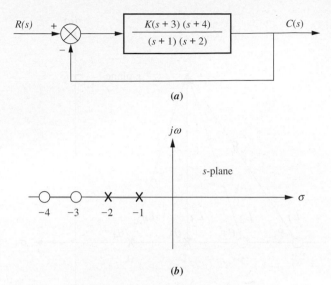

FIGURE 8.6 **a.** Example system; **b.** pole-zero plot of $G(s)$

It is helpful to visualize graphically the meaning of Eq. (8.15). Let us apply the complex number concepts reviewed in Section 8.1 to the root locus of the system shown in Figure 8.6. For this system the open-loop transfer function is

$$KG(s)H(s) = \frac{K(s+3)(s+4)}{(s+1)(s+2)} \tag{8.18}$$

The closed-loop transfer function, $T(s)$, is

$$T(s) = \frac{K(s+3)(s+4)}{(1+K)s^2 + (3+7K)s + (2+12K)} \tag{8.19}$$

If point s is a closed-loop system pole for some value of gain, K, then s must satisfy Eqs. (8.14) and (8.15).

Consider the point $-2 + j3$. If this point is a closed-loop pole for some value of gain, then the angles of the zeros minus the angles of the poles must equal an odd multiple of $180°$. From Figure 8.7,

$$\theta_1 + \theta_2 - \theta_3 - \theta_4 = 56.31° + 71.57° - 90° - 108.43° = -70.55° \tag{8.20}$$

Therefore, $-2 + j3$ is not a point on the root locus, or alternatively, $-2 + j3$ is not a closed-loop pole for any gain.

If these calculations are repeated for the point $-2 + j(\sqrt{2}/2)$, the angles do add up to $180°$. That is, $-2 + j(\sqrt{2}/2)$ is a point on the root locus for some value of gain. We now proceed to evaluate that value of gain.

From Eqs. (8.5) and (8.16),

$$K = \frac{1}{|G(s)H(s)|} = \frac{1}{M} = \frac{\prod \text{pole lengths}}{\prod \text{zero lengths}} \tag{8.21}$$

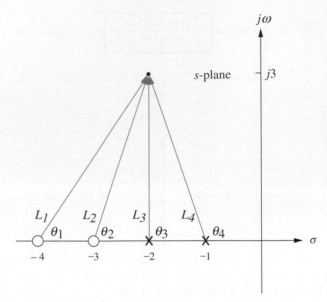

FIGURE 8.7 Vector representation of $G(s)$ from Figure 8.6(a) at $-2 + j3$

Looking at Figure 8.7 with the point $-2 + j3$ replaced by $-2 + j(\sqrt{2}/2)$, the gain, K, is calculated as

$$K = \frac{L_3 L_4}{L_1 L_2} = \frac{\frac{\sqrt{2}}{2}(1.22)}{(2.12)(1.22)} = 0.33 \tag{8.22}$$

Thus, the point $-2 + j(\sqrt{2}/2)$ is a point on the root locus for a gain of 0.33.

We summarize what we have found as follows: Given the poles and zeros of the open-loop transfer function, $KG(s)H(s)$, a point in the s-plane is on the root locus for a particular value of gain, K, if the angles of the zeros minus the angles of the poles, all drawn to the selected point on the s-plane, add up to $(2k + 1)180°$. Furthermore, gain K at that point for which the angles add up to $(2k + 1)180°$ is found by dividing the product of the pole lengths by the product of the zero lengths.

SKILL-ASSESSMENT EXERCISE 8.2

WileyPLUS

Control Solutions

TryIt 8.2

Use MATLAB and the following statements to solve Skill-Assessment Exercise 8.2.

```
s=-3+0j;
G=(s+2)/(s^2+4*s+13);
Theta=(180/pi)*...
    angle(G)
M=abs(G);
K=1/M
```

Problem: Given a unity feedback system that has the forward transfer function

$$G(s) = \frac{K(s + 2)}{(s^2 + 4s + 13)}$$

do the following:

a. Calculate the angle of $G(s)$ at the point $(-3 + j0)$ by finding the algebraic sum of angles of the vectors drawn from the zeros and poles of $G(s)$ to the given point.

b. Determine if the point specified in (a) is on the root locus.

c. If the point specified in (a) is on the root locus, find the gain, K, using the lengths of the vectors.

ANSWERS:

   a. Sum of angles $= 180°$

   b. Point is on the root locus

   c. $K = 10$

The complete solution is at www.wiley.com/college/nise.

8.4 SKETCHING THE ROOT LOCUS

It appears from our previous discussion that the root locus can be obtained by sweeping through every point in the *s*-plane to locate those points for which the angles, as previously described, add up to an odd multiple of $180°$. Although this task is tedious without the aid of a computer, the concept can be used to develop rules that can be used to *sketch* the root locus without the effort required to *plot* the locus. Once a sketch is obtained, it is possible to accurately plot just those points that are of interest to us for a particular problem.

The following five rules allow us to sketch the root locus using minimal calculations. The rules yield a sketch that gives intuitive insight into the behavior of a control system. In the next section we refine the sketch by finding actual points or angles on the root locus. These refinements, however, require some calculations or the use of computer programs such as MATLAB.

1. **Number of branches.** Each closed-loop pole moves as the gain is varied. If we define a *branch* as the path that one pole traverses, then there will be one branch for each closed-loop pole. Our first rule, then, defines the number of branches of the root locus:

   The number of branches of the root locus equals the number of closed-loop poles.

   As an example, look at Figure 8.5(*b*), where the two branches are shown. One originates at the origin, the other at -10.

2. **Symmetry.** If complex closed-loop poles do not exist in conjugate pairs, the resulting polynomial, formed by multiplying the factors containing the closed-loop poles, would have complex coefficients. Physically realizable systems cannot have complex coefficients in their transfer functions. Thus, we conclude:

   The root locus is symmetrical about the real axis.

   An example of symmetry about the real axis is shown in Figure 8.5(*b*).

3. **Real-axis segments.** Let us make use of the angle property, Eq. (8.15), of the points on the root locus to determine where the real-axis segments of the root locus exist. Figure 8.8 shows the poles and zeros of a general open-loop system. If an attempt is made to calculate the angular contribution of the poles and zeros at each point, P_1, P_2, P_3, and P_4, along the real axis, we observe the following: (1) At each point the angular contribution of a pair of open-loop complex poles or zeros is zero, and (2) the contribution of the open-loop poles and open-loop zeros to the left of the respective point is zero. The conclusion is that the only contribution to the angle at any of the points comes from the open-loop, real-axis poles and zeros that exist to the right of the respective point. If we calculate the angle at each point using only the

FIGURE 8.8 Poles and zeros of a general open-loop system with test points, P_i, on the real axis

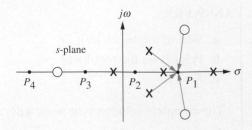

open-loop, real-axis poles and zeros to the right of each point, we note the following: (1) The angles on the real axis alternate between $0°$ and $180°$, and (2) the angle is $180°$ for regions of the real axis that exist to the left of an odd number of poles and/or zeros. The following rule summarizes the findings:

On the real axis, for K > 0 the root locus exists to the left of an odd number of real-axis, finite open-loop poles and/or finite open-loop zeros.

Examine Figure 8.6(*b*). According to the rule just developed, the real-axis segments of the root locus are between -1 and -2 and between -3 and -4 as shown in Figure 8.9.

4. **Starting and ending points.** Where does the root locus begin (zero gain) and end (infinite gain)? The answer to this question will enable us to expand the sketch of the root locus beyond the real-axis segments. Consider the closed-loop transfer function, $T(s)$, described by Eq. (8.3). $T(s)$ can now be evaluated for both large and small gains, K. As K approaches zero (small gain),

$$T(s) \approx \frac{KN_G(s)D_H(s)}{D_G(s)D_H(s) + \epsilon} \tag{8.23}$$

From Eq. (8.23) we see that the closed-loop system poles at small gains approach the combined poles of $G(s)$ and $H(s)$. We conclude that the root locus begins at the poles of $G(s)H(s)$, the open-loop transfer function.

At high gains, where K is approaching infinity,

$$T(s) \approx \frac{KN_G(s)D_H(s)}{\epsilon + KN_G(s)N_H(s)} \tag{8.24}$$

From Eq. (8.24) we see that the closed-loop system poles at large gains approach the combined zeros of $G(s)$ and $H(s)$. Now we conclude that the root locus ends at the zeros of $G(s)H(s)$, the open-loop transfer function.

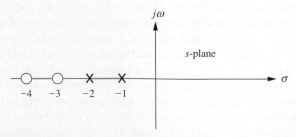

FIGURE 8.9 Real-axis segments of the root locus for the system of Figure 8.6

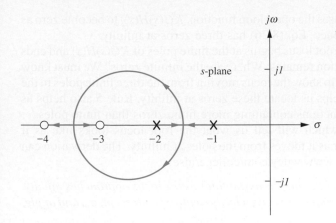

FIGURE 8.10 Complete root locus for the system of Figure 8.6

Summarizing what we have found:

> *The root locus begins at the finite and infinite poles of $G(s)H(s)$ and ends at the finite and infinite zeros of $G(s)H(s)$.*

Remember that these poles and zeros are the open-loop poles and zeros.

In order to demonstrate this rule, look at the system in Figure 8.6(*a*), whose real-axis segments have been sketched in Figure 8.9. Using the rule just derived, we find that the root locus begins at the poles at -1 and -2 and ends at the zeros at -3 and -4 (see Figure 8.10). Thus, the poles start out at -1 and -2 and move through the real-axis space between the two poles. They meet somewhere between the two poles and break out into the complex plane, moving as complex conjugates. The poles return to the real axis somewhere between the zeros at -3 and -4, where their path is completed as they move away from each other, and end up, respectively, at the two zeros of the open-loop system at -3 and -4.

5. **Behavior at infinity.** Consider applying Rule 4 to the following open-loop transfer function:

$$KG(s)H(s) = \frac{K}{s(s+1)(s+2)} \tag{8.25}$$

There are three finite poles, at $s = 0$, -1, and -2, and no finite zeros.

A function can also have *infinite* poles and zeros. If the function approaches infinity as s approaches infinity, then the function has a pole at infinity. If the function approaches zero as s approaches infinity, then the function has a zero at infinity. For example, the function $G(s) = s$ has a pole at infinity, since $G(s)$ approaches infinity as s approaches infinity. On the other hand, $G(s) = 1/s$ has a zero at infinity, since $G(s)$ approaches zero as s approaches infinity.

Every function of s has an equal number of poles and zeros if we include the infinite poles and zeros as well as the finite poles and zeros. In this example, Eq. (8.25) contains three finite poles and three infinite zeros. To illustrate, let s approach infinity. The open-loop transfer function becomes

$$KG(s)H(s) \approx \frac{K}{s^3} = \frac{K}{s \cdot s \cdot s} \tag{8.26}$$

Each s in the denominator causes the open-loop function, $KG(s)H(s)$, to become zero as that s approaches infinity. Hence, Eq. (8.26) has three zeros at infinity.

Thus, for Eq. (8.25), the root locus begins at the finite poles of $KG(s)H(s)$ and ends at the infinite zeros. The question remains: Where are the infinite zeros? We must know where these zeros are in order to show the locus moving from the three finite poles to the three infinite zeros. Rule 5 helps us locate these zeros at infinity. Rule 5 also helps us locate poles at infinity for functions containing more finite zeros than finite poles.[1]

We now state Rule 5, which will tell us what the root locus looks like as it approaches zeros at infinity or as it moves from the poles at infinity. The derivation can be found in Appendix L.1 at www.wiley.com/college/nise.

The root locus approaches straight lines as asymptotes as the locus approaches infinity. Further, the equation of the asymptotes is given by the real-axis intercept, σ_a, and angle, θ_a, as follows:

$$\sigma_a = \frac{\Sigma \text{ finite poles} - \Sigma \text{ finite zeros}}{\#\text{finite poles} - \#\text{finite zeros}} \tag{8.27}$$

$$\theta_a = \frac{(2k+1)\pi}{\#\text{finite poles} - \#\text{finite zeros}} \tag{8.28}$$

where $k = 0, \pm 1, \pm 2, \pm 3$ and the angle is given in radians with respect to the positive extension of the real axis.

Notice that the running index, k, in Eq. (8.28) yields a multiplicity of lines that account for the many branches of a root locus that approach infinity. Let us demonstrate the concepts with an example.

■ EXAMPLE 8.2 ■

Sketching a root locus with asymptotes

Problem: Sketch the root locus for the system shown in Figure 8.11.

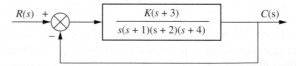

Figure 8.11   System for Example 8.2.

SOLUTION: Let us begin by calculating the asymptotes. Using Eq. (8.27), the real-axis intercept is evaluated as

$$\sigma_a = \frac{(-1 - 2 - 4) - (-3)}{4 - 1} = -\frac{4}{3} \tag{8.29}$$

---

[1] Physical systems, however, have more finite poles than finite zeros, since the implied differentiation yields infinite output for discontinuous input functions, such as step inputs.

The angles of the lines that intersect at $-4/3$, given by Eq. (8.28), are

$$\theta_a = \frac{(2k+1)\pi}{\#\text{finite poles} - \#\text{finite zeros}} \tag{8.30a}$$

$$= \pi/3 \quad \text{for } k = 0 \tag{8.30b}$$

$$= \pi \quad \text{for } k = 1 \tag{8.30c}$$

$$= 5\pi/3 \quad \text{for } k = 2 \tag{8.30d}$$

If the value for k continued to increase, the angles would begin to repeat. The number of lines obtained equals the difference between the number of finite poles and the number of finite zeros.

Rule 4 states that the locus begins at the open-loop poles and ends at the open-loop zeros. For the example there are more open-loop poles than open-loop zeros. Thus, there must be zeros at infinity. The asymptotes tell us how we get to these zeros at infinity.

Figure 8.12 shows the complete root locus as well as the asymptotes that were just calculated. Notice that we have made use of all the rules learned so far. The real-axis segments lie to the left of an odd number of poles and/or zeros. The locus starts at the open-loop poles and ends at the open-loop zeros. For the example there is only one open-loop finite zero and three infinite zeros. Rule 5, then, tells us that the three zeros at infinity are at the ends of the asymptotes.

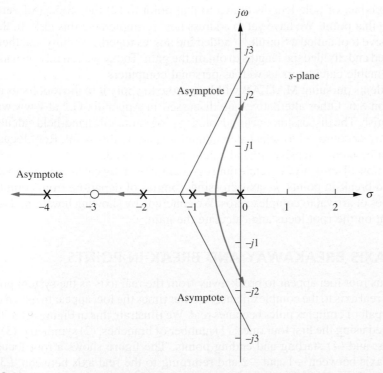

FIGURE 8.12   Root locus and asymptotes for the system of Figure 8.11

SKILL-ASSESSMENT EXERCISE 8.3

Problem: Sketch the root locus and its asymptotes for a unity feedback system that has the forward transfer function

$$G(s) = \frac{K}{(s+2)(s+4)(s+6)}$$

ANSWER: The complete solution is at www.wiley.com/college/nise.

8.5 REFINING THE SKETCH

The rules covered in the previous section permit us to sketch a root locus rapidly. If we want more detail, we must be able to accurately find important points on the root locus along with their associated gain. Points on the real axis where the root locus enters or leaves the complex plane—real-axis breakaway and break-in points—and the $j\omega$-axis crossings are candidates. We can also derive a better picture of the root locus by finding the angles of departure and arrival from complex poles and zeros, respectively.

In this section we discuss the calculations required to obtain specific points on the root locus. Some of these calculations can be made using the basic root locus relationship that the sum of the zero angles minus the sum of the pole angles equals an odd multiple of 180°, and the gain at a point on the root locus is found as the ratio of (1) the product of pole lengths drawn to that point to (2) the product of zero lengths drawn to that point. We have yet to address how to implement this task. In the past an inexpensive tool called a Spirule™ added the angles together rapidly and then quickly multiplied and divided the lengths to obtain the gain. Today we can rely on hand-held or programmable calculators as well as personal computers.

Students pursuing MATLAB will learn how to apply it to the root locus at the end of Section 8.6. Other alternatives are discussed in Appendix G.2 at www.wiley.com/college/nise. The discussion can be adapted to programmable hand-held calculators. All readers are encouraged to select a computational aid at this point. Root locus calculations can be labor intensive if hand calculations are used.

We now discuss how to refine our root locus sketch by calculating real-axis breakaway and break-in points, $j\omega$-axis crossings, angles of departure from complex poles, and angles of arrival to complex zeros. We conclude by showing how to find accurately any point on the root locus and calculate the gain.

REAL-AXIS BREAKAWAY AND BREAK-IN POINTS

Numerous root loci appear to break away from the real axis as the system poles move from the real axis to the complex plane. At other times the loci appear to return to the real axis as a pair of complex poles becomes real. We illustrate this in Figure 8.13. This locus is sketched using the first four rules: (1) number of branches, (2) symmetry, (3) real-axis segments, and (4) starting and ending points. The figure shows a root locus leaving the real axis between −1 and −2 and returning to the real axis between +3 and +5. The point where the locus leaves the real axis, −σ_1, is called the *breakaway point,* and the point where the locus returns to the real axis, σ_2, is called the *break-in point.*

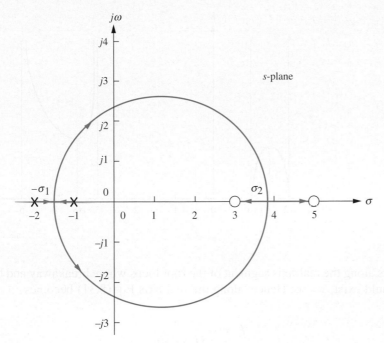

FIGURE 8.13 Root locus example showing real-axis breakaway $(-\sigma_1)$ and break-in points (σ_2)

At the breakaway or break-in point, the branches of the root locus form an angle of $180°/n$ with the real axis, where n is the number of closed-loop poles arriving at or departing from the single breakaway or break-in point on the real axis (*Kuo, 1991*). Thus, for the two poles shown in Figure 8.13, the branches at the breakaway point form $90°$ angles with the real axis.

We now show how to find the breakaway and break-in points. As the two closed-loop poles, which are at -1 and -2 when $K = 0$, move toward each other, the gain increases from a value of zero. We conclude that the gain must be maximum along the real axis at the point where the breakaway occurs, somewhere between -1 and -2. Naturally, the gain increases above this value as the poles move into the complex plane. We conclude that the breakaway point occurs at a point of maximum gain on the real axis between the open-loop poles.

Now let us turn our attention to the break-in point somewhere between $+3$ and $+5$ on the real axis. When the closed-loop complex pair returns to the real axis, the gain will continue to increase to infinity as the closed-loop poles move toward the open-loop zeros. It must be true, then, that the gain at the break-in point is the minimum gain found along the real axis between the two zeros.

The sketch in Figure 8.14 shows the variation of real-axis gain. The breakaway point is found at the maximum gain between -1 and -2, and the break-in point is found at the minimum gain between $+3$ and $+5$.

There are three methods for finding the points at which the root locus breaks away from and breaks into the real axis. The first method is to maximize and minimize the gain, K, using differential calculus. For all points on the root locus, Eq. (8.13) yields

$$K = -\frac{1}{G(s)H(s)} \tag{8.31}$$

FIGURE 8.14   Variation of gain along the real axis for the root locus of Figure 8.13

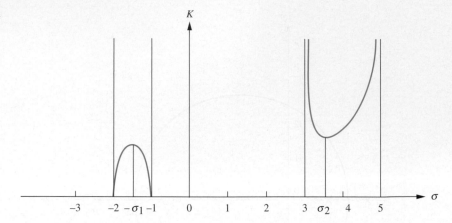

For points along the real-axis segment of the root locus where breakaway and break-in points could exist, $s = \sigma$. Hence, along the real axis Eq. (8.31) becomes

$$K = -\frac{1}{G(\sigma)H(\sigma)} \tag{8.32}$$

This equation then represents a curve of K versus σ similar to that shown in Figure 8.14. Hence, if we differentiate Eq. (8.32) with respect to σ and set the derivative equal to zero, we can find the points of maximum and minimum gain and hence the breakaway and break-in points. Let us demonstrate.

EXAMPLE 8.3

Breakaway and break-in points via differentiation

Problem: Find the breakaway and break-in points for the root locus of Figure 8.13, using differential calculus.

SOLUTION: Using the open-loop poles and zeros, we represent the open-loop system whose root locus is shown in Figure 8.13 as follows:

$$KG(s)H(s) = \frac{K(s-3)(s-5)}{(s+1)(s+2)} = \frac{K(s^2 - 8s + 15)}{(s^2 + 3s + 2)} \tag{8.33}$$

But for all points along the root locus, $KG(s)H(s) = -1$, and along the real axis, $s = \sigma$. Hence,

$$\frac{K(\sigma^2 - 8\sigma + 15)}{(\sigma^2 + 3\sigma + 2)} = -1 \tag{8.34}$$

Solving for K, we find

$$K = \frac{-(\sigma^2 + 3\sigma + 2)}{(\sigma^2 - 8\sigma + 15)} \tag{8.35}$$

Differentiating K with respect to σ and setting the derivative equal to zero yields

$$\frac{dK}{d\sigma} = \frac{(11\sigma^2 - 26\sigma - 61)}{(\sigma^2 - 8\sigma + 15)^2} = 0 \tag{8.36}$$

Solving for σ, we find $\sigma = -1.45$ and 3.82, which are the breakaway and break-in points.

The second method is a variation on the differential calculus method. Called the *transition method*, it eliminates the step of differentiation (*Franklin, 1991*). This method, derived in Appendix L.2 at www.wiley.com/college/nise, is now stated:

Breakaway and break-in points satisfy the relationship

$$\boxed{\sum_{1}^{m} \frac{1}{\sigma + z_i} = \sum_{1}^{n} \frac{1}{\sigma + p_i}} \tag{8.37}$$

where z_i and p_i are the negative of the zero and pole values, respectively, of $G(s)H(s)$.

Solving Eq. (8.37) for σ, the real-axis values that minimize or maximize K, yields the breakaway and break-in points without differentiating. Let us look at an example.

EXAMPLE 8.4

Breakaway and break-in points without differentiation

Problem: Repeat Example 8.3 without differentiating.

SOLUTION: Using Eq. (8.37),

$$\frac{1}{\sigma - 3} + \frac{1}{\sigma - 5} = \frac{1}{\sigma + 1} + \frac{1}{\sigma + 2} \tag{8.38}$$

Simplifying,

$$11\sigma^2 - 26\sigma - 61 = 0 \tag{8.39}$$

Hence, $\sigma = -1.45$ and 3.82, which agrees with Example 8.3.

For the third method the root locus program discussed in Appendix G.2 at www.wiley.com/college/nise can be used to find the breakaway and break-in points. Simply use the program to search for the point of maximum gain between -1 and -2 and to search for the point of minimum gain between $+3$ and $+5$. Table 8.2 shows the results of the search. The locus leaves the axis at -1.45, the point of maximum gain between -1 and -2, and reenters the real axis at $+3.8$, the point of minimum gain between $+3$ and $+5$. These results are the same as those obtained using the first two methods. MATLAB also has the capability of finding breakaway and break-in points.

THE $j\omega$-AXIS CROSSINGS

We now further refine the root locus by finding the imaginary-axis crossings. The importance of the $j\omega$-axis crossings should be readily apparent. Looking at Figure 8.12, we see that the system's poles are in the left half-plane up to a particular value of gain. Above this value

TABLE 8.2   Data for breakaway and break-in points for the root locus of Figure 8.13

Real-axis value	Gain	Comment
−1.41	0.008557	
−1.42	0.008585	
−1.43	0.008605	
−1.44	0.008617	
−1.45	0.008623 ←	Max. gain: breakaway
−1.46	0.008622	
3.3	44.686	
3.4	37.125	
3.5	33.000	
3.6	30.667	
3.7	29.440	
3.8	29.000 ←	Min. gain: break-in
3.9	29.202	

of gain, two of the closed-loop system's poles move into the right half-plane, signifying that the system is unstable. The $j\omega$-axis crossing is a point on the root locus that separates the stable operation of the system from the unstable operation. The value of ω at the axis crossing yields the frequency of oscillation, while the gain at the $j\omega$-axis crossing yields, for this example, the maximum positive gain for system stability. We should note here that other examples illustrate instability at small values of gain and stability at large values of gain. These systems have a root locus starting in the right half-plane (unstable at small values of gain) and ending in the left half-plane (stable for high values of gain).

To find the $j\omega$-axis crossing, we can use the Routh-Hurwitz criterion, covered in Chapter 6, as follows: Forcing a row of zeros in the Routh table will yield the gain; going back one row to the even polynomial equation and solving for the roots yields the frequency at the imaginary-axis crossing.

EXAMPLE 8.5

Frequency and gain at imaginary-axis crossing

Problem: For the system of Figure 8.11, find the frequency and gain, K, for which the root locus crosses the imaginary axis. For what range of K is the system stable?

SOLUTION: The closed-loop transfer function for the system of Figure 8.11 is

$$T(s) = \frac{K(s+3)}{s^4 + 7s^3 + 14s^2 + (8+K)s + 3K} \tag{8.40}$$

Using the denominator and simplifying some of the entries by multiplying any row by a constant, we obtain the Routh array shown in Table 8.3.

A complete row of zeros yields the possibility for imaginary axis roots. For positive values of gain, those for which the root locus is plotted, only the s^1 row can

TABLE 8.3 Routh table for Eq. (8.40)

s^4	1	14	$3K$
s^3	7	$8+K$	
s^2	$90-K$	$21K$	
s^1	$\dfrac{-K^2-65K+720}{90-K}$		
s^0	$21K$		

yield a row of zeros. Thus,

$$-K^2 - 65K + 720 = 0 \tag{8.41}$$

From this equation K is evaluated as

$$K = 9.65 \tag{8.42}$$

Forming the even polynomial by using the s^2 row with $K = 9.65$, we obtain

$$(90 - K)s^2 + 21K = 80.35s^2 + 202.7 = 0 \tag{8.43}$$

and s is found to be equal to $\pm j1.59$. Thus the root locus crosses the $j\omega$-axis at $\pm j1.59$ at a gain of 9.65. We conclude that the system is stable for $0 \leq K < 9.65$.

Another method for finding the $j\omega$-axis crossing (or any point on the root locus, for that matter) uses the fact that at the $j\omega$-axis crossing, the sum of angles from the finite open-loop poles and zeros must add to $(2k + 1)180°$. Thus, we can search the $j\omega$-axis until we find the point that meets this angle condition. A computer program, such as the root locus program discussed in Appendix G.2 at www.wiley.com/college/nise or MATLAB, can be used for this purpose. Subsequent examples in this chapter use this method to determine the $j\omega$-axis crossing.

ANGLES OF DEPARTURE AND ARRIVAL

In this subsection we further refine our sketch of the root locus by finding angles of departure and arrival from complex poles and zeros. Consider Figure 8.15, which shows the open-loop poles and zeros, some of which are complex. The root locus starts at the open-loop poles and ends at the open-loop zeros. In order to sketch the root locus more accurately, we want to calculate the root locus departure angle from the complex poles and the arrival angle to the complex zeros.

If we assume a point on the root locus ϵ close to a complex pole, the sum of angles drawn from all finite poles and zeros to this point is an odd multiple of $180°$. Except for the pole that is ϵ close to the point, we assume all angles drawn from all other poles and zeros are drawn directly to the pole that is near the point. Thus, the only unknown angle in the sum is the angle drawn from the pole that is ϵ close. We can solve for this unknown angle, which is also the angle of departure from this complex pole. Hence, from Figure 8.15(a),

$$-\theta_1 + \theta_2 + \theta_3 - \theta_4 - \theta_5 + \theta_6 = (2k + 1)180° \tag{8.44a}$$

FIGURE 8.15 Open-loop poles and zeros and calculation of
a. angle of departure;
b. angle of arrival

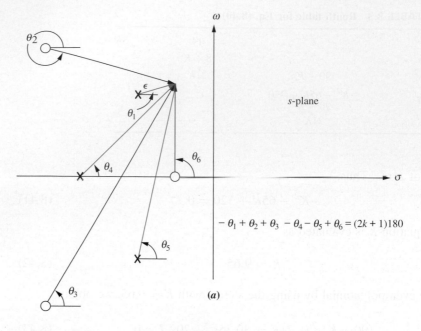

$$-\theta_1 + \theta_2 + \theta_3 - \theta_4 - \theta_5 + \theta_6 = (2k+1)180$$

(a)

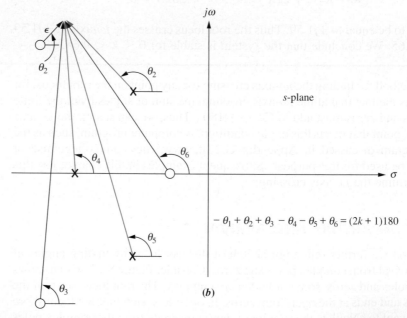

$$-\theta_1 + \theta_2 + \theta_3 - \theta_4 - \theta_5 + \theta_6 = (2k+1)180$$

(b)

or

$$\theta_1 = \theta_2 + \theta_3 - \theta_4 - \theta_5 + \theta_6 - (2k+1)180° \qquad (8.44b)$$

If we assume a point on the root locus ϵ close to a complex zero, the sum of angles drawn from all finite poles and zeros to this point is an odd multiple of $180°$. Except for the zero that is ϵ close to the point, we can assume all angles drawn from all other poles and zeros are drawn directly to the zero that is near the point. Thus, the only unknown angle in the sum is the angle drawn from the zero that is ϵ close. We can solve for this unknown angle, which is also the angle of arrival to this complex zero. Hence, from Figure 8.15(*b*),

$$-\theta_1 + \theta_2 + \theta_3 - \theta_4 - \theta_5 + \theta_6 = (2k+1)180° \tag{8.45a}$$

or

$$\theta_2 = \theta_1 - \theta_3 + \theta_4 + \theta_5 - \theta_6 + (2k+1)180° \tag{8.45b}$$

Let us look at an example.

EXAMPLE 8.6

Angle of departure from a complex pole

Problem: Given the unity feedback system of Figure 8.16, find the angle of departure from the complex poles and sketch the root locus.

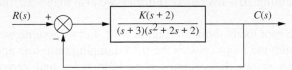

FIGURE 8.16 Unity feedback system with complex poles

SOLUTION: Using the poles and zeros of $G(s) = (s+2)/[(s+3)(s^2 + 2s + 2)]$ as plotted in Figure 8.17, we calculate the sum of angles drawn to a point ϵ close to the

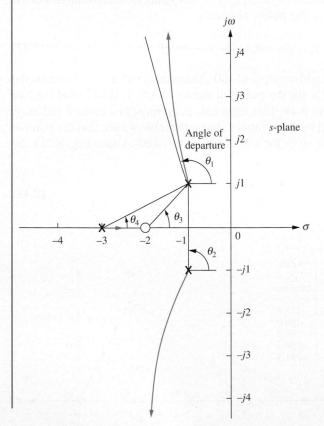

FIGURE 8.17 Root locus for system of Figure 8.16 showing angle of departure

complex pole, $-1 + j1$, in the second quadrant. Thus,

$$-\theta_1 - \theta_2 + \theta_3 - \theta_4 = -\theta_1 - 90° + \tan^{-1}\left(\frac{1}{1}\right) - \tan^{-1}\left(\frac{1}{2}\right) = 180° \quad (8.46)$$

from which $\theta = -251.6° = 108.4°$. A sketch of the root locus is shown in Figure 8.17. Notice how the departure angle from the complex poles helps us to refine the shape.

PLOTTING AND CALIBRATING THE ROOT LOCUS

Once we sketch the root locus using the rules from Section 8.4, we may want to accurately locate points on the root locus as well as find their associated gain. For example, we might want to know the exact coordinates of the root locus as it crosses the radial line representing 20% overshoot. Further, we also may want the value of gain at that point.

Consider the root locus shown in Figure 8.12. Let us assume we want to find the exact point at which the locus crosses the 0.45 damping ratio line and the gain at that point. Figure 8.18 shows the system's open-loop poles and zeros along with the $\zeta = 0.45$ line. If a few test points along the $\zeta = 0.45$ line are selected, we can evaluate their angular sum and locate that point where the angles add up to an odd multiple of $180°$. It is at this point that the root locus exists. Equation (8.20) can then be used to evaluate the gain, K, at that point.

Selecting the point at radius 2 $(r = 2)$ on the $\zeta = 0.45$ line, we add the angles of the zeros and subtract the angles of the poles, obtaining

$$\theta_2 - \theta_1 - \theta_3 - \theta_4 - \theta_5 = -251.5° \quad (8.47)$$

Since the sum is not equal to an odd multiple of $180°$, the point at radius $= 2$ is not on the root locus. Proceeding similarly for the points at radius $= 1.5, 1, 0.747,$ and 0.5, we obtain the table shown in Figure 8.18. This table lists the points, giving their radius, r, and the sum of angles indicated by the symbol $\angle$. From the table we see that the point at radius 0.747 is on the root locus, since the angles add up to $-180°$. Using Eq. (8.21), the gain, K, at this point is

$$K = \frac{|A||C||D|E|}{|B|} = 1.71 \quad (8.48)$$

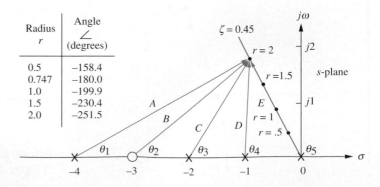

Radius r	Angle $\angle$ (degrees)
0.5	−158.4
0.747	−180.0
1.0	−199.9
1.5	−230.4
2.0	−251.5

FIGURE 8.18 Finding and calibrating exact points on the root locus of Figure 8.12

In summary, *we search a given line for the point yielding a summation of angles (zero angles – pole angles) equal to an odd multiple of* 180°. We conclude that the point is on the root locus. The gain at that point is then found by *multiplying the pole lengths drawn to that point and dividing by the product of the zero lengths drawn to that point.* A computer program, such as that discussed in Appendix G.2 at www.wiley.com/college/nise or MATLAB, can be used.

SKILL-ASSESSMENT EXERCISE 8.4

Problem: Given a unity feedback system that has the forward transfer function

$$G(s) = \frac{K(s+2)}{(s^2 - 4s + 13)}$$

do the following:

a. Sketch the root locus.
b. Find the imaginary-axis crossing.
c. Find the gain, K, at the $j\omega$-axis crossing.
d. Find the break-in point.
e. Find the angle of departure from the complex poles.

ANSWERS:

a. See solution at www.wiley.com/college/nise.
b. $s = \pm j\sqrt{21}$
c. $K = 4$
d. Break-in point $= -7$
e. Angle of departure $= -233.1°$

The complete solution is at www.wiley.com/college/nise.

8.6 AN EXAMPLE

We now review the rules for sketching and finding points on the root locus, as well as present an example. The root locus is the path of the closed-loop poles of a system as a parameter of the system is varied. Each point on the root locus satisfies the angle condition, $\angle G(s)H(s) = (2k + 1)180°$. Using this relationship, rules for sketching and finding points on the root locus were developed and are now summarized:

BASIC RULES FOR SKETCHING THE ROOT LOCUS

Number of branches The number of branches of the root locus equals the number of closed-loop poles.

Symmetry The root locus is symmetrical about the real axis.

Real-axis segments On the real axis, for $K > 0$ the root locus exists to the left of an odd number of real-axis, finite open-loop poles and/or finite open-loop zeros.

Starting and ending points The root locus begins at the finite and infinite poles of $G(s)H(s)$ and ends at the finite and infinite zeros of $G(s)H(s)$.

Behavior at infinity The root locus approaches straight lines as asymptotes as the locus approaches infinity. Further, the equations of the asymptotes are given by the real-axis intercept and angle in radians as follows:

$$\sigma_a = \frac{\sum \text{finite poles} - \sum \text{finite zeros}}{\#\text{finite poles} - \#\text{finite zeros}} \tag{8.49}$$

$$\theta_a = \frac{(2k+1)\pi}{\#\text{finite poles} - \#\text{finite zeros}} \tag{8.50}$$

where $k = 0, \pm 1, \pm 2, \pm 3, \ldots$.

ADDITIONAL RULES FOR REFINING THE SKETCH

Real-axis breakaway and break-in points The root locus breaks away from the real axis at a point where the gain is maximum and breaks into the real axis at a point where the gain is minimum.

Calculation of jω-axis crossings The root locus crosses the $j\omega$-axis at the point where $\angle G(s)H(s) = (2k+1)180°$. Routh-Hurwitz or a search of the $j\omega$-axis for $(2k+1)180°$ can be used to find the $j\omega$-axis crossing.

Angles of departure and arrival The root locus departs from complex, open-loop poles and arrives at complex, open-loop zeros at angles that can be calculated as follows. Assume a point ϵ close to the complex pole or zero. Add all angles drawn from all open-loop poles and zeros to this point. The sum equals $(2k+1)180°$. The only unknown angle is that drawn from the ϵ close pole or zero, since the vectors drawn from all other poles and zeros can be considered drawn to the complex pole or zero that is ϵ close to the point. Solving for the unknown angle yields the angle of departure or arrival.

Plotting and calibrating the root locus All points on the root locus satisfy the relationship $\angle G(s)H(s) = (2k+1)180°$. The gain, K, at any point on the root locus is given by

$$K = \frac{1}{|G(s)H(s)|} = \frac{1}{M} = \frac{\prod \text{finite pole lengths}}{\prod \text{finite zero lengths}} \tag{8.51}$$

Let us now look at a summary example.

EXAMPLE 8.7

Sketching a root locus and finding critical points

Problem: Sketch the root locus for the system shown in Figure 8.19(*a*) and find the following:

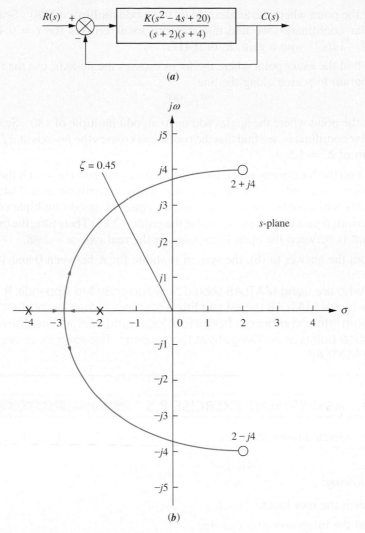

FIGURE 8.19 **a.** System for Example 8.7; **b.** root locus sketch

a. The exact point and gain where the locus crosses the 0.45 damping ratio line
b. The exact point and gain where the locus crosses the $j\omega$-axis
c. The breakaway point on the real axis
d. The range of K within which the system is stable

SOLUTION: The problem solution is shown, in part, in Figure 8.19(b). First sketch the root locus. Using Rule 3, the real-axis segment is found to be between -2 and -4. Rule 4 tells us that the root locus starts at the open-loop poles and ends at the open-loop zeros. These two rules alone give us the general shape of the root locus.

a. To find the exact point where the locus crosses the $\zeta = 0.45$ line, we can use the root locus program discussed in Appendix H.2 at www.wiley.com/college/nise to search along the line

$$\theta = 180° - \cos^{-1} 0.45 = 116.7° \tag{8.52}$$

for the point where the angles add up to an odd multiple of 180°. Searching in polar coordinates, we find that the root locus crosses the $\zeta = 0.45$ line at $3.4 \angle 116.7°$ with a gain, K, of 0.417.

b. To find the exact point where the locus crosses the $j\omega$-axis, use the root locus program to search along the line

$$\theta = 90° \tag{8.53}$$

for the point where the angles add up to an odd multiple of 180°. Searching in polar coordinates, we find that the root locus crosses the $j\omega$-axis at $\pm j3.9$ with a gain of $K = 1.5$.

c. To find the breakaway point, use the root locus program to search the real axis between -2 and -4 for the point that yields maximum gain. Naturally, all points will have the sum of their angles equal to an odd multiple of 180°. A maximum gain of 0.0248 is found at the point -2.88. Therefore, the breakaway point is between the open-loop poles on the real axis at -2.88.

d. From the answer to (b), the system is stable for K between 0 and 1.5.

Students who are using MATLAB should now run ch8p1 in Appendix B. You will learn how to use MATLAB to plot and title a root locus, overlay constant ζ and ω_n curves, zoom into and zoom out from a root locus, and interact with the root locus to find critical points as well as gains at those points. This exercise solves Example 8.7 using MATLAB.

SKILL-ASSESSMENT EXERCISE 8.5

TryIt 8.3

Use MATLAB, the Control System Toolbox, and the following statements to plot the root locus for Skill-Assessment Exercise 8.5. Solve the remaining parts of the problem by clicking on the appropriate points on the plotted root locus.

```
numg=poly([2  4]);
deng=[1 6 25];
G=tf(numg,deng)
rlocus(G)
z=0.5
sgrid(z,0)
```

Problem: Given a unity feedback system that has the forward transfer function

$$G(s) = \frac{K(s - 2)(s - 4)}{(s^2 + 6s + 25)}$$

do the following:

a. Sketch the root locus.

b. Find the imaginary-axis crossing.

c. Find the gain, K, at the $j\omega$-axis crossing.

d. Find the break-in point.

e. Find the point where the locus crosses the 0.5 damping ratio line.

f. Find the gain at the point where the locus crosses the 0.5 damping ratio line.

g. Find the range of gain, K, for which the system is stable.

ANSWERS:

a. See solution at www.wiley.com/college/nise.

b. $s = \pm j4.06$

c. $K = 1$

d. Break-in point $= +2.89$

e. $s = -2.42 + j4.18$

f. $K = 0.108$

g. $K < 1$

The complete solution is at www.wiley.com/college/nise.

8.7 TRANSIENT RESPONSE DESIGN VIA GAIN ADJUSTMENT

Now that we know how to sketch a root locus, we show how to use it for the design of transient response. In the last section we found that the root locus crossed the 0.45 damping ratio line with a gain of 0.417. Does this mean that the system will respond with 20.5% overshoot, the equivalent to a damping ratio of 0.45? It must be emphasized that the formulas describing percent overshoot, settling time, and peak time were derived only for a system with two closed-loop complex poles and no closed-loop zeros. The effect of additional poles and zeros and the conditions for justifying an approximation of a two-pole system were discussed in Sections 4.7 and 4.8 and apply here to closed-loop systems and their root loci. The conditions justifying a second-order approximation are restated here:

1. Higher-order poles are much farther into the left half of the s-plane than the dominant second-order pair of poles. The response that results from a higher-order pole does not appreciably change the transient response expected from the dominant second-order poles.

2. Closed-loop zeros near the closed-loop second-order pole pair are nearly canceled by the close proximity of higher-order closed-loop poles.

3. Closed-loop zeros not canceled by the close proximity of higher-order closed-loop poles are far removed from the closed-loop second-order pole pair.

The first condition as it applies to the root locus is shown graphically in Figure 8.20(a) and (b). Figure 8.20(b) would yield a much better second-order approximation than Figure 8.20(a), since closed-loop pole p_3 is farther from the dominant, closed-loop second-order pair, p_1 and p_2.

The second condition is shown graphically in Figure 8.20(c) and (d). Figure 8.20(d) would yield a much better second-order approximation than Figure 8.20(c), since closed-loop pole p_3 is closer to canceling the closed-loop zero.

Summarizing the design procedure for higher-order systems, we arrive at the following:

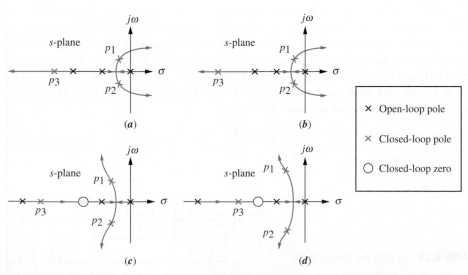

FIGURE 8.20 Making second-order approximations

1. Sketch the root locus for the given system.

2. Assume the system is a second-order system without any zeros and then find the gain to meet the transient response specification.

3. Justify your second-order assumption by finding the location of all higher-order poles and evaluating the fact that they are much farther from the $j\omega$-axis than the dominant second-order pair. As a rule of thumb, this textbook assumes a factor of five times farther. Also, verify that closed-loop zeros are approximately canceled by higher-order poles. If closed-loop zeros are not canceled by higher-order closed-loop poles, be sure that the zero is far removed from the dominant second-order pole pair to yield approximately the same response obtained without the finite zero.

4. If the assumptions cannot be justified, your solution will have to be simulated in order to be sure it meets the transient response specification. It is a good idea to simulate all solutions, anyway.

We now look at a design example to show how to make a second-order approximation and then verify whether or not the approximation is valid.

■■■■■■■■■■■■ **EXAMPLE 8.8** ■■■■■■■■■■■■

Third-order system gain design

Problem: Consider the system shown in Figure 8.21. Design the value of gain, K, to yield 1.52% overshoot. Also estimate the settling time, peak time, and steady-state error.

SOLUTION: The root locus is shown in Figure 8.22. Notice that this is a third-order system with one zero. Breakaway points on the real axis can occur between 0 and −1 and between −1.5 and −10, where the gain reaches a peak. Using the root locus program and searching in these regions for the peaks in gain, breakaway points are found at −0.62 with a gain of 2.511 and at −4.4 with a gain of 28.89. A break-in point on the real axis can occur between −1.5 and −10, where the gain reaches a local minimum. Using the root locus program and searching in these regions for the local minimum gain, a break-in point is found at −2.8 with a gain of 27.91.

Next assume that the system can be approximated by a second-order, underdamped system without any zeros. A 1.52% overshoot corresponds to a damping ratio of 0.8. Sketch this damping ratio line on the root locus, as shown in Figure 8.22.

Use the root locus program to search along the 0.8 damping ratio line for the point where the angles from the open-loop poles and zeros add up to an odd multiple of 180°. This is the point where the root locus crosses the 0.8 damping ratio or 1.52 percent overshoot line. Three points satisfy this criterion: $-0.87 \pm j0.66$, $-1.19 \pm j0.90$, and $-4.6 \pm j3.45$ with respective gains of 7.36, 12.79, and 39.64. For each point the settling time and peak time are evaluated using

$$T_s = \frac{4}{\zeta\omega_n} \tag{8.54}$$

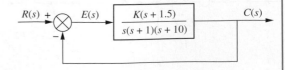

FIGURE 8.21   System for Example 8.8

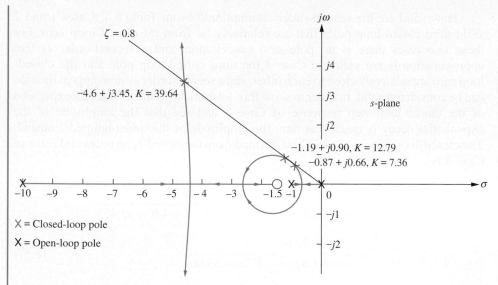

FIGURE 8.22 Root locus for Example 8.8

where $\zeta\omega_n$ is the real part of the closed-loop pole, and also using

$$T_p = \frac{\pi}{\omega_n\sqrt{1-\zeta^2}} \tag{8.55}$$

where $\omega_n\sqrt{1-\zeta^2}$ is the imaginary part of the closed-loop pole.

To test our assumption of a second-order system, we must calculate the location of the third pole. Using the root locus program, search along the negative extension of the real axis between the zero at -1.5 and the pole at -10 for points that match the value of gain found at the second-order dominant poles. For each of the three crossings of the 0.8 damping ratio line, the third closed-loop pole is at -9.25, -8.6, and -1.8, respectively. The results are summarized in Table 8.4.

Finally, let us examine the steady-state error produced in each case. Note that we have little control over the steady-state error at this point. When the gain is set to meet the transient response, we have also designed the steady-state error. For the example, the steady-state error specification is given by K_v and is calculated as

$$K_v = \lim_{s\to 0} sG(s) = \frac{K(1.5)}{(1)(10)} \tag{8.56}$$

The results for each case are shown in Table 8.4.

TABLE 8.4 **Characteristics of the system of Example 8.8**

Case	Closed-loop poles	Closed-loop zero	Gain	Third closed-loop pole	Settling time	Peak time	K_v
1	$-0.87 \pm j0.66$	$-1.5 + j0$	7.36	-9.25	4.60	4.76	1.1
2	$-1.19 \pm j0.90$	$-1.5 + j0$	12.79	-8.61	3.36	3.49	1.9
3	$-4.60 \pm j3.45$	$-1.5 + j0$	39.64	-1.80	0.87	0.91	5.9

How valid are the second-order assumptions? From Table 8.4, Cases 1 and 2 yield third closed-loop poles that are relatively far from the closed-loop zero. For these two cases there is no pole-zero cancellation, and a second-order system approximation is not valid. In Case 3 the third closed-loop pole and the closed-loop zero are relatively close to each other, and a second-order system approximation can be considered valid. In order to show this, let us make a partial-fraction expansion of the closed-loop step response of Case 3 and see that the amplitude of the exponential decay is much less than the amplitude of the underdamped sinusoid. The closed-loop step response, $C_3(s)$, formed from the closed-loop poles and zeros of Case 3 is

$$C_3(s) = \frac{39.64(s + 1.5)}{s(s + 1.8)(s + 4.6 + j3.45)(s + 4.6 - j3.45)}$$

$$= \frac{39.64(s + 1.5)}{s(s + 1.8)(s^2 + 9.2s + 33.06)} \qquad (8.57)$$

$$= \frac{1}{s} + \frac{0.3}{s(s + 1.8)} - \frac{1.3(s + 4.6) + 1.6(3.45)}{(s + 4.6)^2 + 3.45^2}$$

Thus, the amplitude of the exponential decay from the third pole is 0.3, and the amplitude of the underdamped response from the dominant poles is $\sqrt{1.3^2 + 1.6^2} = 2.06$. Hence, the dominant pole response is 6.9 times as large as the nondominant exponential response, and we assume that a second-order approximation is valid.

Using a simulation program, we obtain Figure 8.23, which shows comparisons of step responses for the problem we have just solved. Cases 2 and 3 are plotted for both the third-order response and a second-order response, assuming just the dominant pair of poles calculated in the design problem. Again, the second-order approximation was

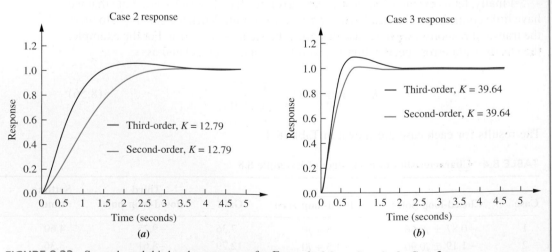

FIGURE 8.23   Second- and third-order responses for Example 8.8: **a.** Case 2; **b.** Case 3

justified for Case 3, where there is a small difference in percent overshoot. The second-order approximation is not valid for Case 2. Other than the excess overshoot, Case 3 responses are similar.

Students who are using MATLAB should now run ch8p2 in Appendix B. You will learn how to use MATLAB to enter a value of percent overshoot from the keyboard. MATLAB will then draw the root locus and overlay the percent over-shoot line requested. You will then interact with MATLAB and select the point of intersection of the root locus with the requested percent overshoot line. MATLAB will respond with the value of gain, all closed-loop poles at that gain, and a closed-loop step response plot corresponding to the selected point. This exercise solves Example 8.8 using MATLAB.

Students who are using MATLAB may want to explore the SISO Design Tool described in Appendix D at www.wiley.com/college/nise. The SISO Design Tool is a convenient and intuitive way to obtain, view, and interact with a system's root locus. Section D.7 describes the advantages of using the tool, while Section D.8 describes how to use it. For practice you may want to apply the SISO Design Tool to some of the problems at the end of this chapter.

SKILL-ASSESSMENT EXERCISE 8.6

Problem: Given a unity feedback system that has the forward-path transfer function

$$G(s) = \frac{K}{(s+2)(s+4)(s+6)}$$

do the following:

a. Sketch the root locus.

b. Using a second-order approximation, design the value of K to yield 10% overshoot for a unit-step input.

c. Estimate the settling time, peak time, rise time, and steady-state error for the value of K designed in (b).

d. Determine the validity of your second-order approximation.

ANSWERS:

a. See solution located at www.wiley.com/college/nise.

b. $K = 45.55$

c. $T_s = 1.97$ s, $T_p = 1.13$ s, $T_r = 0.53$ s, and $e_{step}(\infty) = 0.51$

d. Second-order approximation is not valid.

The complete solution is located at www.wiley.com/college/nise.

8.8 GENERALIZED ROOT LOCUS

Up to this point we have always drawn the root locus as a function of the forward-path gain, K. The control system designer must often know how the closed-loop poles change as a function of another parameter. For example, in Figure 8.24 the parameter of interest is the open-loop pole at $-p_1$. How can we obtain a root locus for variations of the value of p_1?

If the function $KG(s)H(s)$ is formed as

$$KG(s)H(s) = \frac{10}{(s+2)(s+p_1)} \tag{8.58}$$

the problem is that p_1 is not a multiplying factor of the function, as the gain, K, was in all of the previous problems. The solution to this dilemma is to create an equivalent system where p_1 appears as the forward-path gain. Since the closed-loop transfer function's denominator is $1 + KG(s)H(s)$, we effectively want to create an equivalent system whose denominator is $1 + p_1G(s)H(s)$.

For the system of Figure 8.24, the closed-loop transfer function is

$$T(s) = \frac{KG(s)}{1 + KG(s)H(s)} = \frac{10}{s^2 + (p_1 + 2)s + 2p_1 + 10} \tag{8.59}$$

Isolating p_1, we have

$$T(s) = \frac{10}{s^2 + 2s + 10 + p_1(s+2)} \tag{8.60}$$

Converting the denominator to the form $[1 + p_1G(s)H(s)]$ by dividing numerator and denominator by the term not included with p_1, $s^2 + 2s + 10$, we obtain

$$T(s) = \frac{\dfrac{10}{s^2 + 2s + 10}}{1 + \dfrac{p_1(s+2)}{s^2 + 2s + 10}} \tag{8.61}$$

Conceptually, Eq. (8.61) implies that we have a system for which

$$KG(s)H(s) = \frac{p_1(s+2)}{s^2 + 2s + 10} \tag{8.62}$$

The root locus can now be sketched as a function of p_1, assuming the open-loop system of Eq. (8.62). The final result is shown in Figure 8.25.

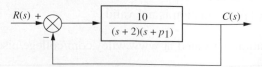

FIGURE 8.24 System requiring a root locus calibrated with p_1 as a parameter

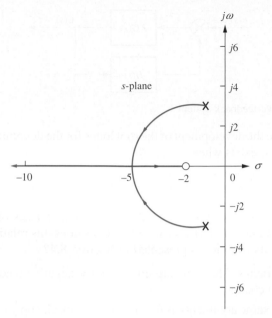

FIGURE 8.25 Root locus for the system of Figure 8.24, with p_1 as a parameter

---

| **SKILL-ASSESSMENT EXERCISE 8.7** |

Problem: Sketch the root locus for variations in the value of p_1, for a unity feedback system that has the following forward transfer function:

$$G(s) = \frac{100}{s(s + p_1)}$$

ANSWER: The complete solution is at www.wiley.com/college/nise.

In this section we learned to plot the root locus as a function of any system parameter. In the next section we will learn how to plot root loci for positive-feedback systems.

8.9 ROOT LOCUS FOR POSITIVE-FEEDBACK SYSTEMS

The properties of the root locus were derived from the system of Figure 8.1. This is a negative-feedback system because of the negative summing of the feedback signal to the input signal. The properties of the root locus change dramatically if the feedback signal is added to the input rather than subtracted. A positive-feedback system can be thought of as a negative-feedback system with a negative value of $H(s)$. Using this concept, we find that the transfer function for the positive-feedback system shown in Figure 8.26 is

$$T(s) = \frac{KG(s)}{1 - KG(s)H(s)} \tag{8.63}$$

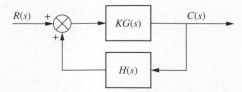

FIGURE 8.26 Positive-feedback system

We now retrace the development of the root locus for the denominator of Eq. (8.63). Obviously, a pole, s, exists when

$$KG(s)H(s) = 1 = 1\angle k360° \qquad k = 0, \pm 1, \pm 2, \pm 3, \ldots \tag{8.64}$$

Therefore, the root locus for positive-feedback systems consists of all points on the s-plane where the angle of $KG(s)H(s) = k360°$. How does this relationship change the rules for sketching the root locus presented in Section 8.4?

1. **Number of branches.** The same arguments as for negative feedback apply to this rule. There is no change.

2. **Symmetry.** The same arguments as for negative feedback apply to this rule. There is no change.

3. **Real-axis segments.** The development in Section 8.4 for the real-axis segments led to the fact that the angles of $G(s)H(s)$ along the real axis added up to either an odd multiple of $180°$ or a multiple of $360°$. Thus, for positive-feedback systems the root locus exists on the real axis along sections where the locus for negative-feedback systems does not exist. The rule follows:

   Real-axis segments: On the real axis, the root locus for positive-feedback systems exists to the left of an even number of real-axis, finite open-loop poles and/or finite open-loop zeros.

   The change in the rule is the word *even*; for negative-feedback systems the locus existed to the left of an *odd* number of real-axis, finite open-loop poles and/or zeros.

4. **Starting and ending points.** You will find no change in the development in Section 8.4 if Eq. (8.63) is used instead of Eq. (8.12). Therefore, we have the following rule.

   Starting and ending points: The root locus for positive-feedback systems begins at the finite and infinite poles of $G(s)H(s)$ and ends at the finite and infinite zeros of $G(s)H(s)$.

5. **Behavior at infinity.** The changes in the development of the asymptotes begin at Eq. (J.4) in Appendix J.1 at www.wiley.com/college/nise since positive-feedback systems follow the relationship in Eq. (8.64). That change yields a different slope for the asymptotes. The value of the real-axis intercept for the asymptotes remains unchanged. The student is encouraged to go through the development in detail and show that the behavior at infinity for positive-feedback systems is given by the following rule:

   The root locus approaches straight lines as asymptotes as the locus approaches infinity. Further, the equations of the asymptotes for positive-feedback systems are given by the real-axis intercept, σ_a, and angle, θ_a, as follows:

$$\sigma_a = \frac{\Sigma \text{ finite poles} - \Sigma \text{ finite zeros}}{\# \text{ finite poles} - \# \text{ finite zeros}} \tag{8.65}$$

$$\theta_a = \frac{k2\pi}{\# \text{ finite poles} - \# \text{ finite zeros}} \qquad (8.66)$$

where $k = 0, \pm 1, \pm 2, \pm 3, \ldots,$ *and the angle is given in radians with respect to the positive extension of the real axis.*

The change we see is that the numerator of Eq. (8.66) is $k2\pi$ instead of $(2k + 1)\pi$.

What about other calculations? The imaginary-axis crossing can be found using the root locus program. In a search of the $j\omega$-axis, you are looking for the point where the angles add up to a multiple of $360°$ instead of an odd multiple of $180°$. The breakaway points are found by looking for the maximum value of K. The break-in points are found by looking for the minimum value of K.

When we were discussing *negative*-feedback systems, we always made the root locus plot for positive values of gain. Since *positive*-feedback systems can also be thought of as *negative*-feedback systems with negative gain, the rules developed in this section apply equally to *negative*-feedback systems with negative gain. Let us look at an example.

EXAMPLE 8.9

Root locus for a positive-feedback system

Problem: Sketch the root locus as a function of negative gain, K, for the system shown in Figure 8.11.

SOLUTION: The equivalent positive-feedback system found by pushing -1, associated with K, to the right past the pickoff point is shown in Figure 8.27(a).

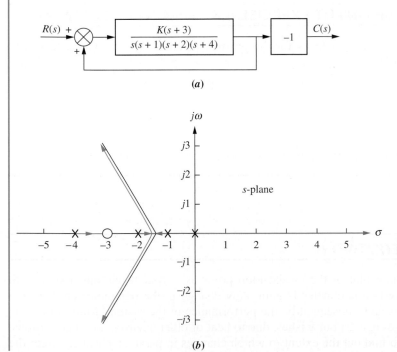

(a)

(b)

FIGURE 8.27 **a.** Equivalent positive-feedback system for Example 8.9; **b.** root locus

Therefore, as the gain of the equivalent system goes through positive values of K, the root locus will be equivalent to that generated by the gain, K, of the original system in Figure 8.11 as it goes through negative values.

The root locus exists on the real axis to the left of an even number of real, finite open-loop poles and/or zeros. Therefore, the locus exists on the entire positive extension of the real axis, between -1 and -2 and between -3 and -4. Using Eq. (8.27), the σ_a intercept is found to be

$$\sigma_a = \frac{(-1-2-4)-(-3)}{4-1} = -\frac{4}{3} \tag{8.67}$$

The angles of the lines that intersect at $-4/3$ are given by

$$\theta_a = \frac{k2\pi}{\#\text{ finite poles} - \#\text{ finite zeros}} \tag{8.68a}$$

$$= 0 \qquad\qquad \text{for } k = 0 \tag{8.68b}$$

$$= 2\pi/3 \qquad\qquad \text{for } k = 1 \tag{8.68c}$$

$$= 4\pi/3 \qquad\qquad \text{for } k = 2 \tag{8.68d}$$

The final root locus sketch is shown in Figure 8.27(b).

SKILL-ASSESSMENT EXERCISE 8.8

Problem: Sketch the root locus for the positive-feedback system whose forward transfer function is

$$G(s) = \frac{K(s+4)}{(s+1)(s+2)(s+3)}$$

The system has unity feedback.

ANSWER: The complete solution is at www.wiley.com/college/nise.

8.10 POLE SENSITIVITY

The root locus is a plot of the closed-loop poles as a system parameter is varied. Typically, that system parameter is gain. Any change in the parameter changes the closed-loop poles and, subsequently, the performance of the system. Many times the parameter changes against our wishes, due to heat or other environmental conditions. We would like to find out the extent to which changes in parameter values affect the performance of our system.

The root locus exhibits a nonlinear relationship between gain and pole location. Along some sections of the root locus, (1) very small changes in gain yield very large changes in pole location and hence performance; along other sections of the root locus, (2) very large changes in gain yield very small changes in pole location. In the first case we say that the system has a high sensitivity to changes in gain. In the second case the system has a low sensitivity to changes in gain. We prefer systems with low sensitivity to changes in gain.

In Section 7.7 we defined sensitivity as the ratio of the fractional change in a function to the fractional change in a parameter as the change in the parameter approaches zero. Applying the same definition to the closed-loop poles of a system that vary with a parameter, we define *root sensitivity* as the ratio of the fractional change in a closed-loop pole to the fractional change in a system parameter, such as gain. Using Eq. (7.75), we calculate the sensitivity of a closed-loop pole, s, to gain, K:

$$S_{s:K} = \frac{K}{s}\frac{\delta s}{\delta K} \tag{8.69}$$

where s is the current pole location, and K is the current gain. Using Eq. (8.69) and converting the partials to finite increments, the actual change in the closed-loop poles can be approximated as

$$\Delta s = s(S_{s:K})\frac{\Delta K}{K} \tag{8.70}$$

where Δs is the change in pole location, and $\Delta K/K$ is the fractional change in the gain, K. Let us demonstrate with an example. We begin with the characteristic equation from which $\delta s/\delta K$ can be found. Then, using Eq. (8.69) with the current closed-loop pole, s, and its associated gain, K, we can find the sensitivity.

EXAMPLE 8.10

Root sensitivity of a closed-loop system to gain variations

Problem: Find the root sensitivity of the system in Figure 8.4 at $s = -9.47$ and $-5 + j5$. Also calculate the change in the pole location for a 10% change in K.

SOLUTION: The system's characteristic equation, found from the closed-loop transfer function denominator, is $s^2 + 10s + K = 0$. Differentiating with respect to K, we have

$$2s\frac{\delta s}{\delta K} + 10\frac{\delta s}{\delta K} + 1 = 0 \tag{8.71}$$

from which

$$\frac{\delta s}{\delta K} = \frac{-1}{2s + 10} \tag{8.72}$$

Substituting Eq. (8.72) into Eq. (8.69), the sensitivity is found to be

$$S_{s:K} = \frac{K}{s}\frac{-1}{2s + 10} \tag{8.73}$$

For $s = -9.47$, Table 8.1 shows $K = 5$. Substituting these values into Eq. (8.73) yields $S_{s:K} = -0.059$. The change in the pole location for a 10% change in K can be found using Eq. (8.70), with $s = -9.47$, $\Delta K/K = 0.1$, and $S_{s:K} = -0.059$. Hence, $\Delta s = 0.056$, or the pole will move to the right by 0.056 units for a 10% change in K.

For $s = -5 + j5$, Table 8.1 shows $K = 50$. Substituting these values into Eq. (8.73) yields $S_{s:K} = 1/(1 + j1) = (1/\sqrt{2})\angle - 45°$. The change in the pole location for a 10% change in K can be found using Eq. (8.70), with $s = -5 + j5$, $\Delta K/K = 0.1$, and $S_{s:K} = (1/\sqrt{2})\angle - 45°$. Hence, $\Delta s = -j5$, or the pole will move vertically by 0.5 unit for a 10% change in K.

In summary, then, at $K = 5$, $S_{s:K} = -0.059$. At $K = 50$, $S_{s:K} = (1/\sqrt{2})\angle - 45°$. Comparing magnitudes, we conclude that the root locus is less sensitive to changes in gain at the lower value of K. Notice that root sensitivity is a complex quantity possessing both the magnitude and direction information from which the change in poles can be calculated.

SKILL-ASSESSMENT EXERCISE 8.9

WileyPLUS

Control Solutions

Problem: A negative unity feedback system has the forward transfer function

$$G(s) = \frac{K(s + 1)}{s(s + 2)}$$

If K is set to 20, find the changes in closed-loop pole location for a 5% change in K.

ANSWER: For the closed-loop pole at -21.05, $\Delta s = -0.9975$; for the closed-loop pole at -0.95, $\Delta s = -0.0025$.

The complete solution is at www.wiley.com/college/nise.

CASE STUDIES

Design

Antenna Control: Transient Design via Gain

The main thrust of this chapter is to demonstrate design of higher-order systems (higher than two) through gain adjustment. Specifically, we are interested in determining the value of gain required to meet transient response requirements, such as percent overshoot, settling time, and peak time. The following case study emphasizes this design procedure, using the root locus.

Problem: Given the antenna azimuth position control system shown on the front endpapers, Configuration 1, find the preamplifier gain required for 25% overshoot.

SOLUTION: The block diagram for the system was derived in the Case Studies section in Chapter 5 and is shown in Figure 5.34(c), where $G(s) = 6.63K/[s(s + 1.71)(s + 100)]$.

First a sketch of the root locus is made to orient the designer. The real-axis segments are between the origin and -1.71 and from -100 to infinity. The locus begins at the open-loop poles, which are all on the real axis at the origin, -1.71, and -100. The locus then moves toward the zeros at infinity by following asymptotes that, from Eqs. (8.27) and (8.28), intersect the real axis at -33.9 at angles of $60°$, $180°$, and $-60°$. A portion of the root locus is shown in Figure 8.28.

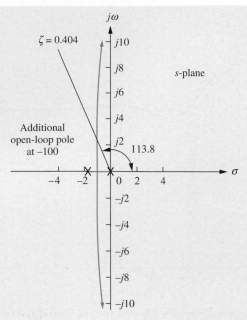

FIGURE 8.28   Portion of the root locus for the antenna control system

From Eq. (4.39), 25% overshoot corresponds to a damping ratio of 0.404. Now draw a radial line from the origin at an angle of $\cos^{-1}\zeta = 113.8$. The intersection of this line with the root locus locates the system's dominant, second-order closed-loop poles. Using the root locus program discussed in Appendix G.2 at www.wiley.com/college/nise to search the radial line for 180° yields the closed-loop dominant poles as $2.063 \angle 113.8° = -0.833 \pm j1.888$. The gain value yields $6.63K = 425.7$, from which $K = 64.21$.

Checking our second-order assumption, the third pole must be to the left of the open-loop pole at -100 and is thus greater than five times the real part of the dominant pole pair, which is -0.833. The second-order approximation is thus valid.

The computer simulation of the closed-loop system's step response in Figure 8.29 shows that the design requirement of 25% overshoot is met.

Challenge: You are now given a problem to test your knowledge of this chapter's objectives. Referring to the antenna azimuth position control system shown on the front endpapers, Configuration 2, do the following:

   a. Find the preamplifier gain, K, required for an 8-second settling time.

   b. Repeat, using MATLAB.

UFSS Vehicle: Transient Design via Gain

In this case study we apply the root locus to the UFSS vehicle pitch control loop. The pitch control loop is shown with both rate and position feedback on the back endpapers. In the example that follows, we plot the root locus without the rate feedback and then with the rate feedback. We will see the stabilizing effect that rate feedback has upon the system.

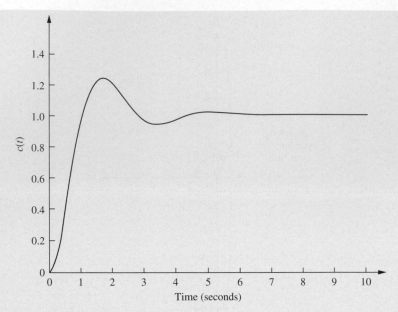

FIGURE 8.29 Step response of the gain-adjusted antenna control system

Problem: Consider the block diagram of the pitch control loop for the UFSS vehicle shown on the back endpapers (*Johnson, 1980*).

    a. If $K_2 = 0$ (no rate feedback), plot the root locus for the system as a function of pitch gain, K_1, and estimate the settling time and peak time of the closed-loop response with 20% overshoot.

    b. Let $K_2 = K_1$ (add rate feedback) and repeat (a).

SOLUTION:

    a. Letting $K_2 = 0$, the open-loop transfer function is

$$G(s)H(s) = \frac{0.25K_1(s + 0.435)}{(s + 1.23)(s + 2)(s^2 + 0.226s + 0.0169)} \tag{8.74}$$

from which the root locus is plotted in Figure 8.30. Searching along the 20% overshoot line evaluated from Eq. (4.39), we find the dominant second-order poles to be $-0.202 \pm j0.394$ with a gain of $K = 0.25K_1 = 0.706$, or $K_1 = 2.824$.

From the real part of the dominant pole, the settling time is estimated to be $T_s = 4/0.202 = 19.8$ seconds. From the imaginary part of the dominant pole, the peak time is estimated to be $T_p = \pi/0.394 = 7.97$ seconds. Since our estimates are based upon a second-order assumption, we now test our assumption by finding the third closed-loop pole location between -0.435 and -1.23 and the fourth closed-loop pole location between -2 and infinity. Searching each of these regions for a gain of $K = 0.706$, we find the third and fourth poles at -0.784 and -2.27, respectively. The third pole, at -0.784, may not be close enough to the zero at -0.435, and thus the system should be simulated. The fourth pole, at -2.27, is 11 times as far from the imaginary axis as the dominant poles and thus meets the requirement of at least five times the real part of the dominant poles.

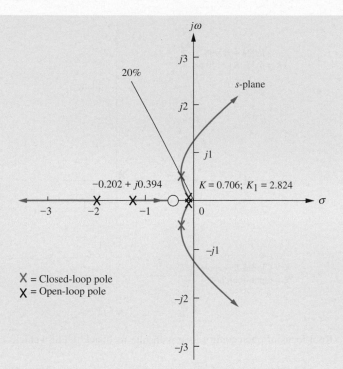

FIGURE 8.30   Root locus of pitch control loop without rate feedback, UFSS vehicle

A computer simulation of the step response for the system, which is shown in Figure 8.31, shows a 29% overshoot above a final value of 0.88, approximately 20-second settling time, and a peak time of approximately 7.5 seconds.

b. Adding rate feedback by letting $K_2 = K_1$ in the pitch control system shown on the back endpapers, we proceed to find the new open-loop transfer function. Pushing $-K_1$ to the right past the summing junction, dividing the pitch rate

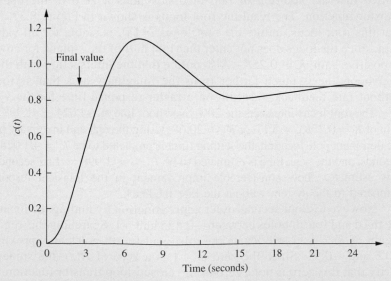

FIGURE 8.31   Computer simulation of step response of pitch control loop without rate feedback, UFSS vehicle

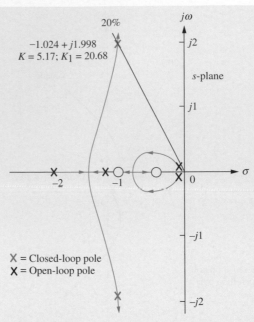

FIGURE 8.32   Root locus of pitch control loop with rate feedback, UFSS vehicle

sensor by $-K_1$, and combining the two resulting feedback paths obtaining $(s + 1)$ give us the following open-loop transfer function:

$$G(s)H(s) = \frac{0.25K_1(s + 0.435)(s + 1)}{(s + 1.23)(s + 2)(s^2 + 0.226s + 0.0169)} \qquad (8.75)$$

Notice that the addition of rate feedback adds a zero to the open-loop transfer function. The resulting root locus is shown in Figure 8.32. Notice that this root locus, unlike the root locus in (a), is stable for all values of gain, since the locus does not enter the right half of the s-plane for any value of positive gain, $K = 0.25K_1$. Also notice that the intersection with the 20% overshoot line is much farther from the imaginary axis than is the case without rate feedback, resulting in a faster response time for the system.

The root locus intersects the 20% overshoot line at $-1.024 \pm j1.998$ with a gain of $K = 0.25K_1 = 5.17$, or $K_1 = 20.68$. Using the real and imaginary parts of the dominant pole location, the settling time is predicted to be $T_s = 4/1.024 = 3.9$ seconds, and the peak time is estimated to be $T_p = \pi/1.998 = 1.57$ seconds. The new estimates show considerable improvement in the transient response as compared to the system without the rate feedback.

Now we test our second-order approximation by finding the location of the third and fourth poles between -0.435 and -1. Searching this region for a gain of $K = 5.17$, we locate the third and fourth poles at approximately -0.5 and -0.91. Since the zero at -1 is a zero of $H(s)$, the student can verify that this zero is not a zero of the closed-loop transfer function. Thus, although there may be pole-zero cancellation between the closed-loop pole

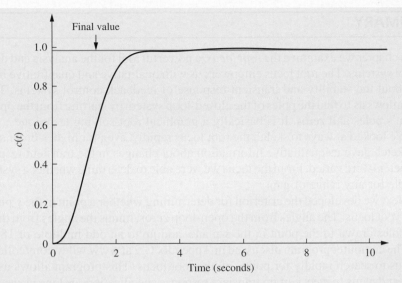

FIGURE 8.33   Computer simulation of step response of pitch control loop with rate feedback, UFSS vehicle

at −0.5 and the closed-loop zero at −0.435, there is no *closed-loop* zero to cancel the closed-loop pole at −0.91.[2] Our second-order approximation is not valid.

A computer simulation of the system with rate feedback is shown in Figure 8.33. Although the response shows that our second-order approximation is invalid, it still represents a considerable improvement in performance over the system without rate feedback; the percent overshoot is small, and the settling time is about 6 seconds instead of about 20 seconds.

Challenge: You are now given a problem to test your knowledge of this chapter's objectives. For the UFSS vehicle (*Johnson, 1980*) heading control system shown on the back endpapers, and introduced in the case study challenge in Chapter 5, do the following:

a. Let $K_2 = K_1$ and find the value of K_1 that yields 10% overshoot.

b. Repeat, using MATLAB.

We have concluded the chapter with two case studies showing the use and application of the root locus. We have seen how to plot a root locus and estimate the transient response by making a second-order approximation. We saw that the second-order approximation held when rate feedback was not used for the UFSS. When rate feedback was used, an open-loop zero from $H(s)$ was introduced. Since it was not a closed-loop zero, there was no pole-zero cancellation, and a second-order approximation could not be justified. In this case, however, the transient response with rate feedback did represent an improvement in transient response over the system without rate feedback. In subsequent chapters we will see why rate feedback yields an improvement. We will also see other methods of improving the transient response.

[2] The zero at −1 shown on the root locus plot of Figure 8.32 is an open-loop zero since it comes from the numerator of $H(s)$.

SUMMARY

In this chapter we examined the *root locus,* a powerful tool for the analysis and design of control systems. The root locus empowers us with qualitative and quantitative information about the stability and transient response of feedback control systems. The root locus allows us to find the poles of the closed-loop system by starting from the open-loop system's poles and zeros. It is basically a graphical root-solving technique.

We looked at ways to sketch the root locus rapidly, even for higher-order systems. The sketch gave us qualitative information about changes in the transient response as parameters were varied. From the locus we were able to determine whether a system was unstable for any range of gain.

Next we developed the criterion for determining whether a point in the s-plane was on the root locus: The angles from the open-loop zeros, minus the angles from the open-loop poles drawn to the point in the s-plane, add up to an odd multiple of $180°$.

The computer program discussed in Appendix G.2 at www.wiley.com/college/nise helps us to search rapidly for points on the root locus. This program allows us to find points and gains to meet certain transient response specifications as long as we are able to justify a second-order assumption for higher-order systems. Other computer programs, such as MATLAB, plot the root locus and allow the user to interact with the display to determine transient response specifications and system parameters.

Our method of design in this chapter is gain adjustment. We are limited to transient responses governed by the poles on the root locus. Transient responses represented by pole locations outside of the root locus cannot be obtained by a simple gain adjustment. Further, once the transient response has been established, the gain is set, and so is the steady-state error performance. In other words, by a simple gain adjustment, we have to trade off between a specified transient response and a specified steady-state error. Transient response and steady-state error cannot be designed independently with a simple gain adjustment.

We also learned how to plot the root locus against system parameters other than gain. In order to make this root locus plot, we must first convert the closed-loop transfer function into an equivalent transfer function that has the desired system parameter in the same position as the gain. The chapter discussion concluded with positive-feedback systems and how to plot the root loci for these systems.

The next chapter extends the concept of the root locus to the design of compensation networks. These networks have as an advantage the separate design of transient performance and steady-state error performance.

REVIEW QUESTIONS

1. What is a root locus?
2. Describe two ways of obtaining the root locus.
3. If $KG(s)H(s) = 5 \angle 180°$, for what value of gain is s a point on the root locus?
4. Do the zeros of a system change with a change in gain?
5. Where are the zeros of the closed-loop transfer function?
6. What are two ways to find where the root locus crosses the imaginary axis?
7. How can you tell from the root locus if a system is unstable?
8. How can you tell from the root locus if the settling time does not change over a region of gain?

9. How can you tell from the root locus that the natural frequency does not change over a region of gain?

10. How would you determine whether or not a root locus plot crossed the real axis?

11. Describe the conditions that must exist for all closed-loop poles and zeros in order to make a second-order approximation.

12. What rules for plotting the root locus are the same whether the system is a positive- or a negative-feedback system?

13. Briefly describe how the zeros of the open-loop system affect the root locus and the transient response.

PROBLEMS

1. For each of the root loci shown in Figure P8.1, tell whether or not the sketch can be a root locus. If the sketch cannot be a root locus, explain why. Give *all* reasons. [Section: 8.4]

2. Sketch the general shape of the root locus for each of the open-loop pole-zero plots shown in Figure P8.2. [Section: 8.4]

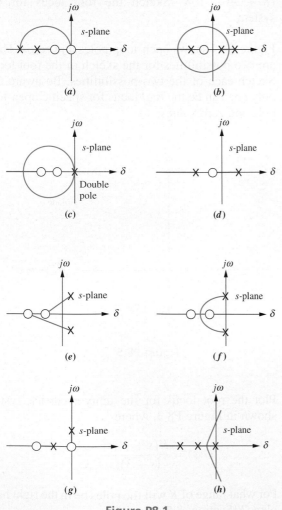

Figure P8.1

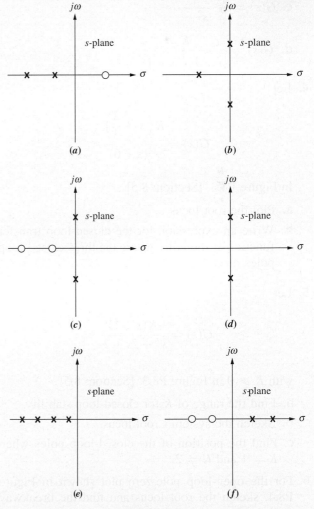

Figure P8.2

3. Sketch the root locus for the unity feedback system shown in Figure P8.3 for the following transfer functions: [Section: 8.4]

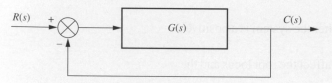

Figure P8.3

a. $G(s) = \dfrac{K(s+2)(s+6)}{s^2+8s+25}$

b. $G(s) = \dfrac{K(s^2+4)}{(s^2+1)}$

c. $G(s) = \dfrac{K(s^2+1)}{s^2}$

d. $G(s) = \dfrac{K}{(s+1)^3(s+4)}$

4. Let

$$G(s) = \dfrac{K\left(s + \dfrac{2}{3}\right)}{s^2(s+6)}$$

in Figure P8.3. [Section: 8.5]

a. Plot the root locus.

b. Write an expression for the closed-loop transfer function at the point where the three closed-loop poles meet.

5. Let

$$G(s) = \dfrac{-K(s+1)^2}{s^2+2s+2}$$

with $K > 0$ in Figure P8.3. [Section: 8.5]

a. Find the range of K for closed-loop stability.

b. Sketch the system's root locus.

c. Find the position of the closed-loop poles when $K = 1$ and $K = 2$.

6. For the open-loop pole-zero plot shown in Figure P8.4, sketch the root locus and find the breakaway point.

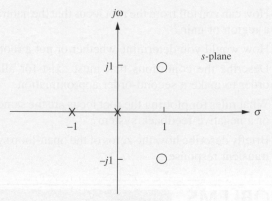

Figure P8.4

7. The characteristic polynomial of a feedback control system, which is the denominator of the closed-loop transfer function, is given by $s^3 + 3s^2 + (K+2)s + 10K$. Sketch the root locus for this system.

8. Figure P8.5 shows open-loop poles and zeros. There are two possibilities for the sketch of the root locus. Sketch each of the two possibilities. Be aware that only one can be the *real* locus for specific open-loop pole and zero values.

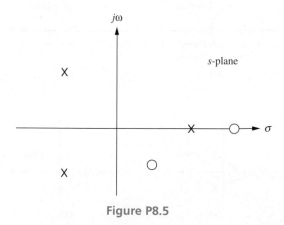

Figure P8.5

9. Plot the root locus for the unity feedback system shown in Figure P8.3, where

$$G(s) = \dfrac{K(s+1)(s^2+2)}{(s+3)(s-3)}$$

For what range of K will the poles be in the right half-plane? [Section: 8.5]

10. For the unity feedback system shown in Figure P8.3, where

$$G(s) = \frac{K(s^2 - 9)}{(s^2 + 4)}$$

sketch the root locus and tell for what values of K the system is stable and unstable. [Section: 8.5]

11. Sketch the root locus for the unity feedback system shown in Figure P8.3, where

$$G(s) = \frac{K(s^2 + 2)}{(s + 3)(s + 4)}$$

Give the values for all critical points of interest. Is the system ever unstable? If so, for what range of K? [Section: 8.5]

12. For each system shown in Figure P8.6, make an accurate plot of the root locus and find the following: [Section: 8.5]

a. The breakaway and break-in points

b. The range of K to keep the system stable

c. The value of K that yields a stable system with critically damped second-order poles

d. The value of K that yields a stable system with a pair of second-order poles that have a damping ratio of 0.707

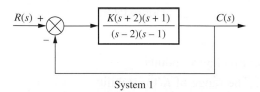

System 1

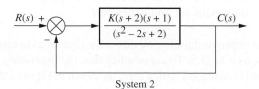

System 2

Figure P8.6

13. Sketch the root locus and find the range of K for stability for the unity feedback system shown in

Figure P8.3 for the following conditions: [Section: 8.5]

a. $G(s) = \dfrac{K(s^2 + 1)}{(s - 1)(s + 2)(s + 3)}$

b. $G(s) = \dfrac{K(s^2 - 2s + 2)}{s(s + 1)(s + 2)}$

14. For the unity feedback system of Figure P8.3, where

$$G(s) = \frac{K(s + 2)}{(s^2 + 1)(s - 1)(s + 4)}$$

sketch the root locus and find the range of K such that there will be only two right-half-plane poles for the closed-loop system.

15. For the unity feedback system of Figure P8.3, where

$$G(s) = \frac{K}{s(s + 6)(s + 9)}$$

plot the root locus and calibrate your plot for gain. Find all the critical points, such as breakaways, asymptotes, $j\omega$-axis crossing, and so forth. [Section: 8.5]

16. Given the unity feedback system of Figure P8.3, make an accurate plot of the root locus for the following:

a. $G(s) = \dfrac{K(s^2 - 2s + 2)}{(s + 1)(s + 2)}$

b. $G(s) = \dfrac{K(s - 1)(s - 2)}{(s + 1)(s + 2)}$

Calibrate the gain for at least four points for each case. Also find the breakaway points, the $j\omega$-axis crossing, and the range of gain for stability for each case. Find the angles of arrival for Part **a**. [Section: 8.5]

17. Given the root locus shown in Figure P8.7, [Section: 8.5]

a. Find the value of gain that will make the system marginally stable.

b. Find the value of gain for which the closed-loop transfer function will have a pole on the real axis at −5.

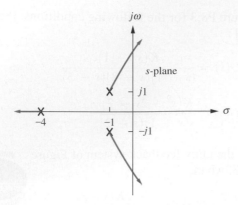

Figure P8.7

18. Given the unity feedback system of Figure P8.3, where

$$G(s) = \frac{K(s+1)}{s(s+2)(s+3)(s+4)}$$

do the following: [Section: 8.5]

a. Sketch the root locus.

b. Find the asymptotes.

c. Find the value of gain that will make the system marginally stable.

d. Find the value of gain for which the closed-loop transfer function will have a pole on the real axis at −0.5.

19. For the unity feedback system of Figure P8.3, where

$$G(s) = \frac{K(s+\alpha)}{s(s+3)(s+6)}$$

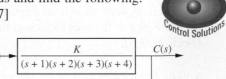

find the values of α and K that will yield a second-order closed-loop pair of poles at $-1 \pm j100$. [Section: 8.5]

20. For the unity feedback system of Figure P8.3, where

$$G(s) = \frac{K(s-1)(s-2)}{s(s+1)}$$

sketch the root locus and find the following: [Section: 8.5]

a. The breakaway and break-in points

b. The $j\omega$-axis crossing

c. The range of gain to keep the system stable

d. The value of K to yield a stable system with second-order complex poles, with a damping ratio of 0.5

21. For the unity feedback system shown in Figure P8.3, where

$$G(s) = \frac{K(s+10)(s+20)}{(s+30)(s^2 - 20s + 200)}$$

do the following: [Section: 8.7]

a. Sketch the root locus.

b. Find the range of gain, K, that makes the system stable.

c. Find the value of K that yields a damping ratio of 0.707 for the system's closed-loop dominant poles.

d. Find the value of K that yields closed-loop critically damped dominant poles.

22. For the system of Figure P8.8 (*a*), sketch the root locus and find the following: [Section: 8.7]

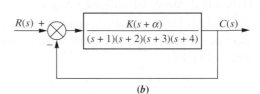

(*a*)

(*b*)

Figure P8.8

a. Asymptotes

b. Breakaway points

c. The range of K for stability

d. The value of K to yield a 0.7 damping ratio for the dominant second-order pair

To improve stability, we desire the root locus to cross the $j\omega$-axis at $j5.5$. To accomplish this, the open-loop function is cascaded with a zero, as shown in Figure P8.8(*b*).

e. Find the value of α and sketch the new root locus.

f. Repeat Part **c** for the new locus.

g. Compare the results of Part **c** and Part **f**. What improvement in transient response do you notice?

23. Sketch the root locus for the positive-feedback system shown in Figure P8.9. [Section: 8.9]

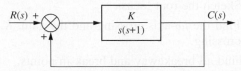

Figure P8.9

24. Root loci are usually plotted for variations in the gain. Sometimes we are interested in the variation of the closed-loop poles as other parameters are changed. For the system shown in Figure P8.10, sketch the root locus as α is varied. [Section: 8.8]

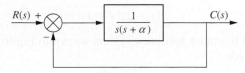

Figure 8.10

25. Given the unity feedback system shown in Figure P8.3, where

$$G(s) = \frac{K}{(s+1)(s+2)(s+3)}$$

do the following problem parts by first making a second-order approximation. After you are finished with all of the parts, justify your second-order approximation. [Section: 8.7]

a. Sketch the root locus.

b. Find K for 20% overshoot.

c. For K found in Part **b**, what is the settling time, and what is the peak time?

d. Find the locations of higher-order poles for K found in Part **b**.

e. Find the range of K for stability.

26. For the unity feedback system shown in Figure P8.3, where

$$G(s) = \frac{K(s^2 - 2s + 2)}{(s+2)(s+4)(s+5)(s+6)}$$

do the following: [Section: 8.7]

a. Sketch the root locus.

b. Find the asymptotes.

c. Find the range of gain, K, that makes the system stable.

d. Find the breakaway points.

e. Find the value of K that yields a closed-loop step response with 25% overshoot.

f. Find the location of higher-order closed-loop poles when the system is operating with 25% overshoot.

g. Discuss the validity of your second-order approximation.

h. Use MATLAB to obtain the closed-loop step response to validate or refute your second-order approximation.

27. The unity feedback system shown in Figure 8.3, where

$$G(s) = \frac{K(s+2)(s+3)}{s(s+1)}$$

is to be designed for minimum damping ratio. Find the following: [Section: 8.7]

a. The value of K that will yield minimum damping ratio

b. The estimated percent overshoot for that case

c. The estimated settling time and peak time for that case

d. The justification of a second-order approximation (discuss)

e. The expected steady-state error for a unit ramp input for the case of minimum damping ratio

28. For the unity feedback system shown in Figure P8.3, where

$$G(s) = \frac{K}{s(s+1)(s+2)}$$

find K to yield a damping ratio of 0.7. Does your solution require a justification of a second-order approximation? Explain.

29. For the unity feedback system shown in Figure P8.3, where

$$G(s) = \frac{K(s+\alpha)}{s(s+1)(s+10)}$$

WileyPLUS

Control Solutions

find the value of α so that the system will have a settling time of 4 seconds for large values of K. Sketch the resulting root locus. [Section: 8.8]

30. For the unity feedback system shown in Figure 8.3, where

$$G(s) = \frac{K(s+6)}{(s^2 + 10s + 26)(s+1)^2(s+\alpha)}$$

design K and α so that the dominant complex poles of the closed-loop function have a damping ratio of 0.45 and a natural frequency of 9/8 rad/s.

31. For the unity feedback system shown in Figure P8.3, where

$$G(s) = \frac{K}{s(s+1)(s+5)(s+6)}$$

do the following:

a. Sketch the root locus.

b. Find the value of K that will yield a 10% overshoot.

c. Locate all nondominant poles. What can you say about the second-order approximation that led to your answer in part (b)?

d. Find the range of K that yields a stable system.

32. Repeat Problem 31 using MATLAB. Use one program to do the following:

a. Display a root locus and pause.

b. Draw a close-up of the root locus where the axes go from -1 to 0 on the real axis and -2 to 2 on the imaginary axis.

c. Overlay the 10% overshoot line on the close-up root locus.

d. Allow you to select interactively the point where the root locus crosses the 10% overshoot line, and respond with the gain at that point as well as all of the closed-loop poles at that gain.

e. Generate the step response at the gain for 10% overshoot.

33. For the unity feedback system shown in Figure 8.3, where

$$G(s) = \frac{K(s^2 + 4s + 5)}{(s^2 + 2s + 5)(s+3)(s+4)}$$

do the following: [Section: 8.7]

a. Find the gain, K, to yield a 1-second peak time if one assumes a second-order approximation.

b. Check the accuracy of the second-order approximation using MATLAB to simulate the system.

34. For the unity feedback system shown in Figure P8.3, where

$$G(s) = \frac{K(s+2)(s+3)}{(s^2 + 2s + 2)(s+4)(s+5)(s+6)}$$

do the following: [Section: 8.7]

a. Sketch the root locus.

b. Find the $j\omega$-axis crossing and the gain, K, at the crossing.

c. Find all breakaway and break-in points.

d. Find angles of departure from the complex poles.

e. Find the gain, K, to yield a damping ratio of 0.3 for the closed-loop dominant poles.

35. Repeat Parts **a** through **c** and **e** of Problem 34 for [Section: 8.7]

$$G(s) = \frac{K(s+8)}{s(s+2)(s+4)(s+6)}$$

36. For the unity feedback system shown in Figure P8.3, where

$$G(s) = \frac{K}{(s+3)(s^2 + 4s + 5)}$$

do the following: [Section: 8.7]

a. Find the location of the closed-loop dominant poles if the system is operating with 15% overshoot.

b. Find the gain for Part **a**.

c. Find all other closed-loop poles.

d. Evaluate the accuracy of your second-order approximation.

37. For the system shown in Figure P8.11, do the following: [Section: 8.7]

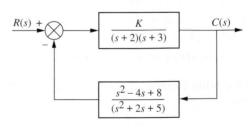

Figure P8.11

a. Sketch the root locus.

b. Find the $j\omega$-axis crossing and the gain, K, at the crossing.

c. Find the real-axis breakaway to two-decimal-place accuracy.

d. Find angles of arrival to the complex zeros.

e. Find the closed-loop zeros.

f. Find the gain, K, for a closed-loop step response with 30% overshoot.

g. Discuss the validity of your second-order approximation.

38. Sketch the root locus for the system of Figure P8.12 and find the following:

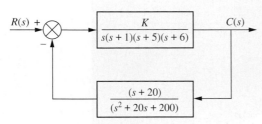

$R(s)$ + $\;\;\;\;\;\;\;$ $\dfrac{K}{s(s+1)(s+5)(s+6)}$ $\;\;\;\;\;$ $C(s)$

$\dfrac{(s+20)}{(s^2+20s+200)}$

Figure P8.12

a. The range of gain to yield stability

b. The value of gain that will yield a damping ratio of 0.707 for the system's dominant poles

c. The value of gain that will yield closed-loop poles that are critically damped

39. Repeat Problem 38 using MATLAB. The program will do the following in one program: MATLAB

a. Display a root locus and pause.

b. Display a close-up of the root locus where the axes go from −2 to 2 on the real axis and −2 to 2 on the imaginary axis.

c. Overlay the 0.707 damping ratio line on the close-up root locus.

d. Allow you to select interactively the point where the root locus crosses the 0.707 damping ratio line, and respond by displaying the gain at that point as well as all of the closed-loop poles at that gain. The program will then allow you to select interactively the imaginary-axis crossing, and respond with a display of the gain at that point as well as all of the closed-loop poles at that gain. Finally, the program will repeat the evaluation for critically damped dominant closed-loop poles.

e. Generate the step response at the gain for 0.707 damping ratio.

40. Given the unity feedback system shown in Figure P8.3, where

$$G(s) = \frac{K(s+z)}{s^2(s+20)}$$

WileyPLUS Control Solutions

do the following: [Section: 8.7]

a. If $z = 6$, find K so that the damped frequency of oscillation of the transient response is 10 rad/s.

b. For the system of Part **a**, what static error constant (finite) can be specified? What is its value?

c. The system is to be redesigned by changing the values of z and K. If the new specifications are $\%OS = 4.32\%$ and $T_s = 0.4$ s, find the new values of z and K.

41. Given the unity feedback system shown in Figure P8.3, where

$$G(s) = \frac{K}{(s+1)(s+3)(s+6)^2}$$

find the following: [Section: 8.7]

a. The value of gain, K, that will yield a settling time of 4 seconds

b. The value of gain, K, that will yield a critically damped system

42. Let

$$G(s) = \frac{K(s-1)}{(s+2)(s+3)}$$

in Figure P8.3. [Section: 8.7].

a. Find the range of K for closed-loop stability.

b. Plot the root locus for $K > 0$.

c. Plot the root locus for $K < 0$.

d. Assuming a step input, what value of K will result in the smallest attainable settling time?

e. Calculate the system's e_{ss} for a unit step input assuming the value of K obtained in Part **d**.

f. Make an approximate hand sketch of the unit step response of the system if K has the value obtained in Part **d**.

43. Given the unity feedback system shown in Figure P8.3, where

$$G(s) = \frac{K}{s(s+1)(s+5)}$$

evaluate the pole sensitivity of the closed-loop system if the second-order, underdamped closed-loop poles are set for [Section: 8.10]

a. $\zeta = 0.591$

b. $\zeta = 0.456$

c. Which of the two previous cases has more desirable sensitivity?

44. Figure P8.13(a) shows a robot equipped to perform arc welding. A similar device can be configured as a six-degrees-of-freedom industrial robot that can transfer objects according to a desired program. Assume the block diagram of the swing motion system shown in Figure P8.13(b). If $K = 64,510$, make a second-order approximation and estimate the following (*Hardy, 1967*):

(*a*)

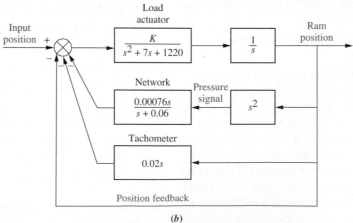

(*b*)

Figure P8.13 **a.** Robot equipped to perform arc welding; **b.** block diagram for swing motion system

a. Damping ratio

b. Percent overshoot

c. Natural frequency

d. Settling time

e. Peak time

What can you say about your original second-order approximation?

45. During ascent the automatic steering program aboard the space shuttle provides the interface between the low-rate processing of guidance (commands) and the high-rate processing of flight control (steering in response to the commands). The function performed is basically that of smoothing. A simplified representation of a maneuver smoother linearized for coplanar maneuvers is shown in Figure P8.14. Here $\theta_{CB}(s)$ is the commanded body angle as calculated by guidance, and $\theta_{CB}(s)$ is the desired body angle sent to flight control after smoothing.[3] Using the methods of Section 8.8, do the following:

a. Sketch a root locus where the roots vary as a function of K_3.

b. Locate the closed-loop zeros.

c. Repeat Parts **a** and **b** for a root locus sketched as a function of K_2.

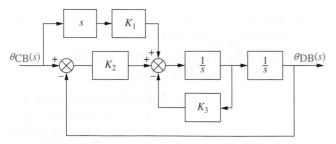

Figure P8.14 Block diagram of smoother

46. Repeat Problem 3 but sketch your root loci for negative values of K. [Section: 8.9]

47. Large structures in space, such as the space station, have to be stabilized against unwanted vibration. One method is to use an active vibration absorber to control the structure, as shown in Figure P8.15(a) (*Bruner, 1992*). Assuming that all values except the

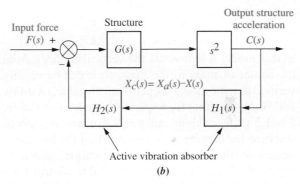

(a)

(b)

Figure P8.15 a. Active vibration absorber (©1992 AIAA); **b.** control system block diagram

mass of the active vibration absorber are known and are equal to unity, do the following:

a. Obtain $G(s)$ and $H(s) = H_1(s)H_2(s)$ in the block diagram representation of the system of Figure 8.15(b), which shows that the active vibration absorber acts as a feedback element to control the structure. (*Hint:* Think of K_c and D_c as producing inputs to the structure.)

b. Find the steady-state position of the structure for a force disturbance input.

c. Sketch the root locus for the system as a function of active vibration absorber mass, M_c.

48. Figure P8.16 shows the block diagram of the closed-loop control of the linearized magnetic levitation

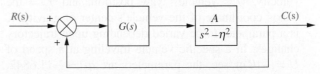

Figure P8.16 Linearized magnetic levitation system block diagram

[3] Source: Rockwell International.

system described in Chapter 2, Problem 56. (*Galvao, 2003*).

Assuming $A = 1300$ and $\eta = 860$, draw the root locus and find the range of K for closed-loop stability when:

a. $G(s) = K$;

b. $G(s) = \dfrac{K(s + 200)}{s + 1000}$

49. The simplified transfer function model from steering angle $\delta(s)$ to tilt angle $\varphi(s)$ in a bicycle is given by

$$G(s) = \frac{\varphi(s)}{\delta(s)} = \frac{aV}{bh} \frac{s + \dfrac{V}{a}}{s^2 - \dfrac{g}{h}}$$

In this model h represents the vertical distance from the center of mass to the floor, so it can be readily verified that the model is open-loop unstable. (*Åström, 2005*). Assume that for a specific bicycle, $a = 0.6$ m, $b = 1.5$ m, $h = 0.8$ m, and $g = 9.8$ m/sec. In order to stabilize the bicycle, it is assumed that the bicycle is placed in the closed-loop configuration shown in Figure P8.3 and that the only available control variable is V, the rear wheel velocity.

a. Find the range of V for closed-loop stability.

b. Explain why the methods presented in this chapter cannot be used to obtain the root locus.

c. Use MATLAB to obtain the system's root locus.

50. A technique to control the steering of a vehicle that follows a line located in the middle of a lane is to define a look-ahead point and measure vehicle deviations with respect to the point. A linearized model for such a vehicle is

$$\begin{bmatrix} \dot{V} \\ \dot{r} \\ \dot{\psi} \\ \dot{Y}_g \end{bmatrix} = \begin{bmatrix} a_{11} & a_{12} & -b_1 K & \dfrac{b_1 K}{d} \\ a_{21} & a_{22} & -b_2 K & \dfrac{b_2 K}{d} \\ 0 & 1 & 0 & 0 \\ 1 & 0 & U & 0 \end{bmatrix} \begin{bmatrix} V \\ r \\ \psi \\ Y_g \end{bmatrix}$$

where $V =$ vehicle's lateral velocity, $r =$ vehicle's yaw velocity, $\psi =$ vehicle's yaw position, and $Y_g =$ the y-axis coordinate of the vehicle's center of gravity. K is a parameter to be varied depending upon trajectory changes. In a specific vehicle traveling at a speed of $U = -10$ m/sec, the parameters are $a_{11} = -11.6842$, $a_{12} = 6.7632$, $b_1 = -61.5789$, $a_{21} = -3.5143$, $a_{22} = 24.0257$, and $b_2 = 66.8571$. $d = 5$ m is the look-ahead

distance (*Ünyelioğlu, 1997*). Assuming the vehicle will be controlled in closed loop:

a. Find the system's characteristic equation as a function of K.

b. Find the system's root locus as K is varied.

c. Using the root locus found in Part **b**, show that the system will be unstable for all values K.

51. It is known that mammals have hormonal regulation mechanisms that help maintain almost constant calcium plasma levels (0.08–0.1 g/L in dairy cows). This control is necessary to maintain healthy functions, as calcium is responsible for diverse physiological functions, such as bone formation, intracellular communications, and blood clotting. It has been postulated that the mechanism of calcium control resembles that of a PI (proportional-plus-integral) controller. PI controllers (discussed in detail in Chapter 9) are placed in cascade with the plant and used to improve steady-state error. Assume that the PI controller has the form $G_c(s) = \left[K_P + \dfrac{K_I}{S} \right]$, where K_P and K_I are constants. Also assume that the mammal's system accumulates calcium in an integrator-like fashion, namely $P(s) = \dfrac{1}{Vs}$, where V is the plasma volume. The closed-loop model is similar to that of Figure P8.3, where $G(s) = G_c(s)P(s)$ (*Khammash, 2004*).

a. Sketch the system's root locus as a function of K_P, assuming $K_I > 0$ is constant.

b. Sketch the system's root locus as a function of K_I, assuming $K_P > 0$ is constant.

52. Problem 62 in Chapter 7 introduced the model of a TCP/IP router whose packet-drop probability is controlled by using a random early detection (RED) algorithm (*Hollot, 2001*). Using Figure P8.3 as a model, a specific router queue's open-loop transfer function is

$$G(s) = \frac{7031250 L e^{-0.2s}}{(s + 0.667)(s + 5)(s + 50)}$$

The function $e^{-0.2s}$ represents delay. To apply the root locus method, the delay function must be replaced with a rational function approximation. A first-order Padé approximation can be used for this purpose. Let $e^{-sD} \approx 1 - Ds$. Using this approximation, plot the root locus of the system as a function of L.

53. For the dynamic voltage restorer (DVR) discussed in Problem 46, Chapter 7, do the following:

a. When $Z_L = \dfrac{1}{sC_L}$, a pure capacitance, the system is more inclined toward instability. Find the system's characteristic equation for this case.

b. Using the characteristic equation found in Part **a**, sketch the root locus of the system as a function of C_L. Let $L = 7.6$ mH, $C = 11$ μF, $\alpha = 26.4$, $\beta = 1$, $K_m = 25$, $K_v = 15$, $K_T = 0.09565$, and $\tau = 2$ ms (*Lam, 2004*).

Design Problems

54. A floppy disk drive is a position control system in which a read/write head is positioned over a magnetic disk. The system responds to a command from a computer to position itself at a particular track on the disk. A physical representation of the system and a block diagram are shown in Figure P8.17.

a. Find K to yield a settling time of 0.1 second.

b. What is the resulting percent overshoot?

c. What is the range of K that keeps the system stable?

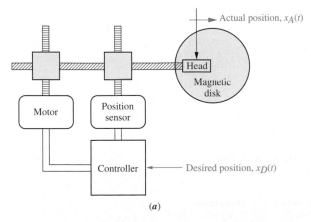

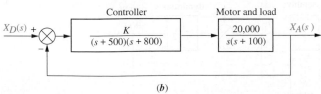

Figure P8.17 Floppy disk drive: **a.** physical representation; **b.** block diagram

55. A simplified block diagram of a human pupil servomechanism is shown in Figure P8.18. The term $e^{-0.18s}$ represents a time delay. This function can be approximated by what is known as a *Pade approximation*. This approximation can take on many increasingly complicated forms, depending upon the degree of accuracy required. If we use the Pade approximation

$$e^{-x} = \frac{1}{1 + x + \dfrac{x^2}{2!}}$$

then

$$e^{-0.18s} = \frac{61.73}{s^2 + 11.11s + 61.73}$$

Since the retinal light flux is a function of the opening of the iris, oscillations in the amount of retinal light flux imply oscillations of the iris (*Guy, 1976*). Find the following:

a. The value of K that will yield oscillations

b. The frequency of these oscillations

c. The settling time for the iris if K is such that the eye is operating with 20% overshoot

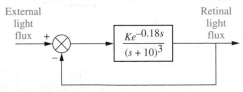

Figure P8.18 Simplified block diagram of pupil servomechanism

56. A possible active suspension system for AMTRAK trains has been proposed. The system uses a pneumatic actuator in parallel with the passive suspension system, as shown in Figure P8.19. The force of the actuator subtracts from the force applied by the ground, as represented by displacement, $y_g(t)$. Acceleration is sensed by an accelerometer, and signals proportional to acceleration and velocity are fed back to the force actuator. The transfer function relating acceleration to ground displacement is

$$\frac{\ddot{Y}_m(s)}{Y_g(s)} = \frac{s^2(Ds + K)}{(C_a + M)s^2 + (C_v + D)s + K}$$

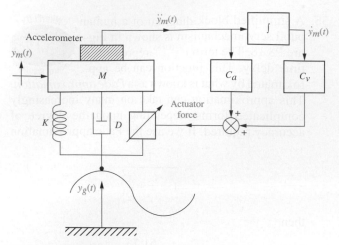

Figure P8.19   Active suspension system

Assuming that $M = 1$ and $D = K = C_v = 2$, do the following (*Cho, 1985*):

a. Sketch a root locus for this system as C_a varies from zero to infinity.

b. Find the value of C_a that would yield a damping ratio of 0.69 for the closed-loop poles.

57. The pitch stabilization loop for an F4-E military aircraft is shown in Figure P8.20. δ_{com} is the elevator

and canard input deflection command to create a pitch rate (see Problem 20, Chapter 3). If

$$G_2(s) = \frac{-508(s + 1.6)}{(s + 14)(s - 1.8)(s + 4.9)}$$

do the following (*Cavallo, 1992*):

a. Sketch the root locus of the inner loop.

b. Find the range of K_2 to keep the inner loop stable with just pitch-rate feedback.

c. Find the value of K_2 that places the inner-loop poles to yield a damping ratio of 0.5.

d. For your answer to Part **c**, find the range of K_1 that keeps the system stable.

e. Find the value of K_1 that yields closed-loop poles with a damping ratio of 0.45.

58. Accurate pointing of spacecraft is required for communication and mapping. Attitude control can be implemented by exchanging angular momentum between the body of the spacecraft and an onboard momentum wheel. The block diagram for the pitch axis attitude control is shown in Figure P8.21, where $\theta_c(s)$ is a commanded pitch angle and $\theta(s)$ is the actual pitch angle of the spacecraft. The compensator, which

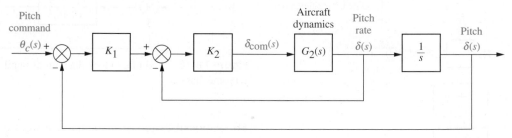

Figure P8.20   F4-E pitch stabilization loop

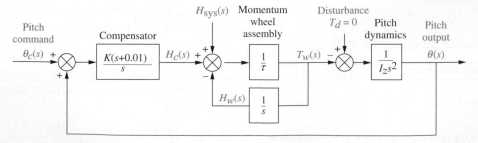

Figure P8.21   Pitch axis attitude control system utilizing momentum wheel

improves pointing accuracy, provides a commanded momentum, $H_c(s)$, to the momentum wheel assembly. The spacecraft momentum, $H_{sys}(s)$, is an additional input to the momentum wheel. This body momentum is given by

$$h_{sys}(t) = I_2\dot{\theta}(t) + h_w(t)$$

where I_2 is the spacecraft moment of inertia about the pitch axis and $h_w(t)$ is the momentum of the wheel. The total torque output from the momentum wheel, T_w, as shown in Figure P8.21, is

$$T_w(t) = \frac{h_{sys}(t) - h_w(t) + h_c(t)}{\tau}$$

If $\tau = 23$ seconds and $I_2 = 9631$ in-lb-s², do the following (*Piper, 1992*):

a. Sketch the root locus for the pitch axis control system.

b. Find the value of K to yield a closed-loop step response with 25% overshoot.

c. Evaluate the accuracy of any second-order approximations that were made.

59. During combustion in such devices as gas turbines and jet engines, acoustic waves are generated. These pressure waves can lead to excessive noise as well as mechanical failure. Active control is proposed to reduce this thermoacoustic effect. Specifically, a microphone is used as a sensor to read the sound waves, while a loudspeaker is used as an actuator to set up opposing pressure waves to reduce the effect. A proposed diagram showing the microphone and loudspeaker positioned in the combustion chamber is shown in Figure P8.22(*a*). A simplified block diagram of the active control system is shown in Figure P8.22(*b*). The transfer functions are dependent upon microphone and loudspeaker placement and parameters as well as flame placement and parameters. The forward-path transfer function is of the form

$$G(s) = KG_1(s)G_c(s)G_m(s)$$
$$= \frac{K(s + z_f)(s^2 + 2\zeta_2\omega_{2s} + \omega_2^2)}{(s + p_f)(s^2 - 2\zeta_1\omega_1 s + \omega_1^2)(s^2 + 2\zeta_2\omega_2 s + \omega_2^2)}$$

where the values for three configurations (A, B, and C) are given in the following table for Part **b** (*Annaswamy, 1995*).

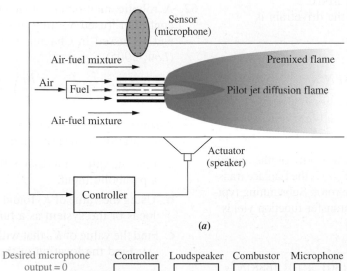

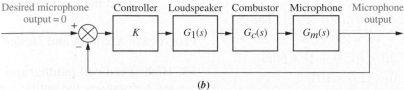

(b)

Figure P8.22   **a.** Combustor with microphone and loudspeaker (©1995 IEEE); **b.** block diagram (©1995 IEEE)

	A	**B**	**C**
z_f	1500	1500	1500
p_f	1000	1000	1000
ζ_z	0.45	0.45	−0.45
ω_z	4500	4500	4500
ζ_1	0.5	−0.5	−0.5
ω_1	995	995	995
ζ_2	0.3	0.3	0.3
ω_2	3500	3500	3500

a. Draw the root locus for each configuration.

b. For those configurations where stable regions of operation are possible, evaluate the range of gain, K, for stability.

60. Wind turbines, such as the one shown in Figure P8.23(*a*), are becoming popular as a way of generating electricity. Feedback control loops are designed to control the output power of the turbine, given an input power demand. Blade-pitch control may be used as part of the control loop for a constant-speed, pitch-controlled wind turbine, as shown in Figure P8.23(*b*). The drivetrain, consisting of the windmill rotor, gearbox, and electric generator (see Figure P8.23(*c*)), is part of the control loop. The torque created by the wind drives the rotor. The windmill rotor is connected to the generator through a gearbox.

The transfer function of the drivetrain is

$$\frac{P_o(s)}{T_R(s)} = G_{dt}(s)$$

$$= \frac{3.92 K_{LSS} K_{HSS} K_G N^2 s}{\{N^2 K_{HSS}(J_R s^2 + K_{LSS})(J_G s^2 [\tau_{el} s + 1]}{+ K_G s) + J_R s^2 K_{LSS}[(J_G s^2 + K_{HSS})}{(\tau_{el} s + 1) + K_G s]\}}$$

where $P_o(s)$ is the Laplace transform of the output power from the generator and $T_R(s)$ is the Laplace transform of the input torque on the rotor. Substituting typical numerical values into the transfer function yields

$$\frac{P_o(s)}{T_R(s)} = G_{dt}(s)$$

$$= \frac{(3.92)(12.6 \times 10^6)(301 \times 10^3)(688)N^2 s}{\{N^2(301 \times 10^3)(190{,}120 s^2 + 12.6 \times 10^6)}$$
$$\times (3.8 s^2 [20 \times 10^{-3} s + 1] + 668 s)$$
$$+ 190{,}120 s^2 (12.6 \times 10^6)$$
$$\times [(3.8 s^2 + 301 \times 10^3)$$
$$\times (20 \times 10^{-3} s + 1) + 668 s]\}$$

(*Anderson, 1998*). Do the following for the drivetrain dynamics, making use of any computational aids at your disposal:

a. Sketch a root locus that shows the pole locations of $G_{dt}(s)$ for different values of gear ratio, N.

b. Find the value of N that yields a pair of complex poles of $G_{dt}(s)$ with a damping ratio of 0.5.

61. A hard disk drive (HDD) arm has an open-loop unstable transfer function,

$$P(s) = \frac{X(s)}{F(s)} = \frac{1}{I_b s^2}$$

where $X(s)$ is arm displacement and $F(s)$ is the applied force (*Yan, 2003*). Assume the arm has an inertia of $I_b = 3 \times 10^{-5}$ kg-m^2 and that a lead controller, $G_c(s)$ (used to improve transient response and discussed in Chapter 9), is placed in cascade to yield

$$P(s) G_c(s) = G(s) = \frac{K}{I_b} \frac{(s+1)}{s^2(s+10)}$$

as in Figure P8.3.

a. Plot the root locus of the system as a function of K.

b. Find the value of K that will result in dominant complex conjugate poles with a $\zeta = 0.7$ damping factor.

62. A robotic manipulator together with a cascade PI controller (used to improve steady-state response and discussed in Chapter 9) has a transfer function (*Low, 2005*)

$$G(s) = \left(K_p + \frac{K_I}{s} \right) \frac{48{,}500}{s^2 + 2.89 s}$$

Assume the robot's joint will be controlled in the configuration shown in Figure P8.3.

a. Find the value of K_I that will result in $e_{ss} = 2\%$ for a parabolic input.

b. Using the value of K_I found in Part **a**, plot the root locus of the system as a function of K_P.

c. Find the value of K_P that will result in a real pole at −1. Find the location of the other two poles.

Progressive Analysis and Design Problems

63. High-speed rail pantograph. Problem 19 in Chapter 1 discusses the active control of a pantograph mechanism for high-speed rail systems. In Problem 72(*a*), Chapter 5, you found the block diagram for the

(a)

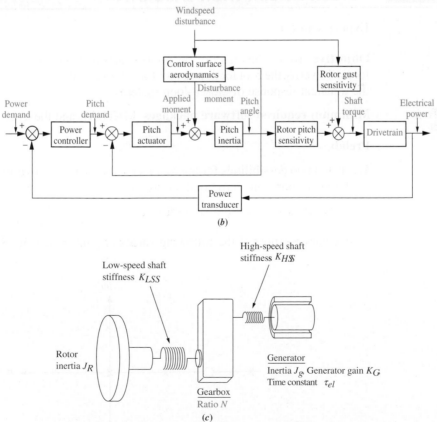

(b)

(c)

FIGURE P8.23 **a.** Wind turbines generating electricity near Palm Springs, California; **b.** control loop for a constant-speed pitch-controlled wind turbine (©1998 IEEE); **c.** drivetrain (©1998 IEEE)

431

active pantograph control system. Use your block diagram to do the following (*O'Connor, 1997*):

a. Sketch the root locus.

b. Assume a second-order approximation and find the gain, K, to yield a closed-loop step response that has 38% overshoot.

c. Estimate settling time and peak time for the response designed in Part **b**.

d. Discuss the validity of your second-order approximation.

e. Use MATLAB to plot the closed-loop step response for the value of K found in Part **b**. Compare the plot to predicted values found in Parts **b** and **c**.

64. Control of HIV/AIDS. In the linearized model of Chapter 6, Problem 64, where virus levels are con-

trolled by means of RTIs, the open-loop plant transfer function was shown to be

$$P(s) = \frac{Y(s)}{U_1(s)} = \frac{-520s - 10.3844}{s^3 + 2.6817s^2 + 0.11s + 0.0126}$$

The amount of RTIs delivered to the patient will automatically be calculated by embedding the patient in the control loop as $G(s)$ shown in Figure P6.19 (*Craig, 2004*).

a. In the simplest case, $G(s) = K$, with $K > 0$. Note that this effectively creates a positive-feedback loop because the negative sign in the numerator of $P(s)$ cancels out with the negative-feedback sign in the summing junction. Use positive-feedback rules to plot the root locus of the system.

b. Now assume $G(s) = -K$ with $K > 0$. The system is now a negative-feedback system. Use negative-feedback rules to draw the root locus. Show that in this case the system will be closed-loop stable for all $K > 0$.

CYBER EXPLORATION LABORATORY

Experiment 8.1

Objective To see the effect of open-loop poles and zeros upon the shape of the root locus. To verify the root locus as a tool for estimating the effect of open-loop gain upon the transient response of closed-loop systems.

Minimum required software packages MATLAB and the Control System Toolbox

Prelab

1. Sketch two possibilities for the root locus of a unity negative-feedback system with the open-loop pole-zero configuration shown in Figure P8.24.

2. If the open-loop system of Prelab 1 is $G(s) = \dfrac{K(s + 1.5)}{s(s + 0.5)(s + 10)}$, estimate the percent overshoot at the following values of gain, K: 20, 50, 85, 200, and 700.

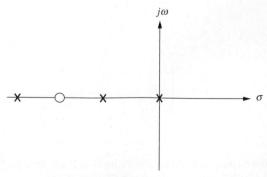

Figure P8.24

Lab

1. Using Matlab's SISO Design Tool, set up a negative unity feedback system with $G(s) = \dfrac{K(s + 6)}{s(s + 0.5)(s + 10)}$ to produce a root locus. For convenience, set up the zero at -6 using SISO Design Tool's compensator function by simply dragging a zero to -6 on the resulting root locus. Print the root locus for the zero at -6. Move the zero to the following locations and print out a root locus at each location: -2, -1.5, -1.37, and -1.2.

2. Using Matlab's SISO Design Tool, set up a negative unity feedback system with $G(s) = \dfrac{K(s + 1.5)}{s(s + 0.5)(s + 10)}$ to produce a root locus. Open the LTI Viewer for SISO Design Tool to show step responses. Using the values of K specified in Prelab 2, record the percent overshoot and settling time and print the root loci and step response for each value of K.

Postlab

1. Discuss your findings from Prelab 1 and Lab 1. What conclusions can you draw?

2. Make a table comparing percent overshoot and settling time from your calculations in Prelab 2 and your experimental values found in Lab 2. Discuss the reasons for any discrepancies. What conclusions can you draw?

BIBLIOGRAPHY

Anderson, C. G., Richon, J.-B., and Campbell, T. J. An Aerodynamic Moment-Controlled Surface for Gust Load Alleviation on Wind Turbine Rotors. *IEEE Transactions on Control System Technology*, vol. 6, no. 5, September 1998, pp. 577–595.

Annaswamy, A. M., and Ghonien, A. F. Active Control in Combustion Systems. *IEEE Control Systems*, December 1995, pp. 49–63.

Åström, K., Klein, R. E., and Lennartsson, A. Bicycle Dynamics and Control. *IEEE Control Systems*, August 2005, pp. 26–47.

Bruner, A. M., Belvin, W. K., Horta, L. G., and Juang, J. Active Vibration Absorber for the CSI Evolutionary Model: Design and Experimental Results. *Journal of Guidance, Control, and Dynamics*, vol. 15, no. 5, September–October 1992, pp. 1253–1257.

Cavallo, A., De Maria, G., and Verde, L. Robust Flight Control Systems: A Parameter Space Design. *Journal of Guidance, Control, and Dynamics*, vol. 15, no. 5, September–October 1992, pp. 1207–1215.

Cho, D., and Hedrick, J. K. Pneumatic Actuators for Vehicle Active Suspension Applications. *Journal of Dynamic Systems, Measurement, and Control*, March 1985, pp. 67–72.

Craig, I. K., Xia, X., and Venter, J. W., Introducing HIV/AIDS Education into the Electrical Engineering Curriculum at the University of Pretoria. *IEEE Transactions on Education*, vol. 47, no. 1, February 2004, pp. 65–73.

Dorf, R. C. *Modern Control Systems*, 5th ed. Addison-Wesley, Reading, MA., 1989.

Evans, W. R. Control System Synthesis by Root Locus Method. *AIEE Transactions*, vol. 69, 1950, pp. 66–69.

Evans, W. R. Graphical Analysis of Control Systems. *AIEE Transactions*, vol. 67, 1948, pp. 547–551.

Franklin, G. F., Powell, J. D., and Emami-Naeini, A. *Feedback Control of Dynamic Systems*, 2d ed. Addison-Wesley, Reading, MA., 1991.

Galvão, K. H. R., Yoneyama, T., and de Araújo, F. M. U. A Simple Technique for Identifying a Linearized Model for a Didactic Magnetic Levitation System. *IEEE Transactions on Education*, vol. 46, no. 1, February 2003, pp. 22–25.

Guy, W., *The Human Pupil Servomechanism.* Computers in Education Division of ASEE, Application Note No. 45, 1976.

Hardy, H. L. Multi-Loop Servo Controls Programmed Robot. *Instruments and Control Systems,* June 1967, pp. 105–111.

Hollot, C. V., Misra, V., Towsley, D., and Gong, W. A Control Theoretic Analysis of RED. *Proceedings of IEEE INFOCOM,* 2001, pp. 1510–1519.

Johnson, H., et al. *Unmanned Free-Swimming Submersible (UFSS) System Description.* NRL Memorandum Report 4393. Naval Research Laboratory, Washington, DC, 1980.

Khammash, M., and El-Samad, H. Systems Biology: From Physiology to Gene Regulation. *IEEE Control Systems,* August 2004, pp. 62–76.

Kuo, B. C. *Automatic Control Systems,* 6th ed. Prentice Hall, Englewood Cliffs, NJ, 1991.

Lam, C. S., Wong, M. C., and Han, Y D. Stability Study on Dynamic Voltage Restorer (DVR). Power Electronics Systems and Applications 2004; Proceedings of the First International Conference on Power Electronics, 2004, pp. 66–71.

Low, K. H., Wang, H., Liew, K. M., and Cai, Y. Modeling and Motion Control of Robotic Hand for Telemanipulation Application. *International Journal of Software Engineering and Knowledge Engineering,* vol. 15, 2005, pp. 147–152.

O'Connor, D. N., Eppinger, S. D., Seering, W. P., and Wormly, D. N. Active Control of a High-Speed Pantograph. *Journal of Dynamic Systems, Measurements, and Control,* vol. 119, March 1997, pp. 1–4.

Piper, G. E., and Kwatny, H. G. Complicated Dynamics in Spacecraft Attitude Control Systems. *Journal of Guidance, Control, and Dynamics,* vol. 15, no. 4, July–August 1992, pp. 825–831.

Ünyelioğlu, K. A., Hatopoğlu, C., and Özgüner, Ü. Design and Stability Analysis of a Lane Following Controller. *IEEE Transactions on Control Systems Technology,* vol. 5, 1997, pp. 127–134.

Yan, T., and Lin, R. Experimental Modeling and Compensation of Pivot Nonlinearity in Hard Disk Drives. *IEEE Transactions on Magnetics,* vol. 39, 2003, pp. 1064–1069.

DESIGN USING THE GRAPHICAL TOOL

9

CHAPTER OBJECTIVES

In this chapter you will learn the following:

- How to use the root locus to design cascade compensators to improve the steady-state error
- How to use the root locus to design cascade compensators to improve the transient response
- How to use the root locus to design cascade compensators to improve both the steady-state error and the transient response
- How to use the root locus to design feedback compensators to improve the transient response
- How to realize the designed compensators physically

CASE STUDY OBJECTIVES

You will be able to demonstrate your knowledge of the chapter objectives with case studies as follows:

- Given the antenna azimuth position control system shown on the front endpapers, you will be able to design a cascade compensator to meet transient response and steady-state error specifications.
- Given the pitch or heading control system for the UFSS vehicle shown on the back endpapers, you will be able to design a cascade or feedback compensator to meet transient response specifications.

9.1 INTRODUCTION

In Chapter 8 we saw that the root locus graphically displayed both transient response and stability information. The locus can be sketched quickly to get a general idea of the changes in transient response generated by changes in gain. Specific points on the locus also can be found accurately to give quantitative design information.

The root locus typically allows us to choose the proper loop gain to meet a transient response specification. As the gain is varied, we move through different regions of response. Setting the gain at a particular value yields the transient response dictated by the poles at that point on the root locus. Thus, *we are limited to those responses that exist along the root locus.*

IMPROVING TRANSIENT RESPONSE

Flexibility in the design of a desired transient response can be increased if we can design for transient responses that are not on the root locus. Figure 9.1(*a*) illustrates the concept. Assume that the desired transient response, defined by percent overshoot and settling time, is represented by point *B*. Unfortunately, on the current root locus at the specified percent overshoot, we only can obtain the settling time represented by point *A* after a simple gain adjustment. Thus, our goal is to speed up the response at *A* to that of *B*, without affecting the percent overshoot. This increase in speed cannot be accomplished by a simple gain adjustment, since point *B* does not lie on the root locus. Figure 9.1(*b*) illustrates the improvement in the transient response we seek: The faster response has the same percent overshoot as the slower response.

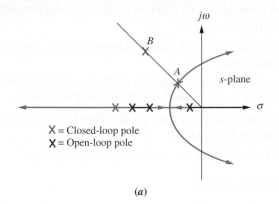

(*a*)

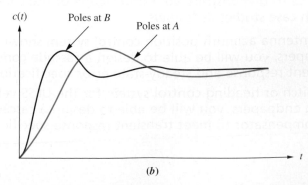

(*b*)

FIGURE 9.1 **a.** Sample root locus, showing possible design point via gain adjustment (*A*) and desired design point that cannot be met via simple gain adjustment (*B*); **b.** responses from poles at *A* and *B*

One way to solve our problem is to replace the existing system with a system whose root locus intersects the desired design point, *B*. Unfortunately, this replacement is expensive and counterproductive. Most systems are chosen for characteristics other than transient response. For example, an elevator cage and motor are chosen for speed and power. Components chosen for their transient response may not necessarily meet, for example, power requirements.

Rather than change the existing system, we augment, or *compensate,* the system with *additional* poles and zeros, so that the compensated system has a root locus that goes through the desired pole location for some value of gain. One of the advantages of compensating a system in this way is that additional poles and zeros can be added at the low-power end of the system before the plant. Addition of compensating poles and zeros need not interfere with the power output requirements of the system or present additional load or design problems. The compensating poles and zeros can be generated with a passive or an active network.

A possible disadvantage of compensating a system with additional open-loop poles and zeros is that the system order can increase, with a subsequent effect on the desired response. In Chapters 4 and 8, we discussed the effect of additional closed-loop poles and zeros on the transient response. At the beginning of the design process discussed in this chapter, we determine the proper location of additional *open-loop* poles and zeros to yield the desired second-order *closed-loop* poles. However, we do not know the location of the higher-order *closed-loop* poles until the end of the design. Thus, we should evaluate the transient response through simulation after the design is complete to be sure the requirements have been met.

In Chapter 2, when we discuss state-space design, the disadvantage of finding the location of higher-order closed-loop poles after the design will be eliminated by techniques that allow the designer to specify and design the location of all the closed-loop poles at the beginning of the design process.

One method of compensating for transient response that will be discussed later is to insert a differentiator in the forward path in parallel with the gain. We can visualize the operation of the differentiator with the following example. Assuming a position control with a step input, we note that the error undergoes an initial large change. Differentiating this rapid change yields a large signal that drives the plant. The output from the differentiator is much larger than the output from the pure gain. This large, initial input to the plant produces a faster response. As the error approaches its final value, its derivative approaches zero, and the output from the differentiator becomes negligible compared to the output from the gain.

IMPROVING STEADY-STATE ERROR

Compensators are not only used to improve the transient response of a system; they are also used *independently* to improve the steady-state error characteristics. Previously, when the system gain was adjusted to meet the transient response specification, steady-state error performance deteriorated, since both the transient response and the static error constant were related to the gain. The higher the gain, the smaller the steady-state error, but the larger the percent overshoot. On the other hand, reducing gain to reduce overshoot increased the steady-state error. If we use dynamic compensators, compensating networks can be designed that will allow us to meet transient and steady-state error specifications *simultaneously.*[1] We no longer need to compromise between

[1] The word *dynamic* describes compensators with noninstantaneous transient response. The transfer functions of such compensators are functions of the Laplace variable, *s*, rather than pure gain.

transient response and steady-state error, as long as the system operates in its linear range.

In Chapter 7 we learned that steady-state error can be improved by adding an open-loop pole at the origin in the forward path, thus increasing the system type and driving the associated steady-state error to zero. This additional pole at the origin requires an integrator for its realization.

In summary, then, transient response is improved with the addition of differentiation, and steady-state error is improved with the addition of integration in the forward path.

CONFIGURATIONS

Two configurations of compensation are covered in this chapter: cascade compensation and feedback compensation. These methods are modeled in Figure 9.2. With cascade compensation, the compensating network, $G_1(s)$, is placed at the low-power end of the forward path in cascade with the plant. If feedback compensation is used, the compensator, $H_1(s)$, is placed in the feedback path. Both methods change the open-loop poles and zeros, thereby creating a new root locus that goes through the desired closed-loop pole location.

COMPENSATORS

Compensators that use pure integration for improving steady-state error or pure differentiation for improving transient response are defined as *ideal compensators*. Ideal compensators must be implemented with active networks, which, in the case of electric networks, require the use of active amplifiers and possible additional power sources. An advantage of ideal integral compensators is that steady-state error is reduced to zero. Electromechanical ideal compensators, such as tachometers, are often used to improve transient response, since they can be conveniently interfaced with the plant.

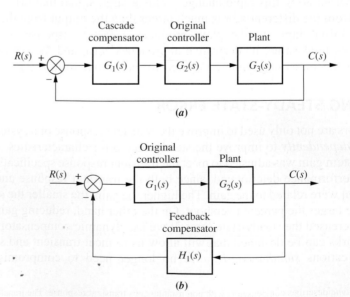

FIGURE 9.2 Compensation techniques: **a.** cascade; **b.** feedback

Other design techniques that preclude the use of active devices for compensation can be adopted. These compensators, which can be implemented with passive elements such as resistors and capacitors, do not use pure integration and differentiation and are not ideal compensators. Advantages of passive networks are that they are less expensive and do not require additional power sources for their operation. Their disadvantage is that the steady-state error is not driven to zero in cases where ideal compensators yield zero error.

Thus, the choice between an active or a passive compensator revolves around cost, weight, desired performance, transfer function, and the interface between the compensator and other hardware. In Sections 9.2, 9.3, and 9.4, we first discuss cascade compensator design using ideal compensation and follow with cascade compensation using compensators that are not implemented with pure integration and differentiation.

9.2 IMPROVING STEADY-STATE ERROR VIA CASCADE COMPENSATION

In this section we discuss two ways to improve the steady-state error of a feedback control system using cascade compensation. One objective of this design is to improve the steady-state error without appreciably affecting the transient response.

The first technique is *ideal integral compensation,* which uses a pure integrator to place an open-loop, forward-path pole at the origin, thus increasing the system type and reducing the error to zero. The second technique does not use pure integration. This compensation technique places the pole near the origin, and although it does not drive the steady-state error to zero, it does yield a measurable reduction in steady-state error.

While the first technique reduces the steady-state error to zero, the compensator must be implemented with active networks, such as amplifiers. The second technique, although it does not reduce the error to zero, does have the advantage that it can be implemented with a less expensive passive network that does not require additional power sources.

The names associated with the compensators come either from the method of implementing the compensator or from the compensator's characteristics. Systems that feed the error forward to the plant are called *proportional control systems*. Systems that feed the integral of the error to the plant are called *integral control systems*. Finally, systems that feed the derivative of the error to the plant are called *derivative control systems*. Thus, in this section we call the ideal integral compensator a *proportional-plus-integral (PI) controller,* since the implementation, as we will see, consists of feeding the error (proportional) plus the integral of the error forward to the plant. The second technique uses what we call a *lag compensator*. The name of this compensator comes from its frequency response characteristics, which will be discussed in Chapter 11. Thus, we use the name *PI controller* interchangeably with *ideal integral compensator,* and we use the name *lag compensator* when the cascade compensator does not employ pure integration.

IDEAL INTEGRAL COMPENSATION (PI)

Steady-state error can be improved by placing an open-loop pole at the origin, because this increases the system type by one. For example, a Type 0 system responding to a step input with a finite error responds with zero error if the system type is increased by one.

Active circuits can be used to place poles at the origin. Later in this chapter we show how to build an integrator with active electronic circuits.

To see how to improve the steady-state error without affecting the transient response, look at Figure 9.3(a). Here we have a system operating with a desirable transient response generated by the closed-loop poles at A. If we add a pole at the origin to increase the system type, the angular contribution of the open-loop poles at point A is no longer 180°, and the root locus no longer goes through point A, as shown in Figure 9.3(b).

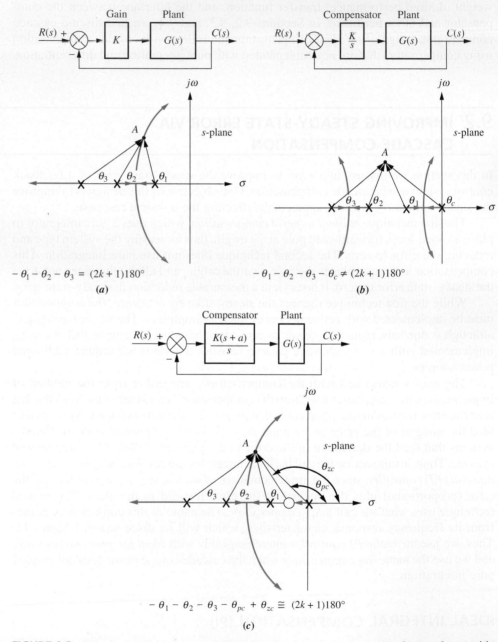

FIGURE 9.3 Pole at A is **a.** on the root locus without compensator; **b.** not on the root locus with compensator pole added; **c.** approximately on the root locus with compensator pole and zero added

To solve the problem, we also add a zero close to the pole at the origin, as shown in Figure 9.3(c). Now the angular contribution of the compensator zero and compensator pole cancel out, point A is still on the root locus, and the system type has been increased. Furthermore, the required gain at the dominant pole is about the same as before compensation, since the ratio of lengths from the compensator pole and the compensator zero is approximately unity. Thus, we have improved the steady-state error without appreciably affecting the transient response. A compensator with a pole at the origin and a zero close to the pole is called an *ideal integral compensator*.

In the example that follows, we demonstrate the effect of ideal integral compensation. An open-loop pole will be placed at the origin to increase the system type and drive the steady-state error to zero. An open-loop zero will be placed very close to the open-loop pole at the origin so that the original closed-loop poles on the original root locus still remain at approximately the same points on the compensated root locus.

EXAMPLE 9.1

Effect of an ideal integral compensator

Problem: Given the system of Figure 9.4(a), operating with a damping ratio of 0.174, show that the addition of the ideal integral compensator shown in Figure 9.4(b) reduces the steady-state error to zero for a step input without appreciably affecting transient response. The compensating network is chosen with a pole at the origin to increase the system type and a zero at -0.1, close to the compensator pole, so that the angular contribution of the compensator evaluated at the original, dominant, second-order poles is approximately zero. Thus, the original, dominant, second-order closed-loop poles are still approximately on the new root locus.

SOLUTION: We first analyze the uncompensated system and determine the location of the dominant, second-order poles. Next we evaluate the uncompensated steady-state error for a unit step input. The root locus for the uncompensated system is shown in Figure 9.5.

A damping ratio of 0.174 is represented by a radial line drawn on the s-plane at 100.02°. Searching along this line with the root locus program discussed in Appendix G.2 at www.wiley.com/college/nise, we find that the dominant poles are

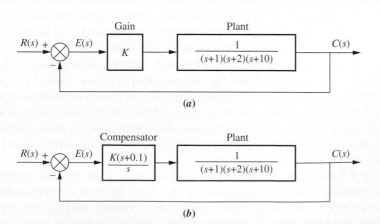

(a)

(b)

FIGURE 9.4 Closed-loop system for Example 9.1: **a.** before compensation; **b.** after ideal integral compensation

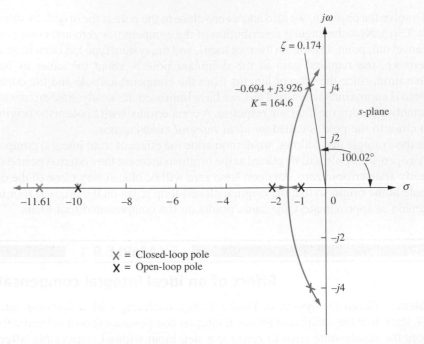

FIGURE 9.5 Root locus for uncompensated system of Figure 9.4(*a*)

−0.694 ± *j*3.926 for a gain, *K*, of 164.6. Now look for the third pole on the root locus beyond −10 on the real axis. Using the root locus program and searching for the same gain as that of the dominant pair, *K* = 164.6, we find that the third pole is approximately at −11.61. This gain yields $K_p = 8.23$. Hence, the steady-state error is

$$e(\infty) = \frac{1}{1 + K_p} = \frac{1}{1 + 8.23} = 0.108 \tag{9.1}$$

Adding an ideal integral compensator with a zero at −0.1, as shown in Figure 9.4(*b*), we obtain the root locus shown in Figure 9.6. The dominant second-order poles, the third pole beyond −10, and the gain are approximately the same as for the uncompensated system. Another section of the compensated root locus is between the origin and −0.1. Searching this region for the same gain at the dominant pair, *K* = 158.2, the fourth closed-loop pole is found at −0.0902, close enough to the zero to cause pole-zero cancellation. Thus, the compensated system's closed-loop poles and gain are approximately the same as the uncompensated system's closed-loop poles and gain, which indicates that the transient response of the compensated system is about the same as the uncompensated system. However, the compensated system, with its pole at the origin, is a Type 1 system; unlike the uncompensated system, it will respond to a step input with zero error.

Figure 9.7 compares the uncompensated response with the ideal integral compensated response. The step response of the ideal integral compensated system approaches unity in the steady state, while the uncompensated system approaches 0.892. Thus, the ideal integral compensated system responds with zero steady-state error. The transient response of both the uncompensated and the ideal integral

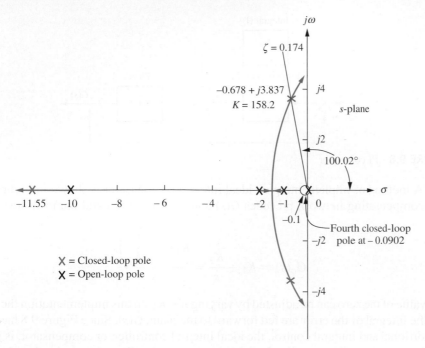

FIGURE 9.6   Root locus for compensated system of Figure 9.4(*b*)

compensated systems is the same up to approximately 3 seconds. After that time the integrator in the compensator, shown in Figure 9.4(*b*), slowly compensates for the error until zero error is finally reached. The simulation shows that it takes 18 seconds for the compensated system to reach to within ±2% of the final value of unity, while the uncompensated system takes about 6 seconds to settle to within ±2% of its final value of 0.892. The compensation at first may appear to yield deterioration in the settling time. However, notice that the compensated system reaches the uncompensated system's final value in about the same time. The remaining time is used to improve the steady-state error over that of the uncompensated system.

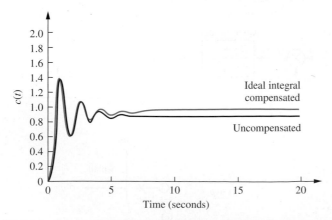

FIGURE 9.7   Ideal integral compensated system response and the uncompensated system response of Example 9.1

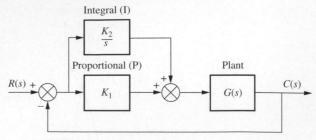

FIGURE 9.8 PI controller

A method of implementing an ideal integral compensator is shown in Figure 9.8. The compensating network precedes $G(s)$ and is an ideal integral compensator since

$$G_c(s) = K_1 + \frac{K_2}{s} = \frac{K_1\left(s + \dfrac{K_2}{K_1}\right)}{s} \tag{9.2}$$

The value of the zero can be adjusted by varying K_2/K_1. In this implementation the error and the integral of the error are fed forward to the plant, $G(s)$. Since Figure 9.8 has both proportional and integral control, the ideal integral controller, or compensator, is given the alternate name *PI controller*. Later in the chapter we will see how to implement each block, K_1 and K_2/s.

LAG COMPENSATION

Ideal integral compensation, with its pole on the origin, requires an active integrator. If we use passive networks, the pole and zero are moved to the left, close to the origin, as

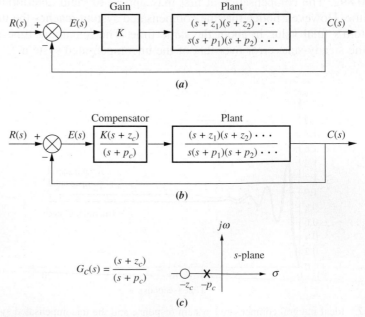

FIGURE 9.9   a. Type 1 uncompensated system; **b.** Type 1 compensated system; **c.** compensator pole-zero plot

shown in Figure 9.9(c). One may guess that this placement of the pole, although it does not increase the system type, does yield an improvement in the static error constant over an uncompensated system. Without loss of generality, we demonstrate that this improvement is indeed realized for a Type 1 system.

Assume the uncompensated system shown in Figure 9.9(a). The static error constant, K_{v_O}, for the system is

$$K_{v_O} = \frac{K\, z_1\, z_2 \cdots}{p_1 p_2 \cdots} \tag{9.3}$$

Assuming the lag compensator shown in Figure 9.9(b) and (c), the new static error constant is

$$K_{v_N} = \frac{(K\, z_1\, z_2 \cdots)(z_c)}{(p_1 p_2 \cdots)(p_c)} \tag{9.4}$$

What is the effect on the transient response? Figure 9.10 shows the effect on the root locus of adding the lag compensator. The uncompensated system's root locus is shown in Figure 9.10(a), where point P is assumed to be the dominant pole. If the lag compensator pole and zero are close together, the angular contribution of the compensator to point P is approximately zero degrees. Thus, in Figure 9.10(b), where the compensator has been added, point P is still at approximately the same location on the compensated root locus.

What is the effect on the required gain, K? After inserting the compensator, we find that K is virtually the same for the uncompensated and compensated systems, since the lengths of the vectors drawn from the lag compensator are approximately equal and all other vectors have not changed appreciably.

Now, what improvement can we expect in the steady-state error? Since we established that the gain, K, is about the same for the uncompensated and compensated systems, we can substitute Eq. (9.3) into (9.4) and obtain

$$K_{v_N} = K_{v_O}\frac{z_c}{p_c} > K_{v_O} \tag{9.5}$$

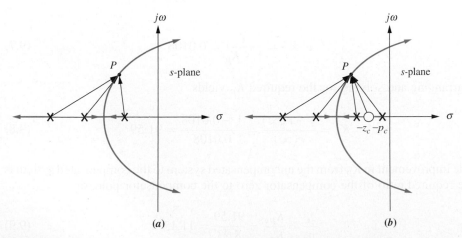

FIGURE 9.10   Root locus: **a.** before lag compensation; **b.** after lag compensation

Equation (9.5) shows that the improvement in the compensated system's K_v over the uncompensated system's K_v is equal to the ratio of the magnitude of the compensator zero to the compensator pole. In order to keep the transient response unchanged, we know the compensator pole and zero must be close to each other. The only way the ratio of z_c to p_c can be large in order to yield an appreciable improvement in steady-state error and simultaneously have the compensator's pole and zero close to each other to minimize the angular contribution is to place the compensator's pole-zero pair close to the origin. For example, the ratio of z_c to p_c can be equal to 10 if the pole is at -0.001 and the zero is at -0.01. Thus, the ratio is 10, yet the pole and zero are very close, and the angular contribution of the compensator is small.

In conclusion, although the ideal compensator drives the steady-state error to zero, a lag compensator with a pole that is not at the origin will improve the static error constant by a factor equal to z_c / p_c. There also will be a minimal effect upon the transient response if the pole-zero pair of the compensator is placed close to the origin. Later in the chapter we show circuit configurations for the lag compensator. These circuit configurations can be obtained with passive networks and thus do not require the active amplifiers and possible additional power supplies that are required by the ideal integral (PI) compensator. In the following example we design a lag compensator to yield a specified improvement in steady-state error.

EXAMPLE 9.2

Lag compensator design

Problem: Compensate the system of Figure 9.4(a), whose root locus is shown in Figure 9.5, to improve the steady-state error by a factor of 10 if the system is operating with a damping ratio of 0.174.

SOLUTION: The uncompensated system error from Example 9.1 was 0.108 with $K_p = 8.23$. A tenfold improvement means a steady-state error of

$$e(\infty) = \frac{0.108}{10} = 0.0108 \tag{9.6}$$

Since

$$e(\infty) = \frac{1}{1 + K_p} = 0.0108 \tag{9.7}$$

rearranging and solving for the required K_p yields

$$K_p = \frac{1 - e(\infty)}{e(\infty)} = \frac{1 - 0.0108}{0.0108} = 91.59 \tag{9.8}$$

The improvement in K_p from the uncompensated system to the compensated system is the required ratio of the compensator zero to the compensator pole, or

$$\frac{z_c}{p_c} = \frac{K_{p_N}}{K_{p_O}} = \frac{91.59}{8.23} = 11.13 \tag{9.9}$$

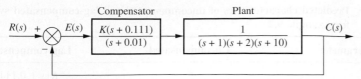

FIGURE 9.11 Compensated system for Example 9.2

Arbitrarily selecting

$$p_c = 0.01 \tag{9.10}$$

we use Eq. (9.9) and find

$$z_c = 11.13\,p_c \approx 0.111 \tag{9.11}$$

Let us now compare the compensated system, shown in Figure 9.11, with the uncompensated system. First sketch the root locus of the compensated system, as shown in Figure 9.12. Next search along the $\zeta = 0.174$ line for a multiple of $180°$ and find that the second-order dominant poles are at $-0.678 \pm j3.836$ with a gain, K, of 158.1. The third and fourth closed-loop poles are at -11.55 and -0.101, respectively, and are found by searching the real axis for a gain equal to that of the dominant poles. All transient and steady-state results for both the uncompensated and the compensated systems are shown in Table 9.1.

The fourth pole of the compensated system cancels its zero. This leaves the remaining three closed-loop poles of the compensated system very close in value to the three closed-loop poles of the uncompensated system. Hence, the transient response of

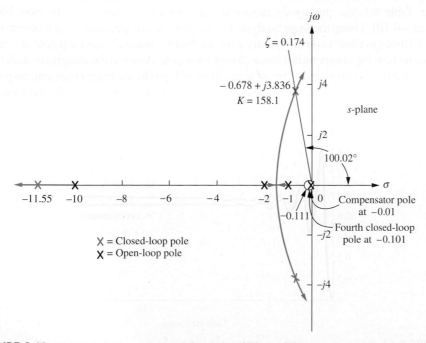

FIGURE 9.12 Root locus for compensated system of Figure 9.11

TABLE 9.1 **Predicted characteristics of uncompensated and lag-compensated systems for Example 9.2**

Parameter	Uncompensated	Lag-compensated
Plant and compensator	$\dfrac{K}{(s+1)(s+2)(s+10)}$	$\dfrac{K(s+0.111)}{(s+1)(s+2)(s+10)(s+0.01)}$
K	164.6	158.1
K_p	8.23	87.75
$e(\infty)$	0.108	0.011
Dominant second-order poles	$-0.694 \pm j3.926$	$-0.678 \pm j3.836$
Third pole	-11.61	-11.55
Fourth pole	None	-0.101
Zero	None	-0.111

TryIt 9.1

Use the following MATLAB and Control System Toolbox statements to reproduce Figure 9.13.

```
Gu = zpk([], ...
[-1 - 2 - 10], 164.6);
Gc = zpk([-0.111], ...
[-0.01], 1);
Gce = Gu*Gc;
Tu = feedback(Gu, 1);
Tc = feedback(Gce, 1);
step(Tu)
hold
step(Tc)
```

both systems is approximately the same, as is the system gain, but notice that the steady-state error of the compensated system is 1/9.818 that of the uncompensated system and is close to the design specification of a tenfold improvement.

Figure 9.13 shows the effect of the lag compensator in the time domain. Even though the transient responses of the uncompensated and lag-compensated systems are the same, the lag-compensated system exhibits less steady-state error by approaching unity more closely than the uncompensated system.

We now examine another design possibility for the lag compensator and compare the response to Figure 9.13. Let us assume a lag compensator whose pole and zero are 10 times as close to the origin as in the previous design. The results are compared in Figure 9.14. Even though both responses will eventually reach approximately the same steady-state value, the lag compensator previously designed, $G_c(s) = (s + 0.111)/(s + 0.01)$, approaches the final value faster than the proposed lag compensator, $G_c(s) = (s + 0.0111)/(s + 0.001)$. We can explain this phenomenon as follows. From Table 9.1, the previously designed lag compensator has a fourth closed-loop pole at -0.101. Using the same analysis for the new lag compensator with its open-loop pole 10 times as close to the imaginary axis, we find its fourth closed-loop pole at -0.01. Thus, the new lag compensator has a closed-loop pole closer to the imaginary axis than the original lag compensator. This pole at -0.01 will produce a longer transient response than the original pole at -0.101, and the steady-state value will not be reached as quickly.

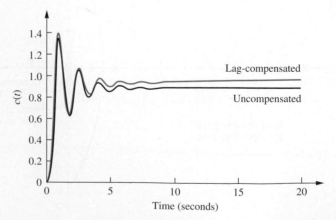

FIGURE 9.13 Step responses of uncompensated and lag-compensated systems for Example 9.2

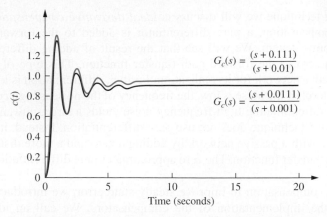

$$G_c(s) = \frac{(s + 0.111)}{(s + 0.01)}$$

$$G_c(s) = \frac{(s + 0.0111)}{(s + 0.001)}$$

FIGURE 9.14 Step responses of the system for Example 9.2 using different lag compensators

---

SKILL-ASSESSMENT EXERCISE 9.1

Problem: A unity feedback system with the forward transfer function

$$G(s) = \frac{K}{s(s + 7)}$$

is operating with a closed-loop step response that has 15% overshoot. Do the following:

a. Evaluate the steady-state error for a unit ramp input.

b. Design a lag compensator to improve the steady-state error by a factor of 20.

c. Evaluate the steady-state error for a unit ramp input to your compensated system.

d. Evaluate how much improvement in steady-state error was realized.

ANSWERS:

a. $e_{\text{ramp}}(\infty) = 0.1527$

b. $G_{\text{lag}}(s) = \dfrac{s + 0.2}{s + 0.01}$

c. $e_{\text{ramp}}(\infty) = 0.0078$

d. 19.58 times improvement

The complete solution is at www.wiley.com/college/nise.

9.3 IMPROVING TRANSIENT RESPONSE VIA CASCADE COMPENSATION

Since we have solved the problem of improving the steady-state error without affecting the transient response, let us now improve the transient response itself. In this section we discuss two ways to improve the transient response of a feedback control system by using cascade compensation. Typically, the objective is to design a response that has a desirable percent overshoot and a shorter settling time than the uncompensated system.

The first technique we will discuss is *ideal derivative compensation*. With ideal derivative compensation, a pure differentiator is added to the forward path of the feedback control system. We will see that the result of adding differentiation is the addition of a zero to the forward-path transfer function. This type of compensation requires an active network for its realization. Further, differentiation is a noisy process; although the level of the noise is low, the frequency of the noise is high compared to the signal. Thus, differentiating high-frequency noise yields a large, unwanted signal.

The second technique does not use pure differentiation. Instead, it approximates differentiation with a passive network by adding a zero and a more distant pole to the forward-path transfer function. The zero approximates pure differentiation as described previously.

As with compensation to improve steady-state error, we introduce names associated with the implementation of the compensators. We call an ideal derivative compensator a *proportional-plus-derivative (PD) controller*, since the implementation, as we will see, consists of feeding the error (proportional) plus the derivative of the error forward to the plant. The second technique uses a passive network called a *lead compensator*. As with the lag compensator, the name comes from its frequency response, which is discussed in Chapter 5. Thus, we use the name *PD controller* interchangeably with *ideal derivative compensator*, and we use the name *lead compensator* when the cascade compensator does not employ pure differentiation.

IDEAL DERIVATIVE COMPENSATION (PD)

The transient response of a system can be selected by choosing an appropriate closed-loop pole location on the *s*-plane. If this point is on the root locus, then a simple gain adjustment is all that is required in order to meet the transient response specification. If the closed-loop pole location is not on the root locus, then the root locus must be reshaped so that the compensated (new) root locus goes through the selected closed-loop pole location. In order to accomplish the latter task, poles and zeros can be added in the forward path to produce a new open-loop function whose root locus goes through the design point on the *s*-plane. One way to speed up the original system that generally works is to add a single zero to the forward path.

This zero can be represented by a compensator whose transfer function is

$$G_c(s) = s + z_c \tag{9.12}$$

This function, the sum of a differentiator and a pure gain, is called an *ideal derivative*, or *PD controller*. Judicious choice of the position of the compensator zero can quicken the response over the uncompensated system. In summary, transient responses unattainable by a simple gain adjustment can be obtained by augmenting the system's poles and zeros with an ideal derivative compensator.

We now show that ideal derivative compensation speeds up the response of a system. Several simple examples are shown in Figure 9.15, where the uncompensated system of Figure 9.15(*a*), operating with a damping ratio of 0.4, becomes a compensated system by the addition of a compensating zero at −2, −3, and −4 in Figures 9.15(*b*), (*c*), and (*d*), respectively. In each design the zero is moved to a different position, and the root locus is shown. For each compensated case the dominant, second-order poles are farther out along the 0.4 damping ratio line than the uncompensated system.

Each of the compensated cases has dominant poles with the same damping ratio as the uncompensated case. Thus, we predict that the percent overshoot will be the same for each case.

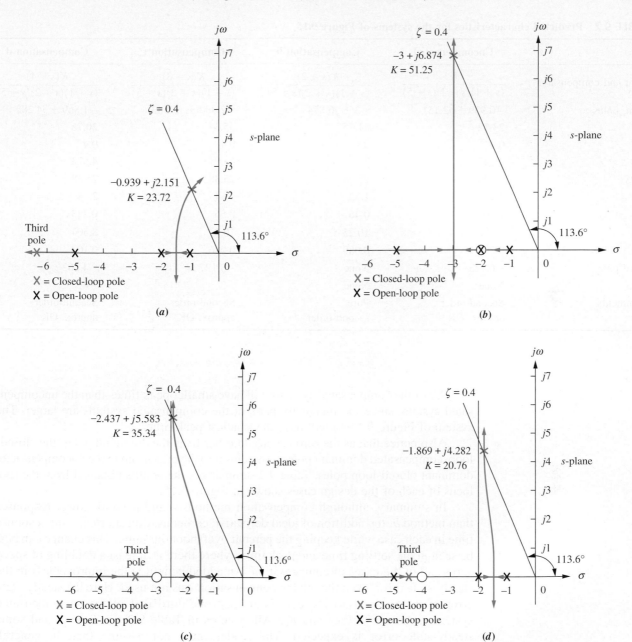

FIGURE 9.15 Using ideal derivative compensation: **a.** uncompensated; **b.** compensator zero at −2; **c.** compensator zero at −3; **d.** compensator zero at −4.

Also, the compensated, dominant, closed-loop poles have more negative real parts than the uncompensated, dominant, closed-loop poles. Hence, we predict that the settling times for the compensated cases will be shorter than for the uncompensated case. The compensated, dominant, closed-loop poles with the more negative real parts will have the shorter settling times. The system in Figure 9.15(*b*) will have the shortest settling time.

TABLE 9.2   Predicted characteristics for the systems of Figure 9.15

	Uncompensated	Compensation b	Compensation c	Compensation d
Plant and compensator	$\dfrac{K}{(s+1)(s+2)(s+5)}$	$\dfrac{K(s+2)}{(s+1)(s+2)(s+5)}$	$\dfrac{K(s+3)}{(s+1)(s+2)(s+5)}$	$\dfrac{K(s+4)}{(s+1)(s+2)(s+5)}$
Dom, poles	$-0.939 \pm j2.151$	$-3 \pm j6.874$	$-2.437 \pm j5.583$	$-1.869 \pm j4.282$
K	23.72	51.25	35.34	20.76
ζ	0.4	0.4	0.4	0.4
ω_n	2.347	7.5	6.091	4.673
%OS	25.38	25.38	25.38	25.38
T_s	4.26	1.33	1.64	2.14
T_p	1.46	0.46	0.56	0.733
K_p	2.372	10.25	10.6	8.304
$e(\infty)$	0.297	0.089	0.086	0.107
Third pole	-6.123	None	-3.127	-4.262
Zero	None	None	-3	-4
Comments	Second-order approx. OK	Pure second-order	Second-order approx. OK	Second-order approx. OK

All of the compensated systems will have smaller peak times than the uncompensated system, since the imaginary parts of the compensated systems are larger. The system of Figure 9.15(b) will have the smallest peak time.

Also notice that as the zero is placed farther from the dominant poles, the closed-loop, compensated dominant poles move closer to the origin and to the uncompensated, dominant closed-loop poles. Table 9.2 summarizes the results obtained from the root locus of each of the design cases shown in Figure 9.15.

In summary, although compensation methods c and d yield slower responses than method b, the addition of ideal derivative compensation shortened the response time in each case while keeping the percent overshoot the same. This change can best be seen in the settling time and peak time, where there is at least a doubling of speed across all of the cases of compensation. An added benefit is the improvement in the steady-state error, even though lag compensation was not used. Here the steady-state error of the compensated system is at least one-third that of the uncompensated system, as seen by $e(\infty)$ and K_p. All systems in Table 9.2 are Type 0, and some steady-state error is expected. The reader must not assume that, in general, improvement in transient response always yields an improvement in steady-state error.

The time response of each case in Table 9.2 is shown in Figure 9.16. We see that the compensated responses are faster and exhibit less error than the uncompensated response.

Now that we have seen what ideal derivative compensation can do, we are ready to design our own ideal derivative compensator to meet a transient response specification. Basically, we will evaluate the sum of angles from the open-loop poles and zeros to a design point that is the closed-loop pole that yields the desired transient response. The difference between $180°$ and the calculated angle must be the angular contribution of the compensator zero. Trigonometry is then used to locate the position of the zero to yield the required difference in angle.

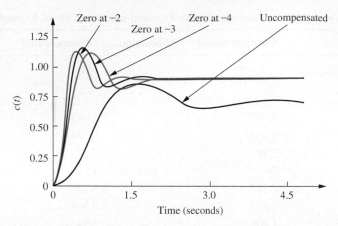

FIGURE 9.16 Uncompensated system and ideal derivative compensation solutions from Table 9.2

EXAMPLE 9.3

Ideal derivative compensator design

Problem: Given the system of Figure 9.17, design an ideal derivative compensator to yield a 16% overshoot, with a threefold reduction in settling time.

SOLUTION: Let us first evaluate the performance of the uncompensated system operating with 16% overshoot. The root locus for the uncompensated system is shown in Figure 9.18. Since 16% overshoot is equivalent to $\zeta = 0.504$, we search along that damping ratio line for an odd multiple of 180° and find that the dominant, second-order pair of poles is at $-1.205 \pm j2.064$. Thus, the settling time of the uncompensated system is

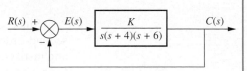

FIGURE 9.17 Feedback control system for Example 9.3

$$T_s = \frac{4}{\zeta\omega_n} = \frac{4}{1.205} = 3.320 \qquad (9.13)$$

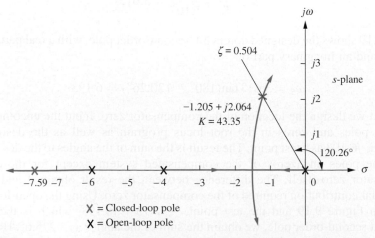

FIGURE 9.18 Root locus for uncompensated system shown in Figure 9.17

TABLE 9.3   **Uncompensated and compensated system characteristic of Example 9.3**

	Uncompensated	Simulation	Compensated	Simulation
Plant and compensator	$\dfrac{K}{s(s+4)(s+6)}$		$\dfrac{K(s+3.006)}{s(s+4)(s+6)}$	
Dominant poles	$-1.205 \pm j2.064$		$-3.613 \pm j6.193$	
K	43.35		47.45	
ζ	0.504		0.504	
ω_n	2.39		7.17	
%OS	16	14.8	16	11.8
T_s	3.320	3.6	1.107	1.2
T_p	1.522	1.7	0.507	0.5
K_v	1.806		5.94	
$e(\infty)$	0.554		0.168	
Third pole	-7.591		-2.775	
Zero	None		-3.006	
Comments	Second-order approx. OK		Pole-zero not canceling	

Since our evaluation of percent overshoot and settling time is based upon a second-order approximation, we must check the assumption by finding the third pole and justifying the second-order approximation. Searching beyond -6 on the real axis for a gain equal to the gain of the dominant, second-order pair, 43.35, we find a third pole at -7.59, which is over six times as far from the $j\omega$-axis as the dominant, second-order pair. We conclude that our approximation is valid. The transient and steady-state error characteristics of the uncompensated system are summarized in Table 9.3.

Now we proceed to compensate the system. First we find the location of the compensated system's dominant poles. In order to have a threefold reduction in the settling time, the compensated system's settling time will be one-third of Eq. (9.13). The new settling time will be 1.107. Therefore, the real part of the compensated system's dominant, second-order pole is

$$\sigma = \frac{4}{T_s} = \frac{4}{1.107} = 3.613 \tag{9.14}$$

Figure 9.19 shows the designed dominant, second-order pole, with a real part equal to -3.613 and an imaginary part of

$$\omega_d = 3.613 \tan(180° - 120.26°) = 6.193 \tag{9.15}$$

Next we design the location of the compensator zero. Input the uncompensated system's poles and zeros in the root locus program as well as the design point $-3.613 \pm j6.193$ as a test point. The result is the sum of the angles to the design point of all the poles and zeros of the compensated system except for those of the compensator zero itself. The difference between the result obtained and $180°$ is the angular contribution required of the compensator zero. Using the open-loop poles shown in Figure 9.19 and the test point, $-3.613 + j6.193$, which is the desired dominant second-order pole, we obtain the sum of the angles as $-275.6°$. Hence, the angular contribution required from the compensator zero for the test point to be on the

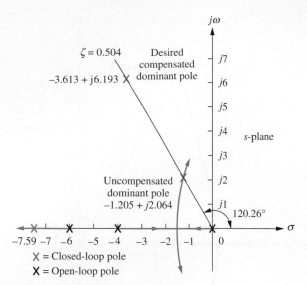

FIGURE 9.19 Compensated dominant pole superimposed over the uncompensated root locus for Example 9.3

root locus is $+275.6° - 180° = 95.6°$. The geometry is shown in Figure 9.20, where we now must solve for $-\sigma$, the location of the compensator zero.

From the figure,

$$\frac{6.193}{3.613 - \sigma} = \tan(180° - 95.6°) \tag{9.16}$$

Thus, $\sigma = 3.006$. The complete root locus for the compensated system is shown in Figure 9.21.

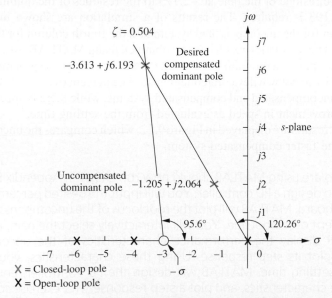

FIGURE 9.20 Evaluating the location of the compensating zero for Example 9.3

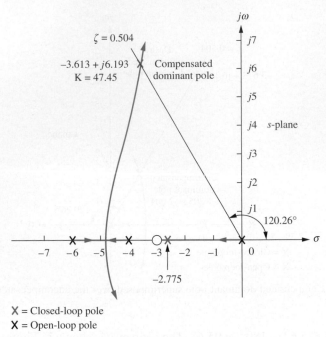

X = Closed-loop pole
X = Open-loop pole

FIGURE 9.21   Root locus for the compensated system of Example 9.3

Table 9.3 summarizes the results for both the uncompensated system and the compensated system. For the uncompensated system the estimate of the transient response is accurate since the third pole is at least five times the real part of the dominant, second-order pair. The second-order approximation for the compensated system, however, may be invalid because there is no approximate closed-loop third-pole and zero cancellation between the closed-loop pole at -2.775 and the closed-loop zero at -3.006. A simulation or a partial-fraction expansion of the closed-loop response to compare the residue of the pole at -2.775 to the residues of the dominant poles at $-3.613 \pm j6.193$ is required. The results of a simulation are shown in the table's second column for the uncompensated system and the fourth column for the compensated system. The simulation results can be obtained using MATLAB (discussed at the end of this example) or a program like the state-space step-response program described in Appendix G.1 at www.wiley.com/college/nise. The percent overshoot differs by 3% between the uncompensated and compensated systems, while there is approximately a threefold improvement in speed as evaluated from the settling time.

The final results are displayed in Figure 9.22, which compares the uncompensated system and the faster compensated system.

Students who are using MATLAB should now run ch9p1 in Appendix B. MATLAB will be used to design a PD controller. You will input the desired percent overshoot from the keyboard. MATLAB will plot the root locus of the uncompensated system and the percent overshoot line. You will interactively select the gain, after which MATLAB will display the performance characteristics of the uncompensated system and plot its step response. Using these characteristics, you will input the desired settling time. MATLAB will design the PD controller, enumerate its performance characteristics, and plot a step response. This exercise solves Example 9.3 using MATLAB.

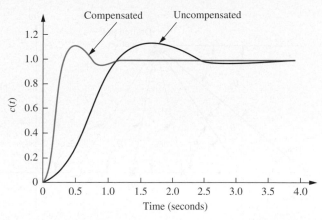

FIGURE 9.22 Uncompensated and compensated system step responses of Example 9.3

Once we decide on the location of the compensating zero, how do we implement the ideal derivative, or PD controller? The ideal integral compensator that improved steady-state error was implemented with a proportional-plus-integral (PI) controller. The ideal derivative compensator used to improve the transient response is implemented with a proportional-plus-derivative (PD) controller. For example, in Figure 9.23 the transfer function of the controller is

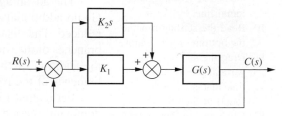

FIGURE 9.23 PD controller

$$G_c(s) = K_2 s + K_1 = K_2 \left(s + \frac{K_1}{K_2} \right) \tag{9.17}$$

Hence, K_1/K_2 is chosen to equal the negative of the compensator zero, and K_2 is chosen to contribute to the required loop-gain value. Later in the chapter we will study circuits that can be used to approximate differentiation and produce gain.

While the ideal derivative compensator can improve the transient response of the system, it has two drawbacks. First, it requires an active circuit to perform the differentiation. Second, as previously mentioned, differentiation is a noisy process: The level of the noise is low, but the frequency of the noise is high compared to the signal. Differentiation of high frequencies can lead to large unwanted signals or saturation of amplifiers and other components. The lead compensator is a passive network used to overcome the disadvantages of ideal differentiation and still retain the ability to improve the transient response.

LEAD COMPENSATION

Just as the active ideal integral compensator can be approximated with a passive lag network, an active ideal derivative compensator can be approximated with a passive lead compensator. When passive networks are used, a single zero cannot be produced; rather, a compensator zero and a pole result. However, if the pole is farther from the imaginary axis than the zero, the angular contribution of the compensator is still positive and thus approximates an equivalent single zero. In other words, the angular contribution of the compensator pole subtracts from the angular contribution of the zero but does not preclude the use of the compensator to improve transient response, since the net angular contribution is positive, just as for a single PD controller zero.

TryIt 9.2

Use MATLAB, the Control System Toolbox, and the following steps to use SISOTOOL to perform the design of Example 9.3.

1. Type **SISOTOOL** in the MATLAB **Command Window**.
2. Select **Import** in the File menu of the **SISO Design for SISO Design Task Window**.
3. In the **Data** field for G, type `zpk([],[0,-4,-6],1)` and hit **ENTER** on the keyboard. Click **OK**.
4. On the **Edit** menu choose **SISO Tool Preferences...** and select **Zero/pole/gain:** under the **Options** tab. Click **OK**.

(TryIt continues)

(continued)

5. Right-click on the root locus white space and choose **Design Requirements/New**…
6. Choose **Percent overshoot** and type in 16. Click **OK**.
7. Right-click on the root locus white space and choose **Design Requirements/New**…
8. Choose **Settling time** and click **OK**.
9. Drag the settling time vertical line to the intersection of the root locus and 16% overshoot radial line.
10. Read the settling time at the bottom of the window.
11. Drag the settling time vertical line to a settling time that is 1/3 of the value found in Step 9.
12. Click on a red zero icon in the menu bar. Place the zero on the root locus real axis by clicking again on the real axis.
13. Left-click on the real-axis zero and drag it along the real axis until the root locus intersects the settling time and percent overshoot lines.
14. Drag a red square along the root locus until it is at the intersection of the root locus, settling time line, and the percent overshoot line.
15. Click the **Compensator Editor** tab of the **Control and Estimation Tools Manager** window to see the resulting compensator, including the gain.

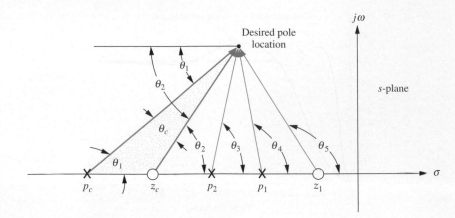

FIGURE 9.24   Geometry of lead compensation

The advantages of a passive lead network over an active PD controller are that (1) no additional power supplies are required and (2) noise due to differentiation is reduced. The disadvantage is that the additional pole does not reduce the number of branches of the root locus that cross the imaginary axis into the right half-plane, while the addition of the single zero of the PD controller tends to reduce the number of branches of the root locus that cross into the right half-plane.

Let us first look at the concept behind lead compensation. If we select a desired dominant, second-order pole on the s-plane, the sum of the angles from the uncompensated system's poles and zeros to the design point can be found. The difference between $180°$ and the sum of the angles must be the angular contribution required of the compensator.

For example, looking at Figure 9.24, we see that

$$\theta_2 - \theta_1 - \theta_3 - \theta_4 + \theta_5 = (2k + 1)180° \qquad (9.18)$$

where $(\theta_2 - \theta_1) = \theta_c$ is the angular contribution of the lead compensator. From Figure 9.24 we see that θ_c is the angle of a ray extending from the design point and intersecting the real axis at the pole value and zero value of the compensator. Now visualize this ray rotating about the desired closed-loop pole location and intersecting the real axis at the compensator pole and zero, as illustrated in Figure 9.25. We realize that an infinite number of lead compensators could be used to meet the transient response requirement.

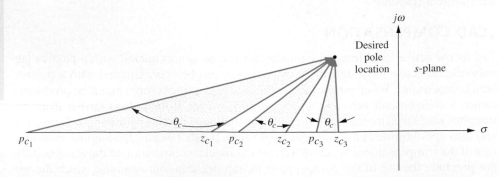

FIGURE 9.25   Three of the infinite possible lead compensator solutions

How do the possible lead compensators differ? The differences are in the values of static error constants, the gain required to reach the design point on the compensated root locus, the difficulty in justifying a second-order approximation when the design is complete, and the ensuing transient response.

For design we arbitrarily select either a lead compensator pole or zero and find the angular contribution at the design point of this pole or zero along with the system's open-loop poles and zeros. The difference between this angle and 180° is the required contribution of the remaining compensator pole or zero. Let us look at an example.

EXAMPLE 9.4

Lead compensator design

Problem: Design three lead compensators for the system of Figure 9.17 that will reduce the settling time by a factor of 2 while maintaining 30% overshoot. Compare the system characteristics between the three designs.

SOLUTION: First determine the characteristics of the uncompensated system operating at 30% overshoot to see what the uncompensated settling time is. Since 30% overshoot is equivalent to a damping ratio of 0.358, we search along the $\zeta = 0.358$ line for the uncompensated dominant poles on the root locus, as shown in Figure 9.26. From the pole's real part, we calculate the uncompensated settling time as $T_s = 4/1.007 = 3.972$ seconds. The remaining characteristics of the uncompensated system are summarized in Table 9.4.

Next we find the design point. A twofold reduction in settling time yields $T_s = 3.972/2 = 1.986$ seconds, from which the real part of the desired pole location is $-\zeta\omega_n = -4/T_s = -2.014$. The imaginary part is $\omega_d = -2.014 \tan(110.98°) = 5.252$.

We continue by designing the lead compensator. Arbitrarily assume a compensator zero at -5 on the real axis as a possible solution. Using the root locus program, sum the angles from both this zero and the uncompensated system's poles and zeros,

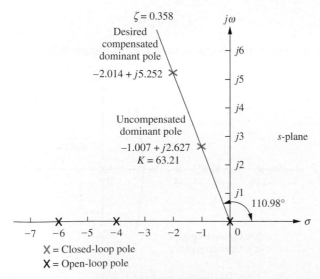

FIGURE 9.26 Lead compensator design, showing evaluation of uncompensated and compensated dominant poles for Example 9.4

TABLE 9.4 **Comparison of lead compensation designs for Example 9.4**

	Uncompensated	Compensation a	Compensation b	Compensation c
Plant and compensator	$\dfrac{K}{s(s+4)(s+6)}$	$\dfrac{K(s+5)}{s(s+4)(s+6)(s+42.96)}$	$\dfrac{K(s+4)}{s(s+4)(s+6)(s+20.09)}$	$\dfrac{K(s+2)}{s(s+4)(s+6)(s+8.971)}$
Dominant poles	$-1.007 \pm j2.627$	$-2.014 \pm j5.252$	$-2.014 \pm j5.252$	$-2.014 \pm j5.252$
K	63.21	1423	698.1	345.6
ζ	0.358	0.358	0.358	0.358
ω_n	2.813	5.625	5.625	5.625
$\%OS^*$	30 (28)	30 (30.7)	30 (28.2)	30 (14.5)
T_s^*	3.972 (4)	1.986 (2)	1.986 (2)	1.986 (1.7)
T_p^*	1.196 (1.3)	0.598 (0.6)	0.598 (0.6)	0.598 (0.7)
K_v	2.634	6.9	5.791	3.21
$e(\infty)$	0.380	0.145	0.173	0.312
Other poles	-7.986	$-43.8, -5.134$	-22.06	$-13.3, -1.642$
Zero	None	-5	None	-2
Comments	Second-order approx. OK	Second-order approx. OK	Second-order approx. OK	No pole-zero cancellation

*Simulation results are shown in parentheses.

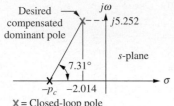

Desired compensated dominant pole

$-p_c$ -2.014 $7.31°$

$j\omega$ $j5.252$

s-plane

σ

X = Closed-loop pole
X = Open-loop pole

Note: This figure is not drawn to scale.

FIGURE 9.27 s-plane picture used to calculate the location of the compensator pole for Example 9.4

using the design point as a test point. The resulting angle is $-172.69°$. The difference between this angle and $180°$ is the angular contribution required from the compensator pole in order to place the design point on the root locus. Hence, an angular contribution of $-7.31°$ is required from the compensator pole.

The geometry shown in Figure 9.27 is used to calculate the location of the compensator pole. From the figure,

$$\frac{5.252}{p_c - 2.014} = \tan 7.31° \tag{9.19}$$

from which the compensator pole is found to be

$$p_c = 42.96 \tag{9.20}$$

The compensated system root locus is sketched in Figure 9.28.

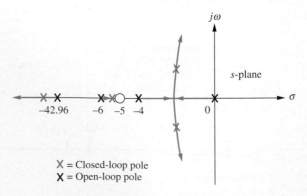

$j\omega$

s-plane

σ

-42.96 -6 -5 -4 0

X = Closed-loop pole
X = Open-loop pole

Note: This figure is not drawn to scale.

FIGURE 9.28 Compensated system root locus

In order to justify our estimates of percent overshoot and settling time, we must show that the second-order approximation is valid. To perform this validity check, we search for the third and fourth closed-loop poles found beyond −42.96 and between −5 and −6 in Figure 9.28. Searching these regions for the gain equal to that of the compensated dominant pole, 1423, we find that the third and fourth poles are at −43.8 and −5.134, respectively. Since −43.8 is more than 20 times the real part of the dominant pole, the effect of the third closed-loop pole is negligible. Since the closed-loop pole at −5.134 is close to the zero at −5, we have pole-zero cancellation, and the second-order approximation is valid.

All results for this design and two other designs, which place the compensator zero arbitrarily at −2 and −4 and follow similar design techniques, are summarized in Table 9.4. Each design should be verified by a simulation, which could consist of using MATLAB (discussed at the end of this example) or the state-space model and the step-response program discussed in Appendix G.1 at www.wiley.com/college/nise. We have performed a simulation for this design problem, and the results are shown by parenthetical entries next to the estimated values in the table. The only design that disagrees with the simulation is the case where the compensator zero is at −2. For this case the closed-loop pole and zero do not cancel.

A sketch of the root locus, which you should generate, shows why the effect of the zero is pronounced, causing the response to be different from that predicted. Placing the zero to the right of the pole at −4 creates a portion of the root locus that is between the origin and the zero. In other words, there is a closed-loop pole closer to the origin than the dominant poles, with little chance of pole-zero cancellation except at high gain. Thus, a quick sketch of the root locus gives us information from which we can make better design decisions. For this example, we want to place the zero on, or to the left of, the pole at −4, which gives a better chance for pole-zero cancellation and for a higher-order pole that is to the left of the dominant poles and subsequently faster. This is verified by the fact that our results show good second-order approximations for the cases where the zero was placed at −4 and −5. Again, decisions about where to place the zero are based on simple rules of thumb and must be verified by simulations at the end of the design.

Let us now summarize the results shown in Table 9.4. First we notice differences in the following:

1. The position of the arbitrarily selected zero
2. The amount of improvement in the steady-state error
3. The amount of required gain, K
4. The position of the third and fourth poles and their relative effect upon the second-order approximation. This effect is measured by their distance from the dominant poles or the degree of cancellation with the closed-loop zero.

Once a simulation verifies desired performance, the choice of compensation can be based upon the amount of gain required or the improvement in steady-state error that can be obtained without a lag compensator.

The results of Table 9.4 are supported by simulations of the step response, shown in Figure 9.29 for the uncompensated system and the three lead compensation solutions.

Students who are using MATLAB should now run ch9p2 in Appendix B. MATLAB will be used to design a lead compensator. You will input the desired percent overshoot from the keyboard. MATLAB will plot the root locus of the

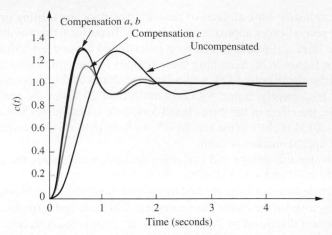

FIGURE 9.29 Uncompensated system and lead compensation responses for Example 9.4

uncompensated system and the percent overshoot line. You will interactively select the gain, after which MATLAB will display the performance characteristics of the uncompensated system and plot its step response. Using these characteristics, you will input the desired settling time and a zero value for the lead compensator. You will then interactively select a value for the compensator pole. MATLAB will respond with a root locus. You can then continue selecting pole values until the root locus goes through the desired point. MATLAB will display the lead compensator, enumerate its performance characteristics, and plot a step response. This exercise solves Example 9.4 using MATLAB.

SKILL-ASSESSMENT EXERCISE 9.2

Problem: A unity feedback system with the forward transfer function

$$G(s) = \frac{K}{s(s + 7)}$$

is operating with a closed-loop step response that has 15% overshoot. Do the following:

a. Evaluate the settling time.

b. Design a lead compensator to decrease the settling time by three times. Choose the compensator's zero to be at -10.

ANSWERS:

a. $T_s = 1.143$ s

b. $G_{\text{lead}}(s) = \dfrac{s + 10}{s + 25.52}$, $K = 476.3$

The complete solution is at www.wiley.com/college/nise.

9.4 IMPROVING STEADY-STATE ERROR AND TRANSIENT RESPONSE

We now combine the design techniques covered in Sections 9.2 and 9.3 to obtain improvement in steady-state error and transient response *independently*. Basically, we first improve the transient response by using the methods of Section 9.3. Then we improve the steady-state error of this compensated system by applying the methods of Section 9.2. A disadvantage of this approach is the slight decrease in the speed of the response when the steady-state error is improved.

As an alternative, we can improve the steady-state error first and then follow with the design to improve the transient response. A disadvantage of this approach is that the improvement in transient response in some cases yields deterioration in the improvement of the steady-state error, which was designed first. In other cases the improvement in transient response yields further improvement in steady-state errors. Thus, a system can be overdesigned with respect to steady-state errors. Overdesign is usually not a problem unless it affects cost or produces other design problems. In this textbook we first design for transient response and then design for steady-state error.

The design can use either active or passive compensators, as previously described. If we design an active PD controller followed by an active PI controller, the resulting compensator is called a *proportional-plus-integral-plus-derivative (PID) controller*. If we first design a passive lead compensator and then design a passive lag compensator, the resulting compensator is called a *lag-lead compensator*.

PID CONTROLLER DESIGN

A PID controller is shown in Figure 9.30. Its transfer function is

$$G_c(s) = K_1 + \frac{K_2}{s} + K_3 s = \frac{K_1 s + K_2 + K_3 s^2}{s} = \frac{K_3 \left(s^2 + \frac{K_1}{K_3} s + \frac{K_2}{K_3} \right)}{s} \quad (9.21)$$

which has two zeros plus a pole at the origin. One zero and the pole at the origin can be designed as the ideal integral compensator; the other zero can be designed as the ideal derivative compensator.

The design technique, which is demonstrated in Example 9.5, consists of the following steps:

1. Evaluate the performance of the uncompensated system to determine how much improvement in transient response is required.

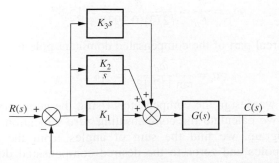

FIGURE 9.30 PID controller

2. Design the PD controller to meet the transient response specifications. The design includes the zero location and the loop gain.

3. Simulate the system to be sure all requirements have been met.

4. Redesign if the simulation shows that requirements have not been met.

5. Design the PI controller to yield the required steady-state error.

6. Determine the gains, K_1, K_2, and K_3, in Figure 9.30.

7. Simulate the system to be sure all requirements have been met.

8. Redesign if simulation shows that requirements have not been met.

■ EXAMPLE 9.5 ■

PID controller design

Problem: Given the system of Figure 9.31, design a PID controller so that the system can operate with a peak time that is two-thirds that of the uncompensated system at 20% overshoot and with zero steady-state error for a step input.

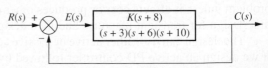

FIGURE 9.31 Uncompensated feedback control system for Example 9.5

SOLUTION: Note that our solution follows the eight-step procedure described earlier.

Step 1 Let us first evaluate the uncompensated system operating at 20% overshoot. Searching along the 20% overshoot line ($\zeta = 0.456$) in Figure 9.32, we find the dominant poles to be $-5.415 \pm j10.57$ with a gain of 121.5. A third pole, which exists at -8.169, is found by searching the region between -8 and -10 for a gain equivalent to that at the dominant poles. The complete performance of the uncompensated system is shown in the first column of Table 9.5, where we compare the calculated values to those obtained through simulation (Figure 9.35). We estimate that the uncompensated system has a peak time of 0.297 second at 20% overshoot.

Step 2 To compensate the system to reduce the peak time to two-thirds of that of the uncompensated system, we must first find the compensated system's dominant pole location. The imaginary part of the compensated dominant pole is

$$\omega_d = \frac{\pi}{T_p} = \frac{\pi}{(2/3)(0.297)} = 15.87 \tag{9.22}$$

Thus, the real part of the compensated dominant pole is

$$\sigma = \frac{\omega_d}{\tan 117.13°} = -8.13 \tag{9.23}$$

Next we design the compensator. Using the geometry shown in Figure 9.33, we calculate the compensating zero's location. Using the root locus program, we find the sum of angles from the uncompensated system's poles and zeros to the desired compensated dominant pole to be $-198.37°$. Thus, the contribution required from the compensator zero

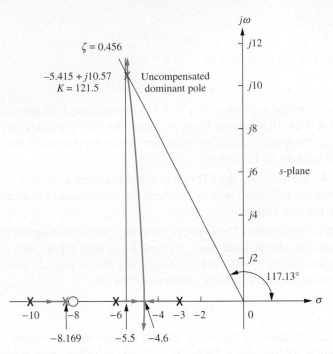

FIGURE 9.32   Root locus for the uncompensated system of Example 9.5

is $198.37° − 180° = 18.37°$. Assume that the compensator zero is located at $−z_c$, as shown in Figure 9.33. Since

$$\frac{15.87}{z_c − 8.13} = \tan 18.37°$$ (9.24)

TABLE 9.5   **Predicated characteristics of uncompensated, PD-, and PID-compensated systems of Example 9.5**

	Uncompensated	**PD-compensated**	**PID-compensated**
Plant and compensator	$\dfrac{K(s+8)}{(s+3)(s+6)(s+10)}$	$\dfrac{K(s+8)(s+55.92)}{(s+3)(s+6)(s+10)}$	$\dfrac{K(s+8)(s+55.92)(s+0.5)}{(s+3)(s+6)(s+10)s}$
Dominant poles	$-5.415 \pm j10.57$	$-8.13 \pm j15.87$	$-7.516 \pm j14.67$
K	121.5	5.34	4.6
ζ	0.456	0.456	0.456
ω_n	11.88	17.83	16.49
$\%OS$	20	20	20
T_s	0.739	0.492	0.532
T_p	0.297	0.198	0.214
K_p	5.4	13.27	∞
$e(\infty)$	0.156	0.070	0
Other poles	-8.169	-8.079	$-8.099, -0.468$
Zeros	-8	$-8, -55.92$	$-8, -55.92, -0.5$
Comments	Second-order approx. OK	Second-order approx. OK	Zeros at -55.92 and -0.5 not canceled

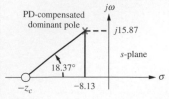

X = Closed-loop pole

Note: This figure is not drawn to scale.

FIGURE 9.33 Calculating the PD compensator zero for Example 9.5

then

$$z_c = 55.92 \qquad (9.25)$$

Thus, the PD controller is

$$G_{PD}(s) = (s + 55.92) \qquad (9.26)$$

The complete root locus for the PD-compensated system is sketched in Figure 9.34. Using a root locus program, the gain at the design point is 5.34. Complete specifications for ideal derivative compensation are shown in the third column of Table 9.5.

Steps 3 and 4 We simulate the PD-compensated system, as shown in Figure 9.35. We see the reduction in peak time and the improvement in steady-state error over the uncompensated system.

Step 5 After we design the PD controller, we design the ideal integral compensator to reduce the steady-state error to zero for a step input. Any ideal integral compensator zero will work, as long as the zero is placed close to the origin. Choosing the ideal integral compensator to be

$$G_{PI}(s) = \frac{s + 0.5}{s} \qquad (9.27)$$

we sketch the root locus for the PID-compensated system, as shown in Figure 9.36. Searching the 0.456 damping ratio line, we find the dominant, second-order poles to be $-7.516 \pm j14.67$, with an associated gain of 4.6. The remaining characteristics for the PID-compensated system are summarized in the fourth column of Table 9.5.

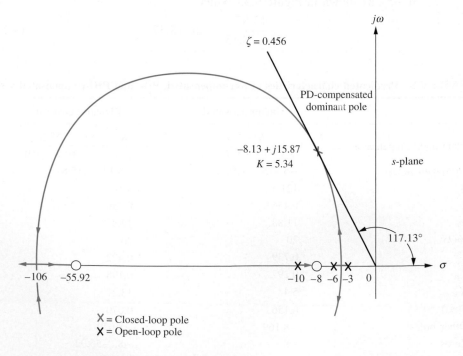

X = Closed-loop pole
X = Open-loop pole

Note: This figure is not drawn to scale.

FIGURE 9.34 Root locus for PD-compensated system of Example 9.5

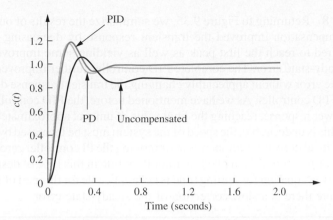

FIGURE 9.35 Step responses for uncompensated, PD-compensated, and PID-compensated systems of Example 9.5

Step 6 Now we determine the gains, K_1, K_2, and K_3, in Figure 9.30. From Eqs. (9.26) and (9.27), the product of the gain and the PID controller is

$$G_{PID}(s) = \frac{K(s + 55.92)(s + 0.5)}{s} = \frac{4.6(s + 55.92)(s + 0.5)}{s}$$

$$= \frac{4.6(s^2 + 56.42s + 27.96)}{s} \tag{9.28}$$

Matching Eqs. (9.21) and (9.28), $K_1 = 259.5$, $K_2 = 128.6$, and $K_3 = 4.6$

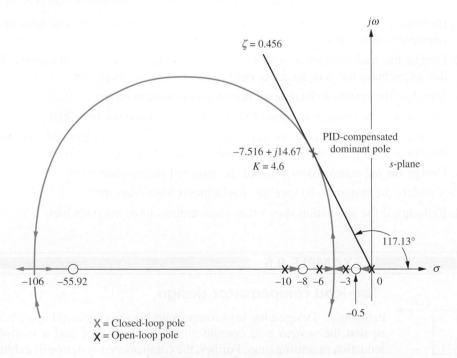

FIGURE 9.36 Root locus for PID-compensated system of Example 9.5

Steps 7 and 8   Returning to Figure 9.35, we summarize the results of our design. PD compensation improved the transient response by decreasing the time required to reach the first peak as well as yielding some improvement in the steady-state error. The complete PID controller further improved the steady-state error without appreciably changing the transient response designed with the PD controller. As we have mentioned before, the PID controller exhibits a slower response, reaching the final value of unity at approximately 3 seconds. If this is undesirable, the speed of the system must be increased by redesigning the ideal derivative compensator or moving the PI controller zero farther from the origin. Simulation plays an important role in this type of design since our derived equation for settling time is not applicable for this part of the response, where there is a slow correction of the steady-state error.

LAG-LEAD COMPENSATOR DESIGN

In the previous example we serially combined the concepts of ideal derivative and ideal integral compensation to arrive at the design of a PID controller that improved both the transient response and the steady-state error performance. In the next example we improve both transient response and the steady-state error by using a lead compensator and a lag compensator rather than the ideal PID. Our compensator is called a *lag-lead compensator*.

We first design the lead compensator to improve the transient response. Next we evaluate the improvement in steady-state error still required. Finally, we design the lag compensator to meet the steady-state error requirement. Later in the chapter we show circuit designs for the passive network. The following steps summarize the design procedure:

1. Evaluate the performance of the uncompensated system to determine how much improvement in transient response is required.
2. Design the lead compensator to meet the transient response specifications. The design includes the zero location, pole location, and the loop gain.
3. Simulate the system to be sure all requirements have been met.
4. Redesign if the simulation shows that requirements have not been met.
5. Evaluate the steady-state error performance for the lead-compensated system to determine how much more improvement in steady-state error is required.
6. Design the lag compensator to yield the required steady-state error.
7. Simulate the system to be sure all requirements have been met.
8. Redesign if the simulation shows that requirements have not been met.

EXAMPLE 9.6

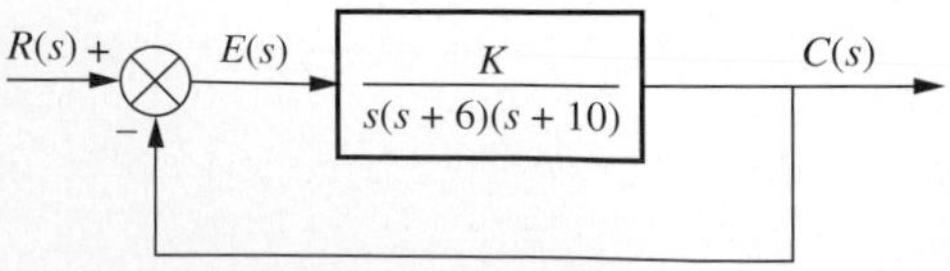

FIGURE 9.37   Uncompensated system for Example 9.6

Lag-lead compensator design

Problem: Design a lag-lead compensator for the system of Figure 9.37 so that the system will operate with 20% overshoot and a twofold reduction in settling time. Further, the compensated system will exhibit a tenfold improvement in steady-state error for a ramp input.

SOLUTION: Again, our solution follows the steps just described.

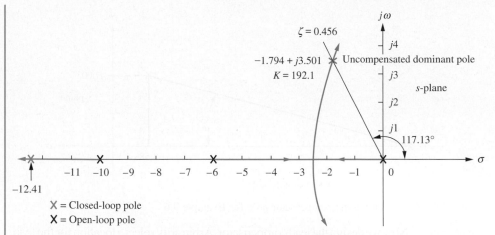

$\zeta = 0.456$

$-1.794 + j3.501$ ✗ Uncompensated dominant pole
$K = 192.1$

s-plane

$117.13°$

✗ = Closed-loop pole
✗ = Open-loop pole

FIGURE 9.38   Root locus for uncompensated system of Example 9.6

Step 1   First we evaluate the performance of the uncompensated system. Searching along the 20% overshoot line ($\zeta = 0.456$) in Figure 9.38, we find the dominant poles at $-1.794 \pm j3.501$, with a gain of 192.1. The performance of the uncompensated system is summarized in Table 9.6.

Step 2   Next we begin the lead compensator design by selecting the location of the compensated system's dominant poles. In order to realize a twofold reduction in settling time, the real part of the dominant pole must be increased by a factor of 2, since the settling time is inversely proportional to the real part. Thus,

$$-\zeta\omega_n = -2(1.794) = -3.588 \qquad (9.29)$$

The imaginary part of the design point is

$$\omega_d = \zeta\omega_n \tan 117.13° = 3.588 \tan 117.13° = 7.003 \qquad (9.30)$$

TABLE 9.6   **Predicated characteristics of uncompensated, lead-compensated, and lag-lead-compensated systems of Example 9.6**

	Uncompensated	Lead-compensated	Lag-lead-compensated
Plant and compensator	$\dfrac{K}{s(s+6)(s+10)}$	$\dfrac{K}{s(s+10)(s+29.1)}$	$\dfrac{K(s+0.04713)}{s(s+10)(s+29.1)(s+0.01)}$
Dominant poles	$-1.794 \pm j3.501$	$-3.588 \pm j7.003$	$-3.574 \pm j6.976$
K	192.1	1977	1971
ζ	0.456	0.456	0.456
ω_n	3.934	7.869	7.838
$\%OS$	20	20	20
T_s	2.230	1.115	1.119
T_p	0.897	0.449	0.450
K_v	3.202	6.794	31.92
$e(\infty)$	0.312	0.147	0.0313
Third pole	-12.41	-31.92	$-31.91, -0.0474$
Zero	None	None	-0.04713
Comments	Second-order approx. OK	Second-order approx. OK	Second-order approx. OK

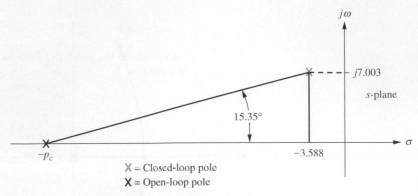

FIGURE 9.39 Evaluating the compensator pole for Example 9.6

Now we design the lead compensator. Arbitrarily select a location for the lead compensator zero. For this example we select the location of the compensator zero coincident with the open-loop pole at −6. This choice will eliminate a zero and leave the lead-compensated system with three poles, the same number that the uncompensated system has.

We complete the design by finding the location of the compensator pole. Using the root locus program, sum the angles to the design point from the uncompensated system's poles and zeros and the compensator zero and get −164.65°. The difference between 180° and this quantity is the angular contribution required from the compensator pole, or −15.35°. Using the geometry shown in Figure 9.39,

$$\frac{7.003}{p_c - 3.588} = \tan 15.35° \tag{9.31}$$

from which the location of the compensator pole, p_c, is found to be −29.1.

The complete root locus for the lead-compensated system is sketched in Figure 9.40. The gain setting at the design point is found to be 1977.

Steps 3 and 4 Check the design with a simulation. (The result for the lead-compensated system is shown in Figure 9.42 and is satisfactory.)

Step 5 Continue by designing the lag compensator to improve the steady-state error. Since the uncompensated system's open-loop transfer function is

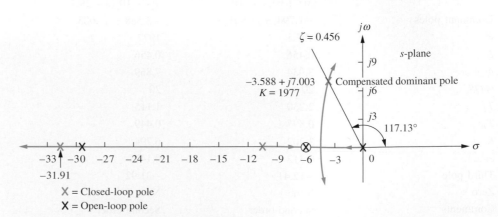

FIGURE 9.40 Root locus for lead-compensated system of Example 9.6

$$G(s) = \frac{192.1}{s(s+6)(s+10)} \tag{9.32}$$

the static error constant, K_v, which is inversely proportional to the steady-state error, is 3.201. Since the open-loop transfer function of the lead-compensated system is

$$G_{\text{LC}}(s) = \frac{1977}{s(s+10)(s+29.1)} \tag{9.33}$$

the static error constant, K_v, which is inversely proportional to the steady-state error, is 6.794. Thus, the addition of lead compensation has improved the steady-state error by a factor of 2.122. Since the requirements of the problem specified a tenfold improvement, the lag compensator must be designed to improve the steady-state error by a factor of 4.713 $(10/2.122 = 4.713)$ over the lead-compensated system.

Step 6 We arbitrarily choose the lag compensator pole at 0.01, which then places the lag compensator zero at 0.04713, yielding

$$G_{\text{lag}}(s) = \frac{(s+0.04713)}{(s+0.01)} \tag{9.34}$$

as the lag compensator. The lag-lead-compensated system's open-loop transfer function is

$$G_{\text{LLC}}(s) = \frac{K(s+0.04713)}{s(s+10)(s+29.1)(s+0.01)} \tag{9.35}$$

where the uncompensated system pole at -6 canceled the lead compensator zero at -6. By drawing the complete root locus for the lag-lead-compensated system and by searching along the 0.456 damping ratio line, we find the

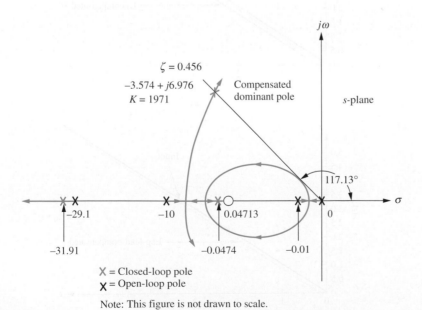

FIGURE 9.41 Root locus for lag-lead-compensated system of Example 9.6

FIGURE 9.42 Improvement in
step response for lag-lead-
compensated system of
Example 9.6

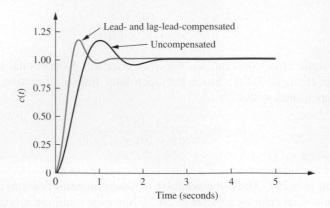

dominant, closed-loop poles to be at $-3.574 \pm j6.976$, with a gain of 1971.
The lag-lead-compensated root locus is shown in Figure 9.41.

A summary of our design is shown in Table 9.6. Notice that the lag-lead
compensation has indeed increased the speed of the system, as witnessed by
the settling time or the peak time. The steady-state error for a ramp input has
also decreased by about 10 times, as seen from $e(\infty)$.

Step 7   The final proof of our designs is shown by the simulations of Figures 9.42 and
9.43. The improvement in the transient response is shown in Figure 9.42,
where we see the peak time occurring sooner in the lag-lead-compensated

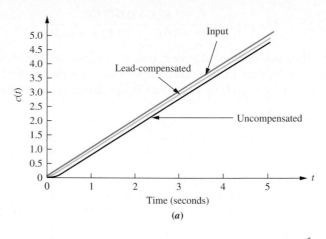

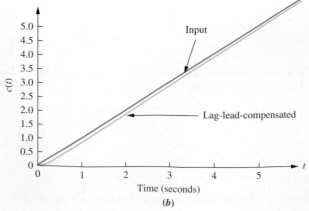

FIGURE 9.43
Improvement in ramp response
error for the system of
Example 9.6:
a. lead-compensated;
b. lag-lead-compensated

system. Improvement in the steady-state error for a ramp input is seen in Figure 9.43, where each step of our design yields more improvement. The improvement for the lead-compensated system is shown in Figure 9.43(*a*), and the final improvement due to the addition of the lag is shown in Figure 9.43(*b*).

In the previous example we canceled the system pole at -6 with the lead compensator zero. The design technique is the same if you place the lead compensator zero at a different location. Placing a zero at a different location and not canceling the open-loop pole yields a system with one more pole than the example. This increased complexity could make it more difficult to justify a second-order approximation. In any case, simulations should be used at each step to verify performance.

NOTCH FILTER

If a plant, such as a mechanical system, has high-frequency vibration modes, then a desired closed-loop response may be difficult to obtain. These high-frequency vibration modes can be modeled as part of the plant's transfer function by pairs of complex poles near the imaginary axis. In a closed-loop configuration, these poles can move closer to the imaginary axis or even cross into the right half-plane, as shown in Figure 9.44(*a*). Instability or high-frequency oscillations superimposed over the desired response can result (see Figure 9.44(*b*)).

One way of eliminating the high-frequency oscillations is to cascade a *notch filter*[2] with the plant (*Kuo, 1995*), as shown in Figure 9.44(*c*). The notch filter has zeros close to the low-damping-ratio poles of the plant as well as two real poles. Figure 9.44(*d*) shows that the root locus branch from the high-frequency poles now goes a short distance from the high-frequency pole to the notch filter's zero. The high-frequency response will now be negligible because of the pole-zero cancellation (see Figure 9.44(*e*)). Other cascade compensators can now be designed to yield a desired response.

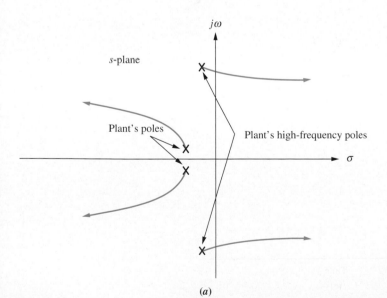

(a)

FIGURE 9.44
a. Root locus before cascading notch filter (figure continues)

---

[2] The name of this filter comes from the shape of its magnitude frequency response characteristics, which shows a dip near the damped frequency of the high-frequency poles. Magnitude frequency response is discussed in Chapter 10.

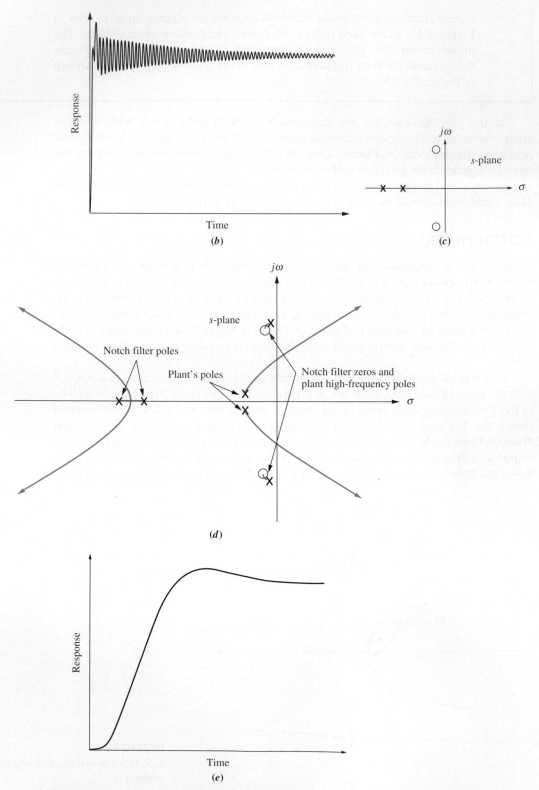

FIGURE 9.44   (Continued) **b.** typical closed-loop step response before cascading notch filter; **c.** pole-zero plot of a notch filter; **d.** root locus after cascading notch filter; **e.** closed-loop step response after cascading notch filter

The notch filter will be applied to Progressive Analysis and Design Problem 52 near the end of this chapter.

SKILL-ASSESSMENT EXERCISE 9.3

Problem: A unity feedback system with forward transfer function

$$G(s) = \frac{K}{s(s+7)}$$

is operating with a closed-loop step response that has 20% overshoot. Do the following:

a. Evaluate the settling time.

b. Evaluate the steady-state error for a unit ramp input.

c. Design a lag-lead compensator to decrease the settling time by 2 times and decrease the steady-state error for a unit ramp input by 10 times. Place the lead zero at -3.

ANSWERS:

a. $T_s = 1.143$ s

b. $e_{\text{ramp}}(\infty) = 0.1189$

c. $G_c(s) = \dfrac{(s+3)(s+0.092)}{(s+9.61)(s+0.01)}$, $K = 205.4$

The complete solution is at www.wiley.com/college/nise.

Before concluding this section, let us briefly summarize our discussion of cascade compensation. In Sections 9.2, 9.3, and 9.4, we used cascade compensators to improve transient response and steady-state error. Table 9.7 itemizes the types, functions, and characteristics of these compensators.

TABLE 9.7 **Types of cascade compensators (table continues)**

Function	Compensator	Transfer function	Characteristics
Improve steady-state error	PI	$K\dfrac{s + z_c}{s}$	1. Increases system type.
			2. Error becomes zero.
			3. Zero at $-z_c$ is small and negative.
			4. Active circuits are required to implement.
Improve steady-state error	Lag	$K\dfrac{s + z_c}{s + p_c}$	1. Error is improved but not driven to zero.
			2. Pole at $-p_c$ is small and negative.
			3. Zero at $-z_c$ is close to, and to the left of, the pole at $-p_c$.
			4. Active circuits are not required to implement.
Improve transient response	PD	$K(s + z_c)$	1. Zero at $-z_c$ is selected to put design point on root locus.
			2. Active circuits are required to implement.
			3. Can cause noise and saturation; implement with rate feedback or with a pole (lead).

TABLE 9.7 (Continued)

Function	Compensator	Transfer function	Characteristics
Improve transient response	Lead	$K\dfrac{s + z_c}{s + p_c}$	1. Zero at $-z_c$ and pole at $-p_c$ are selected to put design point on root locus.
			2. Pole at $-p_c$ is more negative than zero at $-z_c$.
			3. Active circuits are not required to implement.
Improve steady-state error and transient response	PID	$K\dfrac{(s + z_{\text{lag}})(s + z_{\text{lead}})}{s}$	1. Lag zero at $-z_{\text{lag}}$ and pole at origin improve steady-state error.
			2. Lead zero at $-z_{\text{lead}}$ improves transient response.
			3. Lag zero at $-z_{\text{lag}}$ is close to, and to the left of, the origin.
			4. Lag zero at $-z_{\text{lead}}$ is selected to put design point on root locus.
			5. Active circuits required to implement.
			6. Can cause noise and saturation; implement with rate feedback or with an additional pole.
Improve steady-state error and transient response	Lag-lead	$K\dfrac{(s + z_{\text{lag}})(s + z_{\text{lead}})}{(s + p_{\text{lag}})(s + p_{\text{lead}})}$	1. Lag pole at $-p_{\text{lag}}$ and lag zero at $-z_{\text{lag}}$ are used to improve steady-state error.
			2. Lead pole at $-p_{\text{lead}}$ and lead zero at $-z_{\text{lead}}$ are used to improve transient response.
			3. Lag pole at $-p_{\text{lag}}$ is small and negative.
			4. Lag zero at $-z_{\text{lag}}$ is close to, and to the left of, lag pole at $-p_{\text{lag}}$.
			5. Lead zero at $-z_{\text{lead}}$ and lead pole at $-p_{\text{lead}}$ are selected to put design point on root locus.
			6. Lead pole at $-p_{\text{lead}}$ is more negative than lead zero at $-z_{\text{lead}}$.
			7. Active circuits are not required to implement.

9.5 FEEDBACK COMPENSATION

In Section 9.4 we used cascade compensation as a way to improve transient response and steady-state response independently. Cascading a compensator with the plant is not the only way to reshape the root locus to intersect the closed-loop s-plane poles that yield a desired transient response. Transfer functions designed to be placed in a feedback path can also reshape the root locus. Figure 9.45 is a generic configuration showing a compensator, $H_c(s)$, placed in the *minor loop* of a feedback control system. Other configurations arise if we consider K unity, $G_2(s)$ unity, or both unity.

The design procedures for feedback compensation can be more complicated than for cascade compensation. On the other hand, feedback compensation can yield faster responses. Thus, the engineer has the luxury of designing faster responses into portions of a control loop in order to provide isolation. For example, the transient response of the ailerons and rudder control systems of an aircraft can be designed separately to be fast in order to reduce the effect of their dynamic response on the steering control loop. Feedback compensation can be used in cases where noise problems preclude the use of cascade compensation. Also, feedback compensation may not require additional

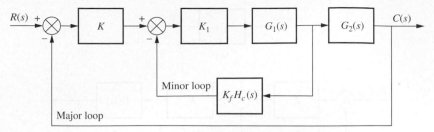

FIGURE 9.45 Generic control system with feedback compensation

amplification, since the signal passing through the compensator originates at the high-level output of the forward path and is delivered to a low-level input in the forward path. For example, let K and $G_2(s)$ in Figure 9.45 be unity. The input to the feedback compensator, $K_f H_c(s)$, is from the high-level output of $G_1(s)$, while the output of $K_f H_c(s)$ is one of the low-level inputs into K_1. Thus, there is a reduction in level through $K_f H_c(s)$, and amplification is usually not required.

A popular feedback compensator is a rate sensor that acts as a differentiator. In aircraft and ship applications, the rate sensor can be a rate gyro that responds with an output voltage proportional to the input angular velocity. In many other systems this rate sensor is implemented with a tachometer. A tachometer is a voltage generator that yields a voltage output proportional to input rotational speed. This compensator can easily be geared to the position output of a system. Figure 9.46 is a position control system showing the gearing of the tachometer to the motor. You can see the input and output potentiometers as well as the motor and inertial load. The block diagram representation of a tachometer is shown in Figure 9.47(*a*), and its typical position within a control loop is shown in Figure 9.47(*b*).

While this section shows methods for designing systems using rate feedback, it also sets the stage for compensation techniques in Chapter 12, where not only rate but all states including position will be fed back for proper control system performance.

We now discuss design procedures. Typically, the design of feedback compensation consists of finding the gains, such as K, K_1, and K_f in Figure 9.45, after establishing a dynamic form for $H_c(s)$. There are two approaches. The first is similar to cascade compensation. Assume a typical feedback system, where $G(s)$ is the forward path and $H(s)$ is the feedback. Now consider that a root locus is plotted from $G(s)H(s)$. With cascade compensation we added poles and zeros to $G(s)$. With feedback compensation, poles and zeros are added via $H(s)$.

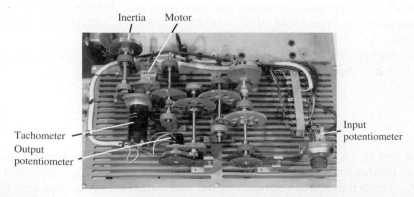

FIGURE 9.46 A position control system that uses a tachometer as a differentiator in the feedback path. Can you see the similarity between this system and the schematic on the front endpapers?

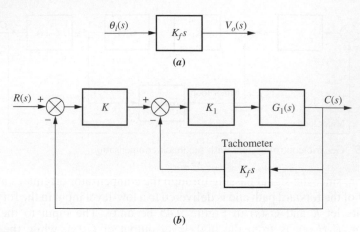

FIGURE 9.47   **a.** Transfer function of a tachometer; **b.** tachometer feed-back compensation

With the second approach we design a specified performance for the minor loop, shown in Figure 9.45, followed by a design of the major loop. Thus, the minor loop, such as ailerons on an aircraft, can be designed with its own performance specifications and operate within the major loop.

APPROACH 1

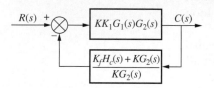

FIGURE 9.48   Equivalent block diagram of Figure 9.45

The first approach consists of reducing Figure 9.45 to Figure 9.48 by pushing K to the right past the summing junction, pushing $G_2(s)$ to the left past the pickoff point, and then adding the two feedback paths. Figure 9.48 shows that the loop gain, $G(s)H(s)$, is

$$G(s)H(s) = K_1G_1(s)[K_fH_c(s) + KG_2(s)] \tag{9.36}$$

Without feedback, $K_fH_c(s)$, the loop gain is

$$G(s)H(s) = KK_1G_1(s)G_2(s) \tag{9.37}$$

Thus, the effect of adding feedback is to replace the poles and zeros of $G_2(s)$ with the poles and zeros of $[K_fH_c(s) + KG_2(s)]$. Hence, this method is similar to cascade compensation in that we add new poles and zeros via $H(s)$ to reshape the root locus to go through the design point. However, one must remember that zeros of the equivalent feedback shown in Figure 9.48, $H(s) = [K_fH_c(s) + KG_2(s)]/KG_2(s)$, are not closed-loop zeros.

For example, if $G_2(s) = 1$ and the minor-loop feedback, $K_fH_c(s)$, is a rate sensor, $K_fH_c(s) = K_fs$, then from Eq. (9.36) the loop gain is

$$G(s)H(s) = K_fK_1G_1(s)\left(s + \frac{K}{K_f}\right) \tag{9.38}$$

Thus, a zero at $-K/K_f$ is added to the existing open-loop poles and zeros. This zero reshapes the root locus to go through the desired design point. A final adjustment of the gain, K_1, yields the desired response. Again, you should verify that this zero is not a closed-loop zero. Let us look at a numerical example.

████ **EXAMPLE 9.7** ████

Compensating zero via rate feedback

Problem: Given the system of Figure 9.49(*a*), design rate feedback compensation, as shown in Figure 9.49(*b*), to reduce the settling time by a factor of 4 while continuing to operate the system with 20% overshoot.

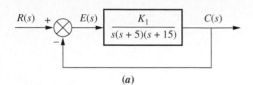

(*a*)

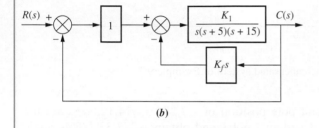

(*b*)

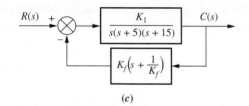

(*c*)

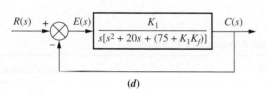

(*d*)

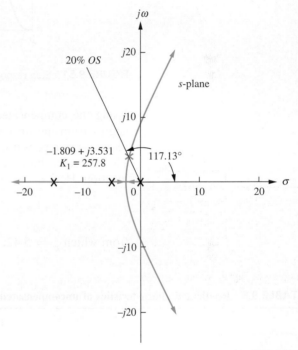

FIGURE 9.49 **a.** System for Example 9.7; **b.** system with rate feedback compensation; **c.** equivalent compensated system; **d.** equivalent compensated system showing unity feedback

FIGURE 9.50 Root locus for uncompensated system of Example 9.7

SOLUTION: First design a PD compensator. For the uncompensated system search along the 20% overshoot line ($\zeta = 0.456$) and find that the dominant poles are at $-1.809 \pm j3.531$, as shown in Figure 9.50. The estimated specifications for the uncompensated system are shown in Table 9.8, and the step response is shown in Figure 9.51. The settling time is 2.21 seconds and must be reduced by a factor of 4 to 0.55 second.

Next determine the location of the dominant poles for the compensated system. To achieve a fourfold decrease in the settling time, the real part of the pole must be increased by a factor of 4. Thus, the compensated pole has a real part of $4(-1.809) = -7.236$. The imaginary part is then

$$\omega_d = -7.236 \tan 117.13° = 14.12 \qquad (9.39)$$

where $117.13°$ is the angle of the 20% overshoot line.

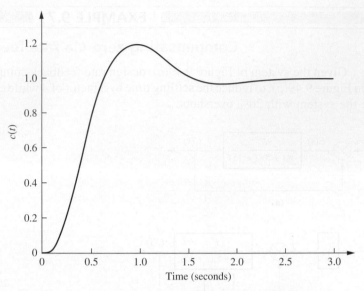

FIGURE 9.51 Step response for uncompensated system of Example 9.7

Using the compensated dominant pole position of $-7.236 \pm j14.12$, we sum the angles from the uncompensated system's poles and obtain $-277.33°$. This angle requires a compensator zero contribution of $+97.33°$ to yield $180°$ at the design point. The geometry shown in Figure 9.52 leads to the calculation of the compensator's zero location. Hence,

$$\frac{14.12}{7.236 - z_c} = \tan(180° - 97.33°) \tag{9.40}$$

from which $z_c = 5.42$.

TABLE 9.8 **Predicated characteristics of uncompensated and compensated systems of Example 9.7**

	Uncompensated	Compensated
Plant and compensator	$\dfrac{K_1}{s(s+5)(s+15)}$	$\dfrac{K_1}{s(s+5)(s+15)}$
Feedback	1	$0.185(s+5.42)$
Dominant poles	$-1.809 \pm j3.531$	$-7.236 \pm j14.12$
K_1	257.8	1388
ζ	0.456	0.456
ω_n	3.97	15.87
%OS	20	20
T_s	2.21	0.55
T_p	0.89	0.22
K_v	3.44	4.18
$e(\infty)$ (ramp)	0.29	0.24
Other poles	-16.4	-5.53
Zero	None	None
Comments	Second-order approx. OK	Simulate

The root locus for the equivalent compensated system of Figure 9.49(c) is shown in Figure 9.53. The gain at the design point, which is $K_1 K_f$ from Figure 9.49(c), is found to be 256.7. Since K_f is the reciprocal of the compensator zero, $K_f = 0.185$. Thus, $K_1 = 1388$.

In order to evaluate the steady-state error characteristic, K_v is found from Figure 9.49(d) to be

$$K_v = \frac{K_1}{75 + K_1 K_f} = 4.18 \tag{9.41}$$

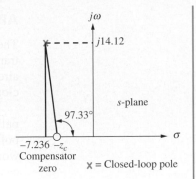

FIGURE 9.52 Finding the compensator zero in Example 9.7

Predicted performance for the compensated system is shown in Table 9.8. Notice that the higher-order pole is not far enough away from the dominant poles and thus cannot be neglected. Further, from Figure 9.49(d), we see that the closed-loop transfer function is

$$T(s) = \frac{G(s)}{1 + G(s)H(s)} = \frac{K_1}{s^3 + 20s^2 + (75 + K_1 K_f)s + K_1} \tag{9.42}$$

Thus, as predicted, the open-loop zero is not a closed-loop zero, and there is no pole-zero cancellation. Hence, the design must be checked by simulation.

The results of the simulation are shown in Figure 9.54 and show an over-damped response with a settling time of 0.75 second, compared to the uncompensated system's settling time of approximately 2.2 seconds. Although not meeting the design requirements, the response still represents an improvement over the uncompensated system of Figure 9.51. Typically, less overshoot is acceptable. The system should be redesigned for further reduction in settling time.

You may want to do Problem 7 at the end of this chapter, where you can repeat this example using PD cascade compensation. You will see that the compensator zero for cascade compensation is a closed-loop zero, yielding the possibility of pole-zero cancellation. However, PD compensation is usually noisy and not always practical.

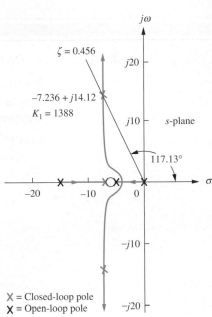

FIGURE 9.53 Root locus for the compensated system of Example 9.7

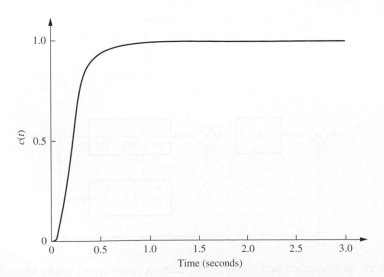

FIGURE 9.54 Step response for the compensated system of Example 9.7

APPROACH 2

The second approach allows us to use feedback compensation to design a minor loop's transient response separately from the closed-loop system response. In the case of an aircraft, the minor loop may control the position of the aerosurfaces, while the entire closed-loop system may control the entire aircraft's pitch angle.

We will see that the minor loop of Figure 9.45 basically represents a forward-path transfer function whose poles can be adjusted with the minor-loop gain. These poles then become the open-loop poles for the entire control system. In other words, rather than reshaping the root locus with additional poles and zeros, as in cascade compensation, we can actually change the plant's poles through a gain adjustment. Finally, the closed-loop poles are set by the loop gain, as in cascade compensation.

▮▮▮▮▮▮ EXAMPLE 9.8 ▮▮▮▮▮▮

Minor-loop feedback compensation

Problem: For the system of Figure 9.55(a), design minor-loop feedback compensation, as shown in Figure 9.55(b), to yield a damping ratio of 0.8 for the minor loop and a damping ratio of 0.6 for the closed-loop system.

SOLUTION: The minor loop is defined as the loop containing the plant, $1/[s(s+5)(s+15)]$, and the feedback compensator, $K_f s$. The value of K_f will be adjusted to set the location of the minor-loop poles, and then K will be adjusted to yield the desired closed-loop response.

The transfer function of the minor loop, $G_{ML}(s)$, is

$$G_{ML}(s) = \frac{1}{s[s^2 + 20s + (75 + K_f)]} \tag{9.43}$$

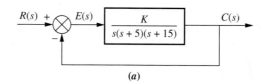

(a)

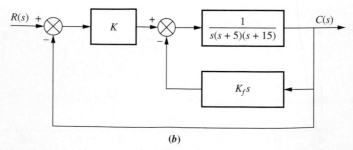

(b)

FIGURE 9.55   **a.** Uncompensated system and **b.** feedback-compensated system for Example 9.8

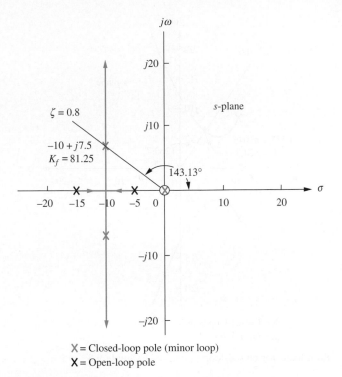

$\zeta = 0.8$

$-10 + j7.5$
$K_f = 81.25$

143.13°

s-plane

X = Closed-loop pole (minor loop)
X = Open-loop pole

FIGURE 9.56 Root locus for minor loop of Example 9.8

The poles of $G_{ML}(s)$ can be found analytically or via the root locus. The root locus for the minor loop, where $K_f s/[s(s+5)(s+15)]$ is the open-loop transfer function, is shown in Figure 9.56. Since the zero at the origin comes from the feedback transfer function of the minor loop, this zero is not a zero of the closed-loop transfer function of the minor loop. Hence, the pole at the origin appears to remain stationary, and there is no pole-zero cancellation at the origin. Eq. (9.43) also shows this phenomenon. We see a stationary pole at the origin and two complex poles that change with gain. Notice that the compensator gain, K_f, varies the natural frequency, ω_n, of the minor-loop poles as seen from Eq. (9.43). Since the real parts of the complex poles are constant at $\zeta \omega_n = -10$, the damping ratio must also be varying to keep $2\zeta \omega_n = 20$, a constant. Drawing the $\zeta = 0.8$ line in Figure 9.56 yields the complex poles at $-10 \pm j7.5$. The gain, K_f, which equals 81.25, places the minor-loop poles in a position to meet the specifications. The poles just found, $-10 \pm j7.5$, as well as the pole at the origin (Eq. (9.43)), act as open-loop poles that generate a root locus for variations of the gain, K.

The final root locus for the system is shown in Figure 9.57. The $\zeta = 0.6$ damping ratio line is drawn and searched. The closed-loop complex poles are found to be $-4.535 \pm j6.046$, with a required gain of 624.3. A third pole is at -10.93.

The results are summarized in Table 9.9. We see that the compensated system, although having the same damping ratio as the uncompensated system, is much faster and also has a smaller steady-state error. The results, however, are predicted results and must be simulated to verify percent overshoot, settling time,

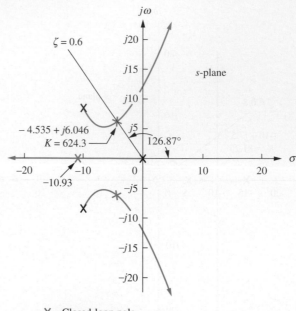

$\zeta = 0.6$

$-4.535 + j6.046$
$K = 624.3$

$126.87°$

-10.93

X = Closed-loop pole
X = Open-loop pole

FIGURE 9.57   Root locus for closed-loop system of Example 9.8

TABLE 9.9   **Predicted characteristics of the uncompensated and compensated systems of Example 9.8**

	Uncompensated	Compensated
Plant and compensator	$\dfrac{K_1}{s(s+5)(s+15)}$	$\dfrac{K}{s(s^2+20s+156.25)}$
Feedback	1	1
Dominant poles	$-1.997 \pm j2.662$	$-4.535 \pm j6.046$
K	177.3	624.3
ζ	0.6	0.6
ω_n	3.328	7.558
%OS	9.48	9.48
T_s	2	0.882
T_p	1.18	0.52
K_v	2.364	3.996
$e(\infty)$ (ramp)	0.423	0.25
Other poles	-16	-10.93
Zero	None	None
Comments	Second-order approx. OK	Simulate

and peak time, since the third pole is not far enough from the dominant poles. The step response is shown in Figure 9.58 and closely matches the predicted performance.

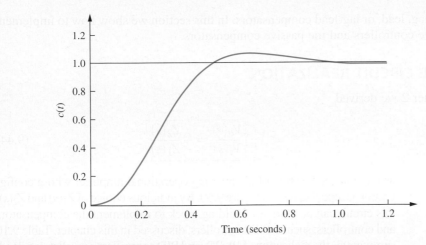

FIGURE 9.58 Step response simulation for Example 9.8

SKILL-ASSESSMENT EXERCISE 9.4

Problem: For the system of Figure 9.59, design minor-loop rate feedback compensation to yield a damping ratio of 0.7 for the minor loop's dominant poles and a damping ratio of 0.5 for the closed-loop system's dominant poles.

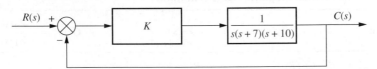

FIGURE 9.59 System for Skill-Assessment Exercise 9.4

ANSWER: The system is configured similar to Figure 9.55(*b*) with $K_f = 77.42$ and $K = 626.3$.

The complete solution is at www.wiley.com/college/nise.

Our discussion of compensation methods is now complete. We studied both cascade and feedback compensation and compared and contrasted them. We are now ready to show how to physically realize the controllers and compensators we designed.

9.6 PHYSICAL REALIZATION OF COMPENSATION

In this chapter we derived compensation to improve transient response and steady-state error in feedback control systems. Transfer functions of compensators used in cascade with the plant or in the feedback path were derived. These compensators were defined by their pole-zero configurations. They were either active PI, PD, or PID controllers or passive lag, lead, or lag-lead compensators. In this section we show how to implement the active controllers and the passive compensators.

ACTIVE-CIRCUIT REALIZATION

In Chapter 2 we derived

$$\frac{V_o(s)}{V_i(s)} = -\frac{Z_2(s)}{Z_1(s)} \tag{9.44}$$

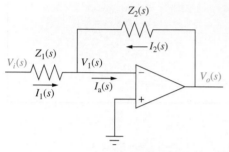

FIGURE 9.60 Operational amplifier configured for transfer function realization

as the transfer function of an inverting operational amplifier whose configuration is repeated here in Figure 9.60. By judicious choice of $Z_1(s)$ and $Z_2(s)$, this circuit can be used as a building block to implement the compensators and controllers, such as PID controllers, discussed in this chapter. Table 9.10 summarizes the realization of PI, PD, and PID controllers as well as lag, lead, and lag-lead compensators using operational amplifiers. You can verify the table by using the methods of Chapter 2 to find the impedances.

Other compensators can be realized by cascading compensators shown in the table. For example, a lag-lead compensator can be formed by cascading the lag compensator with the lead compensator, as shown in Figure 9.61. As an example let us implement one of the controllers we designed earlier in the chapter.

TABLE 9.10 Active realization of controllers and compensators, using an operational amplifier (table continues)

Function	$Z_1(s)$	$Z_2(s)$	$G_c(s) = -\dfrac{Z_2(s)}{Z_1(s)}$
Gain	R_1	R_2	$-\dfrac{R_2}{R_1}$
Integration	R	C	$-\dfrac{\frac{1}{RC}}{s}$
Differentiation	C	R	$-RCs$
PI controller	R_1	R_2 C	$-\dfrac{R_2}{R_1}\dfrac{\left(s+\frac{1}{R_2C}\right)}{s}$
PD controller	C $\parallel$ R_1	R_2	$-R_2C\left(s+\dfrac{1}{R_1C}\right)$
PID controller	C_1 $\parallel$ R_1	R_2 C_2	$-\left[\left(\dfrac{R_2}{R_1}+\dfrac{C_1}{C_2}\right)+R_2C_1s+\dfrac{\frac{1}{R_1C_2}}{s}\right]$

TABLE 9.10 **(Continued)**

Function	$Z_1(s)$	$Z_2(s)$	$G_c(s) = -\dfrac{Z_2(s)}{Z_1(s)}$
Lag compensation	C_1 ‖ R_1	C_2 ‖ R_2	$-\dfrac{C_1}{C_2}\dfrac{\left(s+\dfrac{1}{R_1 C_1}\right)}{\left(s+\dfrac{1}{R_2 C_2}\right)}$ where $R_2 C_2 > R_1 C_1$
Lead compensation	C_1 ‖ R_1	C_2 ‖ R_2	$-\dfrac{C_1}{C_2}\dfrac{\left(s+\dfrac{1}{R_1 C_1}\right)}{\left(s+\dfrac{1}{R_2 C_2}\right)}$ where $R_1 C_1 > R_2 C_2$

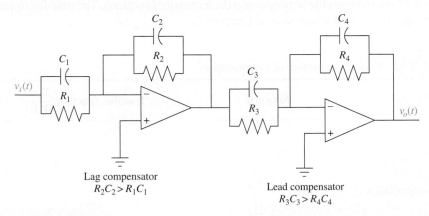

Lag compensator
$R_2 C_2 > R_1 C_1$

Lead compensator
$R_3 C_3 > R_4 C_4$

FIGURE 9.61 Lag-lead compensator implemented with operational amplifiers

EXAMPLE 9.9

Implementing a PID controller

Problem: Implement the PID controller of Example 9.5.

SOLUTION: The transfer function of the PID controller is

$$G_c(s) = \frac{(s+55.92)(s+0.5)}{s} \tag{9.45}$$

which can be put in the form

$$G_c(s) = s + 56.42 + \frac{27.96}{s} \tag{9.46}$$

Comparing the PID controller in Table 9.10 with Eq. (9.46), we obtain the following three relationships:

$$\frac{R_2}{R_1} + \frac{C_1}{C_2} = 56.42 \tag{9.47}$$

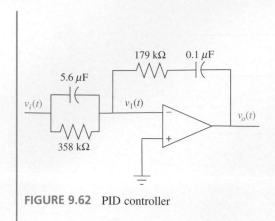

FIGURE 9.62   PID controller

$$R_2C_1 = 1 \qquad (9.48)$$

and

$$\frac{1}{R_1C_2} = 27.96 \qquad (9.49)$$

Since there are four unknowns and three equations, we arbitrarily select a practical value for one of the elements. Selecting $C_2 = 0.1\ \mu F$, the remaining values are found to be $R_1 = 357.65 k\Omega$, $R_2 = 178,891\ k\Omega$, and $C_1 = 5.59\ \mu F$.

The complete circuit is shown in Figure 9.62, where the circuit element values have been rounded off.

PASSIVE-CIRCUIT REALIZATION

Lag, lead, and lag-lead compensators can also be implemented with passive networks. Table 9.11 summarizes the networks and their transfer functions. The transfer functions can be derived with the methods of Chapter 2.

TABLE 9.11   **Passive realization of compensators**

Function	Network	Transfer function, $\dfrac{V_o(s)}{V_i(s)}$
Lag compensation		$\dfrac{R_2}{R_1 + R_2}\dfrac{s + \dfrac{1}{R_2C}}{s + \dfrac{1}{(R_1 + R_2)C}}$
Lead compensation		$\dfrac{s + \dfrac{1}{R_1C}}{s + \dfrac{1}{R_1C} + \dfrac{1}{R_2C}}$
Lag-lead compensation		$\dfrac{\left(s + \dfrac{1}{R_1C_1}\right)\left(s + \dfrac{1}{R_2C_2}\right)}{s^2 + \left(\dfrac{1}{R_1C_1} + \dfrac{1}{R_2C_2} + \dfrac{1}{R_2C_1}\right)s + \dfrac{1}{R_1R_2C_1C_2}}$

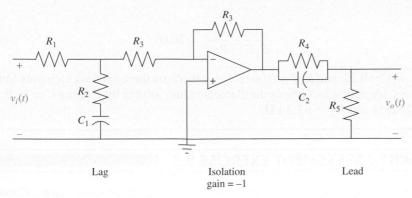

FIGURE 9.63 Lag-lead compensator implemented with cascaded lag and lead networks with isolation

The lag-lead transfer function can be put in the following form:

$$G_c(s) = \frac{\left(s + \dfrac{1}{T_1}\right)\left(s + \dfrac{1}{T_2}\right)}{\left(s + \dfrac{1}{\alpha T_1}\right)\left(s + \dfrac{\alpha}{T_2}\right)} \tag{9.50}$$

where $\alpha < 1$. Thus, the terms with T_1 form the lead compensator, and the terms with T_2 form the lag compensator. Equation (9.50) shows a restriction inherent in using this passive realization. We see that the ratio of the lead compensator zero to the lead compensator pole must be the same as the ratio of the lag compensator pole to the lag compensator zero. In Chapter 11 we design a lag-lead compensator with this restriction.

A lag-lead compensator without this restriction can be realized with an active network as previously shown or with passive networks by cascading the lead and lag networks shown in Table 9.11. Remember, though, that the two networks must be isolated to ensure that one network does not load the other. If the networks load each other, the transfer function will not be the product of the individual transfer functions. A possible realization using the passive networks uses an operational amplifier to provide isolation. The circuit is shown in Figure 9.63. Example 9.10 demonstrates the design of a passive compensator.

EXAMPLE 9.10

Realizing a lead compensator

Problem: Realize the lead compensator designed in Example 9.4 (Compensator b).

SOLUTION: The transfer function of the lead compensator is

$$G_c(s) = \frac{s + 4}{s + 20.09} \tag{9.51}$$

Comparing the transfer function of a lead network shown in Table 9.11 with Eq. (9.51), we obtain the following two relationships:

$$\frac{1}{R_1 C} = 4 \tag{9.52}$$

and

$$\frac{1}{R_1 C} + \frac{1}{R_2 C} = 20.09 \qquad (9.53)$$

Hence, $R_1 C = 0.25$, and $R_2 C = 0.0622$. Since there are three network elements and two equations, we may select one of the element values arbitrarily. Letting $C = 1 \mu F$, then $R_1 = 250\,k\Omega$ and $R_2 = 62.2$ kΩ.

SKILL-ASSESSMENT EXERCISE 9.5

WileyPLUS

Control Solutions

Problem: Implement the compensators shown in (a) and (b) below. Choose a passive realization if possible.

    a. $G_c(s) = \dfrac{(s+0.1)(s+5)}{s}$

    b. $G_c(s) = \dfrac{(s+0.1)(s+2)}{(s+0.01)(s+20)}$

ANSWERS:

    a. $G_c(s)$ is a PID controller and thus requires active realization. Use Figure 9.60 with the PID controller circuits shown in Table 9.10. One possible set of approximate component values is

$$C_1 = 10 \ \mu F, \qquad C_2 = 100 \ \mu F, \qquad R_1 = 20 \ k\Omega, \qquad R_2 = 100 \ k\Omega$$

    b. $G_c(s)$ is a lag-lead compensator that can be implemented with a passive network because the ratio of the lead pole to zero is the inverse of the ratio of the lag pole to zero. Use the lag-lead compensator circuit shown in Table 9.11. One possible set of approximate component values is

$$C_1 = 100 \ \mu F, \qquad C_2 = 900 \ \mu F, \qquad R_1 = 100 \ k\Omega, \qquad R_2 = 560 \ \Omega$$

The complete solution is at www.wiley.com.college/nise.

CASE STUDIES

Design

Antenna Control: Lag-Lead Compensation

For the antenna azimuth position control system case study in Chapter 8, we obtained a 25% overshoot using a simple gain adjustment. Once this percent overshoot was obtained, the settling time was determined. If we try to improve the settling time by increasing the gain, the percent overshoot also increases. In this section we continue with the antenna azimuth position control by designing a cascade compensator that yields 25% overshoot at a reduced settling time. Further, we effect an improvement in the steady-state error performance of the system.

Problem: Given the antenna azimuth position control system shown on the front endpapers, Configuration 1, design cascade compensation to meet the following requirements: (1) 25% overshoot, (2) 2-second settling time, and (3) $K_v = 20$.

SOLUTION: For the case study in Chapter 8, a preamplifier gain of 64.21 yielded 25% overshoot, with the dominant, second-order poles at $-0.833 \pm j1.888$. The settling time is thus $4/\zeta\omega_n = 4/.833 = 4.8$ seconds. The open-loop function for the system as derived in the case study in Chapter 5 is $G(s) = 6.63K/[s(s + 1.71)(s + 100)]$. Hence $K_v = 6.63K/(1.71 \times 100) = 2.49$. Comparing these values to this example's problem statement, we want to improve the settling time by a factor of 2.4, and we want approximately an eightfold improvement in K_v.

Lead compensator design to improve transient response: First locate the dominant second-order pole. To obtain a settling time, T_s, of 2 seconds and a percent overshoot of 25%, the real part of the dominant second-order pole should be at $-4/T_s = -2$. Locating the pole on the $113.83°$ line ($\zeta = 0.404$, corresponding to 25% overshoot) yields an imaginary part of 4.529 (see Figure 9.64).

   Second, assume a lead compensator zero and find the compensator pole. Assuming a compensator zero at -2, along with the uncompensated system's open-loop poles and zeros, use the root locus program in Appendix G.2 at www. wiley.com/college/nise to find that there is an angular contribution of $-120.14°$ at the design point of $-2 \pm j4.529$. Therefore, the compensator's pole must contribute $120.14° - 180° = -59.86°$ for the design point to be on the compensated system's root locus. The geometry is shown in Figure 9.64. To calculate the compensator pole, we use $4.529/(p_c - 2) = \tan 59.86°$ or $p_c = 4.63$.

   Now determine the gain. Using the lead-compensated system's open-loop function,

$$G(s) = \frac{6.63K(s + 2)}{s(s + 1.71)(s + 100)(s + 4.63)} \tag{9.54}$$

and the design point $-2 + j4.529$ as the test point in the root locus program, the gain, $6.63K$, is found to be 2549.

Lag compensator design to improve the steady-state error: K_v for the lead-compensated system is found using Eq. (9.54). Hence,

$$K_v = \frac{2549(2)}{(1.71)(100)(4.63)} = 6.44 \tag{9.55}$$

Since we want $K_v = 20$, the amount of improvement required over the lead-compensated system is $20/6.44 = 3.1$. Choose $p_c = -0.01$ and calculate $z_c - 0.031$, which is 3.1 times larger.

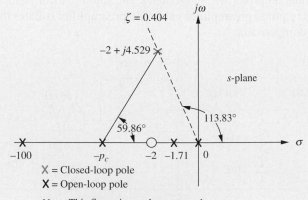

FIGURE 9.64   Locating compensator pole

Determine gain: The complete lag-lead-compensated open-loop function, $G_{\text{LLC}}(s)$, is

$$G_{\text{LLC}}(s) = \frac{6.63K(s+2)(s+0.031)}{s(s+.01)(s+1.71)(s+4.63)(s+100)} \tag{9.56}$$

Using the root locus program in Appendix G.2 at www.wiley.com/college/nise and the poles and zeros of Eq. (9.56), search along the 25% overshoot line (113.83°) for the design point. This point has moved slightly with the addition of the lag compensator to $-1.99 \pm j4.51$. The gain at this point equals 2533, which is $6.63K$. Solving for K yields $K = 382.1$.

Realization of the compensator: A realization of the lag-lead compensator is shown in Figure 9.63. From Table 9.11 the lag portion has the following transfer function:

$$G_{\text{lag}}(s) = \frac{R_2}{R_1+R_2} \frac{s+\dfrac{1}{R_2C}}{s+\dfrac{1}{(R_1+R_2)C}} = \frac{R_2}{R_1+R_2} \frac{(s+0.031)}{(s+0.01)} \tag{9.57}$$

Selecting $C = 10\ \mu\text{F}$, we find $R_2 = 3.2\ \text{M}\Omega$ and $R_1 = 6.8\ \text{M}\Omega$.
From Table 9.11 the lead compensator portion has the following transfer function:

$$G_{\text{lead}}(s) = \frac{s+\dfrac{1}{R_1C}}{s+\dfrac{1}{R_1C}+\dfrac{1}{R_2C}} = \frac{(s+2)}{(s+4.63)} \tag{9.58}$$

Selecting $C = 10\ \mu\text{F}$, we find $R_1 = 50\ \text{k}\Omega$ and $R_2 = 38\ \text{k}\Omega$.
The total loop gain required by the system is 2533. Hence,

$$6.63K \frac{R_2}{R_1+R_2} = 2533 \tag{9.59}$$

where K is the gain of the preamplifier, and $R_2/(R_1 + R_2)$ is the gain of the lag portion. Using the values of R_1 and R_2 found during the realization of the lag portion, we find $K = 1194$.

The final circuit is shown in Figure 9.65, where the preamplifier is implemented with an operational amplifier whose feedback and input resistor ratio approximately equals 1194, the required preamplifier gain. The preamplifier isolates the lag and lead portions of the compensator.

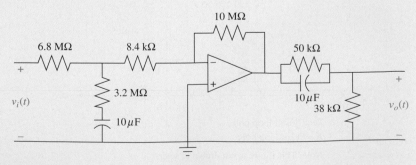

FIGURE 9.65 Realization of lag-lead compensator

Summary of the design results: Using Eq. (9.56) along with $K = 382.1$ yields the compensated value of K_v. Thus,

$$K_v = \lim_{s \to 0} sG_{\text{LLC}}(s) = \frac{2533(2)(0.031)}{(0.01)(1.71)(4.63)(100)} = 19.84 \qquad (9.60)$$

which is an improvement over the gain-compensated system in the case study of Chapter 8, where $K_v = 2.49$. This value is calculated from the uncompensated $G(s)$ by letting $K = 64.21$, as found in the Case Study of Chapter 8.

Finally, checking the second-order approximation via simulation, we see in Figure 9.66 the actual transient response. Compare this to the gain-compensated system response of Figure 8.29 to see the improvement effected by cascade compensation over simple gain adjustment. The gain-compensated system yielded 25%, with a settling time of about 4 seconds. The lag-lead-compensated system yields 28% overshoot, with a settling time of about 2 seconds. If the results are not adequate for the application, the system should be redesigned to reduce the percent overshoot.

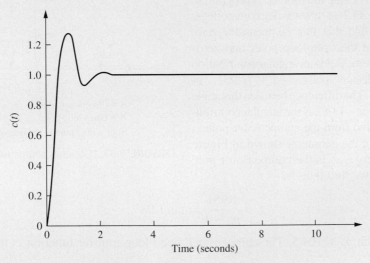

FIGURE 9.66 Step response of lag-lead-compensated antenna control

Challenge: You are now given a problem to test your knowledge of this chapter's objectives. You are given the antenna azimuth position control system shown on the front endpapers, Configuration 2. In the challenge in Chapter 8, you were asked to design, via gain adjustment, an 8-second settling time.

a. For your solution to the challenge in Chapter 8, evaluate the percent overshoot and the value of the appropriate static error constant.

b. Design a cascade compensator to reduce the percent overshoot by a factor of 4 and the settling time by a factor of 2. Also, improve the appropriate static error constant by a factor of 2.

c. Repeat Part **b** using MATLAB.

UFSS Vehicle: Lead and Feedback Compensation

As a final look at this case study, we redesign the pitch control loop for the UFSS vehicle. For the case study in Chapter 8, we saw that rate feedback improved the transient response. In this chapter's case study, we replace the rate feedback with a cascade compensator.

Problem: Given the pitch control loop without rate feedback ($K_2 = 0$) for the UFSS vehicle shown on the back endpapers, design a compensator to yield 20% overshoot and a settling time of 4 seconds (*Johnson, 1980*).

SOLUTION: First determine the location of the dominant closed-loop poles. Using the required 20% overshoot and a 4-second settling time, a second-order approximation shows the dominant closed-loop poles are located at $-1 \pm j1.951$. From the uncompensated system analyzed in the Chapter 8 case study, the estimated settling time was 19.8 seconds for dominant closed-loop poles of $-0.202 \pm j0.394$. Hence, a lead compensator is required to speed up the system.

Arbitrarily assume a lead compensator zero at -1. Using the root locus program in Appendix G.2 at www.wiley.com/college/nise, we find that this compensator zero, along with the open-loop poles and zeros of the system, yields an angular contribution at the design point, $-1 + j1.951$, of $-178.92°$. The difference between this angle and $180°$, or $-1.08°$, is the angular contribution required from the compensator pole.

Using the geometry shown in Figure 9.67, where $-p_c$ is the compensator pole location, we find that

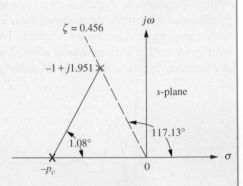

FIGURE 9.67   Locating compensator pole

$$\frac{1.951}{p_c - 1} = \tan 1.08° \tag{9.61}$$

from which $p_c = 104.5$. The compensated open-loop transfer function is thus

$$G(s) = \frac{0.25K_1(s + 0.435)(s + 1)}{(s + 1.23)(s + 2)(s^2 + 0.226s + 0.0169)(s + 104.5)} \tag{9.62}$$

where the compensator is

$$G_c(s) = \frac{(s + 1)}{(s + 104.5)} \tag{9.63}$$

Using all poles and zeros shown in Eq. (9.62), the root locus program shows that a gain of 516.5 is required at the design point, $-1 \pm j1.951$. The root locus of the compensated system is shown in Figure 9.68.

A test of the second-order approximation shows three more closed-loop poles at -0.5, -0.9, and -104.5. Since the open-loop zeros are at -0.435 and -1, simulation is required to see if there is effectively closed-loop pole-zero cancellation with the closed-loop poles at -0.5 and -0.9, respectively. Further, the closed-loop pole at -104.5 is more than five times the real part of the dominant closed-loop pole, $-1 \pm j1.951$, and its effect on the transient response is therefore negligible.

The step response of the closed-loop system is shown in Figure 9.69, where we see a 26% overshoot and a settling time of about 4.5 seconds. Comparing this response

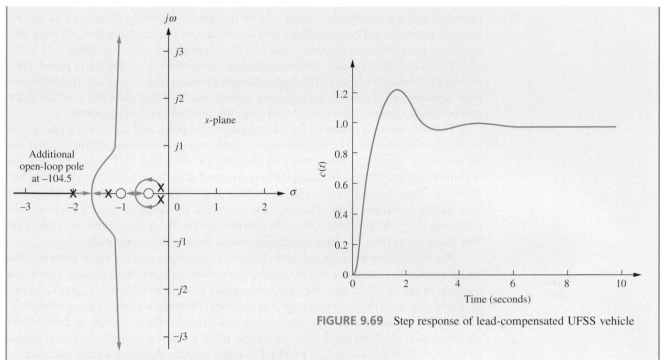

FIGURE 9.68   Root locus for lead-compensated system

FIGURE 9.69   Step response of lead-compensated UFSS vehicle

with Figure 8.31, the response of the uncompensated system, we see considerable improvement in the settling time and steady-state error. However, the transient response performance does not meet the design requirements. Thus, a redesign of the system to reduce the percent overshoot is suggested if required by the application.

Challenge: You are now given a problem to test your knowledge of this chapter's objectives. The heading control system for the UFSS vehicle is shown on the back endpapers. The minor loop contains the rudder and vehicle dynamics, and the major loop relates output and input heading (*Johnson, 1980*).

a. Find the values of K_1 and K_2 so that the minor-loop dominant poles have a damping ratio of 0.6 and the major-loop dominant poles have a damping ratio of 0.5.

b. Repeat, using MATLAB.

MATLAB

SUMMARY

In this chapter we learned how to design a system to meet transient and steady-state specifications. These design techniques overcame limitations in the design methodology covered in Chapter 8, whereby a transient response could be created only if the poles generating that response were on the root locus. Subsequent gain adjustment yielded the desired response. Since this value of gain dictated the amount of steady-state error in the response, a trade-off was required between the desired transient response and the desired steady-state error.

Cascade or *feedback compensation* is used to overcome the disadvantages of gain adjustment as a compensating technique. In this chapter we saw that the transient response and the steady-state error can be designed separately from each other. No longer was a trade-off between these two specifications required. Further, we were able to design for a transient response that was not represented on the original root locus.

The transient response design technique covered in this chapter is based upon reshaping the root locus to go through a desired transient response point, followed by a gain adjustment. Typically, the resulting gain is much higher than the original if the compensated system response is faster than the uncompensated response.

The root locus is reshaped by adding additional poles and zeros via a cascade or feedback compensator. The additional poles and zeros must be checked to see that any second-order approximations used in the design are valid. All poles besides the dominant second-order pair must yield a response that is much faster than the designed response. Thus, nondominant poles must be at least 5 times as far from the imaginary axis as the dominant pair. Further, any zeros of the system must be close to a nondominant pole for pole-zero cancellation, or far from the dominant pole pair. The resulting system can then be approximated by two dominant poles.

The steady-state response design technique is based upon placing a pole on or near the origin in order to increase or nearly increase the system type, and then placing a zero near this pole so that the effect upon the transient response is negligible. However, final reduction of steady-state error occurs with a long time constant. The same arguments about other poles yielding fast responses and about zeros being cancelled in order to validate a second-order approximation also hold true for this technique. If the second-order approximations cannot be justified, then a simulation is required to make sure the design is within tolerance.

Steady-state design compensators are implemented via *PI controllers* or *lag compensators*. PI controllers add a pole at the origin, thereby increasing the system type. Lag compensators, usually implemented with passive networks, place the pole off the origin but near it. Both methods add a zero very close to the pole in order not to affect the transient response.

The transient response design compensators are implemented through *PD controllers* or *lead compensators*. PD controllers add a zero to compensate the transient response; they are considered *ideal*. Lead compensators, on the other hand, are not ideal since they add a pole along with the zero. Lead compensators are usually passive networks.

We can correct both transient response and steady-state error with a *PID* or *lag-lead compensator*. Both of these are simply combinations of the previously described compensators. Table 9.7 summarizes the types of cascade compensators.

Feedback compensation can also be used to improve the transient response. Here the compensator is placed in the feedback path. The feedback gain is used to change the compensator zero or the system's open-loop poles, giving the designer a wide choice of various root loci. The system gain is then varied to move along the selected root locus to the design point. An advantage of feedback compensation is the ability to design a fast response into a subsystem independently of the system's total response.

In the next chapter we look at another method of design, frequency response, which is an alternate method to the root locus.

REVIEW QUESTIONS

1. Briefly distinguish between the design techniques in Chapter 8 and Chapter 9.
2. Name two major advantages of the design techniques of Chapter 9 over the design techniques of Chapter 8.
3. What kind of compensation improves the steady-state error?

4. What kind of compensation improves transient response?

5. What kind of compensation improves both steady-state error and transient response?

6. Cascade compensation to improve the steady-state error is based upon what pole-zero placement of the compensator? Also, state the reasons for this placement.

7. Cascade compensation to improve the transient response is based upon what pole-zero placement of the compensator? Also, state the reasons for this placement.

8. What difference on the *s*-plane is noted between using a PD controller or using a lead network to improve the transient response?

9. In order to speed up a system without changing the percent overshoot, where must the compensated system's poles on the *s*-plane be located in comparison to the uncompensated system's poles?

10. Why is there more improvement in steady-state error if a PI controller is used instead of a lag network?

11. When compensating for steady-state error, what effect is sometimes noted in the transient response?

12. A lag compensator with the zero 25 times as far from the imaginary axis as the compensator pole will yield approximately how much improvement in steady-state error?

13. If the zero of a feedback compensator is at −3 and a closed-loop system pole is at −3.001, can you say there will be pole-zero cancellation? Why?

14. Name two advantages of feedback compensation.

PROBLEMS

1. Design a PI controller to drive the step response error to zero for the unity feedback system shown in Figure P9.1, where

$$G(s) = \frac{K}{(s+1)(s+3)(s+10)}$$

The system operates with a damping ratio of 0.5. Compare the specifications of the uncompensated and compensated systems. [Section: 9.2]

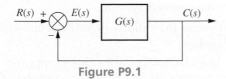

Figure P9.1

2. Consider the unity feedback system shown in Figure P9.1, where

$$G(s) = \frac{K}{s(s+2)(s+5)}$$

  a. Design a PI controller to drive the ramp response error to zero for any *K* that yields stability. [Section: 9.2]

  b. Use MATLAB to simulate your design for *K* = 1. Show both the input ramp and the output response on the same plot.

3. The unity feedback system shown in Figure P9.1 with

$$G(s) = \frac{K}{(s+1)(s+3)(s+5)}$$

  is operating with 10% overshoot. [Section: 9.2]

  a. What is the value of the appropriate static error constant?

  b. Find the transfer function of a lag network so that the appropriate static error constant equals 4 without appreciably changing the dominant poles of the uncompensated system.

  c. Use MATLAB or any other computer program to simulate the system to see the effect of your compensator.

4. Consider the unity feedback system shown in Figure P9.1 with

$$G(s) = \frac{K}{(s+2)(s+4)(s+6)}$$

   a. Design a compensator that will yield $K_p = 20$ without appreciably changing the dominant pole location that yields a 10% overshoot for the uncompensated system. [Section: 9.2]

   b. Use MATLAB or any other computer program to simulate the uncompensated and compensated systems.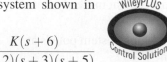

   c. Use MATLAB or any other computer program to determine how much time it takes the slow response of the lag compensator to bring the output to within 2% of its final compensated value.

5. The unity feedback system shown in Figure P9.1 with

$$G(s) = \frac{K(s+6)}{(s+2)(s+3)(s+5)}$$

   is operating with a dominant-pole damping ratio of 0.707. Design a PD controller so that the settling time is reduced by a factor of 2. Compare the transient and steady-state performance of the uncompensated and compensated systems. Describe any problems with your design. [Section: 9.3]

6. Redo Problem 5 using MATLAB in the following way:

   a. MATLAB will generate the root locus for the uncompensated system along with the 0.707 damping ratio line. You will interactively select the operating point. MATLAB will then inform you of the coordinates of the operating point, the gain at the operating point, as well as the estimated %OS, T_s, T_p, ζ, ω_n, and K_p represented by a second-order approximation at the operating point.

   b. MATLAB will display the step response of the uncompensated system.

   c. Without further input, MATLAB will calculate the compensated design point and will then ask you to input a value for the PD compensator zero from the keyboard. MATLAB will respond with a plot of the root locus showing the compensated design point. MATLAB will then allow you to keep changing the PD compensator value from the keyboard until a root locus is plotted that goes through the design point.

   d. For the compensated system, MATLAB will inform you of the coordinates of the operating point, the gain at the operating point, as well as the estimated %OS, T_s, T_p, ζ, ω_n, and K_p represented by a second-order approximation at the operating point.

   e. MATLAB will then display the step response of the compensated system.

7. Design a PD controller for the system shown in Figure P9.2 to reduce the settling time by a factor of 4 while continuing to operate the system with 20% overshoot. Compare your performance to that obtained in Example 9.7.

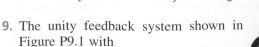
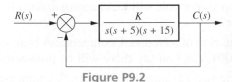

Figure P9.2

8. Consider the unity feedback system shown in Figure P9.1 with

$$G(s) = \frac{K}{(s+2)^2(s+3)}$$

   a. Find the location of the dominant poles to yield a 1.6 seconds settling time and an overshoot of 25%.

   b. If a compensator with a zero at -1 is used to achieve the conditions of (a), what must the angular contribution of the compensator pole be?

   c. Find the location of the compensator pole.

   d. Find the gain required to meet the requirements stated in (a).

   e. Find the location of other closed-loop poles for the compensated system.

   f. Discuss the validity of your second-order approximation.

   g. Use MATLAB or any other computer program to simulate the compensated system to check your design.

9. The unity feedback system shown in Figure P9.1 with

$$G(s) = \frac{K}{s^2}$$

is to be designed for a settling time of 1.667 seconds and a 16.3% overshoot. If the compensator zero is placed at -1, do the following: [Section: 9.3]

a. Find the coordinates of the dominant poles.

b. Find the compensator pole.

c. Find the system gain.

d. Find the location of all nondominant poles.

e. Estimate the accuracy of your second-order approximation.

f. Evaluate the steady-state error characteristics.

g. Use MATLAB or any other computer program to simulate the system and evaluate the actual transient response characteristics for a step input.

10. Given the unity feedback system of Figure P9.1, with

$$G(s) = \frac{K(s+3)}{(s+1)(s+2)(s+4)(s+5)}$$

do the following:

a. Sketch the root locus.

b. Find the coordinates of the dominant poles for which $\zeta = 0.8$.

c. Find the gain for which $\zeta = 0.8$.

d. If the system is to be cascade-compensated so that $T_s = 4/3$ second and $\zeta = 0.8$, find the compensator pole if the compensator zero is at -2.5.

e. Discuss the validity of your second-order approximation.

f. Use MATLAB or any other computer program to simulate the compensated and uncompensated systems and compare the results to those expected.

11. Redo Problem 9 using MATLAB in the following way:

a. MATLAB will generate the root locus for the uncompensated system along with the 0.8 damping-ratio line. You will interactively select the operating point. MATLAB will then inform you of the coordinates of the operating point, the gain at the operating point, as well as the estimated %OS, T_s, T_p, ζ, ω_n, and K_p represented by a second-order approximation at the operating point.

b. MATLAB will display the step response of the uncompensated system.

c. Without further input, MATLAB will calculate the compensated design point and will then ask you to input a value for the lead compensator pole from the keyboard. MATLAB will respond with a plot of the root locus showing the compensated design point. MATLAB will then allow you to keep changing the lead compensator pole value from the keyboard until a root locus is plotted that goes through the design point.

d. For the compensated system, MATLAB will inform you of the coordinates of the operating point, the gain at the operating point, as well as the estimated %OS, T_s, T_p, ζ, ω_n, and K_p represented by a second-order approximation at the operating point.

e. MATLAB will then display the step response of the compensated system.

f. Change the compensator's zero location a few times and collect data on the compensated system to see if any other choices of compensator zero yield advantages over the original design.

12. Consider the unity feedback system of Figure P9.1 with

$$G(s) = \frac{K}{s(s+10)(s+30)}$$

The system is operating at 15% overshoot. Design a compensator to decrease the settling time by a factor of 3 without affecting the percent overshoot and do the following:

a. Evaluate the uncompensated system's dominant poles, gain, and settling time.

b. Evaluate the compensated system's dominant poles and settling time.

c. Evaluate the compensator's pole and zero. Find the required gain.

d. Use MATLAB or any other computer program to simulate the compensated and uncompensated systems' step response.

13. The unity feedback system shown in Figure P9.1 with

$$G(s) = \frac{K}{(s+15)(s^2+6s+13)}$$

is operating with 30% overshoot. [Section: 9.3]

a. Find the transfer function of a cascade compensator, the system gain, and the dominant pole location that will cut the settling time in half if the compensator zero is at -7.

b. Find other poles and zeros and discuss your second-order approximation.

c. Use MATLAB or any other computer program to simulate both the uncompensated and compensated systems to see the effect of your compensator.

14. For the unity feedback system of Figure P9.1 with

$$G(s) = \frac{K}{s(s+1)(s^2+10s+26)}$$

do the following: [Section: 9.3]

a. Find the settling time for the system if it is operating with 15% overshoot.

b. Find the zero of a compensator and the gain, K, so that the settling time is 7 seconds. Assume that the pole of the compensator is located at -15.

c. Use MATLAB or any other computer program to simulate the system's step response to test the compensator.

15. A unity feedback control system has the following forward transfer function:

$$G(s) = \frac{K}{s^2(s+10)}$$

a. Design a compensator to yield dominant poles with a damping ratio of 0.357 and a natural frequency of 1.6 rad/s. Be sure to specify the value of K.

b. Estimate the expected percent overshoot and settling time.

c. Is your second-order approximation valid?

d. Use MATLAB or any other computer program to simulate and compare the transient response of the compensated system to the predicted transient response.

16. For the unity feedback system of Figure P9.1, with

$$G(s) = \frac{K}{(s^2+20s+101)(s+20)}$$

the damping ratio for the dominant poles is to be 0.4, and the settling time is to be 0.5 second. [Section: 9.3]

a. Find the coordinates of the dominant poles.

b. Find the location of the compensator zero if the compensator pole is at -15.

c. Find the required system gain.

d. Compare the performance of the uncompensated and compensated systems.

e. Use MATLAB or any other computer program to simulate the system to check your design. Redesign if necessary.

17. Consider the unity feedback system of Figure P9.1, with

$$G(s) = \frac{K}{(s+3)(s+5)}$$

a. Show that the system cannot operate with a settling time of 2/3 second and a percent overshoot of 1.5% with a simple gain adjustment.

b. Design a lead compensator so that the system meets the transient response characteristics of Part **a.** Specify the compensator's pole, zero, and the required gain.

18. Given the unity feedback system of Figure P9.1 with

$$G(s) = \frac{K}{(s+2)(s+4)(s+6)(s+8)}$$

Find the transfer function of a lag-lead compensator that will yield a settling time 0.5 second shorter than that of the uncompensated system, with a damping ratio of 0.5, and improve the steady-state error by a factor of 30. The compensator zero is at -5. Also, find the compensated system's gain. Justify any second-order approximations or verify the design through simulation. [Section: 9.4]

19. Redo Problem 19 using a lag-lead compensator and MATLAB in the following way:

a. MATLAB will generate the root locus for the uncompensated system along with the 0.5 damping-ratio line. You will interactively select the operating point. MATLAB will then proceed to inform you of the coordinates of the operating point, the gain at the operating point, as well as the estimated %OS, T_s, T_p, ζ, ω_n, and K_p represented by a second-order approximation at the operating point.

b. MATLAB will display the step response of the uncompensated system.

c. Without further input, MATLAB will calculate the compensated design point and will then ask you to input a value for the lead compensator pole from the keyboard. MATLAB will respond with a plot of the root locus showing the compensated design point. MATLAB will then allow you to keep changing the lead compensator pole value from the keyboard until a root locus is plotted that goes through the design point.

d. For the compensated system, MATLAB will inform you of the coordinates of the operating point, the gain at the operating point, as well as the estimated %OS, T_s, T_p, ζ, ω_n, and K_p represented by a second-order approximation at the operating point.

e. MATLAB will then display the step response of the compensated system.

f. Change the compensator's zero location a few times and collect data on the compensated system to see if any other choices of the compensator zero yield advantages over the original design.

g. Using the steady-state error of the uncompensated system, add a lag compensator to yield an improvement of 30 times over the uncompensated system's steady-state error, with minimal effect on the designed transient response. Have MATLAB plot the step response. Try several values for the lag compensator's pole and see the effect on the step response.

20. Given the uncompensated unity feedback system of Figure P9.1, with

$$G(s) = \frac{K}{s(s+1)(s+3)}$$

do the following: [Section: 9.4]

a. Design a compensator to yield the following specifications: settling time = 2.86 seconds; percent overshoot = 4.32%; the steady-state error is to be improved by a factor of 2 over the uncompensated system.

b. Compare the transient and steady-state error specifications of the uncompensated and compensated systems.

c. Compare the gains of the uncompensated and compensated systems.

d. Discuss the validity of your second-order approximation.

e. Use MATLAB or any other computer program to simulate the uncompensated and compensated systems and verify the specifications.

21. For the unity feedback system given in Figure P9.1 with

$$G(s) = \frac{K}{s(s+5)(s+11)}$$

do the following: [Section: 9.4]

a. Find the gain, K, for the uncompensated system to operate with 30% overshoot.

b. Find the peak time and K_v for the uncompensated system.

c. Design a lag-lead compensator to decrease the peak time by a factor of 2, decrease the percent overshoot by a factor of 2, and improve the steady-state error by a factor of 30. Specify all poles, zeros, and gains.

22. The unity feedback system shown in Figure P9.1 with

$$G(s) = \frac{K}{(s^2 + 4s + 8)(s + 10)}$$

is to be designed to meet the following specifications:

Overshoot: Less than 25%
Settling time: Less than 1 second
$K_p = 10$

Do the following: [Section: 9.4]

a. Evaluate the performance of the uncompensated system operating at 10% overshoot.

b. Design a passive compensator to meet the desired specifications.

c. Use MATLAB to simulate the compensated system. Compare the response with the desired specifications.

23. Consider the unity feedback system in Figure P9.1, with

$$G(s) = \frac{K}{(s+2)(s+4)}$$

The system is operated with 4.32% overshoot. In order to improve the steady-state error, K_p is to be increased by at least a factor of 5. A lag compensator of the form

$$G_c(s) = \frac{(s + 0.5)}{(s + 0.1)}$$

is to be used. [Section: 9.4]

a. Find the gain required for both the compensated and the uncompensated systems.

b. Find the value of K_p for both the compensated and the uncompensated systems.

c. Estimate the percent overshoot and settling time for both the compensated and the uncompensated systems.

d. Discuss the validity of the second-order approximation used for your results in Part **c**.

e. Use MATLAB or any other computer program to simulate the step response for the uncompensated and compensated systems. What do you notice about the compensated system's response?

 MATLAB

f. Design a lead compensator that will correct the objection you notice in Part **e**.

24. For the unity feedback system in Figure P9.1, with

$$G(s) = \frac{K}{(s + 1)(s + 4)}$$

design a PID controller that will yield a peak time of 1.047 seconds and a damping ratio of 0.8, with zero error for a step input. [Section: 9.4]

25. For the unity feedback system in Figure P9.1, with

$$G(s) = \frac{K}{(s + 4)(s + 6)(s + 10)}$$

do the following:

WileyPLUS

Control Solutions

a. Design a controller that will yield no more than 25% overshoot and no more than a 2 second settling time for a step input and zero steady-state error for step and ramp inputs.

b. Use MATLAB and verify your design.

 MATLAB

26. Redo Problem 25 using MATLAB in the following way:

MATLAB

a. MATLAB will ask for the desired percent overshoot, settling time, and PI compensator zero.

b. MATLAB will design the PD controller's zero.

c. MATLAB will display the root locus of the PID-compensated system with the desired percent overshoot line.

d. The user will interactively select the intersection of the root locus and the desired percent overshoot line.

e. MATLAB will display the gain and transient response characteristics of the PID-compensated system.

f. MATLAB will display the step response of the PID-compensated system.

g. MATLAB will display the ramp response of the PID-compensated system.

27. If the system of Figure P9.3 operates with a damping ratio of 0.517 for the dominant second-order poles, find the location of all closed-loop poles and zeros.

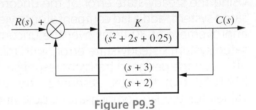

Figure P9.3

28. For the unity feedback system in Figure P9.1, with

$$G(s) = \frac{K}{s(s + 2)(s + 4)(S + 6)}$$

do the following: [Section: 9.5]

a. Design rate feedback to yield a step response with no more than 15% overshoot and no more than 3 seconds settling time. Use Approach 1.

b. Use MATLAB and simulate your compensated system.

MATLAB

29. Given the system of Figure P9.4: [Section: 9.5]

a. Design the value of K_1, as well as a in the feedback path of the minor loop, to yield a settling time of 1 second with 5% overshoot for the step response.

b. Design the value of K to yield a major-loop response with 10% overshoot for a step input.

c. Use MATLAB or any other computer program to simulate the step response to the entire closed-loop system.

d. Add a PI compensator to reduce the major-loop steady-state error to zero and simulate the step response using MATLAB or any other computer program.

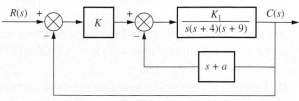

Figure P9.4

30. Identify and realize the following controllers with operational amplifiers. [Section: 9.6]

   a. $\dfrac{s + 0.01}{s}$

   b. $s + 2$

31. Identify and realize the following compensators with passive networks. [Section: 9.6]

   a. $\dfrac{s + 0.1}{s + 0.01}$

   b. $\dfrac{s + 2}{s + 5}$

   c. $\left(\dfrac{s + 0.1}{s + 0.01}\right)\left(\dfrac{s + 1}{s + 10}\right)$

32. Repeat Problem 31 using operational amplifiers. [Section: 9.6]

Design Problems

33. The room temperature of an 11 m^2 room is to be controlled by varying the power of an indoor radiator. For this specific room the open-loop transfer function from radiator power, $\dot{Q}(s)$, to temperature, $T(s)$, is (*Thomas, 2005*)

$$G(s) = \frac{T(s)}{\dot{Q}(s)} = \frac{(1 \times 10^{-6})s^2 + (1.314 \times 10^{-9})s + (2.66 \times 10^{-13})}{s^3 + 0.00163s^2 + (5.272 \times 10^{-7})s + (3.538 \times 10^{-11})}$$

The system is assumed to be in the closed-loop configuration shown in Figure P9.1.

a. For a unit step input, calculate the steady-state error of the system.

b. Try using the procedure of Section 9.2 to design a PI controller to obtain zero steady-state error for step inputs without appreciably changing the transient response. Then explain why it is not possible to do so.

c. Design a PI controller of the form $G_c(s) = \dfrac{K(s + z)}{s}$ that will reduce the step-response error to zero while not changing significantly the transient response. (Hint: Place the zero of the compensator in a position where the closed-loop poles of the uncompensated root locus will not be affected significantly.)

d. Use Simulink to simulate the systems of Parts **b** and **c** and to verify the correctness of your design in Part **c**. *Simulink*

34. Figure P9.5 shows a two-tank system. The liquid inflow to the upper tank can be controlled using a valve and is represented by F_0. The upper tank's outflow equals the lower tank's inflow and is represented by F_1. The outflow of the lower tank is F_2. The objective of the design is to control the liquid level, $y(t)$, in the lower tank. The open-loop transmission for this system is $\dfrac{Y(s)}{F_o(s)} = \dfrac{a_2 a_3}{s^2 + (a_1 + a_4)s + a_1 a_4}$ (*Romagnoli, 2006*). The system will be controlled in a loop analogous to that of Figure P9.1, where the

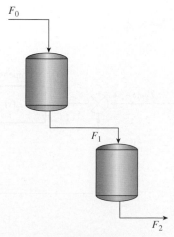

Figure P9.5

lower liquid level will be measured and compared to a set point. The resulting error will be fed to a controller, which in turn will open or close the valve feeding the upper tank.

a. Assuming $a_1 = 0.04$, $a_2 = 0.0187$, $a_3 = 1$, and $a_4 = 0.227$, design a lag compensator to obtain a step-response steady-state error of 10% without affecting the system's transient response appreciably.

b. Verify your design through MATLAB simulations.

35. Figure P9.6(*a*) shows a heat-exchanger process whose purpose is to maintain the temperature of a liquid at a prescribed temperature.

The temperature is measured using a sensor and a transmitter, TT 22, that sends the measurement to a corresponding controller, TC 22, that compares the actual temperature with a desired temperature set point, SP. The controller automatically opens or closes a valve to allow or prevent the flow of steam to change the temperature in the tank. The corresponding block diagram for this system is shown in Figure P9.6(*b*) (*Smith 2002*). Assume the following transfer functions:

$$G_v(s) - \frac{0.02}{4s + 1}; \quad G_p(s) = \frac{70}{50s + 1}; \quad H(s) = \frac{1}{12s + 1}.$$

a. Assuming $G_c(s) = K$, find the value of K that will result in a dominant pole with $\zeta = 0.7$. Obtain the corresponding T_s.

b. Design a PD controller to obtain the same damping factor as Part **a** but with a settling time 20% smaller.

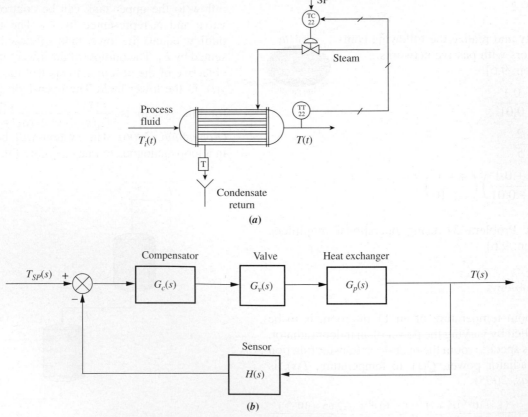

Figure P9.6   **a.** Heat-exchanger process; **b.** block diagram

c. Verify your results through MATLAB simulation.

36. Repeat Problem 35, Parts **b** and **c**, using a lead compensator.

37. a. Find the transfer function of a motor whose torque-speed curve and load are given in Figure P9.7.

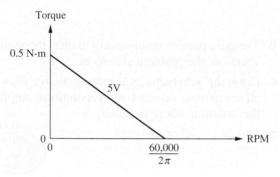

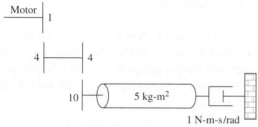

Figure P9.7

b. Design a tachometer compensator to yield a damping ratio of 0.5 for a position control employing a power amplifier of gain 1 and a preamplifier of gain 5000.

c. Compare the transient and steady-state characteristics of the uncompensated system and the compensated system.

38. You are given the motor whose transfer function is shown in Figure P9.8(*a*).

a. If this motor were the forward transfer function of a unity feedback system, calculate the percent overshoot and settling time that could be expected.

b. You want to improve the closed-loop response. Since the motor constants cannot be changed and

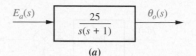

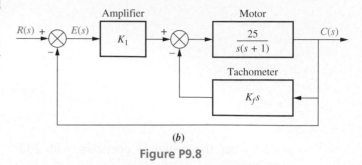

Figure P9.8

you cannot use a different motor, an amplifier and tachometer are inserted into the loop as shown in Figure P9.8(*b*). Find the values of K_1 and K_f to yield a percent overshoot of 25% and a settling time of 0.2 second.

c. Evaluate the steady-state error specifications for both the uncompensated and the compensated systems.

39. A position control is to be designed with a 20% overshoot and a settling time of 2 seconds. You have on hand an amplifier and a power amplifier whose cascaded transfer function is $K_1/(s + 20)$ with which to drive the motor. Two 10-turn pots are available to convert shaft position into voltage. A voltage of $\pm 5\pi$ volts is placed across the pots. A dc motor whose transfer function is of the form

$$\frac{\theta_o(s)}{E_a(s)} = \frac{K}{s(s + a)}$$

is also available. The transfer function of the motor is found experimentally as follows. The motor and geared load are driven open-loop by applying a large, short, rectangular pulse to the armature. An oscillogram of the response shows that the motor reached 63% of its final output value at 1/2 second after the application of the pulse. Further, with a constant 10 volts dc applied to the armature, the constant output speed was 100 rad/s.

a. Draw a complete block diagram of the system, specifying the transfer function of each com-

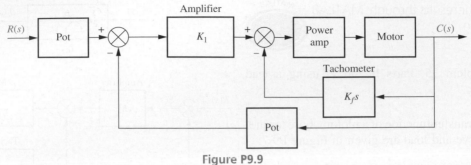

Figure P9.9

ponent when the system is operating with 20% overshoot.

b. What will the steady-state error be for a unit ramp input?

c. Determine the transient response characteristics.

d. If tachometer feedback is used around the motor, as shown in Figure P9.9, find the tachometer and the amplifier gain to meet the original specifications. Summarize the transient and steady-state characteristics.

40. A position control is to be designed with a 10% overshoot, a settling time of 1 second, and $K_v = 1000$. You have on hand an amplifier and a power amplifier whose cascaded transfer function is $K_1/(s + 40)$ with which to drive the motor. Two 10-turn pots are available to convert shaft position into voltage. A voltage of $\pm 20\pi$ volts is placed across the pots. A dc motor whose transfer function is of the form

$$\frac{\theta_o(s)}{E_a(s)} = \frac{K}{s(s + a)}$$

is also available. The following data are observed from a dynamometer test at 50 V. At 25 N-m of torque, the motor turns at 1433 rpm. At 75 N-m of torque, the motor turns at 478 rpm. The speed measured at the load is 0.1 that of the motor. The equivalent inertia, including the load, at the motor armature is 100 kg-m^2, and the equivalent viscous damping, including the load, at the motor armature is 50 N-m-s/rad.

a. Draw a complete block diagram of the system, specifying the transfer function of each component.

b. Design a passive compensator to meet the requirements in the problem statement.

c. Draw the schematic of the compensator showing all component values. Use an operational amplifier for isolation where necessary.

d. Use MATLAB or any other computer program to simulate your system and show that all requirements have been met.

MATLAB

41. Given the system shown in Figure P9.10, find the values of K and K_f so that the closed-loop dominant poles will have a damping ratio of 0.5 and the underdamped poles of the minor loop will have a damping ratio of 0.8.

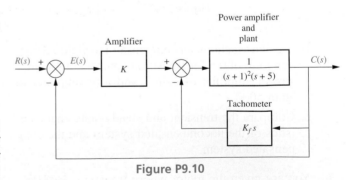

Figure P9.10

42. Given the system in Figure P9.11, find the values of K and K_f so that the closed-loop system will have a 4.32% overshoot and the minor loop will have a damping ratio of 0.8. Compare the expected performance of the system without tachometer compensation to the expected performance with tachometer compensation.

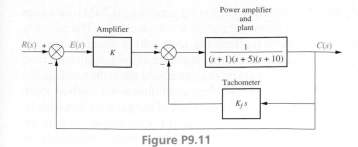

Figure P9.11

43. In Problem 54 of Chapter 8, a head-position control system for a floppy disk drive was designed to yield a settling time of 0.1 second through gain adjustment alone. Design a lead compensator to decrease the settling time to 0.05 second without changing the percent overshoot. Also, find the required loop gain.

44. Consider the temperature control system for a chemical process shown in Figure P9.12. The uncompensated system is operating with a rise time approximately the same as a second-order system with a peak time of 16 seconds and 5% overshoot. There is also considerable steady-state error. Design a PID controller so that the compensated system will have a rise time approximately equivalent to a second-order system with a peak time of 8 seconds and 5% overshoot, and zero steady-state error for a step input. *WileyPLUS Control Solutions*

45. Steam-driven power generators rotate at a constant speed via a governor that maintains constant steam pressure in the turbine. In addition, automatic generation control (AGC) or load frequency control (LFC) is added to ensure reliability and consistency despite load variations or other disturbances that can affect the distribution line frequency output. A specific turbine-governor system can be described only using the block diagram of Figure P9.1 in which $G(s) = G_c(s)G_g(s)G_t(s)G_m(s)$, where (*Khodabakhshian, 2005*)

$G_g(s) = \dfrac{1}{0.2s + 1}$ is the governor's transfer function

$G_t(s) = \dfrac{1}{0.5s + 1}$ is the turbine transfer function

$G_m(s) = \dfrac{1}{10s + 0.8}$ represents the machine and load transfer functions

$G_c(s)$ is the LFC compensation to be designed

a. Assuming $G_c(s) = K$, find the value of K that will result in a dominant pole with $\zeta = 0.7$. Obtain the corresponding T_s.

b. Design a PID controller to obtain the same damping factor as in Part **a**, but with a settling time of 2 seconds and zero steady-state error to step input commands.

c. Verify your results using a MATLAB simuation. **MATLAB**

46. Repeat Problem 45 using a lag-lead compensator instead of a PID controller. Design for a steady-state error of 1% for a step input command.

47. Digital versatile disk (DVD) players incorporate several control systems for their operations. The control tasks include (1) keeping the laser beam focused on the disc surface, (2) fast track selection, (3) disc rotation speed control, and (4) following a track accurately. In order to follow a track, the pickup-head radial position is controlled via a voltage that operates a voice coil embedded in a magnet config-

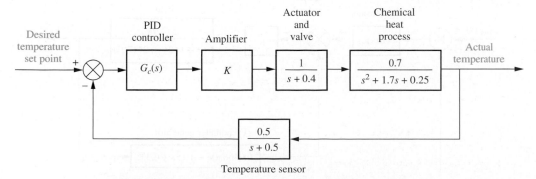

Figure P9.12 Chemical process temperature control system

uration. For a specific DVD player, the transfer function is given by

$$P(s) = \frac{X(s)}{V(s)}$$

$$= \frac{0.63}{\left(1 + \dfrac{0.36}{305.4}s + \dfrac{s^2}{305.4^2}\right)\left(1 + \dfrac{0.04}{248.2}s + \dfrac{s^2}{248.2^2}\right)}$$

where $x(t)$ = radial pickup position and $v(t)$ — the coil input voltage (*Bittanti, 2002*).

a. Assume that the system will be controlled in a closed-loop configuration, such as the one shown in Figure P9.1. Assuming that the plant, $P(s)$, is cascaded with a proportional compensator, $G_c(s)$ = K, plot the root locus of the system.

b. Repeat Part **a** using MATLAB if your root locus plot was created by any other tool. **MATLAB**

c. Find the range of K for closed-loop stability, the resulting damping factor range, and the smallest settling time.

d. Design a notch filter compensator so that the system's dominant poles have a damping factor of $\zeta = 0.7$ with a closed-loop settling time of 0.1 second.

e. Simulate the system's step response for Part **c** using MATLAB. **MATLAB**

f. Add a PI compensator to the system to achieve zero steady-state error for a step input without appreciably affecting the transient response achieved in Part **b**.

g. Simulate the system's step response for Part **e** using MATLAB. **MATLAB**

48. A coordinate measuring machine (CMM) measures coordinates on three-dimensional objects. The accuracy of CMMs is affected by temperature changes as well as by mechanical resonances due to joint elasticity. These resonances are more pronounced when the machine has to go over abrupt changes of dimension, such as sharp corners at high speed. Each of the machine links can be controlled in a closed-loop configuration, such as the one shown in Figure P9.13 for a specific machine with prismatic (sliding) links. In the figure, $X_{ref}(s)$ is the commanded position and $X(s)$ is the actual position. The minor loop uses a tachometer generator to obtain the joint speed, while the main loop controls the joint's position (*Özel, 2003*).

a. Find the value of K that will result in a minor loop with $\zeta = 0.5$.

b. Use a notch filter compensator, $G_c(s)$, for the external loop so that it results in a closed-loop damping factor of $\zeta = 0.7$ with $T_s \approx 4$ seconds.

c. Use MATLAB to simulate the compensated system's closed-loop step response: **MATLAB**

49. Magnetic levitation systems are now used to elevate and propel trains along tracks. A diagram of a demonstration magnetic levitation system is shown in Figure P9.14(*a*). Action between a permanent magnet attached to the Ping-Pong ball, the object to be levitated, and an electromagnet provides the lift. The amount of elevation can be controlled through V_a applied to the electromagnet as shown in Figure P9.14(*a*). The elevation is controlled by using a photodetector pair to detect the elevation of the Ping-Pong ball. Assume that the elevation control system is represented by Figure P9.14(*b*) and do the following (*Cho, 1993*):

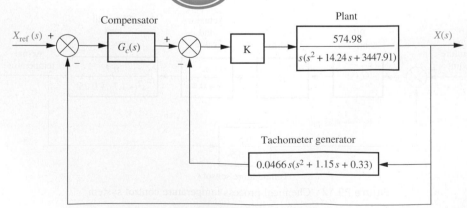

Figure P9.13

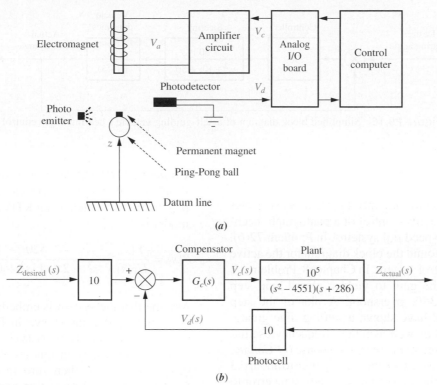

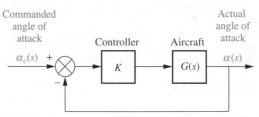

Figure P9.14 **a.** Magnetic levitation system (© 1993 IEEE); **b.** block diagram

a. Design a compensator, $G_c(s)$, to yield a settling time of 0.1 second or less if the step response is to have no more than 1% overshoot. Specify the compensator's poles, zeros, and gain.

b. Cascade another compensator to minimize the steady-state error and have the total settling time not exceed 0.5 second. This compensator should not appreciably affect the transient response designed in Part **a.** Specify the poles and zeros of this compensator.

c. Use MATLAB or any other computer program to simulate the system to check your design.

50. The transfer function for an AFTI/F-16 aircraft relating angle of attack, $\alpha(t)$, to elevator deflection, $\delta_e(t)$, is given by

$$G(s) = \frac{\alpha(s)}{\delta_e(s)}$$

$$= 0.072 \frac{(s+23)(s^2+0.05s+0.04)}{(s-0.7)(s+1.7)(s^2+0.08s+0.04)}$$

Assume the block diagram shown in Figure P9.15 for controlling the angle of attack, α, and do the following (*Monahemi, 1992*):

Figure P9.15 Simplified block diagram for angle of attack control

a. Find the range of K for stability.

b. Plot or sketch a root locus.

c. Design a cascade compensator to yield zero steady-state error, a settling time of about 0.05 second, and a percent overshoot not greater than 20%.

d. Use MATLAB or any other computer program to simulate the system to check your design.

51. Figure P9.16 is a simplified block diagram of a self-guiding vehicle's bearing angle control. Design a lead compensator to yield a closed-loop step response with 10% overshoot and a settling time of 1.5 seconds.

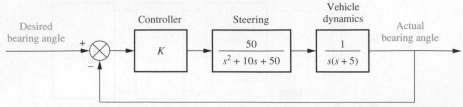

Figure P9.16   Simplified block diagram of a self-guiding vehicle's bearing angle control

Progressive Analysis and Design Problems

52. **High-speed rail pantograph.** Problem 19 in Chapter 1 discusses the active control of a pantograph mechanism for high-speed rail systems. In Problem 72(*b*), Chapter 5, you found the block diagram for the active pantograph control system. In Chapter 8, Problem 63, you designed the gain to yield a closed-loop step response with 38% overshoot. A plot of the step response should have shown a settling time greater than 0.5 second as well as a high-frequency oscillation superimposed over the step response (*O'Conner, 1997*). We want to reduce the settling time to about 0.3 second, reduce the step response steady-state error to zero, and eliminate the high-frequency oscillation. A way of eliminating the high-frequency oscillation is to cascade a notch filter with the plant. Using the notch filter,

$$G_n(s) = \frac{s^2 + 16s + 9200}{(s + 60)^2}$$

do the following:

a. Design a PD controller to yield a settling time of approximately 0.3 second with no more then 60% overshoot.

b. Add a PI controller to yield zero steady-state error for step inputs.

c. Use MATLAB to plot the PID/notch-compensated closed-loop step response.

53. **Control of HIV/AIDS.** It was shown in Chapter 6, Problem 64 that when the virus levels in an HIV/AIDS patient are controlled using RTIs the linearized plant model is

$$P(s) = \frac{Y(s)}{U_1(s)} = \frac{-520s - 10.3844}{s^3 + 2.6817s^2 + 0.11s + 0.0126}$$

Assume that the system is embedded in a configuration, such as the one shown in Figure P9.1, where $G(s) = G_c(s)\,P(s)$. Here, $G_c(s)$ is a cascade compensator. For simplicity in this problem, choose the dc gain of $G_c(s)$ less then zero to obtain a negative-feedback system (the negative signs of $G_c(s)$ and $P(s)$ cancel out) (*Craig, 2004*).

a. Consider the uncompensated system with $G_c(s) = -K$. Find the value of K that will place all closed-loop poles on the real axis.

b. Use MATLAB to simulate the unit step response of the gain-compensated system. Note the %*OS* and the T_s from the simulation.

c. Design a PI compensator so that the steady-state error for step inputs is zero. Choose a gain value to make all poles real.

d. Use MATLAB to simulate the design in Part **c** for a unit step input. Compare the simulation to Part **b.**

CYBER EXPLORATION LABORATORY

Experiment 9.1

Objectives To perform a trade-off study for lead compensation. To design a PI controller and see its effect upon steady-state error.

Minimum required software packages MATLAB, and the Control System Toolbox

Prelab

1. How many lead compensator designs will meet the transient response specifications of a system?

2. What differences do the lead compensators of Prelab 1 make?

3. Design a lead compensator for a unity negative feedback system with a forward transfer function of $G(s) = \dfrac{K}{s(s+3)(s+6)}$ to meet the following specifications: percent overshoot = 20%; settling time = 2 seconds. Specify the required gain, K. Estimate the validity of the second-order approximation.

4. What is the total angular contribution of the lead compensator of Prelab 3?

5. Determine the pole and zero of two more lead compensators that will meet the requirements of Prelab 3.

6. What is the expected steady-state error for a step input for each of the lead-compensated systems?

7. What is the expected steady-state error for a ramp input for each of the lead-compensated systems?

8. Select one of the lead compensator designs and specify a PI controller that can be cascaded with the lead compensator that will produce a system with zero steady-state error for both step and ramp inputs.

Lab

1. Using the SISO Design Tool, create the design in Prelab 3 and plot the root locus, step response, and ramp response. Take data to determine the percent overshoot, settling time, and step and ramp steady-state errors. Record the gain, K.

2. Repeat Lab 1 for each of the designs in Prelab 5.

3. For the design selected in Prelab 8, use the SISO Design Tool and insert the PI controller. Plot the step response and measure the percent overshoot, settling time, and steady-state error. Also, plot the ramp response for the design and measure the steady-state error.

4. Plot the step and ramp responses for two more values of the PI controller zero.

Postlab

1. Make a table showing calculated and actual values for percent overshoot, settling time, gain, K, steady-state error for step inputs, and steady-state error for ramp inputs. Use the three systems without the PI controller and the single system with the PI controller from Lab 3.

2. Itemize the benefits of each system without the PI controller.

3. Choose a final design and discuss the reasons for your choice.

BIBLIOGRAPHY

Bittanti, S., Dell'Orto, F., Di Carlo, A., and Savaresi, S. M. Notch Filtering and Multirate Control for Radial Tracking in High Speed DVD-Players. *IEEE Transactions on Consumer Electronics,* vol. 48, 2002, pp. 56–62.

Budak, A. *Passive and Active Network Analysis and Synthesis.* Houghton Mifflin, Boston, MA, 1974.

Cho, D., Kato, Y., and Spilman, D. Sliding Mode and Classical Controllers in Magnetic Levitation Systems. *IEEE Control Systems,* February 1993, pp. 42–48.

Craig, I. K., Xia, X., and Venter, J. W. Introducing HIV/AIDS Education into the Electrical Engineering Curriculum at the University of Pretoria. *IEEE Transactions on Education,* vol. 47, no. 1, February 2004, pp. 65–73.

D'Azzo, J. J., and Houpis, C. H. *Feedback Control System Analysis and Synthesis,* 2d ed. McGraw-Hill, New York, 1966.

Dorf, R. C. *Modern Control Systems,* 5th ed. Addison-Wesley, Reading, MA, 1989.

Hostetter, G. H., Savant, C. J., Jr., and Stefani, R. T. *Design of Feedback Control Systems,* 2d ed. Saunders College Publishing, New York, 1989.

Johnson, H. et al. *Unmanned Free-Swimming Submersible (UFSS) System Description.* NRL Memorandum Report 4393. Naval Research Laboratory, Washington, DC, 1980.

Khodabakhshian, A., and Golbon, N. Design of a New Load Frequency PID Controller Using QFT. *Proceedings of the 13th Mediterranean Conference on Control and Automation,* 2005, pp. 970–975.

Kuo, B. C. *Automatic Control Systems,* 7th ed. Prentice Hall, Englewood Cliffs, NJ, 1995.

Monahemi, M. M., Barlow, J. B., and O'Leary, D. P. Design of Reduced-Order Observers with Precise Loop Transfer Recovery. *Journal of Guidance, Control, and Dynamics,* vol. 15, no. 6, November–December 1992, pp. 1320–1326.

O'Connor, D. N., Eppinger, S. D., Seering, W. P., and Wormly, D. N. Active Control of a High-Speed Pantograph. *Journal of Dynamic Systems, Measurements, and Control,* vol. 119, March 1997, pp. 1–4.

Ogata, K. *Modern Control Engineering,* 2d ed. Prentice Hall, Englewood Cliffs, NJ, 1990.

Özel, T. Precision Tracking Control of a Horizontal Arm Coordinate Measuring Machine. *Proceedings of the IEEE Conference on Control Applications,* 2003, pp. 103–108.

Romagnoli, J. A., and Palazoglu, A. *Introduction to Process Control.* CRC Press, Boca Raton, FL, 2006.

Smith, C. A. *Automated Continuous Process Control.* Wiley, New York, 2002.

Thomas, B., Soleimani-Mosheni, M., and Fahlén, P. Feed-forward in Temperature Control of Buildings. *Energy and Buildings,* vol. 37, 2005, pp. 755–761.

Van de Vegte, J. *Feedback Control Systems,* 2d ed. Prentice Hall, Englewood Cliffs, NJ, 1990.

SINUSOIDAL TOOLS

10

CHAPTER OBJECTIVES

In this chapter you will learn the following:

- The definition of frequency response
- How to plot frequency response
- How to use frequency response to analyze stability
- How to use frequency response to analyze a system's transient and steady-state error performance
- How to use frequency response to design the gain to meet stability specifications

CASE STUDY OBJECTIVES

You will be able to demonstrate your knowledge of the chapter objectives with a case study as follows:

- Given the antenna azimuth position control system shown on the front endpapers and using frequency response methods, you will be able to find the range of gain, K, for stability. You will also be able to find percent overshoot, settling time, peak time, and rise time, given K.

10.1 INTRODUCTION

The root locus method for transient design, steady-state design, and stability was covered in Chapters 8 and 9. In Chapter 8 we covered the simple case of design through gain adjustment, where a trade-off was made between a desired transient response and a desired steady-state error. In Chapter 9 the need for this trade-off was eliminated by using compensation networks so that transient and steady-state errors could be separately specified and designed. Further, a desired transient response no longer had to be on the original system's root locus.

This chapter and Chapter 11 present the design of feedback control systems through gain adjustment and compensation networks from another perspective — that of frequency response. The results of frequency response compensation techniques are not new or different from the results of root locus techniques.

Frequency response methods, developed by Nyquist and Bode in the 1930s, are older than the root locus method, which was discovered by Evans in 1948 (*Nyquist, 1932; Bode, 1945*). The older method, which is covered in this chapter, is not as intuitive as the root locus. However, frequency response yields a new vantage point from which to view feedback control systems. This technique has distinct advantages in the following situations:

1. When modeling transfer functions from physical data, as shown in Figure 10.1
2. When designing lead compensators to meet a steady-state error requirement and a transient response requirement
3. When finding the stability of nonlinear systems
4. In settling ambiguities when sketching a root locus

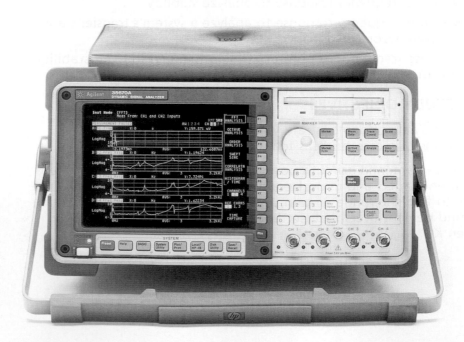

FIGURE 10.1   The Agilent 35670A Dynamic Signal Analyzer obtains frequency response data from a physical system. The displayed data can be used to analyze, design, or determine a mathematical model for the system.

We first discuss the concept of frequency response, define frequency response, derive analytical expressions for the frequency response, plot the frequency response, develop ways of sketching the frequency response, and then apply the concept to control system analysis and design.

THE CONCEPT OF FREQUENCY RESPONSE

In the steady state, sinusoidal inputs to a linear system generate sinusoidal responses of the same frequency. Even though these responses are of the same frequency as the input, they differ in amplitude and phase angle from the input. These differences are functions of frequency.

Before defining frequency response, let us look at a convenient representation of sinusoids. Sinusoids can be represented as complex numbers called *phasors*. The magnitude of the complex number is the amplitude of the sinusoid, and the angle of the complex number is the phase angle of the sinusoid. Thus, $M_1 \cos(\omega t + \phi_1)$ can be represented as $M_1 \angle \phi_1$ where the frequency, ω, is implicit.

Since a system causes both the amplitude and phase angle of the input to be changed, we can think of the system itself as represented by a complex number, defined so that the product of the input phasor and the system function yields the phasor representation of the output.

Consider the mechanical system of Figure 10.2(a). If the input force, $f(t)$, is sinusoidal, the steady-state output response, $x(t)$, of the system is also sinusoidal and at the same frequency as the input. In Figure 10.2(b) the input and output

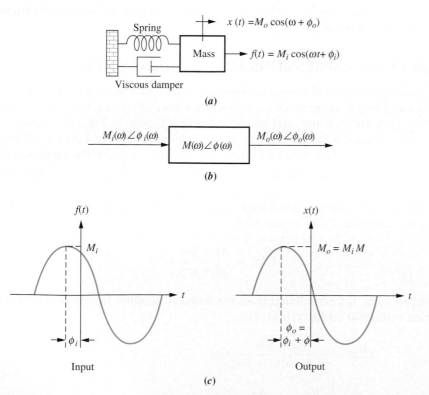

FIGURE 10.2 Sinusoidal frequency response: **a.** system; **b.** transfer function; **c.** input and output waveforms

sinusoids are represented by complex numbers, or phasors, $M_i(\omega)\angle\phi_i(\omega)$ and $M_o(\omega)\angle\phi_o(\omega)$, respectively. Here the M's are the amplitudes of the sinusoids, and the ϕ's are the phase angles of the sinusoids as shown in Figure 10.2(c). Assume that the system is represented by the complex number, $M(\omega)\angle\phi(\omega)$. The output steady-state sinusoid is found by multiplying the complex number representation of the input by the complex number representation of the system. Thus, the steady-state output sinusoid is

$$M_o(\omega)\angle\phi_o(\omega) = M_i(\omega)M(\omega)\angle[\phi_i(\omega) + \phi(\omega)] \tag{10.1}$$

From Eq. (10.1) we see that the system function is given by

$$M(\omega) = \frac{M_o(\omega)}{M_i(\omega)} \tag{10.2}$$

and

$$\phi(\omega) = \phi_o(\omega) - \phi_i(\omega) \tag{10.3}$$

Equations (10.2) and (10.3) form our definition of frequency response. We call $M(\omega)$ the *magnitude frequency response* and $\phi(\omega)$ the *phase frequency response*. The combination of the magnitude and phase frequency responses is called the *frequency response* and is $M(\omega)\angle\phi(\omega)$.

In other words, we define the magnitude frequency response to be the ratio of the output sinusoid's magnitude to the input sinusoid's magnitude. We define the phase response to be the difference in phase angle between the output and the input sinusoids. Both responses are a function of frequency and apply only to the steady-state sinusoidal response of the system.

ANALYTICAL EXPRESSIONS FOR FREQUENCY RESPONSE

Now that we have defined frequency response, let us obtain the analytical expression for it (*Nilsson, 1990*). Later in the chapter we will use this analytical expression to determine stability, transient response, and steady-state error. Figure 10.3 shows a system, $G(s)$, with the Laplace transform of a general sinusoid, $r(t) = A\cos\omega t + B\sin\omega t = \sqrt{A^2 + B^2}\cos[\omega t - \tan^{-1}(B/A)]$ as the input. We can represent the input as a phasor in three ways: (1) in polar form, $M_i\angle\phi_i$, where $M_i = \sqrt{A^2 + B^2}$ and $\phi_i = -\tan^{-1}(B/A)$; (2) in rectangular form, $A - jB$; and (3) using Euler's formula, $M_ie^{j\phi_i}$.

We now solve for the forced response portion of $C(s)$, from which we evaluate the frequency response. From Figure 10.3,

$$C(s) = \frac{As + B\omega}{(s^2 + \omega^2)}G(s) \tag{10.4}$$

We separate the forced solution from the transient solution by performing a partial-fraction expansion on Eq. (10.4). Thus,

$$C(s) = \frac{As + B\omega}{(s + j\omega)(s - j\omega)}G(s)$$

$$\tag{10.5}$$

$$= \frac{K_1}{s + j\omega} + \frac{K_2}{s - j\omega} + \text{Partial fraction terms from } G(s)$$

$R(s) = \dfrac{As + B\omega}{s^2 + \omega^2}$ $\longrightarrow$ $G(s)$ $\longrightarrow$ $C(s)$

FIGURE 10.3 System with sinusoidal input.

where

$$K_1 = \frac{As + B\omega}{s - j\omega} G(s)\Big|_{s \to -j\omega} = \frac{1}{2}(A + jB)G(-j\omega) = \frac{1}{2}M_i e^{-j\phi_i} M_G e^{-j\phi_G}$$

$$= \frac{M_i M_G}{2} e^{-j(\phi_i + \phi_G)}$$

(10.6a)

$$K_2 = \frac{As + B\omega}{s + j\omega} G(s)\Big|_{s \to +j\omega} = \frac{1}{2}(A - jB)G(j\omega) = \frac{1}{2}M_i e^{j\phi_i} M_G e^{j\phi_G}$$

$$= \frac{M_i M_G}{2} e^{j(\phi_i + \phi_G)} = K_1^*$$

(10.6b)

For Eqs. (10.6), K_1^* is the complex conjugate of K_1,

$$M_G = |G(j\omega)|$$

(10.7)

and

$$\phi_G = \text{angle of } G(j\omega)$$

(10.8)

The steady-state response is that portion of the partial-fraction expansion that comes from the input waveform's poles, or just the first two terms of Eq. (10.5). Hence, the sinusoidal steady-state output, $C_{ss}(s)$, is

$$C_{ss}(s) = \frac{K_1}{s + j\omega} + \frac{K_2}{s - j\omega}$$

(10.9)

Substituting Eqs. (10.6) into Eq. (10.9), we obtain

$$C_{ss}(s) = \frac{\dfrac{M_i M_G}{2} e^{-j(\phi_i + \phi_G)}}{s + j\omega} + \frac{\dfrac{M_i M_G}{2} e^{j(\phi_i + \phi_G)}}{s - j\omega}$$

(10.10)

Taking the inverse Laplace transformation, we obtain

$$c(t) = M_i M_G \left(\frac{e^{-j(\omega t + \phi_i + \phi_G)} + e^{j(\omega t + \phi_i + \phi_G)}}{2} \right)$$

(10.11)

$$= M_i M_G \cos(\omega t + \phi_i + \phi_G)$$

which can be represented in phasor form as $M_o \angle \phi_o = (M_1 \angle \phi_1)(M_G \angle \phi_G)$, where $M_G \angle \phi_G$ is the frequency response function. But from Eqs. (10.7) and (10.8), $M_G \angle \phi_G = G(j\omega)$. In other words, the frequency response of a system whose transfer function is $G(s)$ is

$$\boxed{G(j\omega) = G(s)\big|_{s \to j\omega}}$$

(10.12)

PLOTTING FREQUENCY RESPONSE

$G(j\omega) = M_G(\omega) < \phi_G(\omega)$ can be plotted in several ways; two of them are (1) as a function of frequency, with separate magnitude and phase plots; and (2) as a polar plot, where the phasor length is the magnitude and the phasor angle is the phase. When plotting separate magnitude and phase plots, the magnitude curve can be plotted in decibels (dB) vs. log ω, where dB = 20 log M.[1] The phase curve is plotted as phase angle vs. log ω. The motivation for these plots is shown in Section 10.2.

Using the concepts covered in Section 8.1, data for the plots also can be obtained using vectors on the s-plane drawn from the poles and zeros of $G(s)$ to the imaginary axis. Here the magnitude response at a particular frequency is the product of the vector lengths from the zeros of $G(s)$ divided by the product of the vector lengths from the poles of $G(s)$ drawn to points on the imaginary axis. The phase response is the sum of the angles from the zeros of $G(s)$ minus the sum of the angles from the poles of $G(s)$ drawn to points on the imaginary axis. Performing this operation for successive points along the imaginary axis yields the data for the frequency response. Remember, each point is equivalent to substituting that point, $s = j\omega_1$, into $G(s)$ and evaluating its value.

The plots also can be made from a computer program that calculates the frequency response. For example, the root locus program discussed in Appendix G.2 at www.wiley.com/college/nise can be used with test points that are on the imaginary axis. The calculated K value at each frequency is the reciprocal of the scaled magnitude response, and the calculated angle is, directly, the phase angle response at that frequency.

The following example demonstrates how to obtain an analytical expression for frequency response and make a plot of the result.

EXAMPLE 10.1

Frequency response from the transfer function

Problem: Find the analytical expression for the magnitude frequency response and the phase frequency response for a system $G(s) = 1/(s+2)$. Also, plot both the separate magnitude and phase diagrams and the polar plot.

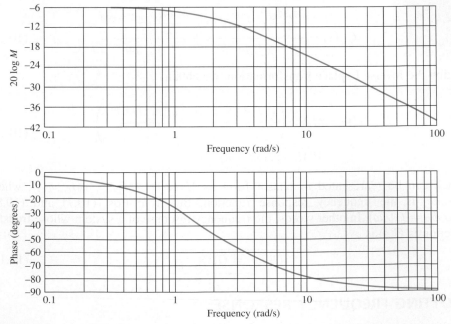

FIGURE 10.4   Frequency response plots for $G(s) = 1/(s+2)$: separate magnitude and phase diagrams

[1] Throughout this book "log" is used to mean $\log_{10}$, or logarithm to the base 10.

SOLUTION: First substitute $s = j\omega$ in the system function and obtain $G(j\omega) = 1/(j\omega + 2) = (2 - j\omega)/(\omega^2 + 4)$. The magnitude of this complex number, $|G(j\omega)| = M(\omega) = 1/\sqrt{(\omega^2 + 4)}$, is the magnitude frequency response. The phase angle of $G(j\omega)$, $\phi(\omega) = -\tan^{-1}(\omega/2)$, is the phase frequency response.

$G(j\omega)$ can be plotted in two ways: (1) in separate magnitude and phase plots and (2) in a polar plot. Figure 10.4 shows separate magnitude and phase diagrams, where the magnitude diagram is $20\log M(\omega) = 20\log(1/\sqrt{\omega^2 + 4})$ vs. $\log \omega$, and the phase diagram is $\phi(\omega) = -\tan^{-1}(\omega/2)$ vs. $\log \omega$. The polar plot, shown in Figure 10.5, is a plot of $M(\omega) < \phi(\omega) = 1/\sqrt{\omega^2 + 4} \ < -\tan^{-1}(\omega/2)$ for different ω.

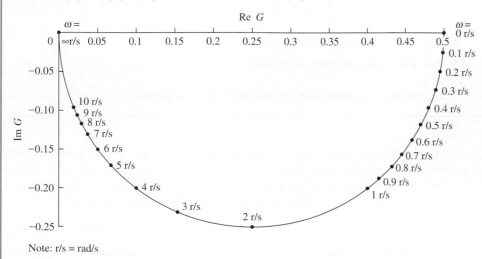

Note: r/s = rad/s

FIGURE 10.5   Frequency response plot for $G(s) = 1/(s + 2)$: polar plot.

In the previous example we plotted the separate magnitude and phase responses, as well as the polar plot, using the mathematical expression for the frequency response. Either of these frequency response presentations can also be obtained from the other. You should practice this conversion by looking at Figure 10.4 and obtaining Figure 10.5 using successive points. For example, at a frequency of 1 rad/s in Figure 10.4, the magnitude is approximately -7 dB, or $10^{-7/20} = 0.447$. The phase plot at 1 rad/s tells us that the phase is about $-26°$. Thus, on the polar plot a point of radius 0.447 at an angle of $-26°$ is plotted and identified as 1 rad/s. Continuing in like manner for other frequencies in Figure 10.4, you can obtain Figure 10.5.

Similarly, Figure 10.4 can be obtained from Figure 10.5 by selecting a sequence of points in Figure 10.5 and translating them to separate magnitude and phase values. For example, drawing a vector from the origin to the point at 2 rad/s in Figure 10.5, we see that the magnitude is $20\log 0.35 = -9.12$ dB and the phase angle is about $-45°$. The magnitude and phase angle are then plotted at 2 rad/s in Figure 10.4 on the separate magnitude and phase curves.

SKILL-ASSESSMENT EXERCISE 10.1

Problem:

a. Find analytical expressions for the magnitude and phase responses of

$$G(s) = \frac{1}{(s + 2)(s + 4)}$$

b. Make plots of the log-magnitude and the phase, using log-frequency in rad/s as the ordinate.

c. Make a polar plot of the frequency response.

ANSWERS:

a. $M(\omega) = \dfrac{1}{\sqrt{(8 - \omega^2)^2 + (6\omega)^2}}$; for $\omega \leq \sqrt{8}$: $\phi(\omega) = -\arctan\left(\dfrac{6\omega}{8 - \omega^2}\right)$, for

$\omega > \sqrt{8}$: $\phi(\omega) = -\left[\pi + \arctan\left(\dfrac{6\omega}{8 - \omega^2}\right)\right]$

b. See the answer at www.wiley.com/college/nise.

c. See the answer at www.wiley.com/college/nise.

The complete solution is at www.wiley.com/college/nise.

In this section we defined frequency response and saw how to obtain an analytical expression for the frequency response of a system simply by substituting $s = j\omega$ into $G(s)$. We also saw how to make a plot of $G(j\omega)$. The next section shows how to approximate the magnitude and phase plots in order to sketch them rapidly.

10.2 ASYMPTOTIC APPROXIMATIONS: BODE PLOTS

The log-magnitude and phase frequency response curves as functions of $\log \omega$ are called Bode plots or Bode diagrams. Sketching Bode plots can be simplified because they can be approximated as a sequence of straight lines. Straight-line approximations simplify the evaluation of the magnitude and phase frequency response.

Consider the following transfer function:

$$G(s) = \frac{K(s + z_1)(s + z_2) \cdots (s + z_k)}{s^m(s + p_1)(s + p_2) \cdots (s + p_n)} \tag{10.13}$$

The magnitude frequency response is the product of the magnitude frequency responses of each term, or

$$|G(j\omega)| = \frac{K|(s + z_1)||(s + z_2)| \cdots |(s + z_k)|}{|s^m||(s + p_1)||(s + p_2)| \cdots |(s + p_n)|}\Bigg|_{s \to j\omega} \tag{10.14}$$

Thus, if we know the magnitude response of each pole and zero term, we can find the total magnitude response. The process can be simplified by working with the logarithm of the magnitude since the zero terms' magnitude responses would be added and the pole terms' magnitude responses subtracted, rather than, respectively, multiplied or divided, to yield the logarithm of the total magnitude response. Converting the magnitude response into dB, we obtain

$$20 \log|G(j\omega)| = 20 \log K + 20 \log|(s + z_1)| + 20 \log|(s + z_2)|$$
$$+ \cdots - 20 \log|s^m| - 20 \log|(s + p_1)| - \cdots|_{s \to j\omega} \tag{10.15}$$

Thus, if we knew the response of each term, the algebraic sum would yield the total response in dB. Further, if we could make an approximation of each term that would consist only of straight lines, graphical addition of terms would be greatly simplified.

Before proceeding, let us look at the phase response. From Eq. (10.13) the phase frequency response is the *sum* of the phase frequency response curves of the zero terms minus the *sum* of the phase frequency response curves of the pole terms. Again, since the phase response is the sum of individual terms, straight-line approximations to these individual responses simplify graphical addition.

Let us now show how to approximate the frequency response of simple pole and zero terms by straight-line approximations. Later we show how to combine these responses to sketch the frequency response of more complicated functions. In subsequent sections, after a discussion of the Nyquist stability criterion, we learn how to use the Bode plots for the analysis and design of stability and transient response.

BODE PLOTS FOR $G(s) = (s + a)$

Consider a function, $G(s) = (s + a)$, for which we want to sketch separate logarithmic magnitude and phase response plots. Letting $s = j\omega$, we have

$$G(j\omega) = (j\omega + a) = a\left(j\frac{\omega}{a} + 1\right) \tag{10.16}$$

At low frequencies when ω approaches zero,

$$G(j\omega) \approx a \tag{10.17}$$

The magnitude response in dB is

$$20\log M = 20\log a \tag{10.18}$$

where $M = |G(j\omega)|$ and is a constant. Eq. (10.18) is shown plotted in Figure 10.6(*a*) from $\omega = 0.01a$ to a.

At high frequencies where $\omega \gg a$, Eq. (10.16) becomes

$$G(j\omega) \approx a\left(\frac{j\omega}{a}\right) = a\left(\frac{\omega}{a}\right) \angle 90° = \omega \angle 90° \tag{10.19}$$

The magnitude response in dB is

$$20\log M = 20\log a + 20\log \frac{\omega}{a} = 20\log \omega \tag{10.20}$$

where $a < \omega < \infty$. Notice from the middle term that the high-frequency approximation is equal to the low-frequency approximation when $\omega = a$, and increases for $\omega > a$.

If we plot dB, $20\log M$, against $\log \omega$, Eq. (10.20) becomes a straight line:

$$y = 20x \tag{10.21}$$

where $y = 20\log M$, and $x = \log \omega$. The line has a slope of 20 when plotted as dB vs. $\log \omega$.

Since each doubling of frequency causes $20\log \omega$ to increase by 6 dB, the line rises at an equivalent slope of 6 dB/octave, where an *octave* is a doubling of frequency. This rise begins at $\omega = a$, where the low-frequency approximation equals the high-frequency approximation.

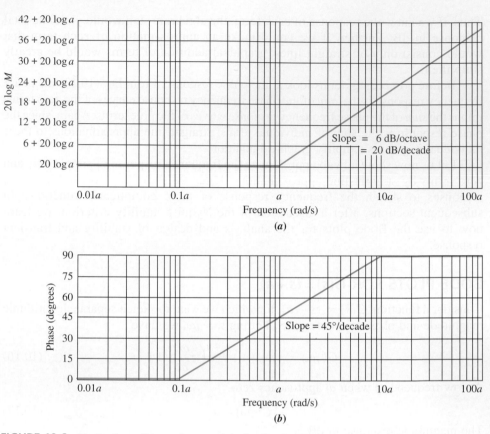

FIGURE 10.6   Bode plots of $(s + a)$: **a.** magnitude plot; **b.** phase plot

We call the straight-line approximations *asymptotes*. The low-frequency approximation is called the *low-frequency asymptote,* and the high-frequency approximation is called the *high-frequency asymptote*. The frequency, a, is called the *break frequency* because it is the break between the low- and the high-frequency asymptotes.

Many times it is convenient to draw the line over a decade rather than an octave, where a *decade* is 10 times the initial frequency. Over one decade, $20 \log \omega$ increases by 20 dB. Thus, a slope of 6 dB/octave is equivalent to a slope of 20 dB/decade. The plot is shown in Figure 10.6(a) from $\omega = 0.01a$ to $100a$.

Let us now turn to the phase response, which can be drawn as follows. At the break frequency, a, Eq. (10.16) shows the phase to be 45°. At low frequencies Eq. (10.17) shows that the phase is 0°. At high frequencies Eq. (10.19) shows that the phase is 90°. To draw the curve, start one decade (1/10) below the break frequency, $0.1a$, with 0° phase, and draw a line of slope $+45°$/decade passing through 45° at the break frequency and continuing to 90° one decade above the break frequency, $10a$. The resulting phase diagram is shown in Figure 10.6(b).

It is often convenient to *normalize* the magnitude and *scale* the frequency so that the log-magnitude plot will be 0 dB at a break frequency of unity. Normalizing and scaling helps in the following applications:

1. When comparing different first- or second-order frequency response plots, each plot will have the same low-frequency asymptote after normalization and the same break frequency after scaling.

2. When sketching the frequency response of a function such as Eq. (10.13), each factor in the numerator and denominator will have the same low-frequency asymptote after normalization. This common low-frequency asymptote makes it easier to add components to obtain the Bode plot.

To normalize $(s + a)$, we factor out the quantity a and form $a[(s/a) + 1]$. The frequency is scaled by defining a new frequency variable, $s_1 = s/a$. Then the magnitude is divided by the quantity a to yield 0 dB at the break frequency. Hence, the normalized and scaled function is $(s_1 + 1)$. To obtain the original frequency response, the magnitude and frequency are multiplied by the quantity a.

We now use the concepts of normalization and scaling to compare the asymptotic approximation to the actual magnitude and phase plot for $(s + a)$. Table 10.1 shows the comparison for the normalized and scaled frequency response of $(s + a)$. Notice that the actual magnitude curve is never greater than 3.01 dB from the asymptotes. This maximum difference occurs at the break frequency. The maximum difference for the phase curve is 5.71°, which occurs at the decades above and below the break frequency. For convenience, the data in Table 10.1 is plotted in Figures 10.7 and 10.8.

We now find the Bode plots for other common transfer functions.

TABLE 10.1 **Asymptotic and actual normalized and scaled frequency response data for $(s + a)$**

Frequency $\dfrac{}{a}$	$20 \log \dfrac{M}{a}$ (dB)		Phase (degrees)	
(rad/s)	Asymptotic	Actual	Asymptotic	Actual
0.01	0	0.00	0.00	0.57
0.02	0	0.00	0.00	1.15
0.04	0	0.01	0.00	2.29
0.06	0	0.02	0.00	3.43
0.08	0	0.03	0.00	4.57
0.1	0	0.04	0.00	5.71
0.2	0	0.17	13.55	11.31
0.4	0	0.64	27.09	21.80
0.6	0	1.34	35.02	30.96
0.8	0	2.15	40.64	38.66
1	0	3.01	45.00	45.00
2	6	6.99	58.55	63.43
4	12	12.30	72.09	75.96
6	15.56	15.68	80.02	80.54
8	18	18.13	85.64	82.87
10	20	20.04	90.00	84.29
20	26.02	26.03	90.00	87.14
40	32.04	32.04	90.00	88.57
60	35.56	35.56	90.00	89.05
80	38.06	38.06	90.00	89.28
100	40	40.00	90.00	89.43

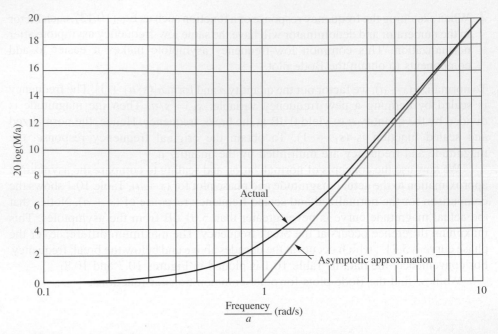

FIGURE 10.7   Asymptotic and actual normalized and scaled magnitude response of $(s + a)$

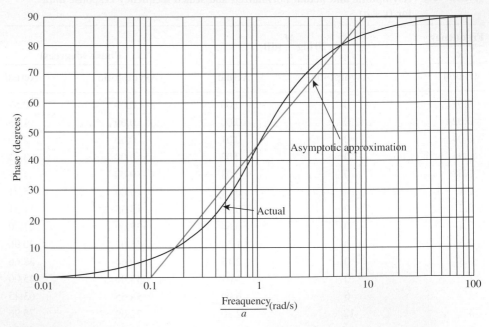

FIGURE 10.8   Asymptotic and actual normalized and scaled phase response of $(s + a)$

BODE PLOTS FOR $G(s) = 1/(s + a)$

Let us find the Bode plots for the transfer function

$$G(s) = \frac{1}{(s + a)} = \frac{1}{a\left(\dfrac{s}{a} + 1\right)} \tag{10.22}$$

This function has a low-frequency asymptote of $20\log(1/a)$, which is found by letting the frequency, s, approach zero. The Bode plot is constant until the break frequency, a rad/s, is reached. The plot is then approximated by the high-frequency asymptote found by letting s approach ∞. Thus, at high frequencies

$$G(j\omega) = \frac{1}{a\left(\dfrac{s}{a}\right)}\Bigg|_{s\to j\omega} = \frac{1}{a\left(\dfrac{j\omega}{a}\right)} = \frac{\dfrac{1}{a}}{\dfrac{\omega}{a}}\angle - 90^\circ = \frac{1}{\omega}\angle - 90^\circ \qquad (10.23)$$

or, in dB,

$$20\log M = 20\log\frac{1}{a} - 20\log\frac{\omega}{a} = -20\log\omega \qquad (10.24)$$

Notice from the middle term that the high-frequency approximation equals the low-frequency approximation when $\omega = a$, and decreases for $\omega > a$. This result is similar to Eq. (10.20), except the slope is negative rather than positive. The Bode log-magnitude diagram will decrease at a rate of 20 dB/decade rather than increase at a rate of 20 dB/decade after the break frequency.

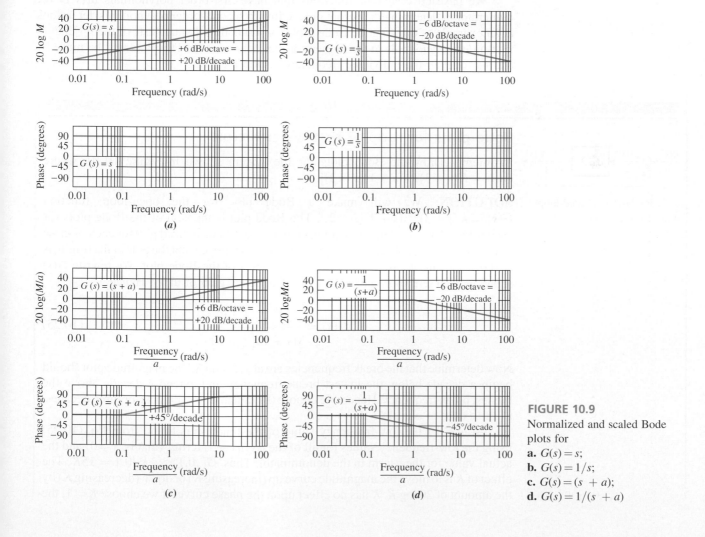

FIGURE 10.9

Normalized and scaled Bode plots for
a. $G(s) = s$;
b. $G(s) = 1/s$;
c. $G(s) = (s + a)$;
d. $G(s) = 1/(s + a)$

The phase plot is the negative of the previous example since the function is the inverse. The phase begins at $0°$ and reaches $-90°$ at high frequencies, going through $-45°$ at the break frequency. Both the Bode normalized and scaled log-magnitude and phase plot are shown in Figure 10.9(d).

BODE PLOTS FOR $G(s) = s$

Our next function, $G(s) = s$, has only a high-frequency asymptote. Letting $s = j\omega$, the magnitude is $20 \log \omega$, which is the same as Eq. (10.20). Hence, the Bode magnitude plot is a straight line drawn with a $+20$ dB/decade slope passing through zero dB when $\omega = 1$. The phase plot, which is a constant $+90°$, is shown with the magnitude plot in Figure 10.9(a).

BODE PLOTS FOR $G(s) = 1/s$

The frequency response of the inverse of the preceding function, $G(s) = 1/s$, is shown in Figure 10.9(b) and is a straight line with a -20 dB/decade slope passing through zero dB at $\omega = 1$. The Bode phase plot is equal to a constant $-90°$.

We have covered four functions that have first-order polynomials in s in the numerator or denominator. Before proceeding to second-order polynomials, let us look at an example of drawing the Bode plots for a function that consists of the product of first-order polynomials in the numerator and denominator. The plots will be made by adding together the individual frequency response curves.

■■■ EXAMPLE 10.2 ■■■

Bode plots for ratio of first-order factors

FIGURE 10.10 Closed-loop unity feedback system

Problem: Draw the Bode plots for the system shown in Figure 10.10, where $G(s) = K(s + 3)/[s(s + 1)(s + 2)]$.

SOLUTION: We will make a Bode plot for the open-loop function $G(s) = K(s + 3)/[s(s + 1)(s + 2)]$. The Bode plot is the sum of the Bode plots for each first-order term. Thus, it is convenient to use the normalized plot for each of these terms so that the low-frequency asymptote of each term, except the pole at the origin, is at 0 dB, making it easier to add the components of the Bode plot. We rewrite $G(s)$ showing each term normalized to a low-frequency gain of unity. Hence,

$$G(s) = \frac{\frac{3}{2}K\left(\frac{s}{3} + 1\right)}{s(s + 1)\left(\frac{s}{2} + 1\right)} \tag{10.25}$$

Now determine that the break frequencies are at 1, 2, and 3. The magnitude plot should begin a decade below the lowest break frequency and extend a decade above the highest break frequency. Hence, we choose 0.1 radian to 100 radians, or three decades, as the extent of our plot.

At $\omega = 0.1$ the low-frequency value of the function is found from Eq. (10.25) using the low-frequency values for all of the $[(s/a) + 1]$ terms, (that is, $s = 0$) and the actual value for the s term in the denominator. Thus, $G(j0.1) \approx \frac{3}{2}K/0.1 = 15K$. The effect of K is to move the magnitude curve up (increasing K) or down (decreasing K) by the amount of $20 \log K$. K has no effect upon the phase curve. If we choose $K = 1$, the

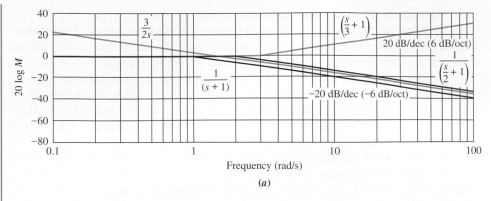

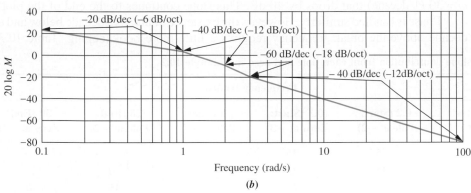

FIGURE 10.11
Bode log-magnitude plot for
Example 10.2:
a. components;
b. composite

magnitude plot can be denormalized later for any value of K that is calculated or known.

Figure 10.11(a) shows each component of the Bode log-magnitude frequency response. Summing the components yields the composite plot shown in Figure 10.11(b). The results are summarized in Table 10.2, which can be used to obtain the slopes. Each pole and zero is itemized in the first column. Reading across the table shows its contribution at each frequency. The last row is the sum of the slopes and correlates with Figure 10.11(b). The Bode magnitude plot for $K = 1$ starts at $\omega = 0.1$ with a value of 20 log 15 = 23.52 dB, and decreases immediately at a rate of -20 dB/decade, due to the s term in the denominator. At $\omega = 1$ the $(s + 1)$ term in the denominator begins its 20 dB/decade downward slope and causes an additional 20 dB/decade negative slope, or a total of -40 dB/decade. At $\omega = 2$ the term $[(s/2) + 1]$ begins its -20 dB/decade slope, adding yet another -20 dB/decade to the resultant

TABLE 10.2 **Bode magnitude plot: slope contribution from each pole and zero in Example 10.2**

	Frequency (rad/s)			
Description	**0.1 (Start: Pole at 0)**	**1 (Start: Pole at -1)**	**2 (Start: Pole at -2)**	**3 (Start: Pole at -3)**
Pole at 0	-20	-20	-20	-20
Pole at -1	0	-20	-20	-20
Pole at -2	0	0	-20	-20
Pole at -3	0	0	0	20
Total slope (dB/dec)	-20	-40	-60	-40

plot, or a total of -60 dB/decade slope that continues until $\omega = 3$. At this frequency the $[(s/3) + 1]$ term in the numerator begins its positive 20 dB/decade slope. The resultant magnitude plot, therefore, changes from a slope of -60 dB/decade to -40 dB/decade at $\omega = 3$, and continues at that slope since there are no other break frequencies.

The slopes are easily drawn by sketching straight-line segments decreasing by 20 dB over a decade. For example, the initial -20 dB/decade slope is drawn from 23.52 dB at $\omega = 0.1$, to 3.52 dB (a 20 dB decrease) at $\omega = 1$. The -40 dB/decade slope starting at $\omega = 1$ is drawn by sketching a line segment from 3.52 dB at $\omega = 1$, to -36.48 dB (a 40 dB decrease) at $\omega = 10$, and using only the portion from $\omega = 1$ to $\omega = 2$. The next slope of -60 dB/decade is drawn by first sketching a line segment from $\omega = 2$ to $\omega = 20$ (1 decade) that drops down by 60 dB, and using only that portion of the line from $\omega = 2$ to $\omega = 3$. The final slope is drawn by sketching a line segment from $\omega = 3$ to $\omega = 30$ (1 decade) that drops by 40 dB. This slope continues to the end of the plot.

Phase is handled similarly. However, the existence of breaks a decade below and a decade above the break frequency requires a little more bookkeeping. Table 10.3

TABLE 10.3 Bode phase plot: slope contribution from each pole and zero in Example 10.2

Description	Frequency (rad/s)					
	0.1 (Start: Pole at -1)	0.2 (Start: Pole at -2)	0.3 (Start: Zero at -3)	0 (End: Pole at -1)	20 (End: Pole at -2)	30 (End: Zero at -3)
Pole at -1	-45	-45	-45	0		
Pole at -2		-45	-45	-45	0	
Pole at -3			45	45	45	0
Total slope (deg/dec)	-45	-90	-45	0	45	0

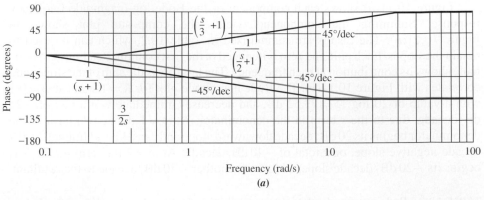

(a)

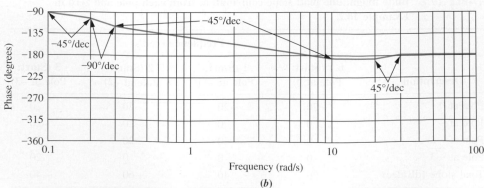

(b)

FIGURE 10.12
Bode phase plot for Example 10.2: **a.** components; **b.** composite

shows the starting and stopping frequencies of the $45°$/decade slope for each of the poles and zeros. For example, reading across for the pole at -2, we see that the $-45°$ slope starts at a frequency of 0.2 and ends at 20. Filling in the rows for each pole and then summing the columns yields the slope portrait of the resulting phase plot. Looking at the row marked *Total slope,* we see that the phase plot will have a slope of $-45°$/decade from a frequency of 0.1 to 0.2. The slope will then increase to $-90°$/decade from 0.2 to 0.3. The slope will return to $-45°$/decade from 0.3 to 10 rad/s. A slope of 0 ensues from 10 to 20 rad/s, followed by a slope of $+45°$/decade from 20 to 30 rad/s. Finally, from 30 rad/s to infinity, the slope is $0°$/decade.

The resulting component and composite phase plots are shown in Figure 10.12. Since the pole at the origin yields a constant $-90°$ phase shift, the plot begins at $-90°$ and follows the slope portrait just described.

BODE PLOTS FOR $G(s) = s^2 + 2\zeta\omega_n s + \omega_n^2$

Now that we have covered Bode plots for first-order systems, we turn to the Bode log-magnitude and phase plots for second-order polynomials in s. The second-order polynomial is of the form

$$G(s) = s^2 + 2\zeta\omega_n s + \omega_n^2 = \omega_n^2\left(\frac{s^2}{\omega_n^2} + 2\zeta\frac{s}{\omega_n} + 1\right) \tag{10.26}$$

Unlike the first-order frequency response approximation, the difference between the asymptotic approximation and the actual frequency response can be great for some values of ζ. A correction to the Bode diagrams can be made to improve the accuracy. We first derive the asymptotic approximation and then show the difference between the asymptotic approximation and the actual frequency response curves.

At low frequencies Eq. (10.26) becomes

$$G(s) \approx \omega_n^2 = \omega_n^2 \angle 0° \tag{10.27}$$

The magnitude, M, in dB at low frequencies therefore is

$$20 \log M = 20 \log|G(j\omega)| = 20 \log \omega_n^2 \tag{10.28}$$

At high frequencies

$$G(s) \approx s^2 \tag{10.29}$$

or

$$G(j\omega) \approx -\omega^2 = \omega^2 \angle 180° \tag{10.30}$$

The log-magnitude is

$$20 \log M = 20 \log|G(j\omega)| = 20 \log \omega^2 = 40 \log \omega \tag{10.31}$$

Equation (10.31) is a straight line with twice the slope of a first-order term (Eq. (10.20)). Its slope is 12 dB/octave, or 40 dB/decade.

FIGURE 10.13

Bode asymptotes for normalized and scaled $G(s) = s^2 + 2\zeta\omega_n s + \omega_n^2$:
a. magnitude;
b. phase

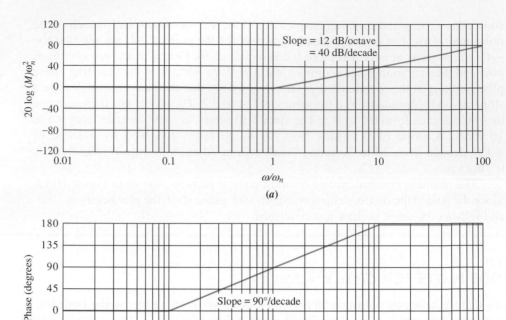

The low-frequency asymptote (Eq. (10.27)) and the high-frequency asymptote (Eq. (10.31)) are equal when $\omega = \omega_n$. Thus, ω_n is the break frequency for the second-order polynomial.

For convenience in representing systems with different ω_n, we normalize and scale our findings before drawing the asymptotes. Using the normalized and scaled term of Eq. (10.26), we normalize the magnitude, dividing by ω_n^2, and scale the frequency, dividing by ω_n. Thus, we plot $G(s_1)/\omega_n^2 = s_1^2 + 2\zeta s_1 + 1$, where $s_1 = s/\omega_n$. $G(s_1)$ has a low-frequency asymptote at 0 dB and a break frequency of 1 rad/s. Figure 10.13(a) shows the asymptotes for the normalized and scaled magnitude plot.

We now draw the phase plot. It is $0°$ at low frequencies (Eq. (10.27)) and $180°$ at high frequencies (Eq. (10.30)). To find the phase at the natural frequency, first evaluate $G(j\omega)$:

$$G(j\omega) = s^2 + 2\zeta\omega_n s + \omega_n^2|_{s \rightarrow j\omega} = (\omega_n^2 - \omega^2) + j2\zeta\omega_n\omega \tag{10.32}$$

Then find the function value at the natural frequency by substituting $\omega = \omega_n$. Since the result is $j2\zeta\omega_n^2$, the phase at the natural frequency is $+90°$. Figure 10.13(b) shows the phase plotted with frequency scaled by ω_n. The phase plot increases at a rate of $90°/\text{decade}$ from 0.1 to 10 and passes through $90°$ at 1.

CORRECTIONS TO SECOND-ORDER BODE PLOTS

Let us now examine the error between the actual response and the asymptotic approximation of the second-order polynomial. Whereas the first-order polynomial has a disparity of no more than 3.01 dB magnitude and 5.71° phase, the second-order function may have a greater disparity, which depends upon the value of ζ.

From Eq. (10.32), the actual magnitude and phase for $G(s) = s^2 + 2\zeta\omega_n s + \omega_n^2$ are, respectively,

$$M = \sqrt{(\omega_n^2 - \omega^2)^2 + (2\zeta\omega_n\omega)^2} \qquad (10.33)$$

$$\text{Phase} = \tan^{-1}\frac{2\zeta\omega_n\omega}{\omega_n^2 - \omega^2} \qquad (10.34)$$

These relationships are tabulated in Table 10.4 for a range of values of ζ and plotted in Figures 10.14 and 10.15 along with the asymptotic approximations for normalized

TABLE 10.4 Data for normalized and scaled log-magnitude and phase plots for $(s^2 + 2\zeta\omega_n s + \omega_n^2)$. Mag $= 20\log(M/\omega_n^2)$

Freq. $\dfrac{\omega}{\omega_n}$	Mag (dB) $\zeta = 0.1$	Phase (deg) $\zeta = 0.1$	Mag (dB) $\zeta = 0.2$	Phase (deg) $\zeta = 0.2$	Mag (dB) $\zeta = 0.3$	Phase (deg) $\zeta = 0.3$
0.10	−0.09	1.16	−0.08	2.31	−0.07	3.47
0.20	−0.35	2.39	−0.32	4.76	−0.29	7.13
0.30	−0.80	3.77	−0.74	7.51	−0.65	11.19
0.40	−1.48	5.44	−1.36	10.78	−1.17	15.95
0.50	−2.42	7.59	−2.20	14.93	−1.85	21.80
0.60	−3.73	10.62	−3.30	20.56	−2.68	29.36
0.70	−5.53	15.35	−4.70	28.77	−3.60	39.47
0.80	−8.09	23.96	−6.35	41.63	−4.44	53.13
0.90	−11.64	43.45	−7.81	62.18	−4.85	70.62
1.00	−13.98	90.00	−7.96	90.00	−4.44	90.00
1.10	−10.34	133.67	−6.24	115.51	−3.19	107.65
1.20	−6.00	151.39	−3.73	132.51	−1.48	121.43
1.30	−2.65	159.35	−1.27	143.00	0.35	131.50
1.40	0.00	163.74	0.92	149.74	2.11	138.81
1.50	2.18	166.50	2.84	154.36	3.75	144.25
1.60	4.04	168.41	4.54	157.69	5.26	148.39
1.70	5.67	169.80	6.06	160.21	6.64	151.65
1.80	7.12	170.87	7.43	162.18	7.91	154.26
1.90	8.42	171.72	8.69	163.77	9.09	156.41
2.00	9.62	172.41	9.84	165.07	10.19	158.20
3.00	18.09	175.71	18.16	171.47	18.28	167.32
4.00	23.53	176.95	23.57	173.91	23.63	170.91
5.00	27.61	177.61	27.63	175.24	27.67	172.87
6.00	30.89	178.04	30.90	176.08	30.93	174.13
7.00	33.63	178.33	33.64	176.66	33.66	175.00
8.00	35.99	178.55	36.00	177.09	36.01	175.64
9.00	38.06	178.71	38.07	177.42	38.08	176.14
10.00	39.91	178.84	39.92	177.69	39.93	176.53

(table continues)

TABLE 10.4   (Continued)

Freq. $\dfrac{\omega}{\omega_n}$	Mag (dB) $\zeta = 0.5$	Phase (deg) $\zeta = 0.5$	Mag (dB) $\zeta = 0.7$	Phase (deg) $\zeta = 0.7$	Mag (dB) $\zeta = 0.1$	Phase (deg) $\zeta = 0.1$
0.10	−0.04	5.77	0.00	8.05	0.09	11.42
0.20	−0.17	11.77	0.00	16.26	0.34	22.62
0.30	−0.37	18.25	0.02	24.78	0.75	33.40
0.40	−0.63	25.46	0.08	33.69	1.29	43.60
0.50	−0.90	33.69	0.22	43.03	1.94	53.13
0.60	−1.14	43.15	0.47	52.70	2.67	61.93
0.70	−1.25	53.92	0.87	62.51	3.46	69.98
0.80	−1.14	65.77	1.41	72.18	4.30	77.32
0.90	−0.73	78.08	2.11	81.42	5.15	83.97
1.00	0.00	90.00	2.92	90.00	6.02	90.00
1.10	0.98	100.81	3.83	97.77	6.89	95.45
1.20	2.13	110.14	4.79	104.68	7.75	100.39
1.30	3.36	117.96	5.78	110.76	8.60	104.86
1.40	4.60	124.44	6.78	116.10	9.43	108.92
1.50	5.81	129.81	7.76	120.76	10.24	112.62
1.60	6.98	134.27	8.72	124.85	11.03	115.99
1.70	8.10	138.03	9.66	128.45	11.80	119.07
1.80	9.17	141.22	10.56	131.63	12.55	121.89
1.90	10.18	143.95	11.43	134.46	13.27	124.48
2.00	11.14	146.31	12.26	136.97	13.98	126.87
3.00	18.63	159.44	19.12	152.30	20.00	143.13
4.00	23.82	165.07	24.09	159.53	24.61	151.93
5.00	27.79	168.23	27.96	163.74	28.30	157.38
6.00	31.01	170.27	31.12	166.50	31.36	161.08
7.00	33.72	171.70	33.80	168.46	33.98	163.74
8.00	36.06	172.76	36.12	169.92	36.26	165.75
9.00	38.12	173.58	38.17	171.05	38.28	167.32
10.00	39.96	174.23	40.00	171.95	40.09	168.58

magnitude and scaled frequency. In Figure 10.14, which is normalized to the square of the natural frequency, the normalized log-magnitude at the scaled natural frequency is $+20 \log 2\zeta$. The student should verify that the actual magnitude at the unscaled natural frequency is $+20 \log 2\zeta\omega_n^2$. Table 10.4 and Figures 10.14 and 10.15 can be used to improve accuracy when drawing Bode plots. For example, a magnitude correction of $+20 \log 2\zeta$ can be made at the natural, or break, frequency on the Bode asymptotic plot.

BODE PLOTS FOR $G(s) = 1/(s^2 + 2\zeta\omega_n s + \omega_n^2)$

Bode plots for $G(s) = 1/(s^2 + 2\zeta\omega_n s + \omega_n^2)$ can be derived similarly to those for $G(s) = s^2 + 2\zeta\omega_n s + \omega_n^2$. We find that the magnitude curve breaks at the natural frequency and decreases at a rate of -40 dB/decade. The phase plot is $0°$ at low frequencies. At $0.1\omega_n$ it begins a decrease of $-90°$/decade and continues until $\omega = 10\omega_n$, where it levels off at $-180°$.

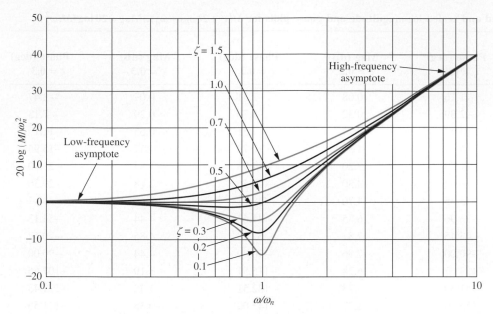

FIGURE 10.14 Normalized and scaled log-magnitude response for $(s^2 + 2\zeta\omega_n s + \omega_n^2)$

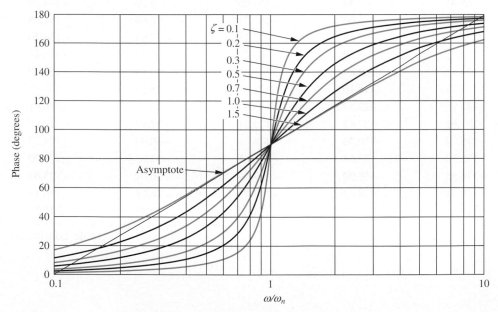

FIGURE 10.15 Scaled phase response for $(s^2 + 2\zeta\omega_n s + \omega_n^2)$

The exact frequency response also follows the same derivation as that of $G(s) = s^2 + 2\zeta\omega_n s + \omega_n^2$. The results are summarized in Table 10.5, as well as Figures 10.16 and 10.17. The exact magnitude is the reciprocal of Eq. (10.33), and the exact phase is the negative of Eq. (10.34). The normalized magnitude at the scaled natural frequency is $-20 \log 2\zeta$, which can be used as a correction at the break frequency on the Bode asymptotic plot.

Let us now look at an example of drawing Bode plots for transfer functions that contain second-order factors.

TABLE 10.5   Data for normalized and scaled log-magnitude and phase plots for $1/(s^2 + 2\zeta\omega_n s + \omega_n^2)$. Mag $= 20 \log (M/\omega_n^2)$

Freq. $\dfrac{\omega}{\omega_n}$	Mag (dB) $\zeta = 0.1$	Phase (deg) $\zeta = 0.1$	Mag (dB) $\zeta = 0.2$	Phase (deg) $\zeta = 0.2$	Mag (dB) $\zeta = 0.3$	Phase (deg) $\zeta = 0.3$
0.10	0.09	−1.16	0.08	−2.31	0.07	−3.47
0.20	0.35	−2.39	0.32	−4.76	0.29	−7.13
0.30	0.80	−3.77	0.74	−7.51	0.65	−11.19
0.40	1.48	−5.44	1.36	−10.78	1.17	−15.95
0.50	2.42	−7.59	2.20	−14.93	1.85	−21.80
0.60	3.73	−10.62	3.30	−20.56	2.68	−29.36
0.70	5.53	−15.35	4.70	−28.77	3.60	−39.47
0.80	8.09	−23.96	6.35	−41.63	4.44	−53.13
0.90	11.64	−43.45	7.81	−62.18	4.85	−70.62
1.00	13.98	−90.00	7.96	−90.00	4.44	−90.00
1.10	10.34	−133.67	6.24	−115.51	3.19	−107.65
1.20	6.00	−151.39	3.73	−132.51	1.48	−121.43
1.30	2.65	−159.35	1.27	−143.00	−0.35	−131.50
1.40	0.00	−163.74	−0.92	−149.74	−2.11	−138.81
1.50	−2.18	−166.50	−2.84	−154.36	−3.75	−144.25
1.60	−4.04	−168.41	−4.54	−157.69	−5.26	−148.39
1.70	−5.67	−169.80	−6.06	−160.21	−6.64	−151.65
1.80	−7.12	−170.87	−7.43	−162.18	−7.91	−154.26
1.90	−8.42	−171.72	−8.69	−163.77	−9.09	−156.41
2.00	−9.62	−172.41	−9.84	−165.07	−10.19	−158.20
3.00	−18.09	−175.71	−18.16	−171.47	−18.28	−167.32
4.00	−23.53	−176.95	−23.57	−173.91	−23.63	−170.91
5.00	−27.61	−177.61	−27.63	−175.24	−27.67	−172.87
6.00	−30.89	−178.04	−30.90	−176.08	−30.93	−174.13
7.00	−33.63	−178.33	−33.64	−176.66	−33.66	−175.00
8.00	−35.99	−178.55	−36.00	−177.09	−36.01	−175.64
9.00	−38.06	−178.71	−38.07	−177.42	−38.08	−176.14
10.00	−39.91	−178.84	−39.92	−177.69	−39.93	−176.53

(table continues)

TABLE 10.5 (Continued)

Freq. $\frac{\omega}{\omega_n}$	Mag (dB) $\zeta = 0.5$	Phase (deg) $\zeta = 0.5$	Mag (dB) $\zeta = 0.7$	Phase (deg) $\zeta = 0.7$	Mag (dB) $\zeta = 0.1$	Phase (deg) $\zeta = 0.1$
0.10	0.04	−5.77	0.00	−8.05	−0.09	−11.42
0.20	0.17	−11.77	0.00	−16.26	−0.34	−22.62
0.30	0.37	−18.25	−0.02	−24.78	−0.75	−33.40
0.40	0.63	−25.46	−0.08	−33.69	−1.29	−43.60
0.50	0.90	−33.69	−0.22	−43.03	−1.94	−53.13
0.60	1.14	−43.15	−0.47	−52.70	−2.67	−61.93
0.70	1.25	−53.92	−0.87	−62.51	−3.46	−69.98
0.80	1.14	−65.77	−1.41	−72.18	−4.30	−77.32
0.90	0.73	−78.08	−2.11	−81.42	−5.15	−83.97
1.00	0.00	−90.00	−2.92	−90.00	−6.02	−90.00
1.10	−0.98	−100.81	−3.93	−97.77	−6.89	−95.45
1.20	−2.13	−110.14	−4.79	−104.68	−7.75	−100.39
1.30	−3.36	−117.96	−5.78	−110.76	−8.60	−104.86
1.40	−4.60	−124.44	−6.78	−116.10	−9.43	−108.92
1.50	−5.81	−129.81	−7.76	−120.76	−10.24	−112.62
1.60	−6.98	−134.27	−8.72	−124.85	−11.03	−115.99
1.70	−8.10	−138.03	−9.66	−128.45	−11.80	−119.07
1.80	−9.17	−141.22	−10.56	−131.63	−12.55	−121.89
1.90	−10.18	−143.95	−11.43	−134.46	−13.27	−124.48
2.00	−11.14	−146.31	−12.26	−136.97	−13.98	−126.87
3.00	−18.63	−159.44	−19.12	−152.30	−20.00	−143.13
4.00	−23.82	−165.07	−24.09	−159.53	−24.61	−151.93
5.00	−27.79	−168.23	−27.96	−163.74	−28.30	−157.38
6.00	−31.01	−170.27	−31.12	−166.50	−31.36	−161.08
7.00	−33.72	−171.70	−33.80	−168.46	−33.98	−163.74
8.00	−36.06	−172.76	−36.12	−169.92	−36.26	−165.75
9.00	−38.12	−173.58	−38.17	−171.05	−38.28	−167.32
10.00	−39.96	−174.23	−40.00	−171.95	−40.09	−168.58

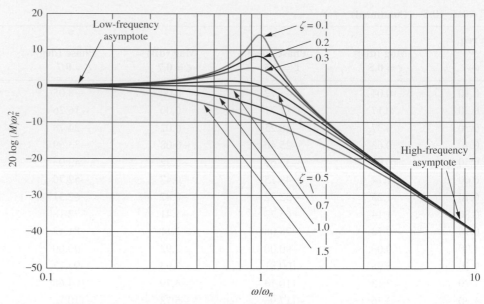

FIGURE 10.16   Normalized and scaled log-magnitude response for $1/(s^2 + 2\zeta\omega_n s + \omega_n^2)$

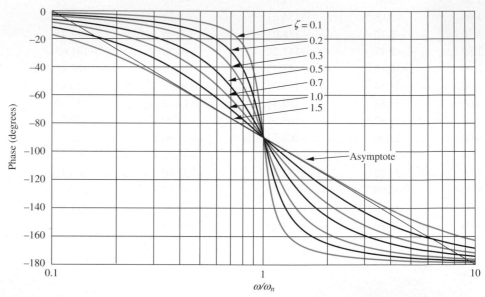

FIGURE 10.17   Scaled phase response for $1/(s^2 + 2\zeta\omega_n s + \omega_n^2)$

EXAMPLE 10.3

Bode plots for ratio of first- and second-order factors

Problem: Draw the Bode log-magnitude and phase plots of $G(s)$ for the unity feedback system shown in Figure 10.10, where $G(s) = (s + 3)/[(s + 2)(s^2 + 2s + 25)]$.

SOLUTION: We first convert $G(s)$ to show the normalized components that have unity low-frequency gain. The second-order term is normalized by factoring

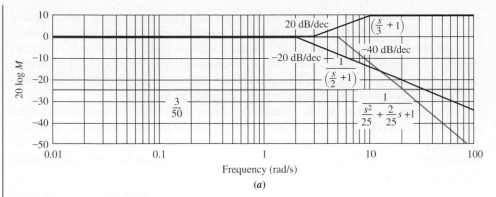

FIGURE 10.18
Bode magnitude plot for
$G(s) = (s + 3)/$
$[(s + 2)(s^2 + 2s + 25)]$:
a. components;
b. composite

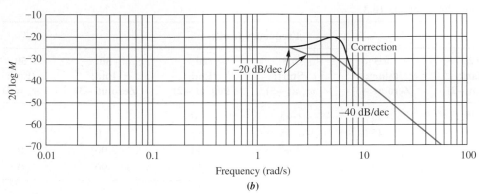

out ω_n^2, forming

$$\frac{s^2}{\omega_n^2} + \frac{2\zeta}{\omega_n}s + 1 \tag{10.35}$$

Thus,

$$G(s) = \frac{3}{(2)(25)} \frac{\left(\dfrac{s}{3} + 1\right)}{\left(\dfrac{s}{2} + 1\right)\left(\dfrac{s^2}{25} + \dfrac{2}{25}s + 1\right)} = \frac{3}{50} \frac{\left(\dfrac{s}{2} + 1\right)}{\left(\dfrac{s}{2} + 1\right)\left(\dfrac{s^2}{25} + \dfrac{2}{25}s + 1\right)} \tag{10.36}$$

The Bode log-magnitude diagram is shown in Figure 10.18(*b*) and is the sum of the individual first- and second-order terms of $G(s)$ shown in Figure 10.18(*a*). We solve this problem by adding the slopes of these component parts, beginning and ending at the appropriate frequencies. The results are summarized in Table 10.6, which can be used to obtain the slopes. The low-frequency value for $G(s)$, found by letting

TABLE 10.6 Magnitude diagram slopes for Example 10.3

	Frequency (rad/s)			
Description	**0.01** (Start: Plot)	**2** (Start: Pole at −2)	**3** (Start: Zero at −3)	**5** (Start: $\omega_n = 5$)
Pole at −2	0	−20	−20	−20
Zero at −3	0	0	20	20
$\omega_n = 5$	0	0	0	−40
Total slope (dB/dec)	0	−20	0	−40

$s = 0$, is 3/50, or -24.44 dB. The Bode magnitude plot starts out at this value and continues until the first break frequency at 2 rad/s. Here the pole at -2 yields a -20 dB/decade slope downward until the next break at 3 rad/s. The zero at -3 causes an upward slope of $+20$ dB/decade, which, when added to the previous -20 dB/decade curve, gives a net slope of 0. At a frequency of 5 rad/s, the second-order term initiates a -40 dB/decade downward slope, which continues to infinity.

The correction to the log-magnitude curve due to the underdamped second-order term can be found by plotting a point $-20 \log 2\zeta$ above the asymptotes at the natural frequency. Since $\zeta = 0.2$ for the second-order term in the denominator of $G(s)$, the correction is 7.96 dB. Points close to the natural frequency can be corrected by taking the values from the curves of Figure 10.16.

TABLE 10.7 **Phase diagram slopes for Example 10.3**

Description	Frequency (rad/s)					
	0.2 (Start: Pole at -2)	0.3 (Start: Zero at -3)	0.5 (Start: ω_n at -5)	20 (End: Pole at -2)	30 (End: Zero at -3)	50 (End: $w_n = 5$)
Pole at -2	-45	-45	-45	0		
Zero at -3		45	45	45	0	
$\omega_n = 5$			-90	-90	-90	0
Total slope (dB/dec)	-45	0	-90	-45	-90	0

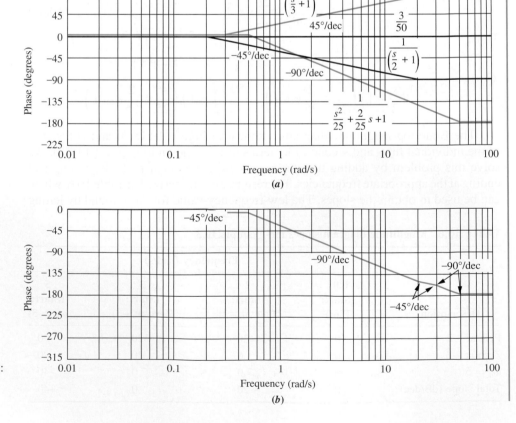

FIGURE 10.19
Bode phase plot for $G(s) = (s + 3)/[(s + 2)(s^2 + 2s + 25)]$:
a. components;
b. composite

We now turn to the phase plot. Table 10.7 is formed to determine the progression of slopes on the phase diagram. The first-order pole at -2 yields a phase angle that starts at $0°$ and ends at $-90°$ via a $-45°$/decade slope starting a decade below its break frequency and ending a decade above its break frequency. The first-order zero yields a phase angle that starts at $0°$ and ends at $+90°$ via a $+45°$/decade slope starting a decade below its break frequency and ending a decade above its break frequency. The second-order poles yield a phase angle that starts at $0°$ and ends at $-180°$ via a $-90°$/decade slope starting a decade below their natural frequency ($\omega_n = 5$) and ending a decade above their natural frequency. The slopes, shown in Figure 10.19(a), are summed over each frequency range, and the final Bode phase plot is shown in Figure 10.19(b).

Students who are using MATLAB should now run ch10p1 in Appendix B. You will learn how to use MATLAB to make Bode plots and list the points on the plots. This exercise solves Example 10.3 using MATLAB.

MATLAB

SKILL-ASSESSMENT EXERCISE 10.2

Problem: Draw the Bode log-magnitude and phase plots for the system shown in Figure 10.10, where

WileyPLUS
Control Solutions

$$G(s) = \frac{(s+20)}{(s+1)(s+7)(s+50)}$$

ANSWER: The complete solution is at www.wiley.com/college/nise.

TryIt 10.1

Use MATLAB, the Control System Toolbox, and the following statements to obtain the Bode plots for the system of Skill-Assessment Exercise 10.2

```
G=zpk([-20],[-1,-7,...
-50],1)
bode (G); grid on
```

After the Bode plots appear, click on the curve and drag to read the coordinates.

In this section we learned how to construct Bode log-magnitude and Bode phase plots. The Bode plots are separate magnitude and phase frequency response curves for a system, $G(s)$. In the next section we develop the Nyquist criterion for stability, which makes use of the frequency response of a system. The Bode plots can then be used to determine the stability of a system.

10.3 INTRODUCTION TO THE NYQUIST CRITERION

The Nyquist criterion relates the stability of a closed-loop system to the open-loop frequency response and open-loop pole location. Thus, knowledge of the open-loop system's frequency response yields information about the stability of the closed-loop system. This concept is similar to the root locus, where we began with information about the open-loop system, its poles and zeros, and developed transient and stability information about the closed-loop system.

Although the Nyquist criterion will yield stability information at first, we will extend the concept to transient response and steady-state errors. Thus, frequency response techniques are an alternate approach to the root locus.

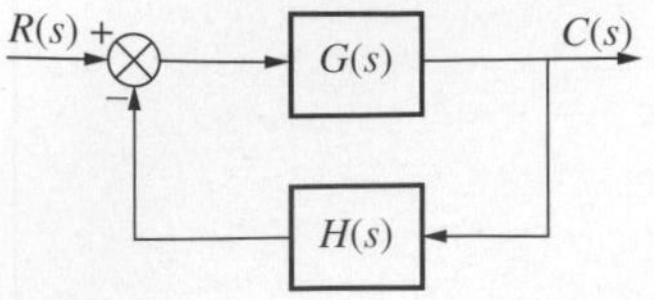

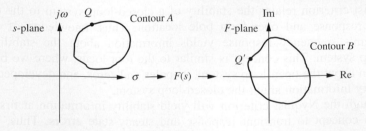

FIGURE 10.20 Closed-loop control system

DERIVATION OF THE NYQUIST CRITERION

Consider the system of Figure 10.20. The Nyquist criterion can tell us how many closed-loop poles are in the right half-plane. Before deriving the criterion, let us establish four important concepts that will be used during the derivation: (1) the relationship between the poles of $1 + G(s)H(s)$ and the poles of $G(s)H(s)$; (2) the relationship between the zeros of $1 + G(s)H(s)$ and the poles of the closed-loop transfer function, $T(s)$; (3) the concept of *mapping* points; and (4) the concept of mapping *contours*.

Letting

$$G(s) = \frac{N_G}{D_G} \tag{10.37a}$$

$$H(s) = \frac{N_H}{D_H} \tag{10.37b}$$

we find

$$G(s)H(s) = \frac{N_G N_H}{D_G D_H} \tag{10.38a}$$

$$1 + G(s)H(s) = 1 + \frac{N_G N_H}{D_G D_H} = \frac{D_G D_H + N_G N_H}{D_G D_H} \tag{10.38b}$$

$$T(s) = \frac{G(s)}{1 + G(s)H(s)} = \frac{N_G D_H}{D_G D_H + N_G N_H} \tag{10.38c}$$

From Eqs. (10.38), we conclude that (1) *the poles of $1 + G(s)H(s)$ are the same as the poles of $G(s)H(s)$, the open-loop system,* and (2) *the zeros of $1 + G(s)H(s)$ are the same as the poles of $T(s)$, the closed-loop system.*

Next, let us define the term *mapping*. If we take a complex number on the s-plane and substitute it into a function, $F(s)$, another complex number results. This process is called *mapping*. For example, substituting $s = 4 + j3$ into the function $(s^2 + 2s + 1)$ yields $16 + j30$. We say that $4 + j3$ maps into $16 + j30$ through the function $(s^2 + 2s + 1)$.

Finally, we discuss the concept of mapping *contours*. Consider the collection of points, called a *contour,* shown in Figure 10.21 as contour A. Also, assume that

$$F(s) = \frac{(s - z_1)(s - z_2) \cdots}{(s - p_1)(s - p_2) \cdots} \tag{10.39}$$

Contour A can be mapped through $F(s)$ into contour B by substituting each point of contour A into the function $F(s)$ and plotting the resulting complex numbers. For example, point Q in Figure 10.21 maps into point Q' through the function $F(s)$.

The vector approach to performing the calculation, covered in Section 8.1, can be used as an alternative. Some examples of contour mapping are shown in Figure 10.22 for some simple $F(s)$. The mapping of each point is defined by complex arithmetic, where the

FIGURE 10.21 Mapping contour A through function $F(s)$ to contour B

FIGURE 10.22 Examples of contour mapping

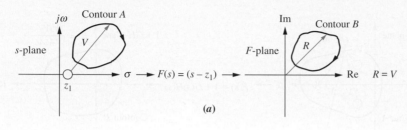

(a)

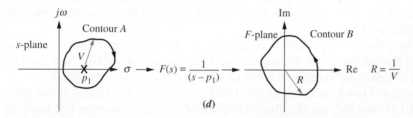

(b)

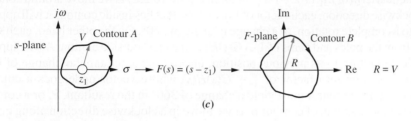

(c)

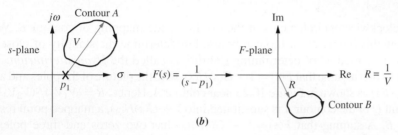

(d)

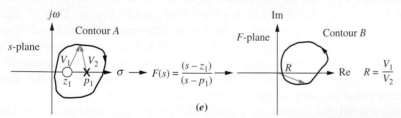

(e)

resulting complex number, R, is evaluated from the complex numbers represented by V, as shown in the last column of Figure 10.22. You should verify that if we assume a clockwise direction for mapping the points on contour A, then contour B maps in a clockwise direc-tion if $F(s)$ in Figure 10.22 has just zeros or has just poles that are not encircled by the contour. The contour B maps in a counterclockwise direction if $F(s)$ has just poles that are encircled by the contour. Also, you should verify that if the pole or zero of $F(s)$ is enclosed by contour A, the mapping encircles the origin. In the last case of Figure 10.22, the pole and zero rotation cancel, and the mapping does not encircle the origin.

Let us now begin the derivation of the Nyquist criterion for stability. We show that a unique relationship exists between the number of poles of $F(s)$ contained inside contour A, the number of zeros of $F(s)$ contained inside contour A, and the number of

FIGURE 10.23 Vector representation of mapping

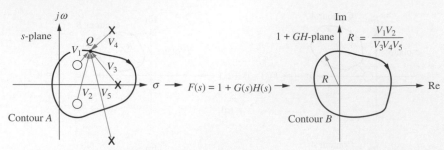

counterclockwise encirclements of the origin for the mapping of contour B. We then show how this interrelationship can be used to determine the stability of closed-loop systems. This method of determining stability is called the *Nyquist criterion*.

Let us first assume that $F(s) = 1 + G(s)H(s)$, with the picture of the poles and zeros of $1 + G(s)H(s)$ as shown in Figure 10.23 near contour A. Hence, $R = (V_1 V_2)/(V_3 V_4 V_5)$. As each point Q of the contour A is substituted into $1 + G(s)H(s)$, a mapped point results on contour B. Assuming that $F(s) = 1 + G(s)H(s)$ has two zeros and three poles, each parenthetical term of Eq. (10.39) is a vector in Figure 10.23. As we move around contour A in a clockwise direction, each vector of Eq. (10.39) that lies inside contour A will appear to undergo a complete rotation, or a change in angle of $360°$. On the other hand, each vector drawn from the poles and zeros of $1 + G(s)H(s)$ that exist outside contour A will appear to oscillate and return to its previous position, undergoing a net angular change of $0°$.

Each pole or zero factor of $1 + G(s)H(s)$ whose vector undergoes a complete rotation around contour A must yield a change of $360°$ in the resultant, R, or a complete rotation of the mapping of contour B. If we move in a clockwise direction along contour A, each zero inside contour A yields a rotation in the clockwise direction, while each pole inside contour A yields a rotation in the counterclockwise direction since poles are in the denominator of Eq. (10.39).

Thus, $N = P - Z$, where N equals the number of counterclockwise rotations of contour B about the origin; P equals the number of poles of $1 + G(s)H(s)$ inside contour A, and Z equals the number of zeros of $1 + G(s)H(s)$ inside contour A.

Since the poles shown in Figure 10.23 are poles of $1 + G(s)H(s)$, we know from Eqs. (10.38) that they are also the poles of $G(s)H(s)$ and are known. But since *the zeros shown in Figure 10.23 are the zeros of* $1 + G(s)H(s)$, we know from Eq. (10.38) that *they are also the poles of the closed-loop system and are not known*. Thus, P equals the number of enclosed open-loop poles, and Z equals the number of enclosed closed-loop poles. Hence, $N = P - Z$, or alternately, $Z = P - N$, tells us that the number of closed-loop poles inside the contour (which is the same as the zeros inside the contour) equals the number of open-loop poles of $G(s)H(s)$ inside the contour minus the number of counterclockwise rotations of the mapping about the origin.

If we extend the contour to include the entire right half-plane, as shown in Figure 10.24, we can count the number of right-half-plane, closed-loop poles inside contour A and determine a system's stability. Since we can count the number of open-loop poles, P, inside the contour, which are the same as the right-half-plane poles of $G(s)H(s)$, the only problem remaining is how to obtain the mapping and find N.

Since all of the poles and zeros of $G(s)H(s)$ are known, what if we map through $G(s)H(s)$ instead of $1 + G(s)H(s)$? The resulting contour is the same as a mapping through $1 + G(s)H(s)$, except that it is translated one unit to the left; thus, we count rotations about -1 instead of rotations about the origin. Hence, the final statement of the Nyquist stability criterion is as follows:

If a contour, A, that encircles the entire right half-plane is mapped through $G(s)H(s)$, then *the number of closed-loop poles, Z, in the right half-plane equals the*

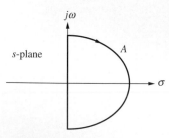

FIGURE 10.24 Contour enclosing right half-plane to determine stability

number of open-loop poles, P, that are in the right half-plane minus the number of counterclockwise revolutions, N, around −1 of the mapping; that is, Z = P − N. The mapping is called the *Nyquist diagram,* or *Nyquist plot, of G(s)H(s).*

We can now see why this method is classified as a frequency response technique. Around contour *A* in Figure 10.24, the mapping of the points on the *jω*-axis through the function $G(s)H(s)$ is the same as substituting $s = j\omega$ into $G(s)H(s)$ to form the frequency response function $G(j\omega)H(j\omega)$. We are thus finding the frequency response of $G(s)H(s)$ over that part of contour *A* on the positive *jω*-axis. In other words, part of the Nyquist diagram is the polar plot of the frequency response of $G(s)H(s)$.

APPLYING THE NYQUIST CRITERION TO DETERMINE STABILITY

Before describing how to sketch a Nyquist diagram, let us look at some typical examples that use the Nyquist criterion to determine the stability of a system. These examples give us a perspective prior to engaging in the details of mapping. Figure 10.25(*a*) shows a contour *A* that does not enclose closed-loop poles, that is, the zeros of $1 + G(s)H(s)$. The contour thus maps through $G(s)H(s)$ into a Nyquist diagram that does not encircle −1. Hence, $P = 0$, $N = 0$, and $Z = P − N = 0$. Since Z is the number of closed-loop poles inside contour *A*, which encircles the right half-plane, this system has no right-half-plane poles and is stable.

On the other hand, Figure 10.25(*b*) shows a contour *A* that, while it does not enclose open-loop poles, does generate two clockwise encirclements of −1. Thus, $P = 0$, $N = −2$, and the system is unstable; it has two closed-loop poles in the right half-plane since $Z = P − N = 2$. The two closed-loop poles are shown inside contour *A* in Figure 10.25(*b*) as zeros of $1 + G(s)H(s)$. You should keep in mind that the existence of these poles is not known a priori.

In this example notice that clockwise encirclements imply a negative value for *N*. The number of encirclements can be determined by drawing a test radius from −1 in any convenient direction and counting the number of times the Nyquist diagram crosses the

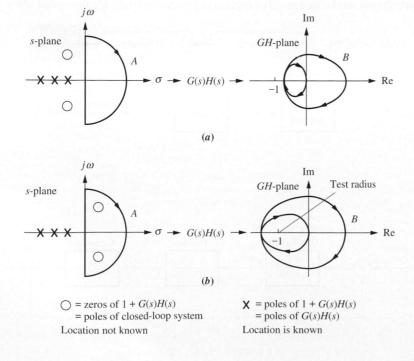

(*a*)

(*b*)

○ = zeros of 1 + G(s)H(s)
  = poles of closed-loop system
Location not known

✕ = poles of 1 + G(s)H(s)
  = poles of G(s)H(s)
Location is known

FIGURE 10.25
Mapping examples:
a. Contour does not enclose closed-loop poles;
b. contour does enclose closed-loop poles

test radius. Counterclockwise crossings are positive, and clockwise crossings are negative. For example, in Figure 10.25(*b*), contour *B* crosses the test radius twice in a clockwise direction. Hence, there are −2 encirclements of the point −1.

Before applying the Nyquist criterion to other examples in order to determine a system's stability, we must first gain experience in sketching Nyquist diagrams. The next section covers the development of this skill.

10.4 SKETCHING THE NYQUIST DIAGRAM

The contour that encloses the right half-plane can be mapped through the function $G(s)H(s)$ by substituting points along the contour into $G(s)H(s)$. The points along the positive extension of the imaginary axis yield the polar frequency response of $G(s)H(s)$. Approximations can be made to $G(s)H(s)$ for points around the infinite semicircle by assuming that the vectors originate at the origin. Thus, their length is infinite, and their angles are easily evaluated.

However, most of the time a simple sketch of the Nyquist diagram is all that is needed. A sketch can be obtained rapidly by looking at the vectors of $G(s)H(s)$ and their motion along the contour. In the examples that follow, we stress this rapid method for sketching the Nyquist diagram. However, the examples also include analytical expressions for $G(s)H(s)$ for each section of the contour to aid you in determining the shape of the Nyquist diagram.

EXAMPLE 10.4

Sketching a Nyquist diagram

Problem: Speed controls find wide application throughout industry and the home. Figure 10.26(*a*) shows one application: output frequency control of electrical power from a turbine and generator pair. By regulating the speed, the control system ensures that the generated frequency remains within tolerance. Deviations from the desired speed are sensed, and a steam valve is changed to compensate for the speed error. The

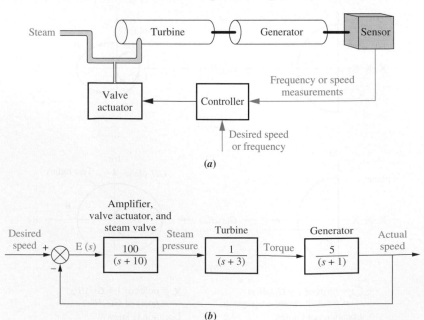

FIGURE 10.26
a. Turbine and generator;
b. block diagram of speed control system for Example 10.4

system block diagram is shown in Figure 10.26(*b*). Sketch the Nyquist diagram for the system of Figure 10.26.

SOLUTION: Conceptually, the Nyquist diagram is plotted by substituting the points of the contour shown in Figure 10.27(*a*) into $G(s) = 500/[(s + 1)(s + 3)(s + 10)]$. This process is equivalent to performing complex arithmetic using the vectors of $G(s)$ drawn to the points of the contour as shown in Figure 10.27(*a*) and (*b*). Each pole and zero term of $G(s)$ shown in Figure 10.26(*b*) is a vector in Figure 10.27(*a*) and (*b*). The resultant vector, R, found at any point along the contour is in general the product of the zero vectors divided by the product of the pole vectors (see Figure 10.27(*c*)). Thus, the magnitude of the resultant is the product of the zero lengths divided by the product of the pole lengths, and the angle of the resultant is the sum of the zero angles minus the sum of the pole angles.

As we move in a clockwise direction around the contour from point A to point C in Figure 10.27(*a*), the resultant angle goes from $0°$ to $-3 \times 90° = -270°$, or from A' to C' in Figure 10.27(*c*). Since the angles emanate from poles in the denominator of $G(s)$, the rotation or increase in angle is really a decrease in angle of the function $G(s)$; the poles gain $270°$ in a counterclockwise direction, which explains why the function loses $270°$.

While the resultant moves from A' to C' in Figure 10.27(*c*), its magnitude changes as the product of the zero lengths divided by the product of the pole lengths. Thus, the

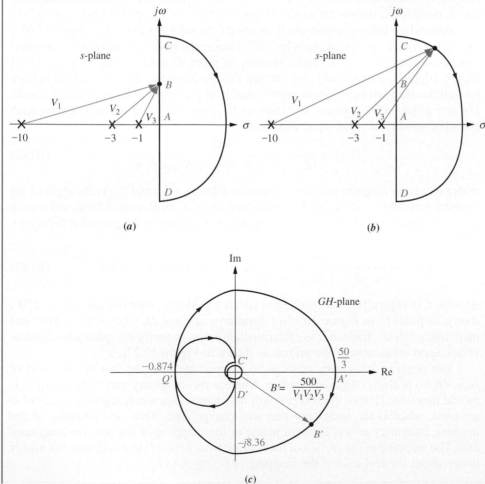

(*a*)

(*b*)

(*c*)

FIGURE 10.27   Vector evaluation of the Nyquist diagram for Example 10.4: **a.** vectors on contour at low frequency; **b.** vectors on contour around infinity; **c.** Nyquist diagram

resultant goes from a finite value at zero frequency (at point A of Figure 10.27(a), there are three finite pole lengths) to zero magnitude at infinite frequency at point C (at point C of Figure 10.27(a), there are three infinite pole lengths).

The mapping from point A to point C can also be explained analytically. From A to C the collection of points along the contour is imaginary. Hence, from A to C, $G(s) = G(j\omega)$, or from Figure 10.26(b),

$$G(j\omega) = \frac{500}{(s+1)(s+3)(s+10)}\bigg|_{s\to j\omega} = \frac{500}{(-14\omega^2 + 30) + j(43\omega - \omega^3)} \quad (10.40)$$

Multiplying the numerator and denominator by the complex conjugate of the denominator, we obtain

$$G(j\omega) = 500\frac{(-14\omega^2 + 30) - j(43\omega - \omega^3)}{(-14\omega^2 + 30)^2 + (43\omega - \omega^3)^2} \quad (10.41)$$

At zero frequency $G(j\omega) = 500/30 = 50/3$. Thus, the Nyquist diagram starts at $50/3$ at an angle of $0°$. As ω increases the real part remains positive, and the imaginary part remains negative. At $\omega = \sqrt{30/14}$, the real part becomes negative. At $\omega = \sqrt{43}$, the Nyquist diagram crosses the negative real axis since the imaginary term goes to zero. The real value at the axis crossing, point Q' in Figure 10.27(c), found by substituting into Eq. (10.41), is -0.874. Continuing toward $\omega = \infty$, the real part is negative, and the imaginary part is positive. At infinite frequency $G(j\omega) \approx 500j/\omega^3$, or approximately zero at $90°$.

Around the infinite semicircle from point C to point D shown in Figure 10.27(b), the vectors rotate clockwise, each by $180°$. Hence, the resultant undergoes a counterclockwise rotation of $3 \times 180°$, starting at point C' and ending at point D' of Figure 10.27(c). Analytically, we can see this by assuming that around the infinite semicircle, the vectors originate approximately at the origin and have infinite length. For any point on the s-plane, the value of $G(s)$ can be found by representing each complex number in polar form, as follows:

$$G(s) = \frac{500}{(R_{-1}e^{j\theta_{-1}})(R_{-3}e^{j\theta_{-3}})(R_{-10}e^{j\theta_{-10}})} \quad (10.42)$$

where R_{-i} is the magnitude of the complex number $(s + 1)$, and θ_{-i} is the angle of the complex number $(s + i)$. Around the infinite semicircle, all R_{-i} are infinite, and we can use our assumption to approximate the angles as if the vectors originated at the origin. Thus, around the infinite semicircle,

$$G(s) = \frac{500}{\infty\angle(\theta_{-1} + \theta_{-3} + \theta_{-10})} = 0\angle-(\theta_{-1} + \theta_{-3} + \theta_{-10}) \quad (10.43)$$

At point C in Figure 10.27(b), the angles are all $90°$. Hence, the resultant is $0 \angle -270°$, shown as point C' in Figure 10.27(c). Similarly, at point D, $G(s) = 0 \angle +270°$ and maps into point D'. You can select intermediate points to verify the spiral whose radius vector approaches zero at the origin, as shown in Figure 10.27(c).

The negative imaginary axis can be mapped by realizing that the real part of $G(j\omega)H(j\omega)$ is always an even function, whereas the imaginary part of $G(j\omega)H(j\omega)$ is an odd function. That is, the real part will not change sign when negative values of ω are used, whereas the imaginary part will change sign. Thus, the mapping of the negative imaginary axis is a mirror image of the mapping of the positive imaginary axis. The mapping of the section of the contour from points D to A is drawn as a mirror image about the real axis of the mapping of points A to C.

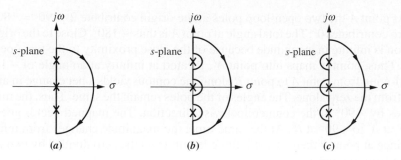

FIGURE 10.28
Detouring around open-loop
poles: **a.** poles on contour;
b. detour right; **c.** detour left

In the previous example there were no open-loop poles situated along the contour enclosing the right half-plane. If such poles exist, then a detour around the poles on the contour is required; otherwise, the mapping would go to infinity in an undetermined way, without angular information. Subsequently, a complete sketch of the Nyquist diagram could not be made, and the number of encirclements of -1 could not be found.

Let us assume a $G(s)H(s) = N(s)/sD(s)$ where $D(s)$ has imaginary roots. The s term in the denominator and the imaginary roots of $D(s)$ are poles of $G(s)H(s)$ that lie on the contour, as shown in Figure 10.28(a). To sketch the Nyquist diagram, the contour must detour around each open-loop pole lying on its path. The detour can be to the right of the pole, as shown in Figure 10.28(b), which makes it clear that each pole's vector rotates through $+180°$ as we move around the contour near that pole. This knowledge of the angular rotation of the poles on the contour permits us to complete the Nyquist diagram. Of course, our detour must carry us only an infinitesimal distance into the right half-plane, or else some closed-loop, right-half-plane poles will be excluded in the count.

We can also detour to the left of the open-loop poles. In this case each pole rotates through an angle of $-180°$ as we detour around it. Again, the detour must be infinitesimally small, or else we might include some left-half-plane poles in the count. Let us look at an example.

EXAMPLE 10.5

Nyquist diagram for open-loop function with poles on contour

Problem: Sketch the Nyquist diagram of the unity feedback system of Figure 10.10, where $G(s) = (s + 2)/s^2$.

SOLUTION: The system's two poles at the origin are on the contour and must be bypassed, as shown in Figure 10.29(a). The mapping starts at point A and continues in a clockwise direction. Points A, B, C, D, E, and F of Figure 10.29(a) map respectively into points A', B', C', D', E', and F' of Figure 10.29(b).

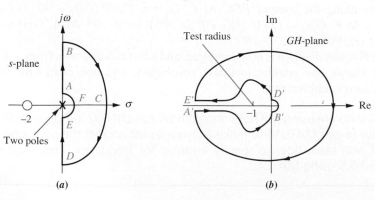

FIGURE 10.29
a. Contour for Example
10.5; **b.** Nyquist diagram for
Example 10.5

At point A the two open-loop poles at the origin contribute $2 \times 90° = 180°$, and the zero contributes $0°$. The total angle at point A is thus $-180°$. Close to the origin, the function is infinite in magnitude because of the close proximity to the two open-loop poles. Thus, point A maps into point A', located at infinity at an angle of $-180°$.

Moving from point A to point B along the contour yields a net change in angle of $+90°$ from the zero alone. The angles of the poles remain the same. Thus, the mapping changes by $+90°$ in the counterclockwise direction. The mapped vector goes from $-180°$ at A' to $-90°$ at B'. At the same time, the magnitude changes from infinity to zero since at point B there is one infinite length from the zero divided by two infinite lengths from the poles.

Alternately, the frequency response can be determined analytically from $G(j\omega) = (2 + j\omega)/(-\omega^2)$, considering ω going from 0 to ∞. At low frequencies $G(j\omega) \approx 2/(-\omega^2)$, or $\infty \angle 180°$. At high frequencies $G(j\omega) \approx j/(-\omega)$, or $0\angle -90°$. Also, the real and imaginary parts are always negative.

As we travel along the contour BCD, the function magnitude stays at zero (one infinite zero length divided by two infinite pole lengths). As the vectors move through BCD, the zero's vector and the two poles' vectors undergo changes of $-180°$ each. Thus, the mapped vector undergoes a net change of $+180°$, which is the angular change of the zero minus the sum of the angular changes of the poles $\{-180 - [2(-180)] = +180\}$. The mapping is shown as $B'C'D'$, where the resultant vector changes by $+180°$ with a magnitude of ϵ that approaches zero.

From the analytical point of view,

$$G(s) = \frac{R_{-2}\angle\theta_{-2}}{(R_0\angle\theta_0)(R_0\angle\theta_0)} \tag{10.44}$$

anywhere on the s-plane where $R_{-2}\angle\theta_{-2}$ is the vector from the zero at -2 to any point on the s-plane, and $R_0\angle\theta_0$ is the vector from a pole at the origin to any point on the s-plane. Around the infinite semicircle, all $R_{-i} = \infty$, and all angles can be approximated as if the vectors originated at the origin. Thus at point B, $G(s) = 0\angle -90°$ since all $\theta_{-i} = 90°$ in Eq. (10.44). At point C all $R_{-i} = \infty$, and all $\theta_{-i} = 0°$ in Eq. (10.44). Thus, $G(s) = 0\angle 0°$. At point D all $R_{-i} = \infty$, and all $\theta_{-i} = -90°$ in Eq. (10.44). Thus, $G(s) = 0\angle 90°$.

The mapping of the section of the contour from D to E is a mirror image of the mapping of A to B. The result is D' to E'.

Finally, over the section EFA, the resultant magnitude approaches infinity. The angle of the zero does not change, but each pole changes by $+180°$. This change yields a change in the function of $-2 \times 180° = -360°$. Thus, the mapping from E' to A' is shown as infinite in length and rotating $-360°$. Analytically, we can use Eq. (10.44) for the points along the contour EFA. At E, $G(s) = (2\angle 0°)/[(\epsilon\angle -90°)(\epsilon\angle -90°)] = \infty\angle 180°$. At F, $G(s) = (2\angle 0°)/[(\epsilon\angle 0°)(\epsilon\angle 0°)] = \infty\angle 0°$. At A, $G(s) = (2\angle 0°)/[(\epsilon\angle 90°)(\epsilon\angle 90°)] = \infty\angle -180°$.

The Nyquist diagram is now complete, and a test radius drawn from -1 in Figure 10.29(b) shows one counterclockwise revolution, and one clockwise revolution, yielding zero encirclements.

Students who are using MATLAB should now run ch10p2 in Appendix B. You will learn how to use MATLAB to make a Nyquist plot and list the points on the plot. You will also learn how to specify a range for frequency. This exercise solves Example 10.5 using MATLAB.

In this section we learned how to sketch a Nyquist diagram. We saw how to calculate the value of the intersection of the Nyquist diagram with the negative real axis. This intersection is important in determining the number of encirclements of -1. Also, we showed how to sketch the Nyquist diagram when open-loop poles exist on the contour; this case required detours around the poles. In the next section we apply the Nyquist criterion to determine the stability of feedback control systems.

10.5 STABILITY VIA THE NYQUIST DIAGRAM

We now use the Nyquist diagram to determine a system's stability, using the simple equation $Z = P - N$. The values of P, the number of open-loop poles of $G(s)H(s)$ enclosed by the contour, and N, the number of encirclements the Nyquist diagram makes about -1, are used to determine Z, the number of right-half-plane poles of the closed-loop system.

If the closed-loop system has a variable gain in the loop, one question we would like to ask is, "For what range of gain is the system stable?" This question, previously answered by the root locus method and the Routh-Hurwitz criterion, is now answered via the Nyquist criterion. The general approach is to set the loop gain equal to unity and draw the Nyquist diagram. Since gain is simply a multiplying factor, the effect of the gain is to multiply the resultant by a constant anywhere along the Nyquist diagram.

For example, consider Figure 10.30, which summarizes the Nyquist approach for a system with variable gain, K. As the gain is varied, we can visualize the Nyquist diagram in Figure 10.30(c) expanding (increased gain) or shrinking (decreased gain) like a balloon.

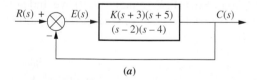

(a)

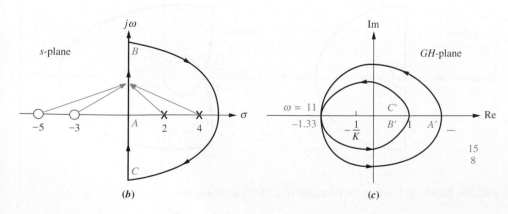

(b)

(c)

FIGURE 10.30 Demonstrating Nyquist stability: **a.** system; **b.** contour; **c.** Nyquist diagram

This motion could move the Nyquist diagram past the -1 point, changing the stability picture. For this system, since $P = 2$, the critical point must be encircled by the Nyquist diagram to yield $N = 2$ and a stable system. A reduction in gain would place the critical point outside the Nyquist diagram where $N = 0$, yielding $Z = 2$, an unstable system.

From another perspective we can think of the Nyquist diagram as remaining stationary and the -1 point moving along the real axis. In order to do this, we set the gain to unity and position the critical point at $-1/K$ rather than -1. Thus, the critical point appears to move closer to the origin as K increases.

Finally, if the Nyquist diagram intersects the real axis at -1, then $G(j\omega)H(j\omega) = -1$. From root locus concepts, when $G(s)H(s) = -1$, the variable s is a closed-loop pole of the system. Thus, the frequency at which the Nyquist diagram intersects -1 is the same frequency at which the root locus crosses the $j\omega$-axis. Hence, the system is marginally stable if the Nyquist diagram intersects the real axis at -1.

In summary, then, if the open-loop system contains a variable gain, K, set $K = 1$ and sketch the Nyquist diagram. Consider the critical point to be at $-1/K$ rather than at -1. Adjust the value of K to yield stability, based upon the Nyquist criterion.

EXAMPLE 10.6

Range of gain for stability via the Nyquist criterion

Problem: For the unity feedback system of Figure 10.10, where $G(s) = K/[s(s + 3)(s + 5)]$, find the range of gain, K, for stability, instability, and the value of gain for marginal stability. For marginal stability also find the frequency of oscillation. Use the Nyquist criterion.

SOLUTION: First set $K = 1$ and sketch the Nyquist diagram for the system, using the contour shown in Figure 10.31(a). For all points on the imaginary axis,

$$G(j\omega)H(j\omega) = \left.\frac{K}{s(s+3)(s+5)}\right|_{\substack{K=1 \\ s=j\omega}} = \frac{-8\omega^2 - j(15\omega - \omega^3)}{64\omega^4 + \omega^2(15 - \omega^2)^2} \qquad (10.45)$$

At $\omega = 0$, $G(j\omega)H(j\omega) = -0.0356 - j\infty$.

Next find the point where the Nyquist diagram intersects the negative real axis. Setting the imaginary part of Eq. (10.45) equal to zero, we find $\omega = \sqrt{15}$. Substituting this value of ω back into Eq. (10.45) yields the real part of -0.0083. Finally, at $\omega = \infty$, $G(j\omega)H(j\omega) = G(s)H(s)|_{s \to j\infty} = 1/(j\infty)^3 = 0 \angle -270°$.

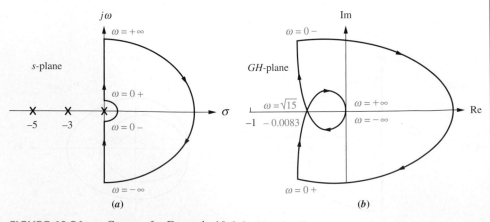

FIGURE 10.31   **a.** Contour for Example 10.6; **b.** Nyquist diagram

From the contour of Figure 10.31(*a*), $P = 0$; for stability N must then be equal to zero. From Figure 10.31(*b*), the system is stable if the critical point lies outside the contour ($N = 0$), so that $Z = P - N = 0$. Thus, K can be increased by $1/0.0083 = 120.5$ before the Nyquist diagram encircles -1. Hence, for stability, $K < 120.5$. For marginal stability $K = 120.5$. At this gain the Nyquist diagram intersects -1, and the frequency of oscillation is $\sqrt{15}$ rad/s.

Now that we have used the Nyquist diagram to determine stability, we can develop a simplified approach that uses only the mapping of the positive $j\omega$-axis.

STABILITY VIA MAPPING ONLY THE POSITIVE $j\omega$-AXIS

Once the stability of a system is determined by the Nyquist criterion, continued evaluation of the system can be simplified by using just the mapping of the positive $j\omega$-axis. This concept plays a major role in the next two sections, where we discuss stability margin and the implementation of the Nyquist criterion with Bode plots.

Consider the system shown in Figure 10.32, which is stable at low values of gain and unstable at high values of gain. Since the contour does not encircle open-loop poles, the Nyquist criterion tells us that we must have no encirclements of -1 for the system to be stable. We can see from the Nyquist diagram that the encirclements of the critical point can be determined from the mapping of the positive $j\omega$-axis alone. If the gain is small, the mapping will pass to the right of -1, and the system will be stable. If the gain is high, the mapping will pass to the left of -1, and the system will be unstable. Thus, this system is stable for the range of loop gain, K, that ensures that the *open-loop magnitude is less than unity at that frequency where the phase angle is 180° (or, equivalently, $-180°$).* This statement is thus an alternative to the Nyquist criterion for this system.

Now consider the system shown in Figure 10.33, which is unstable at low values of gain and stable at high values of gain. Since the contour encloses two open-loop poles, two counterclockwise encirclements of the critical point are required for stability. Thus, for this case the system is stable if the *open-loop magnitude is greater than unity at that frequency where the phase angle is 180° (or, equivalently, $-180°$).*

In summary, first determine stability from the Nyquist criterion and the Nyquist diagram. Next interpret the Nyquist criterion and determine whether the mapping of just the positive imaginary axis should have a gain of less than or greater than unity at 180°. If the Nyquist diagram crosses $\pm180°$ at multiple frequencies, determine the interpretation from the Nyquist criterion.

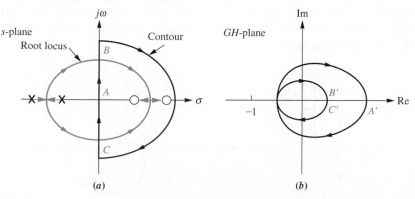

FIGURE 10.32   a. Contour and root locus of system that is stable for small gain and unstable for large gain; **b.** Nyquist diagram

FIGURE 10.33 **a.** Contour and root locus of system that is unstable for small gain and stable for large gain; **b.** Nyquist diagram

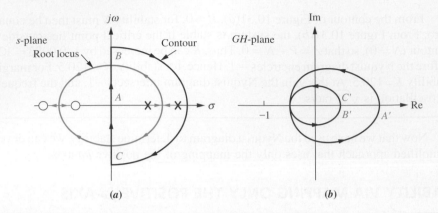

(a)   (b)

EXAMPLE 10.7

Stability design via mapping positive $j\omega$-axis

Problem: Find the range of gain for stability and instability, and the gain for marginal stability, for the unity feedback system shown in Figure 10.10, where $G(s) = K/[(s^2 + 2s + 2)(s + 2)]$. For marginal stability find the radian frequency of oscillation. Use the Nyquist criterion and the mapping of only the positive imaginary axis.

SOLUTION: Since the open-loop poles are only in the left half-plane, the Nyquist criterion tells us that we want no encirclements of -1 for stability. Hence, a gain less than unity at $\pm 180°$ is required. Begin by letting $K = 1$ and draw the portion of the contour along the positive imaginary axis as shown in Figure 10.34(a). In Figure 10.34(b) the intersection with the negative real axis is found by letting $s = j\omega$ in $G(s)H(s)$, setting the imaginary part equal to zero to find the frequency, and then substituting the frequency into the real part of $G(j\omega)H(j\omega)$. Thus, for any point on the positive imaginary axis,

$$
\begin{aligned}
G(j\omega)H(j\omega) &= \left.\frac{1}{(s^2 + 2s + 2)(s + 2)}\right|_{s \to j\omega} \\
&= \frac{4(1 - \omega^2) - j\omega(6 - \omega^2)}{16(1 - \omega^2)^2 + \omega^2(6 - \omega^2)^2}
\end{aligned}
\tag{10.46}
$$

Setting the imaginary part equal to zero, we find $\omega = \sqrt{6}$. Substituting this value back into Eq. (10.46) yields the real part, $-(1/20) = (1/20)\angle 180°$.

This closed-loop system is stable if the magnitude of the frequency response is less than unity at $180°$. Hence, the system is stable for $K < 20$, unstable for $K > 20$, and marginally stable for $K = 20$. When the system is marginally stable, the radian frequency of oscillation is $\sqrt{6}$.

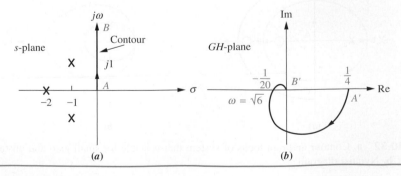

FIGURE 10.34 **a.** Portion of contour to be mapped for Example 10.7; **b.** Nyquist diagram of mapping of positive imaginary axis

(a)   (b)

▬▬▬▬▬ SKILL-ASSESSMENT EXERCISE 10.4 ▬▬▬▬▬

Problem: For the system shown in Figure 10.10, where

$$G(s) = \frac{K}{(s+2)(s+4)(s+6)}$$

do the following:

a. Plot the Nyquist diagram.

b. Use your Nyquist diagram to find the range of gain, K, for stability.

ANSWERS:

a. See the answer at www.wiley.com/college/nise.

b. Stable for $K < 480$

The complete solution is at www.wiley.com/college/nise.

10.6 GAIN MARGIN AND PHASE MARGIN VIA THE NYQUIST DIAGRAM

Now that we know how to sketch and interpret a Nyquist diagram to determine a closed-loop system's stability, let us extend our discussion to concepts that will eventually lead us to the design of transient response characteristics via frequency response techniques.

Using the Nyquist diagram, we define two quantitative measures of how stable a system is. These quantities are called *gain margin* and *phase margin*. Systems with greater gain and phase margins can withstand greater changes in system parameters before becoming unstable. In a sense, gain and phase margins can be qualitatively related to the root locus, in that systems whose poles are farther from the imaginary axis have a greater degree of stability.

In the last section we discussed stability from the point of view of gain at 180° phase shift. This concept leads to the following definitions of gain margin and phase margin:

Gain margin, G_M. The gain margin is the change in open-loop gain, expressed in decibels (dB), required at 180° of phase shift to make the closed-loop system unstable.

Phase margin, Φ_M. The phase margin is the change in open-loop phase shift required at unity gain to make the closed-loop system unstable.

These two definitions are shown graphically on the Nyquist diagram in Figure 10.35.

Assume a system that is stable if there are no encirclements of −1. Using Figure 10.35, let us focus on the definition of gain margin. Here a gain difference between the Nyquist diagram's crossing of the real axis at −1/a and the −1 critical point determines the proximity of the system to instability. Thus, if the gain of the system were multiplied by a units, the Nyquist diagram would intersect the critical point. We then say that the gain margin is a units, or, expressed in dB, $G_M = 20\log a$. Notice that the gain margin is the reciprocal of the real-axis crossing expressed in dB.

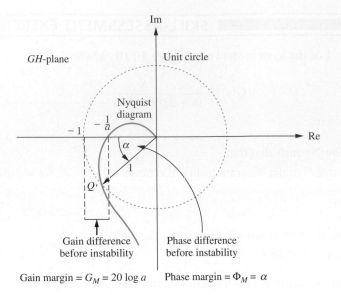

FIGURE 10.35 Nyquist diagram showing gain and phase margins

In Figure 10.35 we also see the phase margin graphically displayed. At point Q', where the gain is unity, a represents the system's proximity to instability. That is, at unity gain, if a phase shift of α degrees occurs, the system becomes unstable. Hence, the amount of phase margin is α. Later in the chapter, we show that phase margin can be related to the damping ratio. Thus, we will be able to relate frequency response characteristics to transient response characteristics as well as stability. We will also show that the calculations of gain and phase margins are more convenient if Bode plots are used rather than a Nyquist diagram, such as that shown in Figure 10.35.

For now let us look at an example that shows the calculation of the gain and phase margins.

EXAMPLE 10.8

Finding gain and phase margins

Problem: Find the gain and phase margin for the system of Example 10.7 if $K = 6$.

SOLUTION: To find the gain margin, first find the frequency where the Nyquist diagram crosses the negative real axis. Finding $G(j\omega)H(j\omega)$, we have

$$
\begin{aligned}
G(j\omega)H(j\omega) &= \left. \frac{6}{(s^2 + 2s + 2)(s + 2)} \right|_{s \to j\omega} \\[2mm]
&= \frac{6[4(1 - \omega^2) - j\omega(6 - \omega^2)]}{16(1 - \omega^2)^2 + \omega^2(6 - \omega^2)^2}
\end{aligned}
\tag{10.47}
$$

The Nyquist diagram crosses the real axis at a frequency of $\sqrt{6}$ rad/s. The real part is calculated to be -0.3. Thus, the gain can be increased by $(1/0.3) = 3.33$ before the real part becomes -1. Hence, the gain margin is

$$
G_M = 20 \log 3.33 = 10.45 \text{ dB}
\tag{10.48}
$$

To find the phase margin, find the frequency in Eq. (10.47) for which the magnitude is unity. As the problem stands, this calculation requires computational tools, such as a function solver or the program described in Appendix G.2. Later in the chapter we will simplify the process by using Bode plots. Eq. (10.47) has unity gain at a frequency of 1.253 rad/s. At this frequency the phase angle is $-112.3°$. The difference between this angle and $-180°$ is $67.7°$, which is the phase margin.

Students who are using MATLAB should now run ch10p3 in Appendix B. You will learn how to use MATLAB to find gain margin, phase margin, zero dB frequency, and 180° frequency. This exercise solves Example 10.8 using MATLAB.

MATLAB

MATLAB's LTI Viewer, with the Nyquist diagram selected, is another method that may be used to find gain margin, phase margin, zero dB frequency, and 180° frequency. You are encouraged to study Appendix D, at www.wiley.com/college/nise, which contains a tutorial on the LTI Viewer as well as some examples. Example D.2 solves Example 10.8 using the LTI Viewer.

GUI Tool

SKILL-ASSESSMENT EXERCISE 10.5

Problem: Find the gain margin and the 180° frequency for the problem in Skill-Assessment Exercise 10.4 if $K = 100$.

WileyPLUS
Control Solutions

ANSWERS: Gain margin = 13.62 dB; 180° frequency = 6.63 rad/s

The complete solution is at www.wiley.com/college/nise.

> **TryIt 10.3**
>
> Use MATLAB, the Control System Toolbox, and the following statements to find the gain and phase margins of $G(s)H(s) = 100/[(s+2)(s+4)(s+6)]$ using the Nyquist diagram.
>
> $G = zpk([], [-2, -4, -6], 100)$
> $nyquist(G)$
>
> After the Nyquist diagram appears:
> 1. Right-click in the graph area.
> 2. Select **Characteristics**.
> 3. Select **All Stability Margins**.
> 4. Let the mouse rest on the margin points to read the gain and phase margins.

In this section we defined gain margin and phase margin and calculated them via the Nyquist diagram. In the next section we show how to use Bode diagrams to implement the stability calculations performed in Sections 10.5 and 10.6 using the

Nyquist diagram. We will see that the Bode plots reduce the time and simplify the calculations required to obtain results.

10.7 STABILITY, GAIN MARGIN, AND PHASE MARGIN VIA BODE PLOTS

In this section we determine stability, gain and phase margins, and the range of gain required for stability. All of these topics were covered previously in this chapter, using Nyquist diagrams as the tool. Now we use Bode plots to determine these characteristics. Bode plots are subsets of the complete Nyquist diagram but in another form. They are a viable alternative to Nyquist plots, since they are easily drawn without the aid of the computational devices or long calculations required for the Nyquist diagram and root locus. You should remember that all calculations applied to stability were derived from and based upon the Nyquist stability criterion. The Bode plots are an alternate way of visualizing and implementing the theoretical concepts.

DETERMINING STABILITY

Let us look at an example and determine the stability of a system, implementing the Nyquist stability criterion using Bode plots. We will draw a Bode log-magnitude plot and then determine the value of gain that ensures that the magnitude is less than 0 dB (unity gain) at that frequency where the phase is $\pm 180°$.

EXAMPLE 10.9

Range of gain for stability via Bode plots

Problem: Use Bode plots to determine the range of K within which the unity feedback system shown in Figure 10.10 is stable. Let $G(s) = K/[(s+2)(s+4)(s+5)]$.

SOLUTION: Since this system has all of its open-loop poles in the left half-plane, the open-loop system is stable. Hence, from the discussion of Section 10.5, the closed-loop system will be stable if the frequency response has a gain less than unity when the phase is $180°$.

Begin by sketching the Bode magnitude and phase diagrams shown in Figure 10.36. In Section 10.2 we summed normalized plots of each factor of $G(s)$ to create the Bode plot. We saw that at each break frequency, the slope of the resultant Bode plot changed by an amount equal to the new slope that was added. Table 10.6 demonstrates this observation. In this example we use this fact to draw the Bode plots faster by avoiding the sketching of the response of each term.

The low-frequency gain of $G(s)H(s)$ is found by setting s to zero. Thus, the Bode magnitude plot starts at $K/40$. For convenience let $K = 40$ so that the log-magnitude plot starts at 0 dB. At each break frequency, 2, 4, and 5, a 20 dB/decade increase in negative slope is drawn, yielding the log-magnitude plot shown in Figure 10.36.

The phase diagram begins at $0°$ until a decade below the first break frequency of 2 rad/s. At 0.2 rad/s the curve decreases at a rate of $-45°$/decade, decreasing an additional $45°$/decade at each subsequent frequency (0.4 and 0.5 rad/s) a decade below

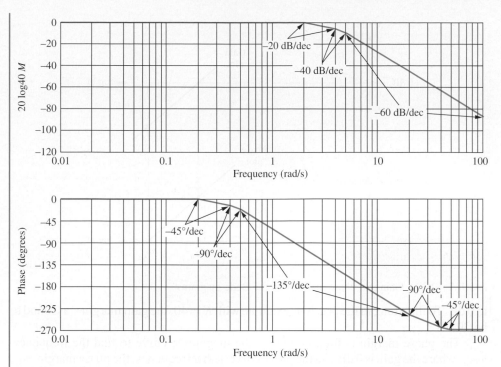

FIGURE 10.36 Bode log-magnitude and phase diagrams for the system of Example 10.9

each break. At a decade above each break frequency, the slopes are reduced by 45°/ decade at each frequency.

The Nyquist criterion for this example tells us that we want zero encirclements of −1 for stability. Thus, we recognize that the Bode log-magnitude plot must be less than unity when the Bode phase plot is 180°. Accordingly, we see that at a frequency of 7 rad/s, when the phase plot is −180°, the magnitude plot is −20 dB. Therefore, an increase in gain of +20 dB is possible before the system becomes unstable. Since the gain plot was scaled for a gain of 40, +20 dB (a gain of 10) represents the required increase in gain above 40. Hence, the gain for instability is $40 \times 10 = 400$. The final result is $0 < K < 400$ for stability.

This result, obtained by approximating the frequency response by Bode asymptotes, can be compared to the result obtained from the actual frequency response, which yields a gain of 378 at a frequency of 6.16 rad/s.

Students who are using MATLAB should now run ch10p4 in Appendix B. You will learn how to use MATLAB to find the range of gain for stability via frequency response methods. This exercise solves Example 10.9 using MATLAB.

EVALUATING GAIN AND PHASE MARGINS

Next we show how to evaluate the gain and phase margins by using Bode plots (Figure 10.37). The gain margin is found by using the phase plot to find the frequency, ω_{GM}, where the phase angle is 180°. At this frequency we look at the magnitude plot to determine the gain margin, G_M, which is the gain required to raise the magnitude curve

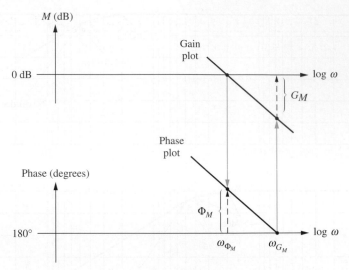

FIGURE 10.37   Gain and phase margins on the Bode diagrams

to 0 dB. To illustrate, in the previous example with $K = 40$, the gain margin was found to be 20 dB.

The phase margin is found by using the magnitude curve to find the frequency, ω_{Φ_M}, where the gain is 0 dB. On the phase curve at that frequency, the phase margin, ϕ_M, is the difference between the phase value and 180°.

EXAMPLE 10.10

Gain and phase margins from Bode plots

Problem: If $K = 200$ in the system of Example 10.9, find the gain margin and the phase margin.

SOLUTION: The Bode plot in Figure 10.36 is scaled to a gain of 40. If $K = 200$ (five times as great), the magnitude plot would be 20 log 5 = 13.98 dB higher.

To find the gain margin, look at the phase plot and find the frequency where the phase is 180°. At this frequency determine from the magnitude plot how much the gain can be increased before reaching 0 dB. In Figure 10.36 the phase angle is 180° at approximately 7 rad/s. On the magnitude plot, the gain is $-20 + 13.98 = -6.02$ dB. Thus, the gain margin is 6.02 dB.

To find the phase margin, we look on the magnitude plot for the frequency where the gain is 0 dB. At this frequency we look on the phase plot to find the difference between the phase and 180°. This difference is the phase margin. Again, remembering that the magnitude plot of Figure 10.36 is 13.98 dB lower than the actual plot, the 0 dB crossing (-13.98 dB for the normalized plot shown in Figure 10.36) occurs at 5.5 rad/s. At this frequency the phase angle is $-165°$. Thus, the phase margin is $-165° - (-180°) = 15°$.

GUI Tool

MATLAB's LTI Viewer, with Bode plots selected, is another method that may be used to find gain margin, phase margin, zero dB frequency, and 180° frequency. You are encouraged to study Appendix D at www.wiley.com/college/nise, which contains a tutorial on the LTI Viewer as well as some examples. Example D.3 solves Example 10.10 using the LTI Viewer.

| SKILL-ASSESSMENT EXERCISE 10.6 |

Problem: For the system shown in Figure 10.10, where

$$G(s) = \frac{K}{(s+5)(s+20)(s+50)}$$

do the following:

a. Draw the Bode log-magnitude and phase plots.

b. Find the range of K for stability from your Bode plots.

c. Evaluate gain margin, phase margin, zero dB frequency, and $180°$ frequency from your Bode plots for $K = 10,000$.

ANSWERS:

a. See the answer at www.wiley.com/college/nise.

b. $K < 96,270$

c. Gain margin $= 19.67$ dB, phase margin $= 92.9°$, zero dB frequency $= 7.74$ rad/s, and $180°$ frequency $= 36.7$ rad/s

The complete solution is at www.wiley.com/college/nise.

TryIt 10.4

Use MATLAB, the Control System Toolbox, and the following statements to solve Skill-Assessment Exercise 10.6(c) using Bode plots.

```
G=zpk([],...
[-5,-20,-50],10000)
bode(G)
grid on
```

After the Bode plot appears:
1. Right-click in the graph area.
2. Select **Characteristics**.
3. Select **All Stability Margins**.
4. Let the mouse rest on the margin points to read the gain and phase margins.

We have seen that the open-loop frequency response curves can be used not only to determine whether a system is stable but to calculate the range of loop gain that will ensure stability. We have also seen how to calculate the gain margin and the phase margin from the Bode diagrams.

Is it then possible to parallel the root locus technique and analyze and design systems for transient response using frequency response methods? We will begin to explore the answer in the next section.

10.8 RELATION BETWEEN CLOSED-LOOP TRANSIENT AND CLOSED-LOOP FREQUENCY RESPONSES

DAMPING RATIO AND CLOSED-LOOP FREQUENCY RESPONSE

In this section we will show that a relationship exists between a system's transient response and its closed-loop frequency response. In particular, consider the second-order feedback control system of Figure 10.38, which we have been using since

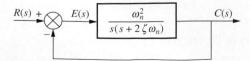

FIGURE 10.38 Second-order closed-loop system

Chapter 4, where we derived relationships between the closed-loop transient response and the poles of the closed-loop transfer function,

$$\frac{C(s)}{R(s)} = T(s) = \frac{\omega_n^2}{s^2 + 2\zeta\omega_n s + \omega_n^2} \tag{10.49}$$

We now derive relationships between the transient response of Eq. (10.49) and characteristics of its frequency response. We define these characteristics and relate them to damping ratio, natural frequency, settling time, peak time, and rise time. In Section 10.10 we will show how to use the frequency response of the open-loop transfer function

$$G(s) = \frac{\omega_n^2}{s(s + 2\zeta\omega_n)} \tag{10.50}$$

shown in Figure 10.38, to obtain the same transient response characteristics.

Let us now find the frequency response of Eq. (10.49), define characteristics of this response, and relate these characteristics to the transient response. Substituting $s = j\omega$ into Eq. (10.49), we evaluate the magnitude of the closed-loop frequency response as

$$M = |T(j\omega)| = \frac{\omega_n^2}{\sqrt{\left(\omega_n^2 - \omega^2\right)^2 + 4\zeta^2\omega_n^2\omega^2}} \tag{10.51}$$

A representative sketch of the log plot of Eq. (10.51) is shown in Figure 10.39.

We now show that a relationship exists between the peak value of the closed-loop magnitude response and the damping ratio. Squaring Eq. (10.51), differentiating with respect to ω^2, and setting the derivative equal to zero yields the maximum value of M, M_p, where

$$M_p = \frac{1}{2\zeta\sqrt{1 - \zeta^2}} \tag{10.52}$$

at a frequency, ω_p, of

$$\omega_p = \omega_n\sqrt{1 - 2\zeta^2} \tag{10.53}$$

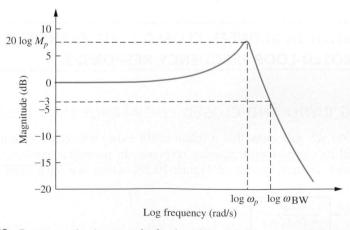

FIGURE 10.39   Representative log-magnitude plot of Eq. (10.51)

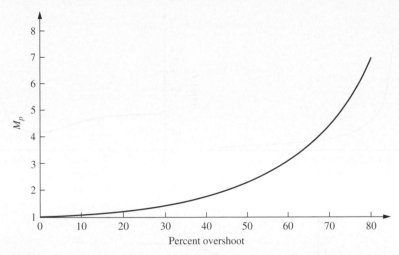

FIGURE 10.40   Closed-loop frequency response peak vs. percent overshoot for a two-pole system

Since ζ is related to percent overshoot, we can plot M_p vs. percent overshoot. The result is shown in Figure 10.40.

Equation (10.52) shows that the maximum magnitude on the frequency response curve is directly related to the damping ratio and, hence, the percent overshoot. Also notice from Eq. (10.53) that the peak frequency, ω_p, is not the natural frequency. However, for low values of damping ratio, we can assume that the peak occurs at the natural frequency. Finally, notice that there will not be a peak at frequencies above zero if $\zeta > 0.707$. This limiting value of ζ for peaking on the magnitude response curve should not be confused with overshoot on the step response, where there is overshoot for $0 < \zeta < 1$.

RESPONSE SPEED AND CLOSED-LOOP FREQUENCY RESPONSE

Another relationship between the frequency response and time response is between the speed of the time response (as measured by settling time, peak time, and rise time) and the *bandwidth* of the closed-loop frequency response, which is defined here as the frequency, ω_{BW}, at which the magnitude response curve is 3 dB down from its value at zero frequency (see Figure 10.39).

The bandwidth of a two-pole system can be found by finding that frequency for which $M = 1/\sqrt{2}$ (that is, -3 dB) in Eq. (10.51). The derivation is left as an exercise for the student. The result is

$$\omega_{BW} = \omega_n \sqrt{(1 - 2\zeta^2) + \sqrt{4\zeta^4 - 4\zeta^2 + 2}} \tag{10.54}$$

To relate ω_{BW} to settling time, we substitute $\omega_n = 4/T_s\zeta$ into Eq. (10.54) and obtain

$$\omega_{BW} = \frac{4}{T_s\zeta} \sqrt{(1 - 2\zeta^2) + \sqrt{4\zeta^4 - 4\zeta^2 + 2}} \tag{10.55}$$

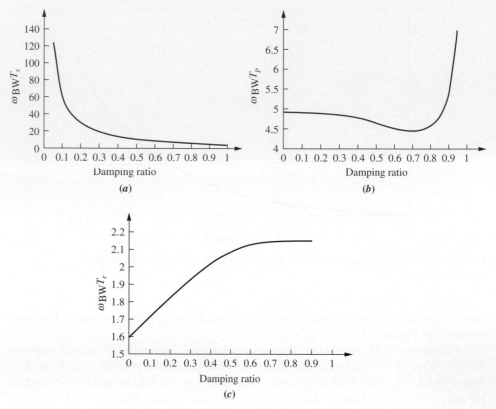

FIGURE 10.41   Normalized bandwidth vs. damping ratio for **a.** settling time; **b.** peak time; **c.** rise time

Similarly, since, $\omega_n = \pi/(T_p\sqrt{1-\zeta^2})$,

$$\omega_{\mathrm{BW}} = \frac{\pi}{T_p\sqrt{1-\zeta^2}}\sqrt{(1-2\zeta^2)+\sqrt{4\zeta^4-4\zeta^2+2}} \qquad (10.56)$$

To relate the bandwidth to rise time, T_r, we use Figure 4.16, knowing the desired ζ and T_r. For example, assume $\zeta = 0.4$ and $T_r = 0.2$ second. Using Figure 4.16, the ordinate $T_r\omega_n = 1.463$, from which $\omega_n = 1.463/0.2 = 7.315$ rad/s. Using Eq. (10.54), $\omega_{\mathrm{BW}} = 10.05$ rad/s. Normalized plots of Eqs. (10.55) and (10.56) and the relationship between bandwidth normalized by rise time and damping ratio are shown in Figure 10.41.

SKILL-ASSESSMENT EXERCISE 10.7

Problem: Find the closed-loop bandwidth required for 20% overshoot and 2 second settling time.

ANSWER: $\omega_{\mathrm{BW}} = 5.79$ rad/s

The complete solution is at www.wiley.com/college/nise.

In this section we related the closed-loop transient response to the closed-loop frequency response via bandwidth. We continue by relating the closed-loop frequency response to the open-loop frequency response and explaining the impetus.

10.9 RELATION BETWEEN CLOSED- AND OPEN-LOOP FREQUENCY RESPONSES

At this point we do not have an easy way of finding the closed-loop frequency response from which we could determine M_p and thus the transient response.[2] As we have seen, we are equipped to rapidly sketch the open-loop frequency response but not the closed-loop frequency response. However, if the open-loop response is related to the closed-loop response, we can combine the ease of sketching the open-loop response with the transient response information contained in the closed-loop response.

CONSTANT *M* CIRCLES AND CONSTANT *N* CIRCLES

Consider a unity feedback system whose closed-loop transfer function is

$$T(s) = \frac{G(s)}{1 + G(s)} \tag{10.57}$$

The frequency response of this closed-loop function is

$$T(j\omega) = \frac{G(j\omega)}{1 + G(j\omega)} \tag{10.58}$$

Since $G(j\omega)$ is a complex number, let $G(j\omega) = P(\omega) + jQ(\omega)$ in Eq. (10.58), which yields

$$T(j\omega) = \frac{P(\omega) + jQ(\omega)}{[(P(\omega) + 1) + jQ(\omega)]} \tag{10.59}$$

Therefore,

$$M^2 = |T^2(j\omega)| = \frac{P^2(\omega) + Q^2(\omega)}{[(P(\omega) + 1)^2 + Q^2(\omega)]} \tag{10.60}$$

Eq. (10.60) can be put into the form

$$\left(P + \frac{M^2}{M^2 - 1}\right)^2 + Q^2 = \frac{M^2}{(M^2 - 1)^2} \tag{10.61}$$

which is the equation of a circle of radius $M/(M^2 - 1)$ centered at $[-M^2/(M^2 - 1), 0]$. These circles, shown plotted in Figure 10.42 for various values of M, are called *constant M circles* and are the locus of the closed-loop magnitude frequency response for unity feedback systems. Thus, if the polar frequency response of an open-loop function, $G(s)$, is plotted and superimposed on top of the constant M circles, the closed-loop magnitude frequency response is determined by each intersection of this polar plot with the constant M circles.

---

[2] At the end of this subsection, we will see how to use MATLAB to obtain closed-loop frequency responses.

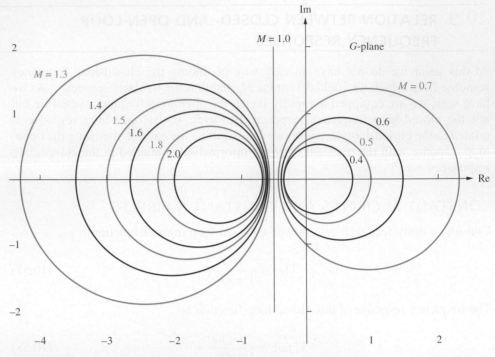

FIGURE 10.42   Constant M circles

Before demonstrating the use of the constant M circles with an example, let us go through a similar development for the closed-loop phase plot, the constant N circles. From Eq. (10.59), the phase angle, ϕ, of the closed-loop response is

$$\phi = \tan^{-1}\frac{Q(\omega)}{P(\omega)} - \tan^{-1}\frac{Q(\omega)}{P(\omega)+1}$$

$$= \tan^{-1}\frac{\dfrac{Q(\omega)}{P(\omega)} - \dfrac{Q(\omega)}{P(\omega)+1}}{1+\dfrac{Q(\omega)}{P(\omega)}\left(\dfrac{Q(\omega)}{P(\omega)+1}\right)} \tag{10.62}$$

after using $\tan(\alpha - \beta) = (\tan\alpha - \tan\beta)/(1 + \tan\alpha\tan\beta)$. Dropping the functional notation,

$$\tan\phi = N = \frac{Q}{P^2 + P + Q^2} \tag{10.63}$$

Equation (10.63) can be put into the form of a circle,

$$\left(P + \frac{1}{2}\right)^2 + \left(Q - \frac{1}{2N}\right)^2 = \frac{N^2 + 1}{4N^2} \tag{10.64}$$

which is plotted in Figure 10.43 for various values of N. The circles of this plot are called *constant N circles*. Superimposing a unity feedback, open-loop frequency response over

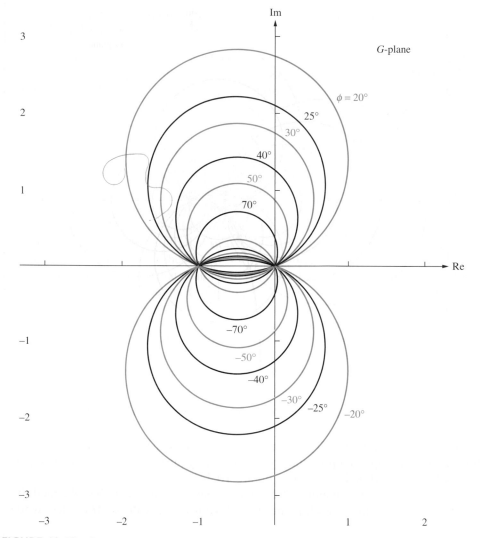

FIGURE 10.43 Constant N circles

the constant N circles yields the closed-loop phase response of the system. Let us now look at an example of the use of the constant M and N circles.

EXAMPLE 10.11

Closed-loop frequency response from open-loop frequency response

Problem: Find the closed-loop frequency response of the unity feedback system shown in Figure 10.10, where $G(s) = 50/[s(s+3)(s+6)]$, using the constant M circles, N circles, and the open-loop polar frequency response curve.

SOLUTION: First evaluate the open-loop frequency function and make a polar frequency response plot superimposed over the constant M and N circles. The open-loop frequency function is

$$G(j\omega) = \frac{50}{-9\omega^2 + j(18\omega - \omega^3)} \qquad (10.65)$$

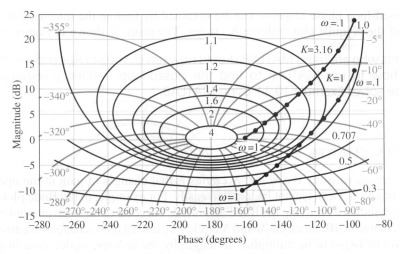

FIGURE 10.47 Nichols chart with frequency response for $G(s) = K/[s(s+1)(s+2)]$ superimposed. Values for $K = 1$ and $K = 3.16$ are shown

we obtain the plot in Figure 10.47 for $K = 1$. If the gain is increased by 10 dB, simply raise the curve for $K = 1$ by 10 dB and obtain the curve for $K = 3.16$ (10 dB). The intersection of the plots of $G(j\omega)$ with the Nichols chart yields the frequency response of the closed-loop system.

Students who are using MATLAB should now run ch10p6 in Appendix B. You will learn how to use MATLAB to make a Nichols plot. This exercise makes a Nichols plot of $G(s) = 1/[s(s + 1)(s + 2)]$ using MATLAB.

MATLAB's LTI Viewer is an alternative method of obtaining the Nichols chart. You are encouraged to study Appendix D at www.wiley.com/college/nise, which contains a tutorial on the LTI Viewer as well as some examples. Example D.4 shows how to obtain Figure 10.47 using the LTI Viewer.

▆▆▆▆ SKILL-ASSESSMENT EXERCISE 10.8 ▆▆▆▆

TryIt 10.5

Use MATLAB, the Control System Toolbox, and the following statements to make a Nichols chart of the system given in Skill-Assessment Exercise 10.8

```
G=zpk([],...
[-5,-20,-50],8000)
nichols(G)
grid on
```

Problem: Given the system shown in Figure 10.10, where

$$G(s) = \frac{8000}{(s+5)(s+20)(s+50)}$$

plot the closed-loop log-magnitude and phase frequency response plots using the following methods:

a. M and N circles

b. Nichols chart

ANSWER: The complete solution is at www.wiley.com/college/nise.

10.10 RELATION BETWEEN CLOSED-LOOP TRANSIENT AND OPEN-LOOP FREQUENCY RESPONSES

DAMPING RATIO FROM *M* CIRCLES

We can use the results of Example 10.11 to estimate the transient response characteristics of the system. We can find the peak of the closed-loop frequency response by finding the maximum *M* curve tangent to the open-loop frequency response. Then we can find the damping ratio, ζ, and subsequently the percent overshoot, via Eq. (10.52). The following example demonstrates the use of the open-loop frequency response and the *M* circles to find the damping ratio or, equivalently, the percent overshoot.

EXAMPLE 10.12

Percent overshoot from open-loop frequency response

Problem: Find the damping ratio and the percent overshoot expected from the system of Example 10.11, using the open-loop frequency response and the *M* circles.

SOLUTION: Equation (10.52) shows that there is a unique relationship between the closed-loop system's damping ratio and the peak value, M_P, of the closed-loop system's magnitude frequency plot. From Figure 10.44, we see that the Nyquist diagram is tangent to the 1.8 *M* circle. We see that this is the maximum value for the closed-loop frequency response. Thus, $M_P = 1.8$.

We can solve for ζ by rearranging Eq. (10.52) into the following form:

$$\zeta^4 - \zeta^2 + \left(1/4M_P^2\right) = 0 \qquad (10.67)$$

Since $M_P = 1.8$, then $\zeta = 0.29$ and 0.96. From Eq. (10.53), a damping ratio larger than 0.707 yields no peak above zero frequency. Thus, we select $\zeta = 0.29$, which is equivalent to 38.6% overshoot. Care must be taken, however, to be sure we can make a second-order approximation when associating the value of percent overshoot to the value of ζ. A computer simulation of the step response shows 36% overshoot.

So far in this section, we have tied together the system's transient response and the peak value of the closed-loop frequency response as obtained from the open-loop frequency response. We used the Nyquist plots and the *M* and *N* circles to obtain the closed-loop transient response. Another association exists between the open-loop frequency response and the closed-loop transient response that is easily implemented with the Bode plots, which are easier to draw than the Nyquist plots.

DAMPING RATIO FROM PHASE MARGIN

Let us now derive the relationship between the phase margin and the damping ratio. This relationship will enable us to evaluate the percent overshoot from the phase margin found from the open-loop frequency response.

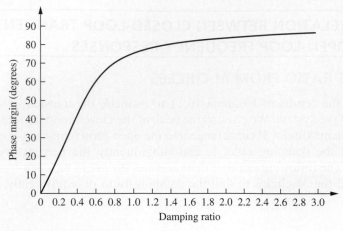

FIGURE 10.48   Phase margin vs. damping ratio

Consider a unity feedback system whose open-loop function

$$G(s) = \frac{\omega_n^2}{s(s + 2\zeta\omega_n)} \tag{10.68}$$

yields the typical second-order, closed-loop transfer function

$$T(s) = \frac{\omega_n^2}{s^2 + 2\zeta\omega_n s + \omega_n^2} \tag{10.69}$$

In order to evaluate the phase margin, we first find the frequency for which $|G(j\omega)| = 1$. Hence,

$$|G(j\omega)| = \frac{\omega_n^2}{|-\omega^2 + j2\zeta\omega_n\omega|} = 1 \tag{10.70}$$

The frequency, ω_1, that satisfies Eq. (10.70) is

$$\omega_1 = \omega_n \sqrt{-2\zeta^2 + \sqrt{1 + 4\zeta^4}} \tag{10.71}$$

The phase angle of $G(j\omega)$ at this frequency is

$$\angle G(j\omega) = -90 - \tan^{-1}\frac{\omega_1}{2\zeta\omega_n}$$

$$= -90 - \tan^{-1}\frac{\sqrt{-2\zeta^2 + \sqrt{4\zeta^4 + 1}}}{2\zeta} \tag{10.72}$$

The difference between the angle of Eq. (10.72) and $-180°$ is the phase margin, ϕ_M. Thus,

$$\Phi_M = 90 - \tan^{-1}\frac{\sqrt{-2\zeta^2 + \sqrt{1 + 4\zeta^4}}}{2\zeta}$$

$$= \tan^{-1}\frac{2\zeta}{\sqrt{-2\zeta^2 + \sqrt{1 + 4\zeta^4}}} \tag{10.73}$$

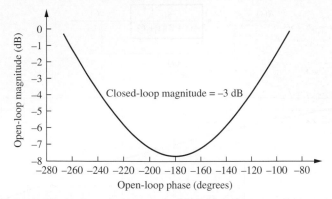

FIGURE 10.49   Open-loop gain vs. open-loop phase angle for −3 dB closed-loop gain

Equation (10.73), plotted in Figure 10.48, shows the relationship between phase margin and damping ratio.

As an example, Eq. (10.53) tells us that there is no peak frequency if $\zeta = 0.707$. Hence, there is no peak to the closed-loop magnitude frequency response curve for this value of damping ratio and larger. Thus, from Figure 10.48, a phase margin of $65.52°$ ($\zeta = 0.707$) or larger is required from the *open-loop* frequency response to ensure there is no peaking in the *closed-loop* frequency response.

RESPONSE SPEED FROM OPEN-LOOP FREQUENCY RESPONSE

Equations (10.55) and (10.56) relate the closed-loop bandwidth to the desired settling or peak time and the damping ratio. We now show that the closed-loop bandwidth can be estimated from the open-loop frequency response. From the Nichols chart in Figure 10.46, we see the relationship between the open-loop gain and the closed-loop gain. The $M = 0.707(−3\,\text{dB})$ curve, replotted in Figure 10.49 for clarity, shows the open-loop gain when the closed-loop gain is −3 dB, which typically occurs at ω_{BW} if the low-frequency closed-loop gain is 0 dB. We can approximate Figure 10.49 by saying that the closed-loop bandwidth, ω_{BW} (the frequency at which the closed-loop magnitude response is −3 dB), equals the frequency at which the open-loop magnitude response is between −6 and −7.5 dB if the open-loop phase response is between $−135°$ and $−225°$. Then, using a second-order system approximation, Eqs. (10.55) and (10.56) can be used, along with the desired damping ratio, ζ, to find settling time and peak time, respectively. Let us look at an example.

EXAMPLE 10.13

Settling and peak times from open-loop frequency response

Problem: Given the system of Figure 10.50(*a*) and the Bode diagrams of Figure 10.50(*b*), estimate the settling time and peak time.

SOLUTION: Using Figure 10.50(*b*), we estimate the closed-loop bandwidth by finding the frequency where the open-loop magnitude response is in the range of − 6 to

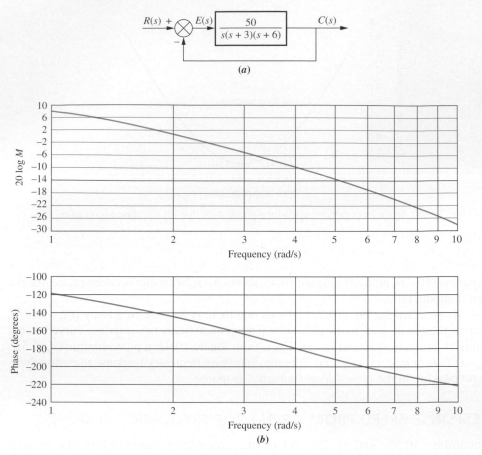

FIGURE 10.50   **a.** Block diagram; **b.** Bode diagrams for system of Example 10.13

−7.5 dB if the phase response is in the range of −135° to −225°. Since Figure 10.50(*b*) shows −6 to −7.5 dB at approximately 3.7 rad/s with a phase response in the stated region, $\omega_{BW} \cong 3.7$ rad/s.

Next find ζ via the phase margin. From Figure 10.50(*b*), the phase margin is found by first finding the frequency at which the magnitude plot is 0 dB. At this frequency, 2.2 rad/s, the phase is about −145°. Hence, the phase margin is approximately $(-145° - (-180°)) = 35°$. Using Figure 10.48, $\zeta = 0.32$. Finally, using Eqs. (10.55) and (10.56), with the values of ω_{BW} and ζ just found, $T_s = 4.86$ seconds and $T_p = 129$ seconds. Checking the analysis with a computer simulation shows $T_s = 5.5$ seconds, and $T_p = 1.43$ seconds.

SKILL-ASSESSMENT EXERCISE 10.9

Problem: Using the open-loop frequency response for the system in Figure 10.10, where

$$G(s) = \frac{100}{s(s+5)}$$

estimate the percent overshoot, settling time, and peak time for the closed-loop step response.

ANSWER: $\%OS = 44\%$, $T_s = 1.64$ s, and $T_P = 0.33$ s

The complete solution is at www.wiley.com/college/nise.

10.11 STEADY-STATE ERROR CHARACTERISTICS FROM FREQUENCY RESPONSE

In this section we show how to use Bode diagrams to find the values of the static error constants for equivalent unity feedback systems: K_p for a Type 0 system, K_v for a Type 1 system, and K_a for a Type 2 system. The results will be obtained from unnormalized and unscaled Bode log-magnitude plots.

POSITION CONSTANT

To find K_p, consider the following Type 0 system:

$$G(s) = K \frac{\prod_{i=1}^{n}(s + z_i)}{\prod_{i=1}^{m}(s + p_i)} \tag{10.74}$$

A typical unnormalized and unscaled Bode log-magnitude plot is shown in Figure 10.51(a). The initial value is

$$20\log M = 20\log K \frac{\prod_{i=1}^{n} z_i}{\prod_{i=1}^{m} p_i} \tag{10.75}$$

But for this system

$$K_p = K \frac{\prod_{i=1}^{n} z_i}{\prod_{i=1}^{m} p_i} \tag{10.76}$$

which is the same as the value of the low-frequency axis. Thus, for an unnormalized and unscaled Bode log-magnitude plot, the low-frequency magnitude is $20\log K_p$ for a Type 0 system.

VELOCITY CONSTANT

To find K_v for a Type 1 system, consider the following open-loop transfer function of a Type 1 system:

$$G(s) = K \frac{\prod_{i=1}^{n}(s + z_i)}{s\prod_{i=1}^{m}(s + p_i)} \tag{10.77}$$

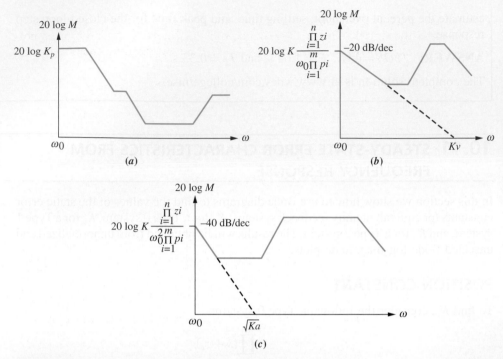

FIGURE 10.51 Typical unnormalized and unscaled Bode log-magnitude plots showing the value of static error constants: **a.** Type 0; **b.** Type 1; **c.** Type 2

A typical unnormalized and unscaled Bode log-magnitude diagram is shown in Figure 10.51(*b*) for this Type 1 system. The Bode plot starts at

$$20 \log M = 20 \log K \frac{\prod_{i=1}^{n} z_i}{\omega_0 \prod_{i=1}^{m} p_i} \tag{10.78}$$

The initial -20 dB/decade slope can be thought of as originating from a function,

$$G'(s) = K \frac{\prod_{i=1}^{n} z_i}{s \prod_{i=1}^{m} p_i} \tag{10.79}$$

$G'(s)$ intersects the frequency axis when

$$\omega = K \frac{\prod_{i=1}^{n} z_i}{\prod_{i=1}^{m} p_i} \tag{10.80}$$

But for the original system (Eq. (10.77)),

$$K_v = K \frac{\prod_{i=1}^{n} z_i}{\prod_{i=1}^{m} p_i} \tag{10.81}$$

which is the same as the frequency-axis intercept, Eq. (10.80). Thus, we can find K_v by extending the initial $-20\,\text{dB/decade}$ slope to the frequency axis on an unnormalized and unscaled Bode diagram. The intersection with the frequency axis is K_v.

ACCELERATION CONSTANT

To find K_a for a Type 2 system, consider the following:

$$G(s) = K\,\frac{\displaystyle\prod_{i=1}^{n}(s+z_i)}{s^2\,\displaystyle\prod_{i=1}^{m}(s+p_i)} \tag{10.82}$$

A typical unnormalized and unscaled Bode plot for a Type 2 system is shown in Figure 10.51(c). The Bode plot starts at

$$20\log M = 20\log K\,\frac{\displaystyle\prod_{i=1}^{n}z_i}{\omega_0^2\,\displaystyle\prod_{i=1}^{m}p_i} \tag{10.83}$$

The initial $-40\,\text{dB/decade}$ slope can be thought of as coming from a function,

$$G'(s) = K\,\frac{\displaystyle\prod_{i=1}^{n}z_i}{s^2\,\displaystyle\prod_{i=1}^{m}p_i} \tag{10.84}$$

$G'(s)$ intersects the frequency axis when

$$\omega = \sqrt{K\,\frac{\displaystyle\prod_{i=1}^{n}z_i}{\displaystyle\prod_{i=1}^{m}p_i}} \tag{10.85}$$

But for the original system (Eq. (10.82)),

$$K_a = K\,\frac{\displaystyle\prod_{i=1}^{n}z_i}{\displaystyle\prod_{i=1}^{m}p_i} \tag{10.86}$$

Thus, the initial $-40\,\text{dB/decade}$ slope intersects the frequency axis at $\sqrt{K_a}$.

EXAMPLE 10.14

Static error constants from Bode plots

Problem: For each unnormalized and unscaled Bode log-magnitude plot shown in Figure 10.52,

    a. Find the system type.
    b. Find the value of the appropriate static error constant.

SOLUTION: Figure 10.52(a) is a Type 0 system since the initial slope is zero. The value of K_p is given by the low-frequency asymptote value. Thus, $20\log K_p = 25$, or $K_p = 17.78$.

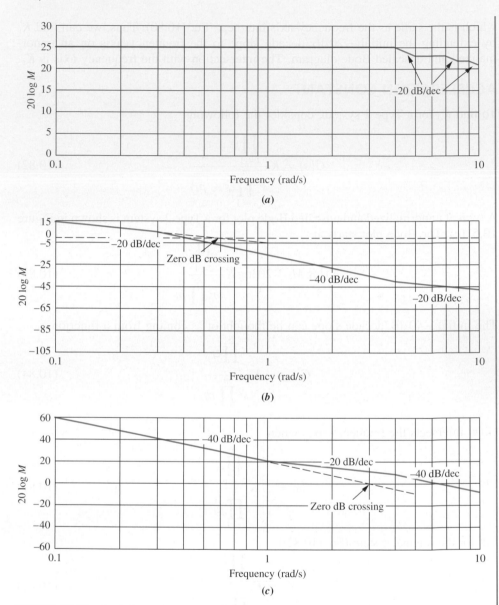

FIGURE 10.52   Bode log-magnitude plots for Example 10.14

Figure 10.52(b) is a Type 1 system since the initial slope is $-20\,\text{dB/decade}$. The value of K_v is the value of the frequency that the initial slope intersects at the zero dB crossing of the frequency axis. Hence, $K_v = 0.55$.

Figure 10.52(c) is a Type 2 system since the initial slope is $-40\,\text{dB/decade}$. The value of $\sqrt{K_a}$ is the value of the frequency that the initial slope intersects at the zero dB crossing of the frequency axis. Hence, $K_a = 3^2 = 9$.

SKILL-ASSESSMENT EXERCISE 10.10

Problem: Find the static error constants for a stable unity feedback system whose open-loop transfer function has the Bode magnitude plot shown in Figure 10.53.

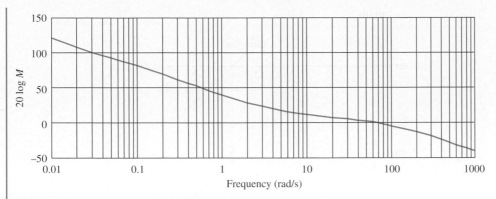

FIGURE 10.53   Bode log-magnitude plot for Skill-Assessment Exercise 10.10

ANSWERS: $K_p = \infty$, $K_v = \infty$, $K_a = 90.25$
The complete solution is www.wiley.com/college/nise.

10.12 SYSTEMS WITH TIME DELAY

Time delay occurs in control systems when there is a delay between the commanded response and the start of the output response. For example, consider a heating system that operates by heating water for pipeline distribution to radiators at distant locations. Since the hot water must flow through the line, the radiators will not begin to get hot until after a specified time delay. In other words, the time between the command for more heat and the commencement of the rise in temperature at a distant location along the pipeline is the time delay. Notice that this is not the same as the transient response or the time it takes the temperature to rise to the desired level. During the time delay, nothing is occurring at the output.

MODELING TIME DELAY

Assume that an input, $R(s)$, to a system, $G(s)$, yields an output, $C(s)$. If another system, $G'(s)$, delays the output by T seconds, the output response is $c(t - T)$. From Table 2.2, Item 5, the Laplace transform of $c(t - T)$ is $e^{-sT}C(s)$. Thus, for the system without delay, $C(s) = R(s)G(s)$, and for the system with delay, $e^{-sT}C(s) = R(s)G'(s)$. Dividing these two equations, $G'(s)/G(s) = e^{-sT}$. Thus, a system with time delay T can be represented in terms of an equivalent system without time delay as follows:

$$G'(s) = e^{-sT}G(s) \tag{10.87}$$

The effect of introducing time delay into a system can also be seen from the perspective of the frequency response by substituting $s = j\omega$ in Eq. (10.87). Hence,

$$G'(j\omega) = e^{-j\omega T}G(j\omega) = |G(j\omega)| \angle \{-\omega T + \angle G(j\omega)\} \tag{10.88}$$

In other words, the time delay does not affect the magnitude frequency response curve of $G(j\omega)$, but it does subtract a linearly increasing phase shift, ωT, from the phase frequency response plot of $G(j\omega)$.

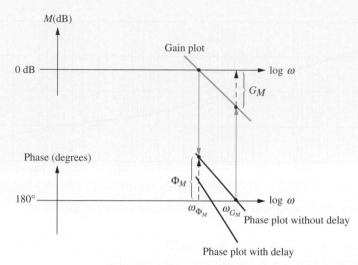

FIGURE 10.54 Effect of delay upon frequency response

The typical effect of adding time delay can be seen in Figure 10.54. Assume that the gain and phase margins as well as the gain- and phase-margin frequencies shown in the figure apply to the system without delay. From the figure, we see that the reduction in phase shift caused by the delay reduces the phase margin. Using a second-order approximation, this reduction in phase margin yields a reduced damping ratio for the closed-loop system and a more oscillatory response. The reduction of phase also leads to a reduced gain-margin frequency. From the magnitude curve, we can see that a reduced gain-margin frequency leads to reduced gain margin, thus moving the system closer to instability.

An example of plotting frequency response curves for systems with delay follows.

EXAMPLE 10.15

Frequency response plots of a system with time delay

Problem: Plot the frequency response for the system $G(s) = K/[s(s+1)(s+10)]$ if there is a time delay of 1 second through the system. Use the Bode plots.

SOLUTION: Since the magnitude curve is not affected by the delay, it can be plotted by the methods previously covered in the chapter and is shown in Figure 10.55(a) for $K = 1$.

The phase plot, however, is affected by the delay. Figure 10.55(b) shows the result. First draw the phase plot for the delay, $e^{-j\omega T} = 1\angle -\omega T = 1\angle -\omega$, since $T = 1$ from the problem statement. Next draw the phase plot of the system, $G(j\omega)$, using the methods previously covered. Finally, add the two phase curves together to obtain the total phase response for $e^{-j\omega T}G(j\omega)$. Be sure to use consistent units for the phase angles of $G(j\omega)$ and the delay; either degrees or radians.

Notice that the delay yields a decreased phase margin, since at any frequency the phase angle is more negative. Using a second-order approximation, this decrease in phase margin implies a lower damping ratio and a more oscillatory response for the closed-loop system.

Further, there is a decrease in the gain-margin frequency. On the magnitude curve, note that a reduction in the gain-margin frequency shows up as reduced gain margin, thus moving the system closer to instability.

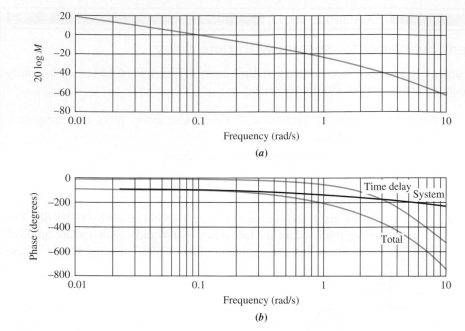

FIGURE 10.55 Frequency response plots for $G(s) = K/[s(s+1)(s+10)]$ with a delay of 1 second and $K = 1$: **a.** magnitude plot; **b.** phase plot

Students who are using MATLAB should now run ch10p7 in Appendix B. You will learn how to use MATLAB to include time delay on Bode plots. You will also use MATLAB to make multiple plots on one graph and label the plots. This exercise solves Example 10.15 using MATLAB.

Let us now use the results of Example 10.15 to design stability and analyze transient response and compare the results to the system without time delay.

EXAMPLE 10.16

Range of gain for stability for system with time delay

Problem: The open-loop system with time delay in Example 10.15 is used in a unity feedback configuration. Do the following:

a. Find the range of gain, K, to yield stability. Use Bode plots and frequency response techniques.

b. Repeat Part **a** for the system without time delay.

SOLUTION:

a. From Figure 10.55, the phase angle is $-180°$ at a frequency of 0.81 rad/s for the system with time delay, marked "Total" on the phase plot. At this frequency the magnitude curve is at -20.39 dB. Thus, K can be raised from its current value of unity to $10^{20.39/20} = 10.46$. Hence, the system is stable for $0 < K \leq 10.46$.

b. If we use the phase curve without delay, marked "System," $-180°$ occurs at a frequency of 3.16 rad/s, and K can be raised 40.84 dB or 110.2. Thus, without delay the system is stable for $0 < K \leq 110.2$, an order of magnitude larger.

EXAMPLE 10.17

Percent overshoot for system with time delay

Problem: The open-loop system with time delay in Example 10.15 is used in a unity feedback configuration. Do the following:

a. Estimate the percent overshoot if $K = 5$. Use Bode plots and frequency response techniques.

b. Repeat Part **a** for the system without time delay.

SOLUTION:

a. Since $K = 5$, the magnitude curve of Figure 10.55 is raised by 13.98 dB. The zero dB crossing then occurs at a frequency of 0.47 rad/s with a phase angle of $-145°$, as seen from the phase plot marked "Total." Therefore, the phase

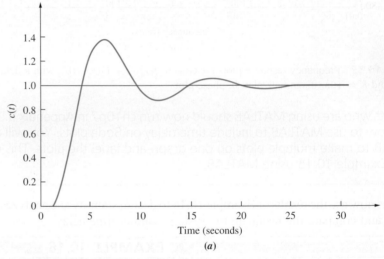

(a)

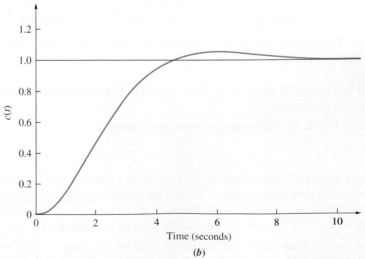

(b)

FIGURE 10.56   Step response for closed-loop system with $G(s) = 5/[s(s+1)(s+10)]$: **a.** with a 1 second delay; **b.** without delay

margin is $(-145° - (-180°)) = 35°$. Assuming a second-order approximation and using Eq. (10.73) or Figure 10.48, we find $\zeta = 0.33$. From Eq. (4.38), $\%OS = 33\%$. The time response, Figure 10.56(a), shows a 38% overshoot instead of the predicted 33%. Notice the time delay at the start of the curve.

b. The zero dB crossing occurs at a frequency of 0.47 rad/s with a phase angle of $-118°$, as seen from the phase plot marked "System." Therefore, the phase margin is $(-118° - (-180°)) = 62°$. Assuming a second-order approximation and using Eq. (10.73) or Figure 10.48, we find $\zeta = 0.64$. From Eq. (4.38), $\%OS = 7.3\%$. The time response is shown in Figure 10.56(b). Notice that the system without delay has less overshoot and a smaller settling time.

SKILL-ASSESSMENT EXERCISE 10.11

Problem: For the system shown in Figure 10.10, where

$$G(s) = \frac{10}{s(s+1)}$$

find the phase margin if there is a delay in the forward path of

a. 0 s

b. 0.1 s

c. 3 s

ANSWERS:

a. $18.0°$

b. $0.35°$

c. $-151.41°$

The complete solution is at www.wiley.com/college/nise.

TryIt 10.6

Use MATLAB, the Control System Toolbox, and the following statements to solve Skill-Assessment Exercise 10.11. For each part of the problem let d = the specified delay.

```
G=zpk([],[0,−1],10)
d=0
[numGd,denGd] = pade...
(d,12)
Gd=tf(numGd,denGd)
Ge=G*Gd
bode(Ge)
grid on
```

After the Bode diagrams appear:
1. Right-click in the graph area.
2. Select **Characteristics.**
3. Select **All Stability Margins.**
4. Let the mouse rest on the margin point on the phase plot to read the phase margin.

In summary, then, systems with time delay can be handled using previously described frequency response techniques if the phase response is adjusted to reflect the time delay. Typically, time delay reduces gain and phase margins, resulting in increased percent overshoot or instability in the closed-loop response.

10.13 OBTAINING TRANSFER FUNCTIONS EXPERIMENTALLY

In Chapter 4 we discussed how to obtain the transfer function of a system through step response testing. In this section we show how to obtain the transfer function using sinusoidal frequency response data.

The analytical determination of a system's transfer function can be difficult. Individual component values may not be known, or the internal configuration of the system may not be accessible. In such cases the frequency response of the system, from input to output, can be obtained experimentally and used to determine the transfer function. To obtain a frequency response plot experimentally, we use a sinusoidal force or signal generator at the input to the system and measure the output steady-state sinusoid amplitude and phase angle (see Figure 10.2). Repeating this process at a number of frequencies yields data for a frequency response plot. Referring to Figure 10.2(*b*), the amplitude response is $M(\omega) = M_o(\omega)/M_i(\omega)$, and the phase response is $\phi(\omega) = \phi_o(\omega) - \phi_i(\omega)$. Once the frequency response is obtained, the transfer function of the system can be estimated from the break frequencies and slopes. Frequency response methods can yield a more refined estimate of the transfer function than the transient response techniques covered in Chapter 4.

Bode plots are a convenient presentation of the frequency response data for the purpose of estimating the transfer function. These plots allow parts of the transfer function to be determined and extracted, leading the way to further refinements to find the remaining parts of the transfer function.

Although experience and intuition are invaluable in the process, the following steps are still offered as a guideline:

1. Look at the Bode magnitude and phase plots and estimate the pole-zero configuration of the system. Look at the initial slope on the magnitude plot to determine system type. Look at phase excursions to get an idea of the difference between the number of poles and the number of zeros.

2. See if portions of the magnitude and phase curves represent obvious first- or second-order pole or zero frequency response plots.

3. See if there is any telltale peaking or depressions in the magnitude response plot that indicate an underdamped second-order pole or zero, respectively.

4. If any pole or zero responses can be identified, overlay appropriate ±20 or ±40 dB/decade lines on the magnitude curve or $\pm45°$/decade lines on the phase curve and estimate the break frequencies. For second-order poles or zeros, estimate the damping ratio and natural frequency from the standard curves given in Section 10.2.

5. Form a transfer function of unity gain using the poles and zeros found. Obtain the frequency response of this transfer function and subtract this response from the previous frequency response (*Franklin, 1991*). You now have a frequency response of reduced complexity from which to begin the process again to extract more of the system's poles and zeros. A computer program such as MATLAB is of invaluable help for this step.

Let us demonstrate.

EXAMPLE 10.18

Transfer function from Bode plots

Problem: Find the transfer function of the subsystem whose Bode plots are shown in Figure 10.57.

SOLUTION: Let us first extract the underdamped poles that we suspect, based on the peaking in the magnitude curve. We estimate the natural frequency to be near the peak frequency, or approximately 5 rad/s. From Figure 10.57, we see a peak of about

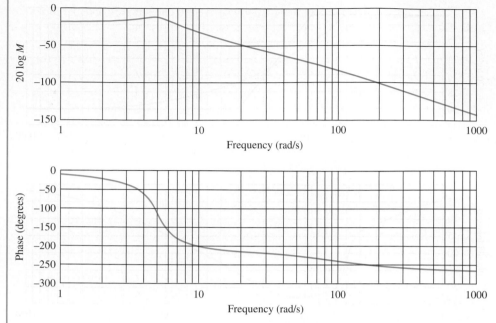

FIGURE 10.57   Bode plots for subsystem with undetermined transfer function

6.5 dB, which translates into a damping ratio of about $\zeta = 0.24$ using Eq. (10.52). The unity gain second-order function is thus $G_1(s) = \omega_n^2/(s^2 + 2\zeta\omega_n s + \omega_n^2) = 25/(s^2 + 2.4s + 25)$. The frequency response plot of this function is made and subtracted from the previous Bode plots to yield the response in Figure 10.58.

   Overlaying a -20 dB/decade line on the magnitude response and a $-45°$/decade line on the phase response, we detect a final pole. From the phase response, we

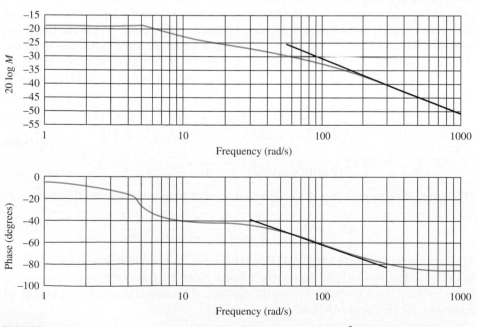

FIGURE 10.58   Original Bode plots minus response of $G_1(s) = 25/(s^2 + 2.4s + 25)$

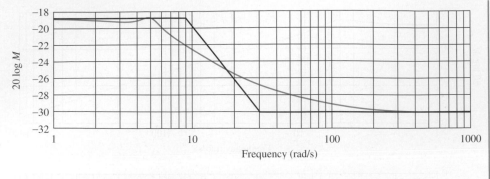

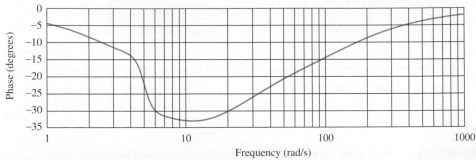

FIGURE 10.59 Original Bode plot minus response of $G_1(s)G_2(s) = [25/(s^2 + 2.4s + 25)][90/(s + 90)]$

estimate the break frequency at 90 rad/s. Subtracting the response of $G_2(s) = 90/(s + 90)$ from the previous response yields the response in Figure 10.59.

Figure 10.59 has a magnitude and phase curve similar to that generated by a lag function. We draw a -20 dB/decade line and fit it to the curves. The break frequencies are read from the figure as 9 and 30 rad/s. A unity gain transfer function containing a pole at -9 and a zero at -30 is $G_3(s) = 0.3(s + 30)/(s + 9)$. Upon subtraction of $G_1(s)G_2(s)G_3(s)$, we find the magnitude frequency response flat ± 1 dB and the phase response flat at $-3° \pm 5°$. We thus conclude that we are finished extracting dynamic transfer functions. The low-frequency, or dc, value of the original curve is -19 dB, or 0.11. Our estimate of the subsystem's transfer function is $G(s) = 0.11G_1(s)G_2(s)G_3(s)$, or

$$G(s) = 0.11\left(\frac{25}{s^2 + 2.4s + 25}\right)\left(90\frac{1}{s + 90}\right)\left(0.3\frac{s + 30}{s + 9}\right)$$

$$= 74.25\frac{s + 30}{(s + 9)(s + 90)(s^2 + 2.4s + 25)} \tag{10.89}$$

It is interesting to note that the original curve was obtained from the function

$$G(s) = 70\frac{s + 20}{(s + 7)(s + 70)(s^2 + 2s + 25)} \tag{10.90}$$

Students who are using MATLAB should now run ch10p8 in Appendix B. You will learn how to use MATLAB to subtract Bode plots for the purpose of estimating transfer functions through sinusoidal testing. This exercise solves a portion of Example 10.18 using MATLAB.

████ SKILL-ASSESSMENT EXERCISE 10.12 ████

Problem: Estimate $G(s)$, whose Bode log-magnitude and phase plots are shown in Figure 10.60.

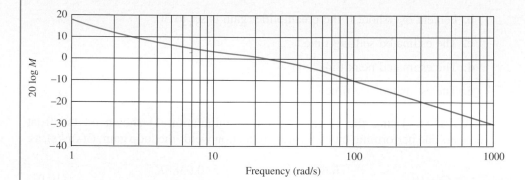

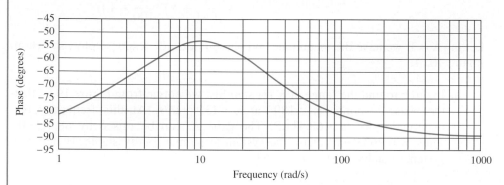

FIGURE 10.60   Bode plots for Skill-Assessment Exercise 10.12

ANSWER: $G(s) = \dfrac{30(s+5)}{s(s+20)}$

The complete solution is at www.wiley.com/college/nisc.

In this chapter we derived the relationships between time response performance and the frequency responses of the open- and closed-loop systems. The methods derived, although yielding a different perspective, are simply alternatives to the root locus and steady-state error analyses previously covered.

████ CASE STUDY ████

Antenna Control: Stability Design and Transient Performance

Our ongoing antenna position control system serves now as an example that summarizes the major objectives of the chapter. The case study demonstrates the use of frequency response methods to find the range of gain for stability and to design a value of gain to meet a percent overshoot requirement for the closed-loop step response.

Problem: Given the antenna azimuth position control system shown on the front endpapers, Configuration 1, use frequency response techniques to find the following:

a. The range of preamplifier gain, K, required for stability

b. Percent overshoot if the preamplifier gain is set to 30

c. The estimated settling time

d. The estimated peak time

e. The estimated rise time

SOLUTION: Using the block diagram (Configuration 1) shown on the front endpapers and performing block diagram reduction yields the loop gain, $G(s)H(s)$, as

$$G(s)H(s) = \frac{6.63K}{s(s+1.71)(s+100)} = \frac{0.0388K}{s\left(\frac{s}{1.71}+1\right)\left(\frac{s}{100}+1\right)} \tag{10.91}$$

Letting $K = 1$, we have the magnitude and phase frequency response plots shown in Figure 10.61.

a. In order to find the range of K for stability, we notice from Figure 10.61 that the phase response is $-180°$ at $\omega = 13.1$ rad/s. At this frequency the magnitude plot is -68.41 dB. The gain, K, can be raised by 68.41 dB. Thus, $K = 2633$ will cause the system to be marginally stable. Hence, the system is stable if $0 < K < 2633$.

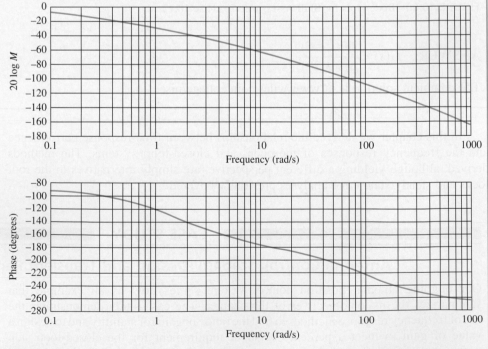

FIGURE 10.61   Open-loop frequency response plots for the antenna control system ($K = 1$)

b. To find the percent overshoot if $K = 30$, we first make a second-order approximation and assume that the second-order transient response equations relating percent overshoot, damping ratio, and phase margin are true for this system. In other words, we assume that Eq. (10.73), which relates damping ratio to phase margin, is valid. If $K = 30$, the magnitude curve of Figure 10.61 is moved up by $20 \log 30 = 29.54$ dB. Therefore, the adjusted magnitude curve goes through zero dB at $\omega = 1$. At this frequency the phase angle is $-120.9°$, yielding a phase margin of $59.1°$. Using Eq. (10.73) or Figure 10.48, $\zeta = 0.6$, or 9.48% overshoot. A computer simulation shows 10%.

c. To estimate the settling time, we make a second-order approximation and use Eq. (10.55). Since $K = 30$ (29.54 dB), the open-loop magnitude response is -7 dB when the normalized magnitude response of Figure 10.61 is -36.54 dB. Thus, the estimated bandwidth is 1.8 rad/s. Using Eq. (10.55), $T_s = 4.25$ seconds. A computer simulation shows a settling time of about 4.4 seconds.

d. Using the estimated bandwidth found in (c), along with Eq. (10.56), and the damping ratio found in (a), we estimate the peak time to be 2.5 seconds. A computer simulation shows a peak time of 2.8 seconds.

e. To estimate the rise time, we use Figure 4.16 and find that the normalized rise time for a damping ratio of 0.6 is 1.854. Using Eq. (10.54), the estimated bandwidth found in (c), and $\zeta = 0.6$, we find $\omega_n = 1.57$. Using the normalized rise time and ω_n, we find $T_r = 1.854/1.57 = 1.18$ seconds. A simulation shows a rise time of 1.2 seconds.

Challenge: You are now given a problem to test your knowledge of this chapter's objectives. You are given the antenna azimuth position control system shown on the front endpapers, Configuration 3. Record the block diagram parameters in the table shown on the front endpapers for Configuration 3 for use in subsequent case study challenge problems. Using frequency response methods, do the following:

a. Find the range of gain for stability.

b. Find the percent overshoot for a step input if the gain, K, equals 3.

c. Repeat Parts **a** and **b** using MATLAB.

SUMMARY

Frequency response methods are an alternative to the root locus for analyzing and designing feedback control systems. Frequency response techniques can be used more effectively than transient response to model physical systems in the laboratory. On the other hand, the root locus is more directly related to the time response.

   The input to a physical system can be sinusoidally varying with known frequency, amplitude, and phase angle. The system's output, which is also sinusoidal in the steady state, can then be measured for amplitude and phase angle at different frequencies. From this data the magnitude frequency response of the system, which is the ratio of the output amplitude to the input amplitude, can be plotted and used in place of an analytically obtained magnitude frequency response. Similarly, we can obtain the phase response by finding the difference between the output phase angle and the input phase angle at different frequencies.

The frequency response of a system can be represented either as a polar plot or as separate magnitude and phase diagrams. As a polar plot, the magnitude response is the length of a vector drawn from the origin to a point on the curve, whereas the phase response is the angle of that vector. In the polar plot, frequency is implicit and is represented by each point on the polar curve. The polar plot of $G(s)H(s)$ is known as a *Nyquist diagram.*

Separate magnitude and phase diagrams, sometimes referred to as *Bode plots,* present the data with frequency explicitly enumerated along the abscissa. The magnitude curve can be a plot of log-magnitude versus log-frequency. The other graph is a plot of phase angle versus log-frequency. An advantage of Bode plots over the Nyquist diagram is that they can easily be drawn using asymptotic approximations to the actual curve.

The Nyquist criterion sets forth the theoretical foundation from which the frequency response can be used to determine a system's stability. Using the Nyquist criterion and Nyquist diagram, or the Nyquist criterion and Bode plots, we can determine a system's stability.

Frequency response methods give us not only stability information but also transient response information. By defining such frequency response quantities as gain margin and phase margin, the transient response can be analyzed or designed. *Gain margin* is the amount that the gain of a system can be increased before instability occurs if the phase angle is constant at $180°$. *Phase margin* is the amount that the phase angle can be changed before instability occurs if the gain is held at unity.

While the open-loop frequency response leads to the results for stability and transient response just described, other design tools relate the closed-loop frequency response peak and bandwidth to the transient response. Since the closed-loop response is not as easy to obtain as the open-loop response because of the unavailability of the closed-loop poles, we use graphical aids in order to obtain the closed-loop frequency response from the open-loop frequency response. These graphical aids are the *M* and *N* circles and the Nichols chart. By superimposing the open-loop frequency response over the *M* and *N* circles or the Nichols chart, we are able to obtain the closed-loop frequency response and then analyze and design for transient response.

Today, with the availability of computers and appropriate software, frequency response plots can be obtained without relying on the graphical techniques described in this chapter. The program used for the root locus calculations and described in Appendix G.2 is one such program. MATLAB is another.

We concluded the chapter discussion by showing how to obtain a reasonable estimate of a transfer function using its frequency response, which can be obtained experimentally. Obtaining transfer functions this way yields more accuracy than transient response testing.

This chapter primarily has examined *analysis* of feedback control systems via frequency response techniques. We developed the relationships between frequency response and both stability and transient response. In the next chapter, we apply the concepts to the *design* of feedback control systems, using the Bode plots.

REVIEW QUESTIONS

1. Name four advantages of frequency response techniques over the root locus.
2. Define frequency response as applied to a physical system.
3. Name two ways to plot the frequency response.
4. Briefly describe how to obtain the frequency response analytically.
5. Define Bode plots.
6. Each pole of a system contributes how much of a slope to the Bode magnitude plot?
7. A system with only four poles and no zeros would exhibit what value of slope at high frequencies in a Bode magnitude plot?
8. A system with four poles and two zeros would exhibit what value of slope at high frequencies in a Bode magnitude plot?
9. Describe the asymptotic phase response of a system with a single pole at -2.
10. What is the major difference between Bode magnitude plots for first-order systems and for second-order systems?
11. For a system with three poles at -4, what is the maximum difference between the asymptotic approximation and the actual magnitude response?
12. Briefly state the Nyquist criterion.
13. What does the Nyquist criterion tell us?
14. What is a Nyquist diagram?
15. Why is the Nyquist criterion called a frequency response method?
16. When sketching a Nyquist diagram, what must be done with open-loop poles on the imaginary axis?
17. What simplification to the Nyquist criterion can we usually make for systems that are open-loop stable?
18. What simplification to the Nyquist criterion can we usually make for systems that are open-loop unstable?
19. Define gain margin.
20. Define phase margin.
21. Name two different frequency response characteristics that can be used to determine a system's transient response.
22. Name three different methods of finding the closed-loop frequency response from the open-loop transfer function.
23. Briefly explain how to find the static error constant from the Bode magnitude plot.
24. Describe the change in the open-loop frequency response magnitude plot if time delay is added to the plant.
25. If the phase response of a pure time delay were plotted on a linear phase versus linear frequency plot, what would be the shape of the curve?
26. When successively extracting component transfer functions from experimental frequency response data, how do you know when you are finished?

12. Use MATLAB's LTI Viewer to find the gain margin, phase margin, zero dB frequency, and 180° frequency for a unity feedback system with

$$G(s) = \frac{10,000}{(s+5)(s+18)(s+30)}$$

Use the following methods:

    a. The Nyquist diagram
    b. Bode plots

13. Derive Eq. (10.54), the closed-loop bandwidth in terms of ζ and ω_n of a two-pole system. [Section: 10.8]

14. For each closed-loop system with the following performance characteristics, find the closed-loop bandwidth.

    a. $\zeta = 0.3$, $T_s = 2$ seconds
    b. $\zeta = 0.3$, $T_p = 2$ seconds
    c. $T_s = 5$ seconds, $T_p = 3$ seconds
    d. $\zeta = 0.38$, $T_r = 2.8$ seconds

15. Consider the unity feedback system of Figure 10.10. For each $G(s)$ that follows, use the M and N circles to make a plot of the closed-loop frequency response: [Section: 10.9]

    a. $G(s) = \dfrac{10}{s(s+1)(s+2)}$

    b. $G(s) = \dfrac{1000}{(s+3)(s+4)(s+5)(s+6)}$

    c. $G(s) = \dfrac{50(s+3)}{s(s+2)(s+4)}$

16. Repeat Problem 15, using the Nichols chart in place of the M and N circles. [Section: 10.9]

17. Using the results of Problem 15, estimate the percent overshoot that can be expected in the step response for each system shown. [Section: 10.10]

18. Use the results of Problem 16 to estimate the percent overshoot if the gain term in the numerator of the forward path of each part of the problem is respectively changed as follows: [Section: 10.10]

    a. From 10 to 30
    b. From 1000 to 2500
    c. From 50 to 75

19. Write a program in MATLAB that will do the following:

    a. Allow a value of gain, K, to be entered from the keyboard
    b. Display the closed-loop magnitude and phase frequency response plots of a unity feedback system with an open-loop transfer function, $KG(s)$
    c. Calculate and display the peak magnitude, frequency of the peak magnitude, and bandwidth for the closed-loop frequency response and the entered value of K

Test your program on the system of Figure P10.5 for $K = 40$.

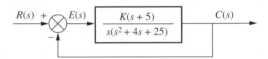

Figure P10.5

20. Use MATLAB's LTI Viewer with the Nichols plot to find the gain margin, phase margin, zero dB frequency, and 180° frequency for a unity feedback system with the forward-path transfer function

$$G(s) = \frac{7(s+5)}{s(s^2+4s+10)}$$

21. Write a program in MATLAB that will do the following:

    a. Make a Nichols plot of an open-loop transfer function
    b. Allow the user to read the Nichols plot display and enter the value of M_p
    c. Make closed-loop magnitude and phase plots
    d. Display the expected values of percent overshoot, settling time, and peak time
    e. Plot the closed-loop step response

Test your program on a unity feedback system with the forward-path transfer function

$$G(s) = \frac{7(s+5)}{s(s^2+4s+10)}$$

22. Using Bode plots, estimate the transient response of the systems in Figure P10.6. [Section: 10.10]

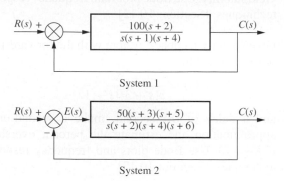

Figure P10.6

Figure P10.6

23. For the system of Figure P10.5, do the following: [Section: 10.10]

a. Plot the Bode magnitude and phase plots.

b. Assuming a second-order approximation, estimate the transient response of the system if $K = 40$.

c. Use MATLAB or any other program to check your assumptions by simulating the step response of the system.

24. The Bode plots for a plant, $G(s)$, used in a unity feedback system are shown in Figure P10.7. Do the following:

a. Find the gain margin, phase margin, zero dB frequency, $180°$ frequency, and the closed-loop bandwidth.

b. Use your results in Part **a** to estimate the damping ratio, percent overshoot, settling time, and peak time.

25. Write a program in MATLAB that will use an open-loop transfer function, $G(s)$, to do the following:

a. Make a Bode plot

b. Use frequency response methods to estimate the percent overshoot, settling time, and peak time

c. Plot the closed-loop step response

Test your program by comparing the results to those obtained for the systems of Problem 22.

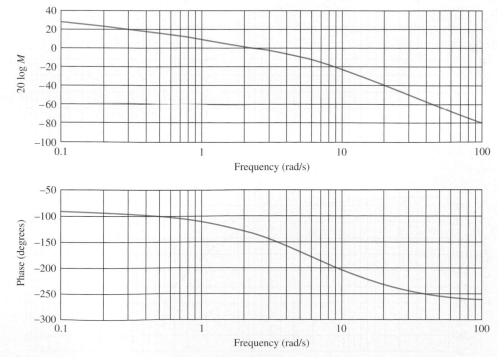

Figure P10.7

26. The open-loop frequency response shown in Figure P10.8 was experimentally obtained from a unity feedback system. Estimate the percent overshoot and steady-state error of the closed-loop system. [Sections: 10.10, 10.11]

27. Consider the system in Figure P10.9.

   a. Find the phase margin if the system is stable for time delays of 0, 2, 3, and 10 seconds.

   b. Find the gain margin if the system is stable for each of the time delays given in (a).

   c. For what time delays mentioned in (a) is the system stable?

   d. For each time delay that makes the system unstable, how much reduction in gain is required for the system to be stable?

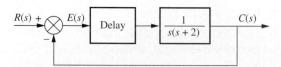

Figure P10.9

28. Given a unity feedback system with the forward-path transfer function

$$G(s) = \frac{K}{(s+1)(s+3)(s+6)}$$

and a delay of 0.5 second, find the range of gain, K, to yield stability. Use Bode plots and frequency response techniques. [Section: 10.12]

29. Given a unity feedback system with the forward-path transfer function

$$G(s) = \frac{K}{s(s+3)(s+12)}$$

and a delay of 0.5 second, make a second-order approximation and estimate the percent overshoot if $K = 40$. Use Bode plots and frequency response techniques. [Section: 10.12]

30. Use the MATLAB function pade(T,n) to model the delay in Problem 29. Obtain the unit step response and evaluate your second-order approximation in Problem 29.

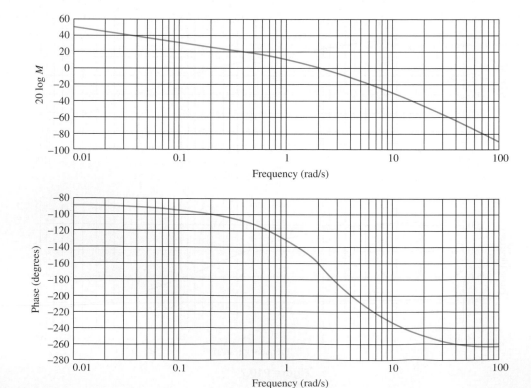

Figure P10.8

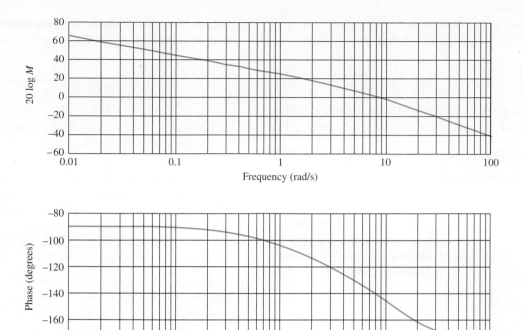

Figure P10.10

31. For the Bode plots shown in Figure P10.10, determine the transfer function by hand or via MATLAB. [Section: 10.13]

32. Repeat Problem 29 for the Bode plots shown in Figure P10.11. [Section: 10.13]

33. An overhead crane consists of a horizontally moving trolley of mass m_T dragging a load of mass m_L, which dangles from its bottom surface at the end of a rope of fixed length, L. The position of the trolley is

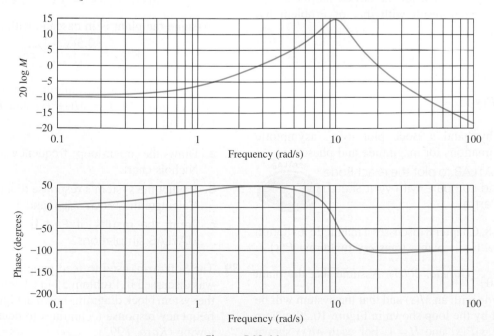

Figure P10.11

controlled in the feedback configuration shown in Figure 10.20. Here, $G(s) = KP(s)$, $H = 1$, and

$$P(s) = \frac{X_T(s)}{F_T(s)} = \frac{1}{m_T} \frac{s^2 + \omega_0^2}{s^2(s^2 + a\omega_0^2)}$$

The input is $f_T(t)$, the input force applied to the trolley. The output is $x_T(t)$, the trolley displacement. Also, $\omega_0 = \sqrt{\dfrac{g}{L}}$ and $a = (m_L + m_T)/m_T$ (*Marttinen, 1990*). Make a qualitative Bode plot of the system assuming $a > 1$.

34. A room's temperature can be controlled by varying the radiator power. In a specific room, the transfer function from indoor radiator power, $\dot{Q}$, to room temperature, T in °C is (*Thomas, 2005*)

$$P(s) = \frac{T(s)}{\dot{Q}(s)}$$
$$= \frac{(1 \times 10^{-6})s^2 + (1.314 \times 10^{-9})s + (2.66 \times 10^{-13})}{s^3 + 0.00163\,s^2 + (5.272 \times 10^{-7})s + (3.538 \times 10^{-11})}$$

The system is controlled in the closed-loop configuration shown in Figure 10.20 with $G(s) = KP(s)$, $H = 1$.

a. Draw the corresponding Nyquist diagram for $K = 1$.

b. Obtain the gain and phase margins.

c. Find the range of K for the closed-loop stability. Compare your result with that of Problem 59, Chapter 6.

35. The open-loop dynamics from dc voltage armature to angular position of a robotic manipulator joint is given by $P(s) = \dfrac{48500}{s^2 + 2.89s}$ (*Low, 2005*).

a. Draw by hand a Bode plot using asymptotic approximations for magnitude and phase.

b. Use MATLAB to plot the exact Bode **MATLAB** plot and compare with your sketch from Part **a**.

36. Problem 48, Chapter 8 discusses a magnetic levitation system with a plant transfer function $P(s) = -\dfrac{1300}{s^2 - 860^2}$ (*Galvão, 2003*). Assume that the plant is in cascade with an $M(s)$ and that the system will be controlled by the loop shown in Figure 10.20, where $G(s) = M(s)P(s)$ and $H = 1$. For each $M(s)$ shown

below, draw the Nyquist diagram when $K = 1$, and find the range of closed-loop stability for $K > 0$.

a. $M(s) = -K$

b. $M(s) = -\dfrac{K(s + 200)}{s + 1000}$

c. Compare your results with those obtained in Problem 48, Chapter 8.

37. The simplified and linearized model for the transfer function of a certain bicycle from steer angle (δ) to roll angle (φ) is given by (*Åstrom, 2005*)

$$P(s) = \frac{\varphi(s)}{\delta(s)} = \frac{10(s + 25)}{s^2 + 25}$$

Assume the rider can be represented by a gain K, and that the closed-loop system is shown in Figure 10.20 with $G(s) = KP(s)$ and $H = 1$. Use the Nyquist stability criterion to find the range of K for closed-loop stability.

38. The control of the radial pickup position of a digital versatile disk (DVD) was discussed in Problem 47, Chapter 9. There, the open-loop transfer function from coil input voltage to radial pickup position was given as (*Bittanti, 2002*)

$$P(s) = \frac{0.63}{\left(1 + \dfrac{0.36}{305.4}s + \dfrac{s^2}{305.4^2}\right)\left(1 + \dfrac{0.04}{248.2}s + \dfrac{s^2}{248.2^2}\right)}$$

Assume the plant is in cascade with a controller,

$$M(s) = \frac{0.5(s + 1.63)}{s(s + 0.27)}$$

and in the closed-loop configuration shown in Figure 10.20, where $G(s) = M(s)P(s)$ and $H = 1$. Do the following:

a. Draw the open-loop frequency response in a Nichols chart.

b. Predict the system's response to a unit step input. Calculate the %OS, c_{final}, and T_s. **MATLAB**

c. Verify the results of Part **b** using MATLAB simulations.

39. The Soft Arm, used to feed people with disabilities, was discussed in Problem 55 in Chapter 6. Assuming the system block diagram shown in Figure P10.12, use frequency response techniques to determine the following (*Kara, 1992*):

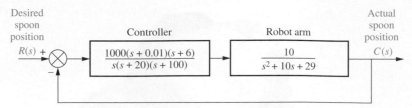

Figure P10.12   Soft Arm position control system block diagram

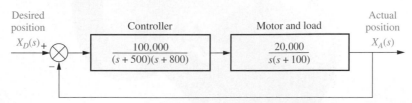

Figure P10.13   Floppy disk drive block diagram

a. Gain margin, phase margin, zero dB frequency, and $180°$ frequency

b. Is the system stable? Why?

40. A floppy disk drive was discussed in Problem 54 in Chapter 8. Assuming the system block diagram shown in Figure P10.13, use frequency response techniques to determine the following:

a. Gain margin, phase margin, zero dB frequency, $180°$ frequency, and closed-loop bandwidth

b. Percent overshoot, settling time, and peak time

c. Use MATLAB to simulate the closed-loop step response and compare the results to those obtained in Part **b.**

41. Industrial robots, such as that shown in Figure P10.14, require accurate models for design of high performance. Many transfer function models for industrial robots assume interconnected rigid bodies with the drive-torque source modeled as a pure gain, or first-order system. Since the motions associated with the robot are connected to the drives through flexible linkages rather than rigid linkages, past modeling does not explain the resonances observed. An accurate, small-motion, linearized model has been developed that takes into consideration the flexible drive. The transfer function

$$G(s) = 999.12 \frac{(s^2 + 8.94s + 44.7^2)}{(s + 20.7)(s^2 + 34.858s + 60.1^2)}$$

relates the angular velocity of the robot base to electrical current commands (*Good, 1985*). Make a

Bode plot of the frequency response and identify the resonant frequencies.

42. The charge-coupled device (CCD) that is used in video movie cameras to convert images into electrical signals can be used as part of an automatic focusing system in cameras. Automatic focusing can be implemented by focusing the center of the image on a charge-coupled device array through two lenses. The separation of the two images on the CCD is related to the focus. The camera senses the separation, and a computer drives the lens and focuses the image. (See

FIGURE P10.14   AdeptOne, a four- or five-axis industrial robot, is used for assembly, packaging, and other manufacturing tasks.

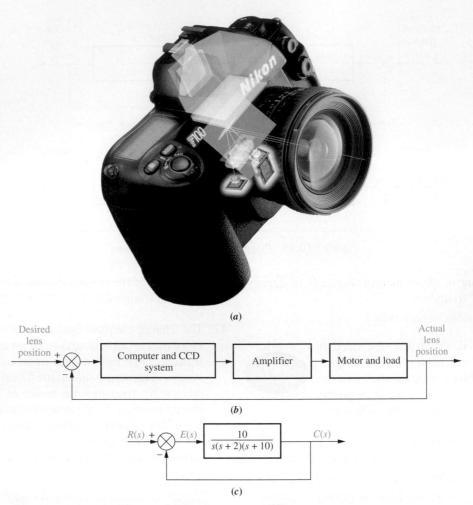

(a)

(b)

(c)

FIGURE P10.15 **a.** A cutaway view of a Nikon 35-mm camera showing parts of the CCD automatic focusing system; **b.** functional block diagram; **c.** block diagram

the three references to *Popular Photography* in this chapter's Bibliography.) The automatic focus system is a position control, where the desired position of the lens is an input selected by pointing the camera at the subject. The output is the actual position of the lens. The Nikon camera in Figure P10.15(a) uses a CCD automatic focusing system. Figure P10.15(b) shows the automatic focusing feature represented as a position control system. Assuming the simplified model shown in Figure P10.15(c), draw the Bode plots and estimate the percent overshoot for a step input.

43. A ship's roll can be stabilized with a control system. A voltage applied to the fins' actuators creates a roll torque that is applied to the ship. The ship, in response to the roll torque, yields a roll angle. Assuming the block diagram for the roll control system shown in Figure P10.16, determine the gain and phase margins for the system.

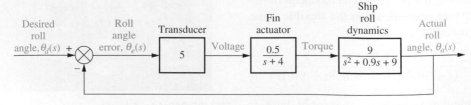

Figure P10.16 Block diagram of a ship's roll-stabilizing system

44. The linearized model of a particular network link working under TCP/IP and controlled using a random early detection (RED) algorithm can be described by Figure 10.20 where $G(s) = M(s)P(s)$, $H = 1$, and (*Hollot, 2001*)

$$M(s) = \frac{0.005L}{s + 0.005}; \qquad P(s) = \frac{140625e^{-0.1s}}{(s + 2.67)(s + 10)}$$

a. Plot the Nichols chart for $L = 1$. Is the system closed-loop stable?

b. Find the range of L for closed-loop stability.

c. Use the Nichols chart to predict %OS and T_s for $L = 0.95$. Make a hand sketch of the expected unit step response.

d. Verify Part **c** with a Simulink unit step response simulation. *Simulink*

45. In the TCP/IP network link of Problem 44, let $L = 0.8$, but assume that the amount of delay is an unknown variable.

a. Plot the Nyquist diagram of the system for zero delay, and obtain the phase margin.

b. Find the maximum delay allowed for closed-loop stability.

46. Thermal flutter of the Hubble Space Telescope (HST) produces errors for the pointing control system. Thermal flutter of the solar arrays occurs when the spacecraft passes from sunlight to darkness and when the spacecraft is in daylight. In passing from daylight to darkness, an end-to-end bending oscillation of frequency f_1 rad/s is experienced. Such oscillations interfere with the pointing control system of the HST. A filter with the transfer function

$$G_f(s) = \frac{1.96(s^2 + s + 0.25)(s^2 + 1.26s + 9.87)}{(s^2 + 0.015s + 0.57)(s^2 + 0.083s + 17.2)}$$

is proposed to be placed in cascade with the PID controller to reduce the bending (*Wie, 1992*).

a. Obtain the frequency response of the filter and estimate the bending frequencies that will be reduced.

b. Explain why this filter will reduce the bending oscillations if these oscillations are thought to be disturbances at the output of the control system.

Progressive Analysis and Design Problems

47. **High-speed rail pantograph.** Problem 19 in Chapter 1 discusses active control of a pantograph mechanism for high-speed rail systems. In Problem 72(a), Chapter 5, you found the block diagram for the active pantograph control system. In Chapter 8, Problem 63, you designed the gain to yield a closed-loop step response with 30% overshoot. A plot of the step response should have shown a settling time greater than 0.5 second as well as a high-frequency oscillation superimposed over the step response. In Chapter 9, Problem 52, we reduced the settling time to about 0.3 second, reduced the step response steady-state error to zero, and eliminated the high-frequency oscillations by using a notch filter (*O'Connor, 1997*). Using the equivalent forward transfer function found in Chapter 5 cascaded with the notch filter specified in Chapter 9, do the following using frequency response techniques:

a. Plot the Bode plots for a total equivalent gain of 1 and find the gain margin, phase margin, and $180°$ frequency.

b. Find the range of K for stability.

c. Compare your answer to Part **b** with your answer to Problem 63, Chapter 6. Explain any differences.

48. **Control of HIV/AIDS.** The linearized model for an HIV/AIDS patient treated with RTIs was obtained in Chapter 6 as (*Craig, 2004*);

$$P(s) = \frac{Y(s)}{U_1(s)} = \frac{-520s - 10.3844}{s^3 + 2.6817s^2 + 0.11s + 0.0126}$$

a. Consider this plant in the feedback configuration in Figure 10.20 with $G(s) = P(s)$ and $H(s) = 1$. Obtain the Nyquist diagram. Evaluate the system for closed-loop stability.

b. Consider this plant in the feedback configuration in Figure 10.20 with $G(s) = -P(s)$ and $H(s) = 1$. Obtain the Nyquist diagram. Evaluate the system for closed-loop stability. Obtain the gain and phase margins.

CYBER EXPLORATION LABORATORY

Experiment 10.1

Objective To examine the relationships between open-loop frequency response and stability, open-loop frequency response and closed-loop transient response, and the effect of additional closed-loop poles and zeros upon the ability to predict closed-loop transient response

Minimum required software packages MATLAB, and the Control System Toolbox

Prelab

1. Sketch the Nyquist diagram for a unity negative feedback system with a forward transfer function of $G(s) = \dfrac{K}{s(s+2)(s+10)}$. From your Nyquist plot, determine the range of gain, K, for stability.

2. Find the phase margins required for second-order closed-loop step responses with the following percent overshoots: 5%, 10%, 20%, 30%.

Lab

1. Using the SISO Design Tool, produce the following plots simultaneously for the system of Prelab 1: root locus, Nyquist diagram, and step response. Make plots for the following values of K: 50, 100, the value for marginal stability found in Prelab 1, and a value above that found for marginal stability. Use the zoom tools when required to produce an illustrative plot. Finally, change the gain by grabbing and moving the closed-loop poles along the root locus and note the changes in the Nyquist diagram and step response.

2. Using the SISO Design Tool, produce Bode plots and closed-loop step responses for a unity negative feedback system with a forward transfer function of $G(s) = \dfrac{K}{s(s+10)^2}$. Produce these plots for each value of phase margin found in Prelab 2. Adjust the gain to arrive at the desired phase margin by grabbing the Bode magnitude curve and moving it up or down. Observe the effects, if any, upon the Bode phase plot. For each case, record the value of gain and the location of the closed-loop poles.

3. Repeat Lab 2 for $G(s) = \dfrac{K}{s(s+10)}$.

Postlab

1. Make a table showing calculated and actual values for the range of gain for stability as found in Prelab 1 and Lab 1.

2. Make a table from the data obtained in Lab 2 itemizing phase margin, percent overshoot, and the location of the closed-loop poles.

3. Make a table from the data obtained in Lab 3 itemizing phase margin, percent overshoot, and the location of the closed-loop poles.

4. For each Postlab task 1 to 3, explain any discrepancies between the actual values obtained and those expected.

BIBLIOGRAPHY

Åstrom, K., Klein, R. E., and Lennartsson, A. Bicycle Dynamics and Control. *IEEE Control System,* August 2005, pp. 26–47.

Auto Focus SLR Update. *Popular Photography,* December 1987, pp. 72–75.

Bittanti, S., Dell'Orto, F., DiCarlo, A., and Savaresi, S. M., Notch Filtering and Multirate Control for Radial Tracking in High Speed DVD-Players. *IEEE Transactions on Consumer Electronics,* vol. 48. 2002, pp. 56–62.

Bode, H. W. *Network Analysis and Feedback Amplifier Design.* Van Nostrand, Princeton, NJ, 1945.

Craig, I. K., Xia, X., and Venter, J. W. Introducing HIV/AIDS Education into the Electrical Engineering Curriculum at the University of Pretoria. *IEEE Transactions on Education,* vol. 47, no. 1, February 2004, pp. 65–73.

Dorf, R. C. *Modern Control Systems,* 5th ed. Addison-Wesley, Reading, MA, 1989.

Franklin, G., Powell, J. D., and Emami-Naeini, A. *Feedback Control of Dynamic Systems,* 2d ed. Addison-Wesley, Reading, MA, 1991.

Galvão, R. K. H., Yoneyama, T., and de Araújo, F. M. U. A Simple Technique for Identifying a Linearized Model for a Didactic Magnetic Levitation System. *IEEE Transactions on Education,* vol. 46, no. 1, February 2003, pp. 22–25.

Goldberg, N., and Frank, M. A. Pop Photo Camera Test of Minolta Maxxum 7000. *Popular Photography,* February 1986, pp. 44–48, 94.

Good, M. C., Sweet, L. M., and Strobel, K. L. Dynamic Models for Control System Design of Integrated Robot and Drive Systems. *Journal of Dynamic Systems, Measurement, and Control,* March 1985, pp. 53–59.

Hollot, C. V., Misra, V., Towsley, D., and Gong, W. A Control Theoretic Analysis of RED. Proceedings of IEEE INFOCOM, 2001, pp. 1510–1519.

Hostetter, G. H., Savant, C. J., Jr., and Stefani, R. T. *Design of Feedback Control Systems,* 2d ed. Saunders College Publishing, New York, 1989.

Kara, A., Kawamura, K., Bagchi, S., and El-Gamal, M. Reflex Control of a Robotic Aid System to Assist the Physically Disabled. *IEEE Control Systems,* June 1992, pp. 71–77.

Kuo, B. C. *Automatic Control Systems,* 5th ed. Prentice Hall, Englewood Cliffs, NJ, 1987.

Kuo, F. F. *Network Analysis and Synthesis.* Wiley, New York, 1966.

Low, K. H., Wang, H., Liew, K. M., and Cai, Y. Modeling and Motion Control of Robotic Hand for Telemanipulation Application. *International Journal of Software Engineering and Knowledge Engineering,* vol. 15, 2005, pp. 147–152.

Marttinen, A., Virkkunen, J., and Salminen, R. T. Control Study with Pilot Crane. *IEEE Transactions on Education,* vol. 33, no. 3, August 1990, pp. 298–305.

Nikon N4004. *Popular Photography,* October 1987, pp. 52–56.

Nilsson, J. W. *Electric Circuits,* 3d ed. Addison-Wesley, Reading, MA, 1990.

Nyquist, H. Regeneration Theory. *Bell Systems Technical Journal,* January 1932, pp. 126–147.

O'Connor, D. N., Eppinger, S. D., Seering, W. P., and Wormly, D. N. Active Control of a High-Speed Pantograph. *Journal of Dynamic Systems, Measurements, and Control,* vol. 119, March 1997, pp. 1–4.

Ogata, K. *Modern Control Engineering,* 2d ed. Prentice Hall, Englewood Cliffs, NJ, 1990.

Thomas, B., Soleimani-Mosheni, M., and Fahlén, P. Feed-forward in Temperature Control of Buildings. *Energy and Buildings,* vol. 37, 2005, pp. 755–761.

Wie, B. Experimental Demonstration to a Classical Approach to Flexible Structure Control. *Journal of Guidance, Control, and Dynamics,* November–December 1992, pp. 1327–1333.

DESIGN USING SINUSOIDAL TOOLS

11

CHAPTER OBJECTIVES

In this chapter you will learn the following:

- How to use frequency response techniques to adjust the gain to meet a transient response specification
- How to use frequency response techniques to design cascade compensators to improve the steady-state error
- How to use frequency response techniques to design cascade compensators to improve the transient response
- How to use frequency response techniques to design cascade compensators to improve both the steady-state error and the transient response

CASE STUDY OBJECTIVES

You will be able to demonstrate your knowledge of the chapter objectives with case studies as follows:

- Given the antenna azimuth position control system shown on the front endpapers, you will be able to use frequency response techniques to design the gain to meet a transient response specification.
- Given the antenna azimuth position control system shown on the front endpapers, you will be able to use frequency response techniques to design a cascade compensator to meet both transient and steady-state error specifications.

11.1 INTRODUCTION

In Chapter 8 we designed the transient response of a control system by adjusting the gain along the root locus. The design process consisted of finding the transient response specification on the root locus, setting the gain accordingly, and settling for the resulting steady-state error. The disadvantage of design by gain adjustment is that only the transient response and steady-state error represented by points along the root locus are available.

In order to meet transient response specifications represented by points not on the root locus and, independently, steady-state error requirements, we designed cascade compensators in Chapter 9. In this chapter, we use Bode plots to parallel the root locus design process from Chapters 8 and 9.

Let us begin by drawing some general comparisons between root locus and frequency response design.

Stability and transient response design via gain adjustment. Frequency response design methods, unlike root locus methods, can be implemented conveniently without a computer or other tool except for testing the design. We can easily draw Bode plots using asymptotic approximations and read the gain from the plots. Root locus requires repeated trials to find the desired design point from which the gain can be obtained. For example, in designing gain to meet a percent overshoot requirement, root locus requires the search of a radial line for the point where the open-loop transfer function yields an angle of 180°. To evaluate the range of gain for stability, root locus requires a search of the $j\omega$-axis for 180°. Of course, if one uses a computer program, such as MATLAB, the computational disadvantage of root locus vanishes.

Transient response design via cascade compensation. Frequency response methods are not as intuitive as the root locus, and it is something of an art to design cascade compensation with the methods of this chapter. With root locus, we can identify a specific point as having a desired transient response characteristic. We can then design cascade compensation to operate at that point and meet the transient response specifications. In Chapter 10, we learned that phase margin is related to percent overshoot (Eq. (10.73)) and bandwidth is related to both damping ratio and settling time or peak time (Eqs. (10.55) and (10.56)). These equations are rather complicated. When we design cascade compensation using frequency response methods to improve the transient response, we strive to reshape the open-loop transfer function's frequency response to meet both the phase-margin requirement (percent overshoot) and the bandwidth requirement (settling or peak time). There is no easy way to relate all the requirements prior to the reshaping task. Thus, the reshaping of the open-loop transfer function's frequency response can lead to several trials until all transient response requirements are met.

Steady-state error design via cascade compensation. An advantage of using frequency design techniques is the ability to design derivative compensation, such as lead compensation, to speed up the system and at the same time build in a desired steady-state error requirement that can be met by the lead compensator alone. Recall that in using root locus there are an infinite number of possible solutions to the design of a lead compensator. One of the differences between these solutions is the steady-state error. We must make numerous tries to arrive at the solution that yields the required steady-state error performance. With frequency response techniques, we build the steady-state error requirement right into the design of the lead compensator.

You are encouraged to reflect on the advantages and disadvantages of root locus and frequency response techniques as you progress through this chapter. Let us take a closer look at frequency response design.

When designing via frequency response methods, we use the concepts of stability, transient response, and steady-state error that we learned in Chapter 10. First, the Nyquist criterion tells us how to determine if a system is stable. Typically, an open-loop stable system is stable in closed-loop if the open-loop magnitude frequency response has a gain of less than 0 dB at the frequency where the phase frequency response is 180°. Second, percent overshoot is reduced by increasing the phase margin, and the speed of the response is increased by increasing the bandwidth. Finally, steady-state error is improved by increasing the low-frequency magnitude responses, even if the high-frequency magnitude response is attenuated.

These, then, are the basic facts underlying our design for stability, transient response, and steady-state error using frequency response methods, where the Nyquist criterion and the Nyquist diagram compose the underlying theory behind the design process. Thus, even though we use the Bode plots for ease in obtaining the frequency response, the design process can be verified with the Nyquist diagram when questions arise about interpreting the Bode plots. In particular, when the structure of the system is changed with additional compensator poles and zeros, the Nyquist diagram can offer a valuable perspective.

The emphasis in this chapter is on the design of lag, lead, and lag-lead compensation. General design concepts are presented first, followed by step-by-step procedures. These procedures are only suggestions, and you are encouraged to develop other procedures to arrive at the same goals. Although the concepts in general apply to the design of PI, PD, and PID controllers, in the interest of brevity, detailed procedures and examples will not be presented. You are encouraged to extrapolate the concepts and designs covered and apply them to problems involving PI, PD, and PID compensation presented at the end of this chapter. Finally, the compensators developed in this chapter can be implemented with the realizations discussed in Section 9.6.

11.2 TRANSIENT RESPONSE VIA GAIN ADJUSTMENT

Let us begin our discussion of design via frequency response methods by discussing the link between phase margin, transient response, and gain. In Section 10.10 the relationship between damping ratio (equivalently percent overshoot) and phase margin was derived for $G(s) = \omega_n^2/s(s + 2\zeta\omega_n)$. Thus, if we can vary the phase margin, we can vary the percent overshoot. Looking at Figure 11.1, we see that if we desire a phase margin, Φ_M, represented by CD, we would have to raise the magnitude curve by AB. Thus, a simple gain adjustment can be used to design phase margin and, hence, percent overshoot.

We now outline a procedure by which we can determine the gain to meet a percent overshoot requirement using the open-loop frequency response and assuming dominant second-order closed-loop poles.

DESIGN PROCEDURE

1. Draw the Bode magnitude and phase plots for a convenient value of gain.

2. Using Eqs. (4.39) and (10.73), determine the required phase margin from the percent overshoot.

3. Find the frequency, ω_{Φ_M}, on the Bode phase diagram that yields the desired phase margin, CD, as shown on Figure 11.1.

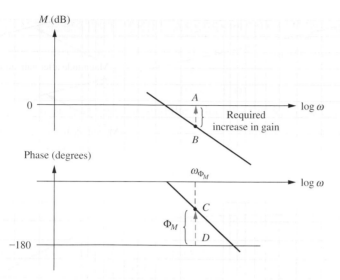

FIGURE 11.1   Bode plots showing gain adjustment for a desired phase margin

4. Change the gain by an amount AB to force the magnitude curve to go through 0 dB at ω_{Φ_M}. The amount of gain adjustment is the additional gain needed to produce the required phase margin.

We now look at an example of designing the gain of a third-order system for percent overshoot.

EXAMPLE 11.1

Transient response design via gain adjustment

Problem: For the position control system shown in Figure 11.2, find the value of preamplifier gain, K, to yield a 9.5% overshoot in the transient response for a step input. Use only frequency response methods.

SOLUTION: We will now follow the previously described gain adjustment design procedure.

1. Choose $K = 3.6$ to start the magnitude plot at 0 dB at $\omega = 0.1$ in Figure 11.3.
2. Using Eq. (4.39), a 9.5% overshoot implies $\zeta = 0.6$ for the closed-loop dominant poles. Equation (10.73) yields a 59.2° phase margin for a damping ratio of 0.6.

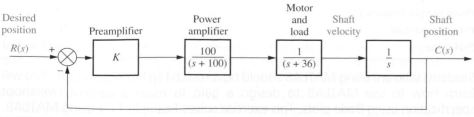

FIGURE 11.2   System for Example 11.1

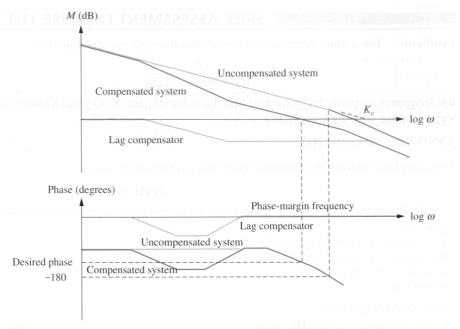

FIGURE 11.4   Visualizing lag compensation

frequency gain.[1] Thus, the low-frequency gain of the system can be made high to yield a large K_v without creating instability. This stabilizing effect of the lag network comes about because the gain at $180°$ of phase is reduced below 0 dB. Through judicious design, the magnitude curve can be reshaped, as shown in Figure 11.4, to go through 0 dB at the desired phase margin. Thus, both K_v and the desired transient response can be obtained. We now enumerate a design procedure.

DESIGN PROCEDURE

1. Set the gain, K, to the value that satisfies the steady-state error specification and plot the Bode magnitude and phase diagrams for this value of gain.

2. Find the frequency where the phase margin is $5°$ to $12°$ greater than the phase margin that yields the desired transient response (*Ogata, 1990*). This step compensates for the fact that the phase of the lag compensator may still contribute anywhere from $-5°$ to $-12°$ of phase at the phase-margin frequency.

3. Select a lag compensator whose magnitude response yields a composite Bode magnitude diagram that goes through 0 dB at the frequency found in Step 2 as follows: Draw the compensator's high-frequency asymptote to yield 0 dB for the compensated system at the frequency found in Step 2. Thus, if the gain at the frequency found in Step 2 is $20 \log K_{PM}$, then the compensator's high-frequency asymptote will be set at $-20 \log K_{PM}$; select the upper break frequency to be 1 decade below the frequency found in Step 2;[2] select the low-frequency asymptote to be at 0 dB; connect the compensator's high- and low-frequency asymptotes with a -20 dB/decade line to locate the lower break frequency.

4. Reset the system gain, K, to compensate for any attenuation in the lag network in order to keep the static error constant the same as that found in Step 1.

---

[1] The name *lag compensator* comes from the fact that the typical phase angle response for the compensator, as shown in Figure 11.4, is always negative, or *lagging* in phase angle.

[2] This value of break frequency ensures that there will be only $-5°$ to $-12°$ phase contribution from the compensator at the frequency found in Step 2.

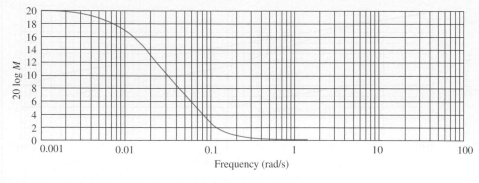

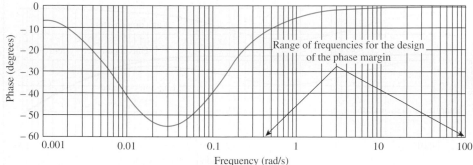

FIGURE 11.5 Frequency response plots of a lag compensator, $G_c(s) = (s + 0.1)/(s + 0.01)$

From these steps, you see that we are relying upon the initial gain setting to meet the steady-state requirements and then relying upon the lag compensator's -20 dB/decade slope to meet the transient response requirement by setting the 0 dB crossing of the magnitude plot.

The transfer function of the lag compensator is

$$G_c(s) = \frac{s + \dfrac{1}{T}}{s + \dfrac{1}{\alpha T}} \tag{11.2}$$

where $\alpha > 1$.

Figure 11.5 shows the frequency response curves for the lag compensator. The range of high frequencies shown in the phase plot is where we will design our phase margin. This region is after the second break frequency of the lag compensator, where we can rely on the attenuation characteristics of the lag network to reduce the total open-loop gain to unity at the phase-margin frequency. Further, in this region the phase response of the compensator will have minimal effect on our design of the phase margin. Since there is still some effect, approximately $5°$ to $12°$, we will add this amount to our phase margin to compensate for the phase response of the lag compensator (see Step 2).

EXAMPLE 11.2

Lag compensation design

Design

Problem: Given the system of Figure 11.2, use Bode diagrams to design a lag compensator to yield a tenfold improvement in steady-state error over the gain-compensated system while keeping the percent overshoot at 9.5%.

SOLUTION: We will follow the previously described lag compensation design procedure.

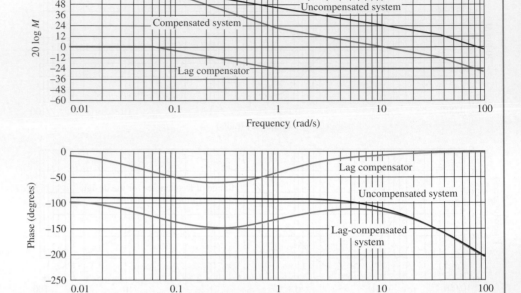

FIGURE 11.6   Bode plots for Example 11.2.

1. From Example 11.1 a gain, K, of 583.9 yields a 9.5% overshoot. Thus, for this system, $K_v = 16.22$. For a tenfold improvement in steady-state error, K_v must increase by a factor of 10, or $K_v = 162.2$. Therefore, the value of K in Figure 11.2 equals 5839, and the open-loop transfer function is

$$G(s) = \frac{583{,}900}{s(s+36)(s+100)} \tag{11.3}$$

The Bode plots for $K = 5839$ are shown in Figure 11.6.

2. The phase margin required for a 9.5% overshoot ($\zeta = 0.6$) is found from Eq. (10.73) to be $59.2°$. We increase this value of phase margin by $10°$ to $69.2°$ in order to compensate for the phase angle contribution of the lag compensator. Now find the frequency where the phase margin is $69.2°$. This frequency occurs at a phase angle of $-180° + 69.2° = -110.8°$ and is $9.8\,\text{rad/s}$. At this frequency the magnitude plot must go through 0 dB. The magnitude at $9.8\,\text{rad/s}$ is now $+24$ dB (exact, that is, nonasymptotic). Thus, the lag compensator must provide -24 dB attenuation at $9.8\,\text{rad/s}$.

3. & 4. We now design the compensator. First draw the high-frequency asymptote at -24 dB. Arbitrarily select the higher break frequency to be about one decade below the phase-margin frequency, or $0.98\,\text{rad/s}$. Starting at the intersection of this frequency with the lag compensator's high-frequency asymptote, draw a $-20\,\text{dB/decade}$ line until 0 dB is reached. The compensator must have a dc gain of unity to retain the value of K_v that we have already designed by setting $K = 5839$. The lower break frequency is found to be $0.062\,\text{rad/s}$. Hence the lag compensator's transfer function is

$$G_c(s) = \frac{0.063(s+0.98)}{(s+0.062)} \tag{11.4}$$

where the gain of the compensator is 0.063 to yield a dc gain of unity.

The compensated system's forward transfer function is thus

$$G(s)G_c(s) = \frac{36,786(s + 0.98)}{s(s + 36)(s + 100)(s + 0.062)} \tag{11.5}$$

The characteristics of the compensated system, found from a simulation and exact frequency response plots, are summarized in Table 11.2.

TABLE 11.2   **Characteristics of the lag-compensated system of Example 11.2**

Parameter	Proposed specification	Actual value
K_v	162.2	161.5
Phase margin	59.2°	62°
Phase-margin frequency	—	11 rad/s
Percent overshoot	9.5	10
Peak time	—	0.25 second

Students who are using MATLAB should now run ch11p2 in Appendix B. You will learn how to use MATLAB to design a lag compensator. You will enter the value of gain to meet the steady-state error requirement as well as the desired percent overshoot. MATLAB then designs a lag compensator using Bode plots, evaluates K_V, and generates a closed-loop step response. This exercise solves Example 11.2 using MATLAB.

MATLAB

SKILL-ASSESSMENT EXERCISE 11.2

Problem: Design a lag compensator for the system in Skill-Assessment Exercise 11.1 that will improve the steady-state error tenfold, while still operating with 20% overshoot.

ANSWER:

$$G_{\text{lag}}(s) = \frac{0.0691(s + 2.04)}{(s + 0.141)}; \quad G(s) = \frac{1,942,000}{s(s + 50)(s + 120)}$$

The complete solution is at www.wiley.com/college/nise.

TryIt 11.2

Use MATLAB, the Control System Toolbox, and the following statements to solve Skill-Assessment Exercise 11.2.

```
pos=20
Ts=0.2
z=(-log(pos/100))/(sqrt(pi^2+log(pos/ 100)^2))
Pm=atan(2*z/(sqrt(-2*z^2+sqrt(1+4*z^4))))*(180/pi)
Wbw=(4/(Ts*z))*sqrt((1-2*z^2)+sqrt(4*z^4-4*z^2+2))
K=1942000
G=zpk([ ], [0, -50, -120], K)
sisotool(G, 1)
```

When the **SISO Design for SISO Design Task Window** appears:
1. Right-click on the Bode plot area and select **Grid**.
2. Note the phase margin shown in the MATLAB **Command Window**.
3. Using the Bode phase plot, estimate the frequency at which the phase margin from Step 2 occurs.
4. On the **SISO Design for SISO Design Task Window toolbar**, click on the red zero.
(TryIt continues)

(continued)

5. Place the zero of the compensator by clicking on the gain plot at a frequency that is 1/10 that found in Step 3.
6. On the **SISO Design for SISO Design Task Window toolbar**, click on the red pole.
7. Place the pole of the compensator by clicking on the gain plot to the left of the compensator zero.
8. Grab the pole with the mouse and move it until the phase plot shows a P.M. equal to that found in Step 2.
9. Right-click in the Bode plot area and select **Edit Compensator**...
10. Read the lag compensator in the **Control and Estimation Tools Manager Window**.

In this section we showed how to design a lag compensator to improve the steady-state error while keeping the transient response relatively unaffected. We next discuss how to improve the transient response using frequency response methods.

11.4 LEAD COMPENSATION

For second-order systems we derived the relationship between phase margin and percent overshoot as well as the relationship between closed-loop bandwidth and other time-domain specifications, such as settling time, peak time, and rise time. When we designed the lag network to improve the steady-state error, we wanted a minimal effect on the phase diagram in order to yield an imperceptible change in the transient response. However, in designing lead compensators via Bode plots, we want to change the phase diagram, increasing the phase margin to reduce the percent overshoot, and increasing the gain crossover to realize a faster transient response.

VISUALIZING LEAD COMPENSATION

The lead compensator increases the bandwidth by increasing the gain crossover frequency. At the same time, the phase diagram is raised at higher frequencies. The result is a larger phase margin and a higher phase-margin frequency. In the time domain, lower percent overshoots (larger phase margins) with smaller peak times (higher phase-margin frequencies) are the results. The concepts are shown in Figure 11.7.

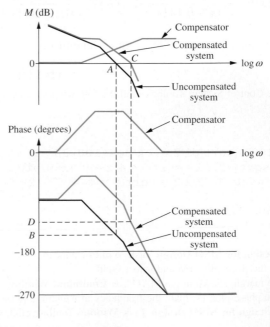

FIGURE 11.7   Visualizing lead compensation

The uncompensated system has a small phase margin (B) and a low phase-margin frequency (A). Using a phase lead compensator, the phase angle plot (compensated system) is raised for higher frequencies.[3] At the same time, the gain crossover frequency in the magnitude plot is increased from A rad/s to C rad/s. These effects yield a larger phase margin (D), a higher phase-margin frequency (C), and a larger bandwidth.

One advantage of the frequency response technique over the root locus is that we can implement a steady-state error requirement and then design a transient response. This specification of transient response with the constraint of a steady-state error is easier to implement with the frequency response technique than with the root locus. Notice that the initial slope, which determines the steady-state error, is not affected by the design for the transient response.

LEAD COMPENSATOR FREQUENCY RESPONSE

Let us first look at the frequency response characteristics of a lead network and derive some valuable relationships that will help us in the design process. Figure 11.8 shows plots of the lead network

$$G_c(s) = \frac{1}{\beta} \frac{s + \dfrac{1}{T}}{s + \dfrac{1}{\beta T}} \tag{11.6}$$

for various values of β, where $\beta < 1$. Notice that the peaks of the phase curve vary in maximum angle and in the frequency at which the maximum occurs. The dc gain of

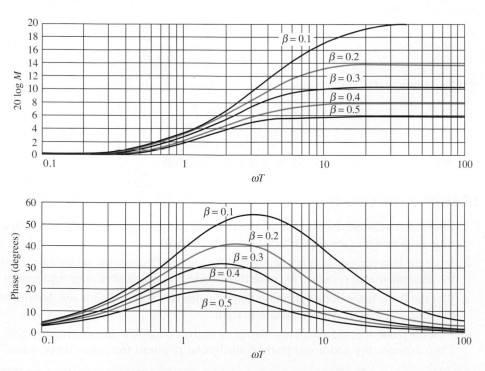

FIGURE 11.8 Frequency response of a lead compensator, $G_c(s) = [1/\beta][(s + 1/T)/(s + 1/\beta T)]$

---

[3] The name *lead compensator* comes from the fact that the typical phase angle response shown in Figure 11.7 is always positive, or *leading* in phase angle.

the compensator is set to unity with the coefficient $1/\beta$, in order not to change the dc gain designed for the static error constant when the compensator is inserted into the system.

In order to design a lead compensator and change both the phase margin and phase-margin frequency, it is helpful to have an analytical expression for the maximum value of phase and the frequency at which the maximum value of phase occurs, as shown in Figure 11.8.

From Eq. (11.6) the phase angle of the lead compensator, ϕ_c, is

$$\phi_c = \tan^{-1}\omega T - \tan^{-1}\omega\beta T \tag{11.7}$$

Differentiating with respect to ω, we obtain

$$\frac{d\phi_c}{d\omega} = \frac{T}{1+(\omega T)^2} - \frac{\beta T}{1+(\omega\beta T)^2} \tag{11.8}$$

Setting Eq. (11.8) equal to zero, we find that the frequency, ω_{max}, at which the maximum phase angle, ϕ_{max}, occurs is

$$\boxed{\omega_{max} = \frac{1}{T\sqrt{\beta}}} \tag{11.9}$$

Substituting Eq. (11.9) into Eq. (11.6) with $s = j\omega_{max}$,

$$G_c(j\omega_{max}) = \frac{1}{\beta}\frac{j\omega_{max}+\dfrac{1}{T}}{j\omega_{max}+\dfrac{1}{\beta T}} = \frac{j\dfrac{1}{\sqrt{\beta}}+1}{j\sqrt{\beta}+1} \tag{11.10}$$

Making use of $\tan(\phi_1 - \phi_2) = (\tan\phi_1 - \tan\phi_2)/(1 + \tan\phi_1\tan\phi_2)$, the maximum phase shift of the compensator, ϕ_{max}, is

$$\boxed{\phi_{max} = \tan^{-1}\frac{1-\beta}{2\sqrt{\beta}} = \sin^{-1}\frac{1-\beta}{1+\beta}} \tag{11.11}$$

and the compensator's magnitude at ω_{max} is

$$\boxed{|G_c(j\omega_{max})| = \frac{1}{\sqrt{\beta}}} \tag{11.12}$$

We are now ready to enumerate a design procedure.

DESIGN PROCEDURE

1. Find the closed-loop bandwidth required to meet the settling time, peak time, or rise time requirement (see Eqs. (10.54) through (10.56)).

2. Since the lead compensator has negligible effect at low frequencies, set the gain, K, of the uncompensated system to the value that satisfies the steady-state error requirement.

3. Plot the Bode magnitude and phase diagrams for this value of gain and determine the uncompensated system's phase margin.

4. Find the phase margin to meet the damping ratio or percent overshoot requirement. Then evaluate the additional phase contribution required from the compensator.[4]

---

[4] We know that the phase-margin frequency will be increased after the insertion of the compensator. At this new phase-margin frequency, the system's phase will be smaller than originally estimated, as seen by comparing points B and E in Figure 11.7. Hence, an additional phase should be added to that provided by the lead compensator to correct for the phase reduction caused by the original system.

5. Determine the value of β (see Eqs. (11.6) and (11.11)) from the lead compensator's required phase contribution.

6. Determine the compensator's magnitude at the peak of the phase curve (Eq. (11.12)).

7. Determine the new phase-margin frequency by finding where the uncompensated system's magnitude curve is the negative of the lead compensator's magnitude at the peak of the compensator's phase curve.

8. Design the lead compensator's break frequencies, using Eqs. (11.6) and (11.9) to find T and the break frequencies.

9. Reset the system gain to compensate for the lead compensator's gain.

10. Check the bandwidth to be sure the speed requirement in Step 1 has been met.

11. Simulate to be sure all requirements are met.

12. Redesign if necessary to meet requirements.

From these steps, we see that we are increasing both the amount of phase margin (improving percent overshoot) and the gain crossover frequency (increasing the speed). Now that we have enumerated a procedure with which we can design a lead compensator to improve the transient response, let us demonstrate.

EXAMPLE 11.3

Lead compensation design

Design

Problem: Given the system of Figure 11.2, design a lead compensator to yield a 20% overshoot and $K_v = 40$, with a peak time of 0.1 second.

SOLUTION: The uncompensated system is $G(s) = 100K/[s(s + 36)(s + 100)]$. We will follow the outlined procedure.

1. We first look at the closed-loop bandwidth needed to meet the speed requirement imposed by $T_p = 0.1$ second. From Eq. (10.56), with $T_p = 0.1$ second and $\zeta = 0.456$ (i.e., 20% overshoot), a closed-loop bandwidth of 46.6 rad/s is required.

2. In order to meet the specification of $K_v = 40$, K must be set at 1440, yielding $G(s) = 144,000/[s(s + 36)(s + 100)]$.

3. The uncompensated system's frequency response plots for $K = 1440$ are shown in Figure 11.9.

4. A 20% overshoot implies a phase margin of 48.1°. The uncompensated system with $K = 1440$ has a phase margin of 34° at a phase-margin frequency of 29.6. To increase the phase margin, we insert a lead network that adds enough phase to yield a 48.1° phase margin. Since we know that the lead network will also increase the phase-margin frequency, we add a correction factor to compensate for the lower uncompensated system's phase angle at this higher phase-margin frequency. Since we do not know the higher phase-margin frequency, we assume a correction factor of 10°. Thus, the total phase contribution required from the compensator is 48.1° − 34° + 10° = 24.1°. In summary, our compensated system should have a phase margin of 48.1° with a bandwidth of 46.6 rad/s. If the system's characteristics are not acceptable after the design, then a redesign with a different correction factor may be necessary.

5. Using Eq. (11.11), $\beta = 0.42$ for $\phi_{max} = 24.1°$.

6. From Eq. (11.12), the lead compensator's magnitude is 3.76 dB at ω_{max}.

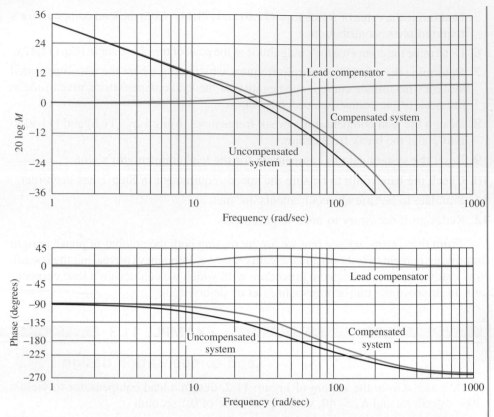

FIGURE 11.9   Bode plots for lead compensation in Example 11.3

7. If we select ω_{max} to be the new phase-margin frequency, the uncompensated system's magnitude at this frequency must be -3.76 dB to yield a 0 dB crossover at ω_{max} for the compensated system. The uncompensated system passes through -3.76 dB at $\omega_{max} = 39$ rad/s. This frequency is thus the new phase-margin frequency.

8. We now find the lead compensator's break frequencies. From Eq. (11.9), $1/T = 25.3$ and $1/\beta T = 60.2$.

9. Hence, the compensator is given by

$$G_c(s) = \frac{1}{\beta}\frac{s + \dfrac{1}{T}}{s + \dfrac{1}{\beta T}} = 2.38\frac{s + 25.3}{s + 60.2} \qquad (11.13)$$

where 2.38 is the gain required to keep the dc gain of the compensator at unity so that $K_v = 40$ after the compensator is inserted.

The final, compensated open-loop transfer function is then

$$G_c(s)G(s) = \frac{342{,}600(s + 25.3)}{s(s + 36)(s + 100)(s + 60.2)} \qquad (11.14)$$

10. From Figure 11.9 the lead-compensated open-loop magnitude response is -7 dB at approximately 68.8 rad/s. Thus, we estimate the closed-loop bandwidth to be 68.8 rad/s. Since this bandwidth exceeds the requirement of 46.6 rad/s, we assume the peak time specification is met. This conclusion about the peak time is

based upon a second-order and asymptotic approximation that will be checked via simulation.

11. Figure 11.9 summarizes the design and shows the effect of the compensation. Final results, obtained from a simulation and the actual (nonasymptotic) frequency response, are shown in Table 11.3. Notice the increase in phase margin, phase-margin frequency, and closed-loop bandwidth after the lead compensator was added to the gain-adjusted system. The peak time and the steady-state error requirements have been met, although the phase margin is less than that proposed and the percent overshoot is 2.6% larger than proposed. Finally, if the performance is not acceptable, a redesign is necessary.

TABLE 11.3 Characteristic of the lead-compensated system of Example 11.3

Parameter	Proposed specification	Actual gain-compensated value	Actual lead-compensated value
K_v	40	40	40
Phase margin	48.1°	34°	45.5°
Phase-margin frequency	—	29.6 rad/s	39 rad/s
Closed-loop bandwidth	46.6 rad/s	50 rad/s	68.8 rad/s
Percent overshoot	20	37	22.6
Peak time	0.1 second	0.1 second	0.075 second

Students who are using MATLAB should now run ch11p3 in Appendix B. You will learn how to use MATLAB to design a lead compensator. You will enter the desired percent overshoot, peak time, and K_v. MATLAB then designs a lead compensator using Bode plots, evaluates K_v, and generates a closed-loop step response. This exercise solves Example 11.3 using MATLAB.

MATLAB

SKILL-ASSESSMENT EXERCISE 11.3

Problem: Design a lead compensator for the system in Skill-Assessment Exercise 11.1 to meet the following specifications: $\%OS = 20\%$, $T_s = 0.2$ s, and $K_v = 50$.

WileyPLUS

Control Solutions

ANSWER: $G_{\text{lead}}(s) = \dfrac{2.27(s + 33.2)}{(s + 75.4)}$; $G(s) = \dfrac{300,000}{s(s + 50)(s + 120)}$

The complete solution is at www.wiley.com/college/nise.

TryIt 11.3

Use MATLAB, the Control System Toolbox, and the following statements to solve Skill-Assessment Exercise 11.3.

```
pos=20
Ts=0.2
z=(-log(pos/100))/(sqrt(pi^2+log(pos/100)^2))
Pm=atan(2*z/(sqrt(-2*z^2+sqrt(1+4*z^4))))*(180/pi)
Wbw=(4/(Ts*z))*sqrt((1-2*z^2)+sqrt(4*z^4-4*z^2+2))
K=50*50*120
G=zpk([],[0,-50,-120],K)
sisotool(G,1)
```

(TryIt continues)

(continued)

When the **SISO Design for SISO Design Task Window appears:**
1. Right-click on the Bode plot area and select **Grid**.
2. Note the phase margin and bandwidth shown in the MATLAB **Command Window**.
3. On the **SISO Design for SISO Design Task Window toolbar,** click on the red pole.
4. Place the pole of the compensator by clicking on the gain plot at a frequency that is to the right of the desired bandwidth found in Step 2.
5. On the **SISO Design for SISO Design Task Window toolbar,** click on the red zero.
6. Place the zero of the compensator by clicking on the gain plot to the left of the desired bandwidth.
7. Reshape the Bode plots: alternately grab the pole and the zero with the mouse and alternately move them along the phase plot until the phase plot show a P.M. equal to that found in Step 2 and a phase-margin frequency close to the bandwidth found in Step 2.
8. Right-click in the Bode plot area and select **Edit Compensator** ...
9. Read the lead compen- sator in the **Control and Estimation Tools Manager Window**.

Keep in mind that the previous examples were designs for third-order systems and must be simulated to ensure the desired transient results. In the next section we look at lag-lead compensation to improve steady-state error and transient response.

11.5 LAG-LEAD COMPENSATION

In Section 9.4, using root locus, we designed lag-lead compensation to improve the transient response and steady-state error. Figure 11.10 is an example of a system to which lag-lead compensation can be applied. In this section we repeat the design, using frequency response techniques. One method is to design the lag compensation to lower the high-frequency gain, stabilize the system, and improve the steady-state error and then design a lead compensator to meet the phase-margin requirements. Let us look at another method.

Section 9.6 describes a passive lag-lead network that can be used in place of separate lag and lead networks. It may be more economical to use a single, passive network that performs both tasks, since the buffer amplifier that separates the lag network from the lead network may be eliminated. In this section, we emphasize lag-lead design, using a single, passive lag-lead network.

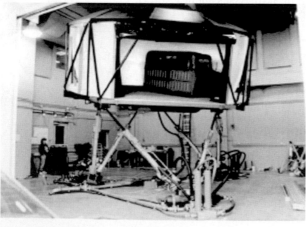

(*a*)   (*b*)

FIGURE 11.10   **a.** The Iowa Driving Simulator; **b.** test driving the simulator with its realistic graphics

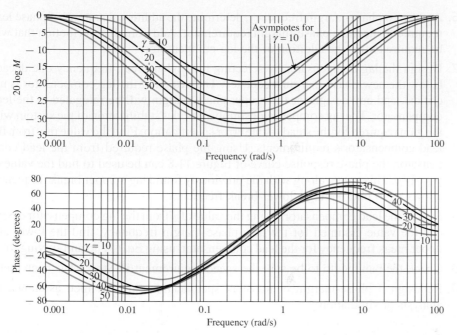

FIGURE 11.11 Sample frequency response curves for a lag-lead compensator, $G_c(s) =$ $[(s+1)(s+0.1)] / \left[(s+\gamma)\left(s + \dfrac{0.1}{\gamma}\right)\right]$

The transfer function of a single, passive lag-lead network is

$$G_c(s) = G_{\text{Lead}}(s)G_{\text{Lag}}(s) = \left(\frac{s + \dfrac{1}{T_1}}{s + \dfrac{\gamma}{T_1}}\right)\left(\frac{s + \dfrac{1}{T_2}}{s + \dfrac{1}{\gamma T_2}}\right) \qquad (11.15)$$

where $\gamma > 1$. The first term in parentheses produces the lead compensation, and the second term in parentheses produces the lag compensation. The constraint that we must follow here is that the single value γ replaces the quantity α for the lag network in Eq. (11.2) and the quantity β for the lead network in Eq. (11.6). For our design, α and β must be reciprocals of each other. An example of the frequency response of the passive lag-lead is shown in Figure 11.11.

We are now ready to enumerate a design procedure.

DESIGN PROCEDURE

1. Using a second-order approximation, find the closed-loop bandwidth required to meet the settling time, peak time, or rise time requirement (see Eqs. (10.55) and (10.56)).
2. Set the gain, K, to the value required by the steady-state error specification.
3. Plot the Bode magnitude and phase diagrams for this value of gain.
4. Using a second-order approximation, calculate the phase margin to meet the damping ratio or percent overshoot requirement, using Eq. (10.73).
5. Select a new phase-margin frequency near ω_{BW}.

6. At the new phase-margin frequency, determine the additional amount of phase lead required to meet the phase-margin requirement. Add a small contribution that will be required after the addition of the lag compensator.

7. Design the lag compensator by selecting the higher break frequency one decade below the new phase-margin frequency. The design of the lag compensator is not critical, and any design for the proper phase margin will be relegated to the lead compensator. The lag compensator simply provides stabilization of the system with the gain required for the steady-state error specification. Find the value of γ from the lead compensator's requirements. Using the phase required from the lead compensator, the phase response curve of Figure 11.8 can be used to find the value of $\gamma = 1/\beta$. This value, along with the previously found lag's upper break frequency, allows us to find the lag's lower break frequency.

8. Design the lead compensator. Using the value of γ from the lag compensator design and the value assumed for the new phase-margin frequency, find the lower and upper break frequency for the lead compensator, using Eq. (11.9) and solving for T.

9. Check the bandwidth to be sure the speed requirement in Step 1 has been met.

10. Redesign if phase-margin or transient specifications are not met, as shown by analysis or simulation.

Let us demonstrate the procedure with an example.

EXAMPLE 11.4

Lag-lead compensation design

Problem: Given a unity feedback system where $G(s) = K/[s(s + 1)(s + 4)]$, design a passive lag-lead compensator using Bode diagrams to yield a 13.25% overshoot, a peak time of 2 seconds, and $K_v = 12$.

SOLUTION: We will follow the steps previously mentioned in this section for lag-lead design.

1. The bandwidth required for a 2 second peak time is 2.29 rad/s.

2. In order to meet the steady-state error requirement, $K_v = 12$, the value of K is 48.

3. The Bode plots for the uncompensated system with $K = 48$ are shown in Figure 11.12. We can see that the system is unstable.

4. The required phase margin to yield a 13.25% overshoot is 55°.

5. Let us select $\omega = 1.8$ rad/s as the new phase-margin frequency.

6. At this frequency, the uncompensated phase is $-176°$ and would require, if we add a $-5°$ contribution from the lag compensator, a 56° contribution from the lead portion of the compensator.

7. The design of the lag compensator is next. The lag compensator allows us to keep the gain of 48 required for $K_v = 12$ and not have to lower the gain to stabilize the system. As long as the lag compensator stabilizes the system, the design parameters are not critical since the phase margin will be designed with the lead compensator. Thus, choose the lag compensator so that its phase response will have minimal effect at the new phase-margin frequency. Let us choose the lag compensator's higher break frequency to be 1 decade below the new phase-margin frequency, at 0.18 rad/s. Since we need to add 56° of phase shift with the lead

compensator at $\omega = 1.8$ rad/s, we estimate from Figure 11.8 that, if $\gamma = 10.6$ (since $\gamma = 1/\beta$, $\beta = 0.094$), we can obtain about 56° of phase shift from the lead compensator. Thus with $\gamma = 10.6$ and a new phase-margin frequency of $\omega = 1.8$ rad/s, the transfer function of the lag compensator is

$$G_{\text{lag}}(s) = \frac{1}{\gamma} \frac{\left(s + \dfrac{1}{T_2}\right)}{\left(s + \dfrac{1}{\gamma T_2}\right)} = \frac{1}{10.6} \frac{(s + 0.183)}{(s + 0.0172)} \qquad (11.16)$$

where the gain term, $1/\gamma$, keeps the dc gain of the lag compensator at 0 dB. The lag-compensated system's open-loop transfer function is

$$G_{\text{lag-comp}}(s) = \frac{4.53(s + 0.183)}{s(s + 1)(s + 4)(s + 0.0172)} \qquad (11.17)$$

8. Now we design the lead compensator. At $\omega = 1.8$, the lag-compensated system has a phase angle of 180°. Using the values of $\omega_{\text{max}} = 1.8$ and $\beta = 0.094$, Eq. (11.9) yields the lower break, $1/T_1 = 0.56$ rad/s. The higher break is then $1/\beta T_1 = 5.96$ rad/s. The lead compensator is

$$G_{\text{lead}}(s) = \gamma \frac{\left(s + \dfrac{1}{T_1}\right)}{\left(s + \dfrac{\gamma}{T_1}\right)} = 10.6 \frac{(s + 0.56)}{(s + 5.96)} \qquad (11.18)$$

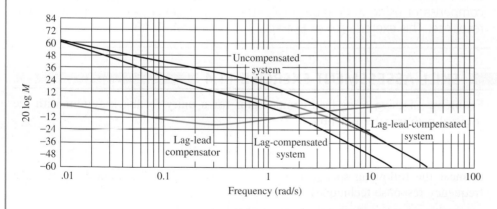

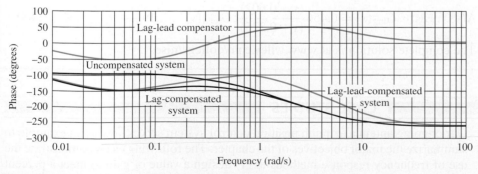

FIGURE 11.12 Bode plots for lag-lead compensation in Example 11.4

The lag-lead-compensated system's open-loop transfer function is

$$G_{\text{lag-lead-comp}}(s) = \frac{48(s+0.183)(s+0.56)}{s(s+1)(s+4)(s+0.0172)(s+5.96)} \tag{11.19}$$

9. Now check the bandwidth. The closed-loop bandwidth is equal to that frequency where the open-loop magnitude response is approximately −7 dB. From Figure 11.12, the magnitude is −7 dB at approximately 3 rad/s. This bandwidth exceeds that required to meet the peak time requirement.

   The design is now checked with a simulation to obtain actual performance values. Table 11.4 summarizes the system's characteristics. The peak time requirement is also met. Again, if the requirements were not met, a redesign would be necessary.

TABLE 11.4 Characteristics of gain-compensated system of Example 11.4

Parameter	Proposed specification	Actual value
K_v	12	12
Phase margin	55°	59.3°
Phase-margin frequency	—	1.63 rad/s
Closed-loop bandwidth	2.29 rad/s	3 rad/s
Percent overshoot	13.25	10.2
Peak time	2.0 seconds	1.61 seconds

MATLAB

Students who are using MATLAB should now run ch11p4 in Appendix B. You will learn how to use MATLAB to design a lag-lead compensator. You will enter the desired percent overshoot, peak time, and K_v. MATLAB then designs a lag-lead compensator using Bode plots, evaluates K_v, and generates a closed-loop step response. This exercise solves Example 11.4 using MATLAB.

SKILL-ASSESSMENT EXERCISE 11.4

Problem: Design a lag-lead compensator for a unity feedback system with the forward-path transfer function

$$G(s) = \frac{K}{s(s+8)(s+30)}$$

to meet the following specifications: %$OS = 10\%$, $T_p = 0.6$ s, and $K_v = 10$. Use frequency response techniques.

ANSWER: $G_{\text{lag}}(s) = 0.456\dfrac{(s+0.602)}{(s+0.275)}$; $G_{\text{lead}}(s) = 2.19\dfrac{(s+4.07)}{(s+8.93)}$; $K = 2400$.

The complete solution is at www.wiley.com/college/nise.

CASE STUDIES

Our ongoing antenna azimuth position control system serves now as an example to summarize the major objectives of the chapter. The following cases demonstrate the use of frequency response methods to (1) design a value of gain to meet a percent overshoot requirement for the closed-loop step response and (2) design cascade compensation to meet both transient and steady-state error requirements.

Design

Antenna Control: Gain Design

Problem: Given the antenna azimuth position control system shown on the front endpapers, Configuration 1, use frequency response techniques to do the following:

a. Find the preamplifier gain required for a closed-loop response of 20% overshoot for a step input.

b. Estimate the settling time.

SOLUTION: The block diagram for the control system is shown on the inside front cover (Configuration 1). The loop gain, after block diagram reduction, is

$$G(s) = \frac{6.63K}{s(s+1.71)(s+100)} = \frac{0.0388K}{s\left(\frac{s}{1.71}+1\right)\left(\frac{s}{100}+1\right)} \qquad (11.20)$$

Letting $K = 1$, the magnitude and phase frequency response plots are shown in Figure 20.

a. To find K to yield a 20% overshoot, we first make a second-order approximation and assume that the second-order transient response equations relating percent overshoot, damping ratio, and phase margin are true for this system. Thus, a 20% overshoot implies a damping ratio of 0.456. Using Eq. (10.73), this damping ratio implies a phase margin of 48.1°. The phase angle should therefore be $(-180° + 48.1°) = -131.9°$. The phase angle is $-131.9°$ at $\omega = 1.49$ rad/s, where the gain is -34.1 dB. Thus $K = 34.1$ dB $= 50.7$ for a 20% overshoot. Since the system is third-order, the second-order approximation should be checked. A computer simulation shows a 20% overshoot for the step response.

b. Adjusting the magnitude plot of Figure 10.61 for $K = 50.7$, we find -7 dB at $\omega = 2.5$ rad/s, which yields a closed-loop bandwidth of 2.5 rad/s. Using Eq. (10.55) with $\zeta = 0.456$ and $\omega_{BW} = 2.5$, we find $T_s = 4.63$ seconds. A computer simulation shows a settling time of approximately 5 seconds.

Challenge: We now give you a problem to test your knowledge of this chapter's objectives. You are given the antenna azimuth position control system shown on the inside front cover (Configuration 3). Using frequency response methods do the following:

a. Find the value of K to yield 25% overshoot for a step input.

b. Repeat Part **a** using MATLAB.

MATLAB

Antenna Control: Cascade Compensation Design

Design

Problem: Given the antenna azimuth position control system block diagram shown on the front endpapers, Configuration 1, use frequency response techniques and design cascade compensation for a closed-loop response of 20% overshoot for a step input, a fivefold improvement in steady-state error over the gain-compensated system operating at 20% overshoot, and a settling time of 3.5 seconds.

SOLUTION: Following the lag-lead design procedure, we first determine the value of gain, K, required to meet the steady-state error requirement.

1. Using Eq. (10.55) with $\zeta = 0.456$, and $T_s = 3.5$ seconds, the required bandwidth is 3.3 rad/s.

2. From the preceding case study, the gain-compensated system's open-loop transfer function was, for $K = 50.7$,

$$G(s)H(s) = \frac{6.63K}{s(s+1.71)(s+100)} = \frac{336.14}{s(s+1.71)(s+100)} \tag{11.21}$$

    This function yields $K_v = 1.97$. If $K - 254$, then $K_v - 9.85$, a fivefold improvement.

3. The frequency response curves of Figure 10.61, which are plotted for $K = 1$, will be used for the solution.

4. Using a second-order approximation, a 20% overshoot requires a phase margin of 48.1°.

5. Select $\omega = 3$ rad/s to be the new phase-margin frequency.

6. The phase angle at the selected phase-margin frequency is $-152°$. This is a phase margin of 28°. Allowing for a 5° contribution from the lag compensator, the lead compensator must contribute $(48.1° - 28° + 5°) = 25.1°$.

7. The design of the lag compensator now follows. Choose the lag compensator upper break one decade below the new phase-margin frequency, or 0.3 rad/s. Figure 11.8 says that we can obtain 25.1° phase shift from the lead if $\beta = 0.4$ or $\gamma = 1/\beta = 2.5$. Thus, the lower break for the lag is at $1/(\gamma T) = 0.3/2.5 = 0.12$ rad/s.
    Hence,

$$G_{\text{lag}}(s) = 0.4\frac{(s+0.3)}{(s+0.12)} \tag{11.22}$$

8. Finally, design the lead compensator. Using Eq. (11.9), we have

$$T = \frac{1}{\omega_{\max}\sqrt{\beta}} = \frac{1}{3\sqrt{0.4}} = 0.527 \tag{11.23}$$

    Therefore the lead compensator lower break frequency is $1/T = 1.9$ rad/s, and the upper break frequency is $1/(\beta T) = 4.75$ rad/s.
    Thus, the lag-lead-compensated forward path is

$$G_{\text{lag-lead-comp}}(s) = \frac{(6.63)(254)(s+0.3)(s+1.9)}{s(s+1.71)(s+100)(s+0.12)(s+4.75)} \tag{11.24}$$

9. A plot of the open-loop frequency response for the lag-lead-compensated system shows -7 dB at 5.3 rad/s. Thus, the bandwidth meets the design requirements for settling time. A simulation of the compensated system shows a 20% overshoot and a settling time of approximately 3.2 seconds, compared to a 20% overshoot for the uncompensated system and a settling time of approximately 5 seconds. K_v for the compensated system is 9.85 compared to the uncompensated system value of 1.97.

Challenge: We now give you a problem to test your knowledge of this chapter's objectives. You are given the antenna azimuth position control system shown on the front endpapers (Configuration 3). Using frequency response methods, do the following:

a. Design a lag-lead compensator to yield a 15% overshoot and $K_v = 20$. In order to speed up the system, the compensated system's phase-margin frequency will be set to 4.6 times the phase-margin frequency of the uncompensated system.

b. Repeat Part **a** using MATLAB.

MATLAB

SUMMARY

This chapter covered the design of feedback control systems using frequency response techniques. We learned how to design by gain adjustment as well as cascaded lag, lead, and lag-lead compensation. Time response characteristics were related to the phase margin, phase-margin frequency, and band-width.

Design by gain adjustment consisted of adjusting the gain to meet a phase-margin specification. We located the phase-margin frequency and adjusted the gain to 0 dB.

A lag compensator is basically a low-pass filter. The low-frequency gain can be raised to improve the steady-state error, and the high-frequency gain is reduced to yield stability. Lag compensation consists of setting the gain to meet the steady-state error requirement and then reducing the high-frequency gain to create stability and meet the phase-margin requirement for the transient response.

A lead compensator is basically a high-pass filter. The lead compensator increases the high-frequency gain while keeping the low-frequency gain the same. Thus, the steady-state error can be designed first. At the same time, the lead compensator increases the phase angle at high frequencies. The effect is to produce a faster, stable system since the uncompensated phase margin now occurs at a higher frequency.

A lag-lead compensator combines the advantages of both the lag and the lead compensator. First, the lag compensator is designed to yield the proper steady-state error with improved stability. Next, the lead compensator is designed to speed up the transient response. If a single network is used as the lag-lead, additional design considerations are applied so that the ratio of the lag zero to the lag pole is the same as the ratio of the lead pole to the lead zero.

In the next chapter we return to state space and develop methods to design desired transient and steady-state error characteristics.

REVIEW QUESTIONS

1. What major advantage does compensator design by frequency response have over root locus design?

2. How is gain adjustment related to the transient response on the Bode diagrams?

3. Briefly explain how a lag network allows the low-frequency gain to be increased to improve steady-state error without having the system become unstable.

4. From the Bode plot perspective, briefly explain how the lag network does not appreciably affect the speed of the transient response.

5. Why is the phase margin increased above that desired when designing a lag compensator?

6. Compare the following for uncompensated and lag-compensated systems designed to yield the same transient response: low-frequency gain, phase-margin frequency, gain curve value around the phase-margin frequency, and phase curve values around the phase-margin frequency.

7. From the Bode diagram viewpoint, briefly explain how a lead network increases the speed of the transient response.

8. Based upon your answer to Question 7, explain why lead networks do not cause instability.

9. Why is a correction factor added to the phase margin required to meet the transient response?

10. When designing a lag-lead network, what difference is there in the design of the lag portion as compared to a separate lag compensator?

PROBLEMS

1. Design the value of gain, K, for a gain margin of 10 dB in the unity feedback system of Figure P11.1 if [Section: 11.2]

   a. $G(s) = \dfrac{K}{(s+3)(s+9)(s+15)}$

   b. $G(s) = \dfrac{K}{s(s+3)(s+9)}$

   c. $G(s) = \dfrac{K(s+2)}{s(s+3)(s+4)(s+5)}$

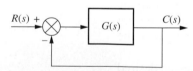

Figure P11.1

2. For each of the systems in Problem 1, design the gain, K, for a phase margin of 40°. [Section: 11.2]

3. Given the unity feedback system of Figure P11.1, use frequency response methods to determine the value of gain, K, to yield a step response with a 20% overshoot if [Section: 11.2]

   a. $G(s) = \dfrac{K}{s(s+6)(s+12)}$

   b. $G(s) = \dfrac{K(s+4)}{s(s+8)(s+10)(s+12)}$

   c. $G(s) = \dfrac{K(s+2)(s+7)}{s(s+4)(s+8)(s+10)(s+15)}$

4. Given the unity feedback system of Figure P11.1 with

$$G(s) = \frac{K(s+10)(s+11)}{s(s+3)(s+6)(s+9)}$$

   do the following:

   a. Use frequency response methods to determine the value of gain, K, to yield a step response with a 15% overshoot. Make any required second-order approximations.

   b. Use MATLAB or any other computer program to test your second-order approximation by simulating the system for your designed value of K.

5. The unity feedback system of Figure P11.1 with

$$G(s) = \frac{K}{s(s+7)}$$

   is operating with 15% overshoot. Using frequency response techniques, design a compensator to yield $K_v = 50$ with the phase-margin frequency and phase margin remaining approximately the same as in the uncompensated system. [Section: 11.3]

6. Given the unity feedback system of Figure P11.1 with

$$G(s) = \frac{K(s+10)(s+11)}{s(s+3)(s+6)(s+9)}$$

do the following: [Section: 11.3]

a. Use frequency response methods to design a lag compensator to yield $K_v = 1000$ and 15% overshoot for the step response. Make any required second-order approximations.

b. Use MATLAB or any other computer program to test your second-order approxima- tion by simulating the system for your designed value of K and lag compensator.

7. The unity feedback system shown in Figure P11.1 with

$$G(s) = \frac{K}{s(s+5)(s+8)}$$

is operating with 20% overshoot. Using frequency response methods, design a compensator to yield a five-fold improvement in steady-state error without appreciably changing the transient response.

8. Design a lag compensator so that the system of Figure P11.1 where

$$G(s) = \frac{K(s+4)}{(s+2)(s+6)(s+8)}$$

operates with a $45°$ phase margin and a static error constant of 100. [Section: 11.3]

9. Design a PI controller for the system of Figure 11.2 that will yield zero steady-state error for a ramp input and a 9.48% overshoot for a step input. [Section: 11.3]

10. For the system of Problem 6, do the following: [Section: 11.3]

a. Use frequency response methods to find the gain, K, required to yield about 15% overshoot. Make any required second-order approximations.

b. Use frequency response methods to design a PI compensator to yield zero steady-state error for a ramp input without appreciably changing the transient response characteristics designed in Part **a**.

c. Use MATLAB or any other computer program to test your second-order approximation by simulating the system for your designed value of K and PI compensator.

11. Write a MATLAB program that will design a PI controller assuming a second-order approximation as follows:

a. Allow the user to input from the keyboard the desired percent overshoot

b. Design a PI controller and gain to yield zero steady-state error for a closed-loop step response as well as meet the percent overshoot specification

c. Display the compensated closed-loop step response

Test your program on

$$G(s) = \frac{K}{(s+5)(s+10)}$$

and 25% overshoot.

12. Design a compensator for the unity feedback system of Figure P11.1 with

$$G(s) = \frac{K}{s(s+2)(s+4)(s+6)}$$

to yield a $K_v = 2$ and a phase margin of $30°$.

13. Consider the unity feedback system of Figure P11.1 with

$$G(s) = \frac{K}{s(s+5)(s+20)}$$

The uncompensated system has about 55% overshoot and a peak time of 0.5 second when $K_v = 10$. Do the following: [Section: 11.4]

a. Use frequency response methods to design a lead compensator to reduce the percent overshoot to 10%, while keeping the peak time and steady-state error about the same or less. Make any required second-order approximations.

b. Use MATLAB or any other computer program to test your second-order approximation by simulating the system for your designed value of K.

14. The unity feedback system of Figure P11.1 with

$$G(s) = \frac{K(s+6)}{(s+2)(s+3)}$$

is operating with 25% overshoot.

 a. Find the settling time.

 b. Find K_v.

 c. Find the phase margin and the phase-margin frequency.

 d. Using frequency response techniques, design a compensator that will yield a threefold improvement in K_v and a twofold reduction in settling time while keeping the overshoot at 25%.

15. Repeat the design of Example 11.3 in the text using a PD controller. [Section: 11.4]

16. Write a MATLAB program that will design a lead compensator assuming second-order approximations as follows:

 a. Allow the user to input from the keyboard the desired percent overshoot, peak time, and gain required to meet a steady-state error specification

 b. Display the gain-compensated Bode plot

 c. Calculate the required phase margin and bandwidth

 d. Display the pole, zero, and gain of the lead compensator

 e. Display the compensated Bode plot

 f. Output the step response of the lead-compensated system to test your second-order approximation

 Test your program on a unity feedback system where

$$G(s) = \frac{K(s+1)}{s(s+2)(s+6)}$$

and the following specifications are to be met: percent overshoot = 10%, peak time = 0.1 second, and $K_v = 30$.

17. Use frequency response methods to design a lag-lead compensator for a unity feedback system where [Section: 11.4]

$$G(s) = \frac{K(s+7)}{s(s+5)(s+15)}$$

and the following specifications are to be met: percent overshoot = 15%, settling time = 0.1 second, and $K_v = 1000$.

18. Write a MATLAB program that will design a lag-lead compensator assuming second-order approximations as follows: [Section: 11.5]

 a. Allow the user to input from the keyboard the desired percent overshoot, settling time, and gain required to meet a steady-state error specification

 b. Display the gain-compensated Bode plot

 c. Calculate the required phase margin and bandwidth

 d. Display the poles, zeros, and the gain of the lag-lead compensator

 e. Display the lag-lead-compensated Bode plot

 f. Display the step response of the lag-lead-compensated system to test your second-order approximation

 Use your program to do Problem 17.

19. Given a unity feedback system with

$$G(s) = \frac{K}{s(s+1)(s+4)}$$

design a PID controller to yield zero steady-state error for a ramp input, as well as a 12% overshoot, and a peak time less than 2 seconds for a step input. Use only frequency response methods.

20. A unity feedback system has

$$G(s) = \frac{K}{s(s+3)(s+6)}$$

If this system has an associated 0.5 second delay, use MATLAB to design the value of K for 20% overshoot. Make any necessary second-order approximations, but test your assumptions by simulating your design. The delay can be represented by cascading the MATLAB function pade (T, n) with $G(s)$, where T is the delay in seconds and

n is the order of the Pade approximation (use 5). Write the program to do the following:

a. Accept your value of percent overshoot from the keyboard

b. Display the Bode plot for $K = 1$

c. Calculate the required phase margin and find the phase-margin frequency and the magnitude at the phase-margin frequency

d. Calculate and display the value of K

Design Problems

21. Aircraft are sometimes used to tow other vehicles. A roll control system for such an aircraft was discussed in Problem 56 in Chapter 6. If Figure P11.2 represents the roll control system, use only frequency response techniques to do the following (*Cochran, 1992*):

a. Find the value of gain, K, to yield a closed-loop step response with 10% overshoot.

b. Estimate peak time and settling time using the gain-compensated frequency response.

c. Use MATLAB to simulate your system. Compare the results of the simulation with the requirements in Part **a** and your estimation of performance in Part **b**.

22. The model for a specific linearized TCP/IP computer network queue working under a random early detection (RED) algorithm has been modeled using the block diagram of Figure P11.1, where $G(s) = M(s)P(s)$, with

$$M(s) = \frac{0.005L}{s + 0.005}$$

and

$$P(s) = \frac{140,625e^{-0.1s}}{(s + 2.67)(s + 10)}$$

Also, L is a parameter to be varied (*Hollot, 2001*).

a. Adjust L to obtain a 15% overshoot in the transient response for step inputs.

b. Verify Part **a** with a Simulink unit step response simulation.

23. An electric ventricular assist device (EVAD) that helps pump blood concurrently to a defective natural heart in sick patients can be shown to have a transfer function

$$G(s) = \frac{P_{ao}(s)}{E_m(s)} = \frac{1361}{s^2 + 69s + 70.85}$$

The input, $E_m(s)$, is the motor's armature voltage, and the output is $P_{ao}(s)$, the aortic blood pressure (*Tasch, 1990*). The EVAD will be controlled in the closed-loop configuration shown in Figure P11.1.

a. Design a phase lag compensator to achieve a tenfold improvement in the steady-state error to step inputs without appreciably affecting the transient response of the uncompensated system.

b. Use MATLAB to simulate the uncompensated and compensated systems for a unit step input.

24. A Tower Trainer 60 Unmanned Aerial Vehicle has a transfer function

$$P(s) = \frac{h(s)}{\delta_e(s)}$$

$$= \frac{-34.16s^3 - 144.4s^2 + 7047s + 557.2}{s^5 + 13.18s^4 + 95.93s^3 + 14.61s^2 + 31.94s}$$

where $\delta_e(s)$ is the elevator angle and $h(s)$ is the change in altitude (*Barkana, 2005*).

a. Assuming the airplane is controlled in the closed-loop configuration of Figure P11.1 with $G(s) = KP(s)$, find the value of K that will result in a $30°$ phase margin.

b. For the value of K calculated in Part **a**, obtain the corresponding gain margin.

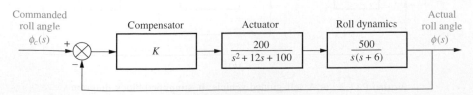

Figure P11.2 Towed-vehicle roll control

c. Obtain estimates for the system's %OS and settling times T_s for step inputs.

d. Simulate the step response of the system using MATLAB.

MATLAB

e. Explain the simulation results and discuss any inaccuracies in the estimates obtained in Part **c**.

25. Self-guided vehicles, such as that shown in Figure P11.3(*a*), are used in factories to transport products from station to station. One method of construction is to embed a wire in the floor to provide guidance. Another method is to use an onboard computer and a laser scanning device. Bar-coded reflective devices at known locations allow the system to determine the vehicle's angular position. This system allows the vehicle to travel anywhere, including between buildings (*Stefanides, 1987*). Figure P11.3(*b*) shows a simplified block diagram of the vehicle's bearing control system. For 11% overshoot, *K* is set equal to 2. Design a lag compensator using frequency response techniques to improve the steady-state error by a factor of 30 over that of the uncompensated system.

26. An aircraft roll control system is shown in Figure P11.4. The torque on the aileron generates a roll rate. The resulting roll angle is then controlled through a feedback system as shown. Design a lead compensator for a 60° phase margin and $K_v = 5$.

27. The transfer function from applied force to arm displacement for the arm of a hard disk drive has been identified as

$$G(s) = \frac{X(s)}{F(s)} = \frac{3.3333 \times 10^4}{s^2}$$

(*a*)

(*b*)

Figure P11.3   **a.** A self-guided vehicle; **b.** simplified block diagram

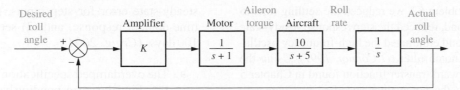

Figure P11.4

The position of the arm will be controlled using the feedback loop shown in Figure P11.1 (*Yan, 2003*).

a. Design a lead compensator to achieve closed-loop stability with a transient response of 16% overshoot and a settling time of 2 msec for a step input.

b. Verify your design through MATLAB simulations.

28. A pitch axis attitude control system utilizing a momentum wheel was the subject of Problem 58 in Chapter 8. In that problem the compensator is shown as a PI compensator. We want to replace the PI compensator with a lag-lead compensator to improve both transient and steady-state error performance. The block diagram for the pitch axis attitude control is shown in Figure P11.5, where $\theta_c(s)$ is a commanded pitch angle and $\theta(s)$ is the actual pitch angle of the spacecraft. If $\tau = 23$ seconds and $I_z = 9631$ in-lb-s^2, do the following (*Piper, 1992*):

a. Design a lag-lead compensator and find $G_c(s)$ and K to yield a system with the following performance specifications: percent overshoot = 20%, settling time = 10 seconds, $K_v = 200$. Make any required second-order approximations.

b. Use MATLAB or any other computer program to test your second-order approximation by simulating the system for your designed value of K and lag-lead compensator.

29. For the heat exchange system described in Problem 35, Chapter 9 (*Smith, 2002*):

a. Design a passive lag-lead compensator to achieve 5% steady-state error with a transient response of 10% overshoot and a settling time of 60 seconds for step inputs.

b. Use MATLAB to simulate and verify your design.

Progressive Analysis and Design Problems

30. **High-speed rail pantograph.** Problem 19 in Chapter 1 discusses active control of a pantograph mechanism for high-speed rail systems. In Problem 72(a), Chapter 5, you found the block diagram for the active pantograph control system. In Chapter 8, Problem 63, you designed the gain to yield a closed-loop step response with 38% overshoot. A plot of the step response should have shown a settling time greater than 0.5 second as well as a high-frequency oscillation superimposed over the step response. In

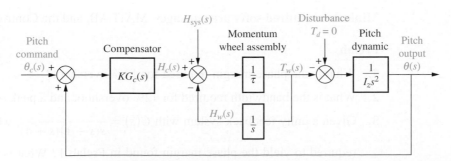

Figure P11.5

Chapter 9, Problem 52, we reduced the settling time to about 0.3 second, reduced the step response steady-state error to zero, and eliminated the high-frequency oscillations using a notch filter (*O'Connor, 1997*). Using the equivalent forward transfer function found in Chapter 5 cascaded with the notch filter specified in Chapter 9, design, using frequency response techniques, a lag-lead compensator to meet the following specifications:

a. At least 35° phase margin

b. A maximum of 10% steady-state error for the closed-loop step response

c. At least 35 rad/s bandwidth

31. Control of HIV/AIDS. In Chapter 6 the model for an HIV/AIDS patient treated with RTIs was linearized and shown to be

$$P(s) = \frac{Y(s)}{U_1(s)} = \frac{-520s - 10.3844}{s^3 + 2.6817s^2 + 0.11s + 0.0126}$$

$$= \frac{-520(s + 0.02)}{(s + 2.2644)(s^2 + 0.04s + 0.0048)}$$

It is assumed here that the patient will be treated and monitored using the closed-loop configuration shown in Figure P11.1 Since the plant has a negative dc gain, assume for simplicity that $G(s) = G_c(s) P(s)$ and $G_c(0) < 0$. Assume also that the specifications for the design are (1) zero steady-state error for step inputs, (2) overdamped time-domain response, and (3) settling time $T_s \approx 100$ days (*Craig, 2004*).

a. The overdamped specification requires a $\Phi_M \approx 90°$. Find the corresponding bandwidth required to satisfy the settling time requirement.

b. The zero steady-state error specification implies that the open-loop transfer function must be augmented to Type 1. The -0.02 zero of the plant adds too much phase lead at low frequencies, and the complex conjugate poles, if left uncompensated within the loop, result in undesired oscillations in the time domain. Thus, as an initial approach to compensation for this system we can try

$$G_c(s) = \frac{-K(s^2 + 0.04s + 0.0048)}{s(s + 0.02)}$$

For $K = 1$, make a Bode plot of the resulting system. Obtain the value of K necessary to achieve the design demands. Check for closed-loop stability.

c. Simulate the unit step response of the system using MATLAB. Adjust K to achieve the desired response.

CYBER EXPLORATION LABORATORY

Experiment 11.1

Objectives: To design a PID controller using MATLAB's SISO Design Tool. To see the effect of a PI and a PD controller on the magnitude and phase responses at each step of the design of a PID controller.

Minimum required software packages MATLAB, and the Control System Toolbox

Prelab

1. What is the phase margin required for 12% overshoot?

2. What is the bandwidth required for 12% overshoot and a peak time of 2 seconds?

3. Given a unity feedback system with $G(s) = \dfrac{K}{s(s + 1)(s + 4)}$, what is the gain, K, required to yield the phase margin found in Prelab 1? What is the phase-margin frequency?

4. Design a PI controller to yield a phase margin 5° more than that found in Prelab 1.

5. Complete the design of a PID controller for the system of Prelab 3.

Lab

1. Using MATLAB's SISO Design Tool, set up the system of Prelab 3 and display the open-loop Bode plots and the closed-loop step response.

2. Drag the Bode magnitude plot in a vertical direction until the phase margin found in Prelab 1 is obtained. Record the gain K, the phase margin, the phase-margin frequency, the percent overshoot, and the peak time. Move the magnitude curve up and down and note the effect upon the phase curve, the phase margin, and the phase-margin frequency.

3. Design the PI controller by adding a pole at the origin and a zero one decade below the phase-margin frequency found in Lab 2. Readjust the gain to yield a phase margin 5° higher than that found in Prelab 1. Record the gain K, the phase margin, the phase-margin frequency, the percent overshoot, and the peak time. Move the zero back and forth in the vicinity of its current location and note the effect on the magnitude and phase curve. Move the magnitude curve up and down and note its effect on the phase curve, the phase margin, and the phase-margin frequency.

4. Design the PD portion of the PID controller by first adjusting the magnitude curve to yield a phase-margin frequency slightly below the bandwidth calculated in Prelab 2. Add a zero to the system and move it until you obtain the phase margin calculated in Prelab 1. Move the zero and note its effect. Move the magnitude curve and note its effect.

Postlab

1. Compare the Prelab PID design with that obtained via the SISO Design Tool. In particular, compare the gain K, the phase margin, the phase-margin frequency, the percent overshoot, and the peak time.

2. For the uncompensated system, describe the effect of changing gain on the phase curve, the phase margin, and the phase-margin frequency.

3. For the PI-compensated system, describe the effect of changing gain on the phase curve, the phase margin, and the phase-margin frequency. Repeat for changes in the zero location.

4. For the PID-compensated system, describe the effect of changing gain on the phase curve, the phase margin, and the phase-margin frequency. Repeat for changes in the PD zero location.

BIBLIOGRAPHY

Barkana, I. Classical and Simple Adaptive Control of Nonminimum Phase Autopilot Design. *Journal of Guidance, Control, and Dynamics,* vol. 28, 2005, pp. 631–638.

Cochran, J. E., Innocenti, M., No, T. S., and Thukral, A. Dynamics and Control of Maneuverable Towed Flight Vehicles. *Journal of Guidance, Control, and Dynamics,* vol. 15, no. 5, September–October 1992, pp. 1245–1252.

Craig, I. K., Xia, X., and Venter, J. W. Introducing HIV/AIDS Education into the Electrical Engineering Curriculum at the University of Pretoria. *IEEE Transactions on Education,* vol. 47, no. 1, February 2004, pp. 65–73.

D'Azzo, J. J., and Houpis, C. H. *Feedback Control System Analysis and Synthesis,* 2d ed. McGraw-Hill, New York, 1966.

Dorf, R. C. *Modern Control Systems,* 5th ed. Addison-Wesley, Reading, MA, 1989.

Flower, T. L., and Son, M. Motor Drive Mechanics and Control Electronics for a High Performance Plotter. *HP Journal,* November 1981, pp. 12–15.

Hollot, C. V., Misra, V., Towsley, D., and Gong, W. A Control Theoretic Analysis of RED. Proceedings of IEEE INFOCOM, 2001, pp. 1510–1519.

Hostetter, G. H., Savant, C. J., and Stefani, R. T. *Design of Feedback Control Systems,* 2d ed. Saunders College Publishing, New York, 1989

Kuo, B. C. *Automatic Control Systems,* 5th ed. Prentice Hall, Englewood Cliffs, NJ, 1987.

O'Connor, D. N., Eppinger, S. D., Seering, W. P., and Wormly, D. N. Active Control of a High-Speed Pantograph. *Journal of Dynamic Systems, Measurements, and Control,* vol. 119, March 1997, pp. 1–4.

Ogata, K. *Modern Control Engineering,* 2d ed. Prentice Hall, Englewood Cliffs, NJ, 1990.

Phillips, C. L., and Harbor, R. D. *Feedback Control Systems.* Prentice Hall, Englewood Cliffs, NJ, 1988.

Piper, G. E., and Kwatny, H. G. Complicated Dynamics in Spacecraft Attitude Control Systems. *Journal of Guidance, Control, and Dynamics,* vol. 15, no. 4, July–August 1992, pp. 825–831.

Raven, F. H. *Automatic Control Engineering,* 4th ed. McGraw-Hill, New York, 1987.

Smith, C. A. *Automated Continuous Process Control.* Wiley, New York, 2002.

Stefanides, E. J. Self-Guided Vehicles Upgrade Materials Handling. *Design News,* 7 December 1987, pp. 80–81.

Tasch, U., Koontz, J. W., Ignatoski, M. A., and Geselowitz, D. B. An Adaptive Aortic Pressure Observer for the Penn State Electric Ventricular Assist Device. *IEEE Transactions on Biomedical Engineering,* vol. 37, 1990, pp. 374–383.

Yan, T., and Lin, R. Experimental Modeling and Compensation of Pivot Nonlinearity in Hard Disk Drives. *IEEE Transactions on Magnetics,* vol. 39, 2003, pp. 1064–1069.

DESIGN USING STATE EQUATIONS

12

State Space

This chapter covers only state-space methods.

CHAPTER OBJECTIVES

In this chapter you will learn the following:

- How to design a state-feedback controller using pole placement to meet transient response specifications
- How to design an observer for systems where the states are not available to the controller
- How to design steady-state error characteristics for systems represented in state space

CASE STUDY OBJECTIVES

You will be able to demonstrate your knowledge of the chapter objectives with case studies as follows:

- Given the antenna azimuth position control system shown on the front endpapers, you will be able to specify all closed-loop poles and then design a state-feedback controller to meet transient response specifications.
- Given the antenna azimuth position control system shown on the front endpapers, you will be able to design an observer to estimate the states.
- Given the antenna azimuth position control system shown on the front endpapers, you will be able to combine the controller and observer designs into a viable compensator for the system.

12.1 INTRODUCTION

Chapter 3 introduced the concepts of state-space analysis and system modeling. We showed that state-space methods, like transform methods, are simply tools for analyzing and designing feedback control systems. However, state-space techniques can be applied to a wider class of systems than transform methods. Systems with nonlinearities, such as that shown in Figure 12.1, and multiple-input, multiple-output systems are just two of the candidates for the state-space approach. In this book, however, we apply the approach only to linear systems.

In Chapters 9 and 11 we applied frequency domain methods to system design. The basic design technique is to create a compensator in cascade with the plant or in the feedback path that has the correct additional poles and zeros to yield a desired transient response and steady-state error.

One of the drawbacks of frequency domain methods of design, using either root locus or frequency response techniques, is that after designing the location of the dominant second-order pair of poles, we keep our fingers crossed, hoping that the higher-order poles do not affect the second-order approximation. What we would like to be able to do is specify *all* closed-loop poles of the higher-order system. Frequency domain methods of design do not allow us to specify all poles in systems of order higher than 2 because they do not allow for a sufficient number of unknown parameters to place all of the closed-loop poles uniquely. One gain to adjust, or compensator pole and zero to select, does not yield a sufficient number of parameters to place all the closed-loop poles at desired locations. Remember, to place n unknown quantities, you need n adjustable parameters. State-space methods solve this problem by introducing into the system (1) other adjustable parameters and (2) the technique for finding these parameter values, so that we can properly place all poles of the closed-loop system.[1]

---

[1] This is an advantage as long as we know where to place the higher-order poles, which is not always the case. One course of action is to place the higher-order poles far from the dominant second-order poles or near a closed-loop zero to keep the second-order system design valid. Another approach is to use optimal control concepts, which are beyond the scope of this text.

On the other hand, state-space methods do not allow the specification of closed-loop zero locations, which frequency domain methods do allow through placement of the lead compensator zero. This is a disadvantage of state-space methods, since the location of the zero does affect the transient response. Also, a state-space design may prove to be very sensitive to parameter changes.

Finally, there is a wide range of computational support for state-space methods; many software packages support the matrix algebra required by the design process. However, as mentioned before, the advantages of computer support are balanced by the loss of graphic insight into a design problem that the frequency domain methods yield.

This chapter should be considered only an introduction to state-space design; we introduce one state-space design technique and apply it only to linear systems. Advanced study is required to apply state-space techniques to the design of systems beyond the scope of this textbook.

12.2 CONTROLLER DESIGN

This section shows how to introduce additional parameters into a system so that we can control the location of all closed-loop poles. An nth-order feedback control system has an nth-order closed-loop characteristic equation of the form

$$s^n + a_{n-1}s^{n-1} + \cdots + a_1 s + a_0 = 0 \tag{12.1}$$

Since the coefficient of the highest power of s is unity, there are n coefficients whose values determine the system's closed-loop pole locations. Thus, if we can introduce n adjustable parameters into the system and relate them to the coefficients in Eq. (12.1), all of the poles of the closed-loop system can be set to any desired location.

TOPOLOGY FOR POLE PLACEMENT

In order to lay the groundwork for the approach, consider a plant represented in state space by

$$\dot{\mathbf{x}} = \mathbf{A}\mathbf{x} + \mathbf{B}u \tag{12.2a}$$

$$y = \mathbf{C}\mathbf{x} \tag{12.2b}$$

and shown pictorially in Figure 12.2(a), where light lines are scalars and the heavy lines are vectors.

In a typical feedback control system, the output, y, is fed back to the summing junction. It is now that the topology of the design changes. Instead of feeding back y, what if we feed back all of the state variables? If each state variable is fed back to the control, u, through a gain, k_i, there would be n gains, k_i, that could be adjusted to yield the required closed-loop pole values. The feedback through the gains, k_i, is represented in Figure 12.2(b) by the feedback vector $-\mathbf{K}$.

The state equations for the closed-loop system of Figure 12.2(b) can be written by inspection as

$$\boxed{\dot{\mathbf{x}} = \mathbf{A}\mathbf{x} + \mathbf{B}u = \mathbf{A}\mathbf{x} + \mathbf{B}(-\mathbf{K}\mathbf{x} + r) = (\mathbf{A} - \mathbf{B}\mathbf{K})\mathbf{x} + \mathbf{B}r} \tag{12.3a}$$

$$\boxed{y = \mathbf{C}\mathbf{x}} \tag{12.3b}$$

Before continuing, you should have a good idea of how the feedback system of Figure 12.2(b) is actually implemented. As an example, assume a plant signal-flow

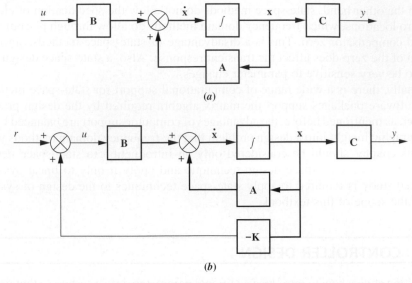

FIGURE 12.2   **a.** State-space representation of a plant; **b.** plant with state-variable feedback

graph in phase-variable form, as shown in Figure 12.3(*a*). Each state variable is then fed back to the plant's input, *u*, through a gain, k_i, as shown in Figure 12.3(*b*). Although we will cover other representations later in the chapter, the phase-variable form, with its typical lower companion system matrix, or the controller canonical form, with its typical upper companion system matrix, yields the simplest evaluation of the feedback gains. In the ensuing discussion, we use the phase-variable form to develop and demonstrate the concepts. End-of-chapter problems will give you an opportunity to develop and test the concepts for the controller canonical form.

The design of state-variable feedback for closed-loop pole placement consists of equating the characteristic equation of a closed-loop system, such as that shown in Figure 12.3(*b*), to a desired characteristic equation and then finding the values of the feedback gains, k_i.

If a plant like that shown in Figure 12.3(*a*) is of high order and not represented in phase-variable or controller canonical form, the solution for the k_i's can be intricate. Thus, it is advisable to transform the system to either of these forms, design the k_i's, and then transform the system back to its original representation. We perform this conversion in Section 12.4, where we develop a method for performing the transformations. Until then, let us direct our attention to plants represented in phase-variable form.

POLE PLACEMENT FOR PLANTS IN PHASE-VARIABLE FORM

To apply pole-placement methodology to plants represented in phase-variable form, we take the following steps:

1. Represent the plant in phase-variable form.

2. Feed back each phase variable to the input of the plant through a gain, k_i.

3. Find the characteristic equation for the closed-loop system represented in Step 2.

4. Decide upon all closed-loop pole locations and determine an equivalent characteristic equation.

5. Equate like coefficients of the characteristic equations from Steps 3 and 4 and solve for k_i.

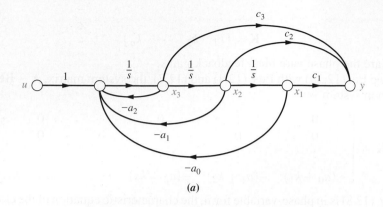

(a)

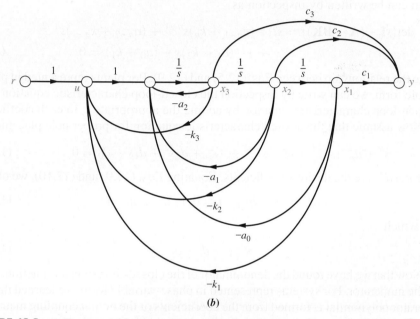

(b)

FIGURE 12.3 **a.** Phase-variable representation for plant; **b.** plant with state-variable feedback

Following these steps, the phase-variable representation of the plant is given by Eq. (12.2), with

$$\mathbf{A} = \begin{bmatrix} 0 & 1 & 0 & \cdots & 0 \\ 0 & 0 & 1 & \cdots & 0 \\ \vdots & \vdots & \vdots & & \vdots \\ -a_0 & -a_1 & -a_2 & \cdots & -a_{n-1} \end{bmatrix}; \quad B = \begin{bmatrix} 0 \\ 0 \\ \vdots \\ 1 \end{bmatrix};$$

$$\mathbf{C} = \begin{bmatrix} c_1 & c_2 & \cdots & c_n \end{bmatrix} \tag{12.4}$$

The characteristic equation of the plant is thus

$$s^n + a_{n-1}s^{n-1} + \cdots + a_1 s + a_0 = 0 \tag{12.5}$$

Now form the closed-loop system by feeding back each state variable to u, forming

$$u = -\mathbf{K}\mathbf{x} \tag{12.6}$$

where

$$\mathbf{K} = \begin{bmatrix} k_1 & k_2 & \cdots & k_n \end{bmatrix} \tag{12.7}$$

The k_i's are the phase variables' feedback gains.

Using Eq. (12.3a) with Eqs. (12.4) and (12.7), the system matrix, $\mathbf{A} - \mathbf{BK}$, for the closed-loop system is

$$\mathbf{A} - \mathbf{BK} = \begin{bmatrix} 0 & 1 & 0 & \cdots & 0 \\ 0 & 0 & 1 & \cdots & 0 \\ \vdots & \vdots & \vdots & \vdots & \vdots \\ -(a_0 + k_1) & -(a_1 + k_2) & -(a_2 + k_3) & \cdots & -(a_{n-1} + k_n) \end{bmatrix} \tag{12.8}$$

Since Eq. (12.8) is in phase-variable form, the characteristic equation of the closed-loop system can be written by inspection as

$$\det(s\mathbf{I} - (\mathbf{A} - \mathbf{BK})) = s^n + (a_{n-1} + k_n)s^{n-1} + (a_{n-2} + k_{n-1})s^{n-2}$$
$$+ \cdots (a_1 + k_2)s + (a_0 + k_1) = 0 \tag{12.9}$$

Notice the relationship between Eqs. (12.5) and (12.9). For plants represented in phase-variable form, we can write by inspection the closed-loop characteristic equation from the open-loop characteristic equation by adding the appropriate k_i to each coefficient.

Now assume that the desired characteristic equation for proper pole placement is

$$s^n + d_{n-1}s^{n-1} + d_{n-2}s^{n-2} + \cdots + d_2 s^2 + d_1 s + d_0 = 0 \tag{12.10}$$

where the d_i's are the desired coefficients. Equating Eqs. (12.9) and (12.10), we obtain

$$d_i = a_i + k_{i+1} \quad i = 0, 1, 2, \ldots, n-1 \tag{12.11}$$

from which

$$k_{i+1} = d_i - a_i \tag{12.12}$$

Now that we have found the denominator of the closed-loop transfer function, let us find the numerator. For systems represented in phase-variable form, we learned that the numerator polynomial is formed from the coefficients of the output coupling matrix, $\mathbf{C}$. Since Figures 12.3(a) and (b) are both in phase-variable form and have the same output coupling matrix, we conclude that the numerators of their transfer functions are the same. Let us look at a design example.

EXAMPLE 12.1

Controller design for phase-variable form

Problem: Given the plant

$$G(s) = \frac{20(s + 5)}{s(s + 1)(s + 4)} \tag{12.13}$$

design the phase-variable feedback gains to yield 9.5% overshoot and a settling time of 0.74 second.

SOLUTION: We begin by calculating the desired closed-loop characteristic equation. Using the transient response requirements, the closed-loop poles are $-5.4 \pm j$ 7.2. Since the system is third-order, we must select another closed-loop pole. The

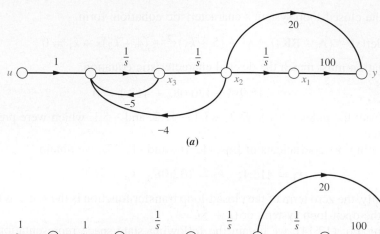

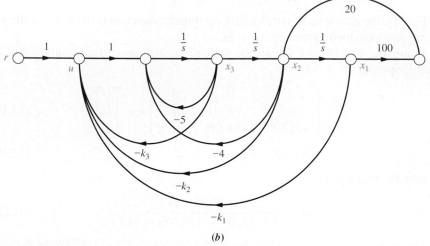

FIGURE 12.4 **a.** Phase-variable representation for plant of Example 12.1; **b.** plant with state-variable feedback

closed-loop system will have a zero at -5, the same as the open-loop system. We could select the third closed-loop pole to cancel the closed-loop zero. However, to demonstrate the effect of the third pole and the design process, including the need for simulation, let us choose -5.1 as the location of the third closed-loop pole.

Now draw the signal-flow diagram for the plant. The result is shown in Figure 12.4(a). Next feed back all state variables to the control, u, through gains k_i, as shown in Figure 12.4(b).

Writing the closed-loop system's state equations from Figure 12.4(b), we have

$$\dot{\mathbf{x}} = \begin{bmatrix} 0 & 1 & 0 \\ 0 & 0 & 1 \\ -k_1 & -(4+k_2) & -(5+k_3) \end{bmatrix} \mathbf{x} + \begin{bmatrix} 0 \\ 0 \\ 1 \end{bmatrix} r \qquad (12.14a)$$

$$y = \begin{bmatrix} 100 & 20 & 0 \end{bmatrix} \mathbf{x} \qquad (12.14b)$$

Comparing Eq. (12.14) to Eq. (12.3), we identify the closed-loop system matrix as

$$\mathbf{A} - \mathbf{BK} = \begin{bmatrix} 0 & 1 & 0 \\ 0 & 0 & 1 \\ -k_1 & -(4+k_2) & -(5+k_3) \end{bmatrix} \qquad (12.15)$$

To find the closed-loop system's characteristic equation, form

$$\det(s\mathbf{I} - (\mathbf{A} - \mathbf{BK})) = s^3 + (5 + k_3)s^2 + (4 + k_2)s + k_1 = 0 \qquad (12.16)$$

This equation must match the desired characteristic equation,

$$s^3 + 15.9s^2 + 136.08s + 413.1 = 0 \qquad (12.17)$$

formed from the poles $-5.4 + j7.2$, $-5.4 - j7.2$, and -5.1, which were previously determined.

Equating the coefficients of Eqs. (12.16) and (12.17), we obtain

$$k_1 = 413.1; \quad k_2 = 132.08; \quad k_3 = 10.9 \qquad (12.18)$$

Finally, the zero term of the closed-loop transfer function is the same as the zero term of the open-loop system, or $(s + 5)$.

Using Eq. (12.14), we obtain the following state-space representation of the closed-loop system:

$$\dot{\mathbf{x}} = \begin{bmatrix} 0 & 1 & 0 \\ 0 & 0 & 1 \\ -413.1 & -136.08 & -15.9 \end{bmatrix} \mathbf{x} + \begin{bmatrix} 0 \\ 0 \\ 1 \end{bmatrix} r \qquad (12.19a)$$

$$y = \begin{bmatrix} 100 & 20 & 0 \end{bmatrix} \mathbf{x} \qquad (12.19b)$$

The transfer function is

$$T(s) = \frac{20(s + 5)}{s^3 + 15.9s^2 + 136.08s + 413.1} \qquad (12.20)$$

Figure 12.5, a simulation of the closed-loop system, shows 11.5% overshoot and a settling time of 0.8 second. A redesign with the third pole canceling the zero at -5 will yield performance equal to the requirements.

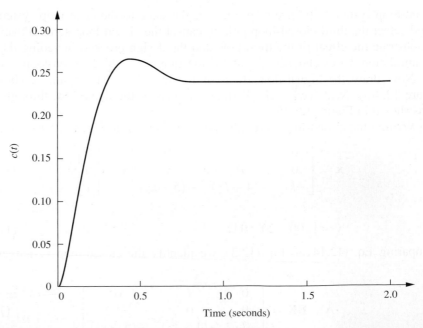

FIGURE 12.5   Simulation of closed-loop system of Example 12.1

Since the steady-state response approaches 0.24 instead of unity, there is a large steady-state error. Design techniques to reduce this error are discussed in Section 12.8.

Students who are using MATLAB should now run ch12p1 in Appendix B. You will learn how to use MATLAB to design a controller for phase variables using pole placement. MATLAB will plot the step response of the designed system. This exercise solves Example 12.1 using MATLAB.

MATLAB

SKILL-ASSESSMENT EXERCISE 12.1

Problems: For the plant

$$G(s) = \frac{100(s+10)}{s(s+3)(s+12)}$$

represented in the state space in phase-variable form by

$$\dot{\mathbf{x}} = \mathbf{Ax} + \mathbf{B}u = \begin{bmatrix} 0 & 1 & 0 \\ 0 & 0 & 1 \\ 0 & -36 & -15 \end{bmatrix} \mathbf{x} + \begin{bmatrix} 0 \\ 0 \\ 1 \end{bmatrix} u$$

$$y = \mathbf{Cx} = \begin{bmatrix} 1000 & 100 & 0 \end{bmatrix} \mathbf{x}$$

design the phase-variable feedback gains to yield 5% overshoot and a peak time of 0.3 second.

ANSWER: $K = \begin{bmatrix} 2094 & 373.1 & 14.97 \end{bmatrix}$

The complete solution is located at www.wiley.com/college/nise.

WileyPLUS

Control Solutions

TryIt 12.1

Use MATLAB, the Control System Toolbox, and the following statements to solve for the phase-variable feedback gains to place the poles of the system in Skill-Assessment Exercise 12.1 at $-3+j5$, $-3-j5$, and -10.

```
A = [0 1 0
     0 0 1
     0 -36 -15]
B = [0;0;1]
poles = [-3+5j,...
         -3-5j,-10]
K = acker(A,B,poles)
```

In this section we showed how to design feedback gains for plants represented in phase-variable form in order to place all of the closed-loop system's poles at desired locations on the s-plane. On the surface it appears that the method should always work for any system. However, this is not the case. The conditions that must exist in order to uniquely place the closed-loop poles where we want them is the topic of the next section.

12.3 CONTROLLABILITY

Consider the parallel form shown in Figure 12.6(*a*). To control the pole location of the closed-loop system, we are saying implicitly that the control signal, u, can control the behavior of each state variable in x. If any one of the state variables cannot be controlled by the control u, then we cannot place the poles of the system where we desire. For example, in Figure 12.6(*b*), if x_1 were not controllable by the control signal and if x_1 also exhibited an unstable response due to a nonzero initial condition, there would be no way to effect a state-feedback design to stabilize x_1; x_1 would perform in its own way regardless of the control signal, u. Thus, in some systems, a state-feedback design is not possible.

FIGURE 12.6 Comparison of
a. controllable and
b. uncontrollable systems

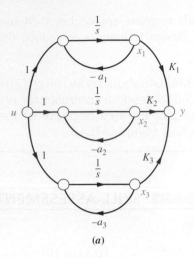

(a)

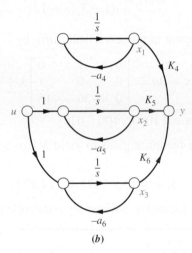

(b)

We now make the following definition based upon the previous discussion:

> If an input to a system can be found that takes every state variable from a desired
> initial state to a desired final state, the system is said to be *controllable;* otherwise,
> the system is *uncontrollable.*

Pole placement is a viable design technique only for systems that are controllable. This
section shows how to determine, a priori, whether pole placement is a viable design
technique for a controller.

CONTROLLABILITY BY INSPECTION

We can explore controllability from another viewpoint: that of the state equation itself.
When the system matrix is diagonal, as it is for the parallel form, it is apparent whether
or not the system is controllable. For example, the state equation for Figure 12.6(a) is

$$\dot{\mathbf{x}} = \begin{bmatrix} -a_1 & 0 & 0 \\ 0 & -a_2 & 0 \\ 0 & 0 & -a_3 \end{bmatrix} \mathbf{x} + \begin{bmatrix} 1 \\ 1 \\ 1 \end{bmatrix} u \qquad (12.21)$$

or

$$\dot{x}_1 = -a_1 x_1 \qquad\qquad\qquad + u \qquad\qquad (12.22a)$$

$$\dot{x}_2 = \qquad\quad -a_2 x_2 \qquad\quad + u \qquad\qquad (12.22b)$$

$$\dot{x}_3 = \qquad\qquad\qquad -a_3 x_3 + u \qquad\qquad (12.22c)$$

Since each of Eqs. (12.22) is independent and decoupled from the rest, the control u affects each of the state variables. This is controllability from another perspective.

Now let us look at the state equations for the system of Figure 12.6(b):

$$\dot{\mathbf{x}} = \begin{bmatrix} -a_4 & 0 & 0 \\ 0 & -a_5 & 0 \\ 0 & 0 & -a_6 \end{bmatrix} \mathbf{x} + \begin{bmatrix} 0 \\ 1 \\ 1 \end{bmatrix} u \qquad\qquad (12.23)$$

or

$$\dot{x}_1 = -a_4 x_1 \qquad\qquad\qquad\qquad\qquad (12.24a)$$

$$\dot{x}_2 = \qquad\quad -a_5 x_2 \qquad\quad + u \qquad\qquad (12.24b)$$

$$\dot{x}_3 = \qquad\qquad\qquad -a_6 x_3 + u \qquad\qquad (12.24c)$$

From the state equations in (12.23) or (12.24), we see that state variable x_1 is not controlled by the control u. Thus, the system is said to be uncontrollable.

In summary, a system with distinct eigenvalues and a diagonal system matrix is controllable if the input coupling matrix **B** does not have any rows that are zero.

THE CONTROLLABILITY MATRIX

Tests for controllability that we have so far explored cannot be used for representations of the system other than the diagonal or parallel form with distinct eigenvalues. The problem of visualizing controllability gets more complicated if the system has multiple poles, even though it is represented in parallel form. Further, one cannot always determine controllability by inspection for systems that are not represented in parallel form. In other forms the existence of paths from the input to the state variables is not a criterion for controllability since the equations are not decoupled.

In order to be able to determine controllability or, alternatively, to design state feedback for a plant under any representation or choice of state variables, a matrix can be derived that must have a particular property if all state variables are to be controlled by the plant input, u. We now state the requirement for controllability, including the form, property, and name of this matrix.[2]

An nth-order plant whose state equation is

$$\dot{\mathbf{x}} = \mathbf{Ax} + \mathbf{Bu} \qquad\qquad (12.25)$$

is completely controllable[3] if the matrix

$$\boxed{\mathbf{C_M} = \begin{bmatrix} \mathbf{B} & \mathbf{AB} & \mathbf{A^2B} & \cdots & \mathbf{A^{n-1}B} \end{bmatrix}} \qquad\qquad (12.26)$$

---

[2] See the work listed in the Bibliography by *Ogata* (*1990: 699–702*) for the derivation.

[3] *Completely controllable* means that all state variables are controllable. This textbook uses *controllable* to mean *completely controllable*.

is of rank n, where $\mathbf{C_M}$ is called the *controllability* matrix.[4] As an example, let us choose a system represented in parallel form with multiple roots.

EXAMPLE 12.2

Controllability via the controllability matrix

Problem: Given the system of Figure 12.7, represented by a signal-flow diagram, determine its controllability.

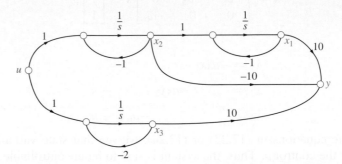

FIGURE 12.7   System for Example 12.2

SOLUTION: The state equation for the system written from the signal-flow diagram is

$$\dot{\mathbf{x}} = \mathbf{Ax} + \mathbf{B}u = \begin{bmatrix} -1 & 1 & 0 \\ 0 & -1 & 0 \\ 0 & 0 & -2 \end{bmatrix} \mathbf{x} + \begin{bmatrix} 0 \\ 1 \\ 1 \end{bmatrix} u \qquad (12.27)$$

At first it would appear that the system is not controllable because of the zero in the $\mathbf{B}$ matrix. Remember, though, that this configuration leads to uncontrollability only if the poles are real and distinct. In this case we have multiple poles at -1.

The controllability matrix is

$$\mathbf{C_M} = \begin{bmatrix} \mathbf{B} & \mathbf{AB} & \mathbf{A^2B} \end{bmatrix} = \begin{bmatrix} 0 & 1 & -2 \\ 1 & -1 & 1 \\ 1 & -2 & 4 \end{bmatrix} \qquad (12.28)$$

The rank of $\mathbf{C_M}$ equals the number of linearly independent rows or columns. The rank can be found by finding the highest-order square submatrix that is nonsingular. The determinant of $\mathbf{C_M} = -1$. Since the determinant is not zero, the 3×3 matrix is nonsingular, and the rank of $\mathbf{C_M}$ is 3. We conclude that the system is controllable since

---

[4] See Appendix F at www.wiley.com/college/nise for the definition of rank. For single-input systems, instead of specifying rank n, we can say that $\mathbf{C_M}$ must be nonsingular, possess an inverse, or have linearly independent rows and columns.

MATLAB

the rank of $\mathbf{C_M}$ equals the system order. Thus, the poles of the system can be placed using state-variable feedback design.

Students who are using MATLAB should now run ch12p2 in Appendix B. You will learn how to use MATLAB to test a system for controllability. This exercise solves Example 12.2 using MATLAB.

In the previous example we found that even though an element of the input coupling matrix was zero, the system was controllable. If we look at Figure 12.7, we can see why. In this figure all of the state variables are driven by the input u.

On the other hand, if we disconnect the input at either dx_1/dt, dx_2/dt, or dx_3/dt, at least one state variable would not be controllable. To see the effect, let us disconnect the input at dx_2/dt. This causes the **B** matrix to become

$$\mathbf{B} = \begin{bmatrix} 0 \\ 0 \\ 1 \end{bmatrix} \tag{12.29}$$

We can see that the system is now uncontrollable, since x_1 and x_2 are no longer controlled by the input. This conclusion is borne out by the controllability matrix, which is now

$$\mathbf{C_M} = \begin{bmatrix} \mathbf{B} & \mathbf{AB} & \mathbf{A}^2\mathbf{B} \end{bmatrix} = \begin{bmatrix} 0 & 0 & 0 \\ 0 & 0 & 0 \\ 1 & -2 & 4 \end{bmatrix} \tag{12.30}$$

Not only is the determinant of this matrix equal to zero, but so is the determinant of any 2 × 2 submatrix. Thus, the rank of Eq. (12.30) is 1. The system is uncontrollable because the rank of $\mathbf{C_M}$ is 1, which is less than the order, 3, of the system.

SKILL-ASSESSMENT EXERCISE 12.2

Problem: Determine whether the system

$$\dot{\mathbf{x}} = \mathbf{Ax} + \mathbf{B}u = \begin{bmatrix} -1 & 1 & 2 \\ 0 & -1 & 5 \\ 0 & 3 & -4 \end{bmatrix} \mathbf{x} + \begin{bmatrix} 2 \\ 1 \\ 1 \end{bmatrix} u$$

is controllable.

ANSWER: Controllable

The complete solution is located at www.wiley.com/college/nise.

TryIt 12.2

Use MATLAB, the Control System Toolbox, and the following statements to solve Skill-Assessment Exercise 12.2.

```
A = [-1   1   2
      0 - 1   5
      0   3 - 4]
B = [2; 1; 1]
Cm = ctrb(A, B)
Rank = rank(Cm)
```

In summary, then, pole-placement design through state-variable feedback is simplified by using the phase-variable form for the plant's state equations. However, controllability, the ability for pole-placement design to succeed, can be visualized best in the parallel form, where the system matrix is diagonal with distinct roots. In any event, the controllability matrix will always tell the designer whether the implementation is viable for state-feedback design.

The next section shows how to design state-variable feedback for systems not represented in phase-variable form. We use the controllability matrix as a tool for transforming a system to phase-variable form for the design of state-variable feedback.

12.4 ALTERNATIVE APPROACHES TO CONTROLLER DESIGN

Section 12.2 showed how to design state-variable feedback to yield desired closed-loop poles. We demonstrated this method using systems represented in phase-variable form and saw how simple it was to calculate the feedback gains. Many times the physics of the problem requires feedback from state variables that are not phase variables. For these systems we have some choices for a design methodology.

The first method consists of matching the coefficients of $\det(s\mathbf{I} - (\mathbf{A} - \mathbf{BK}))$ with the coefficients of the desired characteristic equation, which is the same method we used for systems represented in phase variables. This technique, in general, leads to difficult calculations of the feedback gains, especially for higher-order systems not represented with phase variables. Let us illustrate this technique with an example.

EXAMPLE 12.3

Controller design by matching coefficients

Problem: Given a plant, $Y(s)/U(s) = 10/[(s+1)(s+2)]$, design state feedback for the plant represented in cascade form to yield a 15% overshoot with a settling time of 0.5 second.

SOLUTION: The signal-flow diagram for the plant in cascade form is shown in Figure 12.8(a). Figure 12.8(b) shows the system with state feedback added. Writing the state equations from Figure 12.8(b), we have

$$\dot{\mathbf{x}} = \begin{bmatrix} -2 & 1 \\ -k_1 & -(k_2+1) \end{bmatrix} \mathbf{x} + \begin{bmatrix} 0 \\ 1 \end{bmatrix} r \qquad (12.31a)$$

$$y = \begin{bmatrix} 10 & 0 \end{bmatrix} \mathbf{x} \qquad (12.31b)$$

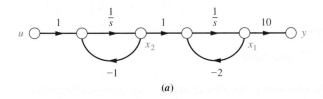

(a)

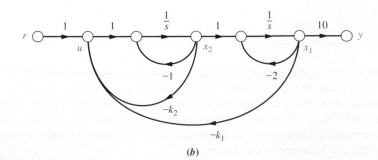

(b)

FIGURE 12.8
a. Signal-flow graph in cascade form for $G(s) = 10/[(s+1)(s+2)]$;
b. system with state feedback added

where the characteristic equation is

$$s^2 + (k_2 + 3)s + (2k_2 + k_1 + 2) = 0 \qquad (12.32)$$

Using the transient response requirements stated in the problem, we obtain the desired characteristic equation

$$s^2 + 16s + 239.5 = 0 \qquad (12.33)$$

Equating the middle coefficients of Eqs. (12.32) and (12.33), we find $k_2 = 13$. Equating the last coefficients of these equations along with the result for k_2 yields $k_1 = 211.5$.

The second method consists of transforming the system to phase variables, designing the feedback gains, and transforming the designed system back to its original state-variable representation.[5] This method requires that we first develop the transformation between a system and its representation in phase-variable form.

Assume a plant not represented in phase-variable form,

$$\dot{\mathbf{z}} = \mathbf{A}\mathbf{z} + \mathbf{B}u \qquad (12.34a)$$

$$y = \mathbf{C}\mathbf{z} \qquad (12.34b)$$

whose controllability matrix is

$$\mathbf{C_{Mz}} = \begin{bmatrix} \mathbf{B} & \mathbf{AB} & \mathbf{A}^2\mathbf{B} & \cdots & \mathbf{A}^{n-1}\mathbf{B} \end{bmatrix} \qquad (12.35)$$

Assume that the system can be transformed into the phase-variable ($\mathbf{x}$) representation with the transformation

$$\boxed{\mathbf{z} = \mathbf{P}\mathbf{x}} \qquad (12.36)$$

Substituting this transformation into Eq. (12.34), we get

$$\dot{\mathbf{x}} = \mathbf{P}^{-1}\mathbf{A}\mathbf{P}\mathbf{x} + \mathbf{P}^{-1}\mathbf{B}u \qquad (12.37a)$$

$$y = \mathbf{C}\mathbf{P}\mathbf{x} \qquad (12.37b)$$

whose controllability matrix is

$$
\begin{aligned}
\mathbf{C_{Mx}} &= \begin{bmatrix} \mathbf{P}^{-1}\mathbf{B} & (\mathbf{P}^{-1}\mathbf{AP})(\mathbf{P}^{-1}\mathbf{B}) & (\mathbf{P}^{-1}\mathbf{AP})^2(\mathbf{P}^{-1}\mathbf{B}) & \cdots & (\mathbf{P}^{-1}\mathbf{AP})^{n-1}(\mathbf{P}^{-1}\mathbf{B}) \end{bmatrix} \\
&= \begin{bmatrix} \mathbf{P}^{-1}\mathbf{B} & (\mathbf{P}^{-1}\mathbf{AP})(\mathbf{P}^{-1}\mathbf{B}) & (\mathbf{P}^{-1}\mathbf{AP})(\mathbf{P}^{-1}\mathbf{AP})(\mathbf{P}^{-1}\mathbf{B}) & \cdots & (\mathbf{P}^{-1}\mathbf{AP}) \end{bmatrix} \\
&\quad (\mathbf{P}^{-1}\mathbf{AP})(\mathbf{P}^{-1}\mathbf{AP}) \quad \cdots \quad (\mathbf{P}^{-1}\mathbf{AP})(\mathbf{P}^{-1}\mathbf{B})] \\
&= \mathbf{P}^{-1}\begin{bmatrix} \mathbf{B} & \mathbf{AB} & \mathbf{A}^2\mathbf{B} & \cdots & \mathbf{A}^{n-1}\mathbf{B} \end{bmatrix} \qquad (12.38)
\end{aligned}
$$

Substituting Eq. (12.35) into (12.38) and solving for $\mathbf{P}$, we obtain

$$\boxed{\mathbf{P} = \mathbf{C_{Mz}}\mathbf{C_{Mx}}^{-1}} \qquad (12.39)$$

Thus, the transformation matrix, $\mathbf{P}$, can be found from the two controllability matrices.

---

[5] See the discussions of Ackermann's formula in *Franklin (1994)* and *Ogata (1990)*, listed in the Bibliography.

After transforming the system to phase variables, we design the feedback gains as in Section 12.2. Hence, including both feedback and input, $u = -\mathbf{K_x x} + r$, Eq. (12.37) becomes

$$\dot{\mathbf{x}} = \mathbf{P}^{-1}\mathbf{APx} - \mathbf{P}^{-1}\mathbf{BK_x x} + \mathbf{P}^{-1}\mathbf{B}r$$

$$= (\mathbf{P}^{-1}\mathbf{AP} - \mathbf{P}^{-1}\mathbf{BK_x})\mathbf{x} + \mathbf{P}^{-1}\mathbf{B}r \qquad (12.40a)$$

$$\mathbf{y} = \mathbf{CPx} \qquad (12.40b)$$

Since this equation is in phase-variable form, the zeros of this closed-loop system are determined from the polynomial formed from the elements of $\mathbf{CP}$, as explained in Section 12.2.

Using $\mathbf{x} = \mathbf{P}^{-1}\mathbf{z}$, we transform Eq. (12.40) from phase variables back to the original representation and get

$$\dot{\mathbf{z}} = \mathbf{Az} - \mathbf{BK_x}\mathbf{P}^{-1}\mathbf{z} + \mathbf{B}r = (\mathbf{A} - \mathbf{BK_x}\mathbf{P}^{-1})\mathbf{z} + \mathbf{B}r \qquad (12.41a)$$

$$\mathbf{y} = \mathbf{Cz} \qquad (12.41b)$$

Comparing Eq. (12.41) with (12.3), the state variable feedback gain, $\mathbf{K_z}$, for the original system is

$$\boxed{\mathbf{K_z} = \mathbf{K_x}\mathbf{P}^{-1}} \qquad (12.42)$$

The transfer function of this closed-loop system is the same as the transfer function for Eq. (12.40), since Eqs. (12.40) and (12.41) represent the same system. Thus, the zeros of the closed-loop transfer function are the same as the zeros of the uncompensated plant, based upon the development in Section 12.2. Let us demonstrate with a design example.

EXAMPLE 12.4

Controller design by transformation

Problem: Design a state-variable feedback controller to yield a 20.8% overshoot and a settling time of 4 seconds for a plant,

$$G(s) = \frac{(s+4)}{(s+1)(s+2)(s+5)} \qquad (12.43)$$

that is represented in cascade form as shown in Figure 12.9.

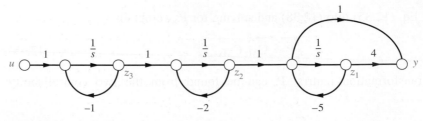

FIGURE 12.9 Signal-flow graph for plant of Example 12.4

SOLUTION: First find the state equations and the controllability matrix. The state equations written from Figure 12.9 are

$$\dot{\mathbf{z}} = \mathbf{A_z z} + \mathbf{B_z} u = \begin{bmatrix} -5 & 1 & 0 \\ 0 & -2 & 1 \\ 0 & 0 & -1 \end{bmatrix} \mathbf{z} + \begin{bmatrix} 0 \\ 0 \\ 1 \end{bmatrix} u \qquad (12.44a)$$

$$y = \mathbf{C_z z} = [-1 \quad 1 \quad 0]\mathbf{z} \qquad (12.44b)$$

from which the controllability matrix is evaluated as

$$\mathbf{C_{Mz}} = [\mathbf{B_z} \quad \mathbf{A_z B_z} \quad \mathbf{A_z^2 B_z}] = \begin{bmatrix} 0 & 0 & 1 \\ 0 & 1 & -3 \\ 1 & -1 & 1 \end{bmatrix} \qquad (12.45)$$

Since the determinant of $\mathbf{C_{Mz}}$ is -1, the system is controllable.

We now convert the system to phase variables by first finding the characteristic equation and using this equation to write the phase-variable form. The characteristic equation, $\det(s\mathbf{I} - \mathbf{A_z})$, is

$$\det(s\mathbf{I} - \mathbf{A_z}) = s^3 + 8s^2 + 17s + 10 = 0 \qquad (12.46)$$

Using the coefficients of Eq. (12.46) and our knowledge of the phase-variable form, we write the phase-variable representation of the system as

$$\dot{\mathbf{x}} = \mathbf{A_x x} + \mathbf{B_x} u = \begin{bmatrix} 0 & 1 & 0 \\ 0 & 0 & 1 \\ -10 & -17 & -8 \end{bmatrix} \mathbf{x} + \begin{bmatrix} 0 \\ 0 \\ 1 \end{bmatrix} u \qquad (12.47a)$$

$$y = [4 \quad 1 \quad 0]\mathbf{x} \qquad (12.47b)$$

The output equation was written using the coefficients of the numerator of Eq.(12.43), since the transfer function must be the same for the two representations. The controllability matrix, $\mathbf{C_{Mx}}$, for the phase-variable system is

$$\mathbf{C_{Mx}} = [\mathbf{B_x} \quad \mathbf{A_x B_x} \quad \mathbf{A_x^2 B_x}] = \begin{bmatrix} 0 & 0 & 1 \\ 0 & 1 & -8 \\ 1 & -8 & 47 \end{bmatrix} \qquad (12.48)$$

Using Eq. (12.39), we can now calculate the transformation matrix between the two systems as

$$\mathbf{P} = \mathbf{C_{Mz} C_{Mx}^{-1}} = \begin{bmatrix} 1 & 0 & 0 \\ 5 & 1 & 0 \\ 10 & 7 & 1 \end{bmatrix} \qquad (12.49)$$

We now design the controller using the phase-variable representation and then use Eq. (12.49) to transform the design back to the original representation. For a 20.8% overshoot and a settling time of 4 seconds, a factor of the characteristic equation of the designed closed-loop system is $s^2 + 2s + 5$. Since the closed-loop zero will be at $s = -4$, we choose the third closed-loop pole to cancel the closed-loop zero. Hence, the total characteristic equation of the desired closed-loop system is

$$D(s) = (s+4)(s^2 + 2s + 5) = s^3 + 6s^2 + 13s + 20 = 0 \qquad (12.50)$$

The state equations for the phase-variable form with state-variable feedback are

$$\dot{\mathbf{x}} = (\mathbf{A_x} - \mathbf{B_x}\mathbf{K_x})\mathbf{x} = \begin{bmatrix} 0 & 1 & 0 \\ 0 & 0 & 1 \\ -(10 + k_{1_x}) & -(17 + k_{2_x}) & -(8 + k_{3_x}) \end{bmatrix}\mathbf{x} \quad (12.51a)$$

$$y = \begin{bmatrix} 4 & 1 & 0 \end{bmatrix}\mathbf{x} \quad (12.51b)$$

The characteristic equation for Eq. (12.51) is

$$\det(s\mathbf{I} - (\mathbf{A_x} - \mathbf{B_x}\mathbf{K_x})) = s^3 + (8 + k_{3_x})s^2 + (17 + k_{2_x})s + (10 + k_{1_x})$$
$$= 0 \quad (12.52)$$

Comparing Eq. (12.50) with (12.52), we see that

$$\mathbf{K_x} = \begin{bmatrix} k_{1_x} & k_{2_x} & k_{3_x} \end{bmatrix} = \begin{bmatrix} 10 & -4 & -2 \end{bmatrix} \quad (12.53)$$

Using Eqs. (12.42) and (12.49), we can transform the controller back to the original system as

$$\mathbf{K_z} = \mathbf{K_x}\mathbf{P}^{-1} = \begin{bmatrix} -20 & 10 & -2 \end{bmatrix} \quad (12.54)$$

The final closed-loop system with state-variable feedback is shown in Figure 12.10, with the input applied as shown.

Let us now verify our design. The state equations for the designed system shown in Figure 12.10 with input r are

$$\dot{\mathbf{z}} = (\mathbf{A_z} - \mathbf{B_z}\mathbf{K_z})\mathbf{z} + \mathbf{B_z}r = \begin{bmatrix} -5 & 1 & 0 \\ 0 & -2 & 1 \\ 20 & -10 & 1 \end{bmatrix}\mathbf{z} + \begin{bmatrix} 0 \\ 0 \\ 1 \end{bmatrix}r \quad (12.55a)$$

$$y = \mathbf{C_z}\mathbf{z} = \begin{bmatrix} -1 & 1 & 0 \end{bmatrix}\mathbf{z} \quad (12.55b)$$

Using Eq. (3.73) to find the closed-loop transfer function, we obtain

$$T(s) = \frac{(s + 4)}{s^3 + 6s^2 + 13s + 20} = \frac{1}{s^2 + 2s + 5} \quad (12.56)$$

The requirements for our design have been met.

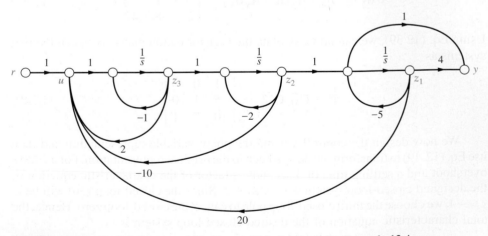

FIGURE 12.10   Designed system with state-variable feedback for Example 12.4

Students who are using MATLAB should now run ch12p3 in Appendix B. You will learn how to use MATLAB to design a controller for a plant not represented in phase-variable form. You will see that MATLAB does not require transformation to phase-variable form. This exercise solves Example 12.4 using MATLAB.

MATLAB

▮ SKILL-ASSESSMENT EXERCISE 12.3 ▮

Problem: Design a linear state-feedback controller to yield 20% overshoot and a settling time of 2 seconds for a plant,

WileyPLUS

Control Solutions

$$G(s) = \frac{(s+6)}{(s+9)(s+8)(s+7)}$$

that is represented in state space in cascade form by

$$\dot{\mathbf{z}} = \mathbf{A}\mathbf{z} + \mathbf{B}u = \begin{bmatrix} -7 & 1 & 0 \\ 0 & -8 & 1 \\ 0 & 0 & -9 \end{bmatrix} \mathbf{z} + \begin{bmatrix} 0 \\ 0 \\ 1 \end{bmatrix} u$$

$$y = \mathbf{C}\mathbf{z} = \begin{bmatrix} -1 & 1 & 0 \end{bmatrix} \mathbf{z}$$

ANSWER:
$$\mathbf{K_z} = \begin{bmatrix} -40.23 & 62.24 & -14 \end{bmatrix}$$

The complete solution is located at www.wiley.com/college/nise.

In this section we saw how to design state-variable feedback for plants not represented in phase-variable form. Using controllability matrices, we were able to transform a plant to phase-variable form, design the controller, and finally transform the controller design back to the plant's original representation. The design of the controller relies on the availability of the states for feedback. In the next section we discuss the design of state-variable feedback when some or all of the states are not available.

12.5 OBSERVER DESIGN

Controller design relies upon access to the state variables for feedback through adjustable gains. This access can be provided by hardware. For example, gyros can measure position and velocity on a space vehicle. Sometimes it is impractical to use this hardware for reasons of cost, accuracy, or availability. For example, in powered flight of space vehicles, inertial measuring units can be used to calculate the acceleration. However, their alignment deteriorates with time; thus, other means of measuring acceleration may be desirable (*Rockwell International, 1984*). In other applications, some of the state variables may not be available at all, or it is too costly to measure them or send them to the controller. If the state variables are not available because of system configuration or cost, it is possible to estimate the states. Estimated states, rather than actual states, are then fed to the controller. One scheme is shown in Figure 12.11(*a*).

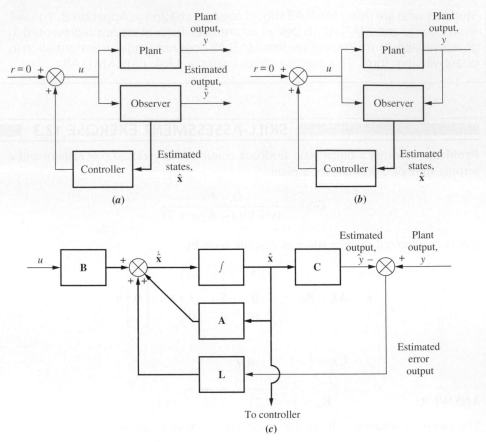

FIGURE 12.11   State-feedback design using an observer to estimate unavailable state variables:
a. open-loop observer; **b.** closed-loop observer; **c.** exploded view of a closed-loop observer,
showing feedback arrangement to reduce state-variable estimation error

An *observer,* sometimes called an *estimator,* is used to calculate state variables that are
not accessible from the plant. Here the observer is a model of the plant.

Let us look at the disadvantages of such a configuration. Assume a plant,

$$\dot{\mathbf{x}} = \mathbf{A}\mathbf{x} + \mathbf{B}u \tag{12.57a}$$

$$y = \mathbf{C}\mathbf{x} \tag{12.57b}$$

and an observer,

$$\dot{\hat{\mathbf{x}}} = \mathbf{A}\hat{\mathbf{x}} + \mathbf{B}u \tag{12.58a}$$

$$\hat{y} = \mathbf{C}\hat{\mathbf{x}} \tag{12.58b}$$

Subtracting Eqs. (12.58) from (12.57), we obtain

$$\dot{\mathbf{x}} - \dot{\hat{\mathbf{x}}} = \mathbf{A}(\mathbf{x} - \hat{\mathbf{x}}) \tag{12.59a}$$

$$y - \hat{y} = \mathbf{C}(\mathbf{x} - \hat{\mathbf{x}}) \tag{12.59b}$$

Thus, the dynamics of the difference between the actual and estimated states is
unforced, and if the plant is stable, this difference, due to differences in initial state
vectors, approaches zero. However, the speed of convergence between the actual state

and the estimated state is the same as the transient response of the plant since the characteristic equation for (12.59a) is the same as for (12.57a). Since the convergence is too slow, we seek a way to speed up the observer and make its response time much faster than that of the controlled closed-loop system, so that, effectively, the controller will receive the estimated states instantaneously.

To increase the speed of convergence between the actual and estimated states, we use feedback, shown conceptually in Figure 12.11(b) and in more detail in Figure 12.11(c). The error between the outputs of the plant and the observer is fed back to the derivatives of the observer's states. The system corrects to drive this error to zero. With feedback we can design a desired transient response into the observer that is much quicker than that of the plant or controlled closed-loop system.

When we implemented the controller, we found that the phase-variable or controller canonical form yielded an easy solution for the controller gains. In designing an observer, it is the observer canonical form that yields the easy solution for the observer gains. Figure 12.12(a) shows an example of a third-order plant represented in

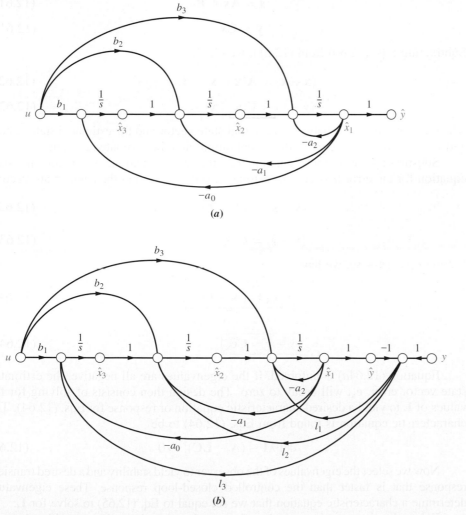

FIGURE 12.12 Third-order observer in observer canonical form: **a.** before the addition of feedback; **b.** after the addition of feedback

observer canonical form. In Figure 12.12(*b*) the plant is configured as an observer with the addition of feedback, as previously described.

The design of the observer is separate from the design of the controller. Similar to the design of the controller vector, **K**, the design of the observer consists of evaluating the constant vector, **L**, so that the transient response of the observer is faster than the response of the controlled loop in order to yield a rapidly updated estimate of the state vector. We now derive the design methodology.

We will first find the state equations for the error between the actual state vector and the estimated state vector, $(\mathbf{x} - \hat{\mathbf{x}})$. Then we will find the characteristic equation for the error system and evaluate the required **L** to meet a rapid transient response for the observer.

Writing the state equations of the observer from Figure 12.11(*c*), we have

$$\dot{\hat{\mathbf{x}}} = \mathbf{A}\hat{\mathbf{x}} + \mathbf{B}u + \mathbf{L}(y - \hat{y}) \tag{12.60a}$$

$$\hat{y} = \mathbf{C}\hat{\mathbf{x}} \tag{12.60b}$$

But the state equations for the plant are

$$\dot{\mathbf{x}} = \mathbf{A}\mathbf{x} + \mathbf{B}u \tag{12.61a}$$

$$y = \mathbf{C}\mathbf{x} \tag{12.61b}$$

Subtracting Eqs. (12.60) from (12.61), we obtain

$$(\dot{\mathbf{x}} - \dot{\hat{\mathbf{x}}}) = \mathbf{A}(\mathbf{x} - \hat{\mathbf{x}}) - \mathbf{L}(y - \hat{y}) \tag{12.62a}$$

$$(y - \hat{y}) = \mathbf{C}(\mathbf{x} - \hat{\mathbf{x}}) \tag{12.62b}$$

where $\mathbf{x} - \hat{\mathbf{x}}$ is the error between the actual state vector and the estimated state vector, and $y - \hat{y}$ is the error between the actual output and the estimated out-put.

Substituting the output equation into the state equation, we obtain the state equation for the error between the estimated state vector and the actual state vector:

$$(\dot{\mathbf{x}} - \dot{\hat{\mathbf{x}}}) = (\mathbf{A} - \mathbf{L}\mathbf{C})(\mathbf{x} - \hat{\mathbf{x}}) \tag{12.63a}$$

$$(y - \hat{y}) = \mathbf{C}(\mathbf{x} - \hat{\mathbf{x}}) \tag{12.63b}$$

Letting $\mathbf{e_x} = (\mathbf{x} - \hat{\mathbf{x}})$, we have

$$\boxed{\dot{\mathbf{e}}_\mathbf{x} = (\mathbf{A} - \mathbf{L}\mathbf{C})\mathbf{e_x}} \tag{12.64a}$$

$$\boxed{y - \hat{y} = \mathbf{C}\mathbf{e_x}} \tag{12.64b}$$

Equation (12.64*a*) is unforced. If the eigenvalues are all negative, the estimated state vector error, $\mathbf{e_x}$, will decay to zero. The design then consists of solving for the values of **L** to yield a desired characteristic equation or response for Eqs. (12.64). The characteristic equation is found from Eqs. (12.64) to be

$$\det[\lambda\mathbf{I} - (\mathbf{A} - \mathbf{L}\mathbf{C})] = 0 \tag{12.65}$$

Now we select the eigenvalues of the observer to yield stability and a desired transient response that is faster than the controlled closed-loop response. These eigenvalues determine a characteristic equation that we set equal to Eq. (12.65) to solve for **L**.

Let us demonstrate the procedure for an *n*th-order plant represented in observer canonical form. We first evaluate $\mathbf{A} - \mathbf{L}\mathbf{C}$. The form of **A**, **L**, and **C** can be derived by extrapolating the form of these matrices from a third-order plant, which you can derive from Figure 12.12. Thus,

$$
\mathbf{A} - \mathbf{LC} = \begin{bmatrix} -a_{n-1} & 1 & 0 & 0 & \cdots & 0 \\ -a_{n-2} & 0 & 1 & 0 & \cdots & 0 \\ \vdots & \vdots & \vdots & \vdots & \vdots & \vdots \\ -a_1 & 0 & 0 & 0 & \cdots & 1 \\ -a_0 & 0 & 0 & 0 & \cdots & 0 \end{bmatrix} - \begin{bmatrix} l_1 \\ l_2 \\ \vdots \\ l_{n-1} \\ l_n \end{bmatrix} \begin{bmatrix} 1 & 0 & 0 & 0 & \cdots & 0 \end{bmatrix}
$$

$$
= \begin{bmatrix} -(a_{n-1}+l_1) & 1 & 0 & 0 & \cdots & 0 \\ -(a_{n-2}+l_2) & 0 & 1 & 0 & \cdots & 0 \\ \vdots & & \vdots & \vdots & \vdots & \vdots \\ -(a_1+l_{n-1}) & 0 & 0 & 0 & \cdots & 1 \\ -(a_0+l_n) & 0 & 0 & 0 & \cdots & 0 \end{bmatrix} \tag{12.66}
$$

The characteristic equation for $\mathbf{A} - \mathbf{LC}$ is

$$
s^n + (a_{n-1}+l_1)s^{n-1} + (a_{n-2}+l_2)s^{n-2} + \cdots + (a_1+l_{n-1})s
$$
$$
+ (a_0+l_n) = 0 \tag{12.67}
$$

Notice the relationship between Eq. (12.67) and the characteristic equation, $\det(s\mathbf{I} - \mathbf{A}) = 0$, for the plant, which is

$$
s^n + a_{n-1}s^{n-1} + a_{n-2}s^{n-2} + \cdots + a_1 s + a_0 = 0 \tag{12.68}
$$

Thus, if desired, Eq. (12.67) can be written by inspection if the plant is represented in observer canonical form. We now equate Eq. (12.67) with the desired closed-loop observer characteristic equation, which is chosen on the basis of a desired transient response. Assume the desired characteristic equation is

$$
s^n + d_{n-1}s^{n-1} + d_{n-2}s^{n-2} + \cdots + d_1 s + d_0 = 0 \tag{12.69}
$$

We can now solve for the l_i's by equating the coefficients of Eqs. (12.67) and (12.69):

$$
l_i = d_{n-i} - a_{n-i} \quad i = 1, 2, \ldots, n \tag{12.70}
$$

Let us demonstrate the design of an observer using the observer canonical form. In subsequent sections we will show how to design the observer for other than observer canonical form.

EXAMPLE 12.5

Observer design for observer canonical form

Problem: Design an observer for the plant

$$
G(s) = \frac{(s+4)}{(s+1)(s+2)(s+5)} = \frac{s+4}{s^3 + 8s^2 + 17s + 10} \tag{12.71}
$$

which is represented in observer canonical form. The observer will respond 10 times faster than the controlled loop designed in Example 12.4.

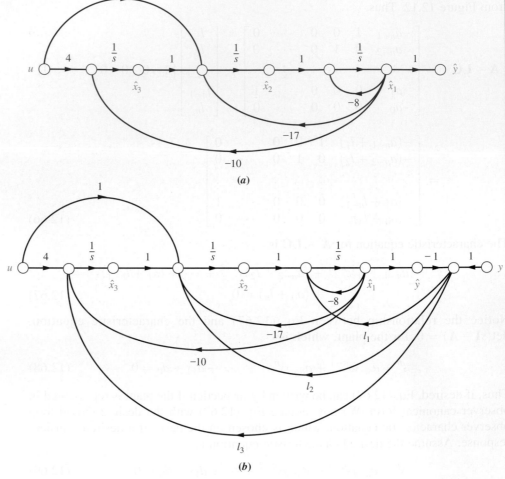

FIGURE 12.13 **a.** Signal-flow graph of a system using observer canonical form variables; **b.** additional feedback to create observer

SOLUTION:

1. First represent the estimated plant in observer canonical form. The result is shown in Figure 12.13(a).

2. Now form the difference between the plant's actual output, y, and the observer's estimated output, ŷ, and add the feedback paths from this difference to the derivative of each state variable. The result is shown in Figure 12.13(b).

3. Next find the characteristic polynomial. The state equations for the estimated plant shown in Figure 12.13(a) are

$$\dot{\mathbf{x}} = \mathbf{A}\hat{\mathbf{x}} + \mathbf{B}u = \begin{bmatrix} -8 & 1 & 0 \\ -17 & 0 & 1 \\ -10 & 0 & 0 \end{bmatrix} \hat{\mathbf{x}} + \begin{bmatrix} 0 \\ 1 \\ 4 \end{bmatrix} u \qquad (12.72a)$$

$$\hat{y} = \mathbf{C}\hat{\mathbf{x}} = \begin{bmatrix} 1 & 0 & 0 \end{bmatrix}\hat{\mathbf{x}} \qquad (12.72b)$$

From Eqs. (12.64) and (12.66), the observer error is

$$\dot{\mathbf{e}}_\mathbf{x} = (\mathbf{A} - \mathbf{LC})\mathbf{e}_\mathbf{x} = \begin{bmatrix} -(8 + l_1) & 1 & 0 \\ -(17 + l_2) & 0 & 1 \\ -(10 + l_3) & 0 & 0 \end{bmatrix} \mathbf{e}_\mathbf{x} \tag{12.73}$$

Using Eq. (12.65), we obtain the characteristic polynomial

$$s^3 + (8 + l_1)s^2 + (17 + l_2)s + (10 + l_3) \tag{12.74}$$

4. Now evaluate the desired polynomial, set the coefficients equal to those of Eq. (12.74), and solve for the gains, l_i. From Eq. (12.50), the closed-loop controlled system has dominant second-order poles at $-1 \pm j2$. To make our observer 10 times faster, we design the observer poles to be at $-10 \pm j20$. We select the third pole to be 10 times the real part of the dominant second-order poles, or -100. Hence, the desired characteristic polynomial is

$$(s + 100)(s^2 + 20s + 500) = s^3 + 120s^2 + 2500s + 50,000 \tag{12.75}$$

Equating Eqs. (12.74) and (12.75), we find $l_1 = 112$, $l_2 = 2483$, and $l_3 = 49,990$.

A simulation of the observer with an input of $r(t) = 100t$ is shown in Figure 12.14. The initial conditions of the plant were all zero, and the initial condition of $\hat{x}_1$ was 0.5.

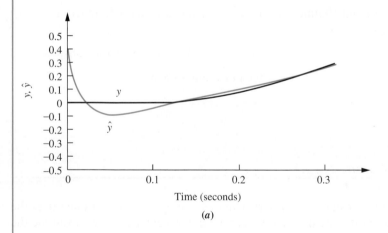

(a)

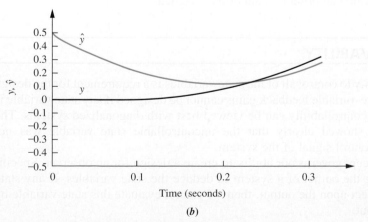

(b)

FIGURE 12.14 Simulation showing response of observer: **a.** closed-loop; **b.** open-loop with observer gains disconnected

MATLAB

Since the dominant pole of the observer is $-10 \pm j20$, the expected settling time should be about 0.4 second. It is interesting to note the slower response in Figure 12.14(b), where the observer gains are disconnected, and the observer is simply a copy of the plant with a different initial condition.

Students who are using MATLAB should now run ch12p4 in Appendix B. You will learn how to use MATLAB to design an observer using pole placement. This exercise solves Example 12.5 using MATLAB.

SKILL-ASSESSMENT EXERCISE 12.4

TryIt 12.3

Use MATLAB, the Control System Toolbox, and the following statements to solve Skill-Assessment Exercise 12.4.

```
A=[-24  1  0
   -191  0  1
   -504  0  0]
C=[1  0  0]
pos=20
Ts=2
z=(-log(pos/100))/...
(sqrt(pi^2+...
log(pos/100)^2));
wn=4/(z*Ts);
r=roots([1,2*z*wn,...
wn^2]);
poles=10*[r' 10*...
real(r(1))]
l=acker(A',C',poles)'
```

Problem: Design an observer for the plant

WileyPLUS

Control Solutions

$$G(s) = \frac{(s+6)}{(s+7)(s+8)(s+9)}$$

whose estimated plant is represented in state space in observer canonical form as

$$\dot{\hat{\mathbf{x}}} = \mathbf{A}\hat{\mathbf{x}} + \mathbf{B}u = \begin{bmatrix} -24 & 1 & 0 \\ -191 & 0 & 1 \\ -504 & 0 & 0 \end{bmatrix} \hat{\mathbf{x}} + \begin{bmatrix} 0 \\ 1 \\ 6 \end{bmatrix} u$$

$$\hat{y} = \mathbf{C}\hat{\mathbf{x}} = \begin{bmatrix} 1 & 0 & 0 \end{bmatrix}\hat{\mathbf{x}}$$

The observer will respond 10 times faster than the controlled loop designed in Skill-Assessment Exercise 12.3.

ANSWER: $L = \begin{bmatrix} 216 & 9730 & 383,696 \end{bmatrix}^{\text{T}}$, where T signifies vector transpose

The complete solution is located at www.wiley.com/college/nise.

In this section we designed an observer in observer canonical form that uses the output of a system to estimate the state variables. In the next section we examine the conditions under which an observer cannot be designed.

12.6 OBSERVABILITY

Recall that the ability to control all of the state variables is a requirement for the design of a controller. State-variable feedback gains cannot be designed if any state variable is uncontrollable. Uncontrollability can be viewed best with diagonalized systems. The signal-flow graph showed clearly that the uncontrollable state variable was not connected to the control signal of the system.

A similar concept governs our ability to create a design for an observer. Specifically, we are using the output of a system to deduce the state variables. If any state variable has no effect upon the output, then we cannot evaluate this state variable by observing the output.

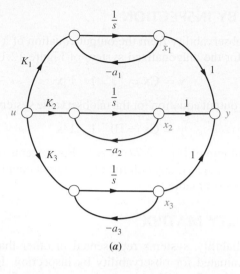

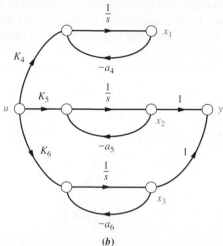

FIGURE 12.15   Comparison of **a.** observable and **b.** unobservable systems

The ability to observe a state variable from the output is best seen from the diagonalized system. Figure 12.15(a) shows a system where each state variable can be observed at the output since each is connected to the output. Figure 12.15(b) is an example of a system where all state variables cannot be observed at the output. Here x_1 is not connected to the output and could not be estimated from a measurement of the output. We now make the following definition based upon the previous discussion:

> If the initial-state vector, $\mathbf{x}(t_0)$, can be found from $u(t)$ and $y(t)$ measured over a finite interval of time from t_0, the system is said to be *observable;* otherwise the system is said to be *unobservable.*

Simply stated, observability is the ability to deduce the state variables from a knowledge of the input, $u(t)$, and the output, $y(t)$. Pole placement for an observer is a viable design technique only for systems that are observable. This section shows how to determine, a priori, whether or not pole placement is a viable design technique for an observer.

OBSERVABILITY BY INSPECTION

We can also explore observability from the output equation of a diagonalized system. The output equation for the diagonalized system of Figure 12.15(a) is

$$y = \mathbf{Cx} = [1 \quad 1 \quad 1]\mathbf{x} \tag{12.76}$$

On the other hand, the output equation for the unobservable system of Figure 12.15(b) is

$$y = \mathbf{Cx} = [0 \quad 1 \quad 1]\mathbf{x} \tag{12.77}$$

Notice that the first column of Eq. (12.77) is zero. For systems represented in parallel form with distinct eigenvalues, if any column of the output coupling matrix is zero, the diagonal system is not observable.

THE OBSERVABILITY MATRIX

Again, as for controllability, systems represented in other than diagonalized form cannot be reliably evaluated for observability by inspection. In order to determine observability for systems under any representation or choice of state variables, a matrix can be derived that must have a particular property if all state variables are to be observed at the output. We now state the requirements for observability, including the form, property, and name of this matrix.

An nth-order plant whose state and output equations are, respectively,

$$\dot{\mathbf{x}} = \mathbf{Ax} + \mathbf{Bu} \tag{12.78a}$$

$$\mathbf{y} = \mathbf{Cx} \tag{12.78b}$$

is completely observable[6] if the matrix

$$\mathbf{O_M} = \begin{bmatrix} \mathbf{C} \\ \mathbf{CA} \\ \vdots \\ \mathbf{CA}^{n-1} \end{bmatrix} \tag{12.79}$$

is of rank n, where $\mathbf{O_M}$ is called the *observability matrix*.[7]

The following two examples illustrate the use of the observability matrix.

EXAMPLE 12.6

Observability via the observability matrix

Problem: Determine if the system of Figure 12.16 is observable.

SOLUTION: The state and output equations for the system are

$$\dot{\mathbf{x}} = \mathbf{Ax} + \mathbf{B}u = \begin{bmatrix} 0 & 1 & 0 \\ 0 & 0 & 1 \\ -4 & -3 & -2 \end{bmatrix}\mathbf{x} + \begin{bmatrix} 0 \\ 0 \\ 1 \end{bmatrix}u \tag{12.80a}$$

$$y = \mathbf{Cx} = [0 \quad 5 \quad 1]\mathbf{x} \tag{12.80b}$$

---

[6] *Completely observable* means that all state variables are observable. This textbook uses *observable* to mean *completely observable*.

[7] See *Ogata (1990: 706–708)* for a derivation.

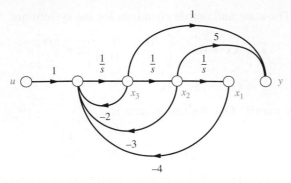

FIGURE 12.16 System of Example 12.6

Thus, the observability matrix, $\mathbf{O_M}$, is

$$\mathbf{O_M} = \begin{bmatrix} \mathbf{C} \\ \mathbf{CA} \\ \mathbf{CA}^2 \end{bmatrix} = \begin{bmatrix} 0 & 5 & 1 \\ -4 & -3 & 3 \\ -12 & -13 & -9 \end{bmatrix} \tag{12.81}$$

Since the determinant of $\mathbf{O_M}$ equals -344, $\mathbf{O_M}$ is of full rank equal to 3. The system is thus observable.

You might have been misled and concluded by inspection that the system is unobservable because the state variable x_1 is not fed *directly* to the output. Remember that conclusions about observability by inspection are valid only for diagonalized systems that have distinct eigenvalues.

Students who are using MATLAB should now run ch12p5 in Appendix B. You will learn how to use MATLAB to test a system for observability. This exercise solves Example 12.6 using MATLAB.

MATLAB

<hr />

EXAMPLE 12.7

Unobservability via the observability matrix

Problem: Determine whether the system of Figure 12.17 is observable.

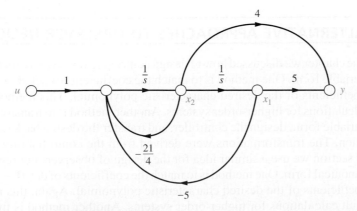

FIGURE 12.17 System of Example 12.7

SOLUTION: The state and output equations for the system are

$$\dot{\mathbf{x}} = \mathbf{A}\mathbf{x} + \mathbf{B}u = \begin{bmatrix} 0 & 1 \\ -5 & -21/4 \end{bmatrix}\mathbf{x} + \begin{bmatrix} 0 \\ 1 \end{bmatrix}u \tag{12.82a}$$

$$y = \mathbf{C}\mathbf{x} = \begin{bmatrix} 5 & 4 \end{bmatrix}\mathbf{x} \tag{12.82b}$$

The observability matrix, $\mathbf{O}_M$, for this system is

$$\mathbf{O}_M = \begin{bmatrix} \mathbf{C} \\ \mathbf{CA} \end{bmatrix} = \begin{bmatrix} 5 & 4 \\ -20 & -16 \end{bmatrix} \tag{12.83}$$

The determinant for this observability matrix equals 0. Thus, the observability matrix does not have full rank, and the system is not observable.

Again, you might conclude by inspection that the system is observable because all states feed the output. Remember that observability by inspection is valid only for a diagonalized representation of a system with distinct eigenvalues.

SKILL-ASSESSMENT EXERCISE 12.5

TryIt 12.4

Use MATLAB, the Control System Toolbox, and the following statements to solve Skill-Assessment Exercise 12.5.

```
A=[-2 -1 -3
    0 -2  1
   -7 -8 -9]
C=[4 6 8]
Om=obsv(A,C)
Rank=rank(Om)
```

Problem: Determine whether the system

$$\dot{\mathbf{x}} = \mathbf{A}\mathbf{x} + \mathbf{B}u = \begin{bmatrix} -2 & -1 & -3 \\ 0 & -2 & 1 \\ -7 & -8 & -9 \end{bmatrix}\mathbf{x} + \begin{bmatrix} 2 \\ 1 \\ 2 \end{bmatrix}u$$

$$y = \mathbf{C}\mathbf{x} = \begin{bmatrix} 4 & 6 & 8 \end{bmatrix}\mathbf{x}$$

is observable.

ANSWER: Observable

The complete solution is located at www.wiley.com/college/nise.

Now that we have discussed observability and the observability matrix, we are ready to talk about the design of an observer for a plant not represented in observer canonical form.

12.7 ALTERNATIVE APPROACHES TO OBSERVER DESIGN

Earlier in the chapter we discussed how to design controllers for systems not represented in phase-variable form. One method is to match the coefficients of $\det[s\mathbf{I} - (\mathbf{A} - \mathbf{BK})]$ with the coefficients of the desired characteristic polynomial. This method can yield difficult calculations for higher-order systems. Another method is to transform the plant to phase-variable form, design the controller, and transfer the design back to its original representation. The transformations were derived from the controllability matrix.

In this section we use a similar idea for the design of observers not represented in observer canonical form. One method is to match the coefficients of $\det[s\mathbf{I} - (\mathbf{A} - \mathbf{LC})]$ with the coefficients of the desired characteristic polynomial. Again, this method can yield difficult calculations for higher-order systems. Another method is first to transform the plant to observer canonical form so that the design equations are simple, then perform the design in observer canonical form, and finally transform the design back to the original representation.

Let us pursue this second method. First we will derive the transformation between a system representation and its representation in observer canonical form. Assume a plant not represented in observer canonical form,

$$\dot{\mathbf{z}} = \mathbf{Az} + \mathbf{B}u \tag{12.84a}$$

$$y = \mathbf{Cz} \tag{12.84b}$$

whose observability matrix is

$$\mathbf{O_{Mz}} = \begin{bmatrix} \mathbf{C} \\ \mathbf{CA} \\ \mathbf{CA}^2 \\ \vdots \\ \mathbf{CA}^{n-2} \\ \mathbf{CA}^{n-1} \end{bmatrix} \tag{12.85}$$

Now assume that the system can be transformed to the observer canonical form, $\mathbf{x}$, with the transformation

$$\mathbf{z} = \mathbf{Px} \tag{12.86}$$

Substituting Eq. (12.86) into Eq. (12.84) and premultiplying the state equation by $\mathbf{P}^{-1}$, we find that the state equations in observer canonical form are

$$\dot{\mathbf{x}} = \mathbf{P}^{-1}\mathbf{APx} + \mathbf{P}^{-1}\mathbf{B}u \tag{12.87a}$$

$$y = \mathbf{CPx} \tag{12.87b}$$

whose observability matrix, $\mathbf{O_{Mx}}$, is

$$\mathbf{O_{Mx}} = \begin{bmatrix} \mathbf{CP} \\ \mathbf{CP}(\mathbf{P}^{-1}\mathbf{AP}) \\ \mathbf{CP}(\mathbf{P}^{-1}\mathbf{AP})(\mathbf{P}^{-1}\mathbf{AP}) \\ \vdots \\ \mathbf{CP}(\mathbf{P}^{-1}\mathbf{AP})(\mathbf{P}^{-1}\mathbf{AP}) \quad \cdots \quad (\mathbf{P}^{-1}\mathbf{AP}) \end{bmatrix} = \begin{bmatrix} \mathbf{C} \\ \mathbf{CA} \\ \mathbf{CA}^2 \\ \vdots \\ \mathbf{CA}^{n-1} \end{bmatrix} P \tag{12.88}$$

Substituting Eq. (12.85) into (12.88) and solving for $\mathbf{P}$, we obtain

$$\mathbf{P} = \mathbf{O_{Mz}}^{-1}\, \mathbf{O_{Mx}} \tag{12.89}$$

Thus, the transformation, $\mathbf{P}$, can be found from the two observability matrices.

After transforming the plant to observer canonical form, we design the feedback gains, $\mathbf{L_x}$, as in Section 12.5. Using the matrices from Eq. (12.87) and the form suggested by Eq. (12.64), we have

$$\dot{\mathbf{e}}_\mathbf{x} = (\mathbf{P}^{-1}\mathbf{AP} - \mathbf{L_x}\mathbf{CP})\mathbf{e}_\mathbf{x} \tag{12.90a}$$

$$y - \hat{y} = \mathbf{CP}\mathbf{e}_\mathbf{x} \tag{12.90b}$$

Since $\mathbf{x} = \mathbf{P}^{-1}\mathbf{z}$, and $\hat{\mathbf{x}} = \mathbf{P}^{-1}\hat{\mathbf{z}}$, then $\mathbf{e}_\mathbf{x} = \mathbf{x} - \hat{\mathbf{x}} = \mathbf{P}^{-1}\mathbf{e}_\mathbf{z}$. Substituting $\mathbf{e}_\mathbf{x} = \mathbf{P}^{-1}\mathbf{e}_\mathbf{z}$ into Eqs. (12.90) transforms Eqs. (12.90) back to the original representation. The result is

$$\dot{\mathbf{e}}_\mathbf{z} = (\mathbf{A} - \mathbf{PL_x}\mathbf{C})\mathbf{e}_\mathbf{z} \tag{12.91a}$$

$$y - \hat{y} = \mathbf{Ce}_\mathbf{z} \tag{12.91b}$$

Comparing Eq. (12.91a) to (12.64a), we see that the observer gain vector is

$$\mathbf{L_z} = \mathbf{PL_x} \tag{12.92}$$

We now demonstrate the design of an observer for a plant not represented in observer canonical form. The first example uses transformations to and from observer canonical form. The second example matches coefficients without the transformation. This method, however, can become difficult if the system order is high.

■ EXAMPLE 12.8 ■

Observer design by transformation

Problem: Design an observer for the plant

$$G(s) = \frac{1}{(s+1)(s+2)(s+5)} \tag{12.93}$$

represented in cascade form. The closed-loop performance of the observer is governed by the characteristic polynomial used in Example 12.5: $s^3 + 120s^2 + 2500s + 50{,}000$.

SOLUTION: First represent the plant in its original cascade form.

$$\dot{\mathbf{z}} = \mathbf{Az} + \mathbf{B}u = \begin{bmatrix} -5 & 1 & 0 \\ 0 & -2 & 1 \\ 0 & 0 & -1 \end{bmatrix} \mathbf{z} + \begin{bmatrix} 0 \\ 0 \\ 1 \end{bmatrix} u \tag{12.94a}$$

$$y = \mathbf{Cz} = \begin{bmatrix} 1 & 0 & 0 \end{bmatrix} \mathbf{z} \tag{12.94b}$$

The observability matrix, $\mathbf{O_{Mz}}$, is

$$\mathbf{O_{Mz}} = \begin{bmatrix} \mathbf{C} \\ \mathbf{CA} \\ \mathbf{CA}^2 \end{bmatrix} = \begin{bmatrix} 1 & 0 & 0 \\ -5 & 1 & 0 \\ 25 & -7 & 1 \end{bmatrix} \tag{12.95}$$

whose determinant equals 1. Hence, the plant is observable.

The characteristic equation for the plant is

$$\det(s\mathbf{I} - \mathbf{A}) = s^3 + 8s^2 + 17s + 10 = 0 \tag{12.96}$$

We can use the coefficients of this characteristic polynomial to form the observer canonical form:

$$\dot{\mathbf{x}} = \mathbf{A_x x} + \mathbf{B_x} u \tag{12.97a}$$

$$y = \mathbf{C_x x} \tag{12.97b}$$

where

$$\mathbf{A_x} = \begin{bmatrix} -8 & 1 & 0 \\ -17 & 0 & 1 \\ -10 & 0 & 0 \end{bmatrix}; \quad \mathbf{C_x} = \begin{bmatrix} 1 & 0 & 0 \end{bmatrix} \tag{12.98}$$

The observability matrix for the observer canonical form is

$$\mathbf{O_{Mx}} = \begin{bmatrix} \mathbf{C_x} \\ \mathbf{C_x A_x} \\ \mathbf{C_x A_x}^2 \end{bmatrix} = \begin{bmatrix} 1 & 0 & 0 \\ -8 & 1 & 0 \\ 47 & -8 & 1 \end{bmatrix} \tag{12.99}$$

We now design the observer for the observer canonical form. First form $(\mathbf{A_x} - \mathbf{L_x C_x})$,

$$\mathbf{A_x} - \mathbf{L_x C_x} = \begin{bmatrix} -8 & 1 & 0 \\ -17 & 0 & 1 \\ -10 & 0 & 0 \end{bmatrix} - \begin{bmatrix} l_1 \\ l_2 \\ l_3 \end{bmatrix} \begin{bmatrix} 1 & 0 & 0 \end{bmatrix} = \begin{bmatrix} -(8+l_1) & 1 & 0 \\ -(17+l_2) & 0 & 1 \\ -(10+l_3) & 0 & 0 \end{bmatrix}$$

$$(12.100)$$

whose characteristic polynomial is

$$\det[s\mathbf{I} - (\mathbf{A_x} - \mathbf{L_x C_x})] = s^3 + (8+l_1)s^2 + (17+l_2)s + (10+l_3) \qquad (12.101)$$

Equating this polynomial to the desired closed-loop observer characteristic equation, $s^3 + 120s^2 + 2500s + 50{,}000$, we find

$$\mathbf{L_x} = \begin{bmatrix} 112 \\ 2483 \\ 49{,}990 \end{bmatrix} \qquad (12.102)$$

Now transform the design back to the original representation. Using Eq. (12.89), the transformation matrix is

$$\mathbf{P} = \mathbf{O_{Mz}}^{-1}\mathbf{O_{Mx}} = \begin{bmatrix} 1 & 0 & 0 \\ -3 & 1 & 0 \\ 1 & -1 & 1 \end{bmatrix} \qquad (12.103)$$

Transforming $\mathbf{L_x}$ to the original representation, we obtain

$$\mathbf{L_z} = \mathbf{P L_x} = \begin{bmatrix} 112 \\ 2147 \\ 47{,}619 \end{bmatrix} \qquad (12.104)$$

The final configuration is shown in Figure 12.18.

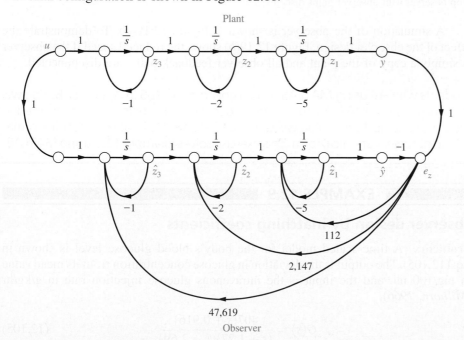

FIGURE 12.18 Observer design

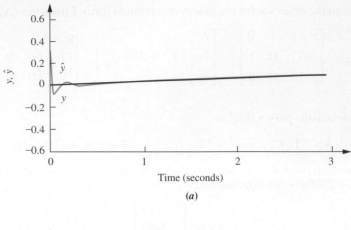

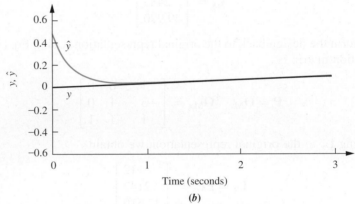

FIGURE 12.19 Observer design step response simulation: **a.** closed-loop observer; **b.** open-loop observer with observer gains disconnected

A simulation of the observer is shown in Figure 12.19(*a*). To demonstrate the effect of the observer design, Figure 12.19(*b*) shows the reduced speed if the observer is simply a copy of the plant and all observer feedback paths are disconnected.

Students who are using MATLAB should now run ch12p6 in Appendix B. You will learn how to use MATLAB to design an observer for a plant not represented in observer canonical form. You will see that MATLAB does not require transformation to observer canonical form. This exercise solves Example 12.8 using MATLAB.

EXAMPLE 12.9

Observer design by matching coefficients

Problem: A time-scaled model for the body's blood glucose level is shown in Eq. (12.105). The output is the deviation in glucose concentration from its mean value in mg/100 ml, and the input is the intravenous glucose injection rate in g/kg/hr (*Milhorn, 1966*).

$$G(s) = \frac{407(s + 0.916)}{(s + 1.27)(s + 2.69)} \tag{12.105}$$

Design an observer for the phase variables with a transient response described by $\zeta =$ 0.7 and $\omega_n = 100$.

SOLUTION: We can first model the plant in phase-variable form. The result is shown in Figure 12.20(a) .

For the plant,

$$\mathbf{A} = \begin{bmatrix} 0 & 1 \\ -3.42 & -3.96 \end{bmatrix}; \quad \mathbf{C} = \begin{bmatrix} 372.81 & 407 \end{bmatrix} \qquad (12.106)$$

Calculation of the observability matrix, $\mathbf{O_M} = \begin{bmatrix} \mathbf{C} & \mathbf{CA} \end{bmatrix}^T$, shows that the plant is observable and we can proceed with the design. Next find the characteristic equation of the observer. First we have

$$\begin{aligned} \mathbf{A} - \mathbf{LC} &= \begin{bmatrix} 0 & 1 \\ -3.42 & -3.96 \end{bmatrix} - \begin{bmatrix} l_1 \\ l_2 \end{bmatrix} \begin{bmatrix} 372.81 & 407 \end{bmatrix} \\ &= \begin{bmatrix} -372.81 l_1 & (1 - 407 l_1) \\ -(3.42 + 372.81 l_2) & -(3.96 + 407 l_2) \end{bmatrix} \end{aligned} \qquad (12.107)$$

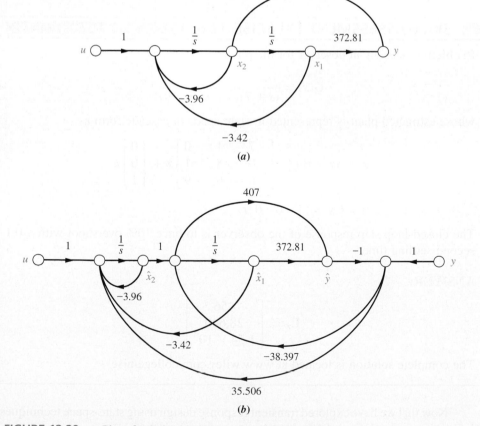

FIGURE 12.20 **a.** Plant; **b.** designed observer for Example 12.9

Now evaluate $\det[\lambda \mathbf{I} - (\mathbf{A} - \mathbf{LC})] = 0$ in order to obtain the characteristic equation:

$$
\begin{aligned}
\det[\lambda \mathbf{I} - (\mathbf{A} - \mathbf{LC})] &= \det \begin{bmatrix} (\lambda + 372.81 l_1) & -(1 - 407 l_1) \\ (3.42 + 372.81 l_2) & (\lambda + 3.96 + 407 l_2) \end{bmatrix} \\
&= \lambda^2 + (3.96 + 372.81 l_1 + 407 l_2)\lambda \\
&\quad + (3.42 + 84.39 l_1 + 372.81 l_2) \\
&= 0
\end{aligned}
\tag{12.108}
$$

From the problem statement, we want $\zeta = 0.7$ and $\omega_n = 100$. Thus,

$$
\lambda^2 + 140\lambda + 10{,}000 = 0
\tag{12.109}
$$

Comparing the coefficients of Eqs. (12.108) and (12.109), we find the values of l_1 and l_2 to be -38.397 and 35.506, respectively. Using Eq. (12.60), where

$$
\mathbf{A} = \begin{bmatrix} 0 & 1 \\ -3.42 & -3.96 \end{bmatrix}; \quad \mathbf{B} = \begin{bmatrix} 0 \\ 1 \end{bmatrix}; \quad \mathbf{C} = [372.81 \quad 407];
$$

$$
\mathbf{L} = \begin{bmatrix} -38.397 \\ 35.506 \end{bmatrix}
\tag{12.110}
$$

the observer is implemented and shown in Figure 12.20(b).

SKILL-ASSESSMENT EXERCISE 12.6

WileyPLUS
Control Solutions

Problem: Design an observer for the plant

$$
G(s) = \frac{1}{(s+7)(s+8)(s+9)}
$$

whose estimated plant is represented in state space in cascade form as

$$
\dot{\hat{\mathbf{z}}} = \mathbf{A}\hat{\mathbf{z}} + \mathbf{B}u = \begin{bmatrix} -7 & 1 & 0 \\ 0 & -8 & 1 \\ 0 & 0 & -9 \end{bmatrix} \hat{\mathbf{z}} + \begin{bmatrix} 0 \\ 0 \\ 1 \end{bmatrix} u
$$

$$
\hat{y} = \mathbf{C}\hat{\mathbf{x}} = [1 \quad 0 \quad 0]\hat{\mathbf{z}}
$$

The closed-loop step response of the observer is to have 10% overshoot with a 0.1 second settling time.

ANSWER:

$$
\mathbf{L_z} = \begin{bmatrix} 456 \\ 28{,}640 \\ 1.54 \times 10^6 \end{bmatrix}
$$

The complete solution is located at www.wiley.com/college/nise.

Now that we have explored transient response design using state-space techniques, let us turn to the design of steady-state error characteristics.

12.8 STEADY-STATE ERROR DESIGN VIA INTEGRAL CONTROL

In Section 7.8 we discussed how to *analyze* systems represented in state space for steady-state error. In this section we discuss how to *design* systems represented in state space for steady-state error.

Consider Figure 12.21. The previously designed controller discussed in Section 12.2 is shown inside the dashed box. A feedback path from the output has been added to form the error, e, which is fed forward to the controlled plant via an integrator. The integrator increases the system type and reduces the previous finite error to zero. We will now derive the form of the state equations for the system of Figure 12.21 and then use that form to design a controller. Thus, we will be able to design a system for zero steady-state error for a step input as well as design the desired transient response.

An additional state variable, x_N, has been added at the output of the leftmost integrator. The error is the derivative of this variable. Now, from Figure 12.21,

$$\dot{x}_N = r - \mathbf{Cx} \tag{12.111}$$

Writing the state equations from Figure 12.21, we have

$$\dot{\mathbf{x}} = \mathbf{Ax} + \mathbf{B}u \tag{12.112a}$$

$$\dot{x}_N = -\mathbf{Cx} + r \tag{12.112b}$$

$$y = \mathbf{Cx} \tag{12.112c}$$

Eqs. (12.112) can be written as augmented vectors and matrices. Hence,

$$\begin{bmatrix} \dot{\mathbf{x}} \\ \dot{x}_N \end{bmatrix} = \begin{bmatrix} \mathbf{A} & \mathbf{0} \\ -\mathbf{C} & 0 \end{bmatrix} \begin{bmatrix} \mathbf{x} \\ x_N \end{bmatrix} + \begin{bmatrix} \mathbf{B} \\ 0 \end{bmatrix} u + \begin{bmatrix} \mathbf{0} \\ 1 \end{bmatrix} r \tag{12.113a}$$

$$y = \begin{bmatrix} \mathbf{C} & 0 \end{bmatrix} \begin{bmatrix} \mathbf{x} \\ x_N \end{bmatrix} \tag{12.113b}$$

But

$$u = -\mathbf{Kx} + K_e x_N = -\begin{bmatrix} \mathbf{K} & -K_e \end{bmatrix} \begin{bmatrix} \mathbf{x} \\ x_N \end{bmatrix} \tag{12.114}$$

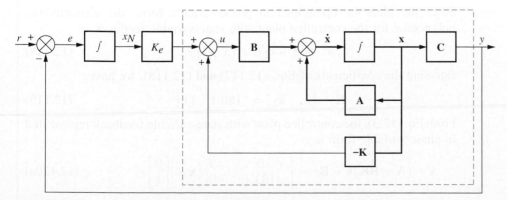

FIGURE 12.21   Integral control for steady-state error design

Substituting Eq. (12.114) into (12.113a) and simplifying, we obtain

$$\begin{bmatrix} \dot{\mathbf{x}} \\ \dot{x}_N \end{bmatrix} = \begin{bmatrix} (\mathbf{A} - \mathbf{BK}) & \mathbf{B}K_e \\ -\mathbf{C} & 0 \end{bmatrix} \begin{bmatrix} \mathbf{x} \\ x_N \end{bmatrix} + \begin{bmatrix} 0 \\ 1 \end{bmatrix} r \qquad (12.115a)$$

$$y = \begin{bmatrix} \mathbf{C} & 0 \end{bmatrix} \begin{bmatrix} \mathbf{x} \\ x_N \end{bmatrix} \qquad (12.115b)$$

Thus, the system type has been increased, and we can use the characteristic equation associated with Eq. (12.115a) to design $\mathbf{K}$ and K_e to yield the desired transient response. Realize, we now have an additional pole to place. The effect on the transient response of any closed-loop zeros in the final design must also be taken into consideration. One possible assumption is that the closed-loop zeros will be the same as those of the open-loop plant. This assumption, which of course must be checked, suggests placing higher-order poles at the closed-loop zero locations. Let us demonstrate with an example.

EXAMPLE 12.10

Design of integral control

Problem: Consider the plant of Eqs. (12.116):

$$\dot{\mathbf{x}} = \begin{bmatrix} 0 & 1 \\ -3 & -5 \end{bmatrix} \mathbf{x} + \begin{bmatrix} 0 \\ 1 \end{bmatrix} u \qquad (12.116a)$$

$$y = \begin{bmatrix} 1 & 0 \end{bmatrix} \mathbf{x} \qquad (12.116b)$$

a. Design a controller without integral control to yield a 10% overshoot and a settling time of 0.5 second. Evaluate the steady-state error for a unit step input.

b. Repeat the design of (a) using integral control. Evaluate the steady-state error for a unit step input.

SOLUTION:

a. Using the requirements for settling time and percent overshoot, we find that the desired characteristic polynomial is

$$s^2 + 16s + 183.1 \qquad (12.117)$$

Since the plant is represented in phase-variable form, the characteristic polynomial for the controlled plant with state-variable feedback is

$$s^2 + (5 + k_2)s + (3 + k_1) \qquad (12.118)$$

Equating the coefficients of Eqs. (12.117) and (12.118), we have

$$\mathbf{K} = \begin{bmatrix} k_1 & k_2 \end{bmatrix} = \begin{bmatrix} 180.1 & 11 \end{bmatrix} \qquad (12.119)$$

From Eq. (12.3), the controlled plant with state-variable feedback represented in phase-variable form is

$$\dot{\mathbf{x}} = (\mathbf{A} - \mathbf{BK})\mathbf{x} + \mathbf{B}r = \begin{bmatrix} 0 & 1 \\ -183.1 & -16 \end{bmatrix} \mathbf{x} + \begin{bmatrix} 0 \\ 1 \end{bmatrix} r \qquad (12.120a)$$

$$y = \mathbf{Cx} = \begin{bmatrix} 1 & 0 \end{bmatrix} \mathbf{x} \qquad (12.120b)$$

Using Eq. (7.96), we find that the steady-state error for a step input is

$$e(\infty) = 1 + \mathbf{C}(\mathbf{A} - \mathbf{BK})^{-1}\mathbf{B}$$

$$= 1 + \begin{bmatrix} 1 & 0 \end{bmatrix} \begin{bmatrix} 0 & 1 \\ -183.1 & -16 \end{bmatrix}^{-1} \begin{bmatrix} 0 \\ 1 \end{bmatrix}$$

$$= 0.995 \tag{12.121}$$

b. We now use Eqs. (12.115) to represent the integral-controlled plant as follows:

$$\begin{bmatrix} \dot{x}_1 \\ \dot{x}_2 \\ \dot{x}_N \end{bmatrix} = \left(\begin{bmatrix} 0 & 1 \\ -3 & -5 \\ & -\begin{bmatrix} 1 & 0 \end{bmatrix} \end{bmatrix} - \begin{bmatrix} 0 \\ 1 \end{bmatrix} \begin{bmatrix} k_1 & k_2 \end{bmatrix} \right) \begin{bmatrix} 0 \\ 1 \\ 0 \end{bmatrix} K_e \begin{bmatrix} x_1 \\ x_2 \\ x_N \end{bmatrix} + \begin{bmatrix} 0 \\ 0 \\ 1 \end{bmatrix} r$$

$$= \begin{bmatrix} 0 & 1 & 0 \\ -(3 + k_1) & -(5 + k_2) & K_e \\ -1 & 0 & 0 \end{bmatrix} \begin{bmatrix} x_1 \\ x_2 \\ x_N \end{bmatrix} + \begin{bmatrix} 0 \\ 0 \\ 1 \end{bmatrix} r \tag{12.122a}$$

$$y = \begin{bmatrix} 1 & 0 & 0 \end{bmatrix} \begin{bmatrix} x_1 \\ x_2 \\ x_N \end{bmatrix} \tag{12.122b}$$

Using Eq. (3.73) and the plant of Eqs. (12.116), we find that the transfer function of the plant is $G(s) = 1/(s^2 + 5s + 3)$. The desired characteristic polynomial for the closed-loop integral-controlled system is shown in Eq. (12.117). Since the plant has no zeros, we assume no zeros for the closed-loop system and augment Eq. (12.117) with a third pole, $(s + 100)$, which has a real part greater than five times that of the desired dominant second-order poles. The desired third-order closed-loop system characteristic polynomial is

$$(s + 100)(s^2 + 16s + 183.1) = s^3 + 116s^2 + 1783.1s + 18{,}310 \tag{12.123}$$

The characteristic polynomial for the system of Eqs. (12.122) is

$$s^3 + (5 + k_2)s^2 + (3 + k_1)s + K_e \tag{12.124}$$

Matching coefficients from Eqs. (12.123) and (12.124), we obtain

$$k_1 = 1780.1 \tag{12.125a}$$

$$k_2 = 111 \tag{12.125b}$$

$$k_e = 18{,}310 \tag{12.125c}$$

Substituting these values into Eqs. (12.122) yields this closed-loop integral-controlled system:

$$\begin{bmatrix} \dot{x}_1 \\ \dot{x}_2 \\ \dot{x}_N \end{bmatrix} - \begin{bmatrix} 0 & 1 & 0 \\ -1783.1 & -116 & 18{,}310 \\ -1 & 0 & 0 \end{bmatrix} \begin{bmatrix} x_1 \\ x_2 \\ x_N \end{bmatrix} + \begin{bmatrix} 0 \\ 0 \\ 1 \end{bmatrix} r \tag{12.126a}$$

$$y = \begin{bmatrix} 1 & 0 & 0 \end{bmatrix} \begin{bmatrix} x_1 \\ x_2 \\ x_N \end{bmatrix} \tag{12.126b}$$

In order to check our assumption for the zero, we now apply Eq. (3.73) to Eqs. (12.126) and find the closed-loop transfer function to be

$$T(s) = \frac{18{,}310}{s^3 + 116s^2 + 1783.1s + 18{,}310} \tag{12.127}$$

Since the transfer function matches our design, we have the desired transient response.

Now let us find the steady-state error for a unit step input. Applying Eq. (7.96) to Eqs. (12.126), we obtain

$$e(\infty) = 1 + \begin{bmatrix} 1 & 0 & 0 \end{bmatrix} \begin{bmatrix} 0 & 1 & 0 \\ -1783.1 & -116 & 18{,}310 \\ -1 & 0 & 0 \end{bmatrix}^{-1} \begin{bmatrix} 0 \\ 0 \\ 1 \end{bmatrix} = 0 \tag{12.128}$$

Thus, the system behaves like a Type 1 system.

■ SKILL-ASSESSMENT EXERCISE 12.7 ■

Problem: Design an integral controller for the plant

$$\dot{\mathbf{x}} = \begin{bmatrix} 0 & 1 \\ -7 & -9 \end{bmatrix} \mathbf{x} + \begin{bmatrix} 0 \\ 1 \end{bmatrix} u$$

$$y = \begin{bmatrix} 4 & 1 \end{bmatrix} \mathbf{x}$$

to yield a step response with 10% overshoot, a peak time of 2 seconds, and zero steady-state error.

ANSWER: $\mathbf{K} = \begin{bmatrix} 2.21 & -2.7 \end{bmatrix}$, $K_e = 3.79$

The complete solution is located at www.wiley.com/college/nise.

Now that we have designed controllers and observers for transient response and steady-state error, we summarize the chapter with a case study demonstrating the design process.

■ CASE STUDY ■

Design

Antenna Control: Design of Controller and Observer

In this case study we use our ongoing antenna azimuth position control system to demonstrate the combined design of a controller and an observer. We will assume that the states are not available and must be estimated from the output. The block diagram of the original system is shown on the front endpapers, Configuration 1. Arbitrarily setting the preamplifier gain to 200 and removing the existing feedback, the forward transfer function is simplified to that shown in Figure 12.22.

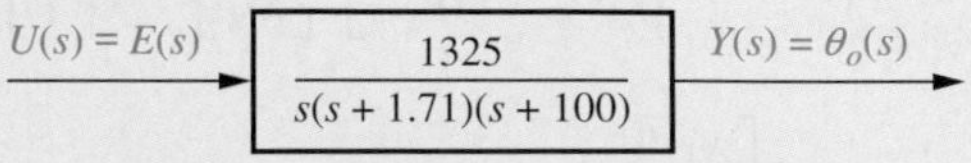

$$U(s) = E(s) \longrightarrow \boxed{\dfrac{1325}{s(s + 1.71)(s + 100)}} \longrightarrow Y(s) = \theta_o(s)$$

FIGURE 12.22   Simplified block diagram of antenna control system shown on the front endpapers (Configuration 1) with $K = 200$

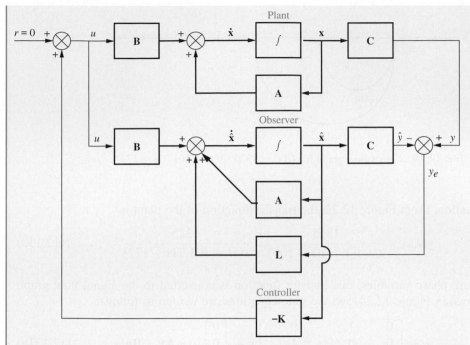

FIGURE 12.23 Conceptual state-space design configuration, showing plant, observer, and controller

The case study will specify a transient response for the system and a faster transient response for the observer. The final design configuration will consist of the plant, the observer, and the controller, as shown conceptually in Figure 12.23. The design of the observer and the controller will be separate.

Problem: Using the simplified block diagram of the plant for the antenna azimuth position control system shown in Figure 12.22, design a controller to yield a 10% overshoot and a settling time of 1 second. Place the third pole 10 times as far from the imaginary axis as the second-order dominant pair.

Assume that the state variables of the plant are not accessible and design an observer to estimate the states. The desired transient response for the observer is a 10% overshoot and a natural frequency 10 times as great as the system response above. As in the case of the controller, place the third pole 10 times as far from the imaginary axis as the observer's dominant second-order pair.

SOLUTION:

Controller Design: We first design the controller by finding the desired characteristic equation. A 10% overshoot and a settling time of 1 second yield $\zeta = 0.591$ and $\omega_n = 6.77$. Thus, the characteristic equation for the dominant poles is $s^2 + 8s + 45.8 = 0$, where the dominant poles are located at $-4 \pm j5.46$. The third pole will be 10 times as far from the imaginary axis, or at -40. Hence, the desired characteristic equation for the closed-loop system is

$$(s^2 + 8s + 45.8)(s + 40) = s^3 + 48s^2 + 365.8s + 1832 = 0 \qquad (12.129)$$

Next we find the actual characteristic equation of the closed-loop system. The first step is to model the closed-loop system in state space and then find its characteristic

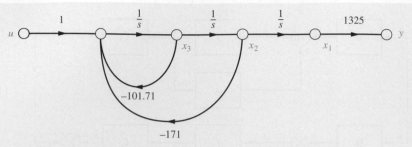

FIGURE 12.24   Signal-flow graph for $G(s) = 1325/[s(s^2 + 101.71s + 171)]$

equation. From Figure 12.22, the transfer function of the plant is

$$G(s) = \frac{1325}{s(s + 1.71)(s + 100)} = \frac{1325}{s(s^2 + 101.71s + 171)} \qquad (12.130)$$

Using phase variables, this transfer function is converted to the signal-flow graph shown in Figure 12.24, and the state equations are written as follows:

$$\dot{\mathbf{x}} = \begin{bmatrix} 0 & 1 & 0 \\ 0 & 0 & 1 \\ 0 & -171 & -101.71 \end{bmatrix} \mathbf{x} + \begin{bmatrix} 0 \\ 0 \\ 1 \end{bmatrix} u = \mathbf{Ax} + \mathbf{B}u \qquad (12.131a)$$

$$y = \begin{bmatrix} 1325 & 0 & 0 \end{bmatrix} \mathbf{x} = \mathbf{Cx} \qquad (12.131b)$$

We now pause in our design to evaluate the controllability of the system. The controllability matrix, $\mathbf{C_M}$, is

$$\mathbf{C_M} = \begin{bmatrix} \mathbf{B} & \mathbf{AB} & \mathbf{A}^2\mathbf{B} \end{bmatrix} \begin{bmatrix} 0 & 0 & 1 \\ 0 & 1 & -101.71 \\ 1 & -101.71 & 10,173.92 \end{bmatrix} \qquad (12.132)$$

The determinant of $\mathbf{C_M}$ is -1; thus, the system is controllable.

Continuing with the design of the controller, we show the controller's configuration with the feedback from all state variables in Figure 12.25. We now find the

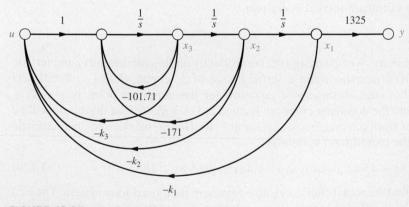

FIGURE 12.25   Plant with state-variable feedback for controller design

characteristic equation of the system of Figure 12.25. From Eq. (12.7) and Eq. (12.131*a*), the system matrix, $\mathbf{A} - \mathbf{BK}$, is

$$\mathbf{A} - \mathbf{BK} = \begin{bmatrix} 0 & 1 & 0 \\ 0 & 0 & 1 \\ -k_1 & -(171 + k_2) & -(101.71 + k_3) \end{bmatrix} \tag{12.133}$$

Thus, the closed-loop system's characteristic equation is

$$\det[s\mathbf{I} - (\mathbf{A} - \mathbf{BK})] = s^3 + (101.71 + k_3)s^2 + (171 + k_2)s + k_1 = 0 \tag{12.134}$$

Matching the coefficients of Eq. (12.129) with those of Eq. (12.134), we evaluate the k_i's as follows:

$$k_1 = 1832 \tag{12.135a}$$

$$k_2 = 194.8 \tag{12.135b}$$

$$k_3 = -53.71 \tag{12.135c}$$

Observer Design: Before designing the observer, we test the system for observability. Using the $\mathbf{A}$ and $\mathbf{C}$ matrices from Eqs. (12.131), the observability matrix, $\mathbf{O_M}$, is

$$\mathbf{O_M} = \begin{bmatrix} \mathbf{C} \\ \mathbf{CA} \\ \mathbf{CA}^2 \end{bmatrix} = \begin{bmatrix} 1325 & 0 & 0 \\ 0 & 1325 & 0 \\ 0 & 0 & 1325 \end{bmatrix} \tag{12.136}$$

The determinant of $\mathbf{O_M}$ is 1325^3. Thus, $\mathbf{O_M}$ is of rank 3, and the system is observable.

We now proceed to design the observer. Since the order of the system is not high, we will design the observer directly without first converting to observer canonical form. From Eq. (12.64*a*) we need first to find $\mathbf{A} - \mathbf{LC}$. $\mathbf{A}$ and $\mathbf{C}$ from Eqs. (12.131) along with

$$\mathbf{L} = \begin{bmatrix} l_1 \\ l_2 \\ l_3 \end{bmatrix} \tag{12.137}$$

are used to evaluate $\mathbf{A} - \mathbf{LC}$ as follows:

$$\mathbf{A} - \mathbf{LC} = \begin{bmatrix} -1325l_1 & 1 & 0 \\ -1325l_2 & 0 & 1 \\ -1325l_3 & -171 & -101.71 \end{bmatrix} \tag{12.138}$$

The characteristic equation for the observer is now evaluated as

$$\begin{aligned} \det[\lambda\mathbf{I} - (\mathbf{A} - \mathbf{LC})] = \ &\lambda^3 + (1325l_1 + 101.71)\lambda^2 \\ &+ (134{,}800l_1 + 1325l_2 + 171)\lambda \\ &+ (226{,}600l_1 + 134{,}800l_2 + 1325l_3) \\ = \ &0 \end{aligned} \tag{12.139}$$

From the problem statement, the poles of the observer are to be placed to yield a 10% overshoot and a natural frequency 10 times that of the system's dominant pair of poles. Thus, the observer's dominant poles yield $[s^2 + (2 \times 0.591 \times 67.7)s + 67.7^2] = (s^2 + 80s + 4583)$. The real part of the roots of this polynomial is -40. The third pole is then placed 10 times farther from the imaginary axis at -400. The composite characteristic equation for the observer is

$$(s^2 + 80s + 4583)(s + 400) = s^3 + 480s^2 + 36{,}580s$$
$$+ 1{,}833{,}000 = 0 \qquad (12.140)$$

Matching coefficients from Eqs. (12.139) and (12.140), we solve for the observer gains:

$$l_1 = 0.286 \qquad (12.141a)$$

$$l_2 = -1.57 \qquad (12.141b)$$

$$l_3 = 1494 \qquad (12.141c)$$

Figure 12.26, which follows the general configuration of Figure 12.23, shows the completed design, including the controller and the observer.

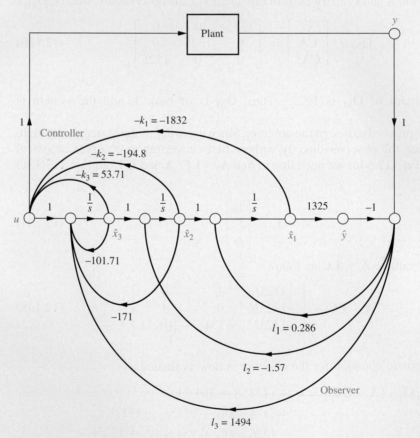

FIGURE 12.26 Completed state-space design for the antenna azimuth position control system, showing controller and observer

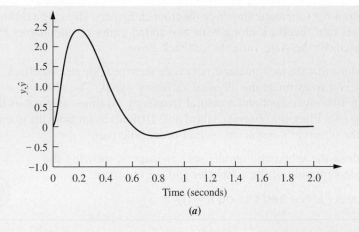

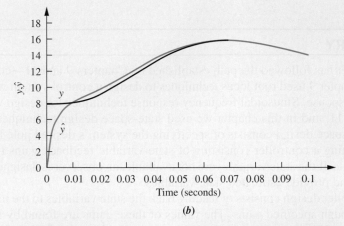

FIGURE 12.27 Designed response of antenna azimuth position control system: **a.** impulse response—plant and observer with the same initial conditions, $x_1(0) = \hat{x}_1(0) = 0$; **b.** portion of impulse response—plant and observer with different initial conditions, $\hat{x}_1(0) = 0.006$ for the plant, $\hat{x}_1(0) = 0$ for the observer

The results of the design are shown in Figure 12.27. Figure 12.27(a) shows the impulse response of the closed-loop system without any difference between the plant and its modeling as an observer. The undershoot and settling time approximately meet the requirements set forth in the problem statement of 10% and 1 second, respectively. In Figure 12.27(b), we see the response designed into the observer. An initial condition of 0.006 was given to x_1 in the plant to make the modeling of the plant and observer different. Notice that the observer's response follows the plant's response by the time 0.06 second is reached.

Challenge: You are now given a case study to test your knowledge of this chapter's objectives: You are given the antenna azimuth position control system shown on the front endpapers, Configuration 3. If the preamplifier gain $K = 20$, do the following:

a. Design a controller to yield 15% overshoot and a settling time of 2 seconds. Place the third pole 10 times as far from the imaginary axis as the second-order dominant pole pair. Use physical variables as follows: power amplifier output, motor angular velocity, and motor displacement.

b. Redraw the schematic shown on the front endpapers, showing a tachometer that yields rate feedback along with any added gains or attenuators required to implement the state-variable feedback gains.

c. Assume that the tachometer is not available to provide rate feedback. Design an observer to estimate the physical variables' states. The observer will respond with 10% overshoot and a natural frequency 10 times as great as the system response. Place the observer's third pole 10 times as far from the imaginary axis as the observer's dominant second-order pole pair.

d. Redraw the schematic on the front endpapers, showing the implementation of the controller and the observer.

e. Repeat Parts **a** and **c** using MATLAB.

SUMMARY

This chapter has followed the path established by Chapters 9 and 11—control system design. Chapter 9 used root locus techniques to design a control system with a desired transient response. Sinusoidal frequency response techniques for design were covered in Chapter 11, and in this chapter we used state-space design techniques.

State-space design consists of specifying the system's desired pole locations and then designing a controller consisting of state-variable feedback gains to meet these requirements. If the state variables are not available, an observer is designed to emulate the plant and provide estimated state variables.

Controller design consists of feeding back the state variables to the input, u, of the system through specified gains. The values of these gains are found by matching the coefficients of the system's characteristic equation with the coefficients of the desired characteristic equation. In some cases the control signal, u, cannot affect one or more state variables. We call such a system *uncontrollable*. For this system a total design is not possible. Using the controllability matrix, a designer can tell whether or not a system is controllable prior to the design.

Observer design consists of feeding back the error between the actual output and the estimated output. This error is fed back through specified gains to the derivatives of the estimated state variables. The values of these gains are also found by matching the coefficients of the observer's characteristic equation with the coefficients of the desired characteristic equation. The response of the observer is designed to be faster than that of the controller, so the estimated state variables effectively appear instantaneously at the controller. For some systems the state variables cannot be deduced from the output of the system, as is required by the observer. We call such systems *unobservable*. Using the observability matrix, the designer can tell whether or not a system is observable. Observers can be designed only for observable systems.

Finally, we discussed ways of improving the steady-state error performance of systems represented in state space. The addition of an integration before the controlled plant yields improvement in the steady-state error. In this chapter this additional integration was incorporated into the controller design.

Three advantages of state-space design are apparent. First, in contrast to the root locus method, all pole locations can be specified to ensure a negligible effect of the nondominant poles upon the transient response. With the root locus, we were forced to justify an assumption that the nondominant poles did not appreciably affect the transient response. We were not always able to do so. Second, with the use of an observer, we are no longer forced to acquire the actual system variables for feedback. The advantage here is that sometimes the variables cannot be physically accessed, or it may be too expensive to provide that access. Finally, the methods shown lend themselves to design automation using the digital computer.

A disadvantage of the design methods covered in this chapter is the designer's inability to design the location of open- or closed-loop zeros that may affect the transient response. In root locus or frequency response design, the zeros of the lag or lead compensator can be specified. Another disadvantage of state-space methods concerns the designer's ability to relate all pole locations to the desired response; this relationship is not always apparent. Also, once the design is completed, we may not be satisfied with the sensitivity to parameter changes.

Finally, as previously discussed, state-space techniques do not satisfy our intuition as much as root locus techniques, where the effect of parameter changes can be immediately seen as changes in closed-loop pole locations.

In the next chapter we return to the frequency domain and design digital systems using gain adjustment and cascade compensation.

REVIEW QUESTIONS

1. Briefly describe an advantage that state-space techniques have over root locus techniques in the placement of closed-loop poles for transient response design.
2. Briefly describe the design procedure for a controller.
3. Different signal-flow graphs can represent the same system. Which form facilitates the calculation of the variable gains during controller design?
4. In order to effect a complete controller design, a system must be controllable. Describe the physical meaning of controllability.
5. Under what conditions can inspection of the signal-flow graph of a system yield immediate determination of controllability?
6. In order to determine controllability mathematically, the controllability matrix is formed, and its rank evaluated. What is the final step in determining controllability if the controllability matrix is a square matrix?
7. What is an observer?
8. Under what conditions would you use an observer in your state-space design of a control system?
9. Briefly describe the configuration of an observer.
10. What plant representation lends itself to easier design of an observer?
11. Briefly describe the design technique for an observer, given the configuration you described in Question 9.
12. Compare the major difference in the transient response of an observer to that of a controller. Why does this difference exist?
13. From what equation do we find the characteristic equation of the controller-compensated system?
14. From what equation do we find the characteristic equation of the observer?
15. In order to effect a complete observer design, a system must be observable. Describe the physical meaning of observability.

16. Under what conditions can inspection of the signal-flow graph of a system yield immediate determination of observability?

17. In order to determine observability mathematically, the observability matrix is formed and its rank evaluated. What is the final step in determining observability if the observability matrix is a square matrix?

PROBLEMS

1. Consider the following open-loop transfer functions, where $G(s) = Y(s)/U(s)$, $Y(s)$ is the Laplace transform of the output, and $U(s)$ is the Laplace transform of the input control signal:

   i. $G(s) = \dfrac{(s+1)}{s(s+2)}$

   ii. $G(s) = \dfrac{(s+2)}{(s+3)(s+4)}$

   iii. $G(s) = \dfrac{10(s+2)(s+3)}{s(s+4)(s+5)}$

   iv. $G(s) = \dfrac{10s}{(s+2)(s+4)(s+6)}$

   v. $G(s) = \dfrac{s^2 + 2s + 10}{(s+7)(s^2 + 3s + 100)}$

   For each of these transfer functions, do the following:

   a. Draw the signal-flow graph in phase-variable form.

   b. Add state-variable feedback to the signal-flow graph.

   c. For each closed-loop signal-flow graph, write the state equations.

   d. Write, *by inspection*, the closed-loop transfer function, $T(s)$, for your closed-loop signal-flow graphs.

   e. Verify your answers for $T(s)$ by finding the closed-loop transfer functions from the state equations and Eq. (3.73).

2. The following open-loop transfer functions can be represented by signal-flow graphs in cascade form.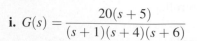

   i. $G(s) = \dfrac{20(s+5)}{(s+1)(s+4)(s+6)}$

   ii. $G(s) = \dfrac{5(s^2 + 3s + 7)}{(s+2)(s^2 + 2s + 10)}$

   For each, do the following:

   a. Draw the signal-flow graph and show the state-variable feedback.

   b. Find the closed-loop transfer function with state-variable feedback.

3. The following open-loop transfer functions can be represented by signal-flow graphs in parallel form.

   i. $G(s) = \dfrac{50(s^2 + 7s + 25)}{s(s+10)(s+20)}$

   ii. $G(s) = \dfrac{50(s+3)(s+4)}{(s+5)(s+6)(s+7)}$

   For each, do the following: [Section: 12.4]

   a. Draw the signal-flow graph and show the state-variable feedback.

   b. Find the closed-loop transfer function with state-variable feedback.

4. Given the following open-loop plant, [Section: 12.2]

   $$G(s) = \frac{20}{(s+1)(s+3)(s+7)}$$

   design a controller to yield a 15% overshoot and a settling time of 0.75 second. Place the third pole 10 times as far from the imaginary axis as the dominant pole pair. Use the phase variables for state-variable feedback.

5. Section 12.2 showed that controller design is easier to implement if the uncompensated system is represented in phase-variable form with its typical lower companion matrix. We alluded to the fact that the design can just as easily progress using the controller canonical form with its upper companion matrix. [Section: 12.2]

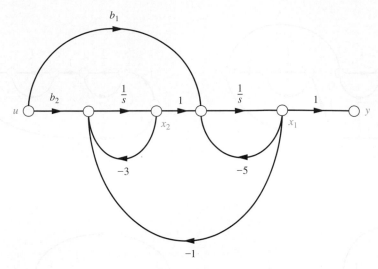

Figure P12.1

a. Redo the general controller design covered in Section 12.2, assuming that the plant is represented in controller canonical form rather than phase-variable form.

b. Apply your derivation to Example 12.1 if the uncompensated plant is represented in controller canonical form.

6. Given the following open-loop plant: [Section: 12.2]

$$G(s) = \frac{100(s+2)(s+20)}{(s+1)(s+3)(s+4)}$$

design a controller to yield 15% overshoot with a peak time of 0.5 second. Use the controller canonical form for state-variable feedback.

7. Given the following open-loop plant: [Section: 12.2]

$$G(s) = \frac{20(s+2)}{s(s+4)(s+6)}$$

design a controller to yield a 10% overshoot and a settling time of 2 seconds. Place the third pole 10 times as far from the imaginary axis as the dominant pole pair. Use the phase variables for state-variable feedback.

8. Repeat Problem 4 assuming that the plant is represented in the cascade form. Do not convert to phase-variable form. [Section: 12.4]

9. Repeat Problem 7 assuming that the plant is represented in the parallel form. Do not convert to phase-variable form. [Section: 12.4]

10. Given the plant shown in Figure P12.1, what relationship exists between b_1 and b_2 to make the system uncontrollable? [Section: 12.3]

11. For each of the plants represented by signal-flow graphs in Figure P12.2, determine the controllability. If the controllability can be determined by inspection, state that it can and then verify your conclusions using the controllability matrix. [Section: 12.3]

12. Use MATLAB to determine the controllability of the systems of Figure P12.2(d) and (f).

13. In Section 12.4 we discussed how to design a controller for systems not represented in phase-variable form with its typical lower companion matrix. We described how to convert the system to phase-variable form, design the controller, and convert back to the original representation. This technique can be applied just as easily if the original representation is converted to controller canonical form with its typical upper companion matrix. Redo Example 12.4 in the text by designing the controller after converting the uncompensated plant to controller canonical form. [Section: 12.4]

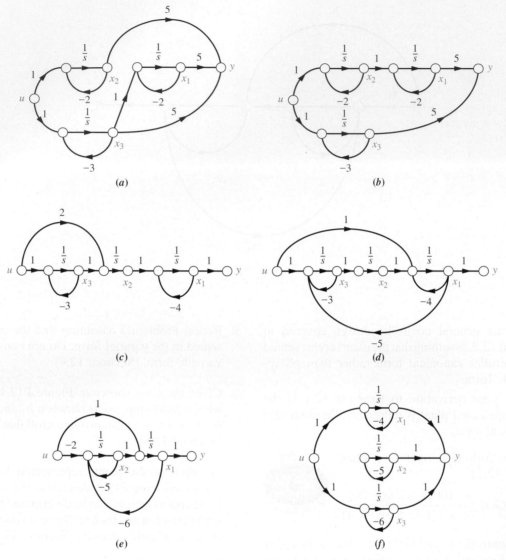

Figure P12.2

14. Consider the following transfer function:

$$G(s) = \frac{(s+6)}{(s+3)(s+8)(s+10)}$$

If the system is represented in cascade form, as shown in Figure P12.3, design a controller to yield a closed-loop response of 10% overshoot with a settling time of 1 second. Design the controller by first transforming the plant to phase variables. [Section: 12.4]

15. Use MATLAB to design the controller gains for the system given in Problem 14.

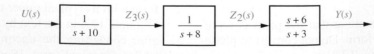

Figure P12.3

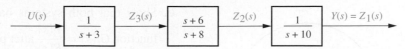

Figure P12.4

16. The open-loop system of Problem 14 is represented as shown in Figure P12.4. If the output of each block is assigned to be a state variable, design the controller gains for feedback from these state variables. [Section: 12.4]

17. If an open-loop plant,

$$G(s) = \frac{100}{s(s+4)(s+8)}$$

is represented in parallel form, design a controller to yield a closed-loop response of 15% overshoot and a peak time of 0.2 second. Design the controller by first transforming the plant to controller canonical form. [Section: 12.4]

18. For a specific individual, the linear time-invariant model of the hypothalamic-pituitary-adrenal axis of the endocrine system with five state variables has been found to be (*Kyrylov, 2005*)

$$\begin{bmatrix} \dot{x}_1 \\ \dot{x}_2 \\ \dot{x}_3 \\ \dot{x}_4 \\ \dot{x}_5 \end{bmatrix} = \begin{bmatrix} -0.014 & 0 & -1.4 & 0 & 0 \\ 0.023 & -0.023 & -0.023 & 0 & 0 \\ 0.134 & 0.67 & -0.67 & 0.38 & 0.003264 \\ 0 & 0 & 0.06 & -0.06 & 0 \\ 0 & 0 & 0.0017 & 0 & -0.001 \end{bmatrix}$$

$$\times \begin{bmatrix} x_1 \\ x_2 \\ x_3 \\ x_4 \\ x_5 \end{bmatrix} + \begin{bmatrix} 1 \\ 0 \\ 0 \\ 0 \\ 0 \end{bmatrix} d_0$$

The state-variable definitions were given in Problem 23, Chapter 3.

a. Use MATLAB to determine if the system is controllable.

b. Use MATLAB to express the matrices A and B in phase-variable form.

19. Consider the plant

$$G(s) = \frac{1}{s(s+2)(s+6)}$$

whose state variables are not available. Design an observer for the observer canonical variables to yield a transient response described by $\zeta = 0.5$ and $\omega_n = 50$. Place the third pole 10 times farther from the imaginary axis than the dominant poles.

20. Design an observer for the plant,

$$G(s) = \frac{10}{(s+1)(s+4)(s+8)}$$

operating with 5% overshoot and 1 second peak time. Design the observer to respond 10 times faster than the plant. Place the observer third pole 20 times farther from the imaginary axis than the observer dominant poles. Assume the plant is represented in observer canonical form.

21. Repeat Problem 18 assuming that the plant is represented in phase-variable form. Do not convert to observer canonical form.

22. Consider the plant

$$G(s) = \frac{(s+1)}{(s+4)(s+6)}$$

whose phase variables are not available. Design an observer for the phase variables with a transient response described by $\zeta = 0.7$ and $\omega_n = 100$. Do not convert to observer canonical form.

23. Determine whether or not each of the systems shown in Figure P12.2 is observable. [Section: 12.6]

24. Given the plant of Figure P12.5, what relationship must exist between c_1 and c_2 in order for the system to be unobservable? [Section: 12.6]

25. Design an observer for the plant

$$G(s) = \frac{1}{(s+5)(s+13)(s+20)}$$

represented in cascade form. Transform the plant to observer canonical form for the design. Then transform the design back to cascade form. The

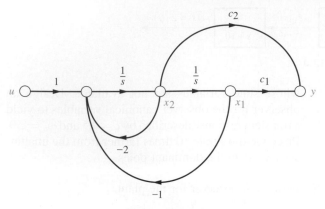

Figure P12.5

characteristic polynomial for the observer is to be
$s^3 + 600s^2 + 40{,}000s + 1{,}500{,}000$.

26. Use MATLAB to design the observer
gains for the system given in Problem
25.

27. Repeat Problem 25 assuming that the plant is represented in parallel form. [Section: 12.7]

28. Design an observer for

$$G(s) = \frac{50}{(s+3)(s+6)(s+9)}$$

represented in phase-variable form with a desired performance of 10% overshoot and a settling time of 0.5 second. The observer will be 10 times as fast as the plant, and the observer's nondominant pole will be 10 times as far from the imaginary axis as the observer's dominant poles. Design the observer by first converting to observer canonical form. [Section: 12.7]

29. Observability and controllability properties depend on the state-space representation chosen for a given system. In general, observability and controllability are affected when pole-zero cancellations are present in the transfer function. Consider the following two systems with representations:

$$\dot{x}_i = A_i x_i + B_i r$$
$$y = C_i x_i;$$

$$A_1 = \begin{bmatrix} 0 & 1 \\ -2 & -3 \end{bmatrix}; \quad B_1 = \begin{bmatrix} 0 \\ 1 \end{bmatrix}; \quad C_1 = [2 \quad 0]$$

$$A_2 = \begin{bmatrix} 0 & 1 & 0 \\ 0 & 0 & 1 \\ -6 & -11 & -6 \end{bmatrix}; \quad B_2 = \begin{bmatrix} 0 \\ 0 \\ 1 \end{bmatrix}; \quad C_2 = [6 \quad 2 \quad 0]$$

a. Show that both systems have the same transfer function $G_i(s) = \dfrac{Y(s)}{R(s)}$ after pole-zero cancellations.

b. Evaluate the observability of both systems.

30. Given the plant
$$\dot{\mathbf{x}} = \begin{bmatrix} -1 & 1 \\ 0 & 2 \end{bmatrix}\mathbf{x} + \begin{bmatrix} 0 \\ 1 \end{bmatrix}u; \quad y = [1 \quad 1]\mathbf{x}$$

design an integral controller to yield a 10% overshoot, 0.5-second settling time, and zero steady-state error for a step input. [Section: 12.8]

31. Repeat Problem 30 for the following plant: [Section: 12.8]

$$\dot{\mathbf{x}} = \begin{bmatrix} -2 & 1 \\ 0 & -5 \end{bmatrix}\mathbf{x} + \begin{bmatrix} 0 \\ 1 \end{bmatrix}u; \quad y = [1 \quad 1]\mathbf{x}$$

Design Problems

32. A magnetic levitation system is described in Problem 49 in Chapter 9 (*Cho, 1993*). Remove the photocell in Figure P9.14(*b*) and design a controller for phase variables to yield a step response with 5% overshoot and a settling time of 0.5 second.

33. Problem 22 in Chapter 3 introduced the model for patients treated under a regimen of a single day of Glargine insulin (*Tarín, 2005*). The model to find the response for a specific patient to medication can be expressed in phase-variable form with

$$\mathbf{A} = \begin{bmatrix} 0 & 1 & 0 \\ 0 & 0 & 1 \\ -501.6 \times 10^{-6} & -128.8 \times 10^{-3} & -854 \times 10^{-3} \end{bmatrix};$$

$$\mathbf{B} = \begin{bmatrix} 1 \\ 0 \\ 0 \end{bmatrix}; \quad \mathbf{C} = [0.78 \times 10^{-4} \quad 41.4 \times 10^{-4} \quad 0.01];$$

$$\mathbf{D} = 0$$

The state variables will take on a different significance in this expression, but the input and the output remain the same. Recall that u = external insulin flow, and y = plasma insulin concentration.

a. Obtain a state-feedback gain matrix so that the closed-loop system will have two of its poles placed at $-1/15$ and the third pole at $-1/2$.

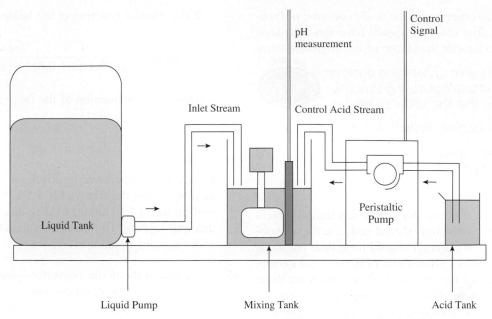

Figure P12.6 (© 2000 IEEE)

b. Use MATLAB to verify that the poles appear at the positions specified in Part **a**. MATLAB

34. Figure P12.6 shows a continuous stirred tank reactor in which an aqueous solution of sodium acetate (CH_3COONa) is neutralized in the mixing tank with hydrochloric acid (HCl) to maintain a particular pH in the mixing tank.

The amount of acid in the mix is controlled by varying the rotational speed of a feeding peristaltic pump. A nominal linearized transfer function from HCl flowrate to pH has been shown to be (*Tadeo, 2000*)

$$G(s) = \frac{-0.9580 \times 10^{-4}s - 0.01197 \times 10^{-4}}{s^3 + 0.5250s^2 + 0.01265s + 0.000078}$$

a. Write the system in state-space phase-variable form.

b. Use state-feedback methods to design a matrix **K** that will yield an overdamped output pH response with a settling time of $T_s \approx 5$ min for a step input change in pH.

c. Simulate the step response of the resulting closed-loop system using MATLAB.

35. In the dc-dc converter of Problem 62, Chapter 4 (*Van Dijk, 1995*) with $L = 6$ mH, $C = 1$ mF, $R = 100\ \Omega$, a 50% PWM duty cycle, and assuming the system's output is the voltage across the capacitor, the model can be expressed as

$$\begin{bmatrix} i_L \\ \dot{u}_C \end{bmatrix} = \begin{bmatrix} 0 & -83.33 \\ 500 & -10 \end{bmatrix} \begin{bmatrix} i_L \\ u_C \end{bmatrix} + \begin{bmatrix} 166.67 \\ 0 \end{bmatrix} E_s$$

$$y = \begin{bmatrix} 0 & 1 \end{bmatrix} \begin{bmatrix} i_L \\ u_C \end{bmatrix}$$

a. Find the system's transfer function.

b. Express the system's state equations in phase-variable form.

c. Find a set of state-feedback gains to obtain 20% overshoot and a settling time of 0.5 second in the phase-variable system.

d. Obtain the corresponding set of state-feedback gains in the original system.

e. Verify that the set of gains in Part **d** places the closed-loop poles at the desired positions.

f. Simulate the unit step response of the system using MATLAB.

36. **a.** Design an observer for the dc-dc converter of Problem 34. The observer should have time constants 10 times smaller than those of the original system.

    b. Simulate your system and observer for a unit step input using Simulink. Assume that the initial conditions for the original system are $\mathbf{x}(0) = \begin{bmatrix} 2 \\ 1 \end{bmatrix}$. The observer should have initial conditions $\hat{\mathbf{x}}(0) = \begin{bmatrix} 0 \\ 0 \end{bmatrix}$.

37. **a.** Design an observer for the neutralization system using the continuous stirred tank reactor of Problem 34. The observer should have time constants 10 times smaller than those of the original system. Assume that the original state variables are those obtained in the phase-variable representation.

    b. Simulate your system and observer for a unit step input using Simulink. Assume that the initial conditions for the original system are $\mathbf{x}(0) = \begin{bmatrix} -1 \\ -10 \\ 3 \end{bmatrix}$. The observer should have initial conditions $\hat{\mathbf{x}}(0) = \begin{bmatrix} 0 \\ 0 \\ 0 \end{bmatrix}$.

38. The conceptual block diagram of a gas-fired heater is shown in Figure P12.7. The commanded fuel pressure is proportional to the desired temperature. The difference between the commanded fuel pressure and a measured pressure related to the output temperature is used to actuate a valve and release fuel to the heater. The rate of fuel flow determines the temperature. When the output temperature equals the equivalent commanded temperature as determined by the commanded fuel pressure, the fuel flow is stopped and the heater shuts off (*Tyner, 1968*).

If the transfer function of the heater, $G_H(s)$, is

$$G_H(s) = \frac{1}{(s + 0.4)(s + 0.8)} \frac{\text{degrees F}}{\text{ft}^3/\text{min}}$$

and the transfer function of the fuel valve, $G_v(s)$, is

$$G_v(s) = \frac{5}{s + 5} \frac{\text{ft}^3/\text{min}}{\text{psi}}$$

replace the temperature feedback path with a phase-variable controller that yields a 5% overshoot and a settling time of 10 minutes. Also, design an observer that will respond 10 times faster than the system but with the same percent overshoot.

39. **a.** Redesign the dc-dc converter system of Problem 35 to include integral control.

    b. Simulate your system for a step input using Simulink and verify that the specifications are met. In particular, verify that the system has zero steady-state error.

40. The floppy disk drive of Problem 54 in Chapter 8 is to be redesigned using state-variable feedback. The controller is replaced by a unity dc gain amplifier, $G_a(s) = 800/(s + 800)$. The plant, $G_p(s) = 20{,}000/[s(s + 100)]$, is in cascade with the amplifier.

    a. Design a controller to yield 10% overshoot and a settling time of 0.05 second. Assume that the state variables are the output position, output velocity, and amplifier output.

    b. Evaluate the steady-state error and redesign the system with an integral controller to reduce the steady-state error to zero. (Use of a program with symbolic capability is highly recommended.)

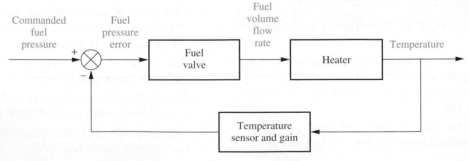

Figure P12.7   Block diagram of a gas-fired heater

c. Simulate the step response for both the controller-compensated and integral controller-compensated systems. Use MATLAB or any other computer program.

41. Given the angle of attack control system for the AFTI/F-16 aircraft shown in Figure P9.15 (*Monahemi, 1992*), use MATLAB to design a controller for the plant to yield 10% overshoot with a settling time of 0.5 second. Assume that the phase variables are accessible. Have the program display the step response of the compensated system.

42. For the angle of attack control system of Problem 41, use MATLAB to design an observer for the phase variables that is 15 times faster than the controller designed system.

43. For the angle of attack control system of Problem 41, do the following:

   a. Design an integral control using phase variables to reduce the steady-state error to zero. (Use of a program with symbolic capability is highly recommended.)
   b. Use MATLAB to obtain the step response.

Progressive Analysis and Design Problems

44. **High-speed rail pantograph.** Problem 19 in Chapter 1 discusses active control of a pantograph mechanism for high-speed rail systems (*O'Connor, 1997*). In Problem 72(a), Chapter 5, you found the block diagram for the active pantograph control system. For the open-loop portion of the pantograph system modeled in Chapter 5, do the following:

   a. Design a controller to yield 20% overshoot and a 1-second settling time.
   b. Repeat Part **a** with a zero steady-state error.

45. **Control of HIV/AIDS.** The linearized model of HIV infection when RTIs are used for treatment was introduced in Chapter 4 and repeated here for convenience (*Craig, 2004*):

$$\begin{bmatrix} \dot{T} \\ \dot{T}^* \\ \dot{v} \end{bmatrix} = \begin{bmatrix} -0.04167 & 0 & -0.0058 \\ 0.0217 & -0.24 & 0.0058 \\ 0 & 100 & -2.4 \end{bmatrix} \begin{bmatrix} T \\ T^* \\ v \end{bmatrix}$$

$$+ \begin{bmatrix} 5.2 \\ -5.2 \\ 0 \end{bmatrix} u_1$$

$$y = \begin{bmatrix} 0 & 0 & 1 \end{bmatrix} \begin{bmatrix} T \\ T^* \\ v \end{bmatrix}$$

T represents the number of healthy T-cells, T^* the number of infected cells, and v the number of free viruses.

   a. Design a state-feedback scheme to obtain
      i. zero steady-state error for step inputs
      ii. 10% overshoot
      iii. a settling time of approximately 100 days

   (Hint: the system's transfer function has an open-loop zero at approximately -0.02. Use one of the poles in the desired closed-loop-pole polynomial to eliminate this zero. Place the higher-order pole 6.25 times further than the dominant pair.)

   b. Simulate the unit step response of your design using Simulink.

CYBER EXPLORATION LABORATORY

Experiment 12.1

Objective To simulate a system that has been designed for transient response via a state-space controller and observer.

Minimum Required Software Packages MATLAB, Simulink, and the Control System Toolbox

Prelab

1. This experiment is based upon your design of a controller and observer as specified in the Case Study Challenge problem in Chapter 12. Once you have completed the controller and observer design in that problem, go on to Prelab 2.

2. What is the controller gain vector for your design of the system specified in the Case Study Challenge problem in Chapter 12?

3. What is the observer gain vector for your design of the system specified in the Case Study Challenge problem in Chapter 12?

4. Draw a Simulink diagram to simulate the system. Show the system, the controller, and the observer using the physical variables specified in the Case Study Challenge problem in Chapter 12.

Lab

1. Using Simulink and your diagram from Prelab 4, produce the Simulink diagram from which you can simulate the response.

2. Produce response plots of the system and the observer for a step input.

3. Measure the percent overshoot and the settling time for both plots.

Postlab

1. Make a table showing the design specifications and the simulation results for percent overshoot and settling time.

2. Compare the design specifications with the simulation results for both the system response and the observer response. Explain any discrepancies.

3. Describe any problems you had implementing your design.

BIBLIOGRAPHY

Cho, D., Kato, Y., and Spilman, D. Sliding Mode and Classical Controllers in Magnetic Levitation Systems. *IEEE Control Systems,* February 1993, pp. 42–48.

Craig, I. K, Xia, X., and Venter, J. W. Introducing HIV/AIDS Education into the Electrical Engineering Curriculum at the University of Pretoria. *IEEE Transactions on Education,* vol. 47, no.1, February 2004, pp. 65–73.

D' Azzo, J. J., and Houpis, C. H. *Linear Control System Analysis and Design: Conventional and Modern,* 3d ed. McGraw-Hill, New York, 1988.

Franklin, G. F, Powell, J. D, and Emami-Naeini, A. *Feedback Control of Dynamic Systems,* 3d ed. Addison-Wesley, Reading, MA, 1994.

Hostetter, G. H, Savant, C. J., Jr., and Stefani, R. T. *Design of Feedback Control Systems,* 2d ed. Saunders College Publishing, New York, 1989.

Kailath, T. *Linear Systems.* Prentice Hall, Englewood Cliffs, NJ, 1980.

Kyrylov, V., Severyanova, L. A., and Vieira, A. Modeling Robust Oscillatory Behavior of the Hypothalamic-Pituitary-Adrenal Axis. *IEEE Transactions on Biomedical Engineering,* vol. 52, no. 12, 2005, pp. 1977–1983.

Luenberger, D. G. Observing the State of a Linear System. *IEEE Transactions on Military Electronics,* vol. MIL-8, April 1964, pp. 74–80.

Milhorn, H. T., Jr., *The Application of Control Theory to Physiological Systems.* W. B. Saunders, Philadelphia, 1966.

Monahemi, M. M, Barlow, J. B, and O'Leary, D. P. Design of Reduced-Order Observers with Precise Loop Transfer Recovery. *Journal of Guidance, Control, and Dynamics,* vol. 15, no. 6, November–December 1992, pp. 1320–1326.

O' Connor, D. N, Eppinger, S. D., Seering, W. P., and Wormly, D. N. Active Control of a High-Speed Pantograph. *Journal of Dynamic Systems, Measurements, and Control,* vol. 119, March 1997, pp. 1–4.

Ogata, K. *Modern Control Engineering,* 2d ed. Prentice Hall, Englewood Cliffs, NJ, 1990.

Ogata, K. *State Space Analysis of Control Systems.* Prentice Hall, Englewood Cliffs, NJ, 1967.

Rockwell International. *Space Shuttle Transportation System.* 1984 (press information).

Shinners, S. M. *Modern Control System Theory and Design.* Wiley, New York, 1992.

Sinha, N. K. *Control Systems.* Holt, Rinehart & Winston, New York, 1986.

Tadeo, F., Pérez López, O., and Alvarez, T., Control of Neutralization Processes by Robust Loop-shaping. *IEEE Transactions on Control Systems Technology,* vol. 8, no. 2, 2000, pp. 236–246.

Tarín, C., Teufel, E., Picó, J., Bondia, J., and Pfleiderer, H. J. Comprehensive Pharmacokinetic Model of Insulin Glargine and other Insulin Formulations. *IEEE Transactions on Biomedical Engineering,* vol. 52, no. 12, 2005, pp. 1994–2005.

Timothy, L. K, and Bona, B. E. *State Space Analysis: An Introduction.* McGraw-Hill, New York, 1968.

Tyner, M., and May, F. P. *Process Engineering Control.* Ronald Press, New York, 1968.

Van Dijk, E., Spruijt, J. N., O' Sullivan, D. M., and Klaasens, J. B. PWM-Switch Modeling of DC-DC Converters. *IEEE Transactions on Power Electronics,* vol. 10, 1995, pp. 659–665.

DISCRETE CONTROL SYSTEMS

13

CHAPTER OBJECTIVES

In this chapter you will learn the following:

■ How to model digital systems
■ How to design the stability of digital systems
■ How to design digital systems to meet steady-state error specifications
■ How to design digital systems to meet transient response specifications using gain adjustment
■ How to design cascade compensation for digital systems

CASE STUDY OBJECTIVES

You will be able to demonstrate your knowledge of the chapter objectives with a case study as follows:

■ Given the analog antenna azimuth position control system shown on the front endpapers and in Figure 13.1(*a*), you will be able to convert the system to a digital system as shown in Figure 13.1(*b*) and then design the gain to meet a transient response specification.
■ Given the digital antenna azimuth position control system shown in Figure 13.1(*b*), you will be able to design a digital cascade compensator to improve the transient response.

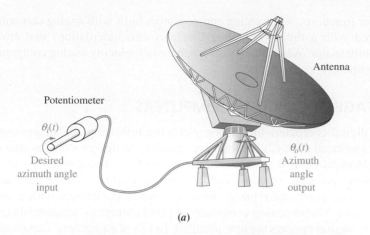

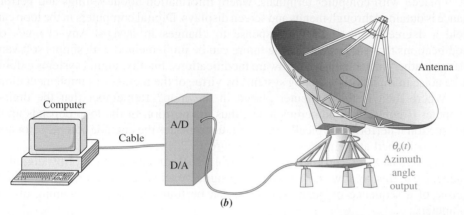

FIGURE 13.1 Conversion of antenna azimuth position control system from **a.** analog control to **b.** digital control

13.1 INTRODUCTION

This chapter is an introduction to digital control systems and will cover only frequency-domain analysis and design. You are encouraged to pursue the study of state-space techniques in an advanced course in sampled-data control systems. In this chapter we introduce analysis and design of stability, steady-state error, and transient response for computer-controlled systems.

   With the development of the minicomputer in the mid-1960s and the micro-computer in the mid-1970s, physical systems need no longer be controlled by expensive mainframe computers. For example, milling operations that required mainframe computers in the past can now be controlled by a personal computer.

   The digital computer can perform two functions: (1) supervisory—external to the feedback loop; and (2) control—internal to the feedback loop. Examples of supervisory functions consist of scheduling tasks, monitoring parameters and variables for out-of-range values, or initiating safety shutdown. Control functions are of primary interest to us, since a computer that performs within the feedback loop replaces the methods of compensation heretofore discussed. Examples of control functions are lead and lag compensation.

Transfer functions, representing compensators built with analog components, are now replaced with a digital computer that performs calculations that emulate the physical compensator. What advantages are there to replacing analog components with a digital computer?

ADVANTAGES OF DIGITAL COMPUTERS

The use of digital computers in the loop yields the following advantages over analog systems: (1) reduced cost, (2) flexibility in response to design changes, and (3) noise immunity. Modern control systems require control of numerous loops at the same time—pressure, position, velocity, and tension, for example. In the steel industry, a single digital computer can replace numerous analog controllers with a subsequent reduction in cost. Where analog controllers implied numerous adjustments and resulting hardware, digital systems are now installed. Banks of equipment, meters, and knobs are replaced with computer terminals, where information about settings and performance is obtained through menus and screen displays. Digital computers in the loop can yield a degree of flexibility in response to changes in design. Any changes or modifications that are required in the future can be implemented with simple software changes rather than expensive hardware modifications. Finally, digital systems exhibit more noise immunity than analog systems by virtue of the methods of implementation.

Where then is the computer placed in the loop? Remember that the digital computer is controlling numerous loops; thus, its position in the loop depends upon the function it performs. Typically, the computer replaces the cascade compensator and is thus positioned at the place shown in Figure 13.2(*a*).

The signals *r, e, f,* and *c* shown in Figure 13.2(*a*) can take on two forms: digital or analog. Up to this point we have used analog signals exclusively. Digital signals, which consist of a sequence of binary numbers, can be found in loops containing digital computers.

Loops containing both analog and digital signals must provide a means for conversion from one form to the other as required by each subsystem. A device that converts analog signals to digital signals is called an *analog-to-digital (A/D) converter.* Conversely, a device that converts digital signals to analog signals is called a *digital-to-analog (D/A) converter.* For example, in Figure 13.2(*b*), if the plant output, *c,* and the system input, *r,* are analog signals, then an analog-to-digital converter must be provided

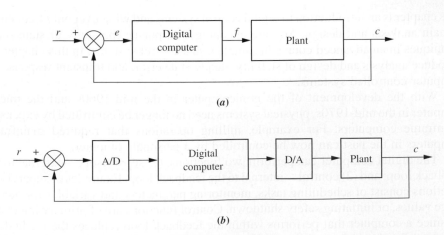

FIGURE 13.2   a. Placement of the digital computer within the loop; **b.** detailed block diagram showing placement of A/D and D/A converters

at the input to the digital computer. Also, if the plant input, f, is an analog signal, then a digital-to-analog converter must be provided at the output of the digital computer.

DIGITAL-TO-ANALOG CONVERSION

Digital-to-analog conversion is simple and effectively instantaneous. Properly weighted voltages are summed together to yield the analog output. For example, in Figure 13.3 three weighted voltages are summed. The three-bit binary code is represented by the switches. Thus, if the binary number is 110_2, the center and bottom switches are on, and the analog output is 6 volts. In actual use the switches are electronic and are set by the input binary code.

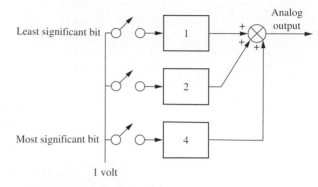

FIGURE 13.3 Digital-to-analog converter

ANALOG-TO-DIGITAL CONVERSION

Analog-to-digital conversion, on the other hand, is a two-step process and is not instantaneous. There is a delay between the input analog voltage and the output digital word. In an analog-to-digital converter, the analog signal is first converted to a sampled signal and then converted to a sequence of binary numbers, the digital signal.

The sampling rate must be at least twice the bandwidth of the signal, or else there will be distortion. This minimum sampling frequency is called the *Nyquist sampling rate*.[1]

In Figure 13.4(*a*) we start with the analog signal. In Figure 13.4(*b*) we see the analog signal sampled at periodic intervals and held over the sampling interval by a device called a *zero-order sample-and-hold* (*z.o.h.*) that yields a staircase approximation to the analog signal. Higher-order holds, such as a first-order hold, generate more complex and more accurate waveshapes between samples. For example, a first-order hold generates a ramp between the samples. Samples are held before being digitized because the analog-to-digital converter converts the voltage to a digital number via a digital counter, which takes time to reach the correct digital number. Hence, the constant analog voltage must be present during the conversion process.

After sampling and holding, the analog-to-digital converter converts the sample to a digital number (as shown in Figure 13.4(*c*)), which is arrived at in the following manner. The dynamic range of the analog signal's voltage is divided into discrete levels, and each level is assigned a digital number. For example, in Figure 13.4(*b*), the analog signal is divided into eight levels. A three-bit digital number can represent each of the eight levels as shown in the figure. Thus, the difference between quantization levels is $M/8$ volts, where M is the maximum analog voltage. In general, for any system, this difference is $M/2^n$ volts, where n is the number of binary bits used for the analog-to-digital conversion.

Looking at Figure 13.4(*b*), we can see that there will be an associated error for each digitized analog value except the voltages at the boundaries such as $M/8$ and $2M/8$. We call this error the *quantization error*. Assuming that the quantization process rounds off the analog voltage to the next higher or lower level, the maximum value of the quantization error is $1/2$ the difference between quantization levels in the range of analog voltages from 0 to $15M/16$. In general, for any system using roundoff, the quantization error will be $(1/2)(M/2^n) = M/2^{n+1}$.

---

[1] See *Ogata (1987: 170–177)* for a detailed discussion.

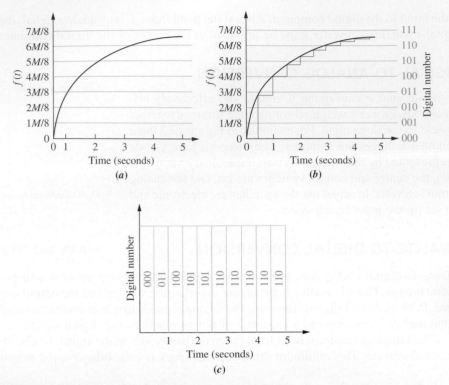

FIGURE 13.4 Steps in analog-to-digital conversion: **a.** analog signal; **b.** analog signal after sample-and-hold; **c.** conversion of samples to digital numbers

We have now covered the basic concepts of digital systems. We found out why they are used, where the digital computer is placed in the loop, and how to convert between analog and digital signals. Since the computer can replace the compensator, we have to realize that the computer is working with a quantized amplitude representation of the analog signal formed from values of the analog signal at discrete intervals of time. Ignoring the quantization error, we see that the computer performs just as the compensator does, except that signals pass through the computer only at the sampled intervals of time. We will find that the sampling of data has an unusual effect upon the performance of a closed-loop feedback system, since stability and transient response are now dependent upon the sampling rate; if it is too slow, the system can be unstable since the values are not being updated rapidly enough. If we are to analyze and design feedback control systems with digital computers in the loop, we must be able to model the digital computer and associated digital-to-analog and analog-to-digital converters. The modeling of the digital computer along with associated converters is covered in the next section.

13.2 MODELING THE DIGITAL COMPUTER

If we think about it, the form of the signals in a loop is not as important as what happens to them. For example, if analog-to-digital conversion could happen instantaneously, and time samples occurred at intervals of time that approached zero, there would be no need to differentiate between the digital signals and the analog signals. Thus, previous analysis and design techniques would be valid regardless of the presence of the digital computer.

The fact that signals are sampled at specified intervals and held causes the system performance to change with changes in sampling rate. Basically, then, the computer's effect upon the signal comes from this sampling and holding. Thus, in order to model digital control systems, we must come up with a mathematical representation of this sample-and-hold process.

MODELING THE SAMPLER

Our objective at this point is to derive a mathematical model for the digital computer as represented by a sampler and zero-order hold. Our goal is to represent the computer as a transfer function similar to that for any subsystem. When signals are sampled, however, the Laplace transform that we have dealt with becomes a bit unwieldy. The Laplace transform can be replaced by another related transform called the *z-transform*. The *z-transform* will arise naturally from our development of the mathematical representation of the computer.

Consider the models for sampling shown in Figure 13.5. The model in Figure 13.5(*a*) is a switch turning on and off at a uniform sampling rate. In Figure 13.5(*b*) sampling can also be considered to be the product of the time waveform to be sampled, $f(t)$, and a sampling function, $s(t)$. If $s(t)$ is a sequence of pulses of width T_W, constant amplitude, and uniform rate as shown, the sampled output, $f^*_{T_W}(t)$, will consist of a sequence of sections of $f(t)$ at regular intervals. This view is equivalent to the switch model of Figure 13.5(*a*).

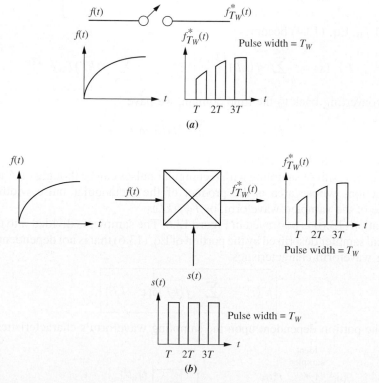

FIGURE 13.5   Two views of uniform-rate sampling: **a.** switch opening and closing; **b.** product of time waveform and sampling waveform

We can now write the time equation of the sampled waveform, $f^*_{T_W}(t)$. Using the model shown in Figure 13.5(b), we have

$$f^*_{T_W}(t) = f(t)s(t) = f(t)\sum_{k=-\infty}^{\infty} u(t - kT) - u(t - kT - T_W) \qquad (13.1)$$

where k is an integer between $-\infty$ and $+\infty$, T is the period of the pulse train, and T_W is the pulse width.

Since Eq. (13.1) is the product of two time functions, taking the Laplace transform in order to find a transfer function is not simple. A simplification can be made if we assume that the pulse width, T_W, is small in comparison to the period, T, such that $f(t)$ can be considered constant during the sampling interval. Over the sampling interval, then, $f(t) = f(kT)$. Hence,

$$f^*_{T_W}(t) = \sum_{k=-\infty}^{\infty} f(kT)[u(t - kT) - u(t - kT - T_W)] \qquad (13.2)$$

for small T_W.

Equation (13.2) can be further simplified through insight provided by the Laplace transform. Taking the Laplace transform of Eq. (13.2), we have

$$F^*_{T_W}(s) = \sum_{k=-\infty}^{\infty} f(kT)\left[\frac{e^{-kTs}}{s} - \frac{e^{-kTs-T_Ws}}{s}\right] = \sum_{k=-\infty}^{\infty} f(kT)\left[\frac{1 - e^{-T_Ws}}{s}\right]e^{-kTs} \qquad (13.3)$$

Replacing e^{-T_Ws} with its series expansion, we obtain

$$F^*_{T_W}(s) = \sum_{k=-\infty}^{\infty} f(kT)\left[\frac{1 - \left\{1 - T_Ws + \dfrac{(T_Ws)^2}{2!} - \cdots\right\}}{s}\right]e^{-kTs} \qquad (13.4)$$

For small T_W, Eq. (13.4) becomes

$$F^*_{T_W}(s) = \sum_{k=-\infty}^{\infty} f(kT)\left[\frac{T_Ws}{s}\right]e^{-kTs} = \sum_{k=-\infty}^{\infty} f(kT)T_We^{-kTs} \qquad (13.5)$$

Finally, converting back to the time domain, we have

$$f^*_{T_W}(t) = T_W\sum_{k=-\infty}^{\infty} f(kT)\delta(t - kT) \qquad (13.6)$$

where $\delta(t - kT)$ are Dirac delta functions.

Thus, the result of sampling with rectangular pulses can be thought of as a series of delta functions whose area is the product of the rectangular pulse width and the amplitude of the sampled waveform, or $T_Wf(kT)$.

Equation (13.6) is portrayed in Figure 13.6. The sampler is divided into two parts: (1) an ideal sampler described by the portion of Eq. (13.6) that is not dependent upon the sampling waveform characteristics,

$$\boxed{f^*(t) = \sum_{k=-\infty}^{\infty} f(kT)\delta(t - kT)} \qquad (13.7)$$

and (2) the portion dependent upon the sampling waveform's characteristics, T_W.

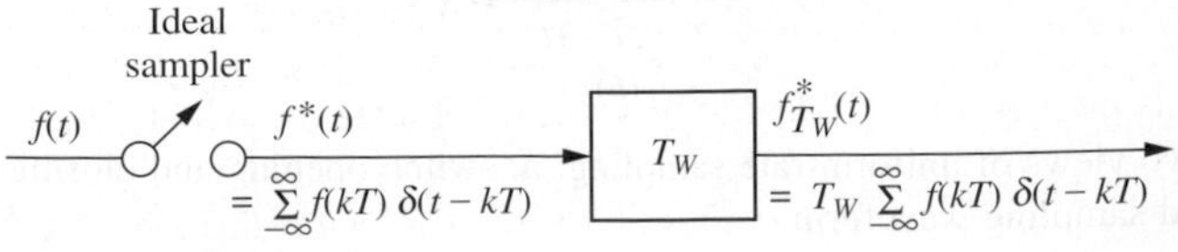

FIGURE 13.6
Model of sampling with a uniform rectangular pulse train

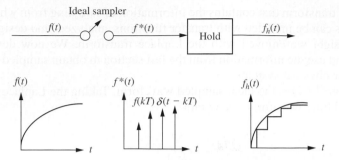

FIGURE 13.7 Ideal sampling and the zero-order hold

MODELING THE ZERO-ORDER HOLD

The final step in modeling the digital computer is modeling the zero-order hold that follows the sampler. Figure 13.7 summarizes the function of the zero-order hold, which is to hold the last sampled value of $f(t)$. If we assume an ideal sampler (equivalent to setting $T_W = 1$), then $f^*(t)$ is represented by a sequence of delta functions. The zero-order hold yields a staircase approximation to $f(t)$. Hence, the output from the hold is a sequence of step functions whose amplitude is $f(t)$ at the sampling instant, or $f(kT)$. We have previously seen that the transfer function of any linear system is identical to the Laplace transform of the impulse response since the Laplace transform of a unit impulse or delta function input is unity. Since a single impulse from the sampler yields a step over the sampling interval, the Laplace transform of this step, $G_h(s)$, which is the impulse response of the zero-order hold, is the transfer function of the zero-order hold. Using an impulse at zero time, the transform of the resulting step that starts at $t = 0$ and ends at $t = T$ is

$$G_h(s) = \frac{1 - e^{-Ts}}{s} \tag{13.8}$$

In a physical system, samples of the input time waveform, $f(kT)$, are held over the sampling interval. We can see from Eq. (13.8) that the hold circuit integrates the input and holds its value over the sampling interval. Since the area under the delta functions coming from the ideal sampler is $f(kT)$, we can then integrate the ideal sampled waveform and obtain the same result as for the physical system. In other words, if the ideal sampled signal, $f^*(t)$, is followed by a hold, we can use the ideal sampled waveform as the input, rather than $f^*_{T_W}(t)$.

In this section we modeled the digital computer by cascading two elements: (1) an ideal sampler and (2) a zero-order hold. Together, the model is known as a *zero-order sample-and-hold*. The ideal sampler is modeled by Eq. (13.7), and the zero-order hold is modeled by Eq. (13.8). In the next section we start to create a transform approach to digital systems by introducing the z-transform.

13.3 THE z-TRANSFORM

The effect of sampling within a system is pronounced. Whereas the stability and transient response of analog systems depend upon gain and component values, sampled-data system stability and transient response also depend upon sampling rate. Our goal is to develop a transform that contains the information of sampling from which sampled-data systems can be modeled with transfer functions, analyzed, and designed with the ease and insight we enjoyed with the Laplace transform. We now develop such a transform and use the information from the last section to obtain sampled-data transfer functions for physical systems.

Equation (13.7) is the ideal sampled waveform. Taking the Laplace transform of this sampled time waveform, we obtain

$$F^*(s) = \sum_{k=0}^{\infty} f(kT)e^{-kTs} \tag{13.9}$$

Now, letting $z = e^{Ts}$, Eq. (13.9) can be written as

$$F(z) = \sum_{k=0}^{\infty} f(kT)z^{-k} \tag{13.10}$$

Equation (13.10) defines the *z-transform*. That is, an $F(z)$ can be transformed to $f(kT)$, or an $f(kT)$ can be transformed to $F(z)$. Alternately, we can write

$$f(kT) \Longleftrightarrow F(z) \tag{13.11}$$

Paralleling the development of the Laplace transform, we can form a table relating $f(kT)$, the value of the sampled time function at the sampling instants, to $F(z)$. Let us look at an example.

◼ EXAMPLE 13.1 ◼

z-transform of a time function

Problem: Find the *z*-transform of a sampled unit ramp.

SOLUTION: For a unit ramp, $f(kT) = kT$. Hence the ideal sampled step can be written from Eq. (13.7) as

$$f^*(t) = \sum_{k=0}^{\infty} kT\delta(t - kT) \tag{13.12}$$

Taking the Laplace transform, we obtain

$$F^*(s) = \sum_{k=0}^{\infty} kTe^{-kTs} \tag{13.13}$$

Converting to the *z*-transform by letting $e^{-kTs} = z^{-k}$, we have

$$F(z) = \sum_{k=0}^{\infty} kTz^{-k} = T\sum_{k=0}^{\infty} kz^{-k} = T(z^{-1} + 2z^{-2} + 3z^{-3} + \cdots) \tag{13.14}$$

Equation (13.14) can be converted to a closed form by forming the series for $zF(z)$ and subtracting $F(z)$. Multiplying Eq. (13.14) by z, we get

$$zF(z) = T(1 + 2z^{-1} + 3z^{-2} + \cdots) \tag{13.15}$$

Subtracting Eq. (13.14) from Eq. (13.15), we obtain

$$zF(z) - F(z) = (z - 1)F(z) = T(1 + z^{-1} + z^{-2} + \cdots) \tag{13.16}$$

But

$$\frac{1}{1 - z^{-1}} = 1 + z^{-1} + z^{-2} + z^{-3} + \cdots \qquad (13.17)$$

which can be verified by performing the indicated division. Substituting Eq. (13.17) into (13.16) and solving for $F(z)$ yields

$$F(z) = T \frac{z}{(z - 1)^2} \qquad (13.18)$$

as the z-transform of $f(kT) = kT$.

Students who are performing the MATLAB exercises and want to explore the added capability of MATLAB's Symbolic Math Toolbox should now run ch13sp1 in Appendix E located at www.wiley.com/college/nise. You will learn how to find the z-transform of time functions. Example 13.1 will be solved using MATLAB and the Symbolic Math Toolbox.

Symbolic Math

The example demonstrates that any function of s, $F^*(s)$, that represents a sampled time waveform can be transformed into a function of z, $F(z)$. The final result, $F(z) = Tz/(z - 1)^2$, is in a closed form, unlike $F^*(s)$. If this is the case for numerous other sampled time waveforms, then we have the convenient transform that we were looking for. In a similar way, z-transforms for other waveforms can be obtained that parallel the table of Laplace transforms in Chapter 2. A partial table of z-transforms is shown in Table 13.1, and a partial table of z-transform theorems is shown in Table 13.2. For functions not in the table, we must perform an inverse z-transform calculation

TABLE 13.1   Partial table of z- and s-transforms

	$f(t)$	$F(s)$	$F(z)$	$f(kT)$
1.	$u(t)$	$\dfrac{1}{s}$	$\dfrac{z}{z - 1}$	$u(KT)$
2.	t	$\dfrac{1}{s^2}$	$\dfrac{Tz}{(z - 1)^2}$	kT
3.	t^n	$\dfrac{n!}{s^{n+1}}$	$\displaystyle\lim_{a \to 0}(-1)^n \dfrac{d^n}{da^n}\left[\dfrac{z}{z - e^{-aT}}\right]$	$(kT)^n$
4.	e^{-at}	$\dfrac{1}{s + a}$	$\dfrac{z}{z - e^{-aT}}$	e^{-akT}
5.	$t^n e^{-at}$	$\dfrac{n!}{(s + a)^{n+1}}$	$(-1)^n \dfrac{d^n}{da^n}\left[\dfrac{z}{z - e^{-aT}}\right]$	$(kT)^n e^{-akT}$
6.	$\sin \omega t$	$\dfrac{\omega}{s^2 + \omega^2}$	$\dfrac{z \sin \omega T}{z^2 - 2z \cos \omega T + 1}$	$\sin \omega kT$
7.	$\cos \omega t$	$\dfrac{s}{s^2 + \omega^2}$	$\dfrac{z(z - \cos \omega T)}{z^2 - 2z \cos \omega T + 1}$	$\cos \omega kT$
8.	$e^{-at}\sin \omega t$	$\dfrac{\omega}{(s + a)^2 + \omega^2}$	$\dfrac{ze^{-aT}\sin \omega T}{z^2 - 2ze^{-aT}\cos \omega T + e^{-2aT}}$	$e^{-akT}\sin \omega kT$
9.	$e^{-at}\cos \omega t$	$\dfrac{s + a}{(s + a)^2 + \omega^2}$	$\dfrac{z^2 - ze^{-aT}\cos \omega T}{z^2 - 2ze^{-aT}\cos \omega T + e^{-2aT}}$	$e^{-akT}\cos \omega kT$

TABLE 13.2 z-transform theorems

	Theorem	Name
1.	$z\{af(t)\} = aF(z)$	Linearity theorem
2.	$z\{f_1(t) + f_2(t)\} = F_1(z) + F_2(z)$	Linearity theorem
3.	$z\{e^{-aT}f(t)\} = F(e^{aT}z)$	Complex differentiation
4.	$z\{f(t - nT)\} = z^{-n}F(z)$	Real translation
5.	$z\{tf(t)\} = -Tz\dfrac{dF(z)}{dz}$	Complex differentiation
6.	$f(0) = \lim\limits_{z \to \infty} F(z)$	Initial value theorem
7.	$f(\infty) = \lim\limits_{z \to 1}(1 - z^{-1})F(z)$	Final value theorem

Note: kT may be substituted for t in the table.

similar to the inverse Laplace transform by partial-fraction expansion. Let us now see how we can work in the reverse direction and find the time function from its z-transform.

THE INVERSE z-Transform

Two methods for finding the inverse z-transform (the sampled time function from its z-transform) will be described: (1) partial-fraction expansion and (2) the power series method. Regardless of the method used, remember that since the z-transform came from the sampled waveform, the inverse z-transform will yield only the values of the time function at the sampling instants. Keep this in mind as we proceed, because even as we obtain closed-form time functions as results, they are valid only at sampling instants.

Inverse z-Transforms via Partial-Fraction Expansion. Recall that the Laplace transform consists of a partial fraction that yields a sum of terms leading to exponentials, that is, $A/(s + a)$. Taking this lead and looking at Table 13.1, we find that sampled exponential time functions are related to their z-transforms as follows:

$$e^{-akT} \Longleftrightarrow \frac{z}{z - e^{aT}} \tag{13.19}$$

We thus predict that a partial-fraction expansion should be of the following form:

$$F(z) = \frac{Az}{z - z_1} + \frac{Bz}{z - z_2} + \cdots \tag{13.20}$$

Since our partial-fraction expansion of $F(s)$ did not contain terms with s in the numerator of the partial fractions, we first form $F(z)/z$ to eliminate the z terms in the numerator, perform a partial-fraction expansion of $F(z)/z$, and finally multiply the result by z to replace the z's in the numerator. An example follows.

EXAMPLE 13.2

Inverse z-transform via partial-fraction expansion

Problem: Given the function in Eq. (13.21), find the sampled time function.

$$F(z) = \frac{0.5z}{(z - 0.5)(z - 0.7)} \tag{13.21}$$

SOLUTION: Begin by dividing Eq. (13.21) by z and performing a partial-fraction expansion.

$$\frac{F(z)}{z} = \frac{0.5}{(z-0.5)(z-0.7)} = \frac{A}{z-0.5} + \frac{B}{z-0.7} = \frac{-2.5}{z-0.5} + \frac{2.5}{z-0.7} \qquad (13.22)$$

Next, multiply through by z.

$$F(z) = \frac{0.5z}{(z-0.5)(z-0.7)} = \frac{-2.5z}{z-0.5} + \frac{2.5z}{z-0.7} \qquad (13.23)$$

Using Table 13.1, we find the inverse z-transform of each partial fraction. Hence, the value of the time function at the sampling instants is

$$f(kT) = -2.5(0.5)^k + 2.5(0.7)^k \qquad (13.24)$$

Also, from Eqs. (13.7) and (13.24), the ideal sampled time function is

$$f^*(t) = \sum_{k=-\infty}^{\infty} f(kT)\delta(t-kT) = \sum_{k=-\infty}^{\infty} \left[-2.5(0.5)^k + 2.5(0.7)^k\right]\delta(t-kT) \qquad (13.25)$$

If we substitute $k = 0, 1, 2$, and 3, we can find the first four samples of the ideal sampled time waveform. Hence,

$$f^*(t) = 0\delta(t) + 0.5\delta(t-T) + 0.6\delta(t-2T) + 0.545\delta(t-3T) \qquad (13.26)$$

Students who are performing the MATLAB exercises and want to explore the added capability of MATLAB's Symbolic Math Toolbox should now run ch13sp2 in Appendix E located at www.wiley.com/college/nise. You will learn how to find the inverse z-transform of sampled time functions. Example 13.2 will be solved using MATLAB and the Symbolic Math Toolbox.

Symbolic Math

Inverse z-Transform via the Power Series Method. The values of the sampled time waveform can also be found directly from $F(z)$. Although this method does not yield closed-form expressions for $f(kT)$, it can be used for plotting. The method consists of performing the indicated division, which yields a power series for $F(z)$. The power series can then be easily transformed into $F^*(s)$ and $f^*(t)$.

EXAMPLE 13.3

Inverse *z*-transform via power series

Problem: Given the function in Eq. (13.21), find the sampled time function.

SOLUTION: Begin by converting the numerator and denominator of $F(z)$ to polynomials in z.

$$F(z) = \frac{0.5z}{(z-0.5)(z-0.7)} = \frac{0.5z}{z^2 - 1.2z + 0.35} \qquad (13.27)$$

Now perform the indicated division.

$$
z^2 - 1.2z + 0.35 \overline{)\begin{array}{l} 0.5z^{-1} + 0.6z^{-2} + 0.545z^{-3} \\ 0.5z \\ \underline{0.5z - 0.6 + 0.175z^{-1}} \\ 0.6 - 0.175z^{-1} \\ \underline{0.6 - 0.720z^{-1} + 0.21} \\ 0.545z^{-1} - 0.21 \end{array}}
\tag{13.28}
$$

Using the numerator and the definition of z, we obtain

$$
F^*(s) = 0.5e^{-Ts} + 0.6e^{-2Ts} + 0.545e^{-3Ts} + \cdots \tag{13.29}
$$

from which

$$
f^*(t) = 0.5\delta(t - T) + 0.6\delta(t - 2T) + 0.545\delta(t - 3T) + \cdots \tag{13.30}
$$

You should compare Eq. (13.30) with Eq. (13.26), the result obtained via partial expansion.

SKILL-ASSESSMENT EXERCISE 13.1

Problem: Derive the z-transform for $f(t) = \sin \omega t\, u(t)$.

ANSWER:
$$
F(z) = \frac{z^{-1}\sin(\omega T)}{1 - 2z^{-1}\cos(\omega T) + z^{-2}}
$$

The complete solution is located at www.wiley.com/college/nise.

SKILL-ASSESSMENT EXERCISE 13.2

Problem: Find $f(kT)$ if $F(z) = \dfrac{z(z+1)(z+2)}{(z-0.5)(z-0.7)(z-0.9)}$.

ANSWER: $f(kT) = 46.875(0.5)^k - 114.75(0.7)^k + 68.875(0.9)^k$

The complete solution is located at www.wiley.com/college/nise.

13.4 TRANSFER FUNCTIONS

Now that we have established the z-transform, let us apply it to physical systems by finding transfer functions of sampled-data systems. Consider the continuous system shown in Figure 13.8(a). If the input is sampled as shown in Figure 13.8(b), the output is still a continuous signal. If, however, we are satisfied with finding the output at the sampling instants and not in between, the representation of the sampled-data system can be greatly simplified. Our assumption is visually described in Figure 13.8(c), where the output is conceptually sampled in synchronization with the input by a phantom sampler. Using the concept described in Figure 13.8(c), we derive the pulse transfer function of $G(s)$.

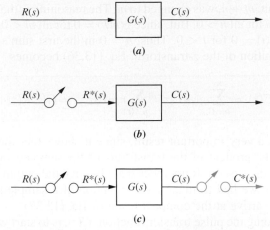

(a)

(b)

(c)

Note: Phantom sampler is shown in color.

FIGURE 13.8 Sampled-data systems: **a.** continuous; **b.** sampled input; **c.** sampled input and output

DERIVATION OF THE PULSE TRANSFER FUNCTION

Using Eq. (13.7), we find that the sampled input, $r^*(t)$, to the system of Figure 13.8(c) is

$$r^*(t) = \sum_{n=0}^{\infty} r(nT)\delta(t - nT) \tag{13.31}$$

which is a sum of impulses. Since the impulse response of a system, $G(s)$, is $g(t)$, we can write the time output of $G(s)$ as the sum of impulse responses generated by the input, Eq. (13.31). Thus,

$$c(t) = \sum_{n=0}^{\infty} r(nT)g(t - nT) \tag{13.32}$$

From Eq. (13.10),

$$C(z) = \sum_{k=0}^{\infty} c(kT)z^{-k} \tag{13.33}$$

Using Eq. (13.32) with $t = kT$, we obtain

$$c(kT) = \sum_{n=0}^{\infty} r(nT)g(kT - nT) \tag{13.34}$$

Substituting Eq. (13.34) into Eq. (13.33), we obtain

$$C(z) = \sum_{k=0}^{\infty} \sum_{n=0}^{\infty} r(nT)g[(k - n)T]z^{-k} \tag{13.35}$$

Letting $m = k - n$, we find

$$C(z) = \sum_{m+n=0}^{\infty} \sum_{n=0}^{\infty} r(nT)g(mT)z^{-(m+n)} \tag{13.36}$$

$$= \left\{ \sum_{m=0}^{\infty} g(mT)z^{-m} \right\} \left\{ \sum_{n=0}^{\infty} r(nT)z^{-n} \right\}$$

where the lower limit, $m + n$, was changed to m. The reasoning is that $m + n = 0$ yields negative values of m for all $n > 0$. But, since $g(mT) = 0$ for all $m < 0$, m is not less than zero. Alternately, $g(t) = 0$ for $t < 0$. Thus, $n = 0$ in the first sum's lower limit.

Using the definition of the z-transform, Eq. (13.36) becomes

$$C(z) = \sum_{m=0}^{\infty} g(mT)z^{-m} \sum_{n=0}^{\infty} r(nT)z^{-n} = G(z)R(z) \qquad (13.37)$$

Equation (13.37) is a very important result, since it shows that the transform of the sampled output is the product of the transforms of the sampled input and the pulse transfer function of the system. Remember that although the output of the system is a continuous function, we had to make an assumption of a sampled output (phantom sampler) in order to arrive at the compact result of Eq. (13.37).

One way of finding the pulse transfer function, $G(z)$, is to start with $G(s)$, find $g(t)$, and then use Table 13.1 to find $G(z)$. Let us look at an example.

EXAMPLE 13.4

Converting $G_1(s)$ in cascade with z.o.h. to $G(z)$

Problem: Given a z.o.h. in cascade with $G_1(s) = (s + 2)/(s + 1)$ or

$$G(s) = \frac{1 - e^{-Ts}}{s} \frac{(s + 2)}{(s + 1)} \qquad (13.38)$$

find the sampled-data transfer function, $G(z)$, if the sampling time, T, is 0.5 second.

SOLUTION: Equation (13.38) represents a common occurrence in digital control systems, namely a transfer function in cascade with a zero-order hold. Specifically, $G_1(s) = (s + 2)/(s + 1)$ is in cascade with a zero-order hold, $(1 - e^{-Ts})/s$. We can formulate a general solution to this type of problem by moving the s in the denominator of the zero-order hold to $G_1(s)$, yielding

$$G(s) = (1 - e^{-Ts}) \frac{G_1(s)}{s} \qquad (13.39)$$

from which

$$G(z) = (1 - z^{-1})z\left\{\frac{G_1(s)}{s}\right\} = \frac{z - 1}{z} z\left\{\frac{G_1(s)}{s}\right\} \qquad (13.40)$$

Thus, begin the solution by finding the impulse response (inverse Laplace transform) of $G_1(s)/s$. Hence,

$$G_2(s) = \frac{G_1(s)}{s} = \frac{s + 2}{s(s + 1)} = \frac{A}{s} + \frac{B}{s + 1} = \frac{2}{s} - \frac{1}{s + 1} \qquad (13.41)$$

Taking the inverse Laplace transform, we get

$$g_2(t) = 2 - e^{-t} \qquad (13.42)$$

from which

$$g_2(kT) = 2 - e^{-kT} \qquad (13.43)$$

Using Table 13.1, we find

$$G_2(z) = \frac{2z}{z-1} - \frac{z}{z-e^{-T}} \tag{13.44}$$

Substituting $T = 0.5$ yields

$$G_2(z) = z\left\{\frac{G_1(s)}{s}\right\} = \frac{2z}{z-1} - \frac{z}{z-0.607} = \frac{z^2 - 0.213z}{(z-1)(z-0.607)} \tag{13.45}$$

From Eq. (13.40),

$$G(z) = \frac{z-1}{z}G_2(z) = \frac{z-0.213}{z-0.607} \tag{13.46}$$

Students who are using MATLAB should now run ch13p1 in Appendix B. You will learn how to use MATLAB to convert $G_1(s)$ in cascade with a zero-order hold to $G(z)$. This exercise solves Example 13.4 using MATLAB.

Students who are performing the MATLAB exercises and want to explore the added capability of MATLAB's Symbolic Math Toolbox should now run ch13sp3 in Appendix E located at www.wiley.com/college/nise. MATLAB's Symbolic Math Toolbox yields an alternative method of finding the z-transform of a transfer function in cascade with a zero-order hold. Example 13.4 will be solved using MATLAB and the Symbolic Math Toolbox with a method that follows closely the hand calculation shown in that example.

Students who are using MATLAB should now run ch13p2 in Appendix B. You will learn how to use MATLAB to convert $G(s)$ to $G(z)$ when $G(s)$ is not in cascade with a zero-order hold. This is the same as finding the z-transform of $G(s)$.

Students who are using MATLAB should now run ch13p3 in Appendix B. You will learn how to create digital transfer functions directly.

Students who are using MATLAB should now run ch13p4 in Appendix B. You will learn how to use MATLAB to convert $G(z)$ to $G(s)$ when $G(s)$ is not in cascade with a zero-order hold. This is the same as finding the Laplace transform of $G(z)$.

> ### TryIt 13.1
>
> Use MATLAB, the Control System Toolbox, and the following statements to find $G_1(s)$ in Example 13.4 given $G(z)$ in Eq. 13.46.
>
> ```
> num=0.213;
> den=0.607;
> K=1;
> T=0.5;
> Gz=zpk(num,den,K,T)
> Gs=d2c(Gz,'zoh')
> ```

MATLAB

Symbolic Math

MATLAB

MATLAB

MATLAB

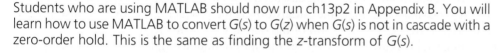

SKILL-ASSESSMENT EXERCISE 13.3

Problem: Find $G(z)$ for $G(s) = 8/(s+4)$ in cascade with a zero-order sample and hold. The sampling period is 0.25 second.

ANSWER: $G(z) = 1.264/(z-0.3679)$

The complete solution is located at www.wiley.com/college/nise.

WileyPLUS
Control Solutions

> ### TryIt 13.2
>
> Use MATLAB, the Control System Toolbox, and the following statements to solve Skill-Assessment Exercise 13.3.
>
> ```
> Gs=zpk([],-4,8)
> Gz=c2d(Gs,0.25,'zoh')
> ```

The major discovery in this section is that once the pulse transfer function, $G(z)$, of a system is obtained, the transform of the sampled output response, $C(z)$, for a given sampled input can be evaluated using the relationship $C(z) = R(z)G(z)$. Finally, the time function can be found by taking the inverse z-transform, as covered in Section 13.3. In the next section we look at block diagram reduction for digital systems.

13.5 BLOCK DIAGRAM REDUCTION

Up to this point, we have defined the z-transform and the sampled-data system transfer function and have shown how to obtain the sampled response. Basically, we are paralleling our discussions of the Laplace transform in Chapters 2 and 4. We now draw a parallel with some of the objectives of Chapter 5, namely block diagram reduction. Our objective here is to be able to find the closed-loop sampled-data transfer function of an arrangement of subsystems that have a computer in the loop.

When manipulating block diagrams for sampled-data systems, you must be careful to remember the definition of the sampled-data system transfer function (derived in the last section) to avoid mistakes. For example, $z\{G_1(s)G_2(s)\} \neq G_1(z)G_2(z)$, where $z\{G_1(s)G_2(s)\}$ denotes the z-transform. The s-domain functions have to be multiplied together before taking the z-transform. In the ensuing discussion, we use the notation $G_1G_2(s)$ to denote a single function that is $G_1(s)G_2(s)$ after evaluating the product. Hence, $z\{G_1(s)G_2(s)\} = z\{G_1G_2(s)\} = G_1G_2(z) \neq G_1(z)G_2(z)$.

Let us look at the sampled-data systems shown in Figure 13.9. The sampled-data systems are shown under the column marked s. Their z-transforms are shown under the column marked z. The standard system that we derived earlier is shown in Figure 13.9(a), where the transform of the output, $C(z)$, is equal to $R(z)G(z)$. This system forms the basis for the other entries in Figure 13.9.

In Figure 13.9(b) there is no sampler between $G_1(s)$ and $G_2(s)$. Thus, we can think of a single function, $G_1(s)G_2(s)$, denoted $G_1G_2(s)$, existing between the two samplers and yielding a single transfer function, as shown in Figure 13.9(a). Hence, the pulse transfer function is $z\{G_1G_2(s)\} = G_1G_2(z)$. The transform of the output, $C(z) = R(z)G_1G_2(z)$.

In Figure 13.9(c) we have the cascaded two subsystems of the type shown in Figure 13.9(a). For this case, then, the z-transform is the product of the two z-transforms, or $G_2(z)G_1(z)$. Hence the transform of the output $C(z) = R(z)G_2(z)G_1(z)$.

Finally, in Figure 13.9(d), we see that the continuous signal entering the sampler is $R(s)G_1(s)$. Thus, the model is the same as Figure 13.9(a) with $R(s)$ replaced by $R(s)G_1(s)$, and $G_2(s)$ in Figure 13.9(d) replacing $G(s)$ in Figure 13.9(a). The z-transform of the input to $G_2(s)$ is $z\{R(s)G_1(s)\} = z\{RG_1(s)\} = RG_1(z)$. The pulse transfer function for the system $G_2(s)$ is $G_2(z)$. Hence, the output $C(z) = RG_1(z)G_2(z)$.

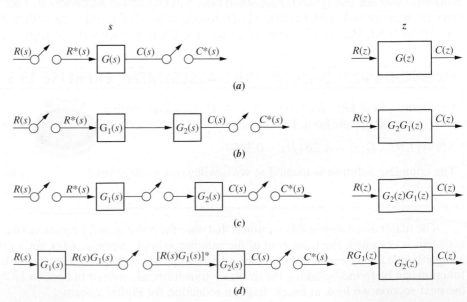

FIGURE 13.9 Sampled-data systems and their z-transforms

Using the basic forms shown in Figure 13.9, we can now find the z-transform of feedback control systems. We have shown that any system, $G(s)$, with sampled input and sampled output, such as that shown in Figure 13.9(a), can be represented as a sampled-data transfer function, $G(z)$. Thus, we want to perform block diagram manipulations that result in subsystems, as well as the entire feedback system, that have sampled inputs and sampled outputs. Then we can make the transformation to sampled-data transfer functions. An example follows.

■ EXAMPLE 13.5 ■

Pulse transfer function of a feedback system

Problem: Find the z-transform of the system shown in Figure 13.10(a).

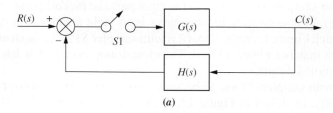

(a)

(b)

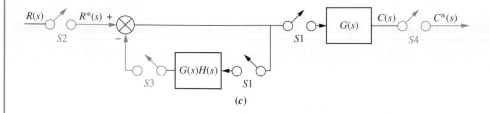

(c)

(d)

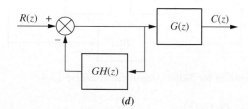

(e)   (f)

Note: Phantom samplers are shown in color.

FIGURE 13.10 Steps in block diagram reduction of a sampled-data system

SOLUTION: The objective of the problem is to proceed in an orderly fashion, starting with the block diagram of Figure 13.10(*a*) and reducing it to the one shown in Figure 13.10(*f*).

One operation we can always perform is to place a phantom sampler at the output of any subsystem that has a sampled input, provided that the nature of the signal sent to any other subsystem is not changed. For example in Figure 13.10(*b*), phantom sampler *S*4 can be added. The justification for this, of course, is that the output of a sampled-data system can only be found at the sampling instants anyway, and the signal is not an input to any other block.

Another operation that can be performed is to add phantom samplers *S*2 and *S*3 at the input to a summing junction whose output is sampled. The justification for this operation is that the sampled sum is equivalent to the sum of the sampled inputs, provided, of course, that all samplers are synchronized.

Next, move sampler *S*1 and $G(s)$ to the right past the pickoff point, as shown in Figure 13.10(*c*). The motivation for this move is to yield a sampler at the input of $G(s)H(s)$ to match Figure 13.9(*b*). Also, $G(s)$ with sampler *S*1 at the input and sampler *S*4 at the output matches Figure 13.9(*a*). The closed-loop system now has a sampled input and a sampled output.

$G(s)H(s)$ with samplers *S*1 and *S*3 becomes $GH(z)$, and $G(s)$ with samplers *S*1 and *S*4 becomes $G(z)$, as shown in Figure 13.10(*d*). Also, converting $R^*(s)$ to $R(z)$ and $C^*(s)$ to $C(z)$, we now have the system represented totally in the z-domain.

The equations derived in Chapter 5 for transfer functions represented with the Laplace transform can be used for sampled-data transfer functions with only a change in variables from s to z. Thus, using the feedback formula, we obtain the first block of Figure 13.10(*e*). Finally, multiplication of the cascaded sampled-data systems yields the final result shown in Figure 13.10(*f*).

▰▰▰▰▰ SKILL-ASSESSMENT EXERCISE 13.4 ▰▰▰▰▰

Problem: Find $T(z) = C(z)/R(z)$ for the system shown in Figure 13.11.

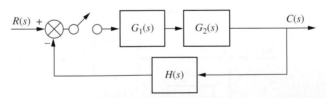

FIGURE 13.11   Digital system for Skill-Assessment Exercise 13.4

ANSWER: $T(z) = \dfrac{G_1 G_2(z)}{1 + H G_1 G_2(z)}$

The complete solution is located at www.wiley.com/college/nise.

This section paralleled Chapter 5 by showing how to obtain the closed-loop, sampled-data transfer function for a collection of subsystems. The next section parallels the discussion of stability in Chapter 6.

13.6 STABILITY

The glaring difference between analog feedback control systems and digital feedback control systems, such as the one shown in Figure 13.12, is the effect that the sampling rate has on the transient response. Changes in sampling rate not only change the nature of the response from overdamped to underdamped, but also can turn a stable system into an unstable one. As we proceed with our discussion, these effects will become apparent. You are encouraged to be on the lookout.

We now discuss the stability of digital systems from two perspectives: (1) z-plane and (2) s-plane. We will see that the Routh-Hurwitz criterion can be used only if we perform our analysis and design on the s-plane.

DIGITAL SYSTEM STABILITY VIA THE z-Plane

In the s-plane, the region of stability is the left half-plane. If the transfer function, $G(s)$, is transformed into a sampled-data transfer function, $G(z)$, the region of stability on the z-plane can be evaluated from the definition, $z = e^{Ts}$. Letting $s = \alpha + j\omega$, we obtain

$$
\begin{aligned}
z = e^{Ts} = e^{T(\alpha + j\omega)} &= e^{\alpha T} e^{j\omega T} \\
&= e^{\alpha T}(\cos \omega T + j \sin \omega T) \\
&= e^{\alpha T} \angle \omega T
\end{aligned}
\tag{13.47}
$$

since $(\cos \omega T + j \sin \omega T) = 1 \angle \omega T$.

Each region of the s-plane can be mapped into a corresponding region on the z-plane (see Figure 13.13). Points that have positive values of α are in the right half of the s-plane, region C. From Eq. (13.47), the magnitudes of the mapped points are

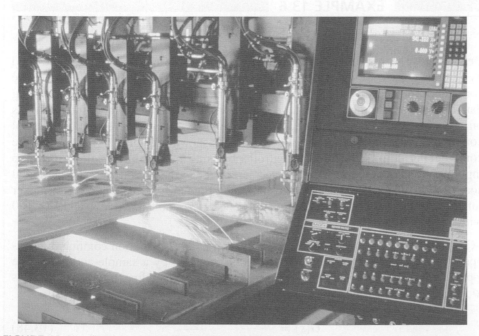

FIGURE 13.12 Computer-controlled torches cut thick sheets of metal used in construction

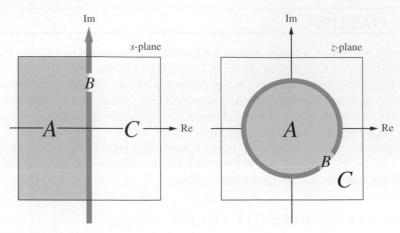

FIGURE 13.13   Mapping regions of the *s*-plane onto the *z*-plane

$e^{\alpha T} > 1$. Thus points in the right half of the *s*-plane map into points outside the unit circle on the *z*-plane.

Points on the $j\omega$-axis, region *B*, have zero values of α and yield points on the *z*-plane with magnitude $= 1$, the unit circle. Hence points on the $j\omega$-axis in the *s*-plane map into points on the unit circle on the *z*-plane.

Finally, points on the *s*-plane that yield negative values of α (left-half-plane roots, region A) map into the inside of the unit circle on the *z*-plane.

Thus, a digital control system is (1) stable if all poles of the closed-loop transfer function, $T(z)$, are inside the unit circle on the *z*-plane, (2) unstable if any pole is outside the unit circle and/or there are poles of multiplicity greater than one on the unit circle, and (3) marginally stable if poles of multiplicity one are on the unit circle and all other poles are inside the unit circle. Let us look at an example.

EXAMPLE 13.6

Modeling and stability

Problem: The missile shown in Figure 13.14(*a*) can be aerodynamically controlled by torques created by the deflection of control surfaces on the missile's body. The commands to deflect these control surfaces come from a computer that uses tracking data along with programmed guidance equations to determine whether the missile is on track. The information from the guidance equations is used to develop flight-control commands for the missile. A simplified model is shown in Figure 13.14(*b*). Here the computer performs the function of controller by using tracking information to develop input commands to the missile. An accelerometer in the missile detects the actual acceleration, which is fed back to the computer. Find the closed-loop digital transfer function for this system and determine if the system is stable for $K = 20$ and $K = 100$ with a sampling interval of $T = 0.1$ second.

SOLUTION: The input to the control system is an acceleration command developed by the computer. The computer can be modeled by a sample-and-hold. The *s*-plane model is shown in Figure 13.14(*c*). The first step in finding the *z*-plane model is to find $G(z)$, the forward-path transfer function. From Figure 13.14(*c*) or (*d*),

$$G(s) = \frac{1 - e^{-Ts}}{s} \frac{Ka}{s(s + a)} \tag{13.48}$$

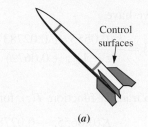

(a)

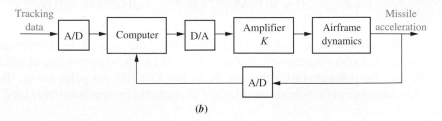

(b)

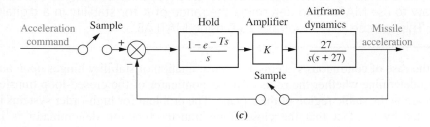

(c)

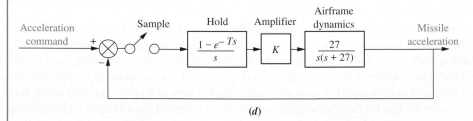

(d)

FIGURE 13.14
Finding stability of a missile control system: **a.** missile; **b.** conceptual block diagram; **c.** block diagram; **d.** block diagram with equivalent single sampler

where $a = 27$. The z-transform, $G(z)$, is $(1 - z^{-1})z\{Ka/[s^2(s + a)]\}$.

The term $Ka/[s^2(s + a)]$ is first expanded by partial fractions, after which we find the z-transform of each term from Table 13.1. Hence,

$$z\left\{\frac{Ka}{s^2(s+a)}\right\} = Kz\left\{\frac{a}{s^2(s+a)}\right\} = Kz\left\{\frac{1}{s^2} - \frac{1/a}{s} + \frac{1/a}{s+a}\right\}$$

$$= K\left\{\frac{Tz}{(z-1)^2} - \frac{z/a}{z-1} + \frac{z/a}{z-e^{-aT}}\right\}$$

$$= K\left\{\frac{Tz}{(z-1)^2} - \frac{(1-e^{-aT})z}{a(z-1)(z-e^{-aT})}\right\} \tag{13.49}$$

Thus,

$$G(z) = K\left\{\frac{T(z - e^{-aT}) - (z-1)\left(\dfrac{1-e^{-aT}}{a}\right)}{(z-1)(z-e^{-aT})}\right\} \tag{13.50}$$

Letting $T = 0.1$ and $a = 27$, we have

$$G(z) = \frac{K(0.0655z + 0.02783)}{(z-1)(z-0.0672)} \tag{13.51}$$

Finally, we find the closed-loop transfer function, $T(z)$, for a unity feedback system:

$$T(z) = \frac{G(z)}{1+G(z)} = \frac{K(0.0655z + 0.02783)}{z^2 + (0.0655K - 1.0672)z + (0.02783K + 0.0672)} \tag{13.52}$$

The stability of the system is found by finding the roots of the denominator. For $K = 20$, the roots of the denominator are $0.12 \pm j0.78$. The system is thus stable for $K = 20$, since the poles are inside the unit circle. For $K = 100$, the poles are at -0.58 and -4.9. Since one of the poles is outside the unit circle, the system is unstable for $K = 100$.

Students who are using MATLAB should now run ch13p5 in Appendix B. You will learn how to use MATLAB to determine the range of K for stability in a digital system. This exercise solves Example 13.6 using MATLAB.

In the case of continuous systems, the determination of stability hinges upon our ability to determine whether the roots of the denominator of the closed-loop transfer function are in the stable region of the s-plane. The problem for high-order systems is complicated by the fact that the closed-loop transfer function denominator is in polynomial form, not factored form. The same problem surfaces with closed-loop sampled-data transfer functions.

Tabular methods for determining stability, such as the Routh-Hurwitz method used for higher-order continuous systems, exist for sampled-data systems. These methods, which are not covered in this introductory chapter to digital control systems, can be used to determine stability in higher-order digital systems. If you wish to go further into the area of digital system stability, you are encouraged to look at Raible's tabular method or Jury's stability test for determining the number of a sampled-data system's closed-loop poles that exist outside the unit circle and thus indicate instability.[2]

The following example demonstrates the effect of sampling rate on the stability of a closed-loop feedback control system. All parameters are constant except for the sampling interval, T. We will see that varying T will lead us through regions of stability and instability just as though we were varying the forward-path gain, K.

EXAMPLE 13.7

Range of T for stability

Problem: Determine the range of sampling interval, T, that will make the system shown in Figure 13.15 stable, and the range that will make it unstable.

SOLUTION: Since $H(s) = 1$, the z-transform of the closed-loop system, $T(z)$, is found from Figure 13.10 to be

$$T(z) = \frac{G(z)}{1+G(z)} \tag{13.53}$$

---

[2] A discussion of Raible's tabular method and Jury's stability test can be found in *Kuo (1980: 278–286)*.

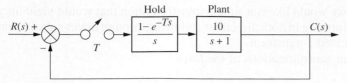

FIGURE 13.15 Digital system for Example 13.7

To find $G(z)$, first find the partial-fraction expansion of $G(s)$.

$$G(s) = 10\frac{1 - e^{-Ts}}{s(s + 1)} = 10(1 - e^{-Ts})\left(\frac{1}{s} - \frac{1}{s + 1}\right) \qquad (13.54)$$

Taking the z-transform, we obtain

$$G(z) = \frac{10(z - 1)}{z}\left[\frac{z}{z - 1} - \frac{z}{z - e^{-T}}\right] = 10\frac{(1 - e^{-T})}{(z - e^{-T})} \qquad (13.55)$$

Substituting Eq. (13.55) into (13.53) yields

$$T(z) = \frac{10(1 - e^{-T})}{z - (11e^{-T} - 10)} \qquad (13.56)$$

The pole of Eq. (13.56), $(11e^{-T} - 10)$, monotonically decreases from $+1$ to -1 for $0 < T < 0.2$. For $0.2 < T < \infty$ $(11e^{-T} - 10)$, monotonically decreases from -1 to -10. Thus, the pole of $T(z)$ will be inside the unit circle, and the system will be stable if $0 < T < 0.2$. In terms of frequency, where $f = 1/T$ the system will be stable as long as the sampling frequency is $1/0.2 = 5$ hertz or greater.

We now have found, via the z-plane, that sampled systems are stable if their poles are inside the unit circle. Unfortunately, this stability criterion precludes the use of the Routh-Hurwitz criterion, which detects roots in the right half-plane rather than outside the unit circle. However, another method exists that allows us to use the familiar s-plane and the Routh-Hurwitz criterion to determine the stability of a sampled system. Let us introduce this topic.

BILINEAR TRANSFORMATIONS

Bilinear transformations give us the ability to apply our s-plane analysis and design techniques to digital systems. We can analyze and design on the s-plane as we have done in Chapters 8 and 9 and then, using these transformations, convert the results to a digital system that contains the same properties. Let us look further into this topic.

We can consider $z = e^{Ts}$ and its inverse, $s = (1/T) \ln z$, as the exact transformations between z and s. Thus, if we have $G(z)$ and substitute $z = e^{Ts}$, we obtain $G(e^{Ts})$ as the result of converting to s. Similarly, if we have $G(s)$ and substitute $s = (1/T)\ln z$, we obtain $G((1/T)\ln z)$ as the result of converting to z. Unfortunately, both transformations yield transcendental functions, which we of course take care of through the rather complicated z-transform.

What we would like is a simple transformation that would yield linear arguments when transforming in both directions (bilinear) through direct substitution and without the complicated z-transform.

Bilinear transformations of the form

$$z = \frac{as + b}{cs + d} \tag{13.57}$$

and its inverse,

$$s = \frac{-dz + b}{cz - a} \tag{13.58}$$

have been derived to yield linear variables in s and z. Different values of a, b, c, and d have been derived for particular applications and yield various degrees of accuracy when comparing properties of the continuous and sampled functions.

For example, in the next subsection we will see that a particular choice of coefficients will take points on the unit circle and map them into points on the $j\omega$-axis. Points outside the unit circle will be mapped into the right half-plane, and points inside the unit circle will be mapped into the left half-plane. Thus, we will be able to make a simple transformation from the z-plane to the s-plane and obtain stability information about the digital system by working in the s-plane.

Since the transformations are not exact, only the property for which they are designed can be relied upon. For the stability transformation just discussed, we cannot expect the resulting $G(s)$ to have the same transient response as $G(z)$. Another transformation will be covered that will retain that property.

DIGITAL SYSTEM STABILITY VIA THE s-PLANE

In this subsection we look at a bilinear transformation that maps $j\omega$-axis points on the s-plane to unit-circle points on the z-plane. Further, the transformation maps right half-plane points on the s-plane to points outside the unit circle on the z-plane. Finally, the transformation maps left-half-plane points on the s-plane to points inside the unit circle on the z-plane. Thus, we are able to transform the denominator of the pulsed transfer function, $D(z)$, to the denominator of a continuous transfer function, $D(s)$, and use the Routh-Hurwitz criterion to determine stability.

The bilinear transformation

$$s = \frac{z + 1}{z - 1} \tag{13.59}$$

and its inverse

$$z = \frac{s + 1}{s - 1} \tag{13.60}$$

perform the required transformation (*Kuo, 1995*). We can show this fact as follows: Letting $s = \alpha + j\omega$ and substituting into Eq. (13.60),

$$z = \frac{(\alpha + 1) + j\omega}{(\alpha - 1) + j\omega} \tag{13.61}$$

from which

$$|z| = \frac{\sqrt{(\alpha + 1)^2 + \omega^2}}{\sqrt{(\alpha - 1)^2 + \omega^2}} \tag{13.62}$$

Thus,

$$|z| < 1 \qquad \text{when } \alpha < 0 \tag{13.63a}$$

$$|z| > 1 \qquad \text{when } \alpha > 0 \tag{13.63b}$$

and

$$|z| = 1 \qquad \text{when } \alpha = 0 \tag{13.63c}$$

Let us look at an example that shows how the stability of sampled systems can be found using this bilinear transformation and the Routh-Hurwit criterion.

EXAMPLE 13.8

Stability via Routh-Hurwitz

Problem: Given $T(z) = N(z)/D(z)$, where $D(z) = z^3 - z^2 - 0.2z + 0.1$, use the Routh-Hurwitz criterion to find the number of z-plane poles of $T(z)$ inside, outside, and on the unit circle. Is the system stable?

SOLUTION: Substitute Eq. (13.60) into $D(z) = 0$ and obtain[3]

$$s^3 - 19s^2 - 45s - 17 = 0 \tag{13.64}$$

The Routh table for Eq. (13.64), Table 13.3, shows one root in the right half-plane and two roots in the left half-plane. Hence, $T(z)$ has one pole outside the unit circle, no poles on the unit circle, and two poles inside the unit circle. The system is unstable because of the pole outside the unit circle.

TABLE 13.3 Routh table for Example 13.8

s^3	1	−45
s^2	19	−17
s^1	−45.89	0
s^0	−17	0

SKILL-ASSESSMENT EXERCISE 13.5

Problem: Determine the range of sampling interval, T, that will make the system shown in Figure 13.16 stable.

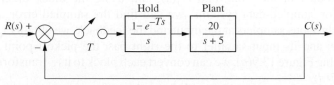

FIGURE 13.16 Digital system for Skill-Assessment Exercise 13.5

ANSWER: $0 < T < 0.1022$ second

The complete solution is located at www.wiley.com/college/nise.

---

[3] Symbolic math software, such as MATLAB's Symbolic Math Toolbox, is recommended to reduce the labor required to perform the transformation.

SKILL-ASSESSMENT EXERCISE 13.6

Problem: Given $T(z) = N(z)/D(z)$, where $D(z) = z^3 - z^2 - 0.5z + 0.3$, use the Routh-Hurwitz criterion to find the number of z-plane poles of $T(z)$ inside, outside, and on the unit circle. Is the system stable?

ANSWER: $T(z)$ has one pole outside the unit circle, no poles on the unit circle, and two poles inside the unit circle. The system is unstable.

The complete solution is located at www.wiley.com/college/nise.

In this section we covered the concepts of stability for digital systems. Both z- and s-plane perspectives were discussed. Using a bilinear transformation, we are able to use the Routh-Hurwitz criterion to determine stability.

The highlight of the section is that sampling rate (along with system parameters, such as gain and component values) helps to determine or destroy the stability of a digital system. In general, if the sampling rate is too slow, the closed-loop digital system will be unstable. We now move from stability to steady-state errors, paralleling our previous discussion of steady-state errors in analog systems.

13.7 STEADY-STATE ERRORS

We now examine the effect of sampling upon the steady-state error for digital systems. Any general conclusion about the steady-state error is difficult because of the dependence of those conclusions upon the placement of the sampler in the loop. Remember that the position of the sampler could change the open-loop transfer function. In the discussion of analog systems, there was only one open-loop transfer function, $G(s)$, upon which the general theory of steady-state error was based and from which came the standard definitions of static error constants. For digital systems, however, the placement of the sampler changes the open-loop transfer function and thus precludes any general conclusions. In this section we assume the typical placement of the sampler after the error and in the position of the cascade controller, and we derive our conclusions accordingly about the steady-state error of digital systems.

Consider the digital system in Figure 13.17(a), where the digital computer is represented by the sampler and zero-order hold. The transfer function of the plant is represented by $G_1(s)$ and the transfer function of the z.o.h. by $(1 - e^{-Ts})/s$. Letting $G(s)$ equal the product of the z.o.h. and $G_1(s)$, and using the block diagram reduction techniques for sampled-data systems, we can find the sampled error, $E^*(s) = E(z)$. Adding synchronous samplers at the input and the feedback, we obtain Figure 13.17(b). Pushing $G(s)$ and its input sampler to the right past the pickoff point yields Figure 13.17(c). Using Figure 13.9(a), we can convert each block to its z-transform, resulting in Figure 13.17(d).

From this figure, $E(z) = R(z) - E(z)G(z)$, or

$$E(z) = \frac{R(z)}{1 + G(z)} \tag{13.65}$$

The final value theorem for discrete signals states that

$$e^*(\infty) = \lim_{z \to 1} (1 - z^{-1})E(z) \tag{13.66}$$

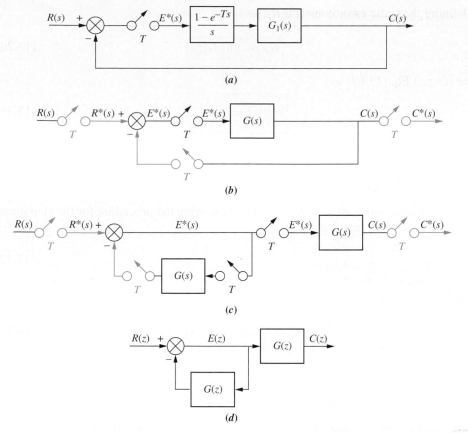

FIGURE 13.17
a. Digital feedback control system for evaluation of steady-state errors; **b.** phantom samplers added; **c.** pushing $G(s)$ and its samplers to the right past the pickoff point; **d.** z-transform equivalent system

Note: Phantom samplers are shown in color.

where $e^*(\infty)$ is the final sampled value of $e(t)$, or (alternatively) the final value of $e(kT)$.[4]

Using the final value theorem on Eq. (13.65), we find that the sampled steady-state error, $e^*(\infty)$, for unity negative-feedback systems is

$$e^*(\infty) = \lim_{z \to 1} (1 - z^{-1}) E(z) = \lim_{z \to 1} (1 - z^{-1}) \frac{R(z)}{1 + G(z)} \qquad (13.67)$$

Equation (13.67) must now be evaluated for each input: step, ramp, and parabola.

UNIT STEP INPUT

For a unit step input, $R(s) = 1/s$. From Table 13.1,

$$R(z) = \frac{z}{z - 1} \qquad (13.68)$$

Substituting Eq. (13.68) into Eq. (13.67), we have

$$e^*(\infty) = \frac{1}{1 + \lim_{z \to 1} G(z)} \qquad (13.69)$$

[4] See *Ogata (1987: 59)* for a derivation.

Defining the static error constant, K_p, as

$$K_p = \lim_{z \to 1} G(z) \tag{13.70}$$

we rewrite Eq. (13.69) as

$$e^*(\infty) = \frac{1}{1 + K_p} \tag{13.71}$$

UNIT RAMP INPUT

For a unit ramp input, $R(z) = Tz/(z-1)^2$. Following the procedure for the step input, you can derive the fact that

$$e^*(\infty) = \frac{1}{K_v} \tag{13.72}$$

where

$$K_v = \frac{1}{T} \lim_{z \to 1} (z-1)G(z) \tag{13.73}$$

UNIT PARABOLIC INPUT

For a unit parabolic input, $R(z) = T^2 z(z+1)/[2(z-1)^3]$. Similarly,

$$e^*(\infty) = \frac{1}{K_a} \tag{13.74}$$

where

$$K_a = \frac{1}{T^2} \lim_{z \to 1} (z-1)^2 G(z) \tag{13.75}$$

SUMMARY OF STEADY-STATE ERRORS

The equations developed above for $e^*(\infty)$, K_p, K_v, and K_a are similar to the equations developed for analog systems. Whereas multiple pole placement at the origin of the s-plane reduced steady-state errors to zero in the analog case, we can see that multiple pole placement at $z = 1$ reduces the steady-state error to zero for digital systems of the type discussed in this section. This conclusion makes sense when one considers that $s = 0$ maps into $z = 1$ under $z = e^{Ts}$.

For example, for a step input, we see that if $G(z)$ in Eq. (13.69) has one pole at $z = 1$, the limit will become infinite, and the steady-state error will reduce to zero.

For a ramp input, if $G(z)$ in Eq. (13.73) has two poles at $z = 1$, the limit will become infinite, and the error will reduce to zero.

Similar conclusions can be drawn for the parabolic input and Eq. (13.75). Here, $G(z)$ needs three poles at $z = 1$ in order for the steady-state error to be zero. Let us look at an example.

EXAMPLE 13.9

Finding steady-state error

Problem: For step, ramp, and parabolic inputs, find the steady-state error for the feedback control system shown in Figure 13.17(a) if

$$G_1(s) = \frac{10}{s(s+1)} \qquad (13.76)$$

SOLUTION: First find $G(s)$, the product of the z.o.h. and the plant.

$$G(s) = \frac{10(1 - e^{-Ts})}{s^2(s+1)} = 10(1 - e^{-Ts})\left[\frac{1}{s^2} - \frac{1}{s} + \frac{1}{s+1}\right] \qquad (13.77)$$

The z-transform is then

$$G(z) = 10(1 - z^{-1})\left[\frac{Tz}{(z-1)^2} - \frac{z}{z-1} + \frac{z}{z-e^{-T}}\right]$$

$$= 10\left[\frac{T}{z-1} - 1 + \frac{z-1}{z-e^{-T}}\right] \qquad (13.78)$$

For a step input,

$$K_p = \lim_{z \to 1} G(z) = \infty; \qquad e^*(\infty) = \frac{1}{1 + K_p} = 0 \qquad (13.79)$$

For a ramp input,

$$K_v = \frac{1}{T}\lim_{z \to 1}(z-1)G(z) = 10; \qquad e^*(\infty) = \frac{1}{K_v} = 0.1 \qquad (13.80)$$

For a parabolic input,

$$K_a = \frac{1}{T^2}\lim_{z \to 1}(z-1)^2 G(z) = 0; \qquad e^*(\infty) = \frac{1}{K_a} = \infty \qquad (13.81)$$

You will notice that the answers obtained are the same as the results obtained for the analog system. However, since stability depends upon the sampling interval, be sure to check the stability of the system after a sampling interval is established before making steady-state error calculations.

Students who are using MATLAB should now run ch13p6 in Appendix B. You will learn how to use MATLAB to determine K_p, K_v, and K_a in a digital system as well as check the stability. This exercise solves Example 13.9 using MATLAB.

MATLAB

SKILL-ASSESSMENT EXERCISE 13.7

Problem: For step, ramp, and parabolic inputs, find the steady-state error for the feedback control system shown in Figure 13.17(a) if

$$G_1(s) = \frac{20(s+3)}{(s+4)(s+5)}$$

Let $T = 0.1$ second. Repeat for $T = 0.5$ second.

ANSWER: For $T = 0.1$ second, $K_p = 3$, $K_v = 0$, and $K_a = 0$; for $T = 0.5$ second, the system is unstable.

The complete solution is located at www.wiley.com/college/nise.

In this section we discussed and evaluated the steady-state error of digital systems for step, ramp, and parabolic inputs. The equations for steady-state error parallel those for analog systems. Even the definitions of the static error constants were similar. Poles at the origin of the s-plane for analog systems were replaced with poles at $+1$ on the z-plane to improve the steady-state error. We continue our parallel discussion by moving into a discussion of transient response and the root locus for digital systems.

13.8 TRANSIENT RESPONSE ON THE *z*-PLANE

Recall that for analog systems a transient response requirement was specified by selecting a closed-loop, s-plane pole. In Chapter 8, the closed-loop pole was on the existing root locus, and the design consisted of a simple gain adjustment. If the closed-loop pole was not on the existing root locus, then a cascade compensator was designed to reshape the original root locus to go through the desired closed-loop pole. A gain adjustment then completed the design.

In the next two sections, we want to parallel the described analog methods and apply similar techniques to digital systems. For this introductory chapter we will parallel the discussion through design via gain adjustment. The design of compensation is left to you to pursue in an advanced course.

Chapter 4 established the relationships between transient response and the s-plane. We saw that vertical lines on the s-plane were lines of constant settling time, horizontal lines were lines of constant peak time, and radial lines were lines of constant percent overshoot. In order to draw equivalent conclusions on the z-plane, we now map those lines through $z = e^{sT}$.

The vertical lines on the s-plane are lines of constant settling time and are characterized by the equation $s = \sigma_1 + j\omega$, where the real part, $\sigma_1 = -4/T_s$, is constant and is in the left half-plane for stability. Substituting this into $z = e^{sT}$, we obtain

$$z = e^{\sigma_1 T} e^{j\omega T} = r_1 e^{j\omega T} \tag{13.82}$$

Equation (13.82) denotes concentric circles of radius r_1. If σ_1 is positive, the circle has a larger radius than the unit circle. On the other hand, if σ_1 is negative, the circle has a smaller radius than the unit circle. The circles of constant settling time, normalized to the sampling interval, are shown in Figure 13.18 with radius $e^{\sigma_1 T} = e^{-4/(T_s/T)}$. Also, $T_s/T = -4/\ln(r)$, where r is the radius of the circle of constant settling time.

The horizontal lines are lines of constant peak time. The lines are characterized by the equation $s = \sigma + j\omega_1$, where the imaginary part, $\omega_1 = \pi/T_p$, is constant. Substituting this into $z = e^{sT}$, we obtain

$$z = e^{\sigma T} e^{j\omega_1 T} = e^{\sigma T} e^{j\theta_1} \tag{13.83}$$

Equation (13.83) represents radial lines at an angle of θ_1. If σ is negative, that section of the radial line lies inside the unit circle. If σ is positive, that section of the radial line lies outside the unit circle. The lines of constant peak time normalized to the sampling interval are shown in Figure 13.18. The angle of each radial line is $\omega_1 T = \theta_1 = \pi/(T_p/T)$, from which $T_p/T = \pi/\theta_1$.

Finally, we map the radial lines of the s-plane onto the z-plane. Remember, these radial lines are lines of constant percent overshoot on the s-plane. From Figure 13.19, these radial lines are represented by

$$\frac{\sigma}{\omega} = -\tan(\sin^{-1}\zeta) = -\frac{\zeta}{\sqrt{1-\zeta^2}} \tag{13.84}$$

Hence,

$$s = \sigma + j\omega = -\omega \frac{\zeta}{\sqrt{1-\zeta^2}} + j\omega \tag{13.85}$$

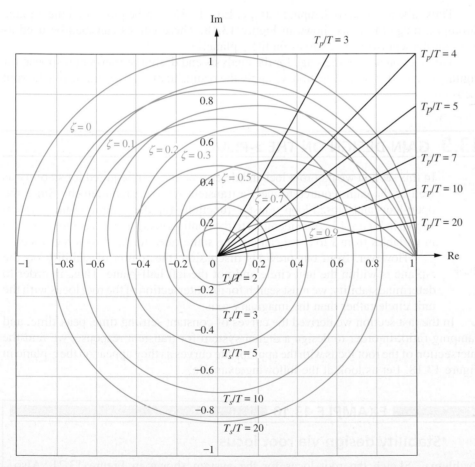

FIGURE 13.18 Constant damping ratio, normalized settling time, and normalized peak time plots on the z-plane

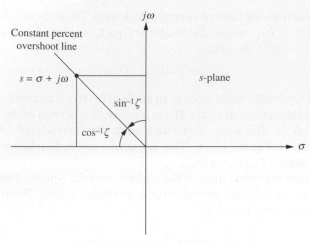

FIGURE 13.19   The *s*-plane sketch of constant percent overshoot line

Transforming Eq. (13.85) to the *z*-plane yields

$$z = e^{sT} = e^{-\omega T(\zeta/\sqrt{1-\zeta^2})}e^{j\omega T} = e^{-\omega T(\zeta/\sqrt{1-\zeta^2})} \angle \omega T \qquad (13.86)$$

Thus, given a desired damping ratio, ζ, Eq. (13.86) can be plotted on the *z*-plane through a range of ωT as shown in Figure 13.18. These curves can then be used as constant percent overshoot curves on the *z*-plane.

This section has set the stage for the analysis and design of transient response for digital systems. In the next section we apply the results to digital systems using the root locus.

13.9   GAIN DESIGN ON THE *z*-PLANE

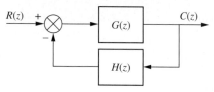

FIGURE 13.20   Generic digital feedback control system

In this section we plot root loci and determine the gain required for stability as well as the gain required to meet a transient response requirement. Since the open-loop and closed-loop transfer functions for the generic digital system shown in Figure 13.20 are identical to the continuous system except for a change in variables from *s* to *z*, we can use the same rules for plotting a root locus.

However, from our previous discussion, the region of stability on the *z*-plane is within the unit circle and not the left half-plane. Thus, in order to determine stability, we must search for the intersection of the root locus with the unit circle rather than the imaginary axis.

In the last section we derived the curves of constant settling time, peak time, and damping ratio. In order to design a digital system for transient response, we find the intersection of the root locus with the appropriate curves as they appear on the *z*-plane in Figure 13.18. Let us look at the following example.

EXAMPLE 13.10

Stability design via root locus

Problem: Sketch the root locus for the system shown in Figure 13.21. Also, determine the range of gain, *K*, for stability from the root locus plot.

SOLUTION: Treat the system as if z were s, and sketch the root locus. The result is shown in Figure 13.22. Using the root locus program discussed in Appendix G.2 at www.wiley.com/college/nise, search along the unit circle for $180°$. Identification of the gain, K, at this point yields the range of gain for stability. Using the program, we find that the intersection of the root locus with the unit circle is $1 \angle 60°$. The gain at this point is 0.5. Hence, the range of gain for stability is $0 < K < 0.5$.

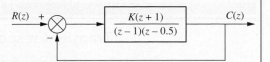

FIGURE 13.21 Digital feedback control for Example 13.10

Students who are using MATLAB should now run ch13p7 in Appendix B. You will learn how to use MATLAB to plot a root locus on the *z*-plane as well as super-impose the unit circle. You will learn how to select interactively the intersection of the root locus and the unit circle to obtain the value of gain for stability. This exercise solves Example 13.10 using MATLAB.

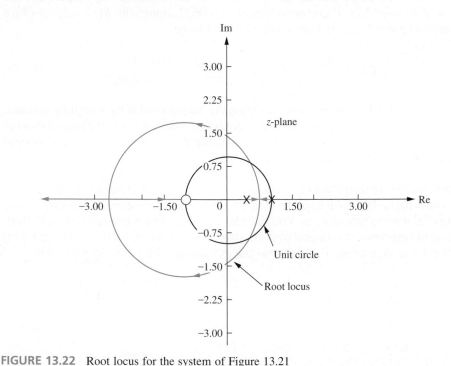

FIGURE 13.22 Root locus for the system of Figure 13.21

In the next example, we design the value of gain, K, in Figure 13.21 to meet a transient response specification. The problem is handled similarly to the analog system design, where we found the gain at the point where the root locus crossed the specified damping ratio, settling time, or peak time curve. In digital systems, these curves are as shown in Figure 13.18. In summary, then, draw the root locus of the digital system and superimpose the curves of Figure 13.18. Then find out where the root locus intersects the desired damping ratio, settling time, or peak time curve and evaluate the gain at that point. In order to simplify the calculations and obtain more accurate results, draw a radial line through the point where the root locus intersects the appropriate curve. Measure the angle of this line and use the root locus program in Appendix G.2 at www.wiley.com/college/nise to search along this radial line for the point of intersection with the root locus.

EXAMPLE 13.11

Transient response design via gain adjustment

Problem: For the system of Figure 13.21, find the value of gain, K, to yield a damping ratio of 0.7.

SOLUTION: Figure 13.23 shows the constant damping ratio curves superimposed over the root locus for the system as determined from the last example. Draw a radial line from the origin to the intersection of the root locus with the 0.7 damping ratio curve (a 16.62° line). The root locus program discussed in Appendix G.2 at www.wiley.com/college/nise can now be used to obtain the gain by searching along a 16.62° line for 180°, the intersection with the root locus. The results of the program show that the gain, K, is 0.0627 at $0.719 + j0.215$, the point where the 0.7 damping ratio curve intersects the root locus.

We can now check our design by finding the unit sampled step response of the system of Figure 13.21. Using our design, $K = 0.0627$, along with $R(z) = z/(z - 1)$, a sampled step input, we find the sampled output to be

$$C(z) = \frac{R(z)G(z)}{1 + G(z)} = \frac{0.0627z^2 + 0.0627z}{z^3 - 2.4373z^2 + 2z - 0.5627} \tag{13.87}$$

Performing the indicated division, we obtain the output valid at the sampling instants, as shown in Figure 13.24. Since the overshoot is approximately 5%, the requirement of a 0.7 damping ratio has been met. You should remember, however, that the plot is valid only at integer values of the sampling instants.

Students who are using MATLAB should now run ch13p8 in Appendix B. You will learn how to use MATLAB to plot a root locus on the z-plane as well as superimpose a grid of damping ratio curves. You will learn how to obtain the gain and a closed-loop step response of a digital system after interactively selecting the operating point on the root locus. This exercise solves Example 13.11 using MATLAB.

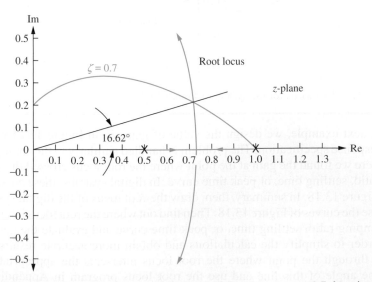

FIGURE 13.23   Root locus for the system of Figure 13.21 with constant 0.7 damping ratio curve

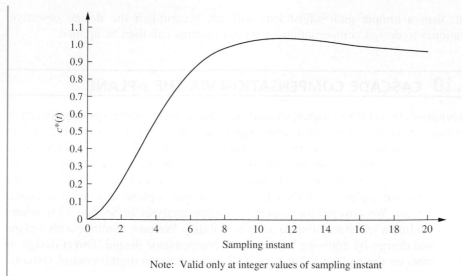

FIGURE 13.24   Sampled step response of the system of Figure 13.21 with $K = 0.0627$

SKILL-ASSESSMENT EXERCISE 13.8

Problem: For the system of Figure 13.20 where $H(z) = 1$ and

$$G(z) = \frac{K(z + 0.5)}{(z - 0.25)(z - 0.75)}$$

find the value of gain, K, to yield a damping ratio of 0.5.

ANSWER: $K = 0.31$

The complete solution is at www.wiley.com/college/nise.

TryIt 13.3

Use MATLAB, the Control System Toolbox, and the following statements to solve Skill-Assessment Exercise 13.8.

```
Gz = zpk (-0.5, [0.25, 0.75],...
    1, [])
rlocus (Gz)
zgrid (0.5, [])
[K,p]=rlocfind (Gz)
```

Note: When the root locus appears, click on the intersection of the 0.5 damping ratio curve and the root locus to calculate the gain.

MATLAB's Simulink provides an alternative method of simulating digital systems to obtain the time response. Students who are performing the MATLAB exercises and want to explore the added capability of Simulink should now consult Appendix C, MATLAB's Simulink Tutorial. Example C.4 in the tutorial shows how to use Simulink to simulate digital systems.

MATLAB's LTI Viewer provides another method of simulating digital systems to obtain the time response. Students who are performing the MATLAB exercises and want to explore the added capability of MATLAB's LTI Viewer should now consult Appendix D at www.wiley.com/college/nise, which contains a tutorial on the LTI Viewer as well as some examples. One of the illustrative examples, Example D.5, finds the closed-loop step response of a digital system using the LTI Viewer.

In this section we used the root locus and gain adjustment to design the transient response of a digital system. This method suffers the same drawbacks as when it was applied to analog systems; namely, if the root locus does not intersect a desired design point, then a simple gain adjustment will not accomplish the design objective. Techniques to design compensation for digital systems can then be applied.

13.10 CASCADE COMPENSATION VIA THE *s*-PLANE

In previous sections of this chapter, we analyzed and designed digital systems directly in the *z*-domain up to and including design via gain adjustment. We are now ready to design digital compensators, such as those covered in Chapters 9 and 11. Rather than continuing on this path of design directly in the *z*-domain, we depart by covering analysis and design techniques that allow us to make use of previous chapters by designing on the *s*-plane and then transforming our *s*-plane design to a digital implementation. We covered one aspect of *s*-plane analysis in Section 13.6, where we used a bilinear transformation to analyze stability. We now continue with *s*-plane analysis and design by applying it to cascade compensator design. Direct design of compensators on the *z*-plane is left for a dedicated course in digital control systems.

CASCADE COMPENSATION

In order to perform design in the *s*-plane and then convert the continuous compensator to a digital compensator, we need a bilinear transformation that will preserve, at the sampling instants, the response of the continuous compensator. The bilinear transformation covered in Section 13.6 will not meet that requirement. A bilinear transformation that can be performed with hand calculations and yields a digital transfer function whose output response at the sampling instants is approximately the same as the equivalent analog transfer function is called the *Tustin transformation*. This transformation is used to transform the continuous compensator, $G_c(s)$, to the digital compensator, $G_c(z)$. The Tustin transformation is given by[5]

$$s = \frac{2(z-1)}{T(z+1)} \tag{13.88}$$

and its inverse by

$$z = \frac{-\left(s + \dfrac{2}{T}\right)}{\left(s - \dfrac{2}{T}\right)} = \frac{1 + \dfrac{T}{2}s}{1 - \dfrac{T}{2}s} \tag{13.89}$$

As the sampling interval, T, gets smaller (higher sampling rate), the designed digital compensator's output yields a closer match to the analog compensator. If the sampling rate is not high enough, there is a discrepancy at higher frequencies between the digital and analog filters' frequency responses. Methods are available to correct the discrepancy, but they are beyond the scope of our discussion. The interested reader should investigate the topic of *prewarping,* covered in books dedicated to digital control and listed in the Bibliography at the end of this chapter.

Astrom and Wittenmark (1984) have developed a guideline for selecting the sampling interval, T. Their conclusion is that the value of T in seconds should be in the range $0.15/\omega_{\Phi_M}$ to $0.5/\omega_{\Phi_M}$, where ω_{Φ_M} is the zero dB frequency (rad/s) of the magnitude frequency response curve for the cascaded analog compensator and plant.

---

[5] See *Ogata (1987: 315–318)* for a derivation.

In the following example, we will design a compensator, $G_c(s)$, to meet the required performance specifications. We will then use the Tustin transformation to obtain the model for an equivalent digital controller. In the next section we will show how to implement the digital controller.

■■■■■■■■■■■■■■■■■■■ EXAMPLE 13.12 ■■■■■■■■■■■■■■■■■■

Digital cascade compensator design

Problem: For the digital control system of Figure 13.25(*a*), where

$$G_p(s) = \frac{1}{s(s+6)(s+10)} \qquad (13.90)$$

design a digital lead compensator, $G_c(z)$, as shown in Figure 13.25(*c*), so that the system will operate with 20% overshoot and a settling time of 1.1 seconds. Create your design in the *s*-domain and transform the compensator to the *z*-domain.

SOLUTION: Using Figure 13.25(*b*), design a lead compensator using the techniques described in Chapter 9 or 11. The design was created as part of Example 9.6,

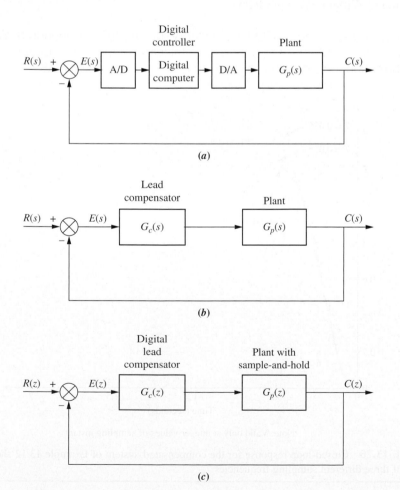

(*a*)

(*b*)

(*c*)

FIGURE 13.25
a. Digital control system showing the digital computer performing compensation;
b. continuous system used for design;
c. transformed digital system

where we found that the lead compensator was

$$G_c(s) = \frac{1977(s+6)}{(s+29.1)} \tag{13.91}$$

Using Eqs. (13.90) and (13.91), we find that the zero dB frequency, ω_{Φ_M}, for $G_p(s)G_c(s)$ is 5.8 rad/s. Using the guideline described by *Astrom and Wittenmark (1984)*, the lowest value of T should be in the range $0.15/\omega_{\Phi_M} = 0.026$ to $0.5/\omega_{\Phi_M} = 0.086$ second. Let us use $T = 0.01$ second.

Substituting Eq. (13.88) into Eq. (13.91) with $T = 0.01$ second yields

$$G_c(z) = \frac{1778z - 1674}{z - 0.746} \tag{13.92}$$

The z-transform of the plant and zero-order hold, found by the method discussed in Section 13.4 with $T = 0.01$ second, is

$$G_p(z) = \frac{(1.602 \times 10^{-7} z^2) + (6.156 \times 10^{-7} z) + (1.478 \times 10^{-7})}{z^3 - 2.847z^2 + 2.699z - 0.8521} \tag{13.93}$$

The time response in Figure 13.26 ($T = 0.01$ s) shows that the compensated closed-loop system meets the transient response requirements. The figure also shows the response for a compensator designed with sampling times at the extremes of Astrom and Wittenmark's guideline.

Students who are using MATLAB should now run ch13p9 in Appendix B. You will learn how to use MATLAB to design a digital lead compensator using the Tustin transformation. This exercise solves Example 13.12 using MATLAB.

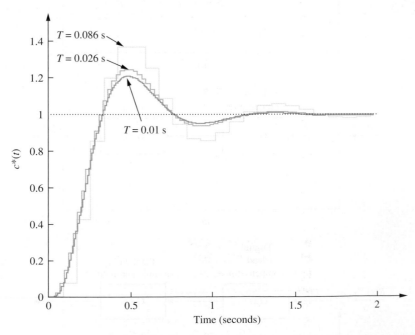

Note: Valid only at integer values of sampling instant

FIGURE 13.26 Closed-loop response for the compensated system of Example 13.12 showing effect of three different sampling frequencies

---

SKILL-ASSESSMENT EXERCISE 13.9

Problem: In Example 11.3 a lead compensator was designed for a unity feedback system whose plant was

$$G(s) = \frac{100K}{s(s+36)(s+100)}$$

The design specifications were as follows: percent overshoot $= 20\%$, peak time $= 0.1$ second, and $K_v = 40$. In order to meet the requirements, the design yielded $K = 1440$ and a lead compensator,

$$G_c(s) = 2.38 \, \frac{s+25.3}{s+60.2}$$

If the system is to be computer controlled, find the digital controller, $G_c(z)$.

ANSWER: $G_c(z) = 2.34 \, \dfrac{z-0.975}{z-0.9416}$, $T = 0.001$ second

The complete solution is at www.wiley.com/college/nise.

Now that we have learned how to design a digital cascade compensator, $G_c(z)$, the next section will teach us how to use the digital computer to implement it.

13.11 IMPLEMENTING THE DIGITAL COMPENSATOR

The controller, $G_c(z)$, can be implemented directly via calculations within the digital computer in the forward path as shown in Figure 13.27. Let us now derive a numerical algorithm that the computer can use to emulate the compensator. We will find an expression for the computer's sampled output, $x^*(t)$, whose transforms are shown in Figure 13.27 as $X(z)$. We will see that this expression can be used to program the digital computer to emulate the compensator.

Consider a second-order compensator, $G_c(z)$,

$$G_c(z) = \frac{X(z)}{E(z)} = \frac{a_3 z^3 + a_2 z^2 + a_1 z + a_0}{b_2 z^2 + b_1 z + b_0} \tag{13.94}$$

Cross-multiplying,

$$(b_2 z^2 + b_1 z + b_0)X(z) = (a_3 z^3 + a_2 z^2 + a_1 z + a_0)E(z) \tag{13.95}$$

Solving for the term with the highest power of z operating on the output, $X(z)$,

$$b_2 z^2 X(z) = (a_3 z^3 + a_2 z^2 + a_1 z + a_0)E(z) - (b_1 z + b_0)X(z) \tag{13.96}$$

Dividing by the coefficient of $X(z)$ on the left-hand side of Eq. (13.96) yields

$$X(z) = \left(\frac{a_3}{b_2}z + \frac{a_2}{b_2} + \frac{a_1}{b_2}z^{-1} + \frac{a_0}{b_2}z^{-2}\right)E(z) - \left(\frac{b_1}{b_2}z^{-1} + \frac{b_0}{b_2}z^{-2}\right)X(z) \tag{13.97}$$

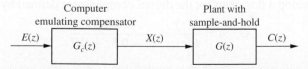

FIGURE 13.27   Block diagram showing computer emulation of a digital compensator

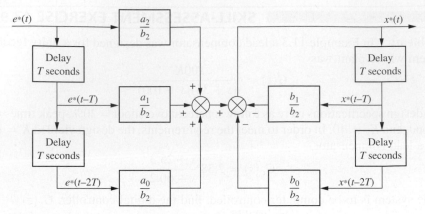

FIGURE 13.28 Flowchart for a second-order digital compensator

Finally, taking the inverse z-transform,

$$x^*(t) = \frac{a_3}{b_2}e^*(t+T) + \frac{a_2}{b_2}e^*(t) + \frac{a_1}{b_2}e^*(t-T) + \frac{a_0}{b_2}e^*(t-2T)$$
$$- \frac{b_1}{b_2}x^*(t-T) - \frac{b_0}{b_2}x^*(t-2T)$$

(13.98)

We can see from this equation that the present sample of the compensator output, $x^*(t)$, is a function of future $(e^*(t+T))$ present $(e^*(t))$ and past $(e^*(t-T)$ and $e^*(t-2T))$ samples of $e(t)$, along with past values of the output, $x^*(t-T)$ and $x^*(t-2T)$. Obviously, if we are to physically realize this compensator, the output sample cannot be dependent upon future values of the input. Hence, to be physically realizable, a_3 must equal zero for the future value of $e(t)$ to be zero. We conclude that the numerator of the compensator's transfer function must be of equal or lower order than the denominator in order that the compensator be physically realizable.

Now assume that a_3 does indeed equal zero. Equation (13.98) now becomes

$$x^*(t) = \frac{a_2}{b_2}e^*(t) + \frac{a_1}{b_2}e^*(t-T) + \frac{a_0}{b_2}e^*(t-2T) - \frac{b_1}{b_2}x^*(t-T) - \frac{b_0}{b_2}x^*(t-2T)$$

(13.99)

Hence, the output sample is a function of current and past input samples of the input as well as past samples of the output. Figure 13.28 shows the flowchart of the compensator from which a program can be written for the digital computer.[6] The figure shows that the compensator can be implemented by storing several successive values of the input and output. The output is then formed by a weighted linear combination of these stored variables. Let us now look at a numerical example.

EXAMPLE 13.13

Digital cascade compensator implementation

Problem: Develop a flowchart for the digital compensator defined by Eq. (13.100).

$$G_c(z) = \frac{X(z)}{E(z)} = \frac{z+0.5}{z^2 - 0.5z + 0.7}$$

(13.100)

[6] For an excellent discussion on basic flowcharts to represent digital compensators, including the representation shown in Figure 13.28 and alternative flowcharts with half as many delays, see *Chassaing (1999, pp. 135–143)*.

SOLUTION: Cross-multiply and obtain

$$(z^2 - 0.5z + 0.7)X(z) = (z + 0.5)E(z) \qquad (13.101)$$

Solve for the highest power of z operating on the output, $X(z)$,

$$z^2 X(z) = (z + 0.5)E(z) - (-0.5z + 0.7)X(z) \qquad (13.102)$$

Solving for $X(z)$ on the left-hand side,

$$X(z) = (z^{-1} + 0.5z^{-2})E(z) - (-0.5z^{-1} + 0.7z^{-2})X(z) \qquad (13.103)$$

Implementing Eq. (13.103) with the flowchart of Figure 13.29 completes the design.

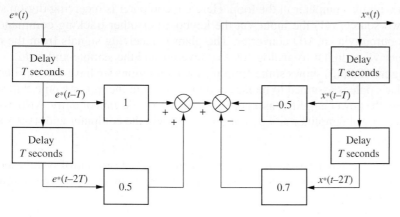

FIGURE 13.29   Flowchart to implement $G_c(z) = \dfrac{z + 0.5}{z^2 - 0.5z + 0.7}$

Problem: Draw a flowchart from which the compensator

$$G_c(z) = \frac{1899z^2 - 3761z + 1861}{z^2 - 1.908z + 0.9075}$$

can be programmed if the sampling interval is 0.1 second.

ANSWER: The complete solution is at www.wiley.com/college/nise.

In this section we learned how to implement a digital compensator. The resulting flowchart can serve as the design of a digital computer program for the computer in the loop. The design consists of delays that can be thought of as storage for each sampled value of input and output. The stored values are weighted and added. The engineer then can implement the design with a computer program.

In the next section we will put together the concepts of this chapter as we apply the principles of digital control system design to our antenna azimuth control system.

CASE STUDIES

Antenna Control: Transient Design via Gain

We now demonstrate the objectives of this chapter by turning to our ongoing antenna azimuth position control system. We will show where the computer is inserted in the loop, model the system, and design the gain to meet a transient response requirement. Later, we will design a digital cascade compensator.

The computer will perform two functions in the loop. First, the computer will be used as the input device. It will receive digital signals from the keyboard in the form of commands, and digital signals from the output for closed-loop control. The keyboard will replace the input potentiometer, and an analog-to-digital (A/D) converter along with a unity gain feedback transducer will replace the output potentiometer.

Figure 13.30(*a*) shows the original analog system, and Figure 13.30(*b*) shows the system with the computer in the loop. Here the computer is receiving digital signals from two sources: (1) the input via the keyboard or other tracking commands and (2) the output via an A/D converter. The plant is receiving signals from the digital computer via a digital-to-analog (D/A) converter and the sample-and-hold.

Figure 13.30(*b*) shows some simplifying assumptions we have made. The power amplifier's pole is assumed to be far enough away from the motor's pole that we can represent the power amplifier as a pure gain equal to its dc gain of unity. Also, we have absorbed any preamplifier and potentiometer gain in the computer and its associated D/A converter.

Problem: Design the gain for the antenna azimuth position control system shown in Figure 13.30(*b*) to yield a closed-loop damping ratio of 0.5. Assume a sampling interval of $T = 0.1$ second.

SOLUTION:

Modeling the System: Our first objective is to model the system in the *z*-domain. The forward transfer function, $G(s)$, which includes the sample-and-hold, power amplifier, motor and load, and the gears, is

$$G(s) = \frac{1 - e^{-Ts}}{s} \frac{0.2083}{s(s + a)} = \frac{0.2083}{a}(1 - e^{Ts})\frac{a}{s^2(s + a)} \tag{13.104}$$

where $a = 1.71$, and $T = 0.1$.

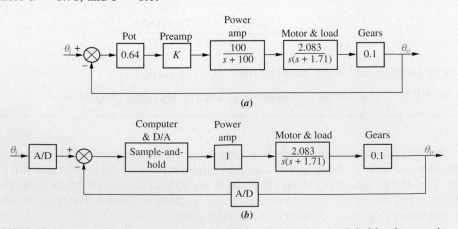

FIGURE 13.30 Antenna control system: **a.** analog implementation; **b.** digital implementation

Since the *z*-transform of $(1 - e^{-Ts})$ is $(1 - z^{-1})$ and, from Example 13.6, the *z*-transform of $a/[s^2(s+a)]$ is

$$z\left\{\frac{a}{s^2(s+a)}\right\} = \left[\frac{Tz}{(z-1)^2} - \frac{(1-e^{-aT})z}{a(z-1)(z-e^{-aT})}\right] \tag{13.105}$$

the *z*-transform of the plant, $G(z)$, is

$$
\begin{aligned}
G(z) &= \frac{0.2083}{a}(1 - z^{-1})z\left\{\frac{a}{s^2(s+a)}\right\} \\
&= \frac{0.2083}{a^2}\left[\frac{[aT - (1-e^{-aT})]z + [(1-e^{-aT}) - aTe^{-aT}]}{(z-1)(z-e^{-aT})}\right]
\end{aligned} \tag{13.106}
$$

Substituting the values for *a* and *T*, we obtain

$$G(z) = \frac{9.846 \times 10^{-4}(z+0.945)}{(z-1)(z-0.843)} \tag{13.107}$$

Figure 13.31 shows the computer and plant as part of the digital feedback control system.

Designing for Transient Response: Now that the modeling in the *z*-domain is complete, we can begin to design the system for the required transient response. We superimpose the root locus over the constant damping ratio curves in the *z*-plane, as shown in Figure 13.32. A line drawn from the origin to the intersection forms an 8.58° angle. Searching along this line for 180°, we find the intersection to be $(0.915 + j0.138)$, with a loop gain, $9.846 \times 10^{-4}K$, of 0.0135. Hence $K = 13.71$.

Checking the design by finding the unit sampled step response of the closed-loop system yields the plot of Figure 13.33, which exhibits 20% over-shoot ($\zeta = 0.456$).

Challenge: We now give you a case study to test your knowledge of this chapter's objectives: You are given the antenna azimuth position control system shown on the front endpapers, Configuration 2. Do the following:

a. Convert the system into a digital system with $T = 0.1$ second. For the purposes of the conversion, assume that the potentiometers are replaced with unity gain transducers. Neglect power amplifier dynamics.

b. Design the gain, K, for 16.3% overshoot.

c. For your designed value of gain, find the steady-state error for a unit ramp input.

d. Repeat Part **b** using MATLAB.

MATLAB

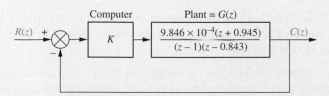

FIGURE 13.31 Analog antenna azimuth position control system converted to a digital system

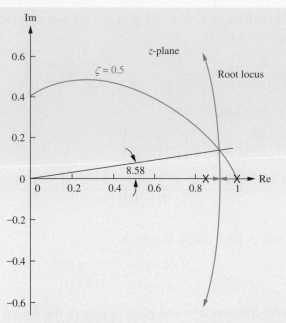

FIGURE 13.32   Root locus superimposed over constant damping ratio curve

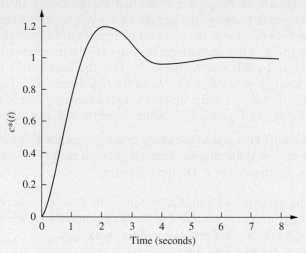

Note: Valid only at integer values of sampling instant

FIGURE 13.33   Sampled step response of the antenna azimuth position control system

Antenna Control: Digital Cascade Compensator Design

Problem: Design a digital lead compensator to reduce the settling time by a factor of 2.5 from that obtained for the antenna azimuth control system in the previous Case Study problem in this chapter.

SOLUTION: Figure 13.34 shows a simplified block diagram of the continuous system, neglecting power amplifier dynamics and assuming that the potentiometers are replaced with unity gain transducers as previously explained.

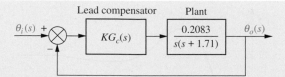

FIGURE 13.34 Simplified block diagram of antenna azimuth control system

We begin with an s-plane design. From Figure 13.33, the settling time is about 5 seconds. Thus, our design requirements are a settling time of 2 seconds and a damping ratio of 0.5. The natural frequency is $\omega_n = 4/(\zeta T_s) = 4$ rad/s. The compensated dominant poles are located at $-\zeta\omega_n \pm j\omega_n\sqrt{1 - \zeta^2} = -2 \pm j3.464$.

Designing a lead compensator zero to cancel the plant pole on the s-plane at -1.71 yields a lead compensator pole at -4. Hence the lead compensator is given by

$$G_c(s) = \frac{s + 1.71}{s + 4} \tag{13.108}$$

Using root locus to evaluate the gain, K, at the design point yields $0.2083K = 16$, or $K = 76.81$.

We now select an appropriate sampling frequency as described in Section 13.10. Using the cascaded compensator,

$$KG_c(s) = \frac{76.81(s + 1.71)}{(s + 4)} \tag{13.109}$$

and plant,

$$G_p(s) = \frac{0.2083}{s(s + 1.71)} \tag{13.110}$$

the equivalent forward-path transfer function, $G_e(s) = KG_c(s)G_p(s)$, is

$$G_e(s) = \frac{16}{s(s + 4)} \tag{13.111}$$

The magnitude frequency response of Eq. (13.111) is 0 dB at 3.1 rad/s. Thus, from Section 13.10, the value of the sampling interval, T, should be in the range $0.15/\omega_{\Phi_M} = 0.05$ to $0.5/\omega_{\Phi_M} = 0.16$ second. Let us choose a smaller value, say $T = 0.025$ second.

Substituting Eq. (13.88) into Eq. (13.111), where $T = 0.025$, yields the digital compensator

$$KG_c(z) = \frac{74.72z - 71.59}{z - 0.9048} \tag{13.112}$$

In order to simulate the digital system, we calculate the z-transform of the plant in Figure 13.34 in cascade with a zero-order sample-and-hold. The z-transform of the sampled plant is evaluated by the method discussed in Section 13.4 using $T = 0.025$. The result is

$$G_p(z) = \frac{6.418 \times 10^{-5}z + 6.327 \times 10^{-5}}{z^2 - 1.958z + 0.9582} \tag{13.113}$$

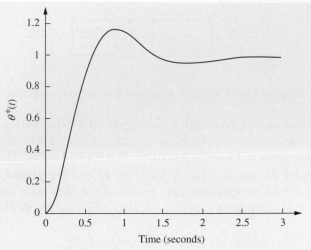

Note: Valid only at integer values of sampling instant

FIGURE 13.35   Closed-loop digital step response for antenna control system with a lead compensator

The step response in Figure 13.35 shows approximately 20% overshoot and a settling time of 2.1 seconds for the closed-loop digital system.

We conclude the design by obtaining a flowchart for the digital compensator. Using Eq. (13.112), where we define $KG_c(z) = X(z)/E(z)$, and cross-multiplying yields

$$(z - 0.9048)X(z) = (74.72z - 71.59)E(z) \qquad (13.114)$$

Solving for the highest power of z operating on $X(z)$,

$$zX(z) = (74.72z - 71.59)E(z) + 0.9048X(z) \qquad (13.115)$$

Solving for $X(z)$,

$$X(z) = (74.72 - 71.59z^{-1})E(z) + 0.9048z^{-1}X(z) \qquad (13.116)$$

Implementing Eq. (13.116) as a flowchart yields Figure 13.36.

Challenge: You are now given a case study to test your knowledge of this chapter's objectives. You are given the antenna azimuth position control system shown on the

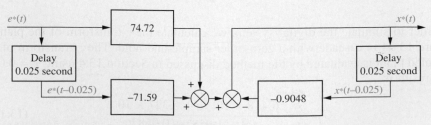

FIGURE 13.36   Flowchart for digital lead compensator

front endpapers, Configuration 2. Replace the potentiometers with unity gain trans-ducers, neglect power amplifier dynamics, and do the following:

a. Design a digital lead compensator to yield 10% overshoot with a 1-second peak time. Design in the *s*-plane and use the Tustin transformation to specify and implement a digital compensator. Choose an appropriate sampling interval.

b. Draw a flowchart for your digital lead compensator.

c. Repeat Part **a** using MATLAB.

MATLAB

SUMMARY

In this chapter we covered the design of digital systems using classical methods. State-space techniques were not covered. However, you are encouraged to pursue this topic in a course dedicated to sampled-data control systems.

We looked at the advantages of digital control systems. These systems can control numerous loops at reduced cost. System modifications can be implemented with software changes rather than hardware changes.

Typically, the digital computer is placed in the forward path preceding the plant. Digital-to-analog and analog-to-digital conversion is required within the system to ensure compatibility of the analog and digital signals throughout the system. The digital computer in the loop is modeled as a sample-and-hold network along with any compensation that it performs.

Throughout the chapter we saw direct parallels to the methods used for *s*-plane analysis of transients, steady-state errors, and the stability of analog systems. The parallel is made possible by the *z*-transform, which replaces the Laplace transform as the transform of choice for analyzing sampled-data systems. The *z*-transform allows us to represent sampled waveforms at the sampling instants. We can handle sampled systems as easily as continuous systems, including block diagram reduction, since both signals and systems can be represented in the *z*-domain and manipulated algebraically. Complex systems can be reduced to a single block through techniques that parallel those used with the *s*-plane. Time responses can be obtained through division of the numerator by the denominator without the partial-fraction expansion required in the *s*-domain.

Digital systems analysis parallels the *s*-plane techniques in the area of stability. The unit circle becomes the boundary of stability, replacing the imaginary axis.

We also found that the concepts of root locus and transient response are easily carried into the *z*-plane. The rules for sketching the root locus do not change. We can map points on the *s*-plane into points on the *z*-plane and attach transient response characteristics to the points. Evaluating a sampled-data system shows that the sampling rate, in addition to gain and load, determines the transient response.

Cascade compensators also can be designed for digital systems. One method is to first design the compensator on the *s*-plane or via frequency response techniques described in Chapters 9 and 11, respectively. Then the resulting design is transformed to a digital compensator using the Tustin transformation. Designing cascade compensation directly on the *z*-plane is an alternative method that can be used. However, these techniques are beyond the scope of this book.

This introductory control systems course is now complete. You have learned how to analyze and design linear control systems using frequency-domain and state-space techniques. This course is only a beginning. You may consider furthering your study of control systems by taking advanced courses in digital, nonlinear, and optimal control, where you will learn new techniques for analyzing and designing classes of systems not covered in this book. We hope we have whetted your appetite to continue your education in control systems engineering.

REVIEW QUESTIONS

1. Name two functions that the digital computer can perform when used with feedback control systems.
2. Name three advantages of using digital computers in the loop.
3. Name two important considerations in analog-to-digital conversion that yield errors.
4. Of what does the block diagram model for a computer consist?
5. What is the z-transform?
6. What does the inverse z-transform of a time waveform actually yield?
7. Name two methods of finding the inverse z-transform.
8. What method for finding the inverse z-transform yields a closed-form expression for the time function?
9. What method for finding the inverse z-transform immediately yields the values of the time waveform at the sampling instants?
10. In order to find the z-transform of a $G(s)$, what must be true of the input and the output?
11. If input $R(z)$ to system $G(z)$ yields output $C(z)$, what is the nature of $c(t)$?
12. If a time waveform, $c(t)$, at the output of system $G(z)$ is plotted using the inverse z-transform, and a typical second-order response with damping ratio $= 0.5$ results, can we say that the system is stable?
13. What must exist in order for cascaded sampled-data systems to be represented by the product of their pulse transfer functions, $G(z)$?
14. Where is the region for stability on the z-plane?
15. What methods for finding the stability of digital systems can replace the Routh-Hurwitz criterion for analog systems?
16. To drive steady-state errors in analog systems to zero, a pole can be placed at the origin of the s-plane. Where on the z-plane should a pole be placed to drive the steady-state error of a sampled system to zero?
17. How do the rules for sketching the root locus on the z-plane differ from those for sketching the root locus on the s-plane?
18. Given a point on the z-plane, how can one determine the associated percent overshoot, settling time, and peak time?
19. Given a desired percent overshoot and settling time, how can one tell which point on the z-plane is the design point?
20. Describe how digital compensators can be designed on the s-plane.
21. What characteristic is common between a cascade compensator designed on the s-plane and the digital compensator to which it is converted?

PROBLEMS

1. Derive the z-transforms for the time functions listed below. Do not use any z-transform tables. Use the plan $f(t) \to f^*(t) \to F^*(s) \to F(z)$, followed by converting $F(z)$ into closed form making use of the fact that $1/(1 - z^{-1}) = 1 + z^{-1} + z^{-2} + z^{-3} + \cdots$. Assume ideal sampling. [Section: 13.3]

   a. $e^{-at}u(t)$

   b. $u(t)$

   c. $t^2 e^{-at}u(t)$

   d. $\cos \omega t \, u(t)$

2. Repeat all parts of Problem 1 using MATLAB and MATLAB's Symbolic Math Toolbox.

3. For each $F(z)$, find $f(kT)$ using partial-fraction expansion. [Section: 13.3]

   a. $F(z) = \dfrac{z(z+3)(z+5)}{(z-0.4)(z-0.6)(z-0.8)}$

   b. $F(z) = \dfrac{(z+0.2)(z+0.4)}{(z-0.1)(z-0.5)(z-0.9)}$

   c. $F(z) = \dfrac{(z+1)(z+0.3)(z+0.4)}{z(z-0.2)(z-0.5)(z-0.7)}$

4. For each $F(z)$ in Problem 3, do the following: [Section: 13.3]

   a. Find $f(kT)$ using the power series expansion.

   b. Check your results against your answers from Problem 3.

5. Using partial-fraction expansion and Table 13.1, find the z-transform for each $G(s)$ shown below if $T = 0.5$ second.

   a. $G(s) = \dfrac{(s+4)}{(s+2)(s+5)}$

   b. $G(s) = \dfrac{(s+1)(s+2)}{s(s+3)(s+4)}$

   c. $G(s) = \dfrac{27}{(s+2)(s^2 + 4s + 13)}$

   d. $G(s) = \dfrac{10}{s(s+2)(s^2 + 12s + 61)}$

6. Repeat all parts of Problem 6 using MATLAB and MATLAB's Symbolic Math Toolbox.

7. Find $G(z) = C(z)/R(z)$ for each of the block diagrams shown in Figure P13.1 if $T = 0.1$ second.

8. Find $T(z) = C(z)/R(z)$ for each of the systems shown in Figure P13.2. [Section: 13.5]

9. Find $C(z)$ in general terms for the digital system shown in Figure P13.3. [Section: 13.5]

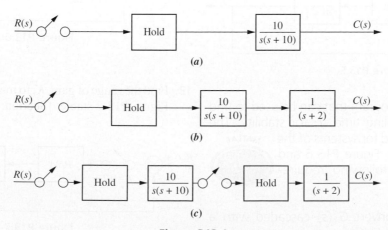

(a)

(b)

(c)

Figure P13.1

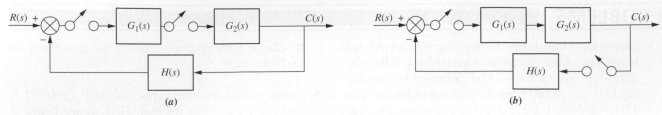

Figure P13.2

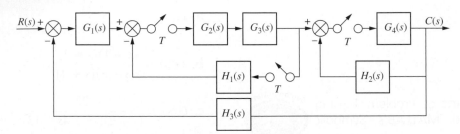

Figure P13.3

10. Find the closed-loop transfer function $T(z) = C(z)/R(z)$, for the system shown in Figure P13.4.

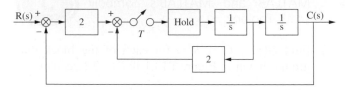

Figure P13.4

11. Given the system in Figure P13.5, find the range of sampling interval, T, that will keep the system stable. [Section: 13.6]

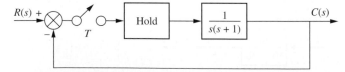

Figure P13.5

12. Write a MATLAB program that can be used to find the range of sampling time, T, for stability. The program will be used for systems of the type represented in Figure P13.6 and should meet the following requirements:

a. MATLAB will convert $G_1(s)$ cascaded with a sample-and-hold to $G(z)$.

b. The program will calculate the z-plane roots of the closed-loop system for a range of T and determine the value of T, if any, below which the system will be stable. MATLAB will display this value of T along with the z-plane poles of the closed-loop transfer function.

Test the program on

$$G_1(s) = \frac{10(s+7)}{(s+1)(s+3)(s+4)(s+5)}$$

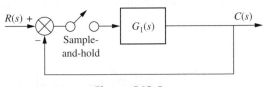

Figure P13.6

13. Find the range of gain, K, to make the system shown in Figure P13.7 stable. [Section: 13.6]

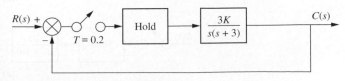

Figure P13.7

14. Find the static error constants and the steady-state error for each of the digital systems shown in Figure P13.8 if the inputs are [Section: 13.7]

a. $u(t)$

b. $tu(t)$

c. $\dfrac{1}{2}t^2u(t)$

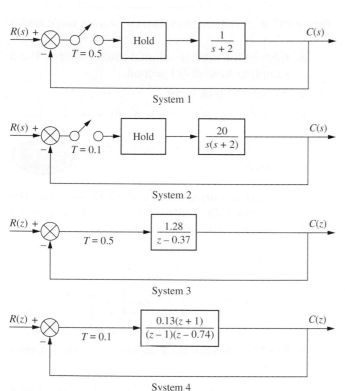

System 1

System 2

System 3

System 4

Figure P13.8

15. Write a MATLAB program that can be used to find K_p, K_v, and K_a for digital systems. The program will be used for systems of the type represented in Figure P13.6. Test your program for

$$G(z) = \frac{0.04406z^3 - 0.03624z^2 - 0.03284z + 0.02857}{z^4 - 3.394z^3 + 4.29z^2 - 2.393z + 0.4966}$$

where $G(z)$ is the pulse transfer function for $G_{(1)}(s)$ in cascade with the z.o.h. and $T = 0.1$ second.

16. For the digital system shown in Figure P13.6, where $G_1(s) = K/[(s + 1) \times (s + 3)]$, find the value of K to yield a 16.3% overshoot. Also find the range of K for stability. Let $T = 0.1$ second. [Section: 13.9]

17. Use Simulink to simulate the step response for the system of Problem 16. Set the value of gain, K, to that designed in Problem 16 for 16.3% overshoot.

18. Use MATLAB's LTI Viewer to determine the peak time and settling time of the closed-loop step response for System 4 in Figure P13.8

19. Write a MATLAB program that can be used to design the gain of a digital control system to meet a percent overshoot requirement. The program will be used for systems of the type represented in Figure P13.6 and meet the following requirements:

a. The user will input the desired percent overshoot.

b. MATLAB will convert $G_1(s)$ cascaded with the sample-and-hold to $G(z)$.

c. MATLAB will display the root locus on the z-plane along with an overlay of the percent overshoot curve.

d. The user will click with the mouse at the intersection of the root locus and percent overshoot overlay and MATLAB will respond with the value of gain followed by a display of the step response of the closed-loop system.

Apply your program to Problem 16 and compare results.

20. For the digital system shown in Figure P13.6, where $G_1(s) = K/[s(s + 1)]$, find the value of K to yield a peak time of 2 seconds if the sampling interval, T, is 0.1 second. Also, find the range of K for stability. [Section: 13.9]

21. For the digital system shown in Figure P13.6, where $G_1(s) = K/[s(s + 1)(s + 3)]$, find the value of K to yield a

20% overshoot if the sampling interval, T, is 0.1 second. Also, find the range of K for stability. [Section: 13.9]

22. For the digital system shown in Figure P13.6, where $G_1(s) = K(s+2) \div [s(s+1)(s+3)]$, find the value of K to yield a settling time of 15 seconds if the sampling interval, T, is 1 second. Also, find the range of K for stability. [Section: 13.9]

23. A PID controller was designed in Example 9.5 for a continuous system with unity feedback. The system's plant was

$$G(s) = \frac{(s+8)}{(s+3)(s+6)(s+10)}$$

The designed PID controller was

$$G_c(s) = 4.6 \frac{(s+55.92)(s+0.5)}{s}$$

Find the digital transfer function, $G_c(z)$, of the PID controller in order for the system to be computer controlled if the sampling interval, T, is 0.01 second. [Section: 13.10]

24. A continuous unity feedback system has a forward transfer function of

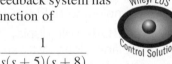

$$G(s) = \frac{1}{s(s+5)(s+8)}$$

The system is to be computer controlled with the following specifications:

Percent overshoot: 10%
Settling time: 2 seconds
Sampling interval: 0.01 second

Design a lead compensator for the digital system to meet the specifications. [Section: 13.10]

Design Problems

25. a. Convert the heading control for the UFSS vehicle shown on the back endpapers (*Johnson, 1980*) into a digitally controlled system.
    b. Find the closed-loop pulse transfer function, $T(z)$, if $T = 0.1$ second.
    c. Find the range of heading gain to keep the digital system stable.

26. A robot equipped to perform arc welding was discussed in Problem 44, Chapter 8. The robot was compensated by feeding back pressure and velocity signals as shown in Figure P8.13(*b*). Eliminating these feedback paths yields the block diagram shown in Figure P13.9 (*Hardy, 1967*).

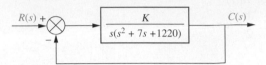

Figure P13.9 Simplified block diagram for robot swing motion

a. Convert the robot to a digital control system. Use a sampling time of 0.1 second.
b. Sketch the root locus.
c. Find the range of gain, K, to keep the digital system stable.
d. Repeat all previous parts using MATLAB.

27. The floppy disk drive of Problem 54, Chapter 8 is to be digitally controlled. If the analog system is as shown in Figure P13.10, do the following:

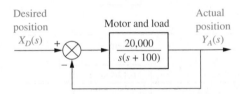

Figure P13.10 Simplified block diagram of a floppy disk drive

a. Convert the disk drive to a digital system. Use a sampling time of 0.01 second.
b. Find the range of digital controller gain to keep the system stable.
c. Find the value of digital controller gain to yield 15% overshoot for a digital step response.
d. Repeat all previous parts and obtain the step response for Part **c** using MATLAB.

28. Scanning probe microscopes are used to visualize samples in the sub-micron dimensional range. They typically use a silica-based probe to physically track the sample topography to create a viable image. However, these devices are very sensitive to external disturbance and vibrations. An approach called

inherent disturbance suppression tries to alleviate the disturbance problem through the addition of a laser interferometer that is used to measure the probe–sample interaction and compensate for undesired probe movements. The technique was implemented in a tapping mode atomic force microscope measuring single DNA molecules. It was shown that for a significant range of frequencies the open-loop transmission from the probe's voltage input to probe's displacement is (*Sparks, 2006*)

$$G_1(s) = \frac{20000}{s}$$

Assuming the probe is digitally controlled in a loop, as shown in Figure P13.6, calculate the sampling period range that will result in a stable closed-loop system.

29. Problem 35, Chapter 9 described a two-tank system where the objective was to maintain a constant liquid level in one of the tanks via control of an inflow valve. Assume for this problem that the transfer function relating liquid-level output, $Y(s)$, to flow rate input $F_\theta(s)$, for the lower tank is (*Romagnoli, 2006*)

$$G(s) = \frac{Y(s)}{F_\theta(s)} = \frac{0.0187}{s^2 + 0.237s + 0.00908}$$

Assume that the system will be controlled in closed loop by means of a digital computer system with a sample period $T = 1$ second, as shown in Figure P13.6, with $G_1(s) = KG(s)$. Use the bilinear transformation and the Routh-Hurwitz method to find the range of K that will result in a stable closed-loop system.

30. Assume that the two-tank system of Problem 29 is controlled by a digital computer in the configuration of Figure P13.6, where $G_1(s) = KG(s)$. If a sampling period of $T = 1$ second is used, do the following (*Romagnoli, 2006*). **MATLAB**

a. Use MATLAB to draw the root locus.

b. Find the value of K that will result in a stable system with a damping factor of $\zeta = 0.7$.

c. Use the root locus of Part **b** to predict the step-response settling time, T_s, and peak time, T_p.

d. Calculate the final value of the closed-loop system to a unit step input.

e. Obtain the step response of the system using Simulink. Verify the predictions you made in Parts **c** and **d**. **Simulink**

31. In Problem 47, Chapter 9, and Problem 38, Chapter 10, we considered the radial pickup position control of a DVD player. A controller was designed and placed in cascade with the plant in a unit feedback configuration to stabilize the system. The controller was given by

$$M(s) = \frac{0.5(s + 1.63)}{s(s + 0.27)}$$

and the plant by (*Bittanti, 2002*)

$$P(s) = \frac{0.63}{\left(1 + \frac{0.36}{305.4}s + \frac{s^2}{305.4^2}\right)\left(1 + \frac{0.04}{248.2}s + \frac{s^2}{248.2^2}\right)}$$

It is desired to replace the continuous system by an equivalent discrete system without appreciably affecting the system performance.

a. Find an appropriate sampling frequency for the discretization.

b. Using the chosen sampling frequency, translate the continuous compensator into a discrete compensator.

c. Use Simulink to simulate the continuous and discrete systems on the same graph. **Simulink** Assume a unit step input. Are there significant differences in the system's performance?

32. In Problem 23, Chapter 11, we discussed an EVAD, a device that works in parallel with the human heart to help pump blood in patients with cardiac conditions. The device has a transfer function

$$G(s) = \frac{P_{ao}(s)}{E_m(s)} = \frac{1361}{s^2 + 69s + 70.85}$$

where $E_m(s)$ is the motor's armature voltage, and $P_{ao}(s)$ is the aortic blood pressure (*Tasch, 1990*). Using continuous techniques, a cascaded compensator is designed in a unity feedback configuration with a transfer function

$$G_c(s) = \frac{0.5(s + 1)}{s + 0.05}$$

Selecting to control the device using a microcontroller, a discrete equivalent has to be found for $G_c(s)$. Do the following.

a. Find an appropriate sampling frequency for the discretization.

b. Translate the continuous compensator into a discrete compensator using the sampling frequency found in Part **a**.

c. Use Simulink to simulate the continuous and discrete systems on the same graph for a unit step input. There should be little difference between the compensated continuous and discrete systems.

33. In Problem 46, Chapter 9, a steam-driven turbine-governor system was implemented by a unity feedback system with a forward-path transfer function (*Khodabakhshian, 2005*)

$$G(s) = \frac{K}{(s+0.08)(s+2)(s+5)}$$

a. Use a sampling period of $T = 0.5\,\text{s}$ and find a discrete equivalent for this system.

b. Use MATLAB to draw the root locus.

c. Find the value of K that will result in a stable system with a damping factor of $\zeta = 0.7$.

d. Use the root locus found in Part **a** to predict the step-response settling time, T_s, and peak time, T_p.

e. Calculate the final value of the closed-loop system unit step response.

f. Obtain the step response of the system using Simulink. Verify the predictions you made in Parts **c** and **d**.

34. If you have not already done so, do Problem 44 in Chapter 9. In this problem, you design a PID controller for a temperature control system. Digitize your PID design and draw a flowchart from which the PID controller can be implemented.

Progressive Analysis and Design Problems

35. **High-speed rail pantograph.** Problem 19 in Chapter 1 discusses active control of a pantograph mechanism for high-speed rail systems (*O'Connor, 1997*). In Problem 72(a), Chapter 5, you found the block dia-

gram for the active pantograph control system. In Chapter 9 you designed a PID controller to yield a settling time of 0.3 second with zero steady-state error. Assuming that the active control system is to be computer controlled, do the following:

a. Convert the PID controller designed in Problem 52, Chapter 9 to a digital controller by specifying its sampled transfer function, $G_c(z)$. Assume that the potentiometers are replaced by a keyboard, A/D converters, and unity gain transducers.

b. Draw a flowchart from which the PID controller can be implemented.

c. Use MATLAB to simulate the step response of the digital active control system.

36. **Control of HIV/AIDS.** In Chapter 11 a continuous cascaded compensator for a unity feedback system was designed for the treatment of the HIV-infected patient treated with RTIs (*Craig, 2004*). The transfer function of the designed compensator was

$$G_c(s) = \frac{-2 \times 10^{-4}(s^2 + 0.04s + 0.0048)}{s(s+0.02)}$$

The linearized plant was given by

$$P(s) = \frac{Y(s)}{U_1(s)} = \frac{-520s - 10.3844}{s^3 + 2.6817s^2 + 0.11s + 0.0126}$$

The compensated system is overdamped with an approximate settling time of 100 seconds. This system must be discretized for practical reasons: (1) HIV patient cannot be monitored continuously and (2) medicine dosage cannot be adjusted continuously.

a. Show that a reasonable sampling period for this system is $T = 8$ days (medicine dosage will be updated on a weekly basis).

b. Use Tustin's method and $T = 8$ days to find a discrete equivalent to $G_c(S)$.

c. Use Simulink to simulate the continuous and discrete compensated systems for a unit step input. Plot both responses on the same graph.

CYBER EXPLORATION LABORATORY

Experiment 13.1

Objective To design the gain of a digital control system to meet a transient response requirement; to simulate a digital control system to test a design; to see the effect of sampling rate upon the time response of a digital system.

Minimum required software packages MATLAB, Simulink, and the Control System Toolbox

Prelab

1. Given the antenna azimuth control system shown on the front endpapers, use Configuration 2 to find the discrete transfer function of the plant. Neglect the dynamics of the power amplifier and include the preamplifier, motor, gears, and load. Assume a zero-order hold and a sampling interval of 0.01 second.

2. Using the digital plant found in Prelab 1, find the preamplifier gain required for a closed-loop digital system response with 10% overshoot and a sampling interval of 0.01 second. What is the peak time?

3. Given the antenna azimuth control system shown on the front endpapers, use Configuration 2 to find the preamplifier gain required for the continuous system to yield a closed-loop step response with 10% overshoot. Consider the open-loop system to be the preamplifier, motor, gears, and load. Neglect the dynamics of the power amplifier.

Lab

1. Verify your value of preamplifier gain found in Prelab 2 using the SISO Design Tool to generate the root locus for the digital open-loop transfer function found in Prelab 1. Use the Design Constraints capability to generate the 10% overshoot curve and place your closed-loop poles at this boundary. Obtain a plot of the root locus and the design boundary. Record the value of gain for 10% overshoot. Also, obtain a plot of the closed-loop step response using the LTI Viewer and record the values of percent overshoot and peak time. Use the same tool to find the range of gain for stability.

2. Using Simulink set up the closed-loop digital system whose plant was found in Prelab 1. Make two diagrams: one with the digital transfer function for the plant and another using the continuous transfer function for the plant preceded by a zero-order sample-and-hold. Use the same step input for both diagrams and obtain the step response of each. Measure the percent overshoot and peak time.

3. Using Simulink, set up both the digital and continuous systems calculated in Prelabs 2 and 3, respectively, to yield 10% overshoot. Build the digital system with a sample-and-hold rather than the z-transform function. Plot the step response of each system and record the percent overshoot and the peak time.

4. For one of the digital systems built in Lab 2, vary the sampling interval and record the responses for a few values of sampling interval above 0.01 second. Record sampling interval, percent overshoot, and peak time. Also, find the value of sampling interval that makes the system unstable.

Postlab

1. Make a table containing the percent overshoot, peak time, and gain for each of the following closed-loop responses: the digital system using the SISO Design Tool; the digital system using Simulink and the digital transfer functions; the digital system using Simulink and the continuous transfer functions with the zero-order sample-and-hold; and the continuous system using Simulink.

2. Using the data from Lab 4, make a table containing sampling interval, percent overshoot, and peak time. Also, state the sampling interval that makes the system unstable.

3. Compare the responses of all of the digital systems with a sampling interval of 0.01 second and the continuous system. Explain any discrepancies.

4. Compare the responses of the digital system at different sampling intervals with the continuous system. Explain the differences.

5. Draw some conclusions about the effect of sampling.

BIBLIOGRAPHY

Astrom, K. J., and Wittenmark, B. *Computer Controlled Systems.* Prentice Hall, Englewood Cliffs, NJ, 1984.

Bittanti, S., Dell'Orto, F., Di Carlo, A., and Savaresi, S. M. Notch Filtering and Multirate Control for Radial Tracking in High Speed DVD-Players. *IEEE Transactions on Consumer Electronics,* vol. 48, 2002, pp. 56–62.

Boyd, M., and Yingst, J. C. PC-Based Operator Control Station Simplifies Process, Saves Time. *Chilton's I & CS,* September 1988, pp. 99–101.

Chassaing, R. *Digital Signal Processing.* Wiley, New York, 1999.

Craig, I. K., Xia, X., and Venter, J. W. Introducing HIV/AIDS Education into the Electrical Engineering Curriculum at the University of Pretoria. *IEEE Transactions on Education,* vol. 47, no. 1, February 2004, pp. 65–73.

Hardy, H. L. Multi-Loop Servo Controls Programmed Robot. *Instruments and Control Systems,* June 1967, pp. 105–111.

Hostetter, G. H. *Digital Control System Design.* Holt, Rinehart & Winston, New York, 1988.

Johnson, H. et al. *Unmanned Free-Swimming Submersible (UFSS) System Description.* NRL Memorandum Report 4393. Naval Research Laboratory, Washington, DC, 1980.

Katz, P. *Digital Control Using Microprocessors.* Prentice Hall, Englewood Cliffs, NJ, 1981.

Khodabakhshian, A., and Golbon, N. Design of a New Load Frequency PID Controller Using QFT. *Proceedings of the 13th Mediterranean Conference on Control and Automation,* 2005, pp. 970–975.

Kuo, B. C. *Automatic Control Systems,* 7th ed. Prentice Hall, Englewood Cliffs, NJ, 1995.

Kuo, B. C. *Digital Control Systems.* Holt, Rinehart & Winston, New York, 1980.

O'Connor, D. N., Eppinger, S. D., Seering, W. P., and Wormly, D. N. Active Control of a High-Speed Pantograph. *Journal of Dynamic Systems, Measurements, and Control,* vol. 119, March 1997, pp. 1–4.

Ogata, K. *Discrete-Time Control Systems.* Prentice Hall, Englewood Cliffs, NJ, 1987.

Phillips, C. L., and Nagle, H. T., Jr. *Digital Control System Analysis and Design.* Prentice Hall, Englewood Cliffs, NJ, 1984.

Romagnoli, J. A., and Palazoglu, A. *Introduction to Process Control.* CRC Press, Boca Raton, FL, 2006.

Smith, C. L. *Digital Computer Process Control.* Intext Educational Publishers, NY, 1972.

Sparks, A. W., and Manalis, S. R. Atomic Force Microscopy with Inherent Disturbance Suppression for Nanostructure Imaging. *Nanotechnology,* vol. 17, 2006, pp. 1574–1579.

Tasch, U., Koontz, J. W., Ignatoski, M. A., and Geselowitz, D. B. An Adaptive Aortic Pressure Observer for the Penn State Electric Ventricular Assist Device. *IEEE Transactions on Biomedical Engineering,* vol. 37, 1990, pp. 374–383.

Tou, J. *Digital and Sampled-Data Control Systems.* McGraw-Hill, New York, 1959.

APPENDIX A: LIST OF SYMBOLS

$\%OS$	Percent overshoot
A	Ampere—unit of electrical current
A	System matrix for state-space representation
a_m	Motor time constant
B	Input matrix for state-space representation
C	Electrical capacitance in farads
C	Output matrix for state-space representation
$C(s)$	Laplace transform of the output of a system
$c(t)$	Output of a system
$\mathbf{C_M}$	Controllability matrix
D	Mechanical rotational coefficient of viscous friction in N-m-s/rad
D	Feedforward matrix for state-space representation
D_a	Motor armature coefficient of viscous damping in N-m-s/rad
D_m	Total coefficient of viscous friction at the armature of a motor, including armature coefficient of viscous friction and reflected load coefficient of viscous friction in N-m-s/rad
E	Energy
$E(s)$	Laplace transform of the error
$e(t)$	Error; electrical voltage
$E_a(s)$	Laplace transform of the motor armature input voltage; Laplace transform of the actuating signal
$e_a(t)$	Motor armature input voltage; actuating signal
F	Farad—unit of electrical capacitance
$F(s)$	Laplace transform of $f(t)$
$f(t)$	Mechanical force in newtons; general time function
f_v	Mechanical translational coefficient of viscous friction
g	Acceleration due to gravity
G	Electrical conductance in mhos

$G(s)$	Forward-path transfer function
$G_c(s)$	Compensator transfer function
$G_c(z)$	Sampled transfer function for a compensator
G_M	Gain margin
$G_p(z)$	Sampled transfer function for a plant
H	Henry—unit of electrical inductance
$H(s)$	Feedback-path transfer function
I	Identity matrix
$i(t)$	Electrical current in amperes
J	Moment of inertia in kg-m^2
J_a	Motor armature moment of inertia in kg-m^2
J_m	Total moment of inertia at the armature of a motor, including armature moment of inertia and reflected load moment of inertia in kg-m^2
K	Controller gain matrix
K	Mechanical translational spring constant in N/m or rotational spring constant in N-m/rad; amplifier gain; residue
k	Controller feedback gain; running index
K_a	Acceleration constant
K_b	Back emf constant in V/rad/s
K_f	Feedback gain
kg	Kilogram = newton seconds^2/meter—unit of mass
kg-m^2	Kilogram meters^2 = newton-meters seconds^2/radian—unit of moment of inertia
K_m	Motor gain
K_p	Position constant
K_t	Motor torque constant relating developed torque to armature current in N-m/A
K_v	Velocity constant
L	Electrical inductance in henries
L	Observer gain matrix
l	Observer feedback gain
M	Mass in kilograms; slope of the root locus asymptotes
m	Meter—unit of mechanical translational displacement
$M(\omega)$	Magnitude of a sinusoidal response
m/s	Meters/second—unit of mechanical translational velocity
M_P	Peak magnitude of the sinusoidal magnitude response
N	Newton—unit of mechanical translational force in kilogram meters/second^2
N-s/m	Newton-seconds/meter—unit of mechanical translational coefficient of viscous friction
n	System type
N/m	Newton/meter—unit of mechanical translational spring constant
N-m	Newton-meter—unit of mechanical torque
N-m-s/rad	Newton-meter-seconds/radian—unit of mechanical rotational coefficient of viscous friction

N-m/A	Newton-meter/ampere—unit of motor torque constant
N-m/rad	Newton-meter/radian—unit of mechanical rotational spring constant
$\mathbf{O_M}$	Observability matrix
$\mathbf{P}$	Similarity transformation matrix
p_c	Compensator pole
Q	Coulomb—unit of electrical charge
$q(t)$	Electrical charge in coulombs
R	Electrical resistance in ohms
$R(s)$	Laplace transform of the input to a system
r	Nonlinear electrical resistance
$r(t)$	Input to a system
R_a	Motor armature resistance in ohms
rad	Radian—unit of angular displacement
rad/s	Radian/second—unit of angular velocity
s	Second—unit of time
s	Complex variable for the Laplace transform
$S_{F:P}$	Sensitivity of F to a fractional change in P
T	Time constant; sampling interval for digital signals
$T(s)$	Closed-loop transfer function; Laplace transform of mechanical torque
$T(t)$	Mechanical torque in N-m
$T_m(t)$	Torque at the armature developed by a motor in N-m
$T_m(s)$	Laplace transform of the torque at the armature developed by a motor
T_p	Peak time in seconds
T_r	Rise time in seconds
T_s	Settling time in seconds
T_w	Pulse width in seconds
$\mathbf{u}$	Input or control vector for state-space representation
u	Input control signal for state-space representation
$u(t)$	Unit step input
V-s/rad	Volt-seconds/radian—unit of motor back emf constant
$v(t)$	Mechanical translation velocity in m/s; electrical voltage
$v_b(t)$	Motor back emf in volts
$v_e(t)$	Error voltage
$v_p(t)$	Power amplifier input in volts
$\mathbf{x}$	State vector for state-space representation
$x(t)$	Mechanical translation displacement in meters; a state variable
$\dot{x}$	Time derivative of a state variable
$\dot{\mathbf{x}}$	Time derivative of the state vector
$\mathbf{y}$	Output vector for state-space representation
$y(t)$	Output scalar for state-space representation
z	Complex variable for the z-transform
z_c	Compensator zero
α	Pole-scaling factor for a lag compensator, where $\alpha > 1$; angle of attack
β	Pole-scaling factor for a lead compensator, where $\beta < 1$

γ	Pole-scaling factor for a lag-lead compensator, where $\gamma > 1$
δ	Thrust angle
ζ	Damping ratio
θ	Angle of a vector with the positive extension of the real axis
$\theta(t)$	Angular displacement
θ_a	Angle of a root locus asymptote with the positive extension of the real axis
θ_c	Angular contribution of a compensator on the s-plane
$\theta_m(t)$	Angular displacement of the armature of a motor
λ	Eigenvalue of a square matrix
σ	Real part of the Laplace transform variable, s
σ_a	Real-axis intercept of the root locus asymptotes
Φ_M	Phase margin
$\Phi(t)$	State transition matrix
ϕ	Sinusoidal phase angle; body angle
ϕ_c	Sinusoidal phase angle of a compensator
ϕ_{max}	Maximum sinusoidal phase angle
Ω	Ohm—unit of electrical resistance
$\mho$	Mho—unit of electrical conductance
ω	Imaginary part of the Laplace transform variable, s
$\omega(t)$	Angular velocity in rad/s
ω_{BW}	Bandwidth in rad/s
ω_d	Damped frequency of oscillation in rad/s
$\omega\phi_M$	Phase-margin frequency in radians
ω_{G_M}	Gain-margin frequency in radians
ω_n	Natural frequency in rad/s
ω_p	Peak-magnitude frequency of the magnitude frequency response in rad/s

APPENDIX B: MATLAB TUTORIAL

B.1 INTRODUCTION

MATLAB is a high-level technical computing environment suitable for solving scientific and engineering problems. When used with routines from its companion software, the Control System Toolbox, MATLAB can be used to analyze and design control systems problems such as those covered in this textbook. MATLAB and the Control System Toolbox are commercial software products available from The Math-Works, Inc., 3 Apple Hill Drive, Natick, MA 01760-2098. Phone: (508) 647-7000. Email: info@mathworks.com. URL: http://www.mathworks.com.

The MATLAB examples in this tutorial consist of solved problems that demonstrate the application of MATLAB to the analysis and design of control systems. Many problems were taken from examples in the text (identified with a **MATLAB** icon) that were solved without MATLAB. A Command Summary at the end of this appendix lists key MATLAB statements and their descriptions.

The code in this tutorial is also available in the Control Systems Engineering Toolbox folder at www.wiley.com/college/nise and at http://www.mathworks.com/matlabcentral/fileexchange. You must have MATLAB Version 7 and the Control System Toolbox Version 8 installed on your machine to execute this appendix's code in the Control Systems Engineering Toolbox Version 5.

To run the M-files, first be sure the files are either added to the search path in **Set Path**... under the **File** menu or appear in the **Current Directory** window, which is part of the **MATLAB** window. To see the computer responses after installing the M-files, run each problem by typing the M-file name, such as ch2p1, after the prompt ($>>$) in the **Command Window**. You may also run the files by right-clicking the file name, if it appears in the **Current Directory** window, and select **Run**.

To view all or part of the M-file in the **Command Window**, enter "type <file name>" or "help <file name>," respectively, after the prompt. You may also view and make changes to the M-file by double-clicking the file in the **Current Directory** window. This action brings up the editor. After editing, be sure to save the revised file before executing.

If you do not have the Control Systems Engineering Toolbox M-files, you can create your own M-files by typing the code for each problem in this appendix into a separate M-file (there is no need to type the final pause statement or comments), and naming each M-file with a .m extension, as in ch2p1.m. You can also type the code for more than one problem into an M-file, including the pause command, and name the M-file with the .m extension. You can then call the file from the **Command Window**, and continue past the pause statements to the next problem by pressing any key.

By its nature, this appendix cannot cover all the background and details necessary for a complete understanding of MATLAB. For further details, you are referred to other sources, including MATLAB reference manuals and instructions specific to your particular computer. The bibliography at the end of this appendix provides a partial listing of references. This appendix should give you enough information to be able to apply MATLAB to the analysis and design problems covered in this book.

The code contained in this appendix and in the Control Systems Engineering Toolbox was developed on a PC using MATLAB Version 7.4 and the Control System Toolbox Version 8.0. The code will also run on workstations that support MATLAB. Consult the MATLAB *Installation Guide* for your platform for minimum system hardware requirements.

B.2 MATLAB EXAMPLES

CHAPTER 2: TRANSFER FUNCTIONS OF PHYSICAL SYSTEMS

ch2p1 Bit strings will be used to identify parts of this tutorial on the computer output. Bit strings are represented by the text enclosed in apostrophes, such as `'ab'`. Comments begin with % and are ignored by MATLAB. Numbers are entered without any other characters. Arithmetic can be performed using the proper arithmetic operator. Numbers can be assigned using a left-hand argument and an equals sign. Finally, we can find the magnitude and angle of a complex number, Q using `abs($Q$)` and `angle($Q$)`, respectively.

```
'(ch2p1)'                  % Display label.
'How are you?'             % Display string.
-3.96                      % Display scalar number -3.96.
-4+7i                      % Display complex number -4+7i.
-5-6j                      % Display complex number -5-6j.
(-4+7i)+(-5-6i)            % Add two complex numbers and
                           % display sum.
(-4+7j)*(-5-6j)            % Multiply two complex numbers and
                           % display product.
M=5                        % Assign 5 to M and display.
N=6                        % Assign 6 to N and display.
P=M+N                      % Assign M+N to P and display.
Q=3+4j                     % Define complex number, Q.
MagQ=abs(Q)                % Find magnitude of Q.
ThetaQ=(180/pi)*angle(Q)   % Find the angle of Q in degrees.
pause
```

ch2p2   Polynomials in s can be represented as row vectors containing the coefficients. Thus $P_1 = s^3 + 7s^2 - 3s + 23$ can be represented by the vector shown below with elements separated by a space or comma. Bit strings can be used to identify each section of this tutorial.

```
'(ch2p2)'                    % Display label.
P1=[1 7 -3 23]               % Store polynomial s^3 + 7s^2 - 3s +
                             % 23 as P1 and display.
pause
```

ch2p3   Running the previous statements causes MATLAB to display the results. Ending the command with a semicolon suppresses the display. Typing an expression without a left-hand assignment and without a semicolon causes the expression to be evaluated and the result displayed. Enter P2 in the **MATLAB Command Window** after execution.

```
'(ch2p3)'                    % Display label.
P2=[3 5 7 8];                % Assign 3s^3 + 5s^2 + 7s + 8 to P2
                             % without displaying.
3*5                          % Evaluate 3*5 and display result.
pause
```

ch2p4   An $F(s)$ in factored form can be represented in polynomial form. Thus $P_3 = (s+2)(s+5)(s+6)$ can be transformed into a polynomial using poly(V), where V is a row vector containing the roots of the polynomial and poly(V) forms the coefficients of the polynomial.

```
'(ch2p4)'                    % Display label.
P3=poly([-2 -5 -6])          % Store polynomial
                             % (s+2)(s+5)(s+6) as P3 and
                             % display the coefficients.
pause
```

ch2p5   We can find roots of polynomials using the roots(V) command. The roots are returned as a column vector. For example, find the roots of $5s^4 + 7s^3 + 9s^2 - 3s + 2 = 0$.

```
'(ch2p5)'                    % Display label.
P4=[5 7 9 -3 2]              % Form 5s^4+7s^3+9s^2-3s+2 and
                             % display.
rootsP4=roots(P4)            % Find roots of 5s^4+7s^3+9s^2
                             % -3s+2,
                             % assign to rootsP4, and display.
pause
```

ch2p6   Polynomials can be multiplied together using the conv(a,b) command (standing for convolve). Thus, $P_5 = (s^3 + 7s^2 + 10s + 9)(s^4 - 3s^3 + 6s^2 + 2s + 1)$ is generated as follows:

```
'(ch2p6)'                          % Display label.
P5=conv([1 7 10 9],[1 -3 6 2 1])   % Form (s^3+7s^2+10s+9)(s^4-
                                   % 3s^3+6s^2+2s+1), assign to P5,
                                   % and display.
pause
```

ch2p7 The partial-fraction expansion for $F(s) = b(s)/a(s)$ can be found using the $[K,p,k] = \text{residue}(b,a)$ command ($K = $ residue; $p = $ roots of denominator; $k = $ direct quotient, which is found by dividing polynomials prior to performing a partial-fraction expansion). We expand $F(s) = (7s^2 + 9s + 12)/[s(s+7)(s^2+10s+100)]$ as an example. Using the results from MATLAB yields: $F(s) = [(0.2554 - 0.3382i)/(s + 5.0000 - 8.6603i)] + [(0.2554 + 0.3382i)/(s + 5.0000 + 8.6603i)] - [0.5280/(s+7)] + [0.0171/s]$.

```
'(ch2p7)'                        % Display label.
numf=[7 9 12]                    % Define numerator of F(s).
denf=conv(poly([0 -7]),[1 10 100];  % Define denominator of F(s).
[K,p,k]=residue(numf,denf)       % Find residues and assign to K;
                                 % find roots of denominator and
                                 % assign to p; find
                                 % constant and assign to k.
pause
```

ch2p8 (Example 2.3) Let us do Example 2.3 in the book using MATLAB.

```
'(ch2p8) Example 2.3'            % Display label.
numy=32;                         % Define numerator.
deny=poly([0 -4 -8]);            % Define denominator.
[r,p,k]=residue(numy,deny)       % Calculate residues, poles, and
                                 % direct quotient.
pause
```

ch2p9 Creating Transfer Functions
Vector Method, Polynomial Form
A transfer function can be expressed as a numerator polynomial divided by a denominator polynomial, that is, $F(s) = N(s)/D(s)$. The numerator, $N(s)$, is represented by a row vector, numf, that contains the coefficients of $N(s)$. Similarly, the denominator, $D(s)$, is represented by a row vector, denf, that contains the coefficients of $D(s)$. We form $F(s)$ with the command, F = tf(numf,denf). F is called a linear time-invariant (LTI) object. This object, or transfer function, can be used as an entity in other operations, such as addition or multiplication. We demonstrate with $F(s) = 150(s^2 + 2s + 7)/[s(s^2 + 5s + 4)]$. Notice after executing the tf command, MATLAB prints the transfer function.

Vector Method, Factored Form
We also can create LTI transfer functions if the numerator and denominator are expressed in factored form. We do this by using row vectors containing the roots of the numerator and denominator. Thus $G(s) = K*N(s)/D(s)$ can be expressed as an LTI object using the command, G = zpk(numg,deng,K), where numg is a row vector containing the

roots of $N(s)$ and `deng` is a row vector containing the roots of $D(s)$. The expression `zpk` stands for zeros (roots of the numerator), poles (roots of the denominator), and gain, K. We demonstrate with $G(s) = 20(s+2)(s+4)/[(s+7)(s+8)(s+9)]$. Notice after executing the `zpk` command, MATLAB prints the transfer function.

Rational Expression in s Method, Polynomial Form
(Requires Control System Toolbox 8.0)

This method allows you to type the transfer function as you normally would write it. The statement `s = tf('s')` must precede the transfer function if you wish to create an LTI transfer function in polynomial form equivalent to using `G = tf(numg,deng)`.

Rational Expression in s Method, Factored Form
(Requires Control System Toolbox 8.0)

This method allows you to type the transfer function as you normally would write it. The statement `s = zpk('s')` must precede the transfer function if you wish to create an LTI transfer function in factored form equivalent to using `G = zpk(numg,deng,K)`.

For both rational expression methods the transfer function can be typed in any form regardless of whether `s = tf('s')` or `s = zpk('s')` is used. The difference is in the created LTI transfer function. We use the same examples above to demonstrate the rational expression in s methods.

```
'(ch2p9)'                              % Display label.
'Vector Method, Polynomial Form'       % Display label.
numf=150*[1 2 7]                       % Store 150 (s^2+2s+7) in numf and
                                       % display.
deng=[1 5 4 0]                         % Store s(s+1)(s+4) in denf and
                                       % display.
'F(s)'                                 % Display label.
F=tf(numf,denf)                        % Form F(s) and display.
clear                                  % Clear previous variables from
                                       % workspace.
'Vector Method, Factored Form'         % Display label.
numg=[-2 -4]                           % Store (s+2)(s+4) in numg and
                                       % display.
deng=[-7 -8 -9]                        % Store (s+7)(s+8)(s+9) in deng
                                       % and display.
K=20                                   % Define K.
'G(s)'                                 % Display label.
G=zpk(numg,deng,K)                     % Form G(s) and display.
clear                                  % Clear previous variables from
                                       % workspace.
'Rational Expression Method, Polynomial Form'
                                       % Display label.
s=tf('s')                              % Define 's' as an LTI object in
                                       % polynomial form.
F=150*(s^2+2*s+7)/[s*(s^2+...          % Form F(s) as an LTI transfer
5*s+4)]                                % function in polynomial form.
G=20*(s+2)*(s+4)/[(s+7)*...            % Form G(s) as an LTI transfer
(s+8)*(s+9)]                           % function in polynomial form.
clear                                  % Clear previous variables from
                                       % workspace.
```

```
'Rational Expression Method, Factored Form'
                          % Display label.
s=zpk('s')                % Define 's' as an LTI object in
                          % factored form.
F=150*(s^2+2*s+7)/[s*(s^2+5*s+4)]
                          % Form F(s) as an LTI transfer
                          % function in factored form.
G=20*(s+2)*(s+4)/[(s+7)*(s+8)*(s+9)]
                          % Form G(s) as an LTI transfer
                          % function in factored form.
pause
```

ch2p10 Transfer function numerator and denominator vectors can be converted between polynomial form containing the coefficients and factored form containing the roots. The MATLAB function, `tf2zp(numtf,dentf)`, converts the numerator and denominator from coefficients to roots. The results are in the form of column vectors. We demonstrate this with $F(s) = (10s^2 + 40s + 60)/(s^3 + 4s^2 + 5s + 7)$. The MATLAB function, `zp2tf(numzp,denzp,K)`, converts the numerator and denominator from roots to coefficients. The arguments `numzp` and `denzp` must be column vectors. In the demonstration that follows, apostrophes signify transpose. We demonstrate the conversion from roots to coefficients with $G(s) = 10(s + 2)(s + 4)/[s(s + 3)(s + 5)]$.

```
'(ch2p10)'                % Display label.
'Coefficients for F(s)'   % Display label.
numftf=[10 40 60]         % Form numerator of F(s)=
                          % (10s^2+40s+60)/(s^3+4s^2+5s
                          % +7).
denftf=[1 4 5 7]          % Form denominator of F(s)=
                          % (10s^2+40s+60)/(s^3+4s^2+5s
                          % +7).
'Roots for F(s)'          % Display label.
[numfzp,denfzp]=tf2zp (numftf,denftf)
                          % Convert F(s) to factored form.
'Roots for G(s)'          % Display label.
numgzp=[-2 -4]            % Form numerator of
K=10                      % G(s)=10(s+2)(s+4)/[s(s+3)
                          % (s+5)].
dengzp=[0 -3 -5]          % Form denominator of
                          %G(s)=10(s+2)(s+4)/[s(s+3)(s+5)].
'Coefficients for G(s)'   % Display label.
[numgtf,dengtf]=zp2tf(numgzp',dengzp',K)
                          % Convert G(s) to polynomial form.
pause
```

ch2p11 LTI models can also be converted between polynomial and factored forms. MATLAB commands `tf` and `zpk` are also used for the conversion between LTI models. If a transfer function, *Fzpk*(*s*), is expressed as factors in the numerator and denominator, then `tf(Fzpk)` converts *Fzpk*(*s*) to a transfer function expressed as coefficients in the numerator and denominator. Similarly, if a transfer function, *Ftf*(*s*), is expressed as coefficients in the numerator and denominator, then `zpk(Ftf)` converts *Ftf*(*s*) to a transfer function expressed as factors in the numerator and denominator. The following example demonstrates the concepts.

```
'(ch2p11)'                          % Display label.
'Fzpk1(s)'                          % Display label.
Fzpk1=zpk([-2 -4], [0 -3 -5],10)    % Form Fzpk1(s)=
                                    % 10(s+2)(s+4)/[s(s+3)(s+5)].
'Ftf1'                              % Display label.
Ftf1=tf(Fzpk1)                      % Convert Fzpk1(s) to
                                    % coefficients form.
'Ftf2'                              % Display label.
Ftf2=tf([10 40 60], [1 4 5 7])      % Form Ftf2(s)=
                                    % (10s^2+40s+60)/(s^3+4s^2+5s
                                    % +7).
'Fzpk2'                             % Display label.
Fzpk2=zpk(Ftf2)                     % Convert Ftf2(s) to
                                    % factored form.
pause
```

ch2p12 Functions of time can be easily plotted using MATLAB's plot(X,Y,S), where X is the independent variable, Y is the dependent variable, and S is a character string describing the plot's color, marker, and line characteristic. Type HELP PLOT in the **Command Window** to see a list of choices for S. Multiple plots also can be obtained using plot (X1,Y1,S1,X2,Y2,S2,X3,Y3,S3,...). In the following example we plot on the same graph sin($5t$) in red and cos($5t$) in green for $t = 0$ to 10 seconds in 0.01 second increments. Time is specified as t = start:increment:final.

```
'(ch2p12)'              % Display label.
t=0:0.01:10;            % Specify time range and increment.
f1=cos(5*t);            % Specify f1 to be cos(5t).
f2=sin(5*t);            % Specify f2 to be sin(5t).
plot(t,f1,'r',t,f2,'g') % Plot f1 in red and f2 in green.
pause
```

CHAPTER 3: STATE EQUATIONS FOR PHYSICAL SYSTEMS

ch3p1 The square system matrix, $\mathbf{A} = \begin{bmatrix} 0 & 1 & 0 \\ 0 & 0 & 1 \\ -9 & -8 & -7 \end{bmatrix}$ is written with a space or comma separating the elements of each row. The next row is indicated with a semicolon or carriage return. The entire matrix is then enclosed in a pair of square brackets.

```
'(ch3p1)'               % Display label.
A=[0 1 0;0 0 1;-9 -8 -7] % Represent A.
'or'
A=[0 1 0                % Represent A.
0 0 1
-9 -8 -7]
pause
```

ch3p2 A row vector, such as the output matrix **C**, can be represented with elements separated by spaces or commas and enclosed in square brackets. A column vector, such as input matrix **B**, can be written as elements separated by semicolons or carriage returns, or as the transpose (') of a row vector.

```
'(ch3p2)'                          % Display label.
C=[2 3 4]                          % Represent row vector C.
B=[7;8;9]                          % Represent column vector B.
'or'
B=[7                               % Represent column vector B.
8
9]
'or'
B=[7 8 9]'                         % Represent column vector B.
pause
```

ch3p3   The state-space representation consists of specifying the **A**, **B**, **C**, and **D** matrices followed by the creation of an LTI state-space object using the MATLAB command, `ss(A,B,C,D)`. Hence, for the matrices in (ch3p1) and (ch3p2), the state-space representation would be:

```
'(ch3p3)'                          % Display label.
A=[0 1 0;0 0 1;-9 -8 -7]           % Represent A.
B=[7;8;9];                         % Represent column vector B.
C=[2 3 4];                         % Represent row vector C.
D=0;                               % Represent D.
F=ss(A,B,C,D)                      % Create an LTI object and display.
```

ch3p4 (Example 3.4)   Transfer functions represented either by numerator and denominator or an LTI object can be converted to state space. For numerator and denominator representation, the conversion can be implemented using `[A,B,C,D]=` `tf2ss(num,den)`. The **A** matrix is returned in a form called the controller canonical form, which will be explained in Chapter 5 in the text. To obtain the phase-variable form, `[Ap, Bp, Cp, Dp]`, we perform the following operations: `Ap=inv` `(P)*A*P; Bp=inv(P)*B; Cp=C*P, Dp=D`, where **P** is a matrix with 1's along the anti-diagonal and 0's elsewhere. These transformations will be explained in Chapter 5. The command `inv(X)` finds the inverse of a square matrix. The symbol `*` signifies multiplication. For systems represented as LTI objects, the command `ss(F)`, where F is an LTI transfer-function object, can be used to convert F to a state-space object. Let us look at Example 3.4 in the text. For the numerator-denominator representation, notice that the MATLAB response associates the gain, 24, with the vector **C** rather than the vector **B** as in the example in the text. Both representations are equivalent. For the LTI transfer-function object, the conversion to state space does not yield the phase-variable form. The result is a balanced model that improves the accuracy of calculating eigenvalues, which are covered in Chapter 4. Since `ss(F)` does not yield familiar forms of the state equations (nor is it possible to easily convert to familiar forms), we will have limited use for that transformation at this time.

```
'(ch3p4) Example 3.4'              % Display label.
'Numerator-denominator representation conversion'
                                   % Display label.
'Controller canonical form'        % Display label.
num=24;                            % Define numerator of
                                   % G(s)=C(s)/R(s).
den=[1 9 26 24];                   % Define denominator of G(s).
```

```
[A,B,C,D]=tf2ss(num,den)          % Convert G(s) to controller
                                  % canonical form, store matrices
                                  % A, B, C, D, and display.
'Phase-variable form'             % Display label.
P=[0 0 1;0 1 0;1 0 0];            % Form transformation matrix.
Ap=inv(P)*A*P                     % Form A matrix, phase-variable
                                  % form.
Bp=inv(P)*B                       % Form B vector, phase-variable
                                  % form.
Cp=C*P                            % Form C vector, phase-variable
                                  % form.
Dp=D                              % Form D phase-variable form.
'LTI object representation'       % Display label.
T=tf(num,den)                     % Represent T(s)=24/(s^3+9s^2+
                                  % 26s+24) as an LTI transfer-
                                  % function object.
Tss=ss(T)                         % Convert T(s) to state space.
pause
```

ch3p5   State-space representations can be converted to transfer functions represented by a numerator and a denominator using [num,den]=ss2tf(A,B,C,D,iu), where iu is the input number for multiple-input systems. For single-input, single-output systems iu = 1. For an LTI state-space system, Tss, the conversion can be implemented using Ttf = tf(Tss) to yield the transfer function in polynomial form or Tzpk = zpk(Tss) to yield the transfer function in factored form. For example, the transfer function represented by the matrices described in (ch3p3) can be found as follows:

```
'(ch3p5)'                         % Display label.
        'Non LTI'                 % Display label.
A=[0 1 0;0 0 1;-9 -8 -7];         % Represent A.
B=[7;8;9];                        % Represent B.
C=[2 3 4]                         % Represent C.
D=0;                              % Represent D.
'Ttf(s)'                          % Display label.
[num,den]=ss2tf(A,B,C,D,1)        % Convert state-space
                                  % representation to a
                                  % transfer function represented as
                                  % a numerator and denominator in
                                  % polynomial form, G(s)=num/den,
                                  % and display num and den.
        'LTI'                     % Display label.
Tss=ss(A,B,C,D)                   % Form LTI state-space model.
'Polynomial form, Ttf(s)'         % Display label.
Ttf=tf(Tss)                       % Transform from state space to
                                  % transfer function in polynomial
                                  % form.
'Factored form, Tzpk(s)'          % Display label.
Tzpk=zpk(Tss)                     % Transform from state space to
                                  % transfer function in factored
                                  % form.

pause
```

CHAPTER 4: TRANSIENT RESPONSE

ch4p1 (Example 4.6) We can use MATLAB to calculate characteristics of a second-order system, such as damping ratio, ζ; natural frequency, ω_n; percent overshoot, %OS (pos); settling time, T_s; and peak time, T_p. Let us look at Example 4.6 in the text.

```
'(ch4p1) Example 4.6'          % Display label.
p1=[1 3+7*i];                  % Define polynomial containing
                               % first pole.
p2=[1 3-7*i];                  % Define polynomial containing
                               % second pole.
deng=conv(p1,p2);             % Multiply the two polynomials to
                               % find the 2nd order polynomial,
                               % as^2+bs+c.
omegan=sqrt(deng(3)/deng(1))   % Calculate the natural frequency,
                               % sqrt(c/a).
zeta=(deng(2)/deng(1))/(2*omegan)
                               % Calculate damping ratio,
                               % ((b/a)/2*wn).
Ts=4/(zeta*omegan)             % Calculate settling time,
                               % (4/z*wn).
Tp=pi/(omegan*sqrt(1-zeta^2))  % Calculate peak time,
                               % pi/wn*sqrt(1-z^2).
pos=100*exp(-zeta*pi/sqrt(1-zeta^2))
                               % Calculate percent overshoot
                               % (100*e^(-z*pi/sqrt(1-z^2)).
pause
```

ch4p2 (Example 4.8) We can use MATLAB to obtain system step responses. These responses are particularly valuable when the system is not a pure two-pole system and has additional poles or zeros. We can obtain a plot of the step response of a transfer function, $T(s) = $ num/den, using the command `step(T)`, where `T` is an LTI transfer-function object. Multiple plots also can be obtained using `step(T`$_1$`,T`$_2$`, ...)`

Information about the plots obtained with `step(T)` can be found by left-clicking the mouse on the curve. You can find the curve's label as well as the coordinates of the point on which you clicked. Right-clicking away from a curve brings up a menu. From this menu you can select (1) system responses to be displayed and (2) response characteristics to be displayed, such as peak response. When selected, a dot appears on the curve at the appropriate point. Let your mouse rest on the point to read the value of the characteristic. You may also select (3) choice for grid on or off, (4) choice to normalize the curve, and (5) properties, such as labels, limits, units, style, and characteristics.

If we add the left-hand side, `[y,t] = step(T)`, we create vectors containing the plot's points, where `y` is the output vector and `t` is the time vector. For this case, a plot is not made until the `plot(t,y)` command is given, where we assume we want to plot the output (`y`) versus time (`t`). We can label the plot, the x-axis, and the y-axis with `title('ab')`, `xlabel('ab')`, and `ylabel('ab')`, respectively. The command `clf` clears the graph prior to plotting. Finally, text can be placed anywhere on the graph using the command `text(X,Y,'text')`, where `(X,Y)` are the graph coordinates where `'text'` will be displayed. Let us look at Example 4.8 in the text.

```
'(ch4p2) Example 4.8'                    % Display label.
'Test Run'                               % Display label.
clf                                      % Clear graph.
numt1=[24.542];                          % Define numerator of T1.
dent1=[1 4 24.542];                      % Define denominator of T1.
'T1(s)'                                  % Display label.
T1=tf(numt1,dent1)                       % Create and display T1(s).
step(T1)                                 % Run a demonstration step response
                                         % plot.
title('Test Run of T1(s)')               % Add title to graph.
pause
'Complete Run'                           % Display label.
[y1,t1]=step(T1);                        % Run step response of T1 and
                                         % collect points.
numt2=[245.42];                          % Define numerator of T2.
p1=[1 10];                               % Define (s+10) in denominator
                                         % of T2.
p2=[1 4 24.542];                         % Define (s^2+4s+24.542) in
                                         % denominator of T2.
dent2=conv(p1,p2);                       % Multiply (s+10)(s^2+4s+24.542)
                                         % for denominator of T2.
'T2(s)'                                  % Display label.
T2=tf(numt2, dent2)                      % Create and display T2.
[y2,t2]=step(T2);                        % Run step response of T2 and
                                         % collect points.
numt3=[73.626];                          % Define numerator of T3.
p3=[1 3];                                % Define (s+3) in denominator
                                         % of T3.
dent3=conv(p3,p2);                       % Multiply (s+3)(s^2+4s+24.542)
                                         % for denominator of T3.
'T3(s)'                                  % Display label.
T3=tf(numt3,dent3)                       % Create and display T3.
[y3,t3]=step(T3);                        % Run step response of T3 and
                                         % collect points.
clf                                      % Clear graph.
plot(t1,y1,t2,y2,t3,y3)                  % Plot acquired points with all
                                         % three plots on one graph.
title('Step Responses of T1(s), T2(s),and T3(s)')
                                         % Add title to graph.
xlabel('Time(seconds)')                  % Add time axis label.
ylabel('Normalized Response')            % Add response axis label.
text(0.7,0.7,'c3(t)')                    % Label step response of T1.
text(0.7,1.1,'c2(t)')                    % Label step response of T2.
text(0.5,1.3,'c1(t)')                    % Label step response of T3.
pause
step(T1,T2,T3)                           % Use alternate method of plotting
                                         % step responses.
title('Step Responses of T1(s),T2(s),and T3(s)')
                                         % Add title to graph.
pause
```

ch4p3   We also can plot the step response of systems represented in state space using the step(T,t) command. Here T is any LTI object and t = a:b:c is the range for the time axis, where a is the initial time, b is the time step size, and c is the final time. For example, t = 0:1:10 means time from 0 to 10 seconds in steps of 1 second. The t field is optional. Finally, in this example we introduce the command grid on, which superimposes a grid over the step response. Place the grid on command after the step(T,t) command.

```
'(ch4p3)'                        % Display label.
clf                              % Clear graph.
A=[0 1 0;0 0 1;−24 −26 −9];      % Generate A matrix.
B=[0;0;1];                       % Generate B vector.
C=[2 7 1];                       % Generate C vector.
D=0;                             % Generate D.
T=ss(A,B,C,D)                    % Generate LTI object, T, in state
                                 % space and display.
t=0:0.1:10;                      % Define range of time for plot.
step(T,t)                        % Plot step response for given
                                 % range of time.
grid on                          % Turn grid on for plot.
pause
```

ch4p4 (Antenna Control Case Study)   We now use MATLAB to plot the step response requested in the Antenna Control Case Study.

```
'(ch4p4) Antenna Control Case Study'
                                 % Display label.
clf                              % Clear graph.
numg=20.83;                      % Define numerator of G(s).
deng=[1 101.71 171];             % Define denominator of G(s).
'G(s)'                           % Display label.
G=tf(numg,deng)                  % Form and display transfer
                                 % Function G(s).
step(G);                         % Generate step response.
title('Angular Velocity Response')
                                 % Add title.
pause
```

ch4p5 (UFSS Case Study)   As a final example, let us use MATLAB to do the UFSS Case Study in the text (*Johnson, 1980*). We introduce table lookup to find the rise time. Using the interp1(y,t,y1) command, we set up a table of values of amplitude, y, and time, t, from the step response and look for the value of time for which the amplitude is y1 = 0.1 and 0.9. We also generate time response data over a defined range of time using t = a:b:c followed by [y,t] = step(G,t). Here G is an LTI transfer-function object and t is the range for the time axis, where a is the initial time, b is the time step size, and c is the final time; y is the output.

```
'(ch4p5) UFSS Case Study'        % Display label.
clf                              % Clear graph.
'(a)'                            % Display label.
numg=0.0169;                     % Define numerator of 2nd order
```

```
                                        % approximation of G(s).
deng=[1 0.226 0.0169];                  % Define 2nd order term of
                                        % denominator of G(s).
'G(s)'                                  % Display label.
G=tf(numg,deng)                         % Create and display G(s).
omegan=sqrt(deng(3))                    % Find natural frequency.
zeta=deng(2)/(2*omegan)                 % Find damping ratio.
Ts=4/(zeta*omegan)                      % Find settling time.
Tp=pi/(omegan*sqrt(1−zeta^2))           % Find peak time.
pos=exp/(−zeta*pi/sqrt(1−zeta^2))*100
                                        % Find percent overshoot.
t=0:0.1:35;                             % Limit time to find rise time. t=0
                                        % to 35 in steps of 0.1.
[y,t]=step(G,t);                        % Generate and save points of step
                                        % response over defined range of t.
Tlow=interp1(y,t,0.1);                  % Search table for time when
                                        % y=0.1*finalvalue.
Thi=interp1(y,t,0.9);                   % Search table for
                                        % time=0.9*finalvalue.
Tr=Thi−Tlow                             % Calculate rise time.
'(b)'                                   % Display label.
numc=0.125*[1 0.435];                   % Define numerator of C(s).
denc=conv(poly([0 −1.23]), [1 0.226 0.0169]);
                                        % Define denominator of C(s).
[K,p,k]=residue(numc, denc)             % Find partial-fraction expansion.
'(d)'                                   % Display label.
numg=0.125*[1 0.435];                   % Define numerator of G(s).
deng=conv([1 1.23], [1 0.226 0.0169]);
                                        % Define denominator of G(s).
'G(s)'                                  % Display label.
G=tf(numg,deng)                         % Create and display G(s).
[y,t]=step(G);                          % Generate complete step response
                                        % and collect points.
plot(t,y)                               % Plot points.
title('Pitch Angle Response')           % Add title.
xlabel ('Time (seconds)')               %label time axis.
ylabel ('Pitch Angle(radians)')         % Label y−axis.
pause
```

CHAPTER 5: EQUIVALENT SYSTEMS

ch5p1 (UFSS Pitch Control System) MATLAB can be used for block diagram reduction. Three methods are available: (1) Solution via Series, Parallel, & Feedback Commands, (2) Solution via Algebraic Operations, and (3) Solution via Append & Connect Commands. Let us look at each of these methods.

1. Solution via Series, Parallel, & Feedback Commands

The closed-loop transfer function is obtained using the following commands successively, where the arguments are LTI objects: `series(G1,G2)` for a cascade connection of $G_1(s)$; and $G_2(s)$; `parallel (G1,G2)` for a parallel connection of $G_1(s)$ and $G_2(s)$; `feedback(G,H,sign)` for a closed-loop connection with $G(s)$ as the forward path, $H(s)$ as the feedback, and `sign` is -1 for negative-feedback systems or $+1$ for positive-feedback systems. The sign is optional for negative-feedback systems.

2. Solution via Algebraic Operations

Another approach is to use arithmetic operations successively on LTI transfer functions as follows: `G2*G1` for a cascade connection of $G_1(s)$ and $G_2(s)$; `G1+G2` for a parallel connection of $G_1(s)$ and $G_2(s)$; `G/(1+G*H)` for a closed-loop negative-feedback connection with $G(s)$ as the forward path and $H(s)$ as the feedback; `G/(1-G*H)` for positive-feedback systems. When using division we follow with the function `minreal(sys)` to cancel common terms in the numerator and denominator.

3. Solution via Append & Connect Commands

The last method, which defines the topology of the system, may be used effectively for complicated systems. First, the subsystems are defined. Second, the subsystems are appended, or gathered, into a multiple-input/multiple-output system. Think of this system as a single system with an input for each of the subsystems and an output for each of the subsystems. Next, the external inputs and outputs are specified. Finally, the subsystems are interconnected. Let us elaborate on each of these steps.

The subsystems are defined by creating LTI transfer functions for each. The subsystems are appended using the command `G = append(G1,G2,G3,G4, .....Gn)`, where the `Gi` are the LTI transfer functions of the subsystems and `G` is the appended system. Each subsystem is now identified by a number based upon its position in the append argument. For example, `G3` is 3, based on the fact that it is the third subsystem in the append argument (not the fact that we write it as `G3`).

Now that we have created an appended system, we form the arguments required to interconnect their inputs and outputs to form our system. The first step identifies which subsystems have the external input signal and which subsystems have the external output signal. For example, we use `inputs = [1 5 6]` and `outputs = [3 4]` to define the external inputs to be the inputs of subsystems 1, 5, and 6 and the external outputs to be the outputs of subsystems 3 and 4. For single-input/single-output systems, these definitions use scalar quantities. Thus `inputs = 5, outputs = 8` define the input to subsystem 5 as the external input and the output of subsystem 8 as the external output.

At this point we tell the program how all of the subsystems are interconnected. We form a Q matrix that has a row for each subsystem whose input comes from another subsystem's output. The first column contains the subsystem's number. Subsequent columns contain the numbers of the subsystems from which the inputs come. Thus, a typical row might be as follows: `[3 6 -7]`, or subsystem 3's input is formed from the sum of the output of subsystem 6 and the negative of the output of subsystem 7.

Finally, all of the interconnection arguments are used in the `connect(G Q inputs,outputs)` command, where all of the arguments have been previously defined.

Let us demonstrate the three methods for finding the total transfer function by looking at the back endpapers and finding the closed-loop transfer function of the pitch control loop for the UFSS with $K_1 = K_2 = 1$ (*Johnson, 1980*). The last method using append and connect requires that all subsystems be proper (the order of the numerator cannot be greater than the order of the denominator). The pitch rate sensor violates this requirement. Thus, for the third method, we perform some block diagram maneuvers by pushing the pitch rate sensor to the left past the summing junction and combining the resulting blocks with the pitch gain and the elevator actuator. These changes are reflected in the program. You should verify all computer results with hand calculations.

```
'(ch5p1) UFSS Pitch Control System'
'& Feedback Commands'
'Solution via Series, Parallel;    % Display labels.
numg1=[-1];                        % Define numerator of G1(s).
deng1=[1];                         % Define denominator of G1(s).
numg2=[0 2];                       % Define numerator of G2(s).
deng2=[1 2];                       % Define denominator of G2(s).
numg3=-0.125*[1 0.435];            % Define numerator of G3(s).
deng3=conv([1 1.23],[1 0.226 0.0169]);
                                   % Define denominator of G3(s).
numh1=[-1 0];                      % Define numerator of H1(s).
denh1=[0 1];                       % Define denominator of H1(s).
G1=tf(numg1,deng1);                % Create LTI transfer function,
                                   % G1(s).
G2=tf(numg2,deng2);                % Create LTI transfer function,
                                   % G2(s).
G3=tf(numg3,deng3);                % Create LTI transfer function,
                                   % G3(s).
H1=tf(numh1,denh1);                % Create LTI transfer function,
                                   % H1(s).
G4=series(G2,G3);                  % Calculate product of elevator
                                   % and vehicle dynamics.
G5=feedback(G4,H1);                % Calculate close-loop transfer
                                   % function of inner loop.
Ge=series(G1,G5);                  % Multiply inner-loop transfer
                                   % function and pitch gain.
'T(s) via Series, Parallel, & Feedback Commands'
                                   % Display label.
T=feedback(Ge,1)                   % Find closed-loop transfer
                                   % function.
'Solution via Algebraic Operations'
                                   % Display label.
clear                              % Clear session.
numg1=[-1];                        % Define numerator of G1(s).
deng1=[1];                         % Define denominator of G1(s).
numg2=[0 2];                       % Define numerator of G2(s).
deng2=[1 2];                       % Define denominator of G2(s).
numg3=-0.125*[1 0.435];            % Define numerator of G3(s).
deng3=conv([1 1.23],[1 0.226 0.0169]);
                                   % Define denominator of G3(s).
numh1=[-1 0];                      % Define numerator of H1(s).
denh1=[0 1];                       % Define denominator of H1(s).
G1=tf(numg1,deng1);                % Create LTI transfer function, G1(s).
G2=tf(numg2,deng2);                % Create LTI transfer function, G2(s).
G3=tf(numg3,deng3);                % Create LTI transfer function, G3(s).
H1=tf(numh1,denh1);                % Create LTI transfer function, H1(s).
G4=G3*G2;                          % Calculate product of elevator and
                                   % vehicle
                                   % dynamics.
```

```
G5=G4/(1+G4*H1);                % Calculate closed-loop transfer
                                % function of inner loop.
G5=minreal(G5);                 % Cancel common terms.
Ge=G5*G1;                       % Multiply inner-loop transfer
                                % functions.
'T(s) via Algebraic Operations' % Display label.
T=Ge/(1+Ge);                    % Find closed-loop transfer function.
T=minreal(T)                    % Cancel common terms.
'Solution via Append & Connect Commands'
                                % Display label.
'G1(s) = (-K1)*(1/(-K2s)) = 1/s' % Display label.
numg1=[1];                      % Define numerator of G1(s).
deng1=[1 0];                    % Define denominator of G1(s).
G1=tf(numg1,deng1)              % Create LTI transfer function,
                                % G1(s) = pitch gain*
                                % 1 (1/Pitch rate sensor).
'G2(s)=(-K2s)*(2/(s + 2)'       % Display label.
numg2=[-2 0];                   % Define numerator of G2(s).
deng2=[1 2];                    % Define denominator of G2(s).
G2=tf(numg2,deng2)              % Create LTI transfer function,
                                % G2(s) = pitch rate sensor*vehicle
                                % dynamics.
'G3(s) = -0.125(s +0.435)/((s+1.23)(s^2+0.226s+0.0169))'
                                % Display label.
numg3=-0.125*[1 0.435];         % Define numerator of G3(s).
deng3=conv([1 1.23],[1 0.226 0.0169]);
                                % Define denominator of G3(s).
G3=tf(numg3,deng3)              % Create LTI transfer function.
                                % G3(s) = vehicle dynamics.
System=append(G1,G2,G3);        % Gather all subsystems.
input=1;                        % Input is at first subsystem,
                                % G1(s).
output=3;                       % Output is output of third
                                % subsystem, G3(s).
Q=[1 -3 0                       % Subsystem 1, G1(s), gets its
                                % input from the negative of the
                                % output of subsystem 3, G3(s).
2 1 -3                          % Subsystem 2, G2(s), gets its
                                % input from subsystem 1, G1(s),
                                % and the negative of the output
                                % of subsystem 3, G3(s).
3 2 0];                         % Subsystem 3, G3(s), gets its
                                % input from subsystem 2, G2(s).
T=connect(System,Q,input,output);
                                % Connect the subsystems.
'T(s) via Append & Connect Commands'
                                % Display label.
T=tf(T);                        % Create LTI closed-loop transfer
                                % function.
T=minreal(T)                    % Cancel common terms.
pause
```

ch5p2 (Example 5.3) We can use MATLAB to calculate the closed-loop character-istics of a second-order system, such as damping ratio, ζ; natural frequency, ω_n; percent overshoot, %*OS* (pos); settling time, T_s; and peak time, T_p. The command [numt, dent] = tfdata(T,'v') extracts the numerator and denominator of $T(s)$ for a single-input/single-output system from which the calculations are based. The argument 'v' returns the numerator and denominator as simple row vectors. Omitting 'v' would return the numerator and denominator as cell arrays requiring more steps to obtain the row vectors. We end by generating a plot of the closed-loop step response. Let us look at Example 5.3 in the text.

```
'(ch5p2) Example 5.3'        % Display label.
numg=[25];                   % Define numerator of G(s).
deng=poly([0 -5]);           % Define denominator of G(s).
'G(s)'                       % Display label.
G=tf(numg,deng)              % Create and display G(s).
'T(s)'                       % Display label.
T=feedback(G,1)              % Find T(s).
[numt,dent]=tfdata(T,'v');   % Extract numerator & denominator
                             % of T(s).
wn=sqrt(dent(3))             % Find natural frequency.
z=dent(2)/(2*wn)             % Find damping ratio.
Ts=4/(z*wn)                  % Find settling time.
Tp=pi/(wn*sqrt(1-z^2))       % Find peak time.
pos=exp(-z*pi/sqrt(1-z^2))*100 % Find percent
                             overshoot.
step(T)                      % Generate step response.
pause
```

ch5p3 MATLAB can be used to convert transfer functions to state space in a specified form. The command [Acc Bcc Ccc Dcc] = tf2ss(num,den) can be used to convert $T(s)$ = num/den into controller canonical form with matrices and vectors Acc, Bcc, Ccc, and Dcc. We can then form an LTI state-space object using Scc = ss(Acc,Bcc,Ccc,Dcc). This object can then be converted into parallel form using Sp = canon(Scc,'type'), where type = modal yields the parallel form. Another choice, not used here, is type = companion, which yields a right companion system matrix. Transformation matrices can be used to convert to other representations. As an example, let us convert $C(s)/R(s) = 24/[(s+2)(s+3)(s+4)]$ into a parallel representation in state space, as is done in Section 5.7 - Parallel Form. Notice that the product of values in the **B** and **C** vectors yields the same product as the results in Eqs. (5.49) and (5.50). Thus, the two solutions are the same, but the state variables are ordered differently, and the gains are split between the **B** and **C** vectors. We can also extract the system matrices from the LTI object using [A,B,C,D] = ssdata(S), where S is a state-space LTI object and A, B, C, D, are its associated matrices and vectors.

```
'(ch5p3)'                    % Display label.
numt=24;                     % Define numerator of T(s).
dent=poly([-2 -3 -4]);       % Define denominator of T(s).
'T(s)'                       % Display label.
T=tf(numt,dent)              % Create and display T(s).
```

```
[Acc Bcc Ccc Dcc]=tf2ss(numt,dent);
                                     % Convert T(s) to controller
                                     % canonical form.
Scc=ss(Acc,Bcc,Ccc,Dcc);            % Create LTI controller canonical
                                     % state-space object.
Sp=canon(Scc,'modal');              % Convert controller canonical form
                                     % to parallel form.
'Controller Canonical Form'         % Display label.
[Acc,Bcc,Ccc,Dcc]=ssdata(Scc)       % Extract and display controller
                                     % canonical form matrices.
'Parallel Form'                     % Display label.
[Ap,Bp,Cp,Dp]=ssdata(Sp)            % Extract and display parallel form
                                     % matrices.
pause
```

ch5p4 (Example 5.9) We can use MATLAB to perform similarity transformations to obtain other forms. Let us look at Example 5.9 in the text.

```
'(ch5p4) Example 5.9'               % Display label.
Pinv=[2 0 0;3 2 0;1 4 5];           % Define P inverse.
P=inv(Pinv)                         % Calculate P.
'Original'                          % Display label.
Ax=[0 1 0;0 0 1;-2 -5 -7]           % Define original A.
Bx=[0 0 1]                          % Define original B.
Cx=[1 0 0]                          % Define original C.
'Transformed'                       % Display label.
Az=Pinv*Ax*P                        % Calculate new A.
Bz=Pinv*Bx                          % Calculate new B.
Cz=Cx*P                             % Calculate new C.
pause
```

ch5p5 Using MATLAB's $[P,d] = eig(A)$ command, where the columns of P are the eigenvectors of A and the diagonal elements of d are the eigenvalues of A, we can find the eigenvectors of the system matrix and then proceed to diagonalize the system. We can also use $canon(S,'modal')$ to diagonalize an LTI object, S, represented in state space.

```
'(ch5p5)'                           % Display label.
A=[3 1 5;4 -2 7;2 3 1];             % Define original A.
B=[1;2;3];                          % Define original B.
C=[2 4 6];                          % Define original C.
[P,d]=eig(A)                        % Generate transformation matrix,
                                    % P, and eigenvalues, d.
'Via Transformation'                % Display label.
Adt=inv(P)*A*P                      % Calculate diagonal system A.
Bdt=inv(P)*B                        % Calculate diagonal system B.
Cdt=C*P                             % Calculate diagonal system C.
'Via Canon Command'                 % Display label.
S=ss(A,B,C,0)                       % Create state-space LTI object
```

```
                                    % for original system.
Sp=canon(S,'modal')                 % Calculate diagonal system via
                                    % canon command.
pause
```

CHAPTER 6: TRANSIENT RESPONSE STABILITY

ch6p1 (Example 6.7)   MATLAB can solve for the poles of a transfer function in order to determine stability. To solve for the poles of $T(s)$ use the `pole(T)` command. Let us look at Example 6.7 in the text.

```
'(ch6p1) Example 6.7'               % Display label.
numg=1;                             % Define numerator of G(s).
deng=conv([1 0],[2 3 2 3 2]);       % Define denominator of G(s).
G=tf(numg,deng);                    % Create G(s) object.
'T(s)'                              % Display label.
T=feedback(G,1)                     % Calculate closed-loop T(s)
                                    % object.
                                    % Negative feedback is default
                                    % when there is no sign parameter.
poles=pole(T)                       % Find poles of T(s).
pause
```

ch6p2 (Example 6.9)   We can use MATLAB to find the range of gain for stability by generating a loop, changing gain, and finding at what gain we obtain right-half-plane poles.

```
'(ch6p2) Example 6.9'               % Display label.
K=[1:1:2000];                       % Define range of K from 1 to 2000
                                    % in steps of 1.

for n=1:length(K);                  % Set up length of DO LOOP to equal
                                    % number of K values to be tested.

       dent=[1 18 77 K(n)];         % Define the denominator of T(s)
                                    % for the nth value of K.

       poles=roots(dent);           % Find the poles for the nth value
                                    % of K.

       r=real(poles);               % Form a vector containing the real
                                    % parts of the poles for K(n).

          if max(r) > = 0,          % Test poles found for the nth
                                    % value of K for a real value ≥ 0.

             poles                  % Display first pole values where
                                    % there is a real part ≥ 0.

             K=K(n)                 % Display corresponding value of K.
             break                  % Stop loop if rhp poles are found.
   end                              % End if.
end                                 % End for.
pause
```

ch6p3 (Example 6.11)   We can use MATLAB to determine the stability of a system represented in state space by using the command `eig(A)` to find the eigenvalues of the system matrix, A. Let us apply the concept to Example 6.11 in the text.

```
'(ch6p3) Example 6.11'          % Display label.
A=[0 3 1;2 8 1;-10 -5 -2]       % Define system matrix, A.
eigenvalues=eig(A)              % Find eigenvalues.
pause
```

CHAPTER 7: FORCED RESPONSE ERRORS

ch7p1 (Example 7.4, sys. b) Static error constants are found using lim $s^n G(s)$ as $s \to 0$. Once the static error constant is found, we can evaluate the steady-state error. To evaluate the static error constant we can use the command $\texttt{dcgain(G)}$, which evaluates $G(s)$ at $s = 0$. Let us look at Example 7.4, system (b), in the text.

```
'(ch7p1) Example 7.4, sys. b'   % Display label.
numg=500*poly([-2 -5 -6]);      % Define numerator of G(s).
deng=poly([0 -8 -10 -12]);      % Define denominator of G(s).
G=tf(numg,deng);                % Form G(s)
'Check Stability'               % Display label.
T=feedback(G,1);                % Form T(s).
poles=pole(T)                   % Display closed-loop poles.
'Step Input'                    % Display label.
Kp=dcgain(G)                    % Evaluate Kp=numg/deng for s=0.
ess=1/(1+Kp)                    % Evaluate ess for step input.
'Ramp Input'                    % Display label.
numsg=conv([1 0],numg);         % Define numerator of sG(s).
densg=poly([0 -8 -10 -12]);     % Define denominator of sG(s).
sG=tf(numsg,densg);             % Create sG(s).
sG=minreal(sG);                 % Cancel common 's' in
                                % numerator(numsg) and
                                % denominator(densg).

Kv=dcgain(sG)                   % Evaluate Kv=sG(s) for s=0.
ess=1/Kv                        % Evaluate steady-state error for
                                % ramp input.

'Parabolic Input'               % Display label.
nums2g=conv([1 0 0],numg);      % Define numerator of s^2G(s).
dens2g=poly([0 -8 -10 -12]);    % Define denominator of s^2G(s).
s2G=tf(nums2g,dens2g);          % Create s^2G(s).
s2G=minreal(s2G);               % Cancel common 's' in
                                % numerator(nums2g) and
                                % denominator(dens2g).

Ka=dcgain(s2G)                  % Evaluate Ka=s^2G(s) for s=0.
ess=1/Ka                        % Evaluate steady-state error for
                                % parabolic input.
pause
```

ch7p2 (Example 7.6) We can use MATLAB to evaluate the gain, K, required to meet a steady-state error specification. Let us look at Example 7.6 in the text.

```
'(ch7p2) Example 7.6'           % Display label.
numgdK=[1 5];                   % Define numerator of G(s)/K.
dengdK=poly([0 -6 -7 -8]);      % Define denominator of G(s)/K.
```

```
GdK=tf(numgdK,dengdK);          % Create G(s)/K.
numgkv=conv([1 0],numgdK);      % Define numerator of sG(s)/K.
dengkv=dengdK;                  % Define denominator of sG(s)/K.
GKv=tf(numgkv,dengkv);          % Create sG(s)/K.
GKv=minreal(GKv);               % Cancel common 's' in numerator
                                % and denominator of sG(s)/K.

KvdK=dcgain(GKv)                % Evaluate (Kv/K)=(numgkv/dengkv)
                                % for s=0.

ess=0.1                         % Enumerate steady-state error.
K=1/(ess*KvdK)                  % Solve for K.
'Check Stability'               % Display label.
T=feedback(K*GdK,1);            % Form T(s).
poles=pole(T)                   % Display closed-loop poles.
pause
```

CHAPTER 8: A GRAPHICAL TOOL

ch8p1 (Example 8.7)   MATLAB allows root loci to be plotted with the `rlocus(GH)` command, where $G(s)H(s) = $ `numgh/dengh` and `GH` is an LTI transfer-function object. Points on the root locus can be selected interactively using the `[K,p] = rlocfind(GH)` command. MATLAB then yields the gain (K) at that point as well as all other poles (p) that have that gain. We can zoom in and out of the root locus by changing the range of axis values using the command `axis([xmin,xmax,ymin,ymax])`. The root locus can be drawn over a grid that shows constant damping ratio (z) and constant natural frequency (wn) curves using the `sgrid(z,wn)` command. To plot multiple ζ and ω_n curves, use `z = zmin:zstep:zmax` and `wn = wnmin:wnstep:wnmax` to specify ranges of values.

```
'(ch8p1) Example 8.7'           % Display label.
clf                             % Clear graph on screen.
numgh=[1 -4 20];                % Define numerator of G(s)H(s).
dengh=poly([-2 -4]);            % Define denominator of G(s)H(s).
'G(s)H(s)'                      % Display label.
GH=tf(numgh,dengh)              % Create G(s)H(s) and display.
rlocus(GH)                      % Draw root locus.
z=0.2:0.05:0.5;                 % Define damping ratio values: 0.2
                                % to 0.5 in steps of 0.05.

wn=0:1:10;                      % Define natural frequency values:
                                % 0 to 10 in steps of 1.

sgrid(z,wn)                     % Generate damping ratio and
                                % natural frequency grid lines for
                                % root locus.

title('Root Locus')            % Define title for root locus.
pause
rlocus(GH)                      % Draw close-up root locus.
axis([-3 1 -4 4])              % Define range on axes for root
                                % locus close-up view.

title('Close-up')              % Define title for close-up root
                                % locus.

z=0.45;                         % Define damping ratio line for
                                % overlay on close-up root locus.
```

```
wn=0;                          % Suppress natural frequency
                               % overlay curves.
sgrid(z,wn)                    % Overlay damping ratio curve on
                               % close-up root locus.
for k=1:3                      % Loop allows 3 points to be
                               % selected as per Example 8.7,
                               % (z=0.45, jw crossing, breakaway).
[K,p]=rlocfind(GH)             % Generate gain, K, and closed-loop
                               % poles, p, for point selected
                               % interactively on the root locus.
end                            % End loop.
pause
```

ch8p2 (Example 8.8)   We can couple the design of gain on the root locus with a step-response simulation for the gain selected. We introduce the command `rlocus(G,K)`, which allows us to specify the range of gain, K, for plotting the root locus. This command will help us smooth the usual root locus plot by equivalently specifying more points via the argument, K. Notice that the first root locus plotted without the argument K is not smooth. We also introduce the command `x = input('prompt')`, which allows keyboard entry of a value for x in response to a prompt. We apply this command to enter the desired percent overshoot. We also add a variable's value to the title of the root locus and step-response plots by inserting another field in the title command and use `num2str(value)` to convert value from a number to a character string for display. Let us apply the concepts to Example 8.8 in the text.

```
'(ch8p2) Example 8.8'          % Display label.
clear                          % Clear variables from workspace.
clf                            % Clear graph on screen.
numg=[1 1.5];                  % Define numerator of G(s).
deng=poly([0 -1 -10]);         % Define denominator of G(s).
'G(s)'                         % Display label.
G=tf(numg,deng)                % Create and display G(s).
rlocus(G)                      % Draw root locus (H(s)=1).
title('Original Root Locus')   % Add title.
pause
K=0.005;                       % Specify range of gain to smooth
                               % root locus.
rlocus(G,K)                    % Draw smoothed root locus
                               % (H(s)=1).
title('Smoothed Root Locus')   % Add title.
pos=input('Type %OS ');        % Input desired percent overshoot
                               % from the keyboard.
z=-log(pos/100)/sqrt(pi^2+[log(pos/100)]^2)
                               % Calculate damping ratio.
sgrid(z,0)                     % Overlay desired damping ratio
                               % line on root locus.
title(['Root Locus with ', num2str(pos),'% overshoot line'])
                               % Define title for root locus
                               % showing percent overshoot used.
```

```
[K, p]=rlocfind(G)              % Generate gain, K, and closed-
                                % loop poles, p, for point selected
                                % interactively on the root locus.
pause
'T(s)'                          % Display label
T=feedback(K*G,1)               % Find closed-loop transfer
                                % function
                                % with selected K and display.
step(T)                         % Generate closed-loop step
                                % response for point select on
                                % root locus.
title(['Step Response for K=',num2str(K)])
                                % Give step response a title which
                                % includes the value of K.
pause
```

CHAPTER 9: DESIGN USING THE GRAPHICAL TOOL

ch9p1 (Example 9.3) We can use MATLAB to design PD controllers. The program allows us to input a desired percent overshoot via the keyboard. MATLAB then produces a root locus for the uncompensated system with an overlay of the percent overshoot line. We interactively select the intersection of the root locus and the desired percent overshoot line to set the gain. MATLAB outputs an estimate of the uncompensated system's performance specifications and a step response of the uncompensated system for us to determine the required settling time. After we input the settling time through the keyboard, MATLAB designs the PD controller and produces a root locus of the PD compensated system from which we can interactively select the gain. Finally, MATLAB produces an estimate of the PD compensated system's performance specifications and a step response of the PD compensated system.

```
'(ch9p1) Example 9.3'           % Display label.
clf                             % Clear graph on screen.
'Uncompensated System'          % Display label.
numg=1;                         % Generate numerator of G(s).
deng=poly([0 -4 -6]);           % Generate denominator of G(s).
'G(s)'                          % Display label.
G=tf(numg,deng)                 % Create and display G(s).
pos=input('Type desired percent overshoot ');
                                % Input desired percent overshoot.
z-log(pos/100)/sqrt(pi^2+[log(pos/100)]^2);
                                % Calculate damping ratio.
rlocus(G)                       % Plot uncompensated root locus.
sgrid(z,0)                      % Overlay desired percent
                                % overshoot line.
title(['Uncompensated Root Locus with ' , num2str(pos),...
Overshoot Line'])               % Title uncompensated root locus.
[K,p]=rlocfind(G);              % Generate gain, K, and closed-loop
                                % poles, p, for point selected
                                % interactively on the root locus.
```

```
'Closed-loop poles = '              % Display label.
p                                   % Display closed-loop poles.
f=input('Give pole number that is operating point ');
                                    % Choose uncompensated system
                                    % dominant pole.
'Summary of estimated specifications for selected point on'
'uncompensated root locus'          % Display label.
operatingpoint=p(f)                 % Display uncompensated dominant
                                    % pole.
gain=K                              % Display uncompensated gain.
estimated_settling_time=4/abs(real(p(f)))
                                    % Display uncompensated settling
                                    % time.
estimated_peak_time=pi/abs(imag(p(f)))
                                    % Display uncompensated peak time.
estimated_percent_overshoot=pos
                                    % Display uncompensated percent
                                    % overshoot.
estimated_damping_ratio=z           % Display uncompensated damping
                                    % ratio.
estimated_natural_frequency=sqrt(real(p(f))^2+imag(p(f))^2)
                                    % Display uncompensated natural
                                    % frequency.
numkv=conv([1 0],numg);             % Set up numerator to evaluate Kv.
denkv=deng;                         % Set up denominator to evaluate Kv.
sG=tf(numkv,denkv);                 % Create sG(s).
sG=minreal(sG);                     % Cancel common poles and zeros.
Kv=dcgain(K*sG)                     % Display uncompensated Kv.
ess=1/Kv                            % Display uncompensated
                                    % steady-state
                                    % error for unit ramp input.
'T(s)'                              % Display label.
T=feedback(K*G,1)                   % Find uncompensated T(s).
step(T)                             % Plot step response of
                                    % uncompensated system.
title(['Uncompensated System Step Response with ',num2str(pos),...
'% Overshoot'])                     % Add title to uncompensated step
                                    % response.
'Press any key to go to PD compensation'
                                    % Display label.
pause
'Compensated system'               % Display label.
Ts=input('Type Desired Settling Time ');
                                    % Input desired settling time from
                                    % the keyboard.
wn=4/(Ts*z);                        % Calculate natural frequency.
desired_pole=(-z*wn)+(wn*sqrt(1-z^2)*i);
                                    % Calculate desired dominant pole
                                    % location.
```

```
angle_at_desired_pole=(180/pi)*...
angle(polyval(numg, desired_pole)/polyval(deng,desired_pole));
                                        % Calculate angular contribution
                                        % to desired pole without PD
                                        % compensator.
PD_angle=180-angle_at_desired_pole;
                                        % Calculate required angular
                                        % contribution from PD
                                        % compensator.
zc=((imag(desired_pole)/tan(PD_angle*pi/180))...
_real (desired_pole));                  % Calculate PD zero location.
'PD' Compensator'                       % Display label.
numc=[1 zc];                            % Calculate numerator of Gc(s).
denc=[0 1];                             % Calculate numerator of Gc(s).
'Gc(s)'                                 % Display label.
Gc=tf(numc, denc)                       % Create and display Gc(s).
'G(s)Gc(s)'                             % Display label.
Ge=G*Gc                                 % Cascade G(s) and Gc(s).
rlocus(Ge,0:0.005:100)                  % Plot root locus of PD compensated
                                        % system.
syrid(z,0)                              % Overlay desired percent
                                        % overshoot line.
title(['PD Compensated Root Locus with ' , num2str(pos),...
'% Overshoot Line'])                    % Add title to PD compensated root
                                        % locus.
[K,p]=rlocfind(Ge);                     % Generate gain, K, and closed-loop
                                        % poles, p, for point selected
                                        % interactively on the root locus.
'Closed-loop poles = '                  % Display label.
p                                       % Display PD compensated system's
                                        % closed-loop poles.
f=input('Give pole number that is operating point ');
                                        % Choose PD compensated system
                                        % dominant pole.
'Summary of estimated specifications for selected point on PD'
'compensated root locus'                % Display label.
operatingpoint=p(f)                     % Display PD compensated dominant
                                        % pole.
gain=K                                  % Display PD compensated gain.
estimated_settling_time=4/abs(real(p(f)))
                                        % Display PD compensated settling
                                        % time.
estimated_peak_time=pi/abs(imag(p(f)))
                                        % Display PD compensated peak time.
estimated_percent_overshoot=pos         % Display PD compensated percent
                                        % overshoot.
estimated_damping_ratio=z               % Display PD compensated damping
                                        % ratio.
```

```
estimated_natural_frequency=sqrt(real(p(f))^2+imag(p(f))^2
                                % Display PD compensated natural
                                % frequency.
s=tf([1 0],1);                  % Created transfer function, 's'.
sGe=s*Ge;                       % Create sGe(s).
sGe=minreal(sGe);               % Cancel common poles and zeros.
Kv=dcgain(K*sGe)                % Display compensated Kv.
ess=1/Kv                        % Display compensated
                                % steady-state error for
                                % unit ramp input.
'T(s)'                          % Display label.
T=feedback(K*Ge,1)              % Create and display PD compensated
                                % T(s).
'Press any key to continue and obtain the PD compensated step'
'response'                      % Display label.
pause
step(T)                         % Plot step response for PD
                                % compensated system.
title(['PD Compensated System Step Response with '...
num2str(pos), '% Overshoot'])   % Add title to step response
                                % of PD compensated system.
pause
```

ch9p2 (Example 9.4)   We can use MATLAB to design a lead compensator. The program allows us to input a desired percent overshoot via the keyboard. MATLAB then produces a root locus for the uncompensated system with an overlay of the percent overshoot line. We interactively select the intersection of the root locus and the desired percent overshoot line to set the gain. MATLAB outputs an estimate of the uncompensated system's performance specifications and a step response of the uncompensated system for us to determine the required settling time. Next we input the settling time and the lead compensator zero through the keyboard. At this point we take a different approach from that of the previous example. Rather than letting MATLAB calculate the lead compensator pole directly, MATLAB produces a root locus for every interactive guess of a lead compensator pole. Each root locus contains the desired damping ratio and natural frequency curves. When our guess is correct, the root locus, the damping ratio line, and the natural frequency curve will intersect. We then interactively select this point of intersection to input the gain. Finally, MATLAB produces an estimate of the lead-compensated system's performance specifications and a step response of the lead-compensated system.

```
'(ch9p2) Example 9.4'           % Display label.
Clf                             % Clear graph on screen.
'Uncompensated System'          % Display label.
numg=1;                         % Generate numerator of G(s).
deng=poly([0 -4 -6]);           % Generate denominator of G(s).
'G(s)'                          % Display label.
G=tf(numg,deng)                 % Create and display G(s).
pos=input('Type desired percent overshoot ');
                                % Input desired percent overshoot.
```

```
z=-log(pos/100)/sqrt(pi^2+[log(pos/100)]^2);
                                   % Calculate damping ratio.
rlocus(G)                          % Plot uncompensated root locus.
sgrid(z,0)                         % Overlay desired percent
                                   % overshoot line.
title(['Uncompensated Root Locus with' , num2str(pos ),...
'% Overshoot Line'])               % Title uncompensated root locus.
[K,p]=rlocfind(G);                 % Generate gain, K, and closed-loop
                                   % poles, p, for point selected
                                   % interactively on the root locus.
'Closed-loop poles ='             % Display label.
p                                  % Display closed-loop poles.
f=input('Give pole number that is operating point ');
                                   % Choose uncompensated system
                                   % dominant pole.
'Summary of estimated specifications for selected point on'
'uncompensated root locus'         % Display label.
operatingpoint=p(f)                % Display uncompensated dominant
                                   % pole.
gain=K                             % Display uncompensated gain.
estimated_settling_time=4/abs(real(p(f)))
                                   % Display uncompensated settling
                                   % time.
estimated_peak_time=pi/abs(imag(p(f)))
                                   % Display uncompensated peak time.
estimated_percent_overshoot=pos  % Display uncompensated percent
                                   % overshoot.
estimated_damping_ratio=z          % Display uncompensated damping
                                   % ratio.
estimated_natural_frequency=sqrt(real(p(f))^2+imag(p(f))^2
                                   % Display uncompensated natural
                                   % frequency.
numkv=conv([1 0],numg);            % Set up numerator to evaluate Kv.
denkv=deng;                        % Set up denominator to evaluate Kv.
sG=tf(numkv,denkv);                % Create sG(s).
sG=minreal(sG);                    % Cancel common poles and zeros.
Kv=dcgain(K*sG)                    % Display uncompensated Kv.
ess=1/Kv                           % Display uncompensated
                                   % steady-state error for
                                   % unit ramp input.

'T(s)'                             % Display label.
T=feedback(K*G,1)                  % Create and display T(s).
step(T)                            % Plot step response of
                                   % uncompensated system.
title([['Uncompensated System Step Response with ',...
num2str(pos),'% Overshoot'])       % Add title to uncompensated step
                                   % response.
```

```
'Press any key to go to lead compensation'
                                % Display label.
pause
Ts=input('Type Desired Settling Time ');
                                % Input desired settling time.
b=input('Type Lead Compensator Zero, (s+b). b= ');
                                % Input lead compensator zero.
done=1;                         % Set loop flag.
while done==1                   % Start loop for trying lead
                                % compensator pole.
a=input('Enter a Test Lead Compensator Pole, (s+a). a = ');
                                % Enter test lead compensator pole.
numge=conv(numg,[1 b]);         % Generate numerator of Gc(s)G(s).
denge=conv([1 a],deng);         % Generate denominator
                                % of Gc(s)G(s).
Ge=tf(numge,denge);             % Create Ge(s)=Gc(s)G(s).
wn=4/(Ts*z);                    % Evaluate desired natural
                                % frequency.
clf                             % Clear graph on screen.
rlocus(Ge)                      % Plot compensated root locus with
                                % test lead compensator pole.
axis([-10,10,-10,10])           % Change lead-compensated
                                % root locus axes.
sgrid(z,wn)                     % Overlay grid on lead-compensated
                                % root locus.
title(['Lead-Compensated Root Locus with ' , num2str(pos),...
% Overshoot Line, Lead Pole at ',...
num2str(-a),' and Required Wn'])  % Add title to lead-compensated
                                % root locus.
done=input('Are you done? (y=0,n=1) ');
                                % Set loop flag.
end                             % End loop for trying compensator
                                % pole.
[K,p]=rlocfind(Ge);             % Generate gain, K, and closed-loop
                                % poles, p, for point selected
                                % interactively on the root locus.
'Gc(s)'                         % Display label.
Gc=tf([1 b],[1 a])              % Display lead compensator.
'Gc(s)G(s)'                     % Display label.
Ge                              % Display Gc(s)G(s).
'Closed-loop poles = '          % Display label.
p                               % Display lead-compensated
                                % system's
                                % closed-loop poles.
f=input('Give pole number that is operating point ');
                                % Choose lead-compensated system
                                % dominant pole.
'Summary of estimated specifications for selected point on lead'
'compensated root locus'        % Display label.
```

```
operatingpoint=p(f)                  % Display lead-compensated
                                     % dominant pole.
gain=K                               % Display lead-compensated gain.
estimated_settling_time=4/abs(real(p(f)))
                                     % Display lead-compensated
                                     % settling time.
estimated_peak_time=pi/abs(imag(p(f)))
                                     % Display lead-compensated
                                     % peak time.
estimated_percent_overshoot=pos% Display lead-compensated
                                     % percent overshoot.
estimated_damping_ratio=z            % Display lead-compensated
                                     % damping ratio.
estimated_natural_frequency=sqrt(real(p(f))^2+imag(p(f))^2)
                                     % Display lead-compensated
                                     % natural frequency.
s=tf([1 0],1);                       % Create transfer Function, 's'.
sGe=s*Ge;                            % Create sGe(s) to evaluate Kv.
sGe=minreal(sGe);                    % Cancel common poles and zeros.
Kv=dcgain(K*sGe)                     % Display lead-compensated Kv.
ess=1/Kv                             % Display lead-compensated steady-
                                     % state error for unit ramp input.
'T(s)'                               % Display label.
t=feedback(K*Ge,1)                   % Create and display lead-
                                     % compensated T(s).
'Press any key to continue and obtain the lead-compensated step'
'response'                           % Display label.
pause
step(T)                              % Plot step response for lead
                                     % compensated system.
title(['Lead-Compensated System Step Response with ',...
num2str(pos),'% Overshoot'])         % Add title to step response
                                     % of lead-compensated system.
pause
```

CHAPTER 10: SINUSOIDAL TOOLS

ch10p1 (Example 10.3)   We can use MATLAB to make Bode plots using bode(G), where G/(s) = numg/deng and G is an LTI transfer-function object. Information about the plots obtained with bode(G) can be found by left-clicking the mouse on the curve. You can find the curve's label, as well as the coordinates of the point on which you clicked. Right-clicking away from a curve brings up a menu if the icons on the menu bar are deselected. From this menu you can select (1) system responses to be displayed and (2) characteristics, such as peak response. When selected, a dot appears on the curve at the appropriate point. Let your mouse rest on the point to read the value of the characteristic. You may also select (3) which curves to view, (4) choice for grid on or off, (5) returning to full view after zooming, and (6) properties, such as labels, limits, units, style, and characteristics. We can obtain points on the plot using [mag,phase,w] =

bode(G), where magnitude, phase, and frequency are stored in `mag`, `phase`, and `w`, respectively. Magnitude and phase are stored as 3-D arrays. We use `mag(:,:)'`, `phase(:,:)'` to convert the arrays to column vectors, where the apostrophe signifies matrix transpose. Let us look at Example 10.3 in the text.

```
'(ch10p1) Example 10.3'          % Display label.
clf                              % Clear graph on screen.
numg=[1 3];                      % Define numerator of G(s).
deng=conv([1 2],[1 2 25]);       % Define denominator of G(s).
'G(s)'                           % Display label.
G=tf(numg,deng)                  % Create and display G(s).
bode(G)                          % Make a Bode plot.
grid on                          % Turn on grid for Bode plot.
title('Open-Loop Frequency Response')
                                 % Add a title to the Bode plot.
[mag,phase,w]=bode(G);           % Store points on the Bode plot.
points=[20*log10(mag(:,:))',phase(:,:)',w]
                                 % List points on Bode plot with
                                 % magnitude in dB.
pause
```

ch10p2 (Example 10.5) We can use MATLAB to make Nyquist diagrams using `nyquist(G)`, where $G(s)$ = `numg`/`deng` and G is an LTI transfer-function object. Information about the plots obtained with `nyquist(G)` can be found by left-clicking the mouse on the curve. You can find the curve's label, as well as the coordinates of the point on which you clicked and the frequency. Right-clicking away from a curve brings up a menu if the icons on the menu bar are deselected. From this menu you can select (1) system responses to be displayed and (2) characteristics, such as peak response. When selected, a dot appears on the curve at the appropriate point. Let your mouse rest on the point to read the value of the characteristic. You may also select (3) whether or not to show negative frequencies, (4) choice for grid on or off, (5) choice for zooming to $(-1,0)$, (6) returning to full view after zooming, and (7) properties, such as labels, limits, units, style, and characteristics. We can obtain points on the plot by using `[re,im,w]` = `nyquist(G)`, where the real part, imaginary part, and frequency are stored in `re`, `im`, and `w`, respectively, and `re` and `im` are 3-D arrays. We can specify a range of `w` by using `[re,im]` = `nyquist(G,w)`. We use `re(:,:)'`, and `im(:,:)'` to convert the arrays to column vectors. Let us look at Example 10.5 in the text.

```
'(ch10p2) Example 10.5'          % Display label.
clf                              % Clear graph on screen.
numg=[1 2];                      % Define numerator of G(s).
deng=[1 0 0];                    % Define denominator of G(s).
'G(s)'                           % Display label.
G=tf(numg,deng)                  % Create and display G(s).
nyquist(G)                       % Make a Nyquist diagram.
grid on                          % Turn on grid for Nyquist diagram.
title('Open-Loop Frequency Response')
                                 % Add a title to the Nyquist
                                 % diagram.
w=0:0.5:10;                      % Let 0 < w < 10 in steps of 0.5.
```

```
[re,im]=nyquist(G,w);          % Get Nyquist diagram points for a
                               % range of w.
points=[re(:,:)',im(:,:)',w']  % List specified range of points
                               % in Nyquist diagram.
pause
```

ch10p3 (Example 10.8)   We can use MATLAB to find gain margin (Gm), phase margin (Pm), the gain margin frequency, where the phase plot goes through 180 degrees (Wcg), and the phase-margin frequency, where the magnitude plot goes through zero dB (Wcp). To find these quantities we use [G_m, P_m, W_{cg}, W_{cp}]=margin(G), where $G(s)$ = numg/deng and G is an LTI transfer-function object. Let us look at Example 10.8 in the text.

```
'(ch10p3) Example 10.8'        % Display label.
clf                            % Clear graph on screen.
numg=6;                        % Define numerator of G(s).
deng=conv([1 2],[1 2 2]);      % Define denominator of G(s).
'G(s)'                         % Display label.
G=tf(numg,deng)                % Create and display G(s).
nyquist(G)                     % Make a Nyquist diagram.
grid on                        % Turn on grid for the Nyquist
                               % diagram.
title('Open-Loop Frequency Response')
                               % Add a title to the Nyquist
                               % diagram.
[Gm,Pm,Wcg,Wcp]=margin(G);     % Find margins and margin
                               % frequencies.
'Gm(dB); Pm(deg.); 180 deg. freq.(r/s); 0 dB freq. (r/s)'
                               % Display label.
margins=[20*log10(Gm),Pm,Wcg,Wcp]
                               % Display margin data.
pause
```

ch10p4 (Example 10.9)   We can use MATLAB to determine the range of *K* for stability using frequency response methods. Let us look at Example 10.9 in the text.

```
'(ch10p4) Example 10.9'        % Display label.
numg=1;                        % Define numerator of G(s).
deng=poly([-2 -4 -5]);         % Define denominator of G(s).
'G(s)'                         % Display label.
G=tf(numg,deng)                % Create and display G(s).
[Gm,Pm,Wcg,Wcp]=margin(G);     % Find margins and margin
                               % frequencies.
K=Gm                           % Display K for stability.
pause
```

ch10p5 (Example 10.11)   We can use MATLAB to find the closed-loop frequency response. Let us look at Example 10.11 in the text.

```
'(ch10p5) Example 10.11'       % Display label.
```

```
clf                                 % Clear graph on screen.
numg=50;                            % Define numerator of G(s).
deng=poly([0 -3 -6]);              % Define denominator of G(s).
'G(s)'                              % Display label.
G=tf(numg,deng)                    % Create and display G(s).
'T(s)'                              % Display label.
T=feedback(G,1)                    % Find and display closed-loop
                                    % transfer function.
bode(T)                            % Make a Bode plot.
grid on                            % Turn on the grid for the plots.
title('Closed-Loop Frequency Response')
                                    % Add a title to the Bode plot.
pause
nyquist(T)                         % Make a Nyquist diagram.
title('Closed-Loop Frequency Response')
                                    % Add a title to the Nyquist
                                    % diagram.
pause
```

ch10p6   We can use MATLAB to plot Nichols charts using `nichols(G)`, where $G(s) =$ `numg/deng` and `G` is an LTI transfer-function object. The Nichols grid can be added using the `ngrid` command after the `nichols(G)` command. Information about the plots obtained with `nichols(G)` can be found by left-clicking the mouse on the curve. You can find the curve's label, as well as the coordinates of the point on which you clicked and the frequency. Right-clicking away from a curve brings up a menu if the icons on the menu bar are deselected. From this menu you can select (1) system responses to be displayed and (2) characteristics, such as peak response. When selected, a dot appears on the curve at the appropriate point. Let your mouse rest on the point to read the value of the characteristic. You may also select (3) choice for grid on or off, (4) returning to full view after zooming, and (5) properties, such as labels, limits, units, style, and characteristics. Let us make a Nichols chart of $G(s)=1/[s(s+1)(s+2)]$.

```
'(ch10p6)'                          % Display label.
clf                                 % Clear graph on screen.
numg=1;                             % Define numerator of G(s).
deng=poly([0 -1 -2]);              % Define denominator of G(s).
'G(s)'                              % Display label.
G=tf(numg,deng)                    % Create and display G(s).
nichols(G)                         % Make a Nichols plot.
ngrid                              % Add Nichols grid.
pause
```

ch10p7 (Example 10.15)   We can use MATLAB and frequency response methods to include time delay in the loop. Time delay is represented by `[numd,dend] = pade(T, n)`, where `T` is the delay time in seconds and `n` is the order. Larger values of `n` give better approximations to the delay, $G_d(s) =$ `numd/dend`. Since we are plotting multiple plots, we first collect the data for the Bode plots by using `[mag,phase] = bode(G,w)`, where `w` is specified as a range of frequencies. We then use the generic plotting command.

Also notice the commands used to label the axes and the plots on the Bode plot (see the MATLAB instruction manual for details). Let us look at Example 10.15 in the text.

```
'(ch10p7) Example 10.15'            % Display label.
clf                                 % Clear graph on screen.
hold off                            % Turn graph hold off.
numg=1;                             % Define numerator of G(s).
deng=poly([0 -1 -10]);              % Define denominator of G(s).
'G(s)'                              % Display label.
G=tf(numg,deng)                     % Create and display G(s).
w=0.01:0.1:10;                      % Let 0.01 < w < 10 in steps of 0.1.
[magg,phaseg]=bode(G,w);            % Collect Bode data for G(s).
[numd,dend]=pade(1,6);              % Represent the delay.
Gd=tf(numd,dend);                   % Create and display the delay,
                                    % Gd(s).
[magd,phased]=bode(Gd,w);           % Collect Bode data for Gd(s).
Ge=Gd*G;                            % Form Gd(s)G(s).
[mage,phasee]=bode(Ge,w);           % Collect Bode data for Gd(s)G(s).
subplot(2,1,1)                      % Subdivide plot area for plot 1.
semilogx(w,20*log10(mage(:,:)))     % Plot magnitude response.
grid on                             % Turn on grid for magnitude plot.
axis([0.01,10,-80,20]);             % Limit Bode plot axes.
title('Magnitude Response with Delay')
                                    % Add title to magnitude response.
xlabel('Frequency (rad/s)')         % Label x-axis of magnitude
                                    % response.
ylabel('20log M')                   % Label y-axis of magnitude
                                    % response.
subplot(2,1,2)                      % Subdivide plot area for plot 2.
semilogx(w,phaseg(:,:),w,phased(:,:),w,phasee(:,:))
                                    % Plot phase response for G(s),
                                    % Gd(s), and G(s)Gd(s) on one
                                    % graph.
grid on                             % Turn on grid for phase plot.
axis([0.01,10,-900,0]);             % Limit Bode plot axes.
title('Phase Response with Delay')
                                    % Add title to phase response.
xlabel('Frequency (rad/s)')         % Label x-axis of phase response.
ylabel('Phase (degrees)')           % Label y-axis of phase response.
text(1.5,-50,'Time Delay')          % Label time delay curve.
text(4,-150,'System')               % Label system curve.
text(2.7,-300,'Total')              % Label total curve.
pause
```

ch10p8 (Example 10.18)   We can use MATLAB and frequency response methods to determine experimentally a transfer function from frequency response data. By determining simple component transfer functions and then successively subtracting their frequency response, we can approximate the complete transfer function. Let us look at Example 10.18 in the text and use MATLAB for a portion of the problem. You can complete the program for practice. For this problem we generate the original frequency response plot via a transfer function. Normally, the data for the original frequency response plot would be tabular, and the program would begin at the step [M0,P0] = bode(G0,w) where the tabular data is generated. In other words, in a real application, the data would consist of column vectors M0, P0, and w'.

```
'(ch10p8) Example 10.18'              % Display label.
clf                                   % Clear graph on screen.
hold off                             % Turn graph hold off.
% Generate the experimental Bode plots for G0(s)=numg0/deng0, that
% is,M0,P0.
numg0=70*[1 20];                     % Define numerator of G0(s).
deng0=conv([1 7],[1 2 25]);          % Partially define denominator of
                                     % G0(s).
deng0=conv(deng0,[1 70]);            % Complete the denominator of
                                     % G0(s).
G0=tf(numg0,deng0);                  % Create G0(s).
w=1:0.5:1000;                        % Let 1 < w < 1000 in steps of 0.5.
[M0,P0]=bode(G0,w);                  % Generate the tabular data.
[20*log10(M0(:,:))',P0(:,:)',w'];
                                     % Convert magnitude data to dB.
bode(G0,w)                           % Generate a Bode plot.
grid on                              % Turn on grid for Bode plot.
title('Experimental')                % Add title.
pause
clf                                  % Clear graph.
% Estimate a component part of the transfer function as
% G1(s)=25/(s^2+2*0.22*5s+5^2) and subtract it from the experimental
% frequency response
numg1=5^2;                           % Define numerator of G1(s).
deng1=[1 2*0.22*5 5^2];              % Define denominator of G1(s).
'First estimate'                     % Display label.
G1=tf(numg1,deng1)                   % Create and display G1(s).
[M1,P1]=bode(G1,w);                  % Generate Bode data for G1(s).
M2=20*log10(M0(:,:))-20*log10(M1(:,:));
                                     % Subtract Bode magnitude data of
                                     % G1 from original magnitude data.
P2=P0(:,:)-P1(:,:);                  % Subtract Bode phase data of G1
                                     % from original phase data.
subplot(2,1,1)                       % Divide plot area in two for
                                     % magnitude plot.
semilogx(w(:,:),M2)                  % Plot magnitude response after
                                     % subtracting.
grid on                              % Turn on grid for magnitude plot.
xlabel('Frequency (rad/sec)')        % Add x-axis label.
ylabel('Gain dB')                    % Add y-axis label.
subplot(2,1,2)                       % Divide plot area in two for phase
                                     % plot.
semilogx(w,P2)                       % Plot the phase response after
                                     % subtracting.
```

```
grid on                                    % Turn on grid for phase plot.
title('Experimental Minus 25/(s^2+2*0.22*5s+5^2)')
                                           % Add title.
xlabel('Frequency (rad/sec)')   % Add x-axis label.
ylabel('Phase deg')             % Add y-axis label.
'This completes a portion of Example 10.18.'
'The student should continue the program for practice.'
pause
```

CHAPTER 11: DESIGN USING SINUSOIDAL TOOLS

ch11p1 (Example 11.1)   We can design via gain adjustment on the Bode plot using MATLAB. You will input the desired percent overshoot from the keyboard. MATLAB will calculate the required phase margin and then search the Bode plot for that phase margin. The magnitude at the phase-margin frequency is the reciprocal of the required gain. MATLAB will then plot a step response for that gain. Let us look at Example 11.1 in the text.

```
'(ch11p1) Example 11.1'         % Display label.
clf                             % Clear graph on screen.
numg=[100];                     % Define numerator of G(s).
deng=poly([0 -36 -100]);        % Define denominator of G(s).
G=tf(numg,deng)                 % Create and display G(s).
pos=input('Type %OS ');         % Input desired percent overshoot.
z=(-log(pos/100))/(sqrt(pi^2+log(pos/100)^2));
                                % Calculate required damping ratio.
Pm=atan(2*z/(sqrt(-2*z^2+sqrt(1+4*z^4))))*(180/pi);
                                % Calculate required phase margin.
w=0.01:0.01:1000;               % Set range of frequency from 0.01
                                % to 1000 in steps of 0.01.
[M,P]=bode(G,w);                % Get Bode data.
Ph=-180+Pm;                     % Calculate required phase angle.
for k=1:1:length(P);            % Search Bode data for required
                                % phase angle.
if P(k)-Ph<=0;                  % If required phase angle is found,
                                % find the value of
M=M(k);                         % magnitude at the same frequency.
'Required K'                    % Display label.
K=1/M                           % Calculate the required gain.
break                           % Stop the loop.
end                             % End if.
end                             % End for.
T=feedback(K*G,1);              % Find T(s) using the calculated K.
step(T)                         % Generate a step response.
title(['Closed-Loop Step Response for K= ',num2str(K)])
                                % Add title to step response.
pause
```

ch11p2 (Example 11.2) Let us use MATLAB to design a lag compensator. The program solves Example 11.2 in the text and follows the same design technique demonstrated in that example. You will input the value of gain to meet the steady-state error requirement followed by the desired percent overshoot. MATLAB then designs a lag compensator, evaluates K_v, and generates a closed-loop step response.

```
'(ch11p2) Example 11.2'          % Display label.
clf                              % Clear graph on screen.
K=input('Type value of K to meet steady-state error requirement ');
                                 % Input K.
pos=input('Type %OS ');          % Input desired percent overshoot.
numg=[100*K];                    % Define numerator of G(s).
deng=poly([0 -36 -100]);         % Define denominator of G(s).
'G(s)'                           % Display label.
G=tf(numg,deng)                  % Create and display G(s).
z=(-log(pos/100))/(sqrt(pi^2+log(pos/100)^2));
                                 % Calculate required damping
                                 % ratio.
Pm=atan(2*z/(sqrt(-2*z^2+sqrt(1+4*z^4))))*(180/pi)+10;
                                 % Calculate required phase margin.
w=0.01:0.01:100;                 % Set range of frequency from 0.01
                                 % to 1000 in steps of 0.01.
[M,P]=bode(G,w);                 % Get Bode data.
Ph=-180+Pm;                      % Calculate required phase angle.
for k=1:1:length(P);            % Search Bode data for required
                                 % phase angle.
if P(k)-Ph<=0;                   % If required phase angle is found,
                                 % find the value of
M=M(k);                          % magnitude at the same frequency.
wf=w(k);                         % At this frequency the magnitude
                                 % plot must go through 0 dB.
break                            % Stop the loop.
end                              % End if.
end                              % End for.
wh=wf/10;                        % Calculate the high-frequency
                                 % break of the lag compensator.
wl=(wh/M);                       % Calculate the low-frequency
                                 % break of the lag compensator;
                                 % found from lag compensator,
                                 % Gc(s)=Kc(s+wh)/(s+wl), high & low
                                 % frequency gain requirements.
                                 % At low w, gain=1. Thus,
                                 % Kc*wh/wl=1. At high w, gain=1/M.
                                 % Thus Kc=1/M. Hence
                                 % Kc=wl/wh=1/M, or wl=wh/M.
numc=[1 wh];                     % Generate numerator of lag
                                 % compensator, Gc(s).
denc=[1 wl];                     % Generate denominator of lag
                                 % compensator, Gc(s).
```

```
Kc=w1/wh;                                % Generate K for Gc(s).
'Lag compensator'                        % Display label.
Kc                                       % Display lag compensator K.
'Gc(s)'                                  % Display label.
Gc=tf(Kc*numc,denc)                      % Create and display Gc(s).
'Gc(s)G(s)'                              % Display label.
GcG=Gc*G                                 % Create and display Gc(s)G(s).
s=tf([1 0],1);                           % Create transfer function, 's'.
sGcG=s*GcG;                              % Create sGc(s)G(s).
sGcG=minreal(sGcG);                      % Cancel common terms.
Kv=dcgain(sGcG)                          % Evaluate Kv.
T=feedback(GcG,1);                       % Create T(s).
step(T)                                  % Generate a closed-loop, lag-
                                         % compensated step response.
title('Closed-Loop Step Response for Lag-Compensated System')
                                         % Add title to step response.

pause
```

ch11p3 (Example 11.3) Let us use MATLAB to design a lead compensator. The
program solves Example 11.3 in the text and follows the same design technique
demonstrated in that example. You will enter desired percent overshoot, peak time, and
K_v. MATLAB then designs the lead compensator using Bode plots, calculates K_v, and
plots a closed-loop step response.

```
'(ch11p3) Example 11.3'                  % Display label.
pos=input('Type %OS  ');                 % Input desired percent overshoot.
Tp=input('Type peak time  ');            % Input desired peak time.
Kv=input('Type value of Kv  ');          % Input Kv.
numg=[100];                              % Define numerator of G(s).
deng=poly([0 -36 -100]);                 % Define denominator of G(s).
G=tf(numg,deng);                         % Create G(s).
s=tf([1 0],1);                           % Create transfer function, 's'.
sG=s*G;                                  % Create sG(s).
sG=minreal(sG);                          % Cancel common factors.
K=dcgain(Kv/sG);                         % Solve for K.
'G(s)'                                   % Display label.
G=zpk(K*G)                               % Put K into G(s), convert to
                                         % factored form, and display.
z=(-log(pos/100))/(sqrt(pi^2+log(pos/100)^2));
                                         % Calculate required damping
                                         % ratio.
Pm=atan(2*z/(sqrt(-2*z^2+sqrt(1+4*z^4))))*(180/pi);
                                         % Calculate required phase margin.
wn=pi/(Tp*sqrt(1-z^2));                  % Calculate required natural
                                         % frequency.
wBW=wn*sqrt((1-2*z^2)+sqrt(4*z^4-4*z^2+2));
                                         % Determine required bandwidth.
w=0.01:0.5:1000;                         % Set range of frequency from 0.01
                                         % to 1000 in steps of 0.5
[M,P]=bode(G,w);                         % Get Bode data.
[Gm,Pm,Wcg,Wcp]=margin(G);               % Find current phase margin.
```

```
Pmreq=atan(2*z/(sqrt(-2*z^2+sqrt(1+4*z^4))))*(180/pi);
                             % Calculate required phase margin.
Pmreqc=Pmreq+10;             % Add a correction factor of 10
                             % degrees.
Pc=Pmreqc-Pm;                % Calculate phase contribution
                             % required from lead compensator.
% Design lead compensator
beta=(1-sin(Pc*pi/180))/(1+sin(Pc*pi/180));
                             % Find compensator beta.
magpc=1/sqrt(beta);          % Find compensator peak magnitude.
for k=1:1:length(M);         % Find frequency at which
                             % uncompensated system has a
                             % magnitude of 1/magpc.
                             % This frequency will be the new
                             % phase margin frequency.
if M(k)-(1/magpc)<=0;        % Look for peak magnitude.
wmax=w(k);                   % This is the frequency at the
                             % peak magnitude.
break                        % Stop the loop.
end                          % End if.
end                          % End for.
% Calculate lead compensator zero, pole, and gain.
zc=wmax*sqrt(beta);          % Calculate the lead compensator's
                             % low break frequency.
pc=zc/beta;                  % Calculate the lead compensator's
                             % high break frequency.
Kc=1/beta;                   % Calculate the lead compensator's
                             % gain.
'Gc(s)'                      % Display label.
Gc=tf(Kc*[1 zc],[1 pc]);     % Create Gc(s).
Gc=zpk(Gc)                   % Convert Gc(s) to factored form
                             % and display.
'Ge(s)=G(s)Gc(s)'            % Display label.
Ge=G*Gc                      % Form Ge(s)=Gc(s)G(s).
sGe=s*Ge;                    % Create sGe(s).
sGe=minreal(sGe);            % Cancel common factors.
Kv=dcgain(sGe)               % Calculate Kv.
T=feedback(Ge,1);            % Find T(s).
step(T)                      % Generate closed-loop, lead-
                             % compensated step response.
title('Lead-Compensated Step Response')
                             % Add title to lead-compensated
                             % step response.
pause
```

ch11p4 (Example 11.4) Let us use MATLAB to design a lag-lead compensator. The program solves Example 11.4 in the text and follows the same design technique demonstrated in that example. You will enter desired percent overshoot, peak time, and K_v. MATLAB then designs the lag-lead compensator using Bode plots, calculates K_v, and plots a closed-loop step response.

```
'(ch11p4) Example 11.4'                    % Display label.
pos=input('Type %OS ');                    % Input desired percent overshoot.
Tp=input('Type peak time ');               % Input desired peak time.
Kv=input('Type value of Kv ');             % Input desired Kv.
numg=[1];                                  % Define numerator of G(s).
deng=poly([0 -1 -4]);                      % Define denominator of G(s).
G=tf(numg,deng);                           % Create G(s) without K.
s=tf([1 0],1);                             % Create transfer function, 's'.
sG=s*G;                                    % Create sG(s).
sG=minreal(sG);                            % Cancel common factors.
K=dcgain(Kv/sG);                           % Solve for K.
'G(s)'                                     % Display label.
G=tf(K*numg,deng);                         % Put K into G(s).
G=zpk(G)                                   % Convert G(s) to factored form and
                                           % display.
z=(-log(pos/100))/(sqrt(pi^2+log(pos/100)^2));
                                           % Calculate required damping ratio.
Pmreq=atan(2*z/(sqrt(-2*z^2+sqrt(1+4*z^4))))*(180/pi);
                                           % Calculate required phase margin.
wn=pi/(Tp*sqrt(1-z^2));                     % Calculate required natural
                                           % frequency.
wBW=wn*sqrt((1-2*z^2)+sqrt(4*z^4-4*z^2+2));
                                           % Determine required bandwidth.
wpm=0.8*wBW;                               % Choose new phase-margin
                                           % frequency.
[M,P]=bode(G,wpm);                         % Get Bode data.
Pmreqc=Pmreq-(180+P)+5;                     % Find phase contribution required
                                           % from lead compensator
                                           % with additional 5 degrees.
beta=(1-sin(Pmreqc*pi/180))/(1+sin(Pmreqc*pi/180));
                                           % Find beta.
                                           % Design lag compensator zero, pole,
                                           % and gain.
zclag=wpm/10;                              % Calculate zero of lag compensator.
pclag=zclag*beta;                          % Calculate pole of lag compensator.
Kclag=beta;                                % Calculate gain of lag compensator.
'Lag compensator, Glag(s)'                 % Display label.
Glag=tf(Kclag*[1zclag],[1pclag]);          % Create lag compensator.
Glag=zpk(Glag)                             % Convert Glag(s) to factored form
                                           % and display.
                                           % Design lead compensator zero,
                                           % pole, and gain.
zclead=wpm*sqrt(beta);                     % Calculate zero of lead
                                           % compensator.
pclead=zclead/beta;                        % Calculate pole of lead
                                           % compensator.
Kclead=1/beta;                             % Calculate gain of lead
                                           % compensator.
'Lead compensator'                         % Display label.
```

```
Glead=tf(Kclead*[1 zclead],[1 pclead]);
                          % Create lead compensator.
Glead=zpk(Glead)          % Convert Glead(s) to factored form
                          % and display.
'Lag-Lead Compensated Ge(s)'    % Display label.
Ge=G*Glag*Glead           % Create compensated system,
                          % Ge(s)=G(s)Glag(s)Glead(s).
sGe=s*Ge;                 % Create sGe(s).
sGe=minreal(sGe);         % Cancel common factors.
Kv=dcgain(sGe)            % Calculate Kv
T=feedback(Ge,1);         % Find T(s).
step(T)                   % Generate closed-loop, lag-lead-
                          % compensated step response.
title('Lag-Lead-Compensated Step Response')
                          % Add title to lag-lead-
                          % compensated
                          % step response.
pause
```

CHAPTER 12: DESIGN USING STATE EQUATIONS

ch12p1 (Example 12.1) We can use MATLAB to design controller gains using pole placement. You will enter the desired percent overshoot and settling time. We introduce the following commands: [num,den] = ord2(wn,z), which produces a second-order system, given the natural frequency (wn) and the damping ratio (z). Then we use the denominator (den) to specify the dominant poles; and K = acker(A,B,-poles), which calculates controller gains from the system matrix (A), the input matrix (B), the desired poles (poles). Let us look at Example 12.1 in the text.

```
'(ch12p1) Example 12.1'   % Display label.
clf                       % Clear graph on screen.
numg=20*[1 5];            % Define numerator of G(s).
deng=poly([0 -1 -4]);     % Define denominator of G(s).
'Uncompensated G(s)'      % Display label.
G=tf(numg,deng)           % Create and display G(s).
pos=input('Type desired %OS  '); % Input desired percent overshoot.
Ts=input('Type desired settling time ');
                          % Input desired settling time.
z=(-log(pos/100))/(sqrt(pi^2+log(pos/100)^2));
                          % Calculate required damping ratio.
wn=4/(z*Ts);              % Calculate required natural
                          % frequency.
[num,den]=ord2(wn,z);     % Produce a second-order system
                          % that meets the transient response
                          % requirements.
r=roots(den);             % Use denominator to specify
                          % dominant poles.
poles=[r(1) r(2) -5.1];   % Specify pole placement for all
                          % poles.
```

```
characteristiceqdesired=poly(poles)
                                    % Form desired characteristic
                                    % polynomial for display.
[Ac Bc Cc Dc]=tf2ss(numg,deng);     % Find controller canonical form
                                    % of state-space representation
                                    % of G(s).
P=[0 0 1;0 1 0;1 0 0];              % Transformation matrix for
                                    % controller canonical to phase-
                                    % variable form.
Ap=inv(P)*Ac*P;                     % Transform Ac to phase-variable
                                    % form.
Bp=inv(P)*Bc;                       % Transform Bc to phase-variable
                                    % form.
Cp=Cc*P;                            % Transform Cc to phase-variable
                                    % form.
Dp=Dc;                              % Transform Dc to phase-variable
                                    % form.
Kp=acker(Ap,Bp,poles)              % Calculate controller gains in
                                    % phase-variable form.
Apnew=Ap-Bp*Kp;                     % Form compensated A matrix.
Bpnew=Bp;                           % Form compensated B matrix.
Cpnew=Cp;                           % Form compensated C matrix.
Dpnew=Dp;                           % Form compensated D matrix.
[numt,dent]=ss2tf(Apnew,Bpnew,Cpnew,Dpnew);
                                    % Form T(s) numerator and
                                    % denominator.
'T(s)'                              % Display label.
T=tf(numt,dent)                     % Create and display T(s).
poles=roots(dent)                   % Display poles of T(s).
Tss=ss(Apnew,Bpnew,Cpnew,Dpnew)    % Create and display Tss, an LTI
                                    % state-space object.
step(Tss)                           % Produce compensated step
                                    % response.
title('Compensated Step Response')
                                    % Add title to compensated step
                                    % response.
pause
```

ch12p2 (Example 12.2) We can test controllability by using the MATLAB command `Cm = ctrb(A,B)` to find the controllability matrix given the system matrix (`A`) and the input matrix (`B`). This command is followed by `rank(Cm)` to test the rank of the controllability matrix (`Cm`). Let us apply the commands to Example 12.2.

```
'(ch12p2) Example 12.2'             % Display label.
A=[-1 1 0;0 -1 0;0 0 -2]            % Define compensated A matrix.
B=[0;1;1]                           % Define compensated B matrix.
Cm=ctrb(A,B)                        % Calculate controllability
                                    % matrix.
```

```
Rank=rank(Cm)                    % Find rank of controllability
                                 % matrix.
pause
```

ch12p3 (Example 12.4)   If we design controller gains using MATLAB, we do not have to convert to phase-variable form. MATLAB will give us the controller gains for any state-space representation we input. Let us look at Example 12.4 in the text.

```
'(ch12p3) Example 12.4'          % Display label.
clf                              % Clear graph on screen.
A=[-5 1 0;0 -2 1;0 0 -1];        % Define system matrix A.
B=[0;0;1];                       % Define input matrix B.
C=[-1 1 0];                      % Define output matrix C.
D=0;                             % Define matrix D.
pos=input('Type desired %OS  '); % Input desired percent overshoot.
Ts=input('Type desired settling time ')
                                 % Input desired settling time.
z=(-log(pos/100))/(sqrt(pi^2+log(pos/100)^2));
                                 % Calculate required damping ratio.
wn=4/(z*Ts);                     % Calculate required natural
                                 % frequency.
[num,den]=ord2(wn,z);            % Produce a second-order system
                                 % that meets the transient
                                 % requirements.
r=roots(den);                    % Use denominator to specify
                                 % dominant poles.
poles=[r(1) r(2) -4];            % Specify pole placement for all
                                 % poles.
K=acker(A,B,poles)               % Calculate controller gains.
Anew=A-B*K;                      % Form compensated A matrix.
Bnew=B;                          % Form compensated B matrix.
Cnew=C;                          % Form compensated C matrix.
Dnew=D;                          % Form compensated D matrix.
Tss=ss(Anew,Bnew,Cnew,Dnew);     % Form LTI state-space object.
'T(s)'                           % Display label.
T=tf(Tss);                       % Create T(s).
T=minreal(T)                     % Cancel common terms and display
                                 % T(s).
poles=pole(T)                    % Display poles of T(s).
step(Tss)                        % Produce compensated step
                                 % response.
title('Compensated Step Response')
                                 % Add title to compensated step
                                 % response.
pause
```

ch12p4 (Example 12.5)   We can design observer gains by using the command `l = acker(A',C',poles)'`. Notice we use the transpose of the system matrix (`A`) and output matrix (`C`) along with the desired poles (`poles`). Let us look at Example 12.5 in the text.

```
'(ch12p4) Example 12.5'          % Display label.
numg=[1 4];                      % Define numerator of G(s).
deng=poly([-1 -2 -5]);           % Define denominator of G(s).
'G(s)'                           % Display label.
G=tf(numg,deng)                  % Create and display G(s).
[Ac,Bc,Cc,Dc]=tf2ss(numg,deng);  % Transform G(s) to controller
                                 % canonical form in state space.
Ao=Ac';                          % Transform Ac to observer
                                 % canonical form.
Bo=Cc';                          % Transform Bc to observer
                                 % canonical form.
Co=Bc';                          % Transform Cc to observer
                                 % canonical form.
Do=Dc;                           % Transform Dc to observer
                                 % canonical form.
r=roots([1 2 5])                 % Find the controller-compensated
                                 % system poles.
poles=10*[r' 10*real(r(1))]      % Make observer poles 10x bigger.
lp=acker(Ao',Co',poles)'         % Find the observer gains in
                                 % observer canonical form.
pause
```

ch12p5 (Example 12.6) We can test observability using the MATLAB command `Om = obsv(A,C)` to find the observability matrix given the system matrix (`A`) and the output matrix (`C`). This command is followed by `rank(Om)` to test the rank of the observability matrix (`Om`). Let us apply the commands to Example 12.6.

```
'(ch12p5) Example 12.6'          % Display label.
A=[0 1 0;0 0 1;-4 -3 -2]         % Define compensated A matrix.
C=[0 5 1]                        % Define compensated C matrix.
Om=obsv(A,C)                     % Form observability matrix.
Rank=rank(Om)                    % Find rank of observability
                                 % matrix.
pause
```

ch12p6 (Example 12.8) We can design observer gains using the command `l = acker(A',C',poles)'` without transforming to observer canonical form. Let us look at Example 12.8 in the text.

```
'(ch12p6) Example 12.8'          % Display label.
A=[-5 1 0;0 -2 1;0 0 -1];        % Define system matrix A.
B=[0;0;1];                       % Define input matrix B.
C=[1 0 0];                       % Define output matrix C.
D=0;                             % Define matrix D.
poles=roots([1 120 2500 50000])  % Specify pole placement for all
                                 % poles.
```

```
l=acker(A',C',poles)'          % Calculate observer gains.
pause
```

CHAPTER 13: DISCRETE CONTROL SYSTEMS

ch13p1 (Example 13.4)   We can convert $G_1(s)$ in cascade with a zero-order hold (z.o.h.) to $G(z)$ using MATLAB's $G = \texttt{c2d(G1,T,'zoh')}$ command, where G1 is an LTI continuous-system object and G is an LTI sampled-system object. T is the sampling interval and `'zoh'` is a method of transformation that assumes $G_1(s)$ in cascade with a z.o.h. We simply put $G_1(s)$ into the command (the z.o.h. is automatically taken care of) and the command returns $G(z)$. Let us apply the concept to Example 13.4. You will enter T through the keyboard.

```
'(ch13p1) Example 13.4'        % Display label.
T=input('Type T ');            % Input sampling interval.
numg1s=[1 2];                  % Define numerator of G1(s).
deng1s=[1 1];                  % Define denominator of G1(s).
'G1(s)'                        % Display label.
G1=tf(numg1s,deng1s)           % Create G1(s) and display.
'G(z)'                         % Display label.
G=c2d(G1,T,'zoh')              % Convert G1(s) in cascade with
                               % z.o.h. to G(z) and display.
pause
```

ch13p2   We also can use MATLAB to convert $G(s)$ to $G(z)$ when $G(s)$ is not in cascade with a z.o.h. The command $H = \texttt{c2d(F,T,'zoh')}$ transforms $F(s)$ in cascade with a z.o.h. to $H(z)$, where $H(z)=((z-1)/z)^*z\{F(s)/s\}$. If we let $F(s) = sG(s)$, the command solves for $H(z)$, where $H(z) = ((z-1)/z)^*z\{G(s)\}$. Hence, $z\{G(s)\} = (z/[z-1])^*H(z)$. In summary, input $F(s) = sG(s)$, and multiply the result of $H = \texttt{c2d(F,T,'zoh')}$ by $(z/[z-1])$. This process is equivalent to finding the z-transform. We convert $G(s) = (s+3)/(s^2+6s+13)$ into $G(z)$. You will enter T, the sampling interval, through the keyboard. T is used to form $H(z)$. We use an unspecified sampling interval, T=[ ], to form $z/(z-1)$.

```
'(ch13p2)'                     % Display label.
T=input('Type T ');            % Input sampling interval.
numgs=[1 3];                   % Define numerator of G(s).
dengs=[1 6 13];                % Define denominator of G(s).
'G(s)'                         % Display label.
Gs=tf(numgs,dengs)             % Create and display G(s).
Fs=Gs*tf([1 0],1)              % Create F(s)=sG(s).
Fs=minreal(Fs);                % Cancel common poles and zeros.
Hz=c2d(Fs,T,'zoh');            % Convert F(s) to H(z) assuming
                               % z.o.h.
Gz=Hz*tf([1 0],[1 -1],[]);     % Form G(z)=H(z)*z/(z-1).
'G(z)'                         % Display label.
Gz=minreal(Gz)                 % Cancel common poles and zeros.
pause
```

ch13p3 Creating Digital Transfer Functions Directly
Vector Method, Polynomial Form

A digital transfer function can be expressed as a numerator polynomial divided by a denominator polynomial, that is, $F(z) = N(z)/D(z)$. The numerator, $N(z)$, is represented by a vector, `numf`, that contains the coefficients of $N(z)$. Similarly, the denominator, $D(z)$, is represented by a vector, `denf`, that contains the coefficients of $D(z)$. We form $F(z)$ with the command, `F = tf(numf,denf,T)`, where `T` is the sampling interval. `F` is called a linear time-invariant (LTI) object. This object, or transfer function, can be used as an entity in other operations, such as addition or multiplication. We demonstrate with $F(z) = 150(z^2 + 2z + 7)/(z^2 - 0.3z + 0.02)$. We use an unspecified sampling interval, `T = [ ]`. Notice after executing the `tf` command, MATLAB prints the transfer function.

Vector Method, Factored Form

We also can create digital LTI transfer functions if the numerator and denominator are expressed in factored form. We do this by using vectors containing the roots of the numerator and denominator. Thus, $G(s) = K^* N(z)/D(z)$ can be expressed as an LTI object using the command, `G = zpk(numg,deng,K,T)`, where `numg` is a vector containing the roots of $N(z)$, `deng` is a vector containing the roots of $D(z)$, `K` is the gain, and `T` is the sampling interval. The expression `zpk` stands for zeros (roots of the numerator), poles (roots of the denominator), and gain, `K`. We demonstrate with $G(z) = 20(z+2)(z+4)/[(z-0.5)(z-0.7)(z-0.8)]$ and an unspecified sampling interval. Notice after executing the `zpk` command, MATLAB prints the transfer function.

Rational Expression in z Method, Polynomial Form
(Requires Control System Toolbox 8)

This method allows you to type the transfer function as you normally would write it. The statement `z = tf('z')` must precede the transfer function if you wish to create a digital LTI transfer function in polynomial form equivalent to using `G = tf(numg, deng,T)`.

Rational Expression in z Method, Factored Form
(Requires Control System Toolbox 8)

This method allows you to type the transfer function as you normally would write it. The statement `z = zpk('z')` must precede the transfer function if you wish to create a digital LTI transfer function in factored form equivalent to using `G=zpk(numg,-deng,K,T)`.

For both rational expression methods the transfer function can be typed in any form regardless of whether `z=tf('z')` or `z=zpk('z')` is used. The difference is in the created digital LTI transfer function. We use the same examples above to demonstrate the rational expression in z methods.

```
'(ch13p3)'                          % Display label.
'Vector Method, Polynomial Form'    % Display label.
numf=150*[1 2 7]                    % Store 150(z^2+2z+7) in numf and
                                    % display.
```

```
denf=[1 -0.3 0.02]              % Store(z^2-0.3z+0.02) in denf and
                                % display.
'F(z)'                          % Display label.
F=tf(numf,denf,[])              % Form F(z) and display.
clear                           % Clear previous variables from
                                % workspace.
'Vector Method, Factored Form'  % Display label.
numg=[-2 -4]                    % Store (s+2)(s+4) in numg and
                                % display.
deng=[0.5 0.7 0.8]              % Store (s-0.5)(s-0.7)(s-0.8) in
                                % deng and display.
K=20                            % Define K.
'G(z)'                          % Display label.
G=zpk(numg,deng,K,[])           % Form G(z) and display.
clear                           % Clear previous variables from
                                % workspace.
'Rational Expression Method, Polynomial Form'
                                % Display label.
z=tf('z')                       % Define z as an LTI object in
                                % polynomial form.
F=150*(z^2+2*z+7)/(z^2-0.3*z+0.02)
                                % Form F(z) as an LTI transfer
                                % function in polynomial form.
G=20*(z+2)*(z+4)/[(z-0.5)*(z-0.7)*(z-0.8)]
                                % Form G(z) as an LTI transfer
                                % function in polynomial form.
clear                           % Clear previous variables from
                                % workspace.
'Rational Expression Method, Factored Form'
                                % Display label.
z=zpk('z')                      % Define z as an LTI object in
                                % factored form.
F=150*(z^2+2*z+7)/(z^2-0.3*z+0.02)
                                % Form F(z) as an LTI transfer
                                % function in factored form.
G=20*(z+2)*(z+4)/[(z-0.5)*(z-0.7)*(z-0.8)]
                                % Form G(z) as an LTI transfer
                                % function in factored form.
pause
```

ch13p4 We also can use MATLAB to convert $G(z)$ to $G(s)$ when $G(s)$ is not in cascade with a z.o.h. First, we create a sampled LTI transfer function, as discussed in ch13p3. The command F = d2c(H,'zoh') transforms $H(z)$ to $F(s)$ in cascade with a z.o.h., where $H(z) = ((z-1)/z)^* z\{F(s)/s\}$. If we consider $F(s) = sG(s)$, the command solves for $sG(s)$ given $H(z)$. Finally, $sG(s)/s = G(s)$ yields the final result. In summary, form $H(z)$, where $H(z) = ((z-1)/z)^* G(z)$. Use F = d2c(H,'zoh') to find $F(s)=sG(s)$. Divide the result by s and obtain $G(s)$. We convert $G(z) = z/(z-0.3)$ into $G(s)$. You will enter T, the sampling interval, through the keyboard.

```
'(ch13p4)'                      % Display label.
T=input('Type T  ');            % Input sampling interval.
```

```
numgz=[1 0];                    % Define numerator of G(z).
dengz=[1 -.3];                  % Define denominator of G(z).
'G(z)'                          % Display label.
Gz=tf(numgz,dengz,T)            % Create and display G(z).
Hz=Gz*tf([1 -1],[1 0],T);       % Create H(z)=((z-1)/z)*G(z).
Hz=minreal(Hz);                 % Cancel common poles and zeros.
Fs=d2c(Hz,'zoh');               % Convert from H(z) to F(s)=sG(s).
Gs=Fs*tf(1,[1 0]);              % Create G(s)=F(s)(1/s).
'G(s)'                          % Display label.
Gs=minreal(Gs)                  % Cancel common poles and zeros.
pause
```

ch13p5 (Example 13.6) We can use MATLAB to find the gain for stability. Let us look at Example 13.6 in the text.

```
'(ch13p5) Example 13.6'         % Display label.
numgas=27;                      % Define numerator of Ga(s).
dengas=[1 27 0];                % Define denominator of Ga(s).
'Ga(s)'                         % Display label.
Ga=tf(numgas,dengas)            % Create and display Ga(s).
'G(z)'                          % Display label.
Gz=c2d(Ga,0.1,'zoh')            % Find G(z) assuming Ga(s) in
                                % cascade with z.o.h. and display.
for K=1:0.1:50;                 % Set range of K to look for
                                % stability.
Tz=feedback(K*Gz,1);            % Find T(z).
r=pole(Tz);                     % Get poles for this value of K.
rm=max(abs(r));                 % Find pole with maximum absolute
                                % value for this value of K.
if rm>=1,                       % See if pole is outside unit
                                % circle.
break;                          % Stop if pole is found outside
                                % unit circle.
end;                            % End if.
end;                            % End for.
K                               % Display K value.
r                               % Display closed-loop poles for
                                % this value of K.
rm                              % Display absolute value of pole.
pause
```

ch13p6 (Example 13.9) We can use MATLAB's command `dcgain(Gz)` to find steady-state errors. The command evaluates the dc gain of `Gz`, a digital LTI transfer function object, by evaluating `Gz` at $z = 1$. We use the dc gain to evaluate K_p, K_v, and K_a. Let us look at Example 13.9 in the text. You will input T, the sampling interval, through the keyboard to test stability.

```
'(ch13p6) Example 13.9'         % Display label.
T=input('Type T ');             % Input sampling interval.
```

```
numg1s=[10];                    % Define numerator of G1(s).
deng1s=poly([0 -1]);            % Define denominator of G1(s).
'G1(s)'                         % Display label.
G1s=tf(numg1s,deng1s)           % Create and display G1(s).
'G(z)'                          % Display label.
Gz=c2d(G1s,T,'zoh')             % Convert G1(s) and z.o.h. to G(z)
                                % and display.
'T(z)'                          % Display label.
Tz=feedback(Gz,1)               % Create and display T(z).
'Closed-Loop z-Plane Poles'     % Display label.
r=pole(Tz)                      % Check stability.
M=abs(r)                        % Display magnitude of roots.
pause
Kp=dcgain(Gz)                   % Calculate Kp.
GzKv=Gz*(1/T)*tf([1 -1],[1 0],T);
                                % Multiply G(z) by (1/T)*(z-1).
                                % Also, divide G(z) by z, which
                                % makes transfer function proper
                                % and yields same Kv.
GzKv=minreal(GzKv,0.00001);     % Cancel common poles and zeros.
Kv=dcgain(GzKv)                 % Calculate Kv.
GzKa=Gz*(1/T^2)*tf([1 -2 1],[1 0 0],T);
                                % Multiply G(z) by (1/T^2)(z-1)^2.
                                % Also, divide G(z) by z^2, which
                                % makes the transfer function
                                % proper and yields the same Ka.
GzKa=minreal(GzKa,0.00001)      % Cancel common poles and zeros.
Ka=dcgain(GzKa)                 % Calculate Ka.
pause
```

ch13p7 (Example 13.10) We now use the root locus to find the gain for stability. First, we create a digital LTI transfer-function object for $G(z) = N(z)/D(z)$, with an unspecified sampling interval. The LTI object is created using tf(numgz,dengz,[ ]), where numgz represents $N(z)$, dengz represents $D(z)$, and [ ] indicates an unspecified sampling interval. MATLAB produces a z-plane root locus along with the unit circle superimposed using the command, zgrid([ ],[ ]). We then interactively select the intersection of the root locus and the unit circle. MATLAB responds with the value of gain and the closed-loop poles. Let us look at Example 13.10.

```
'(ch13p7) Example 13.10'        % Display label.
clf                             % Clear graph.
numgz=[1 1];                    % Define numerator of G(z).
dengz=poly([1 0.5]);            % Define denominator of G(z).
'G(z)'                          % Display label.
Gz=tf(numgz,dengz,[ ])          % Create and display G(z).
rlocus(Gz)                      % Plot root locus.
zgrid([ ],[ ])                  % Add unit circle to root locus.
title(['z-Plane Root Locus'])   % Add title to root locus.
```

```
[K,p]=rlocfind(Gz)                % Allows input of K by selecting
                                  % point on graphic.
pause
```

ch13p8 (Example 13.11) We now use the root locus to find the gain to meet a transient response requirement. After MATLAB produces a *z*-plane root locus, along with damping ratio curves superimposed using the command `zgrid`, we interactively select the desired operating point at a damping ratio of 0.7, thus determining the gain. MATLAB responds with a gain value as well as the step response of the closed-loop sampled system using `step(Tz)`, where `Tz` is a digital LTI transfer-function object. Let us look at Example 13.11.

```
'(ch13p8) Example 13.11'          % Display label.
clf                               % Clear graph.
numgz=[1 1];                      % Define numerator of G(z).
dengz=poly([1 0.5]);              % Define denominator of G(z).
'G(z)'                            % Display label.
Gz=tf(numgz,dengz,[])             % Create and display G(z).
rlocus(Gz)                        % Plot root locus.
axis([0,1,-1,1])                  % Create close-up view.
zgrid                             % Add damping ratio curves to root
                                  % locus.
title(['z-Plane Root Locus'])     % Add title to root locus.
[K,p]=rlocfind(Gz)                % Allows input of K by selecting
                                  % point on graphic.
'T(z)'                            % Display label.
Tz=feedback(K*Gz,1)               % Find T(z).
step(Tz)                          % Find step response of gain-
                                  % compensated system.
title(['Gain Compensated Step Response'])
                                  % Add title to step response of
                                  % gain-compensated system.
pause
```

ch13p9 (Example 13.12) Let us now use MATLAB to design a digital lead compensator. The *s*-plane design was performed in Example 9.6. Here we convert the design to the *z*-plane and run a digital simulation of the step response. Conversion of the *s*-plane lead compensator, $Gc(s) = $ numgcs / dengcs, to the *z*-plane compensator, $Gc(z) = $ numgcz / dengcz, is accomplished using the Gcz = c2d(numgcs, dengcs,T,'tustin') command to perform a Tustin transformation, where T = sampling interval, which for this example is 1/300. This exercise solves Example 13.12 using MATLAB.

```
'(ch13p9) Example 13.12'          % Display label.
clf                               % Clear graph.
T=0.01                            % Define sampling interval.
numgcs=1977*[1 6];                % Define numerator of Gc(s).
dengcs=[1 29.1];                  % Define denominator of Gc(s).
'Gc(s) in polynomial form'        % Print label.
```

```
Gcs=tf(numgcs,dengcs)              % Create Gc(s) in polynomial form
                                   % and display.
'Gc(s) in polynomial form'         % Display label.
Gcszpk=zpk(Gcs)                    % Create Gc(s) in factored form
                                   % and display.
'Gc(z) in polynomial form via Tustin Transformation'
                                   % Display label.
Gcz=c2d(Gcs,T,'tustin')            % Form Gc(z) via Tustin
                                   % transformation.
'Gc(z) in factored form via Tustin Transformation'
                                   % Display label.
Gczzpk=zpk(Gcz)                    % Show Gc(z) in factored form.
numgps=1                           % Define numerator of Gp(s).
dengps=poly([0 -6 -10]);           % Define denominator of Gp(s).
'Gp(s) in polynomial form'         % Display label.
Gps=tf(numgps,dengps)              % Create Gp(s) in polynomial form
                                   % and display.
'Gp(s) in factored form'           % Display label.
Gpszpk=zpk(Gps)                    % Create Gp(s) in factored form
                                   % and display.
'Gp(z) in polynomial form'         % Display label.
Gpz=c2d(Gps,T,'zoh')               % Form Gp(z) via zoh transformation.
'Gp(z) in factored form'           % Display label.
Gpzzpk=zpk(Gpz)                    % Form Gp(z) in factored form.
Gez=Gcz*Gpz                        % Form Ge(z) = Gc(z)Gp(z).
'Ge(z) = Gc(z)Gp(z) in factored form'
                                   % Display label.
Gezzpk=zpk(Gez)                    % Form Ge(z) in factored form
                                   % and display.
'z-1'                              % Display label.
zm1=tf([1 -1],1,T)                 % Form z-1.
zm1Gez=minreal(zm1*Gez,0.00001);   % Cancel common factors.
'(z-1)Ge(z) for finding steady-state error'
                                   % Display label.
zm1Gezzpk=zpk(zm1Gez)              % Form & display (z-1)Ge(z) in
                                   % factored form.
Kv=(1/T)*dcgain(zm1Gez)            % Find Kv.
'T(z) = Ge(z)/(1+Ge(z))'           % Display label.
Tz=feedback(Gez,1)                 % Find closed-loop
                                   % transfer function, T(z)
step(Tz,0:T:2)                     % Find step reponse.
title('Closed-Loop Digital Lead Compensated Step Response')
                                   % Add title to step response.
```

B.3 COMMAND SUMMARY

abs(x)	Obtain absolute value of x.
acker(A,B,poles)	Find gains for pole placement.
angle(x)	Compute the angle of x in radians.

`atan(x)`	Compute arctan(x).
`axis([xmin,xmax,ymin,ymax])`	Define range on axes of a plot.
`bode(G,w)`	Make a Bode plot of transfer function $G(s)$ over a range of frequencies, ω. Field ω is optional.
`break`	Exit loop.
`c2d(G,T,'tustin')`	Convert $G(s)$ to $G(z)$ using the Tustin transformation. T is the sampling interval.
`c2d(G,T,'zoh')`	Convert $G(s)$ in cascade with a zero-order hold to $G(z)$. T is the sampling interval.
`canon(S,'modal')`	Convert an LTI state-space object, S, to parallel form.
`clear`	Clear variables from workspace.
`clf`	Clear current figure.
`conv([a b c d],[e f g h])`	Multiply $(as^3 + bs^2 + cs + d)$ by $(es^3 + fs^2 + gs + h)$.
`ctrb(A,B)`	Find controllability matrix.
`d2c(G,'zoh')`	Convert $G(z)$ to $G(s)$ in cascade with a zero-order hold.
`dcgain(G)`	Find dc gain for $G(s)$ (that is, $s = 0$), or $G(z)$ (that is, $z = 1$).
`eig(A)`	Find eigenvalues of matrix **A**.
`end`	End the loop.
`exp(a)`	Obtain e^a.
`feedback(G,H,sign)`	Find $T(s) = G(s)/[1 \pm G(s)H(s)]$. Sign $= -1$ or is optional for negative feedback systems. Sign $= +1$ for positive feedback systems.
`grid on`	Put grid lines on a graph.
`hold off`	Turn off graph hold; start new graph.
`imag(P)`	Form a matrix of the imaginary parts of the components of matrix **P**.
`input('str')`	Permit variable values to be entered from the keyboard with prompt `str`.
`interp1(x,y,x1)`	Perform table lookup by finding the value of y at the value of $x = x_1$.
`inv(P)`	Find the inverse of matrix **P**.
`length(P)`	Obtain dimension of vector **P**.
`log(x)`	Compute natural log of x.
`log10(x)`	Compute log to the base 10 of x.
`margin(G)`	Find gain and phase margins, and gain and phase margin frequencies of transfer function, $G(s)$. Return [Gain margin, Phase margin, 180° frequency, 0 dB frequency].
`max(P)`	Find the maximum component of **P**.
`minreal(G,tol)`	Cancel common factors from transfer function $G(s)$ within tolerance, tol. If 'tol' field is blank, a default value is used.
`ngrid`	Superimpose grid over a Nichols plot.
`nichols(G,w)`	Make a Nichols plot of transfer function $G(s)$ over a range of frequencies, ω. Field ω is optional.
`nyquist(G,w)`	Make a Nyquist diagram of transfer function $G(s)$ over a range of frequencies, ω. Field ω is optional.
`obsv(A.C)`	Find observability matrix.
`ord2(wn,z)`	Create a second-order system, $G(s) = 1/[s^2 + 2\zeta\omega_n s + \omega_n^2]$.
`pade(T,n)`	Obtain nth order Pade approximation for delay, T.
`pause`	Pause program until any key is pressed.
`plot(t1,y1,t2,y2,t3,y3)`	Plot $y1$ versus $t1$, $y2$ versus $t2$, and $y3$ versus $t3$ on the same graph.
`pole(G)`	Find poles of LTI transfer function object, $G(s)$.
`poly([-a -b -c])`	Form polynomial $(s + a)(s + b)(s + c)$.
`polyval(P,a)`	Find polynomial $P(s)$ evaluated at a, that is, $P(a)$.
`rank(A)`	Find rank of matrix **A**.

`real(P)`	Form a matrix of the real parts of the components of matrix **P**.
`residue(numf,denf)`	Find residues of $F(s) = $ `numf/denf`.
`rlocfind(GH)`	Allow interactive selection of points on a root locus plot for loop gain, $G(s)H(s)$. Return value for K and all closed-loop poles at that K.
`rlocus(GH,K)`	Plot root locus for loop gain, $G(s)H(s)$, over a range of gain, K. The K field is optional.
`roots(P)`	Find roots of polynomial, P.
`semilogx(w,P1)`	Make a semilog plot of P_1 versus $\log_{10}(\omega)$.
`series(G1,G2)`	Find $G_1(s)G_2(s)$.
`sgrid(z,wn)`	Overlay `z`(ζ) and `wn`(ω_n) grid lines on a root locus.
`sin(x)`	Find $\sin(x)$.
`sqrt(a)`	Compute $\sqrt{a}$.
`ss2tf(A,B,C,D,1)`	Convert a state-space representation to a transfer function. Return `[num,den]`.
`ss(A,B,C,D)`	Create an LTI state-space object, S.
`ss(G)`	Convert an LTI transfer function object, $G(s)$, to an LTI state-space object.
`ssdata(S)`	Extract **A**, **B**, **C**, and **D** matrices from LTI state-space object, S.
`step(G1,G2,.. Gn,t)`	Plot step responses of $G_1(s)$ through $G_n(s)$ on one graph over a range of time, t. Field t is optional as are fields G_2 through G_n.
`subplot(xyz)`	Divide plotting area into an x by y grid with z as the window number for the current plot.
`tan(x)`	Find tangent of x radians.
`text(a,b,'str')`	Put `str` on graph at graph coordinates $x = a$, $y = b$.
`tf2ss(numg,deng)`	Convert $G(s) = $ `numg/deng` to state space in controller canonical form. Return `[A,B,C,D]`.
`tf2zp(numg,deng)`	Convert $G(s) = $ `numg/deng` in polynomial form to factored form. Return `[zeros,poles,gains]`.
`tf(numg,deng,T)`	Create an LTI transfer function, $G(s) = $ `numg/deng`, in polynomial form. T is the sampling interval and should be used only if G is a sampled transfer function.
`tf(G)`	Convert an LTI transfer function, $G(s)$, to polynomial form.
`tfdata(G,'v')`	Extract numerator and denominator of an LTI transfer function, $G(s)$, and convert values to a vector. Return `[num,den]`.
`title('str')`	Put title `str` on graph.
`xlabel('str')`	Put label `str` on x axis of graph.
`ylabel('str')`	Put label `str` on y axis of graph.
`zgrid`	Superimpose `z` (ζ) and `wn` (ω_n) grid curves on a z-plane root locus.
`zgrid([],[])`	Superimpose the unit circle on a z-plane root locus.
`zp2tf([-a - b]',[-c -d]',K)`	Convert $F(s) = K(s+a)(s+b)/(s+c)(s+d)$ to polynomial form. Return `[num,den]`.
`zpk(numg,deng,K,T)`	Create an LTI transfer function, $G(s) = $ `numg/deng`, in factored form. T is the sampling interval and should be used only if G is a sampled transfer function.
`zpk(G)`	Convert an LTI transfer function, $G(s)$, to factored form.

BIBLIOGRAPHY

Johnson, H. et al. *Unmanned Free-Swimming Submersible (UFFS) System Description.* NRL Memorandum Report 4393. Naval Research Laboratory, Washington, DC, 1980.

The MathWorks. *Getting Started with Control System Toolbox 8.* The MathWorks, Natick, MA, 2000–2007.

The MathWorks. *Getting Started with MATLAB Version 7.* The MathWorks, Natick, MA, 1984–2004.

The MathWorks. *MATLAB Graphics Version 7*. The MathWorks, Natick, MA, 1984–2004.

The MathWorks. *MATLAB Mathematics Version 7*. The MathWorks, Natick, MA, 1984–2004.

The MathWorks. *MATLAB Programming Version 7*. The MathWorks, Natick, MA, 1984–2004.

The MathWorks. *Using Simulink Version 6*. The MathWorks, Natick, MA, 1990–2004.

APPENDIX C: MATLAB'S SIMULINK TUTORIAL

C.1 INTRODUCTION

Readers who are studying MATLAB may want to explore the functionality and convenience of MATLAB's Simulink. Before proceeding, the reader should have studied Appendix B, the MATLAB Tutorial, including Section B.1, which is applicable to this appendix.

MATLAB's Simulink Version 6 and MATLAB Version 7 are required in order to use Simulink.

The models described in this appendix, which are available at www.wiley.com/college/nise, were developed on a PC using MATLAB Version 7 and Simulink Version 6. The code will also run on workstations that support MATLAB. Consult the MATLAB Installation Guide for your platform for minimum system hardware requirements.

Simulink is used to simulate systems. It uses a graphical user interface (GUI) for you to interact with blocks that represent subsystems. You can position the blocks, resize the blocks, label the blocks, specify block parameters, and interconnect blocks to form complete systems from which simulations can be run.

Simulink has block libraries from which subsystems, sources (that is, function generators), and sinks (that is, scopes) can be copied. Subsystem blocks are available for representing linear, nonlinear, and discrete systems. LTI objects can be generated if the Control System Toolbox is installed.

Help is available on the menu bar of the **MATLAB** Window. Under **Help** select **Full Product Family Help**. When the help screen is available, choose **Simulink** under the **Contents** tab. Help is also available for each block in the block library and is accessed either by right-clicking a block's icon in the **Simulink Library Browser** and selecting **Help for** . . . or by double-clicking the block's icon and then clicking the

Help button. Finally, screen tips are available for some toolbar buttons. Let your mouse's pointer rest on the button for a few seconds to see the explanation.

C.2 USING SIMULINK

The following summarize the steps to take to use Simulink. Section C.3 will present four examples that demonstrate and clarify these steps.

1. **Access Simulink** The **Simulink Library Browser**, from where we begin Simulink, is accessed by typing *simulink* in the **MATLAB Command Window** or by clicking on the **Simulink Library Browser** button on the toolbar, shown circled in Figure C.1.

   In response, MATLAB displays the **Simulink Library Browser** shown in Figure C.2(*a*). We now create an **untitled** window, Figure C.2(*b*), by clicking on the **Create a new model** button (shown circled in Figure C.2(*a*)) on the tool bar of the **Simulink Library Browser**. You will build your system in this window. Existing models may be opened by clicking on the **Open a model** button on the **Simulink Library Browser** toolbar. This button is immediately to the right of the **Create a new model** button. Existing models may also be opened by selecting the **MATLAB Current Directory** shown on the left side of Figure C.1, selecting your file names, and then dragging them to the **MATLAB Command Window**. Double-clicking a file will bring up the model window.

2. **Select blocks** Figure C.2(*a*) shows the **Simulink Library Browser** from which all blocks can be accessed. The left-hand side of the browser shows major libraries, such as **Simulink**, as well as underlying block libraries, such as **Continuous**. The right-hand side of Figure C.2(*a*) also shows the underlying block libraries. To reveal a block library's underlying blocks, select the block library on the left-hand side or

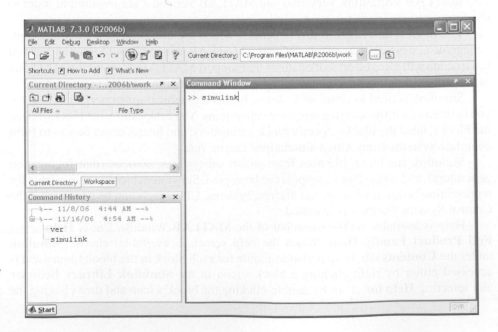

FIGURE C.1   MATLAB Window showing how to access Simulink. The **Simulink Library Browser** button is shown circled.

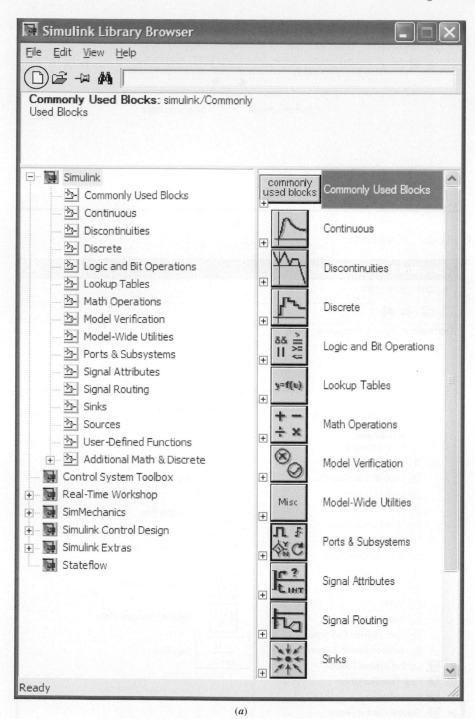

(a)

FIGURE C.2   **a. Simulink Library
Browser** window showing the
Create a new model button
encircled; **b.** resulting **untitled**
model window (figure continues)

double-click the block library on the right-hand side. As an example, the **Continuous**
library blocks under the **Simulink** major library are shown exposed in Figure C.3(*a*).
Figures C.3(*b*) and C.3(*c*) show some of the **Sources** and **Sinks** library blocks,
respectively.

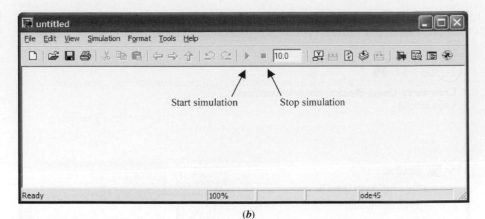

(b)

FIGURE C.2   (Continued)

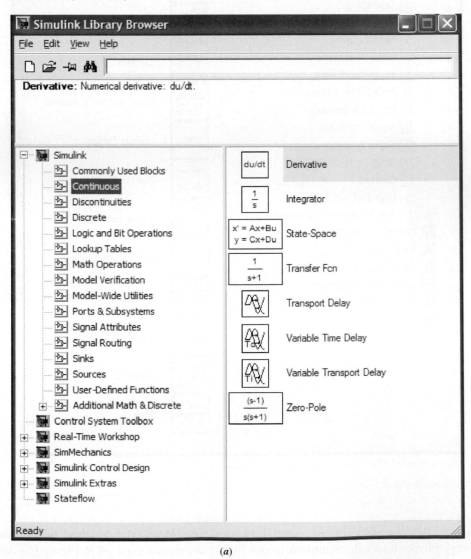

(a)

FIGURE C.3   Simulink block libraries: **a.** Continuous systems; **b.** Sources; **c.** Sinks (figure continues)

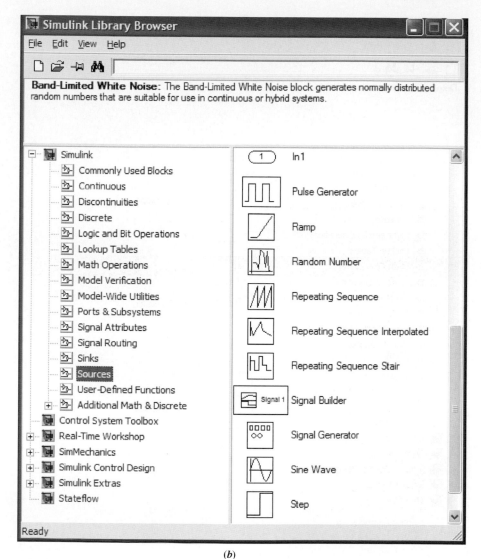

(b)

FIGURE C.3   (figure continues)

Another approach to revealing the Simulink block library is to type *open_system* (*'simulink.mdl'*) in the **MATLAB Command Window**. The window shown in Figure C.4 is the result. Double-clicking any of the libraries in Figure C.4 reveals an individual window containing that library's blocks, equivalent to the right-hand side of the **Simulink Library Browser** as shown in the examples of Figure C.3.

3. **Assemble and label subsystems** Drag required subsystems (blocks) to your model window from the browser, such as those shown in Figure C.3. Also, you may access the blocks by double-clicking the libraries shown in Figure C.4. You can position, resize, and rename the blocks. To position, drag with the mouse; to resize, click on the subsystem and drag the handles; to rename, click on the existing name, select the existing text, and type the new name. The text can also be repositioned to the top of the block by holding the mouse down and dragging the text.

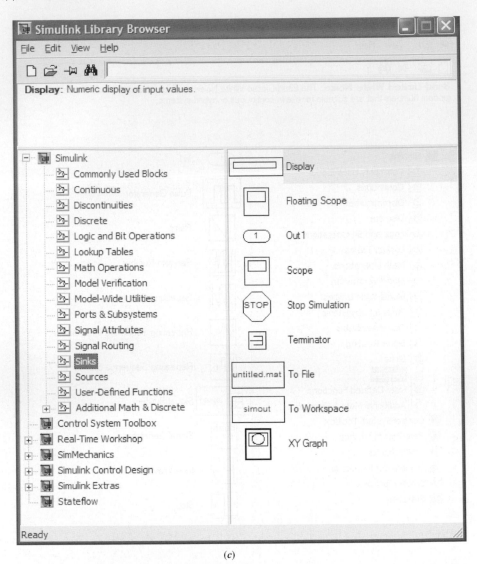

(c)

FIGURE C.3   (continued)

FIGURE C.4   Simulink Block
Library window

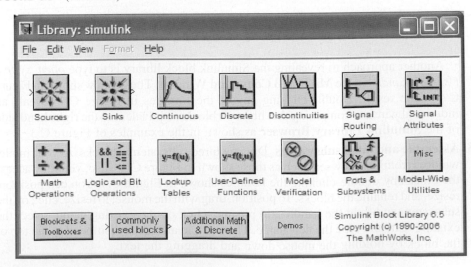

4. **Interconnect subsystems and label signals** Position the pointer on the small arrow on the side of a subsystem, press the mouse button, and drag the resulting cross-hair pointer to the small arrow of the next subsystem. A line will be drawn between the two subsystems. Blocks may also be interconnected by single-clicking the first block followed by single-clicking the second block while holding down the control key. You can move line segments by positioning the pointer on the line, pressing the mouse button, and dragging the resulting four-arrow pointer. Branches to line segments can be drawn by positioning the pointer where you want to create a line segment, holding down the mouse's right button, and dragging the resulting cross hairs. A new line segment will form. Signals can be labeled by double-clicking the line and typing into the resulting box. Finally, labels can be placed anywhere by double-clicking and typing into the resulting box.

5. **Choose parameters for the subsystems** Double-click a subsystem in your model window and type in the desired parameters. Some explanations are provided in the **Function Block Parameters** window. Press the Help button in the **Function Block Parameters** window for more details. The parameters can be read later without opening the block. Let your mouse's pointer rest on the block for a few seconds, and a screen tip will appear, identifying the block and listing its parameters. The information displayed in the screen tip first must be selected in the **Block Data Tips Options** in the model window's **View** menu. Explore other options by right-clicking on a block.

6. **Choose parameters for the simulation** Select **Configuration parameters**. . . under the **Simulation** menu in your model window to set additional parameters, such as simulation time. Press the **Help** button in the **Configuration parameters** window for more details.

7. **Start the simulation** Make your model window the active window. Double-click the **Scope** block (typically, the scope is used to view the simulation results) to display the **Scope** window. Select **Start** under the **Simulation** menu in your model window or click on the **Start simulation** icon on the toolbar of your model window as shown in Figure C.2(*b*). Clicking the **Stop simulation** icon will stop the simulation before completion.

8. **Interact with the plot** In the **Scope** window, using the toolbar buttons, you can zoom in and out, change axes ranges, save axis settings, and print the plot. Right-clicking on the **Scope** window brings up other choices.

9. **Save your model** Saving your model, by choosing **Save** under the **File** menu, creates a file with an .mdl extension, which is required.

C.3 EXAMPLES

This section will present four examples of the use of Simulink to simulate linear, nonlinear, and digital systems. Examples will show the Simulink block diagrams as well as explain the settings of parameters for the blocks. Finally, the results of the simulations will be shown.

EXAMPLE C.1

Simulation of linear systems

Our first example develops a simulation of three linear systems to compare their step responses. In particular, we solve Example 4.8 and reproduce the responses shown in Figure 4.24. Figure C.5 shows a Simulink block diagram formed by following Steps (1) through (5) in Section C.2 as follows:

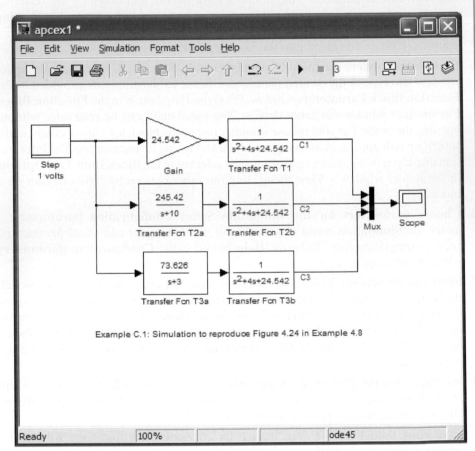

FIGURE C.5   Simulink block diagram for Example C.1

Access Simulink; select, assemble, and label subsystems The source is a 1-volt step input, obtained by dragging the **Step** block from the **Simulink Library Browser** under **Sources** to your model window.

The first system, T1, consists of two blocks, **Gain** and **Transfer Fcn**. Gain is obtained by dragging the **Gain** block from the **Simulink Library Browser** under **Math** to your model window. Transfer function, T1, is obtained by dragging the **Transfer Fcn** block from the **Simulink Library Browser** under **Continuous** to your model window. Systems T2 and T3 are created similarly.

The three output signals, C1, C2, and C3, are multiplexed for display into the single input of a scope. The Mux (multiplexer) is obtained by dragging the **Mux** block from the **Simulink Library Browser** under **Signal Routing** to your model window.

The sink is a scope, obtained by dragging the **Scope** block from the **Simulink Library Browser** under **Sinks** to your model window.

Alternatively, all blocks can be dragged from the **Library: simulink3** window shown in Figure C.4. The **Mux** can be found under **Signals & Systems** in the **Library: simulink3** window.

The labels for the blocks can be changed to those shown in Figure C.5 by following Step (3) in Section C.2.

Interconnect subsystems and label signals Follow Step (4) to interconnect the subsystems and label the signals. You must set the mux's parameters before the wiring can be completed. The Mux is found under **Signal Routing** in the **Simulink Library Browser**. See the next paragraph.

Choose parameters for the subsystems Let us now set the parameters of each block using Step (5). The **Block Parameters** window for each block is accessed by double-clicking the block on your model window. Figure C.6 shows the **Block Parameters** windows for the 1 volt step input, gain, transfer function 1, and mux. Set the parameters to the required values as shown.

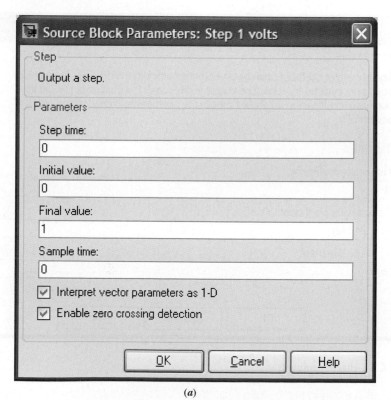

(*a*)

FIGURE C.6 **Block parameters** windows for **a.** 1 volt step source; **b.** gain; **c.** transfer function 1; **d.** mux (figure continues)

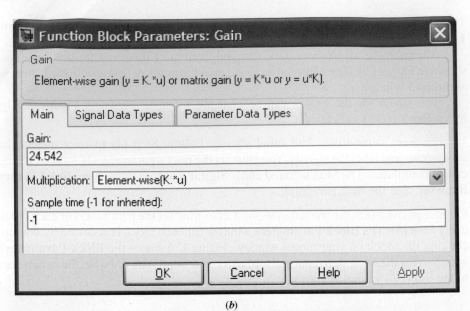

(b)

(c)

FIGURE C.6   (figure continues)

(*d*)

FIGURE C.6   (continued)

The scope requires further explanation. Double-clicking the **Scope** block in your model window accesses the scope's display, Figure C.7(*a*).

Clicking the **Parameters** icon on the **Scope** window toolbar, shown in Figure C.7(*a*), accesses the **'Scope' parameters** window as shown in Figure C.7(*b*). The **'Scope' parameters** window contains two tabs, **General** and **Data history**, as shown in Figure C.7(*b*) and (*c*), respectively. Finally, right-clicking in the plotting area in the **Scope** window and selecting **Axis properties**... reveals the **'Scope' properties:**

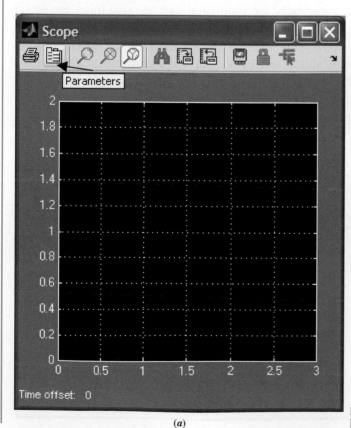

(*a*)

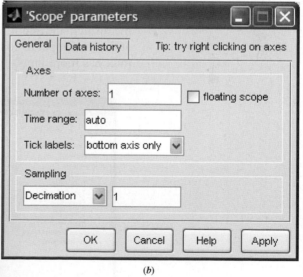

(*b*)

FIGURE C.7   Windows for the scope: **a. Scope; b. 'Scope' parameters, General** tab; **c. 'Scope' parameters, Data history** tab; **d. 'Scope' properties: axis 1** (figure continues)

FIGURE C.7 (continued)

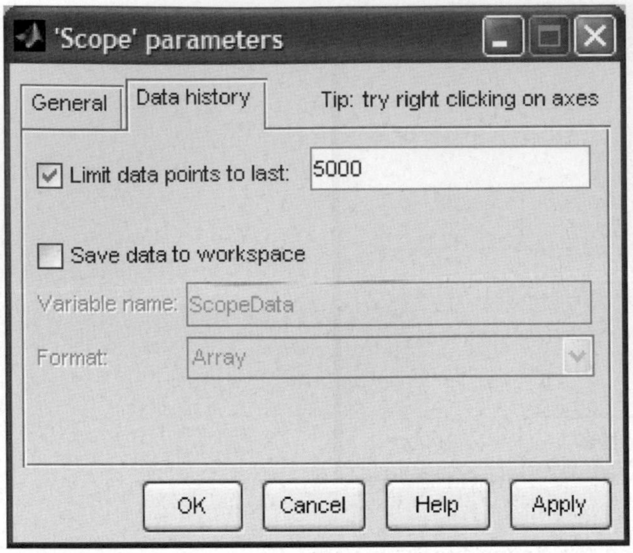

'Scope' parameters

| General | Data history | Tip: try right clicking on axes |

☑ Limit data points to last: 5000

☐ Save data to workspace

Variable name: ScopeData

Format: Array

OK | Cancel | Help | Apply

(*c*)

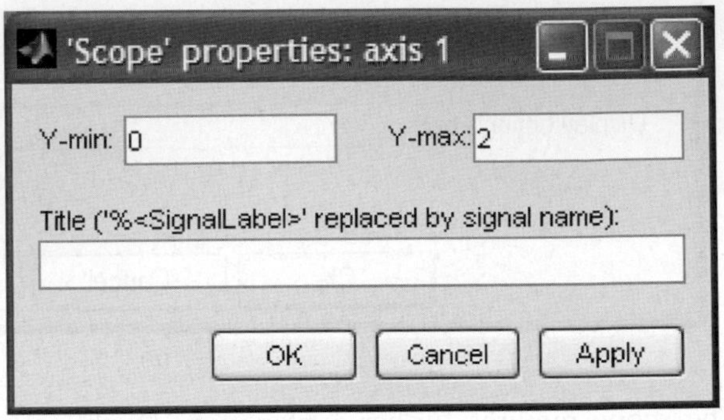

'Scope' properties: axis 1

Y-min: 0   Y-max: 2

Title ('%<SignalLabel>' replaced by signal name):

OK | Cancel | Apply

(*d*)

axis 1 window, Figure C.7(*d*). We now can set the display parameters, such as amplitude range.

Choose parameters for the simulation Follow Step (6) to set simulation parameters. Figure C.8 shows the resulting **Configuration Parameters** window after selecting the **Solver** tab. Among other parameters, the simulation start and stop times can be set.

Start the simulation Now run the simulation by following Step (7). Figure C.9 shows the result in the **Scope** window. Plots are color coded in the order in which they appear at the mux input as follows: yellow, magenta, cyan, red, green, and dark blue. If the mux has more inputs, the colors recycle.

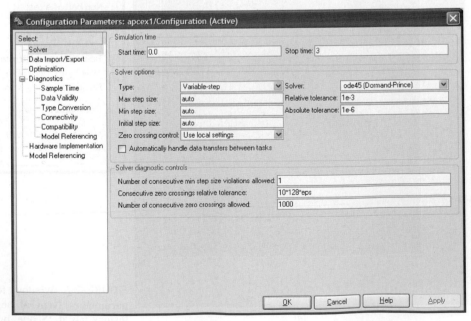

FIGURE C.8 Simulation Parameters window for **Solver** tab

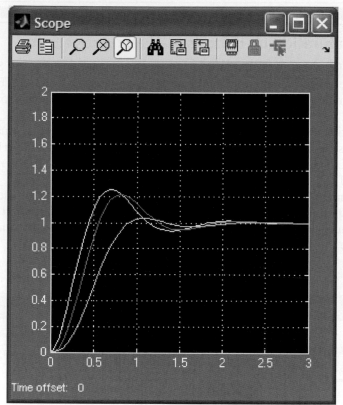

FIGURE C.9   **Scope** window after Example C.1 simulation stops

Interact with the plot The toolbar of the **Scope** window shown in Figure C.9 has
several buttons that can be used to interact with the plot. Let us summarize the function
and operation of each, starting with the left-most button:

Button 1 executes a plot print.
Button 2 has already been explained and is used to set scope parameters.
Button 3 permits zooming into the plot in both the x and y directions. Press the button
and drag a rectangle over the portion of the curve you want to expand.
Button 4 allows zooming in the x direction only. Drag a horizontal line over the plot
covering the extent of x you want to expand.
Button 5 allows zooming in the y direction only. Drag a vertical line over the plot
covering the range of y you want to expand.
Button 6 autoscales axis for use after zooming.
Button 7 saves current axis settings.
Button 8 restores saved axis settings.
Button 9 toggles floating scope. It must be turned off to use zooming. See
documentation for use of floating scopes.
Button 10 toggles lock for current axis selection.
Button 11 allows selection of signals to view when using floating scope.

EXAMPLE C.2

Effect of amplifier saturation on motor's load angular velocity

This example, which generated Figure 4.29 in the text, shows the use of Simulink to simulate the effect of saturation nonlinearity on an open-loop system. Figure C.10 shows a Simulink block diagram formed by following Steps (1) through (5) in Section C.2 above.

Saturation nonlinearity is an additional block that we have not used before. Saturation is obtained by dragging to your model window the **Saturation** block in the **Simulink Library Browser** window under **Discontinuities** as shown in Figure C.11(*a*) and setting its parameters to those shown in Figure C.11(*b*).

Now run the simulation by making your model window active and selecting **Start** under the **Simulation** menu of your model window or clicking on the **Start simulation** button on your model window toolbar. Figure C.12 shows the result in the **Scope** window.

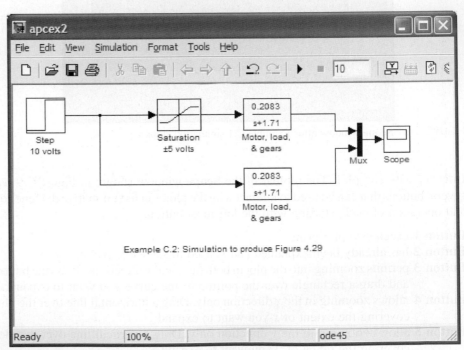

FIGURE C.10 Simulink block diagram for Example C.2

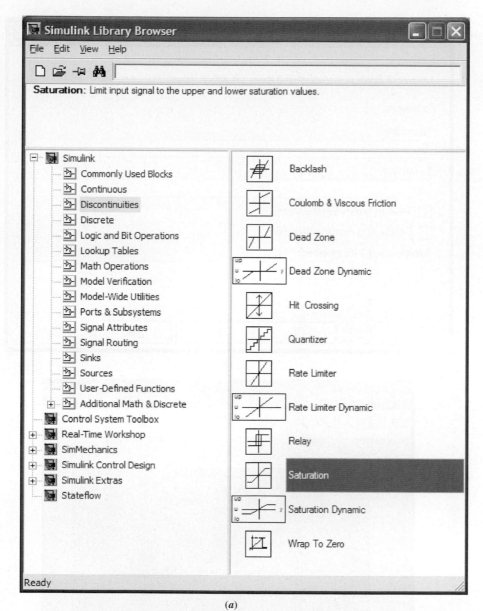

(a)

FIGURE C.11   **a.** Simulink library for nonlinearities; **b.** parameter settings for saturation (figure continues)

FIGURE C.11 (continued)

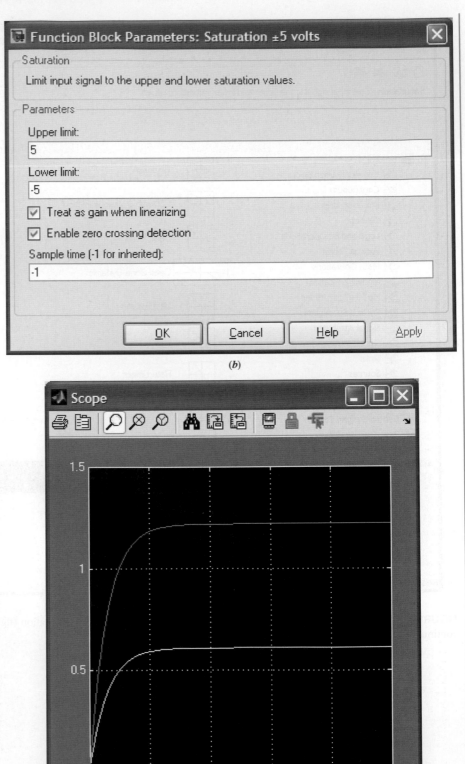

(b)

FIGURE C.12 Scope window
after simulation of Example C.2
stops. The lower curve is the
output with saturation

EXAMPLE C.3

Simulating feedback systems

Simulink can be used for the simulation of feedback systems. Figure C.13(*a*) is an example of a feedback system with saturation.

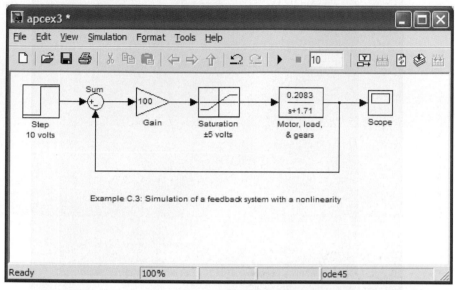

(*a*)

(*b*)

FIGURE C.13   **a.** Simulation block diagram for a feedback system with saturation; **b.** block parameter window for the summer

FIGURE C.14 Simulation output for Example C.3

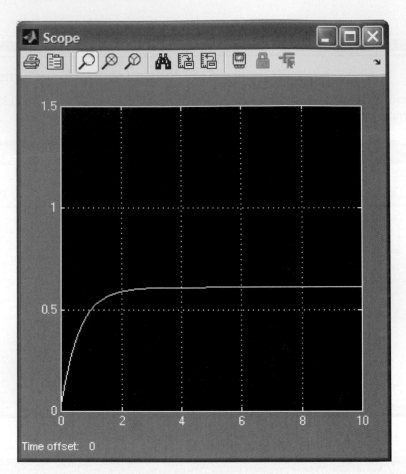

In this example we have added a feedback path (see Step (4) in Section C.2) and a summing junction, which is obtained by dragging the **Sum** block from the **Simulink Library Browser**, contained in the **Math Operations** library, to your model window. The **Function Block Parameters: Sum** window, Figure C.13(*b*), shows the parameter settings for the summer. You can set the shape as well as set the plus and minus inputs. In the list of signs, the "|"symbol signifies a space. We place it at the beginning to start the signs at "nine o'clock," conforming to our standard symbol, rather than at "12 o'clock." The result of the simulation is shown in Figure C.14.

▌ EXAMPLE C.4 ▌

Simulating digital systems

This example demonstrates two methods of generating digital systems via Simulink for the purpose of simulation, as shown in Figure C.15.

The first approach uses a linear transfer function cascaded with a **Zero-Order Hold** block obtained from the **Simulink Library Browser** under the **Discrete** block library, shown on the right-hand side of Figure C.16. The second method uses a discrete transfer function also obtained from the **Simulink Library Browser** under the **Discrete** block library. The remainder of the block diagram was obtained by methods previously described.

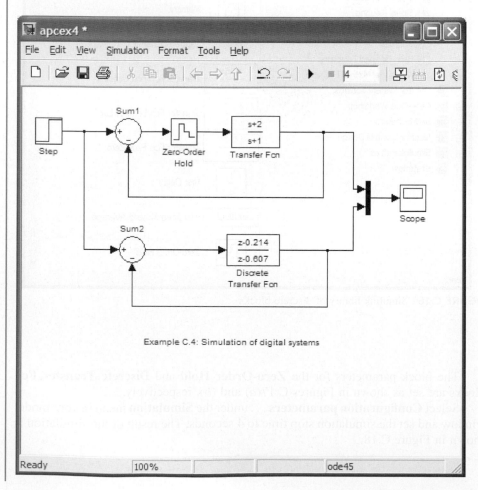

FIGURE C.15 Simulink block diagram for simulating digital systems two ways

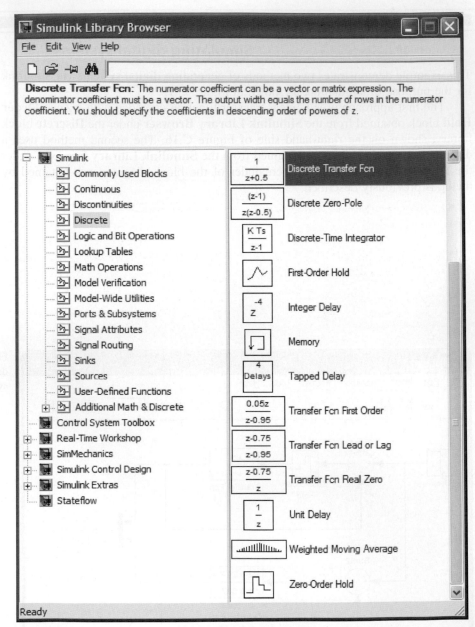

FIGURE C.16   Simulink library of discrete blocks

The block parameters for the **Zero-Order Hold** and **Discrete Transfer Fcn** blocks are set as shown in Figures C.17(*a*) and (*b*), respectively.

Select **Configuration parameters** . . . under the **Simulation** menu in your model window and set the simulation stop time to 4 seconds. The result of the simulation is shown in Figure C.18.

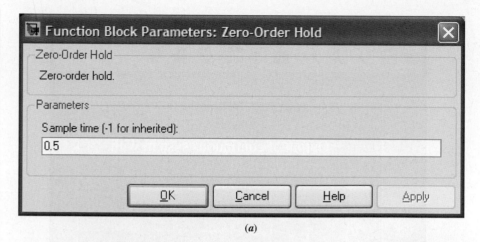

Function Block Parameters: Zero-Order Hold

(a)

Function Block Parameters: Discrete Transfer Fcn

Discrete Transfer Fcn

The numerator coefficient can be a vector or matrix expression. The denominator coefficient must be a vector. The output width equals the number of rows in the numerator coefficient. You should specify the coefficients in descending order of powers of z.

Main   State Properties

Numerator coefficient:

[1 -0.214]

Denominator coefficient:

[1 -0.607]

Sample time (-1 for inherited):

0.5

OK   Cancel   Help   Apply

(b)

FIGURE C.17 Function Block parameter windows for: **a. Zero-Order Hold** block; **b. Discrete Transfer Fcn** block

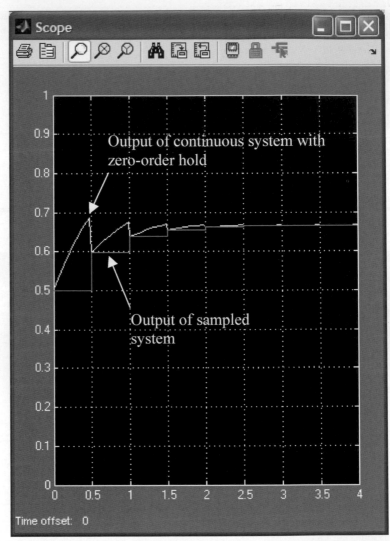

FIGURE C.18   Outputs of the digital systems

C.4 SUMMARY

This appendix explained Simulink, its advantages, and how to use it. Examples were taken from Chapters 4, 5, and 13 and demonstrated the use of Simulink for simulating linear, nonlinear, and digital systems.

The objective of this appendix was to familiarize you with the subject and get you started using Simulink. There are many blocks, parameters, and preferences that could not be covered in this short appendix. You are encouraged to explore and expand your use of Simulink by using the on-screen help that was explained earlier. The references in the Bibliography of this appendix also provide an opportunity to learn more about Simulink.

BIBLIOGRAPHY

The MathWorks. *Getting Started with Control System Toolbox 8*. The MathWorks, Natick, MA, 2000–2007.

The MathWorks. *Getting Started with MATLAB Version 7*. The MathWorks, Natick, MA, 1984–2004.

The MathWorks. *MATLAB Graphics Version 7*. The MathWorks, Natick, MA, 1984–2004.

The MathWorks. *MATLAB Mathematics Version 7*. The MathWorks, Natick, MA, 1984–2004.

The MathWorks. *MATLAB Programming Version 7*. The MathWorks, Natick, MA, 1984–2004.

The MathWorks. *Using Simulink Version 6*. The MathWorks, Natick, MA, 1990–2004.

GLOSSARY

Acceleration constant $\lim_{s \to 0} s^2 G(s)$

Actuating signal The signal that drives the controller. If this signal is the difference between the input and output, it is called the *error*.

Analog-to-digital converter A device that converts analog signals to digital signals.

Armature The rotating member of a dc motor through which a current flows.

Back emf The voltage across the armature of a motor.

Bandwidth The frequency at which the magnitude frequency response is -3 dB below the magnitude at zero frequency.

Basis Linearly independent vectors that define a space.

Bilinear transformation A mapping of the complex plane where one point, s, is mapped into another point, z, through $z = (as + b)/(cs + d)$.

Block diagram A representation of the interconnection of subsystems that form a system. In a linear system the block diagram consists of blocks representing subsystems, arrows representing signals, summing junctions, and pickoff points.

Bode diagram (plot) A sinusoidal frequency response plot where the magnitude response is plotted separately from the phase response. The magnitude plot is dB versus $\log \omega$, and the phase plot is phase versus $\log \omega$. In control systems the Bode plot is usually made for the open-loop transfer function. Bode plots can also be drawn as straight-line approximations.

Branches Lines that represent subsystems in a signal-flow graph.

Break frequency A frequency where the Bode magnitude plot changes slope.

Breakaway point A point on the real axis of the s-plane where the root locus leaves the real axis and enters the complex plane.

Break-in point A point on the real axis of the s-plane where the root locus enters the real axis from the complex plane.

Characteristic equation The equation formed by setting the characteristic polynomial to zero.

Characteristic polynomial The denominator of a transfer function. Equivalently, the unforced differential equation, where the differential operators are replaced by s or λ.

Classical approach to control systems *See* **frequency domain techniques.**

Closed-loop system A system that monitors its output and corrects for disturbances. It is characterized by feedback paths from the output.

Closed-loop transfer function For a generic feedback system with $G(s)$ in the forward path and $H(s)$ in the feedback path, the closed-loop transfer function, $T(s)$, is $G(s)/[1 \pm G(s)H(s)]$, where the $+$ is for negative feedback, and the $-$ is for positive feedback.

Compensation The addition of a transfer function in the forward path or feedback path for the purpose of improving the transient or steady-state performance of a control system.

Compensator A subsystem inserted into the forward or feedback path for the purpose of improving the transient response or steady-state error.

Constant M circles The locus of constant, closed-loop magnitude frequency response for unity feedback systems. It allows the closed-loop magnitude frequency response to be determined from the open-loop magnitude frequency response.

Constant N circles The locus of constant, closed-loop phase frequency response for unity feedback systems. It allows the closed-loop phase frequency response to be determined from the open-loop phase frequency response.

Controllability A property of a system by which an input can be found that takes every state variable from a desired initial state to a desired final state in finite time.

Controlled variable The output of a plant or process that the system is controlling for the purpose of desired transient response, stability, and steady-state error characteristics.

Controller The subsystem that generates the input to the plant or process.

Critically damped response The step response of a second-order system with a given natural frequency that is characterized by no overshoot and a rise time that is faster than any possible overdamped response with the same natural frequency.

Damped frequency of oscillation The sinusoidal frequency of oscillation of an underdamped response.

Damping ratio The ratio of the exponential decay frequency to the natural frequency.

Decade Frequencies that are separated by a factor of 10.

Decibel (dB) The decibel is defined as $10 \log P_G$, where P_G is the power gain of a signal. Equivalently, the decibel is also $20 \log V_G$, where V_G is the voltage gain of a signal.

Decoupled system A state-space representation in which each state equation is a function of only one state variable. Hence, each differential equation can be solved independently of the other equations.

Digital compensator A sampled transfer function used to improve the response of computer-controlled feedback systems. The transfer function can be emulated by a digital computer in the loop.

Digital-to-analog converter A device that converts digital signals to analog signals.

Disturbance An unwanted signal that corrupts the input or output of a plant or process.

Dominant poles The poles that predominantly generate the transient response.

Eigenvalues Any value, λ_i, that satisfies $\mathbf{A}\mathbf{x_i} = \lambda_i\mathbf{x_i}$ for $\mathbf{x_i} \neq 0$. Hence, any value, λ_i, that makes $\mathbf{x_i}$ an eigenvector under the transformation $\mathbf{A}$.

Eigenvector Any vector that is collinear with a new basis vector after a similarity transformation to a diagonal system.

Electric circuit analog An electrical network whose variables and parameters are analogous to another physical system. The electric circuit analog can be used to solve for variables of the other physical system.

Electrical admittance The inverse of electrical impedance. The ratio of the Laplace transform of the current to the Laplace transform of the voltage.

Electrical impedance The ratio of the Laplace transform of the voltage to the Laplace transform of the current.

Equilibrium The steady-state solution characterized by a constant position or oscillation.

Error The difference between the input and the output of a system.

Euler's approximation A method of integration where the area to be integrated is approximated as a sequence of rectangles.

Feedback A path through which a signal flows back to a previous signal in the forward path in order to be added or subtracted.

Feedback compensator A subsystem placed in a feedback path for the purpose of improving the performance of a closed-loop system.

Forced response For linear systems, that part of the total response function due to the input. It is typically of the same form as the input and its derivatives.

Forward-path gain The product of gains found by traversing a path that follows the direction of signal flow from the input node to the output node of a signal-flow graph.

Frequency domain techniques A method of analyzing and designing linear control systems by using transfer functions and the Laplace transform as well as frequency response techniques.

Frequency response techniques A method of analyzing and designing control systems by using the sinusoidal frequency response characteristics of a system.

Gain The ratio of output to input; usually used to describe the amplification in the steady state of the magnitude of sinusoidal inputs, including dc.

Gain margin The amount of additional open-loop gain, expressed in decibels (dB), required at $180°$ of phase shift to make the closed-loop system unstable.

Gain-margin frequency The frequency at which the phase frequency response plot equals $180°$. It is the frequency at which the gain margin is measured.

Homogeneous solution *See* **natural response.**

Ideal derivative compensator *See* **proportional-plus-derivative controller.**

Ideal integral compensator *See* **proportional-plus-integral controller.**

Instability The characteristic of a system defined by a natural response that grows without bounds as time approaches infinity.

Kirchhoff's law The sum of voltages around a closed loop equals zero. Also, the sum of currents at a node equals zero.

Lag compensator A transfer function, characterized by a pole on the negative real axis close to the origin and a zero close and to the left of the pole, that is used for the purpose of improving the steady-state error of a closed-loop system.

Lag-lead compensator A transfer function, characterized by a pole-zero configuration that is the combination of a lag and a lead compensator, that is used for the purpose of improving both the transient response and the steady-state error of a closed-loop system.

Laplace transformation A transformation that transforms linear differential equations into algebraic expressions. The transformation is especially useful for modeling, analyzing, and designing control systems as well as solving linear differential equations.

Lead compensator A transfer function, characterized by a zero on the negative real axis and a pole to the left of the zero, that is used for the purpose of improving the transient response of a closed-loop system.

Linear combination A linear combination of n variables, x_i, for $i = 1$ to n, given by the following sum, S:

$$S = K_n X_n + K_{n-1} X_{n-1} + \cdots + K_1 X_1$$

where each K_i is a constant.

Linear independence The variables x_i, for $i = 1$ to n, are said to be linearly independent if their linear combination, S, equals zero *only* if every $K_i = 0$ and *no* $x_i = 0$. Alternatively, if the x_i's are linearly independent, then $K_n x_n + K_{n-1} x_{n-1} + \cdots + K_1 x_1 = 0$ cannot be solved for any x_k. Thus, no x_k can be expressed as a linear combination of the other x_i's.

Linear system A system possessing the properties of superposition and homogeneity.

Linearization The process of approximating a nonlinear differential equation with a linear differential equation valid for small excursions about equilibrium.

Loop gain For a signal-flow graph, the product of branch gains found by traversing a path that starts at a node and ends at the same node without passing through any other node more than once, and following the direction of the signal flow.

Major-loop compensation A method of feedback compensation that adds a compensating zero to the open-loop transfer function for the purpose of improving the transient response of the closed-loop system.

Marginal stability The characteristic of a system defined by a natural response that neither decays nor grows, but remains constant or oscillates as time approaches infinity as long as the input is not of the same form as the system's natural response.

Mason's rule A formula from which the transfer function of a system consisting of the interconnection of multiple subsystems can be found.

Mechanical rotational impedance The ratio of the Laplace transform of the torque to the Laplace transform of the angular displacement.

Mechanical translational impedance The ratio of the Laplace transform of the force to the Laplace transform of the linear displacement.

Minor-loop compensation A method of feedback compensation that changes the poles of a forward-path transfer function for the purpose of improving the transient response of the closed-loop system.

Modern approach to control systems *See* **state-space representation.**

Natural frequency The frequency of oscillation of a system if all the damping is removed.

Natural response That part of the total response function due to the system and the way the system acquires or dissipates energy.

Negative feedback The case where a feedback signal is subtracted from a previous signal in the forward path.

Newton's law The sum of forces equals zero. Alternatively, after bringing the *ma* force to the other side of the equality, the sum of forces equals the product of mass and acceleration.

Nichols chart The locus of constant closed-loop magnitude and closed-loop phase frequency responses for unity feedback systems plotted on the open-loop dB versus phase-angle plane. It allows the closed-loop frequency response to be determined from the open-loop frequency response.

Nodes Points in a signal-flow diagram that represent signals.

No-load speed The speed produced by a motor with constant input voltage when the torque at the armature is reduced to zero.

Nonminimum-phase system A system whose transfer function has zeros in the right half-plane. The step response is characterized by an initial reversal in direction.

Nontouching-loop gain The product of loop gains from nontouching loops taken two, three, four, and so on at a time.

Nontouching loops Loops that do not have any nodes in common.

Notch filter A filter whose magnitude frequency response dips at a particular sinusoidal frequency. On the s-plane, it is characterized by a pair of complex zeros near the imaginary axis.

Nyquist criterion If a contour, A, that encircles the entire right half-plane is mapped through $G(s)H(s)$, then the number of closed-loop poles, Z, in the right half-plane equals the number of open-loop poles, P, that are in the right half-plane minus the number of counterclockwise revolutions, N, around -1, of the mapping; that is, $Z = P - N$. The mapping is called the *Nyquist diagram* of $G(s)H(s)$.

Nyquist diagram (plot) A polar frequency response plot made for the open-loop transfer function.

Nyquist sampling rate The minimum frequency at which an analog signal should be sampled for correct reconstruction. This frequency is twice the bandwidth of the analog signal.

Observability A property of a system by which an initial state vector, $x(t_0)$, can be found from $u(t)$ and $y(t)$ measured over a finite interval of time from t_0. Simply stated, observability is the property by which the state variables can be estimated from a knowledge of the input, $u(t)$, and output, $y(t)$.

Observer A system configuration from which inaccessible states can be estimated.

Octave Frequencies that are separated by a factor of two.

Ohm's law For dc circuits the ratio of voltage to current is a constant called resistance.

Open-loop system A system that does not monitor its output nor correct for disturbances.

Open-loop transfer function For a generic feedback system with $G(s)$ in the forward path and $H(s)$ in the feedback path, the open-loop transfer function is the product of the forward-path transfer function and the feedback transfer function, or $G(s)H(s)$.

Operational amplifier An amplifier—characterized by a very high input impedance, a very low output impedance, and a high gain—that can be used to implement the transfer function of a compensator.

Output equation For linear systems, the equation that expresses the output variables of a system as linear combinations of the state variables.

Overdamped response A step response of a second-order system that is characterized by no overshoot.

Partial-fraction expansion A mathematical equation where a fraction with n factors in its denominator is represented as the sum of simpler fractions.

Particular solution *See* **forced response**.

Passive network A physical network that only stores or dissipates energy. No energy is produced by the network.

Peak time, T_p The time required for the underdamped step response to reach the first, or maximum, peak.

Percent overshoot, %OS The amount that the underdamped step response overshoots the steady-state, or final, value at the peak time, expressed as a percentage of the steady-state value.

Phase margin The amount of additional open-loop phase shift required at unity gain to make the closed-loop system unstable.

Phase-margin frequency The frequency at which the magnitude frequency response plot equals zero dB. It is the frequency at which the phase margin is measured.

Phase variables State variables such that each subsequent state variable is the derivative of the previous state variable.

Phasor A rotating vector that represents a sinusoid of the form $A\cos(\omega t + \phi)$.

Pickoff point A block diagram symbol that shows the distribution of one signal to multiple subsystems.

Plant or process The subsystem whose output is being controlled by the system.

Poles (1) The values of the Laplace transform variable, s, that cause the transfer function to become infinite; and (2) any roots of factors of the characteristic equation in the denominator that are common to the numerator of the transfer function.

Position constant $\lim_{s \to 0} G(s)$

Positive feedback The case where a feedback signal is added to a previous signal in the forward path.

Proportional-plus-derivative (PD) controller A controller that feeds forward to the plant a proportion of the actuating signal plus its derivative for the purpose of improving the transient response of a closed-loop system.

Proportional-plus-integral (PI) controller A controller that feeds forward to the plant a proportion of the actuating signal plus its integral for the purpose of improving the steady-state error of a closed-loop system.

Proportional-plus-integral-plus-derivative (PID) controller A controller that feeds forward to the plant a proportion of the actuating signal plus its integral plus its derivative for the purpose of improving the transient response and steady-state error of a closed-loop system.

Quantization error For linear systems, the error associated with the digitizing of signals as a result of the finite difference between quantization levels.

Raible's tabular method A tabular method for determining the stability of digital systems that parallels the Routh-Hurwitz method for analog signals.

Rate gyro A device that responds to an angular position input with an output voltage proportional to angular velocity.

Residue The constants in the numerators of the terms in a partial-fraction expansion.

Rise time, T_r The time required for the step response to go from 0.1 of the final value to 0.9 of the final value.

Root locus The locus of closed-loop poles as a system parameter is varied. Typically, the parameter is gain. The locus is obtained from the open-loop poles and zeros.

Routh-Hurwitz criterion A method for determining how many roots of a polynomial in s are in the right half of the s-plane, the left half of the s-plane, and on the imaginary axis. Except in some special cases, the Routh-Hurwitz criterion does not yield the coordinates of the roots.

Sensitivity The fractional change in a system characteristic for a fractional change in a system parameter.

Settling time, T_s The amount of time required for the step response to reach and stay within $\pm 2\%$ of the steady-state value. Strictly speaking, this is the definition of the 2% settling time. Other percentages, for example 5%, also can be used. This book uses the 2% settling time.

Signal-flow graph A representation of the interconnection of subsystems that form a system. It consists of nodes representing signals and lines representing subsystems.

Similarity transformation A transformation from one state-space representation to another state-space representation. Although the state variables are different, each representation is a valid description of the same system and the relationship between the input and the output.

Stability That characteristic of a system defined by a natural response that decays to zero as time approaches infinity.

Stall torque The torque produced at the armature when a motor's speed is reduced to zero under a condition of constant input voltage.

State equations A set of n simultaneous, first-order differential equations with n variables, where the n variables to be solved are the state variables.

State space The n-dimensional space whose axes are the state variables.

State-space representation A mathematical model for a system that consists of simultaneous, first-order differential equations and an output equation.

State-transition matrix The matrix that performs a transformation on $\mathbf{x}(0)$, taking $\mathbf{x}$ from the initial state, $\mathbf{x}(0)$, to the state $\mathbf{x}(t)$ at any time, $t \geq 0$.

State variables The smallest set of linearly independent system variables such that the values of the members of the set at time t_0 along with known forcing functions completely determine the value of all system variables for all $t \geq t_0$.

State vector A vector whose elements are the state variables.

Static error constants The collection of position constant, velocity constant, and acceleration constant.

Steady-state error The difference between the input and the output of a system after the natural response has decayed to zero.

Steady-state response *See* **forced response.**

Subsystem A system that is a portion of a larger system.

Summing junction A block diagram symbol that shows the algebraic summation of two or more signals.

System type The number of pure integrations in the forward path of a unity feedback system.

System variables Any variable that responds to an input or initial conditions in a system.

Tachometer A voltage generator that yields a voltage output proportional to rotational input speed.

Time constant The time for e^{-at} to decay to 37% of its original value at $t = 0$.

Time-domain representation *See* **state-space representation.**

Torque-speed curve The plot that relates a motor's torque to its speed at a constant input voltage.

Transducer A device that converts a signal from one form to another, for example from a mechanical displacement to an electrical voltage.

Transfer function The ratio of the Laplace transform of the output of a system to the Laplace transform of the input.

Transient response That part of the response curve due to the system and the way the system acquires or dissipates energy. In stable systems it is the part of the response plot prior to the steady-state response.

Tustin transformation A bilinear transformation that converts transfer functions from continuous to sampled and vice versa. The important characteristic of the Tustin transformation is that both transfer functions yield the same output response at the sampling instants.

Type *See* **system type**.

Undamped response The step response of a second-order system that is characterized by a pure oscillation.

Underdamped response The step response of a second-order system that is characterized by overshoot.

Velocity constant $\lim_{s \to 0} sG(s)$

z-transformation A transformation related to the Laplace transformation that is used for the representation, analysis, and design of sampled signals and systems.

Zero-input response That part of the response that depends upon only the initial state vector and not the input.

Zero-order sample-and-hold (z.o.h.) A device that yields a staircase approximation to the analog signal.

Zeros (1) Those values of the Laplace transform variable, s, that cause the transfer function to become zero; and (2) any roots of factors of the numerator that are common to the characteristic equation in the denominator of the transfer function.

Zero-state response That part of the response that depends upon only the input and not the initial state vector.

ANSWERS
TO SELECTED PROBLEMS

Chapter 1

17. c. $x(t) = \dfrac{2}{5} - e^{-4t}\left(\dfrac{2}{5}\cos 3t + \dfrac{8}{15}\sin 3t\right)$

18. b. $x(t) = -e^{-t} + 9te^{-t} + 5e^{-2t} + t - 2$

Chapter 2

3. b. $x(t) = \dfrac{15}{26}e^{-2t} - \dfrac{3}{10}e^{-4t} - \dfrac{18}{65}\cos 3t - \dfrac{1}{65}\sin 3t$

7. $\dfrac{Y(s)}{X(s)} = \dfrac{s^3 + 2s^2 + 3s + 7}{s^3 + 5s^2 + 7s + 1}$

8. c. $\dfrac{d^3x}{dt^3} + 8\dfrac{d^2x}{dt^2} + 9\dfrac{dx}{dt} + 15x = \dfrac{df}{dt} + 2f(t)$

16. a. $\dfrac{V_o(s)}{V_i(s)} = \dfrac{1}{s + 2}$

18. b. $\dfrac{V_o(s)}{V_i(s)} = \dfrac{s^2 + 2s + 2}{s^4 + 2s^3 + 3s^2 + 3s + 2}$

32. $\dfrac{\theta_2(s)}{T(s)} = \dfrac{3}{20s^2 + 13s + 4}$

33. $\dfrac{\theta_2(s)}{T(s)} = \dfrac{1/50}{s^2 + 2s + 2}$

42. $\dfrac{\theta_2(s)}{E_a(s)} = \dfrac{0.0833}{s(s + 0.75)}$

Chapter 3

1. $\dot{\mathbf{x}} = \begin{bmatrix} -\dfrac{2}{3} & -\dfrac{1}{3} & \dfrac{1}{3} \\[6pt] -\dfrac{1}{3} & -\dfrac{2}{3} & \dfrac{2}{3} \\[6pt] -\dfrac{1}{3} & -\dfrac{2}{3} & -\dfrac{1}{3} \end{bmatrix} \begin{bmatrix} i_{L_1} \\ i_{L_2} \\ v_o \end{bmatrix} + \begin{bmatrix} \dfrac{2}{3} \\[6pt] \dfrac{1}{3} \\[6pt] \dfrac{1}{3} \end{bmatrix} v_i$

$y = \begin{bmatrix} 0 & 0 & 1 \end{bmatrix} \begin{bmatrix} i_{L_1} \\ i_{L_2} \\ v_o \end{bmatrix}$

Note: L_1 is left-most inductor in Figure P3.1 in the text.

10. a. $\dot{\mathbf{x}} = \begin{bmatrix} 0 & 1 & 0 & 0 \\ 0 & 0 & 1 & 0 \\ 0 & 0 & 0 & 1 \\ -10 & -5 & -1 & -2 \end{bmatrix} \mathbf{x} + \begin{bmatrix} 0 \\ 0 \\ 0 \\ 1 \end{bmatrix} r(t)$

$c(t) = \begin{bmatrix} 10 & 5 & 0 & 0 \end{bmatrix} \mathbf{x}$

12. a. $\dfrac{Y(s)}{R(s)} = \dfrac{10}{s^3 + 5s^2 + 2s + 3}$

17. $\dot{\mathbf{x}} = \begin{bmatrix} -\dfrac{D_{eq}}{J_{eq}} & 0 & \dfrac{K_t N_1}{J_{eq} N_2} \\[8pt] 1 & 0 & 0 \\[8pt] -\dfrac{K_b N_2}{L_a N_1} & 0 & -\dfrac{R_a}{L_a} \end{bmatrix} \begin{bmatrix} \omega_L \\ \theta_L \\ i_a \end{bmatrix} + \begin{bmatrix} 0 \\ 0 \\ \dfrac{1}{L_a} \end{bmatrix} e_a$

$y = \begin{bmatrix} 0 & \dfrac{N_2}{N_1} & 0 \end{bmatrix} \begin{bmatrix} \omega_L \\ \theta_L \\ i_a \end{bmatrix}$

Chapter 4

12. $x(t) = \dfrac{1}{5}\left[1 - \sqrt{\dfrac{20}{19}} e^{-0.5t} \cos\left(\dfrac{\sqrt{19}}{2} t - \arctan \dfrac{1}{\sqrt{19}} \right) \right]$

18. a. $\zeta = 0.375$; $\omega_n = 4$ rad/s; $T_s = 2.67$ s; $T_p = 0.847$ s; $\%OS = 28.06$

21. a. $s = -8 \pm j10.915$;   **b.** $s = -7.589 \pm j12.566$;   **c.** $s = -0.8 \pm j1.57$

33. $s = -5.79, -1.21$

34. a. $s^3 - 5s^2 - 8s + 2 = 0$;   **b.** $s = -1.453, 0.22086, 6.2322$

38. $y(t) = \dfrac{2}{5} - \dfrac{2}{5}e^{-5t}$

41.

$\Phi(t) = \begin{bmatrix} 1.0455e^{-0.20871t} - 0.045545e^{-4.7913t} & 0.21822e^{-0.20871t} - 0.21822e^{-4.7913t} \\ -0.21822e^{-0.20871t} + 0.21822e^{-4.7913t} & -0.045545e^{-0.20871t} + 1.0455e^{-4.7913t} \end{bmatrix}$

$$\mathbf{x}(t) = \begin{bmatrix} 1.0455e^{-0.20871t} - 0.045545e^{-4.7913t} \\ -0.21822e^{-0.20871t} + 0.21822e^{-4.7913t} \end{bmatrix}$$

$$y(t) = 0.60911e^{-0.20871t} + 0.39089e^{-4.7913t}$$

68. $D = 0.143$ N-m-s/rad

71. $R = 912\,\Omega$

Chapter 5

2. $\dfrac{C(s)}{R(s)} = \dfrac{G_3(G_1G_2 + 1)}{1 + G_1H_1}$

4. $\dfrac{C(s)}{R(s)} = \dfrac{G_1G_2 + G_3}{1 + G_3H + G_1G_2H + G_2G_4}$

6. $\dfrac{C(s)}{R(s)} = \dfrac{G_1G_5}{1 + G_1G_2 + G_1G_3G_4G_5 + G_1G_3G_5G_6G_7 + G_1G_5G_8}$

9. $\dfrac{C(s)}{R(s)} = \dfrac{G_4G_6 + G_2G_5G_6 + G_3G_5G_6}{1 + G_6 + G_1G_2 + G_1G_3 + G_1G_2G_6 +}$

$$G_1G_3G_6 + G_4G_6G_7 + G_2G_5G_6G_7 + G_3G_5G_6G_7$$

26. $\dfrac{C(s)}{R(s)} = \dfrac{G_1G_2G_3G_4}{2 + G_2G_3G_4 + 2G_3G_4 + 2G_4}$

27. $\dfrac{C(s)}{R(s)} = \dfrac{G_1G_6G_7(G_2 + G_3)(G_4 + G_5)}{1 - G_6G_7H_3(G_2 + G_3)(G_4 + G_5) - G_6H_1 - G_7H_2 + G_6G_7H_1H_2}$

29. b. $\dot{\mathbf{x}} = \begin{bmatrix} -5 & 1 & 0 & 0 \\ 0 & -5 & 0 & 0 \\ 0 & 0 & -7 & 1 \\ 0 & 0 & 0 & -7 \end{bmatrix} \mathbf{x} + \begin{bmatrix} 0 \\ 1 \\ 0 \\ 1 \end{bmatrix} r(t)$

$$y = \begin{bmatrix} -\dfrac{3}{4} & 1 & -\dfrac{5}{4} & -1 \end{bmatrix} \mathbf{x}$$

35. $\dot{\mathbf{x}} = \begin{bmatrix} 0 & 1 & 0 & 0 \\ -1 & 0 & 1 & 0 \\ 0 & 0 & 0 & 1 \\ 1 & -1 & 0 & 0 \end{bmatrix} \mathbf{x} + \begin{bmatrix} 0 \\ 0 \\ 0 \\ 1 \end{bmatrix} r(t)$

$$c = \begin{bmatrix} -1 & 1 & 0 & 0 \end{bmatrix} \mathbf{x}$$

67. $D_L = 3560$ N-m-s/rad

Chapter 6

1. 2 rhp, 3 lhp, 0 $j\omega$

3. 3 rhp, 2 lhp, 0 $j\omega$

4. 1 rhp, 0 lhp, 4 $j\omega$

5. 0 rhp, 2 lhp, 2 $j\omega$

8. Unstable

15. 1 rhp, 2 lhp, 4 $j\omega$

21. Stable for $0 < K < 140.8$

37. a. $-4 < K < 20.41$; **b.** $1.36\,\text{rad/s}$

39. a. $0 < K < 19.69$; **b.** $K = 19.69$; **c.** $s = \pm\, j1.118, -4.5, -3.5$

40. $-\dfrac{2}{3} < K < 0$

Chapter 7

4. $e_{\text{ss}} = 11.25$

7. $\dot{e}(\infty) = 0.9$

9. a. $\%OS = 4.32$; **b.** $T_s = 0.16\,\text{sec}$; **c.** $e_{\text{ss}} = 0$;

  d. $e_{\text{ss}} = 0.2$; **e.** $e_{\text{ss}} = \infty$

12. a. $K_p = 1, K_v = 0, K_a = 0$; **b.** $e(\infty) = \infty$; **c.** Type 0

19. $K = 110,000$

26. $\beta = 1, K = 1.16, \alpha = 7.76$, or $\beta = -1, K = 5.16, \alpha = 1.74$

30. a. $K = 831,744, a = 831.744$

34. $K_1 = 125,000, K_2 = 0.016$

40. a. Step: $e(\infty) = 1.098$; ramp: $e(\infty) = \infty$

Chapter 8

15. Breakaway point $= -2.333$; asymptotes: $\sigma_a = -5$; $j\omega$-axis crossing $= \pm\, j7.35$

18. b. Asymptotes: $\sigma_a = -\dfrac{8}{3}$; **c.** $K = 140.8$; **d.** $K = 13.12$

19. $K = 9997$; $\alpha = 7$

22. a. $\sigma_a = -\dfrac{5}{2}$; **b.** $s = -1.38, -3.62$; **c.** $0 < K < 126$;

  d. $K = 10.3$

25. b. $K = 9.4$; **c.** $T_s = 4.62\,\text{s}, T_p = 1.86\,\text{s}$; **d.** $s = -4.27$; **e.** $0 < K < 60$

29. $\alpha = 9$

38. a. $K < 834.81$; **b.** $K = 105.129$; **c.** $K = 61.13$

41. a. $K = 170.1$; **b.** $K = 16.95$

Chapter 9

1. $G_c(s) = \dfrac{s + 0.1}{s}$; $K \simeq 72.23$ for both cases; $K_{p_O} = 2.44$; $K_{p_N} = \infty$;

  $\%OS_O = \%OS_N = 16.3$; $T_{s_O} = T_{s_N} = 2.65\,\text{s}$

8. a. $s = -2.5 \pm j5.67$;   **b.** Angle $= -9.78°$;   **c.** $P_c = 35.39$

   d. $K = 1049.41$;   **e.** $s = -36.33, -1.057$

9. a. $s = -2.4 \pm j4.16$;   **b.** $s = -6.06$;   **c.** $K = 29.12$;

   d. $s = -1.263$;   **f.** $K_a = 4.8$

13. a. $G_c(s) = \dfrac{s+7}{s+37.42}$, $K = 5452$; dominant poles $= -4.13 \pm j10.78$

23. a. $K_{uc} = 10$; $K_c = 9.95$;   **b.** $K_{P_{uc}} = 1.25$; $K_{P_c} = 6.22$;

   c. $\%OS_{uc} = \%OS_c = 4.32$;

   d. Uncompensated: exact second-order system, approximation OK; compensated: closed-loop pole at -0.3, closed-loop zero at -0.5, simulate

   e. Approach to final value longer than settling time of uncompensated system

   f. $G_{\text{LLC}}(s) = \dfrac{404.1(s+0.5)(s+4)}{(s+2)(s+4)(s+0.1)(s+28.36)}$ yields approximately a 5 times improvement in speed.

24. $G_c(s) = \dfrac{(s+6.93)(s+0.1)}{s}$, $K = 3.08$

27. Poles $= -0.747 \pm j1.237, -2.51$; zeros—none

Chapter 10

9. System a: $0 < K < 810$; System 2: If $0 < K < 3.94$, the system is unstable. If $K > 3.94$, the system is stable; System 3: If $0 < K < 720$, the system is stable. If $K > 720$, the system is unstable. (Answers are from exact frequency response)

10. a. System 1: Gain margin $= 4$ dB; Phase margin $= 15°$.

14. c. $\omega_{\text{BW}} = 1.5$ rad/s

22. System 2: $T_s = 2.23$ sec, $T_p = 0.476$ s, $\%OS = 42.62$ (Answers are from exact frequency response)

43. $G_M = 1.17$ dB, $\Phi_M = 6.01°$ (Answers are from exact frequency response)

Chapter 11

1. a. $K = 1639$ (Answer is from exact frequency response)

2. a. $K = 1782$ (Answer is from exact frequency response)

3. a. $K = 260$ (Answer is from exact frequency response)

12. The compensated forward path $G(s) = \dfrac{96 \times 3.69(s+1.12)}{s(s+2)(s+4)(s+6) - 4.15}$, $K = 96$

   (Answer is from exact frequency response)

19. $G_{\text{PID}}(s) = 9.62\dfrac{(s+0.042)(s+1.364)}{s^2(s+1)(s+4)}$, $K = 17.14$ dB

   (Answer is from exact frequency response)

Chapter 12

1. d. For function **i:** $T(s) = \dfrac{s+1}{s^2 + (2 + k_2)s + k_1}$

3. b. For function **i**: $G(s) = \dfrac{6.25}{s} - \dfrac{27.5}{s+10} + \dfrac{71.25}{s+20}$, $T(s) = \dfrac{200(s^2 + 7s + 25)}{4s^3 + as^2 + bs + c}$

where $a = (25k_3 - 110k_2 + 285k_1 + 120)$
$\qquad b = (750k_3 - 2200k_2 + 2850k_1 + 800)$
$\qquad c = 5000k_3$

and $\mathbf{C} = \begin{bmatrix} 1 & 1 & 1 \end{bmatrix}$; $\mathbf{B} = \begin{bmatrix} 71.25 & -27.5 & 6.25 \end{bmatrix}^T$ was used

11. a. Uncontrollable;   **b.** Controllable;   **c.** Controllable

14. $\mathbf{K} = \begin{bmatrix} 92.35 & 36.78 & -7 \end{bmatrix}$ for a characteristic polynomial of
$(s+6)(s^2 + 8s + 45.78) = s^3 + 14s^2 + 93.78s + 274.7$

22. $\mathbf{l_1} = -656.4$; $\mathbf{l_2} = 786.4$

Chapter 13

3. a. $f(kT) = 229.5(0.4)^k - 504(0.6)^k + 275.5(0.8)^k$

5. c. $G(z) = 1.02557 \dfrac{z(z + 0.36788)}{(z - 0.36788)(z^2 - 0.052046z + 0.13534)}$

7. b. $G(z) = 0.0012549 \dfrac{(z + 0.19485)(z + 2.821)}{(z - 1)(z - 0.36788)(z - 0.81873)}$

8. a. $T(z) = \dfrac{G_1(z)G_2(z)}{1 + G_1(z)G_2H(z)}$

13. $0 < K < 11.104$

14. a. $K_p = \dfrac{1}{2}$, $e^*(\infty) = \dfrac{2}{3}$; $K_v = 0$, $e^*(\infty) = \infty$; $K_a = 0$, $e^*(\infty) = \infty$

16. $K = 9.68$ for 16.3% of overshoot; $0 < K < 86$ for stability

CREDITS

Figure and Photo Credits

Figures, photos, Case Studies, Examples, and Problems in Chapters 4, 5, 6, 8, 9, 13, Appendix B, and rear endpapers: Adapted from Johnson, H., et al. *Unmanned Free-Swimming Submersible (UFSS) System Description,* NRL Memorandum Report 4393 (Washington, D.C.: Naval Research Laboratory, 1980). MATLAB screen shots in Appendixes C and D were reprinted with permission from The MathWorks.

Chapter 1

1.3: Courtesy of United Technologies Otis Elevator. **1.4:** © Hank Morgan/Rainbow/PNI. **1.5(a):** Rade Lukovic/stockphoto, **(b), (c)** Courtesy of Pioneer Electronics, Inc. **1.7:** Courtesy of Quantum Corp. **1.8:** © Peter Menzel. **P1.3:** Adapted from Ayers, J. Taking the Mystery Out of Winder Controls, *Motion System Design,* April 1988. Penton Media, Inc. **P1.5:** Jenkins, H. E.; Kurfess, T. R.; and Ludwick, S. J. Determination of a Dynamic Grinding Model, *Journal of Dynamic Systems, Measurements and Control,* vol. 119, June 1997, p. 290. 1997 ASME. Reprinted with permission. **P1.6:** Vaughan, N. D., and Gamble, J. B. The Modeling and Simulation of a Proportional Solenoid Valve, *Journal of Dynamic Systems, Measurements and Control,* vol. 118, March 1996, p. 121. 1996 ASME. Reprinted with permission. **P1.7(a), (b), (c):** Reprinted figure with permission from Bechhofer, J., *Feedback for Physicists: A Tutuorial Essay on Control, Reviews of Modern Physics,* pp. 77, 783, 2005. Copyright (2007) by the American Physical Society. **P1.8:** D. A. Weinstein/Custom Medical Stock Photo. **P1.11:** O'Connor, D. N.; Eppinger, S. D.; Seering, W. P.; and Wormly, D. N. Active Control of a High-Speed Pantograph, *Journal of Dynamic Systems, Measurements and Control,* vol. 119, March 1997, p. 2. 1997 ASME. Reprinted with permission.

Chapter 2

2.34: © Debra Lex. **2.51:** Adapted from Milsum, J. H. *Biological Control Systems Analysis* (New York: McGraw-Hill, 1966), p. 182. © 1966 McGraw-Hill, Inc. Used with permission of the publisher. **P2.36:** Lin Jung-Shan, Kanellakopoulos Ioannis. Nonlinear Design of Active Suspensions, *IEEE Control Systems Magazine,* vol. 17, no. 3. June 1997, pp. 45–49. Fig. 1, p. 46. **P2.37:** Marttinen A., Virkkunen J., Salminen R. T. Control Study with Pilot Crane, *IEEE Trans. on Education,* vol. 33, No. 3, August 1990. Fig. 2, p. 300. **P2.38:** Wang J. Z., Tie B., Welkowitz W., Semmlow J. L., Kostis J. B. Modeling Sound Generation in Stenosed Coronary Arteries, *IEEE Trans. on Biomedical Engineering,* vol. 37, no. 11, November 1990. **P2.39(a):** From O'Connor, D. N.; Eppinger, S. D.; Seering, W. P.; and Wormly, D. N. Active Control of a High-Speed Pantograph, *Journal of Dynamic Systems, Measurements and Control,* vol. 119, March 1997, p. 2. 1997 ASME. Reprinted with permission. **P2.39(b):** Adapted from O'Connor, D. N.; Eppinger, S. D.; Seering, W. P.; and Wormly, D. N. Active Control of a High-Speed Pantograph, *Journal of Dynamic Systems, Measurement and Control,* vol. 119, March 1997, p. 3. 1997 ASME. Reprinted with permission. **P2.40:** Craig, I. K., Xia, X., and Venter, J. W. Introducing HIV/AIDS Education into the Electrical Engineering Curriculum at the University of Pretoria. *IEEE Trans. on Education,* vol. 47, no. 1, February 2004, pp. 65–73.

Chapter 3

3.13: Bruce Frisch/S.S./Photo Researchers. **P3.14(a), (b):** Hong, J.; Tan, X.; Pinette, B.; Weiss, R.; and Riseman, E. M. Image-Based Homing, *IEEE Control Systems,* Feb. 1992, pp. 38–45. © 1992 IEEE. **P3.15(a), (b):** Adapted from Cavallo, A.; De Maria, G.; and Verde, L. Robust Flight Control Systems: A Parameter Space Design, *Journal of Guidance, Control, and Dynamics,* vol. 15, no. 5, September–October, 1992, pp. 1210–1211. 1992 AIAA. Reprinted by permission of the American Institute of Aeronautics and Astronautics, Inc. **P3.16:** Adapted from Chiu, D. K., and Lee, S. Design and Experimentation of a Jump Impact Controller, *IEEE Control Systems,* June 1997, Fig. 1, p. 99. 1997 IEEE. Reprinted with permission. **P3.17:** Liceaga-Castro, E., vander Molen G. M. Submarine H∞ Depth Control Under Wave Disturbances, *IEEE Trans. on Control Systems Technology,* vol. 3, no. 3. 1995.

Fig. 1, p. 339. **P3.30(c):** (table) Craig, I. K., Xia, X., and Venter, J. W. Introducing HIV/AIDS Education into the Electrical Engineering Curriculum at the University of Pretoria. *IEEE Trans. on Education,* vol. 47, no. 1, February 2004, pp. 65–73. Table II, p. 67.

Chapter 4

4.22: Courtesy of Cybermotion, Inc. **4.27:** Adapted from Dorf, R. C. *Introduction to Electric Circuits,* 2nd ed. (New York: John Wiley & Sons, 1989, 1993), p. 583. ©1989, 1993 John Wiley & Sons. Reprinted by permission of the publisher. **4.33:** Courtesy of Naval Research Laboratory. **P4.11:** Courtesy of Pacific Robotics, Inc. **P4.12:** Borovic B., Liu A. Q., Popa D., Lewis F. L. *Open-loop versus closed-loop control of MEMS devices: choices and issues.* J. Micromech. Microeng. vol. 15, 2005. Fig. 4, p. 1919. **P4.14:** DiBona G. F. *Physiology in Perspective: The Wisdom of the Body. Neural Control of the Kidney,* Am. J. Physiol. Regul. Integr. Comp. Physiol. vol. 289, 2005. Fig. 6, p. R639. Used with permission. **P4.24:** From Manring, N. D., and Johnson, R. E. Modeling and Designing a Variable Displacement Open-Loop Pump, *Journal of Dynamic Systems, Measurement and Control,* vol. 118, June 1996, p. 268. 1996 ASME. Reprinted with permission.

Chapter 5

5.1: NASA-Houston. **5.33:** © Rob Catanach, Woods Hole Oceanographic Institution. **P5.32:** Tanis, D. *Space Shuttle GN&C Operations Manual* (Downey, CA: Rockwell International), August 1988. **P5.35(a):** Courtesy of Hank Morgan/Rainbow/ PNI. **P5.36(a):** Bailey, F. N.; Cockburn, J. C.; and Dee, A. Robust Control for High-Performance Materials Testing, *IEEE Control Systems,* April 1992, p. 63. © 1992 IEEE. **P5.38:** Lepschy A. M., Mian G. A., Viaro U. Feedback Control in Ancient Water and Mechanical Clocks, *IEEE Trans. on Education,* vol. 35, 1992. Figs. 1 and 2, p. 4. **P5.39:** Ben-Dov D., Salcudean S. E. A Force-Controlled Pneumatic Actuator, *IEEE Trans. on Robotics and Automation,* vol. 11, 1995. Fig. 6, p. 909. **P5.43:** Lin Jung-Shan, Kanellakopoulos Ioannis. Nonlinear Design of Active

Suspensions, *IEEE Control Systems Magazine*, vol. 17, no. 3. June 1997, pp. 45–49. Fig. 3, p. 48. **P5.44:** de Vlugt, Schouten A. C., van der Helm F. C. T. *Adaptation of reflexive feedback during arm posture to different environments,* Biol. Cybern. vol. 87, 2002. Fig. A1, p. 24.

Chapter 6

6.9: Courtesy of Woods Hole Oceanographic Institution. **6.11:** Courtesy of FANUC Robotics North America, Inc. **P6.13(a):** Courtesy of Kazuhiko Kawamura, Vanderbilt University. **P6.16:** From Rober, S. J.; Shin, Y. C.; and Nwokah, O. D. I. A Digital Robust Controller for Cutting Force Control in the End Milling Process, *Journal of Dynamic Systems, Measurement and Control,* vol. 119, June 1997, p. 147. 1997 ASME. Reprinted with permission. **P6.17(a):** © Japan Air Lines/Photo Researchers. **P6.17(b):** Adapted from Bittar, A., and Sales, R. M. H₂ and H∞ Control for MagLev Vehicles, *IEEE Control Systems,* vol. 18, no. 4, August 1998, Equations 7, 8, and Table 2 on pp. 20–21. © 1998 IEEE. Reprinted with permission.

Chapter 7

7.9: Chuck O'Rear/Westlight/Corbis Images. **7.23(a):** Isailovic, J., *Videodisc and Optical Memory Technologies,* © 1985, p. 77. Reprinted by permission of Pearson Education, Inc., Upper Saddle River, N.J. **P7.22:** Lam C. S., Wong M. C., Han Y. D. *Stability Study on Dynamic Voltage Restorer (DVR)* Power Electronics Systems and Applications 2004, Proceedings First International Conference on Power Electronics 2004. Fig. 7, p. 68. **P7.28(a), (c):** From Kumar, R. R.; Cooper, P. A.; and Lim, T. W. Sensitivity of Space Station Alpha Joint Robust Controller to Structural Modal Parameter Variations, *Journal of Guidance, Control, and Dynamics,* vol. 15, no. 6, Nov/Dec 1992, pp. 1427–1428. ©1992 AIAA. Reprinted by permission of the American Institute of Aeronautics and Astronautics, Inc. **P7.31:** Hess, R. A.; Malsbury, T.; and Atencio, A., Jr. Flight Simulator Fidelity Assessment in a Rotorcraft Lateral Translation Maneuver, *Journal of Guidance, Control, and Dynamics,* vol. 16, no. 1 Jan/Feb 1993, p. 80. ©1992 AIAA. Reprinted by permission of the American Institute of Aeronautics and Astronautics, Inc. **P7.32(a), (b):** Ohnishi, K.; Shibata, M.; and Murakami, T. Motion Control for Advanced Mechatronics, *IEEE/ASME Transactions on Mechatronics,* vol. 1, no. 1, March 1996, **(a):** Fig. 14, p. 62, **(b):** Fig. 16, p. 62. © 1996 IEEE. Reprinted with permission.

Chapter 8

8.4(a): Courtesy of ParkerVision. **P8.13(a):** Courtesy of FANUC Robotics North America,

Inc. **P8.13(b):** Adapted from Hardy, H. L. Multi-Loop Servo Controls Programmed Robot, *Instruments and Control Systems,* June 1967, p. 105. **P8.14:** *GNC FSSR FC Ascent,* vol. 1, June 30, 1985 (Downey, CA: Rockwell International). **P8.15(a):** Bruner, A. M.; Belvin, W. K.; Horta, L. G.; and Juang, J. Active Vibration Absorber for the CSI Evolutionary Model: Design and Experimental Results, *Journal of Guidance, Control, and Dynamics,* vol. 15, no. 5, Sept/Oct 1992, p. 1254. © 1992 AIAA. Reprinted by permission of the American Institute of Aeronautics and Astronautics, Inc. **P8.19:** Cho, D., and Hedrick, J. K. Pneumatic Actuators for Vehicle Active Suspension Applications, *ASME Journal of Dynamic Systems, Measurement and Control,* March 1985, p. 68, Fig. 4. **P8.22(a), (b):** Adapted from Annaswamy, A. M., and Ghonien, A. F. Active Control in Combustion Systems, *IEEE Control Systems,* December 1995, p. 50, 51, and 59. ©1995 IEEE. Reprinted with permission. **P8.23(a):** Jim Corwin/Photo Researchers **P8.23(b), (c):** Adapted from Anderson, C. G.; Richon, J.-B.; and Campbell, T. J. An Aerodynamic Moment-Controlled Surface for Gust Load Alleviation on Wind Turbine Rotors, *IEEE transactions on Control System Technology,* vol. 6, no. 5, September 1998, pp. 577–595. ©1998 IEEE.

Chapter 9

9.46: Photo by Mark E. Van Dusen. **P9.5:** Romagnoli, J. A., and Palazoglu, A. *Introduction to Process Control,* CRC Press, Boca Raton, 2006. p. 44, Fig. 3.4. **P9.6:** Smith, C. A. *Automated Continuous Process Control.* John Wiley & Sons, New York, NY, 2002. p. 128, Fig. 6–1.1. **P9.14(a):** Cho, D.; Kato, Y.; and Spilman, D. Sliding Mode and Classical Controllers in Magnetic Levitation Systems, *IEEE Control Systems,* Feb. 1993, p. 43, Fig. 1. ©1993 IEEE. Reprinted with permission.

Chapter 10

10.1: Courtesy of Agilent Technologies. **P10.14:** © 1994 Adept Technology, Inc. All rights reserved. **P10.15(a):** Courtesy of Nikon, Inc.

Chapter 11

11.10(a), (b): Courtesy of Jim Stoner, University of Iowa. **P11.3(a):** Courtesy of Siemens Dematic Automatic Guided Vehicle.

Chapter 12

12.1: ©Dick Blume—Syracuse Newspapers/ The Image Works. **P12.6:** Tadeo F., Pérez, López O., and Alvarez T. Control of Neutralization Processes by Robust Loopsharing. *IEEE Trans. on Cont. Syst. Tech.,* vol. 8, no. 2, 2000. Fig. 2, p. 239.

Chapter 13

13.12: © Blair Steitz/Photo Researchers. **13.28:** Adapted from Chassaing, R. *Digital Signal Processing* (New York: John Wiley & Sons, Inc, 1999), p. 137. © 1999 John Wiley & Sons, Inc. **13.29:** Adapted from Chassaing, R. *Digital Signal Processing* (New York: John Wiley & Sons, Inc., 1999), p. 137. © 1999 John Wiley & Sons, Inc. **13.36:** Adapted from Chassaing, R. *Digital Signal Processing* (New York: John Wiley & Sons, Inc, 1999), p. 137. © 1999 John Wiley & Sons, Inc.

Figure Legend Sources

Copyright page: cover photo caption from Science/PhotoResearch Inc. **1.3(b):** *The World of Otis,* 1991, p. 2, and *Tell Me About Elevators,* 1991, pp. 20–25, United Technologies Otis Elevator Company. ©1991 Otis Elevator Company. **1.8:** Overbye, D. The Big Ear, *OMNI,* Dec. 1990, pp. 41–48. **4.22:** Cybermotion, Inc. advertising brochure. **5.33:** Ballard, R. D. *The Discovery of the Titanic* (New York: Warner Books, Inc., 1987). **6.9:** Ballard, R. D. The Riddle of the Lusitania, *National Geographic,* April 1994, pp. 68–85. **6.11:** M-400 data sheet, FANUC Robotics North America, Inc., **7.9:** Bylinski, G. *Silicon Valley High Tech: Window to the Future* (Hong Kong: Intercontinental Publishing Corp., Ltd., 1985). **8.4(a):** ParkerVision specification sheets and advertising material. **10.1:** *Test & Measurement Catalog* 1998 (Palo Alto, CA: Hewlett-Packard Company, 1997). **P10.14:** Adept Technology, Inc. advertising brochure.

Trademarks

INDEX

UNMANNED FREE-SWIMMING
SUBMERSIBLE VEHICLE

Pitch Control System

Heading Control System

UNMANNED FREE-SWIMMING SUBMERSIBLE VEHICLE

Pitch Control System

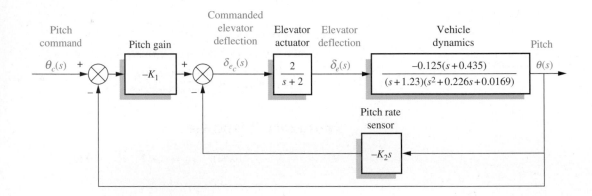

Heading Control System

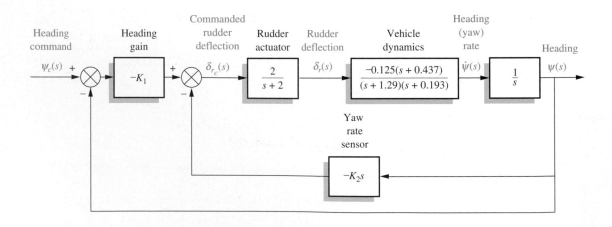

KEY EQUATIONS

Modeling

$$\frac{V_o(s)}{V_i(s)} = -\frac{Z_2(s)}{Z_1(s)} \quad (2.97); \qquad \frac{V_o(s)}{V_i(s)} = \frac{Z_1(s) + Z_2(s)}{Z_1(s)} \quad (2.104)$$

$$\frac{\theta_2}{\theta_1} = \frac{r_1}{r_2} = \frac{N_1}{N_2} \quad (2.133); \qquad \frac{T_2}{T_1} = \frac{\theta_1}{\theta_2} = \frac{N_2}{N_1} \quad (2.135)$$

$$\left(\frac{\text{Number of teeth of gear on } \textit{destination} \text{ shaft}}{\text{Number of teeth of gear on } \textit{source} \text{ shaft}} \right)^2 \quad \text{(see after 2.138)}$$

$$\frac{\theta_m(s)}{E_a(s)} = \frac{K_t/(R_a J_m)}{s\left[s + \frac{1}{J_m}\left(D_m + \frac{K_t K_b}{R_a}\right)\right]} \quad (2.153)$$

$$\frac{K_t}{R_a} = \frac{T_{\text{stall}}}{e_a} \quad (2.162); \quad K_b = \frac{e_a}{\omega_{\text{no-load}}} \quad (2.163)$$

$$T(s) = \frac{Y(s)}{U(s)} = \mathbf{C}(s\mathbf{I} - \mathbf{A})^{-1}\mathbf{B} + \mathbf{D} \quad (3.73)$$

Time Response

$$T_r = \frac{2.2}{a} \quad (4.9); \quad T_s = \frac{4}{a} \quad (4.10)$$

$$G(s) = \frac{\omega_n^2}{s^2 + 2\zeta\omega_n s + \omega_n^2} \quad (4.22)$$

$$\%OS = e^{-(\zeta\pi/\sqrt{1-\zeta^2})} \times 100 \quad (4.38)$$

$$\zeta = \frac{-\ln(\%OS/100)}{\sqrt{\pi^2 + \ln^2(\%OS/100)}} \quad (4.39)$$

$$T_p = \frac{\pi}{\omega_n\sqrt{1-\zeta^2}} \quad (4.34); \quad T_s = \frac{4}{\zeta\omega_n} \quad (4.42)$$

Steady-State Error

$$e(\infty) = e_{\text{step}}(\infty) = \frac{1}{1 + \lim\limits_{s\to 0} G(s)} \quad (7.30); \quad K_p = \lim\limits_{s\to 0} G(s) \quad (7.33)$$

$$e(\infty) = e_{\text{ramp}}(\infty) = \frac{1}{\lim\limits_{s\to 0} sG(s)} \quad (7.31); \quad K_v = \lim\limits_{s\to 0} sG(s) \quad (7.34)$$

$$e(\infty) = e_{\text{parabola}}(\infty) = \frac{1}{\lim\limits_{s\to 0} s^2 G(s)} \quad (7.32); \quad K_a = \lim\limits_{s\to 0} s^2 G(s) \quad (7.35)$$

Root Locus

$$\angle KG(s)H(s) = -1 = 1\angle(2k+1)180° \quad (8.13)$$

$$\sigma_a = \frac{\sum \text{finite poles} - \sum \text{finite zeros}}{\# \text{ finite poles} - \# \text{ finite zeros}} \quad (8.27)$$

$$\theta_a = \frac{(2k+1)\pi}{\# \text{ finite poles} - \# \text{ finite zeros}} \quad (8.28)$$

$$\theta = \sum \text{finite zero angles} - \sum \text{finite pole angles}$$

$$K = \frac{1}{|G(s)H(s)|} = \frac{1}{M} = \frac{\prod \text{finite pole lengths}}{\prod \text{finite zero lengths}} \quad (8.51)$$

Frequency Response

$$M_p = \frac{1}{2\zeta\sqrt{1-\zeta^2}} \quad (10.52); \quad \omega_p = \omega_n\sqrt{1 - 2\zeta^2} \quad (10.53)$$

$$\omega_{\text{BW}} = \omega_n\sqrt{(1 - 2\zeta^2) + \sqrt{4\zeta^4 - 4\zeta^2 + 2}} \quad (10.54)$$

$$\Phi_M = \tan^{-1}\frac{2\zeta}{\sqrt{-2\zeta^2 + \sqrt{1 + 4\zeta^4}}} \quad (10.73)$$

$$\phi_{\max} = \tan^{-1}\frac{1-\beta}{2\sqrt{\beta}} = \sin^{-1}\frac{1-\beta}{1+\beta} \quad (11.11)$$

$$\omega_{\max} = \frac{1}{T\sqrt{\beta}} \quad (11.9); \quad |G_c(j\omega_{\max})| = \frac{1}{\sqrt{\beta}} \quad (11.12)$$

State Space

$$\mathbf{C_M} = \begin{bmatrix} \mathbf{B} & \mathbf{AB} & \mathbf{A}^2\mathbf{B} & \cdots & \mathbf{A}^{n-1}\mathbf{B} \end{bmatrix} \quad (12.26)$$

$$\dot{\mathbf{x}} = (\mathbf{A} - \mathbf{BK})\mathbf{x} + \mathbf{B}r; \quad y = \mathbf{C}\mathbf{x} \quad (12.3); \quad \mathbf{O_M} = \begin{bmatrix} \mathbf{C} \\ \mathbf{CA} \\ \vdots \\ \mathbf{CA}^{n-1} \end{bmatrix} \quad (12.79)$$

$$\dot{\mathbf{e}}_{\mathbf{x}} = (\mathbf{A} - \mathbf{LC})\mathbf{e}_{\mathbf{x}}; \quad y - \hat{y} = \mathbf{C}\mathbf{e}_{\mathbf{x}} \quad (12.64)$$

Digital Control

$$e^*(\infty) = \lim\limits_{z\to 1}(1 - z^{-1})E(z) \quad (13.66)$$

$$K_p = \lim\limits_{z\to 1} G(z) \quad (13.70); \quad K_v = \frac{1}{T}\lim\limits_{z\to 1}(z-1)G(z) \quad (13.73)$$

$$K_a = \frac{1}{T^2}\lim\limits_{z\to 1}(z-1)^2 G(z) \quad (13.75)$$